# DEBTOR-CREDITOR LAW MANUAL

THOMAS D. CRANDALL
*Professor of Law, University of Denver College of Law*

RICHARD B. HAGEDORN
*Visiting Associate Professor of Law, Willamette University College of Law (formerly Associate Professor of Law, Gonzaga University School of Law)*

FRANK W. SMITH, JR.
*Professor of Law, University of Washington School of Law (formerly Professor of Law, J. Reuben Clark School of Law, Brigham Young University)*

WG&L

WARREN, GORHAM & LAMONT
Boston • New York

WARREN, GORHAM & LAMONT, INC.
210 SOUTH STREET
BOSTON, MASSACHUSETTS 02111

---



ISBN 0-88712-189-6

Library of Congress Catalog Card No. 85-50964



PRINTED IN THE UNITED STATES OF AMERICA

*To my parents, Mary and Bob, and my brother Ken,*
*who always knew I could.*

TDC

*To my wife, Claudia, and sons Andy and Scott, whose*
*loving support made my portion of the book possible,*
*and to my parents, Buzz and June Hagedorn,*
*who have given me so much.*

RBH

*To my wife, Susan, who in her caring and unselfish*
*way has made so many things possible.*

FWS

# Preface

THIS BOOK is a comprehensive treatment of the law of debtor-creditor relations, including judicial and nonjudicial collection of debt, consumer credit, suretyship, real and personal property secured transactions, and bankruptcy. It is designed for practical use and addresses both creditor and debtor concerns.

Because it contains comprehensive, one-volume coverage of the law of debtor-creditor relations, this manual should prove valuable for the practicing attorney faced daily with difficult problems related to debt collection, consumer credit, secured transactions, and bankruptcy. The practicing attorney is ordinarily forced to research questions about debtor-creditor law that cut across numerous subtopics of the law that are dealt with only on a piecemeal basis in numerous other reference sources. The uniquely comprehensive coverage of this book can save substantial time for attorneys who need an immediate answer as they research legal problems. The authors believe the book also provides a valuable text for law students and others concerned with acquiring a basic understanding and overview of the areas covered.

There are four areas of discussion in the book. The first reviews the law related to the validity of the debt. Particular emphasis is placed on consumer credit regulation. The second topic is the law of collection of unsecured debts. Coverage of this area of law includes examinations of both extrajudicial and judicial debt collection techniques. The third topic is the law of collection of secured debts. The focus of this discussion is secured transactions in personal property and fixtures (Article 9 of the Uniform Commercial Code), secured transactions in real estate (particularly real estate mortgage law), common law, and statutory and equitable liens (including coverage of federal tax liens). The last topic of discussion is federal bankruptcy and incorporates coverage of the Bankruptcy Amendments and Federal Judgeship Act of 1984.

Whether dealing with federal or uniform state laws, this book provides citation to pertinent primary authority while including occasional references to commentary and other relevant secondary sources. With regard to nonuniform state laws, primary authority is also liberally cited, but a special effort is made to include references to a multitude of excellent secondary sources.

THOMAS D. CRANDALL

RICHARD B. HAGEDORN

FRANK W. SMITH, JR.

July 1985

# Acknowledgments

PROFESSOR CRANDALL would like to thank the staff, faculties, and Deans of the University of Denver College of Law and of Gonzaga University School of Law for their time, encouragement, and support. He also wants to express special gratitude to Patricia Merck, University of Denver '85, whose perseverance and research assistance were invaluable.

PROFESSOR HAGEDORN gratefully acknowledges the valuable assistance received from the following Gonzaga University School of Law students who served as his research assistants: Helen E. Benson, John T. Powers, Terese N. Richmond, and Charles P. Schuerman. He also wishes to express his gratitude for the countless hours spent in preparing the text for his portion of the book by Marge Buck and Sue Newman. Finally, he wishes to express appreciation to all those scholars who have written and published books, articles, comments, and notes in this diverse subject area of the law. They have provided great aid and inspiration and are frequently cited throughout his portion of the book.

PROFESSOR SMITH gratefully acknowledges the outstanding research and support facilities provided by the Law School at Brigham Young University, the encouragement of colleagues at BYU and elsewhere, and the valuable assistance he received from the following law students at Brigham Young University, who, as research assistants, contributed in so many ways: Tamara J. Hauge, Michelle E. Jeans, and Timothy R. Zinnecker.

# Summary of Contents

# Table of Contents

## PART I—VALIDITY OF THE DEBT

## 1 Introduction to Consumer Law



## 2 Problems Arising Before or at the Formation of the Debt

# 3 Regulation of the Substantive Terms of Consumer Credit Transactions

# 4 Regulation of Performance Obligations



# PART II—COLLECTION OF UNSECURED DEBTS

# 5 Extrajudicial Debt Collection

# 6 Judicial Collection

## PART III–COLLECTION OF SECURED DEBTS

## 7 Secured Transactions Under Article 9 of the Uniform Commercial Code

# 8 Mortgages and Other Secured Transactions in Real Estate

# 9 Common-Law, Statutory, and Equitable Liens

## PART IV–FEDERAL BANKRUPTCY

## 10 Bankruptcy as a Method of Dealing With Insolvency



## 11 The Bankruptcy Court System

## 12 Bankruptcy: Commencement of Proceedings

## 13 The Bankruptcy Estate

## 14 Distribution of the Estate

# 15 Bankruptcy: Discharge

# 16 The Trustee's Avoiding Powers and Recovery of Assets for the Estate

# 17 Chapter 13 Plans: Debt Adjustment for Individuals

# I

# VALIDITY OF THE DEBT

# 1

# Introduction to Consumer Law



## ¶ 1.01 THE IMPORTANCE OF CONSUMER LAW IN THE COLLECTION OF DEBTS

Since 1968, there has been an explosion of state and federal legislation and regulation designed to protect a class of debtors–consumers–thought by legislators and regulators to be unable to adequately protect themselves in the marketplace. This consumer law,[1] combined with both an increased representation for low-income consumers by publicly funded lawyers and a greater awareness by the courts of consumer interests, has added a new dimension to disputes between creditor and debtor. Creditors' attempts to enforce obligations now frequently are answered with allegations of consumer law violations.

---

[1] See infra ¶ 1.02 for a discussion of the meaning of "consumer law."

For example, the consumer's counsel may counter with alleged disclosure violations under the federal Truth-in-Lending Act[2] or alleged improper monthly billing under the federal Fair Credit Billing Act.[3] The end result still may be a favorable ruling for the creditor on the issue of liability for the underlying debt, but, if the court finds such a violation, the award to the creditor may be reduced by damages awarded to the consumer.[4] Also, upon the consumer's bankruptcy, the creditor's attorney may be faced with consumer law because of the trustee's power to use the bankrupt's defenses or claims against any creditor.[5] For the consumer debtor's attorney, these laws are important because they may provide the only legal response for the debtor who apparently has defaulted. The effective use of consumer law by the debtor's attorney has prompted more than one settlement favorable to a debtor that might not otherwise have been feasible.

## ¶ 1.02 WHAT IS CONSUMER LAW?

There is no uniformly accepted definition of consumer law. An analysis of federal and state consumer legislation and regulation, popularly called "consumer law," and relevant cases and commentary provide the generally accepted definition: Consumer law is that law designed to protect the natural person when he makes a purchase of personal property or services or borrows money when the primary reason for the purchase or the loan is to satisfy a personal, family, or household purpose.[1] Most consumer law is consumer credit law—that is, law concerned with consumer purchases of goods or services or con-

---

[2] 15 USC §§ 1601–1665a as implemented by Federal Reserve Board Regulation Z, 12 CFR Pt. 226.

[3] 15 USC §§ 1667–1667e as implemented by Federal Reserve Board Regulation Z, 12 CFR Pt. 226.

[4] See, e.g., ¶ 2.04[11] for a discussion of the remedies available to the consumer for a violation of the Truth-in-Lending Act.

[5] The Bankruptcy Reform Act of 1978, Pub. L. No. 95–598, is codified at 11 USC §§ 101 et seq. (hereafter cited as the Bankruptcy Reform Act). The Bankruptcy Reform Act provides in Section 541(e) that the trustee has the benefit of any personal defense that the debtor might have. For a discussion of bankruptcy law, see Part III of this book.

[1] Broadly defined, the term "consumer" encompasses anyone who uses a product or a loan for any purpose. However, the definition of "consumer" in the text is used in the federal Consumer Credit Protection Act (CCPA—which includes the Truth-in-Lending Act and a variety of other statutes discussed directly below) (15 USC §§ 1602(e), 1602(f) and 1602(h) (1976)) and the most recent version of the Uniform Consumer Credit Code (1974 UCCC) (UCCC §§ 1.301(12) and 1.301(15)). Both definitions probably stem from the Uniform Commercial Code (UCC), which for purposes of the classification of collateral in secured transactions defines "consumer goods" as goods "used or bought for use primarily for personal, family or household purposes." UCC § 9-109. Most other state consumer law uses the same definition for consumer. See, e.g., Wis. Stat. Ann. § 421.301.

sumer loans in which the consumer's payment obligation is deferred by agreement.[2]

The primary focus of this chapter and Chapters 2, 3, and 4 is consumer credit law. These chapters, however, also consider the Federal Trade Commission (FTC) Act and similar unfair and deceptive acts based on the FTC Act passed by the states. Although these acts are broad enough to encompass activity outside the definition of consumer credit transactions, consumers in credit transactions are the primary beneficiaries of such laws.

Real property transactions generally are only tangentially covered by consumer law; therefore, only a limited discussion of real estate transactions is necessary here.

One further limitation should be mentioned. In a broad sense, all of the law that relates to warranties and that concerns product liability is consumer law. Both warranty and product liability law, however, have developed independently of other consumer law and historically have been treated separately in all legal forums and commentary. Because of this traditionally independent treatment, and because a discussion of warranty and product liability law alone could easily occupy an entire volume, such discussion is beyond the scope of this work.

## ¶ 1.03 THE SOURCES OF CONSUMER LAW

### [1] Common Law

Most consumer law is statutory, and, to a lesser extent, is implemented by administrative regulation. The courts have made few laws in this area. The first major legislative inroads in the holder-in-due-course area, however, were prompted by some courts' reluctance to allow the holder of a consumer's obligation to escape all liability for defects in or nondelivery of goods purchased.[1] Also, case law on fraud, misrepresentation, and related issues still may be the best source of law for misleading advertising and other solicitations.[2] Cases relating to the holder-in-due-course concept and related doctrines are discussed in Chapter 3.[3] Regulation of advertising is discussed in Chapter 2.[4]

---

[2] More specifically, a transaction is a "credit" transaction under the major consumer credit law—the federal CCPA—when the creditor charges a finance charge or the transaction is payable by written agreement in more than four installments. 15 USC §§ 1602(e), 1602(f). The UCCC uses the same definition for credit. UCCC §§ 1.301(12), 1.301(15). Most other state consumer credit law uses the same definition. See, e.g., Wash. Rev. Code Ann. § 63.14.010.

[1] E.g., Norman v. World Wide Distribs., Inc., 202 Pa. Super. 53, 195 A2d 115 (1963).

[2] See, e.g., Coffin v. Dodge, 146 Me. 3, 76 A2d 541 (1950).

[3] See ¶ 3.03.

[4] See ¶ 2.01.

## [2] Federal Statutes and Regulations

### [a] The Consumer Credit Protection Act—Including the Truth-in-Lending Act

With the enactment of the Consumer Credit Protection Act (CCPA) in 1968,[5] Congress made a major leap into the regulation of consumer credit. As first enacted, CCPA primarily was intended to require creditors to disclose the cost of credit to consumers—the truth-in-lending provisions in Title I of the CCPA.[6] CCPA has been amended several times since its enactment and apparently will remain the major depository of federal consumer credit legislation.

The Truth-in-Lending Act (TILA)[7] remains a major part of CCPA. The basic purpose of TILA is to provide consumers with the opportunity to compare credit prices by requiring the creditor to disclose the costs of credit, including, for example, the total finance charge and annual percentage rate. In 1982, major amendments designed to simplify TILA became effective.[8]

In 1974, Title I was amended to include a new Chapter 4, called the Fair Credit Billing Act (FCBA).[9] FCBA is designed to provide meaningful periodic disclosures of the consumer's obligation and error-resolution procedures.[10]

In 1976, Title I of the CCPA was amended to include a new Chapter 5, which provides for disclosure of relevant terms in consumer leases of goods.[11] Some restrictions on substantive terms of such leases were also included.[12]

The Federal Reserve Board (FRB) has the primary administrative authority for the enforcement of Title I. The FRB has issued Regulation Z to interpret TILA and FCBA provisions.[13] The FRB has issued Regulation M to interpret the Consumer Leasing Act.[14]

It has become common practice for all of Title I, including FCBA, the consumer leasing provisions, and the general disclosure provisions, to be called the "Truth-in-Lending Act."

In 1970, Title VI, the Fair Credit Reporting Act (FCRA), was added to CCPA.[15] Title VI is designed to discourage the use of unreasonably obtained and inaccurate credit information. FCRA regulates the gathering, distribution,

---

[5] Pub. L. No. 90-321, 82 Stat. 146, 15 USC §§ 1601 et seq. (1968).

[6] Truth-in-Lending Act, Pub. L. No. 90-321, 82 Stat. 146, 15 USC §§ 1601–1665a (1968).

[7] Id.

[8] Truth-in-Lending Simplification and Reform Act, Pub. L. No. 96-221, 94 Stat. 168, 15 USC §§ 1601 et seq. (1982).

[9] Pub. L. No. 93-495, 88 Stat. 1511, 15 USC §§ 1601–1666j (1974).

[10] See, e.g., 15 USC § 1666.

[11] Pub. L. No. 94-240, 90 Stat. 257, 15 USC §§ 1667–1667e (1976).

[12] See, e.g., 15 USC § 1667b (limiting amount of consumer's liability for residual value at termination of lease).

[13] 12 CFR §§ 226 et seq.

[14] 12 CFR §§ 213 et seq.

[15] Pub. L. No. 91-508, 84 Stat. 1128, 15 USC §§ 1681 et seq. (1970).

and use of information sought by prospective creditors, employers, and insurers. It further allows some access by individuals who are the subject of credit reports.[16]

Title VII, the Equal Credit Opportunity Act (ECOA), was enacted in 1974 to prohibit discrimination by creditors on the basis of sex and marital status.[17] In 1976, ECOA was amended to prohibit discrimination on the basis of race, color, religion, national origin, certain sources of income, or the exercise of rights under CCPA.[18] Regulation B was issued by the Federal Reserve Board of Governors to interpret ECOA.[19]

Title VIII, the Fair Debt Collection Practices Act (FDCPA), was added to CCPA in 1977.[20] This Act is designed to prohibit harrassing debt-collection activity by debt-collection agencies. FDCPA is discussed in Chapter 5.

The most recent major substantive addition to CCPA occurred in 1978 with the enactment of the Electronic Fund Transfer Act (EFTA) as Title IX.[21] EFTA is intended to protect consumers from difficulties inherent in systems that involve the electronic transfer of funds. For example, EFTA limits the consumer's liability if he loses a card that is designed to enable the consumer to initiate an electronic funds transfer at an automated teller machine.[22] Since EFTA does not cover credit transactions (for example, it does not apply when a Visa card is used solely in a credit transaction), there is no extended discussion of EFTA in this text.[23]

### [b] The National Bank Act and the Monetary Control Act of 1980

Historically, most consumer credit law has been in the form of usury laws–the regulation of the maximum rate of finance charge, or interest rates. Until recently the control of interest rates has been mostly a matter of state control. Since the middle of the last century, however, there has been one major exception. Nationally chartered banks essentially have had a choice of federal or state law. The National Bank Act permits federally chartered banks to charge the highest rate permitted any lender in the state in which the federal bank is located, regardless of what state law provides.[24]

This is sometimes called the "most-favored-lender status." For example, if small loan companies in Minnesota can charge 36 percent for loans granted the

---

[16] 15 USC §§ 1681 et seq.

[17] Pub. L. No. 93-495, 88 Stat. 1521, 15 USC §§ 1691–1691e (1974).

[18] Pub. L. No. 94-239, 90 Stat. 251, 15 USC § 1691 (1976).

[19] 12 CFR §§ 201 et seq.

[20] Pub. L. No. 95-109, 91 Stat. 874, 15 USC §§ 1692 et seq. (1977).

[21] Pub. L. No. 95-630, 92 Stat. 3728, 15 USC §§ 1693 et seq. (1978).

[22] See further discussion of this distinction at ¶ 4.01[3][a] note 13.

[23] Where a card can be used for both an electronic funds transfer and a credit transaction, EFTA or TILA may be applicable. See generally Rohner, The Law of Truth in Lending ¶ 10.09[1] (Warren, Gorham & Lamont, Inc., 1984).

[24] See 12 USC § 85; Marquette Nat'l Bank v. First of Omaha Serv. Corp., 439 US 299 (1978); Tiffany v. Nat'l Bank of Mo., 85 US 409 (1873).

purchase of a consumer product, then national banks located in Minnesota can charge the same rate, regardless of what Minnesota law says the rate should be for bank loans for the purchase of the product. As an alternative, federal banks can charge one percent more than the federal discount rate charged by the Federal Reserve Bank to member banks in the Federal Reserve district in which the federal bank is located.[25]

Under the Federal Credit Union Act, federally chartered credit unions can charge 15 percent per year or a higher amount if allowed by the National Credit Union Administration (NCUA) Board.[26] As with national banks, which can ignore state usury law, federally chartered credit unions may charge the federal credit union rate regardless of state law.

In 1980, Congress usurped much of the states' control of interest rates for other lenders with the enactment of the Depository Institutions Deregulation and Monetary Control Act of 1980.[27] In part, this Act gives to most state-chartered creditors—state-chartered banks, credit unions, and savings and loans if these state-chartered institutions are federally insured—the right to charge the same rates as federally chartered banks even if state law provides otherwise.[28] In addition, the Act removes all interest-rate ceilings for some classes of transactions, such as certain real estate[29] and business transactions.[30] The states had the right to reassert their control over interest rates to the extent of the preemption by the 1980 law,[31] but only if the states acted by the end of 1982. Few decided to do so.[32] The National Bank Act, the Federal Credit Union Act, the Monetary Control Act, and remaining state controls are discussed in Chapter 3.

### [c] The Federal Trade Commission Act

**[i] General Authority.** Although several governmental agencies have authority to protect consumers from a variety of wrongdoings,[33] the federal agency considered to be the primary consumer protector is the FTC. The FTC

---

[25] Id.

[26] 12 USC § 1757(5)(A)(vi).

[27] Pub. L. No. 96-221, 94 Stat. 132, codified in several sections of Titles 12 and 15 of the U.S. Code (1980) (hereinafter cited as the Monetary Control Act).

[28] 12 USC §§ 1730g, 1831d.

[29] 12 USC §§ 1735f–1737.

[30] 12 USC § 86a.

[31] This right does not extend to the National Bank Act or Federal Credit Union Act preemptions.

[32] Only the following states passed legislation reasserting their right to control usury rates: Colorado, Hawaii, Iowa, Kansas, Massachusetts, Minnesota, Nebraska, Nevada, South Carolina, and South Dakota.

[33] See Rothschild & Carroll, Consumer Protection, Text and Materials § 2.01 (Anderson Publishing Co., 2d ed. 1977) for a compilation of such agencies and their authority.

was formed in 1914 with the passage of the FTC Act.[34] Although the FTC has been given authority over the years to enforce a wide spectrum of trade statutes,[35] the FTC's authority to enforce the FTC Act remains its major source of consumer protection power.

When first enacted in 1914, the FTC Act was aimed at controlling monopolies. Judicial enforcement of the Sherman Antitrust Act[36] was thought inadequate. To further the ends of antitrust policy, the FTC Act proscribed "unfair methods of competition."[37]

In *FTC v. Gratz*,[38] the U.S. Supreme Court limited "unfair methods of competition" to acts "previously" considered opposed to good morals or against public policy. This was popularly thought to limit the FTC's authority to practices already considered unfair in 1914. Then in *FTC v. Raladam*,[39] the U.S. Supreme Court held that the FTC could only regulate practices where competitors were harmed, not where only consumers were hurt by the practices.

In *FTC v. Keppel & Bros.*,[40] the U.S. Supreme Court reversed *Gratz*. In 1938, Congress overturned *Raladam* by enacting the Wheeler-Lea Amendments to the FTC Act.[41] The amendments gave the FTC the authority to prohibit "unfair and deceptive acts or practices" in addition to earlier authority with respect to unfair methods of competition.[42] The Wheeler-Lea Amendments are the main consumer protection mandate for the FTC.

In 1941, the U.S. Supreme Court again restricted the exercise of FTC authority in the case of *FTC v. Bunte Bros., Inc.*[43] The Court held that the FTC could regulate prohibited acts only "in interstate commerce." The Court also held that local activity was not covered by the FTC Act, stating that if the FTC was to have the authority to prohibit activity merely "affecting interstate commerce," Congress would have to provide a much clearer manifestation of intent. Congress did so in 1975 with the passage of the Magnuson-Moss Warranty and FTC Improvement Act,[44] which amended Section 5 of the FTC Act to prohibit "unfair methods of competition in or affecting commerce."[45]

---

[34] Ch. 311, 38 Stat. 717, 15 USC §§ 41 et seq. (1914).

[35] See, e.g., Wool Products Labeling Act of 1939, 54 Stat. 1128, 15 USC §§ 68–68j.

[36] Ch. 647, 26 Stat. 209, 15 USC §§ 1 et seq. (1890).

[37] 15 USC § 45.

[38] 253 US 421 (1920).

[39] 283 US 643 (1931).

[40] 291 US 304 (1934).

[41] Ch. 49, 52 Stat. 111, 15 USC §§ 41–58 (1938).

[42] Id. at § 45.

[43] 312 US 349 (1941).

[44] Pub. L. No. 93-637, 88 Stat. 2183 (codified in several sections of Title 15 of the U.S. Code) (hereafter cited as the 1975 FTC Improvement Act).

[45] 15 USC § 45.

**[ii] Trade Regulation Rules and Cease and Desist Orders.** The 1975 FTC Improvement Act made some other major changes with respect to FTC authority. After the original FTC Act was enacted, controversy long surrounded the way in which the FTC was to regulate prohibited acts. Initially, the FTC approached complaints only on a case-by-case basis. The FTC may still do so through its cease and desist procedure. Once a complaint is filed with the FTC alleging a violation of the FTC Act,[46] an investigation is conducted.[47] If the FTC staff concludes that a violation has occurred, the violator may be asked to enter into a consent to a cease and desist order.[48] Such consent applies only to prospective behavior and generally provides that the consent is not an admission of wrongdoing.[49]

If there is a refusal to enter into a consent order or if the FTC decides that the consent order is not in the public interest, the FTC may file a formal complaint and hold a public hearing before an administrative law judge of the FTC. This proceeding is subject to Sections 556 and 557 of Title 5 of the United States Code and Sections 3.11 to 3.55 of Title 16 of the Code of Federal Regulations. After hearing testimony, the administrative judge may issue a cease and desist order. Any party to the initial decision of the administrative judge may appeal to the full FTC.[50] Further appeal may be made to the U.S. court of appeals within any circuit where the method of competition or the act or practice in question was used or where such person resides or carries on his business.[51] Final appeal is to the U.S. Supreme Court upon certiorari.[52]

In order to more efficiently exercise its enforcement powers, the FTC once regularly issued industry guides. A list of these guides can be found in Subchapter B of Title 16 of the Code of Federal Regulations. Guides may relate to a practice common to many industries or to specific practices of a particular industry. The guides do not have force of law, although they obviously have been given some weight both by industry and by the courts.

In 1962, the FTC first showed its intent to enforce Section 5 of the FTC Act by issuing "trade regulation rules." The FTC amended its rules of practice specifically to provide for the issuance of such rules.[53] A violation of the rule was tantamount to a violation of the statutory provision from which the rule

---

[46] FTC investigations may be originated: (1) upon the request of the President, Congress, government agencies, or the Attorney General; (2) upon referrals by the courts; (3) upon complaint by members of the public; or (4) by the FTC upon its own initiative. 16 CFR § 2.1.

[47] Agency procedure for conducting an investigation is found at 16 CFR §§ 2.4–2.16.

[48] The public interest must be served by this process. 16 CFR § 2.31.

[49] 16 CFR § 2.32.

[50] 16 CFR § 3.52.

[51] 15 USC § 45(c).

[52] Id.

[53] 27 Fed. Reg. 4636, 4736, 4796 (1962).

derived. The FTC's power to issue such rules was upheld in *National Petroleum Refiners Association v. FTC.*[54]

The 1975 FTC Improvement Act amendments to the FTC Act confirm the FTC's authority to issue trade regulation rules that have the force of law. The amendments also specify the procedure for the issuance of these rules. The FTC must proceed in accordance with Section 553 of Title 5 of the U.S. Code. In addition, the FTC must (1) publish notice of any proposed rulemaking, stating with particularity the reason for the proposed rule; (2) allow interested persons to submit written data, views, and arguments, and make all such submissions publicly available; (3) provide for an informal hearing; and (4) promulgate, if appropriate, a final rule based on the rulemaking record together with a statement of basis and purpose. Judicial review of rules may be requested by interested persons, including consumers or consumer organizations, not later than sixty days after the promulgation of a rule. Appeal must be to the U.S. Court of Appeals for the District of Columbia Circuit or for the circuit in which the person resides or has his principal place of business. Final appeal is to the U.S. Supreme Court.[55]

The 1975 FTC Improvement Act amendments specifically provide that the FTC has no power to issue rules that regulate banks within the jurisdiction of the FRB, the Federal Deposit Insurance Corporation (FDIC), or the Office of the Comptroller of the Currency (OCC). Within sixty days after the FTC promulgates a trade regulation rule, the FRB must issue "substantially similar" regulations prohibiting acts or practices of banks that are substantially similar to those prohibited by the FTC rules. However, the FRB is not required to issue such rules if it finds that the acts or practices of banks are not unfair or deceptive or that the implementation of similar regulations with respect to banks would seriously conflict with essential monetary and payment systems policies of the FRB.[56]

In 1980, Congress passed another Improvement Act.[57] This legislation gave Congress the power by concurrent resolution of both houses to prohibit a rule promulgated by the FTC from taking effect.[58] This congressional veto power was exercised in May 1982 when the House and Senate knocked down a rule aimed at regulating the sales of used automobiles.[59] In July 1983, however,

---

[54] 482 F2d 672 (DC Cir. 1973).

[55] Pub. L. No. 93-637, 88 Stat. 2193, 15 USC § 57a (1975).

[56] 15 USC § 57a(f)(1).

[57] Pub. L. No. 96-252, 94 Stat. 374, 15 USC §§ 45 et seq. (1980).

[58] 15 USC § 57a-1 (Congress had to veto the rule within ninety days of submission of the rule to Congress. Id.).

[59] S. Con. Res. 60, 128 Cong. Rec. S5402 (daily ed. May 18, 1982), 128 Cong. Rec. H2882 (daily ed. May 26, 1982). The FTC rule, 46 Fed. Reg. 41327 (codified at 16 CFR § 455), was based on a similar Wisconsin rule, which in part required a seller of used cars to disclose certain known defects. Wis. Admin. Code, Ch. 24. The Consumer's Union challenged the authority of Congress to veto the FTC's rules by the resolution process. The Court of Appeals for the D.C. Circuit upheld the challenge, holding that Congress' veto power by resolution was unconstitutional. Consumers Union of U.S., Inc. v. FTC, 691 F2d 575 (1982), aff'd, 51 USLW 3935 (US 1983).

the concurrent resolution disapproving the used-car rule was held to be unconstitutional.[60] The 1980 FTC Improvement Act also limited the FTC's authority with respect to regulating children's advertising and the funeral industry.[61]

Recently, the Court of Appeals for the Ninth Circuit made a significant ruling with respect to the power of the FTC to proceed by cease and desist order rather than by issuing a trade regulation rule.[62] In the mid-1970s, the FTC began an investigation of certain practices by the Big three automobile finance companies and certain automobile dealers in failing to return surpluses after the disposition of repossessed automobiles. The FTC issued a formal complaint requesting that a cease and desist order be issued against a Ford dealer in Portland, Oregon. (The automobile finance companies independently agreed to a consent order in which they admitted no wrongdoing but agreed to cease the practices of concern to the FTC.) Although the administrative law judge held that the Oregon dealer's credit practices had violated Section 5 of the FTC Act, it was also held that the FTC had failed to establish that the dealer's acts were substantially injurious to its customers. Since neither the FTC staff nor the dealer was happy with the judge's order, both appealed to the full Commission. The FTC deleted the portion of the order favorable to the dealer and affirmed the administrative law judge's decision. The order directed the automobile dealer to cease its present credit practices and to adopt the FTC's view of proper practices under Oregon's version of Section 9-504 of the Uniform Commercial Code (UCC).[63]

The Ford dealer appealed to the Court of Appeals for the Ninth Circuit. The FTC's order was vacated because the court held that the FTC should have used its rulemaking authority rather than its cease and desist order authority to move against the practices it found objectionable. The court recognized that the choices among different procedural avenues in exercising agency authority generally belong to the administrative agency. In this instance, however, the court held that the FTC had exceeded its authority for two reasons. First, the court found that the FTC's order requiring the dealer to credit a debtor upon

---

[60] Process Gas Consumers Group v. Consumers Energy Council of Am., 51 USLW 3935 (US 1983). A lawsuit is presently pending challenging the rule. Miller Motor Car Corp. v. FTC, 2d Cir. No. 81-4144. The FTC has decided that the rule will become effective six months after judgment is entered in this lawsuit and has reopened proceedings for reexamination of certain of the rule's provisions. 48 Fed. Reg. 55,874 (1983).

[61] Pub. L. No. 96-252, §§ 11(c), 19, 94 Stat. 374, 15 USC § 57a(1980). The act placed a three-year moratorium on existing FTC authority to promulgate rules for *unfair* commercial advertising. The act also suspended an existing proceeding against children's advertising, which the FTC was pursuing based on its authority to prohibit "unfair" acts or practices. (The distinction between the FTC's authority to proceed against "unfair" acts or practices and the authority to proceed against "deceptive" acts or practices is explored at ¶ 2.01[2].) The Improvement Act specified which activities of funeral directors the FTC could prohibit by rule. The FTC was expressly prohibited from using any authorized funds to promulgate a rule "substantially similar" to its 1975 proposed rule concerning funeral directors.

[62] Ford Motor Co. v. FTC, 673 F2d 1008 (1981), cert. denied, 459 US 999 (1982).

[63] FTC Docket No. 9073, 27 UCC Rep. Serv. 1118 (1979).

disposition of repossessed collateral with the "best possible" value and forbidding the creditor from charging the debtor for overhead and profit was a change of existing law.[64] Second, the court stated that the FTC should have used its rulemaking authority instead of its cease and desist order because the FTC order would have "general application."[65] The FTC's petition for certiorari was denied.[66]

**[iii] Remedies and Penalties.** It is generally accepted that there is no private right of action for a violation of the FTC Act.[67] That is true at least under the federal Act itself. Later in this chapter there is a discussion of "little FTC acts," which often track the prohibitions of the federal Act against "unfair and deceptive" acts.[68] Several of these state acts do allow a private right of action. Generally such states look to FTC trade regulation rules and orders for guidance in determining what is unfair and deceptive under the state acts.[69]

Upon violation of FTC orders and trade regulation rules, the FTC may seek a variety of statutory remedies and penalties. The FTC may obtain preliminary injunctions against unfair or deceptive acts or practices that are unfair or deceptive to consumers.[70] The FTC may bring an action for a civil penalty of up to $10,000 for each violation against any person who is the subject of a cease and desist order.[71] The FTC may also recover a penalty against persons who are not directly covered by an order if they have actual knowledge that acts or practices are unlawful under an existing order against a third party.[72] For

---

[64] Ford Motor Co. v. FTC, 673 F2d 1008 (1981), cert. denied, 459 US 999 (1982). Why this was a change from existing law was not clear from the court's opinion. The court seemed to say that existing law was otherwise because all dealers in the trade used the practice the FTC was opposing and because the FTC could find no cases supporting its view. The court seemed unconcerned with the possibility that a whole trade could engage in an unfair and deceptive practice that had not yet been declared illegal in a previously reported case.

[65] It is unclear whether the court intends the next logical step to be taken from its ruling–the FTC must attack via its rulemaking authority rather than by its cease and desist order authority whenever any practice is used by all or many in a trade. In a dissenting opinion to a denial of a request for a rehearing en banc, Ford Motor Co. v. FTC, 673 F2d 1008 (1982), cert. denied, 459 US 999 (1982). Judge Reinhardt expressed a serious concern that the court's double guessing of the FTC's decision to pursue the cease and desist route was in conflict with the U.S. Supreme Court's decision in NLRB v. Bell Aerospace Co., 416 US 267, 294 (1974).

[66] Ford Motor Co. v. FTC, 673 F2d 1008 (1982), cert. denied, 459 US 999 (1982).

[67] See, e.g., Summey v. Ford Motor Credit Co., 573 F2d 1306 (4th Cir. 1978); Alfred Dunhill Ltd. v. Interstate Cigar Co., 499 F2d 232 (2d Cir. 1974); Carlson v. Coca-Cola Co., 483 F2d 279 (9th Cir. 1973). Contra, Guernsey v. Rich Plan of the Midwest, 408 F. Supp. 582, 586–589 (ND Ind. 1976).

[68] See infra ¶ 1.03[3][b].

[69] Id.

[70] 15 USC § 53.

[71] 15 USC § 45(m)(1)(B).

[72] Id.

example, assume the FTC order discussed above[73] concerning surpluses kept after the disposition of repossessed automobiles by automobile dealers had not been vacated by the Ninth Circuit. Assume further that the FTC notified all dealers that it was unlawful to engage in any practice that is the subject of the order against the Oregon automobile dealer. Subsequent use of the prohibited practice by any dealer receiving the FTC notice would make the dealer potentially subject to the $10,000 penalty.[74]

The FTC also may recover a maximum $10,000 penalty for the violation of trade regulation rules. This is true only if the wrongdoer has "actual knowledge or knowledge fairly implied on the basis of objective circumstances that such act is unfair or deceptive and is prohibited by such rule."[75]

In addition to the above remedies and penalties, on occasion the FTC may seek redress for injured parties. The FTC also may seek redress for a violation of a trade regulation rule.[76] Redress also may be based on a cease and desist order, but only from one against whom the order was issued and only if a reasonable person would have known under the circumstances that the practice was "dishonest or fraudulent."[77]

The question of what specifically constitutes an unfair act or practice is discussed in Chapter 2.[78]

## [3] State Statutes

### [a] Consumer Credit Statutes

Most state consumer law is designed to regulate consumer credit transactions. The earliest state credit laws were usury laws—laws structured to control the maximum rate of charge that a creditor could levy to defer payment. The first usury laws generally were applicable to all transactions, including consumer transactions. These early usury laws provided for low rates. Almost from the beginning, however, exceptions to the general usury rates were recognized.

The courts originally excluded most sales credit when a seller structured a credit sale as a "time-price sale." That is, if the customer paid over a period of time, the retailer could charge a higher time price than the price normally charged if the customer paid for his merchandise in cash at the time of sale. The difference between the normal cash price and the time price, the "time-price differential," generally was not considered an interest or finance charge and, therefore, was not controlled by usury statutes.[79]

---

[73] See supra ¶ 1.03[2][c][ii].

[74] The Ninth Circuit noted that the FTC apparently had planned such notices. Ford Motor Co. v. FTC, 673 F2d 1008, 1010 (1981), cert. denied, 459 US 999 (1982).

[75] 15 USC § 45(m)(1)(A).

[76] 15 USC § 57b.

[77] Id.

[78] See ¶ 2.01.

[79] For an analysis of the time-price dictrine, see State (Wisconsin) v. J.C. Penney Co., 48 Wis. 2d 125, 179 NW2d 641 (1970).

Another early exception to the general usury statutes was for loans to corporations or other legal organizations. Generally this exception was effected through statutes prohibiting such organizations from using the defense of usury.[80]

Over the years the state legislatures were asked to carve out other statutory exceptions from the usury laws. Thus there developed small-loan laws, installment loan laws, credit card laws, and other special legislation originally designed to allow certain types of creditors in certain classes of transactions to avoid the effect of the general usury statutes. Such legislation ultimately served as the depository of the first state legislation to provide for protections beyond controls on interest rates. In most states consumer credit regulation is still scattered among a variety of statutes, including these initial interest-rate statutes. Approximately one quarter of the states have attempted to consolidate into one comprehensive act most of their respective consumer credit legislation.

The following discussion first presents a directory of the types of legislation that one is likely to find in a state with the scattered approach to consumer credit regulation. It then discusses the nature of the comprehensive type of consumer credit statutes. There are no specific examples of particular legislation under either the scattered or comprehensive statutes at this point; that is the subject of the next three chapters, in which types of state legislative controls for various practices are discussed.

**[i] "Scattered" Statutes (e.g., Retail Installment Sales Acts).** The scattered approach to consumer credit regulation prevalent in most states stems from the checkered development of consumer credit granting. During the last century consumer credit was not granted by organized financial institutions. Legal usury rates were too low to attract organized lenders. Consumers were forced to obtain credit from lenders who charged rates far higher than those permitted by usury statutes. In order to curb this loan-sharking, the Russell Sage Foundation proposed that the states adopt a "small-loan law." The proposed law authorized a new class of lender, small-loan companies, to loan up to $300 at a much higher rate than the general usury rate but below that of the loan sharks.[81]

Most states have adopted small-loan statutes that were originally based on the Russell Sage Foundation's proposal. These statutes primarily provide a licensing structure for small-loan companies, limit the amount these companies may loan, and set maximum interest rates at a level substantially above that of most states' general usury rate.[82] Finance companies, as the small-loan compa-

---

[80] See, e.g., Del. Code Ann. tit. 6, § 2306. For a collection of state consumer credit laws see Consumer Cred. Guide (CCH). The set contains five volumes. The first volume contains a chart comparing various interest-rate statutes and other statutes, such as those that regulate maximum time limits, amounts, and licensing requirements. Volumes 2 through 4 contain a collection of the complete text of state statutes. Volume 5 contains new cases and recent developments.

[81] B. Curran, Trends in Consumer Credit Legislation 2 (U.S. Government Printing Office 1965).

[82] Id. at 16.

nies are now more commonly called, still primarily engage in consumer lending under such statutes. Over the years in states that have retained the scattered approach to consumer credit regulation, when the state legislature wished to provide consumer protection provisions for consumers who borrowed from finance companies, such provisions generally have been added to the small-loan acts. The protections added often have been in the form of required disclosures of the terms of the transaction. Small-loan acts also have been amended over the years to allow finance companies to issue loans significantly larger than those originally proposed.[83]

Today, most of the dollar volume of consumer lending is not extended by finance companies. Instead, banks, credit unions, and savings and loans–depository institutions–do most of the consumer lending.[84] The regulation of these institutions is a matter primarily for the states if the institution is state-chartered; federally chartered depository institutions are primarily regulated by the federal government.[85]

The major purpose of state regulation of depository institutions is to protect depositors.[86] Every state has general banking, credit union, and savings and loan laws with which each type of lender must comply. In addition, to provide an exemption from the general usury rates that would otherwise apply in consumer lending, most states with a scattered approach to consumer credit regulation also have other statutes specifically designed to regulate consumer lending by depository institutions.

Industrial loan laws are an example. Industrial banks, first organized in 1910, were designed to enter the consumer lending market. They circumvented the low usury rate limitations by calculating the finance charge by a discount method and by requiring each borrower to become a depositor. Over the years such industrial loans were authorized by statute in nearly half the states. Currently, in most states with industrial loan laws a lender may be organized as a commercial bank or other institution and still be authorized to charge rates permitted in the industrial loan laws. The institutions licensed to grant industrial loans as industrial lenders may be called "industrial loan companies," "industrial loan and thrift companies," "loan and investment companies," or "Morris Plan banks." Very little consumer protection has found its way into such laws. Those that exist do so almost exclusively to provide for interest-rate legislation.[87]

---

[83] See, e.g., Ariz. Rev. Stat. Ann. § 6-601 ($10,000).

[84] At the end of 1981, consumer installment credit totalled $333.4 billion. Of that amount, 44.8 percent was held by commercial banks, 26.9 percent by finance companies, 13.8 percent by credit unions, and 3.5 percent by savings and loans. National Consumer Finance Association Facts Year Book 41 (American Bar Foundation 1981).

[85] The interrelationship of the federal and state regulatory schemes, briefly discussed at supra ¶ 1.03[2][b], is further explored at ¶ 3.01 in the discussion on usury rates.

[86] National Commission on Consumer Finance, Consumer Credit in the United States 46 (U.S. Government Printing Office 1972).

[87] B. Curran, Trends in Consumer Credit Legislation 52–53, 59 (U.S. Government Printing Office 1965).

Commercial banks became heavily involved in consumer lending after the Depression. To avoid the general usury statutes, most states passed installment loan laws, which authorized commercial banks to charge a rate of interest higher than the rate permitted by the general usury statutes. Several states expanded their installment loan laws to authorize installment loans by both industrial and commercial banks. Consumer protection is minimal in installment loan laws. In states without special installment loan laws, state-chartered banks may make consumer loans solely under the general banking and usury laws or industrial loan laws.[88]

Credit unions engage heavily in consumer lending. The primary focus of state laws regulating consumer loans by credit unions, like commercial banks, is to establish a maximum rate of finance charge that is higher than the general usury rate.[89] Consumer protection provisions are rare. In some states there are no special consumer credit laws applicable to credit unions. In such states the credit union is generally subject only to the general usury statute, or, in some states, to installment loan laws.[90]

Unlike laws that regulate loans by other depository institutions, consumer lending laws for savings and loan associations are primarily limited to authorizing such loans. Consumer protection provisions are rarely found in savings and loan laws.[91] The maximum rate of finance charge for a savings and loan association in a scattered-approach state is usually the same as the rate under the general usury statute. In a few states, savings and loans are authorized to lend under installment loan laws.[92]

In addition to general usury, industrial loan, installment loan, general banking, credit union, and savings and loan laws, some states have other specific statutes regulating loans; for example, loans pursuant to bank-issued credit cards[93] or check-credit plans.[94] Once again, the primary function of such statutes is to allow a higher rate of finance charge than would otherwise be allowed by the general usury statute.

Regulation of retail sellers who sell goods pursuant to a consumer credit transaction has a more recent history than the regulation of lenders. Until relatively recently, all aspects of retail consumer credit sales were unregulated. Because of the long-accepted "time-price" doctrine described above,[95] even the charge for credit was generally assumed to be excluded from the coverage of the states' general usury statutes. In 1935, Indiana passed the first retail install-

---

[88] Id. at 66.

[89] Id. at 47.

[90] See, e.g., Tex. Rev. Civ. Stat. Ann. art. 5069-4.01(1).

[91] B. Curran, Trends in Consumer Credit Legislation 60–61 (U.S. Government Printing Office 1965).

[92] See, e.g., Tex. Rev. Civ. Stat. Ann. art. 5069–4.01(1).

[93] See, e.g., Ohio Rev. Code Ann. § 1107.27.

[94] See, e.g., N.J. Stat. Ann. §§ 17:9A-59.6–17:9A-59.8.

[95] See supra ¶ 1.03[3][a].

ment sales act,[96] and now most states with the scattered approach to consumer credit regulation have their own similar versions of this legislation. Initially, consumer protection in such statutes consisted almost exclusively of disclosure requirements on the theory that informed consumers could not be hurt.[97] Although disclosure remains the primary emphasis, most modern retail installment sales acts also prohibit certain abusive practices and limit the maximum rates of finance charge.[98]

Some states have "all goods" retail installment acts that cover all credit sales of consumer goods.[99] Other states have one act for all consumer credit sales of goods other than motor vehicles and another for the credit sale of motor vehicles.[100] The two types of statutes may vary substantially with respect to interest rates and the amount and type of consumer protection law they contain.

In addition to the types of statutes mentioned above, most states with the scattered approach also have separate statutes that regulate consumer credit insurance[101] and insurance premium financing.[102] The first type of statute is directed at controlling the terms and cost of insurance sold to insure the repayment of a credit obligation when the insured dies or is unable to pay the credit obligation because of an accident or illness. Insurance premium financing statutes regulate the credit transaction that arises when an insured wishes to pay insurance premiums in installments through a credit plan.

**[ii] "Comprehensive" Codes (e.g., the Uniform Consumer Credit Code).** Obviously, the scattered approach leads to some confusion, even for those who are used to dealing with consumer credit matters on a regular basis. The problems are compounded for one who must know the credit laws in more than one state because the credit laws in states with the scattered approach differ substantially from state to state. Further, the existence of separate statutes within one state for various types of credit grantors often leads to differing substantive provisions with respect to essentially identical transactions.[103]

Why not create a uniform state law for consumer credit similar to the uniform law for commercial transactions—the UCC? This occurred to the National

---

[96] B. Curran, Trends in Consumer Credit Legislation 9 n.7 (U.S. Government Printing Office 1965).

[97] See Rothschild, & Carroll Consumer Protection: Text and Materials § 1903, at 692 (Anderson Publishing Co., 2d ed. 1977).

[98] See, e.g., Cal. Civ. Code §§ 1807.3 (limiting the use of "balloon payments," payments that are substantially larger than other periodic payments) and 1805.1 (setting interest-rate ceilings in retail installment sales).

[99] See, e.g., Haw. Rev. Stat. §§ 476-1–476-38.

[100] See, e.g., Ariz. Rev. Stat. Ann. §§ 44-281–44-295, 44-6001–44-6006.

[101] See, e.g., Iowa Code Ann. § 509.1(3).

[102] See, e.g., Mich. Stat. Ann. §§ 500.1501–500-1514.

[103] The material on usury at ¶ 3.01 provides some assistance in tracking through statutes in a state with the scattered approach.

Commissioners of Uniform State Laws, who, in 1968, proposed the Uniform Consumer Credit Code (UCCC) for adoption in every state. The 1968 UCCC was revised several times until, in 1974, the final draft was adopted by the National Commissioners.

One of the underlying purposes of the UCCC is "to simplify [and] clarify" consumer credit laws.[104] By consolidating all of a state's consumer credit law into one statute, the UCCC does indeed simplify an enacting state's consumer credit statutes. However, the 1968 version of the UCCC gained substantial acceptance in only six states–Colorado, Idaho, Indiana, Oklahoma, Utah, and Wyoming.[105] Kansas adopted a later version,[106] and the 1974 UCCC has been adopted in only one state–Idaho.[107]

Some states have adopted comprehensive codes other than the UCCC. Wisconsin adopted a major alternative to the 1968 UCCC, the Wisconsin Consumer Act,[108] which gave one major reason for the 1974 redraft of the original UCCC.[109] The Wisconsin act drew in part from the 1968 UCCC and the National Consumer Act.[110] However, since the Wisconsin Consumer Act was the first to be extensively negotiated by both consumer and creditor advocates, the Wisconsin act also presented new statutory approaches. Other state comprehensive codes–those of Iowa, Louisiana, Maine, South Carolina, and West Virginia[111]–are derived primarily from the 1968 UCCC. However, some provisions contained in the 1974 UCCC and its preliminary drafts as well as the National Consumer Act and the Wisconsin Consumer Act have influenced the language of such acts.

From the above it is evident that comprehensive codes have not met with wide acceptance. There are several reasons for this lack of enthusiasm. The UCCC, for example, has regularly met with strong consumer opposition. Creditor groups that favored the passage of the UCCC stopped pushing for its enactment in the late 1970s. Also, comprehensive codes traditionally have been unpopular with state legislators; it has been easier, and politically safer, for state legislatures to deal with consumer credit on a piecemeal basis.

---

[104] Uniform Consumer Credit Code, Prefatory Note (1968 version).

[105] See Colo. Rev. Stat. §§ 5-1-101–5-9-103; Idaho Code §§ 28-31-101 et seq. (since replaced by Idaho Code § 28-41-101 et seq. (1983)); Ind. Code Ann. 24-4.5-1-101–24-4.6-202; Okla. Stat. Ann. tit. 14A, §§ 1-101–9-103; Utah Code Ann. §§ 70B-1-101–70B-9-103; Wyo. Stat. §§ 40-14-101–40-14-702.

[106] Kan. Stat. Ann. §§ 16a-1-101–16a-9-102.

[107] Idaho Code §§ 28-41-101 et seq. (the 1968 version was repealed).

[108] Wis. Stat. Ann. §§ 421.101–428.103.

[109] UCCC § 1.102(2) (1974 version).

[110] The National Consumer Act was a proposed consumer credit code prepared by the National Consumer Law Center. The proposal was never enacted in any state.

[111] Iowa Code Ann. §§ 537.1101–537.7103; La. Rev. Stat. Ann. §§ 9:3510–9:3571; Maine Consumer Credit Code, Me. Rev. Stat. Ann. tit. 9A, §§ 1.101–6-415; S.C. Code §§ 37-1-101–37-10-106; W. Va. Code Ann. §§ 46A-1-101–46A-8-102.

### [b] Consumer Protection Statutes or "Little FTC Acts"

Forty-nine states and the District of Columbia have laws based on the FTC Act's prohibition against deceptive and unfair acts and practices.[112] Alabama is the exception.[113] Such statutes are commonly called "consumer protection statutes" or "little FTC acts." All such statutes prohibit deceptive or misleading acts or practices. Twenty-six jurisdictions also prohibit "unfair" practices in their little FTC acts.[114] Eleven jurisdictions also proscribe "unconscionable" acts in their version of these acts.[115] In addition to the incorporation of broad language that defines prohibited acts or practices, several states itemize various prohibited acts or practices.[116]

The scope of little FTC acts has been the subject of considerable dispute. These acts generally have specific provisions relating to their scope; generally, the statutes cover only the sale of goods or services to a consumer.[117] In the little FTC acts, however, "consumer" is generally used in a broad sense that includes anyone who buys goods or services from the alleged wrongdoer, not just someone who buys for a personal, family, or household purpose. In this interpretation of "consumer," little FTC acts differ from consumer credit laws. Generally, publishers, printers, and broadcasters of deceptive advertising are not liable if they act in good faith.[118] Most jurisdictions exclude practices allowed by or regulated by other state agencies.[119] Some statutes exclude coverage of entire businesses, such as utilities or insurance companies.[120]

---

[112] Most little FTC acts were passed by the states in the 1960s and 1970s. In fact, the first state statutes against deceptive activity were the so-called "Printer's Ink Statutes." These statutes were roughly modeled after a proposal published in 1911 in the trade journal *Printer's Ink*. The statutes adopted prohibited "untrue, deceptive, or misleading" advertising and made the violation of the statute a misdemeanor. Note, "Regulation of Advertising," 56 Colum. L. Rev. 1018, 1058 (1958). The statutes were rarely enforced probably because the sanction was criminal, requiring a greater burden of proof, and because of the apparent reluctance to enforce white-collar crimes.

[113] The footnotes of this section contain a number of lists by jurisdiction of types of substantive provisions. The lists are taken from the chart at page 122 of Sheldon & Zweibel, Survey of Consumer Fraud Law (National Institute of Law Enforcement and Criminal Justice 1978). Obviously, each jurisdiction's law should be consulted.

[114] California, Connecticut, Florida, Georgia, Hawaii, Idaho, Illinois, Kentucky, Louisiana, Maine, Maryland, Massachusetts, Mississippi, Montana, New Hampshire, New Mexico, North Carolina, Oregon, Pennsylvania, Rhode Island, South Carolina, Tennessee, Vermont, Washington, West Virginia, and Wisconsin. See, e.g., Mass. Ann. Laws ch. 93A, § 2. See supra ¶ 1.03[3][b] note 113.

[115] Alaska, District of Columbia, Kansas, Michigan, Nebraska, New Jersey, New Mexico, Ohio, Texas, Utah, and West Virginia. See infra ¶ 1.03[3][b] note 120.

[116] See, e.g., Del. Code Ann. tit. 6, § 2532.

[117] See, e.g., Ill. Ann. Stat. ch. 121 1/2, ¶ 9261, § 1(e).

[118] See, e.g., Colo. Rev. Stat. § 6-1-106.

[119] Id.

[120] See, e.g., Wash. Rev. Code Ann. § 19.86.170.

Problems arise concerning the scope of these exemptions and the coverage of transactions apparently never contemplated by the state legislature. There are a number of cases that have attempted to establish whether the lease of real property or of personalty, sales of insurance, or the providing of credit are covered. However, since such cases are scattered among a few jurisdictions and because state courts do not seem to give much weight to state court decisions from other jurisdictions concerning the scope of their respective statutes, it is deceptive to talk in terms of majority opinions.

The discussion of the FTC Act[121] noted that there is no private right of action under the FTC Act. There is such a right of action, however, under forty-three of the little FTC acts.[122] Since most states give great weight to FTC cease and desist orders and trade regulation rules, the use of a state act's private right of action, along with a substantive finding of deception or unfairness by the FTC in such an action, in effect may give the consumer counsel the private right of action that would otherwise be missing.

All statutes that provide for individual action allow actual damages. About one third of the jurisdictions that allow the private right of action also allow multiple damages.[123] Costs and attorney fees are generally provided.[124] Sixteen jurisdictions specifically authorize class actions.[125]

The public enforcement of most little FTC acts is by a state's attorney general. The enforcing official is generally allowed strong investigatory powers, including the right to subpoena business records and use cease and desist powers, and the power to seek injunctive relief against activity in violation of the state statute.

All but two of the acts provide that the enforcing official may seek restitution for wronged parties.[126] Thirty jurisdictions also provide that the enforcement official may seek civil penalties.[127]

---

[121] See supra ¶ 1.03[2][c].

[122] See, e.g., Mo. Ann. Stat. § 407.025. Arkansas, Iowa, Nevada, New Mexico, New York, North Dakota, and Oklahoma are the exceptions.

[123] Alaska, Delaware, District of Columbia, Georgia, Hawaii, Louisiana, Massachusetts, Montana, New Jersey, North Carolina, Pennsylvania, South Carolina, Tennessee, Texas, Vermont, Washington, and Wisconsin. See, e.g., D.C. Code Ann. § 28-3905(K). See supra ¶ 1.03[3][b] note 120.

[124] See, e.g., Va. Code § 59.1-204.

[125] Alaska, California, Connecticut, Indiana, Kansas, Massachusetts, Michigan, Missouri, New Hampshire, New Jersey, Ohio, Oregon, Rhode Island, Texas, Utah, and Wyoming. See, e.g., Cal. Civ. Code § 1781.

[126] The two exceptions are Indiana and West Virginia. See, e.g., Tenn. Code Ann. § 47-18-108(b).

[127] Alaska, Arizona, California, Connecticut, District of Columbia, Georgia, Hawaii, Illinois, Kansas, Kentucky, Maryland, Michigan, Minnesota, Mississippi, Montana, Nebraska, Nevada, New Hampshire, New Jersey, New Mexico, New York, Oregon, Pennsylvania, South Carolina, South Dakota, Texas, Vermont, Virginia, Washington, and West Virginia. See, e.g., Md. Com. Law Code Ann. § 13-410. See supra ¶ 1.03[3][b] note 113.

# 2

# Problems Arising Before or at the Formation of the Debt

## ¶ 2.01 MISLEADING REPRESENTATIONS IN SOLICITING THE OBLIGATION

### [1] Common-Law Misrepresentation

#### [a] Misrepresentation as Grounds for Avoiding the Contractual Obligation

Misrepresentation in the inducement of a contract generally makes the contract voidable.[1] The wronged party may seek to disaffirm the contract and raise the issue of misrepresentation as a defense for nonperformance of a con-

---

[1] For purposes of determining the effect of misrepresentation on the formation of a contract, the courts have recognized two types of misrepresentation. The most common type is "fraud in the inducement." The other type, rarely found, is "fraud in the factum." Fraud in the inducement is misrepresentation in the bargaining process that fraudulently induces a party to enter into an agreement. An example would be if the seller of an automobile represented it as having been driven only 30,000 miles when in fact the auto had been driven 130,000 miles. Such fraud makes a contract voidable, requiring an affirmative act of avoidance such as rescission. Fraud in the factum exists if there was never a contract because such fraud makes the contract void from its inception. No affirmative act of avoidance is necessary. An example of fraud in the factum is a vendor who convinces a customer to sign a blank form represented as a registration for a gift when in fact the form is an agreement to purchase. Garrett v. Holmes Tuttle Broadway Ford, 5 Ariz. App. 388, 427 P2d 369 (1967). For further discussion of the difference between these two types of misrepresentation, see Federal Deposit Ins. Corp. v. Willis, 497 F. Supp. 272 (SD Ga. 1980); U.S. v. Idlewild Pharmacy, Inc., 308 F. Supp. 19 (ED Va. 1969). The discussion in the text assumes fraud in the inducement.

tractual obligation—for example, to defend nonpayment. Alternatively, the wronged party may seek to avoid the contract by bringing an affirmative action for rescission of the contract. If rescission is allowed, the wronged party may seek restitution. If the plaintiff gave the defendant items of personalty or realty, the property will be returned in kind, if possible.[2] If the plaintiff parted with money, a money judgment for that amount will be the measure of restitution.[3] Some courts also have allowed incidental or consequential damages.[4] Other equitable relief, such as cancelling commercial paper representing the recipient's obligation, also may be granted.[5] In return, the plaintiff who is seeking rescission must return in kind any item of personalty or realty received from the defendant or pay a money judgment in an equivalent amount.[6]

To avoid a contract because of misrepresentation, the debtor must be able to prove the following:

(1) The creditor made an assertion of an existing fact;
(2) The assertion was material or fraudulent;
(3) The debtor justifiably relied on the statement in entering into the contract; and
(4) The debtor suffered because of this reliance.[7]

The first requirement for avoiding a contract is met when a person makes an oral or written statement about a past event or present circumstance. For example, a seller of an encyclopedia might state that his product was "compiled by top experts in the field," although it was written by three student employees who learned as they wrote. The necessary assertion also may take the form of conduct; for example, a seller of goods may actively conceal a known defect from the buyer.[8] Simple nondisclosure also may suffice to meet the first contract avoidance requirement. Generally, however, courts have found simple nondisclosure to result in misrepresentation only when:

---

The distinction between fraud in the inducement and fraud in the factum is generally relevant only when the court tries to determine whether or not a good faith third-party holder of the obligation should collect. Fraud in the factum is a defense against a holder in due course of a negotiable instrument, but fraud in the inducement standing alone is not. See UCC § 3-305(2)(b) and Official Comment 6.

[2] See, e.g., Hart Bros. Music Co. v. Wood, 14 Utah 2d 366, 384 P2d 591 (1963).

[3] See, e.g., Grissom v. Moran, 154 Ind. App. 419, 292 NE2d 627 (1973) (vendor required to return down payment).

[4] Id. at 629.

[5] See, e.g., Beiter v. Decatur Fed. Sav. & Loan Ass'n, 222 Ga. 516, 150 SE2d 687 (1966) (promissory note given by plaintiff was cancelled).

[6] See, e.g., Gage v. Langford, 615 SW2d 934 (Tex. Civ. App. 1981).

[7] See, e.g., Gardner v. Meiling, 280 Ore. 665, 572 P2d 1012 (1977).

[8] See, e.g., Greene v. Gibraltar Mortgage Inv. Corp., 488 F. Supp. 177 (DDC 1980).

(1) There is a relation of trust and confidence between Party *A* and Party *B* that entitles one of them to a disclosure;[9]

(2) Party *A* has made an assertion and later learns it is false;[10] or

(3) Party *A* knows that Party *B* is laboring under a misconception that Party *A* has not caused.

This third scenario can cause problems. For example, assume a prospective buyer of a tract of forested land, who is confident in his knowledge of forestry, thoroughly inspects the tract, which is a stand of bull pine. In this instance, is the seller guilty of misrepresentation if he knows that the buyer is willing to purchase the tract based on the wrong conclusion that the timber is valuable cedar? Under the Restatement (Second) of Contracts, this type of nondisclosure would be misrepresentation only if the nondisclosure "amounts to a failure to act in good faith and in accordance with reasonable standards of fair dealing."[11]

Note that the second requirement for avoiding a contract because of misrepresentation is stated in the alternative; either a material *or* a fraudulent assertion meets the requirement.[12] The assertion is material if it is likely to induce a reasonable person to make the contract.[13] If the assertion would not have so induced a reasonable person, then the assertion is material if the maker of the assertion knew that the assertion would induce the particular recipient to enter the contract.[14] The assertion is fraudulent if it is a consciously false statement (i.e., if there is scienter) and is intended to mislead.[15] Scienter is also a requirement for the tort of intentional misrepresentation.[16]

---

[9] See e.g., Frowen v. Blank, 493 Pa. 137, 425 A2d 412 (981) (necessary relationship was found when defendant was neighbor and close social friend of plaintiff, who was eighty-six years old, feeble, and had little business knowledge).

[10] See, e.g., Strand v. Librascope, Inc., 197 F. Supp. 743 (ED Mich. 1961) (seller told buyer that "noise" in computer components was due to buyer's circuits; later, after only 5 percent of the requisite deliveries had been made, seller learned noise problems were caused by seller's components; not to relay this information to buyer was misrepresentation.)

[11] Restatement (Second) of Contracts § 161(b); see also Obde v. Schlemeyer, 56 Wash. 2d 449, 353 P2d 672, 675 (1960) (vendor failed to act in good faith when he failed to inform real estate purchaser of hidden termites). But see Swinton v. Whitinsville Sav. Bank, 311 Mass. 677, 42 NE2d 808 (1942) (finding no misrepresentation for failure to disclose termites).

[12] Despite the general statement of the requirement in the alternative, a nonmaterial assertion, even if fraudulent, is not likely to be held grounds for rescission. See Farnsworth, Contracts § 4.12, at 244 (Little, Brown 1982).

[13] See, e.g., Cousineau v. Walker, 613 P2d 608 (Alaska 1980).

[14] Brown v. Search, 131 Wis. 109, 111 NW 10 (1907) (father of college student was told that college had enrolled several of child's classmates, which was untrue; misrepresentation was considered material to father because he had made it known that the presence of child's classmates was important).

[15] See, e.g., Poneleit v. Reksmad, 346 So. 2d 615 (Fla. Dist. Ct. App. 1977).

[16] See infra ¶ 2.01[2].

With respect to the justifiable-reliance requirement for avoiding a contract, it is not necessary to show that the assertion was the *primary* factor in assent, only that it was a *substantial* factor.[17] The more material an assertion, the easier it is to show that the assertion was a substantial factor in the formulation of the assent necessary for the formation of an enforceable contract. Evidence that the buyer has more expertise than the party who makes a misrepresentation tends to show no reliance.[18] For example, the more experienced a buyer is about used lawn mowers, the less he will be influenced by a seller's statement, "Now here is a lawn mower that was only used to cut artificial turf." Of course, showing that the buyer has mowed a great number of yards is not the same as showing that he is experienced with lawn mowers. Also, even if the buyer has expertise, it may not mean that he does not rely on the seller's statement. The buyer may feel that the seller is in a better position to know about the truth of his assertion. Showing that a buyer made his own inspection or evaluation of the subject matter of the assertion may lead a court to find that the buyer relied more on the inspection than the seller's assertion.[19] Of course, if the buyer's experience or the nature of the defect is such that a reasonable inspection by the buyer would not disclose the defect, then the fact that there was an inspection does not prohibit a finding of reliance.[20] If a reasonable person would think that the statement by the maker was mere "opinion," the buyer does not justifiably rely on the assertion. Showing that a statement is mere opinion depends on a variety of factors, including the specificity of the assertion.[21] Another important factor is the nature of the relationship between the maker of the statement and the buyer.[22]

### [b] Suing in Tort

Rather than seeking to disaffirm a contract because of misrepresentation, the wronged party instead may bring an affirmative action in tort for intentional misrepresentation or deceit. This action represents an affirmance of the contract and a request for damages for the tort. The plaintiff must establish the existence of essentially the same criteria as those that must exist to avoid a contract because of misrepresentation. The one important distinction is that

---

[17] See, e.g., Pacific Maxon, Inc. v. Wilson, 96 Nev. 867, 619 P2d 816 (1980).

[18] See, e.g., Puget Sound Nat'l Bank v. McMahon, 53 Wash. 2d 51, 330 P2d 559 (1958) (plaintiff was a sophisticated real estate investor alleging that the defendant had misrepresented the gross income of real property sold).

[19] See, e.g., Spudnuts v. Lane, 131 Ariz. 424, 641 P2d 912 (1982).

[20] See, e.g., Fisher v. Mr. Harold's Hair Lab, Inc., 215 Kan. 515, 527 P2d 1026 (1974).

[21] See, e.g., Papile v. Robinson, 4 Conn. Cir. Ct. 307, 231 A2d 91 (1967) ("adequate" was opinion); Ryan v. Collins, 496 SW2d 205 (Tex. Civ. App. 1973) ("unlimited possibilities" was opinion). But see Corona v. Esposito, 4 Conn. Cir. Ct. 296, 230 A2d 624 (1966) ("in good condition" was not opinion).

[22] See, e.g., Hassman v. First State Bank, 183 Minn. 453, 236 NW 921 (1931) (defendant was "financial adviser" making a statement that might have been mere opinion, on which plaintiff could justifiably rely).

the tort of intentional misrepresentation requires that the assertion be proved fraudulent; a mere "material" misrepresentation is not sufficient.[23] To meet this "fraudulent" test, it must be shown that (1) the assertion was consciously false (a showing of scienter) and (2) there was an intent to induce the plaintiff's reliance on the misrepresentation. To show scienter, the plaintiff must show either that the defendant knew that the assertion was false[24] or recklessly disregarded its truth.[25]

Some jurisdictions also recognize the tort of negligent misrepresentation.[26] As with the tort of intentional misrepresentation, the requirements are essentially the same as those that must exist to avoid a contract because of misrepresentation. Fraudulent intent is not necessary. For the tort of negligent misrepresentation, however, it first is necessary to establish a duty of reasonable care to the plaintiff and then to prove that the duty was not met because of negligence. The duty can be established by showing the existence of a fiduciary duty or by establishing that a party has taken it upon itself to offer financial advice in a transaction in which it has a financial interest.

Where the plaintiff has successfully established the tort of intentional misrepresentation, actual damages generally are measured by the "benefit-of-the-bargain" theory.[27] For example, assume the person proving intentional misrepresentation had paid $3,000 for an easement that was intentionally misrepresented as being worth $5,000. In fact, the easement is worth only $2,000. Under the benefit-of-the-bargain theory, the measure of damages is $3,000 ($5,000 less $2,000); that is, the difference between the actual value of the misrepresented easement and the value it would have had were it truthfully represented. This measure of actual damages is the same as actual damages for breach of warranty.[28] A minority of courts measure actual damages for intentional misrepresentation by the "reliance" theory, sometimes called the out-of-pocket rule.[29] Under the out-of-pocket theory, damages in the hypothetical

---

[23] See, e.g., In re Alodex Corp. Sec. Litigation, 533 F2d 372 (8th Cir. 1976); Institute for Professional Dev. v. Regis College, 536 F. Supp. 632 (D. Colo. 1982).

[24] See, e.g., Town & Country Chrysler Plymouth v. Porter, 11 Ariz. App. 369, 464 P2d 815 (1970).

[25] See, e.g., Maxey v. Quintana, 84 NM 38, 499 P2d 356 (1972).

[26] See, e.g., Rosenthal v. Blum, 529 SW2d 102 (Tex. Civ. App. 1975); Restatement (Second) of Torts § 552.

[27] See, e.g., Horne v. Claude Ray Ford Sales, Inc., 162 Ga. App. 329, 290 SE2d 497 (1982).

[28] UCC § 2-714(2). Misrepresentation claims generally are coupled with breach of warranty claims when the alleged misrepresentation arose out of a sale. Depending upon the circumstances, other theories of relief such as negligence and strict tort liability for defective products may accompany the misrepresentation claim. See generally Clark, The Law of Product Warranties (Warren, Gorham & Lamont, Inc. 1984).

[29] See, e.g., Leininger v. Anderson, 255 NW2d 22 (Minn. 1977); Stout v. Turney, 150 Cal. Rptr. 637, 586 P2d 1228 (1978). For a more flexible approach, see Galego v. Knudsen, 281 Ore. 43, 573 P2d 313 (1978) (stating that the benefit-of-the-bargain theory would be applied when there was a misrepresentation as to quality of goods or realty

case would be $1,000 ($3,000 less $2,000); that is, the difference between the value of what was expended and the actual value of what was received.

Where the tort is negligent misrepresentation, there seems to be an inclination to use the out-of-pocket theory to measure actual damages.[30] The use of the out-of-pocket measure has the effect of leaving the wronged party in the same place with respect to actual damages as would rescission plus restitution damages in contractual misrepresentation. The parties are restored to their original position by returning what each received.

Consequential damages also may be recoverable for either intentional or negligent misrepresentation. If a court has awarded actual damages as measured by the benefit-of-the-bargain theory, it must be careful that consequential damages do not represent a double recovery. Consequential damages may be allowed as an alternative to actual damages as measured by the benefit-of-the-bargain theory where an award of both would result in a double recovery.[31] Although attorney fees are not typically recoverable in an action for misrepresentation, they may be awarded if the misrepresentation has caused the wronged party to defend against a third-party lawsuit.[32] As previously indicated, most states have acts prohibiting deceptive trade practices and attorney fees are generally provided in such statutes.[33] Such a statutory claim is often successfully coupled with the common-law claim for misrepresentation.

Punitive (exemplary) damages also may be awarded in a tort action if the defendant's conduct is *intentionally* "malicious, oppressive, or gross"[34] or "willful and wanton."[35] Where the plaintiff is a consumer,[36] however, or the defendant has a fiduciary relationship with the plaintiff,[37] simple intentional fraud may be enough to allow for punitive damages.

Section 2-721 of the Uniform Commercial Code (UCC) states that a claim of rescission is an affirmative action for avoidance of the contract "not inconsistent with a claim for damages." Although the prevailing view at common law appears to be that an action in tort for misrepresentation precludes rescission because the action in tort is an affirmation of the underlying contract, it is likely that the UCC approach will gain favor as it has in so many other areas of the common law of contract.[38] Also, at common law, courts have been quick to

---

but that otherwise the out-of-pocket theory would prevail). See generally 13 A.L.R.3d 875.

[30] See, e.g., Glydenvand v. Schroeder, 90 Wis. 2d 690, 280 NW2d 235 (1979).

[31] Ollerman v. O'Rourke, Inc., 94 Wis. 2d 17, 288 NW2d 95 (1980).

[32] Glendale Fed. Sav. & Loan Ass'n v. Marina View Heights Dev., Inc., 66 Cal. App. 3d 101, 135 Cal. Rptr. 802 (1977).

[33] See ¶ 1.03[3][b].

[34] See, e.g., Winn-Dixie Montgomery, Inc. v. Henderson, 395 So. 2d 475 (Ala. 1981).

[35] Jeffers v. Nysse, 98 Wis. 2d 543, 297 NW2d 495 (1980).

[36] F.D. Borkholder Co., Inc. v. Sandock, 413 NE2d 567 (Ind. 1980).

[37] Ford v. Guarantee Abstract & Title Co., Inc., 220 Kan. 244, 553 P2d 254 (1981).

[38] See Braucher, "Freedom of Contract and the Second Restatement," 78 Yale L.J. 598 (1969).

find no affirmation despite a suit for tort damages where for some reason the tort relief is not available.[39]

The UCC doctrines of unconscionability and good faith may be applicable to complement any misrepresentation claim arising from the sale of goods.[40] Where product quality is at issue, warranty, strict products liability, and/or negligence claims may be involved as well as tort reform statutes or the Magnuson-Moss Warranty Act. Although discussion of these doctrines is beyond the range of the focus here on the too-often overlooked common law of misrepresentation, there is no shortage of excellent works that cover the law relevant to those concerns.[41]

## [2] Deceptive and Unfair Acts and Practices Under the Federal Trade Commission Act

Chapter 1 discusses the Federal Trade Commission's (FTC) authority to regulate against unfair and deceptive acts and practices and the procedure the FTC must follow to exercise that authority.[42] This section discusses these deceptive or unfair acts or practices within the meaning of Section 5 of the FTC Act. It is important not to lose sight of the practical significance of this material in the debtor-creditor dispute. The attorney representing creditors in such disputes may never face the FTC. In an action brought by the creditor for nonpayment, however, the debtor may claim a right of rescission and/or damages because of an alleged deceptive or unfair trade practice. Although there is no private right of action under the FTC Act, most states have acts similar to the FTC Act's prohibition against unfair and deceptive acts or practices.[43] Most of these state acts provide for private remedies, and most state courts give great weight to FTC proceedings. Consequently, the FTC's past activity against deceptive or unfair acts or practices may become relevant.

### [a] Deceptive Acts or Practices

The FTC has the authority to prevent both unfair *and* deceptive acts or practices by use of its adjudicative authority (primarily through the use of the cease and desist order) or its rulemaking authority (by issuing trade regulation rules).[44] Most enforcement by the FTC, however, has been and is likely to

---

[39] See Farnsworth, Contracts 254, at n.4 (Little, Brown 1982).

[40] See UCC § 2-302 for unconscionability and §§ 1-203, 2-103(1)(b) for good faith. The doctrines do not depend on the ability to show misrepresentation. See generally White & Summers, The Uniform Commercial Code Ch. 4 (West, 2d ed. 1980). See also Greene v. Gibraltar Mortgage Inv. Corp., 488 F. Supp. 177 (DDC 1980), which involved companion claims of misrepresentation, unconscionability, and violations of the Truth-in-Lending Act.

[41] See generally supra ¶ 2.01[1][b] note 28.

[42] See ¶ 1.03[2][c].

[43] See ¶ 1.03[3][b].

[44] See generally ¶ 1.03[2][c][ii].

continue to be through its exercise of its adjudicative authority against *deceptive* acts or practices.[45]

Until recently, in deciding whether a deceptive act or practice had been used, the FTC determined whether the act or practice had a capacity or a tendency to deceive.[46] In October 1983, however, the FTC announced a new "enforcement policy statement." Under this new policy, adopted by a vote of three to two, the FTC will find an act or practice deceptive "if there is a misrepresentation, omission, or other practice that is likely to mislead the consumer acting reasonably in the circumstances, to the consumer's detriment."[47] Apparently, the FTC no longer intends to consider the effect the act or practice may have on "the trusting as well as the suspicious."[48]

Courts generally defer to the FTC's finding that an act or practice is deceptive.[49] There must be, however, substantial evidence in the record to support the finding,[50] and the FTC's finding must not be arbitrary or capricious.[51] At times the FTC considers outside sources, such as consumer or expert testimony, surveys, or standard reference definitions.[52]

A defense often raised in a proceeding against alleged deceptive acts or practices is that the representation is merely "puffing." It is difficult to assess the validity of such a defense given the disparate results where apparently similar or identical representations are made.[53] Other defenses that have been raised by defendants in FTC proceedings in which an act or practice is attacked by the FTC as either deceptive or unfair include:[54]

---

[45] Scalia, "Back to Basics: Making Law Without Making Rules," 1981 Regulation 25 (July-Aug.). Note, however, that the FTC may be forced to utilize rulemaking authority. See ¶ 1.03[2][c] notes 64–68 and accompanying text. See also infra ¶ 2.03[2][a] note 46. Also, see the discussion of the FTC Credit Practices Rule, 16 CFR Pt. 444, at ¶ 3.02. The rule, effective March 1, 1985, may indicate an increased willingness to use rulemaking authority.

[46] See, e.g., Trans World Accounts, Inc. v. FTC, 594 F2d 212, 214 (9th Cir. 1979); FTC v. Standard Educ. Soc'y, 302 US 112, 116 (1937).

[47] FTC News (Oct. 24, 1983).

[48] See, e.g., FTC v. Standard Educ. Soc'y, 302 US 112, 116 (1937).

[49] See, e.g., FTC v. Colgate-Palmolive Co., 380 US 374 (1965); Sears, Roebuck & Co. v. FTC, 676 F2d 385 (9th Cir. 1982).

[50] FTC v. Algoma Lumber Co., 291 US 67 (1934).

[51] FTC v. R.F. Keppel & Bros., 291 US 304 (1934).

[52] Posner, Regulation of Advertising by the FTC 12 (American Enterprise Institute 1973).

[53] Compare, e.g., Carlay Co. v. FTC, 153 F2d 49 (1946) ("prime" as puffing) with Goodman v. FTC, 244 F2d 584 (9th Cir. 1957) ("exceptional" as not puffing). For a discussion of other defenses raised in proceedings against alleged deceptive acts or practices and the likely success of such defenses see Rosden, 2 The Law of Advertising, § 18.06 (Matthew Bender 1979).

[54] For a collection of cases in which such defenses have been presented see Trade Reg. Rep. (CCH) ¶¶ 830, 7527 (1981). A collection of other miscellaneous defenses to FTC proceedings raised as both "deceptive" and "unfair" may be found in Trade Reg. Rep. (CCH) ¶ 9641 (1981).

(1) The act or practice is not "in or affecting commerce" as required under Section 5 of the FTC Act;

(2) A proceeding by the Commission is not "to the interest of the public"; and

(3) The defendant is a bank, certain common carrier, or is subject to the Packers and Stockyards Act, and therefore exempt under Section 5 of the FTC Act.

Under the new enforcement policy, defenses in the future will likely include: (1) the practice is not "likely to mislead a consumer acting reasonably in the circumstances"; or (2) the act or practice is not to the "consumer's detriment."[55]

### [b] Unfair Acts or Practices

The FTC only recently has seen fit to exercise its authority to prevent "unfair" acts or practices. The Commission recently stated that

> [t]o justify a finding of unfairness the injury must satisfy three tests. It must be substantial; it must not be outweighed by any countervailing benefits to consumers or competition that the practice produces; and it must be an injury that consumers themselves could not reasonably have avoided.[56]

**[i] Unfairness in Advertising.** The FTC has often used the unfairness requirement to attack two types of advertising: (1) advertising that fails to disclose material terms and (2) advertising that involves unsubstantiated claims.[57] An example of regulation of the first type includes the trade regulation rule requiring the disclosure of insulation efficiency ratings.[58] The decisions of the FTC suggest that a failure to disclose adequate product information may be deemed unfair if: (1) consumers lack the information; (2) consumers would be likely to decide to purchase differently if the information were available; and (3) the benefits of better-informed consumers outweigh the costs of supplying the information.[59]

To regulate against advertising that involves unsubstantiated claims, the FTC has required that advertisers have a "reasonable basis" to substantiate advertising claims and possess such a basis prior to making the claim. The FTC

---

[55] Announced October 24, 1983, in FTC News.

[56] Letter from the Commission to Senators Ford and Danforth (Dec. 17, 1980); Statement of Basis and Purpose, Credit Practices (Feb. 17, 1984), printed in Report 409, Consumer Cred. Guide (CCH) (Mar. 13, 1984).

[57] Craswell, "The Identification of Unfair Acts and Practices by the FTC," 1981 Wis. L. Rev. 107, 109 (1981).

[58] 44 Fed. Reg. 50,218 (1979).

[59] Craswell, "The Identification of Unfair Acts and Practices by the FTC," 1981 Wis. L. Rev. 107.

has said that an advertiser "should have in his possession such information as would satisfy a reasonably prudent businessman, acting in good faith, that such representation was true."[60] FTC activity in the area shows a balance between the potential risks to consumers and economic burdens to the marketplace.[61]

The FTC's authority to regulate any advertising is subject to the First Amendment of the U.S. Constitution. Commercial advertising is protected by the First Amendment subject to a number of exceptions, including restrictions on time, place, and manner, and, most relevant to the FTC, the prohibition of false or misleading advertisments. The U.S. Supreme Court recently has specified the following tests for commercial advertising:

> At the outset, we must determine whether the expression is protected by the First Amendment. For commercial speech to come within that provision, it at least must concern lawful activity and not be misleading. Next, we ask whether the asserted governmental interest is substantial. If both inquiries yield positive answers, we must determine whether the regulation directly advances the governmental interest asserted, and whether it is not more extensive than is necessary to serve that interest.[62]

Congress has separately regulated the advertising of the terms of consumer credit transactions. This regulation is contained in provisions of the Truth-in-Lending Act (TILA), Title 1 of the Consumer Credit Protection Act (CCPA).[63] The credit advertising provisions and other disclosure requirements of TILA are discussed in subsequent sections of this chapter.[64]

**[ii] Unfairness and Trade Regulation Rules.** Outside of advertising, the FTC has exercised its authority to regulate against unfairness in credit practices, door-to-door sales, and the use of practices that deprive consumers of postpurchase rights.[65]

## [3] State Laws Prohibiting Specific Acts or Practices

Chapter 1 introduced various state statutes that, like the FTC Act, contain broad prohibitions against unfair and deceptive acts or practices.[66] In addition to these "little FTC acts," most states have adopted statutes directed toward

---

[60] In re Pfizer, 81 TC 23 (1972).

[61] Craswell, "The Identification of Unfair Acts and Practices by the FTC," 1981 Wis. L. Rev. 107, 126–127.

[62] Central Hudson Gas & Elec. Corp. v. Public Serv. Comm'n, 447 US 557, 566 (1980).

[63] 15 USC §§ 1601 et seq.

[64] Infra ¶ 2.04[9].

[65] See ¶ 3.02 for a discussion of the FTC Credit Practices Rule; infra ¶ 2.02 for a discussion of the Door-to-Door Sales Rule; and ¶ 3.04 for a discussion of the Rule on Preservation of Consumer Claims and Defenses.

[66] See ¶ 1.03[3][b].

specific acts or practices that the state legislature has deemed to be against the public's interest. Two examples follow.

### [a] Bait-and-Switch Advertising

In bait-and-switch advertising, the vendor advertises one product while intending to sell another product that offers a higher profit. Advertising the first product is designed merely to lure the consumer into the store. Several states have statutes prohibiting this practice.[67] Most state statutes, however, give little insight into exactly what activity gives rise to the violation. Instead, these statutes mostly simply state that it is a violation to advertise merchandise as part of a plan to not sell the advertised merchandise.[68]

The following acts or practices are considered by the FTC in determining whether bait and switch has occurred, and are likely to be given considerable weight by state regulators or state courts:[69]

(1) The refusal to show, demonstrate, or sell the product offered in accordance with the terms of the offer;

(2) The disparagement by acts or words of the advertised product or the disparagement of the guarantee, credit terms, availability of service, repairs, or parts, or disparagement in any other respect in connection with the product;

(3) The failure to have available to all outlets listed in the advertisement a sufficient quantity of the advertised product to meet reasonably anticipated demands, unless the advertisement clearly and adequately discloses the supply is limited and/or the merchandise is available only at designated outlets;

(4) The refusal to take orders for the advertised merchandise to be delivered within a reasonable period;

(5) The showing or demonstrating of a product that is defective, unusable, or impractical for the purpose represented or implied in the advertisement;

(6) The use of a sale plan or method of compensation for salespeople, or the penalization of salespeople, to prevent or discourage them from selling the advertised product.

A problem related to bait-and-switch advertising of goods for sale is the underestimation of the cost of repair for services, such as the cost of mechanical work on an automobile. Several states have regulated against such activity.[70]

---

[67] See, e.g., N.Y. Gen. Bus. § 396; Ohio Rev. Code Ann. §§ 4165.02(I), 4165.02(K).

[68] See, e.g., N.J. Stat. Ann. § 56:8-2-2.

[69] FTC Guides Against Bait Advertising, 16 CFR § 238; see also All-State Indus. of N.C. v. FTC, 423 F2d 423 (4th Cir. 1970).

[70] See, e.g., Wash. Rev. Code § 46.71 (if estimate is written, then cost of repairs may not exceed 10 percent of estimate unless prior approval of repairs by customer); Cal. Bus. & Prof. Code § 9884.9.

### [b] Referral Sales Schemes

Referral sales schemes, a first cousin to chain-letter schemes, are prohibited by several states in specific statutes. In a referral sales scheme, the vendor tells the prospective buyer that the product (generally substantially overpriced) will cost the buyer nothing or next to nothing because the buyer will be entitled to a rebate or commission for each purchasing customer the buyer refers to the seller. There are two problems with this sale for the consumer. First, the referrals may not be as gullible as the initial buyer, who is left to pay the full and generally inflated price. Second, a geographical area quickly becomes saturated so that every prospective referral has already been referred or is also seeking referrals. One court, with respect to such a scheme in a city of less than 100,000, demonstrated as follows:[71]

> [R]espondents must earn 12 commissions of $100 each to get, as promised, something for nothing. This means that 12 of respondents' referrals must purchase as respondents did; they, in turn, to get something for nothing, must find 12 more people to purchase, and so forth, as follows:

| | *Number of Purchasers* |
|---|---|
| | 1 |
| 1st round | 12 |
| 2nd round | 144 |
| 3rd round | 1,728 |
| 4th round | 20,736 |
| 5th round | 248,832 |

An example of a statute that prohibits this practice is at Section 2.412 in the 1968 version of the Uniform Consumer Credit Code (UCCC) and Section 3.309 in the 1974 version of that Code.[72]

# ¶ 2.02 COOLING-OFF PERIODS IN DOOR-TO-DOOR SALES

## [1] FTC Rule

### [a] Scope of the FTC Rule

In 1974 the FTC, in accordance with its rulemaking authority, adopted a trade regulation rule making it an unfair and deceptive practice to fail to provide a three-day period in which consumers could rescind a purchase made in a

---

[71] Sherwood & Roberts-Yakima, Inc. v. Leach, 67 Wash. 2d 630, 409 P2d 160, 163 (1965).

[72] For a list of the states having adopted the 1968 UCCC or a later version, see ¶ 1.03[3][a][ii] notes 105 through 110 and accompanying text.

door-to-door sale.[1] Whether or not a buyer in a particular transaction has the rights provided by the rule depends upon the rule's definition of the following terms: "door-to-door sale"; "consumer goods or services"; "seller"; "place of business"; and "purchase price."[2] These definitions demonstrate that a buyer has the rule's protections if *all* of the following six requirements are met:

(1) There is a sale, lease, or rental;
(2) The deal involves consumer goods or services; that is, the sale or lease is made by an individual primarily for personal, family, or household purposes (or for a course of instruction or training without regard to its purpose);
(3) The goods or services have a purchase price of $25 or more whether under one or more contracts (finance charges, postage, freight, insurance, and service charges paid by the consumer are to be included);
(4) The seller or its personal representative personally solicits the sale, lease, or rental;
(5) The buyer's agreement or offer to purchase is made at a place other than the seller's place of business;
(6) The particular transaction is not excluded from coverage under the definition of door-to-door sale.

Excluded under the definition of door-to-door sale, and, therefore, not within the scope of the rule, are the following:[3]

(1) Transactions made pursuant to prior negotiations that are conducted entirely at the seller's regular place of business;
(2) Transactions in which the consumer has a right of rescission under TILA;
(3) Transactions that involve a bona fide emergency and in which the buyer, in a separate signed statement, describes the emergency and expressly recognizes and waives a right to the cooling-off period;
(4) Transactions in which the only contact between the buyer and seller before delivery is by mail or telephome; and
(5) Transactions in which the buyer has initiated contact specifically requesting the seller to visit the buyer's home and perform maintenance on the buyer's personal property.

The rescission right in TILA is for certain transactions in which a security interest is or will be taken in the borrower's residence. The TILA right exists whether or not the sale is away from the creditor's regular place of business.[4]

---

[1] 16 CFR §§ 429.1(a), 429.1(b), 429.1(e).

[2] Id at n.1.

[3] Id.

[4] See infra ¶ 2.04[7].

### [b] Notice to the Buyer

A seller subject to the rule must give notice to the buyer of the right of cancellation in three ways:[5]

(1) Notice in either the contract or receipt
(2) A separate notice of cancellation attached to the contract or receipt, and
(3) Oral notice at the time the buyer signs the contract or purchases the goods or services

The rule provides the actual wording that must be used for the written notice.[6] The language principally used in any oral sales presentation must be used in the notice in the contract or receipt.[7] The seller is prohibited from including any confession of judgment or waiver of any rights permitted under the rule.[8]

### [c] Cancellation by the Buyer

Before midnight of the third business day from the date of the transaction, the buyer may cancel by:[9]

(1) Signing the notice of cancellation form or any other form of written cancellation, inserting the date, and either mailing or delivering it to the seller's place of business; or
(2) Sending a telegram to the seller at the seller's place of business expressing the decision to cancel.

"Business day" excludes Sundays and nine holidays.[10] The notice of cancellation form must specify the date of the last day on which the buyer may cancel.[11]

If the buyer cancels the sale, he must either:[12]

---

[5] 16 CFR § 429.1.

[6] 16 CFR §§ 429.1(a), 429.1(b). The language for the notice in the receipt or contract must be "in substantially the . . . form" specified. The attached Notice of Cancellation "shall contain" the language specified in the rule. Apparently one may use different language than that specified at 16 CFR § 429.1(a), but it does not make much sense to do so. The language in the Notice of Cancellation appears to be mandatory.

[7] 16 CFR §§ 429.1(a), 429.1(b).

[8] 16 CFR § 429.1(d).

[9] See 16 CFR § 429.1(a). The rule does not specifically state that the buyer has the cooling-off period. Instead, the notices that must be given to the buyer state the substantive right.

[10] 16 CFR § 429.1 Note 1(f). The holidays are New Year's Day, Washington's Birthday, Memorial Day, Independence Day, Labor Day, Columbus Day, Veterans Day, Thanksgiving Day, and Christmas Day.

[11] 16 CFR § 429.1(b).

[12] See id. The buyer's duties are contained in the Notice of Cancellation.

(1) Hold the merchandise for at least twenty days after date of cancellation and permit the seller to pick it up in substantially as good condition as when it was received; or

(2) Follow any instructions of the seller for the return of the merchandise at the sole expense and risk of the seller.

The buyer has no further obligations and may keep any goods after the twenty-day period if he has not agreed to hold the goods for a reasonable time.[13]

### [d] Restrictions on the Seller

The rule prohibits the seller from transferring any evidence of indebtedness for five business days after the date the contract was signed or the goods or services were purchased.[14] Within ten business days after receipt of notice of cancellation, the seller must refund any payments made, return any trade-in, cancel and return any negotiable instrument signed by the buyer, take action to terminate promptly any security interest created in the transaction, and notify the buyer whether the seller intends to repossess or to abandon any shipped or delivered goods.[15]

## [2] State Cooling-Off Periods in Door-to-Door Sales

Most states have legislated cooling-off periods in door-to-door sales.[16] These statutes were passed, for the most part, from the mid-1960s to the early 1970s, and generally predate the FTC rule. A transaction may be within the scope of both the state statute and the FTC rule. The presence of an applicable state law does not relieve compliance with the FTC rule. The FTC rule does not exempt compliance with the state law unless the state law is "directly inconsistent" with the provisions of the rule.[17] The FTC issued an advisory opinion in 1976 stating that it will not object to compliance with the state law as long as any language in the state notice that is directly inconsistent with its rule is stricken. The advisory opinion also stated the FTC would find a violation if only a state notice was used and that notice did not inform the consumer of the right to cancel within three days, without penalty or fee.[18] Most states have amended their statutes so that notices required under the state law comply with the FTC rule.[19]

---

[13] See id. This right of the buyer is contained in the Notice of Cancellation.

[14] 16 CFR § 429.1(h).

[15] 16 CFR §§ 429.1(g), 429.1(i).

[16] For a collection of the relevant state statutes, see Consumer Cred. Guide (CCH) ¶ 525 (Mar. 13, 1984).

[17] Id.; 16 CFR § 429.1 Note 2(b).

[18] Advisory Opinion to Direct Selling Association [1974-1980 Transfer Binder], Consumer Cred. Guide (CCH) ¶ 98,425 (Sept. 19, 1980).

[19] See, e.g., Mich. Comp. Laws § 445.113.

# ¶ 2.03 DETERMINING WHO GETS CREDIT

## [1] The Fair Credit Reporting Act

### [a] Purpose of FCRA

Prospective creditors, employers, and insurers have a legitimate need for information about applicants. Potential borrowers, employees, and policyholders, on the other hand, have a legitimate interest in the nature of the information gathered, how it is gathered, and to whom and when such information is disseminated. In 1970, Congress passed the Fair Credit Reporting Act (FCRA) as Title VI of CCPA.[1] FCRA requires consumer reporting agencies (e.g., credit bureaus) to adopt reasonable procedures for supplying consumer credit, personnel, insurance, and other information in a "fair and equitable" manner, "with regard to the confidentiality, accuracy, relevancy, and proper utilization of such information."[2]

### [b] Scope of FCRA

FCRA regulates the preparation of consumer reports by consumer reporting agencies and the use of these reports. A "consumer reporting agency" is defined as any person who regularly engages in the practice of assembling or evaluating information on consumers for the purpose of furnishing consumer reports to third parties.[3] A "consumer report" is any written or oral communication that investigates creditworthiness, credit standing, credit capacity, character, general reputation, personal characteristics, or mode of living, and is used or expected to be used as an evaluation factor for one or more of the following:[4]

(1) Credit or insurance to be used primarily for personal, family, or household purposes;
(2) Employment purposes;
(3) The consumer's eligibility for licenses granted by a governmental instrumentality required by law to consider the applicant's financial responsibility or status; or
(4) A legitimate business need in connection with a business transaction involving an individual.

A number of cases have addressed the issue of whether a report on an individual applicant for business credit is a consumer report. The problem arises because of the ambiguity created by Items 1 and 4 above and because the term "consumer" is broadly defined to include any individual.[5] Most courts

---

[1] Pub. L. No. 91-508, 84 Stat. 1128, 15 USC §§ 1681–1681t.

[2] 15 USC § 1681.

[3] 15 USC § 1681a.

[4] Id.

[5] Id.

have found that a report furnished for the evaluation of business credit for an individual is not covered under the definition of a consumer report.[6]

The motives of a credit reporting agency are relevant in determining whether or not a report is a credit report within the meaning of FCRA. Even though a report actually may be used for a purpose not within the scope of the definition of credit report, a report issued by a credit reporting agency in the expectation that it will be used for a purpose covered in Items 1 through 4 above is a credit report.[7] Also, a credit report originally prepared and first used for such a purpose is still a credit report if it is used later for a purpose not covered.[8]

Specifically excluded from the definition of consumer reports, and therefore excluded under the coverage of FCRA, are the following:

(1) Any report that contains only information between the consumer and the person making the report;
(2) Any approval of a specific extension of credit by the issuer of a credit card or similar device; and
(3) Certain reports to third persons who are not prospective creditors when those persons request that credit be granted to the consumer.[9]

### [c] Requirements for Consumer Reporting Agencies

**[i] Permissible Purposes of Reports.** Unless pursuant either to a written request by the consumer to whom it relates or to a court order,[10] a consumer reporting agency may furnish a consumer report only to a person whom

---

[6] See, e.g., Heath v. Credit Bureau of Sheridan, Inc., 618 F2d 693 (10th Cir. 1980). But see Lee v. Bishop's Serv., Inc., Consumer Cred. Guide CCH ¶ 97,902 (SDNY 1978).

[7] Hansen v. Morgan, 582 F2d 1214 (9th Cir. 1978). But see Henry v. Forbes, 433 F. Supp. 5 (D. Minn. 1976).

[8] Rasor v. Retail Credit Co., 87 Wash. 2d 516, 554 P2d 1041 (1976).

[9] Despite the relative clarity of the exclusion for creditors who report information concerning only their own experiences, courts are still asked with some regularity to apply FCRA in such cases. For example, in Freeman v. Southern Nat'l Bank, 531 F. Supp. 94 (SD Tex. 1982), the plaintiff alleged a violation of the act because the defendant allegedly continued to report a paid loan as unpaid to a local credit bureau. The court held that the bank was not making a consumer report because the bank was only reporting its own experience, albeit wrongly. The court stated that the plaintiff's recourse was to correct the credit bureau's files pursuant to FCRA under 15 USC § 1681i. (The procedure for disputed accuracy applies when there is any dispute with respect to the information in any file held by a consumer reporting agency. "File" is broadly defined to include any information recorded and retained by a consumer reporting agency.) The court also stated that willful false disclosures may be actionable at common law even though the particular disclosure is not covered by FCRA.

[10] The courts have split on the issue of whether a grand jury subpoena is a court order within the meaning of this provision. Compare, e.g., U.S. v. Retail Credit Men's Ass'n of Jacksonville, 501 F. Supp. 21 (D. Fla. 1980) (grand jury subpoena was a court order within the meaning of FCRA) with In re Grand Jury Subpoena Duces Tecum

the agency believes (1) intends to use the information to extend credit or review or collect a credit account; (2) intends to use the information for employment, promotion, reassignment, or retention of an employee;[11] (3) intends to use the information in connection with the underwriting of insurance involving the consumer; (4) intends to use the information to help determine the consumer's eligibility for a government-issued license or other government benefit that requires a consideration of the applicant's financial responsibility or status; or (5) otherwise has a legitimate business need for the information in connection with a business transaction involving the consumer.[12] In addition, an agency may furnish a government agency with identifying information, limited to a consumer's name, address, former addresses, places of employment, or former places of employment.[13]

**[ii] Restrictions on Reporting Obsolete Information.** FCRA prohibits a consumer reporting agency from making any consumer report containing information concerning bankruptcies with a date of adjudication predating the report by more than ten years[14] or other types of adverse information that antedate the report by more than seven years.[15] The restrictions do not apply to (1) a credit transaction involving or reasonably expected to involve a principal of $50,000 or more, (2) the underwriting of insurance with a face amount of $50,000 or more, and (3) the employment of an individual at an annual salary of, or at an annual salary likely to equal, $20,000 or more.[16]

**[iii] Compliance Procedures.** Every consumer reporting agency must maintain procedures designed to avoid reporting obsolete information and furnishing reports for any purposes other than those authorized. In addition, such agencies must follow "reasonable procedures to assure maximum possible accuracy of the information concerning the individual about whom the report relates."[17]

---

Concerning Credit Bureau, Inc. of Ga., 498 F. Supp. 1174 (D. Ga. 1980) (grand jury subpoena was not a court order).

[11] In Hansen v. Morgan, 582 F2d 1214 (9th Cir. 1978), the court held that obtaining a report for political purposes to assist a congressional committee was not for employment purposes within the meaning of FCRA despite the theory advanced that the report had been obtained to evaluate the candidate's fitness for employment as a public official.

[12] 15 USC § 1681b.

[13] 15 USC § 1681f.

[14] 15 USC § 1681c(a)(1).

[15] 15 USC §§ 1681c(a)(2)–1681c(a)(6). Types of adverse information specifically listed in these provisions include: (1) information about suits and judgments; (2) paid tax liens; (3) accounts placed for collection or charged to profit or loss; and (4) records of arrest, indictment, or conviction of crime (dating from date of disposition, release, or parole).

[16] 15 USC § 1681c.

[17] 15 USC § 1681e. If a credit report is in fact accurate, it will be assumed that the procedures used were reasonable. See McPhee v. Chilton Corp., 468 F. Supp. 494 (D.

**[iv] Public Record Information for Employment Purposes.** If a consumer reporting agency furnishes a consumer report for employment purposes and for those purposes compiles and reports items of public record likely to have an adverse effect on the applicant, the agency must (1) notify the consumer that such information is being reported and give the name and address of the recipient or (2) maintain "strict procedures" to ensure that the information is complete and current. The agency can rely on current public records relating to arrest, indictments, convictions, suits, tax liens, and outstanding judgments.[18]

**[v] Restrictions on Investigative Consumer Reports.** An "investigative consumer report" is defined as a consumer report that contains information about a consumer's character, general reputation, personal characteristics, or mode of living, obtained through personal interviews with neighbors, friends, or associates of the consumer. The definition excludes reports containing only factual information about a consumer's credit record obtained directly from a creditor of the consumer or from a consumer reporting agency when the agency obtained information from those sources.[19] Whenever a consumer reporting agency prepares such a report, no adverse information (other than public record information) may be used in a subsequent consumer report unless the information is verified or was received within three months.[20]

**[vi] Disclosures to Consumers.** Upon request and proper identification by a consumer, consumer reporting agencies must clearly and accurately disclose the following information to the consumer:[21]

(1) The nature and substance of all information (except medical information) on file;

(2) The sources for the information. (When the sources supply information acquired solely for investigative consumer reports and this information is actually used for no other purpose, the consumer reporting agency is not required to make disclosure. This exception does not apply, however, if an action is brought and the consumer exercises discovery rights.);

(3) The recipients of consumer reports furnished for employment purposes within the two-year period preceding the request, and for any other purpose within the six-month period preceding the request.

---

Conn. 1978); Roseman v. Retail Credit Co., Inc., 428 F. Supp. 643 (ED Pa. 1977); Bryant v. TRW, Inc., 487 F. Supp. 1234 (ED Mich. 1980), in which the court found a violation of this section when the plaintiff had a history of difficulty with creditors reporting accurately on the status of his accounts, that the history was known to defendant, and the plaintiff had personally alerted defendant to that fact but defendant refused to follow up; see also Morris v. Credit Bureau of Cincinnati, Inc., 563 F. Supp. 962 (SD Ohio 1983).

[18] 15 USC § 1681k.

[19] 15 USC § 1681a(e).

[20] 15 USC § 1681l.

[21] 15 USC § 1681g.

The required disclosures must be made during normal business hours and on reasonable notice. They must be made to the consumer in person or by telephone if the consumer has made a prior written request and pays for any telephone charges. The agency must provide trained personnel to explain to the consumer any required disclosure information. The consumer may be accompanied by another person, but the agency may require the consumer to furnish a written statement stating that the agency may discuss the consumer's file in the presence of the third person.[22]

The agency may not charge for the required disclosures if the consumer requests the disclosures within thirty days after receipt of a notice of adverse action based on a consumer report or notification from a debt-collection agency affiliated with the consumer reporting agency stating that the consumer's credit rating may be or has been adversely affected. Otherwise, the agency may impose a "reasonable charge." The consumer must receive notice of the charge before the agency disclosure. The charge may not exceed the amount that the agency would charge a recipient of the report. There can be no charge for notifying persons of the deletion of information that is inaccurate or unverifiable.[23]

**[vii] Procedure in Cases of Disputed Accuracy.** Unless the consumer reporting agency has reasonable grounds for believing a dispute to be frivolous or irrelevant, any consumer challenge to the completeness or accuracy of a file requires the agency within a reasonable time to reinvestigate and record the current status of the information at issue. If the agency finds that the information is inaccurate or cannot be verified, the information must be promptly deleted from the file.[24] If the reinvestigation does not resolve the dispute, the consumer may have included in the file a statement of 100 words or fewer that sets forth the nature of the dispute.[25] The consumer's statement or a clear and accurate summary of the statement must be furnished in subsequent statements with a notation that the information is disputed.[26] If inaccurate or unverifiable information is deleted from the file, the agency must, at the consumer's request, furnish notification of the deletion to any person specifically designated by the consumer who has received a consumer report for employment purposes within the previous two years. If the report was received for another purpose, the agency must notify the consumer within six months. The consumer must be notified of his or her right to make such a request.[27] However, FCRA does not

---

[22] 15 USC § 1681h.

[23] 15 USC § 1681j.

[24] 15 USC § 1681i(a). The "reasonable grounds" for believing the dispute is frivolous or irrelevant must be something other than the fact that the agency has contra information in the file.

[25] 15 USC § 1681i(b). The 100-word limitation does not apply if the agency does not provide assistance to the consumer in writing a clear summary of the dispute; the statement need only be "brief."

[26] 15 USC § 1681i(c).

[27] 15 USC § 1681i(d).

require the agency to tell a consumer that he has the right to include a statement disputing the information in the report.[28]

### [d] Requirements for Users of Consumer Reports

**[i] Investigative Consumer Reports.** There are limitations on the procurement of investigative consumer reports.[29] Unless the investigative report is to be used for employment for which the consumer has not specifically applied, a consumer must be notified by mail that an investigative report is pending. The notice must be mailed no later than three days after the date on which the report was first requested. If a consumer who receives the notice gives a written request to a user, the user must disclose the nature and scope of the investigation he or she requested. This disclosure must be mailed or delivered no later than five days after the consumer's request.[30]

**[iii] Adverse Action Because of a Report by a Consumer Reporting Agency.** If there is adverse action with respect to the consumer's credit or insurance for personal, family, or household purposes, or if the consumer is denied employment, and such action is based at least in part on information contained in a consumer report from a consumer reporting agency, the user of the report must so advise the consumer, supplying the name and address of the consumer reporting agency that provided the report. There is no liability for failing to meet these requirements if the user can show by a preponderance of evidence that the failure occurred despite the maintenance of procedures reasonably designed to prevent it.[31]

**[iii] Adverse Action Because of a Report by a Person Other Than a Consumer Reporting Agency.** In limited circumstances, users who have obtained information from sources other than consumer reporting agencies must disclose information to consumers. Disclosure in such cases is limited. The first limitation is that disclosure is required only when there is adverse action with respect to credit. Second, no disclosure is required unless the consumer makes a written request within sixty days after learning of the adverse action. The user of such information must disclose to the consumer his right to make a written request at the time the adverse action is communicated to the consumer. If the consumer does make such a request, the user of the report must disclose the nature of the information. The user is not required to disclose the source of the information. There is no liability for failing to meet these requirements if the user can show by a preponderance of evidence that the

---

[28] Roseman v. Retail Credit Co., Inc., 428 F. Supp. 643 (ED Pa. 1977); Middlebooks v. Retail Credit Co., 416 F. Supp. 1013 (ND Ga. 1976).

[29] See supra ¶ 2.03[1][c][v].

[30] 15 USC § 1681d.

[31] 15 USC § 1681m.

failure occurred despite the maintenance of procedures reasonably designed to prevent it.[32]

### [e] Administrative Enforcement of FCRA

Determination of the appropriate administrative agency for the enforcement of FCRA is made in the same way as for enforcement of Title I of CCPA.[33]

### [f] Private Enforcement of FCRA

**[i] Civil Liability for Negligent Noncompliance.** Any consumer reporting agency or user of information who is negligent in failing to comply with any requirement of FCRA is liable to the wronged consumer both for actual damages and for the consumer's costs plus reasonable attorney fees as determined by the court.[34]

**[ii] Civil Liability for Willful Noncompliance.** Any consumer reporting agency or user of information that willfully fails to comply with any requirement of FCRA is liable to the wronged consumer for actual damages, any punitive damages that the court awards, and the consumer's costs and reasonable attorney fees.[35]

**[iii] General Restriction on Actions.** Unless an action is available for liability for negligent or willful noncompliance, the consumer generally may not bring any action or proceeding in the nature of defamation, invasion of privacy, or negligence against any user, consumer reporting agency, or any other person who furnishes information to a consumer reporting agency where such action is based on one of the required disclosures.[36] This restriction does not apply to false information furnished with malice or willful intent to injure the consumer.[37]

---

[32] Id.

[33] See infra ¶ 2.04[10].

[34] 15 USC § 1681o. See infra ¶ 2.04[11][c] for criteria the courts have used to calculate attorney fees in truth-in-lending cases. It is likely the same criteria would be used to calculate such fees under FCRA.

[35] 15 USC § 1681n. In Carroll v. Exxon Co., 434 F. Supp. 557 (ED La. 1977), the court found a willful violation because, pursuant to its regular policy, the creditor purposefully refused to disclose the name and address of the consumer reporting agency. See supra ¶ 2.03[1][d][ii]; see also infra ¶ 2.04[11][c] for criteria the courts have used to calculate attorney fees in truth-in-lending cases. It is likely the same criteria would be used to calculate such fees under FCRA.

[36] 15 USC § 1681h (e). The "required disclosures" referred to are those discussed at supra ¶¶ 2.03[1][c][vi] and 2.03[1][d][i]; i.e., the disclosures required by 15 USC §§ 1681g, 1681h, 1681m of FCRA.

[37] See, e.g., Peller v. Retail Credit Co., 359 F. Supp. 1235 (ND Ga. 1973), aff'd mem., 505 F2d 733 (5th Cir. 1974).

There is no violation of the provision concerning the obligations of the user of investigative consumer reports[38] if the user shows by a preponderance of evidence that at the time of the violation he maintained reasonable procedures to assure compliance with the obligations.[39]

**[iv] Jurisdiction.** There is jurisdiction in federal district courts or "other courts of competent jurisdiction"[40] without regard to the amount in controversy.

**[v] Limitation of Actions.** Generally, an action must be brought within two years of the date on which the liability arises. The action may be brought at any time within two years after discovery when the defendant has materially and willfully misrepresented any information required to be disclosed and the information is material to the defendant's liability.[41]

### [g] Fines and Criminal Liability

Any person who knowingly and willfully obtains information from a consumer reporting agency under false pretenses is subject to a fine of up to $5,000, imprisonment for not more than one year, or both.[42] Any officer or employee of a consumer reporting agency who knowingly and willfully provides information to a person not authorized to receive it also is subject to a fine of up to $5,000, imprisonment for not more than one year, or both.[43]

### [h] Relation of FCRA to State Laws

Fourteen states have credit reporting laws with varying degrees of complexity.[44] FCRA does not exempt compliance with a state act except to the extent that the state law is "inconsistent" with the federal act.[45]

---

[38] See supra ¶ 2.03[1][d][i]; 15 USC § 1681i.

[39] 15 USC § 1681i; see infra ¶ 2.04[12][g][iii] for a discussion of a similar defense in actions under Title I of CCPA (the Truth-in-Lending Act).

[40] 15 USC § 1681p. The quoted phrase includes state courts. Ruth v. Westinghouse Credit Co., Inc., 373 F. Supp. 468 (D. Okla. 1974).

[41] 15 USC § 1681p.

[42] 15 USC § 1681q.

[43] 15 USC § 1681r.

[44] The states are Arizona, California, Connecticut, Florida, Kansas, Kentucky, Maine, Maryland, Massachusetts, Montana, New Hampshire, New Mexico, New York, Oklahoma, Pennsylvania, and Texas. See 1 Consumer Cred. Guide (CCH) ¶ 680 for a summary of the contents of the applicable statutes in those states.

[45] For a discussion of the practical problems created by such a nebulous preemption, see generally Miller, "The Problem of Preemption in Consumer Credit Regulation," 3 Okla. City U.L. Rev. 529 (1979).

## [2] The Equal Credit Opportunity Act

### [a] Purpose of ECOA

The Equal Credit Opportunity Act (ECOA) was passed in 1974 as Title VII of CCPA.[46] The original purpose of the act—to prohibit credit discrimination on the basis of gender and marital status—was expanded in 1976, effective 1977, to prohibit credit discrimination on the basis of race, color, religion, national origin, age, the receipt of public assistance, or the exercise in good faith of any right provided by CCPA.[47] The Federal Reserve Board (FRB) was mandated to prescribe regulations to carry out the purposes of the act,[48] and complied by issuing a comprehensive regulation called Regulation B.[49] A general review of Regulation B provides a good overview of ECOA.[50]

### [b] Regulation B and ECOA

Regulation B attempts to carry out the purposes of ECOA by regulating the following: (1) the questions that may be asked during the application process; (2) the evaluation of credit applications; (3) the granting of credit; and (4) the notifications that must be given to applicants about denial of credit. Additionally, requirements concerning record retention, the supplying of credit information, and special rules for certain classes of transactions have been devised to help meet the desired ends of nondiscrimination. All of Regulation B is directed toward forbidding discrimination on a "prohibited basis."[51] This term is defined as

> race, color, religion, national origin, sex, marital status, or age (provided that the applicant has the capacity to enter into a binding contract), the fact that all or part of the applicant's income derives from any public assistance program, or the fact that the applicant has in good faith exercised any right under the Consumer Credit Protection Act or any State law upon which an exemption has been granted by the Board.[52]

---

[46] Pub. L. No. 93-495, 88 Stat. 1521, 15 USC §§ 1691 et seq. (1968).

[47] Pub. L. No. 94-239, 90 Stat. 251, 15 USC § 1691 (1976).

[48] 15 USC § 1691b.

[49] 12 CFR §§ 202 et seq. (hereafter Reg. B). These regulations are in the process of being revised. The major revision is a requirement for a less specific notification than that now required. Also, the regulation will probably be shorter with an accompanying staff commentary. No revisions are expected to be effective until late summer 1985. 50 Fed. Reg. 10,890 (Mar. 7, 1985).

[50] For a comprehensive work on the subject see Clontz, Equal Credit Opportunity Act (Warren, Gorham & Lamont, Inc. 1984).

[51] See Reg. B § 202.4, containing the "general rule" prohibiting discrimination.

[52] Reg. B § 202.2.

### [c] Scope of ECOA

The scope of ECOA is determined by the definition of key terms used in its substantive provisions. The key terms are "creditor," "credit transaction," and "applicant."[53]

"Creditor" is defined broadly to include not only those who in the ordinary course of business regularly extend, renew, or continue credit, but also those who regularly participate in the decision to grant credit, including a creditor's assignee, transferee, or subrogee. Those who regularly refer customers to a creditor also come within the definition for the purposes of the general rule prohibiting discrimination[54] and the general rule prohibiting a creditor from discouraging applications.[55] Those who merely honor credit cards are not within the definition and are therefore excluded from coverage. Also, a person is not a "creditor" regarding any violation committed by another creditor unless the person knew or had reasonable notice of the act or practice that was in violation.[56]

The term "credit transaction" also is defined broadly. The definition includes every aspect of an applicant's dealings with a creditor, including an original application for credit or application for a further extension of credit. Incidentally, "credit" has its normally accepted definition—the right to defer payment of a debt.[57] In *Dunn v. American Express Co.*,[58] the court refused to find coverage under ECOA because the plaintiff's application was not for "credit." The plaintiff had applied for an access card that would have enabled the applicant to use an automatic teller machine—an electronic funds transfer facility—that only allowed withdrawals from deposit accounts. In *Brothers v. First Leasing*,[59] however, the Court of Appeals for the Ninth Circuit held that ECOA applied to consumer leases. "Applicant" means any person who requests or receives an extension of credit. In addition, the term includes others who may be contractually obligated, except for sureties, endorsers, and similar parties.[60]

It is apparent from the definitions of these key terms that ECOA is not limited to those transactions that are primarily for a personal, family, or household purpose. However, Congress authorized the FRB to exempt from one or more of the provisions of ECOA any class of transaction not primarily for personal, family, or household purposes, if the Board makes an express finding that ECOA's purposes would be substantially met.[61] The FRB has made such

---

[53] Id.

[54] Id.

[55] Reg. B § 202.5(a).

[56] Reg. B § 202.2(i).

[57] Reg. B § 202.2(j).

[58] 529 F. Supp. 633 (D. Colo. 1982).

[59] No. 82-4584 (9th Cir. 1984), printed in 5 Consumer Cred. Guide (CCH) ¶ 96,565 (Feb. 14, 1984).

[60] Reg. B § 202.2(e).

[61] 15 USC § 1691b.

exemptions in varying degrees for business credit, public utilities credit, securities credit, and government credit. There is also special treatment of "incidental credit"; that is, non-credit card transactions or other credit in which there is no finance charge or the obligation is payable in four or fewer installments.[62]

### [d] The Credit Application Procedure

**[i] Discouraging Applications.** A creditor cannot make any statement to applicants or prospective applicants that would discourage on a prohibited basis a reasonable person from making or pursuing an application.

**[ii] Requests for Information.** Although ECOA does not specifically control what may be asked of applicants, Regulation B does. Model application forms are provided,[63] and creditors might do well to use them because proper use automatically ensures compliance.[64] Of course, it sometimes is difficult to know how to use model forms unless the user knows why they are drafted as they are.

The general rule of the regulation concerning requests for information is that anything may be asked on an application as long as the request is not specifically prohibited and as long as the information is not used to discriminate against an applicant on a prohibited basis. A creditor may request an applicant to list any account for which the applicant is liable and to provide the name and address in which the account is carried. A creditor may also ask the names in which an applicant has previously received credit. Questions concerning marital status are not allowed in an application for an individual unsecured account unless (1) the applicant resides in a community-property state, or (2) property upon which the applicant is relying for credit approval is located in a community-property state. Questions about a spouse or former spouse are not generally permitted unless all or part of the applicant's source of income to be used to repay the obligation derives from the spouse's income, alimony, child support, or separate maintenance payments, or the spouse will use the account or be contractually liable for repayment. A creditor may not ask whether any income is derived from alimony, child support, or separate maintenance payments unless the creditor appropriately discloses to the applicant that such income need not be revealed if it is not expected to be used in the consideration of the applicant's creditworthiness. A general inquiry about income must contain a notice stating that the listing of income from such sources is optional. A creditor may not request the gender of an applicant. An applicant may be requested to designate a title such as Miss, Mr., Ms., or Mrs. if the form appropriately discloses that the designation of such a title is optional.[65]

A creditor cannot request information about birth control practices, intentions concerning the bearing or rearing of children, or capability to bear chil-

---

[62] Reg. B § 202.3.

[63] Id. at Appendix B.

[64] Reg. B § 202.5(e).

[65] Reg. B § 202.5.

dren. A creditor may ask about the number and ages of dependents or dependent-related expenditures if the information is requested without regard to gender, marital status, or any other prohibited basis.[66]

A creditor may not ask the race, color, religion, or national origin of an applicant or any other person in connection with a credit transaction. A creditor may inquire, however, about an applicant's permanent residence and immigration status. There is apparently no limitation on asking an applicant's age.[67]

These rules concerning applications are subject to the requirements of Regulation B Section 202.13 on information for monitoring purposes.[68]

### [e] The Evaluation of the Credit Application

There are two types of systems commonly employed by creditors in evaluating creditworthiness: credit scoring and judgmental systems. In credit scoring (called an empirically derived credit system in Regulation B), a creditor assigns positive and negative point values to specific factors that affect credit risk.[69] Such factors may include income, employment status, credit history, and residence. In a judgmental system, the creditor makes a determination on factors other than "a demonstrably and statistically sound, empirically derived credit system"; that is, the creditor makes a subjective evaluation of creditworthiness.

Regardless of which method the creditor uses, the general rule is that a creditor may evaluate any information as long as the information is not used to discriminate against an applicant on a prohibited basis. To accomplish this end, Regulation B lists specific rules for the evaluation of information and subjects all evaluations to the "effects test."[70]

The first of the specific rules concerning the use of information provides that a creditor, unless specifically permitted by Regulation B, cannot take a prohibited basis into account in its evaluation. For example, a creditor cannot give a negative value to an applicant in a credit scoring system because the applicant is a woman.[71] There is a specific rule, however, that allows a creditor

---

[66] Id.

[67] Id.

[68] See infra ¶ 2.03[2][j].

[69] Reg. B § 202.2(p). This system must be a "demonstrably and statistically sound, empirically derived credit system" to meet the definition. This requires such a system to meet the following criteria: (1) the data used to develop the system must be obtained from the applicant pool using appropriate sampling principles; (2) the data must be developed for the purpose of predicting the creditworthiness of applicants with respect to the legitimate business interests of the creditor using the system; (3) the data must separate the noncreditworthy at a statistically significant rate; and (4) the data must be periodically revalidated by the use of appropriate statistical principles. Id. See generally Hsia, "Credit Scoring and the Equal Credit Opportunity Act," 30 Hastings L.J. 371 (1978).

[70] Reg. B § 202.6, Official Note 7.

[71] Id. In footnote 8 to Regulation B, the FRB states that this provision does not prevent a creditor from considering the marital status of an applicant or the source of an applicant's income solely for the purpose of ascertaining the creditor's rights and remedies.

to assign a favorable value to age.[72] Another specific rule prohibits the use of assumptions concerning the likelihood that any group of persons will bear or rear children. Still another specific rule permits the creditor to consider whether the applicant is a permanent resident of this country.[73]

What about all the other criteria that might be used that are not within the specific rules or are not clearly within one of the prohibited bases? This is where the effects test is of use.[74] The effects test was first outlined in the employment discrimination cases of *Griggs v. Duke Power Co.*[75] and *Albemarle Paper Co. v. Moody*.[76] There is little law on the application of the effects test in credit cases.[77] Since the effects test was borrowed from labor discrimination cases, these cases provide useful collateral authority.[78]

### [f] The Extension of Credit

As a general rule, the creditor may not refuse to grant an individual account to a creditworthy applicant on a prohibited basis. Specifically, the creditor may not prohibit an applicant from opening or maintaining an account in a birth-given first name and a surname that is either the applicant's birth-given surname, the spouse's surname, or a combined surname.[79]

---

[72] In a credit scoring system, a creditor may use age as a factor as long as an elderly applicant's age is not assigned a negative value. In a judgmental system, a creditor may use an applicant's age only to determine a "pertinent element of creditworthiness"; for example, the occupation and length of time to retirement of an applicant, to ascertain whether the applicant's income will support the extension of credit until its maturity. Reg. B § 202.6.

[73] Reg. B § 202.6.

[74] Id. at n.7.

[75] 401 US 424 (1971).

[76] 422 US 405 (1975).

[77] In Cherry v. Amoco Oil Co., 481 F. Supp. 727 (ND Ga. 1979), the court agreed with the Griggs decision that a prima facie case was shown for discrimination (in *Cherry* under ECOA) when plaintiff introduced evidence of disparate impact on a protected class. The court stated: "The conventional statistical methodology for showing disparate effect of a facially neutral test or practice is to compare representation of the protected class in the applicant pool with representation in the group actually accepted from the pool. If the statistical disparity is significant, then plaintiff is deemed to have made out a prima facie case." The court found that the plaintiff had failed to make such a showing, and therefore relief was denied. The plaintiff in *Cherry* was attacking the defendant's use of ZIP codes as a factor in a credit scoring system. Interestingly, the defendant entered into a consent decree a month before the reported decision agreeing to drop the use of ZIP codes but not admitting a violation of ECOA. U.S. v. Amoco Oil Co., Civ. No. 80-1071 (DDC 1980). See generally Baer, "The Equal Credit Opportunity Act and the 'Effects Test,'" 95 Banking L.J. 241 (1978).

[78] See, e.g., Washington v. Davis, 426 US 229 (1976).

[79] Reg. B § 202.7. In Anderson v. United Fin. Co., 666 F2d 1274 (9th Cir. 1982), the court remanded the case stating that the creditor may potentially be liable for the full range of remedies, including punitive damages, when the creditor insisted on requiring the spouse's name on an application.

In the absence of evidence of inability or refusal to repay, a creditor may not require a reapplication, change the terms of the account, or terminate the account because the applicant has reached a certain age, has retired, or has changed his or her name or marital status. A creditor was found to violate this regulation when it automatically cancelled a credit card because the applicant's spouse had died—thus changing her marital status from married to widowed.[80]

The signature of a spouse generally may not be required where the applicant's income alone demonstrates creditworthiness. Major exceptions to this stipulation deal with state-law provisions such as community-property laws, which must be considered in determining the independent nature of a person's property interest.[81]

### [g] Special-Purpose Programs

Regulation B authorizes creditors to refuse credit to any applicant who does not fall within certain authorized special-purpose programs. An example of such a program is a loan program for low-income applicants.[82]

### [h] Notification of Action Taken on the Credit Application

If an application for an extension, continuation, or renewal of credit is completed,[83] the creditor generally is required to give notice of any action taken within thirty days of the completion of the application. If the application is approved, notice may be either express or implied where, for example, the creditor issues a credit card, loans money, or otherwise grants what the applicant has requested. If the application is denied, the creditor must provide the applicant with the following information: (1) a written statement of the action taken (oral notice is permitted if the creditor did not receive over 150 applications in the preceding calendar year); (2) notification of the fact that discrimination is prohibited on specific basis; (3) the name and address of the appropriate federal enforcement agency; and (4) either a statement of specific reasons for the action taken or a disclosure of the applicant's right to a statement of reasons within thirty days after receipt by the creditor of a timely

---

[80] Miller v. American Express Co., 688 F2d 1235 (9th Cir. 1982). The creditor may require a reapplication regarding an open-end account because of a change in an applicant's marital status where the credit was based on a spouse's income. Reg. B § 202.7. However, in the case cited the creditor automatically terminated the account before determining whether the survivor's income was sufficient to independently support the account.

[81] Reg. B § 202.7.

[82] Reg. B § 202.8.

[83] Reg. B § 202.2(f). This means the creditor has received all the information regularly obtained from other applicants.

request for such reasons.[84] If multiple creditors are involved, only one notice need be given. Form notices are provided in Regulation B.[85]

An adverse action does not occur where there is a change in the terms agreed to by the applicant or action is taken on an account that is delinquent, inactive, or in default. If the terms or the amount of the credit offered by the creditor are not substantially the same as those applied for, a creditor has ninety days in which to notify the applicant of action taken if, within those ninety days, the applicant has not accepted or used the credit offered.[86]

### [i] Furnishing Credit Information

Regulation B requires that a creditor who reports information to third parties must designate accounts to reflect the participation of both spouses and must furnish information to enable credit reporting agencies to provide information about both spouses. If a creditor receives an inquiry about a particular applicant, it must furnish the information in the name of the spouse about whom the information is requested.[87]

### [j] Record Retention

Creditors are required to retain records regarding the applicant, the application, the evaluation and notification processes, the reasons an adverse action was taken, and any documents received from the applicant alleging a violation until twenty-five months after the creditor has notified the applicant of an action taken on an application. If a creditor is being investigated subject to an enforcement proceeding, or is served with notice of private action under ECOA, the creditor must retain all such records until final disposition of the matter, unless an earlier time is ordered.[88]

### [k] Information for Monitoring Purposes

For the purpose of monitoring compliance with ECOA and Regulation B, any creditor that receives a consumer credit application for the purchase of residential real property,[89] where the extension is to be secured by a lien on such property, must request the following information: (1) race and national origin, using specified categories; (2) gender; (3) marital status, using the categories married, unmarried, or separated; and (4) age. The creditor must state

---

[84] Reg. B § 202.9. The applicant's request is timely if it is received by the creditor within sixty days after the creditor's notice of the adverse action to the applicant. Id.

[85] Id.

[86] Id.

[87] Reg. B § 202.10.

[88] Reg. B § 202.12.

[89] "Residential real property" is defined as improved real property used or intended to be used for residential purposes, including one- to four-family dwellings, cooperatives, and condominiums.

that this information is taken by the federal government to monitor compliance with antidiscrimination statutes and that the applicant need not provide the compliance information.[90]

### [l] Administrative Enforcement of ECOA

Determination of the appropriate administrative agency with authority over creditors subject to ECOA is made in the same way as for enforcement of Title I of CCPA, and is discussed later in this chapter.[91]

If the agency with responsibility for administrative enforcement is unable to obtain compliance with the prohibitions against discrimination on a prohibited basis, the matter may be referred to the U.S. Attorney General with a recommendation that an appropriate civil action be instituted. Upon such referral or if the Attorney General has reason to believe that one or more creditors are in violation of ECOA, the Attorney General may bring a civil action.[92]

### [m] Private Enforcement of ECOA

**[i] Measure of Damages in Individual Actions.** Subject to the success of available defenses, the creditor who fails to comply with any requirement of ECOA is subject to civil liability in an individual action brought by an aggrieved applicant for actual and punitive damages. Liability for punitive damages is restricted to nongovernmental entities and is limited to $10,000 in individual actions.[93] The court also must consider, among other relevant issues, the amount of any actual damages awarded, the frequency and persistence of failures of compliance by the creditor, the resources of the creditor, the number of persons adversely affected, and the extent to which the creditor's failure of compliance was intentional.[94]

**[ii] Measure of Damages in Class Actions.** The creditor's potential liability in class actions for violations of ECOA is the same as that for individual actions, with the exception that in addition to the limitations for punitive damages in individual actions, punitive damages in class actions are limited to $500,000 or one percent of the net worth of the creditor, whichever is less.[95]

**[iii] Equitable Relief.** A court with jurisdiction may grant whatever equitable and declaratory relief is necessary to enforce the requirements imposed under ECOA.[96]

---

[90] Reg. B § 202.13.

[91] See infra ¶ 2.04[10].

[92] Reg. B § 202.1(c).

[93] Id.

[94] 15 USC § 1691e.

[95] Reg. B § 202.1(c); 15 USC § 1691e.

[96] Reg. B § 202.1(c).

**[iv] Attorney Fees and Costs.** In any successful individual or class action, the aggrieved applicant may recover costs and reasonable attorney fees.[97]

**[v] Statutory Defenses.** A creditor is not liable for any act done or omitted in good faith in conformity with any rule, regulation (e.g., Regulation B), or interpretation by the Board of Governors of the Federal Reserve System or with any interpretations or approvals by an authorized employee of the Federal Reserve System (FRS).[98] No person harmed by a violation of ECOA and by the Civil Rights Act of 1968 may recover under both Acts.[99]

**[vi] Limitation of Actions.** The general statute of limitations under ECOA is two years from the date of the violation, unless: (1) an enforcement agency commences an enforcement proceeding within two years of the date of the violation, or (2) the U.S. Attorney General commences a civil action within two years of the date of the violation. Where these exceptions apply, any applicant who has been a victim of the subject discrimination may bring an action no later than one year after the commencement of the administrative proceeding or the action by the U.S. Attorney General.[100]

**[vii] Jurisdiction.** In private actions there is jurisdiction in appropriate state courts and the federal district courts without regard to the amount in controversy. Action by the U.S. Attorney General may be brought in the appropriate federal district court.[101]

## [n] Relation of ECOA to State Laws

Several states have provisions relating to discrimination in the granting of credit.[102] Except as otherwise provided in Section 202.11 of Regulation B, federal law affects state law only to the extent that state law is "inconsistent." State law is not considered inconsistent if the state law is "more protective" of an applicant. Some types of provisions are specifically deemed inconsistent, such as state law provisions that specifically permit a practice prohibited by ECOA. The FRB issues interpretations concerning whether or not a specific

---

[97] Id. See infra ¶ 2.04[11][c] for criteria the courts have used to calculate attorney fees in truth-in-lending cases. It is likely the same criteria would be used to calculate such fees under ECOA.

[98] Id. Unofficial staff interpretations are given great weight but the courts are not bound by such interpretations. See Brothers v. First Leasing, No. 82-4584 (9th Cir. 1984) printed in 5 Consumer Cred. Guide (CCH) ¶ 96,565 (Feb. 14, 1984) at note 15 of the opinion.

[99] 15 USC § 1691e.

[100] Id.

[101] Id.

[102] See, e.g., N.J. Rev. Stat. § 10:5-12(i)(2).

state provision is inconsistent. The procedure for granting such an interpretation is set out in Supplement I to Regulation B.[103]

A state may apply for exemption from ECOA. The procedure for requesting an exemption also is found in Supplement I to Regulation B.[104]

## ¶ 2.04 THE TRUTH-IN-LENDING ACT

### [1] Purpose of TILA

The federal truth-in-lending provisions were enacted in 1968 as Title I of CCPA.[1] Effective October 1, 1982, Title I was substantially amended by the Truth-in-Lending Simplification Act.[2] The purpose of the Truth-in-Lending Act (TILA) provisions is to "assure a meaningful disclosure of credit terms so that the consumer will be able to compare more readily the various credit terms . . . and to protect the consumer against inaccurate and unfair credit billing and credit card practices."[3]

Since the original TILA was passed, the FRB has been mandated to prescribe regulations to carry out the purposes of TILA.[4] These regulations are found in Regulation Z.[5] No act done or omitted in good faith in conformity with Regulation Z will result in liability under TILA.[6] Before 1982, the FRB also regularly issued Official Board Interpretations. These too had the force of law because no good faith compliance with them could result in liability.[7] Also before 1982, numerous Official Staff Interpretations were issued in response to specific inquiries. Although compliance with this type of interpretation was not necessarily tantamount to compliance with TILA, such interpretations were given great deference by the courts.[8] Effective April 1, 1982, the FRB revoked both Official Board Interpretations and Official Staff Interpretations, replacing them with an Official Staff Commentary.[9]

The following discussion focuses on the provisions of Title I of CCPA, which regulate disclosure of the terms of consumer credit transactions. Title I also contains provisions that provide for substantive rights to protect consum-

---

[103] Reg. B § 202.11.

[104] Id.

[1] Pub. L. No. 90-321, §§ 102–145, 82 Stat. 146 (1968), current version at 15 USC §§ 1601–1665.

[2] Pub. L. No. 96-221, 94 Stat. 168 (1980). Additional less substantial amendments became effective in 1982.

[3] 15 USC § 1601.

[4] 15 USC § 1604.

[5] 12 CFR §§ 226.1–226.29 (1983) (hereafter cited as Reg. Z).

[6] 15 USC § 1640.

[7] Id.

[8] See, e.g., Ford Motor Credit v. Milhollin, 444 US 555 (1980).

[9] The Official Staff Commentary is found at 12 CFR § 226 Supp. I.

ers against certain credit billing and credit card practices. For example, under certain circumstances Title I gives the consumer the right to stop paying the credit card issuer when goods purchased with the card prove defective.[10] Provisions that relate to credit billing and credit card practices are discussed in Chapters 3 and 4.[11] Title I also contains some provisions that relate to the consumer leasing of personal property,[12] but an examination of these provisions is beyond the scope of this text.

This section reviews the provisions of Regulation Z to provide an introduction to the TILA disclosure requirements.[13]

Questions concerning compliance with TILA can be directed to the government agency given enforcement authority over the relevant credit grantor.[14]

## [2] Scope of TILA

### [a] Conditions for Coverage by TILA

Except for exempted creditors, TILA generally applies to each individual or business that offers or extends credit where four conditions are met:[15]

(1) The credit is offered or extended to consumers;

(2) The offering or extension of credit is done regularly;

(3) The credit is subject to a finance charge or is payable by a written agreement in more than four installments; and

(4) The credit is primarily for personal, family, or household purposes.

If a credit card is involved, certain provisions apply even if (1) the credit is not subject to a finance charge or is not payable by a written agreement in more than four installments, or (2) the credit card is used for business purposes.[16]

This statement of the scope of TILA stems from the relevant definitions of Regulation Z[17] and its exemption provision.[18] These definitions and the exemption provision are discussed in the following two sections.

---

[10] 15 USC § 1666i.

[11] See ¶¶ 3.04[5], 4.01.

[12] Chapter 5 of Title I of the CCPA, 15 USC § 1667. Regulation M, issued by the FRB (12 CFR Pt. 213), interprets the consumer leasing provisions.

[13] The Official Staff Commentary issued by the FRB and contained in Clontz, Truth-in-Lending Manual (Warren, Gorham & Lamont, Inc., 5th ed. 1982) is particularly helpful.

[14] The relevant agencies and their enforcement authority are discussed at infra ¶ 2.04[10].

[15] Reg. Z § 226.1.

[16] See supra ¶ 2.04[1][b][i].

[17] Reg. Z § 226.2.

[18] Reg. Z § 226.3.

### [b] Key Regulation Z Definitions

**[i] "Creditor."** The Regulation Z definition of "creditor" includes persons who regularly extend consumer credit that is subject to a finance charge[19] or is payable by written agreement in more than four installments (not including a down payment).[20] A further requirement is that the obligation must be initially payable to such a person before that person is defined as a creditor.[21] By specifying a regular extension of credit, Regulation Z means that a creditor must have extended credit more than twenty-five times (or more than five times for transactions secured by a dwelling) in the calendar year preceding the year of the transaction. If the person does not meet these numerical tests for the preceding calendar year, the "regular extension" proviso will be satisfied if the numerical tests are met in the calendar year of the transaction; that is, from January 1 to the date of the transaction.[22]

Persons or businesses who merely honor their customers' credit cards are creditors for the purpose of Regulation Z Section 226.4(c)(8) on discounts, Regulation Z Section 226.9(d) concerning finance charges imposed at the time of the transaction, and Regulation Z Section 226.12(e) concerning prompt notification of returns and crediting of refunds.[23]

Credit card issuers who extend open-end credit (e.g., a bank that issues a Visa card allowing open-end credit) are generally considered creditors for the purpose of complying with open-end disclosure requirements, whether or not a finance charge is levied or the transaction is payable in more than four installments.[24] Credit card issuers who extend closed-end credit that is subject to a finance charge or is payable by written agreement in more than four installments are considered creditors for the purposes of both (1) open-end disclosure requirements (except the finance charge disclosure requirements of Regulation

---

[19] The meaning of "finance charge" is discussed at infra ¶ 2.04[2][b][v].

[20] Reg. Z § 226.2(a)(3)(i). The "four-installment" alternative is based on the assumption that, when a person allows repayment for sales credit in more than four installments, a charge for credit is likely to be buried in the cash price of the goods. See Mourning v. Family Publications Serv., Inc., 411 US 356, 371 (1973). The requirement of a written agreement is designed "to exclude . . . informal arrangements not involving a finance charge, such as those frequently made by doctors, dentists, and other providers of professional services." Official Staff Commentary to Reg. Z § 226.2.

[21] Reg. Z § 226.2. This means that an assignee is not a "creditor" by virtue of an assignment and, therefore, not primarily liable for disclosure. Official Staff Commentary to Reg. Z § 226.2. However, an assignee of a credit obligation may be subject to remedies or penalties for disclosure violations under TILA but only if the violation is "apparent on the face of the disclosure statement. . . ." 15 USC § 1641a.

[22] Reg. Z § 226.2, Official Note 3.

[23] Reg. Z § 226.2.

[24] Reg. Z § 226.2. This serves to include the issuers of so-called travel and entertainment cards that expect repayment at the first billing and do not impose a finance charge. Official Staff Comment to Reg. Z § 226.2.

Z Sections 226.6(a) and 226.7(d) through 226.7(g) and the right of rescission of Regulation Z Section 226.15), and (2) closed-end disclosure requirements.[25]

**[ii] "Consumer Credit."** "Consumer credit" is defined as credit offered or extended to a consumer primarily for "personal, family, or household purposes."[26] "Credit" is defined by Regulation Z as "the right to defer payment of debt or to incur debt and defer its payment."[27] This definition excludes, for example, home-improvement transactions that involve progress payments and most layaway plans in which no finance charge is levied. Both of these transactions, however, would be covered under the Regulation Z definition of "consumer credit" if the consumer has a contractual obligation to continue making payments.[28]

"Consumer" is defined as a cardholder or a natural person to whom consumer credit is offered or extended.[29] For purposes of determining the right to rescission under TILA,[30] the definition also includes a natural person in whose principal dwelling a security interest is or will be retained or acquired, if that person's ownership interest in the dwelling is or will be subject to the security interest.[31]

**[iii] "Open-End" and "Closed-End" Credit.** There are different disclosure requirements for open-end and closed-end credit transactions. A consumer's use of a bank-issued credit card, such as Visa or MasterCard, for a credit purchase of goods from a retailer is an example of open-end credit.[32] The creditor in an open-end credit transaction, however, does not have to be a bank; indeed, no credit card need be used before such credit exists. "Open-end" credit is defined more broadly as consumer credit extended by a creditor under a plan with the following characteristics:[33]

(1) The creditor reasonably contemplates repeated transactions;

---

[25] See infra ¶ 2.04[6] for the disclosure requirements for open-end credit and ¶ 2.04[5] for the disclosure requirements for closed-end credit.

[26] Reg. Z § 226.2(a)(12).

[27] Id.

[28] Official Staff Commentary to Reg. Z § 226.2(a)(14).

[29] Reg. Z § 226.2.

[30] See discussion at infra ¶ 2.04[7].

[31] Reg. Z § 226.2.

[32] Visa, MasterCard, and other such devices sometimes have both a credit feature and a debit feature. That is, the issuer may allow one to use the card both as a credit card (e.g., to buy goods and pay for them over a period of time) and as a debit card (e.g., to buy goods and, at the time of purchase, have the user's checking or savings account automatically debited). The second type of use is not a credit transaction and, therefore, not covered by TILA. Such a transaction, however, may be subject to the Electronic Funds Transfer Act (EFTA), which is found at Title 9 of the federal CCPA. 15 USC §§ 1693–1693r.

[33] Reg. Z § 226.2.

(2) The creditor may impose a finance charge from time to time on an outstanding balance; and

(3) The amount of credit that may be extended to the consumer (up to any limit set by the creditor) generally is made to the extent that any balance is repaid.

In a typical bank-issued credit card transaction, the bank reasonably contemplates repeated transactions by the consumer. Typically, the bank imposes a finance charge on the outstanding balance, usually computed daily and billed monthly. Finally, as long as the consumer's credit purchases are within the previously agreed maximum limit, and the account is current, the consumer generally will be entitled to use the card.

The term "closed-end credit" applies to consumer credit transactions that do not meet the definition of open-end credit.[34] The typical three- or four-year financing arrangement for an automobile or similar big-ticket purchase is an example of closed-end credit. Assume that a consumer agrees to purchase an automobile for $10,000. He or she will finance the purchase over a period of three years and pay a finance charge calculated pursuant to a pre-agreed rate of 18 percent. In such a transaction, it is typically presumed that there will be only one purchase made under the financing arrangement. Thus, the first requirement for open-end credit under Regulation Z (reasonable anticipation of repeated transactions) is not met. Also, since such a transaction is typically structured on the assumption that the consumer would take the full time to pay, the finance charges are calculated once at the beginning of the transaction, not periodically on the outstanding balance, as is required for open-end credit transactions. Finally, in closed-end transactions there typically must be a reapplication for each new credit transaction; thus, the third requirement of open-end credit (credit is extended without reapplication up to the maximum if payments are current) is not met.

**[iv] "Credit Sales."** A "credit sale" is a sale in which the seller is the initial creditor.[35] In a typical credit sale, a retailer allows its customer to purchase goods on credit for a personal, family, or household purpose. A hardware store, for example, may carry its own credit to allow its customer to purchase a water heater on credit for the consumer's home use. The definitions of creditor and credit sale are so worded that the credit granted by the hardware store would be a credit sale even though the business assigned its customer's obligation to a third-party lender such as a bank or finance company (but only if the transaction is initially payable to the retailer).[36] If the contract or other evidence of indebtedness lists someone other than the retailer as the party to whom the obligation is initially payable (e.g., a bank, finance company, or

---

[34] Id.

[35] Id.; see supra ¶ 2.04[2][b][i] for a discussion of the definition of "creditor."

[36] Id.; see the discussion of "creditor" at supra ¶ 2.04[2][b][i].

other third-party lender), the transaction is not a credit sale, even if the retailer and the financial institution are closely related.[37]

Sometimes it may be unclear whether in fact a sale has been made. Regulation Z includes bailments or leases in the definition of credit sale if: (1) the seller is a creditor and the consumer has agreed to pay a sum substantially equivalent to, or more than, the value of the goods or services as compensation for their use; and (2) for no additional (or nominal) consideration, the consumer will become the owner of the property.[38]

**[v] "Finance Charge" and "Annual Percentage Rate."** Of all the disclosures required in TILA, it is the disclosure of the terms "finance charge" and "annual percentage rate" (APR) that best enables the consumer to shop comparatively for credit. Basically, the finance charge is the total amount of the charge for the credit levied on the consumer by the creditor. The APR is the finance charge payable on the declining loan balance stated as an annual percentage. It is a function of time, principal balance, and the total finance charge.

"Finance charge" is defined by Regulation Z as the "cost of consumer credit [expressed] as a dollar amount."[39] The charge includes any indirect or direct charges levied by the creditor as an "incident to or a condition of the extension of credit. It does not include any charge of a type payable in a comparable cash transaction."[40] Regulation Z lists most charges that are likely to arise and specifies whether the charges must be included or excluded in calculating the finance charge.[41]

The following charges are included in calculating the finance charge:

(1) Interest, time-price differential, and any amount payable under an add-on or discount system of additional charges;
(2) Service, transaction, activity, and carrying charges;
(3) Points paid by the buyer, loan fees, assumption fees, finder's fees, and similar charges;
(4) Appraisal, investigation, and credit report fees;
(5) Premiums or other charges for any guarantee or insurance protecting the consumer's default or other credit loss;
(6) Charges paid by the consumer that are levied by a purchaser of the consumer's obligation;

---

[37] Official Staff Commentary to Reg. Z § 226.2.

[38] Reg. Z § 226.2. This language is very similar to language found in the UCC that distinguishes between leases and security interests. UCC § 1–201(37). Therefore, it seems the law under the UCC on this subject is good authority by analogy concerning whether or not in fact a sale or a bailment was involved.

[39] Reg. Z § 226.4.

[40] Id.

[41] Id.

(7) Premiums or other charges for credit life, accident, health, or loss-of-income insurance, written in connection with a credit transaction unless:
   (a) The insurance coverage is not required by the creditor, and this fact is disclosed;
   (b) The premium for the initial term is disclosed (and if the insurance term is less than the term of the credit, the term of the insurance is also disclosed); and
   (c) The consumer signs or initials an affirmative written request for the insurance.

(8) Charges for property insurance written in connection with a credit transaction, unless:
   (a) The consumer may choose the carrier and this fact is disclosed; and
   (b) If the coverage is obtained from or through the creditor, the premium for the initial term of insurance is disclosed.

(9) Discounts for cash unless the discount is offered to all prospective buyers and its availability is disclosed clearly and conspicuously.

The following charges are excluded in calculating the finance charge:

(1) Application fees;

(2) Charges for actual unanticipated late payment, for exceeding a credit limit, or for delinquency, default, or a similar occurrence;

(3) Charges for paying items that overdraw an account, unless the payment and the charge were previously agreed to in writing;

(4) Fees charged for participation in a credit plan (such as a charge for getting a credit card);

(5) Interest forfeited as a result of an interest reduction required by law on a time deposit used as security for an extension of credit;

(6) In a transaction secured by real property or in a residential mortgage transaction if the fees are bona fide and reasonable in amount, the following:
   (a) Fees for title examination, abstract of title, title insurance, property survey, and similar purposes;
   (b) Fees for preparing deeds, mortgages, and reconveyance, settlement, and similar documents;
   (c) Notary, appraisal, and credit report fees;
   (d) Amounts required to be paid into escrow or trustee accounts if the amounts would not otherwise be included in the finance charge.

(7) If itemized and disclosed, the following security interest charges:
   (a) Taxes and fees prescribed by law if actually paid to public officials for determining the existence of or for perfecting, releasing, or satisfying a security interest;
   (b) The premium for insurance in lieu of perfecting a security interest to the extent the premium does not exceed the official fee.

Finally, in calculating the finance charge, interest, dividends, or other income received or to be received by the consumer on deposits or investments must not be deducted in computing the amount of the finance charge.[42]

The rules for the calculation of the APR depend upon whether the credit is open-end or closed-end.[43] Appendices of Regulation Z demonstrate how to compute the correct rate.[44]

**[vi] "Residential Mortgage Transaction" and "Dwelling."** Several provisions of TILA turn on whether the transaction concerns a dwelling or residential mortgage transaction. Regulation Z defines "dwelling" as a residential structure that contains one to four units, whether or not that structure is attached to real property. The term includes "an individual condominium unit, cooperative unit, mobile home, and trailer, if it is used as a residence."[45] "Residential mortgage transaction" is defined by Regulation Z as a transaction in which "a mortgage, deed of trust, purchase money security interest arising under an installment sales contract, or equivalent consensual security interest is created or retained in the consumer's principal dwelling to finance the acquisition or initial construction of that dwelling."[46]

### [c] Exemptions From Coverage Under TILA

Generally, TILA does not apply to the following:[47]

(1) Business, commercial, agricultural, or organizational credit
(2) Credit over $25,000 unless the transaction is secured by any real property or a dwelling (including mobile homes or other personal property used as a principal residence)
(3) Public utility credit for services if the charges are filed or regulated
(4) Securities or commodities accounts credit extended by a registered broker or dealer
(5) Home fuel budget plans
(6) Loans made, insured, or guaranteed pursuant to a program authorized by Title IV of the Higher Education Act of 1965[48]

## [3] General Organization of Disclosure Provisions

The organization of specific disclosure requirements depends upon whether the transaction is open-end or closed-end. Subpart B of Regulation Z

---

[42] Id.

[43] Reg. Z §§ 226.14 and 226.22, respectively.

[44] See Reg. Z Appendix F for APR computations for open-end credit plans, and Reg. Z Appendix J for such computations for closed-end credit transactions.

[45] Reg. Z § 226.2.

[46] Id.

[47] Reg. Z § 226.3.

[48] 20 USC §§ 1070 et seq.

addresses disclosures for open-end credit transactions, and Subpart C addresses disclosures for closed-end credit transactions. Each subpart first sets out general requirements and then requirements for specific disclosures. Subpart D explains miscellaneous requirements concerning such matters as record retention and issues of preemption of state disclosure laws.

## [4] Model Forms

Model forms are published by the FRB.[49] If they are used properly there is no liability under TILA.[50] Of course, in order to determine proper use, the creditor must be familiar with their terminology and know how to calculate the specific disclosures that must be made. The forms, however, present information clearly and concisely and reduce the possibility of oversight and error.

## [5] Closed-End Credit

### [a] General Disclosure Requirements

**[i] Form and Timing of Disclosure.** Under TILA, all required disclosures must be made clearly and conspicuously, in writing, and in a form the consumer can keep. Disclosures must be grouped together and segregated from other information. The specific disclosures require an itemization of the amount financed; that itemization must be separate from any other itemization required in the specific disclosures. When disclosure under specific requirements is necessary, the terms "finance charge" and "annual percentage rate" must be more conspicuous than any other disclosure except for the creditor's identity.[51] The creditor generally must make the required disclosures before the consummation of the transaction.[52] Disclosure can be delayed for certain residential mortgage transactions, mail or telephone transactions, and transactions in which subsequent sales may be added.[53]

**[ii] Basis of Disclosure.** The creditor may assume for disclosure purposes that months have an equal number of days, and that payment dates may be changed because a scheduled date is not a business day. The creditor may disregard any irregularity in the first period and any payment schedule irregularity that results from the irregular first period in certain transactions. In demand obligations, the creditor must make the disclosures based on an assumed maturity of one year unless another maturity date is stated in the obligation. When a multiple-advance loan to finance the construction of a dwelling

---

[49] Reg. Z at Appendix G for open-end credit and Appendix H for closed-end credit.

[50] 15 USC § 1604(b).

[51] Reg. Z § 226.17.

[52] Id.

[53] Id.

is permanently financed by the same creditor, the construction phase and the permanent phase can be treated as one, or more than one, transaction.[54]

**[iii] Estimates of Disclosure.** If any information necessary for disclosure is unavailable, the creditor must make the disclosure based on the best information reasonably available and state that the disclosure is an estimate.[55]

**[iv] Multiple Consumers and Creditors.** If there is more than one consumer, the disclosures may be made to the consumer who is primarily liable on the obligation. However, if there is a right to rescind,[56] each consumer who has the right to rescind is entitled to a separate disclosure. If a transaction involves more than one creditor, only one set of disclosures must be given, and the creditors must agree which creditor must comply with the requirements.[57]

**[v] Interim Student Credit Extensions.** For interim credit extensions under a student credit program, the creditor need not make a disclosure of the finance charge (Regulation Z Section 226.18(d)), the payment schedule (Regulation Z Section 226.18(g)), the total of payments (Regulation Z Section 226.18(h)), or the total sale price (Regulation Z Section 226.18(j)).[58]

### [b] Specific Disclosure Requirements

The following lists the disclosures that are mandated (if applicable) under Regulation Z requirements:[59]

(1) The identity of the creditor;

(2) The "amount financed," using that term and a brief description, such as "the amount of credit provided to you or on your behalf." The amount financed is calculated by:

   (a) Determining the principal loan amount (in a loan) or the cash price less the down payment (in a credit sale);

   (b) Adding any other amounts financed by the creditor that are not part of the finance charge;

   (c) Subtracting any prepaid finance charge. A "prepaid finance charge" is any finance charge paid separately by cash or check before or at the time of consummation, or withheld from the proceeds of the credit at any time.

---

[54] Id.

[55] Id.

[56] See infra ¶ 2.04[7][b][i].

[57] Reg. Z § 226.17.

[58] Id. Most such programs are entirely exempted from coverage. See supra ¶ 2.04[2][c].

[59] Reg. Z § 226.18. Any disclosure not relevant to a particular transaction may be eliminated entirely. For example, in a loan transaction, the creditor may delete disclosure of the total sale price. Official Staff Commentary to Reg. Z § 226.18.

(3) An itemization of the amount financed. Unless the creditor provides a statement to the consumer disclosing a right to an itemization, or the statement has a space to accommodate the itemization and the consumer does not request it, the creditor must itemize the amount financed by listing the following:

(a) The amount of any proceeds distributed directly to the consumer;

(b) The amount credited to the consumer's account;

(c) Any amounts paid to other persons by the creditor on behalf of the consumer;

(d) Good faith estimates of settlement costs provided for transactions subject to the Real Estate Settlement Procedure Act (RESPA).

(4) The "finance charge," using that term and a brief description, such as "the dollar amount the credit will cost you";

(5) The "annual percentage rate," using that term and a brief description, such as "the cost of your credit as a yearly rate";

(6) Any possibility of a variable rate. If the annual percentage rate can increase after consummation, the following disclosures must be made:

(a) The circumstances under which the rate may increase;

(b) Any limitations on the increase;

(c) An example of the payment terms that would result from an increase.

(7) The payment schedule, indicating the number, amounts, and timing of payments scheduled to repay the obligation;

(8) The "total of payments," using that term and a descriptive explanation, such as "the amount you will have paid when you have made all scheduled payments";

(9) If the obligation has a demand feature, that fact shall be disclosed. When the disclosures are based on an assumed maturity of one year, that fact shall also be disclosed;

(10) In a credit sale, the "total sale price" (including the amount of any down payment), using that term and a descriptive explanation, such as "the total price of your purchase on credit, including your down payment of $. . . ." The total sale price is the sum of the cash price, any other amounts financed by the creditor that are not part of the finance charge, and the finance charge that is required to be disclosed under Item 4;

(11) Any prepayment requirements. When the finance charge is computed periodically by applying a rate to the unpaid principal balance, a statement should be included indicating whether or not a penalty may be imposed if the obligation is prepaid in full. When an obligation includes any other finance charge, a statement should be added indicating whether or not the consumer is entitled to a rebate of any finance charge if the obligation is prepaid in full;

(12) Any late payment charges that may be imposed, other than a deferral or extension charge;

(13) The security interest if the creditor has or will acquire a security interest in the property purchased as part of the transaction, or in other property identified by item or type;

(14) The items required by Regulation Z Section 226.4(d) to exclude insurance;[60]

(15) The disclosures required in Regulation Z Section 226.4(e) to exclude official fees with respect to security interest filings and the like or insurance paid for in lieu of such costs;[61]

(16) A statement that the consumer should refer to the underlying contract for information about nonpayment, default, the right to accelerate the maturity of the obligation, and prepayment rebates and penalties. The creditor may choose to disclose other information about security interests; in residential mortgage transactions the creditor may choose to provide the consumer with information about the creditor's policy regarding assumption of the obligation by third parties (e.g., due-on-sale clauses);

(17) The assumption policy. In a residential mortgage transaction, the creditor must state whether or not a subsequent purchaser of the dwelling from the consumer may be permitted to assume the remaining obligation on its original terms;

(18) If the creditor requires the consumer to maintain a deposit as a condition of the specific transaction, a statement that the APR does not reflect the effect of the required deposit. A required deposit need not include, for example:

  (a) An escrow account for items such as taxes, insurance, or repairs; or

  (b) A deposit that earns no less than 5 percent per year.

### [c] Subsequent Disclosure Requirements

New disclosures must be made when there is a refinancing. A refinancing occurs when an existing obligation subject to the closed-end credit disclosures is satisfied and replaced by a new obligation undertaken by the same consumer.[62] The following are not treated as a refinancing:

(1) A renewal of a single-payment obligation with no change in the original terms;

(2) A reduction in the APR with a corresponding change in the payment schedule;

(3) An agreement involving a court proceeding;

(4) A change in the payment schedule or collateral requirements as a result of the consumer's default or delinquency, unless the rate is

---

[60] See supra ¶ 2.04[2][b][v].

[61] Id.

[62] Reg. Z § 226.20.

increased, or the new amount financed exceeds the unpaid balance plus earned finance charges and premiums for allowed insurance;[63]

(5) The renewal of optional insurance purchased by the consumer and added to an existing transaction, if disclosures relating to the initial purchase were provided.[64]

An assumption occurs when a creditor expressly agrees in writing with a subsequent consumer to accept that consumer as a primary obligor on an existing residential mortgage transaction. Before the assumption occurs, the creditor must make new disclosures to the subsequent consumer, based on the remaining obligation.[65]

### [d] Treatment of Credit Balances

Requirements in Regulation Z Section 226.21 for the timing of returns of credit balances such as rebates upon prepayment are discussed in Chapter 4.[66]

## [6] Open-End Credit

The disclosure requirements for open-end credit are organized in much the same way as the disclosures for closed-end credit. As with closed-end credit, general disclosure requirements are established first.[67] Next, specific disclosure requirements are addressed. Unlike closed-end disclosures, however, specific disclosures in open-end credit generally must be given not only at the beginning of a transaction but also periodically in every billing cycle. Specific disclosure requirements for open-end credit are therefore contained in two sections: Regulation Z Section 226.6 for initial disclosures, and Regulation Z Section 226.7 for periodic disclosures.

### [a] General Disclosure Requirements

**[i] Form and Timing of Disclosure.** Disclosures must be in "clear and conspicuous" writing[68] in a form that the consumer can keep.[69]

---

[63] This must be insurance as described in Reg. Z § 226.4(d). See supra ¶ 2.04[2][b][v].

[64] Reg. Z § 226.20(a).

[65] Reg. Z § 226.20(b). If the original finance charge imposed was an add-on or discount finance charge, the creditor need not make all disclosures.

[66] See ¶ 4.01.

[67] Reg. Z § 226.5.

[68] Id. There is an exception. The disclosure of a finance charge imposed by a person honoring a credit card may be oral.

[69] Id. There are exceptions for the alternative summary billing rights statement provided for in Reg. Z § 226.9(a)(2) and the disclosures made under Reg. Z § 226.10(b) about payment requirements. See ¶ 4.01.

The terms "finance charge" and "annual percentage rate," when required to be disclosed with a corresponding amount or percentage rate, must be more conspicuous than any other required disclosure (except on periodic statements required under Regulation Z Section 226.7(d) and under Regulation Z Section 226.16 for advertisements).[70]

For initial disclosures required in Regulation Z Section 226.6, the creditor must furnish the initial disclosure statement before the first transaction is made under the plan.[71] For periodic disclosures, the creditor must mail or deliver required periodic disclosures for each billing cycle in which an account has a debit or credit balance of more than one dollar or on which a finance charge has been levied. The statement need not be sent if the creditor deems that the account is uncollectable, if delinquency collection proceedings have been instituted, or if furnishing the statement would violate federal law. The statement must be mailed at least fourteen days prior to any date or the end of any period required to be disclosed under Regulation Z Section 226.7(j) in order for the consumer to avoid an additional finance or other charge. These periods do not apply if the creditor is unable to meet the requirement because of "an act of God, war, civil disorder, natural disaster, or strike."[72]

**[ii] Estimates of Disclosure.** The rules for estimates are the same as those for closed-end credit transactions.[73]

**[iii] Multiple Consumers and Creditors.** The rules for multiple creditors and multiple consumers are the same as those for closed-end credit transactions.[74]

**[iv] Effect of Subsequent Events.** If a disclosure becomes inaccurate because of an event that occurs after the creditor mails or delivers the disclosures, the resulting inaccuracy is not a violation, although new disclosures may be required.[75]

## [b] Specific Disclosures in the Initial Disclosure Statement

The following are disclosures that must be made (consistent with the terminology to be used in the periodic statements) before the first transaction under the plan:[76]

---

[70] Id. For a discussion of Reg. Z § 226.7(d), see infra ¶ 2.04[6][c]; for Reg. Z § 226.16, see infra ¶ 2.04[8].

[71] Reg. Z § 226.5.

[72] Id. at Official Note 10. Computer malfunction alone is not a valid excuse for delay. Official Staff Commentary to Reg. Z § 226.5.

[73] See Reg. Z § 226.5 and supra ¶ 2.04[5][a][iii].

[74] See Reg. Z § 226.5 and supra ¶ 2.04[5][a][iv].

[75] Reg. Z § 226.5.

[76] Reg. Z § 226.6. See supra ¶ 2.04[6][a][i] concerning the exceptions to the general rules on timing of disclosures.

(1) The circumstances under which a finance charge will be imposed and an explanation of how it will be determined, as follows:

(a) A statement of when finance charges begin to accrue, including a statement of whether there is any free period and, if a free period exists, when payment must be made to avoid finance charges;

(b) A disclosure of the periodic APR that may be used to compute the finance charge, the range of balances to which it is applicable, and the corresponding APR. If the creditor is offering a variable-rate plan, the creditor must also disclose

(i) the circumstances under which the rate(s) increase;

(ii) any limitations on the increase; and

(iii) the effect(s) of an increase.

(c) An explanation of the method used to determine the balance on which the finance charge may be computed;[77]

(d) An explanation of how the amount of any finance charge will be determined, including a description of how any finance charge other than the periodic rate will be determined.

(2) The amount of any charge other than a finance charge that may be imposed as part of the plan and an explanation of how the charge will be determined;

(3) The fact that the creditor has or will acquire a security interest in the property purchased under the plan, or in other property identified by item or type;

(4) A statement that outlines the consumer's rights and the creditor's responsibilities under Regulation Z Sections 226.12(c) and 226.13 and that is substantially similar to the statement found in Regulation Z Appendix G.[78]

### [c] Specific Disclosures in the Periodic Statement

The creditor must furnish the consumer with a periodic statement that, to the extent applicable,[79] discloses the following items:[80]

(1) The account balance outstanding at the beginning of the billing cycle;

---

[77] Reg. Z at Appendix G-1 sets out model clauses.

[78] See ¶¶ 3.04 and 4.01 for a discussion of the billing rights provisions.

[79] The phrase "to the extent applicable" is identical to the language limiting specific disclosures in closed-end transactions. See supra ¶ 2.04[5][v] note 60 for a discussion of the intended effect of this language.

[80] Reg. Z § 226.7; see supra ¶ 2.04[6][a][i] for a discussion of the timing of periodic statements.

(2) An identification of each credit transaction, in accordance with Regulation Z Section 226.8;[81]

(3) Any credit to the account during the billing cycle, including the amount and the date of crediting. The date need not be provided if a delay in crediting does not result in any finance or other charge;

(4) Each periodic rate that may be used to compute the finance charge, the range of balances to which it is applicable, and the corresponding APR. If a variable-rate plan is involved, the creditor must disclose the fact that the periodic rate(s) may vary;

(5) The balance on which the finance charge is computed and an explanation of how that balance was determined;

(6) The amount of finance charge, using the term "finance charge," itemized to show the amount(s) due to the application of any periodic rates and the amount(s) of any other type of finance charge;

(7) The APR (when a finance charge is imposed during the billing cycle) as determined under Regulation Z Section 226.14, using the term "annual percentage rate." Appendix F of Regulation Z assists in the computation of the APR in open-end credit transactions;

(8) The amounts, itemized and identified by type, of any charges other than finance charges debited to the account during the billing cycle. An example of such a charge is an annual membership charge, which would be adequately identified by the simple designation "membership fee";

(9) The closing date of the billing cycle and the new balance;

(10) The date by which or the time period within which the new balance or any portion of the new balance must be paid to avoid additional finance charges. If such a time period is provided, a creditor may, at its option and without disclosure, give a "free ride," even when the payment is not within the disclosed time limit;

(11) The address to be used for notice of billing errors; the address also may be provided on the billing rights statement as permitted by Section 226.9(a)(2) of Regulation Z.

### [d] Subsequent Disclosure Requirements

In addition to annual statements of billing rights (which are discussed in Chapter 4)[82] the creditor must make other disclosures subsequent to the original initial or periodic disclosures. These disclosures include the following:[83]

---

[81] Official Note 16 to Reg. Z § 226.8 provides for no liability for failure to identify under certain circumstances.

[82] See ¶ 4.01.

[83] Reg. Z § 226.9.

(1) Disclosures for supplemental credit devices and additional features added to the consumer's plan if they are added more than thirty days after mailing or delivering the initial disclosures;[84]

(2) A written notice of changes is required whenever any term that is required to be disclosed under Regulation Z Section 226.6[85] is changed or when the required minimum periodic payment is increased. The creditor must mail or deliver a written notice of the change at least fifteen days before the effective date of the change. If the consumer has agreed to the change, the fifteen-day rule does not apply, but the notice must be given before the effective date of the change. No notice of change is necessary when the change involves:

   (a) Late payment charges, charges for documentary evidence, or over-the-limit charges;

   (b) A reduction of any component of a finance charge; or

   (c) Suspension of future credit privileges.

   A notice of change is also unnecessary if the change results from an agreement involving a court proceeding or from the consumer's default or delinquency (other than an increase in the periodic rate or other finance charge).

## [7] Rights of Rescission

### [a] The FTC Right of Rescission vs. the TILA Right of Rescission

The FTC rule on door-to-door sales provides for a three-day period in which consumers can cancel transactions that occur away from the seller's regular place of business.[86] TILA also provides for a right of rescission. When the TILA right of rescission exists, the FTC rule right of rescission is not applicable.[87] The TILA right of rescission generally applies when a consumer credit transaction covered by TILA would result in a security interest in the consumer's principal dwelling regardless of whether the transaction occurs away from the creditor's regular place of business.[88] The TILA right of rescission may exist in both closed-end and open-end consumer credit.[89]

### [b] Characteristics of the Right of Rescission

**[i] Closed-End Credit Transactions.** Except as discussed here, in a closed-end transaction in which a security interest is or will be retained or

---

[84] See supra ¶ 2.04[6][a][i] for a discussion of the timing of the initial disclosures.

[85] See generally supra ¶ 2.04[6][a].

[86] See supra ¶ 2.02.

[87] 16 CFR § 429.1 and Official Note 1(a)(2).

[88] See Reg. Z §§ 226.15(a), 226.23(a).

[89] The right of rescission for closed-end credit is treated in Reg. Z § 226.23. The right of rescission for open-end credit is contained in Reg. Z § 226.15.

acquired in a consumer's principal dwelling, each consumer whose ownership interest is or will be subject to the security interest has the right to rescind the transaction. The right to rescind does *not* extend to the following:

(1) Residential mortgage transactions;

(2) A refinancing or consolidation by the same creditor of an extension of credit already secured by the consumer's principal dwelling (if the new amount financed exceeds the remaining balance, the exemption applies only to the existing debt and its security interest);

(3) A transaction in which a state agency is a creditor;

(4) An advance, other than an initial advance, in a series of advances or certain single-payment obligations if the right of rescission and all material disclosures have been given;

(5) A renewal of optional insurance premiums that are not considered refinancings under Regulation Z Section 226.20(a)(5).[90]

Definitions of the terms "dwelling" and "residential mortgage transaction" are presented above.[91] The effect of the exception for residential mortgage transactions is to remove from coverage any lien created in connection with the acquisition or construction of a dwelling. Note, however, if the consumer is acquiring or constructing a new principal dwelling, any loan secured by the equity in the consumer's current principal dwelling (e.g., a bridge loan) is still subject to the right of rescission regardless of the purpose of that loan.[92] The use of the word "principal" to describe "dwelling" limits the right to rescind to those cases in which the consumer lives most of his or her life in the dwelling at issue.[93]

**[ii] Open-End Credit Transactions.** In an open-end credit transaction in which a security interest is or will be retained or acquired in a consumer's principal dwelling, each consumer whose ownership interest is or will be subject to the security interest has the right to rescind (1) the entire credit plan when it is opened; (2) a security interest when added or increased to secure an existing plan; and (3) the increase when a credit limit on the plan is increased. As with closed-end transactions, the right to rescind does not apply to a residential mortgage transaction or a plan in which a state agency is a creditor.[94]

**[iii] Waiver of the Right of Rescission.** In both open-end and closed-end credit transactions, the consumer can modify or waive the right to rescind. A waiver is effective only when the consumer (1) determines that there is a bona fide personal financial emergency and (2) gives the creditor a

---

[90] Reg. Z § 226.23.

[91] See supra ¶ 2.04[2][b][vi].

[92] Official Staff Commentary to Reg. Z § 226.2.

[93] Id.

[94] TILA § 125(e). See the discussion at supra ¶ 2.04[7][b][i] concerning this type of exclusion.

signed and dated statement that describes the emergency and specifically modifies or waives the right to rescind. Printed forms are prohibited and all consumers who have the right to rescind any particular transaction must sign the waiver.[95]

### [c] Notice of the Right of Rescission

In both open-end and closed-end credit transactions, when the right to rescind exists, the creditor must deliver two copies of the notice of the right to rescind to each consumer entitled to rescind.[96] The notice must identify the transaction or occurrence and clearly and conspicuously disclose the following:

(1) The retention or acquisition of a security interest in the consumer's principal dwelling
(2) The consumer's right to rescind
(3) How to exercise the right to rescind, with a form for that purpose, with the creditor's address
(4) The effects of rescission
(5) The date the rescission period expires

In Appendix G of Regulation Z there are sample notice forms for the right of rescission in open-end credit. Appendix H of Regulation Z has similar sample forms for closed-end credit.

### [d] Exercise of the Right of Rescission

To exercise the right to rescind in either open-end or closed-end credit transactions, the consumer must notify the creditor of the rescission by mail, telegram, or other means of written communication (such as mailing the required disclosure form). Notice is considered given when mailed, when filed for transmission, or, if sent by other means, when delivered to the creditor's designated place of business.[97]

### [e] Determining the Timing of Rescission

**[i] Closed-End Credit Transactions.** The consumer may exercise the right to rescind until midnight of the third business day following consummation, delivery of the notice required,[98] or delivery of all material disclosures (i.e., the APR, the finance charge, the amount financed, the total of payments, and the payment schedule), whichever occurs last. The affirmative right to

---

[95] Reg. Z §§ 226.15(e), 226.23(e).

[96] See supra ¶ 2.04[7][b] for a discussion of who has the rescission right.

[97] Reg. Z §§ 226.15(a)(2), 226.23(a)(2).

[98] See supra ¶ 2.04[7][c].

rescind does not last beyond three years after consummation, transfer of all of the consumer's interest in the property, or sale of the property, whichever occurs first, except when an administrative agency with power to enforce orders a longer time for rescission.[99]

**[ii] Open-End Credit Transactions.** For open-end credit, the time limitations are the same as for closed-end credit transactions, except that the three-day period extends until midnight of the third business day following the occurrence that gave rise to the right of rescission, delivery of the required notice, or delivery of the material disclosures.[100] In open-end credit, these material disclosures mean the information that must be provided to satisfy Regulation Z Section 226.6 with regard to the method of determining the finance charge and the balance upon which a finance charge will be imposed, the APR, and the amount or method of determining the amount of any membership or participation fee that may be imposed as part of the plan.[101]

### [f] Delay of Some Creditor Activities

Unless a consumer waives the right of rescission,[102] the creditor may not disburse any money other than that in escrow, perform any services, or deliver any materials until the rescission period has expired and the creditor is reasonably satisfied that the consumer has not rescinded. In open-end credit the creditor is relieved from liability for failure to delay performance if (1) a third party provides materials or services without knowledge that the rescission right has been activated and (2) any debt incurred for materials or services obtained by the consumer during the rescission period is not secured by a security interest in the consumer's dwelling.[103]

### [g] Effects of Rescission

Most important, upon rescission the security interest that gives rise to the right of rescission becomes void and the consumer is not liable for any amount. Within twenty calendar days after receipt of a notice of rescission, the creditor must return any money or property given to anyone in connection with the transaction and take appropriate action to terminate the security interest. If the creditor has delivered any money or property, the consumer may retain possession until the consumer gets his money or property returned.

After the consumer's money or property has been returned, the consumer must return any of the creditor's property or money given to the consumer. If

---

[99] Reg. Z § 226.23(a)(3). The power of an administrative agency to order a longer time for rescission is found at 15 USC § 1635f. A list of administrative agencies with the power to enforce TILA is found at infra ¶ 2.04[10].

[100] Reg. Z § 226.15(a).

[101] Id. at Official Note 1; supra ¶ 2.04[6].

[102] See supra ¶ 2.04[7][b][iii].

[103] Reg. Z §§ 226.15, 226.23.

the tender of the property is "impracticable or inequitable," the consumer may instead tender its reasonable value. At the consumer's option, tender of property may be where the property is located or at the consumer's residence. Tender of money must be made at the creditor's designated place of business. If the creditor does not take possession of the money or property within twenty calendar days after the consumer's tender, the consumer may keep it without further obligation. A court may modify all procedures.[104]

## [8] Disclosure of Credit Terms in Advertising

Because many consumers shop comparatively by using advertisements, TILA also regulates disclosure of credit terms in advertisements. The creditor need not disclose any credit terms in an advertisement if it avoids *all* disclosure of credit terms. Once it advertises specified terms, however, other disclosures may become necessary. Advertising regulations are found in Regulation Z Section 226.16 for open-end credit transactions and in Regulation Z Section 226.24 for closed-end credit transactions.

### [a] Advertising Correct Terms

For both open-end and closed-end credit transactions, Regulation Z states an obvious requirement: Advertisements that specify terms should only state terms that actually are or will be arranged or offered by the creditor.[105]

### [b] Advertisement of Terms That Require Additional Disclosure

**[i] Closed-End Credit Transactions.** In closed-end credit transactions, if an advertisement states a rate of finance charge, it must state the rate as an "annual percentage rate," using that term. If the APR is subject to increase, the advertisement must state that fact. No other rate may be stated, but a simple annual rate or periodic rate applied to an unpaid balance may be stated in conjunction with the APR. This additional rate, however, cannot be more conspicuous than the APR.[106]

In closed-end credit transactions, the following are the triggering terms:

(1) The amount or percentage of any down payment
(2) The number of payments or period of repayment
(3) The amount of any payment
(4) The amount of any finance charge

If any of the above terms are disclosed, the creditor also must make specific disclosures.[107]

---

[104] Reg. Z §§ 226.15(d), 226.23(d).

[105] Reg. Z §§ 226.16(a), 226.24(a).

[106] Reg. Z § 226.24(b).

[107] Reg. Z § 226.24(c); see infra ¶ 2.04[8][d].

**[ii] Open-End Credit Transactions.** In open-end credit transactions, the terms of Regulation Section Z 226.6[108] are the triggering terms. If any of these terms are used in an advertisement, the advertisement also must include other disclosures.[109]

### [c] Specific Disclosures Required

**[i] Closed-End Credit Transactions.** In closed-end credit transactions, if the creditor uses any of the triggering terms discussed above,[110] the creditor also must state the following terms, as applicable:

(1) The amount or percentage of the down payment
(2) The terms of repayment
(3) The "annual percentage rate," using that term, and, if the rate may be increased after consummation, a statement of that fact[111]

**[ii] Open-End Credit Transactions.** In open-end credit transactions, if the creditor uses any of the triggering terms (i.e., the terms of Regulation Z Section 226.6),[112] the advertisement also must "clearly and conspicuously" set forth the following:

(1) Any minimum, fixed, transaction, activity, or similar charge that could be imposed;
(2) Any periodic rate that may be applied expressed as an APR determined under Section 226.14(b) of Regulation Z. If the plan provides for a variable periodic rate, that fact shall be disclosed;
(3) Any membership or participation fee that could be imposed.[113]

### [d] Catalogs and Multiple-Page Advertisements

In both closed-end and open-end credit transactions, simplified rules apply for catalogs and multiple-page advertisements. When triggering terms are used,[114] disclosures must be made,[115] but only in one place in a table or schedule. The table or schedule must have the disclosures for a representative sampling of amounts if the credit transaction is closed-end.[116] In open-end credit transactions, if the credit terms of a plan vary depending on the amount of

[108] See supra ¶ 2.04[6].

[109] See Reg. Z § 226.16(b) and infra ¶ 2.04[8][d].

[110] See supra ¶ 2.04[8][b][i].

[111] Reg. Z § 226.24(c)(2).

[112] See supra ¶ 2.04[2][b].

[113] Reg. Z § 226.16(b).

[114] See supra ¶ 2.04[8][c].

[115] Id.

[116] Reg. Z § 226.24(d).

balance outstanding rather than on the amount of any property purchased, a table or schedule complies if it includes the required disclosures for representative balances.[117]

## [9] Miscellaneous Provisions of TILA

### [a] Record Retention

Creditors must retain evidence of compliance (other than with respect to advertising requirements)[118] for two years or longer, if the agency responsible for enforcement deems this necessary.[119]

### [b] Spanish-Language Disclosures

All disclosures required by Regulation Z must be made in English, except in Puerto Rico, where creditors may, at their option, make disclosures in Spanish. If Spanish disclosures are made, English disclosures must be provided at the consumer's request. This requirement does not apply to the advertising disclosures of Regulation Z Sections 226.16 and 226.24.[120]

### [c] State Laws

Most states have disclosure requirements for consumer credit transactions. The extent of such regulation varies from full-blown truth-in-lending type statues to scattered provisions that vary with the type of creditor involved.[121] A difficult issue arises when the state disclosures are different from or additional to those required by federal law. Does the creditor disclose under the federal law, the state law, or both? State laws are preempted if they are inconsistent with federal law, but only to the extent of their inconsistency. A state law is inconsistent if it requires a creditor to make disclosures or take actions that contradict the requirements of the federal law.[122] The Official Staff Commentary lists these two examples of inconsistent state laws:

(1) A state law that requires use of the term "finance charge" but defines the term to include fees that the federal law excludes, or to exclude fees the federal law includes.

(2) A state law that requires a label such as "nominal annual interest rate" to be used for what the federal law calls the "annual percentage rate."

---

[117] Reg. Z § 226.16(c).

[118] See supra ¶ 2.04[8].

[119] Reg. Z § 226.25. For a list of the enforcement agencies, see infra ¶ 2.04[11].

[120] Reg. Z § 226.27. For a discussion of the advertising requirements, see supra ¶ 2.04[8].

[121] Cites to these laws can be found at 1 Consumer Cred. Guide (CCH) ¶ 500.

[122] Reg. Z § 226.28.

The Official Staff Commentary to Regulation Z Section 226.28 lists the following as examples of state laws that are not contradictory:

(1) A state law that requires disclosure of the minimum periodic payment for open-end credit even though not required by TILA.

(2) A state law that requires contracts to contain warnings such as: "Read this contract before you sign. Do not sign if any spaces are left blank. You are entitled to a copy of this contract."

A creditor, state, or other interested party may request the FRB to determine whether a state law requirement is inconsistent. The procedures for making such a request are set out in Appendix A of Regulation Z. The Official Staff Commentary states that since the prohibition against giving state disclosures does not apply until the FRB makes its determination, the creditor may choose to give state disclosures until the FRB formally determines that the state law is inconsistent. If the creditor opts instead to ignore state law before such a FRB determination, nothing in TILA protects the creditor from penalties for state violations if the FRB rules that the state law is not inconsistent and therefore not preempted.[123]

The FRB may grant total exemptions from state disclosure laws to any class of credit transactions. The civil liability and liability-of-assignee provisions,[124] however, are not subject to the exemptions.[125]

## [10] Administrative Enforcement of TILA

The federal agencies that enforce TILA are listed below. They should be contacted for any questions concerning compliance.[126]

- *Retail department stores, consumer finance companies, and all other creditors not listed below:*

  Division of Credit Practices
  Bureau of Consumer Protection
  Federal Trade Commission
  Washington, D.C. 20580

---

[123] The tests for inconsistency are different for state laws on the correction of billing errors (TILA § 161) and for state laws on the regulation of credit reports (TILA § 162). For a discussion of the laws pertaining to correction of billing areas see ¶ 4.01; for credit reporting, see supra ¶ 2.03.

[124] 15 USC §§ 1640, 1641.

[125] 15 USC § 1633. Exemptions that vary in scope have been granted in the following states: Connecticut, Maine, Massachusetts, Oklahoma, and Wyoming. See 1 Consumer Cred. Guide (CCH) ¶ 3446 (Feb. 24, 1983).

[126] 15 USC § 1607.

• *National banks:*

Office of Customer and Community Programs
Comptroller of the Currency
Washington, D.C. 20219

• *State-chartered banks that are members of the Federal Reserve System* – The Federal Reserve Bank that serves the district in which the state member bank is located.

• *Banks insured by the Federal Deposit Insurance Corporation but not members of the Federal Reserve System* – The Federal Deposit Insurance Corporation (FDIC) Regional Director for the region in which the nonmember insured bank is located.

• *Savings institutions insured by the FSLIC and members of the FHLBB system (except savings banks insured by the FDIC)* – The Federal Home Loan Bank Board (FHLBB) Supervisory Agent in the district in which the institution is located.

• *Federal Credit Unions* – The regional office of the National Credit Union Administration (NCUA) that serves the area in which the federal credit union is located.

• *Creditors subject to Civil Aeronautics Board:*

Director, Bureau of Consumer Protection
Civil Aeronautics Board
1825 Connecticut Avenue, N.W.
Washington, D.C. 20428

• *Federal Land Banks, Federal Land Bank Associations, Federal Intermediate Credit Banks, and Production Credit Associations:*

Farm Credit Administrations
490 L'Enfant Plaza, S.W.
Washington, D.C. 20578

The above agencies have the authority to enforce TILA pursuant to the specific procedures, remedies, and other substantive provisions of the regulatory acts under which the agencies normally operate.[127] For example, any violation of TILA by federal credit unions will be enforced by the Administrator of the NCUA under the Federal Credit Union Act (FCUA). A violation of TILA by a creditor subject to the enforcement by the FTC is deemed to be a violation of the FTC Act. The FTC may enforce compliance under the FTC Act as it would any other violation of the Act.[128]

---

[127] Id.

[128] Id.

When an APR or finance charge disclosure is inaccurately disclosed, the administrative agency may, in most cases, order restitution. When an agency determines that an error resulted from "(a) a clear and consistent pattern or practice of violations, (b) gross negligence, or (c) a willful violation which was intended to mislead the person to whom the credit was extended," the agency "shall require" restitution. Unless the violation is willful and intended to mislead, however, the agency need not order restitution if certain relatively minor errors have occurred (e.g., "clearly technical and nonsubstantive disclosure violations that do not adversely affect information provided to the consumer and that have not misled"). Also, if any restitution order will have a "significantly adverse impact upon the safety or soundness of the creditor," the enforcement agency has discretion to permit the creditor to make the required adjustments in partial payments over an extended period of time. Another limitation on the exercise of the restitution authority is that there can be no order of restitution if the creditor discovers an error and makes an adjustment that assures that the consumer will not have to pay any charges beyond those disclosed.[129]

## [11] Private Enforcement of TILA

### [a] Measure of Damages in Individual Actions

**[i] Actual Damages.** Subject to the success of available defenses, the consumer is entitled to recover in an individual action any actual damages suffered because of violation of TILA.[130] There have been very few cases awarding actual damages because they are very difficult to assess when the injury is merely a failure to disclose. The statutory penalties discussed below are of more practical consequence.

**[ii] Statutory Penalties.** Subject to the success of available defenses discussed below,[131] and depending upon the nature of the violation of TILA, in an individual action the consumer is entitled to recover, for material violations, statutory penalties equal to twice the amount of the finance charge but not less than $100 or more than $1,000. This penalty may be recovered in closed-end credit transactions only when the violation is of the disclosure requirements for: (1) the amount financed; (2) finance charge; (3) APR; (4) total of payments; (5) number, amount, and due dates of payments; (6) the security interest statement; and (7) any of the disclosure requirements related to the rescission requirements.[132] In open-end credit transactions, statutory

---

[129] 15 USC § 1607(e).

[130] 15 USC § 1640(a).

[131] Infra ¶ 2.04[11][g].

[132] Id. The closed-end disclosures subject to the statutory penalties are found at 15 USC §§ 1638(a)(2)(A), 1638(a)(3), 1638(a)(4), 1638(a)(5), 1638(a)(6), and 1638(a)(9). See supra ¶ 2.04[5][b]. The rescission requirements are at 15 USC § 1635; see supra ¶ 2.04[7].

penalties exist for the violation of most disclosure requirements, including all initial disclosures, and for the violation of the rescission requirements.[133]

### [b] Measure of Damages in Class Actions

Class actions, like individual actions, are subject to the defenses discussed below.[134] When statutory penalties are sought, the court has the discretion to fashion the award, except that the $100-minimum recovery is not applicable to each member of the class. The total recovery for statutory penalties in any class action or series of class actions that arise from the same failure to comply by the same creditor cannot exceed $500,000 or one percent of the net worth of the creditor, whichever is less. There is no specific dollar or percentage limitation of that type with respect to the recovery of actual damages by a class action. In determining the amount of any award in a class action, however, the court must consider, among other relevant factors, the following: (1) the amount of any actual damages awarded; (2) the frequency and persistence of failures of compliance by the creditor; (3) the creditor's resources; (4) the number of persons adversely affected; and (5) the extent to which the creditor's failure of compliance was intentional.[135]

### [c] Costs and Attorney Fees

In the case of any successful action for actual damages or statutory penalties for a violation of specified disclosure provisions, or to enforce the consumer's rescission right, the consumer is entitled to recover costs and reasonable attorney fees to be determined by the court.[136] Courts have used generally accepted methods to arrive at the amount of attorney fees to be awarded, taking into consideration such factors as the amount of time expended, the skill of the attorney, the complexity of the issues, the novelty of the issue, the extent to which the attorney has had to forgo other opportunities, and the customary fee charged by attorneys of comparable skill and experience for bringing similar suits.[137]

### [d] Multiple Obligors and Multiple Violations

Although there may be more than one obligor in a transaction, only one recovery of the statutory penalties is allowed.[138] If multiple violations occur in

---

[133] Id. The open-end disclosures subject to the statutory penalties are found at 15 USC §§ 1637(a) and 1637(b)(4)–1637(b)(10). See supra ¶ 2.04[6][b]. The rescission requirements are found at 15 USC § 1635. See supra ¶ 2.04[7].

[134] See infra ¶ 2.04[11][g].

[135] 15 USC § 1640(a).

[136] Id.

[137] See, e.g., Johnson v. Georgia Highway Express, Inc., 488 F2d 714 (5th Cir. 1974).

[138] 15 USC § 1640(d).

single transactions, and do not occur after recovery has already been granted, there can be recovery for only one violation. The limitation on multiple recoveries, however, does not bar any remedy given for the right of rescission.[139]

### [e] Jurisdiction

In addition to state court jurisdiction, there is jurisdiction in federal district courts without regard to the amount in controversy.[140]

### [f] Right to Setoff

A person may not offset any amount allegedly due to the person as a statutory penalty[141] from any amount the person owes a creditor unless the amount of the liability of the creditor has been determined by a judgment of a court of competent jurisdiction in an action in which such person was a party.[142]

### [g] Defenses

**[i] Limitations of Actions.** A private action for recovery must be brought within one year of the date the violation occurred. In closed-end credit transactions, the courts generally agree that this means the date of consummation of the transaction, even though the violation may be repeated after the date of consummation. In open-end credit transactions, violations may occur with initial disclosures or for the first time in periodic disclosures. The Court of Appeals for the Tenth Circuit has held that, if the violation appears first in a periodic statement, the time limitation period begins at the date of the periodic statement.[143] It also seems that if a violation in a closed-end credit transaction first occurred in a disclosure made subsequent to consummation, the statute of limitations period should date from the time of the subsequent disclosure. The limitation period does not apply when a violation is raised by a matter of defense by way of recoupment or setoff "except as otherwise provided by state law."[144]

**[ii] Voluntary Correction of Errors.** Liability for private recovery may be avoided if the creditor makes timely correction of errors (i.e., makes adjustments to assure that the person will not be required to pay more than the charge actually disclosed or the dollar equivalent of the APR actually disclosed, whichever is lower) and notifies the person concerned of the error. The correction and notification must be within sixty days after discovery of an error and

---

[139] 15 USC § 1640(g).

[140] 15 USC § 1640(e).

[141] See supra ¶ 2.04[11][a][ii].

[142] 15 USC § 1640(h).

[143] Stevens v. Rock Springs Nat'l Bank, 497 F2d 307, 310 (10th Cir. 1974).

[144] 15 USC § 1640(e).

before written notice of an error or the institution of an action for private remedies for the violation of TILA.[145]

**[iii] Bona Fide Error.** The creditor is not liable in any action for private relief if the creditor shows by a "preponderance of evidence that the violation was not intentional and resulted from a bona fide error notwithstanding the maintenance of procedures reasonably adapted to avoid such error." Examples of such bona fide errors include clerical, calculation, computer malfunction, computer programming, and printing errors. But, alas, an error in legal judgment with respect to a person's obligations is not a bona fide error.[146]

**[iv] Good Faith Reliance.** Liability may also be avoided if the creditor engaged in any act or omitted any disclosure in "good faith in conformity with any rule, regulation, or interpretation thereof by the Board or in conformity with any interpretation or approval" by an authorized employee of the FRS.[147]

---

[145] 15 USC § 1640(b).

[146] 15 USC § 1640(c).

[147] 15 USC § 1640(f).

# 3

# Regulation of the Substantive Terms of Consumer Credit Transactions

## ¶ 3.01 CONTROLS ON FINANCE CHARGES: USURY LAWS

### [1] Introduction

Usury is a form of price control on the price of credit in a consumer credit transaction.[1] It is a concept that does not exist in common law; rather, it is a creature of legislation, regulations, or constitutional provisions. Simply put, in a usurious transaction, a creditor charges more "interest" or, in more modern parlance, a greater "finance charge," than that permitted by law.

Remedies for the violation of usury law can be severe. Some state's usury statutes provide that a violation results in a forfeiture of all principal and interest.[2] Another common state remedy provides for all interest to be forfeited and allows the debtor to recover twice the amount of any unlawful interest collected.[3] Federal law provides for a similar penalty.[4]

---

[1] See generally ¶¶ 1.02 and 1.03 concerning the meaning of the term "consumer" and the importance of consumer regulation to debtor-creditor law.

[2] See, e.g, Conn. Gen. Stat. § 37-8.

[3] See, e.g., Fla. Stat. § 687.04.

[4] For national banks, 12 USC § 86; for federally insured depository institutions, §§ 521–523 of the Depository Institutions Deregulation and Monetary Control Act of 1980, Pub. L. No. 96-221, 94 Stat. 161 (codified in various sections of Titles 12 and 15 of the U.S. Code) (hereafter cited as the Monetary Control Act (MCA)). The materials below discuss the applicability of federal or state law.

Although usury historically has been primarily a matter of state law, federal law has become increasingly significant. Overlapping federal and state usury laws present issues of preemption. When state law does control, one must determine which state's law is applicable—a conflicts-of-law issue. The law of any particular state may vary considerably according to the organizational structure of the creditor and other factors. Creditor pressure and economic pressure recently have caused significant change in usury law, with more change to come in the future. This chapter identifies the major issues arising from usury regulation and provides a methodology for resolving them.[5]

## [2] Definition of Usury

In order for usury to occur, all three of the following conditions must be met:

(1) The loan or forbearance of money;

(2) The creditor has extracted a finance charge ("interest") on the loan at a rate prohibited by the applicable law;

(3) The creditor has intended to violate applicable law.[6]

It generally is not difficult to determine when the first and third conditions have been met. If a creditor has loaned money to the debtor, the first condition has been met. Historically, it was assumed that this condition had not been met and there could be no usury when a sale of goods over a period of time was the subject of the transaction. This was the time-price doctrine discussed in Chapter 1.[7] However, most states have adopted specific statutes regulating interest rates on these transactions.[8] If the creditor has intended to impose the finance charge that was in fact levied, whatever the creditor's belief about the legality of the transaction, the third condition is generally met.[9]

In determining whether usury is involved in a transaction, difficulty arises in determining whether the second condition has been met. That inquiry involves two issues: What is the legal rate of finance charge and what is the rate of finance charge actually levied? The following discussion addresses those two issues.

---

[5] The Consumer Credit Guide, published by Commerce Clearing House, compiles federal and state usury statutes.

[6] See generally 45 Am. Jur. 2d Interest and Usury § 5 (1969).

[7] See ¶ 1.03[3][a].

[8] Id.

[9] A programmer's error will typically be considered unintentional assuming the error is not ongoing or caused by poor guidance by management. See Libowsky v. Lakeshore Commercial Fin. Corp., Wis. Ct. App. No. 81-2398, Consumer Cred. Guide (CCH) ¶ 96,770 (Dec. 7, 1982). See generally Leymaster, Consumer Usury and Credit Overcharges 10–11 (National Consumer Law Center 1982).

## [3] What Is the Legal Rate of Finance Charge?

### [a] A Method of Approach

Two basic issues must be resolved to determine the rate of finance charge permitted by law: Does federal or state law apply, and what finance charge does the applicable law allow? A suggested method for approaching these issues is as follows:

(1) Determine the exact organizational structure of the creditor. This is the most important factor for determining generally whether federal or state law applies (as well as which specific federal or state law is applicable). Since federal law also typically preempts with respect to most obligations secured by first liens in residential real property, first liens on residential cooperative housing corporations, or first liens on residential manufactured homes, also determine whether such an obligation is at issue;[10]

(2) Determine whether federal law is applicable to the transaction and, if it is applicable, which specific rate, if any, is the maximum rate for the particular transaction;

(3) If federal law does not apply

(a) Determine which state's law is applicable–a conflicts-of-law issue;

(b) More specifically, characterize the transaction with regard to other factors such as whether the transaction is a loan or credit sale and determine which specific rate, if any, is the maximum rate for the particular transaction.

### [b] Federal Law

Federal usury law is always applicable to credit extended by federally chartered banks. It usually applies to credit extended by federally chartered credit unions, federally insured state-chartered banks and mutual savings banks, federally insured savings and loan associations, and federally insured[11] state-chartered credit unions. Federal usury law also is usually applicable if the transaction results in certain transactions that are secured by a first lien on residential real property, a first lien on a residential cooperative housing corporation, or a first lien on a residential manufactured home.[12] Therefore, organizational structure of the creditor and the nature of the security[13] should be determined in order to decide the applicability of federal law. Federal usury laws are applicable without regard to whether a

---

[10] As is discussed at infra ¶ 3.01[3][b][v], the type of creditor is also important in determining whether these types of transactions are subject to federal preemption.

[11] The applicable federal statutes are discussed in the text that follows.

[12] As is discussed at infra ¶ 3.01[3][b][v], the type of creditor is also important in determining whether these types of transactions are subject to federal preemption.

[13] Id.

transaction is for a consumer or commercial purpose.[14] The primary federal usury laws are contained in certain provisions of the National Bank Act, the Federal Credit Union Act, and the Depository Institutions Deregulation and Monetary Control Act of 1980.[15]

**[i] Federally Chartered Banks.** The National Bank Act (NBA) allows a federally chartered bank (a "national bank") to charge either of the following rates, whichever is greater:

(1) The rate allowed by the laws of the state where the bank is located; or

(2) A rate of one percent greater than the discount rate on ninety-day commercial paper held by the Federal Reserve Bank in the Federal Reserve District where the bank is located.[16]

This federal law preempts state law control of the rates charged by national banks. A state may not override this preemption.

The first rate derives from what is commonly referred to as the "most-favored-lender doctrine." This allows a national bank to charge the highest rate authorized for the lender most favored by the state law in the state in which the bank is located.[17] The most-favored-lender doctrine presents the issue of whether a national bank opting for the most-favored-lender's interest rate opts also for other state controls on that state lender. To illustrate, presume that the Third National Bank decides to charge all its credit card customers a finance charge equivalent to that permitted for finance companies in the state in which the bank is located.[18] Will the Third National Bank be prohibited from making the credit card loan pursuant to the finance company rate if the finance com-

---

[14] With the exception of transactions that are secured by first liens on certain types of real estate and of transactions by federal credit unions, the importance of the federal law is that it enables a covered depository institution to borrow at the rate of a creditor who has the best advantage of a particular state's law. State usury law generally does not cover commercial transactions. See infra ¶ 3.01[3][c]. Therefore, in commercial transactions the effect of allowing most depository institutions to borrow at the state rate is to allow such institutions to charge any rate.

[15] Respectively, 12 USC §§ 85, 1751(5)(A)(vi), and the following sections of the Monetary Control Act: § 501 (certain real estate, cooperative, and manufactured home transactions); § 521 (federally insured state-chartered banks and mutual savings banks); § 522 (federally insured savings and loans); and § 523 (federally insured state-chartered credit unions). See also supra ¶ 3.01[1] note 4.

[16] 12 USC § 85.

[17] See, e.g., Marquette Nat'l Bank of Minneapolis v. First of Omaha Serv. Corp., 439 US 299 (1978); Tiffany v. National Bank of Mo., 85 US 409 (1873).

[18] Finance company rates typically are the highest rates permitted under state law. (In statutes, these are usually called "small loan" statutes because the statutes originally were limited to very small loans.) However, that is not always the case, and there is no need for the bank to choose a rate permitted to traditional competitors of the bank. A national bank, for example, may choose the rate permitted for retail sellers. Northway Lanes v. Gackley Union Nat'l Bank & Trust Co., 464 F2d 855 (6th Cir. 1972).

pany cannot engage in such transactions? There is little relevant law on this subject. The most recent cases hold that the national bank is not subject to such a limitation.[19] Suppose the finance company cannot lend more than $3,000 under state law; would Third National be permitted to do so? The Comptroller of the Currency has ruled that the national bank is limited by such a restriction if it wants to utilize the finance company rate. Loans for amounts exceeding the maximum allowed to the most-favored-lender must be charged another permissible state rate or the one percent above the discount rate permitted by the National Bank Act.[20]

Most-favored-lender status also raises the issue of where a national bank is "located;" that is, whose state law may it utilize? In *Marquette National Bank v. First of Omaha Service Corp.*,[21] the plaintiff asked the Supreme Court to declare unlawful the federally chartered Omaha bank's practice of charging its Minnesota charge card customers the Nebraska rate of finance charge of 18 percent. Minnesota statutes provided that "national banking association[s] doing business in this state" are limited to 12 percent.[22] The Omaha bank clearly was doing business in Minnesota, utilizing agents in Minnesota to offer Minnesota residents charge cards issued by the Omaha bank. The Court, however, refused to declare the practice unlawful, stating that the usury rate for banks in a state where a national bank is doing business is irrelevant. The Court held that the only relevant law is the law of the state in which the bank is located. Since the Omaha bank was located in Nebraska, the Court allowed it to charge the rate permitted in that state.[23]

There is one particularly difficult issue concerning the right of the national banks to charge one percent above the "discount rate on ninety-day commercial paper in the Federal Reserve bank in the Federal Reserve district where the bank is located."[24] In determining the maximum rate, should a simple interest

---

[19] See United Mo. Bank v. Danforth, 394 F. Supp. 774, 783 (ED Mo. 1975) (the court found that the bank's credit card loan to the debtor to buy consumer goods was no different from a finance company loan to buy consumer goods); Equitable Trust Co. v. Sachs, 450 A2d 1273 (Md. 1981) (citing *Danforth*). Contra, Comptroller of the Currency Letter No. 178, Consumer Cred. Guide (CCH) ¶ 97,239 (Jan. 12, 1981).

[20] Comptroller of the Currency Letter No. 178, Consumer Cred. Guide (CCH) ¶ 97,239 (Jan. 12, 1981); see also Deak Nat'l Bank v. Bond, 89 Misc. 2d 95, 390 NYS2d 771 (NY Sup. Ct. 1976). On the subject of the relevance of state restrictions to most-favored lenders, see generally Arnold & Rohner, "The 'Most Favored Lender' Doctrine for Federally Insured Financial Institutions–What Are Its Boundaries?" 31 Catholic U.L. Rev. 1 (1981).

[21] See supra ¶ 3.01[3][b][i] note 16.

[22] Minn. Stat. Ann. § 448.185.

[23] See also Fisher v. First Nat'l Bank of Omaha, 548 F2d 255, 257–258 (8th Cir. 1977); Fisher v. First Nat'l Bank of Chicago, 538 F2d 1284, 1291 (7th Cir. 1976).

[24] 12 USC § 85. This discount rate typically is the same in each of the ten Reserve districts. It is the rate that the Federal Reserve Banks charge its members for large loans. This discount rate has fluctuated substantially over the last few years, rising to as high as 14 percent.

rate–an annual percentage rate–be presumed? Assume, for example, that the federal discount rate is 14 percent. Is a national bank limited to interest calculated at an annual percentage rate of 15 percent (14 plus 1), or may the bank charge interest at a 15 percent discount rate? The significance of this issue is that a 15 percent discount rate is equivalent to an annual percentage rate of 37 percent for a two-year loan or 55 percent for a four-year loan. The issue has not been resolved.[25]

**[ii] Federally Chartered Credit Unions.** The Federal Credit Union Act (FCUA) provides that federally chartered credit unions may impose a finance charge at the rate of 15 percent per year or at a higher rate if allowed by the National Credit Union Administration Board.[26] This law preempts state control of interest rates levied by federally chartered credit unions. The Board has approved rates as high as 20 percent within the last few years.[27]

**[iii] Federally Chartered Savings and Loan Associations.** There is no separate federal usury law for federally chartered savings and loans equivalent to the national bank and national credit union provisions. However, since these institutions are federally insured, they have special privileges under Section 522 of the Monetary Control Act.

**[iv] Federally Insured Depository Institutions.** In 1980, Congress made sweeping changes in the regulation of most financial institutions with the enactment of the Depository Institutions Deregulation and Monetary Control Act of 1980 (MCA).[28] An important part of MCA is its preemption of state usury statutes, subject to an override by the states. Section 521 covers federally insured state-chartered banks and mutual savings banks; Section 522 deals with federally insured savings and loans; and Section 523 covers federally insured state-chartered credit unions.[29]

Contrast a federally "insured" institution with a federally "chartered" institution. Federally chartered financial institutions are organized and licensed by the U.S. government pursuant to federal law. All such institutions and fed-

---

[25] See Evans v. Nat'l Bank, 251 US 108 (1919); First Nat'l Bank in Mena v. Nowlin, 509 F2d 872 (8th Cir. 1975); Northway Lanes v. Hackley Union Nat'l Bank & Trust Co., 464 F2d 855 (6th Cir. 1972) (the latter two cases disagreeing about the effect of *Evans*). See generally Transcript of Program by the Committee on Consumer Financial Services of the American Bar Association 1981 Meeting (ed. W. Burke), "Federal Preemption of Usury Laws," 37 Bus. Law. 747, 762–763 (1982).

[26] 12 USC § 1757(5)(A)(vi).

[27] A national bank may not use the federal credit union rate. Comptroller of the Currency Opinion, Consumer Cred. Guide (CCH) ¶ 96,744 (Jan. 19, 1983). (The rationale behind the National Bank Act was to allow national banks to compete favorably with state creditors. To allow the national banks to use the federal credit union rate would allow the national banks greater rights.)

[28] See supra ¶ 3.01[1] note 4.

[29] Id.

erally chartered savings and loans are also federally insured; that is, federal insurance corporations insure deposits in these institutions. A bank, savings and loan, or credit union may be state-chartered rather than federally chartered (e.g., organized and licensed by a state). State-chartered institutions, like federally chartered institutions, generally have the option to be insured by the appropriate federal insurance corporation.[30]

Sections 521, 522, and 523 of MCA are designed to give federally insured state-chartered banks and mutual savings banks, savings and loans, and state-chartered credit unions the same protection as national banks. These institutions have the same access to the one percent over the discount rate that national banks have.[31] It is generally agreed that Sections 521 through 523 of MCA also give these institutions the most-favored-lender status available to national banks.[32]

Unlike the federal preemption under NBA for federally chartered banks and the law providing rates for federally chartered credit unions, states may override the federal preemptions provided in Sections 521, 522, and 523. This is provided for in Section 525 of MCA.[33] To date, the following states have overridden all or portions of the federal MCA provisions: Colorado, Georgia, Hawaii, Idaho, Iowa, Kansas, Massachusetts, Minnesota, Nebraska, Nevada, North Carolina, South Carolina, South Dakota, and Wisconsin.

**[v] Certain Transactions in Real Estate, Cooperatives, and Manufactured Homes.** Section 501 of MCA preempts most states' usury laws on transactions that are secured by a first lien on residential real property, a first lien on a residential cooperative housing corporation, or a first lien on a residential manufactured home.[34] The creditor must fall within one of the following classes for federal law to be applicable:

(1) Any creditor whose deposits or accounts are federally insured;
(2) Any creditor regulated by any agency of the federal government. (This does not include creditors who are only subject to such federal laws as

---

[30] The relevant insurance provisions are: the Federal Deposit Insurance Act, Pub. L. No. 96-221, 94 Stat. 164, 12 USC § 1831d (1980), for state-chartered banks and mutual savings banks; the National Housing Act, Pub. L. No. 96-221, 94 Stat. 165, 12 USC § 1730g (1980), for savings and loan associations; and the Federal Credit Union Act, Pub. L. No. 97-320, 96 Stat. 1486, 1489, 1540, 12 USC § 1785 (1982), for credit unions.

[31] See supra ¶ 3.01[3][b].

[32] See, e.g., Burke & Kaplinsky, "Unraveling the New Federal Usury Law," 37 Bus. Law. 1079, 1096–1099 (1982). But see Leymaster, Consumer Usury and Credit Overcharges 160–161 (National Consumer Law Center 1982).

[33] See supra ¶ 3.01[1] note 4.

[34] Id. For interpretations of Section 501 of MCA, see regulations issued by the Federal Home Loan Bank Board, 12 CFR Pt. 590.

the Truth-in-Lending Act (TILA) and the Equal Credit Opportunity Act (ECOA).);[35]

(3) Any credit extension made, insured, guaranteed, supplemented, or assisted by the Secretary of Housing and Urban Development (HUD) or any other officer or agency of the federal government or under a housing or urban development program administered by the Secretary of HUD or such other officer or agency;

(4) Any credit extension that is eligible for purchase by the Federal National Mortgage Association, or the Federal Home Loan Mortgage Corporation (FHLMC) or made by any financial institution from which the credit extension could be purchased by the FHLMC;

(5) Any credit extension made by any creditor, as defined in TILA,[36] who makes or invests in residential real estate credit transactions aggregating more than $1 million per year. This dollar requirement does not apply to a creditor selling residential manufactured homes financed by credit secured by first liens on mobile homes if the creditor sells or arranges to sell such loans to a creditor otherwise covered;

(6) Any creditor approved by HUD for participation in any mortgage insurance program under the National Housing Act.

(7) Any individual who finances the sale or exchange of residential real property that the individual owns and occupies or has occupied as his principal residence.

When federal law is applicable to these transactions, there is no limit on the rate of finance charge levied. Section 501 allows states to override the federal preemption with respect to rates on mortgages. The following states have done so: Colorado, Georgia, Hawaii, Idaho, Iowa, Kansas, Massachusetts, Minnesota, Nebraska, Nevada, North Carolina, South Carolina, South Dakota, and Wisconsin. Maine has specifically overridden the preemption in mobile home consumer credit transactions and first lien mortgages on real estate granted by supervised lenders. When state law overrides the federal preemption, state law controls the rates of interest.[37]

**[vi] Trends in Federal Preemptions.** In recent congressional sessions, bills have been introduced to preempt all state usury laws and provide for no limits on interest rates.[38] Although these bills have not passed, it is reasonable to expect further efforts to expand federal preemptions. The success of these efforts depends largely upon whether or not state legislatures keep usury rates above or equal to rates at which creditors are willing to lend.

---

[35] Opinion No. 41 of the General Counsel of Federal Home Loan Bank Board (July 1, 1980).

[36] See ¶ 2.05[2][a].

[37] See infra ¶ 3.01[3][c][ii] notes 49 and 50 and accompanying text.

[38] See, e.g., S. 1406 introduced by Senators Garn, D'Amato, and Proxmire in 1981.

### [c] State Law

**[i] Conflicts-of-Law Issues.** If state usury law is applicable,[39] the first step is to determine which state's laws are applicable—a conflicts-of-law issue. The general rule in usury cases has been that a court should apply the law of the state in which the contract is valid rather than applying the sanctions of the state that would make the contract usurious, provided that the state whose usury law is used bears a normal relationship to the transaction.[40] To protect its residents, some state legislatures have adopted provisions applying their state's law if that state is the domicile of the debtor.[41] In the discussion of federal usury law, it was demonstrated that the most-favored-lender status has the effect of allowing depository institutions entitled to its use to export interest rates from one state to another.[42]

**[ii] Which Usury Law of a State Is Applicable?** It is impossible in the space permitted to specify the applicable rate in each state for every type of transaction. However, the following methodology helps in finding the proper rate:

(1) Characterize the transaction as to a variety of factors. Organizational structure of the creditor, discussed above as the first inquiry in the general method of approach to usury problems,[43] is typically important to a determination of which law of a state is applicable. Other factors that generally must be decided are:

   (a) Whether the transaction is a credit sale of goods or a loan of money;[44]

---

[39] State law may be applicable because federal law is not applicable or because federal law allows a creditor to utilize state law. See the discussion at supra ¶¶ 3.01[3][b][i] and 3.01[3][b][iv] concerning the most-favored-lender status.

[40] Reese, "Choice of Law: Rules or Approach," 57 Cornell L. Rev. 315, 331 (1972); Restatement (Second) of Conflict of Laws § 203 (1971). But see Prebble, "Choice of Law to Determine the Validity and Effect of Contracts," 58 Cornell L. Rev. 635, 681–685 (1973), indicating the disposition of some courts to reject the general rule that protects the state's residents from overreaching out-of-state creditors who may attempt to utilize the higher foreign rate.

[41] E.g., Pa. Stat. Ann. tit. 69, § 21103. This type of statute has survived a number of challenges alleging that it wrongfully interfered with interstate commerce when applied to a mail-order house in Illinois whose only contact with residents of other states was acceptance of orders and distribution of catalogues. E.g., Aldens, Inc. v. LaFollette, 552 F2d 745 (7th Cir.), cert denied, 434 US 880 (1977).

[42] See supra ¶¶ 3.01[3][b][i], 3.01[3][b][iv].

[43] See supra ¶ 3.01[3][a].

[44] ¶ 2.05 concerned TILA and relevant regulations. TILA is federal law that requires disclosure of credit costs in consumer transactions. *The Truth-in-Lending Act does not regulate the amount of finance charge that may be charged. It is not a usury statute.* However, many of the classifications that are important to a determination of the maximum allowable rate of interest under state law are the same types of classifications that need to be made to determine the applicable truth-in-lending disclosures. The

(b) Whether the credit is open-end (revolving) or closed-end;[45]

(c) If a credit sale is involved, the type of goods sold;[46]

(d) The debtor's purpose in obtaining the credit–did the debtor obtain the credit for a personal, family, or household purpose or for a business purpose?[47]

(e) Whether the debtor is a natural person or an organization such as a corporation;

(f) The amount of credit extended–the principal;

(g) Whether the transaction is secured by a first lien in real estate.

(2) Determine the applicable usury law, if any.

If the debtor is a corporation or other legal organization, or the transaction is for a business purpose, state law often provides for no usury limitation.[48] Inquiry concerning the dollar amount of principal is important because some consumer credit statutes (primarily comprehensive codes like the Uniform Consumer Credit Code (UCCC)) do not apply to transactions with a principal above a specified dollar amount, typically $25,000.[49] Determination

---

discussion in Chapter 2 of these classifications, therefore, may be helpful in determining some of the factors set out herein. See, for example, the discussion at ¶ 2.05[3][b] of the difference between a loan and sale under TILA. A word of caution: If state law defines a "credit sale" differently from TILA and if there is some doubt whether a client's transaction fits within the state's usury rate for "credit sales," the state law definition should be followed. The TILA distinctions help when the state law in nonexistent or sketchy.

[45] See id. and ¶ 2.05[3][a].

[46] In states without a comprehensive credit code (see ¶¶ 1.03[3][a][i], 1.03[3][a][ii]) state usury law for credit sales of goods sometimes depends upon whether the sale is for motor vehicles or for other goods. See, e.g., Ariz. Rev. Stat. Ann. §§ 44-281–44-295 and 44-600–44-6006.

[47] See generally ¶ 1.02 concerning the importance of the "consumer" classification to a determination of applicable credit law.

[48] State comprehensive credit codes like the UCCC typically apply only to transactions with natural persons who have engaged in the transaction for a personal, family, or household purpose. See, e.g., Colo. Rev. Stat. §§ 5-2-102, 5-2-104, 3-104. State retail installment sales acts are often limited in the same fashion. See, e.g., Wash. Rev. Code § 63.14.010(1). When these statutes do not apply, the general usury statute of a state is often the only remaining usury law that is arguably applicable. Those statutes generally provide that a business organization cannot raise a defense of usury. See 1 Consumer Cred. Guide (CCH) ¶ 510 (1985) for a chart of the relevant state laws on the subject. Usury statutes of general applicability also sometimes exclude business transactions from coverage. See, e.g., Wash. Rev. Code § 19.52.080. The net effect of these exclusions is that commercial and/or business transactions are not typically subject to usury laws.

[49] See, e.g., Iowa Code § 537.1301. If a particular transaction is normally covered by a comprehensive code but is excluded because the principal is too large, the interest rate of the transaction typically will be covered by a state's usury statute of general applicability, if at all. Some states would provide for no maximum rate on such transactions. See, e.g., Iowa Code § 535.2.

of whether the transaction is secured by a first lien in real estate also is relevant to scope. Federal law serves to preempt most state law that sets rates on transactions secured by a first lien in real estate.[50] In those states that have overridden federal law, state law prevails. The state law that prevails typically is not found in general consumer credit statutes, which usually exclude real estate transactions.[51] In several states that have reasserted their control over real estate transactions, separate statutes setting rates for real estate transactions have been adopted. These statutes typically allow the maximum permissible rate to float depending upon market indicators of the cost of funds to creditors.[52] The following discussion on the applicability of state law presumes a consumer credit transaction in which the debtor is a natural person and the subject of the transaction is not a transaction secured by a first lien in real estate.

After the transaction is classified and it is determined that a consumer credit transaction is involved, one should determine whether the applicable state jurisdiction has a comprehensive form of consumer credit regulation.[53] If the state at issue does have a comprehensive code, the task of finding the specific applicable state law is much simplier than in a state with a scattered approach. For example, if the relevant state law is the UCCC, the applicable usury law for the consumer transaction will generally be found in that statute.

Under the 1968 version of the UCCC, which was chosen by most adopting states,[54] rates depend primarily upon whether the creditor is a supervised lender or nonsupervised lender. Supervised lenders typically include finance ("small loan") companies or any other typical consumer lenders who have received licenses under the UCCC.[55] The loan rate for supervised loans typically is in the form of a step rate–a rate that varies depending upon the balance. For example, in 1984 under Indiana's UCCC, the rate for supervised lenders is 36 percent per year for the part of the unpaid balance of the principal that is $660 or less; 21 percent per year on the part of the unpaid balance of the principal that is more than $660 but does not exceed $2,200; and 15 percent per year on that part of the unpaid balance of the principal that is more than $2,200. In the alternative under the Indiana UCCC, the supervised lender may

---

[50] See supra ¶ 3.01[3][b][v].

[51] See, e.g., Iowa Code § 537.1301(14)(b).

[52] See, e.g., Minn. Stat. § 47.20 (using federal home loan mortgage corporation auction yields as an indicator).

[53] See the discussion at ¶ 1.03[3] concerning those states with comprehensive consumer credit statutes and those with the "scattered" approach to consumer credit.

[54] See ¶ 1.03[3][a][ii] notes 104 and 105 and accompanying text for states adopting the UCCC.

[55] UCCC § 3.503 (1968). Note again that most depository institutions are covered under federal law and because of the most-favored-lender status, may be able to ignore the state rate or choose the highest rate permitted any lender under state law. The supervised lender rate is generally the highest permitted under any adopting state's UCCC. Therefore, a lender that is not obligated to choose this state rate because of the most-favored-lender status may still wish to choose the supervised lender rate. See supra ¶¶ 3.02[3][b][i] and 3.02[3][b][iv] for a discussion of the most-favored-lender status.

charge 21 percent per year.[56] This step rate is not the same in every state. The original UCCC provided for 36 percent on the first $300, 21 percent on the next $700, and 15 percent on any amount over $1,000 or a flat rate of 18 percent.[57] The UCCC further provided that the dollar amounts of the Code were to be subject to change pursuant to the provision's nonadjustment of dollar amounts.[58] The enacting states adopted different provisions initially and adopted differing provisions for the adjustment of dollar amounts.

Rates for loans other than supervised loans under the UCCC also vary by state. In Indiana, for example, the rate is 21 percent per year.[59]

For consumer credit sales under the UCCC, rates also vary from state to state. Typically the rate varies depending upon whether the credit sale is on a revolving plan or nonrevolving plan. For nonrevolving credit sales, the rate generally is identical to the rate for supervised loans.[60] For revolving credit, the rate generally is less than the supervised loan rate and is stated in terms of a percentage charge for each billing cycle and as a step rate. The presumed billing cycle is a monthly cycle.[61] (A typical cycle adopted by creditors is thirty days.) States with versions of the UCCC typically apply the same rate to all consumer credit sales without regard to the type of goods purchased.

In states with a comprehensive code other than the UCCC,[62] there are many different approaches. Most have differentiated their rates much like the UCCC.[63]

In states without a comprehensive code, one finds a variety of laws.[64] Most states have separate retail installment sales acts that regulate the rate of finance charge on consumer credit sales of goods.[65] Rates generally differ for open-end (revolving) and closed-end sales.[66] Some states have rates for the credit sales of motor vehicles that differ from rates for other credit sales.[67]

Finance companies generally have their own statutes for direct loans that they make. Finance company rates generally are the highest authorized rates for consumer loans.[68] Loans by individuals are usually covered by a state's

---

[56] Ind. Code § 24-4.5-3-508.

[57] UCCC § 2.201(2).

[58] UCCC § 2.201(7).

[59] Ind. Code. § 24-4.5-3-201.

[60] See, e.g., Ind. Code § 24-4.5-2-201.

[61] See, e.g., Ind. Code § 24-4.5-2-207 providing for a rate of 2 percent per month on unpaid balances of $500 or less and 1.75 percent per month on any balance of over $500.

[62] See ¶ 1.03[3][a][ii] notes 106 and 109 and accompanying text for states adopting comprehensive codes other than the UCCC.

[63] See, e.g., Iowa Code §§ 537.2201, 537.2301.

[64] See ¶ 1.03[3].

[65] See, e.g., Hawaii Rev. Stat. § 476-1–476-38.

[66] Compare Fla. Stat. § 520.34 with § 520.35.

[67] Fla. Stat. § 520.08.

[68] See, e.g., Wash. Rev. Code § 31.08.160(1) providing for an annual percentage rate of up to 30 percent per year.

general usury statute. Depository institutions that are not covered by federal law[69] are also usually covered by a state's general usury statute. However, these institutions may also be entitled to lend under an "industrial loan law."[70] Occasionally, a separate credit union statute sets rates for state-chartered credit unions.[71]

State laws vary with respect to the form in which maximum interest rates are specified. TILA requires disclosure of interest rates in consumer transactions in the form of an "annual percentage rate,"[72] but it does not mandate that state usury laws use that form. In state comprehensive codes, however, rates are also generally stated in the form of annual percentage rates, and that form clearly is the favored method in all new state legislation.[73] Usury rates of general applicability (e.g., rates that apply within a state when other rates are not applicable) also are expressed as an annual percentage rate.[74]

Interest rates in retail installment sales acts often are stated as an "add-on" rate. For example, for "Class 1" motor vehicles in Florida, the rate of finance charge is expressed as "$10 per $100 per year."[75] For a three-year transaction for a $6,000 auto under such a rate, the finance charge is simply $1,800 (60 × $10 × 3). Ten dollars per one hundred dollars is not the same as a 10 percent annual percentage rate if, as is nearly always the case, the debtor is required to make periodic payments. The classic add-on method of calculating rates is based on the assumption that the borrower has full use of the principal throughout the term of the transaction. In fact, principal is being reduced with each payment. Add-on rates are equivalent to about twice the annual percentage rate. That is, $10 per $100 add-on rate (sometimes expressed as a 10 percent add-on) is close to a 20 percent annual percentage rate.

Finance company rates and industrial loan rates often are expressed in the form of a discount rate. A transaction under a discount rate assumes that the finance charge will be deducted at the beginning of the transaction. For example, a $100 loan for one year at 8 percent discount means the consumer gets the use of only $92. An 8 percent discount rate is equivalent to a 15.7 percent annual percentage rate for one year, 17.3 percent for two years, 18.8 percent for three years, and 22.3 percent for five years.

**[iii] Trends in State Legislation.** In an attempt to meet inflationary and political pressures concerning interest rates, state legislatures have adopted relatively new approaches to the control of interest rates. The most favored approach has been the enactment of new usury laws in which the maximum

---

[69] See supra ¶ 3.01[3][b] listing the institutions covered by federal law and the states that have adopted overrides. Unless a state has overridden federal law, the federal law will prevail.

[70] See, e.g., Wash. Rev. Code §§ 31.04 et seq.

[71] See, e.g., Wash. Rev. Code § 31.12.377.

[72] See generally ¶ 2.04[3][c].

[73] See, e.g., Ind. Code § 28-42-201 (effective 1983).

[74] See, e.g., Wash. Rev. Code § 19.52.020.

[75] See, e.g., Fla. Stat. § 520.08.

rate of interest floats with a specified economic indicator.[76] Theoretically this allows maximum rates to regulate interest rates without unduly restricting the availability of credit during periods of high market rates. A few states have effectively repealed their usury laws.[77]

State legislative activity on usury law will probably arise in the future whenever market pressures near the levels that existed during the early 1980s. Many believe continued high federal deficits will insure such pressure. The most-favored-lender status will serve to pressure state legislatures into making decisions about state usury law. As discussed above, that doctrine allows a depository institution subject to the law to export rates from one state to another.[78] For example, a national bank located in South Dakota may charge a Colorado customer the highest rate permitted in South Dakota. South Dakota essentially does not have any usury limitations[79] and is actively soliciting federal institutions to locate there for this very reason. A state legislature might be persuaded to set higher rates for a federal institution to avoid having that institution move its credit operation to South Dakota.

## [4] What Was the Rate of Finance Charge Actually Levied?

In order to determine whether usury is involved in a particular transaction, it is necessary to compare the rate of finance charge actually levied with the legal rate of finance charge. The rate of finance charge actually levied is a function of the time the credit is outstanding, the principal balance, and the dollar amount of finance charge. Once the value of these elements is determined for a transaction, the rate of finance charge actually levied may be determined by the use of mathematical formulae or commercially available charts, or by programming the values into a calculator or computer equipped to handle such calculations.

The difficulty in determining the rate actually charged is not in making these calculations but in determining the values of the required factors of time, principal, and dollar amount of finance charge. The rate changes according to changes in these values. For example, if a creditor is able to assign a $49 charge to principal, the rate of finance charge will be less than the rate if the creditor includes the charge as part of the finance charge. Since it is important to properly determine the values of principal and amount of finance charge, one would expect state usury laws to clearly define these terms. A charge for a particular item should be defined as a finance charge or part of principal so that the actual rate levied on any particular transaction can be determined and then compared with the maximum permissible rate. The UCCC and other comprehensive state codes that clearly define these terms have borrowed heavily from TILA. In these states, what is part of the finance charge for disclosure purposes

[76] See, e.g., Wash. Rev. Code § 19.52.020 (government bond yields).

[77] See, e.g., S.D. Codified Laws Ann. § 54-3-14; 1982 S.D. Sess. Laws. 178, § 1.

[78] See supra ¶ 3.01[3][b].

[79] Id.

under TILA typically will be part of the finance charge for purposes of calculating whether an excessive rate has been charged.[80]

States without comprehensive codes, however, have sketchy definitions of the important term "finance charge" (or a synonym such as "service charge"). Retail installment sales acts usually are the most specific.[81]

If state statutes or regulations do not define the relevant terms, one must resort to case law. Most common law involves interpretations of usury statutes of general applicability rather than specific statutes such as retail installment sales acts. Nevertheless, if the specific statute is silent with respect to the treatment of a particular charge, common law typically prevails.

Various charges typically are treated in the following manner. As a general rule, any general "service" or other charge can be expected to be considered a part of the finance charge. Charges typically excluded from the finance charge (and therefore to be treated as part of the principal) are any charges specifically excluded by statute or regulation or any separate charge to reimburse the creditor for reasonable and necessary expenditures incurred by the creditor in making the loan.[82] The following types of charges are generally excluded if reasonable and necessary:

(1) Official fees, sales taxes, and other charges actually paid to state officials. An example would be the filing fee paid to a state official to file a financing statement covering secured collateral;[83]

(2) Fees paid to third persons such as attorney fees, credit report charges, and fees for the appraisal of collateral;[84]

(3) Commitment fees (charges for agreeing to lend money in the future) generally are not part of the finance charge if reasonable;[85]

(4) Credit card membership fees;[86]

(5) Delinquency and other late payment or foreclosure charges levied because of the debtor's default. These generally are separately regulated;[87]

---

[80] See, e.g., Wis. Stat. § 421.301.

[81] See, e.g., Wash. Rev. Code § 63.14.010(8).

[82] See, e.g., Opinion of the Michigan Att'y Gen., Consumer Cred. Guide (CCH) ¶ 97,125 (1981). Any specific expenditure that is not reasonable and necessary or a part of general operating expenses such as indirect overhead would typically be considered as part of the finance charge. Id.

[83] See, e.g., Ga. Code § 10-1-2.

[84] See, e.g., Bundrick v. First Nat'l Bank of Jacksonville, 570 SW2d 12 (Tex. Civ. App. 1978) (allowing attorney fees). But see Browne v. Nowlin, 117 Ariz. 73, 570 P2d 1246 (1977) (allowing title examination fees but not attorney fees). Attorney fees available upon default are often separately regulated. See infra ¶ 3.04[2].

[85] See, e.g., Kissell Co. v. Gressley, 591 F2d 47 (9th Cir. 1979).

[86] See, e.g., Equitable Trust Co. v. Sachs, 450 A2d 1273 (Md. 1981).

[87] See, e.g., Cal. Civ. Code § 1803.6.

(6) Credit insurance. These charges generally are separately regulated. Charges in compliance with these regulations typically are excluded from finance charges;[88]

(7) Prepayment penalties. Most usury statutes allow the consumer to prepay without penalty. That is, if the consumer repays a closed-end transaction earlier than originally anticipated, most usury laws provide that the creditor may not charge the debtor for unearned interest. The amount of earned interest on such transactions is generally calculated by the "Rule of 78's."[89] In the absence of such a statute, however, some courts have held that the creditor may levy a prepayment penalty.[90]

If no law can be found in state statutes or case law concerning the treatment of a particular type of charge, it can be argued that TILA treatment of the charge should be adopted. TILA contains the most complete definition of the term "finance charge." Also, it is good policy to adopt methods of calculating rates to determine compliance with usury laws that are the same as those used for disclosure purposes. Finally, TILA represents the "state of the art" on how to treat various charges, as demonstrated by several states' utilization of the TILA meaning of finance charge. It should be emphasized again, however, that TILA does not control usury law, but merely specifies disclosure requirements. If state law clearly specifies that a particular charge is to be excluded from the calculation of finance charges for purposes of a determination concerning usury, the state law must be followed.

## ¶ 3.02 LIMITATIONS ON SECURITY INTERESTS

### [1] Introduction

Article 9 of the Uniform Commercial Code (UCC) is of critical importance in debtor-creditor law.[1] The provisions contained in Article 9 specify the rights and obligations of a creditor with a "security interest" in personal property of the debtor. A creditor can gain important rights under Article 9–rights of self-help repossession against the debtor and priority rights against other claimants in the debtor's property. Chapter 7 specifies the rights and obliga-

---

[88] See, e.g., Wis. Stat. §§ 424.101–424.402.

[89] See, e.g., the following provisions in retail installment sales acts: Ala. Code tit. 5 § 318; Cal. Civ. Code §§ 1803.2, 1806.3; Mass. Gen. Laws Ann. ch. 255D, §§ 9, 13.

[90] See, e.g., Carpenter v. Winn, 39 Colo. App. 238, 566 P2d 370, 371 (1977).

[1] The UCC is the law in forty-nine states. Louisiana has not adopted the entire UCC. There are variations in the UCC as adopted from state to state. These variations are catalogued by state in the Uniform Laws Annotated (West) and the Uniform Commercial Code Reporting Service State Correlation Table (Callaghan). The state variations are minimal in the sections discussed in this part.

tions of both the debtor and creditor upon default and priority rights of the creditor against third-party claimants. This section focuses on the restrictions imposed by Article 9 of the UCC and other state law that limits a creditor's ability to acquire the Article 9 security interest necessary to gain secured creditor status.

Article 9 itself places some restriction on a creditor's ability to take consumer goods as collateral under a security interest. In regard to consumer credit sales and, to a lesser extent, consumer loans, most states have consumer credit laws outside Article 9 that serve to regulate the scope of Article 9 security interests.

## [2] Limitations Under Article 9 of the Uniform Commercial Code

As stated above, and as detailed in Part III, a creditor who properly utilizes Article 9 of the UCC can gain important rights in a debtor's personalty both against the debtor and against third-party claimants. Article 9's right to self-help repossession against the debtor is of chief practical importance to the creditor,[2] as is priority status against third parties.[3] In order to gain these rights, it is essential that the debtor acquire an "attached" security interest.[4] Without this interest, a creditor is not a secured creditor under Article 9 and thus is not entitled to the special rights of self-help repossession and priority status. A creditor who acts as if he has the rights of an Article 9 secured creditor when in fact he does not, may be liable in a conversion action brought by the debtor or by the debtor's representative, including a trustee in bankruptcy, or by other claimants. Further, a violation of Part 5 of Article 9, which includes engaging in self-help repossession without an attached security interest, may give rise to a penalty under UCC Section 9-507.[5]

"Attachment" is a term of art under Article 9. To acquire attachment, a creditor typically must have the debtor execute a proper, written "security agreement." The creditor must give value, and the debtor must have "rights in the collateral."[6] Until these three requirements exist, the creditor is not an Article 9 secured creditor with the accompanying rights of a secured creditor. If the parties so contemplate, a security interest may "attach" to collateral that is acquired at a later date than the collateral that initially is the subject of a secur-

---

[2] See UCC § 9-503.

[3] See UCC Article 9, Part 3.

[4] See UCC § 9-203. Under the 1972 version of Article 9, the version now the law in nearly all states (see Part III), an "enforceable" security interest is obtained at the same time "attachment" occurs. UCC § 9-203(1). "Attachment" will be used here to indicate an "enforceable" and "attached" security interest.

[5] UCC § 9-507(1). The section provides for actual damages. Also, when the collateral is consumer goods (goods held by the debtor for a personal, household, or family purpose (UCC § 9-109(1)), the section provides that the debtor may recover not less than the finance charge plus 10 percent of the principal.

[6] UCC § 9-203(1). Specific agreement may postpone the time of attachment. UCC § 9-203(2).

ity interest. That is, provisions in a security agreement that provide for attachment in "after-acquired" collateral generally are enforceable.[7]

There is, however, an important limitation on the acquisition of an attached interest in after-acquired collateral if the collateral is consumer goods. Such goods are defined as those that the debtor is holding for a "personal, household, or family purpose."[8] No security interest may attach to these consumer goods (other than "accessions") unless the debtor acquires the goods within ten days after the creditor gives value.[9] If the creditor runs afoul of this limitation, the creditor has no Article 9 rights with respect to consumer goods acquired beyond the ten-day limitation.

## [3] Limitations in Consumer Credit Regulation

### [a] Consumer Credit Sales

**[i] Limitations on Type of Collateral.** Under the official UCCC, in a consumer credit sale of goods or services, the creditor generally may not take a security interest in any real or personal property of the debtor other than what was sold.[10] The creditor may, however, take a security interest in goods upon which services are performed or in which goods sold are installed, or to which they are annexed, if the debt secured is $300 or more. In addition, in such a sale, a creditor may take an interest in land to which the sold goods are affixed or which is maintained, repaired, or improved as a result of the sale of the goods or services if the debt secured is $1,000 or more. Under the official UCCC, a security interest in violation of the restrictions is void, and the $300 and $1,000 figures are subject to adjustment.[11] States with other comprehensive codes have similar limitations.[12]

In states with a scattered approach to consumer credit legislation,[13] any legislation on security interests in consumer credit sales are likely to be found in the state's retail installment sales act, if it exists at all. Most states that have

---

[7] UCC § 9-204(1).

[8] UCC § 9-109(1).

[9] UCC § 9-204(2). In the typical consumer case, a creditor makes only one advance of "value"; the advance occurs when the original transaction is consummated or shortly thereafter. In some transactions, however, a creditor may make a series of cash advances beyond the initial advance. These "future advances" are authorized under the UCC whether or not they are subject to a prior commitment by the creditor to make advances. Each of these advances are transfers of value and as long as after-acquired collateral is acquired not more than ten days past any of the advances, there would probably be attachment in the after-acquired collateral.

[10] UCCC §§ 3.301 (1974), 2.407 (1968). See ¶ 1.02(3) for a list of those states adopting the UCCC and the version adopted.

[11] UCCC §§ 3.301 (1974), 2.407 (1968). Within those states adopting the UCCC these amounts vary.

[12] See, e.g., Wis. Stat. Ann. § 422.417.

[13] See ¶ 1.02[3][a][i] for a list of the states with such an approach.

such restrictions have provisions like the UCCC provision discussed above [14] although there generally are no dollar limitations.[15] In a few states, similar provisions are found in retail installment sales acts that cover only the credit sale of motor vehicles.[16]

**[ii] Debt Secured by Cross Collateral.** When a consumer debtor becomes obligated on a subsequent consumer credit sale with the same creditor, it is common for the creditor to consolidate the first and subsequent transactions. A typical provision in consolidated transactions provides that collateral taken in all transactions secures the consolidated transaction. For example, assume a particular consumer purchased a $400 TV on credit in 1983. If the consumer wishes to purchase a $600 refrigerator from the same creditor in 1986, the creditor may consolidate any amounts still due from him on the TV (remaining principal plus unpaid but earned finance charge) with the principal owed on the TV. This would be the principal on the consolidated transaction. In this transaction, a question arises concerning how long the creditor should retain a security interest in both the TV and the refrigerator. Should a security interest be retained in the TV until the consumer pays the entire amount due on the consolidated transaction (principal as calculated above plus a finance charge on the consolidated principal)? Or should the security interest be released on the TV at some earlier time?

In the case of *Williams v. Walker Thomas Furniture Co.*,[17] the creditor allocated the debtor's payments on a pro rata basis in order to keep a security interest on all items as long as any amount was owed. The court remanded to a lower court for a finding as to the unconscionability of the practice.[18] In this case there was no specified procedure for the allocation of the debtor's payments.

Many states specify how payments are to be allocated for purposes of determining the extent of collateral remaining on a consolidated transaction. Both versions of the UCCC provide for a first-in first-out method of allocation. Payments are to be allocated "first to the payment of the debts arising from the sales first made. To the extent debts are paid . . . security interests . . . terminate."[19] Other comprehensive codes have similar provisions.[20]

---

[14] See, e.g., Cal. Civ. Code § 1804.3; Hawaii Rev. Stat. § 476.15; Mass. Gen. Laws Ann. ch. 255D § 15; N.Y. Pers. Prop. Law § 421; Ohio Rev. Code Ann. § 1317.071.

[15] Id. But see N.C. Gen. Stat. § 25-A-23(a) adopting the $300 and $1,000 limitations of the official UCCC.

[16] See, e.g., Cal. Civ. Code § 2984.1(a); Ky. Rev. Stat. Ann. § 190.100(1)(b); Mass. Gen. Laws Ann. ch. 255B, § 201(3); N.J. Stat. Ann. § 17:16C-40.1.

[17] 350 F2d 445 (DC Cir. 1965).

[18] Id. Although the UCC was not effective in the jurisdiction, the court utilized UCC § 2-302 because of its "persuasive authority."

[19] UCCC §§ 2.409 (1968), 3.303 (1974), 3.301 (1974), 2.407 (1968). See ¶ 1.02(3) for a list of those states adopting the UCCC and the version adopted.

[20] See, e.g., Wis. Stat. Ann. § 422.418.

In states with the scattered approach to consumer credit legislation,[21] a few have provisions like the UCCC provision quoted above.[22] The most common allocation required is that all payments prior to a consolidation must be deemed to have been applied to the first purchase, but any payment subsequent to allocation is to be applied in the same ratio as the original cash sale prices of the various purchases bear to the total.[23] This allocation has the effect of allowing the creditor a security interest in earlier obtained collateral not allowed by the UCCC provision quoted above, which requires the allocation of the entire payments to collateral first subject to a security interest of the creditor.

### [b] Consumer Loans

There are relatively few state law restrictions on security interests taken in consumer loans. The UCCC restrictions on security interests in consumer credit sales do not apply in consumer loans. The comprehensive code in Wisconsin—the Wisconsin Consumer Act—does, however, place some restrictions on security interests in loans. The Wisconsin Consumer Act prohibits non-purchase-money security interests[24] in clothing of the debtor and dependents, household goods listed in the relevant section, and real property if the obligation secured is less than $1000.[25]

Retail installment sales acts do not cover direct loans, so the provisions in such statutes in states with the scattered approach provide no limitations for consumer loans. A few states with the scattered approach have other limitations. The most common type of limitation is a provision in some states' small-loan laws (finance company acts) that requires a signature by both spouses before the creditor may obtain a security interest in household goods.[26] New Hampshire's small-loan law prohibits household goods as collateral even in a purchase-money secured transaction unless the loan is over $2,000.[27] Connecti-

---

[21] See ¶ 1.02[3][a][i] for a list of the states with such an approach.

[22] See, e.g., Ala. Code § 5-19-9; W. Va. Code § 46-A-2-109.

[23] See, e.g., Ky. Rev. Stat. Ann. § 371.290(3); Wash. Rev. Code § 63.14.110.

[24] "Purchase-money security interests" are defined in UCC § 9-107. If a seller takes a security interest in the item sold, it is a purchase-money security interest. If a lender lends a debtor money to buy collateral and the money is in fact used, the lender's security interest in such collateral is a purchase-money security interest.

[25] Wis. Stat. Ann. § 422.417(3)(a).

[26] Ariz. Rev. Stat. Ann. § 6-630; Hawaii Rev. Stat. § 409-20; Ill. Rev. Stat. ch. 74, § 35; Mich. Comp. Laws Ann. § 493.17; Minn. Stat. Ann. §§ 56.17, 56.19; N.J. Stat. Ann. § 17:10-18; N.M. Stat. Ann. § 58-15-22; N.D. Cent. Code § 13-03-15(3); Ohio Rev. Code Ann. § 1391.06; R.I. Gen. Laws § 19-25-33; Vt. Stat. Ann. tit. 8, § 2228; Va. Code § 6.1-289.

[27] N.H. Rev. Stat. Ann. § 399-A-7(i)(b). For a discussion of purchase-money security interests, see supra ¶ 3.02[3][b] note 24.

cut seems to have the broadest provision prohibiting non-purchase-money security interests in most consumer credit transactions.[28]

## ¶ 3.03 INSULATION FROM LIABILITY: THE HOLDER-IN-DUE-COURSE DOCTRINE

### [1] Introduction

When goods or services are not of promised quality or if the seller otherwise breaches its performance obligation, the debtor-buyer may have a right to stop paying.[1] If the debtor has a legal reason for nonpayment, there is no default because of nonpayment and the creditor's rights dependent upon default do not arise.

The focus here is on the issue of who is subject to the debtor's defenses. When may the debtor-buyer exercise a right to stop paying for defective goods or services (or raise another defense to nonpayment)—a right that would have been available against the seller—against a third-party financer of the transaction? This third party generally is a bank, finance company, credit union, or other financial institution. Such an institution may be a "financer" of the credit sale because the institution ends up holding the buyer's obligation originally payable to the seller or because the buyer initially borrowed the money from an institution in order to purchase an item from the seller.

Under the UCC and common law, financers are free of the buyer's claims and defenses against the seller if any of three financing arrangements exist. The first of these involves the true "holder in due course," the second concerns the use of a "waiver-of-defense clause," and the third involves a direct loan by a lender to enable the buyer to purchase from the seller.[2]

To illustrate the effect of the true holder in due course doctrine, assume that *A* wishes to purchase an automobile from a car dealer. The seller, *B*, tells *A* that he can do so on credit, so *A* signs a promissory note in which he promises to pay the price of the automobile plus finance charges to *B* or to the "order of *B*." That is, assume *A* executes a negotiable instrument as defined in the

---

[28] Conn. Gen. Stat. § 42-89.

[1] Section 2-717 of the UCC allows the buyer of goods, upon notification to the seller, to deduct from the price owed an amount equivalent to any damages resulting from any breach by the seller. In an Article 2 sale of goods it is not any defect, however, that gives a buyer the right to "cancel" (i.e., stop paying altogether). Under UCC § 2-711, the buyer may do so only in the case of nondelivery or when goods are properly rejected or acceptance is revoked. Even if there is no right to "cancel" because the buyer has finally accepted the goods, the buyer may still be able to deduct part of the price owed—the amount equivalent to any damages resulting from the buyer's breach. Under the law of "conditions" and "setoff," similar principles exist at common law for contracts for the provision of personal services.

[2] Discussions of the insulation from liability of a financer under all three of these concepts often placed together are under the generic term "holder in due course." Clear analysis of existing limitations, however, demands distinguishing among the three.

UCC.[3] If *B* negotiates that note to a third party, typically a bank or finance company, the financer is a holder of the note.[4] If the holder gives value for the note, takes the note in good faith, and without notice of claims and defenses, the financer is a holder in due course under the UCC.[5] This status insulates the financer from any personal defenses the maker, *A*, has against the seller, *B*. Personal defenses may arise from breach of warranty, or other breach relating to quality, quantity, or delivery.[6]

The effect of the "waiver-of-defense clause" under the UCC is the same as that of the holder-in-due-course clause. In the hypothetical situation above, assume that instead of having *A* sign a negotiable instrument, as defined in Article 3 of the UCC, *B* has *A* sign a simple contract to pay the credit obligation to *B*. Further assume that, after consummation of the credit sale, *B* assigns *A*'s contract to a bank. Under the simple contract law of assignments, the bank would be subject to defenses that *A* has against *B*. The bank cannot be a true holder in due course because that requires the execution of a "negotiable instrument."[7] However, if the contract signed by *A* contains a waiver-of-defense clause and the bank takes the contract assignment for value, in good faith, and without notice of claims and defenses, then the bank has the same insulation from liability as if it had the status of a true holder in due course.[8]

To illustrate the insulation from liability of the direct lender, assume that *B* tells *A* that he is not in the credit business. He adds, however, that *A* can probably get a bank loan to purchase a used car. *A* subsequently gets a loan from the bank to use for the purchase of the car from *B*. If the car is not of promised quality, the bank is likely to say that it is not responsible and that it is merely a lender of money and not the seller of goods. Although the UCC is silent as to the bank's status, common law would be on its side.

The following section demonstrates significant limitations on the insulation from liability of financers of consumer credit sales. In commercial transactions, the general insulation discussed above remains the general rule.

---

[3] A promissory note may be one type of negotiable instrument if it meets the requirements for such an instrument under UCC § 3-104. Assume here that the promissory note meets those requirements.

[4] UCC § 3-202.

[5] Id.

[6] See UCC § 3-305. The holder in due course is subject to "real defenses." UCC § 3-306. These are rare. Circumstances that make the contract void rather than merely voidable, such as "fraud in the factum," are such real defenses. See ¶ 2.02[a] note 16.

[7] See UCC § 3-202. A typical installment contract does not meet the definition of "negotiable instrument." It is not payable to order or to bearer and it generally is not conditional–two requirements for negotiability. UCC § 3-104.

[8] If the obligation assigned includes a UCC Article 9 security interest in personal property, the insulation would derive from UCC § 9-206 (subject to any contrary law concerning "consumer goods"). If the obligation is not covered under the UCC, simple contract law would give the same insulation to the assignee who has the benefit of the waiver clause.

## [2] Judicial Limitations

Many cases concern the true holder-in-due-course status and the effect of waiver-of-defense clauses. Most cases have focused on whether there was "value," "good faith," or "notice of claims and defenses." Usually, unless a buyer can show one of these prerequisites has not been met, the assignee or holder in due course is found to be free from the defenses of the buyer. Historically, it has not been an easy task for the buyer. For example, if the buyer is trying to show lack of good faith, it is insufficient to merely demonstrate that the financer has been engaged in practices unacceptable in the trade. The definition of good faith has been said to be "subjective," not dependent upon an objective standard (e.g., a "reasonable lender" standard). Instead, the issue has been whether the particular institution has intentionally acted in bad faith.[9] However, in some states, courts recently have been more ready to deny the holder-in-due-course and waiver-of-defense insulation to creditors. In nearly all such cases, the buyer has been a consumer and there has been some type of close relationship between the seller and financial institution that justified making the lender and seller equally liable for personal defenses.[10] These cases, however, have not heralded any new trend in many jurisdictions[11] and have still involved a case-by-case resolution.

There are almost no common-law cases on the traditional insulation of the direct lender. The reason for this may simply be the general acceptance by debtors' attorneys of direct lenders' insulation from liability.[12]

## [3] Statutory Limitations

### [a] True Holder-in-Due-Course Status

During the 1960s and 1970s, most states placed restrictions on the true holder-in-due-course doctrine in consumer credit transactions.[13] All states with comprehensive consumer credit codes have some control.[14] The official 1968 UCCC position adopted by most enacting states bans the use of negotiable documents (other than currently dated checks) in all consumer credit

---

[9] See, e.g., New Jersey Mortgage & Inv. Co. v. Calvetti, 68 NJ Super. 18, 171 A2d 321 (1961); see also Littlefield, "Good Faith Purchase of Commercial Paper: The Failure of the Subjective Test," 39 S. Cal. L. Rev. 48 (1966).

[10] See, e.g., Unico v. Owens, 50 NJ 101, 232 A2d 405 (1967).

[11] See, e.g., Implement Credit Corp. v. Elsinger, 268 Wis. 143, 66 NW2d 657 (1955).

[12] See generally Note, "Direct Loan Financing of Consumer Purchases," 85 Harv. L. Rev. 1409 (1972).

[13] See Crandall, "The Wisconsin Consumer Act: Wisconsin Consumer Credit Laws Before and After," 1973 Wis. L. Rev. 334, for a collection of state laws on the subject until 1973.

[14] See ¶ 1.03[3][a][ii] for a discussion of the states with such codes.

sales of goods and services.[15] Other comprehensive codes have similar provisions.[16]

In states with a scattered approach to consumer credit regulation, limitations on true holder-in-due-course status are found, if at all, in a state's retail installment sales acts.[17] Limitations in such statutes generally take one of two forms. One type of statute is similar to that of the 1968 UCCC, which provides for a prohibition on the use of negotiable instruments.[18] The other approach provides that any negotiable instrument must have a notation on it providing that the holder is subject to any defenses good against the seller.[19] The latter approach is based on the assumption that, if such notice exists, an otherwise negotiable instrument is not negotiable.[20] Since holder-in-due-course status depends in part upon holding a "negotiable instrument,"[21] there can be no holder in due course of a note with the required notice. A limitation on holder-in-due-course status in some retail installment sales does not insure in every jurisdiction that there is an equivalent limitation on all such sales. Retail installment sales acts vary in scope. In some states, these acts cover all consumer credit sales of goods, but in others there are separate acts for different types of goods, and a limitation in one act may not exist in another.[22]

### [b] Waiver-of-Defense Clause

Most states that have limited the effect of the true holder-in-due-course doctrine in consumer credit sales have also done something about the effect of the waiver-of-defense clause in these transactions. States with the UCCC have taken two approaches.[23] One approach provides that the debtor may raise

---

[15] UCCC § 2.403 (1968).

[16] See, e.g., Wis. Stat. Ann. § 422.406. The Wisconsin Consumer Act provision and the 1974 UCCC clear up a potential problem with the 1968 UCCC provision. Although it was conceptually unlawful for a seller to take a negotiable instrument, a seller could violate the 1968 UCCC prohibition and negotiate the note to a holder-in-due-course who would get the protection of such status. See UCCC § 2.403 (1968) and Official Comment. The Wisconsin Consumer Act and the 1974 UCCC provide that a holder of a negotiable note issued in violation of the prohibition against such notes takes subject to the debtor's defenses. Wis. Stat. Ann. § 422.406; UCCC § 3.404 (1974). Colorado has adopted the 1974 language (Colo. Rev. Stat. § 5-2-403), as well as states with comprehensive codes other than the UCCC. See, e.g., Iowa Code § 537.3404.

[17] See ¶ 1.03[3] for a discussion of consumer legislation in states with a scattered approach.

[18] See, e.g., Minn. Stat. § 325.941(1). For a discussion of a potential problem with this type of language–what if the seller takes such an instrument in violation of the law–see supra ¶ 3.03[3][a] note 16.

[19] See, e.g., Alaska Stat. § 45.50.541(a).

[20] See UCC § 3-104 stating that a "negotiable instrument" must not be conditional. The language of the notice would make a writing conditional.

[21] See UCC § 3-302.

[22] See generally ¶ 1.03[3][b].

[23] This is because the UCCC proposed two alternatives. UCCC § 2.404 (1968).

defenses against the assignee despite a waiver-of-defense clause with no specified time limit within which such a claim must be raised. Utah was the only state to adopt this approach.[24] Another approach, adopted by the other original UCCC states,[25] requires the debtor to raise the defense in writing within a specified time period. Most states with comprehensive codes other than the UCCC have also adopted this approach.[26]

Fewer states with a scattered approach[27] have dealt with the effect of the waiver-of-defense clause than states that have dealt with the true holder-in-due-course doctrine. Such legislation usually is found, if it exists, in a state's retail installment sales act. Typically, such legislation is in the form of an outright ban on the effect of such a clause.[28] Some states, however, have a time limitation like that discussed above as one variation of the 1968 UCCC.[29] Also, note that the coverage of the retail installment sales act containing a limitation must be checked before determining whether the limitation is applicable to any particular credit sale.[30]

An issue with all legislation designed to limit the effect of a waiver-of-defense clause is the extent to which the assignee is liable to the debtor for the debtor's defenses against the seller. When a statute provides that a waiver clause is ineffective to insulate the assignee, does that mean the debtor may bring an affirmative action against the assignee to recover amounts paid before a defense arises or is the assignee's liability limited to only those amounts still owed? Under the 1974 UCCC, the assignee is not liable at all unless the consumer has made a good faith attempt to obtain satisfaction from the seller with respect to the defense. Even then, the amount of liability of the assignee is limited to the amount owed the assignee with respect to the sale at the time the assignee has notice of the defense.[31] Under the Wisconsin Consumer Act, liability includes any amounts already paid to the lender if a judgment against the seller cannot be satisfied.[32] In retail installment sales acts, there is often no specified limitation.[33] However, this probably represents an oversight rather

---

[24] See Utah Code Ann. § 70B-2-404.

[25] See ¶ 1.03[3][a][ii] for a discussion of the states with such codes.

[26] See, e.g., Iowa Code § 537.3404 (thirty days). This is true even though the 1974 UCCC has removed the alternative that specifies a time limit. See UCCC § 3.404 (1974).

[27] See ¶ 1.03[3] for a discussion of consumer legislation in states with a scattered approach.

[28] See, e.g., Wash. Rev. Code §§ 63.14.020, 63.14.150.

[29] See, e.g., Del. Code Ann. tit. 6, §§ 4311(a), 4312 (fifteen days).

[30] See, e.g., Ky. Rev. Stat. Ann. § 371.320 (1969) placing a limitation on all credit sales except motor vehicles. Motor vehicle sales in which the purchase price is less than $5,000 are governed by the Motor Vehicle Installment Sales Act, where there is no similar provision.

[31] UCCC § 3.404 (1974).

[32] Wis. Stat. Ann. § 422.407.

[33] See, e.g., Wash. Rev. Code § 63.14.150.

than a legislative decision to allow unlimited liability. Other retail installment sales acts do limit liability of the assignee.[34]

### [c] Direct Loans

Little state legislation is directed toward making a direct lender subject to defenses the buyer has against the seller—the insulation set out in the third hypothetical situation. State legislation that does so is designed to limit liability in consumer credit sales to situations in which the seller and lender have some type of interlocking relationship.

Since the 1968 UCCC does not have this limitation, the majority of the UCCC states do not have an interlocking loan provision. The 1974 UCCC has such a provision,[35] but as indicated previously, only Idaho has adopted the 1974 UCCC,[36] and Idaho chose not to adopt the interlocking lender provision. One state, Iowa, with a comprehensive code other than the UCCC, however, has borrowed from the 1974 UCCC interlocking loan provision.[37] The Wisconsin Consumer Act also has such a provision.[38] Although all states with interlocking lender provisions have different criteria for the requisite relationship between the lender and seller, the following criteria are typical:

(1) The seller and lender are "related"; that is, they are jointly controlled, or the seller owns the lender, or the lender owns the seller;
(2) The seller uses forms supplied by the lender or prepares documents used by the lender;
(3) The seller refers on a regular basis its customers to the lender;
(4) The lender pays a commission to the seller;
(5) The lender has recourse to the seller under a guaranty or other similar account.[39]

A few states taking the scattered approach[40] have a provision making the interlocking direct lender subject to defenses of the buyer.[41] However, most states, even those that have controlled the true holder-in-due-course status and effect of the waiver-of-defense clause, do not have legislation with respect to the liability of the closely related third-party direct lender.

---

[34] See, e.g., Minn. Stat. § 325.941 (limitation on the amount owing to the assignee at the time the defense is asserted).

[35] UCCC § 3.404 (1974).

[36] See ¶ 1.03[3][a][ii].

[37] See Iowa Code § 537.3405.

[38] Wis. Stat. Ann. § 422.408.

[39] See id. Under the Wisconsin act, knowledge that the seller has a reputation for not remedying complaints may also create the requisite relationship. Id.

[40] See ¶ 1.03[3] for a discussion of consumer legislation in states with a scattered approach.

[41] See, e.g., N.Y. Gen. Bus. Law § 253.

### [4] The Federal Trade Commission Rule

In 1975, the Federal Trade Commission (FTC), pursuant to its rulemaking authority,[42] promulgated the rule on Preservation of Consumer Claims and Defenses.[43] The rule is designed to remove the insulation from liability of the true holder in due course, assignee with a waiver-of-defense clause, and interlocking direct lender in consumer credit transactions for the purchase of goods and services. Before discussing details of the rule, it is important to reemphasize the effect of a rule issued by the FTC. All that such a rule can do is define unfair and deceptive behavior and prohibit it. Enforcement of such a rule is by the FTC. There is no private enforcement under federal law of an FTC rule. In a state with a "little FTC act," one might be able to enforce a state's unfair and deceptive act because of a violation of an FTC rule.[44] Further, the specific rule of concern here only proscribes unfair and deceptive behavior by "sellers" and not "lenders." Under present law, it is not an unfair and deceptive trade practice for a "lender" to fail to do anything required by the rule.[45]

#### [a] General Scope

The FTC rule on Preservation of Consumer Claims and Defenses applies to "consumer credit contracts."[46] The definition of "consumer" under the rule limits the scope of the rule to acquisitions of "goods or services" by one "who seeks or acquires goods or services for personal, family, or household use."[47] The key term further limits the scope of the rule to transactions in which the debt arises from a "financed sale" or a "purchase-money loan."[48] The first of these terms is in turn defined to include most "credit sales" as defined under TILA and under Regulation Z.[49] "Purchase-money loan" is defined to cover certain "consumer loans"–those in which there is a cash advance, in which a "finance charge" is levied within the meaning of TILA and Regulation Z.[50] The cash advance must be used to purchase goods or services from a seller who

---

[42] See generally ¶ 1.03[2][c][ii].

[43] 16 CFR §§ 433.1–433.3.

[44] See generally ¶ 1.03[2][c][iii].

[45] In 1979, the FTC approved in substance an amendment that would make it an unfair or deceptive practice for a creditor to fail to comply with the rule's notice requirements. 44 Fed. Reg. 65,771 (1979). The amendment has never been promulgated. Even if it were promulgated, the FTC has no direct authority over many lenders such as national banks. See ¶ 1.03[2][c][ii] note 59 and accompanying text.

[46] 16 CFR § 433.1(i).

[47] 16 CFR § 433.1(a). See generally ¶ 1.02 concerning the general use of such a test to define "consumer law."

[48] 16 CFR § 433.1(i).

[49] 16 CFR § 433.1(e). See ¶ 2.05[2] for a discussion of the term "credit sale" under TILA and ¶ 2.05[1] for discussion of the relationship between TILA and Regulation Z.

[50] See ¶ 2.05[2][c][i].

refers consumers to the creditor or is affiliated with the creditor by common control, contract, or business arrangement.[51]

"Creditor" is defined to exclude from coverage credit card transactions in which the creditor is acting for the purposes of the particular transaction as a credit card issuer.[52]

### [b] Effect on True Holder-in-Due-Course Status and Effect of Waiver-of-Defense Clause

The "financed sale" contemplated by the rule is the consumer credit sale in which a seller takes a negotiable instrument or simple installment contract. The inclusion of this type of transaction is directed toward the insulation from liability that may arise because of the true holder-in-due-course doctrine or the waiver-of-defense clause. The rule attempts to limit the insulation that may indirectly arise from these concepts in a credit sale by requiring the "seller" to place the following notice (in ten point bold type) in any "consumer credit contract":

**NOTICE**

**ANY HOLDER OF THIS CONSUMER CREDIT CONTRACT IS SUBJECT TO ALL CLAIMS AND DEFENSES WHICH THE DEBTOR COULD ASSERT AGAINST THE SELLER OF GOODS AND SERVICES OBTAINED PURSUANT HERETO OR WITH THE PROCEEDS HEREOF. RECOVERY HEREUNDER BY THE DEBTOR SHALL NOT EXCEED AMOUNTS PAID BY THE DEBTOR HEREUNDER.**

A "consumer credit contract" is broad enough to include a promissory note that the consumer credit seller contemplates negotiating or a simple contract that the consumer credit seller contemplates assigning.[53] If a seller does place the requisite notice in an otherwise negotiable promissory note, the holder of such paper cannot be a holder in due course.[54] If the document representing the debtor's obligation is a retail installment contract and the notice is in the contract, the assignee of the contract is subject to the provisions of the

---

[51] 16 CFR § 433.1(d).

[52] 16 CFR § 433.1(c). The reason for this exclusion is that TILA, an act of Congress, specifically deals with such liability. The liability of credit card issuers is discussed at infra ¶ 3.03[5].

[53] See 16 CFR § 433.1(i), defining "consumer credit contract" in part as "any instrument which evidences or embodies a debt arising from ... [a financed sale or purchase money loan.]"

[54] Holder-in-due-course status depends in part upon holding a "negotiable instrument." See UCC § 3-302. That term is so defined as to exclude a writing with a condition. UCC § 3-104. A writing with the requisite notice would not be negotiable because it could be conditional.

notice as a simple matter of contract law. This is true even if a waiver-of-defense clause has also been inserted.

Note, however, that the existence of the notice does not create any new defenses with respect to the goods or services provided. The substantive rights of the buyer with respect to quality, quantity, and delivery are determined by other law, most notably warranty law. Note also that the effect of the notice, if the notice is the basis of the buyer's claim, is to allow defenses to be raised against the holder of the obligation by alleging a setoff and to limit the further liability of the holder to any amounts already paid.

If the seller does not include the notice when required to do so under the rule, it is unclear what rights the buyer has against the lender who is otherwise a holder in due course or in possession of an otherwise valid waiver-of-defense clause. As already stated, the rule is applicable only to sellers.[55] There may be a state statute or case law making the lender liable.[56] If not, the best argument for the debtor is that the holder of the paper is not acting in good faith, as is required for true holder-in-due-course status or insulation from liability due to the waiver clause.[57] Arguably, purchasers of consumer paper know the requirement of the rule and should recognize that the purchase of paper without the notice is not in good faith.[58] The creditor's best argument is that the rule is not applicable to lenders and should have no effect on its liability.[59] Once again, note that if the relevant state jurisdiction has legislation removing the lender's insulation, the absence of the FTC notice will not save the lender from liability.[60]

### [c] Effect on the Interlocking Lender

The "purchase-money loan" transaction contemplated by the rule is the direct consumer loan by a lender who has an interlocking relationship with the

---

[55] As to the seller's liability for the violation of an FTC rule, see ¶ 1.03[2][c][iii], where it is pointed out that there is no private right of action for a violation of an FTC rule, but that a state "little FTC act" may provide such a right. In 1979, the FTC approved in substance an amendment that would make it an unfair or deceptive practice for a creditor to fail to comply with the rule's notice requirements. 44 Fed. Reg. 65771 (1979). The amendment has never been promulgated. Even if it were promulgated, the FTC has no direct authority over many lenders such as national banks. See ¶ 1.03[2][c][ii] note 59 and accompanying text.

[56] See discussion at supra ¶¶ 3.03[2], 3.03[3].

[57] See supra ¶ 3.03[1] note 5 and accompanying text.

[58] Cf. Alcoa Credit Corp. v. Nickerson, 43 Mass. App. Dec. 1 (1968).

[59] See Capital Bank & Trust Co. v. Lacey, 393 So. 2d 668 (La. 1980) (since a notice was not in the contract, assignee took free of defenses even though consumer credit contract was covered by rule; no determination was made on that issue in the lower court).

[60] What is the effect of the notice on the assignee's liability if the notice is in a contract not within the scope of the rule? In Jefferson Nat'l Bank & Trust Co. v. Stamatiou, 384 So. 2d 388 (La. 1980), although a contract was not within the scope of the rule, the court held that the presence of the notice in the rule made the assignee subject to the buyer's defenses.

seller. Section 433.2 of the rule is aimed at removing the insulation from liability of such a lender. The rule works in an indirect fashion by making it an unfair and deceptive practice for the *seller* to accept any proceeds from a "purchase money loan" unless the loan contract between the lender and the consumer has the requisite notice. The notice is identical to that set out above for financed sales.

In the typical consumer transaction, when a consumer borrows money from a lender to buy specific goods or services from a specified seller, the proceeds of the cash advance go to the seller. Under the rule, the seller is not entitled to accept such proceeds in a "purchase money loan" unless the requisite notice is in the loan contract. Therefore, it is presumed that a seller in such a transaction will persuade the purchase-money lender to place the notice in the loan contract.

"Purchase-money loan" is defined to include only consumer loans in which there is a "referral" of the consumer to the lender or an "affiliation" between seller and lender.[61] "Referral" and "affiliation" are not defined in the rule. The rule does state, however, that such "affiliation" must be by "common control, contract, or business arrangement."[62] "Contract" is defined as any formal or informal agreement that "contemplates . . . cooperative or concerted activity in connection with the sale of goods or services to consumers or the financing thereof."[63] "Business arrangement" means "any understanding, course of dealing . . . formal or informal, between a creditor and a seller, in connection with the sale of goods or services to consumers or the financing thereof."[64]

In addition to the help provided by these definitions in the rule itself, the FTC has issued a "Statement of Enforcement Policy" to clarify the meaning of both "referral" and "affiliation."[65] This "statement" indicates that "referral" is intended to cover those cases in which a seller, in the ordinary course of business, sends its buyers to a particular loan outlet for credit to be used at the seller's. No specific number of referrals is required. The key is whether the seller acts as a conduit, and does not merely engage in a passive information process. For example, when the seller contacts a credit outlet on behalf of the buyer, this would be considered a referral. On the other hand, if the creditor merely "suggests" that there are loan outlets in the vicinity, this is not considered to be a referral. Once a referral relationship exists, all loan contracts must include the notice, provided the specific purchase test is met. This test excludes cases when the loan is used for multiple purchases, and no "substantial part" of the proceeds goes to any specific seller.[66]

The "common control" part of the definition of "affiliation" includes any arrangement in which the creditor and seller are functionally part of the same

---

[61] 16 CFR § 433.1(d).

[62] Id.

[63] 16 CFR § 433.1(f).

[64] 16 CFR § 433.1(g).

[65] 41 Fed. Reg. 20,022 (1976).

[66] Id.

business entity as, for example, when the two companies are owned by a holding company or by substantially the same individuals. The other possible arrangements creating an affiliation are those by "contract" or "business arrangement," which are defined in the rule and set out above. The FTC statement provides these examples of affiliations:

(1) Maintenance of loan application forms in the office of the seller;
(2) Joint participation in the processing of loan documents;
(3) Creditor's referrals of customers to a sales outlet;
(4) Payment of consideration to a seller for furnishing loan customers or to a creditor for furnishing sales prospects;
(5) Floor-planning or inventory financing arrangements that include or contemplate the assignment of indirect paper or the referral of loan customers;
(6) Active creditor participation in a sales program;
(7) Joint advertising efforts;
(8) An agreement to purchase paper on an indirect basis.[67]

Examples of relationships that are not meant to be included in the definition are those involving the mere existence of a commercial checking account, commercial lease, the factoring of accounts receivable, or a general business loan.[68] The FTC statement also points out that there must be some continuity over time; merely conferring over a particular transaction is not enough. Neither is the fact that the seller accepts proceeds from a check issued jointly to the buyer and seller. As with referrals, however, once an affiliation exists, all consumer loan contracts for loans to consumers to buy goods or services from the affiliated seller must contain the notice.[69]

The FTC statement recognizes a further limitation on the scope of "purchase-money loan," providing that there is no unfair and deceptive practice by the seller accepting proceeds from a loan unless the seller is aware that the money he is receiving consists of such proceeds. This is true even if all other parts of the definition such as a "referral" or "affiliation" are met. The seller is not obligated to inquire as to the source of the proceeds from the buyer. Of course, the standard is met when the seller receives a check jointly issued to the seller and buyer.[70]

If the notice is included in the loan contract, as a matter of simple contract law, the lender is subject to the rights set out in the notice. Note the limitations of that right set out above when the notice was discussed with respect to the holder-in-due-course status and the waiver-of-defense clause.

---

[67] Id.

[68] Id.

[69] Id.

[70] Id.

If the notice is not included, the rule is still not applicable to lenders.[71] State statutes or case law may make the lender liable.[72] If there is applicable state law setting out such a right, then state law may be used. The FTC rule does not preempt state law that provides greater rights to the consumer. If there is no such law, however, the best argument for the consumer debtor is the general policy argument that the notice should be read into any contract in which the lender was aware or should have been aware of the applicability of the notice to the particular type of contract. The lender's response may be that the rule does not apply to lenders; reading the notice into a loan contract so as to create liability for the lender rewrites the rule. This important issue has yet to be resolved.[73]

## [5] Credit Card Transactions

Related to the doctrines discussed above is the extent of the credit card issuer's liability for defenses that the cardholder has against the seller who accepts a credit card. Another issue that concerns the relative liability of the card issuer and cardholder is the degree of liability of the cardholder for unauthorized use of a credit card. These issues are discussed below.

### [a] Defective Goods or Services or Other Defenses Arising From the Underlying Transaction

**[i] Federal Law.** TILA and Regulation Z constitute the major law relating to the ability of a debtor to raise defenses against the issuer of a credit card because of defective goods or services or other defenses arising from the

---

[71] In 1979, the FTC approved in substance an amendment that would make it an unfair or deceptive practice for a creditor to fail to comply with the rule's notice requirements. 44 Fed. Reg. 65,771 (1979). The amendment has never been promulgated. Even if it were promulgated, the FTC has no direct authority over many lenders such as national banks. See ¶ 1.03[2][c][ii] note 59 and accompanying text.

As to seller's liability for the violation of an FTC rule see ¶ 1.03[2][c][iii], where it is pointed out that there is no private right of action for a violation of an FTC rule, but that a state "little FTC act" may provide such a right.

[72] See discussion at supra ¶¶ 3.03[2], 3.03[3].

[73] One court has considered the reverse of this issue: What is the liability of a lender who includes the notice in a loan that does not fall within the scope of the rule? The court ruled that the lender is not subject to the rights expressed in the notice. Booth v. K&K Homes, C.A. No. WD-78-21 (Ct. App. Wood Co. Ohio, 1979). The decision appears to be incorrect, however, because as a matter of simple contract law the lender should have been subject to the provisions of the loan contract (i.e., the provisions in the notice, whether or not the lender was compelled by law to put the notice in the document). Further, the court apparently never made a factual inquiry into whether or not there was a referral or affiliation but merely asserted that there was no such relationship. See also, Jefferson Nat'l Bank & Trust Co. v. Stamatiou, 384 So. 2d 388 (La. 1980).

underlying transaction.[74] For example, assume that a consumer purchases a computer for his home, paying with a Visa credit card issued by his bank. The computer does not work. There is clearly a breach of a warranty given by the seller. The seller refuses to repair or replace the computer or otherwise live up to its warranty. Must the buyer continue to pay the bank the total due on the computer or can he deduct some amount equivalent to his damages?

Section 226.12(c) of Regulation Z allows the cardholder, with some limitations, to withhold payment up to the amount of credit outstanding for the property or services that gave rise to the dispute and any finance or other charges imposed on that amount. The scope of the provision is limited to transactions involving the purchase of goods or services by use of a credit card in a "consumer credit transaction."[75] If, for example, a consumer uses a credit card to obtain a cash advance, even if the consumer then uses the money to buy goods or services, the provision would not apply because the card was not directly used for a credit purchase. If a card serves both as an ordinary credit card and also as a check guarantee or debit card, a transaction is subject to the provision when the card is used as an ordinary credit card, but not when used as a check guarantee or debit card. The definition of relevant terms such as "consumer credit transaction" and the exclusion provision of TILA further delineate the scope of the provision.[76]

Another limitation is that the cardholder must first make a good faith attempt to resolve the dispute with the person honoring the credit card. Finally, the right does not exist unless (1) the amount of credit extended exceeds $50, and (2) the disputed transaction occurs in the same state as the cardholder's current designated address or, if not within the same state, within 100 miles from that address. Neither the dollar limitation nor the geographical limitation applies when the person honoring the credit card:

(1) Is the same person as the card issuer (e.g., a Sears card used in a Sears store);
(2) Is controlled by the card issuer directly or indirectly (e.g., the seller is a subsidiary of the issuer);
(3) Is under the direct or indirect control of a third person that also directly controls the card issuer (e.g., the seller and issuer are owned by the same holding company);
(4) Is a franchised dealer of the card issuer's products or services (e.g., a Chevron card used in a franchised Chevron station);
(5) Controls the card issuer directly or indirectly (e.g., a seller forms a company that issues the card to the holder); or

---

[74] See ¶ 2.05[1] for a discussion of the structure of TILA and Regulation Z and their relationship. This discussion cites only relevant provisions of Regulation Z.

[75] Reg. Z § 226.12(c)(1).

[76] See ¶ 2.05[2].

(6) Has obtained the order for the disputed transaction through a mail solicitation made or participated in by the card issuer.[77]

The amount of the defense that the cardholder can assert cannot exceed the amount of credit outstanding for the disputed transaction at the time the cardholder first notifies the card issuer or the person honoring the credit card of the existence of the defense.[78]

If, in accordance with the provision's limitations, the cardholder withholds payment of the amount of credit outstanding, the issuer cannot report that amount as delinquent until the dispute is settled or judgment is rendered.[79]

Further, as a general rule under TILA, a card issuer may not take any action, either before or after termination of credit card privileges, to offset a cardholder's indebtedness arising from a consumer credit transaction against funds of the cardholder held on deposit. This limitation does not affect the right of the issuer to take action under state or federal law to obtain or enforce a consensual security interest (a UCC Article 9 right), to attach or otherwise levy upon the funds, or to obtain or enforce a court order relating to the funds.[80]

**[ii] State Law.** The 1968 UCCC has no provision concerning the liability of card issuers for defenses as against a seller; however, the 1974 version has a provision modeled after the federal law.[81] The few states that have a provision on credit card issuer liability consist mostly of the same states that have their own truth-in-lending acts.[82]

## [b] Liability for the Unauthorized Use of Credit Cards

**[i] Federal Law.** The focus here shifts from the issue of the liability of the card issuer for defenses the cardholder has against a seller to the liability of a cardholder for unauthorized use of a credit card. The major law on this issue is contained in TILA and Regulation Z.[83] Section 226.12(b) of Regulation Z provides that the liability of a cardholder for unauthorized use of a credit card shall not exceed the lesser of (1) $50 or (2) the amount of money, property, labor, or services obtained by the unauthorized use before notification to the card issuer as prescribed in Section 226.12(b)(3).[84] "Unauthorized use" is

---

[77] Reg. Z § 226.12(c)(3).

[78] Reg. Z § 226.12(c)(1).

[79] Reg. Z § 226.12(c)(2).

[80] Reg. Z § 226.12(d).

[81] UCCC § 3.403 (1974).

[82] See, e.g., Substantive and Procedural Rules of Wyoming Administrator of Wyoming's UCCC, § 2.12.

[83] See ¶ 2.05[1] for a discussion of the structure of TILA and Regulation Z and their relationship. This discussion cites only relevant provisions of Regulation Z.

[84] Proper notification is given when "steps have been taken as may be reasonably required in the ordinary course of business to provide the card issuer with the pertinent information about the possible unauthorized use . . . regardless of whether any particu-

defined as the use of credit card by a person, other than the cardholder, who does not have actual, implied, or apparent authority for such use and from whom the cardholder receives no benefit.[85]

The scope of this provision is similar to that of the provision discussed above relating the card issuer's liability for defenses against a seller.[86] Unlike the scope of the provision discussed above, however, this limitation on a cardholder's liability applies even if the unauthorized use was for a business purpose, the cardholder is not a consumer, and the unauthorized use was for other than the purchase of goods or services.[87] However, if ten or more credit cards are issued by one card issuer for use by the employees of an organization, the provision does not prohibit the issuer and the cardholder from agreeing to liability other than that provided for in the section. But liability for unauthorized use by an employee is always subject to the limitation despite any contra agreement between the employer and the card issuer.

There is not even the limited liability set out above for unauthorized use unless:

(1) The credit card is "accepted";

(2) The card issuer has "adequate notice" of the cardholder's maximum potential liability and of means by which the card issuer may be notified of loss or theft of the card;[88]

(3) The card issuer has provided a means to identify the cardholder on the account or the authorized user of the card.[89]

---

lar officer or ... [other agent or employee] ... does, in fact, receive the information. Notification may be given at the time of receipt or ... at the expiration of the time ordinarily required for transmission, whichever is earlier."

[85] Official Note 22 to Reg. Z § 226.12(b).

[86] See supra ¶ 3.03[5][a][i]. Note from the discussion cited that TILA only concerns the relative liability of a cardholder and issuer when the use of the card is for "credit." The same plastic card may have a feature allowing the cardholder access to his or her deposit account; that is, he may use the card as a substitute for cash or check, as a "debit card." If a debit feature of a combination credit/debit card or a card that has only such a feature is used, the provisions of TILA on the liability of the cardholder and issuer do not apply. The issue of a debit cardholder's liability for unauthorized use is covered, if at all, under the Electronic Funds Transfer Act (EFTA), Pub. L. No. 95-630, 92 Stat. 3728, 15 USC §§ 1693 et seq. See EFTA § 906. The scope of EFTA is determined primarily by the definitions of EFTA § 904. For that act to be applicable, an electronic fund transfer would have to take place; if there is none and the card is used as a debit card, neither TILA nor EFTA would be applicable. Liability for unauthorized use of an electronic funds transfer access device can substantially exceed the liability for unauthorized use of a credit card.

[87] Official Staff Commentary to Reg. Z § 226.12(b)(2).

[88] This notice must be printed and must set forth the "pertinent facts so that the cardholder may reasonably be expected" to understand it. Official Note 23 to Reg. Z § 226.12(b).

[89] Reg. Z § 226.12(b)(2). Method of identification could include signature, photograph, or fingerprint on the card, or electronic or mechanical confirmation. Official Staff Commentary to Reg. Z § 226.12(b)(2).

If state law or an agreement between a cardholder and the card issuer provides for lesser liability, the lesser liability prevails.[90]

As a general rule under TILA, a card issuer may not take any action, either before or after termination of credit card privileges, to offset a cardholder's indebtedness arising from a consumer credit transaction against funds of the cardholder held on deposit. This limitation does not affect the right of the issuer to take action under state or federal law to obtain or enforce a consensual security interest (a UCC Article 9 right), to attach or otherwise levy upon the funds; or to obtain or enforce a court order relating to the funds.[91]

**[ii] State Law** Neither the 1968 UCCC nor the 1974 UCCC contains a provision concerning the liability of cardholders for unauthorized use of the credit card. The few states that have a provision on credit card issuer liability are the same states that have their own truth-in-lending acts.[92]

## ¶ 3.04 MISCELLANEOUS LIMITATIONS ON SUBSTANTIVE TERMS

### [1] Introduction

The limitations on substantive terms of consumer credit transactions discussed below are solely a matter of state law. To date, Congress and the FTC have not formulated similar federal limitations.

### [2] Attorney Fees

For some consumer credit contracts, many states have limited the use of contractual provisions that provide for the payment by the debtor of the creditor's attorney fees. The 1968 UCCC proposed a limitation for both consumer credit sales and consumer loans.[1] and it suggested two alternatives for adopting states. Alternative A provided that no consumer credit sale contract or consumer loan contract can contain a provision for attorney fees. Alternative B provided that in either a consumer credit sale or consumer loan contract, a provision could provide for attorney fees if the agreement provided for (1) "reasonable" fees not to exceed 15 percent of the unpaid debt after default, and (2) referral to an attorney who is not a salaried employee of the creditor.[2] None of the states originally adopting the UCCC adopted Alternative A.[3] In fact, none

---

[90] Reg. Z § 226.12(b)(4).

[91] Reg. Z § 226.12(d).

[92] See, e.g., Substantive and Procedural Rules of Wyoming Administrator of Wyoming's UCCC, § 2.12.

[1] UCCC §§ 2.413, 3.404 (1968).

[2] Id.

[3] See ¶ 1.02[3][a][ii] for a list of the states adopting such statutes.

of the adopting states chose Alternative B without modification. The modification typically adopted removed the 15 percent limitation of Alternative B.[4] States with comprehensive codes other than the 1968 UCCC usually have split between adopting provisions entirely prohibiting attorney fees[5] and following the 15 percent limitation of Alternative B of the 1968 UCCC.[6]

In states with a scattered approach to consumer credit legislation,[7] statutes concerning the creditor's use of attorney-fees provisions are usually found, if at all, in retail installment sales acts. Such statutes generally authorize attorney-fees provisions.[8] Limitations on the language allowed in these provisions vary. One common approach has the effect of limiting attorney fees in retail installment contracts to a percentage of the amount due when the contract is referred to an attorney and then only when the attorney is not a salaried employee of the creditor—an approach like that in Alternative A of Section 2.413 of the 1968 UCCC.[9] Another approach simply requires that the attorney not be a salaried employee of the creditor, and does not set any percentage limitation.[10] Yet another approach provides that, if a contract allows attorney fees for the creditor, the contract must also provide attorney fees for the consumer.[11]

### [3] Balloon Payments

In a transaction calling for periodic payments, a "balloon payment" is a payment that is significantly larger than other periodic payments. Some states have limited the use of balloon payments. The most common approach in comprehensive code states[12] is the one proposed by the 1968 UCCC, which requires that when any payment is more than twice as large as the average regular periodic payments, the consumer may refinance the transaction. A further limitation of the UCCC is the requirement that the refinancing be no less favorable than the original transaction.[13] Most comprehensive code states,

---

[4] See, e.g., Ind. Code §§ 24-4.5-2.413, 24-4.5-3.404. Colorado did not entirely delete the 15 percent limitation but added the following to the official language: ". . . or such additional fee as may be directed by the court." Colo. Rev. Stat. §§ 5-2-413, 5-3-404.

[5] See, e.g., Iowa Code § 537.2507; Kan. Stat. Ann. § 16a-2-507.

[6] See, e.g., S.C. Code Ann. §§ 37-2-413, 37-3-404.

[7] See ¶ 1.02[3][a][i] for a list of the states with such an approach.

[8] See, e.g., Cal. Civ. Code § 1810.4.

[9] See, e.g., Mo. Rev. Stat. § 408.330 (15 percent).

[10] See, e.g., Wash. Rev. Code § 63.14.090.

[11] See, e.g., N.H. Rev. Stat. Ann. § 361-C:2 (applicable to both consumer loans and retail installment sales).

[12] See ¶ 1.02[3][a][ii] for a list of the states adopting such statutes.

[13] UCCC §§ 2.405 (credit sales), 3.402 (consumer loans) (1968).

however, allow a refinancing at the current maximum rates and only if the consumer would otherwise then be entitled to credit as an original customer.[14]

A few states with the scattered approach to consumer credit legislation[15] have legislation concerning balloon payments in their retail installment sales acts. A "balloon payment" typically is defined as not "substantially similar" to the average of other regularly scheduled payments. Some of this legislation, like that under the 1968 UCCC, provides that the consumer may refinance under terms no less favorable than those of the first transaction.[16] Other states do not regulate the terms upon refinancing but instead merely prohibit balloon payments in most retail sales.[17]

Exceptions to state limitations on balloon payments generally exist in all legislating states for revolving loan accounts and for transactions in which the payment schedule is adjusted to the seasonal or irregular income of the consumer.[18]

## [4] Wage Assignments

Historically, creditors in retail installment contracts included a provision whereby the debtor agreed to assign future wages as security for the repayment of the obligation. These provisions usually provided that the assignment was contingent upon default. When the debtor defaulted, under the procedure in most states, the creditor with such an assignment could serve the assignment on the employer who then had to transfer the debtor's wages to the creditor. At times, some creditors, mostly credit unions, also included wage assignments that were not contingent on default. Under such an assignment, the employer deducted a portion of the employee-debtor's pay for each pay period in order to pay the creditor.

Wage assignments are now uncommon in most states. Most states have placed some limitation on the use of wage assignments. Limitations are not typically limited to consumer transactions. Most states have limitations on wage assignments in statutes of more general application.[19] The statutes vary in effect. One common approach makes most wage assignments void.[20] Instead of voiding these provisions, many state statutes entirely impose procedural limitations.[21]

---

[14] See, e.g., Colo. Rev. Stat. § 5-2-405.

[15] See ¶ 1.02[3][a][i] for a list of the states with such an approach.

[16] See, e.g., Ohio Rev. Code Ann. § 1317.06.

[17] See, e.g., N.J. Stat. Ann. § 17.16C-26.

[18] See, e.g., Colo. Rev. Stat. § 5-2-405.

[19] See, e.g., Conn. Gen. Stat. § 52.361(g) (providing that assignments of wages are void except as to amounts due for support in public welfare cases).

[20] Id.

[21] See, e.g., Ill. Rev. Stat. ch. 48, §§ 39.1, 39.2, 39.4, 39.5 (includes a common requirement that the spouse must sign a wage assignment). Consumer Cred. Guide (CCH) ¶ 650 contains a compilation of state statutes affecting wage assignments.

In consumer credit transactions, one should determine whether limitations apply that are different from those for other transactions. Under both the 1968 and 1974 UCCC, wage assignments are revocable at will by the consumer.[22] Most states with comprehensive credit codes[23] have adopted a limitation on wage assignments for both consumer credit sales and consumer loans.[24]

In states with the scattered approach to consumer credit regulation,[25] limitations on wage assignments typically are found in both small loan statutes and retail installment sales acts.[26] Limitations in such statutes vary from prohibiting wage assignments entirely[27] to merely providing procedural safeguards such as requiring the spouse's signature and a written statement signed by the consumer.[28]

---

[22] UCCC §§ 2.410 (credit sales), 3.403 (consumer loans) (1968), 3.305 (all covered consumer credit transactions) (1974).

[23] See ¶ 1.02[3][a][ii] for a list of the states adopting such statutes.

[24] See, e.g., Wis. Stat. § 422.404.

[25] See ¶ 1.02[3][a][i] for a list of the states with such an approach.

[26] See, e.g., Hawaii Rev. Stat. § 409-20 (small loan act), 476-13 (retail installment sales act).

[27] See, e.g., Hawaii Rev. Stat. § 476-13 (retail installment sales act); Fla. Stat. § 516.17 (Consumer Finance Act).

[28] See Hawaii Rev. Stat. § 409-20 (small loan act).

# 4

# Regulation of Performance Obligations



## ¶ 4.01 CONTROL OF BILLING PROCEDURES AND RESOLUTION OF BILLING ERRORS

### [1] Federal Credit Billing Act Provisions

Provisions of the Fair Credit Billing Act (FCBA), effective in October 1975, were incorporated into Title I, the Truth-in-Lending Act (TILA), primarily as Chapter 4 of that Title. Some major provisions of FCBA were discussed in Chapter 3: the provisions that (1) establish the rights of a credit card holder to raise defenses against the card issuer for defects in goods or services purchased from one honoring a credit card,[1] and (2) limit the cardholder's liability for unauthorized use of a credit card.[2] This chapter focuses on provisions of FCBA that provide for prompt crediting of payments and treatment of credit balances and billing error resolution.

---

[1] See generally ¶ 3.04[4][a].

[2] See generally ¶ 3.03[4][b].

Generally, the scope of the provisions discussed below is the same as that for most of TILA: consumer credit transactions.[3] Most of the provisions of FCBA are limited in scope to coverage of open-end consumer credit transactions or transactions that involve the use of a credit card by a consumer.[4]

### [2] Crediting of Payments and Treatment of Credit Balances

FCBA provides for a presumption of the validity of payments on an open-end or credit card obligation made at any location where the creditor conducts business, at any time during the creditor's normal business hours, and by cash, money order, draft, or other similar negotiable instrument. The creditor, however, can specify reasonable requirements for making payments in these transactions by disclosing the requirements in the periodic statement or in a separate statement enclosed with the periodic statement. These requirements can provide that payments: (1) be accompanied by the consumer's account number: (2) be made only by check or money order; (3) be sent only by mail; (4) be made only at one address; or (5) be received by a specified cut-off hour for payment.[5]

If the consumer meets the requirements for payment, the creditor must credit a payment to the consumer's account as of the date payment is received, unless a delay in crediting will not result in a finance charge or any other charge. If the consumer does not meet the reasonable requirements for payment but the creditor accepts the nonconforming payment, the creditor must credit the payment within five days of receipt. If a creditor fails to credit a payment as required and charges are improperly imposed, the creditor must adjust the consumer's account in the next billing cycle.[6]

In both open-end and closed-end consumer credit transactions covered by FCBA, the creditor must do the following if a credit balance exceeds one dollar:

(1) Credit the amount of the credit balance to the consumer's account;
(2) Refund any part of the remaining credit balance within seven business days from receipt of a written request from the consumer; and
(3) Make a good faith effort to refund to the consumer any part of the credit balance remaining for more than six months.[7]

### [3] Billing Error Resolution

#### [a] Billing Error and Billing Error Notice

The scope of the billing error resolution provisions of FCBA is determined by the definitions of two relevant terms: "billing error" and "billing error

---

[3] See generally ¶ 2.04[2].

[4] See generally ¶ 2.04[2][b][iii].

[5] Reg. Z § 226.10 and Official Staff Commentary, 12 CFR Pt. 226.

[6] Id.

[7] Reg. Z § 226.11.

notice." A "billing error" includes an indication on the periodic statement that the creditor has billed the consumer:

(1) For expenditures incurred by one who is not authorized to use the consumer's card;[8]
(2) For an improperly identified extension of credit;
(3) For property or services not delivered as agreed,[9] for example, where:
  (a) The consumer refuses to take delivery of goods because they do not comply;
  (b) Delivery of property or services is different from the agreed-upon delivery;
  (c) The wrong quantity is delivered;
  (d) Delivery is late; or
  (e) Delivery is made to the wrong location;
(4) Improperly because of a failure to properly credit a payment or some other credit;
(5) Improperly because of a computational error; and
(6) For an extension of credit for which the consumer requests additional clarification.

The term also includes the creditor's failure to mail or deliver a periodic statement to the consumer's last known address if that address was received by the creditor, in writing, at least twenty days before the end of the billing cycle for which the statement was required.[10]

A "billing error notice" is a written notice from the consumer. This notice must:

(1) Be received by a creditor at the address disclosed by the creditor no later than sixty days after the creditor transmitted the first periodic statement that reflects the alleged billing error;
(2) Enable the creditor to identify the consumer's name and account number; and
(3) To the extent possible, indicate the consumer's belief and the reasons for the belief that a billing error exists, and the type, date, and amount of the error.[11]

---

[8] The requisite authorization exists if the user of the consumer's account has actual, apparent, or implied authority. Reg. Z § 226.12(b) at Official Note 22.

[9] Reg. Z § 226.13(a) and Official Staff Commentary. The billing error resolution procedure does not cover a dispute relating to the quality of goods or services that the consumer "accepts." Protests concerning those disputes may be raised by the consumer only as provided in Reg. Z § 226.12(c), discussed at ¶ 3.04[5][a][i].

[10] Reg. Z § 226.13(a)(7).

[11] Reg. Z § 226.13(b).

The creditor may require that the written notice not be made on the payment medium or on other material that is enclosed with the periodic statement by indicating these stipulations in the billing rights statement.[12]

When the consumer discovers a billing error and gives the appropriate billing error notice, the billing error provisions of FCBA specify the procedure the creditor must follow.[13] The billing error provisions also limit the rights of the creditor during and after the resolution procedure.

### [b] Acknowledgment of the Billing Error Notice

The creditor must mail or deliver written acknowledgment to the consumer within thirty days of receiving a billing error notice, unless within the thirty-day period the creditor has resolved the error or followed the procedures required when no error has been found.[14]

### [c] Required Procedures for Resolution

After receiving the billing error notice, the creditor has two complete billing cycles (but in no event later than ninety days) to take appropriate action. The appropriate action to be taken depends upon whether the creditor deter-

---

[12] Id. at Official Note 29. The requisite disclosures of the billing rights statement are discussed infra at ¶ 4.01[4].

[13] The same plastic card that enables a consumer to engage in credit transactions may give the consumer access to an account by means of electronic fund transfers. For example, some Visa or MasterCard cards may be used to acquire funds on credit or to make a credit purchase and may also be used at an automatic teller machine to withdraw money from a deposit account such as a savings account. If the card is used solely as a credit card in a particular consumer credit transaction and a billing error arises, TILA applies. If the card is used solely to access a deposit account by electronic fund transfers and an error arises, the federal law applicable to error resolution is the Electronic Fund Transfer Act (EFTA), 15 USC §§ 1693 et seq. and Regulation E, promulgated by the Federal Reserve Board. If an error occurs because of credit inadvertently extended incident to an electronic fund transfer (e.g., when the customer uses the debit feature of a card and inadvertently overdraws the deposit account), error resolution is also under EFTA and Regulation E rather than TILA. In many accounts, it is agreed that a consumer may use a card for electronic fund transfers from a deposit account and also that a consumer may exceed the amount of the deposit account; that is, charges beyond the amount in the deposit account may be previously authorized as a line of credit. Where this arrangement exists and an error occurs with respect to the extension of credit, the error resolution is under EFTA and Regulation E. If an electronic funds transfer as defined at Section 903(6) of EFTA (15 USC § 1693(a)(6)) is not involved, when a card is used to access a deposit account (e.g., when a debit card is used at a merchant's to purchase goods and the price is later deducted from a savings account at the issuing institution), the transaction is not subject to EFTA because there is no electronic funds transfer nor is it subject to TILA because there is no credit extension. There is no federal law that regulates such a transaction.

[14] Reg. Z § 226.13(c). The procedure for resolving errors or required procedure for when no error is found are contained in Reg. Z § 226.13(f).

mines that the billing error occurred as asserted or, after reasonable investigation, determines that the billing error did not occur or that a billing error different from that asserted occurred. If it is determined that a billing error was made, the creditor must follow these steps within the two-billing-cycle time limit:

(1) Correct the billing error and credit the account with any disputed amount and related finance or other charges; and
(2) Mail or deliver a correction notice to the consumer.[15]

If after a reasonable investigation the creditor determines that the billing error did not occur, the creditor must, within the time limit stated above:

(1) Mail or deliver to the consumer an explanation that sets forth the reasons for the creditor's belief that the alleged billing error is incorrect in whole or in part;
(2) Furnish copies of documentary evidence of the consumer's indebtedness, if the consumer requests this information; and
(3) If a different billing error occurred, correct the billing error and credit the consumer's account with any disputed amount and related finance or other charges, as applicable.[16]

### [d] Creditor's Rights and Duties During Resolution

Until the billing error is resolved, the consumer need not pay (and the creditor may not try to collect) any portion of any required payment that the consumer believes is related to the disputed amount (including related finance or other charges).[17] If the cardholder maintains a deposit account with the card issuer and has agreed to pay the credit card indebtedness by periodic deduction from the cardholder's deposit account, the card issuer cannot deduct any part of the disputed amount or related finance or other charges if a billing error notice is received any time up to three business days before the scheduled payment date. In addition, the creditor cannot make or threaten to make an adverse report to any person about the consumer's credit standing or report that an amount or account is delinquent because the consumer failed to pay the disputed amount or related finance or other charges.

---

[15] Reg. Z § 226.13(e).

[16] Reg. Z § 226.13(f).

[17] Reg. Z § 226.13(d). The creditor is not prohibited from taking action to collect any disputed amount, deducting the amount from a credit limit, or showing on the periodic statement that the amount is owed if the creditor indicates on or with the periodic statement that payment of any disputed amount is not required pending the creditor's compliance with the billing error resolution procedures. Official Note 30 to Reg. Z § 226.13(d).

### [e] Creditor's Rights and Duties After Resolution

If a creditor, after complying with the duties during resolution,[18] determines that a consumer owes all or part of the disputed amount and related finance or other charges, the creditor has specified rights and responsibilities:

(1) The creditor must promptly notify the consumer in writing of the time when payment is due and the portion of the disputed amount and related finance or other charges that the consumer still owes;

(2) If any free period exists, the creditor must allow for such a period so that the consumer can pay the amount due without incurring additional finance or other charges;

(3) The creditor can report an account or amount as delinquent if the amount remains unpaid after the creditor has allowed any free period or ten days (whichever is longer); and

(4) The creditor cannot report that an amount or account is delinquent because the amount due remains unpaid if the creditor (within the time period specified in (3) above) receives further written notice that any portion of the billing error is still in dispute, unless the creditor also:

   (a) Promptly reports that the amount or account is in dispute;

   (b) Mails or delivers to the consumer (at the same time the report is made) a written notice of the name and address of each person to whom the creditor makes a report; and

   (c) Promptly reports any subsequent resolution of the reported delinquency to all persons to whom the creditor has made a report.[19]

If the creditor has fully complied with these requirements, and the consumer reasserts substantially the same billing error, the creditor has no further responsibilities other than those in Item 4 above.

## [4] Disclosure of Billing Rights

In the initial disclosure statement that the creditor must give to the consumer before the first transaction is made under an open-end credit plan, the creditor must disclose to the consumer the consumer's rights to raise defenses against the card issuer and the billing error rights discussed above.[20] Appendix G of Regulation Z suggests a form for this disclosure and the creditor's disclosure must be substantially similar to this suggested form.[21] In addition, the creditor must mail or deliver an annual statement of billing rights. This state-

---

[18] See supra ¶ 4.01[3][d].

[19] Reg. Z § 226.13(g).

[20] Reg. Z § 226.6(d). See generally ¶ 3.04[5][a] for a discussion of the cardholder's rights to raise defenses against the card issuer, and supra ¶ 4.01[3] for a discussion of the billing error rights.

[21] Reg. Z § 226.6(d).

ment must be given at least once per calendar year, at intervals of not less than six months nor more than eighteen months, and to all consumers (or at least to all consumers entitled to a periodic statement).[22] As an alternative to the annual statement, the creditor may mail or deliver with each periodic statement a statement substantially similar to that in Appendix G of Regulation Z.[23] In the periodic statement required in open-end credit transactions, the creditor must disclose the address to be used for notice of billing errors. Alternatively, the address may be provided on the annual statement of billing rights.[24]

## ¶ 4.02 DEFAULT

Consumer credit statutes in some states restrict a creditor's rights to treat a consumer credit transaction in default. These statutes may do so by defining when a default occurs and/or providing the consumer with a "right to cure"—a right to remedy a default and maintain his or her rights under the transaction. The following sections discuss these state statutes.[1]

### [1] Statutory Definitions of Default

Upon default in a transaction in which the creditor has obtained a security interest in the debtor's collateral—a Uniform Commercial Code (UCC) Article 9 "secured transaction"—the creditor has the right to reduce his claim to judgment, foreclose, or otherwise enforce the security interest.[2] The creditor may repossess collateral with or without judicial process[3] and then sell the repossessed collateral.[4] Article 9 of the UCC does not define default, except to provide that default occurs when the parties' security agreement says that it occurs.[5] A few states have adopted a statutory definition of default applicable

---

[22] Reg. Z § 226.9(a). Reg. Z § 226.5(b)(2) specifies who must receive a periodic statement. See ¶ 2.04[6][c] for a discussion of that provision.

[23] Reg. Z § 226.9(a).

[24] Reg. Z § 226.7(k).

[1] See ¶ 7.05 for a discussion of state statutes that restrict a creditor's method of repossessing personal property and limit the creditor's right to sue for a deficiency judgment after the disposition of repossessed collateral.

[2] UCC § 9-501.

[3] UCC § 9-503.

[4] UCC § 9-504(1). The creditor's rights upon default in a transaction secured by personalty or fixtures are explored in detail at ¶ 7.05.

[5] UCC § 9-501(1). There is one restriction in the UCC on the creditor's right to declare an Article 9 secured transaction in default. UCC Section 1-208 provides that a creditor cannot accelerate an obligation based on a term allowing acceleration "at will" or "when the creditor deems itself insecure" unless he does so in good faith. Also, a creditor may waive his right to exercise a provision providing for default because of inaction or acceptance of previous incidents of default. These concepts are not limited to consumer transactions. They are further discussed at ¶ 7.05[4].

in consumer credit transactions. Two states have attempted to limit when a default may occur because of missed payments. Iowa statutes provide that a default occurs upon the failure to make a required payment within ten days of the due date.[6] Wisconsin statutes also define when a missed payment results in a default, but provide for different time periods for different transactions. For example, in Wisconsin in a closed-end consumer credit transaction with monthly payments, default does not occur because of missed payments until an amount exceeding one full payment has remained unpaid for more than ten days after the scheduled or deferred due dates.[7]

A few states, including Iowa and Wisconsin as well as Kansas, Maine, Massachusetts, and South Carolina, have limited when a default may occur because of incidents of default that involve circumstances other than an actual missed payment. The statutes of Kansas, Maine, and South Carolina are similar in this regard, providing that default may occur in cases other than an actual missed payment only when the prospect of payment, performance, or realization on the collateral is significantly impaired.[8] Iowa, Massachusetts, and Wisconsin require incidents of default to be "material."[9]

### [2] Statutory Right to Cure a Default

About 20 percent of the states have passed statutes mandating that the consumer be given a right to cure some defaults. Typically, these statutes give the right to cure only when the default consists of a missed payment. The Colorado statute is representative of such a statute. It provides that a creditor may not accelerate or proceed against the collateral after a default consisting of a missed payment until it sends notice to the debtor advising him that there are twenty days in which to cure the default by tendering all unpaid sums due at the time of tender, without acceleration, but plus any delinquency or deferral charges. Notice may not be sent until the required payment is ten days past due. Only one cure period is allowed per twelve-month period, except in obligations secured by mobile homes,[10] in which two cure periods are allowed every twelve months.

---

[6] Iowa Code Ann. § 537.5109.

[7] Wis. Stat. § 425.103.

[8] Kan. Stat. § 16a-5-109; Me. Rev. Stat. Ann. tit. 9-A, § 5.109; S.C. Code § 37-5-109.

[9] Iowa Code Ann. § 537.5109; Mass. Ann. Laws ch. 255, § 13I; Wis. Stat. Ann. § 425.103.

[10] Colo. Rev. Stat. §§ 5-5-111–5-5-112; see also Kan. Stat. §§ 16a-5-110–16a-5-111; Me. Rev. Stat. Ann. tit. 9-A, § 5.110–5.111; S.C. Code §§ 37-5-110–37-5-111; W. Va. Code § 46A-2-106. These statutes vary some with respect to time periods, structure of the notice, and how often the notice must be given. However, all are limited to allowing cure when the default is an actual missed payment and all require a notice of the right to cure. Ohio in consumer credit sales (Ohio Rev. Code Ann. § 1317.06(C)), and Virginia in all contracts (Va. Code § 11-4.3), prohibit acceleration until a period of

Iowa, Massachusetts, and Wisconsin allow a right to cure defaults other than those arising because of missed payments and allow more than one right to cure per obligation.[11]

---

time has lapsed (thirty days in Ohio and ten days in Virginia) but do not require any notice of a right to cure.

[11] Iowa Code Ann. § 537.5110; Mass. Ann. Laws ch. 255, § 13I; Wis. Stat. Ann. § 425.105.

# II

# COLLECTION OF UNSECURED DEBTS

# 5

# Extrajudicial Debt Collection

## ¶ 5.01 INTRODUCTION

The remainder of this book usually assumes the validity of the debt and the debtor's default. It focuses on the rights and liabilities of both the debtor and the creditor in and out of bankruptcy within the legal process of collecting a valid debt. The process of collecting an unsecured debt is considered at length in this part.

An "unsecured" debt refers to claims or debts for which the creditor does not yet possess a lien in the debtor's assets. The term "secured" debt refers to debts for which the creditor has a lien in assets of the debtor. A lien is an interest in the debtor's property that affords the creditor the legal power to ultimately satisfy the debt from the assets subject to the lien. A lien may be obtained through agreement with the debtor, through statutory fiat, or through judicial process.[1] Examples of a lien obtained by agreement are the grant of a security interest in personal property or fixtures under Article 9 of the Uniform Commercial Code (UCC) or the grant of a mortgage in real estate under state mortgage law. An example of a statutory lien is a mechanics' or a materialmen's lien granted pursuant to state statute. Finally, examples of judicial liens are attachment, garnishment, execution, and judgment liens. All of these liens are considered at length in Chapter 6 and Part III of this book.

The extrajudicial collection efforts of an unsecured creditor are often crucial to the success of the ultimate collection effort. Initially this chapter will deal more with collection technique and practices than with case and statutory law regulating the collection of an unsecured debt. Practices used in locating the debtor and the assets of the debtor along with actual extrajudicial collection techniques and the debtor's response to such techniques will be considered.[2] Also included are separate sections on setoff[3] and suretyship.[4]

Extrajudicial collection activities of creditors occasionally go beyond the bounds of ethical conduct.[5] Rules have been fashioned by the courts and legislatures that protect the debtor from such collection activity and are considered in the concluding sections of this chapter.[6]

## ¶ 5.02 LOCATING THE DEBTOR

### [1] Beginning the Location Effort

After the validity of the debt and default are ascertained, the creditor and the creditor's attorney must locate the debtor and his assets. This is of extreme practical importance because collection efforts should not begin until the

---

[1] See ¶ 7.01 for a definition and further discussion of the importance of a "secured" debt.

[2] See infra ¶¶ 5.02–5.04, 5.07.

[3] See infra ¶ 5.05.

[4] See infra ¶ 5.06.

[5] See National Commission on Consumer Finance, "Summary of Hearings on Debt Collection Practices," 88 Banking L.J. 291 (1971), for a summary of problems created by overzealous collection efforts of creditors.

[6] See infra ¶¶ 5.08, 5.09.

debtor and his assets are located. The following section describes location techniques commonly used by creditors.[1]

Not all debtors intentionally secrete their location from their creditors. Failure to notify a creditor of a change in location may be inadvertent. The creditor or the creditor's attorney who operates under the assumption that the debtor is an intentional "skip" and rashly accuses the debtor of evasive conduct may serve only to polarize the parties, making extrajudicial collection all the more difficult.

When beginning the location effort, the creditor and the creditor's attorney should first carefully review the documentation of the transaction that led to the creation of the debt and any other related material. If the creditor has a well-kept file, these materials could provide a wealth of location information, including the debtor's former address(es) and employers' names and addresses. As the debtor makes payments during the course of the transaction, the creditor should note the location of the bank account and the debtor. This information is often valuable in locating the debtor who has defaulted. Otherwise, it is generally a good practice for creditors to periodically check the location of the debtor prior to actual default, particularly if payments have been consistently late.

Locating the debtor cannot always be simply resolved by mere reference to the creditor's file. What next? Obviously a private investigator, professional "skip" tracer, or a collection agency could be retained. But this easy way out is often too expensive. Before using such methods, creditors usually try further inexpensive location efforts. Such efforts use resources that can produce helpful information: the postal service, the telephone, personal interviews, and public records. Although using these resources requires little direct expense, it does require substantial amounts of time.

Whatever the resource used, the creditor's attorney should never misrepresent facts pertaining to the collection effort. He should also remember that location efforts should never become abusive or unethical.

To begin, the creditor should double-check the debtor's address contained in the creditor's records, since it may be mistakenly recorded. He should dial any listed phone numbers; or, if the phone is disconnected, check with the information operator for a new telephone number or correct address. Contacting third parties with whom the debtor regularly associates also can be helpful. Third parties include the debtor's employer, landlord, neighbors, relatives, references given by the debtor, motor vehicle bureau, public utilities, schools, and newspapers. A check of public records, including those related to real estate, might also reveal the debtor's new location. Finally, the creditor should investigate any other sources given in the loan application by the debtor to the creditor. If the debtor still cannot be located, using registered mail or other mail devices to locate the debtor should be considered.

---

[1] See the following for other discussion of techniques to locate a debtor: Sherwin, How to Collect a Money Judgement (Attorneys' Aid Publications, rev. ed. 1975); Sherwin, Debtors' and Creditors' Rights and Remedies (Attorneys' Aid Publications 1969); Sherwin, What to Do When Your Bills Exceed Your Paychecks (1974); Sherwin, "Locating the Missing Judgment Debtor," 21 Prac. Law. 13 (1975). See infra ¶¶ 5.08 and 5.09 for discussion of limitations on the creditor's ability to use such techniques.

## [2] Using the Telephone to Locate the Debtor

The telephone is clearly the least expensive and least time-consuming tool to use in locating the debtor. Telephoning third parties is often the most effective means of locating the debtor, since a telephone contact may appear more informal than an "official" personal visit by the creditor or his attorney. Following the guidelines of reputable, professional conduct, the creditor should not be afraid to ask any question regarding the debtor's whereabouts. Any leads obtained can be further pursued with additional telephone calls. Such use of the telephone may be restricted by the Fair Debt Collection Practices Act (FDCPA).[2]

## [3] Using the Mail to Locate the Debtor

While using the mail is more expensive and more time-consuming than using the telephone, many creditors find that it can produce results. The postal superintendent or letter carrier may provide necessary information regarding changes of address. Further, return receipt mail will verify an address; however, the intentional "skip" probably will refuse receipt. One technique that professional collection agencies, creditors, and creditors' attorneys use to locate debtors involves using registered mail addressed to a fictitious name in care of the borrower, and marked "deliver to addressee only." Such a letter will be forwarded to the new address with the new address marked on the envelope. Of course, it will not be delivered when it reaches the new address. When returned, the envelope will bear the new address. Similarly, registered letters sent in the debtor's name to unions and professional organizations of which the debtor is a member marked "deliver to addressee only" will often provide results.[3] Finally, letters can be sent to any of the third parties listed above, who may have information of the debtor's location. The letter can truthfully indicate the importance to the creditor and to the debtor of determining the debtor's location. The creditor should keep in mind that such use of the mail may be restricted by FDCPA.[4]

## [4] Using Legal Process to Locate the Debtor

If all else fails in locating the debtor, the creditor's attorney may have to resort to use of legal process. State statutes often give creditors the right to subpoena in order to locate the debtor. Although this might be the most expensive and time-consuming means of location, it may be the safest method from the standpoint of creditors' liability. For debtors located in another jurisdiction, the reader should refer to subsequent discussion, which considers methods of obtaining and enforcing judgments in the foreign jurisdiction.[5]

---

[2] See infra ¶ 5.09[1].

[3] See Sherwin, Debtors' and Creditors' Rights and Remedies 63 et seq. (Attorneys' Aid Publications 1969), for discussion of these mailing techniques.

[4] See infra ¶ 5.09[1].

[5] See ¶¶ 6.02[2][b], 6.07[4].

## ¶ 5.03 LOCATING THE ASSETS OF THE DEBTOR

The wise creditor will judge the feasibility of the collection effort from a debtor by first determining the extent and location of the debtor's assets. Too often creditors make this determination only after expensive litigation has taken place and a judgment has been obtained against the debtor. Only after a creditor begins to execute is the discovery made that assets are scarce or the location of assets is unknown. The following two sections describe means often employed by creditors and their attorneys to locate the assets of a debtor before instituting judicial action.[1] Short of spending additional money to obtain a private investigator to locate the assets of the debtor, what can the creditor or his attorney do independently?

### [1] Using the Debtor's Financial Statement as a Source of Asset Information

The approach usually taken by creditors to locate the debtor's assets is similar to that taken to locate the debtor.[2] The starting place is the creditor's file on that particular debtor. Too often the information obtained by creditors is sadly lacking in adequate information about the debtor's assets. Within the framework of common business sense, at the inception of the transaction that gives rise to the debt the creditor should carefully obtain information regarding the debtor's assets.

The financial statement is probably the most productive source for asset location information. Information on the statement that identifies other creditors is often helpful, since other creditors may have information regarding the location of the debtor's assets. Finally, the file should reveal the debtor's employer and the location of bank accounts. In regard to bank accounts, as mentioned previously, it is a good creditor's practice to periodically note the location of the debtor's accounts as payments are received.

### [2] Using Public Records as a Source of Asset Information

A second possible source of asset information is public records, particularly real estate filings and UCC-secured transaction filings. Real estate filings in the debtor's own geographic area might reveal new acquisitions of land made since the debtor's financial statement was submitted to the creditor. Filings pursuant to Article 9 of the UCC might also reveal acquisition of personal property or fixtures in which other creditors have acquired a perfected security interest. Although the creditor would be subordinate from a priority standpoint, it is possible the debtor has some equity in the property. These records

---

[1] For other discussion of techniques to locate the assets of a debtor, see Sherwin, Debtors' and Creditors' Rights and Remedies (Attorneys' Aid Publications 1969). See infra ¶¶ 5.08 and 5.09 for a discussion of limitations on the creditor's ability to use such techniques.

[2] See supra ¶ 5.02.

also disclose other creditors who can be contacted to reveal the existence of other assets. Both mortgage filings and UCC filings are considered at length in later chapters of this book.[3]

There is an infinite variety of other third-party sources that are also commonly investigated by creditors. Most of these sources were previously mentioned in the discussion of location of the debtor and need not be reconsidered.[4] Here too the creditor must be careful not to violate FDCPA.[5] Finally, assuming an action is pending or a judgment has been obtained, the use of a supplementary proceeding and its subpoena power can provide results. Supplementary proceedings are considered later.[6]

## ¶ 5.04 GENERAL EXTRAJUDICIAL COLLECTION TECHNIQUES

In most defaults, creditors usually find it advisable to seek voluntary collection without the use of judicial process. The technique used should be adapted to the particular situation, considering the amount due, the nature and personality of the debtor, and past experience with the debtor. Some of these techniques are considered in the following discussion.[1]

The collection letter is sometimes the most effective and cost-efficient method of obtaining collection, at least with a view toward curing a default. If full payment of the debt is not possible, the collection letter may lead to curing a default by bringing payments current or by adopting a new payment schedule. If the letter is improperly written, however, it can serve to polarize and embitter the debtor, thus making future voluntary collection more difficult. Letters often are designed for mailing in sequence—the first being less serious than subsequent letters insofar as possible judicial action is concerned. Initially the creditor should be careful to avoid any reference that the debtor is careless or discourteous, or is intentionally evading payment. On the other hand, most well-written collection letters directly indicate that the debtor has missed a payment, which is expected promptly. The letter should not appear to beg for payment; most creditors believe this weakens their position from a bargaining standpoint. The letter sometimes suggests that the debtor contact the creditor, if possible. A well-written collection letter should be short with a conclusion that calls for prompt action.

Creditors sometimes find that contacting the debtor by telephone can also be effective. Whether the initial contact after default should be by phone or

---

[3] See ¶ 8.09[1].

[4] See supra ¶ 5.02.

[5] See infra ¶ 5.09[1].

[6] See ¶ 6.05[5].

[1] See Sherwin, Debtors' and Creditors' Rights and Remedies (Attorneys' Aid Publications 1969), for a discussion of general extrajudicial collection techniques commonly used by creditors and other attorneys or collection agents. See infra ¶¶ 5.08 and 5.09 for a discussion of limitations on the creditor's ability to use such techniques.

letter is a decision that should be weighed carefully. If the telephone is used, the creditor or the attorney should get the desired facts aggressively and deliver the message that payment must be forthcoming. At the same time, the creditor or attorney should listen carefully to what the debtor has to say. At the conclusion of the call, a memorandum for the file should be prepared detailing the nature and substance of the discussion and including the date on which the call was made. If an attorney makes the call, it may be necessary to advise the debtor to seek the advice of counsel. Once the debtor indicates he wishes the creditor's attorney to contact his own lawyer, any further communication should take place with that lawyer and not directly with the debtor. The creditor and the creditor's attorney must also keep in mind the restrictions of FDCPA.[2]

Either the letter or the telephone call may result in an amicable discussion of the default between the debtor and the creditor. Such personal conferences are often productive, resulting in partial payment and a suggested plan for future payment. Further, they can produce current information about the debtor's financial status and the location of his assets. If the attorney for the creditor is involved in the conference, the debtor should be advised to seek separate counsel. At the conclusion of the conference, a complete statement or memorandum should be prepared for the file. If prudent, a composition-and-extension agreement may be explored.[3]

If personal contacts fail, a creditor then must decide how to proceed. If it is not financially worthwhile to pursue the matter in court, the creditor might consider using a collection agency. The fees of collection agencies vary tremendously. If the matter is worth pursuing judicially, based upon the location of the debtor, his assets, and the amount of the debt, the matter should be referred promptly to the attorney of the creditor for judicial action. The fortunate creditor, however, might have at least two other extrajudicial avenues to pursue. One avenue might be to pursue a third-party guarantor or surety if any exists.[4] The other avenue, setoff, is considered next.

## ¶ 5.05 SETOFF

Banks are usually cognizant (and most appreciative) of their right to set off a delinquent loan against a borrower's bank account. Indeed, it may be the most effective collection technique a bank possesses. However, the creditor's right of setoff is not limited to the bank creditor. This section explores and illustrates the legal basis on which the setoff right rests. The setoff right often appears to be virtually without restriction. Upon close examination of case law, however, one quickly learns that the setoff right should be exercised cautiously.

---

[2] See infra ¶ 5.09[1].

[3] See Hawkland & Loiseaux, Debtor-Creditor Relations 423–426 (Bobbs-Merrill 1979); Shimm, "The Impact of State Law on Bankruptcy," 1971 Duke L.J. 880, 881–888; 2 Nichols, Cyclopedia of Legal Forms 2.406 (1978); 15A Am. Jur. 2d 753; 15A C.J.S. 124.

[4] See infra ¶ 5.06.

This section, therefore, also considers potential legal restrictions to the exercise of the setoff right. Because the right of setoff is most commonly exercised by a bank, this section focuses primarily on the bank setoff.[1]

## [1] The Legal Basis of the Setoff Right

The origins of the setoff right are not entirely clear.[2] Apparently the right originated as one of creditors generally and was not limited to bank creditors. In 1705 an English statute provided that a commissioner in a bankruptcy could adjust accounts when there were mutual credits between the bankrupt and his debtor-creditor, with the debtor-creditor of the bankrupt being compelled to pay merely the balance still owed to the bankrupt.[3] The modern notion of setoff probably began with this statute and similar later English bankruptcy statutes. Apparently the earliest evidence of a *banker's* right of setoff is the case of *Rojerson v. Ladbroke.*[4] In *Rojerson* a banker had deducted funds from a customer's account to pay a bill of exchange that had come due without knowledge of the death of the customer. The validity of the setoff was upheld by the English Court, thus establishing the origins of the banker's right of setoff.

By the second half of the nineteenth century such English law was being cited by a number of American states. The banker's setoff right was given further judicial impetus during several economic depressions in the eighteen hundreds and early nineteen hundreds. It became a right that allowed banks to set off on their own without the need of prior judicial approval. It should be noted that the right of setoff is not rooted in the concept of the general banker's lien that originated in the Law Merchant.[5] What, then, is the legal basis of the setoff right?[6]

The setoff right is available to the creditor as a common-law right. The right usually exists without statutory basis or restriction. The right can be created by contract, although a contractual right is unnecessary. The right is not a lien even when a bank is setting off against an account, as the bank usually has more than a mere lien interest in the deposited funds. Once deposited, the funds become the property of the bank and under the contract of deposit with its depositor the bank becomes a debtor to the depositor. If, for example, a bank has loaned money to a depositor, then the cornerstone of the setoff right that must be present if any creditor wishes to set off–mutuality of indebted-

---

[1] For a similar discussion of setoff, see Hagedorn, "Bank Setoff in Washington–Is It a Right Without Restriction?" 15 Gonz. L. Rev. 989 (1980).

[2] For an excellent discussion of the historical origins of setoff rights, see Murray, "Banks v. Creditors of Their Customers: Setoffs Against Customers' Accounts," 82 Com. L.J. 449 (1977).

[3] 4 Anne, C17, Section XI (1705).

[4] 1 Bing. 94, 130 Eng. Rep. 39 (1822).

[5] See Skilton, "The Secured Party's Rights in a Debtor's Bank Account Under Article 9 of the Uniform Commercial Code," 120 S. Ill. U.L.J. 197 n.128 (1978).

[6] For discussion of the legal basis of setoff, see Hagedorn, "Bank Setoff in Washington–Is It a Right Without Restriction?" 15 Gonz. L. Rev. 989 (1980).

ness—is present; the debtor-depositor is a creditor to the bank regarding the deposit, but regarding the separate loan he is a debtor. For the purpose of efficiency and expediency, if the depositor is in default to the bank on the loan, the bank is allowed by the common law to reduce the debt due it by reducing its obligation to the debtor-depositor under the bank account. For example, assume a borrower opens a checking account and sometime thereafter obtains a $10,000 loan from the same bank. The loan becomes delinquent and the borrower has $2,000 in his checking account. Because of the mutual indebtedness between the borrower and the bank, the bank may set off against its obligation under the borrower's account by reducing the loan outstanding to it by the amount of the account. The result is that the borrower has nothing left in his account and the loan is now outstanding in the amount of $8,000.

A second example of the mutuality principle in the banking context arises when a borrower opens an account at a bank and the borrower and a second debtor obtain a loan from the bank and sign a promissory note on which both the borrower and the debtor are jointly and severally liable. If the note becomes delinquent, the bank may seek to set off the note against the borrower's individual bank account. The bank will probably be unable to set off because the debts due it and its obligation are not mutual.[7] For nonbanking situations the same right of setoff can arise when two parties owe debts to each other, since mutuality of indebtedness is likewise present. In the absence of such mutuality of indebtedness between debtor and creditor, the common-law right of setoff does not arise.

To this point, reference has been made to setoff as a *right* of the creditor. The creditor's attorney and the creditor should recognize that the right is not generally considered a *duty*.[8] For example, courts generally have held the creditor's failure to set off does not operate as a discharge of a surety, although some courts have required a creditor to set off against a debtor or risk a discharge of a surety.[9] Otherwise, setoff is purely a *right* founded on the concept of mutual indebtedness.

## [2] Potential Restrictions to the Assertion of Setoff by the Creditor

### [a] Potential Consequences for Improper Setoff

Creditors sometimes express the opinion that setoff should always be attempted as there is "nothing to lose; you simply reverse the setoff if it turns out it was improper." That attitude can be hazardous, since there are potential

---

[7] See Teeters v. City Nat'l Bank, 214 Ind. 498 14 N.E.2d 1004 (1938); Miles v. Bank of Commerce, 76 Misc. 2d 623, 351 NYS2d 513 (1973); Annot., 68 A.L.R.3d 192 (1976); Annot., 118 A.L.R. 386 (1939).

[8] See, e.g., Schultz v. American Nat'l Bank & Trust Co., 40 Ill. App. 3d 800, 352 NE2d 310 (1980); Overland Nat'l Bank of Grand Island v. Aurora Coop. Elevator Co., 184 Neb. 843, 172 NW2d 786 (1969).

[9] See, e.g., Bank of Am. Nat'l Trust & Sav. Ass'n v. Liberty Nat'l Bank & Trust Co., 116 F. Supp. 233 (WD Okla. 1953), Contra Tatum v. Commercial Bank & Trust Co., 193 Ala. 129, 69 So. 508 (1915).

negative consequences if setoff occurs improperly. This is clearly illustrated in the banking context.

First, a bank could be liable for consequential damages proximately caused the account holder by an improper setoff. Obviously if the account holder can no longer draw on his account due to the setoff, he may suffer loss as a result; that is, he may lose a business investment opportunity. This inability to draw on the account often comes to a head when checks drawn by the account holder are presented for payment to the bank after the account has been depleted by the setoff. For example, assume a bank loans a borrower $10,000. The borrower has a checking account at the bank and the bank mistakenly believes the borrower has defaulted on the loan and sets off against the account, totally depleting it. In these circumstances adverse consequences of improper collection may result. The borrower may have issued a check in payment for goods or services essential to the borrower's business. When the check is presented to the bank for payment it will be dishonored by the bank, since the setoff emptied the account. The payee may immediately sue the borrower. The borrower's credit reputation will be damaged. On top of this, the payee may have the borrower arrested by the police for a criminal offense as a result of the bounced check. Further, the borrower's business may suffer because of the loss of the goods or services for which the check was originally issued. The borrower is given the right to sue the bank, for under UCC Section 4-402 the bank is liable for all actual damages due to the wrongful dishonor of the check.

One other potential consequence of an improper setoff in the banking setting relates to damages suffered by third parties other than the borrower who have an interest in the borrower's account. These include joint account holders, lien holders, and the like. If the bank that sets off did not have the right to do so against the third parties, it also becomes liable to the third parties for damages proximately caused.[10]

### [b] Necessity of a Matured Obligation

Most case law requires that the debt due the creditor from the debtor must have matured prior to the exercise of setoff.[11] This principle is simple when stated in the abstract. In the actual application of the rule, however, the creditor or his attorney must take care to determine that the debt has indeed matured. The question of default will revolve around contractual principles as applied to the loan agreement, promissory note, or other obligation. If setoff occurs prior to maturity, the creditor may suffer the consequences of improper setoff discussed above.

There are a limited number of situations in which setoff in the banking context is usually allowed in the absence of a matured debt. Although there is some contrary authority, this is generally the case when the debtor becomes

---

[10] See infra ¶¶ 5.05[2][l]–5.05[2][q] for discussion of third-party interests.

[11] See, e.g., Kane v. First Nat'l Bank of El Paso, 56 F2d 534 (5th Cir.), cert. denied, 287 US 603 (1932); First City Bank of Oxford v. Long-Lewis Hardware Co., 363 So. 2d 770, on remand, 363 So. 2d 774 (Ala. 1978).

insolvent.[12] Note, however, that an actual bankruptcy of the debtor can limit the exercise of setoff. Such limitations are discussed later in this chapter and in more detail later in the book.[13] In addition, even in the absence of insolvency, there is some authority that will allow the bank to set off upon the death of its debtor, although contrary authority requires insolvency of the estate to allow setoff.[14] Further discussion of the effect of death on the ability of a bank to set off is found later in this chapter.[15] Finally, agreements between the bank and its customer might also broaden the right of setoff in the absence of maturity of the debt; this also is discussed subsequently in this chapter.[16]

### [c] Statute of Limitations on the Debt

If the debt has been "mature" for too long, a creditor may not be able to set off against the obligation it owes the debtor. If the statute of limitations has run on the debt due the creditor, the creditor is precluded from the exercise of its right of setoff. Since a setoff is in essence a counterclaim, the statute of limitations would preclude use of a time-barred claim as a counterclaim. Thus, setoff is also restricted.[17]

### [d] Agreements Affecting the Setoff, Including Special Deposits

It is possible for a creditor to enter into agreements with the debtor that would affect the ability of the creditor to set off. By agreement the creditor's right of setoff could be either expanded or restricted. As an example, one can reconsider the rule forbidding setoff if the debtor's debt is unmatured.[18] The original promissory note signed by the debtor-depositor could provide that a bank could set off prior to maturity or that the bank could accelerate the date of maturity.[19] It would seem, however, that such acceleration or setoff prior to maturity must occur in good faith as defined at UCC Section 1-208.

---

[12] See, e.g., Elizarraras v. Bank of El Paso, 631 F2d 366 (5th Cir. 1980); Schuler v. Israel, 120 US 506 (1887); Kane v. First Nat'l Bank of El Paso, 56 F2d 534 (5th Cir.), cert. denied, 287 US 603 (1932).

[13] See infra ¶ 5.05[2][k] and ¶ 17.08.

[14] See Annot., 7 A.L.R.3d 908 (1966).

[15] See infra ¶ 5.05[2][q].

[16] See infra ¶ 5.05[2][d].

[17] See, e.g., Warren v. Washington Trust Bank, 19 Wash. App. 348, 575 P2d 1077, modified, 92 Wash. 2d 381, 598 P2d 701 (1978); Otto v. Lincoln Sav. Bank of Brooklyn, 268 AD 400, 51 NYS2d 561 (1944), aff'd, 294 NY 798, 62 NE2d 236 (1945).

[18] See ¶ 5.05[1] for a discussion of the rule requiring maturity of a debt before setoff occurs.

[19] See, e.g., U.S. ex rel. Crow Creek Tribe v. Tri-County Bank of Chamberlain, 415 F. Supp. 858 (DSD 1978); Walter v. National City Bank of Cleveland, 42 Ohio St. 2d 524, 330 NE2d 425 (1975); Aetna Casualty & Sur. Co. v. Atlantic Nat'l Bank of W. Palm Beach, 430 F2d 574 (5th Cir. 1970).

The setoff right of the creditor also can be restricted by agreement.[20] The agreement restricting setoff can take many forms, one of which in the banking business concerns a "special deposit." If the debtor-depositor has deposited funds to be used for a special purpose *to the bank's knowledge*, the bank may not set off these funds because they are not a part of the bank's general deposits, but are held by the bank in trust or as a mere bailee.[21]

### [e] Waiver and Estoppel

The creditor's attorney and the creditor should be aware that a creditor can inadvertently restrict its right of setoff where the elements of waiver or estoppel are present. It should first be stated that appellate courts often have not been receptive to arguments of estoppel and waiver without a contractual agreement not to set off. For example, the mere promise by a bank not to set off that is unsupported by consideration will not restrict the bank's ability to set off.[22]

On the other hand, some courts have been more receptive to estoppel arguments against the creditor when some act of the creditor indicating that setoff will not occur is relied upon by the debtor or some third party to its detriment. For example, a delay in exercising setoff can cause a change in position such that estoppel is present. Similarly, acts of a bank that recognize the depositor's control over an account can affect an estoppel. For example, assume a bank is served with notice of garnishment of an account of its debtor-depositor but instead pays over the funds in the account to its debtor. Thereafter it may not plead setoff against the garnishing creditor, since it has waived its right to do so. Some case law illustrating these situations and others in which estoppel is present is cited below.[23]

### [f] Constitutional Considerations

Arguments have been raised that setoff by a bank is subject to the due process of law restrictions of the Fourteenth Amendment to the U.S. Constitu-

---

[20] See, e.g., U.S. ex rel. Crow Creek Tribe v. Tri-County Bank of Chamberlain, 415 F. Supp. 858 (DSD 1976); Filose v. Pecora, 44 Ill. App. 3d 912, 358 NE2d 1213 (1976); First Nat'l Bank of Schulenburg v. Winkler, 139 Tex. 131, 161 SW2d 1053 (1942); Menkes Feuer, Inc. v. Peoples Bank of Johnstown, 43 NYS2d 32 (S. Ct. Fulton Co. 1943).

[21] See, e.g., In re Applied Logic Corp., 576 F2d 952 (2d Cir. 1978); Hudson United Bank v. House of Supreme, Inc., 149 NJ Super. 153, 373 A2d 438 (1977); Houston Nat'l Bank v. Biber, 613 SW2d 771 (Tex. Civ. App. 1981); see also Annot., 50 A.L.R.3d 697 (1973).

[22] See Paine-Erie Hosp. Supply, Inc. v. Lincoln First Bank of Rochester, 82 Misc. 2d 432, 370 NYS2d 370 (NY Sup. Ct. 1975).

[23] See, e.g., Johnson v. Dutch Mill Dairy, 237 Minn. 117 54 NW2d 1 (1952); Peoples Bank v. Gore, 178 Miss. 216, 172 So. 506 (1937); Prudential Loan & Trust Co. v. Metzler, 66 Ore. 224, 133 P 1191 (1913); Niblack v. Park Nat'l Bank, 169 Ill. 517, 48 NE 438 (1897).

tion and similar state constitutional provisions. It has been argued that since setoff by the bank occurs without prior notice and judicial hearing and because there is state action insofar as case law has established the validity of the setoff right, the setoff occurs improperly without due process.[24] Such cases to date uniformly hold that there is insufficient state involvement for the requisite state action and thus the debtor-depositor has no due process rights to assert.[25] On the other hand, that is not to say that notice before setoff is never required; statutes may provide for prior notification. In that regard one should refer to the discussion in this chapter of consumer credit and other statutory restrictions on the offset right.[26]

### [g] Withdrawal of Funds by the Debtor-Depositor or Payment of Funds by the Bank Before Setoff

The timing of setoff is a particularly important matter pertaining to bank setoff; most of this section, therefore, is devoted to setoff in the banking context. A bank may set off against its obligation to its customer under an account only to the extent there is an obligation. There can be no setoff to the extent that the obligation has been discharged or reduced by withdrawals by the customer or by proper payments on presented checks drawn by the customer. In effect, there is a race to the bank account: the first party there obtains rights in the account. Although pinpointing the time of the customer's withdrawal has not generated any legal difficulty, it sometimes is difficult to determine when a presented check is paid.

Determining when setoff is exercised in a timely manner is done by applying UCC Section 4-303. This section provides that a setoff is not timely and cannot affect an account if, before the setoff is exercised, the bank upon presentment has:

(1) Certified a check;
(2) Paid it in cash;
(3) Settled for the item without reserving the right to revoke the settlement and without having such right under statute, clearinghouse rule, or agreement;
(4) Completed the process of posting the check or otherwise has evidenced by examination of the indicated account and by action its decision to pay the item; or
(5) Become accountable for the amount of the item under UCC Sections 4-213(1)(d) and 4-302 dealing with the payor bank's responsibility for late return of items.

---

[24] See Comment, "Banking Setoff: A Study In Commercial Obsolescence," 23 Hastings L.J. 1585 (1972); Annot., 65 A.L.R.3d 1284 (1975).

[25] See, e.g., Allied Sheet Metal Fabricators, Inc. v. Peoples Nat'l Bank of Washington, 10 Wash. App. 530, 518 P2d 734 (1974); Kruger v. Wells Fargo Bank, 11 Cal. 3d 352, 521 P2d 441, 113 Cal. Rptr. 449 (1974).

[26] See infra ¶ 5.05[2][u].

The following example illustrates this timing problem: The bank loans the borrower $10,000. The borrower has a checking account at the bank in which $15,000 is deposited. The bank has been presented for payment a number of checks drawn on the account and has taken the following action with regard to each check:

*Check No. 1:* Bank certified the check.

*Check No. 2:* Bank paid the item in cash "over the counter."

*Check No. 3:* Bank held the item past the bank's midnight deadline and became accountable for it under UCC Section 4-213(d); thus, it has no right to revoke its prior provisional settlement.

*Check No. 4:* Bank posted payment on the item, examined the computer printout showing the posting, found it to be in order, found the check to be in order, and took some other action, such as stamping the check "PAID."

If the bank attempts setoff after the four checks have been handled as indicated, the setoff will not reach the funds in the account affected by each of the four checks due to UCC Section 4-303.[27] It should be noted that the time when the setoff occurs must also be ascertained. In that regard, some jurisdictions deem setoff to have occurred automatically upon the maturity of a mutual debt.[28] Jurisdictions often require some act of the bank such as the making of appropriate bookkeeping entries before setoff is deemed to have occurred.[29]

If a bank can invalidate on some separate theory a transfer of funds out of a customer's account, setoff can occur upon reacquisition of the funds. Such a separate ground could, for example, include that the transfer was a fraudulent conveyance. Without such an ability to invalidate the transfer, the bank will not be allowed to trace the funds to the payee and set off in the hands of the payee.[30]

### [h] Garnishment of the Account Before Setoff

Garnishment of the account again involves a matter usually related to banking. A debtor-depositor of the bank may default on loans made by third-party creditors. If a third-party creditor obtains judgment against the debtor-depositor, the creditor may seek collection of the judgment by garnishing the

---

[27] For an excellent discussion of UCC § 4-303, see Bailey, Brady on Bank Checks 14-56–14-65 (Warren, Gorham & Lamont, Inc., 5th ed. 1979); White & Summers, Uniform Commercial Code 692–703 (West, 2d ed. 1980).

[28] See, e.g., Pittsburgh Nat'l Bank v. U.S., 657 F2d 36 (2d Cir. 1952).

[29] See, e.g., Baker v. National City Bank of Cleveland, 511 F2d 1016 (6th Cir. 1975).

[30] See, e.g., In re Greenwald's Estate, 143 NYS2d 464 (Surrogate Ct. 1955); Trader's Nat'l Bank v. Amsden, 195 NYS2d 291, aff'd, 208 AD 828, 203 NYS 956 (S. Ct. Monroe Co. 1922).

account held by the bank. Assuming the right of setoff is available to the bank (i.e., the loan to the debtor-depositor has matured), can the bank set off even though it has been served with a notice of garnishment?

The garnishing creditor has no greater rights in the bank account than does the debtor-depositor. In effect, the garnishing creditor simply steps into the shoes of the debtor-depositor and is subject to any claim of the bank to which the debtor-depositor is subject. Therefore, the bank may set off even though it has been served with the notice of garnishment.[31] For example, assume that a bank loans a borrower $10,000 and the borrower has a checking account at the bank with $8,000 on deposit. Further assume that the borrower's loan with the bank has "matured" in that the borrower has defaulted under the terms of the loan and a security agreement with the bank. Meanwhile, if the borrower has a judgment entered against him by a creditor and the creditor garnishes the checking account, the bank may wish to set off even though it has not as yet exercised setoff. After serving a notice of garnishment the bank can set off against the account, since the creditor obtained no greater rights in the account than the borrower.[32]

There are some interesting twists in case law regarding the right to set off in the face of a garnishment. Even in the event of a garnishment the bank's claim upon which the setoff is predicated usually must be matured, but some courts have allowed setoff even if the claim is unmatured.[33] Because garnishment in many jurisdictions reaches only funds on deposit at the time that the notice of garnishment is served, deposits made after the notice is served are subject to setoff by the bank even if the bank honors the garnishment.[34] Finally, there is some authority that will allow the bank to set off even after it has answered the garnishment by filing a pleading showing a desire to do so.[35]

### [i] Levy and Assessment by the Internal Revenue Service Before Setoff

Another potential restriction to the creditor's assertion of setoff is posed by the Internal Revenue Service (IRS).[36] The IRS is as aware as the bank and other creditors of the usefulness of the debtor's bank account when seeking

---

[31] See, e.g., Coyle v. Pan Am. Bank of Miami, 377 So. 2d 213 (Fla. Dist. Ct. App. 1979); Aspen Indus., Inc. v. Marine Midland Bank, 52 NY2d 575, 421 NE2d 808, 439 NYS2d 316 (1981); Almi, Inc. v. Dick Corp., 31 Pa. Commw. 36, 375 A2d 1343 (1977); Aarons v. Public Serv. Bldg. & Loan Ass'n, 318 Pa. 113, 178 A 141 (1935); Farmer's & Merchant's State Bank of Teague v. Setzen, Tex., 185 SW 596 (1916).

[32] See Barsco, Inc. v. HWW, Inc., 346 So. 2d 134 (Fla. 1977).

[33] See, e.g., Valley Nat'l Bank v. Harper, 6 Ariz. App. 376, 432 P2d 924 (1967).

[34] See ¶ 6.04[2][d] for discussion of property subsequent to a garnishment.

[35] See, e.g., Smith v. Crocker First Nat'l Bank of San Francisco, 152 Cal. 2d 832, 314 P2d 237 (1957).

[36] For an excellent discussion of this problem area, see Murray, "Banks v. Creditors of Their Customers: Setoffs Against Customers' Accounts," 82 Com. L.J. 449 (1977).

collection,[37] and therefore is another potential creditor. The IRS typically will obtain a lien upon and then seize a taxpayer's bank account when possible to satisfy taxes due. If the bank holding the account has also loaned money to the taxpayer, it may wish to set off if the loan has matured. Resolving who has the first right to the account has been a difficult problem for the courts. Put another way, will the IRS be treated like a garnishing creditor that cannot rise above the rights of the debtor-depositor in the account and is thus subject to the bank's setoff right? Or must the bank have exercised setoff before the IRS even acquires its lien?

Before these questions can be answered, the nature of the IRS collection right must be reviewed.[38] The IRS may levy upon all the taxpayer's property and rights to property upon which it has a lien for payment of taxes.[39] "Rights to property" certainly include the taxpayer's rights in a bank account. The lien is given the IRS if the taxpayer neglects or refuses to pay a tax for which he is liable after assessment and demand. The lien dates from the time of assessment, although some third parties who make claims to the taxpayer's property have priority if the tax lien is unfiled.[40] In summary, the IRS is given priority in the taxpayer's property over all creditors except: (1) creditors who have obtained choate liens *before the tax lien arises*, or (2) creditors who have security interests that are perfected under state law as to judicial lienors *before the tax lien is filed*. The "choateness" doctrine basically requires that the lienor be identified, the property subject to the lien be identified, and the amount of the lien be ascertained at the time the IRS acquires or files its lien.

As discussed above, the setoff right of the bank is not a lien. Even if the bank could establish the right as a lien, the lien would not be choate until setoff were exercised.[41] The other argument in establishing the bank's priority is that the IRS can only acquire the rights of the taxpayer in the account. If so, the IRS' right to the account is restricted by the setoff right of the bank, just as the debtor-depositor's rights are restricted in the account. It has been held, however, that the IRS distraint against the bank account does not put the government in the position of the debtor-depositor against the bank and does not make the government subject to all rights the bank has against the depositor.[42] If the bank is to have priority over the IRS, it must have exercised setoff before a tax lien arises. For example, if the bank is in a particular jurisdiction in which it is deemed to exercise automatically the right of setoff as soon as the debt due from its depositor is overdue, the debtor-depositor has no rights to the account. Therefore, a subsequent IRS lien has nothing to which it can attach.[43] However, if the jurisdiction requires some act of the bank to exercise setoff (e.g.,

---

[37] See supra ¶ 5.05[2][h].

[38] For a detailed consideration of the federal tax lien, see ¶ 9.04.

[39] 26 USC § 6331(a).

[40] 26 USC § 6323(a).

[41] See U.S. v. Sterling Nat'l Bank & Trust Co. of N.Y., 494 F2d 919 (2d Cir. 1974).

[42] U.S. v. Manufacturers Trust Co., 198 F2d 366 (2d Cir. 1952).

[43] See Pittsburgh Nat'l Bank v. U.S., 657 F2d 36 (3d Cir. 1981).

making appropriate bookkeeping entries), the IRS lien takes priority if the lien is acquired before such setoff is so exercised.[44] For example, suppose a bank loans a taxpayer $10,000 and the taxpayer has a checking account at the bank. Assume further that the taxpayer failed to pay taxes and the IRS has made assessment and demand and has filed a tax lien. The IRS now seeks to levy on the bank account. Prior to assessment and demand, the taxpayer defaulted on a loan to the bank. To defeat the IRS levy, the bank must establish that setoff occurred before the IRS acquired its lien. It may do so successfully if setoff actually occurred prior to that time, or if the applicable state law provides that setoff occurs automatically upon default of the taxpayer. Otherwise, the IRS levy will prevail.

### [j] State Insolvency Proceedings of the Debtor Before or After Setoff

As a debtor slides into insolvency, default on debts is a common occurrence. Equally common is a creditor's setoff, particularly by a bank creditor against a debtor's bank account. The setoff may occur just before or shortly after a debtor places his assets in the hands of a custodian under state laws providing for assignments for the benefit of creditors.[45] Setoff shortly before such an assignment might be invalidated as a preference.[46] In essence, it involves the acquisition of the debtor's property by a creditor prior to bankruptcy or a state insolvency proceeding that benefits that creditor to the detriment of other creditors. Setoff after an assignment also may be invalidated, since such collection efforts may be automatically enjoined upon the occurrence of an assignment. Local law must be carefully consulted. Usually, the problem of setoff when the debtor is insolvent does not arise out of a resulting assignment for the benefit of creditors under state laws. Rather, questions related to the timeliness of the setoff in the insolvency setting usually arise when the debtor files federal bankruptcy.

### [k] Federal Bankruptcy of the Debtor Before or After Setoff

Discussion here is limited to a brief outline of the effect a debtor's bankruptcy might have on a creditor's ability to set off before or after a petition in bankruptcy is filed by the debtor or his creditors.[47] Changes to the Bankruptcy Act of 1898 made by the Bankruptcy Reform Act of 1979 (hereafter referred to

---

[44] See Baker v. National City Bank, 511 F2d 1016 (6th Cir. 1975); cf. U.S. v. St. John's Community Bank, 302 F. Supp. 149 (ED Mo. 1969).

[45] See the following for discussion of state laws providing for assignments for the benefit of creditors: Weintraub & Resnick, Bankruptcy Law Manual Ch. 10 (Warren, Gorham & Lamont, Inc. 1981); Greenfield, "Alternatives to Bankruptcy for the Business Debtor," 51 Los Angeles B.J. 135; Shimm, "The Impact of State Law of Bankruptcy," 1971 Duke L.J. 879; 6 Am. Jur. 2d 321; 6A C.J.S. 806.

[46] See infra ¶ 5.05[2][k].

[47] See ¶ 17.08 for a more detailed discussion of setoff in a bankruptcy.

as the "Code") have materially altered the ability of a creditor who wishes to set off.[48]

First, in order to validly set off under Section 553, the debt involved must be a mutual debt. Second, both the debt owed to the debtor and the claim against the debtor must have existed before the petition in bankruptcy is filed. Third, the claim of the creditor must not be disallowed. Fourth, the claim of the creditor cannot have been obtained simply to create the possibility of setoff if the claim was acquired within ninety days of bankruptcy or after petition-filing and the bankrupt was insolvent when the claim was acquired. Fifth, particularly applicable in the banking context, the creditor-bank cannot build up the bankrupt's account to create or increase the right of setoff. More specifically, Section 553 precludes setoff by a bank if money is deposited by the bankrupt within ninety days of petition-filing when the bankrupt was insolvent and where the purpose of the deposit was to create or increase the right of setoff. Sixth, as to prepetition setoffs, the creditor cannot improve his position between the first day of the ninety-day period preceding petition-filing and the date the setoff took place. If this occurs, to the extent of the improvement of position, the setoff will be invalidated. Note that this "improvement of position test" does not reach beyond ninety days prior to bankruptcy. Seventh, as to postpetition setoffs, the filing of the bankruptcy petition under Section 362 will serve to stay setoff until final distribution of the estate, confirmation of a plan in a rehabilitation proceeding, or until relief is obtained from the stay by the creditor who wishes to set off. In addition, it should be emphasized that setoff is unaffected by the preferential transfer provision of the Code, Section 547. Indeed, Section 553 indicates that the Code "does not affect any right of the creditor to offset a mutual debt" except as affected by Sections 362, 363, and 553.

### [l] Claims of Joint Account Holders

A third party may challenge the creditor's ability to set off if the third party possesses some claim in the debt due the creditor. Such third-party challenges typically arise in the banking context. If a bank has made a loan to an individual and the loan is in default, the question is often raised of whether the bank can set off against a joint account held by the individual debtor and some other person. The mutuality requirement discussed above[49] would seem to be violated if setoff is allowed against the nondebtor joint account holder's interest in the account.[50] On the other hand, setoff against the debtor's interest would appear valid. The matter is considerably more complicated than these basic statements reflect, as a review of case law indicates.

Generally a bank can set off against funds in a joint account in which the debtor has an interest. But what is the extent of the debtor's ownership interest

---

[48] 11 USC § 553.

[49] See supra ¶ 5.05[1].

[50] See, e.g., Old S. Life Ins. Co. v. Bank of N.C., N.A., 36 NC App. 18, 244 SE2d 264 (1978); Sandler v. United Indus. Bank, 23 AD2d 567, 256 NYS2d 442 (1965).

in the joint account? Here the results of case law vary.[51] In many jurisdictions there is a presumption that joint accounts are equally held. In other jurisdictions the relative rights of the account holders are determined on the basis of their intentions as evidenced by their actions. In still other jurisdictions, great weight is placed upon statutes that specify the extent of an individual's interest in a joint account. From a practical standpoint, it is quite difficult before or at the time of setoff to ascertain the extent of the debtor's interest in the joint account.

A separate method of handling the problem from the bank-creditor's viewpoint is to contract with the joint depositors for the right to set off the entire account in the event an individual account holder defaults. The agreement could authorize the bank to apply all of the funds in the account to the debt of any one of the joint account holders. One example of a recent extreme case in which such an agreement was upheld is *Simpson v. Georgia State Bank*.[52] In *Simpson*, the bank loaned money to a joint account holder. The joint account holder had opened the joint account with the bank to handle the financial affairs of his elderly mother, who became the other joint account holder. Only the mother's funds were actually placed in the account. It included a provision that allowed the bank to apply all funds in the account to any debt due it of either account holder. The mother, whose eyesight was poor, could not read the fine print of the contract. Her son later defaulted on his loan with the bank and the bank set off against the joint account. The setoff was upheld, for the court concluded the account contract clause was enforceable.

### [m] Claims of Beneficiaries in Trust Accounts

For the account holder the above extreme case illustrates the necessity of using a trust account (or some other form of custodial account) to protect the party for whom the account is actually opened. If the son had merely been the trustee of the account and the mother had been the beneficiary, the bank's setoff against the account of the son's debt would have been impossible. It is clear that if a bank knows or can be charged with knowledge that the account is held in trust by its debtor-depositor, the bank cannot set off the debt against the beneficiary's interest.[53] Such knowledge is clearly present if the account is opened as a trust or custodial type of account. If the funds are held in trust but the bank lacks such knowledge or notice, some courts have allowed setoff while others have not.[54] Generally, a bank should not set off the individual debt of the trustee against the trust account because of the potential liability to the beneficiary.

---

[51] See, e.g., Guilds v. Monroe County Bank, 41 Mich. App. 616, 200 NW2d 769 (1972). For discussion of examples of specific state case law, see also Annot., 68 A.L.R.3d 192 (1976).

[52] 159 Ga. App. 310, 283 SE2d 278 (1981).

[53] See, e.g., Emile v. Bright, 203 So. 2d 328 (Fla. Dist. Ct. App. 1967); Annot., 8 A.L.R.3d 235 (1966).

[54] See, e.g., Arnold v. San Roman Valley Bank, 184 Cal. 632, 194 P 1012 (1921). Contra Cox v. Metropolitan State Bank, Inc., 138 Colo. 576, 336 P2d 742 (1959).

### [n] Claims of the Debtor's Secured Creditors in Bank Account

One of the more challenging third-party claimants in the bank account is the secured creditor of the debtor-depositor. One method by which a creditor can obtain a security interest in the debtor's bank account is by direct grant of the debtor.[55] If this occurs, can the bank set off against the account when the debtor-depositor defaults to it, even though the secured creditor's rights are obviously affected? It would seem that the secured creditor could only obtain the rights of the debtor-depositor in the account and thus would be subject to the setoff. This would be the case if the collateral were any other type of contract right than a bank account. At this writing, however, research fails to disclose a case directly in point.

A second means by which a secured creditor of the debtor-depositor can obtain a security interest in the debtor's bank account arises when proceeds from the sale of other collateral are deposited in the bank account. Of course, here the secured creditor possesses a security interest in the proceeds prior to their deposit and thereafter.[56] Again, can the bank set off against the account upon default of the debtor-depositor and thereby destroy the secured creditor's interest in the account? An answer to this question does not come easily, as it has not been clearly resolved by the UCC. For specific discussions of this problem area and accompanying case citations, refer to the authorities cited below,[57] which are next reviewed.

As reflected in the above discussion, which reflects the case law that considers this problem, there appears to be a split of authority. One position taken by the courts is that if the bank actually knows that funds deposited in the account of one of its debtors are subject to a secured creditor's claim, or has knowledge of circumstances sufficient to necessitate inquiry, it cannot set off against the account to that extent.[58] A second position gives priority to the secured creditor if the creditor possesses a perfected-proceeds security interest before the bank sets off.[59] These holdings rest on the general priority provision of UCC Section 9-201 that provides as follows: "Except as otherwise provided by this Act, a security interest is effective according to its terms between the parties, against purchasers of the collateral and against creditors."

---

[55] However, obtaining security interests in bank accounts is not governed by the UCC Article 9. See UCC § 9-104(k).

[56] See UCC § 9-306.

[57] Skilton, "The Secured Party's Right In The Debtor's Bank Account Under Article 9 of the Uniform Commercial Code," 120 S. Ill. U.L.J. 201–207 (1977); Murray, "Banks v. Creditors of Their Customers: Setoff Against Customers' Accounts," 32 Com. L.J. 449 (1977); Hagedorn, "Bank Setoff In Washington–Is It a Right Without Restriction?" 15 Gonz. L. Rev. 989 (1980); see also Annot., 3 A.L.R.4th 998 (1981).

[58] See, e.g., Commercial Discount Corp. v. Milwaukee W. Bank, 61 Wis. 2d 671, 214 NW2d 37 (Wis. 1974).

[59] See, e.g., Citizens Nat'l Bank v. Mid-States Dev. Co., 177 Ind. App. 548, 380 NE2d 1243 (1978); Associates Discount Corp. v. Fidelity Union Trust Co., 111 NJ Super. 353, 268 A2d 330 (1970); Universal CIT Credit Corp. v. Farmers Bank, 358 F. Supp. 317 (ED Mo. 1973).

### [o] Claims of Beneficiaries to Life Insurance Proceeds Deposited in the Debtor's Account

Another potential impediment to setoff has arisen at least once in American case law.[60] If, for whatever reason, proceeds of a life insurance policy are deposited in an account of someone who is not the proper beneficiary of the policy, can the bank set off against the account a debt due it from the account holder? As the prior discussion of special deposits, trust accounts, and secured creditors reflects, if the bank knows of a third party's valid claim in the account that supersedes the right of the debtor-depositor to the account, it cannot set off against that interest of the third party. The bank, therefore, should not set off if it knows that a party validly claims an interest in the bank account as proceeds of a life insurance policy under which the party is the beneficiary.

### [p] Claims of the Depositor's Surety Company

Although the following potential impediment to the bank right of setoff is very specialized, it occasionally can arise in the course of banking business. Assume a contractor has an account at a bank. The bank lends funds to the contractor and the contractor grants the bank a security interest in construction contracts, accounts arising from the contractor's business, and proceeds derived from the contracts and accounts. Thereafter, the contractor fails to perform a construction contract he has with an owner. A surety has bonded the contractor and now performs the remainder of the construction contract. The owner still owes money to the contractor; however, the surety will now stand in the shoes of the contractor and will have a right under equitable principles to the payment. Further, the surety has priority to the payment over the bank's security interest.[61] If the funds, however, are taken by the contractor and deposited in his account at the bank, and if the contractor has defaulted on the loan with the bank, setoff might be attempted against the account and thus against the surety's interest. The resulting conflict must be resolved.

Although the above illustration raises a technical problem, the basic principles discussed previously again resolve this conflict. The bank can set off against the contractor and his surety until the bank has actual knowledge of sufficient facts to charge it with notice of the surety's interest. Once such knowledge is obtained, the bank cannot set off against the account of the contractor to the extent of the interest of the surety.[62]

---

[60] See Griffin v. Gulf Life Ins. Co., 146 So. 2d 901 (Fla. 1962).

[61] See, e.g., U.S. Fidelity & Guar. Co. v. First State Bank, 208 Kan. 738, 494 P2d 1149 (1972).

[62] See, e.g., Aetna Casualty & Sur. Co. v. Atlantic Nat'l Bank of W. Palm Beach, 430 F2d 574 (5th Cir. 1970); Argonaut Ins. Co. v. C&S Bank of Tifton, 140 Ga. App. 807, 232 SE2d 135 (1976).

### [q] Claims of the Estate or Heirs of the Deceased Debtor-Depositor

All states statutorily regulate the distribution of property of a deceased and the filing of creditors' claims against the estate of the deceased. Under what circumstances can a bank set off against the account of a deceased to whom the bank had made a loan? For example, must the bank file a claim before setoff? Is some of the deceased's estate exempt from creditors' claims?

First recall that as a general rule the debt due to a bank that desires to set off against the account must have matured. But as prior discussion in this chapter of the maturity requirement reflects, the death of a depositor may present an exception.[63] There is some authority that setoff would be allowed even in the absence of maturity of the debt if the estate of the deceased is insolvent. This is the case even if the promissory note or other evidence of indebtedness does not provide for acceleration upon death. Lacking such insolvency or maturity of the debt, the bank probably cannot set off but must file a claim in the deceased depositor's estate. There is some contrary authority that setoff would be allowed without insolvency of the estate or maturity of the debt. In regard to the effect of death on the setoff right of a bank, consult the authorities below.[64] Finally, if the right of setoff is available upon death of the debtor-depositor, the right will not extend to funds deposited by executors of the estate after the death.[65]

Even if the deceased depositor is insolvent or the debt has matured, the bank might be concerned about state statutes that could in effect exempt certain assets from creditors' claims by requiring distribution of certain assets or certain amounts of the estate of a decedent to specific heirs. In short, are the rights of the heirs under such statutes paramount to the otherwise existent setoff right of the bank? The answer is that the bank can set off even against the heir's interest. Put another way, the bank account subject to setoff does not become a part of the estate to that extent. The heir's interest, therefore, never arises.[66]

### [r] Other Security Held by a Creditor

Obviously, many extensions of credit made by a creditor will be at least partially secured by security interests in personal property or mortgages on real estate. This is particularly true with bank loans. An agreement between the bank and its debtor-depositor giving the bank the right to set off even in the

---

[63] See supra ¶ 5.05[2][b].

[64] See, e.g., Sharpe v. Metropolitan Nat'l Bank, 31 Colo. App. 511, 503 P2d 1043 (1972); Ohio Valley Nat'l Bank v. Edwards, 492 SW2d 195 (Ky. 1973); In re Schenck's Estate, 63 Misc. 2d 721, 313 NYS2d 277 (Surrogate Ct. Suffolk Co. 1970); Annot., 7 A.L.R.3d 908 (1966); Annot., 36 A.L.R.3d 693 (1971).

[65] See, e.g., Laighton v. Brookline Trust, 225 Mass. 458, 114 NE 671 (1917).

[66] See, e.g., In re Fucela's Estate, 26 Wis. 2d 476, 132 NW2d 553 (Wis. 1965); Backer v. City Bank & Trust Co., 180 Ga. 672, 180 SE 604 (1935); B.M. Behrends Bank v. Wendt's Estate, 16 Alaska 377 (D. Alaska 1956).

presence of other security would enable the bank to set off if it wishes.[67] But without such an agreement, can the bank ignore other security it holds and set off against the bank account?

The question cannot be answered with certainty because there is a definite split of authority. The attorney must research local law on this issue. Some courts require the bank to exercise its right to other security first.[68] Other states allow setoff only where the bank is not otherwise fully secured.[69] Finally, other jurisdictions allow setoff without first resorting to other security even if the bank is fully secured.[70]

### [s] Exemption Law

Every state (and, to a lesser extent, the federal government) removes certain property of the debtor from a creditor's reach. This is done by the creation of statutorily exempt property, the nature of which is considered later in this book.[71] Such exemption law creates problems for a bank that wishes to set off since it is possible that a portion of a bank account might be exempt. Problems arise when exempt funds are deposited in the debtor's bank account because there are some authorities that have maintained the exemption applies to funds in the bank account that were exempt prior to the deposit.[72] If there are exempt funds in the account of the debtor-depositor, is the bank precluded from setting off against that portion of the account? Although little case law exists that would help the attorney to answer this question, the most definitive case indicates that the bank cannot set off against exempt funds on deposit in the debtor's account.[73] The argument supporting this holding is that in order to fulfill the policy of exemption law, the exempt funds should not lose their exempt character when merely deposited in a bank account. A reasonable contrary argument can be fashioned, however. First, exemption statutes are usually designed to protect the debtor only from creditors pursuing judicial remedies. Second, the debtor, in depositing his funds in the account at a creditor bank, might be seen as waiving any possible exemption by implication. Third, the deposited exempt funds actually become the property of the bank and are

---

[67] See, e.g., Frank Briscoe Co., Inc. v. Suburban Trust Co., 100 NJ Super. 431, 242 A2d 54 (1968).

[68] See, e.g., Melson v. Bank of N.M., 65 NM 70, 332 P2d 472 (1958); Forastiere v. Springfield Inst. for Sav., 303 Mass. 101, 20 NE2d 950 (1939).

[69] See, e.g., Olsen v. Valley Nat'l Bank of Aurora, 91 Ill. App. 2d 365, 234 NE2d 547 (1968); Olsen v. Harlen Nat'l Bank, 162 NW2d 755 (Iowa 1968).

[70] See, e.g., Jensen v. State Bank of Allison, 518 F2d 1 (8th Cir. 1975); Blust v. Yonkers Nat'l Bank & Trust Co., 260 AD 947, 23 NYS2d 512 (1940).

[71] See ¶ 6.07[1].

[72] See, e.g., In re Klein, 10 Bankr. 356 (Bankr. App. Pan. 9th Cir. 1981); Matthews v. Lewis, 617 SW2d 43 (Ky. 1981); Kruger v. Wells Fargo Bank, 11 Cal. 3d 352, 521 P2d 441, 113 Cal. Rptr. 449 (1974).

[73] Kruger v. Wells Fargo Bank, 11 Cal. 3d 352, 521 P2d 441, 113 Cal. Rptr. 449 (1974).

therefore not protected by exemption law designed to protect the property of the debtor.[74]

### [t] Certificates of Deposit

Certificates of deposit are similar to bank accounts in that both involve "debts" owed by the bank to its depositor. However, the certificate of deposit is not a demand deposit, like the typical savings or checking account. Typically, the bank's obligation under a certificate of deposit does not mature until the expiration date of the certificate. Nevertheless, if the bank has made a loan to the holder of a certificate of deposit and the loan is in default, the bank may wish to set off against its obligation under the certificate.

It has been emphasized throughout this discussion of setoff that the right of setoff is founded on the principle that mutual *matured* claims should offset each other. The bank, therefore, cannot set off if the certificate of deposit has not matured.[75] After maturity, it would appear that setoff can occur, assuming the original holder is seeking payment and that the certificate is nonnegotiable. If a certificate is negotiable and has been negotiated to a holder in due course, the holder in due course would be free of most setoff defenses and thereby preclude the bank from exercising setoff.[76]

### [u] Consumer Credit and Other Statutory Restrictions

Earlier in this chapter, it was emphasized that the setoff right is a common-law right. In the great majority of states setoff is neither originated nor regulated by statute. There are, however, statutes that indirectly relate to setoff. For example, setoff is recognized in the UCC at Sections 4-201(1), 4-213(5), and 4-303; these UCC sections, however, do not truly regulate the setoff right. The attorney must research state statutory law to determine if the legislature of a particular state has enacted any regulatory legislation; few states have done so.[77]

In the consumer credit field, one federal statute regulates setoff by a bank. The Fair Credit Billing Act (FCBA)[78] (Chapter 4 of the Truth-in-Lending Act) generally prohibits a bank credit card issuer from exercising setoff against a deposit account for debts arising out of bank credit card plans such as MasterCard

---

[74] In that regard, see Hagedorn, "Bank Setoff In Washington–Is It a Right Without Restriction?" 15 Gonz. L. Rev. 989, 999 (1980).

[75] See, e.g., Marine Midland Bank–N.Y. v. Granbar Elec. Co., Inc., 41 NY2d 703, 363 NE2d 1139, 395 NYS2d 403 (1977); Bonhiver v. State Bank of Clearing, 29 Ill. App. 3d 794, 331 NE2d 390 (1975).

[76] See UCC § 3-305, which defines the rights of a holder in due course of a negotiable instrument.

[77] See, e.g., Cal. Civ. Code § 3054; Cal. Fin. Code §§ 864, 6660; Md. Com. Law Code Ann. § 15-702.

[78] 15 USC §§ 1601 et seq. For a discussion of FCBA, see infra ¶ 5.09[2].

or Visa.[79] Beyond that statutory regulation, case law is the primary regulator of setoff.

## ¶ 5.06 SURETYSHIP

At the beginning of this chapter the distinction between an unsecured and secured debt was considered.[1] The distinction rests on whether or not the creditor has obtained a lien on an asset of the debtor to satisfy the debt. Another means of ensuring that a debt may be satisfied, other than by obtaining a lien in an asset of the debtor, involves suretyship. If a creditor requires someone other than the principal debtor to be committed for the debt, the creditor may pursue the third party for payment. This may be done extrajudicially or judicially.[2]

### [1] The Basic Suretyship Transaction

Suretyship can be defined as the "relation which exists where one person has undertaken an obligation and another person is also under an obligation or other duty to the obligor who is entitled to but one performance, and as between the two who are bound, one rather than the other should perform."[3] A surety is someone who is liable for the debt of another; more specifically, a surety "is one who is liable in form *primarily* on the debt or obligation of another. His obligation is accessorial to that of the principal debtor, but it is direct and not conditioned on the principal debtor's default."[4] The functions of this relationship become more meaningful as the legal relationships among the parties to a contract involving a surety are considered.

---

[79] See Section 169 of the Depository Institutions Amendments of 1974, as implemented by Reg. Z § 226.13(J) of the Fair Credit Billing Act, 15 USC § 1666h (1974). It should be noted that a bank's setoff right *may* be a "security interest" in the debtor's property required to be disclosed under the federal Truth-in-Lending Act. However, there is no definitive case law on this subject. See Fonseca & Teachout, Handling Consumer Credit Cases § 5.15 (Lawyers' Coop. Publishing Co., 2d ed. 1980).

[1] See supra ¶ 5.01.

[2] For other sources that consider suretyship, see Simpson, Suretyship (West 1950); 4 Debtor-Creditor Law Chs. 17–18 (Matthew Bender 1982); Hawkland, Commercial Paper and Bank Deposits and Collections 127–147 (Foundation Press 1967).

[3] See Restatement of Security § 82 (1941); see also UCC § 3-415, which indicates at Official Comment 1 that an "accommodation party" is always a surety. At UCC § 3-415(1), the UCC provides that "an accommodation party is one who signs [an] instrument in any capacity for the purpose of lending his name to another party to it." For a detailed discussion of accommodation parties as sureties on negotiable instruments, see White & Summers, Uniform Commercial Code 516–535 (West, 2d ed. 1980); Bailey, Brady on Bank Checks §§ 6.15, 7.24, 13.16, 7.27 (Warren, Gorham & Lamont, Inc., 5th ed. 1979).

[4] See Simpson, Suretyship 6–8 (West 1950).

One should distinguish between a "surety" and a "guarantor." A guarantor is "one who promises either that another will perform his duty, or that, if another does not perform his duty, he will, nonperformance by the other being a condition precedent to the guarantor's duty to pay."[5] Thus, the technical distinction between a guarantor and a surety is that a guarantor's obligation is collateral and secondary, while that of a surety is primary. The interchangeable use of the terms "guarantor" and "surety" causes confusion; even when a person is both a guarantor and a surety, the legal distinction between the two roles rests on the primary or secondary nature of the obligation. In some states the distinction has been abolished.[6] Since in most cases the legal consequences of suretyship and guarantee are the same,[7] further discussion in this book that refers to a surety will be used to include both a surety and a guarantor.

The best way to analyze the legal relationships within a suretyship transaction is to focus on the various contracts among the parties to the transaction. The party who should perform and who principally benefits from the transaction is the "principal debtor." The party who primarily obligates himself by lending his liability to make payments of the debt or perform the obligation is the "surety." The party who extends credit is naturally known as the "creditor." A minimum of three different contracts arise among the three parties in a suretyship transaction: the contract between the creditor and the principal debtor, the contract between the creditor and the surety, and the contract between the surety and the principal debtor. For each additional surety, three additional contracts are involved. These include the second surety's contracts with the creditor, the principal debtor, and the other surety. The remainder of the discussion of suretyship focuses on these various contractual relationships.

## [2] The Creditor-Principal Debtor Contract

The creditor can pursue the principal debtor once the debt has matured. The question of the creditor's success revolves around contractual principles that need not be considered here. The principal debtor cannot require the creditor to first seek collection from the surety.

There is an important relationship between the creditor-principal debtor contract and the surety's liability to the creditor. First, a judgment in an action against the principal debtor may be res judicata as to the surety.[8] Second, if the creditor-principal debtor contract does not exist, has been discharged, or has been altered, the surety normally will be released from liability. In short, the

[5] Id. at 10.

[6] The distinction between a surety and a guarantor has been abolished in at least some circumstances in California, Texas, and Pennsylvania. See 4 Debtor-Creditor Law ¶¶ 17.03[E][2], 18.03[E][2] (Matthew Bender 1982).

[7] See Simpson, Suretyship 16–23 (West 1950).

[8] See 4 Debtor-Creditor Law ¶ 18.07[E] (Matthew Bender 1982).

surety's obligation to the creditor may be and usually is conditioned on the existence of a particular contract between a creditor and a principal debtor.

If there is no creditor-principal debtor contract, as a basic principle the surety is not liable if the contract was a condition to his liability. This results from the basic concept that the surety is not bound if a condition on which the surety signs is not met.[9] The principal debtor's incapacity to contract is a defense that usually can be raised only by the principal debtor, however.[10] Otherwise, the surety normally can plead any defense available to the principal debtor. For example, the surety may assert as a defense that there is no consideration for the principal contract or that the principal contract is illegal or impossible.[11]

Similarly, if the principal contract has been discharged, the surety is released from liability in most instances. Final payment or performance of the principal obligation obviously discharges the surety.[12] Release of the principal debtor by the creditor also discharges the surety. However, the surety remains obligated where the surety consents to remain liable, and, notwithstanding the release, where the creditor in the release reserves his rights against the surety.[13] The reservation of rights by the creditor has the effect of preserving the surety's rights against the principal debtor.[14] If the principal debtor discharges his obligation in bankruptcy, the surety will not be discharged.[15]

Finally, if the principal contract is materially altered without the consent of the surety, as a general principle the surety will be discharged. If the surety is noncompensated, however, any alteration in the principal contract will be held

---

[9] See, e.g., Michel & Pfeffer v. Oceanside Properties, Inc., 61 Cal. 3d 433, 132 Cal. Rptr. 179 (1976); Kidd-Scruggs Co. v. Tyler Hotel Co., 270 SW 566 (Tex. Civ. App. 1925).

[10] See, e.g., Florida School-Book Depository v. Liddon, 114 Fla. 149, 153 So. 902 (1934). But see Restatement of Security § 125 (1941); Allen v. Small, 129 Vt. 77, 271 A2d 840 (1970); McKee v. Harwood Automotive Co., 204 Ind. 233, 183 NE 646 (1932), which places some limitations on the creditor's ability to enforce the contract against the surety where the principal debtor was legally incapable.

[11] See, e.g., Spear v. Industrial Comm'n, 114 Ariz. 601, 562 P2d 1099 (Ariz. Ct. App. 1977); Taylor & Jennings, Inc. v. Bellino Bros. Constr. Co., Inc., 57 AD2d 42, 393 NYS2d 203 (1977); Stephens v. First Bank & Trust of Richardson, 540 SW2d 572 (Tex. Civ. App. 1976); Stare v. Bi-States Constr. Co., Inc., 269 NW2d 455 (Iowa 1978); Lewis & Queen v. New Mexico Ball Sons, 48 Cal. 2d 141, 308 P2d 713 (1957).

[12] See, e.g., Bonura v. Christiana Bros. Poultry Co. of Gretna, Inc., 336 So. 2d 881 (La. Ct. App. 1976); Koehring Co. v. Hyde Constr. Co., 424 F2d 1200 (7th Cir. 1970); Brunswick Corp. v. Hays, 16 Cal. App. 3d 134, 93 Cal. Rptr. 635 (1971); Baxter v. Continental Ill. Nat'l Bank & Trust Co. of Chicago, 304 Ill. App. 117, 26 NE2d 179 (1940).

[13] See Restatement of Security § 122 (1941); Simpson, Suretyship 296–308 (West 1950); see also UCC § 3-606.

[14] See Restatement of Security § 122 (1941).

[15] See 11 USC § 524(e), which provides in bankruptcy that "discharge of a debt of the debtor does not affect the liability of any other party on, or the property of any other for, such debt."

to operate as a discharge.[16] Typical alterations that result in discharge of the surety include: (1) the addition or substitution of a new party; (2) the allowance of performance not permitted by the creditor–surety contract; (3) the substitution of a new principal contract; (4) the extension of time for performance; and (5) the release of security.[17]

## [3] The Creditor-Surety Contract

In addition to proceeding directly against the principal debtor, the creditor can also proceed under the contract with the surety directly against the surety upon default of the principal debtor.[18] Statutes or case law in a minority of states, however, require the creditor to pursue remedies against the principal debtor before suing the surety; this is the case, for example, in California, Illinois, Ohio, and Texas.[19] The majority position that allows immediate action against the surety simply illustrates the primary nature of the surety's obligation. Recall from the preceding section, however, that the surety can assert most of the defenses that can be asserted by the principal debtor, and that the surety is only liable if the creditor-surety contract is valid and unchanged subsequent to the time the surety obligated himself.

Note that the suretyship relationship can arise in two ways–by operation of law or by contract. Most suretyship relationships, however, are created by express contract. The contract thus defines the specific nature of the surety's obligation. Usually the consideration that supports the principal's promise also supports the surety's promise, the contract being created by a contractual offer and acceptance. If the creditor obtains the surety's promise by fraud or duress the surety may avoid his obligation.[20] The suretyship contract must be in writing, as all states have enacted a Statute of Frauds applicable to suretyship.[21] The statute usually applies to contracts to answer for the debt, default, or mis-

---

[16] See, e.g., Equitable Fire & Mut. Ins. Co. v. Truman Bldg. Corp., 190 So. 2d 197 (Fla. Dist. Ct. App. 1966).

[17] See 4 Debtor-Creditor Law ¶ 18.06 (Matthew Bender 1982).

[18] See, e.g., Warner Lambert Pharmaceutical Co. v. Sylk, 348 F. Supp. 1039 (ED Pa. 1971), aff'd, 475 F2d 1398 (3d Cir. 1973); State Bank of Mt. Horeb v. Banking Comm'n, 240 Wis. 189, 2 NW2d 363 (1942).

[19] See Cal. Civ. Code § 2845; Ill. Ann. Stat. ch. 132, § 1; Ohio Rev. Code Ann. § 1341.04; Tex. Bus. & Comm. Code Ann. § 34.02. Similarly, some states might require that a creditor exhaust all security given by the principal debtor before the creditor can proceed against the surety. See 4 Debtor-Creditor Law ¶ 18.07[D] (Matthew Bender 1982). Finally, it should be noted that if the surety "guarantees collection" the surety has the right to require the creditor to pursue the principal debtor and exhaust all legal remedies against him. In that regard, see Simpson, Suretyship 180 (West 1950).

[20] See, e.g., St. Paul Fire & Marine Ins. Co. v. Commodity Credit Corp., 646 F2d 1064 (5th Cir. 1981); General Ins. Co. of Am. v. Lebowsky, 312 Minn. 370, 252 NW2d 252 (1977); First Nat'l Bank v. Goodwin, 173 Okla. 169, 47 P2d 116 (1935); Rathgaber v. Horton, 52 SD 436, 218 NW 148 (1928).

[21] See, e.g., Colo. Civ. Code Ann. §§ 2793, 2794; N.Y. Gen. Oblig. Law § 5-701.2; Ohio Rev. Code Ann. § 1335.05.

carriage of another. In addition to the general requirement of evidencing the suretyship contract in writing, some statutes specifically require that a description of the consideration also be included in writing.[22] Note that whenever the leading or main object of the surety is to serve some purpose or interest of his own, the consideration agreement is not within the statute.[23]

## [4] The Surety-Principal Debtor Contract

From a liability standpoint, the surety-principal debtor contract is a one-way street. The surety has no liability to the principal debtor. Even if the surety fails to pay the creditor, the principal debtor has no cause of action against the surety. Rather, the surety's liability arises under the creditor-surety contract and only flows to the creditor. The surety might also be liable to another surety. On the other hand, it is the duty of the principal debtor to the surety to satisfy the surety's obligaton by performing his own duty to the creditor in the absence of a defense between himself and the surety, or a defense between himself and the creditor.[24] From this principle there arise three basic rights of the surety against the principal debtor: exoneration, reimbursement, and subrogation.

Exoneration simply involves the right of the surety to require that the principal debtor perform the obligation. The surety can enforce the right by an action for specific performance.[25] In the suit for specific performance the principal debtor is allowed to raise defenses to his obligaton that he has against the creditor.[26]

If the surety pays the debt, he has the right of reimbursement against the principal debtor.[27] The right of reimbursement is subject to at least two notable limitations. First, the surety's outlay that is to be reimbursed must be reasonable.[28] Second, the surety's right to reimbursement is also limited if the principal debtor files bankruptcy, since the principal debtor is discharged from liability in bankruptcy while the surety remains liable to the creditor.[29]

The final right of the surety against the principal debtor is one of subrogation. Upon making payment to the creditor, the surety has the right to be substituted to the position of the creditor against the principal debtor.[30] In effect,

---

[22] See, e.g., Colo. Civ. Code Ann. § 2793.

[23] See, e.g., Schumm by Whyner v. Berg, 37 Cal. 2d 174, 231 P2d 39 (1951).

[24] See Restatement of Security § 103 (1941).

[25] See, e.g., Almi, Inc. v. Dick Corp., 31 Pa. Commw. 36, 375 A2d 1343 (1977); D'Ippolito v. Castoro, 51 NJ 584, 242 A2d 617 (1968); Pinckney v. Wylie, 86 F2d 541 (5th Cir. 1936).

[26] See, e.g., Deems v. Wilson, 114 Ga. App. 341, 151 SE2d 230 (1966).

[27] See, e.g., President & Directors of Georgetown College v. Madden, 505 F. Supp. 557, aff'd in part and dismissed in part, 660 F2d 91 (D. Md. 1980); Republic-Franklin Ins. Co. v. Progressive Casualty Ins. Co., 45 Ohio St. 2d 93, 341 NE2d 600 (1976); Restatement of Security § 104 (1941).

[28] See 4 Debtor-Creditor Law ¶ 18.07[F][2] (Matthew Bender 1982).

[29] See supra ¶ 5.06[2] note 15.

[30] See Simpson, Suretyship 205–206 (West 1950).

this right of subrogation allows the surety to use any remedy against the principal debtor that the creditor could have used. These include the right to use any security or to enjoy any priority, or to enjoy and exercise any rights the creditor has in his relationship with the principal debtor. In short, upon payment to the creditor the surety stands in the shoes of the creditor in relation to the principal debtor.[31] Note, as was previously discussed,[32] that if the creditor unilaterally changes his right in relation to the debtor (e.g., by releasing the debtor or otherwise altering the contract with the debtor), the surety may be discharged.

## [5] The Cosurety and Subsurety Relationship

When more than one surety is involved in a transaction, the ultimate liability of an individual surety may rest on the nature of the relationship between or among the sureties. Assuming recovery cannot be obtained from the principal debtor for payment made by a surety to the creditor, can the surety who made payment seek total reimbursement or partial contribution from another surety? The answer to this question depends upon whether the sureties are "co-" or "sub-" sureties.

Two or more sureties are cosureties if they share a common liability and if one surety has paid more than his proportionate share of the debt.[33] The right of contribution can be enforced by subrogation to the rights of the creditor against the cosurety, limited in recovery to the contributive share.[34] On the other hand, when a suretyship relation exists involving more than one surety, the surety that is entitled to full reimbursement by another surety for any payment he is required to make is called a subsurety.[35] Normally, the parties will be deemed to be cosureties in the absence of an agreement to the contrary. The major exception to the presumption of cosuretyship arises when the sureties have signed a negotiable instrument as endorsers. In this case, the endorsing sureties are presumed to be subsureties liable for reimbursement to each other in order of their endorsements, the earlier signer being liable to the latter.[36] For example, if an individual seeks a loan from a bank, the bank may require the person to first obtain two cosignors. That borrower will be the principal debtor and may sign a note as maker with the two cosignors who are "accommodation parties," signing as endorsers. The first endorser will be presumed liable in the full amount of the note to the latter; thus, if the latter is required to make payment in full by the bank, the first endorser must reimburse the latter in full and then seek reimbursement from the principal debtor.

---

[31] See 4 Debtor-Creditor Law ¶ 18.07[F][3] and Ch. 19 (Matthew Bender 1982).

[32] See supra ¶ 5.06[2].

[33] See Restatement of Security §§ 144, 149 (1941); 4 Debtor-Creditor Law ¶ 18.07[G] (Matthew Bender 1982).

[34] See, e.g., Fithian v. Jamar, 286 Md. 161, 410 A2d 569 (1979); Fazio v. Freedman, 58 AD2d 641, 396 NYS2d 49 (1977); Simpson, Suretyship 222–223 (1980).

[35] See Restatement of Security § 145 (1941).

[36] See UCC §§ 3-414, 3-415.

## ¶ 5.07 ASSISTING THE DEBTOR IMMEDIATELY BEFORE OR AFTER DEFAULT

Thus far, our discussion of extrajudicial collection of unsecured debts has been approached from what may appear to be a creditor's viewpoint. Obviously the preceding discussion in this chapter is also of use to the debtor or the debtor's attorney in assessing debtor strategy immediately before or after default. The remainder of this chapter shifts focus, however. We consider the avenues open at the prejudicial point to a defaulting debtor.[1] The avenue taken largely depends on the individual circumstances of the debtor.

It must be emphasized that the remainder of this chapter continues to assume the validity of the debt and the debtor's impending or actual default. If the debtor has withheld payment because he disputes the validity of the debt on a statutory or contractual basis, his reason for withholding payment should be communicated to the creditor. The basis for disputing such validity, however, is beyond the scope of this text, except as discussed in Part I. This section again concentrates on technique rather than law.

Assuming the debt is valid, the debtor's first step is to consider how to avoid or cure a default. Often the debtor's ability to do so within his particular financial condition depends upon the creditor's willingness to cooperate with the debtor. In turn, a spirit of cooperation can spring only from a reasonable personal relationship between debtor and creditor. In that regard something much less than total hostility between the parties must be fostered. For example, the natural tendency of the debtor may be to hide the reasons that lead to the default from the creditor. That can be a mistake. It often is more productive for the debtor to expose the reasons for the default (e.g., illness, joblessness, unexpected downturns in business, etc). If the creditor can be convinced the debtor will recover from these contingencies and that he is better off working with the debtor, a spirit of cooperation will result.

When a cooperative relationship is fostered, methods of curing the impending or actual default can be explored. These could include a new loan from the creditor; a new loan from a different creditor; a lower payment schedule; a cessation of payments with a later increase in payments; or refinancing of the loan with a charged interest rate. If the debtor's financial difficulties have created problems with numerous creditors, perhaps a composition and extension agreement could be explored.[2] Throughout the negotiation of these proposals, the debtor should be careful to promise only what he is reasonably certain he can perform. The temptation to promise more than can be maintained realistically should be avoided and serious effort should be made to

---

[1] See Hamilton, "Getting Out From Under, or Assisting the Consumer-Debtor in Default," 52 Conn. B.J. 83 (1978), for an excellent practical decision of assisting the defaulting debtor with a focus on Connecticut law.

[2] See Hawkland & Loiseaux, Debtor-Creditor Relations 423–426 (Bobbs-Merrill 1979); Shimm, "The Impact of State Law on Bankruptcy" 1971 Duke L.J. 880, 881–888; 2 Nichols, Cyclopedia of Legal Forms 2.406 (1978); 15A Am. Jur. 2d 753; 15A C.J.S. 124.

adhere to the revised payment schedule. Regular payments, even if small, reassure creditors and can defer legal action on their part.[3] On the other hand, default on a revised payment plan may send the creditor and his attorney scurrying to the courthouse.

If the debtor is insolvent, he may not realistically be able to consider any of the above avenues of relief. In such circumstances, the debtor must avoid panic, which may lead to more serious difficulties (e.g., problems that could result from making a fraudulent conveyance).[4] Instead, legal processes that, in effect, force the creditor to refrain from further collection efforts should be considered. These processes include state local assignments for the benefit of creditors,[5] receiverships,[6] and federal bankruptcy.[7]

There are many legitimate extrajudicial collection efforts that creditors pursue to locate the debtor and his assets and to seek ultimate payment of the debt. Unfortunately, overzealous creditors sometimes go beyond the use of proper and legitimate extrajudicial collection techniques.[8] Such techniques include harassment by repeated calls at inconvenient hours; vulgarity and threats made to embarrass or scare the debtor into paying; and letters sent to the debtor that imitate official government forms, purport to be from a lawyer, reveal that a debt is overdue on the outside of the envelope, or threaten communication with an employer.[9] The debtor's attorney should be aware that both the courts and legislatures have fashioned remedies for debtors injured by such unseemly conduct. The nature of these remedies, explored in the next section, should be considered in assisting the debtor immediately before or after default.

## ¶ 5.08 CREDITORS' COMMON-LAW LIABILITY FOR IMPROPER COLLECTION TECHNIQUES

### [1] Debtor's and Creditor's Interests in the Collection Process

A careful consideration of the creditor's liability for overzealous collection activity requires an initial identification of the parties and their interests that

---

[3] Hamilton, "Getting Out From Under, or Assisting the Consumer-Debtor in Default," 52 Conn. B.J. 83 (1978).

[4] See ¶ 6.07[2] for a discussion of the law of fraudulent conveyances.

[5] See infra ¶ 5.09[4][b] note 43 for a discussion of assignment for the benefit of creditor's law.

[6] See ¶¶ 6.04[4], 8.08[2] for a discussion of receiverships.

[7] See Part III for a discussion of bankruptcy.

[8] See National Commission on Consumer Finance, "Summary of Hearings on Debt Collection Practices," 88 Banking L.J. 291 (1971), for a summary of problems created by overzealous collection efforts of creditors.

[9] Hamilton, "Getting Out From Under, or Assisting the Consumer-Debtor in Default," 52 Conn. B.J. 84 (1978).

might be affected by the creditor's collection methods. This section discusses the common-law theories of liability and statutory rights given the debtor to redress injuries resulting from abusive collection techniques.[1]

The debtor's and creditor's interests are balanced by the courts and legislatures, which have fashioned theories and methods of recovery for the debtor. From the outset one should be reminded of the obvious–that is, the creditor has an interest in collecting the debt with as little expense and effort as possible. Apparently, some creditors feel justified in punishing the debtor or in gaining revenge for the debtor's failure to pay; they think this may deter other debtors from failing to pay their debts.[2]

The debtor's interests in the collection process are somewhat broader than those of the creditor. Clearly the debtor has an interest in protecting his physical, mental, and emotional well-being. This includes freedom from physical attack and freedom from having false statements about him communicated to others. The debtor also has an interest in protecting rights he may have in assets. He also may have an interest in protecting his relationships with third parties such as family, friends, employers, and other creditors. Finally, the debtor has an interest in paying the debt to maintain a good credit rating.[3]

In addition to the creditor and debtor, others may have an interest in the debt-collection process. They may include the debtor's employer,[4] family and friends,[5] neighbors,[6] and other creditors.[7] Finally, the interests of society in general also must be taken into account. Such interests include increasing the welfare of the individual, reducing the congestion of the nation's trial courts, and preventing one person from forcing another to perform an act he is not obligated to perform.[8]

All of these interests probably cannot be fully protected by the courts or legislatures. The question for the interested parties thus becomes: How are the interests balanced by the judicial and legislative branches of government? However, one should not lose sight of the basic interests of the various parties; these interests provide the parties with an analytical means to appraise the judicial and legislative remedies available to the debtor.

---

[1] See Greenfield, "Coercive Collection Tactics–An Analysis of the Interests and the Remedies," 1972 Wash. U.L.Q. 1, for an excellent discussion of creditors' common-law liability for improper extrajudicial collection activity with particular emphasis on the interests of various parties.

[2] Id. at n.19.

[3] Id. at pp. 9–10.

[4] Id. at pp. 11–12.

[5] Id. at p. 13.

[6] Id.

[7] Id.

[8] Id. at p. 14.

## [2] Common-Law Theories of Creditor Liability

### [a] Tort of Defamation

There are numerous common-law theories of creditor liability.[9] The tort of defamation is a theory of creditor liability of long standing in the courts.[10] The tort involves the publication of false matter that results in injury to the debtor's reputation.[11] In most states, if the debtor is not engaged in an activity that requires credit to be extended to him, he cannot recover at all unless he can prove actual damages of a pecuniary nature.[12] The truth of the matter can be used as a defense, and in most states it is an absolute defense, since one element of the tort is falsity.[13] It should be emphasized that "publication" requires

---

[9] For other discussions of various theories of liability, see Cohen, Bankruptcy, Secured Transactions and Other Debtor-Creditor Matters 13–19 (Bobbs-Merrill 1981); Hurt, "Debt Collection Torts," 67 W. Va. L. Rev. 201 (1965); Gloster, "Abuse of Process and Attachment: Toward a Balance of Power," 30 U.C.L.A. L. Rev. 1218 (1983); Leff, "Injury, Ignorance and Spite–The Dynamics of Coercive Collection," 80 Yale L.J. 1 (1970); Sheinfield, "Current Trends in the Restriction of Creditors' Collection Activities," 9 Hous. L. Rev. 615 (1972); Berger, "The Bill Collector and the Law–A Special Tort, at Least for a While," 17 De Paul L. Rev. 327 (1968); Harris, "Improper Methods of Collecting Debts," 58 Com. L.J. 5 (1953); Holman, "Contacting Debtor's Employer Regarding a Delinquent Account," 19 Pers. Fin. Q. Rep. 70 (1964); Smith and Straske, "Collection Procedures and Right of Privacy," 36 Fla. B.J. 1085 (1962); Comment, "Debt Collection Practices: The Need for Comprehensive Legislation," 15 Duq. L. Rev. 971 (1976); Comment, "Debt Collection Practices: Remedies for Abuse," 10 B.C. Ind. & Com. L. Rev. 698 (1969); Comment, "Creditor's Pre-Judgment Communication to Debtor's Employer: An Evaluation," 36 Brooklyn L. Rev. 95 (1969); Comment, "Effectively Regulating Extrajudicial Collection of Debts," 20 Me. L. Rev. 261 (1968); Note, "Credit Transactions–Debtor and Creditor–Improper Collection Practices," 31 N.D.L. Rev. 277 (1955); Comment, "Collection Capers: Liability for Debt Collection Practices," 24 U. Chi. L. Rev. 572 (1957); Note, "Torts: Scope and Adequacy of Existing Remedies for Improper Debt Collection Activity," 1959 Wash. U.L.Q. 410; see also Fritz, "Actions for Harassment of Debtors," 16 Am. Jur. Trials 619–779; the following Annotations that relate to liability for abusive collection activities: 83 A.L.R.3d 598; 42 A.L.R.3d 865; 46 A.L.R.3d 772; 55 A.L.R.3d 911; 56 A.L.R.3d 493; 61 A.L.R.3d 984; 64 A.L.R.3d 1251; 87 A.L.R.3d 201; 97 A.L.R.3d 688; 99 A.L.R.3d 1113; 40 A.L.R.3d 1049; 42 A.L.R.3d 865; 77 A.L.R. 6; 87 A.L.R.3d 201.

[10] See, e.g., Altman v. Amoco Oil Co., 85 Ill. App. 3d 104, 406 NE2d 142 (1980); Information Control Corp. v. Genesis One Computer Corp., 611 F2d 781 (9th Cir. 1980); Green v. Cohutta Banking Co., 156 Ga. App. 292, 247 SE2d 688 (1980); Ragland v. Household Fin. Corp., 254 Iowa 976, 119 NW2d 788 (1963).

[11] Prosser, The Law of Torts § 111 (West, 4th ed. 1971); see also Restatement (Second) of Torts § 559 (1977).

[12] See, e.g., Pirre v. Printing Devs., Inc., 468 F. Supp. 1028, aff'd, 614 F2d 1290 (2d Cir. 1979); Sloan v. Hatton, 66 Ill. App. 3d 41, 383 NE2d 259 (1978); Fennell v. GAC Fin. Corp. of Baltimore, 242 Md. 209, 218 A2d 492 (1966).

[13] See, e.g., Lowenschuss v. West Pub. Co., 542 F2d 180 (3d Cir. 1976); Weingarten v. Block, 102 Cal. App. 3d 129, 162 Cal. Rptr. 701, cert. denied, 101 S. Ct. 267 (1980); Corabi v. Curtis Pub. Co., 411 Pa. 432, 273 A2d 899 (1971).

communication to someone other than the debtor.[14] A communication will be privileged and thus allowed if it involves a matter in which the recipient has an interest. Some examples of such a privilege in the debtor-creditor context are cited below.[15]

### [b] Tort of Invasion of Debtor's Right of Privacy

A second theory of creditor liability is the tort of invasion of the right of privacy.[16] This theory generally protects the debtor's right of privacy and consists of four separate theories, at least two of which have been used by the courts involving cases of debt collection–intrusion upon one's solitude and public disclosure of private facts. The intrusion tort involves an unreasonable intrusion upon the plaintiff's solitude that would be offensive or objectionable to a reasonable person.[17] The disclosure tort involves public disclosure of private facts that would be offensive and objectionable to a reasonable person of ordinary sensibilities.[18] It is a defense to the creditor sued for invasion of the right to privacy if the debtor consented to the invasion. Thus, some courts have held that when a debtor incurs a debt the debtor knows that the creditor will take reasonable steps to collect the debt when it is due (including notification of the debtor's employer) and, therefore, an implied consent might be pre-

---

[14] See, e.g., Pirre v. Printing Devs., Inc., 468 F. Supp. 1028 (SDNY 1979), aff'd, 614 F2d 1290 (2d Cir. 1979); Ray v. Henco Elecs., Inc., 156 Ga. App. 394, 274 SE2d 602 (1980); McKenzie v. Huckaby, 112 F. Supp. 642 (WD Okla. 1953).

[15] Good faith responses by a creditor to third persons who solicit the information from the creditor have been held as privileged. See, e.g., Teichner v. Bellon, 7 AD2d 247, 181 NYS2d 842 (1959); Marshall v. United Fin. & Thrift Corp., 347 SW2d 623 (Tex. Civ. App. 1961).

However, for case examples of creditor communication to the employer of the debtor held as not privileged, see Neigel v. Seaboard Fin. Co., 68 NJ Super. 542, 173 A2d 300 (1961); Evans v. McKay, 212 SW 680 (Tex. Civ. App. 1919); Comment, "Creditor's Pre-Judgment Communication to Debtor's Employer: An Evaluation," 36 Brooklyn L. Rev. 95 (1969); Prosser, The Law of Torts § 115 (West, 4th ed. 1971).

Communications of false matters to a credit reporting agency are privileged at least where the communication is made for a practical purpose in a reasonable manner. See, e.g., Anderson v. Dun & Bradstreet, Inc., 543 F2d 732 (10th Cir. 1976); Thornton v. Equifax Inc., 619 F2d 700, cert. denied, 449 US 835 (8th Cir. 1980); Putnal v. Inman, 76 Fla. 583, 80 So. 316 (1918); Evans, "Legal Immunity for Defamation," 24 Minn. L. Rev. 607 (1940).

[16] See, e.g., Holloway v. Davis, 44 Ala. App. 346, 208 So. 2d 794 (1967); see also Annot., 56 A.L.R.3d 457 (1974); Annot., 33 A.L.R.3d 154 (1970).

[17] See, e.g., Story v. J.M. Fields, Inc., 343 So. 2d 675 (Fla. Dist. Ct. App. 1977); Emerson v. J.F. Shea Co., Inc., 76 Cal. App. 3d 579, 143 Cal. Rptr. 170 (1978); Leonard v. Pioneer Fin. Co., 568 SW2d 937 (Mo. Ct. App. 1978); Guthridge v. Pen-Mod, Inc., 239 A2d 709 (Del. Super. Ct. 1967).

[18] See, e.g., Fogel v. Forbes Inc., 500 F. Supp. 1081 (D. Pa. 1980); Forsher v. Bugliosi, 26 Cal. 3d 792, 163 Cal. Rptr. 628, 608 P2d 716 (1980); Montgomery Ward v. Larragoite, 81 NM 383, 467 P2d 399 (1970).

sent.[19] The creditor's right to communicate the fact of the debt to the debtor's employer has found judicial support for other reasons.[20]

### [c] Tort of Intentional Infliction of Mental Distress

A third theory of creditor liability is the tort of intentional infliction of mental distress.[21] This theory includes protection against mental or emotional injury that results from outrageous conduct intentionally undertaken by the creditor.[22] Cases allowing recovery for abusive collection efforts require the existence of a relationship between the debtor and creditor in which the creditor has the power to damage the debtor's interest. The creditor's outrageous conduct within that relationship results in liability.[23] Mere insults, annoyances, and indignities will not result in liability.[24] Further, the creditor will not be liable if he insists upon payment of his claim in a permissible way although he realizes that such insistence may cause the debtor emotional distress.[25] The courts usually require severe injury.[26] Indeed, in some jurisdictions accompanying physical injury is necessary.[27]

### [d] Tort of Interference With Contractual Relations

A fourth theory of creditor liability involves interference with contractual relations. The elements of this tort cause of action require the existence of a

---

[19] See Timperley v. Chase Collection Serv., 272 Cal. App. 2d 697, 77 Cal. Rptr. 782 (1969); Guthridge v. Pen-Mod, Inc., 239 A2d 709 (Del. Super. Ct. 1967); Prosser, The Law of Torts § 117 (West, 4th ed. 1971).

[20] See Cohen, Bankruptcy, Secured Transactions and Other Debtor-Creditor Matters 16 (Bobbs-Merrill 1981); see also Comment, "The Debtor v. Creditor Dilemma: When Does a Creditor's Communication With the Debtor's Employer Result in an Actionable Invasion of Privacy?" 10 Tulsa L.J. 231 (1974).

[21] See Annot., 87 A.L.R.3d 201 (1978); Annot., 46 A.L.R.3d 772 (1972); Comment, "Intentional Infliction of Mental Stress Within Debtor-Creditor Relationships," 37 Alb. L. Rev. 797 (1973).

[22] See Prosser, The Law of Torts § 12 (West, 4th ed. 1971); Greenfield, "Coercive Collection Tactics–An Analysis of the Interests and Remedies," 1 Wash. U.L.Q. 23, at n.59 (1972).

[23] See Prosser, The Law of Torts § 12, at 57–59 (West, 4th ed. 1971).

[24] See, e.g., Warren v. June's Mobile Home Village & Sales, Inc., 66 Mich. App. 386, 239 NW2d 380 (1976).

[25] See, e.g., Leonard v. Pioneer Fin. Co., 568 SW2d 937 (Mo. Ct. App. 1978); Public Fin. Corp. v. Davis, 66 Ill. 2d 85, 360 NE2d 765 (1976).

[26] See, e.g., Story v. J.M. Fields Inc., 343 So. 2d 675 (Fla. Dist. Ct. App. 1977); McCaskill v. Barr, 92 Ill. App. 3d 157, 414 NE2d 1327 (1980); Doe v. Roe, 93 Misc. 2d 201, 400 NYS2d 668 (NY Sup. Ct. 1977).

[27] See, e.g., Garber v. U.S., 578 F2d 414, (DC Cir. 1978); Bullard v. Central Vt. Ry., Inc. 565 F2d 193 (1st Cir. 1977); Cutler v. Bank of Am. Nat'l Trust & Sav. Ass'n, 441 F. Supp. 863 (ND Cal. 1977); Harned v. E-Z Fin. Co., 151 Tex. 641, 254 SW2d 81 (1953).

contract between the debtor and a third party, the creditor's knowledge of the contract, intent by the creditor to induce a breach of the contract, and a resulting breach.[28] Note that an actual breach is required. Thus, termination of an employment contract with the debtor as a result of some act by the creditor may not be a breach of the employer if the contract was terminable at will.[29] Further, mere impairment of an employment contract as opposed to actual termination is not actionable.[30] Interference is not actionable if the creditor can establish that the interference is justified. In general, the justification defense rests upon the nature of "the creditor's conduct, the debtor's interest, the interest sought to be advanced by the creditor, and the societal interest in protecting the interests of the parties."[31] Finally, note that a creditor's interference, even with a corporate debtor, may result in creditor liability.[32]

### [e] Tort of Abuse of Process

A final major tort theory a debtor might use against a creditor for injuries incurred as a result of overzealous collection practices is abuse of process. Although this theory is beyond the scope of this chapter, for purposes of convenience it should be discussed in relation to the creditor's liability for improper collection techniques. The elements of this tort are the existence of an ulterior purpose in procuring judicial process and some improper use of it after it is issued.[33] Most often the cases involve creditor misuse of criminal pro-

---

[28] See, e.g., South Cent. Livestock Dealers, Inc. v. Security State Bank of Hedley, Tex., 551 F2d 1346, appeal after remand, 614 F2d 1056 (5th Cir. 1977); Fury Imports, Inc. v. Shakespeare Co. 554 F2d 1376, appeal after remand, 625 F2d 585, rehearing denied, 631 F2d 1189, cert. denied, 450 US 921 (11th Cir. 1977); Freed v. Manchester Serv., 165 Cal. App. 2d 186, 331 P2d 689 (1958); see also Prosser, The Law of Torts § 129, at 930, n.64 and accompanying text (West, 4th ed. 1971); Carpenter, "Interference with Contract Relations," 41 Harv. L. Rev. 728 (1928).

[29] See, e.g., Quist v. Guardian Life Ins. Co. of Am., 453 F. Supp. 842 (D. Ariz. 1978); Perfection Subscription Co. v. Kavaler, 427 F. Supp. 1289 (D. Pa. 1977); Malloy v. Bemis Bros. Bag Co., 174 F. Supp. 785 (DNH 1959), aff'd in part, vacated in part on other grounds, 283 F2d 32 (1st Cir. 1960); Terry v. Dairymen's League Coop. Ass'n, 2 AD2d 494, 157 NYS2d 71 (1956). But contrast Gruen Watch Co. v. Artists Alliance, 191 F2d 700 (9th Cir. 1951); Spiegle v. Board of Fire Underwriters, 29 Cal. 2d 34, 172 P2d 867 (1946).

[30] See, e.g., Haggard v. Shaw, 100 Ga. App. 813, 112 SE2d 286 (1959).

[31] See Greenfield, "Coercive Collection Tactics–An Analysis of the Interests and the Remedies," 1972 Wash. U.L.Q. 1, 29 (1972).

[32] See Douglas-Hamilton, "Creditor Liabilities Resulting From Improper Interference With the Management of a Financially Troubled Debtor," 31 Bus. Law. 343 (1975).

[33] See, e.g., Cline v. Flagler Sales Corp., 207 So. 2d 709 (Fla. Dist. Ct. App. 1968); Wood v. Bailey, 144 Mass. 365, 11 NE 567 (1887); Huggins v. Winn-Dixie Greenville, Inc., 249 SC 206, 153 SE2d 693 (1967); see also Prosser, The Law of Torts § 121 (West, 4th ed. 1971); Restatement (Second) of Torts § 682 (1977).

cess.[34] For example, the creditor might obtain an issuance of warrant for arrest and demand payment from the debtor in lieu of arrest. The debtor's action for abuse of process is also available when the creditor misuses civil process.[35] Another cause of action related to abuse of process that may be available to the debtor is malicious prosecution. It adds the element that the creditor must have lacked probable cause in initiating a legal proceeding against the debtor.[36]

### [f] Other Tort Theories

There are other tort theories that might be available to redress injuries incurred by a debtor as a result of improper creditor collection efforts. These include an action by the debtor against a creditor for assault and/or battery. The tort of assault protects the debtor from apprehension of a harmful or offensive contact with the person, but no actual contact is necessary. This is an intentional tort and, along with the tort of battery, is occasionally evidenced as a possible cause of action in the debtor-creditor context.[37] A battery cause of action protects the debtor from intentional and unpermitted contact with the debtor's person. Additionally, the debtor is protected from the creditor's interference with the debtor's freedom of movement by the tort cause of action of false imprisonment.[38] Torts of fraud and extortion have also reared their heads in some cases involving unseemly creditor collection conduct.[39] If the creditor committed a trespass to the debtor's realty or personalty, the common-law tort of trespass may have occurred.[40] Finally, theories of negligence have also been asserted by debtors against creditors for such negligent collection conduct that

---

[34] See Annot., 27 A.L.R.3d 1202 (1969).

[35] For examples of misuse of criminal process, see Baker v. Oklahoma Tire & Supply Co., 344 F. Supp. 780 (D. Ark. 1972); Voytko v. Ramada Inn of Atl. City, 445 F. Supp. 315 (DNJ 1978). For an example of misuse of civil process, see Nevada Credit Rating Bureau, Inc. v. Williams, 503 P2d 9 (Nev. 1972).

[36] See, e.g., Popelka, Allard, McCowen & Jones v. Superior Court of Santa Clara County, 107 Cal. App. 3d 496, 165 Cal. Rptr. 748 (1980); Hulcher v. Archer Daniels Midland Co., 88 Ill. App. 3d 1, 409 NE2d 412 (1980); Neulist v. Nassau County, 108 Misc. 2d 160, 437 NYS2d 239 (NY Sup. Ct. 1981).

[37] For cases involving assault or battery between debtor and creditor, see Deevy v. Tossi, 21 Cal. 2d 109, 130 P2d 388 (1942); Dieas v. Associates Loan Co., 99 So. 2d 279 (Fla. 1957); General Motors Acceptance Corp. v. Cornelius, 424 SW2d 498 (Tex. Civ. App. 1968); see also Annot., 22 A.L.R.2d 1227 (1952).

[38] See, e.g., Gomez v. Garcia, 112 Cal. App. 3d 292, 169 Cal. Rptr. 350 (1980); Fort v. Smith, 35 Ill. App. 3d 479, 407 NE2d 117 (1980); Staebler v. Supermarkets Gen. Corp., 105 Misc. 2d 677, 432 NYS2d 828 (NY Sup. Ct. 1980); Warrem v. Parrish, 436 SW2d 670 (Mo. 1969).

[39] See, e.g., In re Patterson, 6 Bankr. 149 (Bankr. D. Ohio 1980); Dennis v. Dial Fin. & Thrift Co., 401 SW2d 803 (Tex. 1966).

[40] See, e.g., Taylor v. Action Household Rentals, Inc., 351 So. 2d 865 (La. Ct. App. 1977); Kimble v. Universal TV Rental, Inc., 65 Ohio Misc. 17, 417 NE2d 597 (1981); New Morgan Co. Bldg. & Loan Ass'n v. Plemmons, 210 Ala. 286, 98 So. 12 (1923); American Sec. Co. v. Cook, 49 Ga. App. 723, 176 SE 798 (1934).

proximately caused harm to the debtor or his property. The injury incurred under these circumstances, however, must have been reasonably foreseeable.[41]

As the above discussion indicates, many of the tort theories overlap in protecting the interests of the debtor. On the other hand, some interests are not protected under any theory. It has been suggested that a new separate tort theory be developed for the protection of debtors from *unreasonable* creditor collection conduct.[42] This appears to have occurred in at least two states.[43] The response to unreasonable collection conduct usually has been legislative rather than judicial. This legislation goes beyond the basic common-law tort causes of action just discussed. The ensuing discussion considers such legislative activity at both state and federal levels.

## ¶ 5.09 CREDITORS' STATUTORY LIABILITY FOR IMPROPER COLLECTION TECHNIQUES

### [1] The Fair Debt Collection Practices Act

The Fair Debt Collection Practices Act (FDCPA)[1] became effective on March 20, 1978. It was the result of concern over "abusive and unfair debt collection practices by many debt collectors."[2] FDCPA also resulted from the failure of common-law tort theories of creditor liability to adequately protect all interests involved due to the difficulties of proving the many essential elements of such torts. Until the passage of FDCPA there was little federal regulation of abusive debt-collection practices.[3] It remains the principal federal statute that regulates debt collection. This section defines the scope of FDCPA's

---

[41] See, e.g., Story v. J.M. Fields, Inc., 343 So. 2d 675 (Fla. Dist. Ct. App. 1979); Urban v. Hartford Gas Co., 139 Conn. 301, 93 A2d 292 (1952).

[42] See Greenfield, "Coercive Collection Tactics–An Analysis of the Interests and the Remedies," 1972 Wash. U.L.Q. 1, 70–79.

[43] This is clearly the case in Texas. See, e.g., Whatley v. K-Mart Discount Stores, 451 SW2d 568 (Tex. Civ. App. 1970); Note, "Tort–Creditor Harassment–Presenting a Fact Question to the Jury for Unreasonable Collection Efforts," 2 Tex. Tech L. Rev. 177 (1971). This also appears to be the position of the Louisiana Courts. See, e.g., Pack v. Wise, 245 La. 84, 155 So. 2d 909 (1963).

[1] 15 USC §§ 1692 et seq. For other discussions of FDCPA, see Cohen, Bankruptcy, Secured Transactions, and Other Debtor-Creditor Matters 19–25 (Bobbs-Merrill 1981); Fonseca & Teachout, Handling Consumer Credit Cases Ch. 6 (Lawyers' Coop. Publishing Co., 2d ed. 1980); Barron, "An Introduction to the Fair Debt Collection Practices Act," 95 Banking L.J. 500 (1978); Fox, "New Hope for the Harassed Consumers: The Federal Fair Debt Collection Practices Act of 1977," 18 Am. Bus. L.J. 19 (1980); 1 Debtor-Creditor Law Ch. 4 (Matthew Bender 1982).

[2] Cohen, Bankruptcy, Secured Transactions and Other Debtor-Creditor Matters 19 (Bobbs-Merrill 1981).

[3] Hearings on H.R. 29 Before the Subcommittee on Consumer Affairs of House Committee on Banking, Finance and Urban Affairs, 95th Cong., 11th Sess. 1–2 (1977).

application and outlines its substantive provisions. It should be noted from the outset that there is little case law interpreting FDCPA to date.

### [a] Scope of the Act

Perhaps the most important point to be made about FDCPA is that it covers a limited segment of debt-collection activity. For the most part, only a debt collector acting on behalf of, but unaffiliated with, the actual creditor is subject to regulation. In addition, such third-party debt collectors are regulated only when collecting a consumer debt.[4] More specifically, in terms of FDCPA the debt collector is defined as a person who uses any instrumentality of interstate commerce or the mails in any business, the principal purpose of which is the collection of any debt, or as any person who regularly collects or attempts to collect debts due another.[5] Note that the use of an interstate instrumentality is not always required; even where abusive debt-collection practices are purely intrastate in character, they nevertheless directly affect interstate commerce.[6]

Specific exclusions from coverage are also found in FDCPA.[7] However, these exclusions do not eliminate from coverage persons collecting their own debts using a name other than their own, thus giving the impression that a third

---

[4] FDCPA §§ 803(3), 803(5), 15 USC §§ 1692a(3), 1692a(5) (1977), which define the terms "consumer" and "debt." In total, the terms include any natural person who holds an obligation to pay money arising out of the transaction in which the obligation was incurred primarily for personal, family, or household purposes. Thus, a tax collector was not subject to the Act's provisions because delinquent taxes are not FDCPA debts. See Staub v. Harris, 626 F2d 275 (3d Cir. 1980).

[5] FDCPA § 803(6).

[6] FDCPA § 802(d).

[7] See FDCPA § 803(6)(A)–803(6)(G) for the exclusions summarized below:

(1) An employee of a creditor collecting debts in the creditor's name.
(2) A debt collector collecting only the debts of an affiliated creditor.
(3) Any state or federal employee acting in his official capacity. It should be noted that two cases have explored this governmental immunity. See Heredia v. Green, 504 F. Supp. 896 (ED Pa. 1980); Gary v. Spires, 473 F. Supp. 878 (DSC), rev'd on other grounds, 634 F2d 772 (4th Cir. 1979).
(4) A person serving legal process in connection with judicial enforcement of a debt.
(5) Nonprofit consumer counseling agencies.
(6) Attorneys collecting debts in the name of a client.
(7) Trust companies or other fiduciaries.
(8) Persons collecting debts they themselves originated.
(9) Persons servicing debts of another (where the debt servicing began before the debt was in default).
(10) Persons obtaining the debt as collateral in a commercial credit transaction.

As to all of the above, see generally Federal Trade Comm'n v. Shaffner, 626 F2d 32 (7th Cir. 1980).

party is collecting the debt.[8] Finally, as mentioned above, a debt collector taking an assignment of the debt is still subject to regulation under FDCPA.[9]

### [b] General Prohibited Conduct

The debt collector covered by FDCPA cannot engage in three general categories of conduct. First, a collector cannot engage in conduct likely to harass, oppress, or abuse a person in connection with the collection of the debt.[10] Second, a debt collector cannot use any false, deceptive, or misleading representations or means in connection with the collection of any debt.[11] Third, the col-

---

[8] FDCPA § 803(6).

[9] FDCPA § 803(4).

[10] FDCPA § 806. For cases involving this section, see Wright v. Credit Bureau of Ga., Inc., 548 F. Supp. 591 (D. Ga. 1982); Baker v. GC Servs. Corp., 677 F2d 775 (9th Cir. 1982); Bingham v. Collection Bureau, Inc., 505 F. Supp. 864 (DND 1981). This section of FDCPA specifically prohibits the following:

(1) The use or threat of use of violence or other criminal means to harm the physical person, reputation, or property of any person.
(2) The use of obscene or profane language or language whose natural consequence is to abuse the hearer or reader.
(3) The publication of a list of consumers who allegedly refuse to pay debts, except to a consumer reporting agency or to persons meeting the requirements of Section 1681a(f) or 1681b(3) of this Title.
(4) The advertisement or sale of any debt to coerce payment of the debt.
(5) Causing a telephone to ring or engaging any person in telephone conversation repeatedly or continuously with intent to annoy, abuse, or harass any person at the called number.
(6) Except as provided in Section 1692b of this Title, placing telephone calls without meaningful disclosure of the caller's identity.

[11] FDCPA § 807(1). This section of FDCPA specifically prohibits the following:

(1) The false representation or implication that the debt collector is vouched for, bonded by, or affiliated with the United States or any State, including the use of any badge, uniform, or facsimile thereof.
(2) The false representation of
    (a) The character, amount, or legal status of any debt; or
    (b) Any services rendered or compensation that may be lawfully received by any debt collector for the collection of a debt.
(3) The false representation or implication that any individual is an attorney or that any communication is from an attorney.
(4) The representation or implication that nonpayment of any debt will result in the arrest or imprisonment of any person or the seizure, garnishment, attachment, or sale of any property or wages of any person unless such action is lawful and the debt collector or creditor intends to take such action.
(5) The threat to take any action that cannot legally be taken or that is not intended to be taken.
(6) The false representation or implication that a sale, referral, or other transfer of any interest in a debt shall cause the consumer to

lector cannot use any unfair or unconscionable means to collect or attempt to collect any debt.[12] It should be emphasized that each category of general prohibited conduct contains a list of specifically prohibited conduct. Note, however, that FDCPA is careful to provide that this specific listing is not necessarily complete. The possibility that other conduct will fall within the generally

---

(a) Lose any claim or defense to payment of the debt; or
(b) Become subject to any practice prohibited by this Subchapter.

(7) The false representation or implication that the consumer committed any crime or other conduct, in order to disgrace the consumer.
(8) Communicating or threatening to communicate to any person credit information that is known or that should be known to be false, including the failure to communicate that a disputed debt is disputed.
(9) The use or distribution of any written communication that simulates or is falsely represented to be a document authorized, issued, or approved by any court, official, or agency of the United States or any State, or that creates a false impression as to its source, authorization, or approval.
(10) The use of any false representation or deceptive means to collect or attempt to collect any debt or to obtain information concerning a customer.
(11) Except as otherwise provided for communications to acquire location information under Section 1692b of this Title, the failure to disclose clearly in all communications made to collect a debt or to obtain information about a consumer that the debt collector is attempting to collect a debt and that any information obtained will be used for that purpose.
(12) The false representation or implication that accounts have been turned over to innocent purchasers for value.
(13) The false representation or implication that documents are legal process.
(14) The use of any business, company, or organization name other than the true name of the debt collector's business, company, or organization.
(15) The false representation or implication that documents are not legal process forms or do not require action by the consumer.
(16) The false representation or implication that a debt collector operates or is employed by a consumer reporting agency as defined by Section 1681a(f) of this Title.

[12] FDCPA § 800. This section of FDCPA specifically prohibits the following:

(1) The collection of any amount (including any interest, fee, charge, or expense incidental to the principal obligation) unless such amount is expressly authorized by the agreement creating the debt or permitted by law.
(2) The acceptance by a debt collector from any person of a check or other payment instrument postdated by more than five days unless such person is notified in writing of the debt collector's intent to deposit such check or instrument not more than ten or less than three business days prior to such deposit.
(3) The solicitation by a debt collector of any postdated check or other postdated payment instrument for the purpose of threatening or instituting criminal prosecution.
(4) Depositing or threatening to deposit any postdated check or other postdated payment instrument prior to the date on such check or instrument.
(5) Causing charges to be made to any person for communications by concealment of the true purpose of the communication. Such charges include, but are not limited to, collect telephone calls and telegram fees.

defined categories of prohibited conduct and will be prohibited is not limited. In addition, the types of specifically prohibited conduct enumerated by FDCPA have been held by at least one court as nonlimiting.[13]

### [c] Specific Prohibited Conduct

Although the categories of prohibited conduct seem to be rather broad, evidenced by the enumeration of types of conduct that fall within each category, FDCPA further prohibits other specific conduct in two sections.[14] Historically, many form contracts between creditors and consumers grant jurisdiction over the consumer to courts that are located a substantial distance from where the consumer lives. FDCPA requires that the action must be brought in any event in a judicial district in which the consumer signed any contract that is sued upon or in which the consumer resides when the action commences, unless real property secures the debt. In that case the action must be brought where the real property is located.

The other specifically prohibited act involves the furnishing of certain deceptive forms. Creditors sometimes purchase third-party collection forms that are sent to debtors to give the impression the debt has been turned over to a collection agency. This is done in the hope that the debtor will be more likely to make payment if he believes a third party is now seeking collection. FDCPA specifically prohibits the design, compilation, and furnishing of such forms.

### [d] Regulation of Communication With the Debtor and Third Parties

Previously in this chapter[15] various collection techniques of creditors were reviewed. If FDCPA applies to the debt collector, it restricts the debt collector's use of certain collection techniques in specific sections dealing with communication in acquiring location information[16] and communication in connec-

---

(6) Taking or threatening to take any nonjudicial action to effect dispossession or disablement of property if

 (a) There is no present right to possession of the property claimed as collateral through an enforceable security interest;
 (b) There is no present intention to take possession of the property; or
 (c) The property is exempt by law from such dispossession or disablement.

(7) Communicating with a consumer regarding a debt by postcard.

(8) Using any language or symbol, other than the debt collector's address, on any envelope when communicating with a consumer by use of the mails or by telegram, except that a debt collector may use his business name if such name does not indicate that he is in the debt-collection business.

[13] See Rutyna v. Collection Accounts Terminal, Inc., 478 F. Supp. 980, 981–982 (ND Ill. 1979).

[14] FDCPA §§ 811, 812.

[15] See supra ¶¶ 5.02, 5.03, 5.04.

[16] FDCPA § 804.

tion with debt collection.[17] A third section also requires a debt collector to give the debtor certain information in regard to the debt itself.[18]

The section on acquiring location information recognizes a debt collector's need to ascertain the whereabouts of a debtor. "Location information" is defined as "a consumer's place of abode and his telephone number at such place, or his place of employment."[19] On the other hand, to protect the debtor from harassment, FDCPA creates a rule by which the debt collector is limited to only one contact with any third party, unless the third party requests additional contacts or the debt collector reasonably believes that the original information was "erroneous or incomplete" and that the third party now has correct information. In addition, a debt collector must stop contacting third parties for purposes of gaining location information once he knows the debtor is represented by an attorney whose name and address he has or can reasonably ascertain. If the attorney, however, unreasonably fails to respond to the collector's communication, third-party contact can occur. In his communication with third parties the debt collector is prohibited from stating that the debtor owes a debt and must state, in addition to his name, that he is confirming or correcting location information. The debt collector cannot identify his employer unless asked, in which case he must do so. He cannot communicate by postcard or use any language or symbol on any written communication available to third parties that indicates he is attempting to collect a debt.

If a collector has accurately located the debtor and has begun collection efforts, his right to communicate with third parties is virtually at an end. The debt collector can communicate only with the debtor's attorney, his own attorney, the creditor, and the creditor's attorney about the debt or collection process. This is a part of FDCPA designed to protect the debtor from indirect harassment and invasion of privacy. Remember, however, that the debtor or even the court can expressly authorize such communication. The debt collector's direct communication with the debtor without the authorization of the debtor himself or the court is permitted, but restricted. If the debtor is represented by an attorney and the debt collector knows or can determine the lawyer's name and address, the debt collector can communicate only with the debtor's attorney. Once again, however, if the attorney unreasonably fails to respond to his communication, the debt collector can contact a third party. Communication with the debtor cannot be at an inconvenient time unless there are circumstances indicating the contrary. An inconvenient time is deemed to be any time not between 8 A.M. and 9 P.M. of the debtor's local time. Also, the debt collector cannot contact the debtor at

---

[17] FDCPA § 805. For cases interpreting this section, see In re Scrimpsher, 17 Bankr. 999 (Bankr. NDNY 1982); Bingham v. Collection Bureau, Inc., 505 F. Supp., 864 (DND 1981).

[18] FDCPA § 803. For cases involving this section, see Harvey v. United Adjusters, 509 F. Supp. 1248 (D. Ore. 1981); Ost v. Collection Bureau, Inc., 493 F. Supp. 701 (DND 1980).

[19] FDCPA § 803(7).

work if he has reason to know that the debtor's employer prohibits such calls. While there is no specific limitation on the number of contacts the debt collector can have with the debtor, one should keep in mind the previously discussed general prohibition against harassment. If the debtor notifies the debt collector in writing that he does not intend to pay the debt or that he wishes communications to stop, even these limited communications must stop. The debt collector can, however, notify the debtor that his collection efforts will stop, that he may invoke normal specific remedies, and, where required, that he intends to invoke a specific remedy.

A final provision provides the debtor with sufficient information about the alleged debt to enable him to properly determine his obligations and to raise any objections or defenses. The debt collector is required, either in the initial communication with the debtor or within five days of the initial communication, to indicate in writing the amount of the debt and the creditor to whom it is owed, and to state that unless the debtor disputes the debt in writing within thirty days the debt collector will consider the debt valid. The disclosure must also state that if the debtor disputes in writing all or a portion of the debt or requests the name and address of the original creditor, the debt collector will obtain verification of the debt or the name and address of the original creditor and mail it to the debtor. A debtor's dispute of all or part of the debt or a request for the name and address of the original creditor acts as a bar to further collection of the debt, or the disputed part, until verification or original creditor information is supplied.

### [e] Enforcement

FDCPA provides for both civil liability,[20] resulting in enforcement by injured debtors, and administrative enforcement.[21] As to civil liability, FDCPA permits the debtor to recover actual damages, court costs, and attorney fees either by individual or class action, and also provides a statutory damage recovery unrelated to provable loss. FDCPA provides for maximum recoveries but not for minimum recoveries, otherwise leaving the amount of the statutory damages completely at the discretion of the court. The court must consider, among other relevant factors, the frequency and persistence of the noncompliance, the nature of the noncompliance, and whether or not it was intentional. The maximum recovery in an individual action is $1,000; in a class action the maximum recovery is the lesser of $500,000 or one percent of the net worth of the debt collector plus $1,000 for each named plaintiff. FDCPA also requires the court to consider the resources of the debt collector and the number of persons affected in setting the statutory damages in a class action. There is no liability for unintentional errors if procedures have been set up reasonably to avoid such errors. The debtor can also bring suit in federal and state court without regard to the amount in controversy within one year of the date of the violation. FDCPA

---

[20] FDCPA § 813.

[21] FDCPA § 814.

does permit the debt collector to recover the attorney's fees in an unsuccessful debtor action where the court finds the action was brought in bad faith for the purpose of harassment.

The administrative enforcement under the above cited section is given to the Federal Trade Commission (FTC) except in the cases of banks, savings and loans associations, credit unions, common carriers, air carriers, and certain meat-packing entities. Enforcement regarding these entities is handled by the agencies charged with their regulation under existing federal laws.[22] A violation of FDCPA is deemed an unfair or deceptive trade practice under Section 5 of the FTC Act, and the FTC can use its full enforcement powers under the FTC Act regardless of whether or not the activity or the entity meets the other jurisdictional requirements of the FTC Act.

### [f] Miscellaneous Provisions

When the debtor owes more than one debt that the debt collector is attempting to collect, any payment made to the debt collector must be applied according to the debtor's instructions and cannot be applied to any disputed debt.[23] FDCPA requires annual reports to Congress by the FTC assessing the administration of FDCPA and the compliance achieved. The FTC may also make recommendations for change as it deems necessary.[24] Finally, FDCPA also regulates the relationship between FDCPA and state debt-collection law. It expressly permits states to afford consumers greater protection than that provided by the provisions of FDCPA.[25] In addition, FDCPA provides that it does not annul, alter, effect, or exempt any persons subject to its provisions from complying with the laws of any state except to the extent that those laws are inconsistent with FDCPA.[26]

## [2] The Fair Credit Billing Act

A second federal statute that relates to abusive extrajudicial collection practices is the Fair Credit Billing Act (FCBA).[27] FCBA was actually an amendment to the Truth-In-Lending Act (TILA). It became effective in 1975 and, in large part, is directed at billing errors. Because it indirectly relates to

---

[22] For enforcement regarding these entities, see FDCPA § 813.

[23] FDCPA § 810.

[24] FDCPA § 818.

[25] FDCPA §§ 816, 817.

[26] FDCPA § 816. It should be noted that in a state court collection action brought by a creditor, a consumer's claim for violation of FDCPA is not a compulsory counterclaim. See Peterson v. United Accounts, Inc., 638 F2d 1134 (8th Cir. 1981).

[27] 15 USC § 1666. See Chapter 4 for more detailed discussion of and specific citations to FCBA. For other discussion of FCBA, see Fonseca & Teachout, Handling Consumer Credit Cases Ch. 6 (Lawyers' Coop. Publishing Co., 2d ed. 1980).

our present discussion of abusive credit collection tactics, only a brief description of FCBA is necessary here.

FCBA establishes a procedure for correcting billing errors in open-end credit transactions. The term "billing error" is defined in Regulation Z.[28] Prior to a billing error, certain notices must be given by the creditor. The suggested wording for these notices is found in Regulation Z.[29] The notice must be provided when the open-end credit account is opened and must also be sent to all active customers for two billing cycles during the year. The transaction between the creditor and debtor must also be identifiable. In this regard, creditors must have procedures to obtain and disclose primary identifying information related to the transaction.

If the consumer believes there has been a billing error, he must give the creditor written notification of the error to preserve his rights under FCBA. If the error is a simple misunderstanding, a telephone call may suffice to resolve the matter. Otherwise, the creditor must mail a written acknowledgment to the debtor within a designated time. If a billing error has been made, the creditor must make the appropriate correction. The corrections may be sent in the next periodic billing statement. Prior to any action to collect, the billing error dispute must be resolved.

If the creditor fails to comply with the requirements of FCBA, he forfeits any right to collect the disputed amount and any finance charges on it, with a forfeiture limit of fifty dollars. The general TILA penalty provisions also apply to failure to comply.

### [3] Federal Trade Commission Guides Against Debt Collection Deception

As discussed above, FDCPA is primarily limited to debt-collection actions of third-party collectors. When a creditor collects his own debt, FCBA and the FTC Guides Against Debt Collection Deception, both federal provisions, afford the debtor some protection.[30] The FTC Guides identify and prohibit misrepresentation techniques used by debt collectors. In short, the Guides require that the collector use documents that conspicuously disclose that they are being used for collection purposes. In contrast to FDCPA, the Guides apply to all industry members. These FTC regulations are probably valid, since FDCPA only provides that the FTC cannot promulgate regulations with respect to debt collections by debt collectors as defined by FDCPA.[31] Since the creditor's collection of debt on his own is not covered by FDCPA, the FTC Guides appear to be a valid exercise of FTC authority.

---

[28] 12 CFR § 226.13(a).

[29] 12 CFR §§ 226.7, 226.8, 226.9.

[30] 16 CFR § 237.

[31] FDCPA § 814d.

## [4] State Law

As previously discussed in this chapter, the courts have fashioned various tort theories for recovery by debtors injured by the abusive collection conduct of a creditor.[32] Many have argued, however, that these tort theories are not sufficient to provide the debtor with adequate protection.[33] FDCPA is the result of a federal attempt to curb and to redress some abusive collection activities. The state legislatures have also enacted laws to regulate abusive collection practices. Because of their diversity it is difficult to explain the content and application of these statutes on a national scale. The remainder of this chapter attempts to do so, nonetheless, by providing a brief overview of the nature of these statutes and then turning to examples of the specific laws of the states and case law in construing them.

### [a] Overview of State Statutes Regulating Abusive Debt-Collection Practices

State collection regulation statutes today generally tend to resemble the regulatory scheme of the federal FDCPA. A wide variety of creditors' collection conduct is prohibited, as are certain communications with the debtor and third parties. As to prohibited collection practices, state statutes typically prohibit threats to enforce a consumer claim when the debt collector knows the claim is not legitimate. Also typically prohibited are threats to use violence or other criminal means to cause harm to the debtor. A final category of commonly prohibited creditor practices is the use of abusive, harassing, and continuous telephone calls. Many states also limit contact with the employer of the debtor. Communications with the debtor or his family that occur with such frequency that they reasonably can be expected to harass them is also typically prohibited. Finally, state statutes often attempt to restrict communication with a person other than the debtor or his family when the communication would affect the debtor's reputation and when the creditor has knowledge or reason to know the third party does not have a legitimate business need for the information. The specific nature of such statutes and issues arising from them in the case law is further described by examples below.

### [b] Specific Examples of State Statutory Law Regulating Abusive Debt-Collection Practices

Most states have adopted some form of statute that protects at least the consumer debtor from abusive collection practices of creditors.[34] Some state

---

[32] See supra ¶ 5.08[2].

[33] See, e.g., Scott & Strickland, "Abusive Debt Collection–A Model Statute for Virginia," 15 Wm. & Mary L. Rev. 566 (1974); Greenfield, "Coercive Collection Tactics–An Analysis of the Interests and Remedies," 1972 Wash. U.L.Q. 1.

[34] See Fonseca & Teachout, Handling Consumer Credit Cases Ch. 6 (Lawyers' Coop. Publishing Co., 2d ed. 1980) for a discussion of typical state statutes that regulate collection practices of creditors.

statutes only regulate debt-collection agencies, however. Even when FDCPA was enacted in 1977, thirty-seven states and the District of Columbia had such laws, although only a few of these laws contained prohibited practices and private remedy sanctions.[35] Even so, there may be some haven of protection for the harassed debtor in the state statutory law briefly described above. More specifically, such statutes have taken the form of specific debt-collection laws that are unique to the state or that are a part of or are patterned after more comprehensive consumer credit legislation based upon the National Consumer Act (NCA) or the Uniform Consumer Credit Code (UCCC). To begin, some discussion of NCA and UCCC provisions relating to debt collection may be helpful.

NCA was proposed by the National Consumer Law Center at Boston College Law School in 1970. It follows the basic pattern of the UCCC but extends

---

The following is a list of state statutory citations that regulate either debt-collection agencies or debt-collection practices generally. This listing is not intended to be exhaustive. The reader is, of course, reminded to carefully research local statutes to obtain the current status of such legislation.

States that require a collection agency or individual who collects debts to obtain a license as a condition precedent to doing business include the following: Alaska Stat. § 08.24.110; Ariz. Rev. Stat. Ann. § 32-1001; Ark. Stat. Ann. § 71-2001; Cal. Bus. & Prof. Code § 6850; Colo. Rev. Stat. § 12-14-102; Conn. Gen. Stat. Ann. § 42-127a; Fla. Stat. Ann. § 559.55; Hawaii Rev. Stat. § 443-8; Idaho Code § 28-31-101 et seq.; Ill. Ann. Stat. ch. 111, §§ 2007 et seq.; Ind. Code Ann. § 25-11-1-3; Md. Ann. Code art. 56, § 324; Mass. Gen. Laws Ann. ch. 93, § 24; Mich. Stat. Ann. §§ 339.911 et seq.; Minn. Stat. Ann. § 332.33; Neb. Rev. Stat. § 81-8170; Nev. Rev. Stat. § 649.075; N.M. Stat. Ann. § 61-18-33; N.C. Gen. Stat. § 66-49.31; N.D. Cent. Code § 13-05-02; Ore. Rev. Stat. § 697.015; P.R. Laws Ann. tit. 10, §§ 981 et seq.; Tenn. Code Ann. § 62-20-105; Va. Code § 54-729.3; Wash. Rev. Code Ann. § 19.16.110; W. Va. Code § 47-16-4; Wisc. Stat. Ann. § 218.04(2); Wyo. Stat. § 33-11-102.

States that have passed some type of statute otherwise regulating debt-collection practices include the following: Ariz. Rev. Stat. Ann. §§ 32.1001 et seq.; Ark. Stat. Ann. § 71-2001; Cal. Bus & Prof. Code §§ 6850 et seq.; Colo. Rev. Stat. §§ 12-14-101 et seq.; Conn. Gen. Stat. Ann. §§ 42-127 et seq.; Fla. Stat. Ann. § 559.55; Hawaii Rev. Stat. §§ 443-1 et seq.; Idaho Code §§ 28-31-101 et seq.; Ill. Ann. Stat. ch. 111, §§ 2007 et seq.; Ind. Code Ann. §§ 25-11-1-1 et seq.; Iowa Code Ann. § 7.101; La. Rev. Stat. Ann. § 9:3562; Me. Rev. Stat. Ann. tit. 9A, § 5.116; Md. Ann. Code art. 56, §§ 323 et seq.; Mass. Gen. Laws Ann. ch. 93, § 49; Mich. Stat. Ann. §§ 339.911 et seq.; Minn. Stat. Ann. § 322.37; Neb. Rev. Stat. §§ 81-8, 158 et seq.; Nev. Rev. Stat. §§ 649 et seq.; N.H. Rev. Stat. Ann. § 358C; N.J. Stat. Ann. § 45:18-1; N.M. Stat. Ann. §§ 61-18 et seq.; N.Y. Penal Law § 190.50; N.C. Gen. Stat. §§ 66-99.24 et seq.; Ore. Rev. Stat. §§ 697 et seq.; Pa. Cons. Stat. 18 § 7311; P.R. Laws Ann. tit. 10, § 981; Tenn. Code Ann. §§ 62-20 et seq.; Tex. Rev. Civ. Stat. art. 5069-11.01 et seq.; Utah Code Ann. § 12-1-1; Vt. Stat. Ann. tit. 9, § 2453; Va. Code §§ 54-729 et seq.; Wash. Rev. Code §§ 19.16.100 et seq.; W. Va. Code §§ 47-16-1 et seq.; Wisc. Stat. Ann. §§ 218.04 et seq.; Wyo. Stat. §§ 33-11-101 et seq.

[35] See H.R. Rep. No. 95-131, 95th Cong., 1st Sess. 8 (1977) at 3. States without such laws regulating debt collection at the time FDCPA was enacted included Alabama, Delaware, Georgia, Kansas, Kentucky, Mississippi, Missouri, Montana, Ohio, Oklahoma, Rhode Island, South Carolina, and South Dakota.

its regulations into areas the UCCC does not cover. An abbreviated version of NCA entitled the Model Consumer Credit Act was subsequently proposed by the National Consumer Law Center, although the substantive provisions of the new act are basically the same as those of NCA. Specifically NCA provides relief from harassment by collection agencies. While NCA has not been adopted in its entirety by any state, its provisions have resulted in reforms in the UCCC, in individual state laws, and in related federal statutes.

NCA lists and prohibits specific debt-collection abuses. There is substantial overlap between NCA and FDCPA with respect to prohibited practices. The remedies available to a consumer debtor under NCA, however, go beyond those available under FDCPA. If NCA has been violated, NCA gives a consumer debtor a complete defense to payment of the debt, compensatory damages, including damages for emotional distress or mental anguish even though unaccompanied by physical injury, and punitive damages in the discretion of the court.[36]

The UCCC, initially promulgated in 1968, was the first model statute to comprehensively encompass the consumer credit area. The 1974 revision of the UCCC bears some similarity to NCA. The UCCC partially follows NCA approach to debt collection by extending the concept of unconscionability to unreasonable conduct in the collection of consumer debts.[37] A court is given the broad test of whether the conduct is unconscionable, but is directed to consider in making its decision certain factors including use or threat of force, communications with the debtor at unreasonable hours of the night, simulating legal process or governmental authority, and communications with the debtor's employer prior to final judgment. If a court finds that an unconscionable debt-collection practice occurred, the practice may be enjoined,[38] or the aggrieved consumer may be able to have the contract voided, reformed, or otherwise limited by the court. In addition, the consumer debtor may recover attorney's fees in a successful unconscionability action.[39]

Special debt-collection statutes that are not a part of NCA or the UCCC have been adopted in states throughout the country. Many of the statutes are similar to the debt-collection provisions of NCA or the UCCC. New York, Florida, and Wisconsin have adopted such statutes.[40] These statutes cover collection activities arising out of any credit transaction, not just those defined as consumer credit transactions under the UCCC. The remedies available vary greatly. For example, the New York law provides a criminal penalty but no

---

[36] NCA §§ 7.301, 7.302, 7.303.

[37] UCCC § 5.108(2).

[38] UCCC § 6.111.

[39] UCCC § 5.201(8).

[40] One commentator has suggested these states as three good examples of such state statutes. See Fla. Stat. Ann. §§ 559.55 et seq.; Comment, "Fair Debt Collection Practices: Analysis of Florida and Federal Law," 30 U. Fla. L. Rev. 892 (1978); N.Y. Penal Law § 190.50; Wis. Stat. Ann. § 218.04; Heiser, "Wisconsin Consumer Act–A Critical Analysis," 57 Marq. L. Rev. 389 (1974); Fonseca & Teachout, Handling Consumer Credit Cases Ch. 6, at 197 (Lawyers' Coop. Publishing Co., 2d ed. 1980).

civil penalty. The Wisconsin statute provides for a civil penalty of twice the finance charge, with a $100 minimum and a $1,000 maximum. The Florida law makes the defendant liable for actual damages or $500, whichever is greater, and allows actual damages for mental suffering without physical contact. Both Wisconsin and Florida authorize recovery of attorney fees. The list of abusive debt-collection activities also varies from state to state. Finding any one of the factors listed in the Florida, New York, and Wisconsin statutes constitutes a per se violation. The listed abusive collection activity often resembles the list of prohibited conduct under FDCPA. Both the Wisconsin and Florida list of prohibited conduct include a prohibition against use of obscene, threatening, vulgar, or willfully abusive language in attempting to collect a debt, but the New York statute omits this factor entirely.

Another example of a state debt-collection law is the Texas statute.[41] A review of the basic provisions of the statute illustrates the type of debt-collection statute found in some states.[42] The Texas statute contains prohibitions against unreasonable activities by consumer debt collectors. The term "debt collector" is broadly defined to include creditors seeking collection on their own and third-party collection agencies. The statute sets forth a list of deceptive and unconscionable practices, with provisions for injunction, recovery of actual damages for mental anguish (without having to prove physical injury), and attorney fees.[43]

---

[41] Tex. Rev. Civ. Stat. art. 5069-11.01 et seq.

[42] See Fonseca & Teachout, Handling Consumer Credit Cases Ch. 6, at 198–199 (Lawyers' Coop. Publishing Co, 2d ed. 1980).

[43] These practices include the following:

(1) Threats to use violence to collect a debt;
(2) Falsely accusing the debtor of fraud;
(3) Threatening to report that a consumer willfully refuses to pay an undisputed debt when in fact the debt is in dispute;
(4) Threatening to sell a debt with the false representation that the assignee will take free from the defenses the consumer may have;
(5) Threatening the debtor with arrest for nonpayment without proper court proceedings;
(6) Threatening to file criminal charges against the debtor when there has been no violation of criminal law;
(7) Falsely stating that nonpayment will result in repossession or sale of property without court proceedings;
(8) Using profane or obscene language;
(9) Making anonymous phone calls to the debtor without prior disclosure of the collector's identity;
(10) Making repeated phone calls with intent to annoy the debtor;
(11) Obtaining a written statement specifying that the consumer's obligation was incurred for necessaries where this is not the case;
(12) Using a false name in the debt-collection process;
(13) Falsely representing that the debt collector has information in its possession in order to solicit information about the consumer;

Under such debt-collection statutes in Florida, Wisconsin, New York, and Texas, certain common issues have been litigated. The following section summarizes some of the case law arising under these statutes.

### [c] Case Law Involving State Statutes Regulating Abusive Debt-Collection Practices

Cases construing the many state statutes regulating abusive debt collection have focused on a variety of issues.[44] The basic validity (i.e., constitutionality) of such statutes was considered in at least one case in Florida.[45] A creditor had argued that his right to free speech was impaired by a provision in the Florida statute that prohibits the creditor from communicating with the debtor's employer. The court agreed with the trial court's application of the commercial speech doctrine to the facts of the case in finding the statute constitutional. Such commercial speech is more readily curbed in the public interest than speech of a political, social, or religious nature.

The scope of application of an abusive debt-collection statute has also been considered in terms of the persons subject to liability, the persons protected by the statute, and the activity constituting debt collection. In two Florida cases, the relevant Florida statute was held to cover all creditors collecting debts and not just collection agencies.[46] In a Texas case, the party protected under the relevant statute must have been a consumer; the court concluded that a credit card holder can qualify as a consumer.[47] Finally, activity consti-

---

(14) Failing to disclose clearly in any communication that the debt collector is attempting to collect a debt, unless the communication is for location purposes only;
(15) Misrepresenting the character, extent, or amount of a debt against a consumer, or misrepresenting its status in any judicial or governmental proceedings;
(16) Falsely representing that the debt collector is bonded by or affiliated with an agency of government;
(17) False simulation of legal process or governmental documents in the collection of a debt;
(18) Falsely stating that the debt may be increased by attorney fees;
(19) Using any communication that appears to be from an attorney when such is not the case;
(20) Falsely using the term "credit bureau," "retail merchants," or "retail merchants association" to aid in the collection of a debt; and
(21) Knowing use by a creditor of any independent collection agency that repeatedly and continuously engages in acts or practices that violate the statute.

[44] For a discussion of such case law, see Annot., 87 A.L.R.3d 786 (1978). Note that most of the case law has arisen in Florida and Texas to date.

[45] Harris v. Beneficial Fin. Co. of Jacksonville, 338 So. 2d 196 (Fla.), cert. denied, 430 US 950 (1976).

[46] Williams v. Streeps Music Co., 333 So. 2d 65 (Fla. Dist. Ct. App. 1976); Heard v. Mathis, 344 So. 2d 651 (Fla. Dist. Ct. App. 1977).

[47] Ledisco Fin. Servs., Inc. v. Virocole, 553 SW2d 951 (Tex. Civ. App. 1976).

tuting debt collection such that a statute could apply in Texas included efforts to retrieve a credit card.[48]

The elements of a cause of action necessitated by the Florida statute were also considered in another case.[49] The Florida statute provides that no person collecting a consumer claim shall disclose to a person other than the debtor or his family information affecting the debtor's reputation if the collector has knowledge or reason to know that the other person does not have a business need for the information or that the information is false. The court indicated that the debtor must establish all of these elements of the statute, including a demonstration that his reputation was adversely affected.

The standard for determining liability under an abusive debt-collection statute was explored in another Florida case.[50] The statute in question provides that no person shall willfully communicate with the debtor or a member of his family with frequency that can be reasonably expected to amount to harassment. The court emphasized that the trier of fact must consider both the frequency and the purpose of the communication. If there is a legitimate purpose or if the collector seeks merely to obtain legitimate information, there is no violation of the statute. Once the information is obtained, however, further communication becomes harassment if it serves only to exhaust the existing debtor's will.

Some state statutes insulate a creditor from liability if his debt-collection conduct is a result of a good faith error. The defense of good faith error was considered in a Texas case.[51] Under the statute involved, the Texas court emphasized that reasonable procedures must be employed by the debt collector before a good faith error can be excused.

Other cases have considered the nature of damages recoverable and the general recoverability of damages under state debt-collection statutes. One case, for example, held under a Maryland statute that punitive damages were not recoverable.[52] Other cases relate to general recoverability of damages that have arisen under state debt-collection statutes not previously cited or discussed.[53]

---

[48] Id.

[49] Heard v. Mathis, 344 So. 2d 651 (Fla. Dist. Ct. App. 1977).

[50] Story v. J.M. Fields, Inc., 343 So. 2d 675 (Fla. Dist. Ct. App.), cert. denied, 348 So. 2d 954 (Fla. 1977).

[51] Central Adjustment Bureau, Inc. v. Gonzales, 528 SW2d 314 (Tex. Civ. App. 1978).

[52] Cilento v. BT Credit Co., 424 F. Supp. 1 (D. Md. 1977).

[53] See Hatcher v. Budget Rent-A-Car Systs., Inc., 617 F2d 91 (5th Cir. 1980); Moore v. Goodyear Tire & Rubber Co., 369 So. 2d 630 (La. Ct. App. 1978); Baldassari v. Public Fin. Trust, 369 Mass. 33, 337 NE2d 701 (1975); Hansen v. Central Adjustment Bureau, Inc., 348 So. 2d 608 (Fla. Dist. Ct. App. 1977); Pargas of Longview, Inc. v. Jones, 573 SW2d 571 (Tex. Civ. App. 1978); Thomas v. Firestone Tire & Rubber Co., 266 SE2d 905 (W. Va. 1980).

# 6

# Judicial Collection

## ¶ 6.01 INTRODUCTION

This chapter focuses on the collection of unsecured debts[1] by use of judicial process.[2] If the creditor has failed in extrajudicial attempts to collect the

---

[1] For a definition of the term "unsecured debts," see ¶¶ 5.01 and 7.01.

[2] This chapter deals mostly with state law, which varies in content from state to state. However, legal principles common to most states have been extracted such that the discussion contained in this chapter will be useful to all. Additionally, to the extent possible the authors have attempted to provide the reader with illustrative citations to and discussion of particular state law. The reader is cautioned, however, that such citations and discussions are not exhaustive in a national sense and that research of local law is essential. Finally, other secondary sources have been liberally cited, to which the reader may refer for further guidance.

unsecured debt,[3] the creditor may seek collection by bringing a judicial action to obtain a judgment if it is financially prudent to do so. The first portion of this chapter deals with questions relating to judgments that are particularly relevant to the collection of simple debts.[4] The judgment enables the creditor to obtain a judicial lien on assets of the debtor through which the debt may be satisfied. Additionally, the judicial lien may give the creditor priority over other creditors who seek to assert claims in the same asset of the debtor. The methods of obtaining judicial liens, both before[5] and after[6] rendering of judgment, are carefully considered in this chapter. The ultimate effect of the judicially obtained lien is that assets subject to the lien may be sold without the debtor's consent. The law that pertains to these judicial sales is also discussed in this chapter.[7] Finally, miscellaneous matters that generally pertain to judicial collection of unsecured debts are considered in the conclusion of this chapter.[8] Since the basis of this discussion rests on a valid judgment, the law that relates to the obtaining of a judgment is first discussed.

## ¶ 6.02 OBTAINING A JUDGMENT

### [1] Rendition, Entry, and General Effect of a Judgment

This chapter assumes validity of a debt due a creditor and assumes that a judgment will be rendered for the plaintiff-creditor. The rendition of a judgment is simply the pronouncement of a court that judgment has been granted to the plaintiff or defendant.[1] No particular formal act is required to evidence the rendition of a judgment that is common to all jurisdictions.[2] Instead, the "rendition" of a judgment is the subject of many statutes, cases, and court rules.[3] To be effective as a judgment, judicial action is required,[4] which depends upon the intention of the trial judge determined from the judge's acts and the entire rec-

---

[3] See Chapter 5 for discussion of extrajudicial collection of unsecured debts.

[4] See infra ¶ 6.02.

[5] See infra ¶ 6.04.

[6] See infra ¶ 6.05.

[7] See infra ¶ 6.06.

[8] See infra ¶ 6.07.

[1] See, e.g., Allen v. Allen, 129 Ariz. 112, 628 P2d 995 (Ariz. App. 1981); Casati v. Aero Marine Management Co., 43 Ill. App. 3d 1, 536 NE2d 826, appeal after remand, 90 Ill. App. 3d 530, 413 NE2d 122 (1976).

[2] See, e.g., U.S. v. F. & M. Schaefer Brewing Co., 356 US 227 (1958); U.S. v. Hark, 320 US 531, reh'g denied, 321 US 802 (1944).

[3] See, e.g., People ex rel. Schwartz v. Fogerholm, 17 Ill. 2d 131, 161 NE2d 20 (1959).

[4] See, e.g., Safeway Stores v. Brotherhood of Teamsters & Auto Truck Drivers Local No. 70 of Alameda County, 83 Cal. App. 3d 430, 147 Cal. Rptr. 835 (1978); Wakefield v. Kern, 58 Ill. App. 3d 837, 374 NE2d 1074 (1978).

ord.[5] The acts of other judicial officers, attorneys, and the parties may also be considered in this determination.[6] Once the judgment is rendered, it is effective between the parties to the action; however, to be effective as to third parties some other act is often necessary as far as priority disputes involving the debtor's assets are concerned.[7] In short, the creditor must obtain a judicial lien on the assets of the debtor to obtain priority over third parties.

Usually, the prevailing attorney prepares the judgment form for the court. The form of the judgment itself is often regulated by local statutes. Typically, the statutes do not require special language to evidence rendition of the judgment, although the phrase, "It is considered by the court that the plaintiff recover from the defendant $......," or similar language is commonly used.[8] Instead, the substance of the judgment, as opposed to its mere form, will more likely control the legal sufficiency of the rendition of the judgment. Therefore, the creditor's attorney when preparing the judgment form should, at a minimum, ensure that the amount of the judgment is complete and certain.[9] As to the certainty of amount, the judgment form should indicate with reasonable clarity the decision of the court, thus enabling the parties to ascertain their obligations and the judgment to be enforced. There is substantial authority to indicate that a judgment is ineffective and unenforceable if it is ambiguous or silent as to the amount of recovery.[10] For example, if the creditor is awarded attorney fees, the amount of the fee must be included for the fees to be collectible. Similarly, postjudgment interest on the debt must also be included unless the statutory interest rate is applicable and the statute provides for automatic

---

[5] See, e.g., U.S. v. F. & M. Schaefer Brewing Co., 356 US 227 (1958); Fewel v. Fewel, 23 Cal. 2d 431, 144 P2d 592 (1943); Associated Press v. Taft-Ingalls Corp., 323 F2d 114 (6th Cir. 1963); see also Annot., 73 A.L.R.2d 250 (1960).

[6] See, e.g., Bank of Lincolnwood v. Federal Leasing, 622 F2d 944 (7th Cir. 1980); Associated Press v. Taft-Ingalls Corp., 323 F2d 144 (6th Cir. 1963).

[7] See, e.g., Blackledge v. Harrington, 289 Ore. 139, 611 P2d 292 (1980); Cities Serv. Oil v. Village of Oak Brook, 84 Ill. App. 3d 381, 405 NE2d 379 (1980); D'Andrea v. Rende, 123 Conn. 377, 195 A 741 (1937); In re Novotny, 161 Minn. 503, 201 NW 949 (1925); Fleming v. Clark Township, 357 SW2d 940 (Mo. 1962); State v. Capitol City Bank, 31 NM 430, 246 P 899 (1926); Oransky v. Stepanovich, 304 Pa. 84, 155 A 290 (1931).

[8] See, e.g., Pease v. Rathbun-Jones Eng'g Co., 243 US 273 (1917); Jones v. Gablansini, 134 Colo. 64, 299 P2d 503 (1956); U.S. v. F. & M. Schaefer Brewing Co., 356 US 227 (1958); Associated Press v. Taft-Ingalls Corp., 323 F2d 114 (6th Cir. 1963).

[9] See, e.g., People v. W.A. Wiebolt & Co., 357 Ill. 208, 191 NE 689 (1934); Brown v. Brown, 38 Ariz. 459, 300 P 1007 (1931); Shriver v. Superior Court, 48 Colo. App. 576, 192 P 124 (1920); Whatley v. Mueller, 288 SW2d 405 (Mo. Ct. App. 1956); Saline Branch Drainage Dist. v. Urbana-Champaign Sanitary Dist., 395 Ill. 26, 69 NE2d 251 (1946); Taylor v. Taylor, 367 SW2d 58 (Mo. Ct. App. 1963).

[10] See Annot., 55 A.L.R.2d 723 (1957); see also Allison v. Allison, 540 SW2d 635 (Mo. Ct. App. 1976). But see Prince Georges County v. Commonwealth Land Title Ins. Co., 47 Md. App. 380, 423 A2d 270 (1980) (resort to the portions of the record may be had where there is uncertainty or ambiguity as to the amount of a judgment).

recovery of interest on the judgment.[11] Finally, the form should provide for the signature of the court or clerk of the court.

Usually, after rendition, "entry" of the judgment by the clerk occurs. This ministerial act of entering, docketing, or filing the judgment should be distinguished from the rendition of the judgment; the former makes the judgment potentially effective as to third parties, while the latter makes the judgment effective between plaintiff and defendant only.[12] The specific nature of the entry or filing of the judgment varies depending upon the jurisdiction. The judgment might be entered in the journal of the court, in a judgment book, in a minute book, or in other similar records (e.g., judgment dockets, judgment indexes, judges' minutes, or judgment rolls).[13] Entry or filing of the judgment provides the public with information as to the existence and the details of the judgment. In some instances, it may also create liens on the assets of the debtor, particularly if the debtor owns real property in the county in which the judgment is entered.[14] If an error is made or an omission has occurred in the judgment or its entry, the problem may be corrected by amendment, with retroactive application by an entry nunc pro tunc. This may occur when the record of the judgment is not in accord with the judgment as actually announced.[15]

A rendered judgment has the general effect of establishing an indisputable obligation of the judgment debtor to the judgment creditor. It provides a basis for obtaining judicial liens to satisfy the judgment from the debtor's assets. The judgment is a new obligation under which the preexisting obligation of the defendant must be performed.[16] However, the rendition of the judgment does not actually terminate the action even though the trial is terminated; the parties are still regarded as being in court for the purpose of ultimately enforcing the rendered judgment. The judgment creditor is presumed to be the owner of the judgment, although the plaintiff may usually assign his rights to a third person.[17] Even if the cause of action was not assignable, the judgment obtained thereunder is assignable.[18]

When a valid judgment is rendered, the plaintiff cannot thereafter maintain an action on the underlying cause of action; however, in some jurisdictions, the

---

[11] See, e.g., Annot., 1 A.L.R.2d 479 (1948).

[12] See supra ¶ 6.02[1] note 7.

[13] The reader should, of course, consult local law to determine proper procedure for the applicable jurisdiction.

[14] See infra ¶ 6.05[2] for discussion of liens arising from the entry of a judgment.

[15] See, e.g., Harbeck v. Holland, 81 Ill. App. 3d 250, 401 NE2d 9 (1980); Kooyenga v. Hertz Equip. Rentals, Inc., 79 Ill. App. 3d 1051, 399 NE2d 216 (1979); Barros v. Barros, 26 Wash. App. 363, 613 P2d 547 (1980); Chula v. Superior Court, 57 Cal. 2d 199, 368 P2d 107, 18 Cal. Rptr. 507 (1962).

[16] Upon the merger of the cause of action in a judgment, the old debt ceases to exist and the new judgment debt takes its place.

[17] See, e.g., Cuculla v. Hernandez, 103 US 105 (1880); Hunt v. Conrad, 47 Minn. 557, 50 NW 614 (1891).

[18] See, e.g., Brennan v. City of Eugene, 285 Ore. 401, 591 P2d 719 (1979); In re Woods Estate, 144 NYS2d 880 (NY Sur. 1955).

plaintiff may bring an action on the judgment itself.[19] Usually, the principal purpose for bringing an action on the judgment is to extend the effective period of the judgment. An action might also be brought on the judgment in a foreign state in order to obtain full faith and credit of the judgment and thereby make the judgment enforceable in a foreign state. Both of these purposes for bringing an action on the judgment are discussed later in this chapter.[20]

Assuming that complete or partial payment of the judgment occurs, how will this be evidenced in the record? Usually, an entry of satisfaction of judgment is not essential to the discharge of the debtor's obligation thereunder where payment has in fact occurred.[21] However, the debtor will obviously be desirous of "clearing the record" if payment has occurred, and by local law he is usually given the absolute right to have the satisfaction of judgment entered on the record.[22] If the satisfaction is improperly prepared by mistake or by fraud, for example, it usually may be amended or vacated.[23] If the judgment is only partially satisfied, a partial satisfaction may have to be entered. The distinction between a satisfaction of judgment, as opposed to a release of judgment, should be noted. A release of judgment does not provide evidence that a judgment has been paid. Thus, if a judgment creditor accepts less than full payment of the judgment in return for release of the judgment, the creditor should enter a partial satisfaction of judgment and a release of judgment to properly reflect these actions on the record.

## [2] Validity of a Judgment

### [a] Generally

The judgment will be unenforceable if it is invalid, either in the sense of being void or voidable. However, if it is merely voidable, the judgment has all the ordinary attributes of a valid judgment until it is superseded, reversed, or vacated.[24] A judgment when entered is presumed to be valid.[25] This portion of

---

[19] See, e.g., Union Guardian Trust Co. v. Rood, 308 Mich. 168, 13 NW2d 248 (1944).

[20] See infra ¶ 6.07[3] for discussion of bringing an action on the judgment to extend its effective period. For discussion of bringing an action on the judgment for purposes of enforcement in a foreign state, see infra ¶ 6.07[4].

[21] See, e.g., Sherwood ex rel. State Bank v. Collier, 14 NC 380 (App. Div. 1832).

[22] See, e.g., Interstate Bank of Oak Forest v. Sluis, 79 Ill. App. 3d 1039, 398 NE2d 1015 (1979); Nolte Consulting Civil Eng'rs, Inc. v. Magliocco, 93 Cal. App. 190, 155 Cal. Rptr. 348 (1979).

[23] See, e.g., Neustein v. Insurance Placement Facility of Pa., 272 Pa. Super. 126, 412 A2d 608 (1979); City Bank of San Diego v. Ramage, 266 Cal. App. 2d 570, 72 Cal. Rptr. 273 (1968); Cason v. Glass Bottle Blowers Ass'n, 113 Cal. App. 2d 263, 247 P2d 931 (1952).

[24] See, e.g., Cook v. Alexandria Nat'l Bank, 263 Md. 147, 282 A2d 97 (1971); Gunn v. Plant, 94 US 664 (1876); Dodson v. Butler, 101 Ark. 416, 142 SW 503 (1912).

[25] See, e.g., Henderson v. Kibbe, 431 US 145 (1977); People v. Barlow, 103 Cal. App. 3d 351, 163 Cal. Rptr. 664 (1980); Scheller v. Trustees of Schools of Township 41,

the text is not concerned with the appealability of a judgment on the basis of a question of fact or law; rather, it relates to the validity of the judgment from the standpoint of how it was obtained. If invalid methods were used to obtain the judgment, they may be used as the basis for opening, modifying, or vacating the judgment. In that regard, improper methods sometimes used by creditors in obtaining a judgment will be considered generally, followed by a more specific review of the jurisdictional aspects of a valid judgment. Parts of this chapter that relate to default, confession, and consent judgments further illuminate the subject area.[26]

A judgment obtained through fraud or misrepresentation may be opened or vacated.[27] The power of a court to vacate a judgment for fraud is not in need of any statutory support, although some statutes do provide for this authority.[28] To constitute grounds for relief from the judgment, some authority indicates that the fraud must involve "extrinsic," as opposed to "intrinsic," fraud.[29] For example, vacation of the judgment may result from fraud that involves false representations to the court of a jurisdictional fact. A creditor-plaintiff misrepresenting the residence of a debtor-defendant would be an example of such false representation.[30] If the judgment is obtained by a creditor through collusion, grounds for vacating the judgment may also be present.[31] If a judgment is obtained by duress, a basis for setting aside the judgment is also present.[32] Perjury is sometimes also asserted as grounds for vacating a judgment. As a general principal, perjury is not considered to be fraud that would support vacating the judgment.[33] However, if the perjury was material to the outcome of the case and the party against whom the judgment

---

67 Ill. App. 3d 857, 384 NE2d 971 (1978); Haller v. Wallis, 89 Wash. 2d 539, 573 P2d 1302 (1978); Sidran v. Tanenbaum, 391 SW2d 93 (Tex. Civ. App. 1964).

[26] See infra ¶¶ 6.02[4], 6.02[5], 6.02[6].

[27] See, e.g., Scola v. Boat Francis R., Inc. 546 F2d 459 (1st Cir. 1976); Dils v. City of Chicago, 62 Ill. App. 3d 474, 378 NE2d 1130 (1978); Leeper v. Beltrami, 53 Cal. 2d 195, 347 P2d 12, 1 Cal. Rptr. 12 (1959); see also Annot., 78 A.L.R.3d 150 (1977).

[28] See, e.g., Whitfield v. Wakefield, 51 NC App. 124, 275 SE2d 263, review denied, 303 NC 184, 280 SE2d 459 (1981); Haller v. Wallace, 89 Wash. 2d 539, 573 P2d 1302 (1978); Czyewski v. Gleeson, 49 Ill. App. 3d 655, 364 NE2d 557 (1977); Van De Ryt v. Van De Ryt, 6 Ohio St. 2d 31, 215 NE2d 698 (1966); Fed. R. Civ. P. 60(b), 60(b)(3), 60(b)(6).

[29] See, e.g., In re Marriage of Wipson, 113 Cal. App. 3d 136, 169 Cal. Rptr. 664 (1980); Stokley v. Stokley, 30 NC App. 351, 277 SE2d 131 (1976); Mauer v. Rhode, 257 NW2d 489 (Iowa 1977); Scheel v. Superior Mfg. Co., 249 Iowa 873, 89 NW2d 377 (1958).

[30] See, e.g., Davis v. Albritton, 167 Ga. 517, 56 SE 514 (1907).

[31] See, e.g., U.S. v. Johnson, 319 US 302 (1943); Van De Ryt v. Van De Ryt, 6 Ohio St. 2d 31, 315 NE2d 698 (1966).

[32] See, e.g., Hartford v. Hartford, 53 Ohio App. 2d 79, 371 NE2d 591 (1977); Varley v. Varley, 180 Conn. 1, 428 A2d 317 (1980); Chaney v. Chaney, 176 Ore. 203, 156 P2d 559 (1945).

[33] See, e.g., Cates v. Farrington, 423 A2d 539 (Me. 1980); Haner v. Haner, 13 Utah 2d 299, 373 P2d 577 (1962).

was rendered was without fault or negligence in failing to prove the falsity of the perjured testimony, there is authority that a court may vacate the rendered judgment.[34]

Beyond intentional misconduct that leads to obtaining a judgment, there are other grounds for vacating a judgment. These generally include accidental occurrences that resulted in surprise to the party against whom judgment was entered, and which prevented that party from defending itself in the action.[35] Examples include delay or loss of mail or an unauthorized withdrawal of an attorney. Other grounds for vacating the judgment include material mistakes, negligence, inadvertence, and omissions of various sorts.[36] Further, a judgment secured in violation of an agreement not to enter a judgment may be vacated on that ground.[37] Finally, improper or negligent conduct on the part of the judge, clerk, or officer of the court, juror, or attorney for either party can result in grounds for vacation of a judgment.[38]

### [b] Territorial Jurisdiction

The Restatement (Second) of Judgments lists three requirements that must be satisfied for a court to undertake an adjudication properly: notice, subject-matter jurisdiction, and territorial jurisdiction.[39] The latter is of particular importance to the creditor attempting to collect a debt due from a debtor who is located in another state.[40]

The case of *Pennoyer v. Neff* is the starting point in understanding the law that pertains to territorial jurisdiction of courts.[41] In *Pennoyer*, the Court set forth the theoretical framework of the doctrine of territorial jurisdiction in establishing three categories of action.

(1) In personam jurisdiction results in judgments that make the defendant personally liable to the judgment creditor.

---

[34] See, e.g., H & A Inc. v. Gilmore, 172 Ind. App. 10, 359 NE2d 259 (1977); Lark v. Detroit Edison Co., 99 Mich. App. 280, 297 NW2d 653 (1980); Dunn v. Law Offices of Ramon R. Alvarez, P.C., 119 Ariz. 437, 581 P2d 282 (1978).

[35] See, e.g., Ex parte Hartford Ins. Co., 394 So. 2d 933 (Ala. 1981); In re Marriage of Wipson, 113 Cal. App. 3d 136, 169 Cal. Rptr. 664 (1980); Collister v. Inter-State Fidelity Bldg. & Loan Ass'n, 44 Ariz. 427, 38 P2d 626 (1934); Fetting v. Flanigan, 185 Md. 499, 45 A2d 355 (1946).

[36] See 46 Am. Jur. 2d Judgments §§ 717, 718 (1969).

[37] See, e.g., Lawrence v. Grant, 184 So. 2d 412 (Miss. 1966); Baker v. Griffin, 79 Ohio App. 276, 70 NE2d 911 (1946).

[38] See 46 Am. Jur. 2d Judgments §§ 719–738.

[39] Restatement (Second) of Judgments § 1 (1982).

[40] See Clermont, "Restating Territorial Jurisdiction and Venue for State and Federal Courts," 66 Cornell L. Rev. 411 (1981), for an excellent discussion of the law relating to jurisdiction of the courts. See infra ¶ 6.02[5][c] for a discussion of the validity of consenting to jurisdiction by contractual clause.

[41] 95 US 714 (1878).

(2) In rem jurisdiction results in judgments that affect interests of all persons in designated property.

(3) Quasi in rem jurisdiction produces judgments that affect the interests of particular persons in designated property. Quasi in rem jurisdiction might involve the assertion of a preexisting interest in the property or an attempt to apply the defendant's property to satisfaction of a claim against the defendant that is unrelated to the property.

In total, even though a debtor may reside in a foreign state, if the creditor can somehow establish that a court has personal jurisdiction over the debtor, based on a judgment obtained thereunder, the creditor may levy generally on the debtor's assets.[42] On the other hand, enforcement of the judgment will be limited to particular property of the debtor if only in rem or quasi in rem jurisdiction is obtained.

On a constitutional Fourteenth Amendment due process of law theory, *Pennoyer* held that the state asserting jurisdiction must have power over the person or the property for all three types of actions. The authority of a state court is restricted by the territorial limits of the state in which the court is located.[43] As to in rem or quasi in rem jurisdiction, this meant that the property must be physically located within the state. As to in personam jurisdiction, this meant that the debtor must be physically present within the state,[44] or domiciled within the state,[45] or must have consented to the jurisdiction of the court.[46] Other acts committed within the state have also been held to justify exercise of in personam jurisdiction. These have included transacting business,[47] owning real estate,[48] litigating,[49] and committing a tort within the state.[50]

A major turning point in the development of jurisdictional law was the case of *International Shoe Co. v. Washington*.[51] The Court stated that due process of law is constitutionally satisfied in the exercise of in personam jurisdiction only when to do so is "reasonable and just, according to our traditional conception of fair play and substantial justice."[52] To a creditor seeking to obtain a judgment against the debtor, this case meant that the court rendering judgment would have to base jurisdiction on more than mere presence of the debtor. That is to say, the level of the defendant's in-state activity and the

---

[42] See infra ¶ 6.07[4] for related discussion of the enforcement of valid judgments in a foreign state. See also ¶¶ 6.04 and 6.05 for a discussion of enforcement of judgments by levy through attachment, garnishment, execution, and other means.

[43] 95 US 720, 722 (1878).

[44] See, e.g., Fisher, Brown & Co. v. Fielding, 67 Conn. 91, 34 A 716 (1895).

[45] See, e.g., Milliken v. Meyer, 311 US 457 (1940).

[46] See, e.g., Hess v. Pawloski, 274 US 352 (1927).

[47] See, e.g., Henry L. Doherty & Co. v. Goodman, 294 US 623 (1935).

[48] See, e.g., Dubin v. City of Philadelphia, 34 Pa. D. & C. 61 (CP 1937).

[49] See, e.g., Adam v. Saenger, 303 US 59 (1938).

[50] Cf. Olberding v. Illinois Cent. R.R., 346 US 338 (1953).

[51] 326 US 310 (1945).

[52] Id. at 320.

degree of that activity's relatedness to the asserted claim must also be considered. Even though this "reasonableness" test modified the in personam arm of *Pennoyer*, it did not invalidate the territorial power test, nor did it have an effect on the in rem and quasi in rem arms of *Pennoyer*, although the reasonableness test arguably could have been applied to all forms of actions.[53]

A second major turning point in the development of jurisdictional law was in the case of *Shaffer v. Heitner*.[54] The reasonableness test of *International Shoe* was made applicable to quasi in rem and in rem actions. The Court stated that "the case for applying to jurisdiction in rem [or quasi in rem] the same test of fair play and substantial justice as governs assertions of jurisdiction in personam is simple and straightforward."[55] The Court held that "all assertions of state-court jurisdiction must be evaluated according to the standards set forth in *International Shoe* and its progeny."[56] Subsequent cases have confirmed this meaning of *Shaffer*.[57]

Translating the judicial doctrine previously discussed to practical application for use by a creditor or debtor is a heady task at best. In short, "the current law for determining the propriety of state-court jurisdiction under the due process clause is, first, to categorize the action and, second, to apply both the power and the reasonableness tests."[58] If a creditor seeks to have a court assert in personam jurisdiction over a debtor, the court will first apply the power test. If there is power through the physical presence of the debtor or through a long-arm statute, then the court must apply the reasonableness test, focusing on the nature of the contact between the debtor and the foreign state and the relationship of those contacts to the filed action. For in rem or quasi in rem proceedings, the creditor must bring the action where the property is located and, in addition, the reasonableness of the assertion of jurisdiction must be determined. In applying the reasonableness test, the court will consider, for example, whether the claim to the property is the source of the cause of action or not. If the property is not related to the cause of action, it may be less likely that the reasonableness test will be satisfied.

The previous discussion relates primarily to state courts. In regard to territorial jurisdiction of the federal courts, the due process clause of the Fifth Amendment allows the federal courts to assert jurisdiction anywhere within the territorial limits of the United States. Even so, as a general rule, the jurisdiction of the federal courts reaches only as far as the local state courts for several reasons. First, the applicable federal statutes, or rules, may incorporate by ref-

---

[53] See Mullane v. Central Hanover Bank & Trust Co., 339 US 306 (1950); McGee v. International Life Ins. Co., 355 US 220 (1957). But see Hanson v. Denckla, 357 US 235 (1958).

[54] 433 US 186 (1977).

[55] Id. at 207.

[56] Id. at 212.

[57] See Kulko v. Superior Court, 436 US 84 (1978); Rush v. Sauchuk, 444 US 320 (1980); World-Wide Volkswagen Corp. v. Woodson, 444 US 286 (1980).

[58] See Clermont, "Restating Territorial Jurisdiction and Venue for State and Federal Courts," 66 Cornell L. Rev. 411, 423 (1981).

erence the various state jurisdictional limits. Second, the *Erie* Doctrine, which has the effect of placing emphasis on the application of state law, may dictate a similar application of state jurisdictional law. Third, the federal courts may adopt the jurisdictional limitations of state courts for federal court jurisdiction. In short, the jurisdictional doctrine heretofore discussed applies to federal district courts, unless specifically modified by federal statute or rule.[59]

### [c] Venue

Another concern of the creditor related to jurisdiction is that of proper venue. "Venue" is a concept that includes all territorial restrictions on a court's ability to assert jurisdiction other than those found in the U.S. Constitution. These venue restrictions emanate from a variety of sources. First, state provisions regarding venue within the state should be consulted.[60] Second, case law suggests that states sometimes exercise self-restraint in order to distribute judicial business on an interstate level.[61] Third, federal venue provisions must also be considered.[62]

The ability of a court to assert jurisdiction over parties to an action to collect a consumer debt might be specifically inhibited. For example, the Fair Debt Collection Practices Act (FDCPA) protects consumers from suits by collection agencies in inconvenient forums.[63] Actions by "debt collectors" to enforce a lien on real property may be filed only in the county in which the real property is located. Other "debt collector" actions may be brought only where the debtor resides or where the contract is signed.[64] As a second example in the consumer field, venue for collections by a creditor is also occasionally governed by consumer protection state statutes, such as the Uniform Consumer Credit Code (UCCC), the National Consumer Act (NCA), or similar statutes.[65] The UCCC expressly invalidates agreements that determine venue.[66] The NCA limits venue in consumer credit actions to the county where the transaction was entered into, where the consumer resided at the time of the the transaction, or where the consumer resided at the time of commencement of the action.[67] A final example in the consumer field involves the Federal Trade Commission (FTC). *Spiegel, Inc. v. FTC*[68] held that the FTC has the power to prevent credi-

---

[59] Id. at 427–428.

[60] See, e.g., James & Hazard, Civil Procedure § 12.3 (Little, Brown, 2d ed. 1977); Stevens, "Venue Statutes: Diagnosis and Proposed Cure," 49 Mich. L. Rev. 307 (1950).

[61] See Clermont, "Restating of Territorial Jurisdiction and Venue for State and Federal Courts," 66 Cornell L. Rev. 411, 448 (1981).

[62] See, e.g., Fed. R. Civ. P. 4.

[63] See ¶ 5.09[1] for a discussion of the Fair Debt Collection Practices Act, 15 USC § 1692.

[64] FDCPA § 811, 15 USC § 1692(i).

[65] See ¶ 5.09[4] for discussion of the UCCC and the NCA.

[66] UCCC § 1.201(9)(c).

[67] NCA § 5.104.

[68] 540 F2d 287 (7th Cir. 1976).

tors from suing consumers in inconvenient forums. Spiegel, a catalog retailer with its principal place of business in Chicago, regularly sued in Illinois courts to collect delinquent accounts of out-of-state consumer customers. The Illinois long-arm statute granted jurisdiction for these suits. Nevertheless, the FTC issued a "cease-and-desist order." The Court of Appeals for the Seventh Circuit held that the "unfair practice" language of Section 5 of the FTC Act empowered the FTC to enjoin distant forum abuse of consumer debtors.

## [3] Particular Methods of Obtaining a Judgment—Introduction

It is often assumed that the great majority of judgments are obtained only after a long trial on the merits of the complaint, with all the trappings of jury selection, opening arguments, examination and testimony of witnesses, and closing arguments. In fact, this view of the typical debtor-creditor case is distorted. Prolonged litigation is very expensive to the parties and if the debt is clearly due, this expense would be needlessly incurred. A creditor wants to obtain the judgment as quickly as possible and the debtor may see no need to defend if the debt is clearly due. The result is that many actions brought to collect simple debts produce default judgments. The nature of default judgments is considered herein.[69] Creditors may try to avoid even the necessity of obtaining a default judgment by obtaining a judgment by confession, commonly referred to as a cognovit judgment. The law surrounding cognovit judgments is also considered herein.[70] In many situations, the creditor may not be able to obtain a default or a cognovit judgment. Still, the creditor might be able to "settle" the action on the debt by leveraging the debtor into consenting to a judgment by stipulation. Judgments by consent is the last topic considered in this section of the text.[71]

Although these methods of obtaining a judgment are creditor's tools of collection, the debtors' rights in regard to each of these methods must be recognized. The validity of judgments generally has already been reviewed.[72] The following discussion of the methods of obtaining judgments will further consider the validity of judgments by focusing on law peculiar to each of these methods. Assuming the invalidity of a judgment, procedural methods for obtaining relief from such judgments is also undertaken.

## [4] Default Judgments

### [a] Introduction and Basic Procedure

The rendering of a default judgment by a court is one of the most severe sanctions a court can impose on a party. At its most basic level, the rendering of a default judgment usually results from the failure of the debtor-defendant

---

[69] See infra ¶ 6.02[4].

[70] See infra ¶ 6.02[5].

[71] See infra ¶ 6.02[6].

[72] See supra ¶ 6.02[2].

to make a required "appearance" within a legally specified time after the debtor has been properly served with a summons and a copy of the complaint. The policy supporting the use of the default judgment mechanism is to keep the dockets current, to expedite the disposal of cases, and to prevent a procrastinating defendant from impeding the collection of the claim.[73] On the other hand, the purpose of a default judgment should not be one of freeing plaintiffs from potentially valid defenses of the defendant.[74]

A distinction is made between the entry of default and the entry of a default judgment. The mere entry of default serves to preclude the defendant from asserting further defenses, while rendering of a default judgment constitutes a judgment if validly obtained.[75] Typically, the plaintiff may move for an order of default and a default judgment by way of a single motion.[76]

The obtaining of a default judgment begins with the filing of the complaint by the creditor-plaintiff with the appropriate court. A copy of the complaint and summons is then served on the debtor-defendant. The service of process on the defendant, combined with a valid basis for jurisdiction, is crucial to the entry of a default and a default judgment.[77] Unfortunately, some creditors have tried to circumvent the obvious requirement of service of process to increase the likelihood of obtaining a default judgment. In short, service of process never occurs and the creditor, along with a private process server, falsifies the return of service. This so-called sewer service arguably has produced many default judgments over the years.[78] These practices may be attacked by various methods, including criminal prosecution for perjury against the process servers, bar association actions against attorneys involved in fraudulent service, and disciplinary action against public officials who serve process.[79] About half of the states and Rule 4(c) of the Federal Rules of Civil Procedure require court-appointed process servers to ensure that private process servers are not abusing the judicial system.[80]

---

[73] See, e.g., Stoner v. Thompson, 578 SW2d 679 (Tex. 1979); Garrison Carpet Mills v. Lenest, Inc., 65 Ohio App. 2d 251, 417 NE2d 1277 (1979); Mieszkowski v. Norville, 61 Ill. App. 2d 289, 209 NE2d 358 (1965); Rogers v. Lyle Adjustment Co., 70 NM 209, 372 P2d 797 (1962).

[74] See, e.g., Culetsu v. Dix, 149 Conn. 456, 181 A2d 116 (1982).

[75] See, e.g., Peebles v. Moore, 48 NC App. 497, 269 SE2d 694, modified and aff'd, 302 NC 351, 275 SE2d 833 (1980); Board of Transp. v. Williams, 31 NC App. 125, 299 SE2d 37 (1976); Rogers v. Lyle Adjustment Co., 70 NM 209, 372 P2d 797 (1962).

[76] See, e.g., Lewis v. LeBaron, 254 Cal. App. 2d 270, 61 Cal. Rptr. 903 (1967); Catlett v. Chestnut, 107 Fla. 498, 146 So. 241 (1933).

[77] See, e.g., Fonseca & Teachout, Handling Consumer Credit Cases § 6.6 (Lawyers' Coop. Publishing Co., 2d ed. 1980); Note, "Abuse of Process: Sewer Service," 3 Colum. J.L. & Soc. Probs. 17 (1967).

[78] See, e.g., Fonseca & Teachout, Handling Consumer Credit Cases § 6.6 (Lawyers' Coop. Publishing Co., 2d ed. 1980); Tuerkhiemer, "Service of Process in New York City: A Proposed End to Unregulated Criminality," 72 Colum. L. Rev. 847 (1972).

[79] Fonseca & Teachout, Handling Consumer Credit Cases § 6.6 (Lawyers' Coop. Publishing Co., 2d ed. 1980).

[80] Id.

A matter related to service of process and the obtaining of a default judgment concerns statutes that provide for service of process upon a statutory agent. Where the debtor is a foreign corporation, state statutes often provide for the service of process on a statutorially designated agent. Assuming this service is otherwise valid, the statutory agent usually must give the defendant notice of service before the court can properly enter judgment upon a subsequent default.[81]

Upon the proper service of summons, the debtor-defendant will be notified that an appearance must be made within a certain time period or a default and/or a default judgment will be entered. Proof of the service of process by way of a return of service or other documentation will be provided to the plaintiff or the court directly by the process server. Attorneys for creditors will calendar the date after the service of process, upon which an appearance must have been made by the debtor; if no appearance occurs by that date, the creditor's attorney, along with the aid of the creditor client, may enter a motion for default and default judgment with accompanying proof of service of process.[82] The amount of the judgment sought by the motion usually cannot exceed the fair scope of the allegations and prayer of the complaint.[83]

In addition to service of process, failure by the defendant to make an appearance, and a motion for default judgment, a notice of application for default judgment may have to be given to the defendant before a default judgment is granted. This notice may be required by statute or rule.[84] For example, the Federal Rules of Civil Procedure[85] provide that if the party against whom judgment by default is sought has appeared in the action, he must be served with written notice of application for judgment at least three days prior to the hearing on such application.

Assuming the above prerequisites for a default judgment have been satisfied, the court or a clerk of the court will enter the default judgment. However, some statutes or rules limit a clerk's authority to enter a default judgment without direction of the court.[86] As previously noted, a default judgment will be rendered if the clerk of the court is satisfied that service has occurred and the

---

[81] See Annot., 20 A.L.R.2d 1179 (1951).

[82] Note that default judgments are not obtainable against members of the armed forces and that an affidavit indicating the defendant is not in the armed forces must accompany the motion for a default judgment. See Section 200 of the Soldiers' and Sailors' Civil Relief Act, 50 USC app. § 520 (1940); Annot., 35 A.L.R. Fed. 649 (1977).

[83] See, e.g., Southern Ariz. School for Boys v. Chery, 119 Ariz. 277, 580 P2d 738 (1978); Becker v. S.P.V. Constr. Co., 27 Cal. 3d 484, 612 P2d 915, 165 Cal. Rptr. 825 (1980); Dils v. City of Chicago, 62 Ill. App. 3d 474, 378 NE2d 1130 (1978); Columbia Valley Credit Exch., Inc. v. Lampson, 12 Wash. App. 952, 533 P2d 152 (1975).

[84] See, e.g., Ed Martin Ford Co., Inc. v. Martin, 173 Ind. App. 428, 363 NE2d 1292 (1977); Ries Flooring Co., Inc. v. Dileno Constr. Co., 53 Ohio App. 2d 255, 373 NE2d 1266 (1977); U.S. v. Martin, 395 F. Supp. 954 (SDNY 1975); Clark County State Bank v. Bennett, 166 Ind. App. 471, 336 NE2d 663 (1975).

[85] See Fed. R. Civ. P. 55(b)(2). For a discussion of Fed. R. Civ. P. 55(b)(2) and similar state statutes and rules, see Annot., 51 A.L.R.2d 837 (1957).

[86] See Annot., 158 A.L.R. 1091 (1945).

defendant has failed to make an appearance within a specified time period. There is some authority for default based on the withdrawal of an appearance by the defendant or his attorney, failure to appear at trial, and tardy appearance and pleadings.[87] In entering the default judgment when the defendant has failed to appear, proof is not required of the merits of the claim of the plaintiff under the general rule that the material allegations of the complaint are to be taken as true.[88]

### [b] Operation and Effect

As a basic principle, a default judgment will be given the same effect as a judgment validly rendered after a contested proceeding. Thus, the judgment creditor may enforce the judgment as discussed later in this chapter.[89] However, the creditor should recognize that if the validity of the default judgment can be successfully challenged, the creditor may become liable for damages caused by these enforcement efforts. Methods and grounds for obtaining relief from an entered default judgment are next considered. A collateral effect of a default judgment is that it operates as an admission of the truth of all the material allegations set forth in the complaint.[90] Further, a default judgment operates as a basis for applying the doctrine of res judicata[91] and bars a second suit between the same parties involving the same cause of action.[92] Difficult problems arise, however, when a default judgment is relied upon for collateral estoppel.[93]

### [c] Obtaining Relief From Default Judgments

There are two procedures that might be used to obtain relief from a default judgment entered against the debtor. One procedure merely provides for an action for review. Actions for review are special statutory remedies that permit the court to review a judgment in order to prevent an injustice.[94] For example, this method of obtaining relief is available when the default judgment was rendered during the defendant's illness.[95]

---

[87] See generally 47 Am. Jur. 2d Judgments §§ 1165–1172 (1969).

[88] See, e.g., Sheepscot Land Corp. v. Gregory, 383 A2d 16 (Me. 1978); Colonial Pa. Ins. Co. v. Tachibana, 53 Ill. App. 3d 981, 369 NE2d 177 (1977); Pruitt v. Taylor, 247 NC 380, 100 SE2d 841 (1957).

[89] See infra ¶¶ 6.03–6.06.

[90] See Annot., 8 A.L.R.3d 1070, 1073, § 3[a] (1966).

[91] See Annot., 77 A.L.R.2d 1410 (1961).

[92] Id.

[93] Id.

[94] See, e.g., Graziano v. City Council of Canby, 35 Ore. App. 271, 581 P2d 552 (1978); Whalen v. Worcester Elec. Light Co., 307 Mass. 169, 29 NE2d 763 (1940).

[95] See, e.g., Burt v. Hodson, 242 Mass. 302, 136 NE 108 (1922); see also Rowley v. Dairyland Ins. Co., Inc., 44 Ore. App. 333, 605 P2d 1356 (1980).

A second procedure to obtain relief from a default judgment entails motions to have the judgment opened, modified, or vacated.[96] Whether or not these motions will be successful ordinarily depends on the discretion of the court. Because the debtor has not had a trial on the merits, this discretion is often exercised in favor of the defendant.[97] An example of a rule providing for relief from a default judgment is Rule 55(c) of the Federal Rules of Civil Procedure, which provides that if a judgment by default has been entered, it may be set aside in accordance with Rule 60(b).[98] Circumstances where relief might be available from a default judgment generally include fraud in obtaining the default judgment,[99] attorney's error,[100] or reliance by a codefendant on a promise or assumption that another would defend him.[101] If the defendant is successful in obtaining an order that sets aside a default judgment, a majority of cases hold that such an order is not appealable.[102] Similarly, an order denying relief is also not appealable in the absence of a statutory right to do so.[103]

## [5] Cognovit Judgments (Judgments by Confession)

### [a] Introduction and Basic Procedure

A confession of judgment clause in a contract, note, or other document may serve as the basis for a cognovit judgment. Rendition of a judgment based on this clause has the same effect as a judgment obtained by other valid means.[104] The confession of judgment usually occurs when a consumer signs a promissory note[105] or installment sales contract. Cognovit clauses typically include consent to the jurisdiction of a particular state and an authorization by the debtor to allow the creditor's attorney to appear on behalf of the debtor in court to confess judgment for the debtor without prior notice or hearing. State

---

[96] See generally 46 Am. Jur. 2d Judgments §§ 679–684 (1969).

[97] See, e.g., Red Creek Nat'l Bank v. Blue Star Ranch Ltd., 58 AD2d 983, 396 NYS2d 936 (1977); Wagar v. Prudential Ins. Co. of Am., 276 Ore. 827, 556 P2d 658 (1976); North Shore Hosp., Inc. v. Barber, 143 So. 2d 849 (Fla. 1962).

[98] See Bresnan & Cornelis, "Project, Relief From Default Judgments Under Rule 60(b)–A Study of Federal Case Law," 49 Fordham L. Rev. 956 (1981); Annot., 29 A.L.R. Fed. 7 (1976).

[99] See Annot., 78 A.L.R.3d 150 (1977).

[100] See Annot., 21 A.L.R.3d 1255 (1968).

[101] See Annot., 16 A.L.R.2d 1139 (1951).

[102] See Annot., 8 A.L.R.3d 1272 (1966).

[103] Id.

[104] See Fonseca & Teachout, Handling Consumer Credit Cases §§ 6.4, 6.5 (Lawyers' Coop. Publishing Co., 2d ed. 1980), for a discussion of cognovit judgments. See supra ¶ 6.02[1] for discussion of the general effect of a judgment.

[105] Note that the presence of a cognovit clause in a note does not effect the negotiability of the note. See UCC § 3-112(1)(d). Note also that obtaining a judgment by confession may preclude the obtaining of successive judgments on the same debt. In this regard, see Annot., 80 A.L.R.2d 1880 (1961).

statutes often require the cognovit clause to be attested at the time of signature, particularly when the warrant of attorney is a part of the clause.[106] The attorney for the creditor is therefore empowered to confess judgment on behalf of the debtor upon producing the original note or contract containing the cognovit clause.[107] The use of these cognovit clauses is a most attractive collection technique from the creditor's viewpoint and is even faster and less expensive than a default judgment. On the other hand, the clause is particularly onerous to the debtor. The validity of the clause is viewed skeptically by courts and legislatures.[108] Additionally, courts freely grant motions to vacate cognovit judgments, even if the cognovit clause is otherwise valid.[109] Even so, it has been asserted that the cognovit judgment continues to retain some vitality. In particular, low-income consumers who lack legal counsel often make no attempt to have the judgment vacated.[110]

### [b] Waiver of Notice and Hearing

The validity of a judgment rendered pursuant to a cognovit clause is vulnerable to challenge because of the lack of notice or opportunity for hearing given the debtor prior to judgment. The absence of prior notice and hearing in the first instance may be challenged as a denial of rights under the due process clause of the Fourteenth Amendment of the U.S. Constitution.

The principal case dealing with the constitutionality of a cognovit judgment is *D.H. Overmyer Co. v. Frick Co.*[111] Overmyer hired Frick to install equipment at one of Overmyer's warehouses. Because Overmyer defaulted on its payments for the service, another arrangement for payment was negotiated.

---

[106] See Annot., 3 A.L.R.3d 1147 (1965). Note in addition that an agent may also execute a warrant of attorney to confess judgment against his principal. See Annot., 92 A.L.R.2d 952 (1963); see also Annot., 5 A.L.R.3d 426 (1966).

[107] See Annot., 68 A.L.R.2d 1156 (1959).

[108] See infra ¶¶ 6.02[5][b], 6.02[5][c], 6.02[5][d]. Note that there is a considerable split of authority as to what law governs the validity of a cognovit clause where more than one state is involved with the transaction or the enforcement of the debt. The view of some courts is that the validity of the clause is governed by the laws of the state in which it was executed. Other courts conclude that the validity is determined by the law of the place where the obligation was made payable. Still other courts determine validity pursuant to the law of the state in which the judgment is sought or where the judgment is being enforced. See Annot., 19 A.L.R.2d 544 (1951). Finally, at least two states, New York and New Mexico, refuse to enforce foreign notes if executed in the state where cognovit notes are valid. See Atlas Credit Corp. v. Ezrine, 25 NY2d 219, 250 NE2d 474, 303 NYS2d 282 (1969); N.M. Stat. Ann. § 21-9-17. Note, however, that while the cognovit provisions are illegal in New Mexico and unenforceable, judgments on cognovit provisions obtained in other states are entitled to full faith and credit in New Mexico. See Mountain States Fixture Co. v. Daskalos, 61 NM 491, 303 P2d 698 (1956).

[109] See infra ¶ 6.02[5][e].

[110] See Fonseca & Teachout, Handling Consumer Credit Cases § 6.4, at 188 (Lawyers' Coop. Publishing Co., 2d ed. 1980).

[111] 405 US 174 (1972).

Overmyer asked for relief from payments and, as a result of further negotiations, a second promissory note was executed. The second note contained the confession of judgment clause. Overmyer thereafter defaulted on the second note and Frick obtained judgment by confession pursuant to Ohio law. Overmyer moved to vacate the judgment, asserting, among other defenses, a violation of due process rights of notice and opportunity to be heard. The Court acknowledged that the right to a hearing and notice can be waived and cited *National Equipment Rental, Ltd. v. Szukhent*[112] and *Boddie v. Connecticut.*[113] The Court further indicated, however, that "where there is great disparity in bargaining power, and where the debtor receives nothing for the cognovit provision," the enforcement of the cognovit clause would violate the debtor's right to due process of law.[114] However, the Court found that Overmyer had equal bargaining power with Frick and had received substantial benefits from the inclusion of the cognovit clause in the second promissory note. Thus, it concluded that the waiver of due process rights by Overmyer was validated.

A second case of similar importance was decided by the Court on the same day that it handed down the *Overmyer* decision. In *Swarb v. Lennox,*[115] the Court held that a cognovit provision in Pennsylvania was not unconstitutional on its face. *Swarb* involved a three-judge district court opinion, which held that an action challenging the constitutionality of the Pennsylvania cognovit provision could not be maintained as a class action on behalf of *all* Pennsylvania residents who signed cognovit notes. The action could be maintained as a class action for Pennsylvania residents who had signed a cognovit instrument and had earned less than $10,000 annually. Further, the district court had concluded the Pennsylvania procedure of confessing judgment was unconstitutional as applied to that limited class because of lack of a knowing intelligent waiver. The U.S. Supreme Court affirmed the decision but reiterated its position set forth in *Overmyer.* "*Overmyer* necessarily reveals some discomforture on our part with respect to the present case. However that may be, the impact and effect of *Overmyer* upon the Pennsylvania system are not to be delineated in the one-sided appeal in this case and we make no attempt to do so."[116]

In total, *Overmyer* and *Swarb* stand for the principal that the constitutional validity of cognovit clauses depends on the validity of the waiver. If, for example, "a consumer signs a cognovit note without reading and understanding the confession of judgment clause, or if the provision is not voluntarily entered into and bargained for, it seems likely that the note will be held to contravene the Fourteenth Amendment. Since the burden of proving an effective waiver is on the creditor, confessions of judgment seem doomed. . . ."[117]

---

[112] 375 US 311 (1964).

[113] 401 US 371 (1971).

[114] 405 US 174, 188 (1972).

[115] 405 US 191 (1972).

[116] Id. at 201–202.

[117] Fonseca & Teachout, Handling Consumer Credit Cases § 6.4, at 190 (Lawyers' Coop. Publishing Co., 2d ed. 1980).

### [c] Consent to Jurisdiction

Although questions of jurisdiction were previously considered in this chapter,[118] since consent to jurisdiction is often part and parcel of a cognovit clause, the validity of consent to jurisdiction is considered at this point. Consumer notes and installment contract clauses occasionally include, as part of the cognovit clause, a provision by which a consumer consents to service of process in a distant state by means of service on a corporate service organization or on the consumer's agent. In so doing, the consumer has also consented to the jurisdiction of that distant state. Consent has been held to be a constitutionally adequate basis for assertion of jurisdiction. The principal case in this regard is *National Equipment Rental, Ltd. v. Szukhent*,[119] in which a New York resident was designated in an equipment lease as agent for the lessee,[120] a Michigan resident. The agent was a relative of the lessor and was not acquainted with the lessee. A New York action was filed, and the New York agent sent actual notice of the action to the lessee. Because of the actual notice, the Court did not reach the question of due process in the absence of notice.[121] However, the Court did emphasize that "parties to a contract may agree in advance to submit to the jurisdiction of a given court, to prevent notice to be served by the opposing party, or even to waive notice altogether."[122]

Even in light of *Szukhent*, it would seem that, by analogy, *Overmyer*[123] would require the consent to be knowingly, voluntarily, and intelligently made. Particularly in a consumer setting, an argument can be made that contracts with confession clauses and clauses that consent to jurisdiction in a distant state are contracts of adhesion.[124] Further, the debtor may be able to attack the consent to jurisdiction clause on other grounds. Such an attack occurred successfully on a theory of forum non conveniens in the series of *Paragon Homes* cases.[125] A court might also invalidate the clause on a number of other theories, which are considered next in this discussion.

---

[118] See supra ¶ 6.02[2][b].

[119] 375 US 311 (1964).

[120] The New York resident was to serve as an agent under Fed. R. Civ. P. 4.

[121] The court did suggest that actual notice was a prerequisite to a judgment and cited Mullane v. Central Hanover Bank & Trust Co., 339 US 306 (1950).

[122] 375 US 311, 316 (1964).

[123] 485 US 174 (1972), discussed at supra ¶ 6.02[5][b].

[124] See Fonseca & Teachout, Handling Consumer Credit Cases § 6.4, at 188 (Lawyers' Coop. Publishing Co., 2d ed. 1980).

[125] See Paragon Homes of New England, Inc. v. Langlois, 4 UCC Rep. Serv. 16, 157 N.Y.L.J., Mar. 1, 1967, at 23, col. 1 (NY Sup. Ct. 1967); Paragon Homes of Midwest, Inc. v. Crace, 4 UCC Rep. Serv. 19, 157 N.Y.L.J., Mar. 1, 1967, at 23, col. 2 (NY Sup. Ct. 1967); Paragon Homes, Inc. v. Carter, 56 Misc. 2d 463, 288 NYS2d 817, aff'd, 30 AD2d 1052, 295 NYS2d 606 (1968).

### [d] Miscellaneous Restrictions

Both case law and statutory law provide some additional restrictions to the enforcement of a cognovit clause or a judgment obtained thereunder. Administrative regulatory law also may have an impact.

The case law limitations revolve around basic contract law. To be enforceable, the cognovit clause must satisfy the common-law requirements as to the enforceability of any contractual term. Thus, if the contract is void or voidable, the cognovit clause would not seem to be enforceable (e.g., if the debtor signed the contract under duress). The clause alone may also be unenforceable in cases where the clause is unconscionable.[126] Beyond contract law, enforcement of the clause might occur in a manner constituting a tort.[127] There is considerable case law involving the torts of abuse of process or malicious prosecution.[128]

State statutes sometimes prohibit the use of cognovit clauses. Both the UCCC[129] and the NCA [130] prohibit cognovit provisions.[131] In the main, however, most state statutes simply limit or regulate use of confession clauses. It has been suggested that California is a good example of such a state.[132] The California statute prohibits the use of the cognovit clause against a consumer unless an attorney independently representing the consumer certifies that the consumer was advised with respect to the waiver rights involved and has recommended the use of the confession of judgment procedure.[133] The validity of statutes invalidating powers of attorney to confess judgment or invalidating contracts giving such power has produced some interesting case law, which should be carefully researched in one's local jurisdiction.[134]

Finally, regulatory restrictions should be noted. In many jurisdictions, the creditor can obtain a judgment lien[135] on the debtor's real estate immediately after signing a note or contract with a cognovit clause. The Federal Reserve Board (FRB) has ruled that this provision creates an immediate security interest giving the debtor the right to rescind the transaction under the three-day cooling-off period of the Federal Consumer Protection Act.[136]

---

[126] See UCC § 2-302 and infra ¶ 6.02[5][d] note 130.

[127] See ¶ 5.09[4] for a discussion of creditor tort law liability for improper collection techniques.

[128] See Annot., 87 A.L.R.3d 554 (1978).

[129] UCCC § 3.306. The UCCC also prohibits the use of jurisdiction consent clauses. See UCCC § 1.201(8)(e).

[130] NCA § 2.404. The NCA also prohibits use of jurisdiction consent clauses. See NCA § 1.201(9)(b).

[131] The UCCC and NCA are discussed at ¶ 5.09[4].

[132] See Fonseca & Teachout, Handling Consumer Credit Cases § 6.4, at 190 (Lawyers' Coop. Publishing Co., 2d ed. 1980).

[133] Cal Civ. Proc. Code § 1.32(b).

[134] See Annot., 40 A.L.R.3d 1158 (1971).

[135] See infra ¶ 6.05[2] for a discussion of judgment liens.

[136] See Board Interpretation, 34 Fed. Reg. 8698 (May 26, 1969); see also Horwitz, "Confession of Judgment Clauses as Violating Federal Truth-In-Lending Where Credi-

### [e] Obtaining Relief From Cognovit Judgments

Obtaining relief from a cognovit judgment closely resembles the obtaining of relief from default judgments.[137] The debtor may seek an action for review or may attempt to open, modify, or vacate the judgment, although any relief is within the discretion of the court. Perhaps even more than is the case regarding relief from default judgments, courts are inclined to exercise discretion in favor of the debtor where a cognovit judgment has been entered, especially when the judgment is entered under authority of a warrant of attorney to confess judgment.[138] Indeed, courts have held that relief from the cognovit judgment will not be unduly limited.[139]

## [6] Consent Judgments

### [a] Introduction and Basic Procedure

Courts have the authority to render judgments by consent of the parties.[140] A judgment by consent typically results from a compromise settlement of an action and should not be confused with prior discussion in the text relating to cognovit judgments.[141] In the debtor-creditor context, the creditor often may agree to refrain from enforcing the judgment for a period of time in order to permit the debtor to satisfy or to bring the debt current in return for the debtor's stipulation to the judgment. Thus, a judgment by consent is contractual in nature and is acknowledged by a court by rendering judgment accordingly.[142] The validity of the judgment rests on the court's jurisdiction[143] and

---

tors Have Waived Their Right to Have Liens Placed on Obligator's Residence," 66 Ill. B.J. 688 (1978).

[137] See supra ¶ 6.02[4][c].

[138] See, e.g., Pawco Inc. v. Bergman Knitting Mills, Inc., 283 Pa. Super. 443, 424 A2d 891 (1980); Public Fin. Corp. of Toledo v. Chappel, 16 Ohio Misc. 116, 241 NE2d 181 (Ct. CP, Fulton Co., 1967); Westring v. Cheyenne Nat'l Bank, 393 P2d 119 (Wyo. 1964).

[139] See, e.g., First Nat'l Bank of Elgin v. Achilli, 14 Ill. App. 3d 1, 301 NE2d 739 (1973); First Professional Leasing v. Kearney, 129 Ill. App. 2d 101, 262 NE2d 507 (1970); Miles v. Layton, 33 Del. 411, 193 A 567 (1937).

[140] See, e.g., Burton v. Gardner Motors Inc., 117 Cal. App. 3d 426, 172 Cal. Rptr. 647 (1981); State ex rel. State Scholarship Comm. v. Magar, 288 Ore. 635, 607 P2d 167 (1980); Estes v. Estes, 192 Ga. 94, 14 SE2d 681 (1941).

[141] See, e.g., Keystone Fuel Oil Co. v. Del-Way Petroleum, Inc., 364 A2d 826 (Del. 1976); Clark v. Standard Life & Accident Ins. Co., 68 Ill. App. 3d 977, 386 NE2d 890 (1979); Pennsylvania Stave Co.'s Appeal, 225 Pa. 178, 73 A 1107 (1909); Jones v. Baton Rouge Marine Contractors, 127 So. 2d 58 (La. Ct. App. 1961). For discussion of cognovit judgments, see supra ¶ 6.02[5].

[142] See, e.g., People ex rel. Thomas v. Village of Sleepy Hollow, 94 Ill. App. 3d 492, 418 NE2d 466 (1981); Haynes v. Haynes, 45 NC App. 376, 263 SE2d 783 (1980); Nieminen v. Pitzer, 281 Ore. 53, 573 P2d 1227 (1978).

[143] See, e.g., Jones v. World Life Research Inst., 60 Cal. App. 3d 836, 131 Cal. Rptr. 674 (1976); Kam Chin Chun Ming v. Kam Hee Ho, 45 Hawaii 521, 371 P2d 379 (1962).

the law applicable to contracts generally, with the court's authority limited by the consent or stipulation.[144]

One distinction separates the stipulation of judgment from other contracts generally. Some authority indicates that stipulation agreements, even if a binding contract, cannot lead to judgment unless the actual consent to judgment exists at the very moment the court renders judgment; thus, a subsequent withdrawal of consent precludes entry of judgment, although the consent contract may be enforceable in a separate proceeding.[145] Some contrary authority would keep the decision of whether a withdrawal of consent will preclude rendering of judgment within the discretion of the courts.[146]

### [b] Operation and Effect

A judgment by consent of the parties will be given the same effect as a judgment rendered after a trial on the merits of the action.[147] Thus, a judgment by consent is binding and conclusive upon the parties[148] and is res judicata, just as a judgment rendered on the merits[149] and a consent judgment will also raise an estoppel.[150] However, the intention of the parties as indicated by the agreement will be considered.[151] A consent judgment merges the cause of action and bars further action on the cause of action itself.[152]

The appealability of a consent judgment raises some interesting questions. Ordinarily, a consent judgment is not subject to appellate review. That rule is

---

[144] See, e.g., Haller v. Wallis, 89 Wash. 2d 539, 573 P2d 1302 (1978); Cox v. Cox, 43 NC App. 518, 259 SE2d 400, cert. denied, 299 NC 329, 256 SE2d 394 (1979).

[145] See, e.g., Grasso v. Ellis, 608 SW2d 347 (Tex. Civ. App. 1980); Farr v. McKinzie, 477 SW2d 672 (Tex. Civ. App. 1972); Sawyer v. Smith, 552 SW2d 936 (Tex. Civ. App. 1977); Bohlman v. Big River Oil Co., 124 NW2d 835 (ND 1963).

[146] See, e.g., Mubi v. Broomfield, 108 Ariz. 39, 492 P2d 700 (1972); In re Cartnell's Estate, 120 Vt. 234, 138 A2d 592 (1958).

[147] See, e.g., Gunning v. Farm Mut. Auto Ins. Co., 598 SW2d 479 (Mo. App. 1980); McCray v. McCray, 584 SW2d 279 (Tex. 1979); U.S. v. Homestake Mining Co., 595 F2d 421 (8th Cir. 1979); Pollard v. Steffens, 161 Tex. 594, 343 SW2d 234 (1961); Sawyer v. Smith, 552 SW2d 936 (Tex. Civ. App. 1977).

[148] See, e.g., Madison Square Garden Boxing, Inc. v. Shavers, 562 F2d 141 (2d Cir. 1977); Knowlton v. Port Huron, 355 Mich. 448, 94 NW2d 824 (1959); Third Nat'l Bank v. Scribner, 212 Tenn. 400, 370 SW2d 482 (1963).

[149] See, e.g., Quigley v. Braniff Airways, Inc., 487 F. Supp. 393 (ND Tex. 1979); Burlington Data Processing Inc. v. Automated Medical Sys., Inc., 492 F. Supp. 821 (D. Vt. 1980); Agnew v. City Nat'l Bank & Trust Co. of Columbus, 502 F. Supp. 760 (D. Ohio 1979); see also Annot., 2 A.L.R.2d 514 (1948).

[150] See, e.g., Snyder v. Schmoyer, 106 Colo. 290, 104 P2d 612 (1940).

[151] See, e.g., Anderson, Clayton, & Co. v. U.S., 562 F2d 972 (5th Cir.), reh'g denied, 565 F2d 1215, cert. denied, 436 US 944 (1977); Coakley v. Reising, 422 SW2d 502 (Tex. Civ. App. 1967).

[152] See, e.g., Concrete Constructors, Inc. v. Manchester Bank, 117 NH 670, 377 A2d 612 (1977); American Equip. Co. v. Wikomi Mfg. Co., 630 F2d 544 (7th Cir. 1980); Lancaster v. Carelli, 280 Ore. 493, 571 P2d 890 (1977).

subject to some exceptions, such as where the public interest requires a consideration of an appeal, or where the consent judgment affected minors or incompetents. A few courts also allow appeals from inferior courts resulting in trial de novo. If the judgment can be challenged for lack of consent, fraud, collusion, mistake, or jurisdiction, an appeal may be available, although the issue may first have to be raised in the court that initially rendered the consent judgment.[153]

### [c] Obtaining Relief From Consent Judgments

It is considerably more difficult for a debtor to obtain relief from a judgment by consent than it is to obtain relief from a default or cognovit judgment. As a general principle, a judgment rendered by consent cannot be subsequently opened, modified, or vacated; only if fraud, mutual mistake, or absence of consent are present will the consent judgment be attackable, although the parties may subsequently agree to open, vacate, or modify a consent judgment.[154]

## ¶ 6.03 ENFORCEMENT OF THE JUDGMENT–THE IMPORTANCE OF THE JUDICIAL LIEN

Once a valid judgment is obtained or is obtainable, the creditor will seek to coerce satisfaction of the judgment by obtaining a lien in property of the debtor.[1] Without such a lien, the unsecured creditor is limited to the extrajudicial collection techniques discussed previously.[2] A lien is an interest in the debtor's property that gives the creditor the legal power to ultimately satisfy the debt from the assets subject to the lien. A lien may be obtained by a creditor through agreement with the debtor,[3] through statutory fiat,[4] or through judicial process. The remainder of this chapter focuses on methods by which unsecured creditors (i.e., creditors without liens) obtain judicial liens in the assets of the debtor. Opportunities to obtain judicial liens arise both before and after the rendering of the judgment. Liens obtained via such opportunities

---

[153] For a discussion of issues relating to the appealability of a consent judgment, see Annot., 69 A.L.R.2d 755 (1960); Annot., 48 A.L.R. Fed. 663 (1980).

[154] See, e.g., City of Boulder v. Sherrelwood, Inc., 42 Colo. App. 522, 604 P2d 686 (1979); White v. White, 296 NC 661, 252 SE2d 698 (1979). However, for exceptions to the rule, see Annot., 139 A.L.R. 421 (1942).

[1] See ¶¶ 5.01 and 7.01 for further general discussion of the definition of "secured debts" and the importance of securing a debt to the creditor.

[2] See Chapter 5.

[3] For example, a UCC Article 9 security interest in personal property or fixtures, discussed in Chapter 7, or a mortgage in real estate, discussed in Chapter 8.

[4] For example, mechanics' and materialmen's liens. Statutory liens are discussed in Chapter 9.

include liens obtained by attachment,[5] garnishment,[6] judgment,[7] and execution.[8]

The principal effects of obtaining a judicial lien in the debtor's property are twofold. First, the judicial lien provides the creditor with the legal ability to force sale of the property subject to the lien. The proceeds obtained from the sale are then used to satisfy the judgment.

The second effect of obtaining a judicial lien is to provide the lienor with priority over other creditors who may also wish to satisfy claims against the debtor in the same assets. When a debtor defaults on a valid debt, it is often because the debtor lacks sufficient liquid funds with which to pay the creditor. That being the case, it is likely that defaults have occurred on debts that the debtor owes to other creditors. The other creditors also may seek to obtain and assert liens in the assets of the debtor. The assets subject to a single judicial lien might also be sold to a buyer who now wishes to take free of the judicial lien. Finally, the debtor might file bankruptcy, in which case the trustee in bankruptcy will assert claims in the debtor's assets.[9] Whether or not the creditor who has reduced an originally unsecured claim or debt to judgment will succeed in ultimately satisfying the judgment, largely depends on whether the creditor can obtain priority in assets; this, in turn, will rest on the acquisition of a judicial lien. As a general rule of thumb, if the judicial lien is obtained prior to the acquisition of a conflicting interest, the judicial lienor will be accorded priority. Consideration of acquisition of judicial liens and their resulting effects will begin with an analysis of prejudgment methods of obtaining these liens.

## ¶ 6.04 PREJUDGMENT REMEDIES

### [1] Attachment

#### [a] General Nature and Function of Attachment

Attachment involves a judicial process regulated by statute. It results in issuance of a writ of attachment by a court. The court orders a sheriff to levy upon property of a debtor-defendant in order to hold the property for satisfaction of a judgment when obtained by the creditor-plaintiff.[1] The levy functions to create a provisional lien that enables the creditor to obtain liquidation of the

---

[5] For discussion of attachment, see infra ¶ 6.04[1].

[6] For discussion of prejudgment garnishment, see infra ¶ 6.04[2]. For discussion of postjudgment garnishment, see infra ¶ 6.05[4].

[7] For discussion of judgment liens, see infra ¶ 6.05[2].

[8] For discussion of execution, see infra ¶ 6.05[3].

[9] For discussion of the effect of bankruptcy on a judicial lien, see generally Chapter 17.

[1] See, e.g., Hetrick v. Paris Jet, Inc., 64 Cal. App. 3d 158, 134 Cal. Rptr. 285 (1976); Stare v. Friedman, 283 Md. 701, 393 A2d 1356 (1978); I.R.C. Inc. v. Applied Images Inc., 106 Misc. 2d 1034, 431 NYS2d 859 (NY Sup. Ct. 1980).

subject asset upon rendering the judgment.[2] It also provides the creditor with a priority in the assets vis-à-vis other claimants.[3]

Historically, attachment had its origin in the law merchant, in which a debtor's property could be seized prior to judgment for the purpose of forcing the defendant to appear at trial. In the United States, attachment became a part of statutory law compelling the appearance at trial of nonresident defendants. Ultimately, it evolved into a device by which the creditor prior to judgment could secure property from which a future creditor-plaintiff's judgment could be paid.[4]

At the outset, some basic characteristics of attachment should be emphasized.[5] First, the process of attachment is purely a prejudgment judicial remedy that is statutory in nature. Second, because it is a particularly harsh remedy, it is considered extraordinary in nature and the courts will require that specified statutory procedures be carefully followed. Finally, attachment is a provisional remedy—the lien created under it will continue only if judgment is obtained by the creditor-plaintiff; if judgment is rendered for the debtor-defendant, the attachment and lien obtained thereunder become ineffective.

It is helpful initially to distinguish attachment from other forms of judicial collection remedies. Although prejudgment garnishment is similar to attachment, and in some states is treated as a type of attachment, garnishment typically refers to the writ necessitated to reach property of the debtor in the possession of third parties, while attachment reaches property in the possession of the debtor only.[6] The equitable remedy of sequestration is very similar to attachment, although sequestration available in some jurisdictions does not create a lien in property of the debtor and is issued upon different grounds.[7] However, sequestration and attachment are so similar otherwise that some jurisdictions have held the separate bodies of law to apply to both.[8] Attachment also differs from execution[9] and postjudgment garnishment[10] in that both are postjudgment remedies, the latter being limited to reaching property of the debtor in the hands of third parties. Finally, both replevin and receivership are distinguished from attachment and are discussed later in this chapter.[11]

---

[2] See infra ¶¶ 6.04[1][b]–6.04[1][e] and 6.04[1][g] for discussion of the process of attachment and resulting levy.

[3] See infra ¶ 6.04[1][f] for discussion of the creation and priority of an attachment lien.

[4] See 7 Debtor-Creditor Law ¶ 28.01[B][3] (Matthew Bender 1982) for a discussion of the historical origins of attachment.

[5] See 7 Debtor-Creditor Law ¶ 28.01[B][2] (Matthew Bender 1982) for a discussion of the basic characteristics of attachment.

[6] Prejudgment garnishment is discussed at length at infra ¶ 6.04[2].

[7] See, e.g., Jackson v. The Praetorians, 80 SW2d 322 (Tex. Civ. App. 1935).

[8] See, e.g., Chapman v. Chapman, 72 Misc. 2d 436, 339 NYS2d 404 (NY Fam. Ct. 1972).

[9] Execution is discussed at infra ¶ 6.05[3].

[10] Postjudgment garnishment is discussed at infra ¶ 6.05[4].

[11] As to replevin, see infra ¶ 6.04[3]. As to receivership, see infra ¶ 6.04[4].

### [b] Basic Procedure

The authority of a court to issue the writ of attachment[12] rests on statutory provisions.[13] However, assuming this authority exists, one should first be familiar with the basic attachment procedure as it typically exists in most states.[14] The writ of attachment traditionally is issuable under statute by a judge or clerk of the court.[15] The substance of the writ issued includes an order requiring the sheriff to levy upon property of the defendant. The property owned by the debtor must be present within the territorial limits of the court's jurisdiction.[16]

The statutes typically require the plaintiff-creditor (or an agent of the plaintiff-creditor) seeking issuance of attachment to submit a motion and supportive affidavit. The affidavit must establish the plaintiff-creditor's right to attachment, the writ of attachment issuing without the procedural benefits of prior notice and prior hearing being given the defendant. If such ex parte issuance of the writ of attachment is allowed, most statutes provide the debtor with a right to an immediate postseizure hearing.[17] Due to a number of well-known U.S. Supreme Court decisions declaring such procedures to be in violation of the debtor's right to due process of law, prior notice and hearing is most often required by statute or case law.[18] Nevertheless, even if prior notice and prior hearing is required, the affidavit must be made and submitted by the plaintiff or an agent of the plaintiff.[19] It seems advisable for the creditor's attorney not to execute the affidavit, since he seldom has direct knowledge of the essential facts. Rather, it is usually advisable to have the creditor sign the affidavit. Obviously, the required content of the motion and affidavit will be dictated by the applicable attachment statute. As a basic principle, the allegations contained in the motion and affidavit should be specific and factual in nature, as opposed to general conclusions that may not be sufficient to satisfy a court that the extraordinary writ should be issued.

---

[12] For discussion of basic attachment procedure, see Zaretsky, "Attachment Without Seizure: A Proposal for a New Creditor's Remedy," 1978 U. Ill. L.F. 819; Hagedorn, "Prejudgment Attachment in Washington–A Need for Legislative Action," 16 Gonz. L. Rev. 287 (1981); 7 Debtor-Creditor Law ¶ 28.02 (Matthew Bender 1982).

[13] The actions in which attachment is available, the grounds upon which it can issue, and the property that may be subject to attachment are not discussed in this section. For such discussion, see infra ¶¶ 6.04[1][c]–6.04[1][e].

[14] For a discussion of federal attachment and prejudgment garnishment procedure, see infra ¶ 6.04[1][g].

[15] See generally 7 C.J.S. Attachment § 64 (1980).

[16] See, e.g., Land Mfg., Inc. v. Highland Park State Bank, 205 Kan. 526, 470 P2d 782 (1970). For discussion of property subject to attachment, see infra ¶ 6.04[1][e].

[17] Indeed, in general, a defendant may contest a writ of attachment by moving against it at any time before final judgment. See discussion infra within this section.

[18] For a discussion of the debtor's constitutional right to due process, see ¶ 6.04[5][a].

[19] See, e.g., Hitchens, Inc. v. Phillips Packing Co., 42 Del. 393, 35 A2d 502 (1943); Butter v. Nail, 36 SW2d 307 (Tex. Civ. App. 1931).

Assuming prior notice and opportunity for hearing will be given the defendant, creditors are often concerned that the debtor-defendant will dispose of or damage the property that the creditor is seeking to attach between notice and levy under the writ of attachment. In some states, the creditors may seek a temporary restraining order.[20] However, it would seem that even the issuance of such a temporary order will be deemed an extraordinary remedy and will be viewed skeptically by the courts. Thus, the creditor should prepare the motion and affidavit, seeking issuance of the writ of attachment with a view toward possible ex parte issuance of a temporary restraining order by including within the motion and affidavit a specific factual showing of necessity for such relief (e.g., the debtor has already disposed of or has destroyed property).

In addition to the procedural requirement of motion, affidavit, and prior notice and hearing given the debtor-defendant, the creditor may also be required to post a bond. The surety bond is designed to protect the defendant from damages resulting from a wrongful attachment and is payable to the defendant.[21] The amount of the bond is usually fixed based upon the amount of the underlying claim of the creditor.[22] If the bond is not obtained, the attachment is void.[23]

The issuance of the writ directs the sheriff or similar court officer to levy upon as much of the defendant's property as is necessary to satisfy the writ. The levy may occur by actual seizure of personal property of the defendant or by filing of appropriate notice as to real estate.[24] The effect of the levy principally is twofold. First, the levy creates the judicial lien. Second, the sheriff's duty after levy is to safeguard the property until a final judgment is entered for the plaintiff against the defendant. The sheriff is directed by statute to levy within a specified time period, after which the writ is ineffective.[25] After levy, the sheriff must make a return to the issuing court (and sometimes the creditor) indicating whether levy occurred, and if so, upon what property of the debtor.[26] In some states, the sheriff may require the plaintiff to provide a bond to indemnify the sheriff from the liability he may incur as a result of the attachment.[27]

If the levy has occurred pursuant to an issued writ of attachment, it is still possible for the debtor to obtain relief from the attachment. First, the debtor may obtain release of the property in most jurisdictions by posting a bond.[28] Such bonds typically take one or two forms. A forthcoming or delivery bond is

---

[20] See, e.g., Cal. Civ. Proc. Code § 486.010; N.Y. Civ. Prac. Law § 6210.

[21] See, e.g., Fla. Stat. Ann. § 76.12; Tex Civ. Proc. Rules Ann. R. 279, 592.

[22] In Florida, the amount must be at least double the debt and in Texas the amount is fixed by the judge or justice of the peace issuing the attachment. Id.

[23] See, e.g., Ill. Ann. Stat. ch. 11, § 4a; see also Zaretsky, "Attachment Without Seizure: A Proposal for a New Creditor's Remedy," 1978 U. Ill. L.F. 819.

[24] See infra ¶ 6.04[1][f] for discussion of methods of levy and the resulting lien.

[25] See, e.g., Cal. Civ. Proc. Code § 488.070.

[26] See, e.g., Fla. Stat. Ann. § 76.251; 211 So. 2d 206.

[27] See, e.g., Tex. Rev. Civ. Stat. Ann. art. 287.

[28] See Epstein & Landers, Debtors and Creditors 7–8 (West, 2d ed. 1982).

conditioned so that if judgment is obtained by the creditor, the attached property will be forthcoming to satisfy the judgment; if the property is not forthcoming, the surety will be liable to the extent of the value of the property. The attachment lien, however, is retained on the property. A discharging or dissolution bond is conditioned so that the debtor will perform whatever judgment is taken by the creditor. The bond not only obtains release of the property from the possession of the sheriff, but it also releases the property from the attachment lien. The use of bonding has been criticized as a very ineffective form of debtor relief in that creditor's prayers for judgment often are exaggerated and debtors often cannot afford the premium for the bond.[29] Finally, as to release bonds, although there is a division of authority, some courts have held that defects or irregularities in an attachment are waived by the filing of a release bond.[30]

In addition to posting a release bond, the debtor's other means of obtaining relief from an attachment is by challenging the writ of attachment by motion to dissolve, quash, or vacate.[31] Typical grounds for motions include "(1) the fact that the case is not one in which attachment may properly issue; (2) the failure of the complaint, tested by pleading rules, to state any cause of action; (3) defects in the undertaking or affidavit; or (4) issuance of the writ for an amount greater than that stated in the affidavit. Improper levy on the writ–e.g., attaching legally exempt property–may be challenged by a motion to quash or vacate the levy."[32]

### [c] Actions in Which Attachment Is Available

It has been emphasized that attachment is a statutory remedy. The types of actions in which attachment is available, as specified by statute, vary depending upon the particular jurisdiction.[33] However, some useful generalizations that are applicable to most jurisdictions can be made.

To begin, regardless of the type of action in which attachment may issue as specified by statute, the creditor's complaint must state a legally sufficient cause of action in order to support an attachment of the debtor's property,[34]

---

[29] See, Alexander, "Wrongful Attachment Damages Must Be Fixed in the Original Suit," 4 U.S.F.L. Rev. 38, 39–40 (1969).

[30] See Annot., 72 A.L.R. 120, 127 (1931).

[31] See, e.g., Fla. Stat. Ann. § 76.24; N.Y. Civ. Prac. Law § 6223; Tex. Civ. Proc. Rules Ann. R. 608; see also Epstein & Landers, Debtors and Creditors 7 (West, 2d ed. 1982).

[32] Burke v. Superior Court of Sacramento County, 71 Cal. 2d 276, 279, 455 P2d 409, 414, 78 Cal. Rptr. 481, 486 (1969).

[33] For additional discussion of actions in which attachment may issue, see 7 Debtor-Creditor Law ¶ 28.12 (Matthew Bender 1982).

[34] See, e.g., Granmo v. Superior Court ex rel. Pima County, 122 Ariz. 510, 596 P2d 36 (Ariz. Ct. App. 1979); Muth v. Educators Sec. Ins. Co., 114 Cal. App. 3d 749, 170 Cal. Rptr. 849 (1981).

and the court must have subject matter jurisdiction to hear the case.[35] Many statutes also require that the creditor establish the likely success of the creditor's action.[36] The creditor will establish this initially through use of affidavit in support of the motion for attachment, coupled with the showing of fact at the time of hearing, if the hearing occurs. Concerning matters of evidence, the creditor should attempt to make specific factual showings, as opposed to asserting a right to attachment on the basis of mere conclusion.[37]

The use of attachment is designed to secure payment of a money judgment. Therefore, many states require that the action seek a money judgment.[38] If the plaintiff seeks recovery of money damages and some other form of relief, statutory law varies as to the availability of attachment.[39] In addition to seeking a money judgment, the action must often be based on a contract, express or implied;[40] indeed, some statutes require the contract to be for the *direct* payment of the money, thereby distinguishing such contracts from guarantee contracts.[41] From a policy standpoint, limiting use of attachment to actions on contracts seeking money judgments serves to lessen the harshness of attachment by requiring the plaintiff's claims to be asserted in a specific measurable amount from which the amount of property needed to be levied upon may be ascertained. In that vein, the money judgment sought in some states must be based upon a liquidated claim, such that the amount of the claim is ascertainable.[42] A liquidated claim has been defined as one that is fixed as to amount, has been agreed upon, or is capable of ascertainment by mathematical computation or operation of law.[43]

Some attachment statutes preclude the issuance of attachment if the underlying claim is secured because to allow attachment might result in the

---

[35] See, e.g., Schreiber v. Republic Intermodal Corp., 473 Pa. 614, 375 A2d 1285 (1977); Benefield v. Radiator Specialty Co., 116 Ga. App. 588, 158 SE2d 423 (1967).

[36] See, e.g., Cal. Civ. Proc. Code § 484.030; N.Y. Civ. Prac. Law § 6212(a); Board of Educ. of City of N.Y. v. Treyball, 86 AD2d 639, 446 NYS2d 417 (1981).

[37] See, e.g., Bowman v. Dussault, 425 A2d 1325 (Me. 1981).

[38] See, e.g., Great Am. Ins. Co. v. National Health Servs., Inc., 62 Cal. App. 3d 785, 133 Cal. Rptr. 420 (1976); Cal. Civ. Proc. Code § 483.010(a); N.Y. Civ. Prac. Law § 6201; Atlas Garage & Custom Builders, Inc. v. Hurley, 197 Conn. 248, 355 A2d 286 (1974).

[39] See, e.g., Humiston v. Bishop, 29 Conn. Supp. 324, 286 A2d 323 (1971); Samuels v. Superior Court, 276 Cal. App. 2d 264, 81 Cal. Rptr. 216 (1969).

[40] See, e.g., Bank of Ephraim v. Davis, 581 P2d 1001 (Utah 1978); Askew v. Resource Funding Ltd., 94 Cal. App. 3d 402, 156 Cal. Rptr. 208 (1979); Vazquez v. Center Art Gallery, 485 F. Supp. 1015 (D. Hawaii 1980); Cal. Civ. Proc. Code § 483.010; Hawaii Rev. Stat. § 651-2.

[41] See, e.g., Mont. Code Ann. § 27-18-101; Stenwad v. Miners & Merchants Bank of Roundup, 598 P2d 1083 (Mont. 1979); Eaton v. Queen, 78 Cal. App. 2d 571, 177 P2d 997 (1947).

[42] See, e.g., Cal. Civ. Proc. Code § 483.010(a). But see Ill. Ann. Stat. ch. 11, § 1.

[43] See, e.g., V.L. Nicholson Co. v. Transcon Inv. & Fin. Ltd., Inc., 595 SW2d 474 (Tenn. 1980); Robinson v. Loyola Found. Inc., 236 So. 2d 154 (Fla. Dist. Ct. App. 1970).

secured creditor tying up more property than is needed to satisfy the debt.[44] However, such statutes often make an exception if the collateral has become insufficient in value to secure the entire debt.[45] Finally, as to secured claims, other attachment statutes might require the creditor to first exhaust the collateral before turning to other property of the debtor by use of attachment. This is usually done by so-called single-action statutes, which provide that there can be only one action for recovery of any secured debt and that the collateral must be exhausted before turning to other property.[46]

### [d] Grounds for Attachment

State statutes also specify the grounds on which attachment may issue. The burden of proof of the existence of the statutory grounds for attachment is on the creditor-plaintiff;[47] however, if the creditor establishes a prima facie case, the burden of proof shifts to the debtor-defendant.[48] The grounds upon which attachment may issue vary from state to state. A review of legislation nationally does reflect some uniformity.[49] The study of these uniform grounds for issuance illustrates further the rather extraordinary nature of the attachment remedy. In summary, the grounds for issuance common to most states include that the debtor-defendant has absconded or is concealing his location, or that the plaintiff is otherwise unable to serve process on him; that the debtor-defendant is a nonresident; or that the debtor-defendant has fraudulently transferred, removed, or concealed property, or is about to do so. Additionally, there are other less notable miscellaneous grounds for issuance of attachment that frequently are provided for by statute. All these various grounds are discussed next in this section of the text.

Traditionally, the issuance of attachment was thought justified by state legislatures where it could be shown that the defendant either had departed the state or was concealing his location within the state.[50] Since personal service could not be had, the use of prejudgment attachment was seen as an essential jurisdictional tool resulting in the obtaining of quasi in rem jurisdiction over the debtor's property. However, the modern development of long-arm jurisdiction statutes has greatly reduced the necessity of using attachment in these situ-

---

[44] See, e.g., Cal. Civ. Proc. Code § 483.010(b); Jue v. Bass, 299 F2d 374 (9th Cir. 1962).

[45] Cal. Civ. Proc. Code § 483.010(b).

[46] See, e.g., Nev. Rev. Stat. § 40.430; Utah Code Ann. § 78-37-1.

[47] See, e.g., Ice Projects, Inc. v. World Hockey Ass'n, 443 F. Supp. 483 (ED Pa. 1977); Kesslor v. Dugar, 144 So. 2d 733 (La. Ct. App. 1962).

[48] See, e.g., American Jerex Co. v. Universal Aluminum Extrusions, Inc., 340 F. Supp. 524 (EDNY 1972); George A. Fuller Co. v. Vitro Corp. of Am., 26 AD2d 916, 274 NYS2d 600 (1966); Hoffman v. Martin, 226 Ky. 137, 10 SW2d 636 (1928).

[49] For discussion of grounds of attachment, see 7 Debtor-Creditor Law ¶ 28.13 (Matthew Bender 1982).

[50] See, e.g., Fla. Stat. Ann. §§ 76.04(5)–76.04(8), 76.04(11), 76.04(12); Ill. Ann. Stat. ch. 11, § 1; Tex. Rev. Civ. Stat. Ann art. 275(3).

ations. This ground for attachment remains viable where it can be shown that the debtor has permanently left the state and that the long-arm statute is of no assistance to the creditor. The intent to permanently abscond or conceal oneself usually must also be established.[51] A similar ground for the issuance of attachment found in many attachment statutes is that the defendant is simply a nonresident,[52] or that the plaintiff is otherwise unable to serve process on the debtor and thereby to obtain personal jurisdiction without regard to the debtor's intent to conceal.[53] Again, the principal function of attachment on these grounds is to assert quasi in rem jurisdiction over the debtor's property. The use of the writ of attachment for that purpose has been greatly restricted by the U.S. Supreme Court. Because of long-arm statutes and judicial restrictions on the assertion of quasi in rem jurisdiction by the use of attachment of the debtor's property, these grounds for attachment are currently of limited importance.[54]

By contrast, if the creditor can establish that the defendant has or is about to transfer, remove from the state, or otherwise secrete property with the intent to defraud creditors, a useful ground for attachment provided by statute is present.[55] This ground for attachment assists in protecting creditors from fraudulent dissipation of assets from which the attaching creditor might satisfy the judgment when and if obtained. It also reflects the appropriate use of attachment as an extraordinary remedy. The statute usually will require proof that the disposition of the property that is occurring, or will occur, is fraudulent.[56] Actual intent to defraud creditors may have to be established through use of circumstantial evidence.

Other grounds for attachment that can be found in attachment statutes occasionally include that the underlying claim on which the cause of action is based arose from fraudulent conduct of the debtor.[57] Apparently the justification for this ground of attachment is that the debtor is not to be trusted. Similarly, if the creditor's claim arose from a criminal act of the defendant, some

---

[51] See, e.g., International State Bank v. Gamer, 281 NW2d 855 (Minn. 1979); Shelton v. Kindred, 279 So. 2d 642 (Miss. 1973).

[52] See, e.g., Cal. Civ. Proc. Code § 492.010(a); Ill. Ann. Stat. ch. 11, § 1; N.Y. Civ. Proc. Law § 6201.1.

[53] See, e.g., Ill. Ann. Stat. ch. 11, § 1; N.J. Stat. Ann. § 2A:26-2.b.

[54] See supra ¶ 6.02[2][b] for discussion of jurisdiction.

[55] See, e.g., Fla. Stat. Ann. §§ 76.04(1)–76.04(3), 76.04(9), 76.04(10), 76.05, 76.07; N.Y. Civ. Prac. Law § 6201.3; Tex. Rev. Civ. Stat. Ann. art. 275(5)–275(11). For discussion of fraudulent conveyances generally, see infra ¶ 6.07[2]. For discussion of fraudulent conveyances in bankruptcy, see ¶ 17.05.

[56] See, e.g., Ice Projects, Inc. v. World Hockey Ass'n, 443 F. Supp. 483 (ED Pa. 1977); Kazakos v. Soteres, 120 Ga. App. 258, 170 SE2d 50 (1959).

[57] See, e.g., Reeder v. Mastercraft Elecs. Corp., 297 F. Supp. 815, 820 (SDNY 1969); American European Export Co. v. John E. Safran Co., 68 NYS2d 174 (NY Sup. Ct. 1947); Davis v. Shemper, 49 So. 2d 253 (Miss. 1950).

statutes provide for issuance of the writ.[58] Other miscellaneous common grounds for attachment seem to make the use of attachment less extraordinary, if these grounds alone are held sufficient to support issuance of the writ; however, from a practical standpoint, it is unlikely that a court on these sole grounds would issue the writ. Such grounds include that there is insufficient property within the state to satisfy the creditors' claims;[59] or that the claim is not otherwise secured;[60] or simply that the debtor fails or refuses to pay the debt based upon a contract, express or implied.[61]

### [e] Property Subject to Attachment

The initial principle is that all property in which the debtor has an interest is subject to attachment.[62] Nowadays, the writ of attachment reaches equitable, as well as legal, interests of the debtor in property.[63] If the debtor transfers an interest in property that he held, and the transfer is not a "fraudulent conveyance,"[64] the property transferred is not attachable, since attachment of property not belonging to the debtor is ineffective.[65] The principle that all property of the debtor is attachable is subject to various limitations and refinements. For example, if property (tangible or intangible) in which the debtor has an interest is possessed by a third party, use of the writ of garnishment may be necessitated.[66] Otherwise, the basic principle remains that all property of the debtor is subject to attachment.[67]

The basic principle encompasses virtually all forms of personalty and realty in which the debtor has an interest. The levy by the sheriff in the case of

---

[58] See, e.g., Montanari v. Haworth, 180 Ohio St. 8, 140 NE 319 (1923); Brandenstein v. Way, 17 Wash. 293, 49 P 511 (1897).

[59] See, e.g., Paramount Ins., Inc. v. Rayson & Smitley, 86 Nev. 644, 472 P2d 530 (Nev. 1970); Walker v. Grayson County State Bank, 237 Ky. 449, 35 SW2d 850 (1931).

[60] See, e.g., International State Bank v. Gamer, 281 NW2d 855 (Minn. 1979); Jue v. Bass, 299 F2d 374 (9th Cir. 1962); Paramount Ins., Inc. v. Rayson & Smitley, 86 Nev. 644, 472 P2d 530 (1970).

[61] See, e.g., Landry v. Marshall, 243 Cal. App. 2d 170, 52 Cal. Rptr. 119 (1966); S.E. Martin & Son v. Jesse L. Hedden Co., 106 Me. 498, 76 A 935 (1910).

[62] See 7 Debtor-Creditor Law ¶ 28.14 (Matthew Bender 1982) for a discussion of the principles and matters related to the types of property subject to attachment.

[63] Riesenfeld, Creditor's Remedies and Debtors' Protection 283–284 (West, 3d ed. 1979).

[64] See infra ¶ 6.07[2] for a discussion of fraudulent conveyances.

[65] See, e.g., U.R.C. Inc. v. Applied Images, Inc., 106 Misc. 2d 1034, 431 NYS2d 859 (1980); E-Systems, Inc. v. Islamic Republic of Iran, 491 F. Supp. 1294 (ND Tex. 1980); A.C.A. Am. Masters, Inc. v. Wertz, 45 AD2d 838, 358 NYS2d 445 (1974).

[66] For discussion of the difference between attachment and garnishment, see supra ¶ 6.04[1][a].

[67] For discussions of other matters also affecting the choice of assets subject to attachment, see infra ¶¶ 6.07[1], 6.07[2], 6.07[5]. See also infra ¶ 6.05[3][d], which considers the related matter of property subject to execution. Both ¶ 6.05[3][d] and this section, related to property subject to attachment, should be considered by the reader.

personalty will normally be by actual seizure of the property; the levy in the case of realty will normally occur by the filing of notices in court or in real estate records.[68] As to examples of personalty, a creditor's "shopping list" for attachable property for which there is some authority for attachment includes fixtures,[69] memberships in organizations,[70] commingled goods;[71] money,[72] alimony (when received),[73] crops,[74] goods in transit,[75] corporate stock,[76] and interests of heirs and devisees.[77] In order to describe the property interests subject to attachment that most commonly raise legal difficulties, a specific discussion of these interests is required.

Contingent interests that a debtor has in property or contracts may not be subject to attachment. The interest is "contingent" if the debtor's right to the property may never vest, because the right depends on the occurrence of a future uncertain event. In such a case, there is authority that the interest is not attachable because it is too remote–a mere expectancy of an interest in property.[78] On the other hand, attachment of a debt or account receivable (assuming garnishment is not necessitated) will lie for the creditor as long as the existence of the debt does not depend on a contingency.[79] Once a contingent interest is vested, the interest is attachable.[80]

The attachment of investment securities[81] has provided state legislatures with a peculiar problem: If allowed at all, should attachment occur by service

---

[68] See infra ¶ 6.04[1][f] for a discussion of methods of levy on personalty and realty under a writ of attachment.

[69] See, e.g., Morey v. Hoyt, 62 Conn. 542, 26 A 127 (1893).

[70] See, e.g., Wagner v. Farmer's Coop. Exch. Co. of Good Thunder, 147 Minn. 376, 180 NW 231 (1920).

[71] See, e.g., Kelly-Goodfellow Shoe Co. v. Sally, 114 Mo. App. 222, 89 SW 889 (1905).

[72] See, e.g., U.R.C. Inc. v. Applied Images, Inc., 106 Misc. 2d 1034, 431 NYS2d 859 (NY Sup. Ct. 1980).

[73] See, e.g., Ex parte Dunaway, 174 Misc. 735, 22 NYS2d 69 (Jefferson Co. Ct. 1940); Zander v. Bright, 142 Kan. 833, 52 P2d 368 (1935).

[74] See, e.g., Lofton v. Mooney, 652 SW2d 617 (Ky. 1970); Johnston v. Cunningham, 12 Cal. App. 3d 123, 90 Cal. Rptr. 487 (1970).

[75] See, e.g., Sante Fe Pac. R.R. v. Bossut, 10 NM 322, 62 P 977 (1900).

[76] See, e.g., In re Southwest Restaurant Sys., Inc., 607 F2d 1243 (9th Cir.), cert. denied, Stockton & Hing v. Evans, 444 US 1081 (1979).

[77] See, e.g., Harry Winston Inc. v. Adreson, 144 NYS2d 972 (NY Sup. Ct. 1958).

[78] See, e.g., E-Systems, Inc. v. Islamic Republic of Iran, 491 F. Supp. 1294 (ND Tex. 1980).

[79] See, e.g., Bata Shoe Co. v. Silvestre Segarra E. Hijos, S.A., 58 AD2d 133, 396 NYS2d 369 (1977).

[80] See, e.g., Everson v. Everson, 264 Pa. Super. 563, 400 A2d 887 (1979), aff'd, 431 A2d 889 (Pa. 1981).

[81] See generally Kennedy, "The Rights of Levying Creditors Against Negotiable Property Under the Uniform Commercial Code," 31 Bus. Law. 1517 (1976); Austin & Nelson, "Attaching and Levying on Corporate Shares," 16 Bus. Law. 336 (1961).

of a stop-transfer notice on the corporate transfer agent, or should it occur by seizure of the stock certificate? Under common law, investment securities were not subject to attachment.[82] However, states ultimately enacted legislation providing for levy by serving the corporate home office.[83] In 1909, the Uniform Stock Transfer Act, as enacted by most states, provided in Sections 13 and 14 for levy either by seizure of the stock or by an injunction against its negotiation, unless the stock was previously surrendered to the issuing corporation. Today, Section 8-317 of the Uniform Commercial Code (UCC) regulates attachment of securities in most states. This section requires actual seizure of the stock certificate.[84] This action appears desirable, in that stock can be negotiable; by seizing the stock, it can no longer pass into the hands of a bona fide purchaser. It should be noted that Delaware has not adopted Section 8-317 of the UCC. Thus, stock in a Delaware corporation may be levied upon without seizure of the stock by giving notice to the issuer of the stock.[85]

The attachment of negotiable instruments creates problems of a nature similar to attachment of investment securities. For example, if the debtor holds a negotiable promissory note, does the attaching creditor instruct the sheriff to seize the note or must the debt evidenced by the note be garnished by service of notice of garnishment on the maker of the note? Curiously, the UCC, which regulates negotiable instruments generally in Article 3, does not answer this question. It would seem however, that seizure of the instrument must occur due to the negotiable character of the property.[86]

Property in which the debtor has an interest may become subject to liens of other creditors. The debtor's remaining interest in the property is still attachable. Perhaps the best example of this principle involves UCC Article 9, security interests. If the debtor's property is subject to a UCC Article 9 security interest, the property is still attachable. Section 9-311 of the UCC makes it clear that the debtor has an interest in the collateral, which may be subjected to levy.[87] However, since the attaching creditor's interest will be later in time, the lien created by the attachment will probably be subordinate to the existing lien of the other creditor.[88]

---

[82] See, e.g., Denton v. Livingston, 9 Johns. 96, 99 (NY Sup. Ct. 1812).

[83] See Kennedy, "The Rights of Levying Creditors Against Negotiable Property Under the Uniform Commercial Code," 31 Bus. Law. 1522 (1976).

[84] Note that levy upon a document of title also must occur under the UCC by actual seizure of the document. See UCC § 7-602; Manufacturers' Mercantile Co. v. Monarch Refrigeration Co., 266 Ill. 584, 107 NE 885 (1915).

[85] See, e.g., Baker v. Gotz, 387 F. Supp. 1381 (D. Del.), aff'd, 523 F2d 1050 (3d Cir. 1975); Brainard v. Canaday, 49 Del. 182, 112 A2d 862 (1955).

[86] See 7 Debtor-Creditor Law ¶ 28.14[A][4] (Matthew Bender 1982); Kennedy, "The Rights of Levying Creditors Against Negotiable Property Under the Uniform Commercial Code," 31 Bus. Law. 1517 (1976).

[87] UCC § 9-311 provides: "The debtor's right in collateral may be voluntarily or involuntarily transferred (by way of sale, creation of a security interest, attachment, levy, garnishment or other judicial process) notwithstanding a provision in the security agreement prohibiting any transfer or making the transfer constitute a default."

[88] Cf. UCC § 9-301.

Occasionally, the debtor may have an interest in a trust or may hold an interest of an heir or legatee in an estate of a deceased. As to interests of the debtor in trusts, it is clear that the creditor may not attach the debtor's interest as a trustee.[89] On the other hand, as a general principle, the creditor may levy upon the interests of the debtor in a trust as a beneficiary.[90] Such a beneficiary's interest may be levied provided the interest is assignable, releaseable, or alienable.[91] The beneficiary's interest may not be reached if it is a spendthrift trust. In a spendthrift trust, the trustor creates the trust so that the benefit of the trust will be free of the reach of the beneficiary's creditors; this intent will be enforced by the courts.[92] However, once trust property or income is received from the spendthrift trust by the beneficiary, creditors may attach the property received.[93] As to interests of heirs and legatees in an estate, such interests are subject to attachment.[94] However, as a general rule, interests in the estate must be vested before attachment can occur, such as when there has been a decree of distribution from the estate.[95]

A final problem area is raised when the debtor assigns his property for the benefit of creditors.[96] When this occurs, the property is said to be in custodia legis (i.e., in the custody of the law). Creditor's bills[97] and receiverships[98] may also have the same effect. As a basic principle, the property that is in custodia legis is not subject to attachment.[99] Therefore, creditors will have to await release of the property after its purpose to the court has been fulfilled.

---

[89] Cf. Helmsley-Spear, Inc. v. Winter, 47 AD2d 195, 426 NYS2d 778 (1980).

[90] See, e.g., Everson v. Everson, 264 Pa. Super. 563, 400 A2d 887 (1979); Lawrence's Estate v. Lawrence, 267 Cal. App. 2d 77, 72 Cal. Rptr. 851 (1968).

[91] See, e.g., Judis v. Martin, 218 AD 402, 218 NYS2d 423 (1926), motion granted, 244 NY 605, 155 NE 916 (1927).

[92] See, e.g., Pray v. Boissevain, 27 Misc. 2d 703, 212 NYS2d 432 (NY Sup. Ct. 1963); Lowe v. Jones, 414 Pa. 466, 200 A2d 880 (1964); Sproul-Bolton v. Sproul-Bolton, 383 Pa. 85, 117 A2d 688 (1955).

[93] See, e.g., Pray v. Boissevain, 27 Misc. 2d 703, 212 NYS2d 432 (NY Sup. Ct. 1963).

[94] See, e.g., In re Lawrence's Estate, 267 Cal. App. 2d 77, 72 Cal. Rptr. 851 (1968); Fount-Wip, Inc. v. Golstein, 29 Cal. 3d 751, 105 Cal. Rptr. 780 (1972).

[95] See, e.g., In re Silverman's Estate, 249 Cal. App. 2d 180, 57 Cal. Rptr. 379 (1967); Meadows v. Russell, 203 SW2d 647 (Tex. Civ. App. 1947); In re Brennan's Estate, 433 P2d 512 (Wyo. 1967).

[96] For a discussion of assignment for the benefit of creditors, see 6 Am. Jur. 2d § 321 (1963); 6A C.J.S. § 806 (1975).

[97] See infra ¶ 6.05[5] for discussion of creditor's bills.

[98] See infra ¶ 6.04[4] for discussion of receiverships.

[99] See, e.g., Meadows v. Holiday, 264 SE2d 461 (W. Va. 1980); Ice Projects, Inc. v. World Hockey Ass'n, 443 F. Supp. 483 (ED Pa. 1977); Gende v. Fleming, 55 Ill. App. 3d 659, 371 NE2d 191 (1977).

### [f] The Creation, Nature, and Effect of an Attachment Lien

It has been previously emphasized that use of the writ of attachment can produce a lien in the debtor's property and a resulting priority in the subject asset over other parties asserting claims in it. Assuming a writ of attachment is validly issued,[100] as previously indicated, the sheriff is ordered to "levy" upon the debtor's assets. Because attachment statutes provide that the levy creates the attachment lien,[101] discussion of how levy occurs is presented in the following paragraphs.

Levy under writs of attachment occurs differently depending upon whether the property is personal or real property. Levy by the sheriff on personalty requires the sheriff to assume dominion over the property, that is, the sheriff must actually seize the property or take other necessary action in order to establish his physical control over it.[102] Thus, the sheriff's possession or control of the property should enable him to know if other parties are asserting an interest in the property subsequent to levy. The sheriff then can notify the subsequent claimant that attachment has already occurred. More importantly, the sheriff's levy also makes it physically apparent to subsequent claimants that the levy has occurred. As a result, a form of public notice is present.

Actual seizure of real property is a physical impossibility. Additionally, third parties place great emphasis on public records to evidence the state of title in the case of real estate. Recognizing this, a levy of attachment on real estate will statutorily occur by notice and recording, as opposed to seizure in a physical sense.[103] Thus, the statutes may require posting of a notice on the real estate,[104] or a filing in a designated public record of a copy of the writ of attachment, certificate of attachment, or the like, combined with a description of the property.[105]

---

[100] See supra ¶ 6.04[1][b] for discussion of basic attachment procedure. For similar discussion regarding creation of liens pursuant to the writ of execution, see infra ¶ 6.05[3][e].

[101] See, e.g., Fla. Stat. Ann. § 76.14; Ill. Ann. Stat. ch. 11, §§ 8, 9; Tex. Rev. Civ. Stat. Ann. art. 300; see also Wright v. Standard Eng'g Corp., 28 Cal. App. 3d 244, 104 Cal. Rptr. 539 (1972); Williams, "Creditors' Prejudgment Remedies: Expanding Strictures on Traditional Rights, 25 U. Fla. L. Rev. 60 (1972); Gulf Oil, U.S. v. First Nat'l Bank of Hereford, 503 SW2d 300 (Tex. Civ. App. 1973); Amoco Overseas Oil Co. v. Compagnie Nationale Algerienne de Navigation ("C.N.A.N."), 605 F2d 648 (SDNY 1978).

[102] See, e.g., U.S. v. Southern Growth Indus., Inc., 251 SC 404, 162 SE2d 849 (1968); State ex rel. Mather v. Carnes, 551 SW2d 272 (Mo. Ct. App. 1977). If the property is bulky or cumbersome and actual seizure would be impractical, levy does not require actual seizure. See, e.g., Brunswick Corp. v. Haerter, 182 NW2d 852 (ND 1971).

[103] See, e.g., In re Maier Brewing Co., 65 F2d 673 (9th Cir. 1933), cert. denied, Wells v. Simons, 290 US 695 (1934).

[104] See, e.g., Jock Dev. Inc. v. Howard Eales, Inc., 388 A2d 466 (DC 1978); cf. San Leandro Collection Serv. v. Dunbar, 259 Cal. App. 2d Supp. 933, 66 Cal. Rptr. 495 (Cal. App. Dep't Super. 1968); Phillips v. Loberg, 607 P2d 561 (Mont. 1980).

[105] See, e.g., Jack Dev. Inc. v. Howard Eales, Inc., 388 A2d 466 (DC App. 1978); First Auburn Trust Co. v. Buck, 137 Me. 172, 16 A2d 258 (1940).

Once the levy occurs and the lien is thereby created, the basic purpose of prejudgment attachment becomes apparent: It is meant to aid in collection when the money judgment is obtained. The property subject to the lien serves as security for the judgment, thus giving the creditor priority over subsequent claimants.[106] This lien is provisional, inchoate, and contingent until such time as judgment is obtained, thereby making the lien final. Rendering of judgment against the creditor vacates the lien.[107]

From a priority standpoint, interests obtained by third parties subsequent to the acquisition of the attachment lien are usually subordinate to the attaching creditor's lien due to the standard priority rule of "first in time, first in right."[108] This is true even though the third-party interest is asserted before the attaching creditors obtain judgment. In essence, upon the obtaining of judgment, the lien becomes choate and relates back to when it was obtained.[109] In some jurisdictions, the priority reaches all the way back to when the writ of attachment was issued or delivered to the sheriff, even though levy must occur to create the lien.[110]

### [g] Attachment and Prejudgment Garnishment in Federal Courts

The enforcement of federal judgments occurs pursuant to state law due to Rule 64 of the Federal Rules of Civil Procedure.[111] Therefore, attachment and

---

[106] See, e.g., Duncan Box & Lumber Co. v. Applied Energies, Inc., 270 SE2d 140 (W. Va. 1980); State v. Friedman, 283 Md. 701, 393 A2d 1356 (1978).

[107] See, e.g., State v. Friedman, 283 Md. 701, 393 A2d 1356 (1978); Hartford Provision Co. v. U.S., 579 F2d 7 (2d Cir. 1978).

[108] See, e.g., Garcia v. Atmajian, 113 Cal. App. 3d 516, 169 Cal. Rptr. 845 (1980); Mahalko v. Arctic Trading Co., Inc., 29 Wash. App. 411, 628 P2d 859 (1981); U.S. v. County of Los Angeles, 336 F. Supp. 1014 (CD Cal. 1972).

[109] See, e.g., State v. Friedman, 283 Md. 701, 393 A2d 1356 (1978); Investors Capital Corp. v. Schmidt, 29 Conn. Supp. 444, 291 A2d 248 (1972); Spunt v. Brumby, 518 SW2d 345 (Tenn. 1974). However, this is not the case where the subsequent claim is a federal tax claim. In that regard, see ¶ 9.04[6].

[110] See, e.g., Ark. Stat. Ann. § 31-122; Ind. Code Ann. § 34-1-11-10; New York Civ. Prac. Law & R. § 6203.

[111] Rule 64 provides:

> "At the commencement of and during the course of an action, all remedies providing for seizure of person or property for the purpose of securing satisfaction of the judgment ultimately to be entered in the action are available under the circumstances and in the manner provided by the law of the state in which the district court is held, existing at the time the remedy is sought, subject to the following qualifications: (1) any existing statute of the United States governs to the extent which it is applicable; (2) the action in which any of the foregoing remedies is used shall be commenced and prosecuted or, if removed from a state court, shall be prosecuted after removal, pursuant to these rules. The remedies thus available include arrest, attachment, garnishment, replevin, sequestration, and other corresponding or equivalent remedies, however designated and regardless of whether by

prejudgment garnishment law of the state in which the federal court is located regulates the availability and use of the writs, as long as the state law is not preempted by federal statutes (which rarely happens)[112] and as long as the action in which the attachment is issued is commenced and prosecuted pursuant to the Federal Rules of Civil Procedure.[113] When an action is commenced in state court and an attachment or prejudgment garnishment is validly obtained, if the action is removed thereafter to federal court, the attachment or garnishment remains valid.[114] Finally, if the federal case is removed to bankruptcy court, the removal does not as a general rule affect an attachment or prejudgment garnishment obtained in the earlier proceeding.[115]

## [2] Prejudgment Garnishment

### [a] General Nature and Function of Prejudgment Garnishment

The writ of garnishment modernly is used by creditors to obtain satisfaction of a judgment (either obtained or to be obtained) from personal property owned by the debtor and in the possession of a third party, or from an indebtedness of a third party that is due the debtor.[116] Thus, the remedy is used both before and after a judgment is obtained.[117] This portion of the text considers prejudgment garnishment, although most matters discussed here also apply to

---

state procedure the remedy is ancillary to an action or must be obtained by an independent action."

[112] See 7 Moore's Federal Practice ¶ 64.07[3] (Matthew Bender 1979).

[113] See supra ¶ 6.04[1][g] note 111.

[114] 28 USC § 1450. Section 1450 attachment or sequestration; securities, provides:

"Whenever any action is removed from a State court to a district court of the United States, any attachment or sequestration of the goods or estate of the defendant in such action in the State court shall hold the goods or estate to answer the final judgment or decree in the same manner as they would have been held to answer final judgment or decree had it been rendered by the State court.

"All bonds, undertakings, or security given by either party in such action prior to its removal shall remain valid and effectual notwithstanding such removal.

"All injunctions, orders, and other proceedings had in such action prior to its removal shall remain in full force and effect until dissolved or modified by the district court."

[115] 28 USC § 1479.

[116] See, e.g., Smith v. Ethyl Corp. 417 F. Supp. 669 (SD Tex. 1976); Rocky Mountain Ass'n of Credit Management v. Hessler Mfg. Corp. 37 Colo. App. 531, 553 P2d 840 (1976); Ray Lein Constr., Inc. v. Wainwright, 346 So. 2d 1029 (Fla. 1977); Goodspeeds Book Shop, Inc. v. State Street Bank & Trust Co., 8 Mass. App. Ct. 147, 391 NE2d 1262 (1979); Blessing v. Ocean Accident & Guar. Corp., 152 Ore 632, 54 P2d 300 (1936). The creditor is referred to as the "garnishor," and the third party who holds the debtor's property or owes a debt to the debtor is referred to as the "garnishee."

[117] See infra ¶ 6.05[4] for discussion of postjudgment garnishment.

postjudgment garnishment. Indeed, some of the authority cited here equally relates to matters involving both prejudgment and postjudgment garnishment.

Garnishment originally was the procedure by which "foreign attachment" of personal property of the debtor in the hands of third parties or of debts owed to him by third parties was effectuated.[118] However, as attachment was used for means other than to establish jurisdiction over the debtor, garnishment also become coupled with "domestic attachment."[119] It evolved that garnishment was used also in connection with postjudgment executions.[120] Due to this historical development, in which garnishment was an outgrowth of attachment and execution, it resulted that in the majority of jurisdictions garnishment is a process in the aid of or for the execution of either a writ of attachment or a writ of execution that reaches assets of the debtor in the hands of third parties, or debts owed to the debtor by third parties. On the other hand, in some jurisdictions, garnishment is a separate remedy independent of attachment or execution altogether.[121]

In some jurisdictions, garnishment goes by different names. For example, some states refer to the remedy that assists the creditor in reaching property in the hands of third parties as a form of attachment or execution.[122] In New England states other than Connecticut,[123] garnishment is referred to as "trustee process."[124] However, the purpose of trustee process is the same as that of garnishment—to reach property not subject to levy under a writ of attachment or execution, such as property in the hands of a third party or debts owed to the debtor by third parties.

A final comment should be made about garnishment in general and its coverage at this point in the text. There are numerous other aspects of the law that affect garnishment, not the least of which is the law of exemptions. Exemption law and other matters that particularly affect prejudgment garnishment are considered later in this book.[125]

---

[118] See Riesenfeld, Creditors' Remedies and Debtors' Protection 255 (West, 3d ed. 1979).

[119] Id.; see 15 Va. (5 Hen. & M.) 59 (1819).

[120] See infra ¶ 6.05[4] for discussion of postjudgment garnishment.

[121] See, e.g., Ala. R. Civ. P. 64; Ala. Code §§ 6-6-353–6-6-484; Ariz. R. Civ. P. 64; Ariz. Rev. Stat. Ann. §§ 12-1521–12-1539, 12-1571–12-1595; Tex. Rev. Civ. Stat. Ann. art. 4076(2); Tex. Civ. Proc. Rules Ann. R. 658a.

[122] See, e.g., N.Y. Civ. Prac. Law § 62; Fla. Stat. Ann. §§ 76.01–76.37, 77.51–77.28.

[123] In Connecticut, garnishment is referred to as "foreign attachment." See Conn. Gen. Stat. Ann. §§ 52-329–52-346, 52-381–52-393.

[124] See Mass. Gen. Laws Ann. ch. 246; Mass. R. Civ. P. 4.2; Me. Rev. Stat. Ann. tit. 14, §§ 2601–3105, Me. R. Civ. P. 4B; N.H. Rev. Stat. Ann. §§ 511-A, 512:50; N.H. Sup. Ct. R. 8, 81; R.I. Gen. Laws 10-5-2, 10-5-19, 10-17-1–10-17-22; R.I. R. Civ. P. 4(j); Vt. Stat. Ann. tit. 12, §§ 3011–3166; Vt. R. Civ. P. 4.2.

[125] See infra ¶¶ 6.07[1], 6.07[2], 6.07[5].

### [b] Basic Procedure

Garnishment, like attachment, is a purely statutory remedy.[126] Garnishment may be statutorily treated as a writ in aid of attachment or execution, or, under other jurisdictions' statutes, as an altogether separate procedure.[127] This distinction is most important from a procedural standpoint, since substantively there is little effect that results from these different types of garnishment statutes. This section of the text considers the basic procedure by which the writ of prejudgment garnishment will issue and discusses specific procedural issues.

The basic procedure for issuance of the writ of garnishment prior to judgment closely resembles the statutory procedure for issuance of the writ of attachment.[128] If garnishment is treated as a writ in aid of attachment, then the writ of attachment must be issued prior to, or concurrently with, the issuance of the writ of garnishment. Alternatively, if garnishment is statutorily separated from attachment, the issuance of attachment is unnecessary to the validity of the issued writ of garnishment. Regardless of the type of garnishment statute with which the parties are dealing, the judgment creditor must file a motion with supportive affidavits stating that the grounds for issuance of the writ of prejudgment garnishment are present.[129] In addition, he usually must post a bond.[130] Traditionally, prejudgment garnishment statutes did not provide the debtor with prior notice or an opportunity for a hearing regarding the issuance of the writ. If ex parte issuance of the writ occurred, a postissuance hearing often was provided the debtor. Due to a line of U.S. Supreme Court cases declaring these procedures to be in violation of the debtor's right to due process of law,[131] prior notice and hearing is most often required by statute or case law.[132] Nevertheless, as was the case with attachment, the notice and supportive affidavits must be filed to initiate the proceeding. The same guidelines for the preparation and filing of the motion and affidavit discussed in relation to attachment apply to prejudgment garnishment procedure.[133]

Assuming the statutory grounds of issuance of the writ of garnishment have been satisfied, the court or clerk of the court will issue the writ directing the sheriff to serve the garnishment on the third-party garnishee who holds

---

[126] See, e.g., Marcheschi v. P.I. Corp., 84 Ill. App. 3d 873, 405 NE2d 1230 (1980); Chandler v. Cashwan Bldg. Materials Inc., 584 SW2d 950 (Tex. Civ. App. 1979).

[127] See supra ¶ 6.04[2][a] & note 121.

[128] See supra ¶ 6.04[1][b] for discussion of basic attachment procedure.

[129] See, e.g., C & S Plumbing Inc. v. Live Supply Inc., 397 So. 2d 998 (Fla. App. 1981); Dale Jewelers, Inc. v. Walker, 44 Ill. App. 2d 224, 194 NE2d 509 (1963).

[130] See, e.g., American Fidelity Fire Ins. Co. v. Paste-Ups Unlimited, Inc., 368 F. Supp. 219 (SDNY 1973); Wilson v. Polacek, 15 Ariz. App. 139, 486 P2d 819 (1971); Wilson v. Fulton Metal Bed Mfg. Co., 88 Ga. App. 884, 78 SE2d 360 (1953).

[131] For a discussion of a debtor's constitutional right to due process, see infra ¶ 6.04[5][a].

[132] See, e.g., Cal. Civ. Proc. Code §§ 484.090, 485.240, 492.050; Tex. Civ. Proc. Rules Ann. R. 592, 608, 658, 664a.

[133] See supra ¶ 6.04[1][b] for discussion of such guidelines.

property of the debtor or owes a debt to the debtor.[134] State statutes sometimes also provide that the debtor should be notified after issuance of the writ.[135] Upon service, prejudgment garnishment becomes a warning or notice to the garnishee that the garnishor claims to have the property or debt applied to the satisfaction of the garnishor's claim when reduced to judgment. The content of the writ typically orders the garnishee to hold the property until the creditor's action has been tried and the resulting judgment is satisfied.

After the service of the summons or notice of garnishment upon the garnishee, the garnishee is required to "answer" the garnishment within a statutory stated time period. In its answer, the garnishee must provide information regarding the assets or debts, if any, that he holds for, or owes to, the debtor. As a part of the answer, the garnishee is given an opportunity to defend against the garnishment. The nature of such possible defenses is considered in connection with postjudgment garnishment.[136] If the garnishee's answer is unsatisfactory to the garnishor, the latter may controvert the answer and have the matter litigated. If the garnishment results in "freezing" property of the debtor or in forestalling payment of a debt to the debtor, the garnishee is usually protected by statute or case law from double liability to the garnishor and debtor.[137]

Concerning liability to the debtor, the question might be raised as to whether the garnishee must assert the debtor's exemptions for him. As a general rule, the garnishee has only an obligation of fair play with respect to the debtor,[138] including the duty to keep him apprised of any occurrence that affects the debtor's rights to an exemption.[139] However, authority is divided on the issue of whether the garnishee owes a duty to the debtor to claim a known exemption so that failure to do so would deprive the garnishee of the right to plead the garnishment in payment as a defense in a subsequent action brought against the garnishee by the debtor.[140]

The consequences to the garnishee of the failure to properly answer the garnishment or otherwise to comply with the garnishment order are twofold. First, the garnishee could be held in contempt of court. In that regard, penalties

---

[134] Under many state statutes, prejudgment garnishment can no longer be issued by a clerk but must be issued by a "judicial officer." See, e.g., Conn. Gen. Stat. §§ 52-278c, 52-278d; Md. Real Prop. Code Ann. § 44; Tex. Civ. Proc. Rules Ann. R. 592, 658.

[135] See, e.g., Kan. Stat. Ann. § 60-717(b); Mich. Stat. Ann. § 600.4011(3), as amended in 1974, Mich. Gen. Ct. R. 738.4(3); Minn. Stat. Ann. §§ 571.47(4)–571.51.

[136] See infra ¶ 6.05[4].

[137] See Hawkland & Loiseaux, Debtor-Creditor Relations 76–77 (Bobbs-Merrill 1979), for discussion of protections afforded the garnishee.

[138] See Riesenfeld, Creditors' Remedies and Debtors' Protection 252 (West 3d ed. 1979).

[139] See, e.g., Bowie v. Union Bank, 11 Cal. App. 3d 807, 90 Cal. Rptr. 103 (1970).

[140] See Annot., 45 A.L.R. 646 (1926); Annot., 166 A.L.R. 272, 304 (1947), for cases imposing such a duty. See Miss. Code Ann. § 11-35-33 and Wis. Stat. Ann. § 812.11(4) for statutes authorizing the garnishee to claim exemptions. Finally, see 7A Colo. R. Civ. P. 103(h), which provides that a garnishee need not claim an exemption for the debtor.

and other sanctions might be issued by the court to the garnishee. Secondly, the garnishment also makes the garnishee personally liable to the garnishor. In that regard, the failure of the garnishee to properly comply with the writ may result in judgment against the garnishee personally.[141] The judgment against the garnishee may not exceed the amount of liability of the debtor to the garnishor.[142] The effect of judgment against the garnishee on the debtor has posed difficult problems. Generally, the issues revolve around whether the judgment bars further action, or is res judicata to further action against the garnishee. A judgment against the garnishee by a court having jurisdiction over both parties liberates the garnishee to that extent from liability to the debtor; conversely, a judgment discharging a garnishee will not bar a subsequent action by the debtor unless the debtor has litigated the issue of the garnishee's liability by becoming involved with the garnishment itself. A judgment against the garnishee in favor of the garnishor will not bar an action by the debtor for any excess and is not res judicata with respect to the total amount owed by the garnishee, unless the debtor has become a party to the garnishment itself and is bound by the outcome or has litigated the matter.[143]

In addition to the garnishee and garnishor, other parties can become involved in the garnishment proceeding. In the absence of a statute or rule that provides otherwise, the debtor is not a party to the garnishment; however, he can intervene. For example, many statutes or rules allow the debtor to controvert the garnishee's disclosure as to the amount owed by him[144] or may allow intervention to claim an exemption.[145] Additionally, the debtor might become involved by being interpleaded by the garnishee. Finally, the debtor does become involved where the applicable statute provides for service of a copy of the writ of garnishment on the debtor. Beyond the debtor, third parties who claim interests in the garnished property may become involved with the garnishment proceeding. Third parties may usually intervene or might be interpleaded by the garnishee.[146]

---

[141] See, e.g., Ill. Ann. Stat. ch. 62, § 47; Mich. Gen. Ct. R. 738.13(3)(c); N.Y. Civ. Prac. Law & R. 5225(b), 5102.

[142] See Riesenfeld, Creditors' Remedies and Debtors' Protection 245 (West, 3d ed. 1979). Note that garnishment may result in permissible splitting of causes of action. See, e.g., Ariz. Rev. Stat. Ann. §§ 12-1585, 12-1592; Tex. Civ. Proc. Rules Ann. R. 668, 678; Wash. Rev. Code Ann. § 7.33.300.

[143] For an excellent summary of the law relating to the effect of a judgment against the garnishee on the debtor, see Riesenfeld, Creditors' Remedies and Debtors' Protection 245–246 (West, 3d ed. 1979).

[144] See, e.g., Ariz. Rev. Stat. Ann. § 12-1589; Tex. Civ. Proc. Rules Ann. R. 673; Wis. Stat. Ann. § 812.15; Miss. Code Ann. § 11-35-47.

[145] See, e.g., Iowa Code Ann. § 642.15; Erwin v. Erwin, 251 Iowa 1344, 105 NW2d 238 (1982); Born v. Williams, 81 Ga. 796, 7 SE 868 (1888).

[146] See, e.g., Cal. Civ. Proc. Code § 689; Ill. Ann. Stat. ch. 62, § 42; Wis. Stat. Ann. § 812.17.

### [c] Prejudgment Garnishment: Actions and Grounds Available

The actions in which and the grounds on which prejudgment garnishment may statutorily issue will first depend upon whether garnishment is statutorily in aid of attachment or is simply a writ that is separately issued.[147] However, the grounds for issuance of attachment and prejudgment garnishment are strikingly similar.

If the statute provides for issuance of prejudgment garnishment as an aid to attachment, the writ of attachment must first be validly issued. Although the action in which and the grounds on which attachment can typically issue were previously discussed at length,[148] a brief review of that discussion is helpful at this time. In summary, attachment is an extraordinary prejudgment statutory remedy based upon a legally sufficient complaint that will likely result in money judgment for the plaintiff-creditor. Often, the complaint must be based upon a contract, express or implied, with the claim of the creditor being "liquidated." Additionally, attachment will usually not issue unless at least one of the following grounds is present:

(1) The debtor has absconded or is concealing his location, or the creditor is unable to locate the debtor;
(2) The debtor is a nonresident;
(3) The debtor has fraudulently transferred, removed, or concealed property, or is about to do so; or
(4) Other miscellaneous grounds, discussed previously,[149] are present.

If prejudgment garnishment is issued by statute separately from issuance of attachment, a separate basis for its issuance must be established. Alternatively, even if prejudgment garnishment is issued in aid of attachment, separate grounds may have to be established to enable the issuance of the garnishment writ.[150] Even so, the issuance of prejudgment garnishment occurs in similar actions and on similar grounds to that of issuance of attachment. The issuance of garnishment is statutorily regulated. Thus, garnishment may be had only if the action and grounds statutorily proscribed are established by the creditor's

---

[147] See supra ¶¶ 6.04[2][a] and 6.04[2][b] for discussion of the two different statutory treatments of garnishment as an aid to attachment or as a totally separate writ.

[148] See supra ¶¶ 6.04[1][c] and 6.04[1][d] with accompanying citations to authority.

[149] Id.

[150] See supra ¶ 6.04[2][a] note 121 and Riesenfeld, Creditors' Remedies and Debtors' Protection 268–269 (West, 3d ed. 1979). Note that this distinction between garnishment in aid of attachment as opposed to a garnishment issued separately can have a substantive as well as a procedural impact in at least the situation where the defendant-debtor in the main action dies. In some jurisdictions death of the defendant dissolves the attachment. See, e.g., Mass. Gen. Laws Ann. ch. 223, § 116. Thus, if the attachment dissolves, so too does the garnishment in aid of the attachment. Further, a statute providing for the survival of attachment proceedings has been held to not include garnishment proceedings. See, e.g., Ionian Bank Ltd. v. Mamatos, 340 Pa. 52, 16 A2d 397 (1940).

complaint, motion, and affidavit.[151] The statutory law in this regard evidences the extraordinary nature of prejudgment garnishment. Prejudgment garnishment is typically available only when the judgment sought is for money damages.[152] Statutes sometimes specify that the underlying action must be a proceeding in personam, as opposed to proceedings in rem.[153] The action underlying the issuance of the writ of garnishment also must usually be one in contract, express or implied;[154] prejudgment garnishment is usually not available in actions for tort.[155] Generally, most statutes require the claim of the creditor to be liquidated.[156] As is the general rule with regard to the requirement of liquidation of the debt in the case of attachment, the test of liquidation is whether the demand for money judgment itself is capable of definite ascertainment at the time of the action.[157] To support the issuance of prejudgment garnishment, the complaint in which the creditor seeks judgment to collect the debt must be one in which judgment on the merits may be and is likely to be rendered; other grounds on which attachment may issue typically are also found in the garnishment statutes with regard to issuance of prejudgment garnishment.[158]

In the absence of a contrary statute, other remedies do not need to be exhausted before garnishment is available,[159] although there is some contrary authority.[160] For example, it has been held that other security for the claim sued upon by the creditor will not preclude issuance of garnishment.[161]

---

[151] See, e.g., Mary v. Lewis, 399 Mich. 401, 249 NW2d 102 (1976); Cerone v. Clark, 110 Ill. App. 2d 301, 249 NE2d 186 (1969).

[152] See, e.g., Kahn v. Friedman, 329 Mich. 164, 45 NW2d 18 (1950); Hisel v. Chrysler Corp., 90 F. Supp. 655 (WD Mo. 1950); Dunham v. Kauffman, 319 Ill. App. 229, 48 NE2d 777, rev'd on other grounds, 385 Ill. 79, 52 NE2d 1431 (1944).

[153] See, e.g., Grubbs v. Atlanta Newspapers, Inc., 129 Ga. App. 595, 200 SE2d 335 (1973); Marcheschi v. P.I. Corp., 84 Ill. App. 3d 873, 405 NE2d 1230 (1980).

[154] See, e.g., Chernin v. International Oil Co., 261 Wis. 308, 52 NW2d 785 (1952); Bieker v. National Furniture Serv., 327 Mich. 66, 41 NW2d 335 (1950).

[155] See, e.g., McGill v. Robbins, 231 Ark. 411, 329 SW2d 540 (1959); Welch v. Renfro, 42 Tex. Civ. App. 460, 94 SW 107 (1906).

[156] See, e.g., Frank F. Fasi Supply Co. v. Wigwam Inv. Co., 308 F. Supp. 59 (D. Hawaii 1969); Talbert v. Solventol Chem. Prods., 304 Mich. 557, 8 NW2d 637 (1943). For further discussion of the garnishability of both liquidated and unliquidated claims, see infra ¶ 6.04[2][d].

[157] See, e.g., Frank F. Fasi Supply Co. v. Wigwam Inv. Co., 308 F. Supp. 59 (D. Hawaii 1969); Cleveland v. San Antonio Bldg. & Loan Ass'n, 223 SW2d 226 (Tex. Civ. App. 1949).

[158] See supra ¶¶ 6.04[1][c], 6.04[1][d].

[159] See, e.g., Simpson v. Loehmann; 81 Misc. 2d 386, 365 NYS2d 368 (NY Sup. Ct. 1975); E.I. du Pont de Nemours Co. v. Lednum, 82 Colo. 472, 260 P 1017 (1927).

[160] See, e.g., G-W-L, Inc. v. Juneau, 486 SW2d 812 (Tex. Civ. App. 1972); Iron Cliff Co. v. Lahais, 52 Mich. 394, 18 NW 121 (1884).

[161] See, e.g., Pilette Indus., Inc. v. Alexander, 17 Mich. App. 226, 169 NW2d 149 (1969); Kaminski v. Walpole, 10 Ariz. App. 260, 458 P2d 127 (1969).

### [d] Property Subject to Prejudgment Garnishment

Up to this point in the text, garnishment has been described as a writ that assists the creditor in reaching property of the debtor in the possession of third parties or in reaching debts due the debtor from third parties. This portion of the text explores more specifically the nature of property subject to prejudgment garnishment and considers both tangible and intangible classes of property interests.[162] The discussion begins with a consideration of matters that pertain to both classes and follows with a separate consideration of each class.

In order for property to be garnishable, the defendant must have an interest in the property, tangible or intangible. If the interest is such that the defendant has a right of action against the third-party garnishee for the recovery of property or payment of a claim or debt, this interest is usually garnishable.[163] Only the interest of the debtor is garnishable.[164]

In all jurisdictions, garnishment impounds tangible property in the possession of the garnishee or an indebtedness of the garnishee existing at the time of the service of the garnishment notice.[165] In some jurisdictions, however, the effect of the garnishment is determined *solely* as of the date of the service of the notice of garishment upon the garnishee.[166] In other jurisdictions, the garnishment also reaches property that comes into the possession of the garnishee (and the indebtedness of the garnishee that it incurred) *after* the service of the notice upon the garnishee up to the date set for the garnishee's answer, or up to the date of the actual answer of the garnishee.[167] In yet other jurisdictions, the period from service of the notice upon the garnishee to the determination controls if the garnishee's answer is controverted.[168]

As to tangible property, virtually all forms held by a third party are garnishable, as would be the case of attachment of tangible property if it were possessed by the debtor.[169] The interest of the debtor in the tangible property

---

[162] This portion of the text does not consider the relation of exemption law to the question of what property is garnishable. For a discussion of exemption law, see infra ¶ 6.07[1].

[163] See, e.g., Diaz v. Diaz, 83 Ill. App. 3d 341, 403 NE2d 1219 (1980); Escambia Chem. Corp. v. Chemical Constr. Corp., 444 F. Supp. 925 (D. Miss. 1977); Powell v. Prudence Mut. Casualty Co., 88 Ill. App. 2d 343, 232 NE2d 155 (1967).

[164] See, e.g., Rocky Mountain Ass'n of Credit Management v. Hessler Mfg. Co., 37 Colo. App. 551, 553 P2d 840 (1976); James Talcott, Inc. v. Valley Fed. Sav. & Loan Ass'n, 611 SW2d 692 (Tex. Civ. App. 1980); Best T.V., Inc. v. Simberg, 413 Pa. 101, 196 A2d 332 (1964); Matsuda v. Noble, 184 Ore. 686, 200 P2d 962 (1948).

[165] See Riesenfeld, Creditors' Remedies and Debtors' Protection 234–235 (West, 3d ed. 1979).

[166] See, e.g., Colo. Rev. Stat. Ann., Colo. R. Civ. P. Rule 103 (semble); Mich. Gen. Ct. R. 738.5; Helms v. State ex rel. Mifflin, 137 Okla. 55, 280 P 416 (1929).

[167] See, e.g., Ariz. Rev. Stat. Ann. §§ 12-1574, 12-1581, 12-1584 (semble); Kan. Stat. Ann. § 60-717(c); N.H. Rev. Stat. Ann. § 512.20.

[168] See, e.g., Md. Ann. Code, Md. R. P. 71, G.45, G.55b.

[169] See supra ¶ 6.04[1][e] for discussion of the types of property subject to attachment.

held by the garnishee must be assignable,[170] although the question of which type of property interests are garnishable is subject to statute, since garnishment is strictly a statutory remedy.[171] A "shopping list" for creditors seeking to garnish tangible property for which there is some authority could include both real and personal property. Real property is garnishable if so provided by the statute.[172] Otherwise, it is not within the general scope of a garnishment statute.[173] Innumerable types of tangible personalty are, of course, garnishable.

The most common target of the creditor's garnishment efforts is intangible property. Normally, the intangible asset involves some type of indebtedness that the third-party garnishee owes the debtor. The most common types of debts include those related to the debtor's income (e.g., wages, salaries, and commissions) and bank accounts. Determining what indebtedness is garnishable has caused difficulty. As is the case with regard to tangible property, the courts often look to the assignability of the intangible sought to be garnished, especially in the case of tort claims.[174] There is agreement among the jurisdictions that a tort claim for personal injury is not garnishable prior to its reduction to final nonappealable judgment.[175] The same rule appears to prevail as to tort claims for libel, slander,[176] fraud, and deceit.[177] An insurer's tort liability, which results from its failure to settle a suit defended by it, also appears to be subject to the same rule.[178] As to the garnishability of claims in contract, in the majority of jurisdictions, statutes or case law allow garnishment if the claim is unconditionally due and is fixed in amount, even though it is payable at a future date.[179] Authority is split as to the garnishability of contract claims that depend on future contingencies or that are otherwise unliquidated. Generally,

---

[170] See, e.g., Garvey v. Parrish, 84 Ill. App. 3d 578, 405 NE2d 1105 (1980); Baumgarden v. Reconstruction Fin. Corp., 131 F2d 741 (7th Cir. 1942).

[171] See, e.g., Javorek v. Superior Court of Monterey County, 17 Cal. 3d 629, 552 P2d 728, 131 Cal. Rptr. 768 (1976); Haines v. Public Fin. Corp., 7 Ohio App. 2d 89, 218 NE2d 727 (1966).

[172] See, e.g., Allied Prods., Inc. v. Peterson, 233 Ga. 266, 211 SE2d 123 (1974); Selig v. Selig, 217 Pa. Super. 7, 268 A2d 215 (1970); Citizens State Bank v. Carda, 47 SD 29, 195 NW 828 (1923).

[173] See, e.g., Berar Enters., Inc. v. Harmon, 93 Mich. App. 1, 285 NW2d 774 (1979); Fitzgerald v. Brown, Smith & Marsh Bros., 283 SW 576 (Tex. Civ. App. 1926).

[174] See Riesenfeld, Creditors' Remedies and Debtors' Protection 235 (West, 3d ed. 1979).

[175] See, e.g., Pacific Gas & Elec. Co. v. Nakano, 12 Cal. 2d 711, 87 P2d 700 (1939); Kreisle v. Campbell, 32 SW 581 (Tex. Civ. App. 1895).

[176] See, e.g., Detroit Post & Tribune Co. v. Reilly, 46 Mich. 459, 9 NW 492 (1881).

[177] See, e.g., Braniff Inv. Co. v. Carter, 181 Okla. 599, 75 P2d 439 (1937).

[178] See, e.g., Murphy v. Allstate Ins. Co., 17 Cal. 3d 937, 553 P2d 584, 132 Cal. Rptr. 424 (1976).

[179] See, e.g., Bell v. West, 241 Ark. 89, 406 SW2d 316 (Ark. 1966); State ex rel. Government Employees Ins. Co. v. Lasky, 454 SW2d 942 (Mo. Ct. App. 1970); Iran Express Lines v. Sumatrop, 563 F2d 648 (4th Cir. 1977).

unliquidated contract claims are not garnishable, although some exceptions have been made.[180]

Garnishment of income-producing debts has proven to be a field of garnishment law in itself.[181] Wages cannot be garnished before they are earned, except under special statutes that provide for garnishment of future earnings.[182] Some statutes have provided procedures to reach future earnings by mandatory withholdings, either in favor of ordinary judgment creditors or of persons entitled to alimony or child support.[183] Use of a receiver, however, may offer the creditor an alternate means of reaching future earnings.[184]

### [e] The Creation, Nature, and Effect of a Prejudgment Garnishment Lien

In most jurisdictions, but not all, a garnishment (pre- or postjudgment) creates a lien on the indebtedness or the tangible property subject to the garnishment in the possession of the garnishee or due from the garnishee.[185] The prejudgment garnishment lien is provisional, existing permanently provided that the creditor-garnishor obtains judgment, and, at the least, creates a lien on all personalty in the possession of the garnishee and all debts owed to the garnishee by the debtor at the time of service of the writ.[186] In some jurisdictions, the lien attaches also to property of the debtor coming into the possession of the garnishee, or to debts incurred by him and due the debtor, before the garnishee's answer or before judgment.[187]

The lien has three effects. First, in jurisdictions that provide for creation of the lien by garnishment, it is the basis of the garnishee's liability.[188] The liability of the garnishee is said to lapse when the lien expires. The lien continues

---

[180] See, e.g., Cummings Gen. Tire Co. v. Volpe Constr. Co., 230 A2d 712 (DC App. 1967); Annot., 134 A.L.R. 853 (1941).

[181] See, e.g., the discussion at 7 Debtor-Creditor Law ¶¶ 29.01–29.12 (Matthew Bender 1982).

[182] See, e.g., In re Stone, 194 Colo. 394, 573 P2d 98 (1977); U.S. v. Williams, 279 Md. 673, 370 A2d 1134 (1977); Miami Herald Publishing Co. v. Payne, 345 So. 2d 730, quashed, 358 So. 2d 541, adopted, 360 So. 2d 122 (Fla. Dist. Ct. App. 1977). It might be noted that the same rule applies to future rent. See, e.g., Hustead v. Superior Court, 2 Cal. App. 3d 780, 83 Cal. Rptr. 26 (1969); Glassman v. Hyder, 23 NY2d 354, 244 NE2d 259, 296 NYS2d 783 (1968).

[183] See, e.g., Cal. Civ. Proc. Code § 723.030.

[184] See infra ¶ 6.04[4] for discussion of receivership.

[185] See, e.g., Equifax, Inc. v. Luster, 463 F. Supp. 352 (D. Ark.), aff'd, Arkansas La. Gas Co. v. Luster, 604 F2d 31 (8th Cir.), cert. denied, 445 US 916 (1978); Northwestern Nat'l Ins. Co. v. Wetherall, Inc. 267 Md. 378, 298 A2d 1 (1972); see also Riesenfeld, Creditors' Remedies and Debtors' Protection 241 (West, 3d ed. 1979).

[186] See supra ¶ 6.04[2][d] notes 165, 166.

[187] See supra ¶ 6.04[2][d] notes 167, 168; 42 Pa. R. Civ. P. 1258.

[188] See supra ¶ 6.04[2][b].

until recovery of judgment and a reasonable period thereafter.[189] The lien on the garnished property or debt even provides the garnishor with the ability to file a claim against the administration of a deceased garnishee.[190] If the debtor-defendant dies, the lien survives in most jurisdictions. However, it may not survive in others.[191]

The second effect of the lien is that it provides the creditor with legal ability to force a sale of the assets subject to garnishment or to apply cash received from the garnishment to the principal debt—once judgment is obtained.[192] The nature of execution and judicial sales is discussed elsewhere in this book.[193]

The final effect of the garnishment lien is that it provides the garnishee with a priority as to other parties who assert claims in the assets subject to the garnishment (e.g., third-party purchasers and other creditors of the debtor-defendant). The "priority date" accorded the lien varies from state to state. In the majority of states, the lien obtained by the garnishment must date from the time of service of the writ on the garnishee.[194] Other states, for example, relate the priority date back in time to the date the sheriff received the garnishment order.[195] The priority rule applicable to judicial liens generally applies to prejudgment garnishment liens—"first in time, first in right."[196] Thus, a person who obtains a claim in the garnished asset subsequent to one of the established priority dates described previously would be subordinate to the creditor's prejudgment garnishment lien. On the other hand, if the claim was acquired prior to the established priority date described previously, the third-party claimant would be awarded priority. For example, the assignee under an assignment made before the priority date of garnishment has priority over the garnishor.[197]

---

[189] See Riesenfeld, Creditors' Remedies and Debtors' Protection 271 (West, 3d ed. 1979).

[190] See, e.g., Chapman v. Cole, 32 NH 141 (1853).

[191] For discussion of cases on the survival of garnishment and attachment liens, see Annot., 131 A.L.R. 1146 (1941); Annot., 21 A.L.R. 272 (1922).

[192] See discussion at supra ¶ 6.04[2][a].

[193] See infra ¶ 6.06.

[194] See, e.g., Cal. Civ. Proc. Code § 723.023(a); N.J. Stat. Ann. § 2A:17-52; see also 7 Debtor-Creditor Law ¶ 29.05[B] (Matthew Bender 1982).

[195] See, e.g., Schwartz v. Goldberg, 58 Misc. 2d 308, 295 NYS2d 245 (Bronx Sup. Ct. 1968); N.Y. Civ. Prac. Law § 5231(h).

[196] See, e.g., Cal. Civ. Proc. Code § 723.023(a)(b)(c); N.J. Stat. Ann. § 2A:17-52; N.Y. Civ. Prac. Law § 5231(h).

[197] See Riesenfeld, Creditors' Remedies and Debtors' Protection 241 (West, 3d ed. 1979). Note, however, that to the extent that an assignment of account needs to be filed under UCC Sections 9-104(f) and 9-302(1)(e), a garnishing creditor is protected against a prior unperfected assignment and that a garnishee without notice of a prior assignment may make payment to the garnishing creditor of the assignor with the same effect as payment to the assignor himself.

In jurisdictions that do not provide the garnishee with a lien, the garnishment still has the effect of conferring upon the garnishor a right to force sale of the subject property or to apply cash received to satisfaction of the debt upon the obtaining of judgment. The garnishee is also liable to the garnishor, even in the absence of a lien in such states.[198] However, from a priority standpoint, if no lien is attached, no priority is established. Thus, if the garnishee sells the garnished property to a bona fide purchaser, the purchaser will take the property free of the garnishor's claim, although the garnishee would remain liable to the garnishor.[199]

Where more than one creditor has garnished the same property or debt, the "first in time, first in right" rule gives priority to the garnishment with the earliest priority date (e.g., the garnishment served first).[200] Occasionally, garnishment writs of various creditors are served simultaneously. In this situation, there is authority that the creditors will share pro rata or equally in the property or indebtedness garnished.[201] One state, however, in the simultaneous service situation, would accord priority to the garnishor whose judgment was first entered; if the judgments were entered on the same day, the employer-garnishee is allowed to choose between the competing garnishments.[202]

## [3] Replevin and Its Relationship to Prejudgment Remedies

### [a] General Nature and Function of Replevin as Compared to Attachment and Prejudgment Garnishment

Replevin is an action brought by a plaintiff to obtain possession of specific property from the defendant in which the plaintiff has an existing interest.[203] The writs of attachment and prejudgment garnishment are used to establish, in the first instance, an interest of the creditor in the property of the debtor in order to secure payment of the judgment when obtained. Use of these writs is ancillary to the main cause of action. Replevin, by contrast, is itself a possessory action brought by a plaintiff who already claims to have an existing interest in specific property of the defendant. In the debtor-creditor context, replevin is not used to collect unsecured debts; rather, the action is one means of enforcing a UCC Article 9 security interest, whereby the secured creditor attempts to obtain possession of the collateral and to satisfy the secured debt through it.[204]

---

[198] See prior discussion within this section and supra ¶ 6.04[2][b].

[199] See, e.g., Benedict v. T.L.V. Land & Cattle Co., 66 Neb. 236, 92 NW 210 (1902).

[200] See supra ¶ 6.04[2][e] note 194.

[201] See, e.g., Guilford v. Reeves, 103 Ala. 301, 15 So. 661 (1894).

[202] See Cal. Civ. Proc. Code § 723.023(b).

[203] See 7 Debtor-Creditor Law Ch. 30 (Matthew Bender 1982) for an excellent discussion of replevin generally and as applied to specific states.

[204] See ¶ 7.05 for discussion of enforcement of UCC Article 9 security interests.

Even though this chapter discusses judicial collection of unsecured debts, it is useful to consider the subject of replevin at this juncture for three reasons. First, even though replevin differs from the writs of attachment and prejudgment garnishment, case law related to limitations on prejudgment remedies often involves replevin actions. To facilitate a discussion of such case law, some background regarding replevin is desirable.[205] Second, some background regarding replevin aids in understanding its use in enforcing UCC Article 9 security interests. Finally, because replevin is a prejudgment "remedy" in a sense, it should be defined and, as already done, distinguished from the use of the writ of attachment and prejudgment garnishment.

Before considering modern replevin procedure, a brief historical note regarding the action might be useful. The action originated in the common law, although nowadays it is a statutory action.[206] Under the common law, replevin was available to a party only when the property was wrongfully taken *and* detained by the defendant. If only a wrongful detention occurred, replevin did not lie for the plaintiff;[207] rather, the proper remedy was detinue.[208] Statutory law has, in essence, combined the two remedies, providing for its availability to a party who is simply seeking recovery of specific personal property in which the plaintiff asserts an existing interest.[209]

### [b] Grounds on Which Replevin May Be Based

The replevin action involves the determination of who has a better right to possession of the personal property that is the subject of the action. The plaintiff must show the existence of a superior right to possession,[210] although proof of title is unnecessary as illustrated by the use of replevin in enforcing a valid UCC Article 9 security interest.[211] As to the right of possession, it has been said that the plaintiff must establish an exclusive right to possession—or at least, a right that excludes the defendant.[212] Also, the plaintiff must establish the right to immediate possession without the existence of a condition prece-

---

[205] See infra ¶ 6.04[5] for discussion of limitations on the use of prejudgment remedies.

[206] See 7 Debtor-Creditor Law 30-4 (Matthew Bender 1982).

[207] See, e.g., Baron v. Peoples Nat'l Bank of Secaucus, 9 NJ 249, 87 A2d 898 (1952).

[208] Id.

[209] See, e.g., Jim's Furniture Mart, Inc. v. Harris, 42 Ill. App. 3d 488, 356 NE2d 175 (1976); Waltenberger v. Pearson, 81 Ohio App. 51, 77 NE2d 491 (1946).

[210] See, e.g., Brandywine Lanes, Inc. v. Pittsburgh Nat'l Bank, 437 Pa. 499, 264 A2d 377 (1970); In re Estate of Schneier, 98 Misc. 2d 183, 413 NYS2d 568 (NY Sur. 1979), modified, 74 AD2d 22, 426 NYS2d 624 (1980).

[211] See, e.g., Brandywine Lanes, Inc. v. Pittsburgh Nat'l Bank, 437 Pa. 499, 264 A2d 377 (1970); for discussion of UCC Article 9 security interests, see ¶ 7.05.

[212] See, e.g., Aircraft Acceptance Corp. v. Jolly, 141 Ind. App. 515, 230 NE2d 446 (1967); Robinson v. Tool-O-Matic, 216 Pa. Super. 258, 263 A2d 914 (1970).

dent to the right of possession.[213] That right must be present at the time a replevin action is filed.[214]

Replevin, again by contrast to attachment, reaches only personal property.[215] If the property is a fixture, it may be replevied only if the property is severable from the real estate to which it is affixed.[216] Further, the property must be tangible and specifically identifiable.[217] In claims for money, unless the actual money is identified, other remedies are appropriate.[218] Shares of stock, which are an intangible interest, are not subject to replevin; however, the stock certificate may be the subject of replevin.[219]

The replevin action must also establish that the defendant is in possession of the personal property. In other words, the defendant must have the ability to restore possession to the plaintiff.[220] The possession may be actual or constructive. The existence of constructive possession has been considered by the courts.[221] At the least, the defendant must have the legal ability by way of the possession, actual or constructive, to give the plaintiff possession of the property. The possession of the defendant must be wrongful, either in the sense that the possession was originally wrongfully obtained, or in the sense that the pos-

---

[213] Robinson v. Tool-O-Matic, 216 Pa. Super. 258, 263 A2d 914 (1970); Fisher v. Bernard's Surf, 217 So. 2d 576 (Fla. Dist. Ct. App. 1969).

[214] See, e.g., Scutti Pontiac, Inc. v. Rund, 192 Misc. 2d 881, 402 NYS2d 144 (NY Sup. Ct. 1978); Schiller Park Compressed Steel Corp. v. Boerema, 45 Ill. App. 3d 434, 359 NE2d 852 (1977); Akins v. Pierce, 263 Ark. 15, 563 SW2d 406 (1978); Teater v. Good Hope Dev. Corp., 14 Cal. 2d 196, 93 P2d 112 (1939).

[215] See, e.g., International Elec. Co. v. NST Metal Prods. Co., 370 Pa. 213, 88 A2d 40 (1952); Commonwealth v. Dean, 245 Pa. Super. 322, 369 A2d 423 (1976).

[216] See, e.g., Isham v. Dudlip, 33 Ill. App. 2d 254, 179 NE2d 25 (1962).

[217] See, e.g., Equitable Life Assurance Soc'y of the U.S. v. Branch, 32 AD2d 959, 302 NYS2d 958 (1969).

[218] Id. The other appropriate actions might include actions for damages, money had and received, and unjust enrichment. Some modern courts, however, have allowed replevin of money. "Historically replevin is an action undertaken to regain possession of goods and chattels from the defendants; however, money may be the proper subject of replevin action if it is easily susceptible to ready and positive identification." Commonwealth v. Dean, 245 Pa. Super. 322, 369 A2d 423 (1976). But such *ready* identification may be a tough test. "Money is not the subject of replevin unless it is so marked or labeled as to be capable of identification; it must be specific identifiable money." 1967 Senior Class of Pekin High School v. Tharp, 261 Iowa 359, 154 NW2d 874 (1967).

[219] See, e.g., Lamus v. Engwicht, 39 Cal. App. 523, 179 P 435 (1919); Baron v. Peoples Nat'l Bank of Secaucus, 16 NJ Super. 243, 84 A2d 492 (1951), appeal dismissed, 9 NJ 249, 87 A2d 989 (1952).

[220] See, e.g., Commonwealth v. Dean, 245 Pa. Super. 322, 369 A2d 423 (1976); Huber Pontiac, Inc. v. Wells, 59 Ill. App. 3d 14, 375 NE2d 149 (1978).

[221] See, e.g., Lou Leventhal Auto Co., Inc. v. Munas, 164 Ind. App. 368, 328 NE2d 734 (1975); Piner v. Pender, 83 NM 502, 494 P2d 164 (1972); Bush v. Belenke, 381 So. 2d 315 (Fla. Dist. Ct. App. 1980).

session is wrongfully detained.[222] In the case of wrongful detention, where the property was first obtained lawfully by the defendant, a demand for possession must usually be made[223] unless demand would be futile[224] or the defendant admits that the plaintiff has a superior right to possession.[225] The demand requirement has been further eroded by case law that suggests that demand is not necessitated if, prior to seizure of the property, the defendant has notice and opportunity to judicially challenge the taking.[226] Other courts, although generally requiring a demand for possession, have held that the failure of demand may be otherwise immaterial and not fatal to replevin.[227] Finally, as to the requirement that the defendant should be in possession, where he has wrongfully transferred the property, possession of the defendant is not required, since he is not allowed to plead such misconduct as a defense.[228]

### [c] Basic Procedure

A replevin action is considered an action at law, as opposed to a suit in equity.[229] The action is often seen as an action in rem,[230] although many courts have characterized the action as a "mixed remedy."[231] Although the difference between replevin and the prejudgment remedies of attachment and garnishment has been emphasized, with regard to basic replevin procedure, the remedies are quite similar. This is the case, since replevin traditionally involves

---

[222] See, e.g., Ethiopian Zion Coptic Church v. City of Miami Beach, 376 So. 2d 925 (Fla. Dist. Ct. App. 1979).

[223] See, e.g., Houser v. Ohio Historical Soc'y, 55 Ohio App. 2d 241, 380 NE2d 728 (1977); N.J. Civ. Prac. Rule 4:61-2.

[224] See, e.g., Iovinella v. General Elec. Credit Corp., 79 AD2d 748, 343 NYS2d 806 (1980); White Motor Credit Corp. v. Sapp Bros. Truck Plaza, Inc., 197 Neb. 421, 249 NW2d 489 (1977); Rochester Gas & Elec. Corp. v. Chatterton, 81 Misc. 2d 522, 366 NYS2d 323 (Monroe Co. Ct. 1975).

[225] See, e.g., Trager v. Trager, 43 Misc. 2d 829, 252 NYS2d 480 (NY Sup. Ct. 1964).

[226] See, e.g., Harris-Intertype Corp. v. Donley Bindery Co., 26 Ill. App. 3d 140, 324 NE2d 668 (1975); Schanbarger v. Edward Dott's Garage, Inc., 61 AD2d 243, 402 NYS2d 72 (1978); Rochester Gas & Elec. Corp. v. Chatterton, 81 Misc. 2d 522, 366 NYS2d 323 (Monroe Co. Ct. 1975).

[227] See, e.g., International Packaging Corp. v. Marshall, 68 Misc. 2d 575, 326 NYS2d 462 (NYC Civ. Ct. 1971).

[228] See, e.g., Rozen v. Redco Corp., 362 P2d 1095 (Okla. 1960); Black v. City of Cleveland, 58 Ohio App. 2d 29, 387 NE2d 1388 (1978).

[229] See, e.g., Delacruz v. Peninsula State Bank, 221 So. 2d 772 (Fla. Dist. Ct. App. 1969); Blum v. City of Chicago, 126 Ill. App. 2d 228, 261 NE2d 457 (1970); Van Hoose v. Robbins, 165 So. 2d 209 (Fla. Dist. Ct. App. 1964); Brandt v. Hershey, 198 Pa. Super. 539, 182 A2d 219 (1962).

[230] See, e.g., Neil v. South Fla. Auto Painters, Inc., 397 So. 2d 1160 (Fla. Dist. Ct. App. 1961).

[231] See, e.g., In re Patenorte's Estate, 16 Misc. 2d 64, 153 NYS2d 375 (NY Sur. 1956).

a prejudgment seizure of the subject property. The seizure is provisional, like attachment and prejudgment garnishment, pending final judgment on the replevin action itself.[232]

In order to obtain a writ of replevin, the plaintiff must file a complaint, application, or affidavit in which the statutory grounds for replevin are set forth. The content of the complaint seeks both the property and a money judgment. As to obtaining possession of the property, the statutes typically provide for prejudgment seizure. Such seizure brings into play issues related to the defendant's constitutional right to due process of law.[233] Therefore, whether by case law or modern statutory requirement, notice and hearing before seizure is often required. At the least, an immediate postseizure hearing will be necessitated.[234] Subsequent to the prejudgment seizure, the plaintiff will move forward to obtain judgment in the action.

The complaint, application, or affidavit must specifically identify the property.[235] The description most often should include the location of the property to be replevied, at least to the best information and belief of the plaintiff.[236] Statutes also require a recitation of the value of the property, since allegations are needed to support recovery of its value as an alternate remedy if the property is not available.[237]

The pleadings and supportive affidavits also must set forth the facts upon which the plaintiff's claim is based. As was emphasized in regard to prejudgment attachment and garnishment, the facts must be stated with particularity; it is not sufficient to make a mere conclusory statement that the plaintiff is entitled to possession.[238] This is particularly important if the plaintiff is seeking a prejudgment seizure of the property. The specific factual allegations must state the basis of the plaintiff's claim; that the plaintiff is entitled to immediate possession of the property claimed; and that the defendant is improperly detaining the property.[239] Other specific allegations might also be required

---

[232] See, e.g., Fuentes v. Shevin, 407 US 67 (1972); Mitchell v. W.T. Grant Co., 416 US 600 (1974); Weigh Less for Life, Inc. v. Barnett Bank of Orange Park, 399 So. 2d 88 (Fla. Dist. Ct. App. 1981); Goldie v. Bauchet Properties, 15 Cal. 3d 307, 540 P2d 1, 124 Cal. Rptr. 161 (1975).

[233] See infra ¶ 6.04[5][a].

[234] See, e.g., Cal. Civ. Proc. Code Ann. § 512.020(b); N.Y. Civ. Prac. Law § 7102(d)4.

[235] See, e.g., Commonwealth v. Dean, 245 Pa. Super. 322, 369 A2d 423 (1976); N.Y. Civ. Prac. Law § 7102; Cal. Civ. Proc. Code Ann. § 512.010(b)(4).

[236] See, e.g., Fla. Stat. Ann. § 78.055(1).

[237] See, e.g., Cal. Civ. Proc. Code Ann. § 512.010(b)(3); Tex Civ. Proc. Rules Ann. R. 696.

[238] See, e.g., Fuentes v. Shevin, 407 US 67 (1972); Mitchell v. W.T. Grant Co., 416 US 600 (1974).

[239] See, e.g., Cal. Civ. Proc. Code Ann. §§ 512.010(b)(1), 512.010(b)(2); N.Y. Civ. Prac. Law § 7102(c).

depending upon local statute, particularly where an ex parte seizure is sought.[240]

Bonding is an important aspect of replevin procedure, as is the case with attachment and prejudgment garnishment. Most statutes require that the plaintiff post a bond before replevin results in prejudgment seizure of property.[241] Typically, the bond must be in an amount twice the value of the property or twice the amount owed.[242] The plaintiff's bond serves as security for damage that the defendant might incur if the resulting seizure is wrongful. In some cases, the bond also protects the sheriff. The defendant may also file a counterbond.[243] If this is posted, it enables the defendant to retain or regain possession of the property. Typically, the amount of the counterbond is twice the value of the property.

As has been emphasized, the principal purpose of replevin is to obtain possession of the subject property. Additionally, the plaintiff's complaint may also seek recovery of a monetary judgment as an alternate remedy. The judgment may provide for recovery of damages for any injury to the plaintiff's interest in the property[244] and for the value of the property if the property itself cannot be recovered.[245] The damage award may even include recovery of punitive damages.[246]

## [4] Receivership and Its Relationship to Judicial Remedies

### [a] General Nature and Function of Receivership

A receiver is a disinterested party appointed by a court pursuant to its equitable powers[247] or appointed by a court pursuant to statutory authority.[248] The receiver characteristically functions to administer the property of another. The party whose property the receiver obtains by appointment is usually in financial difficulty. The receiver cares for, collects, and disposes of the

---

[240] See 7 Debtor-Creditor Law ¶¶ 30.05 et seq. (Matthew Bender 1982) for discussion of such additional required allegations in the situation of an attempted ex parte seizure.

[241] See, e.g., Fla. Stat. Ann. § 78.068(3); Mich. Gen. Ct. R. 757.5(d)(3).

[242] See, e.g., Cal. Civ. Proc. Ann. § 515.010; Tex. Civ. Proc. Rules Ann. R. 698.

[243] See, e.g., N.Y. Civ. Prac. Law § 7103(a); Tex. Civ. Proc. Rules Ann. R. 701.

[244] See, e.g., Nichols v. Martin, 121 Ariz. 208, 589 P2d 451 (1978); Rocky Mountain Turbines, Inc. v. 660 Syndicate, Inc., 623 P2d 758 (Wyo. 1981); Cottrell v. Gerson, 296 Ill. App. 412, 16 NE2d 529 (1938), aff'd, 371 Ill. 174, 20 NE2d 74 (1939).

[245] See, e.g., Cal. Civ. Proc. Code § 667; N.Y. Civ. Prac. Law § 7108; Tex. Civ. Proc. Rules Ann. R. 704.

[246] See, e.g., Miller v. Bank of Pecatonica, 83 Ill. App. 3d 424, 403 NE2d 1262 (1980); Haskins v. Shelden, 558 P2d 487 (Alaska 1976).

[247] See, e.g., Bassett v. Merchant's Trust Co., 115 Conn. 530, 161 A 789 (1932); Grayson v. Grayson, 222 Ore. 507, 352 P2d 738 (1960).

[248] See, e.g., Cal. Civ. Proc. Code § 564; Wash. Rev. Code Ann. § 6.32.390; Boonville Nat'l Bank v. Blakey, 107 F 891 (7th Cir. 1901).

property or the proceeds of property of the debtor over which the receiver has been given authority.[249] In the absence of a statutory provision, the appointment of the receiver only results in possession of the property passing to the receiver. Title to the property does not pass to the receiver.[250] Once the receiver is appointed, he may be required to simply preserve the property. However, the court may direct how to continue a business, collect rents and profits, and liquidate property.

From the creditor's point of view, one of the more important uses of receivership arises prior to judgment.[251] The appointment of a receiver pendente lite before judgment will assist the creditor in preserving the property of the debtor pending final judgment. As a prejudgment remedy, receivership is considered a harsh remedy.[252] When invoked, it provides the creditors with tremendous leverage over the debtor. On the other hand, the creditors typically do not obtain a lien in the debtor's assets by mere appointment of a receiver. To the extent appointment of a receiver can affect priorities in the debtor's assets among creditors, the majority of states determine the priorities among creditors by the order of serving the notice to appear on the debtor.[253] Further, a receiver pedente lite generally does not effect title to the property received, in that existing liens remain valid.[254] However, although creditors can obtain some leverage over the debtor, the property cannot be liquidated by a levying creditor; the receiver's possession without consent of the court will not be disturbed.[255]

The use of a receiver postjudgment may also be advantageous from the creditor's point of view. Supplementary proceedings often will terminate in the appointment of a receiver charged with the collection of debts or property that

---

[249] See, e.g., Hankin v. Hankin, 279 Pa. Super. 179, 420 A2d 1090, appeal after remand, 302 Pa. Super. 295, 448 A2d 1049 (1980); Pearson Mfg. Co. v. Pittsburgh Steamboat Co., 309 Pa. 340, 163 A 680 (1932); Sinclair v. Moore Cent. R.R. Co., 228 NC 389, 45 SE2d 555 (1947).

[250] See, e.g., Riesenfeld, "Creditors' Remedies and the Conflict of Laws," 60 Colum. L. Rev. 659, 680 (1960); Booth v. Clark, 58 US (17 How.) 322 (1854); Hale v. Allinson, 188 US 56, 68 (1903). It should be noted, however, in Washington a supplementary proceeding receiver is invested with title. Wash. Rev. Code Ann. § 6.32.330; Morse Electro Prod. Corp. v. Beneficial Indus. Loan Co., 90 Wash. 2d 195, 579 P2d 1341 (1978).

[251] Receivership may be used as either a prejudgment or postjudgment collection remedy.

[252] See infra ¶ 6.04[4][b] for discussion of grounds for appointment of a receiver.

[253] See, e.g., Kellogg v. Coller, 47 Wis. 649, 3 NW 433 (1879); Annot., 92 A.L.R. 1435, 1448 (1934).

[254] This is true of receivership generally. See, e.g., PSL Realty Co. v. Granite Inv. Co., 76 Ill. App. 3d 978, 395 NE2d 641, aff'd in part, rev'd in part, 86 Ill. App. 2d 291, 427 NE2d 563 (1979).

[255] See, e.g., Turner v. Superior Court of Kern County, 72 Cal. App. 3d 804, 140 Cal. Rptr. 475 (1977); Securities & Exch. Comm'n v. United Fin. Group, Inc., 576 F2d 217 (9th Cir. 1978); Wiswall v. Sampson, 55 US (14 How.) 52, 68 (1852); Erikson v. Hewlett, 212 Ga. 423, 93 SE2d 563 (1956).

cannot be reached by ordinary postjudgment remedies, such as execution and postjudgment garnishment.[256] The appointment of a receiver in connection with postjudgment supplementary proceedings may also result in creating liens in specific assets of the debtor in favor of the specific creditors seeking satisfaction of a judgment.

A controversial problem related to receiverships involves the extraterritorial reach of a receiver's authority to a state other than the state in which the receiver has been appointed. The U.S. Supreme Court has frequently held that a receiver is not vested with title to assets. In that vein, the Court has held that a receiver cannot dispose of property located in another state unless he is appointed as an ancillary receiver or on principles of comity.[257]

### [b] Grounds for Appointment—Equitable and Statutory

The legal basis on which appointment of a receiver may rest originated in the courts of equity.[258] New York adopted pioneering legislation that set forth the cases in which a receiver could be appointed,[259] and many other states have subsequently followed this precedent.[260] However, for the most part, this statutory law is a codification of rules of equity, except with regard to corporations.

Three basic principles underlie judicial decisions to appoint or not to appoint receivers. First, the appointment is primarily a matter of discretion with the court.[261] Second, courts are very reluctant to appoint receivers prior to the judgment, since such appointments are a harsh remedy. It would seem that a creditor prior to judgment could only obtain an appointment of a receiver if it is shown that, in the absence of appointment, irreparable damage will result to the creditor's ability to recover a judgment.[262] Third, since the

---

[256] See, e.g., Cal. Civ. Proc. Code § 564(4); Mich. Gen. Ct. R. 741.5; Mich. Comp. Laws Ann. § 600.6104(4); Wash. Rev. Code Ann. § 6.32.290.

[257] See, e.g., Booth v. Clark, 58 US (17 How.) 322 (1854); Hale v. Allinson, 188 US 56 (1902); Great W. Min. & Mfg. Co. v. Harris, 198 US 561 (1905); Keatley v. Furey, 226 US 399 (1912). For discussion of receivership with regard to enforcement of mortgages, see ¶ 8.08[3].

[258] See, e.g., Levin v. Garfinkle, 514 F. Supp. 1160 (ED Pa. 1981); Petitpren v. Taylors School Dist., 104 Mich. App. 283, 304 NW2d 553 (1981); Hughes v. Marshall Nat'l Bank, 538 SW2d 820 (Tex. Civ. App. 1976); Rodgers v. Carson Lake Road Improvement Dist., 191 Ark. 112, 85 SW2d 716 (1935).

[259] Cf. 1825 N.Y. Laws 325, which became part of the revised statutes of 1829, N.Y. Rev. Stat. pt. III, ch. 8, art. 2.

[260] See Note, "State Statute Providing for Appointment of a Receiver Upon Return of Execution Unsatisfied as Insolvency Statute," 30 Minn. L. Rev. 638 (1946).

[261] See, e.g., Greater Fort Worth v. Mims, 574 SW2d 870, error dismissed (Tex. Civ. App. 1978); Ginsberg v. Davis, 191 Minn. 12, 252 NW 669 (1934).

[262] See, e.g., Bracco v. Lackner, 462 F. Supp. 436 (ND Cal. 1978); Poulakidas v. Charalidis, 68 Ill. App. 3d 610, 386 NE2d 405 (1979); see also Riesenfeld, Creditors' Remedies and Debtors' Protection 306–307 (West, 3d ed. 1979).

remedy is basically equitable in nature, receivership will not lie if there is an adequate legal remedy, such as attachment, garnishment, and execution.[263]

In total, a simple contract creditor ordinarily will not be able to obtain appointment of a receiver prior to judgment. Such a creditor may be able to obtain appointment of a receiver to aid in the enforcement of a money judgment (e.g., in aid of supplementary proceedings) if a court concludes that resort to relief is warranted. Even as to postjudgment receiverships, courts are reluctant to appoint receivers. The decision to appoint a receiver rarely will be upset by higher courts upon appeal.[264]

### [c] Use in Corporate Liquidations

If a corporate debtor is involved, statutory law is more commonly found to be at variance with the basic equitable principles previously discussed. In 1825, New York passed what was, in effect, a corporate receivership law. It was an "act to prevent fraudulent bankruptcies by incorporated companies, to facilitate proceedings against them and for other purposes."[265] The New York statute was adopted by many jurisdictions. More recently, similar provisions for the involuntary dissolution or liquidation of a corporation on petition of unsatisfied creditors have been included in many corporation codes.[266] Because of the similarity between state involuntary corporate receiverships and involuntary bankruptcy petitions, the validity of these provisions is in doubt. This is due to the fact that the U.S. Constitution grants Congress the authority to regulate bankruptcy[267] and that some courts find, with regard to corporations, that the receivership statutes are "tantamount to bankruptcy."[268] It should be emphasized, however, that receiverships in dissolutions begun by stockholders are not affected by the Bankruptcy Code.[269] In any event, the inclusion of

---

[263] See, e.g., Mintzer v. Arthur L. Wright & Co., 263 F2d 823 (3d Cir. 1959); Leighton v. One William St. Fund, Inc., 343 F2d 565 (2d Cir. 1965)

[264] See, e.g., supra ¶ 6.04[4][b] note 261.

[265] See supra ¶ 6.04[4][b] note 259.

[266] See, e.g., Model Business Corporation Act (American Law Institute (A.L.I.)) §§ 97(b)(1), 97(b)(2); Del. Corp. Code § 291; Ill. Bus. Corp. Act § 157.86(b); N.Y. Bus. Corp. Law §§ 1201, 1202.

[267] U.S. Constitution, article 1, section 8, clause 4.

[268] See, e.g., Straton v. New, 283 US 318 (1931); Emil v. Hanley, 318 US 515 (1943). However, there is contrary authority. See First Nat'l Bank in Albuquerque v. Robinson, 107 F2d 50 (10th Cir. 1939). Many state courts seem to assume the validity of corporate receivership statutes. See, e.g., Ebling Brewing Co. v. Heirloom, Inc., 1 NJ 71 61 A2d 885 (1948); Commercial Trading Co. v. Detroit Gray Iron & Steel Foundries, Inc., 69 Mich. App. 204, 244 NW2d 413 (1976); see also Felix, "The Effect of the National Bankruptcy Code Upon the Uniform Business Corporation Act," 23 Wash. L. Rev. 60 (1948); Glenn, Liquidations §§ 247–248 (Boker, Voorhis & Co. 1935).

[269] See, e.g., Compton v. Paul K. Harding Realty Co., 6 Ill. App. 3d 488, 285 NE2d 574 (1972); Lust v. Kolbe, 31 Md. App. 483, 356 A2d 592 (1976).

corporate reorganization provisions in bankruptcy law has resulted in a demise of liquidation or reorganization receiverships.[270]

## [5] Limitations Common to Prejudgment Remedies

### [a] Constitutional Due Process Limitations

**[i] The *Sniadach* Decision and Other Case Law.** During the last decade, state statutes providing for prejudgment remedies[271] have undergone a rapid evolution with respect to the procedure for issuance of writs of attachment, prejudgment garnishment, and replevin. This portion of the text considers the principal national case law that has caused this evolution. As a result of the decision in *Sniadach*, prior notice and opportunity for hearing now are usually afforded the debtor before a creditor may obtain issuance of writs of attachment and prejudgment garnishment.[272] The case law also relates to the use of replevin, although with arguably less impact on traditional replevin procedure. The principal impetus for this change has been the Fourteenth Amendment of the U.S. Constitution as applied by the U.S. Supreme Court through a well-known series of cases beginning with *Sniadach v. Family Finance Corp.*[273] Before consideration of these cases, a brief review of pre-*Sniadach* attachment, prejudgment garnishment, and replevin statutes should be undertaken.

The typical pre-*Sniadach* attachment, prejudgment garnishment, and replevin statutes allow a plaintiff to obtain issuance of writs ordering the sheriff to levy on the defendant's property. The issuance of the writs and subsequent levy can usually occur without prior notice or prior opportunity to a hearing being given the defendant. Thus, the plaintiff is typically allowed to submit a motion and affidavit delineating the statutory requirements for issuance of the writs. In the case of personal property, "levy" occurs by way of seizure and retention by the sheriff of the property of the defendant. As to real property, levy occurs by a sheriff filing a notice in real estate records or posting of a notice on the real property itself. In order to obtain issuance of the writs, the plaintiff must usually post a bond. The defendant is then given a subsequent opportunity to challenge the levy or to post a bond in order to obtain a release

---

[270] See Riesenfeld, Creditors' Remedies and Debtors' Protection 497–498 (West, 3d ed. 1979); see also, 7 Moore's Federal Practice ¶¶ 66.05[1], 66.09[2] (Matthew Bender 1972). There still is a need for general receiverships at the federal level to conserve assets in the public interest. See Smallwood v. U.S., 358 F. Supp. 398 (ED Mo. 1973).

[271] Other limitations common to prejudgment remedies have already been considered or will be considered in other parts of the text. See, e.g., supra ¶¶ 6.04[1], 6.04[2]; see also infra ¶ 6.07[1] for discussion of exemption law and infra ¶ 6.07[3] for discussion of the duration of judicial liens.

[272] The ensuing discussion of the constitutional due process considerations relevant to prejudgment remedies is largely adopted from Hagedorn, "Prejudgment Attachment in Washington–A Need for Legislative Action," 16 Gonz. L. Rev. 287 (1981).

[273] 395 US 337 (1969); see also North Ga. Finishing, Inc. v. Di-Chem, Inc., 419 US 601 (1975); Mitchell v. W.T. Grant Co., 416 US 600 (1974); Fuentes v. Shevin, 407 US 67, reh'g denied, 409 US 902 (1972).

of the seized property. The levy often creates a lien on the property through which the plaintiff may satisfy a judgment when it is ultimately obtained. The levy, through creation of a lien, also often establishes priority in the plaintiff as against other claimants to the property. In short, pre-*Sniadach* attachment and prejudgment garnishment are procedures that normally provide plaintiff-creditors with an ex parte means of easily securing collection of a judgment when ultimately obtained. However, the very advantage that these summary procedures offered a creditor ultimately caused the procedures to run afoul of the U.S. Constitution.

The death knell to such ex parte procedures initially rang in *Sniadach*, which involved a wage garnishment that occurred without the defendant receiving prior notice or an opportunity for a hearing. The U.S. Supreme Court held that the procedure violated the due process requirements of the Fourteenth Amendment. More specifically, the Court held that a garnishment statute must require notice and opportunity to be heard before a creditor can garnish a debtor's wages, noting that wages are a specialized type of property presenting distinct problems in our economic system. Finally, the Court indicated that such a summary procedure might be acceptable in certain extraordinary situations not present in *Sniadach*. The nature of these was left undefined by the Court except for the following four situations. Three involved summary seizure or impounding of property by a governmental agency to protect the public welfare;[274] the fourth involved the attachment of property of a nonresident debtor.[275]

*Fuentes v. Shevin*[276] provided the next relevant decision. The case involved the statutory replevin procedures of two states, whereby the clerk of a court could issue a writ of replevin upon the filing of an application and the posting of a bond by the person seeking the writ. The seizure occurred prior to judgment and deprived the defendants of their property unless they posted a bond to obtain its release. The writs were issued under the statutes without the requirement of a convincing showing by the plaintiffs that they were entitled to the property in question. The Court held that the replevin statutes violated due process because notice of deprivation did not occur at a meaningful time prior to seizure of the property. The Court emphasized that any significant taking of property by the state is within the purview of the due process clause. Further, the Court held that the *Sniadach* requirement of prior notice and hearing applicable to wages also applied to all other types of property. The Court again referred to the possibility that an ex parte seizure may be justified under extraordinary circumstances (e.g., where the seizure is directly necessary to secure an important governmental or general public interest). There is dictum

---

[274] See Ewing v. Mytinger & Casselberry, Inc., 339 US 594, 598–600 (1949); Fahey v. Mallonee, 332 US 245, 253–254 (1947); Coffin Bros. & Co. v. Bennett, 277 US 29, 31 (1928); Ownbey v. Morgan, 256 US 94, 110–112 (1920).

[275] Note that after *Sniadach*, the case of Shaffer v. Heitner, 433 US 186 (1977), has greatly diminished the use of prejudgment remedies to obtain quasi in rem jurisdiction, thus reducing in importance the extraordinary circumstances justifying ex parte seizure alluded to by the *Sniadach* Court. For a discussion of *Shaffer*, see supra ¶ 6.02[2][b].

[276] 407 US 67 (1972).

indicating that a showing of immediate danger (a debtor's intent to destroy or conceal property) would suffice to constitutionally justify an ex parte seizure.

The third U.S. Supreme Court case relevant to the constitutionality of summary prejudgment remedies is *Mitchell v. W.T. Grant Co.*[277] The holding of *Mitchell* stands in contrast to *Sniadach* and *Fuentes*. The Court upheld the constitutionality of a sequestration procedure, whereby a creditor could obtain a writ of sequestration by filing a petition and posting a sufficient bond, even though prior notice and hearing were not provided the debtor. The creditor, in *Mitchell*, had a lien on the subject property. The statute under scrutiny required the creditor to allege specific facts supporting its claim, as opposed to mere conclusory allegations. The debtor also had a right to an immediate postseizure hearing. A clerk did not issue the writ under the statute; rather, a magistrate had to authorize its issuance. The Court "balanced" the rights of the debtor and creditor, holding that, as long as safeguards are present, the interest of the creditor in preserving the property allegedly subject to his lien would override the interest of the debtor in continued use and possession. The safeguards deemed sufficient by the *Mitchell* Court included the following previously mentioned requirements that

(1) The creditor sign an affidavit alleging specific facts;
(2) A magistrate issue the writ;
(3) The creditor post bond; and
(4) A prompt postseizure hearing be made available.

The latest U.S. Supreme Court decision in point is *North Georgia Finishing, Inc. v. Di-Chem, Inc.*[278] This case involved a garnishment of the defendant's bank account. The state garnishment procedure permitted a clerk of the court to issue a writ of garnishment upon the filing of an affidavit by the plaintiff without the defendant receiving prior notice or an opportunity for a hearing. The Court, with emphasis on the *Fuentes* rationale, held that the procedure violated due process of law because the defendant was deprived of a substantial property interest without notice and opportunity for an early hearing and without participation of a judicial officer. Further, the Court reaffirmed its reliance on the *Mitchell* rationale by noting that the statute under scrutiny had none of the saving characteristics of the statute involved in the *Mitchell* sequestration.

The relationship of the four cases remains unclear, thus presenting a necessity for further development in the field based on a case-by-case analysis of ex parte prejudgment remedies. In terms of prejudgment remedies, generally only four conclusions can safely be reached from the four cases:

(1) Prejudgment remedies are not unconstitutional per se;
(2) The use of prejudgment remedies is subject to due process limitations;
(3) Due process requires notice and opportunity for an adversary proceeding; and

---

[277] 416 US 600 (1974).

[278] 419 US 601 (1975).

(4) In at least some situations, a preseizure ex parte hearing, coupled with the opportunity for a prompt postseizure adversary proceeding, will satisfy due process, where, for example, the creditor asserts an Article 9 security interest in assets to be replevied.

The confusion engendered by these four cases is particularly troublesome to parties litigating in a state where the state legislature clings to traditional pre-*Sniadach* collection statutes, the nature of which enhance the uncertainty evoked by these important cases. Unlike the situation in *Mitchell*, where the creditor had a vendor's lien on the sequestered property, the use of a pre-*Sniadach* attachment or prejudgment garnishment statute is not predicated upon a preexisting interest of the plaintiff-creditor in the attached or garnished asset. Thus, it would seem that the debtor's constitutional rights concerning unsecured debts are better judged through the *Sniadach* and *North Georgia* situations, in which the equities seemed to fall strongly in favor of the defendant-debtor.

The prejudgment attachment of real property necessarily differs procedurally from attachment of personal property. Whereas attachment of personal property creates a lien at the time of the sheriff's levy through actual seizure of the debtor's property, attachment of real property creates a lien at the time of levy by the sheriff filing an appropriate notice of attachment in the real estate records in the county where the real estate is located. This may also be accomplished by posting notice on the real property itself. The "taking" is, therefore, of an arguably lesser nature in the case of real property since the debtor may continue to use and enjoy it. Of course, any transfer of property will be encumbered by the attachment lien. Since the impact of prejudgment attachment on a real property owner is arguably less than that on an owner of personal property, the question is raised whether the attachment of real estate without notice or opportunity to be heard can be distinguished from such attachment of personal property from a due process standpoint.[279]

The U.S. Supreme Court came close to considering this question in *Spielman-Fond, Inc. v. Hanson's Inc.*[280] The Court affirmed the holding of an Arizona federal district court that a mechanic's and materialman's lien on real property did not deprive the owner of a property interest recognizable under the Fourteenth Amendment.[281] Interestingly, the decision was affirmed only two weeks after *Mitchell* was decided. At the district court level, Spielman-Fond argued that the defendant's perfection of a mechanic's and materialman's lien without prior notice and without an opportunity to be heard violated due process of law. The district court concluded, however, that the debtor's due process rights were not in question because only the economic interest of the

---

[279] The *Sniadach, Fuentes, Mitchell,* and *North Georgia* cases all involved personal property, and the debtor suffered an *actual loss of possession* of the property through the prejudgment remedy involved in each of the cases.

[280] 379 F. Supp. 997 (D. Ariz. 1973) (per curiam), aff'd mem., 417 US 901 (1974).

[281] For discussion of *Spielman-Fond,* see Note, "Real Property Attachment–Property or Economic Interest?" 52 Wash. L. Rev. 767, 777 (1977); Zaretsky, "Attachment Without Seizure: A Proposal for a New Creditors' Remedy," 1978 U. Ill. L.F. 819.

debtor was at stake; no property interest was lost, in that the debtor retained use and enjoyment of his property. The Court summarily affirmed the decision. Such affirmance is considered a decision on the merits and is binding on the inferior federal courts.[282]

Beyond this indication from the Court, other courts are split on the specific question of whether attachment of real estate can be distinguished from attachment of personal property, insofar as due process of law is concerned. In real property attachment cases, some courts have held that the deprivation created by the resulting lien is such a minor deprivation that it is not constitutionally protected.[283] Other courts have held that a resulting lien alone is of sufficient significance to be protected by the Fourteenth Amendment.[284] As a consequence, the question of the constitutionality of summary attachment of real estate awaits a future definitive resolution.

**[ii] State Legislative Responses.** In response to the previously mentioned case law, many state legislatures have revised their prejudgment remedial statutes.[285] Attorneys should carefully review local law to determine if applicable prejudgment remedial statutes require prior notice and hearing before issuance of a prejudgment remedial writ. In the absence of statutory requirements, local case law should be carefully reviewed to determine if state case law has provided further guidance, since lack of legislative guidance makes such procedural vagaries difficult to resolve.[286] Examples of states that have made legislative changes to conform the law to the constitutional mandate are

---

282 See Hicks v. Miranda, 422 US 332 (1975).

283 See, e.g., In re Northwest Homes of Chehalis, Inc., 526 F2d 505 (9th Cir. 1975), cert. denied, 425 US 907 (1976); In re Oronoka, 393 F. Supp. 1311 (D. Me. 1975); Central Sec. Nat'l Bank of Lorain County v. Royal Homes, Inc., 371 F. Supp. 476 (ED Mich. 1974); Harrison v. Morris, 370 F. Supp. 142 (DSC 1974); Black Watch Farms, Inc. v. Dick, 323 F. Supp. 100 (D. Conn. 1971); First Recreation Corp. v. Amoroso, 113 Ariz. 572, 558 P2d 917 (1976); Robinson v. Loyola Found., Inc., 236 So. 2d 154 (Fla. Dist. Ct. App. 1970).

284 See, e.g., MPI Inc. v. McCullough, 463 F. Supp. 887 (ND Miss. 1978); Terranova v. AVCO Fin. Servs., Inc., 396 F. Supp. 1402 (D. Vt. 1975); Bay State Harness Horse Racing & Breeding Ass'n, Inc. v. PPG Indus., Inc., 365 F. Supp. 1299 (D. Mass. 1973); Clement v. Four N. State St. Corp., 360 F. Supp. 933 (DNH 1973); Connolly Dev., Inc. v. Superior Court, 17 Cal. 3d 803, 553 P2d 637, 132 Cal. Rptr. 477 (1976), appeal dismissed, 429 US 1056 (1977); see also Comment, "Non-Possessory Prejudgment Attachment of Real and Personal Property in Vermont," 3 Vt. L. Rev. 217 (1978); Note, "Prejudgment Attachment of Real Property–Mississippi's Chancery Attachment Statutes Violate Due Process," 50 Miss. L.J. 183 (1979).

285 See 7 Debtor-Creditor Law ¶ 27.04 (Matthew Bender 1982) for an excellent review of state legislative responses to the due process problem in the states of California, Florida, Illinois, Michigan, New Jersey, New York, Ohio, Pennsylvania, and Texas.

286 See Hagedorn, "Prejudgment Attachment in Washington–A Need for Legislative Action," 16 Gonz. L. Rev. 287 (1981), for a discussion that illustrates the difficulties creditors and debtors face in a state that has not legislated changes to prejudgment remedial procedures.

California,[287] Florida,[288] Illinois,[289] New York,[290] Pennsylvania,[291] and Texas.[292]

### [b] Other Practical Limitations

In addition to procedural limitations on the use of prejudgment remedies, there are other negative factors inherent in the use of prejudgment remedies from the point of view of the creditor. There are expenses related to most prejudgment remedies resulting in seizure of property. As indicated previously in this chapter, in the case of attachment, a bond may be required of the creditor. The sheriff will often require an indemnity bond before levying on the property in order to protect himself from liability should he wrongfully seize property. The sheriff may seek reimbursement of expenses incurred in levying on the property and in preserving the attached property. Finally, the creditor will incur attorney fees.

Seizure of the debtor's property prior to judgment may induce him to file voluntary bankruptcy proceedings or to induce other creditors to file involuntary proceedings. Under Section 547 of the Bankruptcy Code, most attachments within ninety days of the bankruptcy filing may be avoided as a preference.[293] By attaching a substantial portion of his debtor's property, a creditor may induce competing creditors to file a petition in bankruptcy to avoid the attachment lien priority.

Perhaps the greatest practical limitation to the use of prejudgment remedies by a creditor lies in potential liability, if seizure of an asset is wrongful.[294] This is particularly a concern with regard to prejudgment remedies, since the plaintiff-creditor may not ultimately obtain a judgment, thus potentially making prejudgment seizure wrongful. The nature of such liability is considered in this portion of the text, particularly in the instance of a wrongful attachment.

Liability might be predicated on statutory grounds for wrongful attachment. For example, a creditor was held liable for damages when he attached property without satisfying the statutory requirements for attachment when he seized two trailers on display at a trade show to collect a small debt. The court held him liable for substantial damages because the creditor's attorney failed to allege, as required, that no officer was available to execute the affidavit, that

[287] Cal. Civ. Proc. Code Ann. §§ 481.010–493.060.

[288] Fla. Stat. Ann. §§ 76.03, 76.08, 76.18, 76.24.

[289] Ill. Rev. Stat. ch. 11, § 2.

[290] N.Y. Civ. Prac. Law §§ 6201, 6223, 7102.

[291] Pa. R. Civ. P. 1075.1, 1075.2.

[292] Tex. Civ. Proc. Rules Ann. R. 592-609, 657-679, 696-716.

[293] See ¶ 17.04 for discussion of avoidance of preferential transfers in bankruptcy.

[294] Note that the sheriff involved in a wrongful attachment might also incur liability to the debtor whose property is seized. He could also incur liability to third parties who claim interests in the seized property. See Riesenfeld, Creditors' Remedies and Debtors' Protection 361–364 (West, 3d ed. 1979).

the claim was just, or what amount the affiant thought the creditor should recover, and then failed to object to overly broad jury instructions.[295]

Tort liability may also arise due to wrongful attachment. This liability may be asserted under a bond. However, apart from liability under a bond, to which damages may be limited, usually the attaching plaintiff is not liable to the defendant simply because the attachment is later invalidated.[296] However, the attachment plaintiff may be held liable if the attachment is both malicious and wrongful as the following suggests:[297]

> [The debtor] may sue for malicious and wrongful attachment if the essential elements of that tort are present. He may even maintain an action for abuse of process if the attachment plaintiff maliciously perverts and employs a regularly issued order of attachment to accomplish a result not lawfully or properly obtainable under it.
>
> Where the attachment defendant sues . . . for malicious and wrongful attachment, it is incumbent upon him to establish these essential elements of the tort: (1) That the attachment plaintiff sued out an order of attachment against the property of the attachment defendant without probable cause for believing that the alleged ground for attachment existed; (2) that the attachment plaintiff sued out such order of attachment maliciously; (3) that the order of attachment was actually levied on the property of the attachment defendant, who was thereby deprived of his right to use his property . . . ; (4) that the attachment proceeding has legally terminated in favor of the attachment defendant; and (5) that the attachment defendant suffered damage as a result of the levy of the order of attachment upon his property.[298]

There are other twists in the law regarding tort liability for wrongful attachment. As indicated, liability for wrongful attachment may be limited to the amount of the bond supplied by the plaintiff as a condition to obtaining the writ.[299] Local statutes must be consulted, since damages normally are limited by the bond unless the statute provides otherwise.[300] For example, in some states punitive damages are authorized by statute where the attachment is mali-

---

[295] Duo-Therm Div., Motor Wheel Corp. v. Sheergrain, Inc., 504 SW2d 689 (Ky. 1973).

[296] See, e.g., Audit Servs., Inc. v. Haugen, 181 Mont. 9, 591 P2d 1105 (1979); Delisi v. Garnett, 257 Md. 4, 261 A2d 784 (1970); Clarence E. Morris, Inc. v. Vitek, 85 Nev. 652, 461 P2d 864 (1969); Brown v. Peoples Nat'l Bank of Wash., 39 Wash. 2d 776, 238 P2d 1191 (1951).

[297] See Annot., 83 A.L.R.3d 598 (1978).

[298] Brown v. Guaranty Estates Corp., 239 NC 595, 599–601, 80 SE2d 645, 649–651 (1954).

[299] See, e.g., Finn v. Witherbee, 126 Cal. App. 2d 45, 271 P2d 606 (1954) (bond). But see Minnehoma Fin. Co. v. Johnson, 152 Tex. 386, 258 SW2d 78 (1953) (damages); Commonwealth Tire Co., 193 SE2d 544 (W. Va. 1972) (damages).

[300] See, e.g., Cal. Civ. Proc. Code §§ 489.210–489.220; Wash. Rev. Code § 7.12.060; Iowa Code Ann. § 639.11.

cious.[301] On the other hand, in some states, a lack of malice or bad faith is not a defense to the plaintiff where the levy is improper,[302] but an improper levy by a sheriff that the plaintiff did not direct, consent to, or ratify, usually is not actionable.[303] Further, the defendant may not in some states recover on a wrongful attachment if it is shown that the writ was obtained with probable cause.[304]

It should be emphasized that the right to proceed on a bond does not usually depend on a showing of malice and want of probable cause. In *Brown v. Guaranty Estates Corp.*, the court stated:

> Since the attachment bond is conditioned that if the order of attachment is dissolved, dismissed or set aside by the court, or if the attachment plaintiff fails to obtain judgment against the attachment defendant, the attachment plaintiff will pay all costs that may be awarded to the attachment defendant and all damages that the attachment defendant may sustain by reason of the attachment, the attachment defendant may bring the statutory proceeding to enforce liability on the bond under two conditions, namely, where the order of attachment is dissolved, dismissed or set aside by the court, or where the attachment plaintiff fails to obtain judgment against him. . . . The liability of the surety . . . is limited to the amount of the attachment bond.[305]

In total, the use of prejudgment remedies should be carefully considered by an attorney or creditor. The attorney must advise the creditor of both the potential advantages and disadvantages of using these provisional remedies and then proceed with caution.

## ¶ 6.05 POSTJUDGMENT REMEDIES

### [1] Introduction to Postjudgment Remedies

The creditor who has successfully obtained a judgment will usually enforce the judgment by use of postjudgment remedies. Prejudgment remedies are con-

---

[301] See, e.g., Iowa Code Ann. § 639.14; Arthur Elevator Co. v. Grove, 236 NW2d 383 (Iowa 1975); Cal. Civ. Proc. Code § 3294.

[302] See, e.g., Peterson v. Wiesner, 62 Nev. 184, 146 P2d 789 (1944); Crouter v. United Adjusters, Inc., 259 Ore. 348, 485 P2d 1208, appeal after remand, 266 Ore. 6, 510 P2d 1328 (1971).

[303] See, e.g., Peterson v. Wiesner, 62 Nev. 184, 146 P2d 789 (1944); Snyder v. Stokes, 34 SW2d 918 (Tex. Civ. App. 1930), aff'd, Stokes v. Snyder, 55 SW2d 557 (Tex. Civ. App. 1932); Adams v. Savery House Hotel, 107 Wis. 109, 82 NW 703 (1900).

[304] See, e.g., Braun v. Pepper, 224 Kan. 56, 578 P2d 695 (1978); Marsella's Appliance Sales & Serv., Inc. v. General Elec. Credit Corp., 76 AD2d 990, 429 NYS2d 86 (1980); Hiers v. Cohen, 31 Conn. Supp. 305, 329 A2d 609 (1973).

[305] 239 NC 595, 600–601, 80 SE2d 645 (1954).

sidered extraordinary by the courts,[1] and modernly by the legislatures,[2] and thus often are not available to the creditor. In turning to postjudgment remedies, the judgment creditor whose claim is unsecured seeks to accomplish the same goals that were relevant to prejudgment remedies.[3] That is to say, he seeks to obtain a judicial lien in the debtor's property through which the property may be liquidated with the proceeds used to satisfy the claim, and to obtain priority over other parties who may also seek to acquire interests in the debtor's same property.

As was the case regarding prejudgment remedies, there is considerable variation among the states as to the law relating to postjudgment remedies. Therefore, the lawyer must carefully review local applicable law. Nationwide, the judgment lien,[4] writ of execution,[5] and postjudgment writ of garnishment,[6] constitute the typical postjudgment remedies available to a judgment creditor.[7] Many basic principles common to these three remedies are explored throughout this portion of the text. Continuing through the chronology of a judicial proceeding, the text first considers judgment liens.[8]

## [2] Judgment Liens

### [a] History and Basic Function of the Judgment Lien

The terms "judgment lien" and "judicial lien" are often confused. A judgment lien is a type of judicial lien, as are liens arising from writs of attachment, garnishment, and execution. The judgment lien exists in most jurisdictions and is created by docketing or recording of the judgment.[9] The lien usually attaches to all real estate in which the debtor has an interest located in the county in which docketing or recording has occurred.[10] Only in the New England states (with the exclusion of Connecticut)[11] and in Kentucky and Michigan are there no judgment liens.[12] All other states provide for a judgment lien on real estate.

---

[1] See supra ¶¶ 6.04[1][a]–6.04[1][d], 6.04[2][a]–6.04[2][c], 6.04[5][a][i], 6.04[5][b].

[2] See supra ¶ 6.04[5][a][ii].

[3] See supra ¶ 6.03.

[4] See infra ¶ 6.05[2].

[5] See infra ¶ 6.05[3].

[6] See infra ¶ 6.05[4].

[7] Other common postjudgment remedies considered include creditor's bills and supplementary proceedings. See infra ¶ 6.05[5].

[8] Note that collateral matters pertaining to postjudgment remedies are considered in a later portion of the text. See, e.g., infra ¶ 6.07.

[9] See infra ¶ 6.05[2][c] for a discussion of how the judgment lien is acquired.

[10] See infra ¶¶ 6.05[2][d] and 6.05[2][e] for discussion of the property that is subject to the judgment lien.

[11] See Conn. Gen. Stat. Ann. §§ 49-44–49-50.

[12] See Riesenfeld, "Creditors' Remedies and the Conflict of Laws–Part One: Individual Collection of Claims," 60 Colum. L. Rev. 659, 665 (1960).

In a few states, the lien also reaches the personal property of the debtor. These states include Alabama,[13] Georgia,[14] and Mississippi.[15] In Louisiana, money judgments upon recordation create judicial mortgages upon real property of the debtor then owned or thereafter acquired.[16] This judicial mortgage is the equivalent to the judgment lien of common-law jurisdictions.[17]

Historically,

> [A]t common law, except for debts due the king, the lands of the debtor were not liable to the satisfaction of a judgment against him, and consequently no lien thereon was acquired by a judgment. This was in accordance with the policy of the feudal law introduced into England after the Conquest, which, did not permit the feudatory to charge, or to be deprived, of his lands for his debts, lest thereby he should be disabled from performing his stipulated military service, and which moreover, forbid the alienation of a feud without the lord's consent.[18]

That common law continued in force until the Statute of Westminster II was passed in 1285. This statute created the writ of elegit, which entitled a judgment creditor to a statutory tenancy in half of the judgment debtor's land. From that statute, the judgment lien evolved in the United States. This occurred when a judgment creditor became authorized to sell the judgment debtor's land in satisfaction of his judgment, and most jurisdictions kept the judgment lien as a part of the new procedure.[19] Sale of land situated in the colonies in favor of a judgment creditor was provided for by an English statute in 1732.[20] Thus, from the beginning, judgment liens were statutory in nature and primarily related to the sale of real estate only. Consideration of the judgment lien will, however, be postponed in order to first distinguish the concept of lis pendens.

### [b] Lis Pendens Distinguished

The judgment lien and a notice of lis pendens are very different remedies and yet are often confused. As previously indicated, the judgment lien is a lien that arises after judgment is obtained. The filing of a notice of lis pendens does not create a lien but rather serves to give a plaintiff priority over subsequent

---

[13] See Ala. Code §§ 6-9-210, 6-9-211.

[14] See Ga. Code Ann. § 9-12-80, as qualified vis-à-vis bona fide purchasers by Ga. Code Ann. § 18-2-23; cf. Griffith v. Posey, 98 Ga. 475, 25 SE 515 (1896).

[15] See Miss. Code Ann. § 11-7-191.

[16] See La. Civ. Code Ann. art. 3321, 3322, 3328.

[17] See Comment, "The Judicial Mortgage," 34 Tul. L. Rev. 768 (1960).

[18] See Hutcheson v. Grubbs, 80 Va. 251, 254 (1885).

[19] See Riesenfeld, "Enforcement of Money Judgments in Early American History," 71 Mich. L. Rev. 691 (1973).

[20] See 5 Geo. 2 ch. 7.

purchasers of or lienors in a defendant's property. Further, use of a notice of lis pendens usually arises prior to judgment. For that reason, lis pendens could have been discussed in previous text that dealt with prejudgment remedies. To distinguish between the concept of lis pendens and the judgment lien, lis pendens is considered at this point.

The doctrine of lis pendens (notice of pendency) is that a purchaser (or a subsequent lienor) of property that is the subject of a pending action from a party to that action, is bound by the judgment.[21] "To have a lis pendens there must be property subject to the lis pendens, jurisdiction of the person, jurisdiction of the res, and pleadings which describe the property with particularity. The doctrine only applies to actions directly affecting property, and not to an action for money judgment."[22]

The doctrine of lis pendens evolved from the common law. Originally, it meant that, as to property involved in litigation, the purchaser or subsequent lienor took subject to the outcome of the action or suit, even though public notice was available only by search of the docket of the court in which the action or suit was pending.[23] Apparently, the doctrine applied to the judgment of a trial court and to the ultimate outcome on appeal.[24] The notice resulted from the requirement that the plaintiff describe the property involved in the pleading.[25] However, priority created by lis pendens could be lost for failure to diligently prosecute the action or suit.[26]

The doctrine principally affected real property,[27] although some jurisdictions extended the doctrine to personalty under some circumstances. Thus, there is authority that the doctrine applies to suits to foreclose chattel mort-

---

[21] See Moore, Phillips & D'Agostino, Debtors' and Creditors' Rights 5-79–5-83 (Matthew Bender, 5th ed. 1979) for an excellent summary of the doctrine of lis pendens. See also, e.g., E & E Hauling, Inc. v. County of DePage, 77 Ill. App. 3d 1017, 396 NE2d 1260 (1979); Angelos v. Maryland Cas. Co., 38 Md. App. 265, 380 A2d 646 (1977).

[22] Epstein & Landers, Debtors and Creditors 17 (West, 2d ed. 1982). See also, e.g., Bramall v. Wales, 29 Wash. App. 390, 628 P2d 511 (1981); Polk v. Schwartz, 166 NJ Super. 292, 399 A2d 1001 (1979); N.J. Stat. Ann. 2A:15-6; Angelos v. Maryland Casualty Co., 38 Md. App. 265, 380 A2d 646 (1977).

[23] See Note, "Lis Pendens—Filing and Cross Indexing—Statutory Requirements in North Carolina," 20 N.C.L. Rev. 311, 312 (1942); Note, "Immovables—Lis Pendens—Notice to Third Parties of Suit Affecting Little-Louisiana Act 22 of 1904," 12 Tul. L. Rev. 308 (1938).

[24] See, e.g., Pachner v. Hoppas, 119 Kan. 415, 239 P 967 (1925); noted, 39 Harv. L. Rev. 511 (1926).

[25] See 2 Pomeroy, Equity Jurisprudence § 634c (Lawyers' Coop. Publishing Co., 5th ed. 1941). See, e.g., Bowles v. Middletown Collateral Loan Co., 71 Ohio Op. 110, 328 NE2d 821 (1974); Herman v. Goetz, 204 Kan. 91, 460 P2d 554 (1969).

[26] See Annot., 8 A.L.R.2d 986 (1949).

[27] See Moore, Phillips & D'Agostino, Debtors' and Creditors' Rights 5-82 (Matthew Bender, 5th ed. 1979); Kirk v. Baumann, 336 So. 2d 125 (Fla. Dist. Ct. App. 1976).

gages and other liens;[28] to recover possession of chattels;[29] to enforce a trust on chattels;[30] to enjoin issuance of bonds;[31] and for specific performance of a contract to sell stocks and bonds.[32] The doctrine is particularly important with regard to both realty and personalty in a creditor's bill or supplementary proceeding.[33] This is the case where the creditor's bill is used to reach property of the debtor generally,[34] or where the creditor's bill is used for the specific purpose of reaching the debtor's property that was fraudulently conveyed.[35] The doctrine, however, is not usually applied to negotiable instruments.[36]

Today, most states have statutes requiring the recording of a notice of lis pendens for the protection of a third-party buyer or encumbrancer.[37] These

---

[28] See, e.g., Poole v. Frank, 11 SW2d 611 (Tex. Civ. App. 1928); Hubbard v. Johnson, 89 Wash. 310, 154 P 457 (1916).

[29] See, e.g., In re Washington, 623 F2d 1169 (6th Cir. 1980), cert. denied, 449 US 1101 (1981); P.A. Stark Piano Co. v. Fannin, 212 Ky. 640, 279 SW 1080 (1926); Citizens' State Bank v. Alexander, 274 SW 184 (Tex. Civ. App. 1925).

[30] See, e.g., Fletcher v. Ferrell, 39 Ky. 372 (1840); Mechanics' Bank of Alexandria v. Sexton, 26 US (1 Pet.) 299 (1828); Murray v. Lylburn, 2 Johns. Ch. 441 (NY Ch. 1817). But see Parker v. Superior Court, Riverside County, 9 Cal. App. 3d 397, 88 Cal. Rptr. 352 (1970).

[31] See, e.g., City of LaPorte, Inc. v. Northern Trust Co., 187 F 20 (7th Cir. 1911); Diamond v. Lawrence County, 37 Pa. 353 (1860).

[32] See, e.g., People's Bank v. Columbia Collieries Co., 75 W. Va. 309, 84 SE 914 (1914).

[33] See infra ¶ 6.05[5].

[34] See, e.g., Wilkerson v. Phillips, 118 Ky. 559, 81 SW 691 (1904); Hacker v. White, 23 Ky. 849, 64 SW 446 (1901); Burnham, Manger & Co. v. Smith, 82 Mo. App. 35 (1899).

[35] See, e.g., North Carolina Nat'l Bank v. Evans, 296 NC 374, 250 SE2d 231, (1979); Fidelity & Casualty Co. of N.Y. v. Schachter, 37 Misc. 2d 61, 233 NYS2d 251 (NY Sup. Ct. 1962); Blitman Constr. Corp. v. Denbel Realty & Constr. Co., 13 Misc. 2d 888, 178 NYS2d 249 (NY Sup. Ct. 1958).

[36] See Graubert, "Should Lis Pendens Prevent the Performance of an Executory Contract?" 44 Dick. L. Rev. 59 (1940); Note, "The Application of Lis Pendens to Personalty," 47 Harv. L. Rev. 1023, 1026 (1934); Massie v. Massie, 41 Ohio App. 169, 101 NE2d 222 (1951).

[37] An example of such a statute or rule of procedure is the Connecticut lis pendens statute, Conn. Gen. Stat. § 52-325.20, which provides:

> "In any action in a court of this state or in a court of the United States the plaintiff or his attorney, at the time the action is commended or afterwards, or a defendant, when he sets up an affirmative cause of action in his answer and demands substantive relief at the time the answer is filed, if the same is intended to affect real estate, may cause to be recorded in the office of the town clerk of each town in which the property is situated a notice of the pendency of the action, containing the names of the parties, the nature and object of the action, the court to which it is returnable and the term, session or return day thereof, the date of the process and the description of the property. Such notice shall, from the time of the recording only, be notice to any person thereafter acquiring any interest in such property of the pendency of the action; and each person whose conveyance or encumbrance is subse-

statutes usually relate to real property only, although many courts have decided that in cases not covered by statute the common-law doctrine of lis pendens still applies.[38] The notice of lis pendens and not the pleadings give constructive notice of pending litigation affecting the interest or realty. Thus, the effective time of filing of the notice operates to make subordinate any subsequently acquired interest.[39] Finally, the property affected by the notice is usually limited to property located in the county in which the notice is filed, although there is contrary authority.[40]

In total, lis pendens is significantly different than the judgment lien. The priority of the notice is provided to the plaintiff, who files the notice out of necessity to protect the court's ultimate decree as to the disposition of the subject property.[41] Even if it successfully provides a party with a priority, it does not provide the party with a means of liquidating the property to satisfy a debt or claim.

### [c] Basic Procedure and Nature of the Judgment Lien

As previously indicated, in all states except Kentucky and Michigan, and in all the New England States other than Connecticut, a judgment may result in a lien in real property, or even in the personal property, of the debtor after compliance with certain statutory procedures.[42] This portion of the text is not

---

quently executed or subsequently recorded or whose interest is thereafter obtained, by descent or otherwise, shall be deemed to be a subsequent purchaser or encumbrancer, and shall be bound by all proceedings taken after the recording of such notice to the same extent as if he were made a party to the action. For the purpose of this section an action shall be deemed to be pending from the time of the recording of such notice; provided such notice shall be of no avail unless service of the process is completed within the time provided by law. This section shall be construed to apply to mechanics' liens and all other inchoate liens, certificates of which are recorded subsequent to the recording of the notice of the pendency of the action; and, in suits to foreclose mortgages or other liens, the persons whose conveyances or encumbrances are subsequently executed or subsequently recorded shall forfeit their rights thereunder, unless they apply to the court in which such action is brought to be made parties thereto, prior to the date when the judgment or decree in such action is rendered."

[38] See Note, "Lis Pendens–Filing and Cross Indexing–Statutory Requirements in North Carolina," 20 N.C.L. Rev. 311 (1942); Note, "Immovables–Lis Pendens–Notice to Third Parties of Suit Affecting Little-Louisiana Act 22 of 1904," 12 Tul. L. Rev. 308 (1938); Note, "Statutory Lis Pendens," 20 Iowa L. Rev. 476 (1935); see also Annot., 10 A.L.R. 306 (1921); Freeman, Judgments § 521 (Bancroft-Whitney, 5th ed. 1925).

[39] See Annot., 130 A.L.R. 943 (1941); see also Chrysler Corp. v. Fedders Corp., 670 F2d 1316 (3d Cir. 1982); Schwartz v. Grunwald, 174 NJ Super. 164, 415 A2d 1203 (N.J. Super. Ct. 1980); Wendy's of S. Jersey, Inc. v. Blanchard Management Corp. of N.J., 170 NJ Super. 491, 406 A2d 1337 (1979).

[40] See Annot., 71 A.L.R. 1085 (1931); see also Walker v. Houston, 176 Ga. 878, 169 SE 107 (1933); Ludvik v. James S. Jackson Co., Inc., 635 P2d 1135 (Wyo. 1981).

[41] See supra ¶ 6.05[2][b] note 39.

[42] See supra ¶ 6.05[2][a].

concerned with the question of what property is subject to the judgment lien.[43] Rather, it focuses on the procedures by which judgment liens are obtained and the basic rights it gives the creditor in the debtor's property. The mechanics of obtaining a judgment lien vary from state to state and are discussed first.

Before there can be a valid judgment lien, there must be a judgment that is valid and final.[44] Typically, one associates judgment liens with judgments from a court of law for a definite and certain sum of money.[45] However, there is authority that a decree in equity may create a judgment lien if the equitable decree is for payment of a definite and liquidated sum of money.[46] Unless a statute or order of a court specifies otherwise, the preponderant authority is to the effect that judgments payable in installments for an indefinite period, such as alimony and child support decrees, do not create judgment liens.[47] However, some jurisdictions now have statutes specifically governing judgment liens for alimony and child support.[48] In the absence of a specific statute, no lien is created even as to arrears in accrued installments unless a decree for arrears has been entered and docketed.[49] Finally, as a general rule, the judgment lien arises only in courts of record.[50]

Assuming that a valid and final judgment or decree for a sum of money has been rendered by a court of record, local statutes must be consulted to determine how and when the lien is created. There are basically three different types of statutes:

(1) Statutes that provide that the lien is created upon rendering of the judgment;
(2) Statutes that provide that the lien is created upon docketing of the judgment; and
(3) Statutes that provide that the lien is created upon recording of the judgment.

---

[43] See infra ¶ 6.05[2][d] for discussion of the types of property subject to judgment liens.

[44] See, e.g., Uhrick v. Uhrick, 173 Ind. App. 133, 362 NE2d 1163 (1977); Newstead Bldrs. v. First Merchants Nat'l Bank, 146 NJ Super. 295, 369 A2d 951 (1977); Roach v. Roach, 164 Ohio St. 587, 132 NE2d 742 (1956).

[45] See, e.g., Uhrick v. Uhrick, 173 Ind. App. 133, 362 NE2d 1163 (1977); McClanahan v. Hawkins, 90 Ariz. 139, 367 P2d 196 (1961); Newstead Builder's v. First Merchants' Nat'l Bank, 146 NJ Super. 295, 369 A2d 951 (1977).

[46] See, e.g., Miles v. Gay, 280 Ala. 131, 190 So. 2d 686 (1966).

[47] See, e.g., Black v. Miller, 219 So. 2d 106 (Fla. 1969); Brieger v. Brieger, 197 Kan. 756, 421 P2d 1 (1966); Boyle v. Baggs, 10 Utah 2d 203, 350 P2d 622 (1960).

[48] See, e.g., Cal. Civ. Proc. Code § 674.5; Neb. Rev. Stat. §§ 42-371(2), 42-371(3); Ore. Rev. Stat. § 107.126.

[49] See, e.g., Willoughby v. King, 21 Ariz. App. 589, 522 P2d 54 (1974); Boyle v. Baggs, 10 Utah 2d 203, 350 P2d 622 (1960); Joseph Harris & Sons v. Van Loan, 23 NJ 466, 129 A2d 571 (1957).

[50] See, e.g., First Am. Title Co. v. Howe, 281 NW2d 605 (SD 1979); Etna Auto Fin., Inc. v. Kirby, 240 Ala. 228, 198 So. 356 (1940).

Statutes that provide for creation of the lien merely upon rendering[51] of the judgment are in a small minority.[52] The obvious difficulty with these statutes is that they provide little notice to the public of the creation of the judgment lien. Tennessee was an example of a state that granted a judgment lien to the judgment creditor the moment the judgment was rendered.[53] The Tennessee statute provided that judgments and decrees obtained in any court of record of the state in the county where the debtor resided at the time of rendition, were liens upon the debtor's land in that county from the time that judgment was rendered. This seemed to be a hardship on parties who in good faith obtained interests in the judgment debtor's property subsequent to the judgment.[54]

In most states, the judgment lien attaches only after the judgment creditor has docketed[55] or recorded his judgment in the place specified by the statute.[56] These types of statutes seem preferable to the former Tennessee statute described in the previous paragraph in that they provide a better means of public notice. In those states that require docketing, usually the docketing occurs in a special docket book kept by a court official; in those states that require recording, the recording usually must be made with the recorder of deeds or with a local official who keeps land records.[57] If the judgment is properly docketed or recorded (depending on the type of statute), it typically creates a lien on the debtor's land in the county in which the judgment is docketed or recorded. To acquire liens in other counties of the state in which the judgment is rendered, statutes frequently require further docketing or recording of a transcript or abstract of the judgment in the foreign county. This is true even if the judgment lien is created upon rendering alone in the original county in which the judgment is obtained.[58]

The recording acts differ as to the impact of notice of an existing unrecorded interest of a third party in the property of the judgment debtor. In most states, constructive or actual notice of a third-party interest in the land of the judgment debtor that was acquired before the judgment lien has the effect of defeating or subordinating the judgment lien to the noticed interest. For example, it is usually held that possession by an unrecorded grantee is notice to the judgment creditor and defeats or subordinates his interest.[59]

---

[51] See supra ¶ 6.02[1] for discussion of "rendition."

[52] See Hawkland & Loiseaux, Debtor-Creditor Relations 16 (Bobbs-Merrill 1979).

[53] See Tenn. Code Ann. § 25-501. But see Tenn. Code Ann. § 25-5-101.

[54] For cases involving the former Tennessee statute in which priority disputes arose with third parties, see, e.g., Homes v. Archer Paper Co., 45 Tenn. App. 1, 319 SW2d 252 (1958); Bridges v. Cooper, 98 Tenn. 394, 39 SW 723 (1897).

[55] See supra ¶ 6.02[1] for discussion of entry by "docketing."

[56] See supra ¶ 6.02[1] for examples of typical filing places as required by local statutes.

[57] See supra ¶ 6.02[1].

[58] See, e.g., Tenn. Code Ann. § 25-502; Tenn. Code Ann. § 25-5-102.

[59] See, e.g., Jensen v. Bryson, 614 SW2d 930 (Tex. Civ. App. 1981); In re Investors Funding Corp. of N.Y., 452 F. Supp. 771 (SDNY 1978); Michalski v. U.S., 49 NJ Super.

In states where recording (or filing transcripts or abstracts of judgments) or docketing is required to create the judgment lien, what is recorded or docketed must be legally sufficient. Substantial compliance with the required content of the filing must occur regarding names of the parties and the amount of the judgment.[60] Further, the indexing by the public official must also occur properly.[61] Major errors in docketing or recording the judgment will prevent the lien from attaching. An error by the recording officer will prevent the lien from attaching under most statutes,[62] although such an error may give rise to a cause of action against the recording officer by the harmed judgment creditor.

The judgment lien is such that it "only confers a right to levy on the same, to the exclusion of other adverse interests, subsequent to the judgment. . . ."[63] Thus, the judgment lien only provides a means to liquidate the subject property of the debtor and obtain a priority over interests subsequently asserted by other parties in the same property. The judgment lien does not create an estate in the property in favor of the judgment creditor. Because the judgment lien creates only an encumbrance, the judgment debtor may continue to possess and enjoy the property. The judgment creditor cannot sue for waste or on any impairment of security theory.[64]

### [d] Property Interests Subject to the Judgment Lien

The property interests of the debtor that are subject to the judgment lien (in almost all states) include only interests in real estate; only in Alabama, Georgia, and Mississippi does the judgment lien also reach interests in personal property.[65] Obviously, the property cannot be exempt property.[66] Further, recall that the lien typically only reaches the debtor's interest in real property

---

104, 139 A2d 324 (1958). For further discussion of the relative priority of a judgment lien and an unrecorded interest, see infra ¶ 6.05[2][f].

[60] See, e.g., Jones v. Parker, 107 NJ Super. 235, 258 A2d 26 (1969); McIntire v. Sawichi, 353 SW2d 952 (Tex. Civ. App. 1962); Jaczyszyn v. Paslawski, 147 Pa. Super. 97, 24 A2d 116 (1942); 49 C.J.S. Judgments § 462d(1) (1947).

[61] See, e.g., Day v. Day, 610 SW2d 195 (Tex. Civ. App. 1980); Ostroff v. Brandywine Lock & Safe Co., 428 A2d 8 (Del. 1981); see also 49 C.J.S. Judgments §§ 462d(2), 462d(3) (1947).

[62] See, e.g., Commonwealth ex rel. Orris v. Roberts, 183 Pa. Super. 204, 130 A2d 226, rev'd, 392 Pa. 572, 141 A2d 393 (1956). But see American Nat'l Bank & Trust Co. v. Wilds, 545 SW2d 749 (Tenn. 1977)

[63] See Conard v. Atlantic Ins. Co., 7 US (1 Pet.) 386, 443 (1828).

[64] See, e.g., Onyx Ref. Co. v. Evans Prod. Corp., 182 F. Supp. 253 (ND Tex. 1959). In *Onyx*, there was a judgment lien in a lessor's interest in an oil and gas lease. The court held that proceeds derived from sale of oil should be paid to the judgment debtor who was the lessee and not the judgment creditor who held the judgment lien.

[65] See supra ¶¶ 6.04[2][a], 6.05[2][a] notes 13–15.

[66] See, e.g., Rochford v. Laser, 91 Ill. App. 3d 169, 414 NE2d 1096 (1980); Tpea No. 5 Credit Union v. Solis, 605 SW2d 381 (Tex. Civ. App. 1980). However, the judgment lien can attach to the surplus in value above a homestead exemption. See Annot., 32 A.L.R. 1333 (1924); see also infra ¶ 6.07[1] for discussion of exemption law.

located in the county in which the judgment is rendered, docketed, or recorded.[67] Thus, if the property interest held by the debtor is transferred prior to attachment of the judgment lien, the judgment lien cannot usually reach the transferred property. However, a prior unrecorded conveyance of the judgment debtor is subordinate to a subsequent judgment lien.[68] A few jurisdictions would not protect judgment creditors in the case of a prior unrecorded conveyance by the judgment debtor, although such statutes do protect subsequent bona fide purchasers.[69] Arguably, the judgment creditor who purchases at a judicial sale could qualify as a bona fide purchaser and take free of the unrecorded interest even though no judgment lien technically is attached to the property.[70] If the prior conveyance was a fraudulent conveyance,[71] the states are divided on the question of whether a judgment lien attaches to land fraudulently conveyed. Some states allow for automatic attachment of the judgment lien in the fraudulently conveyed property,[72] while others require the judgment creditor to first avoid the fraudulent conveyance, with the judgment lien thereafter attaching.[73]

There is substantial litigation nationwide as to what constitutes an interest in "real property" for judgment lien purposes, particularly in three problem areas. First, there is a split of authority among the jurisdictions with regard to whether the judgment lien reaches an equitable interest in land.[74] Equitable

---

[67] See supra ¶ 6.05[2][c].

[68] See, e.g., Ill. Ann. Stat. ch. 30, § 29; N.J. Stat. Ann. § 46:22-1. Note that if the judgment debtor holds unrecorded title to real property, the judgment lien will attach to his interest, whatever that may be. See Annot., 43 A.L.R. 44 (1926); Tpea No. 5 Credit Union v. Solis, 605 SW2d 381 (Tex. Civ. App. 1980); Sky Harbor, Inc. v. Jenner, 164 Colo. 490, 435 P2d 894 (1968); U.S. v. Texas E. Transmission Corp., 254 F. Supp. 114 (WD La. 1965). However, if the judgment creditor has active notice of an unrecorded interest, he may be subordinate to the unrecorded interest. See supra ¶ 6.05[2][c] & note 59. For further discussion of the relative priority of a judgment lien and an unrecorded interest, see infra ¶ 6.05[2][f].

[69] See, e.g., Ind. Code Ann. § 32-1-2-16; Kan. Stat. Ann. § 58-2222.

[70] See Hawkland & Loiseaux, Debtor-Creditor Relations 18 (Bobbs-Merrill, 2d ed. 1979). But see In re Urban Dev. Co. & Assocs., 452 F. Supp. 902 (D. Md. 1978); Soloman v. Bolt, 74 Cal. App. 3d 907, 141 Cal. Rptr. 841 (1977); University Assocs. v. Sterling Fin. Co., 37 Ohio App. 2d 17, 305 NE2d 924 (1973); Buell Cabinet Co., Inc. v. Sudduth, 608 F2d 431 (10th Cir. 1979).

[71] See infra ¶ 6.07[2] for discussion of fraudulent conveyances.

[72] See, e.g., Montana Ass'n of Credit Management v. Hergert, 181 Mont. 442, 593 P2d 1059 (1979); Gagne v. Bailey, 17 Wash. App. 599, 564 P2d 348 (1977); Hyde Properties v. McCoy, 507 F2d 301 (6th Cir. 1974); McLaughlin v. Whaland, 127 NJ Eq. 393, 13 A2d 573 (NJ Ch. 1940).

[73] See, e.g., De Martini v. De Martini, 385 Ill. 128, 52 NE2d 139 (1943).

[74] The following representative jurisdictions hold that only legal interests in land are subject to a judgment lien: California, Hawaii, Indiana, New Jersey, Ohio, Oregon, and South Carolina. Examples of jurisdictions that do subject equitable estates to judgment liens are Connecticut, District of Columbia, Florida, Illinois, Iowa, New Mexico, North Carolina, Pennsylvania, Washington, and Texas. See Riesenfeld, Creditors' Rem-

interests include the estate of a beneficiary under a trust or the estate of a vendee under a contract of sale when either the trust or contract involves real property. Most often, in states that provide for judgment liens in a vendee's interest, the vendee must have paid part of the purchase price.[75] If the vendee acquires legal title, the lien will attach to the legal title.[76] However, if the vendor validly forecloses or terminates the contract for sale of the land, the judgment lien terminates, since the judgment debtor no longer possesses even an equitable interest.[77] If the judgment lien does not reach equitable interests, in some of these states the judgment creditor may nevertheless use other means of reaching the equitable interest (e.g., levy by way of the writ of execution).[78] Conversely, judgment liens do attach to legal interests of a vendor holding title as security for an unpaid portion of the purchase price, to the extent of the vendor's interest and subject to the equitable interest of the vendee.[79]

A second problem regarding the reach of the judgment lien to real property involves a judgment debtor's leasehold interest in real estate. At common law, leaseholds are personal property–chattels are real property. Because of this common-law distinction, there is some split of authority among the courts as to whether a judgment lien attaches to the judgment debtor's leasehold interest in real estate. Some states statutorily list leaseholds as subject to judgment liens or include leaseholds within the definition of real property.[80] Other juris-

---

edies and Debtors' Protection 117 (West, 3d ed. 1979); FCX, Inc. v. Long Meadow Farm, Inc., 269 SC 202, 237 SE2d 50 (1977); Cascade Sec. Bank v. Butler, 88 Wash. 2d 777, 567 P2d 631 (1977); Wilkenson v. Wilkenson, 51 Cal. App. 3d 382, 124 Cal. Rptr. 870 (1975); Annot., 30 A.L.R. 504 (1924); Annot., 1 A.L.R. 2d 727, 740 (1948); Bowers v. Mazingo, 399 So. 2d 492 (Fla. Dist. Ct. App. 1981); Cochran v. Cutler, 39 Ill. App. 602, 350 NE2d 59 (1976); Action Realty Co., Inc. v. Miller, 191 Neb. 38, 215 NW2d 629 (1974). As to New York, see Weinstein, Korn & Miller, 6 New York Civil Practice ¶¶ 5201.07, 5205.04 (Matthew Bender 1973).

[75] See, e.g., Joseph v. Donovan, 114 Conn. 79, 157 A 638 (1931). Contra Rand v. Garner, 75 Iowa 311, 39 NW 515 (1888).

[76] See, e.g., Brown v. Jones, 52 Minn. 484, 55 NW 54 (1892) and infra ¶ 6.05[2][e].

[77] See, e.g., Hedlund v. Brellenthin, 520 F. Supp. 81 (WD Wash. 1981); Petrakes v. Krasnow, 54 NM 39, 213 P2d 220 (1949); Eckley v. Bonded Adjustment Co., 30 Wash. 2d 96, 190 P2d 718 (1948).

[78] See, e.g., U.S. v. Fidelity & Deposit Co. of Maryland, 244 F. Supp. 19 (WD Mo. 1965); Greenwich Trust Co. v. Tyson, 129 Conn. 211, 27 A2d 166 (1942); Hansen v. d'Artenay, 13 Cal. App. 2d 293, 57 P2d 202 (1936).

[79] See, e.g., Uffenheiner v. Rob Con Enter., Inc., 74 AD2d 899, 425 NYS2d 856 (1980); Monroe v. Lincoln City Employees Credit Union, 203 Neb. 702, 279 NW2d 866 (1979); Monegan v. Pacific Nat'l Bank of Wash., 16 Wash. App. 280, 556 P2d 226 (1976); Rural Acceptance Corp. v. Pierce, 157 Ind. App. 90, 298 NE2d 499 (1973). Contra Carefree Homes, Inc. v. Production Credit Ass'n, 81 Wis. 2d 541, 260 NW2d 759 (1977); Marks v. City of Tucumcari, 94 NM 4, 595 P2d 1199 (1979).

[80] See, e.g., Tex. Rev. Civ. Stat. Ann. art 5449; U.S. v. Texas E. Transmission Corp., 254 F. Supp. 114 (WD La. 1965); Ill. Ann. Stat. ch. 77, § 3; Hammes v. Esposito, 10 Ill. App. 3d 6, 293 NE2d 641 (1973); Ind. Code Ann. § 34-1-45-2; Commer v. Light, 174 Ind. 367, 93 NE 660, reh'g denied, 175 Ind. 367, 94 NE 325 (1911); Md. R. P. 620a; In re Carton, 4 Bankr. 401 (Md. 1980); N.Y. Civ. Prac. Law & R. §§ 105(5), 5203(a);

dictions consider leaseholds to be covered by the broad language of a statute creating judgment liens.[81] Still other states provide that judgment liens do not reach leasehold interests.[82]

A third problem involves the situation where a judgment debtor holds a security interest in real estate. A security interest in land, such as a mechanic's lien, mortgage, or interest granted by a trust deed, is not real property within the meaning of the judgment lien statutes. The judgment creditor will have to reach such interests by garnishment or creditor's bill.[83]

Assuming that the interest of the debtor is in real property, issues have been raised regarding the effect of coownership of the real property between the judgment debtor and third parties.[84] In most jurisdictions, the judgment debtor's share in real property as a tenant in common or as a joint tenant is subject to the judgment lien.[85] With reference to joint tenancy, most states also agree that the attachment of a judgment lien will not sever the joint tenancy; if the judgment debtor dies, the lien is terminated as the debtor's interest passes to the joint tenant. Apparently, attachment of the judgment lien serves to sever the joint tenancy in only two states.[86] Within other states, an apparent split of authority has developed as to whether severance results subsequent to attachment of the judgment lien upon levy of an execution, foreclosure judgment, sheriff's sale, or expiration of the redemption period, in order to protect the judgment lienor from loss of lien upon death of the judgment debtor. In some states, the issuance of the writ of execution is the final point at which the joint

---

Lacaille v. Feldman, 44 Misc. 2d 370, 253 NYS2d 937 (NY Sup. Ct. Special Term, 1964).

[81] See, e.g., In re Day, 22 F. Supp. (D. Md. 1938); Ives v. Beecher, 75 Conn. 564, 54 A 207 (1903); First Nat'l Bank of Davenport v. Bennett, 40 Iowa 537 (1875).

[82] See, e.g., Hinds v. Phillips Petroleum Co., 591 P2d 697 (Okla. 1979); State Tax Comm'r v. Shor, 43 NY2d 151, 371 NE2d 523, 400 NYS2d 805 (1977); Arnett v. Peterson, 15 Cal. App. 3d 170, 92 Cal. Rptr. 913 (1971); Shaeffer v. Baeringer, 346 Pa. 32, 29 A2d 697 (1943). A related problem area involves a debtor's right to mineral royalties. See Montague v. Brascull, 443 SW2d 706 (Tex. Civ. App. 1969); Donley v. Youngstown Sheet & Tube Co., 328 SW2d 192 (Tex. Civ. App. 1959); Annot., 68 A.L.R.2d 728, 735 (1959); Annot., 52 A.L.R. 135 (1928); see also Annot., 122 A.L.R. 517 (1939).

[83] See, e.g., Galeano v. Galeano, 21 Md. App. 208, 319 A2d 129 (1974); First Fed. Sav. & Loan Ass'n v. Pogue, 27 Ill. Dec. 588, 389 NE2d 653 (1979); Sterling Sav. & Loan Ass'n v. Schultz, 70 Ill. App. 2d 487, 218 NE2d 53 (1966).

[84] See infra ¶ 6.07[5] for further discussion of a creditor's ability to reach property a debtor holds with nondebtors.

[85] See, e.g., First Nat'l Bank of Southglenn v. Energy Fuels Corp., 200 Colo. 540, 618 P2d 1115 (1980); Wirtz v. Phillips, 251 F. Supp. 789 (WD Pa. 1965); see Riesenfeld, Creditors' Remedies and Debtors' Protection 113 (West, 3d ed. 1979); Hawkland & Loiseaux, Debtor-Creditor Relations 21 (Bobbs-Merrill, 2d ed. 1979).

[86] Nebraska and Hawaii. See Note, "Severance by Attachment of Liens to Joint Tenants Interest," 34 Neb. L. Rev. 293 (1954); Coelho v. Fernandez, 46 Hawaii 578, 384 P2d 527 (1963).

tenancy is severed.[87] Other courts hold that severance does not occur until levy is made.[88] Most states hold that severance occurs when the joint interest is sold at execution.[89] One state provides for severance only after the redemption period has run following an execution sale.[90] If redemption occurs after severance, under the common law only a tenancy in common is restored.[91] However, one state provides that redemption reinstates the former joint tenancy.[92]

Another coownership problem arises when the judgment debtor owns real estate as a tenant by the entirety. In those jurisdictions that recognize tenancies by the entirety, most have held that a creditor of one spouse cannot obtain a judgment or execution lien on his or her share in the realty.[93] In some states, the creditor of one spouse may reach the debtor's right to survivorship with the judgment lien attaching thereto.[94] Obviously, a judgment against both spouses

---

[87] Maryland, Massachusetts, and Wisconsin. See Note, "Joint Tenancy Is Not Severed by Judgment Lien–Execution Is Necessary," 14 Md. L. Rev. 151 (1954); Eastern Shore Bldg. & Loan Corp. v. Bank of Somerset, 253 Md. 525, 253 A2d 367 (1969); Musa v. Segelke & Kohlhaus Co., 224 Wis. 432, 272 NW 657 (1937); see also Annot., 161 A.L.R. 1139 (1946).

[88] Alabama, Connecticut, Kentucky, Maine, New Hampshire, and Pennsylvania. See Herbert v. State Oil & Gas Board, 287 Ala. 215, 250 So. 2d 592 (1971); Albright v. Creel, 236 Ala. 286, 182 So. 10 (1938); New Haven Trolley & Bus Employees Credit Union v. Hill, 145 Conn. 332, 142 A2d 730 (1958); N.H. Rev. Stat. Ann. § 529-8; American Oil Co. v. Falconer, 136 Pa. Super. 598, 8 A2d 418 (1939).

[89] E.g., California, Iowa. Kansas, Michigan, Minnesota, New York, North Carolina, Oklahoma, Oregon, and Tennessee; see, e.g., First Nat'l Bank of Southglenn v. Energy Fuels Corp., 200 Colo. 540, 618 P2d 1115 (1980); Jamestown Terminal Elevator, Inc. v. Knapp, 246 NW2d 612 (ND 1976); Russell v. Lescalet, 248 Cal. App. 2d 369, 56 Cal. Rptr. 399 (1967); Ex parte Rauer's Collection Co., 81 Cal. App. 2d 248, 196 P2d 803 (1948); Comment, "Severance of a Joint Tenancy in California," 8 Hastings L.J. 290 (1957); see also Hawkland & Loiseaux, Debtor-Creditor Relations 22 (Bobbs-Merrill, 2d ed. 1979).

[90] Cf. Jackson v. Lacey, 408 Ill. 530, 97 NE2d 839 (1951); Frederick v. Shorman, 259 Iowa 1050, 147 NW2d 478 (1966).

[91] See Hawkland & Loiseaux, Debtor-Creditor Relations 23 (Bobbs-Merrill, 2d ed. 1979).

[92] Cal. Civ. Proc. Code § 703; see Comment, "Severance of a Joint Tenancy in California," 8 Hastings L.J. 290, 396 (1957). As to the equity of redemption, such equity held by the judgment debtor may itself be subject to the judgment lien. See Annot., 91 A.L.R. 647 (1934).

[93] See, e.g., In re Bulter, 5 Bankr. 360 (Bankr. D. Md. 1980); In re Foreclosure of Deed of Trust, 303 NC 514, 279 SE2d 566 (1981); Watterson v. Edgerly, 40 Md. App. 47, 388 A2d 934 (1978); Hinchee v. Security Nat'l Bank, 624 P2d 821 (Alaska 1981); Masonry Prods., Inc. v. Tees, 280 F. Supp. 654 (DVI 1968); see also Annot., 75 A.L.R.2d 1172 (1961).

[94] See, e.g., In re Dawson, 10 Bankr. 680, aff'd, Ray v. Dawson, 14 Bankr. 822 (Bankr. ED Tenn. 1981); Citizens & S. Nat'l Bank v. Auer, 640 F2d 837 (6th Cir. 1981); Napotik v. Equibank & Parkvale Sav. Ass'n, 679 F2d 316 (3d Cir. 1982); Wolfe v. Seniuk, 76 Misc. 2d 860, 352 NYS2d 88 (NY Sup. Ct., Special Term 1973).

results in a judgment lien on the entire property.[95] Finally, a judgment against one spouse will create a lien in the spouse's interest if the tenancy by the entirety is converted to a tenancy in common.[96] Reaching property interests that one debtor has in common with another is discussed later in this book.[97]

Estates in reversion and remainder of a judgment debtor have also created some controversy regarding the attachment of a judgment lien. If vested, the judgment lien will attach to the interest; however, at least half of the states hold that contingent remainders are not subject to the reach of creditors.[98] A final problem regarding the property interest of the debtor that is subject to a judgment lien is considered separately in the following paragraphs.

### [e] After-Acquired Property Interests

Once the judgment has been rendered, docketed, or recorded (depending on the jurisdiction), the judgment lien has been created. After judgment, the judgment debtor may acquire property of a type that is potentially subject to judgment liens. With regard to this "after-acquired" property, two separate issues arise. First, does the judgment lien encompass such after-acquired property? Second, if there is more than one judgment against the debtor and the property is acquired after both judgments are in existence, what are the relative priorities of the judgment liens?[99] Although priority of the judgment lien is considered below,[100] this second issue is so entangled with the first after-acquired property issue that it is presently considered.

The well-known case of *Hulbert v. Hulbert*[101] serves as an excellent example and illustrates the involvement of both the previously mentioned issues. In the *Hulbert* case, *A* docketed a judgment against Hulbert on March 7, 1904, and *B* docketed a judgment against him on April 21, 1904. At this time, Hulbert was without property. In 1910, on the death of his father, Hulbert inherited some valuable real estate in the county in which *A* and *B* had docketed their judgments. Thereafter, *A* executed against this property, but the proceeds

---

[95] See, e.g., In re Magee, 415 F. Supp. 521 (WD Mo. 1976); Napotik v. Equibank & Parkvale Sav. Ass'n, 679 F2d 316 (3d Cir. 1982); Swope v. Turner, 193 Pa. Super. 217, 163 A2d 714 (1960).

[96] See, e.g., U.S. v. Gurley, 415 F2d 144 (5th Cir. 1969).

[97] ¶ 6.07[5]. Also as to judgment liens on community property, see Annot., 10 A.L.R.2d 988 (1950).

[98] See, e.g., Halbach, "Creditor's Rights in Future Interests," 43 Minn. L. Rev. 217 (1958); Note, "Creditor's Rights Against Contingent Remainders," 32 Colum. L. Rev. 1043 (1932); Annot., 60 A.L.R. 803 (1929). But see, for opposite rule, N.Y. Civ. Proc. Law & R. §§ 5201(b), 5203(a); Cibro Petroleum Prods., Inc. v. Fowler Finishing Co., Inc., 92 Misc. 2d 450, 400 NYS2d 322 (NY Sup. Ct. 1977); Brown v. Anderson, 288 Ala. 111, 257 So. 2d 356 (1972); State ex rel. Cooper v. Cloyd, 461 SW2d 833 (Mo. 1971).

[99] For an excellent discussion of both issues, see Hawkland & Loiseaux, Debtor-Creditor Relations 24–26 (Bobbs-Merrill, 2d ed. 1979); see also Annot., 67 A.L.R. 1301 (1930).

[100] See infra ¶ 6.05[2][f] for discussion of priority of the judgment lien.

[101] 216 NY 430, 111 NE 70 (1916).

at the execution sale were insufficient to pay both *A* and *B*. The question arose as to whether *A* was to be paid first, with the remainder going to *B*, or whether the proceeds should be applied pro rata. The Court of Appeals of the State of New York held that the judgment liens of *A* and *B* ranked equally and that the proceeds should be divided pro rata. As this text has emphasized, judgment liens are the creatures of statute, and many states have statutes providing that the docketing or recording of the judgment shall constitute a lien as of the moment of docketing or recording. No lien can exist if the judgment debtor is without property, because a lien does not exist in isolation but is an encumbrance on property.[102] However, if the judgment debtor subsequently acquires property, the previously recorded or docketed judgments immediately attach liens to it.[103] The *Hulbert* case illustrates that point. The judgment lien is often said to be a general lien, as opposed to other forms of judicial liens that are specific in nature; that is, other judicial liens are limited to the property against which levy has occurred or where service of notice, in the case of garnishment, has taken place.

As to the priority issue illustrated in the *Hulbert* fact situation, it would be possible to hold, in view of the wording of the judgment lien statutes, that the first recorded or docketed judgment has the first priority.[104] Indeed, in some states it is held that two or more previously recorded or docketed judgments create equal liens on after-acquired property, but that property is awarded to the diligent creditor who takes out execution first.[105] This apparently is the

---

[102] See, e.g., Merchants Nat'l Bank of Aurora v. Olson, 27 Ill. App. 3d 432, 325 NE2d 633 (1975).

[103] See, e.g., In re Ingram, 475 F. Supp. 1089 (D. Va. 1979); Hohemath v. Wallach, 37 AD2d 248, 323 NYS2d 560 (1971); see also Hawkland & Loiseaux, Debtor Creditor Relations 24–25 (Bobbs-Merrill, 2d ed. 1979); Riesenfeld, Creditors' Remedies and Debtors' Protection 124 (West, 3d ed. 1979). States providing that judgment liens do not attach to after-acquired property are the exception. They include Connecticut, Ohio, and Pennsylvania. Conn. Gen. Stat. Ann. § 49-45; Souers, "Judgment Liens in Ohio," 16 Ohio St. L.J. 1, 14 (1955); Philadelphia Nat'l Bank v. Taylor, 421 Pa. 35, 218 A2d 246 (1966). Note also that the judgment lien will attach to all subsequent increases in land values. See, e.g., Kinney v. Valentine, 15 Cal. 3d 475, 541 P2d 537, 124 Cal. Rptr. 897 (1975); Smith v. Poplan, 266 Ore. 625, 513 P2d 1172 (1973).

[104] See Lowe v. Reierson, 201 Minn. 280, 276 NW 224 (1937), in which the court said:

> "Clearly, if the debtor's interest in real property were in existence at the time of the entry of the judgment, there could be no doubt about priority going with the date of docket entry . . . . [T]he legislative intent was to place all judgment creditors in the same relative position to each other no matter when or by what means the debtor acquired his property. . . . The statute makes no distinction [between presently-owned and after-acquired property], neither should we."

Id. at 277. For an excellent comment on this case, see 23 Minn. L. Rev. 97 (1938).

[105] See, e.g., Smith v. Lind, 29 Ill. 24 (1862), in which the court said: "On principal and authority we are satisfied, where liens of judgment are equal, one judgment creditor can get a priority over another, by superior vigilance in executing his judgment. . . ." Id. at 31.

majority rule in this country.[106] However, there are a number of cases, including *Hulbert v. Hulbert,* which hold that the diligence of one creditor in executing does not change the priority of the parties.[107] The rule adopted by the majority of courts rewarding diligence was criticized in a comment in the *Harvard Law Review* that applauded the decision of *Hulbert v. Hulbert.*[108] The danger in rewarding diligence is that it may force hasty executions. Many judgment debtors are able to pay off the judgments that have been rendered against them if they are given a little time to collect their assets or to borrow funds. "There is no point in seizing the property of such debtors, and where priority is given in accordance with the rank of the various liens, the judgment creditors are amply protected even where they wait for the satisfaction of their judgments."[109]

It should be emphasized, however, that although most courts give priority to the diligent judgment creditor where his lien is equal in rank with another judgment lien, diligence is not similarly rewarded where the liens are of unequal rank. Thus, the diligence of a junior judgment lienor in executing before such action is taken by a senior judgment lienor does not subordinate the latter to the former.[110]

### [f] Priority of the Judgment Lien

As is the case with judicial liens generally, the priority of a judgment lien,[111] relative to others who claim interests in the same property of the judgment debtor, is determined on a "first-in-time, first-in-right" basis.[112] For example, the relative priority among competing judgment liens depends upon

---

[106] See Hawkland & Loiseaux, Debtor-Creditor Relations 25 (Bobbs-Merrill, 2d ed. 1979).

[107] See, e.g., In re Robbin's Estate, 74 Misc. 2d 793, 346 NYS2d 86 (NY Sur. Ct. 1973); Zink v. James River Nat'l Bank, 58 ND 1, 224 NW 901 (1929).

[108] See Comment, "Does Execution by One Judgment Creditor Give a Preference Over Equal Judgment Liens?" 29 Harv. L. Rev. 755 (1915), which states:

> "The cases representing the weight of authority were influenced, presumably, by a fancied analogy to the equitable principle that a creditor who has pursued into equity property of the debtor which cannot be reached at all is entitled to a preference as reward for his diligence, for they continually talk of diligence creating a preference among equal legal claims. The analogy is apt in that the execution reaches no assets which are in danger of extinction by the act of a third party. It subjects no property to the payment of this judgment which is not already irrevocably bound to the satisfaction of all judgments against the owner." Id. at 756.

[109] See Hawkland & Loiseaux, Debtor-Creditor Relations 25 (Bobbs-Merrill, 2d ed. 1979).

[110] See, e.g., Rankin & Schatzell v. Scott, 25 US (12 Wheat.) 177 (1827); see also Okla. Stat. Ann. tit. 42, § 15 (other things being equal, different liens upon the same property have priority according to the time of their creation).

[111] For priority matters pertaining to tax liens and judgment liens, see ¶ 9.04[6].

[112] For discussion of priority of other judicial liens, see supra ¶ 6.01[1][f] (attachment), supra ¶ 6.04[2][e] (prejudgment garnishment), infra ¶ 6.05[3][e] (execution), and infra ¶ 6.05[4] (postjudgment garnishment).

the time at which the judgment lien attaches, with the first to attach being granted priority.[113] There is authority for the opinion that fractions or parts of days are not to be considered; thus, the judgment lien acquired during a particular day is said to begin with the first moment of the day on which it attaches.[114] Probably because judgment liens in most states only attach to real property, and because of the importance placed upon recordation of interests in real estate, some troublesome priority issures have arisen of a specialized nature. Although these issues could also arise in regard to a levy on real estate pursuant to attachment and execution, they are still of sufficient importance to be considered in this discussion.

Issues have been raised as to whether a judgment lien is affected by unrecorded, latent interests in the debtor's real estate.[115] The common-law principle holds that a creditor is not protected against latent equities against the judgment debtor, and that he stands in the shoes of the judgment debtor.[116] Many states, in derogation of the common law, have extended their recording statutes to protect creditors who obtain a lien on real estate by judicial means, including obtaining a judgment lien.[117] In other jurisdictions, creditors without notice acquiring judicial liens, including judgment liens, have been held to be protected by the applicable recording statute.[118] However, some recording acts are clear in that they expressly protect only purchasers and mortgagees.[119] In those states where the judgment lienor is protected from prior unrecorded interests, there are other latent equities not capable of recording, or there are other defects in the debtor's title to which the judgment creditor is subject. Such situations include fraud, for example, which gives rise to a constructive trust incapable of recordation.[120] Another example includes a record title of a judgment debtor that is not based upon conveyance.[121]

---

[113] See, e.g., Massaker v. Petraitis, 173 NJ Super. 459, 414 A2d 590 (1980); Krauth v. First Continental Dev-Con, Inc., 351 So. 2d 1106 (Fla. Dist. Ct. App. 1977); Heller Properties, Inc. v. Rothschild, 11 Cal. App. 3d 705, 90 Cal. Rptr. 133 (1970). But see the discussion regarding after-acquired property in supra ¶ 6.05[2][e].

[114] In general, see 46 Am. Jur. 2d Judgments §§ 165, 280, 286 (1969). But see, for contrary authority, Annot., 37 A.L.R. 268 (1925).

[115] In regard to this problem, see also supra ¶ 6.05[2][d] notes 68–70.

[116] See, e.g., Wells Fargo Bank v. Pal Invs., Inc., 96 Cal. App. 3d 434, 157 Cal. Rptr. 818 (1979); In re Destro, 675 F2d 1037 (9th Cir. 1982); Davis v. Johnson, 241 Ga. 436, 246 SE2d 297 (1978).

[117] See, e.g., Ill. Ann. Stat. ch. 30, § 29; Mich. Comp. Laws Ann. § 600.6051; Minn. Stat. Ann. § 507.34; N.J. Stat. Ann. § 46.22-1; Pa. Stat. Ann. tit. 21, § 351; Tex. Rev. Civ. Stat. Ann. art. 6627; Tpea No. 5 Credit Union v. Solis, 605 SW2d 381 (Tex. Civ. App. 1980); see also Annot., 4 A.L.R. 434 (1919).

[118] See, e.g., Hughes v. Williams, 218 Mass. 448, 105 NE 1056 (1914); Coffin v. Ray, 42 Mass. 212 (1853).

[119] See, e.g., Cal. Civ. Code § 1214; N.Y. Real Prop. Law § 291.

[120] Osin v. Johnson, 243 F2d 653 (DC Cir. 1957).

[121] See, e.g., Farmers & Mercantile State Bank v. Stageberg, 161 Minn. 413, 201 NW 612 (1925); Note, "Execution Sales–Rights of Bona Fide Purchasers," 24 Minn. L.

There is an important exception regarding priority of a judgment lien and the "first-in-time, first-in-right" rule. There is general agreement that a purchase-money mortgage on after-acquired property has priority over a judgment lien based on a judgment docketed before the acquisition of title.[122] Arguably, the purchase-money mortgagee comes later in time and thus normally would be subordinate were it not for the exception.

A final special priority problem regarding judgment liens relates to the timing of a judgment debtor's conveyance of title to a third party. As indicated previously, a conveyance by the judgment debtor before judgment will keep the property free of the judgment lien unless, perhaps, the conveyance is fraudulent.[123] However, what happens if the debtor conveys by deed realty to a third party before the judgment debtor actually holds title, and thereafter the judgment is entered followed by acquisition of title by the debtor? At least one court concludes in that situation that a judgment lien cannot attach to the already conveyed real estate.[124] On the other hand, at least one court has felt that if a judgment is docketed and the debtor then makes the conveyance before he has title and thereafter obtains title, the judgment lien does attach and the transferee takes subject thereto.[125]

### [g] Loss of the Judgment Lien

The judgment lien, as is the case with all judicial liens and the judgment itself, may be lost as a result of the passage of time. In that regard, a subsequent portion of the text focuses upon the duration of judicial liens.[126] This section of the text deals with specific matters relating uniquely to judgment liens. These matters are unique to judgment liens, largely due to the fact that judgment liens typically reach only real property.[127]

To begin, does the judgment lien somehow dissolve upon the death of the judgment debtor? Under common law, the judgment lien does not dissolve and is enforceable in the subject property. This can occur even after the land descends to the heir, as long as the judgment is revived against the heir by various procedural means, including issuance of the common-law writs of scire facias and elegit.[128] Today, a judgment lien obtained during the judgment

---

Rev. 805, 808–809 (1940); First State Bank of Amarillo v. Jones, 107 Tex. 623, 183 SW 874 (1916).

[122] See, e.g., Sarmiento v. Stockton, Whatley, Davin & Co., 399 So. 2d 1057 (Fla. Dist. Ct. App. 1981); Northern State Bank v. Toal, 69 Wis. 2d 50, 230 NW2d 153 (1975); Walley v. P.M.C. Inv. Co., 262 Cal. App. 2d 218, 68 Cal. Rptr. 711 (1968); see ¶ 8.09 for discussion of priorities and mortgages in real estate.

[123] See supra ¶ 6.05[2][d].

[124] Lamprey v. Pike, 28 F 30 (D. Minn. 1886).

[125] Bliss v. Brown, 78 Kan. 467, 96 P 945 (1908).

[126] See infra ¶ 6.07[3].

[127] See supra ¶ 6.05[2][d].

[128] See Riesenfeld, "Enforcement of Money Judgments in Early American History," 71 Mich. L. Rev. 691, 694 (1973).

debtor's life is not dissolved by his death. However, the creditor must recognize that there is no uniformity nationwide on the proper method of enforcement of the existing judgment lien when the judgment debtor dies.[129] Indeed, there appear to be at least four different approaches taken by the various states. Some states permit the issuance of an execution after a certain interval following the death or by leave of the probate court.[130] Other states continue the common-law approach previously described and require some form of revival against the heir.[131] Still other states require a foreclosure proceeding to be brought against the heir in enforcing the judgment lien.[132] Finally, a few states require assertion of the lien during the administration of the deceased judgment debtor's estate.[133] A separate problem arises when the verdict or decision is rendered prior to death but the judgment is not entered at death. Some jurisdictions allow postdeath entry of judgment, but in these cases the judgment does not create a lien on the decedent's real estate.[134]

There are some situations in which the judgment lien is lost. Obviously the judgment creditor could voluntarily release the lien.[135] The lien can also be terminated by satisfaction of the judgment.[136] The vacating of the judgment,[137] as opposed to mere opening of the judgment,[138] also releases the judgment lien. Various forms of waiver or estoppel may be asserted against the judgment lienor, such as where the creditor represents to purchasers or subsequent encumbrancers that he has no claim or that he has abandoned his claim

---

[129] See Annot., 114 A.L.R. 1165 (1938).

[130] See, e.g., Ala. Code § 6-9-63; Colo. Rev. Stat. § 13-58-101; Minn. Stat. Ann. § 550.06; N.Y. Civ. Prac. Law & R. § 5208. But see Willis v. Neilson, 32 Colo. App. 129, 507 P2d 1106 (1973).

[131] See, e.g., McHugh v. Martin, 198 Md. 173, 81 A2d 623 (1951); Dougherty v. White, 112 Neb. 675, 200 NW 884 (1924). But see Rich v. Cooper, 136 Neb. 463, 286 NW 383 (1939).

[132] See, e.g., Cal. Civ. Proc. Code § 686; Cal. Prob. Code § 732.5; Utah R. Civ. P. 69a; Corporation of Am. v. Marks, 10 Cal. 2d 218, 73 P2d 1215 (1937). But see Federal Farm Mortgage Co. v. Walker, 115 Utah 461, 206 P2d 146 (1949).

[133] See, e.g., James v. St. Francis Hosp. & School, 225 Kan. 649, 594 P2d 162 (1979); Long v. Castaneda, 475 SW2d 578 (Tex. Civ. App. 1971); Fla. Stat. Ann. § 733.19; Cumberland & Liberty Mills v. Keggin, 139 Fla. 133, 190 So. 492 (1939).

[134] See, e.g., Cal. Civ. Proc. Code § 669; Cal. Prob. Code § 731; N.Y. Civ. Prac. Law & R. § 5203(a)(4).

[135] See, e.g., Hulke v. International Mfg. Co., 14 Ill. App. 2d 5, 142 NE2d 717 (1957); Moore v. McKay, 439 SW2d 407 (Tex. Civ. App. 1969); City of Houston v. Darland, 264 SW2d 783 (Tex. Civ. App. 1954). Note that a judgment lien by agreement can also be subordinated as to subsequent encumbrances.

[136] See, e.g., Harrison v. Carpenter, 225 Ala. 297, 142 So. 772 (1932); Patterson v. Clark, 96 Ga. 494, 23 SE 496 (1895).

[137] See, e.g., In re Syleecau Mgf. Co., 17 F2d 503 (DSC 1922); Giles v. Ryan, 317 Pa. 65, 176 A 1 (1935).

[138] A mere opening of the judgment will not destroy the judgment lien. Cf. In re Distribution of Proceeds From Sheriff's Sale, 236 Pa. Super. 258, 345 A2d 921 (1975); Joseph Melnick Bldg. & Loan Ass'n v. Melnick, 361 Pa. 328, 64 A2d 773 (1940).

to the subject real estate.[139] If the judgment debtor appeals the judgment, the judgment lien will not be discharged,[140] although there may be some contrary statutory authority.[141] Although the judgment lien obviously continues in real estate upon sale to a buyer, a difficult analogous problem can be raised regarding adverse possession of a debtor's property by a third party. It would seem that the adverse possessor could acquire only the rights of the debtor and would be treated by analogy as a buyer. Thus, he would take subject to the judgment lien.[142]

### [h] Judgment Liens in Federal Court

A federal court judgment[143] is a lien on property of the judgment debtor "in the same manner, to the same extent, and under the same conditions" as state judgments.[144] The states, pursuant to Section 1962 of Title 28 of the U.S. Code, are thus given the power to regulate the liens of federal judgments, provided the states do not discriminate against those judgments. In effect, the states cannot require more of the federal judgment creditor to acquire a judgment lien than would be required if the judgment had been obtained in state court.[145] Thus, if mere rendition of a judgment in state court creates a lien in a

---

[139] See, e.g., Winter v. Allstate Mortgage Corp. of Fla., 303 So. 2d 399 (Fla. Dist. Ct. App. 1974); Valley Title Co. v. Parish Egg Basket, Inc., 31 Cal. 3d 776, 107 Cal. Rptr. 717 (1973); Blackburn v. Venice Inlet Co., 38 So. 2d 43 (Fla. 1949).

[140] See, e.g., Stetson v. Sheehan, 52 Cal. App. 353, 200 P 387 (1921).

[141] See, e.g., Misner v. Strange, 203 Mich. 411, 169 NW 938 (1918); Wrankow v. Oakley, 133 NY 505, 31 NE 521 (1892).

[142] Cf. Eaton v. Daub, 190 NC 14, 128 SE 494 (1925); Moses v. Major, 201 NC 613, 160 SE 890 (1931). But see Hillsborough Inv. Co. v. Lawyers Trust Co., 148 Fla. 224, 3 So. 2d 870 (1941); Spellbrink v. Bramberg, 245 Wis. 322, 14 NW2d 38 (1944).

[143] See supra ¶ 6.04[1][g] for discussion of attachment and prejudgment garnishment in federal courts. See infra ¶ 6.05[3][f] for discussion of execution and postgarnishment in federal courts.

[144] 28 USC § 1962 (1970). The section is set forth below:

> "Every judgment rendered by a district court within a State shall be a lien on the property located in such State in the same manner, to the same extent and under the same conditions as a judgment of a court of general jurisdiction in such State, and shall cease to be a lien in the same manner and time. Whenever the law of any State requires a judgment of a State court to be registered, recorded, docketed or indexed, or any other act to be done, in a particular manner, or in a certain office or county or parish before such lien attached, such requirements shall apply only if the law of such State authorized the judgment of a court of the United States to be registered, recorded, docketed, indexed or otherwise conformed to rules and requirements relating judgments of the courts of the State."

For an excellent treatment of Section 1692, see Annot., 18 A.L.R. Fed. 568 (1974).

[145] See Rhea v. Smith, 274 US 434, (1927). *Rhea* established the so-called "conformity" standard. The case involved a Missouri statute that required federal judgments rendered within Missouri to be filed in the office of the clerk of any Missouri circuit court to be a lien on the real estate of the judgment-debtor situated in the county in

particular state, a judgment lien would also be created upon rendition in the federal court. On the other hand, if a state judgment creditor must record the judgment in an appropriate real estate record, the federal judgment creditor must do the same to acquire a judgment lien. However, if the federal judgment is obtained in a state other than where the debtor's property is located, the judgment creditor will have to take steps to register the judgment in a district court in the state where the property is located.[146]

## [3] Execution

### [a] General Nature and Function of Execution

Execution involves a judicial process regulated by statute, which results in issuance of a writ of execution by a court. The court orders a sheriff to levy upon property of a judgment debtor and to sell the property for the purpose of satisfying a judgment already obtained by a creditor.[147] The levy creates a lien that enables the judgment creditor to obtain liquidation of the subject property and provides the judgment creditor with a priority in the property vis-à-vis other claimants.[148] Prejudgment remedies, such as attachment and prejudgment garnishment, are not always available to a creditor; similarly, the judgment lien usually only reaches the real estate of a debtor. If a creditor has a judgment and has located assets of the debtor, his next step is to obtain the issuance of a writ of execution.[149] Thus, the use of execution (and postjudgment garnishment) perhaps constitutes the most commonly used procedural vehicle by which creditors satisfy judgments.

Under early common law, execution took four different forms.[150] A writ of elegit resulted in transfer of a debtor's personal property to his creditor at an appraised price. If that did not satisfy the debt, the assignment of the use of one half of the debtor's land to the creditor or tenant by elegit resulted, but for

---

which the judgment was filed. Another Missouri statute provided that any judgment rendered by a state court was to be a lien on the real estate of the person against whom it was rendered, situated in the county for which the court was held, and that the lien should commence on the date of rendition of the judgment. The Supreme Court held that these Missouri statutes did not provide the needed conformity as specified in 28 USC § 1962 and that the filing of the judgment in the federal district court created a lien on all the lands of the judgment-debtor lying in the counties over which the court had jurisdiction, notwithstanding the fact that the judgment-creditor did not file copies of his judgment in those counties.

[146] See infra ¶ 6.07[4] for a discussion of the registration process within the federal courts.

[147] See, e.g., Kiker v. National Structures, Inc., 342 So. 2d 746 (Ala. 1977); Wieboldt Stores v. Sturdy, 384 Ill. 271, 51 NE2d 268 (1943); First Nat'l Bank of Everett v. Tiffany, 40 Wash. 2d 193, 242 P2d 169 (1952).

[148] See infra ¶ 6.05[3][e] for discussion of the execution lien.

[149] See supra ¶ 5.03 for discussion of location of the debtor's assets.

[150] For a brief discussion of the common-law forms of execution, see Epstein & Landers, Debtors and Creditors 77 (West, 2d ed. 1982).

a term based upon appraisal of its value. Today, elegit is of historical importance only. Similarly, capis ad satisfacundum is of historical importance only. Capis required a sheriff to arrest the judgment debtor and to keep him imprisoned until the debt was paid. Today, a majority of states have constitutional provisions that invalidate imprisonment for debt—at least, contract debts. Two other common-law writs represent the roots of execution: the writs of fieri facias and levari facias. Fieri facias resulted in an order to the sheriff to seize and sell the debtor's personal property; similarly, levari facias could reach the debtor's real property. Today, the two common-law writs have been merged by statutes to form the writ of execution.

Execution is the postjudgment "equivalent" to attachment. Thus, much of the preceding discussion concerning attachment also applies to execution.[151] Like attachment, execution produces a levy on the property of the debtor. Unlike attachment, execution is not an extraordinary remedy, in that it occurs postjudgment; further, the writ of execution incorporates an order to the sheriff to sell the property of the debtor. Postjudgment garnishment may be necessitated, however, if property in which the debtor has an interest is possessed by a third party.[152]

### [b] Basic Procedure

Assuming that an executable judgment and appropriate grounds are present,[153] and the creditor has located assets of the debtor that are capable of being executed upon,[154] the basic execution procedure is rather simple. The procedural difficulties faced by a creditor without a judgment in the use of attachment have been largely erased by the rendering of judgment.

Execution as a postjudgment remedy involves a four-step procedure.[155] First, as mentioned, the creditor must have an executable judgment.[156] Second, the judgment creditor asks the clerk of the court that rendered the judgment to direct the sheriff to satisfy the judgment by taking land and personalty of the debtor to the extent necessary and by selling the property and paying over the proceeds to the creditor. The request by the creditor usually takes the form of a motion to the court, with a supportive affidavit that establishes the existence of an unsatisfied judgment. Unless a statute otherwise provides, the writ of execution is issued by the clerk of the court where the judgment is entered and is directed to the sheriff of the county where the assets of the debtor are located. Usually, transfer of the judgment itself to the county where the assets are

---

[151] See supra ¶ 6.04[1] for consideration of attachment.

[152] See infra ¶ 6.05[4] for discussion of postjudgment garnishment.

[153] See infra ¶ 6.05[3][c].

[154] See ¶ 5.03 for discussion of location of the debtor's assets.

[155] See Hawkland & Loiseaux, Debtor-Creditor Relations 36–37 (Bobbs-Merrill, 2d ed. 1979) for a brief summary of execution procedure.

[156] See, e.g., State ex rel. Specialty Foam Prods. v. Keet, 579 SW2d 650 (Mo. Ct. App. 1979); Montford v. Cordell Lumber Co., Inc. 147 Ga. App. 720, 250 SE2d 173 (1978); Vorhof v. Vorhof, 532 SW2d 830 (Mo. Ct. App. 1975).

located is not required or even possible in most jurisdictions,[157] although some states make transfer possible, but optional.[158] The writ of execution has a maximum life span of sixty or ninety days, beyond which time the writ becomes functus officis regardless of whether it is returned or not.[159]

Third, the sheriff to whom the writ of execution is issued, must levy upon the judgment debtor's property.[160] Although the nature of the levy is discussed later in the text,[161] it should be noted that levy on personal property usually takes the form of the sheriff actually seizing the property and taking it into his possession. If the personal property cannot actually be taken, the sheriff may tag or mark the property and make it unusable to the judgment debtor. As to real estate, since it cannot be physically taken, a form of public notice is usually required. For example, filing of a certificate of levy with a recorder of deeds or other county officer must occur. This certificate simply states that levy has occurred at a certain time on the land. The effect of levy on personalty or realty is that it creates a lien[162] on behalf of the judgment creditor and places the property in custodia legis (in the custody of the law).[163] This procedure makes possible the ultimate liquidation of the subject property. Once levy has taken place or once the sheriff believes no property of the debtor can be located, the writ of execution must be "returned" to the clerk by the return date specified in the writ. If no assets are levied upon, the return is said to be "nulla bona." If the writ fails to satisfy the judgment, further writs may issue until sufficient property has been levied upon to satisfy the judgment. These later writs are often called alias or pluries writs.[164] Obviously, only one writ should be outstanding in a particular county at any one time.

The final step of the execution process involves the sale of the property levied upon.[165] There are some special procedural problems that might arise in connection with the previously mentioned maximum life span of the writ. When both levy and sale occur after the required return date, no rights are

---

[157] See, e.g., Hickory White Trucks, Inc. v. Green, 34 NC App. 279, 237 SE2d 862 (1977); Md. Cts. & Jud. Proc. Code Ann. § 2-302(b).

[158] See, e.g., Wilson v. Craite, 60 Wis. 2d 350, 210 NW2d 700 (1973).

[159] See, e.g., Cal. Civ. Proc. Code § 683(a); Minn. Stat. Ann. § 550.05; N.Y. Civ. Prac. Law & R. § 5230(c); Mich. Comp. Laws Ann. § 600.6002(2); Pa. R. Civ. P. 3106(d); Tex. Civ. Proc. Rules Ann. R. 621; Va. Sup. Ct. R. 3:2.

[160] See Hawkland & Loiseaux, Debtor-Creditor Relations 37 (Bobbs-Merrill, 2d ed. 1979). See, e.g., Patterson v. Hopkins, 247 Pa. Super. 159, 371 A2d 1378 (1976); Travelers Ins. Co. v. Lawrence, 509 F2d 83 (9th Cir. 1979). But see Oysterman's Bank & Trust Co. v. Weeks, 35 AD2d 580, 513 NYS2d 535 (1970).

[161] For discussion of the nature of the levy, see infra ¶ 6.05[3][e].

[162] For discussion of the execution lien, see infra ¶ 6.05[3][e].

[163] See, e.g., Travelers Ins. Co. v. Lawrence, 509 F2d 83 (9th Cir. 1974).

[164] See, e.g., Vitale v. Hotel Cal., Inc., 184 NJ Super. 512, 446 A2d 880 (1982); see Riesenfeld, Creditors' Remedies and Debtors' Protections 86 (West, 3d ed. 1979).

[165] See infra ¶ 6.06 for a separate discussion of execution sales.

acquired by the judgment creditor or the purchaser at the execution sale.[166] When the levy has taken place before the expiration of the writ, but a sale has not yet occurred, the jurisdictions differ as to the proper procedure to be followed and the consequences of a failure to comply. As to real property, some states still adhere to a common-law procedure that requires a separate writ of venditioni exponas[167] to enable the sheriff to move forward with the sale of the subject property.[168] In other states, the returned writ of execution is merely redelivered to the sheriff for purposes of holding the sale,[169] or it is automatically extended,[170] or it is extended by the clerk of the court.[171] However, in at least one state, the writ is valid during the life of the judgment, or until it is satisfied.[172] Whatever the procedure, many states have held that a sale of property is valid even if it occurs after the required return date, as long as levy occurred before the return date.[173] Some states treat realty differently from personalty. These states would require sale of the real estate before the return date but would allow for the sale of personalty after the return date.[174]

It is sometimes possible for the debtor to stay, quash, vacate, or obtain other relief from an execution.[175] A court may temporarily stay execution whenever necessary to accomplish the ends of justice[176] if there are equitable grounds for a stay,[177] or if there has been a garnishment of the debtor.[178] If certain other proceedings are pending, execution may also be stayed.[179] Further, execution may be stayed where the debtor can furnish security for pay-

---

[166] See, e.g., In re Wendling Bros., Inc., 8 Bankr. 254 (Bankr. ND Ill. 1981); Illi, Inc. v. Margolis, 267 Md. 30, 296 A2d 412 (1972); Smith v. Adams, 333 SW2d 892 (Tex. Civ. App. 1960).

[167] See Gilbert, Execution 22 (1963); Tedd's Practice 930 (3d ed. 1803).

[168] See, e.g., Tex. Civ. Proc. Rules Ann. R. 647.

[169] See, e.g., Cal. Civ. Proc. Code § 683(c).

[170] See, e.g., Minn. Stat. Ann. § 550.05; Pa. R. Civ. P. 3106(d).

[171] See, e.g., N.Y. Civ. Prac. Law & R. § 5230.

[172] See Fla. Stat. Ann. §§ 56.021, 56.041.

[173] See, e.g., Riesenfeld, Creditors' Remedies and Debtors' Protection 87 (West, 3d ed. 1979).

[174] See, e.g., Murphree v. International Shoe Co., 246 Ala. 384, 20 So. 2d 782 (1945); Smith v. Adams, 333 SW2d 892 (Tex. Civ. App. 1960); see also Annot., 2 A.L.R. 189, 193 (1919).

[175] See generally 33 C.J.S. Executions §§ 139 et seq. (1942).

[176] See, e.g., Cutler Assocs., Inc. v. Merrill Trust Co., 395 A2d 453 (Me. 1978); Taylor Nat'l, Inc. v. Jensen Bros. Constr. Co., 641 P2d 150 (Utah 1982); Gilbert v. Gilbert, 628 P2d 1088 (Mont. 1981); see also Annot., 75 A.L.R.2d 1062 (1961).

[177] See, e.g., Goodlotte v. Liberty Mut. Ins. Co., 27 Conn. Supp. 382, 239 A2d 546 (1967); Moskin v. Midland Bank & Trust Co., 96 Misc. 2d 600, 409 NYS2d 327 (NY Sup. Ct. 1978).

[178] See, e.g., Lerno v. Obergfell, 144 Cal. 2d 221, 300 P2d 846 (1956).

[179] See, e.g., Nelson V. Powroznik, 329 Ill. App. 647, 70 NE2d 218 (1946).

ment of the judgment, such as in the form of a bond.[180] A creditor's right to proceed with execution is also often subject to various stays during the pendency of motion for a new trial or for appeals.[181] Some states provide that the stay is automatic upon the filing of motions or appeals.[182] Other states provide that execution may be stayed "upon motion and for cause shown."[183] Again, bonding may be required.[184] One state stays only the sale of the debtor's property; levy is allowed.[185] Quashing the execution is, at best, difficult, although there is authority for quashing an execution in which there is a lack of authority to issue the writ or where the judgment can be successfully attacked.[186] Other forms of relief might also be present, although this would rarely seem to be the case in the postjudgment setting.[187] Third persons may claim an interest in the property levied upon. They may have grounds to successfully intervene, which might indirectly produce some relief for the judgment debtor.[188]

### [c] Grounds for Issuance of Execution

The grounds for issuance of the writ of execution are relatively simple. There must be a valid, unsatisfied judgment rendered against the debtor and the motion and affidavit of the creditor must so indicate. The judgment must be a valid, final, viable, money judgment. To be executable, the judgment must be valid in the sense that it is not barred by the statute of limitations, nor stayed pending appeal or further proceedings, nor dormant.[189]

To support an execution, the judgment must be "obtained." At what stage a judgment is obtained for purposes of supporting issuance of a writ of execution varies somewhat among the jurisdictions. Under some statutes, it is clear

---

[180] See, e.g., Chapman v. Rose, 295 So. 2d 667 (Fla. Dist. Ct. App. 1974); Ferris v. Mancine, 22 NJ Misc. 145, 36 A2d 759 (D. Camden 1944).

[181] See, e.g., Ex parte Osborn, 357 So. 2d 467 (Ala. 1979); Chapman v. Rose, 295 So. 2d 667 (Fla. Dist. Ct. App. 1974); Kurek v. Kavanagh, Sculley, Sudow, White & Frederick, 50 Ill. App. 3d 1033, 365 NE2d 1191 (1977).

[182] See, e.g., 5A Tenn. Code Ann. (R. Civ. P.) 62.02.

[183] See, e.g., R.I. Gen. Laws § 9-25-4.

[184] See, e.g., S.D. Comp. Laws Ann. § 15-27-1; N.Y. Civ. Prac. Law & R. § 5519(a)(2); Minn. Stat. Ann. § 550.36; Ill. Ann. Stat. ch. 110A, § 305(a)(1); 42 Pa. Cons. Stat. Ann. (R. Civ. P.) 3121(a)(2). But see the following statutes, which do not require bonding; Mass. Ann. Laws ch. 231, § 96; R.I. Gen. Laws § 9-25-4; 5A Tenn. Code Ann. (R. Civ. P.) 62.02.

[185] Michigan; see Mich. Comp. Laws Ann. § 600.6011.

[186] In general, see 33 C.J.S. Executions §§ 142–145 (1942). See, e.g., Murphree v. Baykowski, 615 SW2d 463 (Mo. Ct. App. 1981); W.H. Powell Lumber Co., Inc. v. Federal Land Bank Ass'n of Mountain Grove Rolla, 561 SW2d 700 (Mo. Ct. App. 1978).

[187] 33 C.J.S. Executions §§ 147–163 (1942).

[188] Id. at §§ 165–195.

[189] See infra ¶ 6.07[3] regarding duration of the judgment or judicial lien obtained thereunder.

that the judgment must be docketed or recorded as a requisite of execution.[190] Difficult issues are raised, however, when a clerk of a court issues the writ of execution under such a statute prior to the recording or docketing. If this occurs, a levy pursuant to the prematurely issued writ of execution would seem to be ineffective.[191] Other states, however, permit execution prior to any formal entry or docketing.[192]

As indicated previously, the judgment must be valid. Put another way, a "void" judgment is no judgment; thus, execution issued pursuant to it is also void.[193] One must distinguish between a void and an erroneous judgment. For example, if a court has jurisdiction but makes a mistake of law, the judgment is valid, although erroneous. The error is to be corrected upon appeal. In some jurisdictions, executions are stayed upon appeal.[194] However, if, upon appeal, there is no stay, execution may occur, even though the judgment is reversed upon appeal.[195] Of course, once the judgment is reversed, the execution becomes ineffective.

The judgment must be final and it must be for payment in money. For example, execution may not be issued upon an interlocutory order.[196] Equitable and other decrees that do not require payment in money are not executable due to the fact that the writ of execution only gives the sheriff the power to levy upon and liquidate assets of the judgment debtor to satisfy a money judgment. The amount of the judgment must be fairly certain. The distinction between money and nonmoney judgments can become blurred when the amount due under the court order is somewhat uncertain.[197] This is the case, for example,

---

[190] See, e.g., N.Y. Civ. Prac. Law & R. §§ 5016(a), 5230; 42 Pa. Cons. Stat. Ann. (R. Civ. P.) 3101.

[191] See, e.g., Jackson v. Sears, Roebuck & Co., 83 Ariz. 20, 315 P2d 871 (1957); Moreno v. Victor, 261 Iowa 806, 156 NW2d 305 (1968).

[192] See, e.g., State ex rel. Turner v. Sloan, 595 SW2d 778 (Mo. Ct. App. 1980); Industrial Indem. Co. v. Levine, 49 Cal. App. 3d 698, 122 Cal. Rptr. 712 (1975); Wickiser v. Powers, 324 Ill. App. 130, 57 NE2d 522 (1944); Cinebar Coal & Coke Co. v. Robinson, 1 Wash. 2d 620, 97 P2d 128 (1939) See cases cited in Annot., 65 A.L.R.2d 1162, 1164–1166 (1959).

[193] See, e.g., Nalder v. Crest Corp., 93 Idaho 744, 472 P2d 310 (1970); Morris v. American Bankers Ins. Co. of Fla., 184 So. 2d 906 (Fla. Dist. Ct. App. 1966); Roosevelt Hardware v. Green, 94 Misc. 2d 654, 405 NYS2d 220 (NY Sup. Ct.), rev'd, 72 AD2d 261, 424 NYS2d 276 261 (1978); Apple v. Edwards, 123 Mont. 135, 211 P2d 138 (1949).

[194] See supra ¶ 6.05[3][b].

[195] Harrington v. Vandalia-Butler Bd. of Educ., 649 F2d 434 (6th Cir. 1981); Fender v. St. Louis S.W. Ry. Co., 73 Ill. App. 3d 522, 392 NE2d 82 (1974); Rooney v. Tufano Contracting Corp., 43 Misc. 2d 358, 251 NYS2d 392 (NY Sup. Ct. 1964).

[196] See, e.g., State ex rel. Turner v. Sloan, 545 SW2d 778 (Mo. Ct. App. 1980); Grant v. Ward, 109 RI 605, 288 A2d 708 (1972).

[197] See, e.g., Harte v. County of Los Angeles, 87 Cal. App. 3d 419, 151 Cal. Rptr. 88 (1978); Pinecrest Prods., Inc. v. RKO Teleradio Pictures, Inc., 14 Cal. App. 3d 6, 92 Cal. Rptr. 44 (1970); McKay v. Coca-Cola Bottling Co., 110 Cal. App. 2d 672, 243 P2d 35 (1952); Bank of Am. Nat'l Trust & Sav. Ass'n v. Standard Oil of Cal., 10 Cal. 2d 90, 73 P2d 903 (1937); County of Cook v. Malysa, 39 Ill. 2d 376, 235 NE2d 598 (1968).

with support orders issued as a part of the decrees of divorce or separation, with the courts divided as to whether execution may issue on account of such orders.[198]

An executing judgment creditor may obtain partial satisfaction of the judgment by some other means, including a prior execution. In such a case, the creditor's motion for issuance of the writ of execution should reflect that partial satisfaction has occurred. On the other hand, the creditor should keep in mind that local statutes allow him to seek recovery for certain expenses related to each execution, a procedure that increases the amount of debt to be satisfied by the issued execution.

### [d] Property Subject to Execution

The property subject to levy pursuant to a writ of execution is basically the same as property that is subject to levy pursuant to the writ of attachment.[199] The initial principle is that all nonexempt personal property, and real property that a judgment debtor possesses and in which the judgment debtor has an interest, is leviable pursuant to the writ of execution. Because of the common presence of the judgment lien on real estate in most jurisdictions,[200] the use of the writ of execution as to real estate is somewhat perplexing. Thus, the following discussion distinguishes execution upon interests in real estate from personalty.

Since real property is subject to a judgment lien in most jurisdictions, the writ of execution as to real property generally is used to force a sale of the real property instead of creating an execution lien, the latter being unnecessary due to the existence of the judgment lien.[201] Even so, in some situations, execution on real estate may be necessitated in order to initially create a judicial lien in the real estate. It has been suggested, and appropriately so, that the

> date of levy of the writ of execution on real property is material when there is no existing judgment lien, because (a) the judgment is of a type that in a particular jurisdiction does not create a lien, such as an installment judgment, (b) the interest is of a type that in a particular jurisdiction is not subject to a judgment lien, such as an equitable title, (c) the judgment lien has expired but an execution may still issue and be levied on the real prop-

---

[198] See, e.g., Roach v. Roach, 164 Ohio St. 587, 132 NE2d 742 (1956); compare Foust v. Foust, 47 Cal. 2d 121, 302 P2d 11 (1956). However, there are special statutes in many states that deal with collection of support orders.

[199] The property subject to execution closely resembles the property subject to attachment. In this regard, see supra ¶ 6.04[1][e]. For other sections of the text that concern matters also affecting the choice of assets subject to execution, see infra ¶¶ 6.07[1] (exempt property), 6.07[2] (fraudulent conveyances), 6.07[5] (reaching property in which the debtor shares title with a nondebtor).

[200] See supra ¶ 6.05[2] for discussion of the judgment lien.

[201] See infra ¶ 6.06[2][a] for discussion of the use of execution as a procedural means of getting realty subject to a judgment lien to sale.

erty, (d) the judgment was not docketed or recorded in the county where the property is located.[202]

Recognizing the possible importance of executing on real estate raises questions as to the nature of the interest of the debtor in real estate that is subject to levy. For example, vested remainders, even though a nonpossessory interest, are subject to execution.[203] However, in some states, contingent remainders cannot be reached by any process because they are not alienable under local property law,[204] although wherever alienable a contingent remainder is leviable by execution.[205] If the debtor possesses a seller's contractual interest in real estate, some states require the interest to be garnished, the notice being served on the buyer-garnishee.[206] In the same vein, many states prohibit execution upon the interest of a mortgagee prior to foreclosure; again, garnishment is necessitated.[207] Finally, leasehold interests are typically subject to execution, at least where the judgment debtor is the lessee;[208] otherwise, garnishment served upon the lessor in order to reach lease payments may be necessitated.

As to personal property, the general principle is that all forms of personalty that can be described as "chattel," and as not exempt, will be subject to execution.[209] The potential "shopping list" for the judgment creditor is end-

---

[202] Riesenfeld, Creditors' Remedies and Debtors' Protection 130 (West, 3d ed. 1979). Professor Riesenfeld cites the following as examples of each category: Walters v. Walters, 231 Iowa 1267, 3 NW2d 595 (1942); Lean v. Givens, 146 Cal. 739, 81 P 128 (1905); Collins v. Smith, 75 Wis. 392, 44 NW 510 (1890); Clark v. City of Salem, 61 Ore. 116, 121 P 416 (1912). In New York the levy of a writ of execution on land creates a lien, but such levy is not mandatory as long as a judgment lien can be obtained. N.Y. Civ. Prac. Law & R. §§ 5203(a), 5235.

[203] See, e.g., Aetna Ins. Co. v. LaGasse, 223 So. 2d 727 (Fla. 1969); Anemaet v. Martin-Senour Co. 114 So. 2d 23 (Fla. 1959); Stombaugh v. Morey, 388 Ill. 392, 58 NE2d 545, 549 (1944).

[204] See, e.g., Harris v. Bittikofer, 562 SW2d 815 (Tenn. 1978); Brown v. Andrews, 288 Ala. 111, 257 So. 2d 356 (1972); Shrout v. Seale, 278 Ala. 15, 250 So. 2d 592 (1971).

[205] See, e.g., In re Zuben's Estate, 146 Cal. App. 2d 584, 304 P2d 247 (1956); Kay v. Polittle, 344 Mo. 805, 129 SW 863 (1939).

[206] See, e.g., U.S. v. Cohen, 271 F. Supp. 709 (SD Fla. 1969); Culp v. Jacobs, 123 Ohio St. 109, 174 NE 242 (1930). But see Hansen v. d'Artenay, 13 Cal. App. 2d 293, 57 P2d 202 (1936).

[207] See, e.g., U.S. v. Cohen, 271 F. Supp. 709 (SD Fla. 1969); Galeano v. Galeano, 21 Md. App. 208, 319 A2d 129 (1974).

[208] See Hawkland & Loiseaux, Debtor-Creditor Relations 43–44 (Bobbs-Merrill, 2d ed. 1979).

[209] See, e.g., Rochford v. Laser, 91 Ill. App. 3d 769, 414 NE2d 1096 (1980); Coldren v. American Milling Research, Inc., 378 NE2d 870 (Ind. 1978); Asher v. U.S., 436 F. Supp. 22 (ND Ill. 1976), aff'd, 570 F2d 682 (1976). Recall that in a few jurisdictions the judgment lien also reaches personal property. These states include Alabama, Georgia, and Mississippi. See supra ¶ 6.05[2][a] notes 13–15.

less; examples include crops, trees, fruits, and money franchises.[210] It has been said that intangible personal property is not subject to execution;[211] it seems, however, that intangible property is not subject to execution because it most often is a debt due the judgment debtor, in which case use of garnishment is required.[212] Specific problem areas that apply to execution are considered in the following paragraphs.

As previously mentioned in regard to attachment,[213] the method of levy on a judgment debtor's corporate stock has created difficulty over the years. Section 8-317 of the UCC indicates that no levy is valid on any investment security until the security is actually seized by the officer making the levy. However, since Delaware has not adopted UCC Section 8-317, stock in a Delaware corporation may be levied upon without seizure of the stock by giving notice to the issuer of the stock.[214]

A matter related to investment securities involves levy upon documents of title. UCC Section 7-602 deals with this issue by providing that no levy will be effective on any document of title until the document is actually seized by the officer making the levy. It is important to note that, if the judgment debtor owns goods covered by a negotiable document of title, the judgment creditor cannot reach the goods without first obtaining the document of title.[215]

Execution upon negotiable instruments has raised similar troublesome issues. Due to the negotiable character of the property, levy must occur by seizing the negotiable instrument, as opposed to serving notice of garnishment upon the obligor of the instrument.[216] If a third party holds the negotiable instrument as a pledgee or bailee on behalf of the judgment debtor, garnishment may be necessitated.[217] As to negotiable instruments, the UCC is curi-

---

[210] See generally 33 C.J.S. Executions §§ 19 et seq. (1942); Annot., 103 A.L.R. 464 (1936).

[211] See, e.g., Rochford v. Laser, 91 Ill. App. 3d 769, 414 NE2d 1096 (1980).

[212] See, e.g., Ohio Rev. Code Ann. § 2333.01; Colo. Rev. Stat. § 13-52-102; Fallon v. Worthington, 13 Colo. 559, 22 P 960 (1889); Minn. Stat. Ann. § 550.10. But see Minn. Stat. Ann. § 550.39.

[213] See supra ¶ 6.04[1][e].

[214] See, e.g., Baker v. Gotz, 387 F. Supp. 1381 (D. Del. 1975); Brainard v. Canady, 49 Del. 182, 112 A2d 862 (1955).

[215] Cf. American Express Co. v. Vella, 92 NJ Super. 380, 223 A2d 515, aff'd, 94 NJ Super. 258, 227 A2d 711 (1966); Manufacturer's Mercantile Co. v. Monarch Refrigeration Co., 266 Ill. 584, 197 NE 885 (1915).

[216] See Riesenfeld, Creditors' Remedies and Debtors' Protection 173–174 (West, 3d ed. 1979), for an excellent discussion of levy upon negotiable instruments. Professor Riesenfeld comments in part as follows: "This is in accord with the increasingly accepted modern rule that a levy on negotiable instruments, at least while in the possession of the payee, can and must be made by seizure of the instrument and not by garnishment of the maker."

[217] See, e.g., Jubelt v. Sketers, 84 Cal. App. 2d 653, 656, 191 P2d 460, 462 (1948); Carter v. Bush, 79 Tex. 29, 15 SW 167 (1890). As to levy upon negotiable property generally, see also Kennedy, "The Rights of Levying Creditors Against Negotiable Property Under the UCC," 31 Bus. Law. 1517 (1976).

ously silent as to a method of levy in contrast to the specific provisions previously mentioned regarding investment securities and documents of title.

If the judgment debtor holds a divided interest in personal property, the judgment creditor usually can reach whatever interest his debtor may have in the property, subject to the interest of the other claimant.[218] This has been particularly troublesome in cases where the judgment debtor grants a security interest in his property. UCC Section 9-311 has clarified issues consistently with the preceding rule, which pertains generally to levy on property in which the judgment debtor has a divided interest. UCC Section 9-311 permits an execution sale of the debtor's interest, subject to a perfected security interest.[219] However, UCC Section 9-311 has been construed as not impairing the secured party's right to possession, where the secured debt is in default at time of levy or thereafter because of nonpayment or a clause providing that levy on collateral is a default.[220]

Another perplexing specialized problem involves property of a judgment debtor held in a safe deposit box rented by the debtor, with the debtor and the bank possessing the only two keys. May the sheriff, pursuant to execution (or attachment), open the box by force? Some states answer in the affirmative;[221] in other jurisdictions, the creditor is forced to open the box by garnishment.[222] The latter procedure would seem most appropriate, since the property within the box is in the custody of the bank; normally, property of a judgment debtor held by a third party must be garnished.

### [e] The Creation, Nature, and Effect of an Execution Lien

It has previously been emphasized that use of the writ of execution can produce a lien in the debtor's property and a resulting priority in the subject property over other parties asserting claims in it. This is also true as to liens created by use of the writ of attachment.[223] Assuming a writ of execution is validly issued,[224] the sheriff is ordered to "levy" upon the debtor's assets.

---

[218] See Hawkland & Loiseaux, Debtor-Creditor Relations 42–43 (Bobbs-Merrill, 2d ed. 1979); Madison v. General Acceptance Corp., 26 Wash. App. 387, 612 P2d 826 (1980); Schwaller Lumber Co. Inc. v. Watson, 211 Kan. 141, 505 P2d 640 (1973).

[219] See, e.g., Citizens Bank of Lavaca v. Perrin & Sons, Inc., 253 Ark. 639, 488 SW2d 14 (1972); National Shawmut Bank of Boston v. Vera, 352 Mass. 11, 223 NE2d 515 (1967).

[220] See, e.g., Murdock v. Blake, 26 Utah 2d 22, 484 P2d 164 (1971); General Motors Acceptance Corp. v. Stotsky, 60 Misc. 2d 451, 303 NYS2d 463 (NY Sup. Ct. 1969).

[221] See, e.g., Watwood v. Steur, 89 Cal. App. 2d 620, 201 P2d 460 (1949); Williams v. Ricca, 324 Pa. 33, 187 A 722 (1936). See generally Annot., 11 A.L.R. 225, 19 A.L.R. Supp. 863, 39 A.L.R. 1215 (1925).

[222] See, e.g., Morris v. Beatty, 323 Ill. App. 390, 55 NE2d 830 (1944); Texlite v. Liberty State Bank, 150 SW2d 822 (Tex. Civ. App. 1941).

[223] See supra ¶ 6.04[1][f].

[224] See supra ¶ 6.04[3][b] for discussion of execution procedure.

Many execution statutes provide that levy creates the execution lien.[225] A discussion of how levy occurs is undertaken in the following paragraphs.

Levy under writ of execution occurs differently depending upon whether the property is personal or real property. Levy by the sheriff on personalty requires the sheriff to take the property into his custody. Although this may be done either by actual taking or the employment of a keeper, a mere declaration by the sheriff that levy has occurred has been held to be insufficient.[226] The taking of personalty by the sheriff manifests to the world that the judgment creditor is asserting an interest in the property levied upon. There is, however, some authority that indicates an execution levy is valid when the sheriff has appointed the judgment debtor as bailee, provided that the sheriff has properly viewed and inventoried the chattels levied upon and proceeds promptly to sale.[227] This would seem to be appropriate, at least where only the judgment debtor disputes the validity of the levy as opposed to third parties who assert a claim in the chattel and have no notice of the levy.[228] If the chattel cannot be conveniently removed because of bulk or affixation to real estate, some statutes allow for levy by notice to the debtor and appropriate return.[229] Often the levying officer will have to leave notice on the property itself and will make its use inaccessible to the debtor. Some statutes provide for the method of levy on different types of chattels with great specificity; in these cases, the creditor must carefully consult the applicable statute.[230]

Actual seizure as to real estate is a physical impossibility. Additionally, third parties place great emphasis on public records to evidence the state of title in the case of real estate. As a result, many states require recordation or posting of notice on the real estate as a means of providing public notice of the levy. Apparently there is, however, considerable variety in exactly what procedure is to be followed.[231]

---

[225] See, e.g., Cal. Civ. Proc. Code § 688; Va. Code § 8.01-478.

[226] See, e.g., State ex rel. Mather v. Carnes, 551 SW2d 272 (Mo. Ct. App. 1977); Knox v. Binkowski, 99 Conn. 582, 122 A 400 (1923).

[227] See, e.g., Illi, Inc. v. Margolis, 267 Md. 30, 296 A2d 412 (1972); Cumberland Bank v. Hann, 19 NJL 166 (NJ Super. Ct. 1842); Annot., 22 A.L.R.2d 1276 (1952); Annot., 86 A.L.R. 1412 (1933).

[228] See, e.g., Nevada Credit Rating Bureau, Inc. v. Williams, 88 Nev. 601, 503 P2d 9 (1972); Mickelson v. Williams, 50 Wash. 2d 402, 312 P2d 656 (1957).

[229] See, e.g., Ore. Rev. Stat. § 23.410(4); Minn. Stat. Ann. § 550.13. Similar rules apply to crops. See Cal. Civ. Proc. Code §§ 488.360c, 688; Minn. Stat. Ann. §§ 550.13, 550.17.

[230] See Cal. Civ. Proc. Code §§ 488.310–488.430, 688; N.Y. Civ. Prac. Law & R. §§ 5201(c)(4)–5232.

[231] Professor Stefan Riesenfeld summarizes the various statutes as follows:

> "The governing statutes differ greatly as to the requisite form of a levy on real property, such as the recordation thereof in certain offices or the posting of notices, etc. In the absence of specific statutory or court rules it has been held that any overt act will suffice, Hutchins v. Commissioners of Carver County, 16 Minn. 13 (1870), construing Minn. Gen. Stat. 1866, ch. 66, §§ 269, 270, now Minn. Stat. Ann. §§ 550.10 and 11; Hyman v. Landry, 135 Wis. 598, 116 N.W. 236 (1908). In

Once the levy occurs and the lien is thereby created, the basic purpose of the execution becomes apparent: to aid in the collection of the obtained money judgment by giving the judgment creditor the ability to force sale, while obtaining priority over most subsequent interests asserted in the subject property. However, as to the priority of the lien, matters become somewhat complicated when viewed on a national scale. Although the "first-in-time, first-in-right" rule applies, there is considerable variety among the states as to the priority date of the execution lien. A substantial number of jurisdictions follow the rule that delivery of a writ of execution to the sheriff creates a lien and thus a priority date on the judgment debtor's chattels. Jurisdictions following this rule are Arkansas,[232] Colorado,[233] District of Columbia,[234] Florida,[235] Illinois,[236] Indiana,[237] Kentucky,[238] New Jersey,[239] and West Virginia.[240] In some of these jurisdictions, the rule does not operate against bona fide purchasers for value[241] or in case of executions in the hands of different officers.[242] Many states provide for the creation of a lien, and thus a priority date upon actual levy, without distinguishing between classes of third parties affected

---

Pennsylvania and Texas mere endorsement of the levy on the writ (so-called paper levy) suffices, Pa. R. Civ. P. 3108(f); Tex. R. Civ. P. 639. In California the courts have differentiated between levies on real property subject to a judgment lien and interests in land not subject to such liens, Lehnhardt v. Jennings, 119 Cal. 192, 48 Pac. 56 (1897); Lean v. Givens, 146 Cal. 739, 81 P 128 (1905). In New York a formal levy is necessary only if the real property is not or no longer subject to a judgment lien, N.Y., McKinney's C.P.L.R. §§ 5203(a) and 5235. In Illinois no execution lien arises unless a certificate of levy is recorded, Ill., Smith-Hurd Ann. Stat. ch. 77 § 37, cf. Reconstruction Finance Corp. v. Maley, 125 F.2d 131 (7th Cir. 1942), construing an older version of the statute."

Riesenfeld, Creditors' Remedies and Debtors' Protection 131 (West, 3d ed. 1979).

[232] Ark. Stat. Ann. § 30-116.

[233] Colo. Rev. Stat. § 13-52-111.

[234] D.C. Code Ann. § 15-307.

[235] See Flagship State Bank of Jacksonville v. Carantzas, 352 So. 2d 1259 (Fla. Dist. Ct. App. 1977); In re Vero Cooling & Heating, Inc., 11 Bankr. 359 (Bankr. SD Fla. 1981); Brown, "Some Incidents of Execution on Florida Judgments," 12 Fla. L.J. 364 (1938).

[236] Ill. Ann. Stat. ch. 77, § 9, construed in Century Pipe & Supply Co. v. Empire Factors, 19 Ill. App. 2d 165, 153 NE2d 298 (1958); Asher v. U.S., 436 F. Supp. 22 (ND Ill.), aff'd, 570 F2d 682 (7th Cir. 1976).

[237] Ind. Code Ann. § 34-1-34-9; Dragstrem v. Obermeyer, 549 F2d 20 (7th Cir. 1977).

[238] Ky. Rev. Stat. § 426.120; Ky. R. Civ. P. 69.03.

[239] N.J. Stat. Ann. § 2A:17-10, construed in Walton v. Hillier, 128 NJL 119, 24 A2d 219 (NJ 1942); In re Blease, C.A., 605 F2d 97 (3d Cir. 1979).

[240] W. Va. Code § 38-4-8; Birch River Boom & Lumber Co. v. Glendon Boom & Lumber Co., 71 W. Va. 507, 76 SE 972 (1912).

[241] N.J. Stat. Ann. § 2A:17-14; W. Va. Code § 38-4-9.

[242] Ind. Code Ann. § 34-1-34-9.

by the execution. States using this rule include Alaska,[243] California,[244] Delaware,[245] Idaho,[246] Iowa,[247] Kansas,[248] Louisiana,[249] Maryland,[250] Michigan,[251] Minnesota,[252] Missouri,[253] Montana,[254] Nebraska,[255] Nevada,[256] New Mexico,[257] North Dakota,[258] Ohio,[259] Oklahoma,[260] Oregon,[261] South Carolina,[262] South Dakota,[263] Texas,[264] Utah,[265] Virginia,[266] Washington,[267] Wisconsin,[268] and Wyoming.[269] In North Carolina, the statute

---

[243] Alaska Stat. § 09-35-110.

[244] Cal. Civ. Proc. Code § 688.

[245] Del. Code Ann. tit. 10, § 5081, which dated the lien from the time of the delivery of the unit, was held to be amended by the adoption of the UCC. Flemming v. Thompson, 343 A2d 599 (Del. 1975).

[246] Idaho Code § 11-201.

[247] Iowa R. Civ. P. 260.

[248] Kan. Stat. Ann. §§ 60-2401(e), 60-2402 (semble; a specific provision to that effect was not transferred into the new code or procedure).

[249] La. Code Civ. Proc. Ann. art. 2292.

[250] Md. Cts. & Jud. Proc. Code Ann. § 11-403; In re Urban Dev. Co. & Assocs., 452 F. Supp. 902 (D. Md. 1976). Before 1973, delivery of the writ of execution to the sheriff created a lien on chattels. American Sec. & Trust Co. v. New Amsterdam Casualty Co., 246 Md. 36, 227 A2d 214 (1967).

[251] Mich. Comp. Laws Ann. § 600.6012.

[252] Minn. Stat. Ann. § 550.10.

[253] Mo. Ann. Stat. § 513.085.

[254] Mont. Code Ann. § 25-13-501.

[255] Neb. Rev. Stat. § 25.1504.

[256] Nev. Rev. Stat. § 21.080.

[257] N.M. Stat. Ann. § 39-4-1; Van Segerlund v. Dysart, 137 F2d 755 (9th Cir. 1943).

[258] N.D. Cent. Code § 28-21-13; Towne v. Sautter, 326 NW2d 694 (ND 1982).

[259] Butz v. Bancohio Nat'l Bank, 13 Bankr. 425 (Bankr. D. Ohio 1981); Johnson v. Graham Lighter Corp., 83 Ohio App. 489, 80 NE2d 690 (1948).

[260] Okla. Stat. Ann. tit. 12, § 734; Storrie v. McAlester Fuel Co., 133 F2d 1003 (10th Cir. 1943).

[261] Ore. Rev. Stat. § 23.410(5).

[262] S.C. Code Ann. § 15-39-100; U.S. v. Southern Growth Indus., Inc., 251 SC 404, 162 SE2d 849 (1968).

[263] S.D. Code Ann. § 15-18-30.

[264] Brown v. Chambers, 63 Tex. 131 (1885); Herndon v. Cocke, 138 SW2d 298 (Tex. Civ. App. 1940).

[265] Utah Code Ann. § 104-37-0, repealed without change in law by 1951 Utah Laws ch. 58, § 3.

[266] Va. Code § 8.01-478; In re Stoddard, 23 Bankr. 226 (Bankr. SDNY 1982).

[267] Wash. Rev. Code Ann. § 6.04.100(5).

[268] Wis. Stat. Ann. § 815.19.

[269] Wyo. Stat. § 1-17-302.

requires a levy in order to create priority over bona fide purchasers for value and other execution creditors.[270] In three states (Alabama, Georgia, and Mississippi), the governing statutes provide for a judgment lien upon the judgment debtor's chattels, either upon entry[271] or upon recording an abstract thereof.[272] In Georgia, however, the priority does not affect bona fide purchasers. They are subordinate only to an execution docketed prior to transfer.[273] In the absence of recordation, Alabama and Mississippi do not require levy to create a lien.[274] Tennessee is the only state where the execution lien is created and the priority date is established as of the date of issuance of the writ.[275] Finally, New York provides that delivery of an execution to the sheriff gives the judgment creditor priority in the judgment debtor's chattels or debts owed to the judgment debtor. Exceptions arise as to a transferee for fair consideration prior to the levy, or a transferee acquiring rights in chattels not capable of delivery, or in debts owed to the judgment debtor for fair consideration after a levy without knowledge.[276]

#### [f] Execution and Postjudgment Garnishment in the Federal Courts

As indicated previously,[277] the enforcement of federal judgments occurs pursuant to state law due to Rule 64 of the Federal Rules of Civil Procedure.[278] Therefore, execution and postjudgment garnishment law of the state in which the federal court is located regulates the availability and use of the writs. This can occur as long as the state law is not preempted by federal statutes (which is a rarity)[279] and as long as the action in which the execution and postjudgment garnishment is issued is commenced and prosecuted pursuant to the Federal Rules of Civil Procedure.[280]

### [4] Postjudgment Garnishment

This book has previously considered use of the writ of garnishment as a prejudgment method of reaching assets of the debtor held by third parties or

---

[270] N.C. Gen. Stat. § 1-313(1).

[271] Ga. Code Ann. § 9-12-80.

[272] Ala. Code § 6-9-211; Miss. Code Ann. § 11-7-191.

[273] Ga. Code Ann. § 18-2-23.

[274] Ala. Code § 6-9-60; Miss. Code Ann. § 13-3-139.

[275] For details, see Rich, "Enforcing Money Judgments in Tennessee," 4 Mem. St. U.L. Rev. 65, 70 (1973).

[276] N.Y. Civ. Prac. Law & R. § 5202.

[277] See supra ¶ 6.04[1][g] for discussion of attachment and prejudgment garnishment in the federal courts. See supra ¶ 6.05[2][h] for discussion of judgment liens in federal courts.

[278] See supra ¶ 6.04[1][g] note 111 for the text of Rule 64.

[279] See 7 Moore's Federal Practice ¶ 64.07[3] (Matthew Bender 1979).

[280] See supra ¶ 6.04[1][g] note 111.

debts owed the debtor by third parties.[281] As previously indicated, the writ of garnishment is also used in the postjudgment setting to reach such property or debts. Just as execution is the postjudgment procedural equivalent of prejudgment attachment, so too is postjudgment garnishment the procedural equivalent to prejudgment garnishment. Thus, much of the basic postjudgment garnishment law was considered in the discussion of prejudgment garnishment. Even so, in order to continue coverage of judicial remedies in a chronological format, a brief discussion on differences and similarities between postjudgment and prejudgment garnishment is essential at this point.

As was the case with prejudgment garnishment, the use of postjudgment garnishment historically grew out of another writ. As to postjudgment garnishment, the writ developed as a proceeding in aid of the writ of execution.[282] It was necessitated by the fact that the writ of execution could not reach the judgment debtor's property possessed by third parties; nor could execution usually reach debts owed by third parties to the judgment debtor.[283] On the other hand, in a few jurisdictions, postjudgment garnishment is seen as completely separate from execution.[284] Finally, some states treat postjudgment garnishment as a form of execution.[285] Today garnishment, or its equivalent, is purely a statutory remedy.

From a procedural standpoint, whether garnishment is in aid of execution or is completely separate, there are some obvious differences between postjudgment and prejudgment garnishment. The principal difference lies in the simple fact that the creditor has obtained a judgment. As a result, the procedural impediments faced by a creditor seeking prejudgment garnishment of the debtor's property or debts are in large part removed. As is the case regarding issuance of the writ of execution, the judgment creditor basically only needs to establish the existence of an unsatisfied judgment and the reasonable belief that a third party possesses assets of the judgment debtor or owes a debt to the judgment debtor.

Beyond the simplified grounds for obtaining issuance of the postjudgment writ of garnishment, the use and effect of a postjudgment garnishment for the most part parallels prejudgment garnishment. Once notice of garnishment is served on the third party (known as the garnishee), the garnishee is required to answer the complaint within a stated time; failure to do so may result in a default judgment.[286] In some states, default judgments are not easily obtained against a garnishee.[287] In his answer to the complaint, the garnishee indicates

---

[281] See supra ¶ 6.04[2] for complete coverage of garnishment.

[282] See supra ¶ 6.04[2][a].

[283] See supra ¶ 6.05[3][d].

[284] See supra ¶ 6.04[2][a].

[285] Id.

[286] See, e.g., Kan. Stat. Ann. § 60-718 (twenty days); Wash. Rev. Code tit. 7, § 7.32.170; Minn. Stat. Ann. § 571.53 (twenty days).

[287] See, e.g., Nev. Rev. Stat. § 31.320; N.C. Gen. Stat. § 1-440.27 (conditional judgment).

that he holds property belonging to the debtor or that he is otherwise indebted to him.[288] In the alternative, the garnishee might defend himself by asserting that he holds such property but has an interest in it that is paramount to the debtor's interest. He might also indicate that there is no property in his possession[289] or that no debt is due the judgment debtor. Such defenses can include setoff defenses that the garnishee has to assert against the judgment debtor.[290] The garnishee may also use the defense that the debtor's property in his hands is exempt.[291] If the garnishee admits holding the debtor's property, the court will order that it be turned over to the court or sheriff to satisfy the judgment. In the case of prejudgment garnishment, the garnishee may not be required to actually turn over the garnished property until he receives a further order following judgment against the debtor. If the garnishee does not admit the existence of such property or debt or otherwise contends that the judgment creditor is not entitled to it, the judgment creditor may controvert the answer, and in this case the controverted issue is tried like any other civil matter.[292]

Postjudgment garnishment will reach the same property that is reached by a prejudgment garnishment.[293] Similarly a garnishment lien may also be created as in the case of prejudgment garnishment.[294] However, postjudgment garnishment liens will not be provisional in nature due to the already obtained judgment. Otherwise, the effect of the lien will parallel that of a lien obtained by way of prejudgment garnishment.[295]

## [5] Proceedings in Aid of Execution—Creditor's Bills and Supplementary Proceedings

### [a] Historical Background and Purpose of Proceedings in Aid of Execution

It is often assumed that once a writ of execution or the like is issued the sheriff will locate property of the debtor on which to levy. If the sheriff is unable to easily locate property, however, he normally will not serve as a detective for the judgment creditor. Extrajudicial efforts of the judgment creditor to

---

[288] See, e.g., W. Va. Code § 38-7-24.

[289] See, e.g., N.C. Gen. Stat. § 1-440.28; Minn. Stat. Ann. § 541.495.

[290] For discussion of setoff in the face of a garnishment, see ¶ 5.05[2][h]. See generally Annot., 106 A.L.R. 62; 110 A.L.R. Supp. 1268 (1937); Annot., 65 A.L.R.3d 1284 (1975).

[291] See, e.g., Milne v. Shell Oil Co., 129 Vt. 375, 278 A2d 741 (1971); Vt. R. Civ. P. 4.2(j), Vt. Stat. Ann. tit. 12, § 3013. But cf. Conley v. Chilcote, 25 Ohio St. 320, 36 Ohio St. 545 (1881)

[292] See, e.g., W. Va. Code § 38-7-28; Tex. Civ. Proc. Rules Ann. R. 674.

[293] See supra ¶ 6.04[2][d].

[294] See supra ¶ 6.04[2][e].

[295] Id.

locate property of the debtor also may have proven unsuccessful,[296] or if successful, perhaps the various means of reaching that property discussed to this point of the text have proven unsatisfactory due to procedural or practical impediments. Recognizing these problems, the law has provided creditors with additional procedures to aid the creditor in executing upon the debtor's property.

The common law originated the creditor's bill to assist the creditor who is having difficulty in locating property of the debtor. The creditor's bill was particularly essential at common law in that writs of elegit and fieri facis were narrow in scope.[297] In particular, equitable interests and certain intangibles were not subject to levy pursuant to those common-law writs. In any event, the creditor perhaps could not locate assets of the debtor because the debtor secreted them or transferred them in fraud of his creditor.[298] In response to these problems, the English Chancery developed the equitable remedy of the creditor's bill to serve three principal functions: (1) discovery of assets; (2) application of "equitable" assets to the payment of money judgments; and (3) avoidance of fraudulent conveyances.[299]

The creditor's bill proved to be less than satisfactory. It was "available, if at all, only to creditors who had unsuccessfully resorted to elegit or fieri facis. The remedy thus was cumbersome and, in addition, spotty."[300] Today, the creditor's bill is largely only of historical importance. First, the legal writs of execution and garnishment were expanded to reach virtually all forms of property.[301] Second, in many jurisdictions, law and equity have been combined, and statutes have been passed to that effect.[302] Third, the advent of supple-

---

[296] See ¶ 5.03 for discussion of extrajudicial methods of discovering the debtor's assets.

[297] See supra ¶ 6.05[3][a] for a brief discussion of these common-law writs.

[298] The subject of fraudulent conveyances is considered at infra ¶ 6.07[2].

[299] See Riesenfeld, "Collection of Money Judgments in American Law—A Historical Inventory and Prospectus," 42 Iowa L. Rev. 155, 160 (1957).

[300] Riesenfeld, Creditors' Remedies and Debtors' Protection 283 (West, 3d ed. 1979). Professor Riesenfeld cites in support of that conclusion his own article at supra ¶ 6.05[5][a] note 299, and Millar, Civil Procedure of the Trial Court in Historical Perspective 437 (N.Y.U. Law Center 1952).

[301] For discussion of property subject to attachment, see supra ¶ 6.04[1][e]; garnishment, supra ¶¶ 6.04[2][d], 6.05[4]; the judgment lien, supra ¶ 6.05[2][d]. However, a creditor still may use a creditor's bill if, for example, the writ of execution cannot reach certain property. See, e.g., Burchett v. Roncari, 181 Conn. 125, 434 A2d 941 (1980).

[302] For example, Rule 18 of the Federal Rules of Civil Procedure:

> "(a) Joinder of Claims. A party asserting a claim to relief as an original claim, counterclaim, cross-claim, or third-party claim, may join, either as independent or as alternate claims, as many claims, legal, equitable, or maritime, as he has against an opposing party.
>
> "(b) Joinder of Remedies; Fraudulent Conveyances. Whenever a claim is one heretofore cognizable only after another claim has been prosecuted to a conclusion, the two claims may be joined in a single action; but the court shall grant relief in that action only in accordance with the relative substantive rights of the parties.

mentary proceedings, discussed in the following paragraphs, has, in large part, replaced some of the functions of the creditor's bill. However, due to the limitations on the scope of supplementary proceedings in some jurisdictions, the creditor's bill may still be a last resort.[303] Further, the creditor's bill is still the principal procedural vehicle through which fraudulent conveyances are attacked.[304] However, the attorney should be aware that some jurisdictions have abolished use of the creditor's bill altogether.[305] Although the existence of supplementary proceedings does not in itself abolish the creditor's bill,[306] use of supplementary proceedings is the most attractive alternative for most purposes.

---

> In particular, a plaintiff may state a claim for money and a claim to have set aside a conveyance fraudulent as to him, without first having obtained a judgment establishing the claim for money."

See also U.S. ex rel. Goldman v. Meredith, 596 F2d 1353 (8th Cir.), cert. denied, Goldman v. Merrill, Lynch, Pierce, Fenner & Smith, 444 US 838 (1979); Huntress v. Huntress' Estate, 235 F2d 205 (7th Cir. 1956).

[303] See, e.g., U.S. ex rel. Goldman v. Meredith, 596 F2d 1353 (8th Cir.), cert. denied, Goldman v. Merrill, Lynch, Pierce, Fenner & Smith, 444 US 838 (1979); Bond v. Bulgheroni, 215 Cal. 7, 8 P2d 130 (1932); Burchett v. Roncari, 181 Conn. 125, 434 A2d 941 (1980).

[304] For a discussion on fraudulent conveyances, see infra ¶ 6.07[2]. To understand why the creditor's bill is used to set aside fraudulent conveyances, consider the following:

> "It seems to have been the intention of the framers of that statute [creating supplementary proceedings] to provide a summary process for the discovery and application to the judgment, of property subject to execution, concealed and withheld by the debtor, or others in collusion with him, without pretending, when it came to a test under oath, to assert any substantial ground therefor. But where the property alleged to belong to the judgment debtor is claimed by others, either by way of absolute title or pledge or mortgage, or debts claimed to be owing to the judgment debtor are disputed by his alleged debtor, such claims of ownership, lien or denial of indebtedness cannot be adjudicated and determined summarily, and the property ordered applied to the judgment, with none of the usual formalities of forming issues and trial guaranteed as applicable to the determination of property rights."

Ryan v. Maxey, 14 Mont. 81, 84, 35 P 515, 516 (1894). A few states have amended supplementary proceedings statutes so that the court can adjudicate rights and interests in the debt or property that is the subject of the proceeding. However, the language in *Ryan* reflects the state of law in most jurisdictions.

[305] See 6 Weinstein, Korn & Miller, New York Civil Practice ¶ 5201.02 (Matthew Bender 1973).

[306] Cf. 1 Pomeroy, Equity Jurisprudence § 279, at 380 (Lawyers' Coop. Publishing Co., 5th ed. 1941):

> "Where . . . new power is conferred upon the law courts by statutory legislation, the rule is well settled that unless the statute contains negative words or other language expressly taking away the pre-existing equity jurisdiction, or unless the whole scope of the statute, by its reasonable construction and its operation, shows a clear legislative intent to abolish that jurisdiction, the former jurisdiction of equity to grant its relief under the circumstances remains unabridged."

The attempt to develop a procedure to aid creditors in executing upon assets of a judgment debtor beyond the creditor's bill took a somewhat haphazard route from a historical standpoint. Initially, attempts were made to codify extension of equity proceedings.[307] Thereafter, as mentioned previously, the writ of execution was expanded to encompass equitable assets and choses in action and in creation of a new form of levy made by notice to appropriate third parties.[308] At about the same time, garnishment proceedings were expanded to encompass collection of money judgments.[309] Finally, supplementary proceedings, as they are known today, evolved in New York.[310] Using New York as an example, many states followed suit.[311] Today, most supplementary proceedings statutes provide for the following:

(1) Discovery of assets through the right of examination of the debtor and others;
(2) Issuance of injunctions to prevent disposition of property;
(3) Discretionary power to appoint receivers;
(4) Creation of liens on the debtor's property;[312] and
(5) Orders for the sale of the subject property.[313]

### [b] Procedural Nature of Creditor's Bills and Supplementary Proceedings

The creditor's bill, itself, is an equitable quasi in rem proceeding based on a summons and complaint seeking discovery and application of the debtor's property to the creditor's judgment. A creditor may file a creditor's bill for his own benefit; additionally, he may file a creditor's bill as a class

---

[307] See, e.g., N.Y., 2 Rev. Stat. 1829, pt. III, ch. 1, tit. 2, art. 2, §§ 38, 39, copied, for example, in Mich. Rev. Stat. 1838, pt. III, tit. 1, ch. 2, §§ 25, 26.

[308] See Riesenfeld, Creditors' Remedies and Debtors' Protection 284 (West, 3d ed. 1979); see also, e.g., N.Y. Civ. Proc. Code (reported complete) §§ 729, 837 (1850).

[309] Riesenfeld, Creditors' Remedies and Debtors' Protection 284 (West, 3d ed. 1979).

[310] N.Y. Civ. Proc. Code (reported complete) §§ 853–865 (1850).

[311] N.Y. Civ. Proc. Code §§ 292–302 (1849), serving as model for Cal. Civ. Prac. Act §§ 238–245 (1851); Iowa Code §§ 1953–1959; Ky. Code of Prac. ch. 5, §§ 474–478 (1854); Mich. Laws No. 184, at 316 (1851); Ohio Civ. Proc. Code tit. 14, ch. 2, §§ 458–476 (1853); Va. Code tit. 53, ch. 188, §§ 5, 10–15 (1849); Wis. Rev. Stat. ch. 34, §§ 88–99 (1858).

[312] The nature of lien arising under both creditor's bills and supplementary proceedings is considered at infra ¶ 6.05[5][c].

[313] In New York, the state that originated comprehensive supplementary proceedings, the supplementary proceeding is now broken up into a set of separate special remedies. See 6 Weinstein, Korn & Miller, New York Civil Practice ¶¶ 5222.01, 5228.03 (Matthew Bender 1964); N.Y. Civ. Prac. Law & R. §§ 5222, 5225, 5227, 5228.

action for the benefit of all creditors by joining all creditors of the debtor known to him.[314]

Because the creditor's bill was an equitable proceeding offering the creditor equitable remedies, the creditor had to establish that he had a judgment and an unsatisfied execution. This was the rule, regardless of whether the creditor was attempting to discover assets, reach assets not subject to execution, or reach assets conveyed in fraud of creditors.[315] Indeed, the rule was transformed into statute in many jurisdictions.[316] Some variety in this rule can be found; for example, some states merely require issuance of execution without the necessity of an unsatisfied return if the property to be reached by the creditor's bill is not reachable by execution.[317] Similarly, it has been held that only a judgment is needed to reach an equitable interest in land on which the judgment creates a lien.[318] Courts also have allowed filing of creditor's bills where the debtor was a nonresident and was not subject to the jurisdiction of the court, where the debtor was insolvent, or where the debtor had died prior to issuance of execution.[319] As to setting aside fraudulent conveyances, some statutes and rules of procedure have eliminated the need for a judgment creditor's bill, which has had the effect of making an unsatisfied execution also irrelevant.[320] Once the creditor has filed the creditor's bill, the remedies discussed in the next section are available to him.

By contrast, supplementary proceedings are not new actions but are considered a summary process in aid of the original lawsuit.[321] As a result, the "creditor's bill is generally regarded as more onerous and cumbersome for cred-

---

[314] See, e.g., Hefferman v. Bennett & Armour, 110 Cal. App. 2d 564, 243 P2d 846 (1952); Blick v. Nimmo, 121 Md. 139, 88 A 116 (1913); Hutchinson v. Maxwell, 100 Va. 169, 40 SE 655 (1902). A special type of creditor's bill is the charging order provided in Section 28 of the Uniform Partnership Act.

[315] See, e.g., Schaeffer v. Zaltsman, 29 Ill. App. 3d 1011, 331 NE2d 212 (1975); State Bank of Ceresco v. Belk, 68 Neb. 517, 94 NW 617 (1903); Dunham v. Kauffman, 385 Ill. 79, 52 NE2d 143 (1944); 4 Pomeroy, Equity Jurisprudence 1067, 1068 (Lawyers' Coop. Publishing Co., 5th ed. 1941); 1 Glenn, Fraudulent Conveyances 145 (Boker, Voorhis, rev. ed. 1940). But see Morgan v. U.S. Fidelity & Guar. Co., 222 So. 2d 820 (Miss. 1969).

[316] See, e.g., N.Y. Rev. Stat. pt. III, ch. 1, tit. 2, art. 2, § 38 (1829); Ill. Rev. Stat. ch. 21 § 36 (1845).

[317] See, e.g., Freedman's Sav. & Trust Co. v. Earle, 110 US 710 (1884); Hutchinson v. Maxwell, 100 Va. 169, 40 SE 655 (1902).

[318] See Coleman v. Alcock, 272 F2d 618 (5th Cir. 1960).

[319] See, e.g., Miller v. Maryland Casualty Co., 207 Ark. 312, 180 SW2d 581 (1944); Shuck v. Quackenbush, 75 Colo. 592, 277 P. 1041 (1924); Annot., 38 A.L.R. 269 (1925).

[320] See, e.g., Uniform Fraudulent Conveyance Act § 9; Ark. Stat. Ann. § 68-1308; Ga. Code Ann. § 18-2-21.

[321] See, e.g., State Dep't. of Revenue v. Milwaukee Mack Sales, Inc., 91 Wis. 2d 1, 280 NW2d 274 (1979); Florida Guaranteed Sec., Inc. v. McAllister, 47 F2d 762 (SD Fla. 1931).

itors than supplementary proceedings."[322] The supplementary proceeding typically commences upon the motion of the judgment creditor followed by an order of the court. Some supplementary proceeding statutes reflect the law related to creditor's bills in requiring satisfaction of some conditions precedent. The field draft of a Code of Civil Procedure for New York is typical. It retained the need for the return of an unsatisfied execution; however, it did relax the requirement by making it applicable only for the examination of the judgment debtor. Otherwise, the mere issuance of an execution was sufficient for other forms of relief provided by the supplementary proceeding.[323] Other states followed suit.[324] Currently, many states have dispensed with the need for the requirement of the return of an unsatisfied execution.[325] Once the judgment creditor has procured issuance of an order from the court for a supplementary proceeding, he may use the remedies discussed in the next section.

### [c] Remedies Available to Creditors in Proceedings in Aid of Execution

The discussion of proceedings in aid of execution has emphasized that these proceedings function principally to discover assets, to apply them to the judgment, and in so doing create a lien therein, and to avoid fraudulent conveyances (at least with regard to creditor's bills). Once the proceeding in aid of execution commences, the court has at its disposal the usual judicial powers to enable the creditor to examine the debtor and others in an effort to discover assets and have those assets applied to the judgment. In that regard, the subpoena power of the court is of obvious importance. So, too, are other judicial powers to order or enjoin certain actions of parties or nonparties within its jurisdiction. All of these powers when used to assist the creditor's collection efforts can be viewed as remedies available to the creditor in proceedings in aid of execution. In addition to these, three other matters that might be characterized as creditor's remedies that are particularly crucial to a creditor in these proceedings should be separately considered. These include the contempt power; the potential of such a proceeding to create liens in the debtor's property; and the power of the court to appoint receivers.

Although the contempt power perhaps is not unique to proceedings in aid of execution, it is nevertheless particularly central to the effectiveness of such a proceeding. For example, creditors using such proceedings are often protected by injunctions enjoining the debtor from transferring or encumbering his property. If the debtor violates such injunctions, he stands in contempt of court. However, even if in contempt, a transfer of property in violation of the injunc-

---

[322] Hawkland & Loiseaux, Debtor-Creditor Relations 105 (Bobbs-Merrill, 2d ed. 1979).

[323] Commissioners' Report, N.Y. Civ. Proc. Code §§ 853, 854, 857 (1850).

[324] 1851 Cal. Stat. ch. 5, §§ 238, 239, 241; N.Y. Code of Proc. §§ 292, 294 (1851); 1853 Ohio Laws. §§ 459, 460, 464, at 136.

[325] See, e.g., Ga. Code Ann. § 81A-169; Ill. Sup. Ct. R. 277; Ohio Rev. Code Ann. § 2333.13; Utah R. Civ. P. 69(k), 69(l).

tion to a bona fide purchaser allows the purchaser to take free of any claim of the judgment creditor, unless the creditor has obtained a lien in the assets transferred.[326] One noted author suggests that this rule "imposes greater risks in most states on creditors using supplementary proceedings than on those using the creditor's bill."[327] The same contempt power is also useful to "induce" the judgment debtor and others to answer interrogatories concerning the location of assets. The majority of states refuse, however, to impose compensatory fines on the debtor who is in contempt.[328] Some states do give their courts statutory power to impose such fines.[329] Additionally, the federal courts and the courts of a few states have this power as a result of case law.[330] It has been suggested that the rationale of the federal courts regarding compensatory contempt fines is best explained as follows:

> Proceedings in civil contempt are between the original parties and are instituted and tried as a part of the main cause. Though such proceedings are 'nominally those of contempt,' the real purpose of the court order is purely remedial—to coerce obedience to a decree passed in complainant's favor or to compensate plaintiff for a loss caused by respondent's disobedience. . . . If complainant makes a showing that respondent has disobeyed a decree in complainant's favor, and that damages have resulted to complainant thereby, complainant is entitled as of right to an order in civil contempt imposing a compensatory fine.[331]

In spite of this quoted authority, most courts probably continue to use contempt as a means of protecting the courts' authority and not as a remedial procedure designed to compensate parties injured by the conduct that gave rise to the contempt.[332]

A second matter that relates to available remedies in proceedings in aid of execution involves the creation of liens in the debtor's property as a result of institution of a creditor's bill or supplementary proceeding. Such liens have engendered much confusion. Professor Stefan Riesenfeld describes the status of the law as follows:

---

[326] See discussion immediately below regarding creation of liens in proceedings in aid of execution.

[327] Hawkland & Loiseaux, Debtor-Creditor Relations 107 (Bobbs-Merrill, 2d ed. 1979).

[328] Id.

[329] See, e.g., Ind. Code Ann. § 34-4-7-6; N.Y. Jud. Law § 773; Wash. Rev. Code § 7.20.100.

[330] See, e.g., Gompers v. Bucks Stove & Range Co., 211 US 418 (1911); Laurie v. Ryan, 130 NJ Eq. 248, 22 A2d 6 (NJ Ch. 1941); Brocker v. Brocker, 429 Pa. 513, 241 A2d 336 (1968).

[331] Parker v. U.S., 153 F2d 66, 70 (1st Cir. 1946).

[332] See Hawkland & Loiseaux, Debtor-Creditor Relations 108 (Bobbs-Merrill, 2d ed. 1979).

> The question as to whether, as of what time, on what kinds of assets, and with what effect creditors' bills or supplementary proceedings create liens has perplexed the courts greatly and produced a vast amount of confused and conflicting case law and patchwork legislation. The problem arises in the contest of priorities among creditors, relations between creditors initiating creditors' actions or supplementary proceedings and supervening purchasers, and the survival of such liens under the ... Bankruptcy Act. ...[333]

Most statutes relating to creditor's bills and supplementary proceedings do provide for creation of liens in the debtor's property. The jurisdictions differ with respect to the time at which the lien is created and its effect on third parties.[334] Some states have given special attention to the problem, either by statute or case law.[335] Professor Riesenfeld has concluded that

> Apparently the majority rule which can be deduced from these cases is to the effect that the initiation of creditors' suits or supplementary proceedings against the judgment debtor creates a lien on all assets which are discovered thereby or are ordered to be applied to the payment of the judgment, whereas initiation of supplementary proceedings against a third party creates a lien on the debts owed by him to the judgment debtor and on such other assets of the judgment debtor as are held by him.[336]

One final note regarding liens arising from creditor's bills should be made. A creditor's bill may be filed by one creditor for himself or it may be filed as a class action for the benefit of all creditors.[337] If the creditor's bill is filed as a class action, all creditors would maintain equal priority as a result of any obtained lien. If, however, the creditor files the bill for himself only, he would obtain a priority over subsequent asserted interests.[338]

The appointment of a receiver is the final remedy of special import to proceedings in aid of execution. This is particularly relevant to supplemental proceedings because many states provide for the possible appointment of a

---

[333] Riesenfeld, Creditors' Remedies and Debtors' Protection 303 (West, 3d ed. 1979).

[334] See Annot., 153 A.L.R. 211 (1944); Annot., 92 A.L.R. 1435 (1934).

[335] See, e.g., N.Y. Civ. Prac. Law & R. § 5202(b); cf. 6 Weinstein, Korn & Miller, New York Civil Practice ¶¶ 5202.26–5202.29, 5234.17–5234.19 (Matthew Bender 1964); Canfield v. Security-First Nat'l Bank of L.A., 13 Cal. 2d 1, 87 P2d 830 (1939); Bank of Lyons v. Schultz, 22 Ill. App. 3d 410, 318 NE2d 52 (1974); Bunge & Bunge, "Proceedings in Aid of Execution," 16 Ohio St. L.J. 17, 21 (1955).

[336] Riesenfeld, Creditors' Remedies and Debtors' Protection 304 (West, 3d ed. 1979); see also Billson v. Lenderberg, 66 Minn. 66, 70, 68 NW 771, 773 (1896).

[337] See supra ¶ 6.05[5][b].

[338] See, e.g., Traveler's Indem. Co. v. First Nat'l Bank, 368 So. 2d 836 (Miss. 1979); Bluestein v. Davis, 86 Ill. App. 2d 61, 230 NE2d 61 (1967); Salena Mfg. Co. v. Diner's Club, Inc., 382 So. 2d 1309 (Fla. Dist. Ct. App. 1980).

receiver within the context of a supplementary proceeding.[339] Since the subject of receivership is dealt with in other portions of the text, it will only be noted here as a remedy particularly relevant to proceedings in aid of execution. For examples of use of a receiver in supplementary proceedings, the reader should consult the cases cited below.[340]

## ¶ 6.06 EXECUTION AND JUDICIAL SALES

### [1] Introduction and Basic Definitions

Obtaining a judicial lien in a debtor's assets permits a creditor to force a sale of the subject asset.[1] Through the sale of the asset, proceeds are obtained and applied to the satisfaction of the debt that has been reduced to judgment. This portion of the text surveys the law that pertains to execution and judicial sales. The basic procedure typical of sales nationwide is reviewed,[2] with particular emphasis placed upon law that determines the title in the sold property received by the buyer,[3] and upon law that seeks to protect the judgment debtor from potential abuses that might arise in connection with the sale.[4]

A definitional distinction must first be emphasized separating "execution sales" from "judicial sales." An execution sale is a sale of the debtor's property usually conducted by a sheriff. Authority is given the sheriff by a clerk-issued writ of execution that directs the sheriff to sell property previously levied upon.[5] The execution sale is technically different from a judicial sale in that a judicial sale is conducted pursuant to a court order that directs the sale of specifically designated property through which the court gives directions and usually must confirm the sale.[6] On the other hand, there are obvious similarities between the two types of forced sales. To facilitate discussion of principles

---

[339] See supra ¶ 6.04[4].

[340] See, e.g., Melba Investors Atl., Inc. v. Mimi Selig Homes, Inc., 44 Md. App. 234, 407 A2d 808 (1979); Olsan v. Comora, 73 Cal. App. 3d 642, 140 Cal. Rptr. 835 (1977); Candee v. Egan, 84 Wis. 2d 348, 267 NW2d 890 (1978); Annot., 92 A.L.R. 1435 (1935).

[1] See supra ¶¶ 6.01, 6.03, 6.05.

[2] See infra ¶ 6.06[2].

[3] See infra ¶ 6.06[3].

[4] See infra ¶ 6.06[4].

[5] See, e.g., Cochran v. Cochran, 39 Ill. App. 2d 602, 350 NE2d 59 (1926); Chittam v. Armco Steel Corp., 407 P2d 1015 (Wyo. 1965); State ex rel. Roulerson v. Sloan, 134 Fla. 632, 184 So. 128 (1938).

[6] See, e.g., Borman v. Simpson, 45 Ill. App. 3d 176, 359 NE2d 824 (1977); U.S. v. Branch Coal Corp., 340 F2d 7 (3d Cir.), cert. denied, Sun Protection Co. of Am. v. U.S., 391 US 966 (1968).

common to both, and to avoid redundancy, the text does not emphasize the distinction.[7]

## [2] Procedure

### [a] Getting the Property From Lien to Sale

Judicial liens may be acquired in a debtor's assets prior to judgment by way of the writ of attachment[8] and writ of garnishment,[9] and after judgment by way of the judgment lien,[10] writ of execution,[11] and writ of garnishment.[12] Liens obtained by postjudgment execution and garnishment result in sale of the subject asset (or collection of a debt, as discussed in the following paragraphs) by way of the content of those writs. In short, the writs incorporate an order to sell the property levied upon. This may not be the case in regard to prejudgment attachment or garnishment, which, in turn, may necessitate a postjudgment writ of execution or order of the court to sell the property. The order might be incorporated into the judgment itself. Special procedural problems regarding movement of the property from lien status to sale have particularly arisen with regard to garnishment and judgment liens.

Garnishment most often involves debts owed by third parties to the judgment debtor.[13] With regard to garnished debts owed to the judgment debtor by a third party, "the procedure is not to have the debt *sold* but *collected* by garnishment proceedings . . . pursuant to which the garnishee is ordered to pay over to the judgment creditor the amount of the judgment debtor's claim against the garnishee."[14] Nevertheless, issues have occasionally arisen as to whether the debt being garnished should be sold (assigned for a price) pursuant to a writ of garnishment, or whether the garnishee is merely required to make payment of the debt owed to the judgment debtor directly to the sheriff. Although, as just indicated, garnishment of a debt traditionally seeks collection of the debt, there is some authority that stands for the proposition that garnishment of a debt is like a levy on the debt itself, equivalent to seizure of tangible property. Therefore, the garnishor may have the debt itself sold.[15]

---

[7] For examples of separate treatments of judicial and execution sales, see 30 Am. Jur. 2d Executions §§ 303 et seq. (1967); 47 Am. Jur. 2d Judicial Sales §§ 1–402 (1969); 33 C.J.S. Executions §§ 196 et seq. (1942); 50 C.J.S. Judicial Sales §§ 1–71 (1947); Annot., 2 A.L.R.2d 6 (1948).

[8] See supra ¶ 6.04[1][f].

[9] See supra ¶ 6.04[2][e].

[10] See supra ¶ 6.05[2].

[11] See supra ¶ 6.05[3][e].

[12] See supra ¶ 6.05[4].

[13] See supra ¶ 6.04[2][e].

[14] Warren & Hogan, Debtor-Creditor Law, 106–107 (Foundation Press, 2d ed. 1981).

[15] See, e.g., Meacham v. Meacham, 262 Cal. App. 2d 248, 68 Cal. Rptr. 746 (1968); Pavlovich v. Watts, 46 Cal. App. 2d 103, 115 P2d 511 (1941).

The judgment lien clearly contemplates sale of the property subject to the lien. Thus, the question is not whether the property should be sold, but rather how one procedurally gets the property to sale. In other words, how does one enforce a judgment lien? The proper method of enforcing the judgment lien varies significantly among the jurisdictions. First, some jurisdictions require a foreclosure proceeding before the property subject to the judgment lien can be sold.[16] Second, some states require levy and sale pursuant to an issued writ of execution.[17] In these states, the judgment lien seems to create a priority for the judgment creditor but is not an independent means of getting the property to sale, thus necessitating the writ of execution. Third, some jurisdictions provide the judgment creditor with the option of foreclosure or levy under execution as a means of forcing the sale of the property that is subject to the judgment lien.[18] Finally, "a number of jurisdictions permit foreclosure proceedings when the judgment lien subsists but the death of the judgment debtor bars issuance of an execution or requires revival of the judgment against the heir. . . ."[19]

### [b] Conduct of the Sale

The content of statutes that regulate execution sales varies significantly from state to state. However, the typical procedures related to conducting the sale can be outlined, with emphasis placed upon problem areas that have commonly arisen.[20] The typical sales procedure includes matters pertaining to notice of sale, the time and place of sale, the manner of sale, the eligible purchaser, payment of the sales price, confirmation of the sale, and certificates or other conveyances to the purchaser.

Public notification of sale characterizes the effort of legislatures to ensure that the highest price possible can be obtained for the benefit of all interested parties (i.e., the judgment creditor, other encumbrancers, and the debtor alike).[21] Failure to properly give notice may result in invalidating the sale,[22]

---

[16] See, e.g., Hobbs v. Simonds, 61 Conn. 235, 23 A2d 962 (1891); Hutcheson v. Grubbs, 80 Va. 251 (1885).

[17] See, e.g., Belnap v. Blain, 575 P2d 696 (Utah 1978); Gantz v. First Nat'l Bank of Miami, 138 So. 2d 367 (Fla. Dist. Ct. App. 1962); Thompson v. Dole, 58 Minn. 365, 59 NW 1086 (1894).

[18] See, e.g., N.M. Stat. Ann. §§ 39-4-1, 39-4-13; Walker v. Davies, 113 Ariz. 233, 550 P2d 230 (1976); Baker v. West, 120 Tex. 113, 36 SW2d 695 (1931); Ala. Code §§ 6-9-210, 6-9-211; Erlenbach v. Cox, 206 Ala. 298, 89 So. 465 (1921).

[19] Riesenfeld, Creditors' Remedies and Debtors' Protection 103 (West, 3d ed. 1979); see, e.g., Corporation of Am. v. Marks, 10 Cal. 2d 218, 73 P2d 1215 (1937); Federal Farm Mortgage Corp. v. Walker, 115 Utah 461, 206 P2d 146 (1949).

[20] See supra ¶ 6.05[3][b] for discussion of whether a sheriff may proceed to sale where the effective statutory time period of a writ of execution has expired.

[21] See, e.g., Frazee v. Nelson, 179 Mass. 456, 61 NE 40 (1901); Farmers Sec. Bank v. Wood, 132 Neb. 175, 271 NW 349 (1937); Annot., 5 A.L.R.4th 794 (1981); McCartney v. Frost, 37 Md. App. 495, 378 A2d 170 (1977).

[22] See, e.g., Wofford v. Dykes, 67 Fla. 118, 64 So. 451 (1914).

although there is contrary authority.[23] Often, personal notice of the time and location of the sale must be given the judgment debtor.[24] The content of the notice must not be materially in error. Obviously, the notice should accurately specify the terms, place, and time of the sale, and the property must usually be described without a material error.[25] Typically, the notice of the sale must be given in newspapers, be posted, or both.[26] Statutes also specify the length of time that the notice of sale must be given.[27] On the other hand, sales on short notice are sometimes allowed, particularly when the property is perishable.[28]

As a rule of thumb, an execution sale should take place at the time and place named in the public notice.[29] As to the time of the sale, under appropriate circumstances the sale may be delayed, for example, where a delay is ordered for the purpose of obtaining a higher price.[30] The sale may even be adjourned under a variety of circumstances.[31] If adjournment occurs, a re-advertisement, with a new notice of sale, may be required.[32] As to the place of the sale, statutes may proscribe that the sale occur at a specified place. Typical statutes may require sale at the courthouse or courthouse door.[33] In some instances, the sale may occur at the location of the property. If personal property is involved, there is authority that the personalty must be present at the place of sale.[34]

---

[23] See, e.g., Nixon v. Treber, 100 Idaho 198, 595 P2d 1093 (1979); Frink v. Roe, 70 Cal. 296, 11 P 820 (1886). There can be contrary rules by statute that invalidate a sale due to lack of proper notice.

[24] See, e.g., Neff v. Ford Motor Credit Co., 347 So. 2d 1228 (La. Ct. App. 1977); Annas v. Davis, 40 NC App. 51, 252 SE2d 28 (1979); Dearnley v. Survetneck, 360 Pa. 572, 62 A2d 66 (1949).

[25] See, e.g., Butler v. Daum, 245 Md. 447, 226 A2d 261 (1967); Small Equip. Co. v. Walker, 129 Ga. App. 710, 200 SE2d 904 (1973); Griggs v. Miller, 374 SW2d 119 (Mo. 1963).

[26] See, e.g., McCartney v. Frost, 37 Md. App. 495, 378 A2d 170 (1977); Williams v. Continental Sec. Corp., 22 Wash. 2d 1, 153 P2d 847 (1944).

[27] See, e.g., N.Y. Civ. Prac. Law § 5236(c); Wash. Rev. Code § 6.24.010(1).

[28] See, e.g., Cuban Air Force, F.A.R. v. Bergstresser, 135 So. 2d 752 (Fla. Dist. Ct. App. 1961); Annot., 3 A.L.R.3d 593 (1965).

[29] See, e.g., Sparling v. Todd, 27 Ohio St. 521 (1875); McLaury v. Miller, 64 Tex. 381 (1855).

[30] See, e.g., Industries Sales Corp. v. Reliance Mfg. Co., 86 Miss. 658, 138 So. 2d 484 (1962); Short v. Landes, 42 Del. 510, 39 A2d 17 (1944).

[31] See, e.g., Bertonazzi v. Mechanics Nat'l Bank, 379 Mass. 920, 400 NE2d 867 (1980); Williams v. Continental Sec. Corp., 22 Wash. 2d 1, 153 P2d 847 (1944).

[32] See, e.g., Tourles v. Hall, 344 Mass. 299, 168 NE2d 505 (1960); Fraaman v. Fraaman, 64 Neb. 472, 90 NW 245 (1902).

[33] See, e.g., Williams v. Continental Sec. Corp., 22 Wash. 2d 1, 153 P2d 847 (1944). Wash. Rev. Code § 6.24.020; Annot., 1 A.L.R. 1431 (1919).

[34] See, e.g., Garren v. Butigan, 96 Idaho 906, 539 P2d 259 (1975); Manhattan Taxi Serv. Corp. v. Checker Cab Mfg. Corp., 253 NY 455, 171 NE 705 (1930); Annot., 69 A.L.R. 1194 (1930).

The manner of conducting an execution sale will be primarily controlled by statute.[35] Violation of a statutory mandate regarding the conduct of the sale may result in an invalidated sale.[36] For the most part, statutes require that an execution sale be a public auction sale,[37] and not a private or secret sale at which only the sheriff and executing creditor are present.[38] Use of public auction sales is supported in order to increase the number of bidders and thus the price received as a result of bidding competition. A secret sale can be held fraudulent and void, thus transferring no title.[39] To further the policy of obtaining the highest price possible, a sale of personal property usually must occur separately or in parcels, as opposed to en masse,[40] although there may be circumstances that justify en masse sales.[41] In that regard, sale of real estate is treated similarly. Where possible, the real estate not only may but should be sold in parcels.[42] The judgment debtor and the creditor might otherwise agree to sell the property en masse, at least as against generally unsecured creditors.[43]

Basically, any person who is competent to contract may be a purchaser at the sale. The fact that a person has a lien on the property being sold does not disqualify him from being a purchaser.[44] Similarly, the execution creditor[45] or

---

[35] See, e.g., Gilbert v. Watts-De Golyer Co., 169 Ill. 129, 48 NE 430 (1897). However, recall the distinction between "execution" and "judicial" sales discussed at supra ¶ 6.06[1]. Thus, statutes relating to judicial sales may not apply to an execution sale. See, e.g., Yazoo & Miss. Valley R.R. Co. v. Clarksdale, 257 US 10 (1921); McCartney v. Frost, 37 Md. 495, 378 A2d 170 (1977) (execution sale).

[36] See, e.g., City of St. Louis v. Peck, 319 SW2d 678 (Mo. Ct. App. 1959). But see Rio Delta Land Co. v. Johnson, 566 SW2d 710 (Tex. Civ. App. 1978); Wynn v. Treasure Co., 146 Cal. App. 2d 69, 303 P2d 1067 (1956).

[37] See, e.g., Sparling v. Todd, 27 Ohio St. 521 (1875); Williams v. Continental Sec. Corp., 22 Wash. 2d 1, 153 P2d 847 (1944); Annot., 4 A.L.R.2d 575 (1949).

[38] See, e.g., Neblett v. Slosson, 223 SW2d 938 (Tex. Civ. App. 1949); Cargle v. Knox, 143 Ga. 597, 85 SE 764 (1915).

[39] See, e.g., Neblett v. Slosson, 223 SW2d 938 (Tex. Civ. App. 1949).

[40] See, e.g., Brock v. Berry, 132 Ala. 95, 31 So. 517 (1901); Annot., 1 A.L.R. 1431, 1443 (1919).

[41] See, e.g., Sterling v. Colvard, 284 Ala. 378, 225 So. 2d 790 (1969); Knutson v. Rosenberger, 81 Neb. 761, 116 NW 687 (1908).

[42] See, e.g., Wein v. U.S., 339 F2d 82 (8th Cir. 1964); Taliaferro v. Taliaferro, 203 Cal. App. 649, 21 Cal. Rptr. 868 (1962); Anniston Pipe Works v. Williams, 106 Ala. 324, 18 So. 111 (1895); Griggs v. Miller, 374 SW2d 119 (Mo. 1963).

[43] See, e.g., Grim v. Reinbold, 148 Pa. 446, 23 A 1129 (1892); Fox v. Curry, 96 Mont. 212, 29 P2d 663 (1934).

[44] See, e.g., Steffens v. American Standard Ins. Co. of Wis., 181 NW2d 174 (Iowa 1970); Corporation of Am. v. Eustace, 217 Cal. 102, 17 P2d 723 (1932); Braden v. First Nat'l Bank of Clarion, 183 Pa. 462, 28 A 1023 (1898).

[45] See, e.g., Prudential Corp. v. Bazaman, 512 SW2d 85 (Tex. Civ. App. 1924); McDowell v. State, 243 Ala. 87, 8 So. 2d 569 (1942).

the debtor[46] are qualified purchasers. Some problems arise as to whether a coplaintiff or codefendant may individually purchase the property. As to a codefendant, it is held that he is entitled to be a purchaser.[47] Concerning a coplaintiff, the courts may not permit the coplaintiff to be a purchaser for his own benefit, unless the whole amount of the claim is bid.[48] The principal class of persons who may not be purchasers at the sale are those in a fiduciary relationship with the judgment debtor. The courts usually hold that a fiduciary cannot be a purchaser on his own account.[49] This would include trustees,[50] guardians,[51] as well as other types of fiduciaries.[52] However, there is some authority suggesting that a fiduciary, under some circumstances, is qualified to purchase. This can occur when the property has nothing to do with his fiduciary relationship with the debtor.[53] Even if a purchaser is qualified as such, the sheriff can refuse his bid if the bidder refuses or fails upon request to give evidence of his ability to pay the purchase price.[54]

As previously indicated, execution sales are conducted by public auction. Matters pertaining to bids and payment of bids are of great consequence.[55] Also, as indicated previously, it is the policy of the law to multiply bidders and to promote competition in order to sell the property to the highest bidder. Any act that prevents competition is improper and vitiates the sale.[56] Occasionally, the issue arises as to whether an absent bidder may have a bid placed on his behalf by the officer conducting the sale. There is authority that allows this to occur;[57] however, if the bidding officer is required to exercise any discretion, the bid may not be entered.[58] Other authority would not allow the bid to be entered by the sheriff under any

---

[46] See, e.g., Dick v. Cooper, 24 Pa. 217 (1855); Smith v. Boquet, 27 Tex. 507 (1864).

[47] See, e.g., Kilgo v. Castleberry, 38 Ga. 512 (1868); Barnard v. Barnard, 391 So. 2d 939 (La. Ct. App. 1980).

[48] See, e.g., Leisenring v. Black, 5 Watts 303 (Pa. 1836).

[49] See, e.g., Word v. Davis, 107 Ga. 780, 33 SE 691 (1899); Annot., 77 A.L.R. 1513 (1932).

[50] See, e.g., Annot., 37 A.L.R.2d 1381, 1387 (1954); Kenworthy v. Equitable Trust Co., 218 Pa. 286, 67 A 469 (1907).

[51] See, e.g., Taylor v. Calvert, 138 Ind. 67, 37 NE 531 (1894).

[52] See, e.g., San Francisco Water Co. v. Pattee, 86 Cal. 623, 25 P 135 (1890); Annot., 77 A.L.R. 1513 (1932).

[53] See, e.g., Gibbs v. Gibbs, 151 Ga. 745, 108 SE 214 (1921); Annot., 77 A.L.R. 1513 (1932).

[54] See, e.g., Hobbs v. Beavers, 2 Ind. 142 (1850).

[55] For discussion of issues relating to adequacy of price and debtor protection, see infra ¶ 6.06[4].

[56] See, e.g., Rankin v. Carpenter, 568 SW2d 198 (Tex. Civ. App. 1978); Annot., 5 A.L.R.4th 786 (1981); Hoy's Estate, 159 Pa. 381, 28 A 158 (1893).

[57] See, e.g., Brannin v. Broadus, 94 Ky. 33, 21 SW 344 (1893).

[58] See, e.g., Caswell v. Jones, 65 Vt. 457, 26 A 529 (1893).

circumstances.[59] Any bid entered by a party present or absent must be unconditional,[60] although the bid may be withdrawn at any time before the property is "struck off" to the bidder.[61] The acceptance of a bid creates an executory contract, and the bidder becomes bound to comply with his or her bid. Unless the interested parties otherwise agree, or unless a statute otherwise provides, payment by the winning bidder must take place at once, or within a reasonable time, or the bid may be disregarded.[62] Further, in the absence of a contrary agreement among the interested parties, the general rule is that payment must be in money,[63] although certified checks, bank drafts, and cashier's checks probably constitute the most common exceptions to that general rule.[64] Where the judgment creditor is the purchaser at the sale, payment may occur by crediting the amount of his claim on the execution.[65] Assuming the property is of a value that at least is equal to the judgment and costs related to the sale, the judgment creditor will usually bid the amount of the judgment plus sales costs. On the other hand, a credit bid by a junior lienholder intended to be applied to the junior lien to the exclusion of senior liens that were specifically mentioned in the notice of the sale, is improper.[66] A successful bidder who fails to comply with the bid breaches his contract and has no cause of action to acquire the purchased property; indeed, the successful bidder who does not perform acquires no interest in the property and will be subject to action against him to obtain the balance of the purchase price bid.[67] If the bid price is never acquired, the bid may be disregarded and the property resold.[68] Upon resale, the defaulting original

---

[59] See, e.g., Harrison v. McHenry, 9 Ga. 164 (1850); Sparling v. Todd, 27 Ohio St. 521 (1875).

[60] See, e.g., Dorris v. Johnson, 363 Ill. 236, 2 NE2d 74 (1936); Annot., 104 A.L.R. 632 (1936).

[61] See, e.g., Hibernia Sav. & Loan Soc'y v. Behnke, 121 Cal. 339, 53 P 812 (1898); Pennsylvania Co. v. Broad St. Hosp., 356 Pa. 123, 47 A2d 281 (1946).

[62] See, e.g., Flagship State Bank of Jacksonville v. Carantzas, 352 So. 2d 1259 (Fla. Dist. Ct. App. 1977); Buckeye Dev. Corp. v. Brown & Shilling, Inc., 243 Md. 224, 220 A2d 922 (1966); Williams v. Continental Sec. Corp., 22 Wash. 2d 1, 153 P2d 847 (1944).

[63] See, e.g., Barnard v. Barnard, 391 So. 2d 939 (La. Ct. App. 1980); Buckeye Dev. Corp. v. Brown & Shilling, Inc., 243 Md. 224, 220 A2d 922 (1966); Kleckner v. Bank of Am. Nat'l Trust & Sav. Ass'n, 97 Cal. App. 2d 30, 217 P2d 28 (1950).

[64] See, e.g., McCartney v. Frost, 37 Md. App. 495, 378 A2d 170 (1977); Buckeye Dev. Corp. v. Brown & Shilling, Inc., 243 Md. 224, 220 A2d 922 (1966).

[65] See, e.g., Turner v. Donovan, 64 Col. App. 2d 375, 148 P2d 912 (1944); Prudential Corp. v. Bazaman, 512 SW2d 85 (Tex. Civ. App. 1974).

[66] See, e.g., Flagship State Bank of Jacksonville v. Carantzas, 352 So. 2d 1259 (Fla. Dist. Ct. App. 1977).

[67] See, e.g., Jackson v. Universal Life Ins. Co., 582 SW2d 207 (Tex. Civ. App. 1979); G.A.C. Commercial Corp. v. Aurora Trucking Co., 404 F2d 761 (6th Cir. 1968); Acker v. Snyder, 250 Pa. 57, 95 A 325 (1915).

[68] See, e.g., Ponder v. Vernon, 357 So. 2d 622 (La. Ct. App. 1978); May v. Sturdivant, 75 Iowa 116, 39 NW 221 (1888); Dunlap v. Whitmer, 133 La. 317, 62 So. 938 (1913).

successful bidder may be subject to action for any loss resulting from his failure to pay the bid price.[69]

The concluding act of the sale varies, depending upon whether the sale is a judicial or execution sale.[70] For the most part, an execution sale does not need judicial confirmation to conclude it;[71] however, judicial confirmation is sometimes required by statute, particularly when real estate is involved.[72] If judicial confirmation is required, the sale by definition is a judicial sale.[73] If confirmation is required and does occur, the order of confirmation is treated like any other adjudication by a court and is appealable.[74] Assuming the sale is purely an execution sale and the order of confirmation is not required, the sale concludes by issuance of a certificate of sale by the sheriff.[75] As to real property, a sheriff's deed is also part of the execution procedure.[76] The purchaser who receives the certificate of sale may assign it to a third party and, if this occurs, the sheriff's deed may be issued to the assignee.[77] The purchaser has a right to the deed immediately after payment of the bid price, or upon judicial confirmation if this is required, or upon expiration of any required period of redemption.[78] The certificate of sale of property sold at an execution sale gives to the purchaser color of title. The sheriff's deed may be introduced as evidence of title to real estate in any judicial proceeding,[79]

---

[69] See, e.g., Credit Alliance Corp. v. Ingram & Sons, Inc., 116 NJ Super. 497, 282 A2d 788 (1971); G.A.C. Commercial Corp. v. Aurora Trucking Co., 404 F2d 761 (6th Cir. 1968).

[70] For discussion of the difference between judicial and execution sales, see supra ¶ 6.06[1].

[71] See, e.g., McCartney v. Frost, 37 Md. App. 495, 378 A2d 170 (1977); Wein v. U.S., 339 F2d 82 (8th Cir. 1965); Orton v. Brown, 113 Cal. 561, 45 P 835 (1896).

[72] See, e.g., Ferry County Title Co. v. Fogle's Inc., 4 Wash. App. 874, 484 P2d 458 (1971); Yazoo & Miss. Valley R.R. Co. v. Clarksdale, 257 US 10 (1921); Williams v. Continental Sec. Corp., 22 Wash. 2d 1, 153 P2d 847 (1944).

[73] For discussion of the definitions of judicial and execution sales, see supra ¶ 6.06[1].

[74] See, e.g., Northern Commercial Co. v. E.J. Hermann Co., 22 Wash. App. 963, 593 P2d 1332 (1979); Holden v. Byrd, 204 Kan. 113, 460 P2d 559 (1969); Duptron v. Young, 134 US 241 (1890).

[75] See, e.g., Bird v. Kitchens, 215 Ark. 609, 221 SW2d 795 (1949); Reynolds v. Reynolds, 54 Cal. 2d 669, 355 P2d 481, 7 Cal. Rptr. 737 (1960).

[76] See, e.g., Northern Commercial Co. v. E.J. Hermann Co., 22 Wash. App. 963, 593 P2d 1332 (1979); Bird v. Kitchens, 215 Ark. 609, 221 SW2d 795 (1949).

[77] See, e.g., Thompson v. Thompson, 233 Ore. 262, 378 P2d 281 (1932).

[78] See, e.g., Keaton v. Thomasson, 32 Tenn. (2 Swan) 138 (1852); McBain v. McBain, 15 Ohio St. 337 (1855); Bessinger v. Grotz, 66 Cal. App. 2d 947, 153 P2d 369 (1945).

[79] See, e.g., May v. Finnerty, 104 Misc. 2d 450, 428 NYS2d 570 (NY Sup. Ct. 1980); Thomas v. Goodbread, 78 Fla. 278, 82 So. 835 (1919); Consolidated Rendering Co. v. Martin, 128 Me. 96, 145 A 896 (1929).

although proof of the validity of the judgment and execution may be required to establish title.[80]

### [c] Distribution of Proceeds of the Sale

Two categories of issues have traditionally arisen as to the distribution of the proceeds derived from the forced sale. First, who can share in the proceeds and what is the priority of these eligible parties? Second, if there are questions regarding which parties may share or what order they take, how is the question procedurally resolved?

The question of who may share, and in what order, is intertwined with the question of the state of the title received by the buyer.[81] In general, an execution sale does not affect a prior legal estate that a third party has in the property; thus, these third parties generally do not share in the proceeds of the sale.[82] With this in mind, it should be noted that as a general rule the proceeds of an execution sale will be first allocated to legal costs and expenses related to the sale,[83] with the priority not extending to the general costs of the action in which the judgment was rendered. Next, the proceeds will be distributed to the executing creditor who forced the liquidation; all prior interests that are not discharged by an execution sale receive none of the proceeds.[84] On the other hand, all subsequent interests that are discharged by the sale are entitled to be satisfied out of the proceeds of the sale according to their priority as of the time of the sale.[85] These subsequent interests will be satisfied after the executing creditor's interest is fully paid. For example, where a sale is held under a senior execution, the proceeds of the sale may be applied to a junior writ after satisfaction of the senior; where the sale is held under the junior writ, the junior writ is satisfied and the senior writ receives nothing, since the senior lien is not avoided by the sale. The same can be said regarding mortgagees or vendors who are senior or junior to the execution writ under which the sale is being conducted. If interests of various claimants are found to be of equal rank and

---

[80] See, e.g., Kahn v. Marik, 286 SW2d 639 (Tex. Civ. App. 1956); Megahee v. Megahee, 143 Ga. 738, 85 SE 877 (1915). But see Ellis v. Lyford, 270 Mass. 96, 169 NE 800 (1930); see also Annot., 36 A.L.R. 986 (1925); 108 A.L.R. 667 (1937).

[81] See infra ¶ 6.06[3] for discussion of title received by the buyer.

[82] For two old cases in point, see Bush's Appeal, 65 Pa. 363 (1870); Hopkins v. Forsyth, 14 Pa. 34 (1850); see also, e.g., Security Commercial & Sav. Bank v. Imperial Water Co., 183 Cal. 488, 192 P 22 (1920); Roddenberry v. Simpson, 171 Ga. 715, 156 SE 583 (1931).

[83] See, e.g., Monroeville Tire Serv. v. Jessup, 260 Pa. Super. 157, 393 A2d 1060 (1978).

[84] See, e.g., Haak's Appeal, 100 Pa. 59 (1882). But see May v. Finnerty, 104 Misc. 2d 450, 428 NYS2d 570 (NY Sup. Ct. 1980).

[85] See, e.g., Tisch v. Utz, 142 Pa. 186, 21 A 808 (1891); Farmers Nat'l Bank v. Kern, 194 Pa. Super. 479, 168 A2d 620 (1961); Forbes v. Evans, 256 Pa. 586, 100 A 943 (1917).

priority, the proceeds are distributed pro rata to such claimants.[86] For example, where a levy is made under several executions and there is no priority, a pro rata distribution will occur. After all interests subordinate to the executing creditor are satisfied, any remaining proceeds are distributed to the judgment debtor.[87] Unsecured creditors of an execution debtor–creditors without liens in the subject asset–receive nothing from the proceeds of the forced sale.

The doctrine of marshalling assets can skew the distribution scheme previously described. This doctrine is an equitable doctrine applied to satisfy competing claims to a debtor's property. If a creditor has a junior lien in only part of the debtor's property, before a prior creditor may resort to the property subject to the junior interest, the prior creditor may be required to satisfy his claim from other assets in which he has an interest, but in which the junior lienor has no interest.[88] Thus, the distribution of proceeds from an execution sale may be effected. This marshalling of property will not occur where equity would consider the marshalling unjust.[89]

If there is a question regarding who may share and in what order they may take, there must be a procedural mechanism to resolve any dispute. The parties in interest would include the selling officer, the debtor, and the various parties asserting claims in the subject property. The exception is the purchaser, who would appear to have no interest in the disposition of the sales price he paid. The determination of the validity and priority of the various claims initially is the duty of the selling officer.[90] However, from a practical standpoint, it would seem he would prefer to defer involvement in such disputes and turn the proceeds over to the court for further determination of the validity and priority of the claims.[91] If a specific procedure is not provided for by statute, the selling officer could possibly use a bill of interpleader.[92] Third persons seeking to assert claims might also intervene in the action in which the execution was issued.[93] If the proceeds are improperly distributed, the intervenor has a cause

[86] See, e.g., Hagan v. Lucas, 35 US (10 Pet.) 400 (1836); Ladley v. Creighton, 70 Pa. 490 (1872).

[87] See, e.g., Preston Farms, Inc. v. Nacri, 42 AD2d 668, 345 NYS2d 696 (1973); U.S. v. Harris & Co. Advertising, Inc., 149 So. 2d 384 (Fla. Dist. Ct. App. 1963).

[88] See, e.g., Latimer v. Ballew, 41 SC 517, 19 SE 792 (1894); Vernon, "Marshalling of Real Security Interests," 1 How. L.J. 172 (1955).

[89] See, e.g., Francis v. Herren, 101 NC 497, 8 SE 353 (1888).

[90] See, e.g., Preston Farms, Inc. v. Nacri, 42 AD2d 668, 345 NYS2d 696 (1973); Keystone Bank v. Nuclear Magnetic Resonance Specialties, 243 Pa. Super. 471, 366 A2d 251 (1976); De La Garza v. Booth, 28 Tex. 478 (1866).

[91] See, e.g., Keystone Bank v. Nuclear Magnetic Resonance Specialties, 243 Pa. Super. 471, 366 A2d 251 (1976); George W. McAlpin Co. v. Finsterwald, 57 Ohio St. 524, 49 NE 784 (1898).

[92] See Annot., 97 A.L.R. 996, 1003 (1935); see also, for general interpleader requirements, Walker Process Equip. Co. v. Cooley Bldg. Corp., 129 Vt. 333, 278 A2d 714 (1971).

[93] See, e.g., Powers v. Large, 75 Wis. 494, 43 NW 1120 (1889).

of action against the selling officer and the wrongful recipient of the proceeds.[94]

### [3] Title and Other Rights Received by the Buyer

As a general principle, the buyer acquires the interest held by the judgment debtor in the subject property.[95] Even though the sheriff administers the sale on behalf of the judgment creditor, it is the judgment debtor's interest that is being sold. "[I]t has long been established that, in an execution sale, the doctrine of caveat emptor applies; where title fails, the purchaser is not entitled to a return from the judgment creditor of the amount paid."[96] Although there is some contrary authority, this rule of caveat emptor remains intact, subject to one major exception. The buyer is usually protected by recording statutes as to sales of real property. Thus, a

> purchaser at a sale on execution stands, in most jurisdictions, in the position of any other purchaser for value, and takes free from any . . . claims based on unrecorded instruments, of which he has no notice. . . . Even though the purchaser at execution sale has notice of the adverse claim of another, he takes the land uneffected [sic] thereby, if the rights of the judgment creditors were superior thereto, his position being analogous to that of a purchaser with notice from a purchaser without notice.[97]

Arguably, the same principle could be applied to personal property, insofar as security interests acquired pursuant to Article 9 of the UCC are concerned. Otherwise, the doctrine of caveat emptor consistently applies and execution sales are also made without implied or expressed warranties.[98] The doctrine of caveat emptor is seen in its most extreme application where the judgment debtor has no title to the property sold, since the majority of cases have denied recovery in actions by the purchaser against either the sheriff or the judgment creditor for the purchase price paid.[99] However, the purchaser will be subrogated to the creditor's claim against the debtor.

---

[94] See, e.g., Meherin v. Saunders, 131 Cal. 681, 63 P 1084 (1901).

[95] See, in general, 30 Am. Jur. 2d Executions § 427 (1967); 33 C.J.S. Executions § 284 (1942); see also In re Federal's Inc., 553 F2d 509 (6th Cir. 1977); Sisco v. New Jersey Bank, 151 NJ Super. 353, 376 A2d 1287 (1977).

[96] Dixon v. City Nat'l Bank, 81 Ill. 2d 429, 410 NE2d 843 (1980); see also Epstein & Landers, Debtors and Creditors 146–147 (West, 2d ed. 1982) (citing Dixon v. City Nat'l Bank, 81 Ill. 2d 429, 410 NE2d 843, 844 (1980)).

[97] 5 Tiffany, Real Property § 1309, at 100–101 (Callaghan, 3d ed. 1939).

[98] See, e.g., McCartney v. Frost, 37 Md. App. 495, 378 A2d 170 (1977); Moser v. Thorp Sales Corp., 256 NW2d 900 (Iowa 1977); Reynolds v. Reynolds, 54 Cal. 2d 699, 355 P2d 481, 7 Cal. Rptr. 737 (1960).

[99] See, e.g., Household Fin. Corp. v. Ensley, 127 Ga. App. 876, 195 SE2d 236 (1973); Meherin v. Saunders, 131 Cal. 681, 63 P 1084 (1981); Dickson v. McCartney, 226 Pa. 552, 75 A 735 (1910).

Irregularities in the proceeding relating to the sale may affect the title obtained by the buyer. The general rule is that the purchaser is not affected by irregularities in the proceedings leading to a sale on execution if the irregularity merely makes the sale voidable rather than void and if the purchaser is a bona fide purchaser.[100] On the other hand, if the execution is void, the purchaser acquires no title.[101] Voidness would result, for example, where the irregularity nullifies the jurisdiction of the court and makes the judgment itself void.[102] The reversal or vacation of a judgment that is merely erroneous and voidable has been held to have no effect upon the title of the purchaser.[103] However,

> [w]hen [the judgment debtor] fails to take steps to suspend or supersede the judgment pending appeal or writ of error, he cannot disturb one who, not being a party to the suit, purchases under execution issued on the judgment.... The rule is, of course, different where the [judgment creditor] became the execution purchaser. It is plain that he can buy no greater right than he is litigating and, inasmuch as the property in such a case has not passed into innocent hands, he must make restitution.[104]

An important aspect of the execution or judicial sale that relates to the title obtained by the purchaser, is the effect of the sale on existing third-party interests in the property that are superior to or inferior to the lien of the execution creditor. The basic principle concerning third-party interests that are superior to the lien of the execution creditor is that these interests are not discharged by the execution sale.[105] This assumes that the execution creditor has not purchased the position of the superior interest. Senior interests in the prop-

---

[100] See, e.g., Garrison v. Erb, 424 Pa. 306, 227 A2d 848 (1967); Wamsley v. Snow, 331 Mo. 261, 53 SW2d 258 (1932); Swaney v. Hasara, 164 Minn. 416, 205 NW 274 (1925).

[101] See, e.g., Raniere v. I. & M. Inv., Inc., 159 NJ Super. 329, 387 A2d 1254, aff'd, 172 NJ Super. 206, 411 A2d 719 (1978); Roberts v. Gibson, 214 Pa. Super. 220, 251 A2d 799 (1969); Lamaster v. Keeler, 123 US 376 (1887).

[102] See, e.g., Roosevelt Hardware v. Green, 94 Misc. 2d 654, 405 NYS2d 220 (1978); Lincoln-Mercury-Phoenix, Inc. v. Base, 84 Ariz. 9, 322 P2d 891 (1958); Janove v. Bacon, 6 Ill. 2d 245, 128 NE2d 706 (1955).

[103] See, e.g., Merrel v. Fanning & Harper, 597 SW2d 945 (Tex. Civ. App. 1980); Sundie v. Haren, 253 So. 2d 857 (Fla. 1971); People v. Evanuk, 320 Ill. 336, 150 NE 634 (1926); see also Annot., 29 A.L.R. 1071 (1924); Annot., 32 A.L.R.3d 1019 (1970).

[104] Glaze v. Johnson, 27 Tex. Civ. App. 116, 65 SW 662 (1901); see also Moore, Phillips & D'Agostino, Debtor's and Creditor's Rights 5-27–5-28 (Matthew Bender, 5th ed. 1979); Northern Commercial Co. v. E.J. Hermann Co., Inc. 22 Wash. App. 963, 593 P2d 1332 (1979); Rio Delta Land Co. v. Johnson, 475 SW2d 346 (Tex. Civ. App. 1971).

[105] See, e.g., Northern Commercial Co. v. E.J. Hermann Co., 22 Wash. App. 963, 593 P2d 1332 (1971); Commercial Credit Equip. Corp. v. People's Loan Serv., 351 So. 2d 852 (La. Ct. App. 1977); see also 30 Am. Jur. 2d Executions §§ 443 et seq. (1967); 33 C.J.S. Executions § 291 (1942).

erty may not forbid the sale being forced by the junior execution creditor.[106] The basic principle concerning third-party interests that are inferior to the lien of the executing creditor is that these interests are extinguished by the sale.[107] Thus, as was discussed previously,[108] the senior lienor receives nothing from the proceeds of the sale, since his lien continues in the asset after sale; the junior lienor may receive proceeds, if sufficient proceeds are available, since the junior lien will be extinguished. Title of the execution purchaser relates back to the inception of the judgment or execution lien so as to cut off any interest acquired thereafter.[109]

In addition to acquiring title to the property as just outlined, the buyer at an execution sale may acquire other rights of note. A purchaser is bound by the terms or conditions of the sale that may control these rights.[110] He has a right to use and possession of the property and can enjoy the profits derived from it.[111] The general rule is that a purchaser of land acquires title to crops growing on the land that have not been severed and that were owned by the judgment debtor.[112] Timber is treated similarly.[113] If the execution purchaser pays a debt secured by a lien that is not extinguished by the sale, the purchaser is subrogated to the lien.[114] Similarly, the purchaser acquires any right to redeem property that the debtor possessed from unextinguished liens.[115] Encumbant with the title interest, the purchaser also acquires the right to bring action for conversion or trespass.[116]

Where the judgment debtor has the right to redeem the property after the execution sale, both the title and incidental rights of the purchaser may be materially affected. If redemption occurs, the property and title revert back to the redeeming party. During the period of redemption, the buyer may be liable

---

[106] See, e.g., Bernhardt v. Brown, 118 NC 700, 24 SE 527, reh'g dismissed, 119 NC 502, 26 SE 162 (1896).

[107] See, e.g., Preston Farms, Inc. v. Nacri, 42 AD2d 668, 345 NYS2d 696 (1973).

[108] See supra ¶ 6.06[2][c].

[109] See, e.g., Mahalko v. Arctic Trading Co., Inc., 29 Wash. App. 411, 628 P2d 859 (1981); Black v. Miller, 219 So. 2d 106 (Fla. Dist. Ct. App. 1969); Call v. Thunderbird Mortgage Co., 58 Cal. 2d 542, 375 P2d 169, 25 Cal. Rptr. 265 (1962).

[110] See, e.g., Cable v. Byrne, 38 Minn. 534, 38 NW 620 (1888).

[111] See, e.g., Jordan v. Phoenix Fin. Co., 8 Ariz. App. 106, 443 P2d 921 (1968); Black v. Miller, 219 So. 2d 106 (Fla. Dist. Ct. App. 1969); Carpenter v. Hamilton, 24 Cal. 2d 95, 147 P2d 563 (1944).

[112] See, e.g., Schuler-Olsen Ranchers, Inc. v. Garvin, 197 Neb. 746, 250 NW2d 906 (1977); Groves v. Hanks, 546 SW2d 638 (Tex. Civ. App. 1976).

[113] See, e.g., Havens v. Pearson, 334 Pa. 570, 6 A2d 84 (1939).

[114] See, e.g., Swain v. Stockton Sav. & Loan Soc'y, 78 Cal. 600, 21 P 365 (1889).

[115] Id.

[116] See, e.g., Cann v. George B. Williams Land & Livestock Co., 56 Nev. 242, 48 P2d 887 (1935); Moseby v. Fleck, 233 Pa. 102, 81 A 930 (1911).

for any waste committed[117] and may not be able to retain profits obtained during the redemption period.[118] The effect of redemption is to revive previously extinguished liens.[119]

## [4] Debtor Protection From Low-Price Sales

### [a] Generally

Prior discussion in this text of the typical required conduct of sale reflects the legislative and judicial desire to obtain the best price possible for the property that is being sold;[120] thus, the requirements of public notice of sale and competitive public bidding are important. These procedures represent an attempt to protect all interested parties, including the debtor, from loss of property for an inadequate price. Nevertheless, due to the forced nature of the sale, execution sales rarely bring a price that approximates the market value of the property. In protecting the debtor from low-price sales, legislatures and courts have also been cognizant that a judgment has been entered on behalf of the creditor and yet the claim remains unsatisfied. This realization compels these decision-making bodies to balance the debtor's interest in not having his property liquidated for an inadequate price with that of the creditor whose claim should rightfully be satisfied from the property. Basically, three different issues arise in regard to this balancing of interests. First, under what circumstances will a sale be set aside due to inadequacy of price?[121] Second, do state statutes prior to sale ever require appraisal of the property and sale at the appraised price or some percentage thereof?[122] Third, can the debtor (or other interested parties) redeem the property after the sale?[123]

As to the first issue,[124] the general rule is that mere inadequacy of price alone does not justify the setting aside of an execution sale.[125] However, the sale may be set aside if the sale brings a grossly inadequate price combined with other circumstances indicating irregularity. These additional circum-

---

[117] There is a split of authority on this question. For authority that the purchaser is liable for waste, see, e.g., Gray v. C.A. Harris & Son, 200 Wash. 181, 93 P2d 385 (1939). But see O'Connor v. Attalla Bank, 116 Ala. 585, 22 So. 902 (1897).

[118] See, e.g., Griffiths v. Hammon, 560 P2d 1375 (Utah 1977); In re Martinson, 26 Bankr. 648 (Bankr. DND 1983).

[119] See, e.g., Call v. Thunderbird Mortgage Co., 58 Cal. 2d 542, 375 P2d 169, 225 Cal. Rptr. 265 (1962). The judicial lien under which the original sale was commenced will also be revived if the redemption price is not sufficient to satisfy the judgment. See, e.g., Damascus Milk Co. v. Moriss, 1 Wash. App. 501, 463 P2d 212 (1969).

[120] See supra ¶ 6.06[2][b].

[121] See infra ¶ 6.06[4][a].

[122] See infra ¶ 6.06[4][b].

[123] See infra ¶ 6.06[4][c].

[124] For an excellent discussion of this issue, see Annot., 5 A.L.R.4th 794 (1981).

[125] See, e.g., Moore v. Dade Glass & Mirror Co., Inc., 357 So. 2d 221 (Fla. Dist. Ct. App. 1978); Levine v. Berlin, 46 AD2d 902, 362 NYS2d 186 (1974).

stances can include fraud, unfairness, or mistake.[126] Some authorities indicate that the additional irregular circumstance need only be slight if the price was grossly inadequate.[127] Many courts relate the inadequacy of the price with the irregularity; the grosser the inadequacy of price obtained, the slighter the circumstances of irregularity that accompany it need to be.[128] Other courts require a causal connection between the inadequacy of price and the irregularity.[129] Finally, some courts have been willing to set aside sales if inadequacy of price is so gross as to shock the judicial conscience without the need of additional irregularity.[130]

Due to the limited ability of the debtor to have a sale overturned if an inadequate price is obtained, some legislatures provide the debtor (and occasionally other parties with interests in the property) with other protection. This protection takes two forms: appraisal and redemption statutes.

### [b] Appraisal Statutes

Appraisal of the value of a property is required by some statutes as a means of protecting the debtor from loss of property at an inadequate price. These statutes also protect other parties whose liens, for example, were subordinate to the lien of the creditor who has forced the sale and, thus, will be terminated by the sale.[131] Such statutes may require that a certain proportion of the appraised value of the property to be sold at an execution sale must be bid before the sale can occur.[132] Inability to obtain the minimum price will result in adjournment of the sale. Under other appraisal statutes, the sale may take place, but the debtor will be given the right to redeem the property by payment of a specified proportion of the appraised value that was not obtained at the sale.[133] As to federal judicial sales, in which real property is involved

---

[126] See, e.g., Wilson v. Citizens Bank Peach County, 143 Ga. App. 402, 238 SE2d 754 (1977); Weir v. U.S., 339 F2d 82 (8th Cir. 1965); Reed v. Westland Indus. Bank, 484 P2d 1247 (Colo. App. 1971); Mauer v. Butter, 55 AD2d 784, 389 NYS2d 483 (1976).

[127] See, e.g., Mason v. Wilson, 116 Ariz. 255, 568 P2d 1153 (1977); Melner v. Denman, 21 Ill. 2d 182, 171 NE2d 654 (1961); McCartney v. Frost, 282 Md. 631, 386 A2d 784 (1978).

[128] See, e.g., Rio Delta Land Co. v. Johnson, 566 SW2d 710 (Tex. Civ. App. 1978); Prudential Corp. v. Bazaman, 512 SW2d 85 (Tex. Civ. App. 1974).

[129] See, e.g., Reed v. Westland Indus. Bank, 484 P2d 1247 (Colo. App. 1971).

[130] See, e.g., Scott v. Adal Corp., 276 Pa. Super. 459, 419 A2d 548 (1980); McCartney v. Frost, 282 Md. 631, 386 A2d 784 (1978); Sbarp v. Yniguiz, 324 SW2d 291 (Tex. Civ. App. 1959).

[131] See supra ¶ 6.06[3] for discussion of termination of subordinate liens.

[132] As to case examples involving execution sales, see, e.g., Smith v. Cockrill, 73 US (6 Wall.) 756 (1868); Bollman v. Gemmill, 155 Ind. 33, 57 NE 542 (1900). As to case examples involving judicial sales, see, e.g., Stockmeyer v. Tobin, 139 US 176 (1891); Crowley Bank & Trust Co. v. Hurd, 138 La. 978, 71 So. 128 (1916).

[133] See, e.g., Wakenva Coal Co. v. Johnson, 234 Ky. 558, 28 SW2d 737 (1930). See generally 50 C.J.S. Judicial Sales § 9 (1947); 30 Am. Jur. 2d Executions § 371 (1967); 47 Am. Jur. 2d Judicial Sales § 27 (1969).

and sold under an order or decree of the federal court, the court must appoint three disinterested persons to appraise the property. Another option is to appoint different groups of three appraisers each to appraise properties of different classes or that is situated in different localities.[134] The statutory provisions relating to judicial sales of real property ordered by the federal courts also apply to sales of personal property unless the court otherwise orders.[135]

### [c] Right of Redemption

The right of redemption is the most common statutory device used to protect the debtor (and sometimes subordinate lienors) from sale of property for an inadequate price. Approximately thirty states protect the judgment debtor by giving the debtor the right to redeem property from properly conducted execution or judicial sales.[136] Many of these statutes have extremely complicated provisions pertaining to redemption. Specific coverage of individual state redemption statutes is beyond the scope of this text. The attorney is cautioned to familiarize himself carefully with local law. However, numerous issues common to these statutes can be reviewed to alert the reader to the problem areas he may encounter with a local redemption statute. These issues include the distinction between "statutory" and "equitable" redemption; who may redeem property; the amount that must be paid to redeem; the length of the redemption period; and the effect of redemption.

Statutory redemption is a right conferred by statute "given to the debtor (and sometimes to junior creditors and mortgagees) to recover land after it has been sold on execution or foreclosure."[137] Although redemption statutes normally are limited to land, some states do provide for redemption of personal property. By contrast, the "equity of redemption" means that a debtor can always prevent an execution or judicial sale by "paying off his debt *before* these sales are made."[138] Equitable redemption is something different yet. Equitable principles may permit a redemption of land sold under execution, on the ground of improper conduct on the part of the sheriff and purchaser or upon a showing of fraud, mistake, or other conditions that appeal to a court of equity.[139] This text only considers the statutory right of redemption, although the practitioner should realize that in the absence of, or in addition to, the statutory right of redemption, the "equity of redemption" or the right to "equitable redemption" may be available.

---

[134] 28 USC § 2001(b).

[135] 28 USC § 2004.

[136] See Hawkland & Loiseaux, Debtor-Creditor Relatons 348 (Bobbs-Merrill, 2d ed. 1979); see also ¶ 8.08[10].

[137] Id.; see also Wayne Sav. & Loan Co. v. Young, 49 Ohio App. 2d 35, 358 NE2d 1380 (1976).

[138] Id.

[139] See, e.g., Smith v. Kessler, 43 Cal. App. 3d 26, 117 Cal. Rptr. 470 (1974); Kimtruss Corp. v. Westland Manor Nursing Home N., Inc., 39 Colo. App. 542, 568 P2d 105 (1977); Powers v. Powers, 221 Cal. App. 2d 746, 34 Cal. Rptr. 835 (1963); see also, for discussion of equitable redemption, 30 Am. Jur. 2d Executions § 550 (1967).

Under the redemption statutes, there is some variety among the states as to who may redeem. For example, in addition to the debtor, successors to the debtor's interest and other creditors may redeem the property.[140] It should be recalled that creditors' liens that are subordinate to the interest of the creditor who has forced the sale will be terminated by the sale. As a result, some statutes permit such creditors to redeem the property. On the other hand, other redemption statutes are more restrictive and limit redemption to the debtor.[141]

Assuming the right of redemption is available to a particular party, the amount of payment that will be required must be ascertained. As a general rule, the amount to be paid to redeem is the amount of the successful bid plus expenses of the sale.[142] In addition, interest thereon from the date of the sale must be paid.[143] For example, Michigan provides that the interest that accrues is the legal interest of the year of the sale.[144] Washington provides for the sales price, plus eight percent per annum to the time of redemption and for any assessments or taxes that the purchaser or his successor in interest may have paid thereon after purchase and like interest on this amount.[145]

The time period to redeem the sold property is fixed by statute. Typically, as to real property, the period of redemption is twelve months after the date of sale. The time period may vary depending upon who is redeeming the property. For example, a specified time period may be allowed a particular party. If that party redeems, a further period may be given other parties who have the right to redemption.[146] As an example of a statute that specifies a longer period of redemption, in Tennessee "real estate sold for a debt and made redeemable shall continue redeemable to the debtor and his creditor for two years after the sale, upon the terms set forth in this Chapter no matter how often it has previously been redeemed."[147]

Redemption has the basic effect of defeating the interest of the original purchaser. In fact, the redemption is typically memorialized by giving the redemptioner a deed,[148] or by making any title as evidenced in an original deed given the execution purchaser null and void.[149] A collateral effect of redemption is that the redemption leaves property still subject to junior liens that otherwise would have been cut off by the sale.[150]

Finally, it should be noted that redemption statutes have been the subject of considerable criticism. The statutes have been described as "a baffling com-

---

140 See, e.g., Wash. Rev. Code § 6.24.130.

141 See, e.g., Mass. Gen. Laws Ann. ch. 236, § 33.

142 See, e.g., Smith v. Kessler, 43 Cal. App. 3d 26, 117 Cal. Rptr. 470 (1974); Christensen v. Forst, 153 Cal. App. 2d 465, 314 P2d 746 (1957).

143 Id.

144 Mich. Comp. Laws Ann. § 600.6062(1).

145 Wash. Rev. Code § 6.24.140.

146 See, e.g., Clark v. Cuin, 46 Cal. 2d 386, 295 P2d 401 (1956); Gaffney v. Harman, 405 Ill. 273, 90 NE2d 785 (1950).

147 Tenn. Code Ann. § 66-8-102.

148 See, e.g., Mass. Gen. Laws Ann. ch. 236, § 33.

149 See, e.g., Mich. Comp. Laws Ann. § 600.6062(3).

150 See supra ¶ 6.06[3] note 119.

plex of pitfalls."[151] Similarly, statutory redemption has been criticized as being too complicated to work.[152] Professors David Epstein and Jonathan Landers have commented as follows:

> Such statutes may be criticized on the ground that (a) they are primarily designed to ensure adequate bids and such an objective can be achieved more readily by setting reasonable upset prices or antideficiency legislation; (b) they tend to chill the bidding since purchasers will not get anything in the event of redemption and because enjoyment is postponed for a year with attendant dangers of waste and misuse; and (c) the debtor will rarely experience the necessary reversal of fortune to redeem within the statutory period.[153]

In response to these and similar concerns, some states have repealed their statutory redemption laws.[154] However, the complete absence of a statutory redemption right seems less preferable from the debtor's point of view regardless of the shortcomings of many redemption statutes.[155]

## ¶ 6.07 MISCELLANEOUS MATTERS REGARDING ENFORCEMENT OF THE JUDGMENT

### [1] Exempt Property

Exemption law is a matter that significantly cuts across all prior discussion in this text regarding collection of unsecured debts and resulting judgments.[1] All states, by constitutional or statutory provision, and the federal government insulate certain property of the debtor by restricting creditor recourse to this property. The property is referred to as exempt property; if property is exempt and the debtor has done all that is required to take advantage of the exemption, creditors cannot satisfy debts due them to the extent of the exemption without the consent of the debtor. In effect, the debtor retains all rights of ownership of exempt property (i.e., the right to possess, sell, encumber, and use the property).[2] The purpose of exemption law is usually said to be threefold: (1) protection of the debtor; (2) protection of the debtor's family; and (3) protection of

---

[151] Note, "Redemption from Judicial Sales: A Study of the Illinois Statute," 5 U. Chi. L. Rev. 625 (1938).

[152] Id.

[153] Epstein & Landers, Debtors and Creditors 148 (West, 2d ed. 1982).

[154] Ill. Ann. Stat. ch. 77, § 18, repealed effective July 1, 1982; Cal. Civ. Proc. Code § 701, repealed effective July 1, 1983.

[155] See Hawkland & Loiseaux, Debtor-Creditor Relations 349 (Bobbs-Merrill, 2d ed. 1979).

[1] This portion of the text is concerned with nonbankruptcy exemption law. For discussion of exemptions in bankruptcy, see ¶ 14.07.

[2] See Vukowich, "Debtors' Exemption Rights," 62 Geo. L.J. 779, 792 (1974).

society.[3] To attempt to cover exemption law on a national scale in something less than a multivolume treatise is difficult at best due to the tremendous variety of laws that exist from state to state.[4] Indeed, the only apparent commonality among the jurisdictions is that many exemptions are painfully obsolete.[5] Nevertheless, this portion of the text provides the reader with an overview of exemption law.[6]

### [a] Identification of Exempt Property—Type and Value

Exemption statutes[7] identify exempt property by type, by value, or by both type and value.[8] Although it is difficult to summarize the typical types of property designated as exempt, it can be said that some of the most typical property types include personal exemptions, such as clothing, food, and house-

---

[3] See, e.g., Epstein & Landers, Debtors and Creditors 107 (West, 2d ed. 1982); Bankruptcy Law Revision, Report of the Committee on the Judiciary, H.R. Rep. No. 595, 95th Cong., 1st Sess. 126 (1977); Vukowich, "Debtors' Exemption Rights," 62 Geo. L.J. 779 (1974).

[4] Due to the extreme variety among the states and the obsolescence of some state exemption provisions, the Uniform Exemptions Act (UEA) was approved by the National Conference of Commissioners on Uniform State Laws in 1976. It was approved by the American Bar Association in 1977. In 1979, UEA was amended by the National Conference, but to date, no state has adopted it. Section 522 of the Bankruptcy Reform Act of 1978 (11 USC § 522), considered at ¶ 14.07, is very similar to UEA.

[5] See Moore, Phillips & D'Agostino, Debtors' and Creditors' Rights 5-50–5-51 (Matthew Bender, 5th ed. 1979), in which the authors indicate "[m]any of the exemption statutes currently in force are geared to the economy of an earlier day." In their examples, the authors cite only recently repealed Conn. Gen. Stat. § 52-352, which conferred upon each household an exemption for, among other things, "two tons of coal, two tons of hay, five bushels each of potatoes and turnips, two hundred pounds of wheat flour, two cords of wood, ten bushels each of Indian corn and rye or the meal or flour manufactured therefrom. . . ." For cases illustrating the application of exemptions based on historical exemptions, see also Cox v. Smith, 275 So. 2d 459 (La. Ct. App. 1973); Frudden Lumber Co. v. Clifton, 183 NW2d 201 (Iowa 1971); In re Canutt, 264 F. Supp. 919 (D. Ore. 1967); In re Hahn, 5 Bankr. 242 (Bankr. D. Iowa 1980); In re Rash, 81 F. Supp. 389 (WD Wash. 1948). Regarding the need to update exemption provisions, see also Vukowich, "Debtors' Exemption Rights," 62 Geo. L.J. 779 (1974); Joslin, "Debtors' Exemption Laws: Time for Modernization," 34 Ind. L.J. 355 (1959).

[6] For a brief discussion of the historical evolution of exemption law, see Riesenfeld, Creditors' Remedies and Debtors' Protection 308–309 (West, 3d ed. 1979).

[7] Exemption statutes theoretically can be separated into three categories. First, a number of laws use the word "exempt" to describe the property that the debtor may retain. These laws are held to protect listed property from all forms of legal process. Second, a group of statutes do not use the word "exempt" but do provide that listed property shall not be sold to satisfy the owner's debts. Finally, other statutes and constitutions refer to the exemption of property from "all process." For discussion of these categories of exemption statutes and citation to illustrations of statutory and constitutional provisions, see Vukowich, "Debtors' Exemption Rights," 62 Geo. L.J. 779, 788 (1974).

[8] See, Karlen, "Exemptions from Execution," 22 Bus. Law. 1167 (1967).

hold furnishings; tools of the trade; automobiles; life insurance; health aids; income, such as wages, social security, and veterans benefits; and homesteads. Additionally, many exemption statutes include a "catchall" provision that allows the debtor to exempt property at his selection up to a certain value.[9] Three of the more important and common types of exempt property are separately considered at a later point in this text.[10]

Although some types of property are exempt without regard to their value under some statutes,[11] usually the asset is exempt only up to a certain value.[12] This would allow, as a general rule, a creditor to levy upon property that is only partially exempt. However, upon sale, the proceeds first would be distributed to the debtor-owner up to the amount or value of the exemption. Without placing a value limit on the type of property that is exempt, some exemption laws exempt certain types of property only to the extent *necessary* to the judgment debtor or his family.[13] To the extent that courts have dealt with the meaning of "necessary," they have tended to define it in terms of the judgment debtor's accustomed standard of living rather than in terms of the bare minimum needed for survival.[14]

Three further points should be made regarding identification of exempt property. First, other property not designated in exemption statutes may be indirectly protected from the reach of creditors. In this vein, Professor Stefan Riesenfeld has stated that "there exists assets which are exempt on common law grounds, such as tenancies by the entireties. Sometimes assets cannot be reached for want of applicable procedures. Finally it is an accepted judicial tenet that property in custodia legis is not subject to attachment and garnish-

---

[9] See, e.g., Section 522(d) of the Bankruptcy Reform Act of 1978 (11 USC § 522(d)). Exemptions in bankruptcy are not considered at this point of the text but at a later point; see ¶ 14.07. Section 522(d) was an attempt to unify exemption law nationally; as such, it represents a summary of categories of types of exempt property. Very similar is UEA, which has not been enacted as yet in any state.

[10] See infra ¶¶ 6.07[1][d] (homesteads), 6.07[1][g] (income), 6.07[1][h] (life insurance).

[11] See, e.g., N.Y. Civ. Prac. Law & R. § 5205.

[12] See N.Y. Civ. Prac. Law & R. § 5206.

[13] Id.

[14] See Karlen, "Exemptions from Execution," 22 Bus. Law. 1167, 1169 (1967). There is little case law relating to "necessities." Most of the law on this topic is derived from the spendthrift trust area:

> "In determining what is necessary for . . . support . . . courts developed a 'station in life' rule. A high living beneficiary was given a larger exemption than a frugal beneficiary. Spendthrift trusts are usually created only by persons of considerable wealth who have raised their children in considerable luxury. The accustomed manner of living of the child-beneficiary is likely to require the full income of the trust."

Dukeminier & Johanson, Family Wealth Transactions 665 (Little, Brown 1972). See also 2 Scott, Trusts § 152.1 (Little, Brown, 3d ed. 1967); American Sec. & Trust Co. v. Utley, 382 F2d 451 (DC Cir. 1967).

ment."[15] Second, the designation of an asset as exempt may not serve to exempt the asset from all claims of creditors. For example, the federal tax lien reaches and may be satisfied from otherwise exempt property, since the federal tax lien law has its own set of exemptions.[16] Similarly, a number of states make exceptions for state taxes, claims for alimony and child support, and materialmen's and mechanics' liens.[17] Third, if an exempt asset is sold, it might be questioned whether or not the proceeds retain the exempt character of the sold asset. Similarly, if exempt wages are received, it might be questioned if the wage retains an exempt status once it is in the possession of the debtor. This is particularly important when the proceeds or wages are deposited in a bank account of a debtor, and a creditor is seeking to garnish the account. Some statutes and/or cases provide for the retention of an exemption in proceeds or income received by the debtor, and there is some authority indicating the exemption may be traced into the debtor's bank account. However, this is not a universal rule. Thus, the creditor must focus on both the particular exemption statute and the case law thereunder to determine the resolution of these issues.[18]

### [b] Asserting or Waiving the Right to Exemptions

The right to exempt property bestowed on debtors by statute may not be self-executing. The debtor may have to assert the right to the exemption in a timely fashion. As a general principle, in the absence of an express requirement in the exemption statute, notice of claim of exemption is unnecessary.[19] This would especially be the case where a separate and distinct article of property is exempt and where the sheriff knows, or reasonably should know, that the property is exempt.[20] However, there may be contrary authority requiring assertion

---

[15] Riesenfeld, Creditors' Remedies and Debtors' Protection 310 (West, 3d ed. 1979). See particularly notes 16 through 18 on p. 310.

[16] See 26 USC § 6334. For discussion of federal tax liens, see ¶ 9.04.

[17] See Vukowich, "Debtors' Exemption Rights," 62 Geo. L.J. 779, 852 et seq. (1974). For discussion of statutory liens, see generally Chapter 9.

[18] For authority regarding these issues, see, e.g., Annot., 67 A.L.R. 1203 (1930); In re Klein, 10 Bankr. 356 (Bankr. App. Pan. 9th Cir. 1981); Holmes v. B.F.S. Inc., 369 So. 2d 987 (Fla. Dist. Ct. App. 1979); Anderson v. First Nat'l Bank of Atlanta, 151 Ga. App. 573, 260 SE2d 501 (1979); Collier v. C.C. Co., 591 SW2d 391 (Mo. Ct. App. 1980); Board of Educ. v. Treyball, 86 AD2d 639, 446 NYS2d 417 (1982); Household Fin. Corp. v. C.M.B.N.A., 91 Misc. 2d 141, 397 NYS2d 564 (NY Sup. Ct. 1977); McCabe v. Fee, 279 Ore. 437, 568 P2d 661 (1977); Stinner v. Stinner, 300 Pa. Super. 351, 446 A2d 651 (1982); John O. Melby & Co. Bank v. Anderson, 88 Wis. 2d 252, 276 NW2d 274 (1979); Kruger v. Wells Fargo Bank, 113 Cal. Rptr. 449, 521 P2d 441 (1974); Philputt v. Essex County Welfare Bd., 409 US 413 (1973); Dunlop v. First Nat'l Bank, 399 F. Supp. 855 (D. Ariz. 1975).

[19] See, e.g., Smith v. Rhea, 72 Cal. App. 3d 361, 140 Cal. Rptr. 116 (1977). See generally 31 Am. Jur. 2d Exemptions §§ 142 et seq. (1967).

[20] See, e.g., In re Livingston's Estate, 12 AD2d 380, 211 NYS2d 897 (NY Sur. Ct. 1961).

of the right to an exemption, even though the exemption statute does not expressly require assertion of the right.[21] On the other hand, many statutes do expressly require the debtor to claim a right to an exemption. This has traditionally been the case with regard to the homestead exemption, which may require formal declaration of homestead to be recorded in real estate records.[22]

Assuming that the debtor must by statute assert the claim to an exemption, the claim must be asserted within the statutorily prescribed time period.[23] If the statute that requires the debtor to claim the exemption does not specify an applicable time period, or if the need to assert the claim to exemption is founded upon case law, the claim must be asserted within a reasonable time.[24] Typically, the claim is timely if the claim is made before sale under levy.[25] If the claim is not made at all, or if it is made in an untimely fashion, the right to the exemption will be lost,[26] unless there is some legally recognizable excuse.[27] All of this is particularly important for the debtor and the debtor's attorney, since often the uncounseled debtor is unaware of the potential need to assert claims to exemptions.

Failure to claim an exemption in a timely fashion when required, is a form of waiver of exemption. There are other situations in which waiver of an exemption may occur.[28] Although many examples could be cited, perhaps the most common example of waiver of an exemption involves the homestead exemption that typically may be waived by the debtor granting a creditor a mortgage.[29] Exemptions can also be circumvented by grants of UCC Article 9 security interests in personal property or fixtures that are otherwise exempt property. As to waiver of a right to assert an exemption in property that may generally be described as basic living items and subsistence income, some states

---

[21] See, e.g., Phillips v. Bartolomie, 46 Cal. App. 3d 346, 121 Cal. Rptr. 56 (1975).

[22] See infra ¶ 6.07[1][f] for discussion of declaration of homestead. For case examples of statutory requirements to assert right to exemptions, see State v. Smith, 129 Ariz. 28, 628 P2d 65 (1981); Phillips v. Bartolomie, 46 Cal. App. 3d 346, 121 Cal. Rptr. 56 (1975).

[23] See, e.g., Anchor Sav. & Loan Ass'n v. Week, 62 Wis. 2d 169, 213 NW2d 737 (1974).

[24] See, e.g., Arbogast v. Linz, 180 Wash. 315, 39 P2d 615 (1935).

[25] See, e.g., Anchor Sav. & Loan Ass'n v. Week, 62 Wis. 2d 169, 213 NW2d 737 (1974); Wilson v. Virginia Nat'l Bank, 214 Va. 14, 196 SE2d 920 (1973); Garrison v. Seiber, 266 Ore. 368, 513 P2d 1180 (1973); In re Hamill, 317 F. Supp. 909 (D. Kan. 1970).

[26] See, e.g., Russell v. Waller, 283 Ala. 385, 217 So. 2d 534 (1969); Home Bank v. Becker, 48 Wis. 2d 1, 179 NW2d 855 (1970); Westervelt v. Robertson, 122 Cal. App. 3d Supp. 1, 176 Cal. Rptr. 94 (1981); Annot., 82 A.L.R. 648 (1933).

[27] See, e.g., Drigg's Bank v. Norwood, 49 Ark. 136, 4 SW 448 (1887).

[28] See Vukowich, "Debtors' Exemption Rights," 62 Geo. L.J. 779, 848 et seq. (1974).

[29] See, e.g., Ariz. Rev. Stat. Ann. § 33-1103(A)(1) (1976); In re Kelley, 7 Bankr. 384 (Bankr. SD 1980); Englander Co. v. Kennedy, 424 SW2d 305, application for writ of error refused, no reversible error, 428 SW2d 806 (Tex. Civ. App. 1968).

expressly invalidate waiver of exemptions.[30] Case law may also invalidate agreements to waive exemptions as violating public policy and as unenforceable if in the nature of an adhesion contract.[31] Many states explicitly prohibit waiver of a debtor's earnings exemption,[32] although wage assignments may not be affected by such prohibitions.[33] As a side matter, it might be noted that the Bankruptcy Reform Act of 1978 prohibits waiver of exemptions[34] and also provides the bankrupt with the power to avoid non-purchase-money and non-possessory security interests in some types of exempt property.[35]

### [c] Liability for Levy Upon Exempt Property

Up to this point, the discussion of exemption law has emphasized that exemptions have the impact of protecting the debtor's property from the reach of creditors. From the creditor's viewpoint, the presence of exempt property will stifle the collection effort. In addition, the creditor must also be aware of potential exemptions because levy upon exempt property may result in liability for damages caused the debtor.[36]

If the sheriff levies upon exempt property, the creditor may argue successfully that the creditor is not liable; after all, it was the sheriff who committed the unlawful act. Traditionally, "when the plaintiff places the execution in the hands of an officer for service, he is presumed to intend that no action will be taken thereunder not authorized by the terms of the writ. . . . But the principle may be rebutted. The injured party may show that the plaintiff was a co-trespasser with the officer. . . ."[37] There are a number of ways by which the creditor could be shown as a "co-trespasser." This may occur where the plaintiff is present at the levy, or where he advises or directs the levy to be made upon the exempt property. It may also occur by subsequent ratification of the levy upon the exempt property that took place.[38]

Even if the plaintiff-creditor has no liability as a "co-trespasser," from the debtor's point of view, the sheriff may be liable for the unlawful execution upon the exempt property. Where the debtor has not lost his right to claim

---

[30] See, e.g., Va. Code § 34-22; N.Y. Lab. Law § 595(2).

[31] See, e.g., Mayhugh v. Coon, 460 Pa. 128, 331 A2d 452 (1975).

[32] See, e.g., Ore. Rev. Stat. § 23.185(4); Va. Code §§ 34-22, 34-29(c); Resolute Ins. Co. v. Pennington, 423 Pa. 472, 224 A2d 757 (Pa. 1966).

[33] See, e.g., Epps v. Cortese, 326 F. Supp. 127, 135 (ED Pa. 1971); Wis. Stat. Ann. § 241.09; Comment, "Wage Assignments; A Creditor's Remedy in Need of Reform," 18 Wayne L. Rev. 1535 (1972); Comment, "Wisconsin's Personal Receivership Statute–Evaluation and Recommendations," 1968 Wis. L. Rev. 210.

[34] 11 USC § 522(e).

[35] 11 USC § 552(f)(2). See ¶ 14.07 for discussion of exemptions in bankruptcy.

[36] See Moore, Phillips & D'Agostino, Debtors' and Creditors' Rights 5-48–5-50 (Matthew Bender, 5th ed. 1979).

[37] 2 Freeman, Executions § 273 (Whitney & Co., 3d ed. 1900)

[38] Id.

exemptions, an action for damages against the levying officer is present,[39] or the debtor may seek to recover the property,[40] or enjoin any sale of exempt property.[41] However, if the debtor fails to assert exemptions as required, the sheriff will incur no liability.[42]

### [d] Homestead Exemptions

The homestead exemption[43] requires special emphasis due to its importance nationwide. The great majority of states have enacted homestead exemption laws.[44] Apparently, the homestead exemption originated in Texas[45] in 1839 and quickly spread to other jurisdictions.[46] Although most states have exemption laws, there is wide disparity as to the substance of the law among these jurisdictions. This portion of the text focuses on the basics of homestead law nationally, with emphasis placed on those issues on which there is considerable disagreement among the states.

In many states, only families may claim the homestead exemption; single persons may not.[47] Once a "family" is created (i.e., a marriage has occurred

---

[39] See, e.g., Winstead v. Hicks, 135 Ky. 154, 12 SW 1018 (1909).

[40] See, e.g., Wilcox v. Wynn, 52 Abs. 340, 83 NE2d 411 (Ohio Mun. 1948); Tibbs v. Zimmerman, 26 Tenn. App. 321, 71 SW2d 832 (1943).

[41] See, e.g., Evans Division-Royal Indus. v. Jeffries, 511 SW2d 71 (Tex. Civ. App. 1979).

[42] See, e.g., Sterling v. Colvard, 284 Ala. 730, 225 So. 2d 790 (1969); Phillips v. Bartolomie, 46 Cal. App. 3d 346, 121 Cal. Rptr. 56 (1975); Mims v. Commercial Credit Corp., 261 Ind. 591, 307 NE2d 867 (Ind. 1974).

[43] For two excellent and concise summaries of homestead law on a national scale, see Riesenfeld, Creditors' Remedies and Debtors' Protection 311–317, 323–326, 331–332 (West, 3d ed. 1979); Vukowich, "Debtors' Exemption Rights," 62 Geo. L.J. 779, 797–807 (1974); see also Healey, "The Judgment Creditor Encounters Homestead Problems," 27 L.A. B. Bull. 361 (1952); Haskins, "Homestead Exemptions," 63 Harv. L. Rev. 1289 (1950); Vance, "Homestead Exemption Laws," 7 Encyc. Soc. Sci. 441 (1932).

[44] According to Professor Stefan Riesenfeld, all states provide for a homestead exemption except Connecticut, Delaware, Indiana, Maryland, New Jersey, Pennsylvania, and Rhode Island. Indiana has a general exemption for the benefit of resident householders—which is in the nature of a quasi-homestead. Ind. Stat. Ann. Code Ed. § 34-2-28-1 (1973). See Riesenfeld, Creditors' Remedies and Debtors' Protection 312 (West, 3d ed. 1979). Note that homestead exemptions may not be effective as to all debts (e.g., debts resulting from acquisition, construction, or repair of the homestead; claims for alimony; claims for fraud in the investment of the homestead; claims for torts). See, e.g., Annot., 54 A.L.R.2d 1422, 1428 (1957); In re Marriage of De Lotel, 73 Cal. App. 3d 21, 140 Cal. Rptr. 533, 576 (1977); Waddell v. Schwartz, 405 So. 2d 978 (Fla. 1981); Pope v. Pope, 283 Md. 531, 390 A2d 1128 (1978).

[45] 3 Laws of the Republic of Texas 113 (1839).

[46] See, e.g., 1841-1842 Ga. Laws 134; 1841 Miss. Laws ch. 15, at 113; 1848 Mich. Pub. Acts No. 109, at 124; 1848 Wis. Laws 40, amended 1850 Wis. Laws 159, ch. 198; 1850 Ohio Laws 29; 1851 Cal. Stat. ch. 31, at 296; 1851 Ill. Laws 25.

[47] See Hawkland & Loiseaux, Debtor-Creditor Relations 366 (Bobbs-Merrill, 2d ed. 1979).

and the spouses are residing on the subject property), the homestead exemption can survive death[48] and possibly divorce.[49] Although most homestead laws initially were available exclusively to heads of the family,[50] some states now make the homestead available to single persons.[51] Originally, only the husband could select the property to be exempt. However, at the present time either spouse may do so.[52] A removal from the homestead may destroy the homestead, and whether removal constitutes an "abandonment" is a question of fact that is considered on a case-by-case basis.[53] In most states, the person claiming the exemption must have a present possessory interest in land that may be in fee, life estate, leasehold, legal or equitable, held in severalty, joint tenancy, tenancy in common, tenancy by the entirety, or as community property.[54]

The value, size, and type of property that is eligible for homestead exemption protection varies greatly depending upon the jurisdiction. Most homestead laws do limit the exemption by size, value, or both. The originator of the homestead exemption, Texas, has perhaps the most liberal statute in this regard.[55] Texas has a homestead exemption of 200 acres in rural areas without regard to value, and of $10,000 in value at time of acquisition of urban property without regard to subsequent improvements. Under this urban exemption, a $10,000 vacant lot, bought as a homestead and improved by a $100,000 house, is completely exempt. Similarly, a $100,000 house built on rural property would be completely exempt. In other states, the amount of the exemption is not tied to the amount of acreage but only to the dollar value.[56] As to the type of property, the homestead is, of course, associated to real estate on which the claimant permanently resides. However, many states now include such dwellings as

---

[48] See, e.g., Iowa Code Ann. § 561.11; Cal. Civ. Proc. Code § 704.930(b)(1), effective June 30, 1983. However, there is contrary authority. See, e.g., Heard v. Mathis, 344 So. 2d 651 (Fla. Dist. Ct. App. 1977).

[49] See, e.g., Cal. Civ. Proc. Code § 4800(a); Bonner v. Superior Court for the City of L.A., 63 Cal. App. 3d 156, 133 Cal. Rptr. 592 (1976); In re Jordan, 16 Bankr. 590 (Bankr. WD Ky. 1981). Divorce will destroy the homestead exemption if the statute requires the party claiming the exemption to be a householder with dependents and the taking spouse no longer qualifies. See Annot., 84 A.L.R.2d 703, 711 (1962).

[50] See, e.g., Mass. Gen. Laws Ann. ch. 188, § 1; Va. Code §§ 34-1, 34-4.

[51] See, e.g., Cal. Civ. Proc. Code § 704.910; Wis. Stat. Ann. § 815.20.

[52] See, e.g., Kan. Stat. Ann. § 60-2302; Nev. Rev. Stat. § 115.020.1.

[53] See, e.g., Burdick v. Burdick, 399 So. 2d 410 (Fla. Dist. Ct. App. 1981); H.D. Snow Housemoving, Inc. v. Moyers, 581 SW2d 809 (Tex. Civ. App. 1979); In re Joy, 5 Bankr. 681 (Bankr. D. Minn. 1980).

[54] See, e.g., Annot., 74 A.L.R.2d 1357 (1960); Wambeke v. Hopkins, 372 P2d 470 (Wyo. 1962); Annot., 89 A.L.R. 511, 540 (1934).

[55] Tex. Rev. Civ. Stat. Ann. art 3833.

[56] See, e.g., N.D. Cent. Code § 47-18-04; Cal. Civ. Proc. Code § 704.730. Note also that nearly all states protect proceeds from the sale of the homestead for a specific duration. See, e.g., Iowa Code Ann. § 561.20; Annot., 46 A.L.R. 814 (1927); Annot., 161 A.L.R. 1256 (1946). The same protection is also often applied to insurance proceeds. See, e.g., Annot., 63 A.L.R. 1286 (1929).

mobile homes and houseboats.[57] If the property is used in part for nonresidential purposes, the homestead, nevertheless, may still be available.[58]

The debtor-claimant is often required to assert the right to the homestead exemption.[59] In many states, the debtor must record a homestead declaration in the real estate records.[60] However, some states now provide for an automatic exemption (i.e., the exemption is automatically present upon occupancy as a principal residence).[61] Other states provide for some combination of required declaration or automatic exemption, or some other variation.[62] A question related to a declaration of homestead involves the timing of the declaration. Although in many jurisdictions the exemption must be declared prior to execution sale,[63] in some jurisdictions the exemption may be asserted after the sale against the purchaser.[64] In many states, a subsequent declaration of homestead will not defeat judicial liens that have attached prior to that declaration,[65] although there is some contrary authority.[66] Finally, concerning the timing of the declaration, some states make the exemption ineffective as to debts or claims that were incurred prior to the time the debtor acquired the homestead or declared the exemption.[67]

Yet another category of issues involving homesteads arises when only part of the real estate owned by the debtor is protected by the homestead exemption. Obviously, the creditor may wish to assert claims in the nonexempt portion of the property. Most homestead statutes have provisions that provide for the partition of property to enable creditors to pursue satisfaction of the debt in the property and yet save the homestead portion of the property from sale.[68]

---

[57] See, e.g., Cal. Civ. Proc. Code § 704.730; Ore. Rev. Stat. § 23.164.

[58] See Annot., 114 A.L.R. 209 (1938). In Texas, there is a pure business homestead–the claimant need not reside on the premises. See Texas Rev. Civ. Stat. Ann. art. 3833.

[59] See supra ¶ 6.07[1][b] for a general discussion of the need to assert exemption rights.

[60] See, e.g., Idaho Sess. Laws §§ 55-1203–55-1205, 55-1301–55-1304; Wash. Rev. Code §§ 6.12.045, 6.12.070.

[61] See, e.g., Colo. Rev. Stat. § 38-41-202; N.Y. Civ. Prac. Law & R. § 5206.

[62] See, e.g., Cal. Civ. Proc. Code §§ 704.710–704.730, 704.910–704.920; Ala. Code tit. 6, § 6-10-41; Ga. Code Ann. § 44-13-100.

[63] See, e.g., Ala. Code § 6-10-26.

[64] See, e.g., Dixon v. Moller, 42 Ill. App. 3d 688, 356 NE2d 599 (1976).

[65] See, e.g., Shepler v. Kubena, 563 SW2d 382 (Tex. Civ. App. 1982); San Diego County Carpenters Group Ins. v. Loren, 112 Cal. App. 3d 221, 109 Cal. Rptr. 157 (1980); Automotive Supply Inc. v. Powell, 269 Ark. 255, 599 SW2d 735 (1980); Cal. C.C.P. § 704.950; Rusch v. Lagerman, 194 Minn. 469, 261 NW 186 (1935).

[66] See, e.g., Citibanc of Alabama/Tuskegee v. Potter, 379 So. 2d 553 (Ala. 1979); Sanders v. Cassity, 586 P2d 423 (Utah 1978); see also Annot., 110 A.L.R. 883 (1937).

[67] See, e.g., Iowa Code Ann. § 561.21; Mo. Ann. Stat. § 513.510; W. Va. Code § 38-9-3.

[68] See Riesenfeld, Creditors' Remedies and Debtors' Protection 314, 325 n.3 (West, 3d ed. 1979).

If partition is impossible, the entire property will be sold and the debtor will receive the value of his exemption from the proceeds.[69]

The relationship between judgment lien law and the homestead has resulted in some perplexing issues. Most states provide that a judgment lien[70] does not attach to homestead property. Thus, a purchaser of the homestead property takes it free of the judgment creditor's claim, even though the purchaser claims no homestead exemption in the purchased property.[71] On the other hand, the judgment lien usually does attach to the property, to the extent that the property exceeds the size or value of the allowed homestead exemption.[72]

### [e] Income Exemptions

Both federal and state legislation exempt specified income from the reach of creditors by use of garnishment or other judicial process. This portion of the text provides the reader with an overview of such income exemptions beginning with a discussion of federal legislation.[73]

Federal legislation provides a basic wage exemption pursuant to Title III of the Consumer Credit Protection Act (CCPA)[74] and provides some specific exemptions principally related to federal payments and the Employee Retirement Income Security Act (ERISA). The specific exemptions for federal payments include exemptions for federal judiciary annuities,[75] railroad employee annuities,[76] civil service workers' retirement annuities and pensions,[77] military service survivors and retirement benefits,[78] lighthouse service personnel annui-

---

[69] See, e.g., Engelman v. Gordon, 82 Cal. App. 3d 174, 146 Cal. Rptr. 835 (1978); Van Bogaevt v. Amery, 271 Cal. App. 2d 492, 76 Cal. Rptr. 608 (1969); Clement v. First Nat'l Bank of Paris, 115 Tex. 342, 282 SW 558 (1926).

[70] See supra ¶ 6.05[2] for discussion of judgment liens.

[71] See, e.g., Cochran v. Cutler, 39 Ill. App. 2d 602, 350 NE2d 59 (1967); Hoffman v. Love, 494 SW2d 591, application for writ of error refused, no reversible error (Tex. Civ. App. 1973); Lien v. Hoffman, 49 Wash. 2d 642, 306 P2d 240 (1957). A prominent exception is North Carolina, where the lien attaches but is unenforceable until sale, at which time the lien becomes enforceable. See, e.g., Stokes v. Smith, 246 NC 694, 100 SE2d 85 (1957).

[72] See, e.g., Bank of Tex. v. Laguarta, 565 SW2d 363 (Tex. Civ. App. 1978); Ball v. Ball, 27 Ill. App. 3d 678, 326 NE2d 782 (1975); Clawson v. Anderson, 248 Ore. 347, 434 P2d 462 (1967).

[73] For an excellent summary of income garnishment law including income exemption law, see 7 Debtor-Creditor Law 29-1–29-64 (Matthew Bender 1982).

[74] 15 USC §§ 1671–1677.

[75] 28 USC § 376(n).

[76] 45 USC § 231(m).

[77] 5 USC § 8345.

[78] 10 USC §§ 1450(i), 1440.

ties,[79] foreign service employee[80] and Central Intelligence Agency[81] annuity benefits, and veterans' benefits.[82] The predominant view on ERISA pensions is that they cannot be garnished,[83] although a New York court issued a contrary opinion.[84] Congress has legislated a major exemption to these specific federal income exemptions. Pursuant to the Child Support Enforcement Act of 1975, the income exemptions are not applicable as to enforcement of alimony or child support decrees.[85]

The major federal wage exemption mentioned above is found in Title III of CCPA.[86] In large part, the statute was enacted to unify wage exemption law and to counter harsh state garnishment laws.[87] The restriction on garnishment established by CCPA is that the maximum part of the aggregate disposable earnings of an individual for any work week that is subject to garnishment may not exceed the lesser of (1) 25 percent of his disposable earnings for that week or (2) the amount by which his disposable earnings for the week exceeds thirty times the federal minimum hourly wage.[88] For pay periods other than one week, the Secretary of Labor has set forth multiples of the federal minimum wage equivalent in effect to the weekly multiple.[89] CCPA does permit a greater garnishment to enforce court support orders.[90] "Disposable" earnings are defined as that part of an individual's gross compensation for personal services that remains after deduction of amounts required by law to be withheld.[91]

---

[79] Central Intelligence Agency Retirement Act of 1964 (for certain employees), Pub. L. No. 88-643, § 263, 78 Stat. 1043 (1964), reprinted in 50 USC § 403, app. at 86 (Supp. 1981), as amended by Exec. Order No. 12,023, 42 Fed. Reg. 61,443 (1977), reprinted in 50 USC § 403, app. at 90 (Supp. 1981).

[80] 22 USC § 4060(c).

[81] 33 USC § 775.

[82] 38 USC § 3101.

[83] See, e.g, Standard Oil Co. of Cal. v. Agsalud, 633 F2d 760 (9th Cir. 1980); Utility Workers Union of Am. AFL-CIO v. Consumers Power Co., 637 F. Supp. 1082 (ED Mich.), 663 F2d 1074 (6th Cir. 1981); see also Employee Retirement Income Security Act of 1974, 29 USC §§ 2001 et seq.; 7 Debtor-Creditor Law ¶ 29.03[B][2] (Matthew Bender 1982).

[84] National Bank of N. Am. v. IBEW, 69 AD2d 679, 419 NYS2d 679 (1979).

[85] 42 USC § 659(a); see also Annot., 44 A.L.R. Fed. 494 (1979).

[86] 15 USC §§ 1671–1677; see also Annot., 14 A.L.R. Fed. 447 (1973).

[87] See 15 USC § 1671; Hodgson v. Christopher, 365 F. Supp. 583 (DND 1973).

[88] 15 USC § 1673(a).

[89] See 29 CFR Pt. 870.

[90] If the debtor is already supporting a spouse or dependent child, 50 percent of the debtor's aggregate disposable earnings are subject to garnishment. 15 USC § 1673(b)(2)(A). If the debtor is not already supporting a spouse or dependent child, 60 percent of disposable earnings per work week are subject to garnishment for support. 15 USC § 1673(b)(2)(B).

[91] 15 USC §§ 1672(a), 1672(b). For a case that considers the definition of disposable earnings, see Long Island Trust Co. v. U.S. Postal Serv., 647 F2d 336 (2d Cir. 1981); see also Annot., 38 A.L.R. Fed. 546 (1978).

Although CCPA preempts state garnishment laws that permit greater garnishment than that provided by CCPA, more protective state exemption law still can apply instead of CCPA.[92] The Secretary of Labor enforces the provisions of CCPA.[93] Authority is divided as to whether there is an implied private remedy for the debtor.[94]

Under exemption law, states also limit the access of creditors to the debtor's income. Indeed, a few states flatly prohibit garnishment of wages.[95] The state wage exemption statutes affect various forms of income, including wages, pensions, and public assistance payments.[96] Some states have merely enacted in substance Title III of CCPA previously discussed.[97]

### [f] Life Insurance Exemptions

The first life insurance exemption[98] was enacted in 1840.[99] Currently, every state grants important exemptions for life insurance from collection by the owner's creditors. In many states, the exemption also operates against creditors of the beneficiary.[100] Even in the absence of an exemption statute for life insurance, various collection laws "may prevent or at least dissuade a creditor from attempting to reach his debtor's interests in a life insurance policy."[101] In

---

[92] 15 USC § 1677; see, e.g., Hodgson v. Hamilton Municipal Court, 349 F. Supp. 1125 (SD Ohio 1972); Evans v. Evans, 429 F. Supp. 580 (WD Okla. 1976); Pa. Stat. Ann. tit. 42, § 8127; Tex. Const. art. 16, § 28; Tex. Rev. Civ. Stat. Ann. art. 4099; Fla. Stat. Ann. § 222.1.

[93] 15 USC § 1676.

[94] For authority denying a right of action, see, e.g., Simpson v. Sperry Rand Corp., 350 F. Supp. 1057 (WD La. 1972); Smith v. Colton Bros. Baking Co., 609 F2d 738 (5th Cir.), cert. denied, 449 US 821 (1980); McCabe v. Eureka, 500 F. Supp. 59 (ED Mo. 1980); Oldham v. Oldham, 337 F. Supp. 1039 (ND Iowa 1972). For authority allowing a right of action, see, e.g., Stewart v. Travelers Corp., 503 F2d 108 (9th Cir. 1974); Maple v. Citizens Nat'l Bank & Trust Co., 437 F. Supp. 66 (WD Okla. 1977).

[95] See the Pennsylvania, Texas, and Florida provisions cited in supra ¶ 6.07[1][e] note 92.

[96] For a table of such exemption statutes for California, Florida, Illinois, Michigan, New Jersey, New York, Ohio, Pennsylvania, and Texas, see 7 Debtor-Creditor Law ¶ 29D (Matthew Bender 1982).

[97] See, e.g., Cal. Civ. Proc. Code Ann. § 723.050; Ohio Rev. Code Ann. § 2329.66(A)(13); Ill. Ann. Stat. ch. 62, § 73.

[98] For concise reviews of national life insurance exemption law, see Riesenfeld, "Life Insurance and Creditors' Remedies in the United States," 4 U.C.L.A. L. Rev. 583 (1957); Vukowich, "Debtors' Exemption Rights," 62 Geo. L.J. 779, 807–813 (1974).

[99] Verplanck Act, 1840 N.Y. Laws 80.

[100] See, e.g., Cal. Civ. Proc. Code § 704.100; Tex. Ins. Code Ann. art. 21.22; Wash. Rev. Code Ann. § 48.18.410.

[101] Vukowich, "Debtors' Exemption Rights," 62 Geo. L.J. 779, 807, at n.60 (1974); see, e.g., Estate of Williams, 508 F. Supp. 978 (DC Cir. 1981); Sinsel v. Sinsel, 47 Ore. App. 153, 614 P2d 115 (1980); Pope Photo Records, Inc. v. Malone, 539 SW2d 224 (Tex. 1976); Sachs v. U.S., 412 F2d 357 (8th Cir.), cert. denied, 396 US 906 (1969); Kaufman

addition to exemptions for individual life insurance policies, many states provide for exemption of group life insurance.[102] An understanding of these life insurance exemption provisions is aided by a brief review of the different types of life insurance available today.

There are basically three different types of life insurance policies. Term life insurance is a contract between the insured and the insurer, in which the insurer promises to pay the amount of the policy to the beneficiary should the insured die within a given period. If death does not occur within the given period, the contract expires. Little or no cash value is accumulated as a savings to the policyholder. A second type of life insurance policy is whole life insurance. This type of life insurance contract covers the subject of the insurance for his entire life regardless of the number of premiums to be paid. The most common plan of whole life insurance is known as "ordinary life" or "straight life." In such policies, the insured pays a level rate for his entire life and the beneficiaries receive the proceeds upon his death. In the early years of the policy, the premiums are greatly in excess of the actuarial risk rate. The excess amount, together with interest, is considered to be the cash value that belongs to the insured. Thus, the insured can cancel the policy and receive the cash surrender value or he can borrow this reserve. The third common type of life insurance is usually called endowment insurance. Under this insurance contract, the insurer promises to pay a stated amount of money to the beneficiary at once or to the insured if he survives the endowment. Premiums are usually paid over a specified time period. In effect, under this type of insurance, the insured has a contingent right to the face amount of the policy if he survives the endowment period in addition to the usual interest of his beneficiary. A related type of insurance is the annuity contract, which really is not life insurance. Under these contracts, the annuitant pays the insurer a set amount and the insurer agrees to make periodic payments to the annuitant for a specified period.

As to each type of insurance policy described above, the insured-owner has an interest to be protected if he has retained the right to change the beneficiary.[103] Where no right to change the beneficiary has been reserved, the beneficiary has a vested interest that cannot be reached by creditors of the insured.[104] Assuming the usual situation in which the insured does have a right to change the beneficiary, creditors may reach whatever ownership rights the insured has in the policy. "Fearing that the general effect of the doctrine might deprive a bankrupt's dependent of life insurance protection . . . most states have now enacted exemption statutes. . . ."[105] These exemption protections

---

v. New York Life Ins. Co., 32 AD2d 79, 299 NYS2d 269 (1969); Plymouth Cordage Co. v. Ward, 202 So. 2d 600 (Fla. Dist. Ct. App. 1967).

[102] See, e.g., Ariz. Rev. Stat. Ann. § 20-1132; Cal. Civ. Proc. Code § 704.100; Ohio Rev. Code Ann. § 3917.05; Okla. Stat. Ann. tit. 36, § 3632.

[103] See, e.g., Cohen v. Samuels, 245 US 50 (1917).

[104] See Central Bank of Wash. v. Hume, 128 US 195 (1888).

[105] Hawkland & Loiseaux, Debtor-Creditor Relations 376 (Bobbs-Merrill, 2d ed. 1979).

have even been extended to situations in which the insured has not reserved the right to change beneficiaries.[106]

An overview of national life insurance exemption law indicates that many states do not limit the amount of life insurance that is exempt,[107] although some states do limit the exemption by placing a dollar limit on the face amount of the policy.[108] Some states place a dollar ceiling on the annual premium, so that if the premium is greater than that ceiling, the exemption reaches only the part of the insurance that could be bought with the maximum premium allowed by the exemption statute.[109] The statutes exempt the proceeds payable to a qualified beneficiary.[110] The exemption may also protect the cash surrender value of the policy.[111] As stated previously, many states exempt the proceeds paid to the beneficiary from creditors of the beneficiary.[112]

Since the basic purpose of the life insurance exemption is to protect the dependents of the debtor, many statutes require the beneficiary to be a dependent or a close relative of the insured[113] or one having an insurable interest in the insured's life.[114] Other variations include statutes that provide greater protection if the beneficiary is the wife or dependent of the insured;[115] some statutes provide that the exemption is available only if the insured or the owner is not the beneficiary.[116] Others provide for the exemption if the proceeds are payable to the insured's estate or trustee, as long as the ultimate recipient is a relative or dependent.[117]

## [2] Fraudulent Conveyances

If a creditor is seeking collection of a delinquent debt or claim, it is likely that the debtor may be delinquent with other creditors. The debtor may attempt to protect his assets from the reach of creditors by secreting them or by

---

[106] Id.; see, e.g., W. Va. Code ch. 33, art. 6 (27(a)).

[107] See, e.g., Mich. Comp. Laws Ann. § 550.37; Ore. Rev. Stat. § 743.102(1); Tex. Rev. Civ. Stat. Ann. art. 3836(a)(6).

[108] See, e.g., Miss. Code Ann. § 85-3-11.

[109] See, e.g., Cal. Civ. Proc. Code § 704.100; Mont. Code Ann. § 33-15-511-514; Jackson v. Fisher, 56 Cal. 2d 196, 201, 363 P2d 479, 482, 14 Cal. Rptr. 439, 442 (1961).

[110] See, e.g., Mich. Comp. Laws Ann. § 500.2207(1); Ill. Ann. Stat. ch. 73, § 850 (deferred repeal date of Dec. 31, 1987).

[111] See, e.g., Ill. Ann. Stat. ch. 73, § 850 (deferred repeal date of Dec. 31, 1987); N.Y. Ins. Law § 166(1); In re Hygrade Envelope Corp. 272 F. Supp. 451 (EDNY 1967), cert. denied, 89 S. Ct. 114 (1968).

[112] See supra ¶ 6.07[1][f] note 100.

[113] See, e.g., Ill. Ann. Stat. ch. 73, § 850; Tex. Rev. Civ. Stat. Ann. art. 3836(a).

[114] See, e.g., Mass. Gen. Laws Ann. ch. 175, § 125; Ore. Rev. Stat. § 743.099(1); Duffy v. Duffy, 13 Mass. App. 992, 433 NE2d 91 (1982).

[115] See, e.g., Cal. Civ. Proc. Code § 704.100(c); N.Y. Ins. Law § 166(1).

[116] See, e.g., Fla. Stat. Ann. § 222.13(1); Neb. Rev. Stat. § 44-371.

[117] See, e.g., Ohio Rev. Code Ann. § 3911.10; S.D. Comp. Laws Ann. § 43-45-6; Neb. Rev. Stat. § 44-503.01.

transferring them to third parties. If transfer occurs, it may be for less than fair consideration, with a "string" attached to enable the debtor to reclaim the property after the financial woes have disappeared. If the debtor were legally capable of doing this, creditors' collection efforts would often be thwarted. However, beginning in the sixteenth century with the Statute of Elizabeth,[118] creditors have been able to set aside these or similar transfers as "fraudulent conveyances."[119] In the United States, basically two types of fraudulent conveyance statutes have been adopted by the various states. One is the direct descendant of the Statute of Elizabeth; the other, adopted by about half the states, is the Uniform Fraudulent Conveyance Act.[120] Several issues under both types of statutes will be hereinafter considered, beginning with a review of the "Statute of Elizabeth" fraudulent conveyance statutes.[121]

### [a] "Statute of Elizabeth" Jurisdictions

The law of fraudulent conveyances has its roots in the Statute of Elizabeth. It provides that "covinous and fraudulent feoffments, gifts, grants, alienations, conveyances, bonds, suits, judgments and executions, as well of lands of tenements as of goods and chattels. . . devised and contrived of malice, fraud, covin, collusion or guile, to the end, purpose and intent, to delay, hinder or defraud creditors and others . . . shall be utterly void, frustrate and of no effect. . . ."[122] The statute was read to mean that conveyances made with the intent to hinder, delay, or defraud creditors are not actually void, but rather are only voidable as to creditors who were hindered, delayed, or defrauded, the conveyance remaining valid as between grantor and grantee. However, from an early point, the courts concluded that the creditor need not actually have the transfer voided but rather could proceed directly in the transferred property.[123]

The courts quickly recognized the difficulty creditors faced in proving actual fraudulent intent to hinder or delay creditors' collection efforts. Beginning in *Twyne's Case*,[124] the courts began to develop so-called "badges of

[118] 13 Eliz., ch. 5 (1570).

[119] For an excellent and comprehensive treatment of fraudulent conveyance law on a national scale, see 5 Debtor-Creditor Law 22-1–22-88 (Matthew Bender 1982).

[120] The following jurisdictions have adopted the Uniform Fraudulent Conveyance Act (UFCA): Arizona, California, Delaware, Idaho, Maryland, Massachusetts, Michigan, Minnesota, Montana, Nevada, New Hampshire, New Jersey, New Mexico, New York, North Dakota, Ohio, Oklahoma, Pennsylvania, South Dakota, Tennessee, Utah, Virgin Islands, Washington, Wisconsin, and Wyoming. The most recent adoption occurred in 1969.

[121] See ¶ 17.05 for a consideration of the relationship of fraudulent conveyance law to federal bankruptcy.

[122] 13 Eliz., ch. 5 (1570).

[123] Mannochke's Case, 3 Dyer 293b (1571).

[124] 3 Coke 80b, 76 Eng. Rep. 809 (1601).

fraud" to assist creditors in carrying their weighty burden of proof. The badges of fraud simply refer to circumstances indicative of the intent to defraud. Specifically, in *Twyne's Case*, the court held that the transfer involved in the matter was fraudulent, noting the following badges of fraud: that the conveyance was secretly made; that it was made pending litigation; that the transfer was general; and that the debtor retained possession and use of the property "transferred."

The law emanating from the Statute of Elizabeth ultimately found its way into jurisdictions of the United States and remains intact in roughly one half of the states today. The fraudulent conveyance statutes in these states are basically modernized versions of the Statute of Elizabeth, providing creditors with the ability to avoid transfers made by debtors with the intent to hinder, delay, or defraud creditors' collection efforts.[125]

One issue that constantly arises under traditional fraudulent conveyance statutes harks back to *Twyne's Case*. Intent to defraud, hinder, or delay often is difficult to prove by direct evidence. In some states that have not adopted the Uniform Fraudulent Conveyances Act, fraud may be established without proof of actual intent to defraud.[126] In these states, the courts have developed categories of presumptions of intent to defraud where, for example, a transfer is made for less than fair value by a debtor who is or was thereby made insolvent in the sense of having insufficient assets to pay his debts.[127] The majority of the courts hold that the creditor must initially establish that the debtor did not receive fair value for the transfer or that the debtor thereafter was unable to pay his debts.[128] As to what constitutes fair value, it appears the receipt of near equivalent value property or the satisfaction of an antecedent debt will only suffice.[129] In regard to proof of intent, other states hold that a conveyance made whereby the debtor retains possession and use of the property or retains rights in the property may be prima facie or conclusively fraudulent.[130] Still other states require proof of actual fraudulent intent, although the "badges of fraud" may sometimes be employed to support an inference of intent to

---

[125] See, e.g., Fla. Stat. Ann. §§ 726.01, 726.07–726.09; Ill. Ann. Stat. ch. 59, §§ 4–8.

[126] See 5 Debtor-Creditor Law 22-77 (Matthew Bender 1982).

[127] See, e.g., In re Kassuba, 10 Bankr. 309 (SD Fla. 1981); Tri-Star Cabinet & Top Co., v. Heatherwood Homes, Inc., 41 Ill. App. 3d 11, 354 NE2d 4 (1976); Nelson v. Hansen, 278 Ore. 571, 565 P2d 727 (1977); Whipp v. Grider, 330 Ill. App. 131, 70 NE2d 262 (1947).

[128] See, e.g., In re Russo, 1 Bankr. 369 (EDNY 1979); Kailbab Indus., Inc. v. Family Ready Homes, Inc., 80 Ill. App. 3d 782, 372 NE2d 139 (1978); Chambers v. Citizens & S. Nat'l Bank, 242 Ga. 498, 249 SE2d 214 (1978).

[129] See, e.g., Continental Bank v. Marcus, 242 Pa. Super. 371, 363 A2d 1318 (1976); West Gate Bank of Lincoln v. Eberhardt, 202 Neb. 762, 277 NW2d 104 (1979); In re Checkmate Stereo & Elecs. Ltd., 9 Bankr. 585 (Bankr. EDNY 1981); John Ownben Co. Inc. v. Comm'r, 645 F2d 540 (6th Cir. 1981).

[130] See 5 Debtor-Creditor Law 22-81–22-83 (Matthew Bender 1982), and authorities cited therein.

defraud.[131] These badges might include transfers pending litigation,[132] transfers for grossly inadequate consideration,[133] and transfers made outside the usual mode of business[134] or under unusually secretive circumstances.[135]

A second issue that arises under traditional fraudulent conveyance statutes involves parties who become creditors of the debtor after the alleged fraudulent conveyance has occurred. It is possible that these creditors can also establish the requisite proof of intent to defraud if they can prove the transfer was made with the intent to defraud *subsequent* creditors.[136] Although the same basic principles related to proof of intent previously discussed apply,[137] it would appear that establishing intent to defraud subsequent creditors is a much more difficult task, as it would seem that a required showing of anticipated future debts at the time of the conveyance must be established.[138]

A third issue that must be considered under traditional fraudulent conveyance statutes, is whether a good faith purchaser for value is protected as against the creditor of the transferor when the transferor made the conveyance with the intent to hinder, delay, or defraud creditors. The law does protect good faith purchasers for value without notice of the transferor's fraudulent intent.[139] The purchaser is not made to investigate the transferor's business and motives, and the burden of establishing bad faith is on the creditor.[140] As to what constitutes "good faith," there is authority that it is not present where the purchaser has actual knowledge of facts sufficient to put a reasonable person on inquiry, which in turn would lead to the discovery of the fraud.[141] The transferee who is in bad faith not only will be subject to loss of the asset transferred, but might also be liable for damages if, for example, the creditor can establish a tort was committed as against the creditor by the transferee.[142]

---

131 Id. at 22-83–22-84.

132 See, e.g., In re Reed's Estate, 566 P2d 587 (Wyo. 1977).

133 See, e.g., Arnold v. Dirrim, 398 NE2d 442 (Ind. App. 1979).

134 See, e.g., Universal C.I.T. Credit Corp. v. Farmers Bank of Portageville, 358 F. Supp. 317 (ED Mo. 1973).

135 See, e.g., Rees v. Craighead Inv. Co., 251 Ark. 336, 472 SW2d 92 (1971).

136 See, e.g., Fla. Stat. Ann. § 726.07; Ill. Ann. Stat. ch. 59, § 4; Tex. Bus. & Com. Code § 24.02.

137 See, e.g., DeWest Realty Corp. v. Internal Revenue Serv. of U.S., 418 F. Supp. 1274 (SDNY 1976); Waukesha County Dep't. of Social & Health Servs. v. Loper, 53 Wis. 2d 713, 193 NW2d 679 (1974).

138 See, e.g., State Bank of Haines City v. Lockhardt, 120 Fla. 278, 162 So. 691 (1935).

139 See, e.g., Wallin v. Scottsdale Plumbing Co., Inc. 27 Ariz. App. 591, 557 P2d 190 (1976); First S. Properties, Inc. v. Gregory, 538 SW2d 454 (Tex. Civ. App. 1976).

140 See, e.g., Bank of Commerce v. Rosemary & Thyme Inc., 218 Va. 781, 239 SE2d 909 (1981).

141 Id.

142 See, e.g., Jahner v. Jacob, 252 NW2d 1 (ND 1977); Alan Drey Co., Inc. v. Generation, Inc., 22 Ill. App. 3d 611, 317 NE2d 673 (1974).

Although prior discussion reflects that even subsequent creditors can challenge a transfer as fraudulent, it should be emphasized that in order to attack the transfer, a "creditor" must ultimately have a valid claim against the debtor-transferor, whether the claim is absolute and fixed, or whether it is liquidated and contingent.[143] The procedural remedy used by such creditors is also of practical importance. As noted previously, the creditor may simply ignore the transfer and go directly after the transferred asset in the hands of the transferee.[144] That can be a perilous course to take unless the creditor is certain that the transfer was a fraudulent conveyance; if his conclusion was incorrect, liability to the transferee could result. Instead, the more cautious route is to have the transfer avoided and then levy thereafter. In that regard, the use of the creditor's bill often serves as the procedural mechanism through which the conveyance is avoided.[145] Finally, even if a creditor holds an unliquidated and unmatured claim, provisional relief in the form of injunctions or receiverships is available.[146]

### [b] Uniform Fraudulent Conveyance Act Jurisdictions

Approximately one half of the jurisdictions have adopted the Uniform Fraudulent Conveyance Act (UFCA).[147] UFCA was formulated and enacted in an effort to clarify the law of fraudulent conveyances as it existed under the traditional Statute of Elizabeth.[148] UFCA is currently undergoing a redrafting by the National Conference of Commissioners on Uniform Laws. This portion of the text is devoted to UFCA as it presently exists in the jurisdictions that have enacted it.

Two principal sections of UFCA enable creditors to avoid fraudulent conveyances. One section is based upon actual fraud,[149] and the other is based upon "constructive fraud."[150] Section 4 of UFCA, which contains the principal constructive fraud provision, is as follows:

---

[143] See, e.g., 5 Debtor-Creditor Law 22-87 (Matthew Bender 1982).

[144] See supra ¶ 6.07[2][a] note 124.

[145] See supra ¶ 6.05[5] for discussion of creditors' bills.

[146] See, e.g., Douglas v. First Nat'l Realty Corp., 164 US App. DC 363 (DC Cir. 1972); Charton Corp. v. Brockette, 534 SW2d 401 (Tex. Civ. App. 1976).

[147] See supra ¶ 6.07[2] note 120 for a listing of jurisdictions that have adopted UFCA.

[148] See, e.g., Linder v. Lewis, Roca, Scoville, & Beauchamp, 85 Ariz. 118, 333 P2d 286 (1958); 5 Debtor-Creditor Law 22-6 (Matthew Bender 1982).

[149] UFCA § 7.

[150] UFCA § 4. It should be noted that Sections 5, 6, and 8 of UFCA attack conveyances on constructive fraud theories. Section 5 protects creditors from undercapitalized debtors who make conveyances for less than a fair consideration and protects subsequent as well as existing creditors. See, e.g., In re Knox Kreations, Inc., 474 F. Supp. 567 (ED Tenn. 1979); U.S. v. 58th St. Plaza Theater, Inc., 287 F. Supp. 475 (SDNY 1968); 5 Debtor-Creditor Law ¶ 22.04[C] (Matthew Bender 1982). Section 6 is similar to Section 4: It allows an attack on every conveyance and obligation incurred without fair consideration when the person making the conveyance or entering the obligation

> Every conveyance made and every obligation incurred by a person, who is or will be thereby rendered insolvent is fraudulent as to creditors without regard to his actual intent if the conveyance is made or the obligation is incurred without a fair consideration.

UFCA Section 4 protects creditors who have claims against the debtor that exist at the time of the alleged fraudulent conveyance.[151] Additionally, this constructive fraud provision also lends certainty and predictability to the law as proof of actual intent to defraud, hinder, or delay is made irrelevant.[152] Obviously, an understanding of UFCA Section 4 requires an understanding of each of its basic elements.

First, there must be a "conveyance," as defined in UFCA Section 1 to include "any payment in money, assignment, release, transfer, lease, mortgage or pledge of tangible or intangible property, and also the creation of a lien or encumbrance." Thus, the term "conveyance" is broadly defined and has been so interpreted by the courts.[153] Second, the conveyance must have been made or the obligation incurred without a "fair consideration," as defined in UFCA Section 3. Whether the consideration is fair is a question of law for the court.[154] UFCA Section 3 provides two separate definitions. The first defines fair consideration as when an exchange for the property transferred, or obligation incurred, is given as a fair equivalent thereof and in good faith. The second definition relates to security transfers, as opposed to outright transfers. In security transfers, the consideration transferred must not be disproportionately small compared to the value of the property or obligation obtained. Again, the transferee must have acted in good faith. The issue of fair consideration often has been litigated and should be researched carefully.[155] Finally, the debtor-transferor must have been insolvent, or must have become insolvent as a result

---

intends or believes that he will incur debts beyond his ability to pay. Section 6 protects both present and future creditors. Thus, Section 6 is a blend of both intentional and constructive fraud. See, e.g., U.S. v. Ressler, 433 F. Supp. 459 (SD Fla. 1977); Lackawanna Pants Mfg. Co. v. Wiseman, 133 F2d 482 (6th Cir. 1943); 5 Debtor-Creditor Law ¶ 22.05[B] (Matthew Bender 1982). Section 8 provides that every conveyance of partnership property and every partnership obligation incurred when the partnership is or will thereby be rendered insolvent is fraudulent as to partnership creditors if made to a partner or to a person not a partner without fair consideration given the partnership. See, e.g., Hartnett v. Doyle, 16 Tenn. App. 302, 64 SW2d 227 (1932).

[151] See, e.g., In re Flanzbaum, 10 Bankr. 420 (Bankr. SD Fla. 1981).

[152] See, e.g., Commodity Futures Trading Comm'n v. Probber Int'l Equities Corp., 504 F. Supp. 1154 (SDNY 1981); Nelson v. Hansen, 278 Ore. 571, 565 P2d 727 (1977).

[153] See, e.g., Chambers v. Citizens & S. Nat'l Bank, 242 Ga. 498, 249 SE2d 214 (1978); Tuttle v. Tuttle, 38 NC App. 651, 248 SE2d 896 (1978); Dodson v. Temple Hill Baptist Church, Inc., 248 Md. 697, 238 A2d 239 (1968); Cellar Lumber Co. v. Hollen, 9 Ohio App. 288, 224 NE2d 360 (1967).

[154] See, e.g., Town Bank & Trust Co. v. Benson, 176 Conn. 304, 407 A2d 971 (1978).

[155] For discussion of the meaning of "fair consideration" and case law thereunder, see 5 Debtor-Creditor Law ¶ 22.03[D] (Matthew Bender 1982).

of the transfer, in order for UFCA Section 4 grounds for avoidance to be present. "Insolvency" is principally defined in UFCA Section 2 as existing when the "present fair salable value of [the debtor-transferor's] assets is less than the amount that will be required to pay his probable liability on his existing debts as they become absolute and matured."[156] There is nothing in UFCA Section 4 regarding burden of proof, although it would seem that the creditor would have the burden of establishing these various elements. However, the case law indicates that the allocation of the burden of proof varies dramatically from jurisdiction to jurisdiction and should be researched carefully by the lawyer in the applicable jurisdiction on a case-by-case basis.[157]

Section 7 of UFCA deals with actual or intentional fraud as follows:

> Every conveyance made and every obligation incurred with actual intent, as distinguished from intent presumed in law, to hinder, delay, or defraud either present or future creditors, is fraudulent as to both present and future creditors.

This means of avoiding a fraudulent conveyance closely resembles the Statute of Elizabeth, since both require a showing of actual intent.[158] Unlike UFCA Section 4, both present or future creditors may avoid a conveyance as fraudulent under UFCA Section 7.[159] Parties who become creditors after the transfer occurs need not show that the debtor specifically intended to defraud subsequent creditors, nor are they required to show an intent to defraud a particular subsequent creditor. In short, "a general actual intent to defraud existing creditors is sufficient to create rights in all subsequent creditors."[160] As the section indicates, a transfer intended to defraud either present or future creditors is fraudulent as to both.[161]

As discussion of the Statute of Elizabeth indicated,[162] direct evidence of fraudulent intent is often difficult, if not impossible, to produce. Thus, the concept of badges of fraud that originated under the Statute of Elizabeth has carried over to assist creditors in proving fraudulent intent under Section 7 of the UFCA. Again, badges of fraud are really circumstantial evidence of fraud, the badges being those facts that commonly are associated with a fraudulent con-

---

[156] For discussion of the meaning of "insolvency" and case law thereunder, see 5 Debtor-Creditor Law ¶ 22.03[E] (Matthew Bender 1982).

[157] For an excellent national summary of law related to the burden of proof question, see 5 Debtor-Creditor Law ¶ 22.04[E] (Matthew Bender 1982).

[158] See supra ¶ 6.07[2][a] for discussion of the Statute of Elizabeth.

[159] See, e.g., Neubauer v. Cloutier, 265 Minn. 539, 122 NW2d 623 (1963); Elliott v. Elliott, 365 F. Supp. 450 (SDNY 1973).

[160] 5 Debtor-Creditor Law 22-54 (Matthew Bender 1982).

[161] See, e.g., Pettit v. North Am. Stock Exch., 217 F. Supp. 21 (DCNY 1963); T.W.M. Homes Inc. v. Atherwood Realty & Inv. Co., 214 Cal. App. 2d 826, 29 Cal. Rptr. 887 (1963); Yeiser v. Rogers, 19 NJ 284, 116 A2d 3 (1955); Masomi Sasaki v. Yana Kai, 56 Cal. App. 2d 406, 133 P2d 18 (1943).

[162] See supra ¶ 6.07[2][a].

veyance, such as a general transfer of assets, intra-family transfers, transfers for less than fair consideration, and transfers with retention of use or possession.[163] However, existence of various badges of fraud will usually not be conclusive of fraud and may not even establish a prima facie case for the creditor under UFCA.[164] An issue related to proof of fraudulent intent arises if the transfer, in any event, did not damage the creditor. There is at least some authority that avoidance of the transfer cannot occur unless the creditor's collection effort was in fact hindered or delayed, or was otherwise made unsuccessful by the transfer.[165] Finally, the burden of proof of intentional fraud is on the creditor seeking avoidance of the transfer.[166] Again, badges of fraud may result in inference of fraud, direct evidence being unnecessary.

Whether avoidance of a transfer occurs under either UFCA Section 4 or 7, some transferees may nevertheless be protected under other sections of UFCA.[167] First, the transferee is completely protected if the transferee acted in good faith and paid equivalent value due to Section 9 of UFCA. Second, a purchaser who, without actual fraudulent intent, has given less than fair consideration may reclaim the property as security for repayment due to Section 9(2) of UFCA. It should also be noted that the transferee may receive protection if he lacked good faith but did not subjectively intend to defraud.[168]

The creditor's remedies should be considered in the event of a voidable fraudulent conveyance under UFCA. Assuming the creditor has a mature claim, the creditor may have the conveyance avoided, or obligation annulled, to the extent necessary to satisfy his claim.[169] The avoidance would occur through whatever procedural vehicle is appropriate in the applicable jurisdiction, most notably the creditor's bill.[170] Alternatively, the creditor may simply disregard the transfer and levy on the property in the hands of the transferee.[171] Direct levy may be dangerous unless the creditor is certain that the transfer was fraudulent and, in any event, it might be better to clear the property of the cloud

---

[163] See, e.g., Arnold v. Dirrim, 398 NE2d 442 (Ind. App. 1979); U.S. v. Fernon, 640 F2d 609 (11th Cir. 1981). For a summary of various badges of fraud under Section 7 of UFCA, see 5 Debtor-Creditor Law 22-57–22-58 (Matthew Bender 1982).

[164] See, e.g., U.S. v. Leggett, 292 F2d 423 (6th Cir.), cert. denied, 368 US 914 (1961). See discussion at supra ¶ 6.07[2][a] of the effect of the badges of fraud in Statute of Elizabeth jurisdictions.

[165] See, e.g., In re Knox Kreations, Inc., 474 F. Supp. 567 (ED Tenn.), aff'd in part, rev'd in part, 656 F2d 230 (6th Cir. 1978).

[166] See, e.g., Wilk Enters., Inc. v. J.I.B. Realty Corp., 72 Misc. 2d 507, 339 NYS2d 75 (NY Civ. Ct. 1972); Berger v. Hi-Gear Tire & Auto Supply Inc., 257 Md. 470, 263 A2d 507 (1970).

[167] See UFCA §§ 9, 10.

[168] See, e.g., O'Neill v. Little, 107 NJ Super. 426, 258 A2d 731 (1969); Southern Indus., Inc. v. Jeremias, 56 AD2d 178, 411 NYS2d 945 (1978); see also 5 Debtor-Creditor Law 22-67 (Matthew Bender 1982).

[169] UFCA § 9(1)(a).

[170] See supra ¶ 6.05[5] for discussion of creditors' bills.

[171] UFCA § 9(1)(b).

created by the alleged fraud.[172] If the creditor's claim is unmatured, UFCA does give the creditor some remedies.[173] The court may mold any remedy to protect the creditor's interest by appointing a receiver, by restraining disposition of the property, and by other methods.[174] Beyond avoiding or enjoining the transfer, a defrauded creditor might also have an action for damages against the transferee based upon common-law tort principles.[175]

### [c] Pending Redraft of the Uniform Fraudulent Conveyance Act

UFCA is presently being rewritten by the National Conference of Commissioners on Uniform State Laws. At this writing, the new UFCA is in draft form only and undoubtedly will undergo further close scrutiny that will result in changes from its present form.[176] Further, it will be some time before UFCA states enact the revisions. Therefore, only a brief comment will be made at the time of this writing regarding the pending redraft.

The redraft in its present form has been organized into eight sections.[177] The redraft appears, in large part to be an attempt to reorganize UFCA. At the

---

[172] See, e.g., Computer Sciences Corp. v. Sci-Tek, Inc., 367 A2d 658 (Del. Super. Ct. 1976); Gagne v. Bailey, 17 Wash. App. 599, 654 P2d 348 (1977); Patterson v. Hopkins, 247 Pa. Super. 163, 371 A2d 1378 (1977).

[173] UFCA § 10.

[174] Cf. H.L.C. Imports Corp. v. M. & L. Siegel, Inc., 98 Misc. 2d 179, 413 NYS2d 605 (NY Civ. Ct. 1979).

[175] See Section 11 of UFCA, which provides as follows:

> "Cases Not Provided for in Act. In any case not provided for in this act the rules of law and equity including the law merchant, and in particular the rules relating to the law of principal and agent, and the effect of fraud, misrepresentation, duress or coercion, mistake, bankruptcy or other invalidating cause shall govern."

See also, e.g., Flowers & Sons Dev. Corp. v. Municipal Court of City & County of San Francisco, 86 Cal. App. 3d 818, 150 Cal. Rptr. 555 (1978); Jones v. Spindel, 239 Ga. 68, 235 SE2d 486 (1977); Spaziano v. Spaziano, 410 A2d 113 (RI 1980); Winter & Welker, 174 F. Supp. 836 (ED Pa. 1959).

[176] Indeed, the present draft includes a cover page that in part states as follows:

> "The ideas and conclusions herein set forth, including drafts of proposed legislation, have not been passed upon by the Commissioners on Uniform State Laws. They do not necessarily reflect the views of the Committee, Reporters or Commissioners. Proposed statutory language, if any, may not be used to ascertain legislative meaning of any promulgated final law."

[177] The section titles and numbers are as follows:

Section 1 Definitions
Section 2 Insolvency
Section 3 Value
Section 4 Transfers Fraudulent as to Present and Future Creditors
Section 5 Transfers Fraudulent as to Present Creditors
Section 6 Remedies of Creditors
Section 7 Liability and Protection of Transferees
Section 8 Time When Transfer Occurs; Limitations

same time, some provisions of other statutes, notably the Bankruptcy Reform Act of 1978, have been incorporated into the proposed draft, which will result in some significant and substantive changes. The present Section 4 of the draft is a combination of Sections 5, 6, and 7 of the present UFCA, the most important point being that a present and future creditor may still attack a conveyance as fraudulent if it was done with an actual intent to hinder, delay, or defraud any creditor of the debtor. In assisting the creditor to prove actual intent, UFCA Section 4(b) of the proposed draft sets forth "factors" to be given consideration in the determination of actual intent. The "factors" are actually the type of facts that have been characterized as "badges of fraud" in existing fraudulent conveyance law.[178] Section 5(a) of the proposed draft is derived from Section 4 of the present UFCA and remains the principal constructive fraud provision. It adheres to the requirement that a creditor must have been such at the time of the transfer to be able to set aside the transfer. The proposed draft, however, substitutes "reasonably equivalent value" for "fair consideration" and then defines "value" at Section 3. Additionally, the term "insolvency" is redefined at proposed UFCA Section 2 to include both the present balance sheet test of insolvency (liabilities exceed assets) and, in effect, a new equity insolvency test derived primarily from UCC Section 1-201(23).[179] Section 6 of the proposed UFCA draft reorganizes the remedies of

---

[178] Section 4(b) of the proposed draft of UFCA lists the following factors:

"In determining actual intent under subsection (a)(1), consideration may be given, among other factors, to the fact that:

"(1) the relationship between the transferor and the transferee was close;

"(2) the transferor retained possession or dominion after the transfer;

"(3) the transfer was concealed;

"(4) prior to the transfer a creditor has sued, or was threatening to sue, the transferor;

"(5) the transfer was of substantially all the debtor's assets;

"(6) the debtor has absconded or has removed or changed the form of the assets remaining in his possession so as to make the assets less subject to creditor process;

"(7) the value of the consideration received by the debtor was not reasonably equivalent to the value of the asset transferred or the amount of the obligation incurred;

"(8) the debtor was insolvent or heavily indebted or reasonably should have expected to become so indebted;

"(9) the transfer occurred shortly before or after a substantial debt was incurred. Proof of the existence of any one of the factors listed in this subsection does not in itself constitute prima facie proof that the debtor has made a fraudulent transfer or incurred a fraudulent obligation."

[179] UFCA Section 2(a) is as follows:

"(a) A person is 'insolvent' if:

"(1) the person is generally not paying the person's debts as they become due,

"(2) the person cannot pay the person's debts as they become due, or

"(3) the sum of the person's debts is greater than the fair value of all of the person's assets."

creditors found in the present UFCA at Sections 9 and 10. Basically, creditors who hold mature claims would be given the additional remedies of those with unmatured claims, as presently provided in Section 10 of UFCA. Section 7 of the proposed UFCA draft spells out potential liability of transferees and is primarily derived from Sections 550(a) and 548(c) of the Bankruptcy Code. Finally, Section 8 of the proposed UFCA draft pinpoints the time of the transfer in a provision that is derived from Section 548(d) of the Bankruptcy Code. Section 8 of the proposed UFCA draft also provides a statute of limitations, within which a creditor must avoid a conveyance as fraudulent.

### [3] Duration of the Judgment

A judgment in all jurisdictions does not have an unlimited period of existence. Under common law, a judgment became dormant after a year and a day of its signing, if the creditor failed to take out a fieri facias within, or to enter an elegit on the roll "as of," such period.[180] To satisfy the judgment under those circumstances, under common law, the creditor could either bring an action of debt on the judgment and obtain a new judgment or he could sue out a writ of scire facias from the court and obtain an execution on the old judgment.[181] Today, in the United States, there are both statutory and modern common-law limitations on the effective duration of a judgment. Professor Stefan Riesenfeld has emphasized that

> [s]ince in the United States actionability, executability and operation as a lien become three separate effects of a judgment, statutory actions with respect to each of these aspects, though often taken simultaneously, must be differentiated.[182]

Similarly, Professors David Epstein and Jonathan Landers have described the kind of issues confronted by lawyers in this regard as follows:

> Today, the lawyer confronting the problem of keeping a judgment alive in the hope that the debtor will acquire some assets in the future faces at least some of the following questions. (1) Is it possible to keep the judgment alive by periodically obtaining writs of execution? (2) If the judgment becomes dormant, may it be revived by motion (scire facias), action, or both? What statutes of limitation govern these proceedings, and what are the rules as to the jurisdiction and venue (if any)? (3) If revival is by motion, is there a 'defense' based on laches or undue delay? (4) If a judgment is revived or renewed, what priority does the revived judgment lien

---

[180] See Riesenfeld, "Collection of Money Judgments in American Law–A Historical Inventory and a Prospectus," 42 Iowa L. Rev. 155, 172 (1957), and authorities cited therein, including 2 Tedd's Practice 1004 (3d ed. 1803); Seymour v. Greenvill, 90 Eng. Rep. 768 (KB 1694); Taylor's Adm'r v. Spindle, 43 Va. (2 Gratt.) 44 (1845).

[181] Riesenfeld, "Collection of Money Judgments in American Law–A Historical Inventory and a Prospectus," 42 Iowa L. Rev. 155, 172 (1957).

[182] Id. at 173.

have? (5) Are there any limits on the number of renewals and/or revivals which may be obtained? (6) Is there an outside limit of, for example twenty years, on collecting the judgment or obtaining a renewal and/or revival of the judgment? (7) To what extent can the judgment be enforced in a state other than the one which rendered the judgment? What must be done to enforce the judgment in such a state, and what rules as to jurisdiction, venue, and limitations apply?[183]

Although a complete review of the law nationwide that relates to the above issues is beyond the scope of this text, an overview of both the statutory and the common-law limits presently in effect can be undertaken with particular focus on the duration of judgment liens[184] and the duration of liens acquired by levy.[185] Before this overview can occur, a basic definitional distinction must be made.

Judgments may be "revived" or "renewed" depending upon the provisions of the applicable statute. Revival typically occurs by judicial decree or by issuance of a writ of execution, the revival occurring after the judgment by statute has lapsed into a period of "dormancy." By contrast, renewal typically consists of a new money judgment on the original judgment itself. The new judgment stands on its own as far as actionability, executability, and creation of a lien are concerned. The effect on a judgment lien of a revivor is therefore quite different from that of a renewal. If revivor occurs, the judgment lien under the original judgment is extended; the original priority date of the judgment lien is typically maintained. If renewal occurs, a new judgment lien arises and with it a new priority date.[186]

As to the duration of judgment liens, the states nationwide exhibit great variety.[187] Many jurisdictions use the revivor-type statute with the effect that a revivor prolongs the life of the existing judgment lien. However, many other jurisdictions require the taking of a renewal judgment within a specified time period from rendition of the original judgment, which has the effect of creating a new judgment lien.[188] As to revivor statutes, they seem to take different forms upon closer scrutiny. For example, some revivor statutes hold that revivor proceedings will continue the judgment lien for another period if revivor occurs prior to the expiration of the dormancy period; however, if revivor occurs after that time, the judgment lien will be subordinated to intervening interests.[189]

---

[183] Epstein & Landers, Debtors and Creditors 97–98 (West, 2d ed. 1982).

[184] See supra ¶ 6.05[2] for discussion of judgment liens.

[185] See supra ¶¶ 6.04[1][f], 6.04[2][e], 6.05[3][e], and 6.05[4] for discussion of acquisition of liens by levy or service of notice of garnishment.

[186] See generally Riesenfeld, Creditors' Remedies and Debtors' Protection 101 (West, 3d ed. 1979).

[187] See generally Annot., 77 A.L.R.2d 1064 (1961); Annot., 52 A.L.R.2d 672 (1957).

[188] Riesenfeld, Creditors' Remedies and Debtors' Protection 101 (West, 3d ed. 1979); see, e.g., Trend Mills v. Socher, 4 Bankr. 465 (DNJ 1980). But see Breiger v. Breiger, 197 Kan. 756, 421 P2d 1 (1966); Provisor v. Nelson, 234 Cal. App. 2d 876, 44 Cal. Rptr. 894 (1964).

[189] See, e.g., Ark. Stat. Ann. §§ 29-131, 29-607, construed in Alsron v. Bitely, 252 Ark. 74, 447 SW2d 466 (1972); Colo. Rev. Stat. § 7A-1-2; Colo. R. Civ. P. 54(h); Kan.

Revivor in other jurisdictions may occur only after expiration or dormancy of the original lien, resulting in a lien that is new and separate.[190] Still other jurisdictions allow the creditor to avoid having the judgment lapse into dormancy by issuance of the writ of execution or some other or additional procedure.[191] Finally, there are some states that cannot be characterized as either renewal or revivor states. These states limit the enforceability of judgments, and thus judgment liens, to one period only, or perhaps to one extension only.[192]

Some jurisdictions have enacted relevant legislation concerning duration of liens created by levy under writ of execution or attachment, or by service of notice of garnishment.[193] Under common law, these liens would continue from creation until sale of the asset, unless the creditor did something that resulted in loss of lien by implied abandonment or similar actions.[194] In derogation of this common law, states have enacted statutes that call for periods of limitation. The sale must occur within this period or the lien will become ineffective.[195]

---

Stat. Ann. §§ 60-2403, 60-2404, construed in Clark v. Glazer, 4 Kan. App. 2d 658, 609 P2d 1177 (1980); Mo. Ann. Stat. §§ 511.380, 511.390; Mo. R. Civ. P. 74.37, 74.38, construed in Purellage v. De Seaton, 407 SW2d 36 (Mo. Ct. App. 1966); N.M. Stat. Ann. §§ 39-1-19, 39-1-20, construed in Western States Collection Co. v. Shain, 83 NM 203, 490 P2d 461 (1971).

[190] See, e.g., Ga. Code Ann. §§ 9-12-60–9-12-64, applied in Turner v. Wood, 162 Ga. App. 674, 292 SE2d 558 (1982); Ill. Ann. Stat. ch. 110, §§ 2-1601, 13-218; Neb. Rev. Stat. §§ 25-1420, 25-1512, 25-1542, applied in Campagna v. Home Owner's Loan Corp., 141 Neb. 429, 3 NW2d 750 (1942); Ohio Rev. Code Ann. §§ 2325.17, 2325.18, 2329.07, discussed by McLesky & McLesky, "Dormancy and Revival of Ohio Judgments," 16 Ohio St. L.J. 81 (1955).

[191] See, e.g., Ga. Code Ann. §§ 9-12-60–9-12-64, applied in O'Neil v. Williams, 232 Ga. 170, 205 SE2d 226 (1974), and Fielding v. M. Rich & Bros. Co. 46 Ga. App. 785, 169 SE 383 (1933); Kan. Stat. Ann. § 60-2403, construed in Riney v. Riney, 205 Kan. 671, 473 P2d 77 (1970); Neb. Rev. Stat. §§ 25-1515, 25-1542, construed in Hein v. W.T. Rawleigh Co., 167 Neb. 176, 92 NW2d 185 (1958); Ohio Rev. Code Ann. § 2329.07, construed in Kelley v. Vincent, 8 Ohio St. 415 (1858). In Texas, perpetuation of a judgment lien is possible by means of periodic issuance of an execution followed by filing of successive abstracts. See Tex. Rev. Civ. Stat. Ann. art. 5532 (Vernon 1966); see also Hudspeth, "Judgment Liens and Abstracts of Judgments in Texas," 32 Tex. B.J. 520 (1969); Mitchell, "Perpetuating the Force of Judgments and Judgment Liens in Texas," 29 Tex. L. Rev. 530 (1951).

[192] See, e.g., Wash. Rev. Code § 4.56.210, applied in Hathaway v. Hathaway, 19 Wash. App. 449, 576 P2d 919 (1978); Ore. Rev. Stat. §§ 18.360, 12.070 as construed in Ames v. Ames, 60 Ore. App. 50, 652 P2d 1284 (1982), and Newhouse v. Newhouse, 271 Ore. 109, 530 P2d 848 (1975); N.D. Cent. Code §§ 28-20-35, 28-20-23, 28-01-15; see Groth v. Ness, 65 ND 580, 260 NW 700 (1935); Ariz. Rev. Stat. Ann. §§ 12-1611–12-1613.

[193] See supra ¶ 6.07[3] note 185.

[194] See, immediately below, discussion of common-law methods of losing judicial liens.

[195] See, e.g., Cal. Civ. Proc. Code § 688; Tri-County Elevator Co., Inc. v. Superior Court of Santa Barbara County, 135 Cal. App. 3d 271, 185 Cal. Rptr. 209 (1982); N.J. Stat. Ann. § 2A:18-27; In re Hiawatha Do It Yourself, Inc., 82 NJ Super. 399, 197 A2d 715 (1964); N.Y. Civ. Prac. Law & R. § 5232(a); Va. Code § 8.01-505.

In addition to loss of liens due to statutory periods of limitation, creditors can also lose judicial liens by way of common-law doctrine. Discussion of such common law usually focuses on the leading case of *Excelsior Needle Co. v. Globe Cycle Works*,[196] in which it was said:

> The law is quite clear that the object of the execution is to enforce the judgment debt, and not to convert it into a security upon the property, and still allow the judgment debtor to prosecute his business regardless of the lien of execution. As was said in Freeman Executions § 206: 'In other words, it is not the mere issuing or delivery of the writ which creates a lien, but an issuing and delivery for the purpose of execution. The execution of a writ for the purpose of making or keeping it effective as a lien cannot stop with a mere levy upon the property. If the officer is instructed by the plaintiff not to sell till further orders, the lien of the execution and levy becomes subordinate to that of any subsequent writ placed in the officers' hands for service.' . . . The law, therefore, seems to be settled that any direction by the execution creditor to the sheriff which suspends the lien or delays the enforcement of the levy renders the execution dormant against subsequent creditors or bona fide purchasers. However veiled may be the direction, however much it may be founded on humane desire to protect the debtor, if it is tantamount to a mandate or instruction to the sheriff to withhold the execution of his process, during the interim that he accedes to this demand the levy ceases to be effective.[197]

Although this quotation from *Excelsior* indicates that *any* direction by the creditor to the sheriff that delays enforcement renders the execution dormant, there is some contrary authority. For example, where levied upon, goods were permitted to remain with the debtor and the forced sale was delayed by the creditor. Where the delay was for the good faith purpose to enable the debtor to pay the debt before liquidation, it was held that the lien remained valid.[198] Even so, creditors who are concerned about maintaining a priority position in a debtor's assets should be cautious about delaying enforcement of a judicial lien for any reason, due to the *Excelsior* doctrine.

## [4] Enforcement of Foreign Judgments

As creditors often discover, collection efforts are compounded in difficulty if the debtor moves to a "foreign" state after judgment has been rendered. Due to the federal system, numerous issues evolve in such a situation. The U.S. Constitution requires that full faith and credit be given in each state to judg-

---

[196] 48 AD 304, 62 NYS 538 (1900).

[197] Id. at 309–310, 540–541.

[198] See, e.g., Illi, Inc. v. Margolis, 267 Md. 30, 296 A2d 412 (1972), and authorities cited therein.

ments rendered in a sister state.[199] The problem from the judgment creditor's point of view is how full faith and credit may be obtained in a procedural sense. To obtain full faith and credit, the foreign judgment must be "domesticated," since an early American case held that the full faith and credit clause of the Constitution did not require states to directly enforce judgments rendered by sister states.[200] There are basically two different methods of domestication adopted by the various jurisdictions.

The common law originated one method of domesticating the foreign judgment that is still used by approximately three fifths of the states today. The common-law procedure requires the judgment creditor to bring an action in the second state based on the judgment obtained in the first state.[201] The same procedure applies with regard to judgments rendered by a court of a foreign nation.[202] As to domesticating judgments of sister states by this common-law procedure, although jurisdiction must be established over the debtor, the debtor may not relitigate the basic cause of action. However, he is limited to challenging the foreign judgment on jurisdictional grounds or by showing that the judgment is satisfied or that it is barred. Assuming the debtor fails, the second state will render a new judgment upon the old judgment. The new judgment is then enforceable within the second state.[203] If the foreign judgment was rendered in another nation, the debtor may resist its domestication on a variety of other grounds.[204]

A second method of enforcing foreign judgments appeared upon the adoption of the Uniform Enforcement of Foreign Judgments Act by approximately two fifths of the states.[205] This Act provides a summary procedure for domesticating an out-of state judgment. Registration procedures have been substituted

---

[199] U.S. Constitution, article 4, section 8. However, states are not required to give full faith and credit to foreign state exemption statutes and may place judicial liens on choses in action that are exempt in the state of origin. See, e.g., Rhode Island & Pac. Ry. Co. v. Sturm, 174 US 710 (1899); Sanders v. Armour Fertilizer Works, 292 US 190 (1934). Further, states may apply their own limitation periods applicable to their own judgments against the judgment of a foreign state. See, e.g., McElmoyle ex rel. Bailey v. Cohen, 38 US 312 (1829); Roche v. McDonald, 275 US 449 (1928).

[200] McElmoyle ex rel. Bailey v. Cohen, 38 US 312 (1839).

[201] See, e.g., Old Dominion Copper Mining & Smelting Co. v. Bigelow, 203 Mass. 159, 89 NE 193, aff'd, 225 US 111 (1911); Stewart v. Eaton, 287 Mich. 466, 283 NW 651 (1939); Cook v. Brown, 346 Mo. 281, 140 SW2d 42 (1940); State of N.Y. v. Rooney, 115 NH 603, 347 A2d 172 (1975); National Equip. Rental Ltd. v. Collidge Bank & Trust Co., 348 So. 2d 1236 (Fla. Dist. Ct. App. 1977); Viguerire Co. v. Noble, 101 Cal. App. 3d 62, 161 Cal. Rptr. 435 (1980).

[202] See, e.g., Hilton v. Guyot, 159 US 113 (1895).

[203] For a concise discussion of the common-law procedure of domestication, see Hawkland & Loiseaux, Debtor-Creditor Relations 33 (Bobbs-Merrill, 2d ed. 1979).

[204] Id. at 34.

[205] The original 1948 version of the Act was adopted in Arkansas, Illinois, Missouri, Nebraska, Oregon, and Washington. The revised 1964 version of the Act was adopted in Alaska, Arizona, Colorado, Connecticut, Idaho, Kansas, Maine, New York, North Dakota, Oklahoma, Pennsylvania, South Dakota, Wisconsin, and Wyoming.

for suit.[206] This provides some rapid relief for the creditor, in that it is far less complicated than a traditional lawsuit. The constitutionality of the Act has been upheld.[207] As to judgments obtained in foreign countries, the Uniform Foreign Money-Judgments Recognition Act has been adopted in several states.[208] It "somewhat reduces the burdens of a foreign judgment-creditor in seeking to domesticate his judgment, but it preserves many of the grounds which debtors have used successfully to prevent domestication."[209]

A final note regarding enforcement of foreign judgments should be made as to federal court judgments. From the creditor's point of view, the federal court judgment certainly provides an advantage over a state judgment, in that the former is easily transferred from one court to another. The revision of the Federal Judicial Code in 1948 authorized the registration in any other district of final judgments for the recovery of money or property entered in any district court. It also provided that a "judgment so registered shall have the same effect as a judgment of the court of the district where registered and may be enforced in like manner."[210] It should be recalled from prior discussion in the text[211] that a federal judgment is otherwise enforceable pursuant to the law of the state in which the federal district court sits.[212]

### [5] Reaching Property in Which the Debtor Shares Title With a Nondebtor

Throughout most of the discussion of judicial debt collection in the text, it has been assumed that the debtor is the only titleholder to property subjected to the various judicial liens.[213] Obviously, this will not always be the case. Matters from the creditor's point of view are significantly complicated if the debtor holds title with a third party by way of a tenancy in common, joint tenancy, tenancy by the entirety, as community property, or as partnership

---

[206] See, e.g., Burchett v. Roncari, 181 Conn. 125, 434 A2d 941 (1980); Evans v. Advance Schools, Inc., 70 Ill. App. 3d 947, 388 NE2d 1003 (1979); Multibanco Comermex, S.A. v. Gonzales H, 129 Ariz. 321, 630 P2d 1053 (1981); see Annot., 72 A.L.R.2d 1255 (1960); Annot., 100 A.L.R.3d 792 (1980); Annot., 13 A.L.R.4th 1109 (1982).

[207] See, e.g., Sullivan v. Sullivan, 168 Neb. 850, 97 NW2d 348 (1950).

[208] Alaska Stat. §§ 09.30.100–09.30.180; Cal. Civ. Proc. Code §§ 1713–1713.8; Ill. Ann. Stat. ch. 77, §§ 121–129; Md. Cts. & Jud. Proc. Code Ann. §§ 10-701–10-709; Mass. Gen. Laws Ann. ch. 235, § 23A; Mich. Comp. Laws Ann. §§ 691.1151–691.1159; N.Y. Civ. Prac. Law & R. §§ 5301–5309; Okla. Stat. Ann. tit. 12, §§ 710–718; Wash. Rev. Code Ann. §§ 6.40.010–6.40.915.

[209] Hawkland & Loiseaux, Debtor-Creditor Relations 34 (Bobbs-Merrill, 2d ed. 1979).

[210] 28 USC § 1963.

[211] See supra ¶¶ 6.04[1][g], 6.05[2][h], 6.05[3][f].

[212] See 28 USC § 1962; Fed. R. Civ. P. 65, 69.

[213] However, see supra ¶ 6.05[2][d], in which there is discussion of the judgment lien's ability to reach property held in co-ownership.

property. If all the titleholders are obligated on the debt or claim to the creditor, no particular difficulty arises. On the other hand, if not all the titleholders are obligated to the creditor, the issue is raised as to whether the interest of the debtor is subject to judicial process. That issue is considered in this portion of the text.

### [a] Tenancy in Common

In a tenancy in common, two or more persons are entitled to property in such manner that they have undivided possession, but several freeholds or interests.[214] The tenancy in common exists as to real property; it also exists as to personal property.[215] The prevailing rule is that if two or more persons own undivided possessory estates or interests in property, they are presumably tenants in common.[216] Tenants in common have an equal right to possession but, upon the death of one tenant, the deceased's interest passes to his estate or as directed in his will.[217] It is clear that the interest of a tenant in common may be subjected to levy and sale for his individual debt. This is true as to real property[218] and personal property.[219]

### [b] Joint Tenancy

In a joint tenancy, each joint tenant is considered to be the owner of the whole estate and also of an undivided part. This is due to the fact that there is unity in ownership with respect to time, title, interest, and possession. Upon the death of one joint tenant, the surviving joint tenant or tenants continue as owners of the whole estate, a characteristic that differentiates a joint tenancy from the tenancy in common.[220] Statutes commonly provide that the creation of a joint tenancy requires an express declaration that the parties are to take as joint tenants.[221] Although joint tenancy is most often associated with real property, there can be joint tenancy in almost any kind of personal property.[222] Previous discussion in this text pertaining to judgment liens indicates

---

[214] See, e.g., Perkins v. Chad Dev. Corp., 95 Cal. App. 3d 645, 157 Cal. Rptr. 201 (1979); In re Hurlbuttis Estate, 36 Ore. App. 721, 585 P2d 724 (1978); 20 Am. Jur. 2d Co-tenancy and Joint Ownership § 22.

[215] See, e.g., Graver v. Illinois Dep't of Public Aid, 64 Ill. App. 3d 820, 381 NE2d 1044 (1978); Walnut Valley State Bank v. Stovall, 223 Kan. 459, 574 P2d 1382 (1978).

[216] See Burby, Real Property 228 (West, 3d ed. 1965).

[217] Id.

[218] See, e.g., Scott ex rel. Stevenson v. Hatch, 41 Ore. App. 609, 598 P2d 1234 (1979); Madison v. General Acceptance Corp., 26 Wash. App. 387, 612 P2d 826 (1980).

[219] See, e.g., First Nat'l Bank v. Geiger, 61 Ga. App. 865, 7 SE2d 756 (1940).

[220] See Burby, Real Property 215 (West, 3d ed. 1965).

[221] Id.

[222] See, e.g., Estate of Barnhart, 194 Colo. 505, 574 P2d 500 (1978); Constance v. Constance, 366 So. 2d 804 (Fla. Dist. Ct. App. 1979); Hines, "Personal Property Joint Tenancies: More Law, Fact, and Fancy," 54 Minn. L. Rev. 509 (1970).

that a debtor's individual interest in the joint tenancy can be reached by his creditors.[223] As to judicial liens generally, the undivided interest of a joint tenant is subject to the claims of his creditors, although it may not be asserted against a surviving joint tenant; to satisfy the claim, the creditor must execute during the lifetime of the debtor, or the surviving joint tenant is entitled to the property free from the creditor's claim.[224]

### [c] Tenancy by the Entirety

A tenancy by the entirety is a type of concurrent ownership that originated in the common law from the concept of unity of husband and wife.[225] Although it is usually associated with real property, it may also be applied to personal property.[226] Approximately twenty-five jurisdictions recognize tenancy by the entirety.[227] In these jurisdictions, the general rule is that a conveyance to a husband and wife creates a tenancy by the entirety, unless a contrary intention is expressed; however, the "preferred" view is that one spouse cannot create a tenancy by the entirety by conveying property to himself and to the other spouse.[228] Even though at common law, the husband was seen as the sole manager of the property, Married Women's Acts confer upon a married woman equal rights in management.[229] The tenancy by the entirety is similar to a joint tenancy, as discussed previously; however, an important difference affects the ability of a creditor of an individual tenant to reach any interest in the tenancy by the entirety. As one commentator notes,

---

[223] See supra ¶ 6.05[2][d].

[224] See, e.g., In re Estelle's Estate, 122 Ariz. 109, 593 P2d 663 (1979); U.S. v. Mosolowitz, 269 F. Supp. 12 (D. Conn. 1967); Burby, Real Property 227 (West, 3d ed. 1965); Annot., 111 A.L.R. 171 (1937).

[225] For a basic definition and description of tenancy by the entirety, see Burby, Real Property 221–228 (West, 3d ed. 1965). See also Huber, "Creditors' Rights in Tenancies by the Entireties," 1 B.C. Indus. & Com. L. Rev. 197 (1961).

[226] See, e.g., Gibson v. Marr, 395 So. 2d 1278 (Fla. Dist. Ct. App. 1981); In re Barsotti, 7 Bankr. 205 (Bankr. WD Pa. 1980); In re Garretson, 6 Bankr. 127 (Bankr. ED Tenn. 1980); National Bank & Trust Co. of Norwich v. Rickard, 57 AD2d 156, 393 NYS2d 801 (1977); Parslow v. Parslow, 47 NC App. 84, 266 SE2d 746 (1980).

[227] See Riesenfeld, Creditors' Remedies and Debtors' Protection 310, at n.16 (West, 3d ed. 1979), at which the author lists the following jurisdictions as recognizing tenancies by the entirety: Alabama, Arkansas, Delaware, District of Columbia, Florida, Hawaii, Indiana, Kentucky, Massachusetts, Maryland, Michigan, Mississippi, Missouri, New Jersey, New York, North Carolina, Oklahoma, Oregon, Pennsylvania, Rhode Island, Tennessee, Vermont, Virginia, the Virgin Islands, and Wyoming.

[228] See, e.g., Rothschild v. Rothschild, 288 So. 2d 582 (Fla. Dist. Ct. App. 1974). However, there are exceptions to this rule. See, e.g., Stone v. Culver, 286 Mich. 263, 282 NW 142 (1938). There is also contrary authority to the rule stated in the text. See, e.g., Cayce v. Carter Oil Co., 618 F2d 669 (10th Cir. 1980); Liberman v. Kelso, 354 So. 2d 137 (Fla. Dist Ct. App. 1978).

[229] See, e.g., Niglio v. New Jersey Racing Comm'n, 158 NJ Super. 182, 385 A2d 925 (1978).

> [T]he manner of holding the estate was said to be different–joint tenants were seized of a share and of the whole (*per my et per tout*), but tenants by the entirety were seized of the whole and not of a share (*per tout et non per my*). As in the case of joint tenancy, the incident of survivorship attached to a tenancy by the entirety but it was an indestructible right of survivorship. Both spouses could join in a conveyance of the property to a third person but neither alone could create a severance of the tenancy or by any act defeat the right of survivorship of the other spouse.[230]

Most jurisdictions that recognize tenancies by the entirety hold that a creditor of one spouse cannot reach the debtor spouse's share in the property.[231] This rule is thought to be necessary from a policy point of view to preserve the rights of the nondebtor spouse. There are, however, a number of refinements to this rule that exist in various states. For example, there is some authority in a few jurisdictions that a creditor of either spouse can reach his or her right of survivorship and a judgment lien will attach thereon.[232] In this vein, one noted authority[233] has stated that in a number of states a tenancy by the entirety is considered to be in the nature of a tenancy in common, but without a right to compel partition. Thus, there is a remainder or executory interest in the survivor that is alienable, and it may be subjected to the claims of individual creditors of the husband or wife. In one jurisdiction, a judgment lien attaches but is inchoate and unenforceable until survivorship of the judgment debtor.[234]

If the tenancy by the entirety terminates and is converted into some other form of ownership, the creditors of one spouse may now be able to reach the property. For example, the lien of a judgment against one of the spouses will attach upon conversion of the tenancy by the entirety into a tenancy in common resulting from a divorce.[235] Similarly, if the debtor spouse acquires the exclusive right to the property as a result of the death of the other spouse, the creditor may now reach the property.[236] If the nondebtor spouse acquires the exclusive right to the property, the creditor may not reach the property.

Finally, it should be reemphasized that this discussion is predicated upon the assumption that the creditor only has a claim against one spouse; if the

---

[230] Moynihan, Introduction to the Law of Real Property 229–230 (West 1962).

[231] See, e.g., Watterson v. Edgerly, 40 Md. App. 1230, 388 A2d 934 (1978); Thummel v. Thummel, 609 SW2d 175 (Mo. Ct. App. 1980); Sawada v. Endo, 57 Hawaii 608, 561 P2d 1291 (1977).

[232] See, e.g., Wolfe v. Seniuk, 76 Misc. 2d 860, 352 NYS2d 88 (NY Sup. Ct., Special Term 1973); In re Dawson, 10 Bankr. 680, aff'd, Ray v. Dawson, 14 Bankr. 822 (Bankr. ED Tenn. 1981); Cherry v. Cherry, 168 NJ Super. 386, 403 A2d 45 (1979).

[233] Burby, Real Property 226–227 (West, 3d ed. 1965).

[234] See C.I.T. Corp. v. Flint, 330 Pa. 350, 5 A2d 126 (1939).

[235] See, e.g., McDonald v. Driscoll, 103 Misc. 2d 567, 426 NYS2d 678 (NY Fam. Ct. 1980).

[236] See, e.g., In re Houghton's Estate, 75 NJ 462, 383 A2d 713 (1978).

creditor can obtain a judgment against both spouses, the entire property may be reached.[237]

### [d] Community Property

The subject of creditor-debtor rights in relationship to community property nationally is extraordinarily complex.[238] Although there are only eight community-property states,[239] there is great variety among them with regard to debt collection. It is impossible to survey the law of the eight states in a few paragraphs. Even so, an attempt to touch on some of the basic principles is appropriate in providing the reader with some background in this complex area to assist in researching local law.

The origin of community-property ownership in the United States came from the Spanish and can be traced in written form to the Visigothic Code of 698 A.D.[240] In the United States, spouses may possess separate and community property. Separate property includes property that a spouse brought into the marriage, and gifts, bequests, and inheritances received during the marriage; all other property is community property.[241] When a spouse incurs a debt in a community-property state, the debt is characterized as a "separate" debt or "community" debt. The separate debt is the obligation of only one spouse, while a community debt is the obligation of both. Some statutory law defines the distinction between separate and community debts,[242] while other states rely solely upon case law.[243]

A creditor to whom a spouse owes a "separate" debt may reach the separate property of that spouse.[244] The creditor, however, cannot reach the sepa-

---

[237] See, e.g., In re Foreclosure of Deed of Trust, 50 NC App. 69, 272 SE2d 893, rev'd, 303 NC 514, 279 SE2d 566 (1980).

[238] For an excellent discussion of debt collection in community-property states, see McClanahan, Community Property Law in the United States Ch. 10 (Lawyers' Coop. Publishing Co. 1982); see also Reppy & deFuniak, Community Property in the United States (Bobbs-Merrill 1975); deFuniak & Vaughn, Principles of Community Property (Univ. of Ariz. Press, 2d ed. 1971); 5 Debtor-Creditor Law Ch. 20 (Matthew Bender 1972). Those who are uninitiated in the law of community property should see Mennell, Community Property in a Nutshell (West 1982), which provides an excellent introduction to community property with considerable discussion of the status of the law of individual community property states.

[239] The eight community property law states are Arizona, California, Idaho, Louisiana, Nevada, New Mexico, Texas, and Washington.

[240] See generally de Funiak & Vaughn, Principles of Community Property (Univ. of Ariz. Press, 2d ed. 1971).

[241] See McClanahan, Community Property Law in the United States 483 (Lawyers' Coop. Publishing Co. 1982).

[242] See N.M. Stat. Ann. § 40-3-9; La. Civ. Code. Ann. art. 2359–2360, 2363.

[243] See, e.g., In re Marriage of Epstein, 24 Cal. 3d 76, 592 P2d 1165, 154 Cal. Rptr. 413 (1979).

[244] See, e.g., Cal. Civ. Proc. Code § 5121; Idaho Code § 32-911.

rate property of the nondebtor spouse.[245] As a review of the law of the eight community-property states reflects, the law is considerably more complex as to whether or not a creditor holding a separate debt may reach community property. Arizona allows a premarriage creditor to reach community property but not a postmarriage creditor or a creditor who holds a separate tort claim.[246] California allows creditors on separate debts to reach community property if the debt is incurred during marriage; as to premarriage separate debts, the matter is less than clear.[247] In Idaho, a creditor may reach the community property to satisfy a separate debt.[248] Louisiana provides that separate creditors may reach community property, although the nondebtor spouse may seek reimbursement if a marital dissolution occurs.[249] The resolution of the issue is uncertain in Nevada.[250] Yet another variation exists in New Mexico, where separate creditors may reach only the debtor spouse's one-half interest in community property.[251] In Texas, a separate creditor on a contract debt may reach the community property that is under the sole control of the debtor spouse or under the joint control of both; as to tort claims, the separate creditor may also reach the community property under the sole control of the nondebtor spouse if the tort occurred during the marriage.[252] Finally, in Washington, a statute enables premarriage separate creditors, tort or contract, to reach earnings of the debtor spouse; otherwise, community property is insulated from creditors' reach if the separate debt is in contract, but is reachable by separate creditors if the debt is in tort.[253]

As to community debts, the creditor may reach community property.[254] However, whether the creditor who holds a community debt may reach the

---

[245] See, e.g., La. Civ. Code. Ann. art. 2345; Tex. Fam. Code Ann. § 5.61; Wash. Rev. Code §§ 26.16.010, 26.16.020, 26.16.190. There are some exceptions to the principle (e.g., debts incurred for necessities in California and Nevada). See Cal. Civ. Proc. Code § 5120; Nev. Rev. Stat. § 123.090.

[246] See Ariz. Rev. Stat. Ann. § 25-215; Schilling v. Embree, 118 Ariz. 236, 575 P2d 1262 (1977). But creditors may not reach community property for the separate intentional torts of a spouse. See Selby v. Savorel, 134 Ariz. 222, 655 P2d 342 (1982).

[247] As to debts incurred during marriage, see Cal. Civ. Proc. Code § 5116. As to premarriage debts, see Cal. Civ. Proc. Code §§ 5120, 5126.

[248] See, e.g., Gusten v. Bryan, 41 Idaho 538, 240 P 600 (1925); Williams v. Paxton, 98 Idaho 155, 559 P2d 1123 (1976).

[249] See La. Civ. Code Ann. art. 2345, 2364.

[250] See Randono v. Turks, 86 Nev. 123, 466 P2d 218 (1970). But see McClanahan, Community Property Law in the United States 493 (Lawyers' Coop. Publishing Co. 1982).

[251] See, N.M. Stat. Ann. § 40-3-10.

[252] See Tex. Fam. Code Ann. §§ 5.01, 522, 5.61(b), 5.61(c); Lawrence v. Hardy, 583 SW2d 795 (Tex. Civ. App. 1979).

[253] See Wash. Rev. Code § 26.16.200; Nat'l Bank of Commerce v. Green, 1 Wash. App. 713, 463 P2d 187 (1969); De Elche v. Jacobsen, 95 Wash. 2d 236, 622 P2d 835 (1980).

[254] See de Funiak & Vaughn, Principles of Community Property § 159 (Univ. of Ariz. Press, 2d ed. 1971); McClanahan, Community Property Law in the United States 495 (Lawyers' Coop. Publishing Co. 1982).

separate property of a spouse is considerably more complex. The basic principle is that a community debt may be satisfied out of separate property; however, the creditor may be required first to exhaust community property before a resort to separate property will be allowed.[255]

## [e] Partnership Property

An individual partner of a general partnership may incur debts for personal, nonpartnership purposes. The creditor may have difficulty in obtaining satisfaction of the individual debt and may obtain judgment and attempt to have it satisfied by judicial means from the debtor's personal assets. If the debtor's personal assets are insufficient to satisfy the judgment, the issue may arise as to whether the creditor may reach either the partnership assets or the interest of the individual in the partnership. Two noted commentators have stated that "[N]o partnership property question has been more confused by the decisions than the right of a partner's separate creditor to attach or levy execution on the share or interest in the firm's property."[256] Although most states have adopted the Uniform Partnership Act (UPA),[257] discussion of this issue will first examine the common law and then will turn to applicable UPA provisions.

The common law provided that a creditor of a partner could "levy" upon his share in partnership property by use of attachment or execution. On the other hand, the rights of nondebtor copartners to have specific partnership property protected and applied only to partnership purposes was given some protection.[258] In effect, the courts began to separate the ownership of the partnership in specific partnership property from the interest of the partner, the latter being only that which is reachable by separate creditors of an individual partner.[259] The question arose of how the individual partner's interest in the partnership could be reached procedurally, since what the sheriff sells at the execution sale is only that interest and not specific assets of the partnership.[260] To have the partnership interest identified, a partnership accounting was necessitated in a court of equity.[261] Pre-UPA legislation attempted to allow separate

---

[255] See id. For authority in the various community property states on this issue, see Ariz. Rev. Stat. Ann. § 25-215; Cal. Civ. Proc. Code § 5122; La. Civ. Code Ann. art. 2345; N.M. Stat. Ann. § 40-3-11; Tex. Fam. Code Ann. § 5.61; National Bank of Commerce v. Green, 1 Wash. App. 713, 463 P2d 187 (1969); Young, "Joint Management and Control of Community Property in Idaho: A Prognosis," 11 Idaho L. Rev. 1 (1974); Crapo, "Equal Management of Community Property: Creditor's Rights," 13 Idaho L. Rev. 177 (1976).

[256] Crane & Bromberg, Law of Partnership 241 (West 1968). See generally on this topic id. at 241–249.

[257] All states have adopted UPA except Georgia, Louisiana, and Mississippi.

[258] See, e.g., Fox v. Hanbury, 2 Comp. 445, 98 Eng. Rep. 1179 (1776).

[259] See, e.g., Darnell v. State Nat'l Bank of Okla. City, 158 P 921, 59 Okla. 204 (1916); R.A. Myles & Co. v. A.D. Davis Packing Co., 17 Ala. App. 85, 81 So. 863 (1919).

[260] See, e.g., Deal v. Bogue, 20 Pa. 228 (1853); Rainey v. Nance, 54 Ill. 29 (1870).

[261] See, e.g., Johnson v. Wingfield, 42 SW 203 (Tenn. Ch. App. 1897); Eighth Nat'l Bank v. Fitch, 49 NY 539 (1872).

creditors to reach a partner's interest without disturbing, to the extent possible, the rights of other partners. These statutes provided that the individual partner's interest could be reached by such measures as garnishment, bill in equity, and constructive seizure by notice served on a partner of the partnership.[262]

UPA has substantially cleared the muddy waters of the common law in prohibiting any attachment or execution of specific partnership property by a creditor of an individual partner.[263] UPA seeks to protect the partnership use of specific partnership property from interference of creditors of individual partners. On the other hand, these creditors are given a procedural vehicle, known as a charging order, that reaches the partnership interest of the individual partner-debtor.[264] The charging order produces a type of lien on the interest in the partnership resulting in payments due the partner-debtor from the partnership being paid to the creditor of the partner-debtor. The charging order has been interpreted as the exclusive means of reaching the individual partnership interest.[265]

---

[262] See, e.g., Ga. Civ. Code § 6022 (1910); Edmunds Shoe Co. v. Colson, 41 Ga. App. 283, 152 SE 608 (1930); Savings & Loan Corp. v. Bear, 155 Va. 312, 154 SE 587 (1930); Karchiones v. Mitsias, 257 Ill. App. 95 (1931); First Nat'l Bank v. White, 268 Ill. App. 414 (1933).

[263] UPA § 25(2)(c). Cf. Buckman v. Goldblatt, 39 Ohio App. 2d 1, 314 NE2d 188 (1974); Weisman v. Martorano, 405 Pa. 369, 175 A2d 873 (1962). Section 25(2)(c) is as follows:

"A partner's right in specific partnership property is not subject to attachment or execution, except on a claim against the partnership. When a partnership property is attached for a partnership debt the partners, or any of them, or the representatives of a deceased partner, cannot claim any right under the homestead or exemption laws."

[264] UPA § 28. Section 28 is as follows:

"[Partner's Interest Subject to Charging Order.] (1) On due application to a competent court by any judgment creditor of a partner, the court which entered the judgment, order, or decree, or any other court, may charge the interest of the debtor partner with payment of the unsatisfied amount of such judgment debt with interest thereon; and may then or later appoint a receiver of his share of the profits, and of any other money due or to fall due to him in respect of the partnership, and make all other orders, directions, accounts and inquiries which the debtor partner might have made, or which the circumstances of the case may require. *See* Reiger v. Reiger, 243 Ark. 113, 419 SW2d 311 (1967).

"(2) The interest charged may be redeemed at any time before foreclosure, or in case of a sale being directed by the court may be purchased without thereby causing a dissolution:

"(a) With separate property, by any one or more of the partners, or

"(b) With partnership property, by any one or more of the partners with the consent of all the partners whose interests are not so charged or sold.

"(3) Nothing in this act shall be held to deprive a partner of his right, if any, under the exemption laws, as regards his interest in the partnership."

[265] See, e.g., Krauth v. First Continental Dev-Con, Inc. 351 So. 2d 1106 (Fla. Dist. Ct. App. 1977).

# III

# COLLECTION OF SECURED DEBTS

# 7

# Secured Transactions Under Article 9 of the Uniform Commercial Code

## ¶ 7.01 INTRODUCTION

### [1] Importance of Being an Article 9 Secured Creditor

This chapter focuses on secured transactions, covered in Article 9 of the Uniform Commercial Code (UCC). Article 9 enables a creditor to obtain a special interest–a "security interest"–in personal property and fixtures of a debtor. This secured creditor has special rights to the debtor's property that are greater than those of the unsecured creditor. These special rights are important both in disputes between the secured creditor and the debtor and in "priority" disputes–disputes between the secured creditor and third-party claimants. As against the debtor, Article 9 gives the secured creditor various rights, one of which is the special right to self-help repossess property subject to a security interest–collateral. As against third-party claimants, a secured creditor generally has a better chance of winning a priority dispute than an unsecured creditor does.

## [2] Legislative Status of Article 9–Use of 1972 Text

Article 9 has been adopted in all states but Louisiana. There are two major versions: the 1962 Text and the 1972 Text.[1] The 1972 Text was a major redraft of the earlier version,[2] and has been adopted in all jurisdictions except Indiana, Kentucky, Louisiana, Missouri, South Carolina, Tennessee, and Vermont. Unless otherwise noted, the discussion here presumes that the 1972 Text is in effect.[3] Article 9 is not completely uniform. State variations, although they are relatively few, do affect the resolution of a number of issues.

## [3] Historical Personal Property Secured Transactions

Devices for securing obligations with an interest in the debtor's personal property existed before the enactment of Article 9. The state laws regulating such pre-UCC security devices were confusing and diverse. Although Article 9 replaces all pre-UCC devices with the unitary security interest,[4] the following brief review of the pre-UCC devices is offered because pre-UCC terminology is often used by both courts and creditors.[5]

### [a] Pledge and Field Warehouse

The earliest and conceptually simplest pre-Article 9 device was the "pledge." The debtor-pledgor gave to the creditor-pledgee personalty that the

---

[1] These are the most frequently used terms to designate the two versions. In fact, the so-called 1962 Text was officially amended in 1966 and most states first adopting the UCC after that date included those amendments.

[2] It was drafted by the Article 9 Review Committee and the Permanent Editorial Board for the UCC under the joint sponsorship of the National Conference of Commissioners of Uniform State Laws and the American Law Institute.

[3] The 1972 Amendments did not completely replace the language of the 1962 Text. Case law before the 1972 version becomes effective may still offer guidance where language has not changed.

[4] See Official Comment 1 to UCC § 9-102.

[5] For more about pre-UCC security devices, see 1 Gilmore, Security Interests in Personal Property 1–288 (Little, Brown 1965).

pledgee was entitled to retain until the debtor paid the underlying obligation. If the debtor defaulted, the pledgee merely retained possession of the debtor's personal property. In addition to securing repayment, possession of the debtor's personal property served to give other potential creditors notice of the first creditor's interest in the debtor's property. The "secret lien" has long been of concern to courts.[6]

At times, instead of taking possession of the debtor's personalty, the pledgee would take possession of documents that represented control over the debtor's personal property. For example, the creditor might accept the pledge of a warehouse receipt issued by an independent warehouse operator. Since the holder of a warehouse receipt is the only party entitled to possession of the goods located in the warehouse, the possession of the document is tantamount to possession of these goods. The creditor's possession of such a document also served to give notice to third parties of the creditor's interest.

The concept of "field warehousing" was developed to avoid the inconvenience and expense of debtors' having to place goods in the hands of the creditor or an independent warehouse operator. The creditor would set up a field warehouse that he controlled wherever the goods were located. However, to protect the collateral from third parties, the operator of the field warehouse had to exercise "open, unequivocal, exclusive possession," or else the creditor's interest in the debtor's property were not likely to be protected against third parties. Thus, creditors generally were forced to physically cordon off part of the debtor's business place as a warehouse and hire agents (sometimes also employees of the debtor) to watch over the warehouse goods.[7]

### [b] Chattel Mortgage

Obviously, neither the pledge nor field warehousing were advisable when the debtor needed free use of personalty such as equipment used in the manufacturing process or as inventory. Thus was introduced the chattel mortgage. The concept of the chattel mortgage was patterned after the law of real estate mortgages. The borrower would retain possession and use of the collateral. If the borrower defaulted, the mortgage gave the creditor the right to seize the chattels and sell them, using the net proceeds of the sale to reduce the indebtedness. The creditor was required to repay any surplus from the sale of the collateral to the borrower, and the borrower in turn was liable for any deficiency if the proceeds from the sale did not cover the debt.

Since the borrower remained in possession of the chattels with no notice to third parties of the creditor's interest, many states passed legislation requiring public recording of chattel mortgages modeled on real estate recording laws. Chattel mortgage laws were diverse and were interpreted differently from state

[6] See, e.g., Clow v. Woods, 5 Serg. & Rawle 275 (Pa. 1819).

[7] See generally Skilton, "Field Warehousing as a Financing Device," 1961 Wis. L. Rev. 221.

to state on important issues such as the ability of a filed mortgage to attach to property acquired by the debtor after the initial transaction.[8]

### [c] Conditional Sales Contract

The "conditional sale" was used in both commercial and consumer sales transactions. The seller retained legal title to the property sold until the buyer paid the full purchase price plus any finance charges. If a debtor-buyer failed to pay, the contract provided that possession of the property would revert to the seller.

The conditional sales contract differed in several respects from the chattel mortgage. First, it had to arise out of a sales transaction and could not include as collateral any property not already owned by the debtor. Second, a seller had to elect either to repossess the collateral with no claim to any amount due or to sue for the balance of the purchase price without repossession. Third, in many states only a seller and not a lender could use the device.

Some state legislatures abolished the requirement of election of remedies since chattel mortgagees were not faced with the same choice. The majority of states required the public filing of conditional sales contracts.[9]

### [d] Trust Receipt

The trust receipt grew out of the need for a type of security device for a loan made to a borrower to enable him to purchase goods for resale. Chattel mortgage financing was impractical in most states because a new filing was required either when any piece of inventory was acquired or to discharge collateral that was sold. Conditional sales contracts generally did not preserve the seller's interest when the debtor sold inventory, and they did not provide security for lenders. In trust receipt financing, the borrower acknowledged that the creditor, having paid the party who sold the goods to the debtor, held legal title to the goods. The borrower further agreed that the goods were received and held in trust for the creditor, and upon resale the creditor was to receive the proceeds received by the debtor upon sale. The creditor was entitled to possession of the collateral upon the debtor's default.[10]

### [e] Accounts Receivable

A major asset of some businesses is the amount of money owed to them on open account–simple accounts receivable. *X*, for example, promises to buy 30,000 widgets from *Y* and to pay for the widgets within thirty days of delivery. The amounts owed to *Y* are valuable property rights, which, if accepted as collateral, could broaden *Y*'s ability to borrow. In fact, "accounts receivable

---

[8] See Cohen & Gerber, "The After-Acquired Property Clause," 87 U. Pa. L. Rev. 635 (1939).

[9] See generally 1 Gilmore, Security Interests in Personal Property 62–75 (Little, Brown 1965).

[10] Id. at 86–127.

financing" became a major form of lending in this century. Most state statutes on this type of financing were enacted in the late 1940s and 1950s. These statutes influenced the UCC's treatment of intangibles.[11]

### [f] Factor's Lien

The factor's lien arose through the use of independent commissioned sales agents ("factors") by textile manufacturers in the Northeast. From time to time, factors would loan money to the principal for processing more inventory. The factors then would apply the proceeds of any sales made against the debt owed by the manufacturer. As textile manufacturers (and later, other manufacturers) that were financed by factors began to use their own sales forces instead of independent agents, factors no longer worked as selling agents, although they continued to loan money for financing the manufacturer's business. They used the manufacturer's existing and future inventory as collateral for their loans.

In everyday practice, the factor's lien was similar to field warehousing in that the manufacturer segregated the inventory subject to the lien and an independent warehouseman had control over the collateral. The practice of factor financing became so widespread that states passed legislation to control its operation. "Factor" was statutorily defined as one who advanced money with only goods or merchandise as collateral; equipment, machinery, and trade fixtures were excluded.[12]

## [4] Where to Find the Law

### [a] Overview of Article 9

Article 9 of the UCC replaced the previously discussed devices with a unitary "security interest" in personal property and fixtures. The major provisions of Article 9 do the following:

(1) Define the scope of Article 9;
(2) Specify how a creditor gains a security interest;
(3) Provide for resolution of disputes between the creditor and debtor;
(4) Specify how a secured creditor "perfects" its security interest (generally a prerequisite for a secured creditor to win priority against third-party claimants); and
(5) Provide for a resolution of priority disputes over collateral between a secured creditor and third-party claimants.

In analyzing the provisions of Article 9 (or for that matter, any other article of the UCC), Article 1 also may be critical. Article 1 applies generally throughout the UCC. It provides most of the UCC's definitions,[13] emphasizes

---

[11] Id. at 250–286.

[12] Id. at 128–145.

[13] See, e.g., UCC § 1-201.

the importance of trade usage and course of dealing,[14] incorporates concepts of common law (unless UCC provisions are in conflict),[15] and indicates the underlying requirement of good faith throughout all transactions.[16]

### [b] Relevance of Law Outside Article 9

**[i] Other Provisions of the Uniform Commercial Code.** There is a significant overlap of Article 9 of the UCC with Article 2, which regulates the sale of goods.[17] There also is some minor overlap with Articles 5 through 8, mostly involving Article 9's use of relevant definitions from those Articles.[18] When necessary, reference will be made to the appropriate sections outside Article 9.

**[ii] Consumer Law.** Chapters 1 through 4 of this book address the nature of protections for debtors in consumer transactions. Such transactions are generally defined under most state and federal laws as transactions in which the debtor has purchased or services or has received a loan for personal, family, or houschold purposes. Article 9 defers to such consumer law. If a consumer protection law gives a consumer rights in a particular transaction, those rights exist regardless of what the language of Article 9 appears to say about the rights of the debtor.[19] Consumer law controlling secured transaction issues is of greatest importance with respect to:

(1) Certain disclosures that must be made to consumers at the time of the consummation of a consumer credit transaction;
(2) Limitations on types of collateral that can be subject to a security interest;
(3) Rights of the debtor upon an alleged default, including:
   (a) Whether a default exists;
   (b) Rights to repossess the collateral; and
   (c) Limitations on deficiency judgments.

This chapter refers to relevant consumer law. Of course, research is never complete until relevant state and federal consumer law has been reviewed.

**[iii] Federal Law and State Variations.** As with all state laws, there is the possibility of federal preemption of Article 9 provisions.[20] The UCC

---

14 See UCC § 1-205.

15 See UCC § 1-103.

16 See UCC § 1-203.

17 The major overlap concerns the status of an unpaid seller against a creditor with a security interest in the buyer's goods. This dispute is addressed at infra ¶ 7.07[11].

18 For example, a "transferee in bulk" may have priority as against an unperfected secured creditor. UCC § 9-301(1)(c). For the definition of bulk transfers, see UCC § 6-102.

19 Official Note to UCC §§ 9-102, 9-203.

20 See infra ¶ 7.02[4][a].

explicitly recognizes this in Section 9-104(a). In addition, Article 9 of the UCC is not the same in each state. As previously discussed,[21] most states have adopted the 1972 version of Article 9, but since specific provisions may vary, the reader is advised to check local law.

### [c] Official Comments

When the drafters of Article 9 prepared the official language of the proposed statutory provisions, they also prepared Official Comments. However, no state has adopted these comments as law. The statutory language of the section is the law. The Official Comments represent the drafters' interpretations of the statues. Sometimes the comments are very helpful, and, as might be expected, judges often look to such comments for guidance. However, the comments often are not helpful because they are unclear; frequently they are also simply ignored. The Official Comments may seem to go beyond the meaning of the statutory language. In such cases, courts may or may not take the direction suggested by the comments. Obviously, the law practitioner cannot ignore them, and may find them helpful to her understanding of a provision. More importantly, lawyers involved in litigation should be prepared to use the comments to their advantage and to rebut any opponent's use of them.

### [d] Case Law

Occasionally, pre-UCC cases assist in understanding how a particular jurisdiction might interpret a UCC provision. A review of the form of the particular transaction at issue and the introduction to pre-UCC security devices at the beginning of this chapter gives some indication as to the relevancy of pre-UCC cases.[22] Research of case law interpreting the UCC is facilitated by the *Uniform Commercial Code Reporting Service*.[23]

## ¶ 7.02 SCOPE OF ARTICLE 9

### [1] Introduction

Correct determination of whether Article 9 is applicable to a specific transaction can have great practical significance. For example, if a creditor wrongly assumes that Article 9 is applicable and takes possession of a debtor's

---

[21] See supra ¶ 7.01[2].

[22] For example, if a secured creditor is arguing perfection was obtained by possession, pre-UCC cases as to when a creditor had possession under pre-UCC law on pledges might be of assistance. Pre-UCC cases are of less importance now because of the increasing number of well-reasoned opinions interpreting the UCC.

[23] This publication, by Callaghan, consists of over forty hardbound volumes with looseleaf advance sheets that purport to contain all reported decisions interpreting the UCC. See also the Commerce Clearing House (CCH) Secured Transactions Guide, which contains, among other services, summaries of UCC decisions.

property without judicial process, the debtor may have an action in conversion against the creditor. Self-help repossession is a right available only to an Article 9 secured creditor. On the other hand, if the creditor wrongly assumes that Article 9 is *not* applicable, the creditor may fail to take steps—steps to perfect a security interest, for example—that would have protected the creditor from third parties in a priority dispute.

In order to determine whether Article 9 is applicable the creditor should:

(1) Determine whether there is an intent to create a security interest in personal property or fixtures.[1] This will require a determination of:
    (a) Whether the definition of "security interest" has been met; and
    (b) Whether the interest is in "personal property or fixtures."
(2) Determine whether there is a sale of "accounts" or "chattel paper."
(3) Regardless of whether the first or second steps have been met, determine whether the transaction is excluded by UCC Section 9-104.

## [2] Intent to Create a Security Interest in Personal Property or Fixtures

It is usually not difficult to determine whether personal property or fixtures are involved: The physical form of the collateral will typically make this evident. Occasionally, however, it is difficult to distinguish between real property and personal property and to determine the meaning of "fixtures" adopted in the relevant jurisdiction.[2]

"Intent" to create an Article 9 security interest typically will be shown in most secured transactions by the existence of a security agreement with a provision stating that the debtor gives an interest in the debtor's personal property or fixtures to secure the obligation.[3] In personal property leases and consignments, it may be difficult to determine whether the requisite intent exists.

### [a] Personal Property Leases

**[i] Reasons for Leasing.** Leasing of personal property is a multi-billion-dollar business. Although it is an old concept, its major growth began after World War II, probably because of the tax advantages of leasing over outright purchase. Although many of these tax advantages are now minor,[4] leasing continues to grow because of other perceived advantages. For example, leasing may require a smaller initial cash outlay for needed equipment. Leasing may

---

[1] UCC § 9-102.

[2] See the discussion of the real property exclusion at 7.02[4][j] and the discussion of the meaning of the term "fixture" at infra ¶ 7.07[8][a].

[3] Security agreements are discussed at infra ¶ 7.04[2].

[4] See generally Coogan, "Is There a Difference Between a Long-Term Lease and an Installment Sale of Personal Property," 56 N.Y.U. L. Rev. 1036 (1981).

also enable the lessee to more quickly and cheaply adapt to technical advances in needed equipment.

**[ii] Reasons for Distinguishing Between Leases and Other Transactions.** Whatever the commercial advantages, leasing poses a potential headache for the lawyer. Distinguishing between the lease that is not really a lease and the true lease is important because applicable law may vary. To illustrate the difference in the legal consequences, first consider two types of leases. One type of lease may arise when a manufacturer leases its product rather than selling it. A lease may also arise between a financial institution, as the lessor, and a party seeking the manufacturer's product, as the lessee. Because the party who wants the equipment is better able to judge its own needs, the financial institution may have that party choose the equipment. The financial institution may then purchase the equipment and lease it to the party seeking the equipment—a leaseback.

In disputes between a "lessor" and a "lessee," whether or not a true lease is involved may determine whether Article 2 of the UCC—Sales—is applicable. Assume there is a lease of the first type described above between a manufacturer, *M*, and contractor, *C*. If the equipment is destroyed through no fault of either party while the goods are in shipment, who should bear the risk of loss, *M* or *C*? Should the risk issue be decided by the rules of the UCC Article 2 on sales of goods or should the risk issue be decided by resorting to the laws on personal property leasing?[5] Whether or not a true lease is involved may also determine the applicability of laws outside the UCC. In the leasing arrangement with a financial institution as the lessor, should the financial institution be concerned about the laws of usury? If the lease is in fact merely a loan of money to allow the lessee to acquire the goods, usury may be relevant. If a true lease is involved, usury probably is not relevant.[6]

---

[5] See, e.g., Centurian Corp. v. Cripps, 624 P2d 706, 34 UCC Rep. Serv. 525 (Utah 1981) (involving risk-of-loss issue). Personal property leasing law was historically included within "bailment for hire" decisions. More recently courts have looked to real estate and landlord-tenant law by analogy. See Mooney, "Personal Property Leasing: A Challenge," 36 Bus. Law. 1605, 1606–1607.

[6] Usury is discussed at ¶ 3.01. In many states there is no usury limitation on commercial transactions. However, leasing has become a popular way for individuals to acquire automobiles for their own personal use, and usury still is of relevance in most consumer transactions.

In consumer transactions, a variety of other laws may be relevant to a lease; for example, the Consumer Leasing Act of the federal Consumer Credit Protection Act (CCPA), Pub. L. No. 94-240, 15 USC §§ 1667 et seq. Also, some states have provisions that apply equally to consumer leases and sales and loans. See, e.g., Wis. Stat. Ann. § 425.105. Where a lease is involved, and a consumer alleges protections under consumer law not directly applicable to true leases, the lessor is likely to argue that the state consumer law is inapplicable. Recently, state courts appear to more carefully scrutinize consumer leases in order to determine whether the lease was really a disguised sale or a loan subject to the state's consumer protection laws.

The focus of this part is the applicability of UCC Article 9 to leases.[7] In the example of the leasing by the manufacturer, if there is not a true lease, there is a sale and the interest of the manufacturer in the "leased" goods is at best a security interest subject to Article 9. In the second example, if a true lease is not involved, there is a loan and the financial institution's interest in the goods is a security interest subject to Article 9.[8]

Most cases involving the issue of the true lease versus the Article 9 secured transaction involve priority disputes, where a "lessor" is claiming the right to keep "leased" goods as against claims of third parties. In such cases, the lessor generally has failed to perfect a security interest because he did not anticipate the applicability of Article 9. If Article 9 is found to be applicable, the lessor-creditor who has failed to perfect his security interest is likely to lose the priority dispute with third-party claimants. If a true lease is involved, the lessor is likely to win any dispute with third parties; perfection is irrelevant in such a case.

Another type of case involving the true lease versus the Article 9 secured transaction concerns a dispute between the lessor and lessee. The lessee has defaulted on the lease agreement and the lessor acquires possession of the leased goods. An action arises when the lessor sues the lessee for damages for breach of the lease. As part of his defense, the lessee claims that the lessor did not follow the rules of Article 9 concerning the disposition of repossessed collateral. If Article 9 is applicable, the lessor must follow the Article 9 disposition rules. If a true lease is involved, the Article 9 procedure is not directly applicable.[9]

**[iii] Perfecting a Security Interest Whether or Not a Lease Exists.** The 1972 Amendments provide some relief for the lessor who is uncertain whether or not there is a true lease. The lessor may file a financing statement, and thus generally achieve perfected status, even if a true lease exists. The UCC provides that this act of filing does not prejudice a decision on whether a transaction involves a lease or a transaction covered by Article 9.[10] In states that have adopted the 1972 Amendments, the lessor should take advantage of this permissive filing.

---

[7] The case law on a true lease versus an Article 9 secured transaction is often used to assist a court in resolving the types of disputes raised in the last paragraph. For example, case law demonstrating that a particular type of lease between a manufacturer and a lessee involves a secured transaction is relevant in a case concerning the applicability of Article 2 on a sale of goods. This is because a decision that the manufacturer's interest in the leased goods is really an Article 9 security interest in the goods in tantamount to a finding that the manufacturer had sold the goods to the lessee.

[8] See generally Mooney, "Personal Property Leasing: A Challenge," 36 Bus. Law. 1605 (1981).

[9] But see W.L. Scott, Inc. v. Madras Aerotech, Inc., 103 Idaho 736, 653 P2d 791, 35 UCC Rep. Serv. 956 (1982) (true lease found but UCC § 9-504(3) still applied by analogy).

[10] UCC § 9-408.

The permissive filing provision is not helpful if there is a dispute between a creditor and a debtor over the disposition of leased goods. Perfection is relevant only with respect to disputes with third-party claimants; it does not affect the rights of a secured creditor and a debtor. To hedge his bets concerning the obligations toward the lessee, the lessor who is unsure of whether he has a true lease might, instead of perfecting, follow the commercial-reasonableness restraints of Article 9 on the disposition of collateral. If the court finds that there was an Article 9 secured transaction, the Article 9 restrictions on disposition will have been met. If the court finds a true lease, the lessor will not be in violation of leasing law merely because he has followed the Article 9 restrictions.[11]

**[iv] Determining Whether a Lease Is Meant for Security.** There has been a good deal of litigation concerning whether a lease of personal property is in fact a true lease or one intended for security. The issue is resolved by determining whether the parties involved intended to create a security interest. However, a phrase in a lease stating that it is intended to be a true lease is not controlling.[12]

Case law demonstrates that the decisive factor in determining whether a security interest exists is whether, under the purported lease, the lessee will ultimately gain de facto ownership of the leased property.[13] Consistent with this approach, some courts have found that when a lease covers a period that matches the useful life of the personal property leased, a security interest presumably is intended.[14]

Open-end leases often provide that at the end of the lease term the lessor will sell the leased goods. These leases also generally provide that if the resale price is less than a specified figure, the lessee must account for the deficiency. If the resale price is greater than that figure, the lessee is entitled to a surplus. Several courts have held that this type of arrangement indicates the acquisition by the lessee of an ownership interest in the leased goods and, therefore, indicates that a security interest was intended.[15]

---

[11] See, e.g., American Standard Credit, Inc. v. National Cement Co., 643 F2d 248, 31 UCC Rep. Serv. 229 (5th Cir. 1981).

[12] See, e.g., In re Coors of Cumberland, Inc., 19 Bankr. 313, 34 UCC Rep. Serv. 241 (MD Tenn. 1982).

[13] See, e.g., id.; U.S. Fidelity & Guar. Co. v. Thompson & Green Mach. Co., 568 SW2d 821, 23 UCC Rep. Serv. 849 (Tenn. 1978); W.L. Scott, Inc. v. Madras Aerotech, Inc., 103 Idaho 736, 653 P2d 791, 35 UCC Rep. Serv. 956 (1982) (true lease found but UCC § 9-504(3) still applied by analogy); In re Coors of Cumberland, Inc., 19 Bankr. 313, 34 UCC Rep. Serv. 241 (MD Tenn. 1982).

[14] See, e.g., National Equip. Rental, Ltd. v. Priority Elecs. Corp., 435 F. Supp. 236, 22 UCC Rep. Serv. 280 (EDNY 1977).

[15] See, e.g., In re Tulsa Port Warehouse Co., Inc., 690 F2d 809, 34 UCC Rep. Serv. 1357 (10th Cir. 1982) (one factor among others showing security interest intended); In re Tillery, 571 F2d 1361, 23 UCC Rep. Serv. 1335 (5th Cir. 1978) (this was one factor among others that the court felt showed that a security interest was intended).

The UCC also recognizes that acquisition of de facto ownership over the period of the lease is important in determining whether a security interest was intended. Under the UCC, the one factor specified as demonstrating that the parties intended a security interest is a provision that the lessee "shall become or has the option to become the owner of the property for no additional consideration or for a nominal consideration."[16] Not surprisingly, in trying to determine whether a lease is in fact a true lease or an Article 9 security interest, most courts start with whether or not there is an option to purchase and, if so, whether it can be exercised for no additional consideration or for a nominal consideration.

Generally, if the lessee has an option to purchase, the option is evident on the face of the lease. If not, courts have been willing to find that one exists on the basis of evidence of a side oral agreement for the option.[17] In a recent case decided by the Court of Appeals for the Seventh Circuit, the court held that, when there is a right by the lessee to terminate the lease before the date when the option arises under the lease agreement, there is no option to purchase within the meaning of the UCC.[18]

When there is an option to purchase, the next question is whether the option allows the lessee to purchase the leased goods for no consideration or for a nominal consideration. If the lessee must pay the fair market value for the goods at the time of the exercise of the option, courts are generally agreed that the option price is not "nominal." However, although the option price is set at "fair market value," it may be that the lease has run long enough that the fair market value is itself nominal.[19] The courts have adopted the following three approaches in determining whether the option price is nominal:

(1) Comparing the price needed to exercise the option with the original list price or cost of the property;

---

[16] UCC § 1-201(37). The provision also states that an option to purchase in itself (with the option price something other than nominal consideration) is not determinative of the existence of a security interest.

[17] See, e.g., In re Brookside Drug Store, Inc., 3 Bankr. 120, 29 UCC Rep. Serv. 230 (D. Conn. 1980); see also FMA Fin. Corp. v. Pro-Printers, 590 P2d 803, 25 UCC Rep. Serv. 950 (Utah 1979) (evidence of trade usage and course of dealing showing that lessor always offering customers an oral option to purchase was admissible even though the written agreement contained an integration clause excluding all parol evidence; such evidence is generally recognized as outside the parol evidence rule and therefore not subject to the effect of integration clauses). But cf. NBC Leasing Co. v. Stilwell, 334 NW2d 496, 36 UCC Rep. Serv. 625 (SD 1983) (no option to purchase found where there was no oral or written option and lessor's past dealings with other lessees was sometimes to offer leased goods for sale but other times to demand their return).

[18] In re Marhoefer Packing Co., 674 F2d 1139, 33 UCC Rep. Serv. 370 (7th Cir. 1982); see also Union Bank v. John Deere Indus. Dev. Co., 387 So. 2d 787, 29 UCC Rep. Serv. 1436 (Ala. 1980); Arnold Mach. Co. v. Balls, 624 P2d 678, 34 UCC Rep. Serv. 236 (Utah 1981).

[19] See, e.g., American Standard Credit, Inc. v. National Cement Co., 643 F2d 248, 31 UCC Rep. Serv. 229 (5th Cir. 1981); In re Coors of Cumberland, Inc., 19 Bankr. 313, 34 UCC Rep. Serv. 241 (MD Tenn. 1982).

(2) Comparing the option price with "sensible alternatives";

(3) Comparing the option price to the fair market value of the property at the time the option is to be exercised.[20]

Under the first test the courts have generally found that, if the option price is over 25 percent of the original price, the option price is not "nominal."[21] The sensible-alternative test requires a determination of whether the lessee, as a reasonable commercial entity, would have no reasonable economic alternative but to exercise the option and buy the leased goods. If the only sensible alternative would be to exercise the option, the courts using this test would find that the option price was nominal and a security interest was intended. There are fewer cases in which the court has applied the third test. No percentage tests have been suggested. Recently the Alaska Supreme Court refused to overturn as clearly erroneous a lower court holding that an option price of 20 percent of the fair market value at the time of the exercise of the option was not nominal.[22]

Courts often use all three tests in reaching their conclusion. Generally, if the court finds a nominal consideration under one test it finds nominal consideration under the other tests.[23] However, recently one court that had previously assumed that the three tests would yield the same result renounced its position and chose instead to compare the option price with the value of the property at the time the option was to be exercised.[24]

Even if there is no option to purchase, or there is an option to purchase and the consideration is more than nominal, the court may still find that the lease is intended for security. Above, there was a discussion of the general importance of factors indicating that the lessee is acquiring an ownership interest in the leased goods. Some other factors that have been found to be of importance in showing an intended security interest rather than a lease are:

(1) Status of the lessor as a financer[25]

(2) Acceleration of rental payments upon default[26]

---

[20] Federal Sign & Signal Corp. v. Berry, 601 SW2d 137, 29 UCC Rep. Serv. 1404 (Tex. Civ. App. 1980).

[21] See, e.g., In re AAA Mach. Co., Inc., 30 Bankr. 323, 36 UCC Rep. Serv. 287 (Bankr. SD Fla. 1983); In re International Plastic, Inc., 18 Bankr. 583, 33 UCC Rep. Serv. 1080 (D. Kan. 1982).

[22] Western Enters., Inc. v. Arctic Office Mach., Inc., 667 P2d 1232, 36 UCC Rep. Serv. 1331 (Alaska 1983).

[23] See, e.g., FMA Fin. Corp. v. Pro-Printers, 590 P2d 803, 25 UCC Rep. Serv. 950 (Utah 1979).

[24] Western Enters., Inc. v. Arctic Office Mach., Inc., 667 P2d 1232, 36 UCC Rep. Serv. 1331 (Alaska 1983).

[25] See, e.g., In re Lockwood, 16 UCC Rep. Serv. 195 (Bankr. D. Conn. 1973).

[26] See, e.g., All-States Leasing Co. v. Ochs, 42 Ore. App. 319, 600 P2d 899, 27 UCC Rep. Serv. 808 (1979).

(3) The lessee is to bear the risk of loss[27]
(4) The lessee is to pay for taxes and repairs[28]
(5) The goods are fixtures that are difficult to remove[29]

### [b] Consignments

There are various forms of consignment arrangements between sellers and buyers of goods. The most typical is a type of bailment arrangement in which the buyer takes possession of the seller's goods with the understanding that the buyer will resell the goods to her own customers. The UCC has two major provisions concerning consignments.[30] These sections specify certain duties for the true consignor-seller who desires to have rights over the consigned goods that are superior to claims by other creditors of the buyer-consignee. The rights of the consignor, and steps necessary to protect these rights, are not unlike those for the secured creditor. For example, in almost every case in which a true consignor wants to win against third-party claimants, the consignor must file notice of his consignment interest.[31] The filings that are required for the true consignor are essentially the same as those that are required for the Article 9 secured creditor.

Section 9-114 requires that a consignor who wants to win against prior secured creditors claiming an interest in after-acquired inventory must also meet other requirements that are equivalent to those required of a purchase-money secured creditor who wants priority against such secured creditors.[32] But there are also differences: An unperfected secured creditor wins priority disputes against unsecured general creditors.[33] Apparently, a true consignor who has not filed would generally lose against even unsecured creditors.[34]

Given the differing treatment of the consignment and security interest, it is important to distinguish between them. Whether or not a consignment is considered a true consignment or a security interest depends, as with personal property leases, on whether the consignor and consignee intended the creation of a security interest or whether a true consignment was intended.[35] Before the

---

[27] See, e.g., id.; Leasing Service Corp. v. American Nat'l Bank & Trust Co., 19 UCC Rep. Serv. 252 (DNJ 1976).

[28] See, e.g., All-States Leasing Co. v. Ochs, 42 Ore. App. 319, 600 P2d 899, 27 UCC Rep. Serv. 808 (1979); National Equip. Rental v. Priority Elecs. Corp., 435 F. Supp. 236, 22 UCC Rep. Serv. 280 (EDNY 1977).

[29] See, e.g., WOCO v. Benjamin Franklin Corp., 20 UCC 1015 (DNH 1976), aff'd, 562 F2d 1339 (1st Cir. 1977).

[30] UCC §§ 2-326, 9-114.

[31] Id.

[32] See UCC § 9-312(3), discussed at infra ¶ 7.07[4][c]. Unless otherwise specified, in the text of this chapter "Section" refers to a section of the UCC.

[33] UCC § 9-201, discussed at infra ¶ 7.07[2].

[34] UCC § 2-326(3). See generally Dolan, "The UCC's Consignment Rule Needs an Exception for Consumer," 44 Ohio St. L.J. 21 (1983).

[35] UCC §§ 9-102, 1-201(37). But see Limor Diamonds, Inc. v. D'Oro by Christopher, 558 F. Supp. 709, 35 UCC Rep. Serv. 1509 (SDNY 1983); Bufkor, Inc. v. Star

UCC was drafted, the key criterion was whether the consignee-buyer had a right to return the goods that could not be denied by the consignor.[36] This is still recognized as an important test.[37] (It has been suggested that the test should be whether the consignment is one that is functionally equivalent to floor plan financing.[38]) Another classic test was whether the consignment was done in order to fix prices—once the major reason for true consignments. If so, the consignment was a true consignment.[39] Because price control in this form is now generally disallowed, the price-fixing test no longer seems relevant. However, the consignor may still engage in consignments primarily to control the buyer for other purposes (e.g., controlling service facilities). If so, the consignment should not normally be considered as one intended for security.

Section 9-408 offers some protection for the consignor who is uncertain about the status of the consignment. The consignor may file a financing statement. If the consignment is later found to be a secured transaction, the filing will help to establish the priority of the creditor. The filing does not establish per se that the consignment was intended as security.[40]

### [c] Security Interests Arising Under Article 2—Sales

A seller of goods on credit can, like any other creditor, obtain a security interest that arises under the provisions of Article 9.[41] The seller and buyer and other parties can also obtain security interests arising solely under Article 2—Sales. A seller of goods can obtain a security interest arising solely from Article 2:

(1) By reserving title in goods sold;[42]

---

Jewelry Co., Inc., 552 SW2d 522, 22 UCC Rep. Serv. 388 (Tex. Civ. App. 1977) (holding that intent is irrelevant).

[36] See 1 Gilmore, Security Interests in Personal Property 338 (Little, Brown 1965).

[37] See, e.g., Allsop v. Ernst, 20 Bankr. 627, 34 UCC Rep. Serv. 85 (SD Ohio 1982).

[38] White & Summers, Uniform Commercial Code 887 (West, 2d ed. 1980).

[39] Columbia Int'l Corp. v. Kempler, 46 Wis. 2d 550, 175 NW2d 465, 7 UCC Rep. Serv. 650 (1970); see also In re A & T Kwik-N-Handi, Inc., 13 UCC Rep. Serv. 779 (Bankr. MD Ga. 1973); Clark Oil & Ref. Co. v. Liddicoat, 65 Wis. 2d 612, 223 NW2d 530, 15 UCC Rep. Serv. 1145 (1974).

[40] A note of caution, however: If a true consignment does exist, more than simple filing is necessary to protect the consignor against secured creditors who are financing the inventory of the buyer-consignee. UCC § 9-114.

Also, the permissive filing provision is not helpful if there is a dispute between a creditor and a debtor over the disposition of consigned goods. Perfection is relevant only with respect to disputes with third-party claimants. Instead of perfecting, to hedge its bets concerning the obligations toward the consignee, the consignor who is unsure of whether it has a true consignment might follow the commercial-reasonableness restraints of Article 9 on the disposition of collateral. See infra ¶ 7.05.

[41] These provisions are discussed at infra ¶ 7.04.

[42] UCC § 2-401.

(2) By procurement of a negotiable bill of lading[43] or of a nonnegotiable bill of lading issued to the seller's order;[44]

(3) Through the seller's rights of stoppage of goods in transit and resale rights.[45]

A buyer, on rightful rejection or justifiable revocation of acceptance, obtains an Article 2 security interest in the goods purchased for any payments made and other costs incurred.[46] A financing agent may obtain a security interest arising solely under Article 2 by purchasing for value a draft relating to goods sold.[47] Certain agents "in the position of a seller" may obtain a security interest arising solely under Article 2 that is like that of the seller.[48]

The use of the term "security interest" in Article 2 was meant to bring these interests within the scope of Article 9. Section 9-113 provides:

> A security interest arising solely under the Article on Sales (Article 2) is subject to the provisions of this Article except that to the extent that and so long as the debtor does not have or does not lawfully obtain possession of the goods
>
> (a) no security agreement is necessary to make the security interest enforceable;
>
> (b) no filing is required to perfect the security interest; and
>
> (c) the rights of the secured party on default by the debtor are governed by the Article on Sales (Article 2).

The effect of this provision is to place the same rights and restrictions on the Article 2 security interest as on the Article 9 security interest except that the Article 2 security interest holder is entitled to the special rights of Section 9-113. These special rights exist only so long as the "debtor" (the buyer in the case of the seller's security interest; the seller in the case of the buyer's security interest) does not get possession of the goods. Once possession is gained from the debtor, the Article 2 security interest is treated the same as one that is taken under Article 9.

## [3] Sale of Accounts and Chattel Paper

Accounts or chattel paper may be intentionally assigned as security for an obligation. If so, the obligation is covered by Section 9-102(1)(a), which requires an intent to create a security interest. Without regard to intent, sales of

---

[43] UCC § 2505(1)(a).

[44] UCC § 2-505(1)(b).

[45] UCC §§ 2-703, 2-705, 2-706. Official Comment 1 to UCC § 9-113 states that these rights are similar to the rights of a secured party.

[46] UCC § 2-711.

[47] UCC § 2-506.

[48] UCC § 2-707.

accounts and chattel paper are also normally included within the scope of Article 9.[49] The drafters of the UCC included these sales because it is often unclear when the parties have intended to create a security interest or have conducted a simple sale of such intangibles.[50]

"Account" is one classification of collateral under Article 9.[51] The term is defined as a "right to payment for goods sold or for services rendered which is not evidenced by an instrument or chattel paper."[52] The account, then, is simply the long-recognized right to payment for goods sold or for services rendered, commonly called the "account receivable." Chattel paper is a writing or writings that "evidence both a monetary obligation and a security interest in or a lease of specific goods."[53]

**EXAMPLE 1:** *A* sells 5,000 bolts on credit to *B*. *B*'s obligation to pay is not evidenced by an "instrument" (under Section 9-105, typically a negotiable instrument such as a promissory note or check) or by chattel paper. If *A* used *B*'s obligation to pay as collateral securing *A*'s loan from the bank, or sold the obligation to the bank, the bank would have a security interest in an account.[54]

**EXAMPLE 2:** In Example 1, if *B* had signed a written contract with *A* for the purchase of the 5,000 bolts, and with the contract *B* had also granted *A* a security interest in specific goods to insure *B*'s payment for the bolts, the paper containing the obligation plus the grant of the interest is chattel paper. That is, if *A* uses this combination document, representing both a monetary obligation for goods sold and a security interest in the goods, as security for *A*'s loan from bank, the bank has a security interest in chattel paper.[55]

---

[49] UCC § 9-102(1)(b). Note that this is subject to the exclusions of UCC § 9-104. See in particular UCC § 9-104(f), which relates to accounts and chattel paper discussed at infra ¶ 7.02[4][f].

[50] Official Comment 2 to UCC § 9-102.

[51] Collateral, the personal property or fixtures subject to a security interest, may fall within any one of several classifications depending primarily on the debtor's use of the collateral. The importance of classifications, the types, and the definitions of the other classifications are discussed at infra ¶ 7.03.

[52] UCC § 9-106.

[53] UCC § 9-105(1)(b). Charters or other contracts involving the use or hire of a vessel are not included within the definition.

[54] Under the 1962 Text, the UCC had another classification, "contract rights," which was very similar to "accounts." The distinction was that the contract right was a right to payment when the right had not yet been earned by performance. The contract right classification was deleted in the 1972 Text because rarely did it make a difference in the UCC whether an "account" or "contract right" was involved.

[55] Another example of chattel paper is the retail installment contract or conditional sales contract. This contract typically contains a contractual obligation to pay plus a grant of a security interest in the goods sold. If the seller used this contract as

Note that the collateral cannot be both an account and chattel paper. An account does not exist if it is represented by chattel paper.[56]

## [4] Specific Statutory Exclusions From Coverage

Before a final determination is made concerning the coverage of Article 9, it must be determined whether the transaction at issue is excluded from coverage by the terms of Section 9-104. The twelve exclusions listed under Section 9-104 are discussed in the following sections in the order in which they appear in the UCC.

### [a] Federal Preemption

Because the UCC is state law, federal law prevails to the extent that Congress has shown its intent to preempt the UCC. Congress has not seen fit to totally preempt Article 9 coverage. On the contrary, where a federal statute does not directly conflict with the UCC, the UCC as adopted in the state where the transaction took place will be the controlling law in a federal forum.[57]

There are some federal statutes that do control over Article 9 provisions. For the most part such statutes are restricted to dictating how to perfect with respect to certain types of collateral.[58] These statutes provide that perfection is to be accomplished by following the federal statute; thus, they preempt Article 9's perfection rules.

**[i] Federal Aviation Act.** Most litigation concerning federal preemption concerns the coverage of the Federal Aviation Act (FAA) of 1958.[59] The FAA controls how to perfect an interest in aircraft; state law determines who has priority in the aircraft.[60] A secured creditor cannot win against innocent third-party claimants unless the creditor has recorded pursuant to the FAA.[61]

**[ii] Ship Mortgage Act.** The Ship Mortgage Act of 1920[62] controls how a creditor must perfect and foreclose on an interest in any federally docu-

---

security for a loan from the seller's bank, the bank would have a security interest in chattel paper.

[56] UCC § 9-106.

[57] U.S. v. Kimbell Foods, Inc., 440 US 715 (1979).

[58] Perfection is explored in detail at infra ¶ 7.06. UCC § 9-302(3)(a) specifically defers to federal rules concerning federal or international perfection.

[59] See 49 USC § 1403.

[60] Philko Aviation, Inc. v. Shacket, 103 S. Ct. 2476 (1983); South Shore Bank v. Tony Mat, Inc., 712 F2d 896, 36 UCC Rep. Serv. 801 (3d Cir. 1983); In re Gary Aircraft Corp., 681 F2d 365, 34 UCC Rep. Serv. 722 (5th Cir. 1982).

[61] The Secretary of Transportation is charged with setting up the recording scheme. 49 USC § 1403(a). Recording is done with the Federal Aviation Administration. Philko Aviation, Inc. v. Shacket, 103 S. Ct. 2476, 2480 (1983).

[62] 46 USC §§ 911–961.

mented vessel.[63] An interest in such vessels must be recorded with the Collector of Customs[64] in order to protect the interest holder from innocent third-party claimants. Perfection under Article 9 is preempted.[65] If such a vessel is covered by a lien with a preferred status under the federal Act, federal admiralty law controls priority as well.[66]

**[iii] Federal Tax Liens.** Federal law controls priority issues between the United States as a holder of certain tax liens and private parties claiming liens (including security interests) in the same property subject to the tax lien.[67] These priority disputes are discussed elsewhere in this book.[68]

**[iv] Miscellaneous Federal Acts.** Perfection of equipment trusts in railway rolling stock must be by recording pursuant to the Interstate Commerce Act.[69] This Act also provides for perfection of security interests in motor vehicles held by carriers with a certificate issued by the Interstate Commerce Commission.[70] However, the Interstate Commerce Act defers to state certificate-of-title laws,[71] which must also be followed in order to perfect under Article 9.[72]

Other federal recordation rules that prevail over Article 9's perfection scheme are those for copyrights,[73] patents,[74] and registered trademarks.[75]

The Packers and Stockyards Act gives sellers of livestock who sell to packers for cash or check greater priority rights as against secured creditors of the packers than the rights afforded such sellers under Article 9.[76]

---

[63] Small pleasure craft would be excluded. Clark, Law of Secured Transactions ¶ 1.08[1][a], at 1-44 (Warren, Gorham & Lamont, Inc. 1980).

[64] 46 USC § 921(a).

[65] McCorkle v. First Pa. Banking & Trust Co., 321 F. Supp. 149, 8 UCC Rep. Serv. 981 (D. Md. 1970).

[66] 46 USC §§ 951, 953. Security Bank of Ore. v. Levens, 257 Ore. 630, 480 P2d 706, 8 UCC Rep. Serv. 977 (1971).

[67] Federal Tax Lien Act, 26 USC §§ 6321 et seq. (1966); Valley Bank of Nevada v. City of Henderson, 528 F. Supp. 907, 33 UCC Rep. Serv. 382 (D. Nev. 1981).

[68] See ¶ 9.04.

[69] 49 USC § 11303; see In re Auto-Train Corp., 9 Bankr. 207, 31 UCC Rep. Serv. 1711 (Bankr. DDC 1981) (holding that the language of the Interstate Commerce Act whereby a holder of an equipment trust "may" file under the federal act did not mean that the holder must also file under Article 9).

[70] 49 USC § 11304.

[71] Id.

[72] See infra ¶ 7.06[3][b].

[73] Federal Copyright Act, 17 USC § 205 (1976).

[74] 35 USC § 261.

[75] Lanham Act, 15 USC § 1060.

[76] 7 USC §§ 196, 228(c); Fillippo v. S. Bonaccurso & Sons, Inc., 466 F. Supp. 1008, 26 UCC Rep. Serv. 1003 (ED Pa. 1979).

Under the Federal Assignment of Claims Act, in order for an assignment of a claim to have an effect on the rights of the U.S. government, the claim must be allowed, the amount must be decided, and there must be a warrant for payment issued.[77] Article 9 controls where the Act is not applicable: for example, where there is simply a dispute between private parties not affecting the rights of the United States.[78]

Federal liens arise from federal lending programs such as that conducted by the Small Business Administration. In the absence of a congressional directive, priority disputes involving such liens have been decided under Article 9's provisions.[79]

### [b] Landlord's Liens

Section 9-104[80] omits coverage of nonconsensual liens arising from common law or statutes giving a real property landlord a lien in the tenant's personal property for the payment of rent. If a landlord has asked a tenant to agree to give a security interest in his personal property to secure his obligation to pay rent, and the tenant has agreed to do so in writing,[81] there is apparently an Article 9 security interest that is not excluded by Section 9-104.

### [c] Materialman's Liens

By case law or statute, all jurisdictions provide for nonconsensual liens for suppliers of services or materials. Such liens are known by a variety of names, including "artisan's liens," "materialman's liens," "repairman's liens," and "garageman's liens." Except for priority disputes under Section 9-310, Article 9 is not applicable to such liens. Section 9-310 provides for the resolution of priority disputes between a secured creditor and holders of such liens.[82]

### [d] Wage Assignments

Until fairly recently it was common practice for some creditors to require an assignment of the debtor's wages to secure repayment. This was a form of wage checkoff, the debtor agreeing that the creditor would be paid directly a portion of the debtor's wages. A number of states and the Federal Trade Commission (FTC) now regulate such assignments.[83] Whatever the form of local

---

[77] 31 USC § 3727.

[78] See, e.g., In re Metric Metals Int'l, Inc., 20 Bankr. 633, 33 UCC Rep. Serv. 1495 (SDNY 1981); Centron Corp. v. U.S., 585 F2d 982 (Ct. Cl. 1978).

[79] U.S. v. Kimbell Foods, Inc., 440 US 715 (1979).

[80] UCC § 9-104(b).

[81] See discussion at infra ¶ 7.04[2][b] setting out the general requirement of a written security agreement for a valid security interest.

[82] UCC § 9-310. This section is discussed at infra ¶ 7.07[7].

[83] See, e.g., Ala. Code of tit. 39, § 201, making such assignments void; FTC Rule on Credit Practices, 16 CFR § 444.2(3) and discussion at ¶ 3.05.

consumer statutes, Article 9 does not cover assignments of wages, salary, or other compensation of an employee.[84]

### [e] Governmental Transfers

Where the debtor is a government or a governmental agency (local, state, or federal) transferring an interest in its property, Article 9 does not apply.[85]

### [f] Certain Sales of Accounts or Chattel Paper

A transfer of sales of accounts or chattel paper[86] as security and an outright sale of such collateral is included within the scope of Article 9.[87] However, Article 9 does exclude such transfers or sales if there is:

(1) A sale of accounts or chattel paper as part of a sale of the business out of which they arose;
(2) An assignment of such collateral for the purpose of collection only;
(3) A transfer of a right to payment under a contract to an assignee and that assignee is to do the performance under the contract; or
(4) A transfer of a single account to an assignee in whole or partial satisfaction of a preexisting indebtedness.[88]

### [g] Interests or Claims Under Insurance Policies

Section 9-104 excludes a transfer of a cash surrender value by an insured party. It also excludes a transfer by an insured of monies owed the insured by the insurance company because of casualty to the insured's property or an accident, if the insured attempted a transfer of the right to this insurance payment after the insurance company became liable for the payment.[89] However, Section 9-104 does not exclude insurance monies due an insured if the monies are proceeds as defined under Article 9. Article 9 proceeds include insurance payable by reason of loss or damage to collateral that is the subject of a security interest if the secured creditor or debtor are the named insured.[90]

---

[84] UCC § 9-104(d); see Massachusetts Mut. Life Ins. Co. v. Central Pa. Nat'l Bank, 372 F. Supp. 1027, 14 UCC Rep. Serv. 212 (ED Pa. 1974) (holding that an independent insurance agent was an independent contractor and not an employee, therefore making an assignment of commissions due the insurance agent not excluded under the wage-assignment exclusion).

[85] UCC § 9-104(e).

[86] See supra ¶ 7.02[3], which discusses the classification of collateral as accounts and chattel paper.

[87] Supra ¶ 7.02[3].

[88] UCC § 9-104(f).

[89] See Clark, Law of Secured Transactions ¶ 1.08[7], at 1-60 (Warren, Gorham & Lamont, Inc. 1980).

[90] UCC § 9-306(1).

### [h] Rights Represented by a Judgment

Assume that *A* sues *B* for trespass and receives a judgment. Article 9 would not apply to *A*'s transfer of the right represented by the judgment to the bank as security for a loan by the bank to *A*. Article 9 generally excludes such transfers of a right represented by a judgment.[91] There is an exception under which Article 9 applies to the transfer of a right represented by a judgment if the judgment was taken on a right to payment that was collateral.

EXAMPLE: Secured creditor, *SC*, has a valid security interest in the accounts of debtor, *D*. One of these accounts consists of an obligation by *X* to pay *D* for some bolts that *X* bought from *D*. *X* does not pay and *D* sues and recovers a judgment against *X*. *SC's* security interest would extend to the right to payment to *D* that is now represented by a judgment.

### [i] Rights of Setoff

Setoff rights are discussed in detail elsewhere in this book.[92] Article 9 does not apply to such rights. When there is a priority dispute between a bank claiming a right to setoff and an Article 9 secured creditor over the debtor's deposit account in the bank, most courts have held that the Section 9-104(i) exclusion of bank setoff rights means that a holder of a setoff right does not automatically lose priority. Priority rules are generally decided outside Article 9.[93]

### [j] Interests in Real Property

Article 9 does not apply to interests in real estate except for fixtures.[94] Article 9 does cover some collateral related to real estate. Security interests in crops are covered by Article 9 if the crops are growing crops[95] or harvested crops.[96] Security interests in timber are covered if the timber is to be cut and

---

[91] UCC § 9-104(h).

[92] See ¶ 5.05.

[93] Bank of Crystal Springs v. First Nat'l Bank of Jackson, 427 So. 2d 968, 35 UCC Rep. Serv. 1630 (Miss. 1983); State Bank of Rose Creek v. First State Bank of Austin, 320 NW2d 723, 33 UCC Rep. Serv. 1755 (Minn. 1982); Citizens Nat'l Bank of Orlando v. Bornstein, 374 So. 2d 6, 27 UCC Rep. Serv. 242 (Fla. 1979). But see Citizens Bank of Whitly County v. Mid-States Dev. Co., Inc., 177 Ind. App. 548, 380 NE2d 1243, 24 UCC Rep. Serv. 1321 (1978) (UCC § 9-201 used as one argument in support of position that security interest had priority). See also Clark, Law of Secured Transactions ¶ 3.11 (Warren, Gorham & Lamont, Inc., 1982 Cum. Supp. 1).

[94] UCC §§ 9-104(j), 9-102(1); see infra ¶ 7.07[8] for a discussion of fixtures.

[95] This is because growing crops fall within the definition of goods. See UCC § 9-105(1)(h); Flona Corp. v. U.S., 218 F. Supp. 354 (SD Fla. 1963) (discussing the meaning of "growing crops").

[96] See generally Meyer, "Crops As Collateral Under Article 9," 15 U.C.C. L.J. 3, 4–5 (1982).

removed under a conveyance or contract for sale. It makes no difference who is to do the cutting.[97] Security interests in minerals (including oil and gas) are covered if the minerals are extracted.[98]

An issue that has caused much speculation is whether Article 9 applies where the debtor uses as collateral an obligation owed to the debtor by a third person where that obligation is secured by real estate.

> **EXAMPLE:** A seller sells real property to a buyer. The buyer executes a real estate contract. The real estate contract contains a promise by the buyer to pay principal plus interest, and indicates that the seller (as is required in most states) retains title to the real estate until such time as the buyer pays for the real estate.[99] The seller borrows money from a bank. As security, the seller gives the bank an interest in the real estate contract that the seller holds from the buyer.
>
> Most courts would treat the bank's interest in the seller's right to receive payments under the land contract as a security interest covered by Article 9.[100]
>
> The bank would have to follow Article 9 to perfect its interest in that personal property. If the assignment of the real estate contract also contains an assignment of the seller's interest in the real estate, the bank's interest in the real estate would have to be recorded under real estate law to protect the bank against third parties.[101]

---

[97] This is because such timber is included within the definition of goods. See UCC § 9-105(1)(h).

[98] This is because extracted minerals are included within the definition of goods. See UCC § 9-105(1)(h).

[99] To this point, the transaction is entirely outside Article 9 because of both UCC §§ 9-102(1) and 9-104(j); the transaction is a real estate transaction.

[100] See, e.g., In re Freeborn, 94 Wash. 2d 336, 617 P2d 424, 29 UCC Rep. Serv. 1625 (1980) (holding that the collateral in a similar transaction was an account); In re Southworth, 22 Bankr. 376, 34 UCC Rep. Serv. 1372 (D. Kan. 1982) (security interest in rights to receive payment under a contract of deed). This approach is authorized by UCC § 9-102(3) and Official Comment 4. See also U.S. v. Wood, 28 Bankr. 383, 35 UCC Rep. Serv. 1625 (ND Ga. 1983), in which the debtor made a personal guaranty on a loan, secured by a deed on the debtor's residence. The court stated that the deed on the residence was excluded because it was an interest in real estate; however, the debtor had sold his home and the creditor had a security interest in proceeds. The proceeds were personal property, mainly money, and the court held that the real estate exclusion did not exclude the coverage of Article 9 to the secured creditor's security interest in proceeds.

[101] See, e.g., id.; Official Comment 4 to UCC § 9-102 (Comment 4 gives a similar example involving promise to pay plus real estate mortgage used by mortgagee as collateral in loan to mortgagee). See Garnett State Sav. Bank v. Tush, 232 Kan. 447, 657 P2d 508, 35 UCC Rep. Serv. 608 (1983) (assignment of buyer's equity interest under a land contract is an assignment of a real estate interest and not subject to Article 9). Proceeds are discussed at infra ¶ 7.06[7].

### [k] Claims Arising Out of Tort

Article 9 does not apply to any interest in claims arising out of tort. For example, if a party is injured and wishes to assign to a creditor an interest in any claim he may have against the tort-feasor who injured him, Article 9 is not applicable.[102]

### [l] Interests in Deposit Accounts

Deposit accounts are defined as "demand, time, savings, passbook or like accounts maintained with a bank, savings and loan association, credit union or like organization, other than an account evidenced by a certificate of deposit." Note that a deposit account is not the same as an "account"[103] Article 9 is not applicable to a transfer of an interest in a deposit account unless the account represents proceeds.[104] However, since Article 9 defines deposit account to exclude certificates of deposit, this exclusion of Section 9-104(l) does not operate to exclude interests in certificates of deposit. Therefore, Article 9 does apply to security interests in such collateral.

## ¶ 7.03 CLASSIFYING THE COLLATERAL

### [1] Importance of Classifying the Collateral

The property subject to an Article 9 security interest is known as collateral.[1] Determining the applicable provision of Article 9 on all major issues–scope, obtainment of a valid security interest, perfection of the security interest (where to file, for example), determination of priorities, and rights between the creditor and debtor–often requires a classification of collateral.[2] Consequently, classifying collateral is an important early step both in the planning stage and when disputes arise between a secured creditor and a debtor or between a secured creditor and other claimants.

### [2] Official Classifications

#### [a] Introduction

Classifying collateral usually is not difficult, but it does require a careful analysis of the UCC's definitions of collateral. The UCC recognizes nine types

---

[102] UCC § 9-104(k).

[103] See the discussion of the definition of accounts at supra ¶ 7.02[3].

[104] UCC § 9-104(1). Proceeds are discussed at infra ¶ 7.06[7].

[1] UCC § 9-105(1)(c). As already discussed, the sale of accounts and chattel paper may also result in coverage by Article 9. See supra ¶ 7.02[3].

[2] See Official Comment 5 to UCC § 9-102, which contains an index to the various Article 9 sections by type of collateral.

of collateral. Four types–Consumer goods, equipment, farm products, and inventory–are grouped together as "goods." These types of collateral are defined in Section 9-109.[3]

The other five types of collateral are types of intangible collateral:[4] accounts and general intangibles,[5] documents,[6] instruments,[7] and chattel paper.[8] Some commentators have further divided this intangible collateral into (1) pure intangibles: accounts and general intangibles, and (2) semi-intangibles: documents, instruments, and chattel paper.[9]

With respect to the nine official classifications of collateral it is important to recognize that collateral may have only one classification at any one time; the classifications are mutually exclusive. Classifications are made by determining the nature of the collateral in the hands of the debtor. When the determination of the classification should be made can be critical.[10]

It is sometimes necessary to further classify the collateral as fixtures,[11] proceeds,[12] mobile goods,[13] minerals,[14] money,[15] crops,[16] or timber,[17] although these categories are not officially recognized as separate classifications of collateral.

### [b] Goods

**[i] Consumer Goods.** Consumer goods are defined in Section 9-109(1) as goods used or bought for use primarily for "personal, family or

---

[3] A few times Article 9 uses the term "goods," which would include any one of the four types of collateral in UCC § 9-109. See, e.g., UCC §§ 9-306(5), 9-307.

[4] See Official Comment 3 to UCC § 9-105.

[5] See UCC § 9-106.

[6] See UCC § 9-105(1)(f).

[7] See UCC § 9-105(1)(i).

[8] See UCC § 9-105(1)(c).

[9] See e.g., Henson, Secured Transactions 31 (West, 2d ed. 1979). The UCC sections do not use this distinction.

[10] For example, where to file a financing statement within a particular state depends mostly upon the classification of collateral. See infra ¶ 7.06[3][d]. There is some dispute as to what time the classification should be made. See the discussion at infra ¶ 7.03[2][b][v].

[11] See UCC § 9-113, specifying priorities among claims by the secured creditor and real property interest holders, and discussed at infra ¶ 7.07[8].

[12] See, e.g., UCC § 9-306, specifying steps for perfection in proceeds and discussed at infra ¶ 7.06[7].

[13] See UCC § 9-103(3), specifying how to perfect a security interest in mobile goods and discussed at infra ¶ 7.06[6][d].

[14] See UCC § 9-103(5), specifying how to perfect a security interest in minerals and discussed at infra ¶ 7.06[6][f].

[15] See UCC §§ 9-304(1), 9-305.

[16] See UCC § 9-312(2), resolving certain priority disputes in crops and discussed at infra ¶ 7.07[4][d].

[17] See, e.g., UCC § 9-203(1)(a).

household purposes." A television set held by a debtor primarily for use by the family is a consumer good, but if the debtor uses the television set primarily for the waiting room in a business office, the television would be classified as equipment.

It has been argued that the classification of consumer goods was not meant to include high-priced items such as an aircraft even if the aircraft is held by the debtor for a "personal, family or household" use. The basis of the argument is that the consumer-goods classification was meant for smaller nondurable items rather than for expensive items such as aircraft. However, courts usually have not been sympathetic to this argument.[18]

**[ii] Inventory.** Goods are defined as inventory if they are held for sale or lease in the ordinary course of business of the debtor.[19] The definition also includes goods that are to be furnished or have been furnished under a contract of service.[20] Finally, goods are inventory if they are raw materials, work in process, or materials used or consumed in a business. For example, the red paint of a debtor-manufacturer who produces red tractors is inventory. The inclusion of this last type of collateral is intended to include goods that are consumed in a relatively short period of time in the production of some end product.[21]

**[iii] Farm Products.** There are two tests to determine whether goods are farm products. The first requires the goods to be (1) crops or livestock produced in farming operations, (2) supplies used in farming operations, or (3) products of crops or livestock in their unmanufactured states (such as ginned cotton, wool clip, maple syrup, milk, and eggs). The second test requires a determination of whether the goods are in the possession of a debtor engaged in farming operations such as raising, fattening, or grazing livestock.

Most cases concerning whether or not collateral is considered "farm products" have involved whether the debtor was engaged in farming operations. In a case involving nursery stock, *In re Frazier*,[22] the debtor grew nursery seedlings from seed and purchased other seedlings. The debtor allowed the seedlings to grow from one to seven years, depending upon the type of seedling, before he sold them. The court held that the cultivation process of tending and caring for the trees, shrubs, and plants was a farming operation and that the products of the operation were farm products.[23]

---

[18] See, e.g., Commercial Credit Equip. Corp. v. Carter, 83 Wash. 2d 136, 516 P2d 767, 13 UCC Rep. Serv. 1212 (1973); Atlas Credit Corp. v. Dolbow, 193 Pa. Super. 649, 165 A2d 704, 1 UCC Rep. Serv. 5 (1960). Contra In re Sprague, 4 UCC Rep. Serv. 702 (NDNY 1966).

[19] See UCC § 9-109(4) and Official Comment 3.

[20] Id.

[21] Official Comment 3 to UCC § 9-109(4).

[22] 16 Bankr. 674, 33 UCC Rep. Serv. 1150 (MD Tenn. 1981).

[23] Citing, in part, Mountain Credit v. Michiana Lumber & Supply, Inc., 31 Colo. App. 112, 498 P2d 967, 10 UCC Rep. Serv. 1347 (1972).

However, the court held that the nursery stock that was mature and available for sale was inventory.[24]

**[iv] Equipment.** Goods are considered "equipment" if they are used in a business and cannot be classified as invenotry or farm products.[25] Examples are vehicles, machinery, tools, and furniture used in a business.

**[v] Change of Use of Collateral.** The primary test in determining the classifications of inventory, consumer goods, and equipment is how the debtor uses the goods. Does a change of use of the collateral by the debtor, and therefore an apparent change in the classification, affect the rights of the secured creditor? The UCC answers "no" where the issue is whether a filing within the proper state remains effective upon a change of use. The UCC provides that if a filing within a jurisdiction was initially correct, the filing remains effective despite a change in use.[26]

When the issue is other than whether perfection by filing remains valid after the change of use, the UCC is silient concerning the effect of the change. In *Commercial Credit Equipment Corp. v. Carter*,[27] the debtor had bought an airplane primarily for personal use and after purchase changed the use to primarily one for business. Under Washington's version of Article 9, the creditor was restricted from suing for a deficiency judgment if the collateral was consumer goods but not if the collateral was equipment. The Washington Supreme Court ruled that the change of use of collateral should not affect the rights of the creditor and debtor. The relevant classification was the classification at the time of attachment. At that time the collateral was consumer goods; therefore, the court ruled that the creditor was limited by the state law concerning the right to sue for deficiency upon repossession of consumer goods.

Contrast *Commercial Credit* with *First Dallas County Bank v. General Motors Acceptance Corp.*[28] In *First Dallas*, the debtor, an automobile dealer, purchased a car for his personal use, and then sold the car on his used-car lot. The court felt that this resulted in a change in the classification from consumer goods to inventory. This change in classification resulted in the secured creditor losing a priority dispute with a buyer in the ordinary course of business under Section 9-307(1).[29]

---

[24] See also Farmers State Bank v. Webel, 113 Ill. App. 3d 87, 446 NE2d 525, 36 UCC Rep. Serv. 319 (1983) (mere fact that party kept and fed pigs for a time when market conditions dictated did not make the pigs farm products where feeding was incidental to marketing operation).

[25] UCC § 9-109(2) and Official Comment 5.

[26] UCC § 9-401(3); see discussion at infra ¶ 7.06[3][d].

[27] 83 Wash. 2d 136, 516 P2d 767, 13 UCC Rep. Serv. 1212 (1973).

[28] 425 So. 2d 464, 35 UCC Rep. Serv. 701 (Ala. 1983).

[29] See infra ¶ 7.07[5][b].

Of the two cases, the better decision is that adopted in *Commercial Credit.*[30] The nature of the collateral should be determined at the time the security interest attaches and a later change of use should not affect the rights of the secured creditor as against the debtor or a third party. This is consistent with the UCC's rule concerning the effect of a change in use on the duty to change the place of filing a financing statement.

### [c] Intangibles

As previously mentioned, accounts and chattel paper are two types of intangible collateral.[31] The following discussion considers the other three types of intangible collateral–instruments, documents, and general intangibles.

**[i] Instruments.** "Instruments" includes three types of writings.[32] One type is negotiable instruments such as promissory notes, checks, or certificates of deposit that meet the Article 3 definition of negotiable instruments in Section 3-104. A second type is a certificated security as defined in Section 8-102. The third type is a catch-all: any other writing that "evidences a right to the payment of money and is not itself a security agreement or lease" if it is "of a type which is in the ordinary course of business transferred by delivery with any necessary indorsement or assignment."

**[ii] Documents.** "Document" means a document of title as defined in Section 1-201 and receipts as defined in Section 7-201(1). Principal documents are negotiable and nonnegotiable bills of lading and warehouse receipts.

**[iii] General Intangibles.** Just as "equipment" is a catchall for business goods that do not fit within other classifications of goods, "general intangible" is a catchall for intangibles that do not fit within the other classifications of intangibles. The UCC defines these as any "personal property (including things in action) other than goods, accounts, chattel paper, documents, instruments, and money."[33] An important type of collateral that comes within this definition is the right of the debtor to receive payments that are not classified as accounts. Rights to payment for goods sold or leased or for services rendered come within the classification of accounts if the right is not represented by an instrument or chattel paper. However, if such rights to payment are not for goods sold or leased or for services rendered, the classification is "general

---

[30] See, e.g., In re Benton Trucking Serv., Inc., 21 Bankr. 574, 34 UCC Rep. Serv. 332 (ED Mich. 1982); In re Barnes, 11 UCC Rep. Serv. 670 (Bankr. D. Me. 1972); In re Morton, 9 UCC Rep Serv. 1147 (Bankr. D. Me. 1971); see also White & Summers, Uniform Commercial Code § 23-13 (West, 2d ed. 1980).

[31] See supra ¶ 7.02[3] for a definition of accounts. See supra ¶ 7.02[4] for a definition of chattel paper.

[32] UCC § 9-105(1)(i).

[33] UCC § 9-106.

intangible." An example is the right to be repaid for a loan where this right is represented by an instrument or chattel paper. Some items recently found to be within the classification of "general intangible" include:

(1) Rights to a trade name[34]
(2) Amount due in settlement of a lawsuit[35]
(3) Credit union member's capital reserve account[36]
(4) Liquor license[37]

## ¶ 7.04 ATTACHMENT–GETTING SECURED CREDITOR STATUS

### [1] Introduction

Unless a creditor complies with Section 9-203, she has neither an enforceable nor an attached security interest arising under Article 9.[1] Without attachment, a creditor cannot have a perfected security interest, a status generally necessary to win priority disputes against third-party claimants.[2] Even more basic to the creditor's rights is that, without an enforceable, attached security interest, a creditor does not have Article 9 rights, including rights against the debtor such as self-help repossession. Section 9-203(1) provides that an Article 9 security interest is not enforceable and does not attach unless:

(1) The creditor has possession of collateral by agreement with the debtor, or has a written security agreement that
  (a) Is signed by the debtor;
  (b) Contains a description of the collateral; or
  (c) Contains a description of the land concerned if the security interest covers crops growing or to be grown or timber to be cut;
(2) The creditor has given value; and

---

[34] Reis v. Ralls, 250 Ga. 721, 301 SE2d 40, 35 UCC Rep. Serv. 951 (1983). See also Official Comment to UCC § 9-106, listing patents, goodwill, literary rights, and copyrights.

[35] In re Phoenix Marine Corp., 20 Bankr. 424, 34 UCC Rep. Serv. 280 (ED Va. 1982) (since security interest was in the right to the proceeds of a settlement, not the claim itself, it made no difference that original lawsuit involved a tort claim); see supra ¶ 7.02[4][k].

[36] In re Cosner, 3 Bankr. 445, 29 UCC Rep. Serv. 674 (D. Ore. 1980).

[37] In re Matto's, 9 Bankr. 89, 30 UCC Rep. Serv. 1684 (ED Mich. 1981).

[1] The following security interests may arise outside Article 9: (1) an interest of a collecting bank in the item being collected under UCC § 4-208; (2) interests in securities under UCC § 8-321; and (3) security interests arising under Article 2 on Sales. When a security interest arises under Article 2 is discussed at supra ¶ 7.02[2][c].

[2] See UCC § 9-203.

(3) The debtor has rights in the collateral.

Attachment normally occurs at the moment that all these requirements are met. However, the creditor and debtor may agree that attachment occurs at a later date.[3]

## [2] Security Agreement Requirement

### [a] Possession With Oral Agreement

An Article 9 security interest typically does not attach unless the secured creditor has a written security agreement. The one exception is when the secured creditor has possession of the collateral by agreement.[4] Thus, in a transaction like the classic pledge, where the debtor agrees to let the creditor retain possession of the collateral to secure the obligation, no written security agreement is needed.

When no written security agreement exists, two issues are relevant: (1) when possession occurs; and (2) whether there is possession by an agreement. The degree of control necessary by the creditor to constitute possession also may be an issue concerning perfection by possession.[5] The issue of what is a necessary agreement for possession has generated no litigation. The reason is simply that since there is no written security agreement demonstrating an intent by the debtor to give the creditor a security interest in the collateral, there must be an oral agreement that shows such intent. Thus, mere possession obtained by self-help repossession is not typically possession by agreement.

### [b] Written Security Agreement

**[i] Financing Statement Contrasted.** Most commercial secured transactions do not involve a pledge of the debtor's collateral to the secured creditor. Consequently, in most commercial secured transactions one document used is a security agreement. One purpose of the security agreement is evidentiary, to prevent disputes about what items of property are subject to the security interest. The other purpose is to serve as a Statute of Frauds, preventing the enforcement of claims based on wholly oral representations.[6]

In most secured transactions, another document used is a financing statement. The financing statement is the document filed when the creditor wants to perfect by filing public notice of the security interest.[7]

---

[3] UCC § 9-203(2).

[4] UCC § 9-203(1)(a).

[5] See infra ¶ 7.06[4][b]. An agreement for possession is not necessary if the issue is not attachment but whether the creditor took an applicable step for perfection.

[6] Official Comments 3, 5 to UCC § 9-203; In re Numeric, 485 F2d 1328, 13 UCC Rep. Serv. 416 (1st Cir. 1973).

[7] UCC § 9-302(1).

Section 9-203 specifies the requirements for the security agreement, while Section 9-402(1) specifies the requirements for the financing statement. Among other items, the financing statement must contain all of the types of information specified by Section 9-203(1) for a written security agreement. This has given rise to a number of cases addressing the question of whether the financing statement will also serve as a requisite security agreement. The leading case holding that the financing statement alone is not sufficient is *American Card Co. v. H.M.H. Co.*[8] Although the *American Card* decision has been criticized by some commentators,[9] the courts remain unanimous in finding that the financing statement alone is not sufficient. On the other hand, a majority of decisions now indicate that, if the creditor can demonstrate the existence of documents that show an intent to grant a security interest, a security agreement will be found even if there is no single document clearly specifying an intent to give a security interest.[10] Such other documents have taken a variety of forms, such as a promissory note,[11] a directors' resolution,[12] and a letter from the creditor upon which a debtor has written "Agreed."[13]

A creditor who wishes to have secured creditor status should have the debtor sign a document entitled "Security Agreement" that clearly contains a statement that the debtor intends to give the creditor a security interest.

**[ii] Signature of the Debtor.** The signature requirement for a written security agreement rarely creates a problem. "Signed" is broadly defined in Section 1-201(39) to include "any symbol executed or adopted by a party with present intention to authenticate a writing." A typewritten name, for example, could meet the requirement if there were a present intent to authenticate it as a signature. Parol evidence could be used to establish that intent;[14] occasionally,

---

[8] 97 RI 59, 196 A2d 150, 1 UCC Rep. Serv. 447 (1963).

[9] See, e.g., White & Summers, Uniform Commercial Code 907 (West, 2d ed. 1980).

[10] Some courts have refused to allow this use of such documents with the financing statement to meet the written security agreement requirement. A few courts have done this because they have taken a restrictive view that only a formal security agreement should suffice. See, e.g., In re Taylor Mobile Homes, Inc., 17 UCC Rep. Serv. 565 (Bankr. ED Mich. 1975). Generally, however, when courts have refused to read documents together, they have done so because the particular documents were not clearly relevant to show the intent of the debtor, not because of a general aversion to their use. See, e.g., In re Summit Creek Plywood Co., Inc., 27 Bankr. 209, 36 UCC Rep. Serv. 537 (D. Ore. 1982) (financing statement together with interoffice memo between two of creditor's employees and notations made on the desk pad of another of creditor's employees).

[11] In re Harmon, 6 UCC Rep. Serv. 1280 (Bankr. D. Conn. 1969) (note contained the legend, "This note is secured by a certain financing statement").

[12] In re Numeric, 485 F2d 1328, 13 UCC Rep. Serv. 416 (1st Cir. 1973).

[13] In re Carmichael Enters. Inc., 334 F. Supp. 94, 9 UCC Rep. Serv. 990 (ND Ga. 1971).

[14] See, e.g., Rinaldi Estate v. Rinaldi, 112 Mich. App. 25, 314 NW2d 788, 34 UCC Rep. Serv. 998 (1981).

however, the creditor's carelessness in getting a signature results in a finding of no security interest.[15]

**[iii] Description of the Collateral.** Article 9 requires a description of collateral in both a written security agreement and a financing statement that is filed for perfection. The collateral description requirement is discussed elsewhere in this book.[16]

**[iv] Description of the Real Estate.** When the collateral consists of crops or timber to be cut, the written security agreement must contain a description of the real estate concerned in addition to a description of the collateral. No legal description is needed.[17] Section 9-110 provides that descriptions of both collateral and real estate must only "reasonably identify" what is described. Courts have become lenient in the real estate descriptions allowed for the security agreement.[18] Clearly, a security agreement is sufficient if it gives the name of the owner or lessor of the real estate, acreage, county, township, and range of the real estate where the crops or timber are growing.[19] Creditors, therefore, should provide all of this information in their descriptions.

---

[15] See, e.g., In re Nedeau, 24 Bankr. 1, 34 UCC Rep. Serv. 1408 (SD Fla. 1982) (debtor opened a charge account line with creditor; there was a "master security agreement" on the back of credit application; however, the application was signed only by debtor's wife; one of three later invoices was signed by debtor but this signature did not suffice as a signature on the "security agreement"); Pontchartrain State Bank v. Poulson, 684 F2d 704, 34 UCC Rep. Serv. 693 (10th Cir. 1982) (a letter from the debtor's attorney stating that the debtor was vesting the bank with "a security interest in certain business equipment" was not a signed security agreement because the court held that the attorney was not acting as the agent for the debtor in setting up the security agreement; the existence of a signed financing statement did not impress the court, which held that the security agreement must have the signature). A concurring opinion disagreed with the conclusion in *Pontchartrain*, holding that under the relevant state law of Oklahoma, the attorney was an agent of the debtor because the debtor had asked the attorney to notify the creditor of its security interest. Compare In re Mid-Atlantic Piping Prods. of Charlotte, Inc., 24 Bankr. 314, 35 UCC Rep. Serv. 618 (WDNC 1982) (allowing the signature of a corporate agent to suffice as that of the corporation when parol evidence showed the intent to sign in a representative capacity; court also combined promissory notes and financing statement to find requisite signature).

[16] Infra ¶ 7.06[3][c][v].

[17] See, e.g., In re Lovelady, 21 Bankr. 182, 34 UCC Rep. Serv. 713 (D. Ore. 1982); 67 A.L.R.3d 308 (1975).

[18] Real estate descriptions are sometimes required to be on financing statements as well. See infra ¶ 7.06[3][c].

[19] See, e.g., U.S. v. Oakley, 483 F. Supp. 762, 28 UCC Rep. Serv. 199 (ED Ark. 1980); U.S. v. Smith, 22 UCC Rep. Serv. 502 (ND Miss. 1977); In re Colbert, 22 UCC Rep. Serv. 511 (Bankr. ND Miss. 1977); U.S. v. Big Z. Warehouse, 311 F. Supp. 283, 7 UCC Rep. Serv. 1061 (SD Ga. 1970); Production Credit Ass'n v. Columbia Mills, 22 UCC Rep. Serv. 228 (7th Cir. 1977).

Descriptions that have provided less information often have sufficed,[20] but more than one secured creditor has gotten into trouble for being overly general.[21]

**[v] After-Acquired Collateral.** Security interests may attach to property in which the debtor obtains rights after the original security interest has attached. This is referred to as "after-acquired" collateral. There is one limitation on such collateral: No security interest may attach in consumer goods other than accessions when given as additional security unless the debtor acquires rights in such consumer goods within ten days after the secured creditor gives value.[22]

Although the UCC does not clearly indicate whether a security agreement must specify that the security interest attaches to after-acquired collateral, most courts have held that such language or similar language (e.g., "hereafter acquired," "now owned or later owned") must exist in the security agreement.[23] However, when the collateral is inventory or accounts, authority is divided concerning the requirement of an after-acquired clause in the security agreement. The majority of the courts have looked at the parties' intent, utilizing a "reasonable person" test. If a reasonable person were to look at the entire security agreement and financing statement and feel that the creditor and debtor intended the interest to secure after-acquired inventory, the security agreement is adequate without the after-acquired clause. In every case where this test has been used, the court has found that the parties intended to secure

---

[20] See, e.g., In re Johnson, 21 Bankr. 484, 34 UCC Rep. Serv. 708 (WD Mo. 1982) ("310 acres of wheat on home place and land rented" was sufficient description); Bank of Danville v. Farmers Nat'l Bank, 602 SW2d 160, 29 UCC Rep. Serv. 1020 (Ky. 1980) ("Dale Wilson farm located on Lancaster Road, four miles from Danville, Ky." was sufficient description).

[21] See, e.g., Chanute Prod. Credit Ass'n v. Weir Grain Supply, Inc., 210 Kan. 181, 499 P2d 517, 10 UCC Rep. Serv. 1351 (1972) ("land owned or leased by debtor in Cherokee County, Kansas" was not sufficient description).

[22] UCC § 9-204(2). The 1962 limitation on crops that become growing crops more than one year after the execution of the security agreement was removed by the 1972 Amendments. The limitation on attachment in after-acquired consumer goods, and other limitations on security interests in consumer goods imposed by consumer law outside the UCC are discussed at ¶ 3.03.

[23] John Deere Co. v. Butler County Implement, Inc., 232 Kan. 273, 655 P2d 124, 36 UCC Rep. Serv. 957 (1982) (by a list of specific items of collateral by description with no reference to after-acquired collateral, court held that it could not by implication infer any interest in after-acquired collateral); Idaho Bank & Trust Co. v. Cargill, Inc. 105 Idaho 83, 665 P2d 1093, 36 UCC Rep. Serv. 691 (Idaho App. 1983) ("all monies now due or to become due under certain Grain Contracts held in your Warehouse" did not cover accounts that were after-acquired because one could reasonably construe description to be a security interest only in monies due and coming due on existing contracts); Boulder Bank & Trust Co. v. U.S., 26 UCC Rep. Serv. 774 (ND Okla. 1979); In re World Wide Perfume, Inc., 7 UCC Rep. Serv. 616 (Bankr. MD Ala. 1969).

after-acquired inventory.[24] However, other courts have taken different views;[25] with regard to this issue, caution also is advised. If the creditor intends to take a security interest in after-acquired collateral, the security agreement should specify this intent, using the words "after-acquired," whatever the type of collateral involved.[26]

**[vi] Securing Future Advances of Value.** In addition to the original advance of value, the creditor may wish to make a future advance of value. For example, if the creditor initially made a simple loan of money, he may wish to loan more money. The creditor will want to ensure that the debtor's obligation is secured not only to the extent of the amounts owing on the original advance but also to the extent of any amounts owing on the future advance. This requires a security agreement that demonstrates the debtor's intent to give a security interest in the collateral to cover these future advances. The following provision typically is included in the initial security agreement to indicate that intent:

> THE DEBTOR AGREES THAT THE COLLATERAL DESCRIBED ABOVE SECURES ANY ADVANCES OF VALUE MADE BY THE CREDITOR WHENEVER THE ADVANCES ARE MADE.

If there is no future advance clause in the original security agreement, the creditor generally must have the debtor issue a new security agreement that shows the intent to have the security interest secure the entire obligation, including any later advance.

An important issue not yet fully resolved is whether a broadly drafted future advance clause in the security agreement covers all future advances regardless of the purpose for the later advance. Several respected courts have held that, unless the future advance clause is ambiguous, it encompasses all future advances and parol evidence is inadmissible to contradict the clear language of the clause.[27] Other courts insist upon looking at both the security

---

[24] See, e.g., In re Fibre Glass Boat Corp., 324 F. Supp. 1054, 9 UCC Rep. Serv. 118 (SD Fla. 1971); In re Gary & Connie Jones Drugs, Inc., 35 Bankr. 608, 37 UCC Rep. Serv. 563 (D. Kan. 1983); In re Page, 16 UCC Rep. Serv. 501 (MD Fla. 1974); In re Beverage, 30 UCC Rep. Serv. 373 (Bankr. MD Pa. 1980).

[25] See, e.g., In re Middle Atl. Stud Welding Co, 503 F2d 1133, 14 UCC Rep. Serv. 1233 (3d Cir. 1974); In re Taylored Prod., Inc., 5 UCC Rep. Serv. 286 (WD Mich. 1968); Evans Prods. Co. v. Jorgensen, 245 Ore. 362, 421 P2d 978, 3 UCC Rep. Serv. 1099 (Ore. 1966).

[26] Concerning the requirement of the term "after-acquired" or its equivalent in the description of collateral required in the financing statement, see infra ¶ 7.06[3][c][ix].

[27] See e.g., Kimbell Foods, Inc. v. Republic Nat'l Bank of Dallas, 557 F2d 491, 23 UCC Rep. Serv. 177 (5th Cir. 1977), aff'd, 440 US 715, 26 UCC Rep. Serv. (1979); First Nat'l Bank in Dallas v. Rozelle, 493 F2d 1196 (10th Cir. 1974); State Bank of Albany v. U.S., 468 F2d 1211, 11 UCC Rep. Serv. 601 (2d Cir. 1972); Kenneally v. Standard Elec. Corp., 364 F2d 642 (8th Cir. 1966); Thorp Sales Corp. v. Dolese Bros. Co., 453 F. Supp. 196, 24 UCC Rep. Serv. 981 (WD Okla. 1978); Sturdevant v. First Sec. Bank, 186 Mont. 91, 606 P2d 525, 28 UCC Rep. Serv. 569 (1980).

agreement and parol evidence to ensure that the parties intended the future advance clause to cover the particular type of subsequent advance. For example, if parol evidence shows that the initial transaction was for one class of obligation, such as a consumer loan, and the later advance was for another class of loan originally unanticipated by the debtor, such as a business loan, these courts would refuse to find the debtor intended the security interest to cover the later advance.[28] As a planning measure, the initial security agreement should include a provision that indicates the intent that all future advances, whatever their nature, are to be secured. A subsequent security agreement showing the intent to secure a later advance should be taken whenever there is any doubt concerning the validity of a future advance clause.

### [3] Value Requirement

Before attachment can occur, the creditor must also give "value."[29] Value is broadly defined to include any consideration sufficient to support a simple contract.[30] This encompasses the typical extension of value–the advance of money as a loan or the sale of goods on credit. Specifically included in the definition is any binding commitment to extend credit or to extend immediately available credit, whether or not it is drawn upon and whether or not a chargeback is provided for in the event of difficulties in collection.[31] Unlike traditional contract doctrine on consideration, value also includes taking as security collateral for, or in total or partial satisfaction of, a preexisting obligation.[32]

### [4] Requirement of Debtor's Rights in the Collateral

There cannot be an attached or enforceable Article 9 security interest unless the debtor has "rights in the collateral."[33] Article 9 does not delineate what degree of the debtor's interest in collateral is necessary to meet this requirement. Clearly, if the debtor has outright ownership of collateral, the debtor has sufficient rights in the collateral.

Much recent litigation has arisen in cases were the debtor has something less than outright ownership of collateral. In most of these cases, although the debtor has possession of the collateral that is alleged to be subject to the secur-

---

[28] See, e.g., Kitmitto v. First Pa. Bank, N.A., 518 F. Supp. 297, 31 UCC Rep. Serv. 1751 (ED Pa. 1981); Marine Nat'l Bank v. Airco, Inc., 389 F. Supp. 231, 17 UCC Rep. Serv. 291 (WD Pa. 1975); National Bank v. Blankenship, 177 F. Supp. 667 (ED Ark. 1959); In re Smith & West Constr., Inc., 28 Bankr. 682, 36 UCC Rep. Serv. 989 (D. Ore. 1983); Blurton v. Dyersburg Prod. Credit Ass'n, 26 Bankr. 508 (WD Tenn. 1983); In re Grizaffi, 23 Bankr. 137, 34 UCC Rep. Serv. 1398 (D. Colo. 1982).

[29] UCC § 9-203(1)(b).

[30] UCC § 1-201(44)(d).

[31] UCC § 1-201(44)(a).

[32] UCC § 1-201(44)(b).

[33] UCC § 9-203(1)(c).

ity interest, he has something less than free and clear ownership. If the debtor purchases goods under a contract for sale and has possession of the goods, it is clear that he has sufficient rights for the security interest to attach, even though he has not fully paid for the goods.[34] When vehicles are involved, authority is divided concerning whether a buyer has sufficient rights in the vehicle before a certificate of title has been properly assigned to the buyer.[35] If the buyer has paid by a bad check, courts generally have agreed that the buyer still has sufficient rights in the collateral for a security interest to attach, at least if the seller has failed to reclaim the sold goods within the ten-day period provided by Section 2-702.[36]

When the debtor has possession of the collateral but has not purchased the goods, courts have had more difficulty in determining whether sufficient rights exist. In such cases, mere possession of goods, without some other indication of ownership, does not create sufficient rights in the collateral.[37] However, on a number of occasions, courts have found sufficient rights because of the circumstances of the debtor's possession. For example, in the case of *In re Pubs*,[38] the court held that a corporate debtor was estopped from denying the existence of sufficient rights in the collateral. The reason for the corporation's claim was a mix-up in a transfer of assets to the corporation, which was caused by two

---

[34] Amfac Mortgage Corp. v. Arizona Mall of Tempe, Inc., 127 Ariz. 70, 618 P2d 240, 30 UCC Rep. Serv. 744 (Ariz. Ct. App. 1980) (court held that no payments need be made); see also In re Automated Bookbinding Servs., Inc., 336 F. Supp. 1128, 10 UCC Rep. Serv. (D. Md. 1972), rev'd on other grounds, 471 F2d 546, 11 UCC Rep. Serv. 897 (4th Cir. 1972); In re Ultra Precision Indus. Inc., 503 F2d 414, 15 UCC Rep. Serv. 281 (9th Cir. 1974); In re South Atl. Packers Ass'n, Inc., 30 Bankr. 836, 36 UCC Rep. Serv. 1040 (DSC 1983) (collateral consisted of several components to be delivered over period of time; at least by possession of all parts there were sufficient rights).

[35] Compare the following, which held the certificate did not control: In re Emergency Beacon Corp., 665 F2d 36, 32 UCC Rep. Serv. 788 (2d Cir. 1981); First Nat'l Bank of Ariz. v. Carbajal, 132 Ariz. 263, 645 P2d 778, 33 UCC Rep. Serv. 1523 (1982) (although no certificate had been issued, court assumed there had been an attachment); Sanford, "Debtor's Rights in Collateral as a Requirement for Attachment of a Security Interest Under the UCC," 26 S.D.L. Rev. 163, 176 (arguing that South Dakota law so provides) with the following, which held that the debtor could not have sufficient rights until the certificate was assigned under appropriate state law: Gicinto v. Credithrift of Am., No. 3, Inc., 219 Kan. 766, 549 P2d 870, 19 UCC Rep. Serv. 784 (1976); Guy Martin Buick, Inc. v. Colorado Springs Nat'l Bank, 184 Colo. 166, 519 P2d 354, 14 UCC Rep. Serv. 40 (1974).

[36] Holiday Rambler Corp. v. Morris, 32 UCC Rep. Serv. 1222 (D. Kan. 1981); Stowers v. Mahon, 526 F2d 1238, 18 UCC Rep. Serv. 545 (5th Cir. 1976); Swets Motor Sales, Inc. v. Pruisner, 236 NW2d 299, 18 UCC Rep. Serv. 371 (Iowa 1975).

[37] In re Crouthamel Potato Chip Co., Inc., 6 Bankr. 501, 30 UCC Rep. Serv. 346 (ED Pa. 1980) (agent held for principal used goods as collateral for loan; court found that agent typically did not have authority); Chrysler Corp. v. Adamatic, Inc., 59 Wis. 2d 219, 208 NW2d 97, 12 UCC Rep. Serv. 849 (1973) (bailee's possessory interest for limited purpose of repair not sufficient rights in the collateral); dictum Pontchartrain State Bank v. Poulson, 684 F2d 704, 34 UCC Rep. Serv. 693 (10th Cir. 1982).

[38] 618 F2d 432, 28 UCC Rep. Serv. 279 (7th Cir. 1980).

principals of the corporation. In *Kinetics Technology International Corp. v. Fourth National Bank of Tulsa,*[39] a contractor agreed to build machinery for *X*, who in turn agreed to furnish to the contractor some of the supplies necessary to build the machinery. The contractor borrowed money from a third party and gave "inventory" as collateral. The court found that the contractor had sufficient rights in the goods furnished by *X* for the security interest to attach to these supplies. The court held that for the debtor to have sufficient rights over goods in its possession, the debtor must have had some degree of control or authority over the goods; there must have been some agreement giving the debtor something more than "naked possession." The additional authority existed when *X* supplied materials to the contractor. The court was concerned that a different holding would be unfair to third parties who would have no way of determining which of the supplies in the hands of their debtor, if any, were really owned by someone other than the debtor.[40]

Sufficient rights still may exist if the debtor is purchasing items that are to be collateral, but does not yet have possession of collateral. Most courts agree that the debtor acquires sufficient rights in the purchased goods even if she does not have possession, when title passes under Section 2-401. When title passes depends upon delivery requirements and identification of the goods under Section 2-501.[41]

## [5] Proceeds

"Proceeds" are defined at Section 9-306(1) as "whatever is received upon the sale, exchange, collection or disposition of collateral or proceeds." For example, assume that J.A. Supplies is a debtor of Grant County Bank and that Grant County has a security interest in J.A.'s equipment. If J.A. sells an item of equipment subject to the security interest and takes a trade-in auto, $300 cash, and chattel paper from its buyer as consideration for the sale, all are proceeds arising from the disposition of the collateral. If J.A. uses the $300 to buy inventory, the inventory purchased is defined as proceeds arising from the disposition of proceeds. Insurance that is payable by reason of loss or damage to the collateral is also considered to be proceeds, except to the extent that it is payable to some person not a party to the security agreement. Money, checks, and deposit accounts are "cash proceeds." All other proceeds are "noncash proceeds."[42]

A security interest attached to original collateral also becomes attached to any identifiable proceeds.[43] In the previous example, Grant County Bank

---

[39] 705 F2d 396, 36 UCC Rep. Serv. 292 (10th Cir. 1983).

[40] See also Morton Booth Co. v. Tiara Furniture, Inc., 564 P2d 210 (Okla. 1977).

[41] See, e.g., Rex Fin. Corp. v. Mobile Am. Corp., 119 Ariz. 176, 580 P2d 8, 23 UCC Rep. Serv. 788 (Ariz. Ct. App. 1978); International Harvester Credit Corp. v. Associates Fin. Serv. Co., 133 Ga. App. 488, 211 SE2d 430, 16 UCC Rep. Serv. 396 (1974).

[42] UCC § 9-306(1).

[43] UCC § 9-306(2). Perfection in proceeds is discussed at infra ¶ 7.06[7].

has no attached security interest in the trade-in, cash, or chattel paper unless it can identify that each arises from the disposition of the collateral subject to its interest.[44] For creditors trying to identify proceeds, the greatest difficulties arise when cash has been commingled by deposit in a checking account or some other demand account. In such instances, courts have been liberal in allowing creditors to trace cash proceeds. Nearly all of the courts have adopted the "intermediate balance" rule from the law of trusts. It is assumed that a deposit of proceeds into a commingled account remains identifiable where the commingled account has equaled or exceeded the amount of the deposit at all times since the intermingling. For example, assume that J.A. deposits the $300 in its checking account, which contains funds from other sources. The balance after the deposit is $9,000. As long as J.A.'s balance remains above $300, the cash proceeds are deemed identifiable. If J.A.'s balance dips to $200, the maximum amount of cash proceeds identifiable is $200, even though other monies subsequently deposited may raise the balance in the account to above $300.[45]

## ¶ 7.05 RIGHTS AND OBLIGATIONS OF THE CREDITOR AND DEBTOR UPON DEFAULT

### [1] Introduction

Upon default, an Article 9 secured creditor[1] and debtor have the rights and obligations that are contained in Sections 9-501 through 9-507. Most important among the creditor's rights in these sections are the rights to repossess collateral without judicial process (self-help repossession), to dispose of the collateral, and to seek from the debtor any deficiency remaining after disposition.[2] Most important among the debtor's rights in these sections are the right to enforce the UCC's limitations on the creditor's method of repossession and disposition of the collateral, and the right to any surplus remaining after disposition.[3]

---

[44] See In re Nivens, 22 Bankr. 287, 34 UCC Rep. Serv. 1711 (ND Tex. 1982) (interest in deficiency and disaster payments made to debtor included because they were considered proceeds); In re Munger, 498 F2d 511, 14 UCC Rep. Serv. 790 (9th Cir. 1974) (federal subsidy payments to sugar beet grower also abandonment payments).

[45] See e.g., In re Martin, 25 Bankr. 25, 36 UCC Rep. Serv. 671 (ND Tex. 1982); Universal CIT Credit Corp. v. Farmers Bank of Portageville, 358 F. Supp. 317, 13 UCC Rep. Serv. 109 (ED Mo. 1973); In re Guaranteed Muffler Supply Co., 1 UCC Rep. Serv. 324, 27 UCC Rep. Serv. 1228 (ND Ga. 1980).

[1] A creditor does not have this status unless he has an attached security interest. See supra ¶ 7.04.

[2] UCC §§ 9-503, 9-504.

[3] Id.

## [2] Waiver of Rights

Most rights of the debtor and obligations of the secured creditor cannot be waived or varied by agreement of the parties. Section 9-501(3) lists the following sections that cannot be waived or varied:

(1) Sections 9-502(2) and 9-504, to the extent that they require accounting for surplus proceeds;
(2) Sections 9-504(3) and 9-505, which deal with disposition (except to the extent that these sections specifically allow waivers);
(3) Section 9-505(2), concerning the effect of strict foreclosure on the right of the creditor to sue the debtor for any amount still owing on the collateral;
(4) Section 9-506, concerning redemption of collateral; and
(5) Section 9-507(1), concerning the secured creditor's liability for violation of Sections 9-501 through 9-507.[4]

The UCC does provide, however, that the parties may "determine the standards by which the fulfillment of these rights and duties is to be measured if such standards are not manifestly unreasonable."[5] Creditors often attempt to define the period for reasonable notification to the debtor of the disposition of collateral under Section 9-504. The specified notification period must meet the quoted standard.[6]

## [3] The Debtor

A person claiming the rights of a "debtor" under Article 9 of the UCC must be able to show that he falls into the category of "debtor," as defined by Article 9. Most disputes about whether a party meets this definition concern a guarantor or surety. In most cases, courts have held that a guarantor or surety can be considered to be a debtor under Article 9.[7]

---

[4] See, e.g., Carney v. Central Nat'l Bank of Greencastle, 450 NE2d 1034, 36 UCC Rep. Serv. 894 (Ind. Ct. App. 1983); Bank of Forest Park v. Gray, 159 Ga. App. 42, 282 SE2d 692, 32 UCC Rep. Serv. 644 (1981) (holding that a surety was not entitled to the anti-waiver protection of UCC § 9-501(3)).

[5] UCC § 9-501(3).

[6] The notification requirement is in UCC § 9-504(3). The debtor must get a commercially reasonable notification of the disposition of collateral unless the debtor waives this right after default. The UCC does not define "commercially reasonable." See generally infra ¶ 7.05[7][c][i]. In Liberty Bank v. Honolulu Providoring, Inc., 65 Hawaii 273, 650 P2d 576, 34 UCC Rep. Serv. 1025 (1982), the court cited UCC § 9-501(3) as authorizing a security agreement provision setting five days for the notice period. However, the creditor was found to have violated the notice requirement because the notice was not given within the period specified in the security agreement.

[7] See, e.g., Chemlease Worldwide, Inc. v. Brace, Inc., 338 NW2d 428, 37 UCC Rep. Serv. 647 (Minn. 1983); Liberty Bank v. Honolulu Providoring, Inc., 65 Hawaii 273, 650 P2d 576, 34 UCC Rep. Serv. 1025 (1982); Chase Manhattan Bank v. Natarelli, 93 Misc.

## [4] Default

### [a] Definition

The rights and obligations contained in Sections 9-501 through 9-507 do not arise unless a default occurs. In some states, statutes other than the UCC specify when a default occurs; however, these statutes are limited to consumer credit transactions. The UCC does not define default, deferring instead to the terms of a security agreement. Subject to the limitations discussed below, when a debtor acts, or fails to act, in a manner that the security agreement defines as an incident of default, he is in default under Article 9.[8]

A well-drafted security agreement will contain a definition of default that includes as incidents of default (1) missed payment, (2) evidence of inability to pay, (3) occurrences that indicate a decrease in the value of collateral or the unjustifiable removal of the collateral from the location in which the collateral is to be kept, and (4) failure to adequately care for the collateral.[9] In transactions in which accounts or chattel paper are collateral, a common provision provides that the debtor guarantees the validity of the underlying obligations and that the breach of this guarantee is a default.

### [b] Limits of a Creditor's Ability to React to the Debtor's Default

**[i] Exercise of "Insecurity Clauses."** In addition to limitations that may exist in any particular state's consumer credit laws,[10] there are some other general limitations on the creditor's ability to treat the debtor as in default, with one limitation specifically stated in the UCC. Most security agreements contain a provision stating that the creditor may accelerate the entire obliga-

---

2d 78, 401 NYS2d 404, 23 UCC Rep. Serv. 539 (NY Sup. Ct. 1977); DeLay First Nat'l Bank & Trust Co. v. Jacobson Appliance Co., 196 Neb. 398, 243 NW2d 745, 19 UCC Rep. Serv. 994 (1976).

Sureties may pose special problems because of law outside Article 9. A surety is discharged on its obligation on a negotiable instrument "to the extent that without such party's consent the holder unjustifiably impairs any collateral for the instrument. . . ." UCC § 3-606(1)(b). For a discussion of the decisions on when such discharge occurs and how a creditor may prevent such a discharge see Clark, Law of Secured Transactions ¶ 4.03[3] (Warren, Gorham & Lamont, Inc. 1980).

[8] See UCC § 9-501(1).

[9] See generally Clark, Law of Secured Transactions ¶ 4.02[1] (Warren, Gorham & Lamont, Inc. 1980).

[10] See ¶ 4.02. Such restrictions typically are limited to transactions involving the extension of credit to an individual for a personal, family, or household purpose. A few states have by statute limited the definition of default in such transactions by requiring defaults other than those for missed payments to significantly or materially impair the prospect of payment, performance, or realization of collateral. Two states legislate when missed payments may be considered as a default. About 20 percent of the states require a creditor to give a consumer a right to cure a default before the creditor may exercise any rights based on the default. See id. for a list of such states and further discussion.

tion upon an event of default. This enables the creditor to treat the consumer as in default of the entire obligation and seek the enforcement of the entire obligation rather than pursuing a remedy for only the specific default such as one missed payment.[11] The UCC provides that a term allowing an acceleration of payment or performance or additional collateral "at will," or "when the creditor or the creditor's successor in interest deems himself insecure," and language of similar import, will be construed to mean that the creditor has the power to do so only if he in good faith believes that the prospect of payment or performance is impaired.[12]

The debtor has the burden of establishing lack of good faith.[13] Not many debtors have been able to meet this burden. Good faith is defined at Section 1-201(19) as "honesty in fact"–a subjective test for determining whether the particular creditor had an honest intent given its actual knowledge and not whether this intent was reasonable for a creditor with imputed knowledge.[14] However, despite the UCC's adoption of the "honesty in fact" test of good faith, the creditor should attempt to be reasonable, and follow trade practice, in exercising an acceleration clause at will or where he deems himself insecure. Some courts have indicated they favor a test of reasonableness despite the UCC's apparent adoption of a subjective test.[15] In addition, even if the court finds that the subjective test is controlling because of Section 1-201(19), there is a fine line between the application of a subjective test and the application of an objective test that requires a consideration of the reasonableness of the creditor's behavior. That is, it is difficult for a court to believe a creditor is truly honest in fact when the behavior is in fact unreasonable.

Some debtors have argued that the good faith limitation of Section 1-208 applies when the creditor attempts to accelerate due to the occurrence of events specifically defined as incidents of default. For example, a security agreement typically requires the debtor to insure the collateral and further provides that the creditor may accelerate the entire obligation if the debtor defaults by failing to provide the insurance. It has been argued that a creditor cannot accelerate an obligation even though the debtor has failed to comply with such a provision unless the creditor does so in "good faith." Courts have not been sympathetic to these arguments and have generally limited the good faith requirement of Section 1-108 to the exercise of the broadly drafted "at will" or "insecurity

[11] If the creditor has no agreement for acceleration of an entire obligation upon default, she may not accelerate unless the debtor's default rises to the status of an anticipatory repudiation. See, e.g., Sheet Metal Workers Local #76 C.U. v. Hufnagle, 295 NW2d 259, 29 UCC Rep. Serv. 1087 (Minn. 1980). However, it has been held that the right to accelerate is independent of the right to repossess. Ford Motor Credit Co. v. Hunt, 241 Ga. 342, 245 SE2d 295, 24 UCC Rep. Serv. 251 (1978).

[12] UCC § 1-208.

[13] Id.

[14] See, e.g., Salsbery v. Ford Motor Credit Co., 54 Ore. App. 522, 635 P2d 669, 32 UCC Rep. Serv. 1677 (1981) applying such a test.

[15] Cf. Clayton v. Crossroads Equip. Co., 655 P2d 1125, 34 UCC Rep. Serv. 1448 (Utah 1982) (court determined what was "reasonable," not whether the subjective test of honesty in fact was met).

clauses."[16] It has also been argued that the general good faith limitation of Section 1-203 should be applied as a limitation to a creditor's exercise of an acceleration clause upon the violation of a specific default provision. Courts have not been sympathetic to this argument either.[17]

The creditor who accelerates based on the exercise of a demand feature of a note that represents the debtor's obligation need not worry about the use of the good faith argument. The courts have held that there are no good faith limitations on the exercise of the right to require full payment of a demand obligation.[18]

**[ii] Waiver of Right to Claim a Default.** Even if the debtor has violated a default provision, the creditor may not be able to treat the debtor as in default because of principles of waiver and estoppel. This issue typically arises in cases that involve repeated occasions of late payment by the debtor. In such situations, although late payment is listed as an element of default in the security agreement, the creditor has failed to exercise its rights upon default because of the missed payments. Instead, the creditor has accepted late payments and occasionally has levied a late charge depending upon the length of missed payment. At some point, however, the creditor no longer ignores the late payment and repossesses the collateral. The debtor alleges the creditor is estopped to exercise its rights upon default because the creditor's behavior has induced the debtor to rely upon the creditor's past activity in allowing the debtor to cure the late payment.

Article 9 says nothing about the principle of estoppel. However, Section 1-103, which generally applies throughout the UCC, provides that common-law principles, including estoppel, survive the enactment of the UCC unless they are specifically displaced by UCC provisions. This provision has been utilized by some courts, which found in the type of case described above that the creditor is in fact estopped from exercising its rights arising from a default. Classic

---

[16] See, e.g., Bowen v. Danna, 276 Ark. 528, 637 SW2d 560, 34 UCC Rep. Serv. 1095 (1982); see also Brummund v. First Nat'l Bank of Clovis, 99 NM 221, 656 P2d 884, 35 UCC Rep. Serv. 1311 (1983) (involving acceleration after a breach of a default provision prohibiting the debtor from transferring collateral); In re Sutton Invs., Inc., 46 NC App. 654, 266 SE2d 686, 29 UCC Rep. Serv. 395 (1980); Don Anderson Enters., Inc. v. Entertainment Enters., Inc., 589 SW2d 70, 27 UCC Rep. Serv. 1238 (Mo. Ct. App. 1979) (the last two cases involved real estate sales but discussed UCC § 1-208). Whatever the applicability of UCC § 1-208, a court may exercise its equitable powers to relieve the debtor of the hardships of acceleration where the court finds a mistake, fraud, or inequitable conduct of the creditor. See, e.g., Bowen v. Danna, 276 Ark. 528, 637 SW2d 560, 34 UCC Rep. Serv. 1095 (1982) (the majority and dissent split on this issue, the majority finding that the debtor failed to show any inequitable grounds). But see Brummund v. First Nat'l Bank of Clovis, 99 NM 221, 656 P2d 884, 35 UCC Rep. Serv. 1311 (1983); Foreman v. Myers, 79 NM 403, 444 P2d 589 (1968).

[17] See, e.g., Layne v. Fort Carson Nat'l Bank, 655 P2d 856, 34 UCC Rep. Serv. 1728 (Colo. Ct. App. 1982).

[18] See, e.g., Fulton Nat'l Bank v. Willis Denney Ford, Inc., 154 Ga. App. 846, 269 SE2d 916, 31 UCC Rep. Serv. 428 (1980).

equitable estoppel requires a misleading act that results in justifiable reliance by the other party. In decisions that have found the creditor estopped, the inducement is said to be the conduct in accepting the late payments. The reliance is said to be evidenced by the continued pattern of late payments.[19] Generally, despite earlier conduct, the creditor may strictly enforce the payment provision at a later date by giving the debtor notice that late payments will no longer be tolerated.

Security agreements often contain an "anti-waiver clause" that provides that the failure to strictly enforce any provisions upon default will not result in a waiver of the right to strictly enforce such a provision at a later date. These provisions do not necessarily have their intended effect: Some courts refuse to give them effect because at common law such "anti-waiver clauses" may also be waived. In addition, at common law and under Article 2 of the UCC (covering the sale of goods), repeated acts under a contract may result in the modification of the specific terms of the contract.[20]

**[iii] Legislated Definitions of Default and Rights to Cure.** Some states have placed restrictions on when a secured creditor may treat the debtor as in default, and have mandated a period within which the debtor may cure a default. These restrictions are limited primarily to consumer credit transactions and are reviewed elsewhere in this book.[21]

## [5] Basic Creditor Alternatives Upon Default

### [a] Rights Against the Debtor

Upon default, the creditor typically first seeks to work out a mutually agreeable arrangement that will avoid the complete breakdown of the transaction. If that fails, or if the creditor does not want the transaction to continue, the creditor has two basic alternatives. First, the creditor may simply sue for breach of the underlying obligation, seek a judgment, and proceed to satisfy the judgment like any other judgment for breach of a contractual obligation—by execution and levy.[22] Alternatively, the creditor may seek to enforce the secur-

---

[19] See, e.g., Cobb v. Midwest Recovery Bureau Co., 295 NW2d 232, 28 UCC Rep. Serv. 941 (Minn. 1980).

[20] Compare Van Bibber v. Norris, 419 NE2d 115, 31 UCC Rep. Serv. 1522 (Ind. 1981); McAllister v. Langford Investigators, Inc., 380 So. 2d 299, 28 UCC Rep. Serv. 1205 (Ala. Civ. App. 1980) (giving effect to an anti-waiver clause); Williams v. Ford Motor Credit Co., 435 So. 2d 66, 36 UCC Rep. Serv. 1799 (Ala. 1983) (holding that oral acceptance of late payment did not affect creditor's rights to treat the debtor in default when a provision of the contract provided that any modification had to be in writing) with Westinghouse Credit Corp. v. Shelton, 645 F2d 869, 31 UCC Rep. Serv. 410 (10th Cir. 1981), holding that the anti-waiver clause may be waived by course of performance under UCC §§ 2-208 and 2-209).

[21] See ¶ 4.02.

[22] Any judgment lien obtained in this fashion relates back to the date of perfection of the security interest. UCC § 9-501(5). A judicial sale pursuant to such execution is

ity interest under Article 9: (1) by taking possession of the collateral with judicial action or by self-help, (2) by disposing of the collateral (generally by sale) or keeping the collateral in satisfaction of the obligation, and (3) if there is a disposition, by seeking a deficiency judgment after allocation of the proceeds or by returning any surplus to the debtor. If the security agreement covers both real and personal property, the creditor may proceed as to both types of property under real property law.

The creditor's alternative rights to reduce the claim to judgment and execute on that judgment or to proceed under Article 9 are cumulative. Under pre-UCC law, courts often held that a secured creditor who sued on the debt irrevocably elected to seek the sole remedy by that method.[23] However, there is no election-of-remedies doctrine under Article 9. Proceeding under one alternative will not foreclose the other remedy. For example, a creditor could sue on the debt, obtain a judgment—rights outside Article 9—and then take possession of the collateral pursuant to the rights under Article 9.[24]

A secured creditor typically wishes to proceed under Article 9 because it provides direct access to the collateral. Because of depreciation, however, the collateral may not have significant value. If so, the creditor may prefer to proceed by judgment and execution because he can reach assets of the debtor beyond the collateral and avoid the two-step process of Article 9 of first disposing of the collateral and then suing for a deficiency.

### [b] Collection Rights Against Account Debtors or Obligors

Collateral may be in the form of accounts or instruments that have been assigned to the creditor. If so, the creditor upon default may notify the account debtor or the obligor on the instrument and demand that payment be made directly to the secured creditor assignee.[25] This is true even if, before default, payments were to be made directly to the assignor of the accounts or the original payee on the instrument.[26] The secured creditor may also take control of any proceeds to which he is entitled under Section 9-306.[27]

A creditor who is entitled to recourse against the debtor and who undertakes to collect directly from account debtors or obligors on an instrument must proceed in a "commercially reasonable" manner. The creditor may deduct reasonable expenses of realization from the collections. If the underlying transaction involved a sale of accounts or chattel paper, the debtor is entitled to any surplus or is liable for any deficiency only if the security agreement

---

considered a foreclosure of the security interest by judicial procedure, and the secured party may purchase at the sale and ignore any other requirements of Article 9.

[23] White & Summers, Uniform Commercial Code § 26-4, at 1093 (West, 2d ed. 1980).

[24] See, e.g., Ruidoso State Bank v. Garcia, 92 NM 288, 587 P2d 435, 25 UCC Rep. Serv. 614 (1978).

[25] UCC § 9-502(1).

[26] Id.

[27] Id.

so provides. In other cases, the secured party must account to the debtor for any surplus, and unless otherwise agreed, the debtor is liable for any deficiency.[28]

### [6] Obtaining Possession of Collateral

#### [a] Overview

After default, the creditor typically wants to obtain possession of any collateral not already in his possession. Unless otherwise agreed, upon default, Article 9 allows the creditor to repossess by judicial process or without judicial process. The latter method—called "self-help repossession"—cannot involve a "breach of the peace." Some jurisdictions have limitations outside Article 9 that further restrict the creditor's ability to repossess without judicial action.

Whatever method of repossession is chosen, if the security agreement so provides, the secured party may require the debtor to assemble the collateral and make it available to the secured party at a place convenient to both parties.[29] This provision may be enforced by an injunction.[30] Also, without removal, a secured creditor may render equipment incapable of use, and may dispose of collateral on the debtor's premises.[31]

#### [b] Repossession by Judicial Action

If a creditor decides to gain possession by judicial action, the exact nature of the process depends upon state law outside Article 9 of the UCC. In most states, the judicial process for obtaining property subject to a security interest is called "replevin," "claim and delivery," or "sequestration." Historically, statutes authorizing such a process required only the filing of a brief form with a clerk of the court. The form alleged that the property was subject to a security interest to secure payment of an obligation and that the debtor had failed to pay the obligation. Occasionally, the posting of a bond was also required. Upon filing of the complaint and posting of any required bond, the clerk was empowered to issue a writ of replevin (or similar writ) ordering the sheriff to pick up the collateral. The sheriff was authorized to use force, if necessary. Under most state statutes, the debtor could recover seized collateral only by furnishing a bond equal to twice the value of the collateral. A postseizure hearing date sometimes would be set; typically, this occurred only if requested by the debtor.

---

[28] UCC § 9-502(2).

[29] UCC § 9-503.

[30] See, e.g., Clark Equip. Co. v. Armstrong Equip. Co., 431 F2d 54, 7 UCC Rep. Serv. 1249 (5th Cir. 1970), cert. denied, 402 US 909 (1971) (debtor required to assemble road-building equipment located in several states; the court looked to UCC § 9-501(1), the security agreement, and the assembly provisions of UCC § 9-503).

[31] UCC § 9-503.

In *Fuentes v. Shevin*,[32] replevin procedures like those described were held to be unconstitutional by the U.S. Supreme Court because they allowed a taking of property without prior notice and hearing, in violation of the Fourteenth Amendment. However, in *Mitchell v. W.T. Grant Co.*,[33] the Supreme Court upheld a writ of sequestration statute in Louisiana that was very similar to the replevin statute struck down in *Fuentes*. The Court noted that, unlike the statute in *Fuentes*, the Louisiana statute at issue required that: (1) the application for a writ state the specific factual grounds forming the basis for the writ, (2) the writ be approved by a judicial officer, and (3) an immediate hearing be held following seizure at which time the creditor must prove his claim. In *North Georgia Finishing, Inc. v. Di-Chem, Inc.*,[34] the Court found a Georgia garnishment statute unconstitutional because the Georgia statute did not have the "saving" characteristics of the Louisiana statute in *Mitchell*.

In response to these cases, most states have amended their procedures for reposession by judicial action. One type of statute adopted provides for a probable cause hearing before the taking of the collateral. Such a statute appears to go beyond what is required by the cases previously discussed. Replevin and similar proceedings are discussed elsewhere in this book.[35]

### [c] Self-Help Repossession

The right of the creditor to repossess collateral upon default without judicial action is the creditor's right to "self-help repossession." Under Article 9, there is no requirement for a prior notice to the debtor or a right to a prior hearing on the issue of default. The only limitation under the UCC is that the self-help repossession be "without breach of the peace." As discussed below, constitutional challenges have failed. However, in a few jurisdictions, statutes other than the UCC may place some restriction on the creditor's right to repossess.

**[i] Constitutional Limitation.** The courts have agreed that self-help repossession under Article 9 is not unconstitutional under the Fourteenth Amendment of the U.S. Constitution. The cases previously discussed with respect to repossession with judicial action are not applicable because in self-help repossession there is no state action as required for the applicability of the Fourteenth Amendment.[36]

---

[32] 407 US 67, 10 UCC Rep. Serv. 913 (1972).

[33] 416 US 600, 15 UCC Rep. Serv. 263 (1974).

[34] 419 US 601 (1975).

[35] See ¶ 6.04[3].

[36] See, e.g., Gibson v. Dixon, 579 F2d 1071, 24 UCC Rep. Serv. 1345 (7th Cir. 1978); Turner v. Impala Motors, 503 F2d 607, 15 UCC Rep. Serv. 533 (6th Cir. 1974); Nowlin v. Professional Auto Sales, Inc., 496 F2d 16, 14 UCC Rep. Serv. 846 (8th Cir. 1974), cert. denied, 419 US 1009 (1974); Adams v. Southern Cal. First Nat'l Bank, 492 F2d 324, 13 UCC Rep. Serv. 161 (9th Cir. 1973), cert. denied, 419 US 1006 (1974); James v. Pinnix, 495 F2d 206 (5th Cir. 1974); see also Flagg Bros. v. Brooks, 436 US

A recent case suggests that self-help repossession under Article 9 may be unconstitutional under a state constitutional provision.[37] It is unlikely, however, that this decision will become a precedent for subsequent decisions.[38]

**[ii] "Without Breach of the Peace" Limitation.** The creditor cannot self-help repossess if such action will result in a breach of the peace. The UCC does not define the term; however, courts have defined it as any "act of violence or an act likely to produce violence,"[39] or any act that "by causing consternation and alarm, disturbs the peace and quiet of the community."[40] Creditor activity does not need to rise to the status of a criminal breach of the peace to meeet the definition under the UCC.[41]

Decisions concerning the issue of breach of peace in an Article 9 repossession turn closely on the particular facts involved. Nevertheless, a review of case law indicates that the following acts are likely to give rise to a finding of breach of the peace:

(1) The creditor's use of actual force against the debtor;[42]

(2) The creditor's use of threats and intimidation;[43]

---

149, 23 UCC Rep. Serv. 1105 (1978) (involving the sale of goods by a warehouseman without prior notice and hearing pursuant to UCC § 7-210 was an unconstitutional deprivation of due process).

[37] Fox v. First Bank, 33 UCC Rep. Serv. 1166 (Conn. Super. Ct. 1982).

[38] See, e.g., Crouse v. First Trust Union Bank, 86 AD2d 978, 448 NYS2d 329, 33 UCC Rep. Serv. 1170 (1982).

[39] Morris v. First Nat'l Bank & Trust Co. of Ravenna, 21 Ohio St. 2d 25, 254 NE2d 683, 7 UCC Rep. Serv. 131 (1970).

[40] People v. Chesnick, 302 NY 58, 96 NE2d 87 (1950).

[41] Deavers v. Standridge, 144 Ga. App. 673, 242 SE2d 331, 23 UCC Rep. Serv. 834 (1978).

[42] See, e.g., Big Three Motors, Inc. v. Rutherford, 432 So. 2d 483, 36 UCC Rep. Serv. 338 (Ala. 1983) (creditor's employees forced debtor off highway, blocked her reentry onto the road with their truck, and "escorted" her back to the car dealer's office); Ford Motor Credit Co. v. Garcia, 595 SW2d 602, 28 UCC Rep. Serv. 1213 (Tex. Civ. App. 1980); Nicholson's Mobile Home Sales, Inc. v. Schramm, 164 Ind. App. 598, 330 NE2d 785 (1975).

[43] Morris v. First Nat'l Bank & Trust Co. of Ravenna, 21 Ohio St. 2d 25, 254 NE2d 683, 7 UCC Rep. Serv. 131 (1970) (debtor not present but his son was; son testified that he was "surrounded" by creditor's agents and in fear of "being beaten"). But see Williams v. Ford Motor Credit Co., 674 F2d 717, 33 UCC Rep. Serv. (8th Cir. 1982) (woman alone with two children in mobile home heard noises at 4:00 A.M. and discovered that creditor was repossessing her auto; she told the creditor to no avail that she was trying to pay for the auto; the court found no breach of the peace because the debtor failed to object to the repossession and because it felt there was no incident that might provoke violence; a dissent argued breach of the peace on the intimidation grounds).

(3) The creditor's accompaniment by a police officer;[44]

(4) The creditor's continued repossession after the debtor threatens violence or places himself in a position of potential bodily danger;[45]

(5) Entry into a residence without the voluntary consent of the debtor at the time of repossession.[46]

It is less clear whether entry into structures other than residences constitutes a breach of the peace. Forcible entry generally results in a finding of a breach of the peace as, for example, when the creditor breaks into a locked garage.[47] A few courts apparently have made a distinction between residential and commercial structures and have not found a breach of the peace even where there has been a forcible entry into a commercial structure.[48] On the other hand, forcible entry by breaking a lock to gain entrance has been found to be a breach of the peace, even if entry is into an open fenced area.[49] Entry into an open area, including the debtor's property, without forced entry or any

---

[44] The rationale used is that this is the use of constructive force. See, e.g., Walker v. Walthall, 121 Ariz. 121, 588 P2d 863, 25 UCC Rep. Serv. 918 (1978); Stone Mach. Co. v. Kessler, 1 Wash. App. 750, 463 P2d 651, 7 UCC Rep. Serv. 135 (1970). But see Harris v. Cantwell, 47 Ore. App. 211, 614 P2d 124, 29 UCC Rep. Serv. 1097 (1980) (although there was a police officer present, the court was silent on the constructive-force theory).

[45] See, e.g., Deavers v. Standridge, 144 Ga. App. 673, 242 SE2d 331, 23 UCC Rep. Serv. 834 (1978). However, it is unlikely that a breach of the peace would be found if the protests come after the incident of repossession or a long time before. See e.g., Jordan v. Citizens & S. Nat'l Bank of S.C., 278 SC 449, 298 SE2d 213, 35 UCC Rep. Serv. 722 (1982); Wade v. Ford Motor Credit Co., 8 Kan. App. 2d 737, 298 SE2d 213, 36 UCC Rep. Serv. 1433 (1983) (repossession one month after threat of future deadly violence was not a breach of the peace).

[46] See, e.g., Evers-Jordan Furniture Co. v. Hartzog, 237 Ala. 407, 187 So. 491 (1939); Girard v. Anderson, 219 Iowa 142, 257 NW 400 (1934); Kimble v. Universal T.V. Rental, Inc., 65 Ohio Misc. 17, 417 NE2d 597 (1980); see also General Elec. Credit Corp. v. Timbrook, 291 SE2d 383, 33 UCC Rep. Serv. 1583 (W. Va. 1982) (breach of the peace when the creditor broke a lock on a mobile home being repossessed to release a household pet).

[47] See, e.g., Henderson v. Security Nat'l Bank, 72 Cal. App. 3d 764, 140 Cal. Rptr. 388, 22 UCC Rep. Serv. 846 (1977).

[48] See, e.g., Global Casting Indus., Inc. v. Daley-Hodkin Corp., 105 Misc. 2d 517, 432 NYS2d 453, 31 UCC Rep. Serv. 377 (NY Sup. Ct. 1980). Cherno v. Bank of Babylon, 54 Misc. 2d 277, 282 NYS2d 114, 4 UCC Rep. Serv 505 (NY Sup. Ct. 1967), aff'd, 29 AD2d 767, 288 NYS2d 862 (1968); Wirth v. Heavey, 508 SW2d 263, 14 UCC Rep. Serv. 873 (Mo. Ct. App. 1974).

[49] See, e.g., Laurel Coal Co. v. Walter E. Heller & Co., 539 F. Supp. 1006 33 UCC Rep. Serv. 1580 (WD Pa. 1982); see also Rogers v. Allis-Chalmers Credit Corp., 679 F2d 138, 33 UCC Rep. Serv. 1574 (8th Cir. 1982) (holding that the breach of the peace issue was a jury question because creditor had to pass through at least one gate to get to the collateral).

of the acts described above, such as threatened violence or debtor resistance, would probably not be found to be a breach of the peace.[50]

A few decisions have concerned whether the use of trickery alone is enough for a finding of breach of the peace. The cases have not been uniform; two recent cases have split on this issue. In one case, a creditor repossessed an auto from a garage where the debtor had taken it for repairs. The creditor falsely represented to the garage owner that he had the debtor's permission to repossess the car. A federal district court applying Alabama law found no breach of the peace.[51] A few months later, the Alabama Supreme Court found a breach of the peace where the debtor, at the creditor's invitation, had driven the auto subject to the security interest to the creditor's to discuss the alleged default by the debtor. In finding a breach of the peace, the court held that a distinguishing factor in the case was the existence of a bona fide dispute concerning the debtor's default, even though is was later determined that the debtor was in default.[52]

Whatever the rights of the creditor to repossess the collateral, the creditor's rights to repossess do not extend to any property not subject to a security interest. For example, upon repossession of an auto, the creditor should not take any personalty contained in the trunk of the auto. If the creditor does so, and such property is lost or destroyed, the creditor may be liable in a conversion action.[53]

Whenever the creditor is unsure about whether repossession will result in a finding of breach of the peace,[54] it is best to repossess by judicial process. Several jurisdictions have imposed limitations outside Article 9 on self-help repossession, as discussed in the following section.

---

[50] See, e.g., the following decisions finding no breach of the peace: C.I.T. Corp. v. Short, 273 Ky. 190, 115 SW2d 899, (1938) (open garage; there are no cases involving an unlocked garage door that is closed; the creditor would be pushing his luck to enter a closed, unlocked garage); Marine Midland Bank–Cent. v. Cote 351 So. 2d 750, 22 UCC Rep. Serv. 1298 (Fla. Dist. Ct. App. 1977) (carport); Kroeger v. Ogsden, 429 P2d 781 (Okla. 1967) (airport hangar); Ford Motor Credit Co. v. Herring, 267 Ark. 201, 589 SW2d 584, 27 UCC Rep. Serv. 1448 (1979) (debtor's driveway); Thompson v. Ford Motor Credit Co., 324 F. Supp. 108, 9 UCC Rep. Serv. 128 (DSC 1971) (premises of a third party); McWaters v. Gardner, 37 Ala. App. 418, 69 So. 2d 724 (1954) (from a public place).

[51] Thompson v. Ford Motor Credit Co., 550 F2d 256, 21 UCC Rep. Serv. 907 (5th Cir. 1977).

[52] Ford Motor Credit Co. v. Byrd, 351 So. 2d 557, 22 UCC Rep. Serv. 1294 (Ala. 1977).

[53] See, e.g., Ford Motor Credit Co. v. Cole, 503 SW2d 853, 14 UCC Rep. Serv. 259 (Tex. Civ. App. 1973).

[54] If the creditor does breach the peace, the remedies of UCC § 9-507(1) are applicable. Infra ¶ 7.05[9][b]. Furthermore, a court may award punitive damages if the creditor's actions are particularly egregious. See, e.g., Big Three Motors, Inc. v. Rutherford, 432 So. 2d 483, 36 UCC Rep. Serv. 338 (Ala. 1983).

**[iii] Statutory Limitations.** A few states have provisions that regulate the creditor's right to repossession even after default. Like the state provisions defining default, state legislation of the manner of repossession is generally limited in application to consumer credit transactions.[55]

Some states specifically prohibit repossession from a consumer's home without the voluntary consent of the consumer.[56] In retail installment sales in Connecticut, Hawaii, Maryland, and Ohio, the creditor has the option of either sending a notice indicating that the creditor is going to repossess or not sending such a notice. If the creditor does not send the notice, he must hold the collateral for a specified period. During this period, the debtor may recover the collateral and rights under the contract by curing the default through payment of the unaccelerated amount due and the expenses of retaking.[57]

Of all the states, Wisconsin has the most sweeping limitation. In consumer credit transactions, the Wisconsin Consumer Act requires a prior notice and gives a right to a judicial hearing before self-help repossession, unlesss the consumer voluntarily surrenders the collateral.[58] District of Columbia law provides that the parties to a consumer credit transaction may agree that the creditor has the right to self-help repossess only if it can be done without breach of the peace and with the consent of the debtor.[59]

In *Babbitt Ford, Inc. v. Navajo Indian Tribe*,[60] the Court of Appeals for the Circuit held that the Navajo tribe had the sovereign power to enact and enforce a law providing that self-help repossession of Navajo Indains may be effected only with the written consent of the debtor.

### [d] Care of Collateral in the Creditor's Possession

Whether the creditor gains possession of collateral by repossession or has possession of the collateral with the debtor's consent in the typical pledge arrangement, the creditor has the duties with respect to the collateral specified in Section 9-207. The general duty is one of reasonable care.[61] In the case of an instrument or chattel paper this includes taking necessary steps to preserve rights against prior parties unless otherwise agreed.[62]

In many cases a secured party may satisfy the duty of reasonable care by notifying the debtor of any act that must be taken and allowing the debtor to perform the act. The creditor may add reasonable expenses incurred in the cus-

---

[55] State legislation concerning default in consumer credit transactions is discussed at ¶ 4.02.

[56] See, e.g., Mass. Ann. Laws ch. 255D, § 22(a).

[57] Conn. Gen. Stat. Ann. §§ 42-83–42-100a; Hawaii Rev. Stat. §§ 476-1–476-38; Md. Com. Law Code Ann. §§ 12-601–12-636; Ohio Rev. Code Ann. §§ 1317.01–1317.99. Other costs may also be levied depending upon the jurisdiction.

[58] Wis. Stat. Ann. §§ 425.203–425.208.

[59] D.C. Code Ann. §§ 28–3812.

[60] 710 F2d 587, 36 UCC Rep. Serv. 1809 (9th Cir. 1983).

[61] UCC § 9-207(1).

[62] Id.

tody, preservation, use, or operation of the collateral to the debtor's obligation.[63]

The secured creditor is liable for any loss caused by the failure to meet the obligation of reasonable care.[64] However, the risk of accidental loss or damage is on the debtor to the extent of any deficiency in any effective insurance coverage.[65]

### [e] Repossession of Fixtures and Accessions

Where the creditor has priority in fixtures,[66] she may, upon default, remove the collateral from the real estate. The creditor must reimburse any encumbrancer or owner of the real estate (who is not the debtor and who has not otherwise agreed) for the cost of repair for any physical damage. However, the creditor need not reimburse for any loss of value of the real estate caused by the absence of the fixtures. A person entitled to reimbursement may refuse permission for removal until the creditor gives adequate security for performance of this obligation.[67]

A secured creditor with priority in an accession[68] has the same rights and obligations with respect to those with an interest in the whole personal property as the secured creditor with an interest in fixtures has to the real estate claimant.[69]

## [7] Disposition of Collateral

After default and the creditor's repossession of collateral, the creditor generally has two alternatives concerning the disposition of the collateral. The creditor generally has the option of strict foreclosure of the collateral pursuant to Section 9-505. Under this option, the creditor is not entitled to sue the debtor for any deficiency still owing on the obligation or for any expenses incurred in the retaking or storing of the collateral. The debtor is not entitled to any surplus upon strict foreclosure. Alternatively, the creditor may choose to dispose of the repossessed collateral (or be forced to do so if strict foreclosure is prohibited) pursuant to Section 9-504. Under that section, the creditor must

---

[63] UCC § 9-207(2)(a). A secured party may use the collateral for the purpose of preservation, pursuant to a court order, or, except in the case of consumer goods, as provided in the security agreement. UCC § 9-207(4). Collateral must be kept identifiable but fungible collateral may be commingled. UCC § 9-207(2)(d).

[64] UCC § 9-207(3).

[65] UCC § 9-207(2)(b). See generally Clark, Law of Secured Transactions ¶ 7.14 (Warren, Gorham & Lamont, Inc. 1980).

[66] The meaning of the term "fixtures" and priority in fixtures are discussed at infra ¶ 7.07[8].

[67] UCC § 9-313(8).

[68] The meaning of the term "accession" and priority in accessions are discussed at infra ¶ 7.07[9].

[69] UCC § 9-314(4).

dispose of the collateral pursuant to Section 9-504(3) and apply the proceeds of disposition according to Section 9-504(1). After application of the proceeds, the debtor may be entitled to a return of a surplus or may be liable for a deficiency under Section 9-504(2).

### [a] Retention by Strict Foreclosure Under Section 9-505

**[i] Availability of Strict Foreclosure.** The secured creditor who has repossessed collateral after default generally has the right to strictly foreclose the collateral. However, this right is not available in certain cases where the collateral is consumer goods. In the case of a purchase-money security interest in consumer goods, the creditor is not entitled to strict foreclosure if the debtor has paid 60 percent of the cash price of the goods. Similarly, in the case of loans in which there is a non-purchase-money security interest in consumer goods, the creditor is not entitled to strict foreclosure if the debtor has paid 60 percent of the loan obligation. In either case (subject to the limitation discussed in the next paragraph), the creditor must dispose of the collateral under Section 9-504 within 90 days after the creditor takes possession. If the creditor fails to do so, the debtor may recover in conversion or under Section 9-507(1).[70]

These limitations do not apply if the debtor signs a written statement "renouncing or modifying his rights." However, the debtor must sign such a statement after default for the waiver or modification to be effective.[71]

The advantages of strict foreclosure to the creditor are apparent upon review of the restricitons on a disposition under Section 9-504. Every aspect of such a disposition must be "commercially reasonable." This requirement has given rise to a great deal of litigation. The strict foreclosure route saves the creditor from concerns about the reasonableness of a later disposition of collateral in which strict foreclosure was properly exercised. Strict foreclosure also saves the creditor the costs of foreclosure.[72]

**[ii] Procedure for Strict Foreclosure.** The creditor who is entitled to strict foreclosure must follow the procedure of Section 9-505(2). This requires the creditor to send written notice of the creditor's plan to retain the collateral in satisfaction of the debtor's obligation. The debtor must be given this notice, unless he has signed, after a default, a statement renouncing or modifying his rights to a notice. Unless the collateral is consumer goods, the creditor must also send notice to other secured creditors from whom the secured creditor has received written notice of a claim of an interest in the collateral. The notice must be received by the secured creditor proposing strict foreclosure before the

---

[70] UCC § 9-505(1). Remedies are discussed at infra ¶ 7.05[9].

[71] UCC § 9-505(1).

[72] It is unclear under UCC § 9-505 whether the creditor should be able to strictly foreclose as to part of the collateral and exercise rights under UCC § 9-504 as to other items of collateral. See, e.g., American City Bank of Tullahoma v. Western Auto Supply Co., 631 SW2d 410, 32 UCC Rep. Serv. 1251 (Tenn. Ct. App. 1981).

creditor has sent the debtor's notice or before the debtor has renounced its rights.

If the secured creditor receives notice of an objection from the debtor or other secured parties entitled to notice within twenty-one days after the secured creditor in possession sent notice, the secured party must dispose of the collateral under Section 9-504. If no objection is received from such parties, the creditor may keep the collateral in lieu of resale or other disposition. The exercise of the strict foreclosure right pursuant to this procedure results in a discharge of the obligation. The debtor has no right to a surplus and the creditor has no right to sue for a deficiency.

**[iii] Forced Strict Foreclosure.** Under Section 9-504, the creditor is generally able to sue for any deficiency remaining after she has properly allocated the proceeds of any disposition under the section. The creditor has no right to sue for a deficiency judgment after strict foreclosure. It is occasionally argued that a commercially unreasonable delay in disposing of collateral under Section 9-504 implies an exercise of strict foreclosure under Section 9-505, and thus no right to a deficiency, even though the creditor has not sent notice that it intended a strict foreclosure. The courts are almost evenly split on the validity of such an argument.[73]

### [b] Sale or Other Disposition Under Section 9-504: Generally

If a secured creditor decides not to strictly foreclose under Section 9-505, or if that alternative is not available, disposition of the collateral is governed by Section 9-504. Typically, such a disposition will be by a public or private sale, but the disposition may also be by a lease. The creditor must follow the procedure of Section 9-504(3), under which the disposition may be of the entire collateral or in units or parcels. Generally, the creditor must give notice of the disposition both to other secured creditors who have given timely written

---

[73] Compare, e.g., the following cases finding strict foreclosure may exist although not intended by the creditor: Service Chevrolet, Inc. v. Sparks, 99 Wash. 2d 199, 660 P2d 760, 35 UCC Rep. Serv. 1371 (1983) (remanded for determination of whether retention of auto for four weeks was unreasonable delay); Tanenbaum v. Economics Laboratory, Inc., 628 SW2d 769, 33 UCC Rep. Serv. 124 (Tex. 1982) (destruction of the collateral without any notification to the debtor was an elected UCC § 9-505 strict foreclosure); National Equip. Rental Ltd. v. Priority Elecs. Corp., 435 F. Supp. 236, 22 UCC Rep. Serv. 280 (EDNY 1977) with Chrysler Credit Corp. v. Mitchell, 94 AD2d 971, 464 NYS2d 96, 36 UCC Rep. Serv. 1451 (1983) (stating that strict foreclosure will not be implied when there is no notice by the creditor proposing it); Nelson v. Armstrong, 99 Idaho 422, 582 P2d 1100, 24 UCC Rep. Serv. 1378 (1978); Jones v. Morgan, 58 Mich. App. 455, 228 NW2d 419, 16 UCC Rep. Serv. 1450 (1975) (simply allowing damages under UCC § 9-507(1) for unreasonable delay in disposing of collateral under UCC § 9-504). See Clark, Law of Secured Transactions ¶ 4.10[5] (Warren, Gorham & Lamont, Inc. 1980), arguing against forced strict foreclosure and stating that an unreasonable delay in disposition where the creditor is proceeding under UCC § 9-504 should only give rise to damages under UCC § 9-507(1) and not the loss of the right to sue for a deficiency.

notice of their claims to the secured creditor and to the debtor. Every aspect of the disposition must be "commercially reasonable."[74] Purchasers of the collateral upon disposition are given special protection from the debtor and other claimants.[75]

The creditor must apply proceeds of the disposition according to Section 9-504(1). This allows the creditor to deduct from the proceeds reasonable expenses involved in the repossession and the disposition and then to apply the proceeds to the satisfaction of the secured obligation. After applying the proceeds, Section 9-504(2) provides that the secured creditor must account to the debtor for any surplus and that the debtor is liable for any deficiency (except when the underlying transaction was a sale of accounts or chattel paper and there is no provision in the security agreement so providing). Where a deficiency is owing, this must be sought in a separate deficiency judgment action.

If the creditor fails to follow the procedure of Section 9-504, the debtor may be entitled to the remedies of Section 9-507(1). In addition, in most jurisdictions, a violation of the disposition procedure of Section 9-504(3) will affect the creditor's deficiency judgment action.

## [c] Notification Required Under Section 9-504

**[i] When Notice Is Required.** Section 9-504(3) provides that the secured creditor must give notification of any disposition unless:

(1) The collateral is "perishable or threatens to decline speedily in value";
(2) The collateral is of a type customarily sold on a recognized market; or
(3) The debtor has signed, after default, a statement "renouncing or modifying his right to notification."

One purpose of the notification requirement is to allow the debtor and other secured creditors entitled to notice the opportunity to bid or to encourage others to bid on the collateral.[76] The purpose for the exclusion for perishable goods or goods that will decline rapidly in value is obvious: to exclude notification where the delay occasioned by notification may cause a significant loss in the value of the collateral. The customary market exclusion exists because the price set in these markets represents the fair market value of the collateral. Fungible collateral such as grain fits within this category. Corporate stock also falls within this category.[77] It has sometimes been argued that automobiles or

---

[74] UCC § 9-504(3).

[75] UCC § 9-504(4).

[76] See, e.g., Ocean Nat'l Bank of Kennebunk v. Odell, 444 A2d 422, 33 UCC Rep. Serv. 1803 (Me. 1982); State Bank of Towner v. Hansen, 302 NW2d 760, 30 UCC Rep. Serv. 1493 (ND 1981).

[77] See, e.g., Ocean Nat'l Bank of Kennebunk v. Odell, 444 A2d 422, 33 UCC Rep. Serv. 1803 (Me. 1982); LeRoy v. Marquette Nat'l Bank of Minneapolis, 306 NW2d 815, 32 UCC Rep. Serv. 1310 (Minn. 1981).

trucks are "of a type customarily sold on a recognized market." Courts, however, have rejected this argument.[78]

The validity of a debtor's waiver has not often been questioned. The language of Section 9-504(3) clearly requires that the waiver be given after default; therefore, a waiver in the security agreement is invalid. The creditor should not rely upon any statements or conduct that does not unequivocally indicate a specific waiver of the right to notification.[79]

**[ii] Who Is Entitled to Notice.** In addition to sending notice to the debtor except where the collateral is consumer goods, the creditor must also send a notice of the disposition to other secured creditors from whom the secured creditor has received written notice of a claim of interest in the collateral. The secured creditor conducting the disposition must receive such notice of the other secured creditors' claims either before the creditor has sent the notification to the debtor, or before any waiver of notification by the debtor. The term "debtor" includes a guarantor of the obligation.[80]

**[iii] "Sent" vs. "Received."** Section 9-504(3) requires only that notification of the disposition be sent. There is no requirement that the notice be received.[81] Section 1-201(26) defines "notifies" as follows:

> A person "notifies" or "gives" a notice or notification to another by taking such steps as may be reasonably required to inform the other in ordinary course whether or not such other actually comes to know of it.

Of course, this requires that the creditor use the proper address, if known, and proper postage.[82] The courts have not restricted notice to certified or registered letters. However, it is advisable to use certified mail because of the evidentiary

---

[78] See, e.g., Nelson v. Monarch Inv. Plan of Henderson, Inc., 452 SW2d 375, 7 UCC Rep. Serv. 394 (Ky. 1970); Carter v. Ryburn Ford Sales, Inc., 248 Ark. 236, 451 SW2d 199, 7 UCC Rep. Serv. 386 (1970).

[79] Compare Simmons Mach. Co., v. M&M Brokerage, Inc., 409 So. 2d 743, 33 UCC Rep. Serv. 419 (Ala. 1981) (where debtor agreed to surrender collateral and agreed to the sale, no sufficient waiver) with Nelson v. Monarch Inv. Plan of Henderson, Inc., 452 SW2d 375, 7 UCC Rep. Serv. 394 (Ky. 1970) (voluntary return of the collateral coupled with a statement by the debtor that the debtor did not want it back was a sufficient waiver of notification of sale).

[80] See, e.g., Liberty Bank v. Honolulu Providoring Inc., 65 Hawaii 273, 650 P2d 576, 34 UCC Rep. Serv. 1025 (1982) and discussion at supra ¶ 7.05[3]. As a consequence, the guarantor's waiver of a right to notice of disposition in the security agreement should not be effective, because the debtor cannot waive the right to notice until default. See, e.g., Borg-Warner Acceptance Corp. v. Watton, 215 Neb. 318, 36 UCC Rep. Serv. 1831 (1983).

[81] See, e.g., Leasing Serv. Corp. v. Diamond Timber, Inc., 559 F. Supp. 972, 36 UCC Rep. Serv. 1075 (SDNY 1983)

[82] Edmondson v. Air Serv., 123 Ga. App. 263, 180 SE2d 589, 8 UCC Rep. Serv. 916 (1971) (notice not considered sent when notice was returned because amount of postage was not correct and notice was returned).

value of the return receipt. When the creditor's notice is returned without delivery, it has been held that the creditor should make another reasonable effort to notify.[83] A provision for alternative notice when the notice is returned is advisable.[84]

Although Section 9-504 does not specify that notification of a disposition must be in writing, it does state that notice must be sent. This requirement has led most courts to find that the notice must be in writing.[85] Although some courts have upheld an oral notice,[86] the creditor should give written notice.

**[iv] Timing of Notice.** The UCC does not specify when notice must be sent to the debtor or other creditors. It does provide, however, that the notification must be "commercially reasonable." The notice should be sent early enough to allow the recipients sufficient time to arrange an appearance at any public sale, to encourage others to purchase the collateral, or to otherwise take appropriate steps to protect their interest in the sale or other disposition.[87] The amount of time sufficient to carry out these actions varies with the circumstances, including the nature of the collateral and the location of the sale.[88] Professor Barkley Clark suggests at least ten days' notice, or to be "supersafe,"

---

[83] See, e.g., ITT Indus. Credit Co. v. Rector, SW2d, 34 UCC 379 (Tenn. Ct. App. 1982) (when notice returned unclaimed after being properly sent to debtor's post office box, secured creditor held to have duty to make a second try); In re Carter, 511 F2d 1203, 16 UCC Rep. Serv. 874 (9th Cir. 1975) certified letter returned unclaimed and officer in large bank knew of whereabouts). But see Leasing Serv. Corp. v. Diamond Timber, Inc., 559 F. Supp. 972, 36 UCC Rep. Serv. 1075 (SDNY 1983).

[84] See, e.g., Dougherty v. 425 Dev. Assocs., 93 AD2d 438, 462 NYS2d 851, 36 UCC Rep. Serv. 354 (1983).

[85] See, e.g., Executive Fin. Servs., Inc. v. Garrison, 535 F. Supp. 263, 33 UCC Rep. Serv. 1188 (Bankr. WD Mo. 1982); DeLay First Nat'l Bank & Trust Co. v. Jacobson Appliance Co., 196 Neb. 398, 243 NW2d 745, 19 UCC Rep. Serv. 944 (1976).

[86] See, e.g., Fairchild v. Williams Feed, Inc., 169 Mont. 18, 544 P2d 1216 18 UCC Rep. Serv. 822 (Mont. 1976); Hall v. Owen City State Bank, 175 Ind. App. 150, 370 NE2d 918, 23 UCC Rep. Serv. 267 (1977) (dictum that oral notice should not invalidate the notice as a matter of law but should instead be one of the factors considered in deciding whether or not the notice was reasonable).

[87] Official Comment 5 to UCC § 9-504.

[88] See, e.g., Chemlease Worldwide, Inc. v. Brace, Inc., 338 NW2d 428, 37 UCC Rep. Serv. 647 (Minn. 1983) ("In the absence of contrary evidence, a mailing ten days prior to the sale date does not per se appear commercially unreasonable. Accordingly, the burden of producing evidence shifts to [the debtor] ... Had the [debtors] initiated some protective action which they could not complete prior to the proposed sale date [such as trying to find buyers or seeking a restraining order], such would be specific evidence that the notice was not commercially reasonable"); Hall v. Owen County State Bank, 175 Ind. App. 150, 370 NE2d 918, 23 UCC Rep. Serv. (1977). But see DeLay First Nat'l Bank & Trust Co. v. Jacobson Appliance Co., 196 Neb. 398, 243 NW2d 745, 19 UCC Rep. Serv. 994 (1976). (apparently finding that no period of less than three days would be reasonable notification when the disposition was by private sale; court did not consider the nature of the collateral or other circumstances).

a minimum of seven business days prior to the sale.[89] The period runs from the date when notice is given to the date of the sale. When the sale occurs depends upon an interpretation of Section 2-106, which defines the time when a sale occurs, and Section 2-401, which specifies when title passes.[90]

Provisions in a security agreement specifying when the notification must be given will be given effect if not patently unreasonable. The creditor who has included such a provision in the security agreement should, however, take care to comply with the provision.[91]

**[v] Content of Notice.** The UCC specifies some minimum requirements for the content of the notice of disposition. If the disposition is by public sale, the notification must contain the time and place of the public sale. If the sale is to be by private sale or other disposition, the notice must specify the time after which such a disposition is to be made.[92] If the notice indicates that a public sale will be conducted and a private sale is conducted instead, a creditor cannot successfully claim that the notice sufficiently meets the requirements for a private sale.[93]

Some cases have held that the notice should warn the debtor of the possibility of a deficiency judgment.[94] Professor Barkley Clark suggests that the notice should also contain the following (1) a statement of whether or not the sale is to be by private or public sale, (2) a description of the event of default, (3) reference to the note and security agreement, (4) the unpaid balance of the debt and the amount necessary to redeem, (5) the terms of the intended disposition, and (6) a statement of the right to inspect the collateral prior to sale.[95]

### [d] Commercial Reasonableness

**[i] Presumptions of Reasonableness.** The UCC does not dictate how a disposition must be conducted. However, Section 9-504(3) states that every

---

[89] Clark, Law of Secured Transactions ¶ 4.08[7][c] (Warren, Gorham & Lamont, Inc. 1980).

[90] See, e.g., Chemlease Worldwide, Inc. v. Brace, Inc., 338 NW2d 428, 37 UCC Rep. Serv. 647 (Minn. 1983) ("sale" occurred in shipment contract when the carrier received possession of the goods).

[91] See, e.g., Liberty Bank v. Honolulu Providoring, Inc., 65 Hawaii 273, 650 P2d 576, 34 UCC Rep. Serv. 1025 (1982) (failure to meet five-day period specified in agreement made two-day notice insufficient).

[92] UCC § 9-504(3); see Brown v. Ford, 280 Ark. 261, 658 SW2d 355, 36 UCC Rep. Serv. 1819 (1983) (even though the private sale was not conducted until sixteen months after the notification, no new notice was necessary).

[93] See, e.g., Hayes v. Ring Power Corp., 431 So. 2d 266. 36 UCC Rep. Serv. 1452 (Fla. Dist. Ct. App. 1983).

[94] See, e.g., First Nat'l Bank & Trust Co. of Fremont v. Hughes, 214 Neb. 42, 332 NW2d 674, 36 UCC Rep. Serv. 364 (1983).

[95] Clark, Law of Secured Transactions ¶ 7.04[7][e] (Warren, Gorham & Lamont, Inc. 1980).

aspect of a disposition "including the method, manner, time, place and terms must be commercially reasonable."[96] Section 9-507(2) provides that a sale of collateral is a commercially reasonable disposition when the secured party sells the collateral:

(1) In the usual manner in any recognized market for such collateral;[97]
(2) At the price current in such market at the time of sale;[98]
(3) In conformity with reasonable commercial practices among dealers in the type of property sold.[99]

Also, Section 9-507(2) provides that any disposition is conclusively presumed to be commercially reasonable if the disposition has been approved in any judicial proceeding[100] or by any bona fide creditors' committee or representative of creditors.

**[ii] Effect of Price on Commercial Reasonableness.** Another presumption of Section 9-507(2) is stated in the negative:

> The fact that a better price could have been obtained by a sale at a different time or in a different method from that selected by the secured party is not of itself sufficient to establish that the sale was not made in a commercially reasonable manner.

---

[96] See generally Annot., 7 A.L.R.4th 308 (1981).

[97] See supra ¶ 7.05[7][c][i] for a discussion of the meaning of "recognized market."

[98] Id.

[99] If a sale at wholesale is an accepted method of selling the type of goods involved, a retail sale will not be required. See, e.g., Piper Acceptance Corp. v. Yarbrough, 702 F2d 733, 35 UCC Rep. Serv. 1704 (8th Cir. 1983); Cessna Fin. Corp. v. Bielenberg Masonry Contracting, Inc., 35 UCC Rep. Serv. 315 (D. Kan. 1982), aff'd, 715 F2d 1442 (10th Cir. 1983) (wholesale sale to dealers of plane commercially reasonable because that was industry practice). But see California Airmotive Corp. v. Jones, 415 F2d 554, 6 UCC Rep. Serv. 1007 (6th Cir. 1969) (seems to suggest that sale of plane should be on retail basis because that was the way plane was purchased); Clark Leasing Corp. v. White Sands Forest Prods., 87 NM 451, 535 P2d 1077, 16 UCC Rep. Serv. 1442 (1975); Lamb Bros., Inc. v. First State Bank, 285 Ore. 39, 589 P2d 1094, 26 UCC Rep. Serv. 1395 (1979); Marine Midland Bank–Rochester v. Vaeth, 88 Misc. 2d 657, 388 NYS2d 548, 20 UCC Rep. Serv. 1132 (1976) (holding that sale of shares of stock on the New York Stock Exchange showed commercial reasonableness).

[100] Compare In re Appalachian Pocahontas Coal Co., Inc., 31 Bankr. 579, 36 UCC Rep. Serv. 1803 (SD W. Va. 1983) (parties stipulated to the sale of equipment including four basic aspects of the sale; court entered the stipulation as an order; however, the order was held not to constitute judicial approval under UCC § 9-507(2) because it did not indicate that it was entered into pursuant to a statute or that it was meant to serve as an advance judicial approval) with In re Zsa Zsa, Ltd., 352 F. Supp. 665, 11 UCC Rep. Serv. 1116 (SDNY 1972) (sale conducted according to a plan developed in a hearing before referee in bankruptcy was held to meet this test since all parties in interest had an opportunity to comment upon the arrangement and the plan had passed through a "judicial filter" at the hearing).

Most courts, assume, however, that a low price upon disposition is a factor to be determined in making a decision on commercial reasonableness.[101] This factor will lead a court to scrutinize the sales procedures closely.[102] Where the creditor purchases the collateral and then resells it at a much higher price, courts have found this fact important in determining commercial reasonableness.[103] Several cases have found a disposition to be commercially unreasonable when apparently there was little wrong with the disposition other than the low price received.[104] Where low price is an apparent problem, evidence of reasons for the low price will help the creditor to avoid a finding of commercial unreasonableness.[105]

**[iii] Private or Public Sale.** A "public sale" envisions a broader market than a "private sale." The most common type of public sale is a public auction. The primary distinguishing characteristic of a public sale is bona fide competitive bidding.[106] Section 9-504(3) seems to give the secured party absolute discretion in choosing between a public or private sale where the disposition is by sale. However, the courts have held that the choice is subject to the commercial reasonableness test of Section 9-504(3).[107]

---

[101] Dulan v. Montana Nat'l Bank of Roundup, 661 P2d 28, 36 UCC Rep. Serv. 346 (Mont. 1983); Hall v. Owen County State Bank, 175 Ind. App. 150, 370 NE2d 918, 23 UCC Rep. Serv. 267 (1977); Mercantile Fin. Corp. v. Miller, 292 F. Supp. 797, 7 UCC Rep. Serv. 402 (ED Pa. 1968); Annot., 7 A.L.R.4th 359 (1981). But see Leasing Serv. Corp. v. Diamond Timber, Inc., 559 F. Supp. 972, 36 UCC Rep. Serv. 1075 (SDNY 1983).

[102] See, e.g., Levers v. Rio King Land & Invest. Co., 93 Nev. 95, 560 P2d 917, 21 UCC Rep. Serv. 344 (1977); Connex Press, Inc. v. International Airmotive, Inc., 436 F. Supp. 51, 22 UCC Rep. Serv. 1310 (DDC 1977); Hall v. Owen County State Bank, 175 Ind. App. 150, 370 NE2d 918, 23 UCC Rep. Serv. 267 (1977).

[103] See, e.g., Kobuk Eng'g & Contracting Servs., Inc. v. Superior Tank & Constr. Co.-Alaska, Inc., 568 P2d 1007, 22 UCC Rep. Serv. 854 (Alaska 1977) (purchase by the secured party for $16,000 and resale for $25,000).

[104] White & Summers, Uniform Commercial Code § 26-11, at 1116 (West, 2d ed. 1980).

[105] See, e.g., Federal Deposit Ins. Corp. v. Herald Square Fabrics Corp., 81 AD2d 168, 439 NYS2d 944, 32 UCC Rep. Serv. 558 (1981).

[106] See, e.g., DeLay First Nat'l Bank & Trust Co. v. Jacobson Appliance Co., 196 Neb. 398, 243 NW2d 745, 19 UCC Rep. Serv. 994 (1976) (dissent).

[107] See, e.g., U.S. v. Willis, 593 F2d 247, 25 UCC Rep. Serv. 1178 (6th Cir. 1979) (applied Ohio UCC as federal law in finding public auction sale commercially unreasonable when the creditor had firm offers of $200,000 and $210,000 and, before the auction, the auctioneer had estimated the return from the auction at $45,000); Morrell Employees Credit Union v. Uselton, 28 UCC Rep. Serv. 269 (Tenn. Ct. App. 1979) (sale limited to credit union employees was a private sale, which court felt was not commercially reasonable); Appleton St. Bank v. Van Dyke Ford, Inc., 90 Wis. 2d 200, 279 NW2d 443, 26 UCC Rep. Serv. 1035 (1979) (secured party's "semi-private" sale to Ford dealers of a number of autos was commercially reasonable where twenty-three notices were sent and four appeared to bid).

**[iv] Sale as a Unit or in Parcels.** The secured party's choice of whether to dispose of repossessed collateral as a unit or in parcels may be a factor in the court's consideration of whether or not the sale is commercially reasonable. The key to the reasonableness of the choice is the trade practice with respect to the sale of such goods. For example, if the customary method of selling inventory of a bankrupt distributor is by a sale in bulk, the secured party's decision to sell in bulk is likely to be upheld.[108] On the other hand, if the customary method is sale in parcels (e.g., if it is the practice to sell a drilling rig piece-by-piece), it may be commercially unreasonable to sell as a unit.[109]

**[v] Time Between Repossession and Disposition.** The length of time between repossession and disposition is a factor in determining the commercial reasonableness of the disposition. If the lapse of time from repossession to disposition is either too long or too short, the disposition is not commercially reasonable. The appropriate length of time depends in part upon the specific type of collateral. Some items take longer to sell than others.[110] The more likely the collateral is to depreciate in value over time, the more quickly the disposition must be conducted.[111] Of course, there may be mitigating circumstances, such as the institution of insolvency proceedings, which will give a longer period than that which might otherwise be reasonable.[112] If storage facilities are inadequate to protect the collateral,[113] or the creditor is levying storage charges,[114] the period will be shorter. Whatever the specific facts concerning storage, the disposition probably will be found to be within a reasonable time if the disposition time is similar to the time needed for the regular sale of the particular product. A period of time that is too short will be held to be

---

[108] Fedders Corp. v. Taylor, 473 F. Supp. 961, 27 UCC Rep. Serv. 305 (D. Minn. 1979) (sale of inventory of distributor of air conditioning equipment and parts in bulk at three public sales was proper).

[109] Liberty Nat'l Bank & Trust Co. of Okla. v. Acme Tool Div. of Rucker Co., 540 F2d 1375, 19 UCC Rep. Serv. 1288 (10th Cir. 1976).

[110] See, e.g., Ace Parts & Distribs., Inc. v. First Nat'l Bank of Atlanta, 146 Ga. App. 4, 245 SE2d 314, 23 UCC Rep. Serv. 1370 (1978) (collateral consisted of thousands of automobile parts, which had to be separately inventoried, evaluated, and priced).

[111] See, e.g., In re Myers, 20 UCC Rep. Serv. 1420 (Bankr. WD Va. 1976).

[112] See, e.g., Sparkle Laundry & Cleaners, Inc. v. Kelton, 595 SW2d 88, 28 UCC Rep. Serv. 1531 (Tenn. Ct. App. 1979) (delay caused by the pending of a bankruptcy action); First Nat'l Bank of Kenosha v. Hinrichs, 90 Wis. 2d 214, 279 NW2d 449, 26 UCC Rep. Serv. 1044 (1979) (seven months to sell stock not too long when the creditor had waited to accommodate the debtor who had requested the delay).

[113] See, e.g., Bank Josephine v. Conn, 599 SW2d 773, UCC Rep. Serv. 1226 (Ky. Ct. App. 1980).

[114] See, e.g., FMA Fin. Corp. v. Pro-Printers, 590 P2d 803, 25 UCC Rep. Serv. 950 (Utah 1979) (item sat in storage for six months while creditor made no effort to dispose of the collateral); Ace Parts & Distribs., Inc. v. First Nat'l Bank of Atlanta, 146 Ga. App. 4, 245 SE2d 314, 23 UCC Rep. Serv. 1370 (1978) (fact that creditor provided free storage was important to court in finding that period was not too long).

commercially unreasonable because it indicates that the secured party did not take the time necessary to conduct a reasonable disposition and because the debtor and other secured parties may be denied the chance to protect their interests.[115]

**[vi] Preparation of Collateral.** The UCC does not impose a specific duty on the creditor to recondition or enhance the value of repossessed collateral.[116] However, if the creditor, by making minor repairs or engaging in minor reconditioning, can be assured of higher disposition proceeds, the expenditures should be made. Several courts have found the failure to repair to be an important factor in determining the commercial reasonableness of a disposition in cases where it was the practice in the trade to clean and repair before sale.[117]

**[vii] Time and Place of Sale.** The time of day, week, and year, and the physical location of a sale, have been considered as factors in determining commercial reasonableness.[118]

**[viii] Publication of Sale.** The creditor should take care to publicize any disposition of collateral through the use of advertising.[119] Any advertisement should be designed to reach the audience that is most likely to be interested in purchasing the type of collateral offered. This requires attention to the frequency of the advertising, the placement of the advertisements, and the

---

[115] See, e.g., In re Bryan, 20 UCC Rep. Serv. 571 (Bankr. SD Ohio 1976) (three weeks after repossession was too short for sale of mobile home when usual commercial practice among dealers indicated a normal time of three to six months);

[116] See, e.g., C.I.T. Corp. v. Duncan Grading & Constr., Inc., 36 UCC Rep. Serv. 1809 (ED Mo. 1983); Eaton, Yale & Towne, Inc. v. Sherman Indus. Equip. Co., 316 F. Supp. 435 (ED Mo. 1970).

[117] See, e.g., In re Bryan, 20 UCC Rep. Serv. 571 (Bankr. SD Ohio 1976) (failure to repair and clean mobile home was commercially unreasonable when that was the trade practice); Liberty Nat'l Bank & Trust Co. of Okla. v. Acme Tool Div. of Rucker Co., 540 F2d 1375, 19 UCC Rep. Serv. 1288 (10th Cir. 1976).

[118] See, e.g., General Elec. Credit Corp. v. Bo-Mar Co., 72 Cal. App. 3d 887, 140 Cal. Rptr. 417 (1977) (a public sale of reposessed collateral should ordinarily be held during normal business hours); International Paper Credit Corp. v. Columbia Wax Prods. Co., 102 Misc. 2d 738, 424 NYS2d 827, 28 UCC Rep. Serv. 1484 (1980) (fact that sale of candlemaking machine was held on a day of inclement weather and a forecast of potentially hazardous conditions having an effect upon attendance at the sale was one factor the court looked at in deciding that the sale was not commercially reasonable).

[119] See, e.g., Pioneer Dodge Center, Inc. v. Glaubensklee, 649 P2d 28, 33 UCC Rep. Serv. 1588 (Utah 1982) (creditor took repossessed truck to a few lots and obtained oral bids of undisclosed amounts, placed the truck on the lot for a few days and announced the sale over the loudspeader immediately before the sale; court held this to be inadequate because of failure to advertise in newspaper of general circulation); Wilkerson Motor Co. v. Johnson, 580 P2d 505, 34 UCC Rep. Serv. 842 (Okla. 1978) (although posting a notice on poles is not per se unreasonable notice of the sale of an auto, posting on two utility poles in two alleys and on the side of a building was inadequate).

selection of an appropriate form of publication.[120] It also requires attention to the content of the advertisement, which should list the time, place, and terms of sale, and describe the collateral available. In a private sale, the creditor is not required to publish notice of the sale or to necessarily contact more than one individual.[121] The creditor should, however, contact all those who would reasonably be interested in purchasing the collateral.

**[ix] Other Factors.** Failure to allow prospective bidders an opportunity to conduct an adequate inspection is a factor in commercial reasonableness.[122] Although there are fewer cases on the subject, some courts have also held that the failure to conduct an appraisal of collateral is also a factor in determining commercial reasonableness.[123] A sale of sophisticated equipment by a creditor or creditor's representative who has no familiarity with the type of equipment sold is sometimes considered a factor in determining commercial reasonableness.[124]

### [e] Right of Creditor to Buy

The secured party may purchase the collateral at any *public* sale.[125] If the secured party is the only prospective purchaser at a public sale, however, the courts will more closely scrutinize the sale to determine its commercial reasona-

---

[120] See, e.g., Leasing Serv. Corp. v. Diamond Timber, Inc., 559 F. Supp. 972, 36 UCC Rep. Serv. 1075 (SDNY 1983) (advertising four times in three newspapers and publication in "Contractor's Hotline" of sale of a log loader was adequate); Smith v. Daniels, 634 SW2d 276, 34 UCC Rep. Serv. 355 (Tenn. Ct. App. 1982) (advertising in county newspaper, posting notice on courthouse, and making phone calls to amusement equipment dealers in yellow pages was insufficient for sale of amusement equipment, where standard practice was to advertise in major newspapers in state and in trade magazines and circulate flyers to dealers).

[121] See, e.g., Hall v. Owen County State Bank, 175 Ind. App. 150, 370 NE2d 918, 23 UCC Rep. Serv. 267 (1977) (reasonable sale, although there was only one solicitation, where collateral dropped at bank's door and on that same day a prospective purchaser made an offer to purchase collateral on a one-day take-it-or-leave-it basis); In re Nellis, 22 UCC Rep. Serv. 1318 (Bankr. ED Pa. 1977) (contact of single prospective buyer reasonable, where collateral was attractive to only a limited class of potential buyers and there was a network of informal communication among class of buyers).

[122] See, e.g., Connex Press, Inc. v. International Airmotive, Inc., 436 F. Supp. 51, 22 UCC Rep. Serv. 1310 (DDC 1977).

[123] See, e.g., Granite Equip. Leasing Corp. v. Marine Dev. Corp., 139 Ga. App. 778, 230 SE2d 43, 20 UCC Rep. Serv. 568 (1976); Hall v. Owen County State Bank, 175 Ind. App. 150, 370 NE2d 918, 23 UCC Rep. Serv. 267 (1977); In re Bishop, 482 F2d 381, 12 UCC Rep. Serv. 1256 (4th Cir. 1973).

[124] See, e.g., U.S. v. Bass, 618 F2d 500, 29 UCC Rep. Serv. 717 (8th Cir. 1980); Granite Equip. Leasing Corp. v. Marine Dev. Corp., 139 Ga. App. 778, 230 SE2d 43, 20 UCC Rep. Serv. 568 (1976); Hall v. Owen County State Bank, 175 Ind. App. 150, 370 NE2d 918, 23 UCC Rep. Serv. 267 (1977).

[125] UCC § 9-504(3).

bleness.[126] The secured party cannot purchase at a *private* sale unless the collateral is "of a type customarily sold in a recognized market or is of a type which is the subject of widely distributed standard price quotations."[127]

### [f] Rights of Purchasers

The disposition of collateral after default has these effects:

(1) Transfers to a purchaser for value all of the debtor's rights therein;
(2) Discharges the security interest which the disposition is made; and
(3) Discharges any security interest or subordinate lien.[128]

The purchaser takes the collateral free of all such rights and interests even if the secured party failed to follow the restrictions of Part 5 of Article 9, including the restrictions of Section 9-504(3) on disposition. The purchaser also takes the collateral even if the creditor failed to comply with any judicial proceedings if:

(1) In the case of any public sale, the purchaser has no knowledge of any defects in the sale and if the purchaser does not buy in collusion with the secured party, other bidders or the person conducting the sale; or
(2) In any other case, the purchaser acts in good faith.[129]

### [g] Application of Proceeds

Under Section 9-504(1), the secured creditor must apply the proceeds of any disposition in the following order:

(1) To the reasonable expenses of retaking, holding, preparing for sale or lease, selling, leasing or otherwise disposing of the collateral, and, to the extent provided for in the agreement and not prohibited by law, the reasonable attorney fees and legal expenses incurred by the secured party;[130]
(2) To the satisfaction of the indebtedness secured by the security interest under which the disposition is made;

---

[126] See, e.g., Bank Josephine v. Conn, 599 SW2d 773, 28 UCC Rep. Serv. 1226 (Ky. Ct. App. 1980); Connex Press, Inc. v. International Airmotive, Inc., 436 F. Supp. 51, 22 UCC Rep. Serv. 1310 (DDC 1977).

[127] UCC § 9-504(3); see supra ¶ 7.05[7][c][i]. If the purchaser and secured party are in effect the same entity, a private sale not meeting either of the two exceptions will be considered commercially unreasonable. See, e.g., Dougherty v. 425 Dev. Assocs., 93 AD2d 438, 462 NYS2d 851, 36 UCC Rep. Serv. 354 (1983) (purchaser was a nominee of the creditor and the purchaser and creditor shared the same business address).

[128] UCC § 9-504(4).

[129] Id.

[130] See ¶ 3.04[2] for a discussion of consumer credit statutes limiting attorney fees.

(3) To the satisfaction of indebtedness secured by any subordinate security interest in the collateral if written notification of demand for such application is received before distribution of the proceeds is completed.[131]

### [h] Debtor's Right to a Surplus

After the creditor has applied proceeds in the order set out above, if there is a surplus of proceeds from the disposition, the debtor is generally entitled to the surplus.[132] If the underlying transaction was a sale of accounts or chattel paper, however, the debtor is entitled to any surplus only if the security agreement so provides.[133]

### [i] Creditor's Right to Sue for a Deficiency

If the proceeds are insufficient to satisfy the reasonable expenses of the taking, the disposition, permissible attorney fees, and the indebtedness owed the secured creditor on the underlying transaction, the creditor may be entitled to a deficiency judgment in an independent action.[134] If the underlying transaction was a sale of accounts or chattel paper, the creditor is entitled to a deficiency only if the security agreement so provides.[135] The failure of the secured party to follow the restrictions of Sections 9-501 to 9-507 of Article 9 may also result in a judicially imposed restraint or prohibition of the right to a deficiency judgment.[136]

Finally, about one half of the jurisdictions have imposed limitations on deficiency judgments in consumer credit sales. For example, the Uniform Consumer Credit Code (UCCC) provides that if the cash sale price of consumer goods in a credit sale exceeds a specified amount,[137] the creditor is not entitled to a deficiency judgment. Since deficiency judgments are rarely sought on low-priced consumer goods, the UCCC provision has had little real effect. In the state of Washington, deficiency judgments are prohibited if a seller takes consumer goods by self-help repossession.[138]

---

[131] The secured party can demand reasonable proof of the subordinate interest. If not given within a reasonable time, the secured party need not apply proceeds to the subordinate lien. UCC § 9-504(1).

[132] UCC § 9-504(2).

[133] Id.

[134] Id.

[135] Id.

[136] See supra ¶ 7.05[9][c] for a discussion of such limitations.

[137] This amount varies in the adopting states, but generally it is around $2,000.

[138] Wash. Rev. Code § 62A.9-501. Jurisdictions with provisions limiting deficiency judgments in consumer credit sales include: Alabama, Arizona, California, Colorado, Connecticut, Florida, Georgia, Hawaii, Idaho, Illinois, Indiana, Kansas, Maine, Massachusetts, Minnesota, Ohio, Oklahoma, Oregon, South Carolina, Utah, Washington, West Virginia, Wisconsin, Wyoming. See Consumer Cred. Guide ¶ 4310.

## [8] Debtor's Right to Redeem

### [a] Length of Time for Redemption

The debtor[139] or any other secured party may have the right to redeem (recover) collateral. The redemption must occur before any of the following events:[140]

(1) The secured party disposes of the collateral under Section 9-504(3);
(2) The secured party makes a contract for the disposal of the collateral under Section 9-504(3);
(3) The secured party has exercised the right to strict foreclosure under Section 9-505(2); or
(4) The debtor has agreed in writing after default to waive the redemption right.[141]

### [b] Cost of Redemption

In order to redeem, the debtor or secured party seeking to redeem must "tender fulfillment" of:

(1) All obligations secured by the collateral;
(2) Reasonable expenses incurred by the secured party in retaking, holding, and preparing the collateral;
(3) The costs of the actual disposition; and
(4) To the extent provided by agreement, and not prohibited by law, reasonable attorney fees.[142]

"Tendering fulfillment" of an obligation means more than just making a new promise; it requires payment in full of all monetary obligations and all other obligations then due. If in an installment transaction the debtor has missed one or more installment payments, the amount due on the obligation consists of the outstanding installments unless the creditor has exercised an acceleration as provided for in the agreement. If the obligation to pay is accel-

---

[139] See supra ¶ 7.03[3] for a discussion of the parties that meet this definition; see also In re Bialac, 712 F2d 426, 36 UCC Rep. Serv. 1467 (9th Cir. 1983) (debtor who had a one-sixth interest in a note that was collateral and who was jointly and severally liable on the entire judgment had the right to redeem the entire note).

[140] UCC § 9-506. If the events below occur with respect to only some commercial units of the collateral, the redemption right may be exercised with respect to the other commercial units. Official Comment to UCC § 9-506.

[141] It has been held that such a waiver must also be signed. Kellos v. Parker-Sharpe, Inc., 245 Ga. 130, 263 SE2D 138, 28 UCC Rep. Serv. 266 (1980).

[142] See ¶ 3.04[2] for a discussion of state limitations on attorney fees in some consumer credit transactions.

erated, the entire obligation must be paid to redeem.[143] Any monetary obligation should also include any earned but unpaid interest.[144]

The reasonableness of costs of repossession, preparing for disposition, and the costs of the disposition are issues that may also arise in the creditor's action for a deficiency or the debtor's action for a surplus.[145] The creditor has a good deal of discretion in such expenditures,[146] but expenses will not be considered reasonable if they are disproportionate to the reasonable value of the collateral, the expected return upon disposition of the collateral, or actual out-of-pocket expenses.[147]

## [9] Recovery for Creditor's Wrongful Actions

### [a] Tort Actions

Common-law remedies may exist because of a creditor's unlawful behavior in repossessing or disposing of the collateral. Conversion is the most common type of tort action brought. Courts generally have upheld such a claim where the creditor either has repossessed collateral when there was no default or has disposed of collateral without notice to the debtor or other secured parties to notice.[148] The measure of general damages used in such a conversion action generally is the difference between the reasonable market value of the collateral and the balance due on the debt at the time of conversion.[149] Special damages

---

[143] Rogers v. Associates Commercial Corp., 632 P2d 1002, 32 UCC Rep. Serv. 635 (Ariz. Ct. App. 1981).

[144] See Credit Alliance Corp. v. Adams Constr. Corp., 570 SW2d 283, 25 UCC Rep. Serv. 338 (Ky. 1978) (refusing to require the debtor to pay interest to the creditor that had not yet been earned by the creditor).

[145] See UCC §§ 9-504(1)(a), 9-504(2).

[146] See, e.g., Brown v. Ford, 280 Ark. 261, 658 SW2d 355, 36 UCC Rep. Serv. 1819 (1983).

[147] See, e.g., Thomas v. International Harvester Credit Corp., 636 SW2d 296, 34 UCC Rep. Serv. 1050 (Ark. Ct. App. 1982) (15 percent handling charge not item for recovery in calculating the deficiency, if any, when the equipment was put on the lot by the debtor at his own expense, when it was resold quickly, and when no evidence was presented supporting the charge).

[148] See, e.g., Warren v. Ford Motor Credit Co., 693 F2d 1373, 35 UCC Rep. Serv. 306 (11th Cir. 1982). Where the conversion action is brought because of a failure of the creditor to give the notice of a disposition to the debtor under UCC § 9-507(4), the majority of courts hold that the action is not adversely affected if the debtor is in fact in default. See, e.g., Wells v. Central Bank of Ala., 347 So. 2d 114, 21 UCC Rep. Serv. 1504 (Ala. Civ. App. 1977); State v. Weber, 76 NM 636, 417 P2d 444, 3 UCC Rep. Serv. 907 (1966) . Contra William Iselin & Co. v. Burgess & Leigh, Ltd., 52 Misc. 2d 821, 276 NYS2d 659, 3 UCC Rep. Serv. 1168 (1967).

[149] See, e.g., id.; Allard v. Ford Motor Credit Co., 139 Vt. 162, 422 A2d 940, 30 UCC Rep. Serv. 1180 (1980) (no actual damages were awarded because amount of remaining obligation was greater than reasonable market value). But see Clayton v. Crossroads Equip. Co., 655 P2d 1125, 34 UCC Rep. Serv. 1448 (Utah 1982). The court upheld a jury award that in essence allowed rescission, giving the debtor all amounts

in the form of exemplary or punitive damages may also be awarded but only if the creditor's conduct is particularly objectionable.[150]

Wrongful conduct during repossession can give rise to other tort actions. Breach of the peace during repossession might give rise to trespass action when, for example, the creditor or the creditor's agent wrongfully enters a residence. Wrongful physical contact might give rise to an assault-and-battery action.

### [b] Statutory Remedies Under Section 9-507(1)

Section 9-507(1) provides for the following remedies for a violation of Sections 9-501 to 9-507:

(1) The right to recover from the secured party "any loss caused by a failure to comply" with those sections;
(2) Order for, or restraint of, disposition; and
(3) The right of the debtor to recover as a minimum penalty the finance charge plus 10 percent of the principal if the collateral is consumer goods.

Actions under Section 9-507(1) are most often brought because the creditor has allegedly failed to conduct a commercially reasonable disposition under Section 9-504(3).[151] The measure of general damages for the failure to conduct

---

paid on the obligation and punitive damages and giving the creditor the collateral. The debtor had sued for damages for loss of use of the collateral. Two justices dissented from the decision concerning damages giving three reasons: (1) the plaintiff had elected its remedy by suing for loss of use and the court should not have allowed the substitution of an inconsistent remedy; (2) the damages should have been reduced by the value of the debtor's use of the collateral; (3) punitive damages are only recoverable for a tort, but rescission is a contractual remedy.

[150] See, e.g., Warren v. Ford Motor Credit Co., 693 F2d 1376, 35 UCC Rep. Serv. 306 (11th Cir. 1982) (under Alabama law the evidence must show "legal malice, willfulness, insult or other aggravating circumstances"; court by remititur reduced exemplary damage award of $54,100 to $20,000); Clayton v. Crossroads Equip. Co., 655 P2d 1125, 34 UCC Rep. Serv. 1448 (Utah 1982) ("willful or malicious" conduct or "such gross neglect of duty as to evidence a reckless indifference to the rights of others on the part of the wrongdoer, and an entire want of care so as to raise the presumption that the person at fault is conscious of the consequences of his carelessness" will give rise to exemplary damages); Beneficial Fin. Co. v. Young, 612 P2d 1357, 29 UCC Rep. Serv. 359 (Okla. 1980) (punitive damages award set aside where court found no "wanton or oppressive action"). But see Allard v. Ford Motor Credit Co., 139 Vt. 162, 422 A2d 940, 30 UCC Rep. Serv. 1180 (1980) (court found no actual damages because, by application of general measure, fair market value and amount owing cancelled each other; since there were no actual damages, the court refused to award exemplary damages).

[151] Although Official Comment 2 indicates that the statutory remedy of UCC § 9-507(1) also may be used when the creditor has conducted a wrongful repossession, actions for wrongful repossessions are generally brought for conversion—a common-law tort action. See supra ¶ 7.05[9][a]. Actions brought because the creditor has failed to give appropriate notice of the disposition may also be structured as tort actions for conversion or under UCC § 9-507(1). Both types of action are utilized. See UCC § 1-106; Ben-

a commercially reasonable resale typically is the difference between the actual resale price of the collateral and the probable price the collateral would have brought had the resale been commercially reasonable. The burden of proof is on the debtor to show that actual damage did in fact result. In the case of consumer goods, Section 9-507(1) entitles the debtor to a minimum recovery regardless of the debtor's ability to show actual damages. Therefore, the minimum recovery is, in effect, a penalty. This minimum is 10 percent of the principal plus the finance charge.

When there is a failure to conduct a commercially reasonable disposition of collateral other than consumer goods, there is no minimum recovery. If the debtor is unable to meet the burden of proof as to actual damages, there is no recovery.[152]

### [c] Effect on Deficiency Judgments

The drafters of the UCC did not address the question of whether a creditor's failure to follow the restrictions of Sections 9-501 to 9-507 should have an effect on the creditor's right to recover a deficiency. The courts have taken three positions. One approach, held by a minority of jurisdictions, is that Section 9-507(1) is the exclusive remedy of the debtor. Since it says nothing about deficiency judgments, creditor misbehavior has no effect on the creditor's right to sue for a deficiency.[153] The sole remedy of the debtor is the right to set off actual damages for any losses suffered by the debtor.

Another minority approach bars the deficiency judgment entirely if the creditor fails to follow the provisions of Sections 9-501 through 9-507.[154] Since failure to follow the UCC's restriction harms the debtor by denying the debtor

---

eficial Fin. Co. v. Young, 612 P2d 1357, 29 UCC Rep. Serv. 359 (Okla. 1980) (if an action is brought under UCC § 9-507(1), no punitive damages may be awarded).

[152] UCC § 9-507(1).

[153] See, e.g., Chapman v. Field, 124 Ariz. 100, 602 P2d 481, 27 UCC Rep. Serv. 861 (1979); Commercial Credit Corp. v. Wollgast, 11 Wash. App. 117, 521 P2d 1191, 14 UCC Rep. Serv. 1498 (1974). But see U.S. v. Cawley, 464 F. Supp. 189, 25 UCC Rep. Serv. 1481 (ED Wash. 1979).

[154] See, e.g., Atlas Thrift Co. v. Horan, 27 Cal. App. 3d 999, 104 Cal. Rptr. 315, 11 UCC Rep. Serv. 417 (1972); Randolph v. Franklin Inv. Co., 398 A2d 340, 25 UCC Rep. Serv. 1199 (DC App. 1979); Wilmington Trust Co. v. Conner, 415 A2d 773, 28 UCC Rep. Serv. 900 (Del. 1980); Turk v. St. Petersburg Bank & Trust Co., 281 So. 2d 534, 13 UCC Rep. Serv. 383 (Fla. Dist. Ct. App. 1973); Gurwitch v. Luxurest Furniture Mfg. Co., 233 Ga. 934, 214 SE2d 373, 16 UCC Rep. Serv. 878 (1975); Stensel v. Stensel, 63 Ill. App. 3d 639, 380 NE2d 526, 24 UCC Rep. Serv. 1373 (1978); Herman Ford-Mercury, Inc. v. Betts, 251 NW2d 492, 21 UCC Rep. Serv. 684 (Iowa 1977); DeLay First Nat'l Bank & Trust Co. v. Jacobson Appliance Co., 196 Neb. 398, 243 NW2d 745, 19 UCC Rep. Serv. 994 (1976); Vic Hansen & Sons, Inc. v. Crowley, 57 Wis. 2d 106, 203 NW2d 728, 11 UCC Rep. Serv. 1089 (1973); Aimonetto v. Keepes, 501 P2d 1017, 11 UCC Rep. Serv. 1081 (Wyo. 1972). Note that just because a jurisdiction has denied a deficiency because of a failure to notify the debtor of a disposition, it is not necessarily true that this jurisdiction would deny a deficiency for another violation (e.g., a commercially unreasonable disposition).

the right to redeem and the benefit of the most favorable disposition possible, these courts hold that such violations should be deterred. It is felt that denial of the deficiency is the best deterrent for creditor misbehavior.

A third position is now recognized to be the majority approach. Under this approach, the failure of the creditor to follow the restrictions of Part 5 of Article 9, such as the failure to conduct a commercially reasonable resale, creates a rebuttable presumption that the value that should have been received by the disposition of the collateral equals the balance due on the outstanding debt—a presumption that there is nothing owing the creditor.[155] The courts adopting this approach feel that it places the burden on the person who is in a better position to have knowledge of the facts to go forward with the evidence—the creditor. On the other hand, the majority approach also represents a feeling that absolute denial of the right to a deficiency is too harsh a penalty. If the creditor can show by credible evidence that the collateral was not worth an amount equivalent to the deficiency, the creditor will be able to recover the lesser of either: (1) the difference between the debt (plus reasonable expenses of repossession and other expenses, as spelled out in Section 9-504(1)); or (2) the difference between the unpaid debt (plus expenses allowed under Section 9-507(1)) and the proceeds of resale.[156] The debtor would still be entitled to deduct any damages recoverable under Section 9-507(1) or under common-law tort actions from the deficiency amount even if the creditor was able to rebut the presumption.[157] Creditor evidence necessary to rebut the presumption must be something more than the resale price itself.[158] In addition, testimony

---

[155] Valley Mining Corp., Inc. v. Metro Bank, 383 So. 2d 158, 28 UCC Rep. Serv. 123 (Ala. 1980); Kobuk Eng'g & Contracting Servs., Inc. v. Superior Tank & Constr. Co.-Alaska, Inc., 568 P2d 1007, 22 UCC Rep. Serv. 854 (Alaska 1977); Universal C.I.T. Credit Co. v. Rone, 248 Ark. 665, 453 SW2d 37, 7 UCC Rep. Serv. 847 (1970); Community Management Ass'n of Colorado Springs, Inc. v. Tousley, 32 Colo. App. 33, 505 P2d 1314, 11 UCC Rep. Serv. 1101 (1973); Savings Bank of New Britain v. Booze, 34 Conn. Supp. 632, 382 A2d 226, 23 UCC Rep. Serv. 556 (1977); Liberty Bank v. Honolulu Providoring, Inc., 65 Hawaii 273, 650 P2d 576, 34 UCC Rep. Serv. 1025 (1982); Hall v. Owen County State Bank, 175 Ind. App. 150, 370 NE2d 918, 23 UCC Rep. Serv. 267 (1977); Westgate State Bank v. Clark, 231 Kan. 81, 642 P2d 961, 33 UCC Rep. Serv. 1172 (1982); Levers v. Rio King Land & Inv. Co., 93 Nev. 95, 560 P2d 917, 21 UCC Rep. Serv. 344 (1977); Conti Causeway Ford v. Jarossy, 114 NJ Super. 382, 276 A2d 402, 8 UCC Rep. Serv. 1348 (1971), aff'd, 118 NJ Super. 521, 288 A2d 872 (1972); Clark Leasing Corp. v. White Sands Forest Prods., Inc., 87 NM 451, 535 P2d 1077, 16 UCC Rep. Serv. 1442 (1975); Hodges v. Norton, 29 NC App. 193, 223 SE2d 848, 19 UCC Rep. Serv. 714 (1976); Associates Capital Servs. Corp. v. Riccardi, 408 A2d 930, 27 UCC Rep. Serv. 1457 (RI 1979).

[156] Clark, Law of Secured Transactions ¶ 4.12[4] (Warren, Gorham & Lamont, Inc. 1980). Clark feels that the courts should refuse the deficiency judgment for creditors misbehavior in a consumer case and follow the majority presumption approach in commercial transactions. Id.

[157] Liberty Bank v. Honolulu Providoring, Inc., 65 Hawaii 273, 650 P2d 576, 34 UCC Rep. Serv. 1025 (1982).

[158] See, e.g., Hall v. Owen County State Bank, 175 Ind. App. 150, 370 NE2d 918, 23 UCC Rep. Serv. 267 (1977).

by the creditor's employee alone will not suffice to overcome the presumption.[159] The creditor who desires to overcome the presumption should introduce independent evidence of the fair market value. Such evidence generally would be the testimony of someone with expertise about the value of the type of collateral involved.

## ¶ 7.06 PERFECTING THE SECURITY INTEREST

### [1] Introduction

"Perfection" is not a status that is relevant with respect to the creditor's rights against the debtor. However, a secured creditor generally must be perfected to have priority against third-party claimants. For example, a secured creditor who is unperfected at the time the debtor files a petition in bankruptcy will lose a priority dispute with the trustee in bankruptcy.[1]

Perfection is achieved when, and only when, the creditor can show:

(1) The security interest is "attached"; and
(2) The creditor has taken a permissible "applicable step"–filed a financial statement, taken possession of the collateral, or has achieved "automatic perfection."[2]

Rather than covering the requirements for "attachment,"[3] this section instead concentrates on the applicable steps for perfection–what they are and how they are achieved. It cannot be overemphasized that attachment is a critical part of the perfection formula. Without attachment, all the filing or other applicable steps are useless.

### [2] Applicable Steps–Overview

The potential harm of secret liens in property has long been of concern. A creditor's secret interest in the debtor's property may deceive third parties into thinking that the debtor's property is unencumbered. Most priority laws are designed to favor secured creditors who have taken steps to give public notice of their interest. Filing a financial statement or possessing the collateral are two applicable steps for perfection under Article 9 of the UCC–a preferable status for the creditor–because they are designed to give such notice. The third applicable step–automatic perfection–does not provide public notice; therefore, its use is limited to transactions in which other policy concerns outweigh the policies favoring public notice.

---

[159] Id.

[1] See Section 544(a) of the Bankruptcy Code of 1978; UCC §§ 9-301(3), 9-301(1).

[2] UCC § 9-303(1).

[3] The requirements for attachment are discussed at supra ¶ 7.04.

## [3] Applicable Step–Filing

### [a] Overview

Filing a financing statement is the UCC's preferred method of perfection[4] because it is most likely to give notice to third parties of the creditor's interest. It is also the method of perfection preferred by commercial parties because, in contrast to the applicable step of possession by the creditor, filing allows the debtor to retain possession of the collateral.

With respect to accounts and general intangibles, filing a financing statement under Article 9 is not merely an alternative method of perfection; typically, it is the only permissible method for perfection.[5] On the other hand, with respect to instruments and money, perfection generally requires possession of the collateral.[6]

With respect to vehicles covered by certificate-of-title legislation and some types of collateral covered by federal law, filing under Article 9 is not effective. Instead, filing must be accomplished under state certificate-of-title law or applicable federal law, discussed below.

### [b] Filing Outside Article 9

**[i] Collateral Subject to Certificate-of-Title Legislation.** Every state except Kentucky has certificate-of-title legislation.[7] Most of this legislation is similar to the Uniform Motor Vehicle Certificate of Title Act.[8] With the exception of a vehicle owned by a manufacturer or a dealer and held for sale, or a vehicle owned by a nonresident of the state and not required by law to register the vehicle, the Uniform Act requires that vehicles be covered by a certificate of title.[9] Where the collateral is such a vehicle, perfection must be under the certificate-of-title statute. Perfection under Article 9 is without effect.[10]

---

[4] See UCC § 9-302(1). The presumption of this section is that filing is the typical method of perfecting.

[5] The only exception is where a security interest in certain accounts is perfected upon attachment–automatic perfection. UCC § 9-302(1)(e). That method of perfection of certain accounts is discussed at infra ¶ 7.06[5][c].

[6] A creditor may achieve temporary automatic perfection in instruments under UCC § 9-304(4) or 9-304(5). Infra ¶ 7.06[5][e]. Also, a perfected security interest, without possession, may arise in money and instruments as "proceeds." UCC § 306. See infra ¶ 7.06[7].

[7] Clark, Law of Secured Transactions ¶ 2.08[2] (Warren, Gorham & Lamont, Inc. 1980).

[8] The laws are compiled at 1 Secured Transactions Guide (CCH) ¶ 24. Each state's laws should be carefully reviewed for variations.

[9] The definition of vehicle and thus the coverage of certificate-of-title acts, varies some from state to state. Id. Of course, automobiles and trucks used for personal or commercial purpose are typically covered unless they are held as inventory by a manufacturer or dealer.

[10] UCC §§ 9-302(3)(b), 9-302(3)(c).

Perfection under the Uniform Motor Vehicle Certificate of Title Act is obtained by the delivery to the Department of Motor Vehicles, or its equivalent, an application for the certificate containing the name of the lienholder, the date of the security agreement, and the required fee and registration card.[11]

**[ii] Federal Perfection.** Federal law on perfection, which preempts the rules of Article 9, is discussed earlier in this chapter.[12]

### [c] Document Filed—The Financing Statement

**[i] Overview.** The filing system of the UCC is a notice filing system. It is assumed that prospective creditors will have to make further inquiry from the creditor and debtor.[13] The filed document is called a "financing statement." The financing statement, also called a "UCC 1," must contain the following:

(1) The names of the debtor and the secured party;
(2) The debtor's signature;
(3) An address of the secured party from which information concerning the security interest may be obtained;
(4) A mailing address of the debtor; and
(5) An indication of the types of collateral or a description of the items of collateral.[14]

If the financing statement covers crops, there also must be a description of the real estate upon which the crops are growing or will be grown. Additional information is needed if the financing statement covers timber to be cut, minerals or the like (including oil and gas) or accounts arising from the sale of such collateral at the wellhead or minehead, or if the financing statement is filed as a so-called "fixture filing."[15]

A copy of the security agreement is sufficient as a financing statement if it contains all the required information and is signed by the debtor. A carbon, photographic, or other reproduction of a security agreement is sufficient if the security agreement so provides or if the original has been filed in the controlling jurisdiction.[16]

**[ii] Names of Parties; Change in Name or Organizational Status.** The financing statement must include both the name of the debtor and the secured

---

[11] Variations exist. The laws of Michigan and Wyoming represent significant variations. Perfection in those states requires compliance with the certificate-of-title law and a separate chattel filing. 1 Secured Transactions Guide (CCH) ¶ 24; Clark, Law of Secured Transactions ¶ 2.08[2] (Warren, Gorham & Lamont, Inc. 1980).

[12] See supra ¶ 7.02[4][a].

[13] See Official Comment 2 to UCC § 9-402.

[14] UCC § 9-402(1).

[15] Id.

[16] Id.

creditor.[17] Creditors have often been found to be unperfected because of carelessness in stating the debtor's name. Great care should be taken in: (1) determining the person obligated, (2) determining the legal name of the organization or individual debtor (or both, if both are debtors), and (3) assuring the inclusion of that name, properly spelled, on the financing statement.[18] A financing statement sufficiently shows the name of the debtor if it gives the true name of the debtor whether an individual, partnership, corporation, or other organization name.[19] For example, if the debtor is a natural person, the individual's name must be used. This is true even if the obligation is incurred for an unorganized sole proprietorship that operates under an assumed trade name.[20] Although the creditor may use the trade name along with the name of the individual, several creditors have been found to be unperfected because they listed only an assumed trade name as the debtor's name.[21] Occasionally, creditors have been saved in such cases by the operation of Section 9-402(8), which excuses "minor errors that are not seriously misleading." However, this generally occurs only in cases in which the trade name was nearly identical to or similar to the individual's.[22]

If the debtor is a corporation, the use of the corporate name is required. If both the corporation and an individual (e.g., an officer of the corporation) are obligors, both names should be used. If a partnership operates under an

---

[17] Id. The critical nature of the debtor's name is indicated by UCC § 9-403(4), which provides that the filing officer must file the financing statement according to the debtor's name.

[18] "Debtor" is defined as the person who owes the payment of the obligation. UCC § 9-105(1)(d). The UCC defines a "person" as including an individual or organization. UCC § 1-201(30). "Organization" is defined as including corporations, business trusts, estates, trusts, partnerships or associations, two or more persons having a joint or common interest, or any other legal or commercial entity. UCC § 1-201(28).

[19] UCC § 9-402(7).

[20] See Official Comment 7 to UCC § 9-402.

[21] See, e.g., In re Leichter, 471 F2d 785, 11 UCC Rep. Serv. 673 (2d Cir. 1972); In re Thomas, 466 F2d 51, 11 UCC Rep. Serv. 257 (9th Cir. 1972).

[22] The leading case is In re Platt, 257 F. Supp. 478, 3 UCC Rep. Serv. 719 (ED Pa. 1966) (debtor was listed as "Platt Fur Co.," where the true debtor was "Henry Platt"). Although decided under the 1962 UCC, a jurisdiction favorable to that approach could find the same decision under the 1972 UCC given UCC § 9-402(8), which forgives minor errors that are not seriously misleading. The *Platt* line of authority has attracted a good deal of criticism. See, e.g., Citizens Bank v. Ansley, 467 F. Supp. 51, 26 UCC Rep. Serv. 223 (MD Ga. 1979) (name of "Ansley Farms" was incorrect when debtor was "Emory Ansley"); see also Official Comment 7 to UCC § 9-402.

On the other hand, a recent Fifth Circuit Court of Appeals case shows a willingness to stretch the applicability of UCC § 9-402(8) beyond the limited approach of *Platt*. In re McBee, 714 F2d 1316, 36 UCC Rep. Serv. 1473 (5th Cir. 1983) (debtor was an individual but creditor's filing under "Oak Hill Gun Shop" was upheld; the court stated that the critical inquiry is whether a "reasonably prudent subsequent creditor would have discovered the prior security interest"; the court felt the standard was met even though there was no similarity between the assumed name and the individual debtor's name).

adopted partnership name and the partnership is the debtor, the partnership name should be used. However, the addition of a partner's name in such a case is permissible.[23] Here, too, minor errors that are not "seriously misleading" will not defeat the filing.[24]

Section 9-402(7) determines the effect of changes in the debtor's name. If an individual debtor changes his name or an organization debtor changes its name, identity, or corporate structure, the filing remains effective unless the filed financing statement becomes seriously misleading because of the change.[25] Even if the change is made to a name that does not apparently make the statement misleading, if the secured creditor had knowledge of the impending name change, courts have been more likely to require that a filing reflect the change.[26] If the change does make the financing statement seriously misleading, the creditor's filing is not effective to perfect a security interest in after-acquired collateral that is acquired more than four months after the change, unless a new financing statement is filed before the end of the four months.[27]

**[iii] Addresses.** Section 9-402(1) indicates that the financing statement must contain: (1) an address of the secured creditor from which information concerning the security interest may be obtained, and (2) a mailing address of the debtor. Minor errors in either type of address are tolerated. Section 9-402(8) provides that a financing statement substantially complying with the requirements of the section is effective even if it contains minor errors, as long as errors are not "seriously misleading." Errors or omissions in addresses are

---

[23] UCC § 9-402(7).

[24] See, e.g., In re Excel Stores, Inc., 341 F2d 961, 2 UCC Rep. Serv. 316 (2d Cir. 1965) ("Excel Department Stores" used instead of "Excel Stores, Inc."). But see In re Tyler, 23 Bankr. 806, 34 UCC Rep. Serv. 1428 (SD Fla. 1982). The court held that a change from "Tri-State Moulded Plastics, Inc." to "Tri-State Molded Plastics, Inc." was held to be seriously misleading because computerized search of records under new name would not reveal financing statements under old name. This decision may herald a stricter approach to approving incorrect names occasioned by the use of computerized searching rather than the personal approach. See also In re McCauley's Reprographics, Inc., 638 F2d 117, 30 UCC Rep. Serv. 801 (9th Cir. 1981) (use of predecessor partnership's name "McCauley's Reprographics and Mapping" was held misleading when true name was "McCauley's Reprographics, Inc."). The *McCauley's* decision is criticized as too conservative in DeKoven, "Secured Transactions," 37 Bus. Law. 1033 (1982).

[25] Most courts would hold that the change makes the filing "seriously misleading" unless the new name is very similar to the old. See, e.g., the following cases in which name changes were held to be not seriously misleading: In re Kittyhawk Television Corp., 516 F2d 24, 16 UCC Rep. Serv. 1401 (6th Cir. 1975) (from "Kittyhawk Broadcasting Corp." to "Kittyhawk Television Corp."); White Motor Credit Corp. v. Euclid Nat'l Bank, 17 Ohio App. 312, 409 NE2d 1063, 30 UCC Rep. Serv. 331 (1978) (from "A.A.A. Lift Truck, Inc." to "A.A.A. Lift Truck Leasing, Inc."). But see In re Tyler, 23 Bankr. 806, 34 UCC Rep. Serv. 1428 (SD Fla. 1982).

[26] In re D. G. & Assocs., Inc., 9 Bankr. 94, 31 UCC Rep. Serv. 347 (ED Tenn. 1981); In re Thermal Barriers, Inc., 8 Bankr. 294, 31 UCC Rep. Serv. 364 (ED Mich. 1981).

[27] UCC § 9-402(7).

more likely to be excused if the creditor or debtor are well known[28] or if the geographical area is small in population.[29] Two cases have held that a financing statement may be adequate even though the addresses of both creditor and debtor were missing. The courts in those cases ruled that the financing statement would be adequate without the addresses as long as it was not seriously misleading.[30] However, most courts have held that a complete omission of an address is always seriously misleading.[31]

**[iv] Signature of Debtor.** The debtor must sign the financing statement.[32] If the financing statement is amended, both the secured creditor and debtor must sign the amendment. A financing statement otherwise complying with Section 9-402(1) can be signed by only the secured creditor instead of the debtor if a security interest is to be perfected in:

(1) Collateral already subject to a security interest when brought into a new state or when the debtor's location changes to such state (such a financing statement must also state that the collateral was brought into the new state or that the debtor's location was changed to the new state);
(2) Proceeds under Section 9-306 if the security interest in the original collateral was perfected (such a financing statement must describe the original collateral);
(3) Collateral for which the filing has lapsed; or
(4) Collateral acquired after a change of name, identity, or corporate structure of the debtor.[33]

**[v] Description of Collateral.** There must be a description of collateral in the financing statement. The description must indicate the types or

---

[28] See, e.g., In re Wood, 33 Bankr. 320, 37 UCC Rep. Serv. 627 (D. Idaho 1983) ("Utah Power & Light Co. of Rigby, Idaho" was acceptable because the creditor was a business entity and the town listed was where the creditor's relevant office was located).

[29] See, e.g., In re Davison, 29 Bankr. 987, 36 UCC Rep. Serv. 717 (WD Mo. 1983) (minor error when address listed was "118 N. Cedar," although correct business address of debtor was "122 1/2 N. Cedar"; business district of town with population of only 10,000).

[30] Rooney v. Mason, 394 F2d 250, 5 UCC Rep. Serv. 308 (10th Cir. 1968); In re French, 317 F. Supp. 1226, 8 UCC Rep. Serv. 580 (ED Tenn. 1970); White & Summers, Uniform Commercial Code § 23-16 (West, 2d ed. 1980); see also In re Blier Cedar Co., 28 UCC Rep. Serv. 1202 (Bankr. D. Me. 1980) (holding that the secured party's address need not be as explicit as the debtor's).

[31] See, e.g., In re L & K Transp. Co., 8 Bankr. 921, 30 UCC Rep. Serv. 1745 (D. Mass. 1981) and cases cited therein.

[32] See supra ¶ 7.04[2][b][ii] for a discussion of "signed" and supra ¶ 7.05[3] for a discussion of "debtor."

[33] UCC § 9-401(2).

describe the items of collateral.[34] Section 9-110 provides that a description of personal property is sufficient, whether or not it is specific, if it reasonably identifies what is described. Courts generally approve the creditor's use of the appropriate generic term utilized by the UCC drafters to classify collateral.[35] For example, if a creditor has a security interest in all equipment, inventory, or accounts, an indication of the type of collateral as equipment, inventory, or accounts is an adequate description.[36] Of course, the use of the wrong classification—for example, equipment when the collateral is inventory—would be a fatal error. In addition, if the creditor uses a further descriptive term, such as "located at 110 Vine," and the collateral is actually located elsewhere, the description will fail.[37] Only a few courts have refused to accept the use of UCC classification terms.[38]

Other courts have found the use of terms that represent a broader class, such as "all personal property," to be unacceptable.[39] Although decisions are rare that refuse to accept the use of property descriptions that are broader in scope than the UCC's classification terms, decisions approving broad property descriptions are equally rare. The creditor runs a greater risk using general, sweeping terms than he would if the UCC's classification terms were used.

---

[34] UCC § 9-402(1). There must also be a description of collateral in a written security agreement for there to be attachment under UCC § 9-203(1)(a). "Attachment" is discussed at supra ¶ 7.04. It is generally presumed that the description of collateral for the security agreement requires the same degree of specificity as the description of collateral in the financing statement. But see American Restaurant Supply Co. v. Wilson, 371 So. 2d 489, 25 UCC Rep. Serv. 1159 (Fla. Dist. Ct. App. 1979) (in finding a description of collateral in a security agreement defective, the court stated that the description in the security agreement was held to a greater specificity test because of the purpose of the security agreement; given the facts of the case, however, the description utilized would probably have been defective whether in the financing statement or in the security agreement).

[35] The classifications are listed and defined at supra ¶ 7.03.

[36] See, e.g., In re Buttram, 2 Bankr. 92, 28 UCC Rep. Serv. 874 (ND Okla. 1979) (laundry equipment); Biggins v. Southwest Bank, 490 F2d 1304 (9th Cir. 1973) (inventory); South County Sand & Gravel Co. v. Bituminous Pavers Co., 106 RI 178, 256 A2d 514, 6 UCC Rep. Serv. 901 (1969) (accounts receivable); In re Kendrick & King Lumber, Inc., 14 Bankr. 764, 32 UCC Rep. Serv. 575 (WD Okla. 1981) (general intangibles).

[37] See, e.g., In re California Pump & Mfg. Co., 588 F2d 717, 25 UCC Rep. Serv. 576 (9th Cir. 1978). Contra In re Little Puffer Billy, Inc., 16 Bankr. 174, 32 UCC Rep. Serv. 975 (D. Ore. 1981) ("All inventory of [debtor], Valley River Center" did not limit security interest to inventory at that location but covered inventory at other stores that were later opened by the debtor; court felt that the location was listed as a place where inquiry could be made, not as a limitation on the collateral).

[38] See, e.g., Mammoth Cave Prod. Credit Ass'n v. York, 429 SW2d 26, 5 UCC 11 (Ky. 1968); In re Werth, 443 F. Supp. 738, 23 UCC Rep. Serv. 489 (D. Kan. 1977).

[39] Compare In re Fuqua, 461 F2d 1186, 10 UCC Rep. Serv. 936 (10th Cir. 1972) ("all personal property" too broad) with Leasing Serv. Corp. v. American Nat'l Bank & Trust Co., 19 UCC Rep. Serv. 252 (DNJ 1976) ("any and all property, wherever located" was adequate).

The creditor can use a description that is more specific than the UCC's classification terms. Typically, this is accomplished by the use of a serial number or other form of specific identification. The risk is that the creditor may make a mistake, for example, using an incorrect serial number. Whether such a description will stand depends on the significance of the error.[40] Although one erroneous digit in a serial number with several digits will probably be considered a minor error,[41] the use of a number that bears no resemblance to the true number when the debtor owns many pieces of equipment probably will not be considered minor.[42]

Occasionally, the description of collateral in the financing statement differs from that in the security agreement. Where the description in the financing statement covers more collateral than the description in the security agreement, the security interest is defined by the narrower description of the security agreement.[43] Where the description in the financing statement is narrower, the secured creditor would have a security interest that attaches to the broader collateral described in the security agreement. However, if filing is relied upon for perfection, there would be no perfection in collateral not described in the financing statement.

**[vi] Real Estate Description for Crops.** If the collateral consists of crops that are growing or to be grown, the financing statement also must contain a description of real estate.[44] Real estate descriptions are also required for a written security agreement covering crops or timber to be cut.[45] Case law on the sufficiency of real estate descriptions for security agreements should be valid authority on the sufficiency of real estate descriptions for financing statements.[46]

**[vii] Special Requirements for Fixtures.** A "fixture filing" may give the creditor greater protection in certain priority disputes.[47] In addition to the

---

[40] UCC § 9-402(8) provides that a financing statement substantially complying with the requirements of the section is effective even if it contains minor errors that are not "seriously misleading."

[41] City Bank & Trust Co. v. Warthen Serv. Co., 91 Nev. 293, 535 P2d 162, 16 UCC Rep. Serv. 1370 (1975); (one-digit error in twelve-digit serial number was minor error); In re Blier Cedar Co., 4 Bankr. 669, 29 UCC Rep. Serv. 1085 (D. Me. 1980) (omission of final letter a minor error when numbers correct).

[42] Bank of Middletown v. Town & Country Ford Tractor, Inc., 27 UCC Rep. Serv. 588 (7th Cir. 1979) (one-digit error in twelve-digit serial number was minor error).

[43] See, e.g., Allis-Chalmers Corp. v. Staggs, 117 Ill. App. 3d 428, 453 NE2d 145, 37 UCC Rep. Serv. 262 (1983); In re Mitchell, 458 F2d 700, 10 UCC Rep. Serv. 737 (10th Cir. 1972).

[44] Real estate descriptions are also required for financing statements used to perfect in fixture filings, and financing statements used to perfect an interest in timber to be cut, minerals (including oil and gas), and accounts arising from the sale of minerals at the wellhead or minehead. See discussion at infra ¶¶ 7.06[3][c][vi], 7.06[3][c][viii].

[45] UCC § 9-203(1)(a).

[46] See supra ¶ 7.04[2][b][iv].

[47] Priority in fixtures and the relevance of the fixture filing to such disputes is discussed at infra ¶ 7.07[8].

requirements for a standard financing statement discussed above, the financing statement used for a fixture filing must contain the following:

(1) A statement that it covers fixtures or goods that are to become fixtures;
(2) Provision that it is to be filed in the real estate records;
(3) A description of the real estate;
(4) The name of the record owner if the debtor does not have an interest of record in the real estate.[48]

A transmitting utility is defined to include railroads, electric utilities, electronic communications companies, and oil and gas pipeline companies. If the debtor meets this definition, the financing statement necessary for a fixture filing need not meet the above special requirements for a fixture filing.[49] The drafters recognized the difficulty, for example, of a secured party describing all the real estate that is crossed by an oil pipeline when the pipeline fixtures are collateral.

A real estate mortgage may be filed as a fixture filing if:

(1) The goods are described in the mortgage by item or type;[50]
(2) The goods are or are to become fixtures related to the real estate described in the mortgage;
(3) The mortgage complies with the requirements for a financing statement in this section other than a recital that it is to be filed in the real estate records;
(4) The mortgage is duly recorded.[51]

---

[48] UCC § 9-402(5). Real estate descriptions are also required in: (1) written security agreements (which are generally necessary for attachment and thus perfection) where the collateral is crops or timber to be cut (see supra ¶ 7.04[2][b][iv]); and (2) financing statements filed to perfect crops. See supra ¶ 7.06[3][c][vi]. However, case law on the adequacy of these real estate descriptions may not be good authority with respect to the nature of the real estate description required in UCC § 9-402(5) for a fixture filing. The 1972 Amendments to UCC § 9-402(5) proposed alternative language to UCC § 9-402(5). This alternative language provides that an adequate real estate description required under this section would have to be "sufficient if it were contained in a mortgage of the real estate to give constructive notice of the mortgage under the law of this state." This is a more stringent test than that adopted by most courts for a real estate description for written security agreements in crops and timber to be cut and for the real estate description required at UCC § 9-402(1). If the forum jurisdiction has not adopted the alternative language of UCC § 9-402(5) quoted above, the case law on the adequacy of the real estate description in security agreements should be good authority on the adequacy of the real estate description required under UCC § 9-402(5).

[49] UCC § 9-402(5).

[50] See supra ¶ 7.06[3][c][v].

[51] UCC § 9-402(6). No fee is required other than the regular recording and satisfaction fees with respect to the mortgage. Id.

**[viii] Special Requirements for Timber, Minerals, and Certain Accounts.** If the collateral is timber, minerals (including oil and gas), or accounts arising from the sale of minerals at the wellhead or minehead, the financing statement must meet essentially the same requirements listed above[52] for a fixture filing. Instead of listing the type of collateral as fixtures, the secured party should, where appropriate, substitute either "The above timber is standing on . . ." or "The above minerals or the like (including oil and gas) or accounts will be financed at the wellhead or minehead of the well or mine located on . . ."[53]

**[ix] Mention of After-Acquired Collateral.** A security agreement may attach to collateral acquired by the debtor after the date of the original attachment. Generally, this requires that the security agreement contain a clause stating that it covers such after-acquired collateral.[54] The UCC is unclear concerning whether the financing statement also needs an after-acquired collateral clause in order for the filing to cover such later acquisitions. A majority of courts have found that the financing statement need not mention after-acquired collateral if the collateral is accounts or inventory because it is generally assumed that in such transactions the creditor intended to have an interest in acquisitions of after-acquired collateral.[55] Recently, courts have also seemed inclined to hold that the after-acquired collateral clause is not necessary even if the collateral is other than inventory or accounts.[56] This is consistent with the UCC's adoption of a notice system of filing. The prospective creditor can always seek further information from the creditor or debtor in determining the extent of the obligation. Despite the apparently liberal approach taken by

---

[52] Supra ¶ 7.06[3][c][vii].

[53] This will meet the requirement of UCC § 9-402(5) stating that the description "must show that it covers this type of collateral."

[54] See discussion at supra ¶ 7.04[2][b][v].

[55] See, e.g., In re Stofko, 17 Bankr. 115, 34 UCC Rep. Serv. 1437 (WD Pa. 1982) (description in financing statement included forty types of goods that were a part of debtor's inventory; the word "inventory" was not used and no reference was made to after-acquired inventory; however, court allowed financing statement to perfect security interest in after-acquired inventory); South County Sand & Gravel Co. v. Bituminous Pavers Co., 106 RI 178, 256 A2d 514, 6 UCC Rep. Serv. 901 (1969) (accounts receivable); In re Varney Wood Prods., Inc., 458 F2d 435, 10 UCC Rep. Serv. 513 (4th Cir. 1972) (accounts receivable). This is generally true with respect to security agreements as well. See supra ¶ 7.04[2][b][5]. Contra In re Middle Atl. Stud Welding Co., 503 F2d 1133, 14 UCC Rep. Serv. 1233 (3d Cir. 1974) (accounts receivable).

[56] See, e.g., Pinkerton's Inc. v. John A. Roebling Steel Corp., 186 NJ Super. 10, 450 A2d 1336, 34 UCC Rep. Serv. 1755 (1982) (financing statement served to help perfect security interest in later-acquired instruments although no mention of after-acquired instruments in financing statement); U.S. v. Southeast Miss. Livestock Farmers Ass'n, 619 F2d 435, 29 UCC Rep. Serv. 311 (5th Cir. 1980) (description "livestock" sufficient for financing statement to cover after-acquired hogs). This approach has not been generally adopted where the collateral is other than inventory and accounts, and where the issue is whether the "after-acquired" clause must be in the security agreement. See supra ¶ 7.04[2][b][v].

many courts, the financing statement should include an "after-acquired collateral" clause when such collateral is anticipated.

**[x] Mention of Future Advances.** In addition to the original advance of value, the creditor may later extend new value in the form of a loan of additional funds. The creditor will want to assure that the debtor's obligation is secured to the extent of not only the amounts owing on the original advance but also to the extent of any amounts owing on the future advance as well. The requirement for a written security agreement in order to achieve attachment to the extent of the future advance is discussed elsewhere in this book.[57]

Whatever the need for a mention of future advances in the security agreement, nearly every court has agreed that the financing statement does not need to mention future advances in order for it to cover future advances.

> EXAMPLE: A creditor makes a loan to a debtor for $300,000 on May 14, 1984, and takes an attached security interest. On the same date, the creditor properly files a financing statement that meets all the requirements of Section 9-402(1). No mention is made of future advances in the financing statement. On June 1, 1986, the debtor borrows $1 million from the creditor. No new financing statement is filed.
>
> The original financing statement will suffice as an appropriate filing to the extent of the total amount owing, including the amounts owing on the $1 million future advance despite the failure to mention future advances in the financing statement.[58] This is true if the original financing statement remains current and on file even if there is a period of time between the original advance and the later advance in which no money is owed the creditor.[59]

**[xi] Mention of Proceeds.** The meaning of "proceeds" and "attachment in proceeds" is discussed earlier in the chapter.[60] There is no requirement that the financing statement indicate that the creditor claim a security interest in proceeds. However, a separate financing statement has to be filed in some special circumstances. In other cases, perfection is automatic. The special rules for perfecting a security interest in proceeds are discussed below.[61]

---

[57] Supra ¶ 7.04[2][b][vi].

[58] See, e.g., UCC § 9-312(7), James Talcott, Inc., v. Franklin Natl'l Bank of Minneapolis, 292 Minn. 277, 194 NW2d 775, 10 UCC Rep. Serv. 11 (1972); In re Bates, 37 UCC Rep. Serv. 554 (Bankr. MD Tenn. 1983). Contra Coin-O-Matic Serv. Co. v. Rhode Island Hosp. Trust Co., 3 UCC Rep. Serv. 1112 (RI 1966). This case's reasoning was recently been rejected by the bankruptcy court in the same jurisdiction. In re Nason, 31 UCC 1739 (Bankr. DRI 1981). Also, only one case directly followed *Coin-O-Matic:* Texas Kenworth Co. v. First Nat'l Bank of Bethany, 564 P2d 222, 21 UCC Rep. Serv. 1512 (Okla. 1977).

[59] See, e.g., In re Gilchrist Co., 403 F. Supp. 197, 16 UCC Rep. Serv. 1384 (ED Pa. 1975); In re Lawrence Peska Assocs., Inc., 27 UCC Rep. Serv. 272 (Bankr. SDNY 1979).

[60] See supra ¶ 7.04[5].

[61] See infra ¶ 7.06[7].

### [d] Where to File Within a State

**[i] State Alternatives.** Section 9-401(1) discusses where to file the financing statement within a state.[62] Unfortunately, the UCC drafters proposed three alternatives of this subsection for state adoption and each of the three alternatives was selected by different states. The states also freely amended the official language.[63]

The official first alternative to Section 9-401(1) requires central filing in most transactions (in most states, filing takes place in the office of the Secretary of State or its equivalent). Local filing (where a real estate mortgage would be filed in the county) is required where: (1) the collateral is timber to be cut; (2) the collateral is minerals (including oil or gas) and accounts arising from the sale of minerals at the wellhead or minehead; or (3) the filing is a "fixture filing."

The official second and third alternatives to Section 9-401(1) also require local filing for those types of collateral. In addition, the second alternative requires local filing (in a county office where the debtor resides)[64] where the collateral is: (1) farm equipment; (2) farm products (or accounts and general intangibles arising from such products); and (3) consumer goods. If the collateral consists of crops that are growing or to be grown, filing under this alternative must be local in the county in which the crops are located.[65] With respect to other types of collateral, under the second alternative to Section 9-401(1), the filing must be central (generally at the Secretary of State's office).

The official third alternative to Section 9-401(1) requires local filing for all the transactions in which local filing is required under the second alternative. All other filings must be central. In addition, there also must be a local filing in the county in which the debtor resides if the debtor has no place of business in the state but resides in the state.[66] If the debtor has a place of business in more than one county of the state, there also must be a local filing in all the counties where the place of business is located.

When first adopting the UCC, most states adopted a version of the second alternative to Section 9-401(1). Of course, the version adopted by another state

---

[62] UCC § 9-103 on multi-state transactions determines which is the proper state. See infra ¶ 7.06[6].

[63] See volume 1 of the Secured Transactions Guide (CCH) for a list of state amendments.

[64] For the purposes of determining the proper place to file within a state, the residence of an organization is its place of business or, if it has more than one place of business, its chief executive office. UCC § 9-401(6).

[65] Under the second alternative, filing for crops must be in two local county offices if the debtor resides in one county and the crops are located in another county.

[66] For the purposes of determining the proper place to file within a state, the residence of an organization is its place of business, or, if it has more than one place of business, its chief executive office. UCC § 9-401(6).

is irrelevant if the forum state has adopted another alternative. Each state's version of Section 9-401(1) must be studied.[67]

Whatever the alternative adopted, the importance of proper identification of collateral is evident. Improper classification may lead the creditor to file locally when filing should be statewide, and vice versa. The classifications of "consumer goods," "equipment," and "equipment used in farming operations" depend upon the debtor's use of collateral. In determining the proper place for the initial filing, some courts have held the intended use of the debtor to be controlling while other courts have looked to the actual use by the debtor.[68] Another case has looked to the normal use for such collateral.[69] Given these differing opinions, if there is a possibility that intended initial use and actual initial use will vary, the creditor should take no chances and file according to each of the classifications for the collateral. For example, assume a debtor-farmer purchases a snowplow blade on credit. The debtor states that the blade is to be used primarily for grading streets for hire—equipment. If there is any possibility that the plow may instead be used primarily for moving manure on the debtor's farm, the creditor should make dual filings as if the collateral is both equipment and equipment used in farming operations. The effect of a change in use of the collateral on a filing that was originally filed in the proper place is discussed below.[70]

**[ii] When Debtor Is a Transmitting Utility.** Special rules apply when the debtor is a transmitting utility. "Transmitting utility" is defined at Section 9-105(1)(n) to include any person primarily engaged in the (1) railroad or bus business; (2) electric or electronic communications transmission business; (3) pipeline transmission of goods; (4) the transmission or production of electricity, steam, gas, or water; or (5) the provision of sewer service. Financing statements covering collateral of a transmitting utility must be filed centrally (typically this is in the office of the Secretary of State).[71]

### [e] Change in Use of Collateral

The test for the classifications of "equipment" and "consumer goods" and one alternative test for "farm products" turn on the debtor's use.[72] Under the official second and third alternatives to Section 9-401(1), consumer goods and farm products require local filing. However, under both alternatives, a financing statement covering equipment is centrally filed (under the third alternative, both central and local filing is required for such collateral). If the use of the

---

[67] See volume 1 of the Secured Transactions Guide (CCH) for a list of state enactments of UCC § 9-401(1).

[68] See White & Summers, Uniform Commercial Code § 23-13, at 944 (West, 2d ed. 1980).

[69] In re Burgess, 30 Bankr. 364, 36 UCC Rep. Serv. 708 (WD Okla. 1983).

[70] See infra ¶ 7.06[3][e].

[71] UCC § 9-401(5).

[72] See supra ¶ 7.04.

collateral changes from consumer goods or farm products to equipment or vice versa, the classification change raises the issue of whether a new filing is necessary. Section 9-401(3) indicates that the change of use of the collateral does not affect a filing that is properly filed before the change.[73]

### [f] Effect of Change in Debtor's Residence, Place of Business, or Location of Collateral

When local filing is required under Section 9-401(1), the county for local filing may be determined by the debtor's residence, place of business, or location of collateral. If the county for local filing is initially determined by one of these factors, and, after proper original filing there is a change in this factor, the original filing remains effective under Section 9-401(3). For example, under the third alternative to Section 9-401(1), both central and local filing are required in most transactions. Local filing is to be in the appropriate county office in the county of the debtor's place of business. If the debtor has no place of business but resides in the state, then local filing takes place in the appropriate county office in the county in which the debtor resides. Assume the debtor's place of business is in Wayne County when the transaction is first perfected. Six months later, the debtor moves his business to Mississinewa County in the same state. There is no requirement under Section 9-401(3) for the creditor to file in Mississinewa County.

An official alternative to Section 9-401(3) has been adopted in a few states.[74] Under this alternative, if the county of the place of business, residence, or location of collateral changes and one of those factors controlled the original filing, the creditor must file in the new county within four months.

---

[73] The UCC does not specify at what time the creditor should initially make a determination of the proper place to file within the state. If the creditor chooses the wrong time and determines the place of filing based on the then current use of the collateral (or the then current residence or place of business of the debtor if that is controlling), the filing may be improper if, at the correct time for determining filing, the collateral is within a different classification (or the debtor's address has changed when the debtor's residence originally controlled the place of filing). The courts have split. Some have assumed the relevant facts existing at the time of attachment should control. See, e.g., In re Knapp, 575 F2d 341, 23 UCC Rep. Serv. 1354 (2d Cir. 1978). Others have assumed the relevant time is at the time for filing. See Kripke, "The Last Event Test for Perfection of Security Interests Under Article 9 of the Uniform Commercial Code," 50 N.Y.U. L. Rev. 47 (1975) supporting this approach and the cases cited therein. However, Official Comment 4 to UCC § 9-401 suggests that the relevant time is the time when the last event occurs upon which perfection is based. This may be filing or attachment depending upon which occurs last. It is the same test used in UCC § 9-103(1) for determining which state is proper for filing in certain multi-state transactions. See infra ¶ 7.06[6]. The "last-event" test for UCC § 9-401(1) on where to file within a particular state has recently been adopted by the Fifth Circuit Court of Appeals. In re Hammons, 614 F2d 399, 23 UCC Rep. Serv. 857 (5th Cir. 1980). Because of the existence of Official Comment 4 to UCC § 9-401, the last-event approach will likely be the precedent for future cases.

[74] See volume 1 of the Secured Transactions Guide (CCH).

### [g] Effect of Creditor's Filing Errors

If more than one type of collateral is involved, the filing may be in the proper place with respect to one type of collateral but not to the others. If the filing was made in good faith, it is effective with respect to the type of collateral for which the filing properly complied.[75] For example, under the second alternative to Section 9-401(1), filing as to farm products must be in the county in which the debtor resides, while filing as to equipment used in a business must be central.[76] Assume that a creditor takes a security interest in farm products and equipment used in another business of the debtor, but files only locally in the county where the debtor resides. The filing is proper with respect to the farm products, if the filing was in good faith. However, it is improper with respect to the equipment.

Improper filing as to collateral is effective only as against a person "who has knowledge of the contents of such financing statement."[77] This means that the person has actual knowledge rather than reason to know.[78] However, the nature of the knowledge required by the courts varies. No court has required that the party actually see the financing statement. Most courts have found that knowledge of the minimum facts contained in a typical financing statement—the names of the debtors and creditors and a description of the collateral—is sufficient.[79]

### [h] Duties of Filing Officer and Effect of Mistakes

The filing officer's duties with respect to fixture filings and filings for timber to be cut, minerals, and accounts arising upon the sale of minerals at the wellhead or minehead are determined by Section 9-403(7). The filing officer must index such a financing statement under the names of the debtor, and any owner of record shown on the financing statement, in the same fashion as if they were the mortgagors in a real estate mortgage on the described real estate. Also, if the state provides for indexing by a mortgagee index under the name of the secured party as mortgagee, the filing officer must index under the name of the secured party as mortgagee.

In all other filings under Article 9, upon receipt of the financing statement and filing fee, the filing officer must mark each statement with a file number

---

[75] UCC § 9-401(2).

[76] See supra ¶ 7.06[3][d].

[77] UCC § 9-401(2). However, under the 1972 Text, knowledge of a lien creditor (which includes the trustee in bankruptcy) is not relevant.

[78] See, e.g., In re Mistura, Inc., 705 F2d 1496 (9th Cir. 1983).

[79] See, e.g., id.; In re Davidoff, 351 F. Supp. 440, 11 UCC Rep. Serv. 609 (SDNY 1972). But see U.S. v. Waterford No. 2 Office Center, 246 Ga. 475, 271 SE2d 790, 29 UCC Rep. Serv. 1680, 1681 (1980); (third party knew of names of debtor and creditor and property in which secured party claimed a security interest, but court stated that "[k]nowledge of the claim of a security interest is not equivalent to knowledge of the contents of the financing statement"); In re County Green Ltd. Partnership, 438 F. Supp. 693, 23 UCC Rep. Serv. 168 (WD Va. 1977).

and with the date and hour of filing. The filing officer must also hold the statement or a copy for public inspection. In addition, the filing officer must index the statement according to the name of the debtor and note in the index the file number and the address of the debtor given in the statement.

Occasionally, the filing officer does not properly file the financing statement. Under Section 9-403(1):

> Presentation for filing of a financing statement and tender of the filing fee or acceptance of the statement by the filing officer constitutes filing under this Article.

Courts have taken this to mean that the burden of misfiling by the filing officer will generally fall on the searching party and not on the party who filed the statement.[80] But the secured party will not be protected where an ambiguous or a multipurpose document is filed.[81] A party misled by improper filing may have an action against the state or county who employed the filing officer.[82]

### [i] Amendments to the Financing Statement

A financing statement may be amended by filing a written statement signed by both the debtor and the secured party. An amendment does not extend the length of time the financing statement is effective. If any amendment adds collateral, the financing statement is effective as to the added collateral only from the filing date of the amendment.[83]

### [j] Duration of the Filing

A filed financing statement typically is effective for five years from the date of filing.[84] The secured party may extend the effective period by filing a

---

[80] See, e.g., In re Wood, 33 Bankr. 320, 37 UCC Rep. Serv. 627 (D. Idaho 1983); In re Flagstaff Foodservice Corp., 16 Bankr. 132, 32 UCC Rep. Serv. 1666 (SDNY 1981).

[81] See, e.g., U.S. v. Globe Corp., 113 Ariz. 44, 546 P2d 11, 18 UCC Rep. Serv. 789 (1976); Whitworth v. Krueger, 98 Idaho 65, 558 P2d 1026, 20 UCC Rep. Serv. 1368 (1976).

[82] See, e.g., Mobile Enters., Inc. v. Conrad, 177 Ind. App. 475, 380 NE2d 100, 24 UCC 1031 (1978).

[83] UCC § 9-402(4).

[84] UCC § 9-403(2). Under the 1962 Text, the expiration date could be an earlier date if an earlier date was specified in the financing statement. Under the 1972 Text of the section, the effective period is five years unless: (1) the debtor is a "transmitting utility" (see supra ¶ 7.06[3][d][ii]); or (2) a real estate mortgage is effective as a fixture filing (see supra ¶ 7.03[3][c][vii]). In the first case, the filing is effective until a termination statement is filed and in the second case until the mortgage of record is released, satisfied, or its effectiveness otherwise terminates as to the real estate. UCC § 9-403(6). Also, under the 1972 Text the expiration period may be longer if insolvency proceedings are instituted. In such a case, the filing remains effective until termination of the insol-

continuation statement before the expiration date. The continuation statement cannot be filed until six months before the expiration of the five-year period. The continuation statement must be signed by the secured party, identify the original statement by file number, and state that the original statement is still effective. If the continuation statement is timely filed, the secured creditor has another five years from the date of the termination of the original statement.[85]

Upon lapse of a filing, the security interest becomes unperfected unless perfection is by possession or there is automatic perfection. If the security interest becomes unperfected because of a lapse in filing, it is deemed to have been unperfected as against a person who became a purchaser or lien creditor before lapse.[86]

### [k] Assignments and the Effect on Filing

The originally filed financing statement may disclose an assignment of a security interest by including: (1) the name and address of the assignee, (2) the assignment itself, or (3) a copy of the assignment on the face or back of the financing statement (although this is not necessary for an assignee to have perfection in collateral).[87] Although the following is not necessary for the assignee to have a perfected security interest, a later assignment may be noted by filing, in the place where the original financing statement was filed, a separate written statement of assignment that:

(1) Is signed by the secured party of record;
(2) Lists the name of the secured party of record and the debtor;
(3) Lists the file number and the date of filing of the original financing statement;
(4) Lists the name and address of the assignee; and
(5) Describes the collateral.[88]

Upon receipt of such a separate written assignment, the filing officer typically must mark the assignment with the date and hour of filing and note the assignment on the index of the financing statement. However, if the filing is a fixture filing or a filing for timber to be cut or minerals (and accounts arising from their sale at the wellhead or minehead), the filing officer must index the assignment under the name of the assignor as grantor. If the state law provides

---

vency proceedings and beyond for sixty days, or the expiration of the five-year period, whichever is later.

[85] UCC § 9-403(3).

[86] UCC § 9-403(2). "Purchaser" includes a secured creditor. See UCC § 1-201(32).

[87] UCC § 9-405(1) & Official Comment. The reason given by the Official Comment for the permissive filing of the section is that: "A secured party who has assigned his interest might wish to have the fact noted of record, so that inquiries concerning the transaction would be addressed not to him but to the assignee. . . ."

[88] UCC § 9-405(2) & Official Comment.

for indexing under the name of the assignee, the officer must also index under the name of the assignee.[89]

### [l] Termination of Perfection by Filing

In consumer-goods transactions, the creditor must always file a termination statement where there is no outstanding secured obligation and no commitment to give value. The termination statement must indicate that the creditor no longer claims a security interest under the financing statement, and must identify the financing statement by file number. The statement must be filed with all filing officers where the financing statement was filed and must be filed within one month after the obligation or any commitment to give value has expired. The termination statement may have to be filed earlier than that date if, after the obligation or any commitment ceases, the debtor files a written demand. In such a case, the termination statement must be filed within ten days after the demand but not, in any event, before the secured obligation is paid or while there is any commitment to extend value.[90]

In non-consumer-goods cases, wherever there is no outstanding secured obligation or commitment to extend value, the secured party must, upon written demand, send a termination statement. The statement must take the same form as the termination statement described above and sent to each filing officer with whom a financing statement was filed. The creditor need not file the termination statement in non-consumer-goods transactions or provide one to the debtor without written demand by the debtor.[91]

A failure to file or provide a termination statement as required by Section 9-404 gives rise to actual damages plus a penalty of $100.[92]

Upon presentation to the filing officer of the termination statement, the filing officer must note it on the index. If the statement is received in duplicate, he must return a copy stamped with the time of receipt.[93]

## [4] Applicable Step—Possession

### [a] When Possession Is Required or Permitted

If the collateral consists of accounts or general intangibles, possession is not an appropriate applicable step for perfection.[94] On the other hand, with the exception of brief periods for automatic perfection, possession is the only applicable step for perfecting a security interest in original collateral classified

---

[89] Id.

[90] UCC § 9-404(1).

[91] Id.

[92] Id.

[93] UCC § 9-404(2).

[94] See UCC § 9-305.

as "instruments" or "money."[95] In all other cases, possession is a permissible applicable step for perfection.[96]

Of course, it is important to remember that some types of security interests must be perfected outside Article 9.[97] For example, motor vehicles generally must be perfected by compliance with state certificate-of-title laws. This typically allows perfection only by notation on a certificate of title of the interest; therefore, possession under Article 9 will not suffice.[98] If there is law outside Article 9 regarding perfection in the type of collateral involved, that law must be followed. The controlling statute outside Article 9 may or may not independently allow perfection by possession.[99]

### [b] Meaning of "Possession"

A security interest is perfected by possession from the time possession is taken without relation back.[100] Except for short periods of temporary automatic perfection under Section 9-304,[101] perfection by possession continues only as long as possession is retained.[102] If collateral perfected by possession is held by a bailee in control of the creditor, the secured party is deemed to have possession from the time the bailee receives notification of the secured party's interest.[103]

The extent of physical control by the creditor, or agent of the creditor, that is necessary for the status of possession was an issue left by the drafters to be covered under other law. It is not an issue that has created a great deal of litigation. Clearly, the debtor cannot have control of the collateral under any circumstances; the debtor cannot qualify as the creditor's agent.[104]

---

[95] UCC § 9-304(1). Proceeds arising upon the disposition of original collateral may consist of instruments or money. When this occurs, perfection is still accomplished under the proceeds section discussed at infra ¶ 7.06[7].

[96] UCC § 9-305. If the secured creditor has possession of the collateral by agreement, no written security agreement is necessary for attachment. UCC § 9-203(1)(a).

[97] See generally supra ¶ 7.06[3][b].

[98] See, e.g., Milwaukee Mack Sales, Inc. v. First Wis. Nat'l Bank of Milwaukee, 93 Wis. 2d 589, 287 NW2d 708, 28 UCC Rep. Serv. 540 (1980). But see In re King, 10 Bankr. 685, 31 UCC Rep. Serv. 697 (Bankr. ED Tenn. 1981).(This decision was criticized in Clark, Law of Secured Transactions ¶ 2.06[1] (Warren, Gorham & Lamont, Inc. 1980), in part for failure to consider state certificate-of-title law to determine whether possession was permissible method of perfection under that law.)

[99] See generally supra ¶ 7.06[3][b].

[100] UCC § 9-305.

[101] See discussion at infra ¶ 7.06[5][d].

[102] UCC § 9-305.

[103] The only exception is when the goods are covered by a negotiable document. Id.

[104] See, e.g., In re Maryville Sav. & Loan Corp., 27 Bankr. 701, 35 UCC Rep. Serv. 983 (ED Tenn. 1983); see also In re Lee, 28 Bankr. 319, 35 UCC Rep. Serv. 1000 (DRI 1983) (control by cousin of debtor's wife).

### [c] Secured Creditor's Duties as to Collateral Within Its Possession

The duties and rights of the creditor in possession of collateral are specified in Section 9-207. The general duty is one of reasonable care.[105] In the case of an instrument or chattel paper, this includes taking necessary steps to preserve rights against prior parties unless otherwise agreed.[106]

In many transactions, a secured party may satisfy the duty of reasonable care by notifying the debtor of any act that must be taken and allowing the debtor to perform the act. The creditor may add reasonable expenses incurred in the custody, preservation, use, or operation of the collateral to the debtor's obligation.[107]

The secured creditor is liable for any loss caused by the failure to meet the obligation of reasonable care.[108] However, the risk of accidental loss or damage is on the debtor to the extent of any deficiency in any effective insurance coverage.[109]

## [5] Applicable Step—Automatic Perfection

### [a] Overview

At times, perfection may automatically occur the moment that the security interest becomes attached; the secured creditor does not need to file a financing statement or take possession of the collateral. Where automatic perfection exists, there is the risk that prospective third-party creditors will not receive notice of the secured creditor's claim. Nevertheless, automatic perfection is allowed in certain instances where the UCC drafters believed that the burdens of requiring filing or possession by the creditor outweighed the benefit achieved from the notice to the public. Automatic perfection is the exception rather than the rule, it is allowed in only limited cases.

### [b] Purchase-Money Security Interests in Consumer Goods

A secured creditor is generally entitled to automatic perfection if the security interest is a purchase-money security interest in consumer goods.[110]

---

[105] UCC § 9-207(1).

[106] Id.

[107] UCC § 9-207(2)(a). A secured party may use the collateral for the purpose of preservation, pursuant to a court order, or, except in the case of consumer goods, as provided in the security agreement. UCC § 9-207(4). Collateral must be kept identifiable but fungible collateral may be commingled. UCC § 9-207(2)(d).

[108] UCC § 9-207(3). See Clark, Law of Secured Transactions ¶ 7.14 (Warren, Gorham & Lamont, Inc. 1980) for an extended discussion of the creditor's duty under UCC § 9-207.

[109] UCC § 9-207(2)(b).

[110] UCC § 9-302(1)(d). If the collateral is a motor vehicle covered by certificate-of-title legislation, perfection is accomplished only by complying with the certificate-of-

"Consumer goods" is collateral classified as goods used by the debtor primarily for a personal, family, or household purpose.[111] A purchase-money security interest in goods may arise in two ways under Section 9-107. In the first type, the secured creditor is a seller who allows the debtor to purchase goods on credit. The seller takes a security interest in the goods sold.[112] In the second type, the secured creditor is a lender who loans money to a debtor for the purchase of goods, the debtor does in fact purchase the goods with the money lent, and the lender takes a security interest in the goods purchased.

In either type of purchase-money security interest, if the collateral is consumer goods, the security interest is automatically perfected. The creditor need not file a financing statement or take possession of the collateral to perfect.[113]

### [c] Certain Assignments of Accounts

The mere assignment of accounts may create an Article 9 security interest even if the assignee and assignor were unaware of this effect.[114] Perfection of a security interest in accounts can typically be accomplished only by filing a financing statement pursuant to Article 9.[115] However, automatic perfection exists where the assignment of accounts "does not alone or in conjunction with

---

title laws. See supra ¶ 7.06[3][b][i]. Priority disputes over security interests in fixtures are sometimes resolved under UCC § 9-313 depending upon whether the secured creditor has made a fixture filing. If the collateral is fixtures and such a filing is necessary for priority, the security interest in fixtures is not automatically perfected; a fixture filing is necessary for perfection. See supra ¶ 7.06[3][c][vii].

[111] UCC § 9-109(1); see supra ¶ 7.03[2][b].

[112] Occasionally, a creditor fails to establish the existence of a purchase-money security interest when the security agreement fails to provide a method for release of collateral as the consumer pays the amount of credit extended for that item. The most frequently cited case in this line is In re Manuel, 507 F2d 990, 16 UCC Rep. Serv. 493 (5th Cir. 1975). In this case, the debtor had bought a number of items over a period of time. When a new credit purchase was made, the creditor had the debtor enter into a new consolidated obligation. The security agreement was structured so that every item purchased was kept as collateral regardless of the amount paid. No item of collateral whenever purchased was released from the security interest. The court in *Manuel* found that the secured creditor had no purchase-money security interest in items originally purchased where a new item was purchased and the old obligation was consolidated into the new obligation. The court reasoned that the value extended pursuant to the new transaction was not extended to allow acquisition of the old items because the debtor had already acquired those items. Compare In re Breakiron, 32 Bankr. 400, 37 UCC Rep. Serv. 257 (WD Pa. 1983) (upholding the creditor's claim of automatic perfection where the security agreement provided that each item purchased secured only the debt on that item).

[113] The creditor may wish to file to perfect. A consumer buyer who takes from a consumer seller will generally defeat a secured creditor unless the creditor has perfected by filing. UCC § 9-307(2). See infra ¶ 7.07[5][b][ii].

[114] For a discussion of the applicablity of Article 9 to accounts, see supra ¶ 7.02[3].

[115] UCC § 9-305 & Official Comment 1.

other assignments to the same assignee transfer a significant part of the outstanding accounts of the assignor."[116]

The UCC does not define "significant part." The courts seem to have adopted two tests in determining whether this condition has been met. One test comes from Official Comment 5 to Section 9-302. That test requires the court to examine the circumstances surrounding the transaction, including the status of the assignee, to determine whether the assignment was "casual or isolated." If the court finds that the transaction was not part of a regular course of commercial financing, the assignment is considered to be automatically perfected and filing is not required. In the words of one court, the adoption of this test

> tells commercial lenders that they fail to file at their peril and at the same time does not penalize a casual onetime lender who, in genuine innocence, accepts an assignment of over a certain percentage of a business' accounts.[117]

The other test is a percentage test in which the court looks to the size of the assignment in relation to all of the assignor's outstanding accounts. The larger the value of the assignment as a percentage of the total accounts, the more likely the court will find that the assignment is "significant."[118] The percentage test does not inherently take into consideration the sophistication of the assignee as a lender engaged in financing with accounts as security. The percentage test also raises the issue of whether all accounts should be taken into consideration in determining the percentage; for example, should the debtor's total accounts be considered to include uncollectible accounts?[119]

Some courts have used both tests.[120] Wherever a party takes an assignment of accounts not clearly outside of Article 9's scope,[121] the party should file a financing statement to perfect and not rely on automatic perfection.

---

[116] UCC § 9-302(1)(e).

[117] In re Barrington, 37 UCC Rep. Serv. 540, 544 (Bankr. MD Fla. 1983).

[118] The courts have never set an absolute percentage beyond which the assignment is deemed "significant." Compare Standard Lumber Co. v. Chamber Frames, Inc., 317 F. Supp. 837, 8 UCC Rep. Serv. 139 (ED Ark. 1970) (automatic perfection available where accounts assigned only 16 percent of total of debtor's accounts); In re Sun Air Int'l, Inc., 24 Bankr. 135, 34 UCC Rep. Serv. 1369 (SD Fla. 1982) (14 percent was not "significant") with Miller v. Wells Fargo Bank Int'l Corp., 406 F. Supp. 452, 18 UCC Rep. Serv. 489 (SDNY 1975), aff'd, 540 F2d 548 (2d Cir. 1976) (just under 20 percent was "significant" and therefore filing was required).

[119] See, e.g., In re B. Hollis Knight Co., 605 F2d 397, 27 UCC Rep. Serv. 337 (8th Cir. 1979).

[120] See, e.g., id. (stating that the combination of the two would require a filing if the creditor received a large part of the accounts of the debtor and would also require filing if the creditor regularly took such assignments regardless of the percentage represented by the particular assignment); City of Vermillion, S.D. v. Stan Houston Equip. Co., 341 F. Supp. 707, 10 UCC Rep. Serv. 1246 (DSD 1972).

[121] UCC § 9-104; supra ¶ 7.02[3].

### [d] Temporary Automatic Perfection in Instruments, Documents, and Certain Goods in the Possession of Bailee

A security interest in instruments (other than certificated securities) or negotiable documents is perfected automatically for twenty-one days from the time of attachment to the extent it arises for new value given under a written security agreement.[122] An additional twenty-one-day automatic perfection exists where a secured party having a perfected security interest in a negotiable document, or goods in the possession of a bailee who has not issued a negotiable document, makes available to the debtor the goods or documents representing the goods for the purpose of ultimate sale or exchange, or for the purpose of loading, unloading, storing, shipping, manufacturing, processing, or otherwise dealing with them preparatory to sale or exchange.[123] For instruments (other than certificated securities), an additional twenty-one-day period is allowed if the creditor who has possession of the instrument delivers the instrument to the debtor for the purpose of ultimate sale or exchange or of presentation, collection, renewal, or registration of transfer.[124]

### [e] Article 2 Security Interests

Security interests may arise solely under Article 2.[125] Until the debtor gets the possession (the "debtor" is the buyer when the security interest arises under Article 2 in favor of the seller), no filing is necessary under Article 2 for perfection.[126]

### [f] Miscellaneous Security Interests in Assignees and Banks

If a secured party assigns a perfected security interest, no filing is necessary in order to continue the perfected status as against creditors of and transferees from the original debtor.[127] Automatic perfection also exists for the assignee of a beneficial interest in a trust or a decedent's estate.[128] Creditors who receive an assignment for the benefit of all the creditors of the transferor, and subsequent transferees, also have automatic perfection.[129]

During the process of collecting commercial paper, including checks, banks receive a security interest arising solely under Section 4-208(1). A bank has automatic perfection in such an item.[130]

---

[122] UCC §§ 9-302(1)(b), 9-304(4).

[123] UCC § 9-304(5)(a).

[124] UCC § 9-304(5)(b).

[125] See supra ¶ 7.02[2][c].

[126] UCC §§ 9-302(1)(f), 9-113(b).

[127] UCC § 9-302(2).

[128] UCC § 9-302(1)(c).

[129] UCC § 9-302(1)(g).

[130] UCC § 9-302(1)(f).

### [g] Proceeds

Automatic perfection may also be achieved in proceeds. Perfection in proceeds is discussed below.[131]

## [6] Multi-State Collateral: Where to File

### [a] Overview

As previously discussed, the location for filing is either central (in a statewide office) or local (in a particular county office).[132] The issue here is which state's law governs perfection; that is, in which state should the secured creditor file? If the secured creditor, the debtor, and the collateral are all located in the same state, if there is no contact with another state, and if the goods are not "mobile goods," the answer is an easy one. But given the mobility of parties to a secured transaction, and of collateral, determining the right state for perfection or for additional perfection when the collateral or debtor move may be difficult.

Although the UCC has a general choice-of-laws provision at Section 1-105, it is not applicable when the issue is one of proper perfection or priority.[133] Whatever the agreement of the parties, Section 9-103 contains the applicable choice-of-law provision for determining which state's laws control on perfection and the effect of perfection (i.e., priority).[134]

### [b] Determining the Appropriate Subsection of Section 9-103

Since the applicability of the rules of Section 9-103 depends on the type of collateral involved, the creditor initially must determine the nature of the collateral. It is critical to classify collateral appropriately. The choice-of-law rules for each subsection of Section 9-103 are mutually exclusive. The various types of collateral are discussed in the following subsections:

(1) Section 9-103(1): "Documents, instruments and ordinary goods";

(2) Section 9-103(2): Goods "covered by a certificate of title";

---

[131] See infra ¶ 7.06[7].

[132] See supra ¶ 7.06[3][d] for a discussion.

[133] UCC § 1-105 is of importance where the issue is which state's law is applicable to other Article 9 issues such as the rights of the creditor and debtor upon default. The section allows the parties to agree that the law of the forum state or another state or nation may apply where a transaction bears a reasonable relationship to such states or nations. Failing such agreement, Article 9 of the forum state applies if the transaction bears an "appropriate relation to this state."

[134] There is not a great deal of difference in the priority rules from state to state; therefore, applying one state's priority rules over those of another state may not give a different result. However, determining which state's law of perfection controls is always important to a resolution of perfection issues. If State *X*'s law of perfection controls, filing is in State *X*. If State *Y*'s law of perfection controls, filing is in State *Y*.

(3) Section 9-103(3): "Accounts, general intangibles and mobile goods";
(4) Section 9-103(4): "Chattel paper";
(5) Section 9-103(5): "Minerals (including oil and gas); and accounts resulting from the sale of minerals at the wellhead or minehead"; and
(6) Section 9-103(6) (as under the 1978 proposed amendments to Article 9): "Uncertificated securities."

Most of the classifications used in Section 9-103 have been discussed previously and will not be defined here.[135] The following classifications are unique to Section 9-103: "ordinary goods," "goods covered by a certificate of title," and "mobile goods."

Goods collateral subject to Section 9-103(1)—"ordinary goods"—are goods other than those that meet the definition of "goods covered by a certificate of title" under Section 9-103(2), "mobile goods" under Section 9-103(3), and "minerals" under Section 9-103(5).

The collateral subject to the rules of Section 9-103(2)—goods covered by a certificate of title—are goods for which the forum state or another state have issued a certificate of title and the law of the issuing state requires a notation of a security interest on the title.[136] As previously discussed, automobiles and other motor vehicles other than those held for inventory must be titled under the law of every state but Kentucky.[137] In addition, under the law of each state except Kentucky, a security interest in a motor vehicle that is titled cannot be perfected under Article 9. Perfection of these vehicles must be pursuant to state title law; this law generally limits perfection to notation of the interest on the certificate of title.[138] Such titled motor vehicles are subject to the choice-of-law rules of Section 9-103(2).[139]

Goods collateral subject to the rules of Section 9-103(3)—mobile goods—are defined as

> goods which are of a type normally used in more than one jurisdiction,[140] such as motor vehicles, trailers, rolling stock, airplanes, shipping contain-

---

[135] Supra ¶ 7.03. Uncertificated securities, defined in proposed UCC § 8-102(b) (1978) as securities not represented by an instrument that "may be treated as the property it represents," are outside the scope of this work. See generally Coogan, "Security Interests in Investment Securities Under Revised Article 8 of the Uniform Commercial Code," 92 Harv. L. Rev. 1013 (1979).

[136] To trigger UCC § 9-103(2), the certificate need not be issued to the debtor but may be issued to the seller of the goods. Payment Plans, Inc. v. Strell, 717 F2d 25, 36 UCC Rep. Serv. 1337 (2d Cir. 1983).

[137] Supra ¶ 7.06[3][b][i].

[138] Id.

[139] There is some dispute about whether a vehicle is covered by the certificate-of-title law of a particular state where that state issues a certificate, although it is improper under the law of the state to do so. See White & Summers, Uniform Commercial Code 977 n.286 (West, 2d ed. 1980).

[140] It makes no difference if the specific collateral has never been moved or will probably never be moved. The issue is whether it is of a "type normally used in more

ers, road building and construction machinery and commercial harvesting machinery and the like

BUT ONLY IF

(1) the goods are "equipment" or "inventory leased or held for lease";[141] and

(2) are not "goods covered by a certificate of title."

To determine which subsection of Section 9-103 covers goods, it is easiest to begin with Section 9-103(5). If the goods are minerals (including oil and gas), Section 9-103(5) is the applicable section. If minerals are not involved, go to Section 9-103(2). If the goods meet the definition there of "goods covered by a certificate of title," Section 9-103(2) is applicable. If the goods are neither minerals nor goods covered by a certificate of title, determine if they meet the definition of mobile goods under Section 9-103(3). If so, that section is applicable. Finally, if the goods are neither minerals under Section 9-103(5), goods covered by a certificate of title under Section 9-103(2), nor mobile goods under Section 9-103(3), then they are ordinary goods under Section 9-103(1).

### [c] Documents, Instruments, and Ordinary Goods

**[i] The "Last-Event" Rule.** When the collateral is "documents," "instruments," or "ordinary goods," Section 9-103(1)(a) is the starting point for determining which state's law governs perfection and priority.[142] The rule there basically is a situs rule. If the other subsections of Section 9-103(1) (discussed below) are not applicable, the law of perfection and priority are determined by the law of the jurisdiction "where the last event occurs on which is based the assertion that the security interest is perfected or unperfected."

Which "events" determine perfection? Before perfection occurs, there must be "attachment" and an "applicable step."[143] Attachment requires: (1) a written security agreement unless the creditor has possession of the collateral; (2) debtor rights in the collateral; and (3) value given by the creditor.[144] An applicable step for perfection may typically be either filing or possession. Alternatively, perfection may occur automatically upon attachment.[145] If the collateral is ordinary goods, however, the creditor normally perfects by filing a

---

than one jurisdiction." See, e.g., In re Utah Agricorp, Inc., 12 Bankr. 573, 31 UCC Rep. Serv. 1712 (D. Utah 1980).

[141] Note that mobile goods do not exist if they are classed as inventory because the goods are held for sale.

[142] The meaning of "documents" and "instruments" is discussed at supra ¶ 7.03. The meaning of "ordinary goods" is discussed at supra ¶ 7.06[6][b].

[143] UCC § 9-303.

[144] See supra ¶ 7.04.

[145] See supra ¶ 7.06[2]. If the collateral is "instruments," perfection must be by possession, except in very limited circumstances where automatic perfection suffices. UCC § 9-304(1).

financing statement. Therefore, if the collateral is "ordinary goods," perfection generally requires the occurrence of all of the following four events:

(1) A written security agreement;
(2) Debtor rights in the collateral;
(3) Value given by the creditor; and
(4) Filing of a financing statement by the creditor.

If the ordinary goods remain in one state while all of these events occur, the last-event rule poses no problems. The law of perfection and priority is determined by the state where the collateral is located. The last-event test also seems to work smoothly when the last event is filing a financing statement. The relevant law is that of the state where the collateral is located when the financing statement is filed. However, the four events need not occur in any particular order. It is possible, for example, that the collateral may be in one state when the first and third events occur, and in another state when the second and fourth occur.

> **EXAMPLE:** First Bank loans H. Garage $300,000. H executes a valid security agreement granting a security interest in metal lathes now owned and hereafter acquired. (Assume this collateral meets the definition of ordinary goods.) All of this takes place in State *X*, and First Bank also files a financing statement in State *X*. Ten days later, H acquires a metal lathe by sending a cash order to a seller in State *Y*. The seller then immediately sets the lathe aside for H. When the last event upon which perfection is based occurs, the collateral is in State *Y*. In this example, the last event for perfection occurs when the debtor acquires rights in the collateral.[146]
>
> Under the last-event test, the law of State *Y* apparently should control perfection. If so, the filing of the financing statement should be in State *Y* and not in State *X*.[147]

The result arising from the facts in this example makes little sense and has been criticized as requiring filing in a state that really does not have much connection with the transaction.[148] However, regardless of the illogical nature of the result, Section 9-103(1) seems to dictate this conclusion.

**[ii] The Thirty-Day Rule.** The last-event test is subject to the thirty-day rule of Section 9-103(1)(c). The thirty-day rule controls when:

(1) The security interest is a purchase-money security interest entered into in one jurisdiction; and

---

[146] See supra ¶ 7.04[4].

[147] If State *Y*'s law is applicable, then State *Y*'s version of UCC § 9-401(1) determines where to file. If filing is central, filing is in a statewide office of State *Y*.

[148] See Coogan, "The New UCC Article 9," 86 Harv. L. Rev. 477, 539–542 (1973); Kripke, "The Last Event Test for Perfection of Security Interests Under Article 9 of the Uniform Commercial Code," 50 N.Y.U. L. Rev. 47, 48–49 (1975).

(2) The secured creditor and debtor understand at the time the security interest attaches that the collateral will be kept in another jurisdiction.[149]

Since the subsection is limited to purchase-money security interests, it is limited to the transaction in which the collateral is "ordinary goods."

> **EXAMPLE:** A creditor loans money to a debtor in State *X* and takes an attached purchase-money security interest in a conveyor belt. (Assume that the belt is ordinary goods.) It is understood at the time of attachment that the conveyor belt will be kept in State *Y* rather than the state of purchase.
>
> Section 9-103(1)(c) applies in such a case and provides that the law of State *Y* is controlling. In effect, the creditor need only perfect in State *Y*.

Section 9-103(1)(c) is subject to an important time limitation. Perfection is valid in the state in which the goods are to be kept (State *Y* in the example), for only thirty days after the debtor receives possession, unless the goods are in fact moved to the other jurisdiction (from State *X* to State *Y* in the example). Although the goods are in the first state, perfection exists only in the state to which the goods will be moved. The time limitation was imposed because third parties in the first state may not be aware of the security interest. The thirty-day limitation, requiring the goods to be moved from State *X* to State *Y* in that period, at least shortens the time during which the secret lien exists.

**[iii] The Four-Month Rule.** The last-event test of Section 9-103(1)(b) is also subject to the four-month rule of Section 9-103(1)(d). The four-month rule is designed to deal with the movement of documents, instruments, or ordinary goods from one jurisdiction to another when the collateral is perfected in the state from which it is moved. The rule generally gives the creditor four months to perfect in the state to which the collateral is moved.

> **EXAMPLE:** A creditor has a security interest in ordinary goods that is perfected in State *X*. After perfection, the collateral is moved to State *Y* and kept in State *Y*.[150]
>
> Section 9-103(1)(d) gives the creditor four months after the collateral is brought into State *Y* within which to perfect in the new state.[151] Perfec-

---

[149] The UCC is unclear as to what kind of evidence shows that the parties understood this to be the case. If the security agreement indicates that the goods are to be kept in another state, that should suffice. See, e.g., In re SSC Corp., 27 UCC Rep. Serv. 828 (Bankr. D. Utah 1979).

[150] Transit through a state, even if there is temporary storage, does not cause the section to apply. The removal must be intended to be permanent. In re Potomac School of Law, Inc., 16 Bankr. 102, 32 UCC Rep. Serv. 1598 (DDC 1981).

[151] The time period is not ended by the filing of a suit for reclamation of the collateral or insolvency proceedings. In re Utah Agricorp, Inc., 12 Bankr. 573, 31 UCC Rep. Serv. 1712 (D. Utah 1980).

tion in State *Y* depends upon State *Y*'s version of Article 9. If the creditor does not get possession of the goods, or there is no automatic perfection of the goods in the new state, the creditor must perfect by filing a financing statement in the place dictated by State *Y*'s version of Section 9-401(1) within the four-month period. If the creditor perfects in State *Y*, he remains perfected in the new state.[152]

A creditor may get less than four months to perfect in the new state. Assume that the collateral in the example was perfected by a filing in State *X* and the filing was to lapse under Section 9-403(2) in State *X* on January 22, 1986. The collateral is moved from State *X* to State *Y* on January 2, 1986. In this case, the four-month rule would not apply. Instead, the creditor would have only until January 22, 1986 to perfect in the new state. The four-month rule does not extend the duration of perfection beyond the time when the filing in the original state was due to lapse.[153]

### [d] Goods Covered by a Certificate of Title

**[i] The Flexible Four-Month Rule.** If the collateral is goods covered by a certificate of title,[154] the choice-of-law provision is Section 9-103(2). It provides, in part:

> Except as otherwise provided in this subsection, perfection and the effect of perfection or non-perfection of the security interest are governed by the law (including the conflict of laws rules) of the jurisdiction issuing the certificate until four months after the goods are removed from that jurisdiction and thereafter until the goods are registered in another jurisdiction, but in any event not beyond surrender of the certificate. After the expiration of that period, the goods are not covered by the certificate of title within the meaning of this section.

Under this provision, the creditor with a security interest noted on the title may have four months after the collateral is removed from the state of perfec-

---

[152] If the creditor does not perfect within the time period, the security interest becomes unperfected at the end of the period, and is thereafter deemed unperfected as against any person who became a "purchaser" after removal. UCC § 9-103(1)(d). This includes any subsequent secured creditor, but it is unclear whether or not the interest is thereafter deemed unperfected as against a lien creditor (including the trustee in bankruptcy). White & Summers, Uniform Commercial Code § 23-18, at 974–976 (West, 2d ed. 1980); see also In re Bob Schwermer & Assoc., Inc. 27 Bankr. 304, 36 UCC Rep. Serv. 1400 (ND Ill. 1983) (race horses were kept in more than one state but returned to the home state of Illinois before the debtor filed bankruptcy, court held that the creditor's perfection remained valid because at no time had there been any intervening creditors in the other states).

[153] UCC § 9-103(1)(d).

[154] See supra ¶ 7.06[3][b][i] for a discussion of the applicability of this term.

tion to become perfected in a state to which collateral is moved. More time may be provided if registration in the new state occurs after the four-month period;[155] however, the time period will never extend beyond the time when the certificate of title issued in the original state is surrendered in the new state.[156]

> **EXAMPLE:** A debtor owns an automobile covered by a certificate of title issued by State *X*. A creditor loans the debtor money and takes a security interest in the auto. Pursuant to the law of State *X*, the creditor has the Department of Motor Vehicles in State *X* note the existence of the security interest on the certificate. The debtor moves from State *X* on May 1 and arrives in State *Y* with the automobile on May 10. State *Y*'s certificate-of-title legislation also covers the type of vehicle.[157] The debtor registers the auto in State *Y* on May 10.
>
> If State *X*'s certificate of title has not been surrendered, the security interest remains perfected until the expiration of four months from May 1–the date that the goods were removed from State *X*.[158] However, if the certificate is not surrendered and the vehicle is not registered in the new state until November 1, the original perfection remains valid until Novem-

---

[155] Registration of a vehicle may or may not be accomplished at the same time a certificate is issued. Registration, which varies with each state, is a procedure generally necessary before a vehicle may be licensed. A vehicle may be registered for a period of time in a state without a certificate being issued in the state. See In re Hartberg, 25 UCC Rep. Serv. 1429 (Bankr. ED Wis. 1979). But see Brewton Trading Corp. v. Midland Bank & Trust Co., 115 Misc. 2d 475, 454 NYS2d 510, 34 UCC Rep. Serv. 980 (NY Sup. Ct. 1982) (holding that "registration" means the issuance of a title certificate and not merely the procurement of nontitle registration to operate a motor vehicle).

[156] Typically, the creditor will retain possession of the certificate so that surrender of the certificate will not normally occur.

[157] This is considered movement from a title state to a title state. There can be movement from a nontitle state to a title state and vice versa. Since Kentucky is the only noncertificate state, this is not a frequent occurrence where the collateral is of a type (such as privately owned automobiles) that is covered under every state's title laws. Rules concerning movement from a nontitle state to a title state are applicable, however, if collateral such as an automobile is not covered under the law of one state (perhaps because it is within that state's inventory exclusion) but is moved to another state where it is covered under the title law. Movement from a nontitle state to a title state or the reverse also can occur where the collateral is boats, mobile homes, or other collateral that is covered by one state's title laws. Where collateral moves from one state, in which it is perfected by some other method than by notation upon certificate of title, to another state, in which it does become covered by a certificate of title issued by the new state, the rules of UCC § 9-103(1)(d) apply. UCC § 9-103(1)(c). For movement from title to nontitle states, see generally White & Summers, Uniform Commercial Code 982–985 (West, 2d ed. 1980).

[158] Contrast the date from which the four-month period begins to run under UCC § 9-103(2)(b) (the date of removal) with the date the four-month period begins to run under UCC § 9-103(1)(d) (the date the collateral arrives in the new state).

ber 1. In such a case, the validity of the original perfection extends to the date of registration. If the certificate was surrendered upon May 11, however, the perfection would terminate at the time of the surrender without regard to the time of registration in the new state.[159]

**[ii] The Innocent Buyer.** Section 9-103 is sometimes thought of as a priority section. However, the section is not directed primarily toward the resolution of priority disputes. It almost exclusively deals with the issue of which state's law of perfection and priority controls. Of course, perfection in the wrong state is generally tantamount to losing priority. However, the priority resolution must still be effected through the priority sections previously discussed, with one exception. Section 9-103(2)(d) directly resolves one priority dispute that has long existed. Under that section, certain innocent buyers of vehicles that have been titled in a new state may have priority against a secured creditor that has not had its security interest noted on the new certificate.

> **EXAMPLE:** A creditor takes an attached security interest in a debtor's auto in State *X*. The creditor has the interest noted on the certificate of title. The debtor takes auto to State *Y* and has a new certificate issued by State *Y*. The new certificate does not list the creditor's interest.[160] The debtor sells the auto to a neighbor in State *Y*. The creditor claims priority in the auto.
>
> State *Y*'s version of Section 9-103(2)(d) controls. Under the official version of that section, priority depends upon the status of the neighbor and what he knows. The neighbor has priority over the creditor if:
>
> (1) The new certificate does not show that the goods are subject to the security interest or that they may be subject to security interests not shown on the certificate;[161]
>
> (2) The neighbor is not in the business of selling goods of that kind; and
>
> (3) The neighbor gives value and receives delivery both after issuance of the certificate and without knowledge of the security interest.[162]

---

[159] UCC § 9-103(2)(b).

[160] This is no easy feat. Officials in the relevant state agencies do not normally issue a certificate of title without surrender of the existing certificate. However, it sometimes happens through oversight or fraud.

[161] Sometimes a new certificate is issued without the surrender of the old certificate because of a claim that the old certificate is lost or stolen. It is the practice in some states to include a legend on the new certificate that it has been issued to replace a lost or stolen certificate and that the vehicle may be subject to liens not noted on the certificate. This legend would seem to show that the vehicle "may be subject to security interests not shown on the certificate" and keep the buyer from winning priority.

[162] UCC § 103(2)(d).

### [e] Accounts, General Intangibles, and Mobile Goods

**[i] General Rule.** When the collateral is accounts, general intangibles,[163] or mobile goods,[164] the choice-of-law rule is under Section 9-103(3). The controlling law on perfection and priority is that of the jurisdiction where the debtor is located.

**EXAMPLE:** A creditor loans money to a debtor to finance a steam roller used in highway construction (assume that this collateral is mobile goods) and takes an attached security interest in the roller.[165] The steam roller is located in State *X*. The debtor is located in State *Y*. The transaction was entered into in State *Z*.

The proper place to file would be in State *Y* according to the law of State *Y* because that is where the debtor is located.[166]

**[ii] Determining Debtor's Location.** The location of the debtor is the debtor's place of business if the debtor has one, or the chief executive office if it has more than one place of business. If the debtor has no place of business, the location of the debtor is the debtor's residence.[167]

**[iii] Change in Debtor's Location.** If the debtor moves its location to another state, the creditor has a maximum of four months after the debtor's change of location to reperfect in the new state.[168] The creditor has less than four months to perfect in the new state if he had perfected by filing in the first state and the filing was to lapse in that state before the end of the four-month period. The four-month grace period does not extend the dura-

---

[163] See supra ¶¶ 7.02[4], 7.03[2][c][v].

[164] See supra ¶ 7.06[6][b]. It should be emphasized that collateral does not fit the classification of mobile goods if it consists of goods "covered by a certificate of title" within the meaning of UCC § 9-103(2)(a). See supra ¶ 7.06[6][b]. Also, although there is no reference in UCC § 9-103(3), certain accounts arising from the sale of minerals are instead covered under UCC § 9-103(5). If the secured creditor's interest attaches to accounts resulting from the sale of minerals at the wellhead or minehead, the choice of law is determined under UCC § 9-103(5). See discussion at infra ¶ 7.06[6][f].

[165] Such an item would be "mobile goods" under the definition of UCC § 9-103(3)(a) if it is not covered by a certificate of title.

[166] If the debtor is located in a jurisdiction outside the United States (the "United States" includes its territories and possessions and Puerto Rico) and such jurisdiction does not provide for perfection by filing or recording in that jurisdiction, the law of the jurisdiction in the United States in which the debtor has its "major executive office" would control.

[167] UCC § 9-103(3)(d). If the debtor is a foreign air carrier under the Federal Aviation Act of 1958, as amended, the debtor is deemed located at the designated office of the agent upon whom service of process may be made on the carrier. Id.

[168] UCC § 9-103(1)(e).

tion of perfection beyond the time when the filing in the original state was due to lapse.[169]

### [f] Chattel Paper

If the collateral is chattel paper, the choice-of-law rule is determined by whether the creditor has possession of the chattel paper. If the creditor has possession of the chattel paper, the rules for perfection are determined by Section 9-103(1), which contains the rules for documents, instruments, and ordinary goods.[170] If the creditor does not have possession of the chattel paper, the same rules for accounts under Section 9-103(3) apply.[171]

### [g] Minerals (Including Oil and Gas) and Certain Accounts

If the interest is in minerals (including oil and gas), which attaches to the minerals as extracted or which attaches to an account resulting from the sale of the minerals at the wellhead or minehead, the choice-of-law rule is determined under Section 9-103(5). Perfection and priority are determined by the law of the jurisdiction where the wellhead or minehead is located.

## [7] Perfection in Proceeds

### [a] Overview

Proceeds include whatever is received upon the disposition of original collateral or proceeds. Money, checks, deposit accounts, and the like are cash proceeds. All other proceeds are noncash proceeds.[172] Attachment in proceeds occurs when the proceeds are identifiable.[173] Basically, the creditor must be able to show that the items claimed as proceeds arose from the disposition of the collateral subject to the creditor's security interest—a tracing rule.[174]

Perfection of a security interest in original collateral requires attachment plus an applicable step, which typically consists of possession of the collateral or filing a financing statement.[175] However, perfection may also occur at the time of attachment when there is automatic perfection. Perfection in proceeds may be executed in the same way as perfection in original collateral. The primary rules for perfection of a security interest in proceeds are not, however,

---

[169] Id.

[170] See supra ¶ 7.06[6][b] for a discussion of those rules.

[171] See supra ¶ 7.06[6][d] for a discussion of those rules. UCC § 9-103(4) adds that notice to the account debtor is of no effect for protection.

[172] UCC § 9-306(1). For further discussion of the meaning of "proceeds" and examples, see supra ¶ 7.04[5].

[173] UCC § 9-306(2).

[174] For further discussion of the meaning of "proceeds" and examples, see supra ¶ 7.04[5].

[175] UCC § 9-303(1).

located in the same sections as the provisions for perfection in original collateral. The primary provisions for perfection in proceeds are contained in Sections 9-306(3) and 9-306(4). Section 9-306(3) specifies when perfection in proceeds occurs when there are no insolvency proceedings (such as bankruptcy) instituted by or against the debtor. Section 9-306(4) specifies when perfection in proceeds occurs when such proceedings have been instituted.

It should be emphasized that Section 9-306 concerns only perfection. Priority may, and generally does, ultimately turn on the question of whether perfection exists and when it occurred. Although a creditor may be perfected, this does not necessarily mean it will have priority.[176]

### [b] When No Insolvency Proceedings Are Instituted

When no insolvency proceedings are instituted by or against the debtor (such as the filing of a bankruptcy petition), whether any further action is necessary for perfection in proceeds is determined under Section 9-306(3).[177] Under this section, perfection extends to proceeds arising from the disposition of original collateral or other proceeds for only ten days unless:

(1) There is a filed financing statement covering the original collateral and the proceeds are collateral in which a security interest may be perfected by filing in the office or offices where the financing statements has been filed;[178]

(2) A filed financing statement covers the original collateral and the proceeds are identifiable cash proceeds;[179] or

(3) The security interest in proceeds is perfected before the expiration of ten days after receipt of the proceeds by the debtor.[180]

An example of the first type of perfection in proceeds follows:

**EXAMPLE 1:** A creditor, *Y*, takes an attached security interest in inventory and files an appropriate financing statement centrally with the Secretary of State. The debtor, *X*, sells the inventory and takes the buyer's obligation to pay and security interest to assure payment. In *X*'s hands this is chattel paper.

---

[176] See infra ¶ 7.07 for a discussion of priority disputes.

[177] For purposes of this discussion it is assumed that the proceeds are identifiable. This is required for attachment under UCC § 9-306(2) and thus is also a requirement for perfection. For a discussion of the meaning of "identifiable" and examples, see supra ¶ 7.04[5].

[178] UCC § 9-306(3)(a).

[179] UCC § 9-306(3)(b).

[180] UCC § 9-306(3)(c).

If filing a financing statement with the Secretary of State would perfect a security interest in chattel paper as original collateral,[181] the perfection continues in the chattel paper as proceeds without further action by the creditor.

The following is an example of the second type of perfection in proceeds.

**EXAMPLE 2:** Creditor *X* takes an attached security interest in inventory and properly files with the Secretary of State. Debtor *Y* sells an item of inventory for cash. (The cash, of course, is cash proceeds.) Debtor *Y* uses the cash proceeds to purchase equipment. Creditor *X* must perfect its interest in the proceeds within ten days after debtor *Y* received possession of the equipment unless the original filed financing statement included equipment in the description of collateral.[182]

Where further action is necessary to perfect, the security interest must be perfected by use of the methods or under the circumstances permitted in Article 9 for original collateral of the same type.[183] In Example 2, if perfection were necessary to perfect the interest in the equipment proceeds, the creditor would perfect as if the equipment were original collateral.

### [c] When Insolvency Proceedings Are Instituted

When insolvency proceedings are instituted by or against the debtor (such as the filing of a bankruptcy petition),[184] perfection in proceeds is determined primarily by Section 9-306(4).[185] Under Section 9-306(4), two primary classifications of the proceeds must be made before determining the extent of perfection: (1) Are the proceeds cash proceeds or noncash proceeds? and (2) If cash proceeds are involved, have the cash proceeds been commingled?[186] There is perfection in noncash proceeds if the proceeds are identifiable,[187] and if the

---

[181] This would require a look at the state's version of UCC § 9-401(1). See generally supra ¶ 7.06[3].

[182] See, e.g., In re A.E.I. Corp., 11 Bankr. 97, 31 UCC Rep. Serv. 1467 (ED Pa. 1981) (creditor lost proceeds when specific description of items of inventory used when items were sold, cash received, and cash was used to purchase other items of inventory; the specific descriptions of items of inventory in financing statement did not indicate the new items constituting the proceeds).

[183] UCC § 9-306(3).

[184] "Insolvency proceedings" means "any assignment for the benefit of creditors or other proceedings intended to liquidate or rehabilitate the estate of the person involved." UCC § 1-201(22).

[185] There is some relationship to UCC § 9-306(3), as is demonstrated below.

[186] For the distinction between cash proceeds and noncash proceeds, see supra ¶ 7.04[5].

[187] For example, if the creditor is claiming perfection in chattel paper as proceeds, the creditor must be able to show that the particular chattel paper in fact arose from the

creditor can show that any action required under Section 9-306(3) has been taken.[188]

If the proceeds are cash proceeds and *not commingled*, perfection is allowed if the cash proceeds are identifiable and if:

(1) The cash proceeds are deposited in a separate deposit account;[189]

(2) The cash proceeds are money and not placed in a deposit account;[190] or

(3) The cash proceeds are in the form of checks and the like that are not deposited in a deposit account prior to the institution of the insolvency proceedings.[191]

If the proceeds are commingled with other funds (e.g., the debtor deposits proceeds in the form of checks or money in a general checking account of the debtor), perfection is determined by following these steps:[192]

(1) Determine the amount of proceeds received by the debtor within ten days before the institution of the insolvency proceedings;[193]

(2) Deduct the amount of any proceeds received and paid over to the secured party during the ten days;

---

disposition of the original collateral covered by the security interest or other identifiable proceeds.

[188] The UCC is not very clear in establishing this requirement. However, it can be implied from the following introductory language of UCC § 9-306(4): "[A] secured party with a *perfected* security interest in proceeds has a perfected security interest only in the following proceeds." (Emphasis added.) The first use of the term "perfected" in the quoted language requires a reference to UCC § 9-306(3). For the meaning of this section, see supra ¶ 7.07[7][b].

[189] UCC § 9-306(4)(a). It is common in floor planning and other transactions in which cash proceeds are expected for the creditor to require the maintenance of a separate deposit account, such as a checking account, that will contain only cash proceeds.

[190] UCC § 9-306(4)(b). This includes, for example, money set aside in a safe that is clearly identified as proceeds from the disposition of the original collateral covered by the creditor's security interest.

[191] UCC § 9-306(4)(c). This means, for example, that checks representing proceeds arising from disposition of the original collateral or proceeds that are not yet deposited for collection by the debtor.

[192] UCC § 9-306(4)(d); Gilmore, Security Interests in Personal Property, § 45.9, at 1339 (Little, Brown 1965).

[193] It is unclear from the UCC whether this amount should include proceeds received from any source or only identifiable proceeds, (e.g., those that can be shown as arising only from the disposition of the collateral or proceeds that are covered by the creditor's security interest). See generally White & Summers, Uniform Commercial Code 1014–1017 (West, 2d ed. 1980).

(3) Deduct any amount to which the depositary institution is entitled to as a matter of setoff.[194]

The amount remaining is the amount of cash in which the secured creditor has a perfected security interest.

## ¶ 7.07 RESOLUTION OF PRIORITY DISPUTES

### [1] Introduction

If the debtor defaults, more than one party may claim an interest in the debtor's personal property or fixtures. Where one of the claimants has an attached Article 9 security interest, disputes between the Article 9 claimant and other claimants are generally resolved pursuant to the priority provisions of Article 9.

To determine the applicable priority section of Article 9, the collateral should first be classified.[1] Then the status of each of the claimants should be identified. For Article 9 to apply, one of the claimants must have an attached Article 9 security interest.[2] Once the attached secured creditor is identified, other questions must be answered concerning the status of the secured creditor:

(1) Is the security interest properly perfected in the proper place in the proper state and in the proper manner?
(2) When was it perfected?
(3) Is the security interest a purchase-money security interest?[3]

The other claimants may take a variety of different forms. The second claimant may be a general unsecured creditor, a lien creditor, another secured creditor, a trustee in bankruptcy, a statutory lien holder, a purchaser, a real estate claimant claiming an interest in fixtures, a party claiming a security interest arising solely under Article 2 of the UCC, or the Internal Revenue Service. If the second claimant is another secured creditor, the questions posed above for the first secured creditor claimant must also be answered with respect to the other secured creditor. If the second claimant fits one of the other classes of claimants, it is necessary to determine when its status became fixed. For example, if the other claimant is a lien creditor, it is necessary to determine when the lien creditor status arose.[4]

---

[194] This does not add to the bank's right of setoff. Whether the bank has such a right is discussed at supra ¶ 7.02[4][i].

[1] See generally supra ¶ 7.03.

[2] See generally supra ¶ 7.04.

[3] Perfection is discussed at supra ¶ 7.06.

[4] The status of the various types of claimants is discussed below in conjunction with the discussion of the resolution of the various types of priority disputes. For exam-

Once these steps are completed, the appropriate priority section of Article 9 must be applied. Application of the Article 9 priority provisions is the primary focus of the following material.

## [2] Secured Creditor vs. General Unsecured Creditor

Section 9-201 provides: "Except as otherwise provided by this Act a security agreement is effective according to its terms between the parties against purchasers of the collateral and against creditors." At first glance, this statement seems to give the secured creditor broad protection from other claimants. However, the phrase "Except as otherwise provided," indicates that there are exceptions to the general rule, and in practice, the exceptions far outweigh the general rule. Section 9-201 does apply to give the Article 9 secured creditor priority over: (1) general unsecured creditors (those without lien creditor or statutory lien status), and (2) those who have purchased collateral from the debtor if such purchasers cannot find another priority section that will award them priority. The secured creditor has the priority even if unperfected.[5]

For example, a general unsecured creditor loses priority by the operation of Section 9-201 if he has loaned money to the debtor and failed to: (1) take an attached Article 9 security interest, or (2) achieve lien creditor status under Section 9-301(3).[6]

## [3] Secured Creditor vs. Lien Creditor

### [a] The Lien Creditor

A lien creditor is defined in Section 9-301(3) as:

> a creditor who has acquired a lien on the property involved by attachment, levy, or the like and includes an assignee for benefit of creditors from the time of assignment, and a trustee in bankruptcy from the date of the filing of the petition or a receiver in equity from the time of appointment.

---

ple, the status of the lien creditor claimant is discussed at infra ¶ 7.07[3], which concerns priority disputes between secured creditors and lien creditors.

[5] The security interest must be attached pursuant to UCC §§ 9-203, 9-204. Without attachment, the creditor is not a secured creditor under Article 9 and has no secured creditor rights as against the debtor or third parties. See supra ¶ 7.04.

[6] A secured creditor may be claiming monies in a deposit account as proceeds arising from the disposition of original collateral, whereas the bank in which the deposit account is located may be claiming the same monies through the exercise of its right of setoff. There is an issue as to whether this dispute is covered at all under Article 9. Most courts hold that Article 9 is not applicable. See supra ¶ 7.02[4][i]. However, if the court does apply Article 9, the bank is likely to lose the dispute under UCC § 9-201. See, e.g., Citizens Nat'l Bank of Whitley County v. Mid-States Dev. Co., 177 Ind. App. 548, 380 NE2d 1243, 24 UCC Rep. Serv. 1321 (1978). See generally Clark, Law of Secured Transactions ¶ 3.11 (Warren, Gorham & Lamont, Inc., 1983 Cum. Supp. 2).

A lien creditor is a common priority claimant. The trustee in bankruptcy using this status often leads the charge against the debtor's collateral. The trustee gains lien creditor status upon the filing of the bankruptcy petition. Priority disputes between the secured creditor and trustee are discussed elsewhere in this book.[7]

The claimant who has obtained a judgment on an obligation and then obtained a lien by "levy or the like" also is a common claimant with lien creditor status. To determine exactly when lien creditor status arises with respect to such a claimant, it is necessary to look at state law outside Article 9. Typically, state law provides for lien creditor status for judgment creditors after execution is levied by the sheriff.

### [b] General Priority Rule

The Article 9 secured creditor has priority against a lien creditor if he is perfected at the time the lien status arises; if not perfected at that time, the lien creditor has priority.

> **EXAMPLE 1:** A secured creditor, *SC*, loans a debtor, *D*, money so *D* can purchase a new trampoline for his backyard. *SC* takes an attached security interest in the trampoline on September 1.[8] On September 2, a lien creditor, *LC*, wins an action against *D* for a breach of contract on an unsecured obligation. On September 3, the sheriff levies execution on the trampoline to satisfy *LC*'s judgment.
>
> *SC* would have priority over *LC* if the trampoline were purchased for a personal, family, or household use. Typically, there is automatic perfection when the security interest is a purchase-money security interest in consumer goods.[9] Since *SC*'s security interest was perfected before the lien creditor status arose (lien creditor status would arise on September 3 in most states because that was the date the sheriff levied), *SC* has priority under Section 9-301(1)(b).

> **EXAMPLE 2:** In Example 1 above, if the trampoline had been purchased primarily for a business purpose, *LC* would win. The trampoline would be equipment. Perfection would not be achieved until *SC* filed a financing statement or obtained possession of the trampoline. There is no automatic perfection when the collateral is equipment.[10] Since *LC* achieved its lien creditor status before perfection, *LC* has priority over *SC* pursuant to Section 9-301(1)(b).

In limited circumstances, an unperfected secured creditor with a purchase-money security interest in non-consumer goods may win against a lien creditor. If the secured party files with respect to a purchase-money security interest

---

[7] See ¶¶ 16.02, 16.05.

[8] See generally supra ¶ 7.04.

[9] See supra ¶ 7.06[5][c].

[10] Supra ¶ 7.06.

before or within ten days after the debtor receives possession of the collateral, the secured creditor takes priority over a lien creditor if this status arises between the time the security interest attaches and the time of filing.[11]

### [c] Future Advances

Future advances have previously been discussed in this chapter,[12] in regard to the extent that perfection can extend to advances of value that are made after the date of the original transaction. Even where a secured creditor can show perfection to the extent of future advances, the secured creditor's priority against the lien creditor is limited with respect to the future advances. The secured creditor loses priority in the future advance if the advance is made with knowledge of the lien or if it is made more than forty-five days after the lien creditor status arises.[13]

## [4] Secured Creditor vs. Secured Creditor

### [a] First-in-Time Rule

Section 9-312 generally applies where there is a priority dispute between two creditors with attached Article 9 security interests.[14] In such disputes, (1) Section 9-312(2) establishes priority in a very limited case involving perfected security interests in crops when new value has been given to allow production of the crops; (2) Section 9-312(3) controls priority when one of the secured creditors has a perfected purchase-money security interest in inventory and follows the procedural rules of the subsection; and (3) Section 9-312(4) controls when one of the secured creditors has a perfected purchase-money security interest in collateral other than inventory and follows the procedural rules of the subsection. However, the great majority of cases involving priority disputes

---

[11] UCC § 9-301(2). This rule also gives the secured creditor priority over any transferee in bulk (defined in UCC § 6-102). If perfection can be obtained by filing under Article 9, filing must meet the requirements for proper filing under Article 9. However, if the type of collateral must be perfected outside Article 9, such as for vehicles covered by certificate-of-title laws or subject to federal perfection rules, the filing must be pursuant to those laws. See supra ¶ 7.06[3][b].

[12] Supra ¶ 7.07[3][c][x].

[13] UCC § 9-301(4). The secured creditor also has priority with respect to extensions made after forty-five days if they are pursuant to a binding commitment made within the forty-five-day period and without knowledge of the lien. Id.

[14] As indicated in the introduction to this section (supra ¶ 7.07[1]), other sections relating to attachment and applicable steps for perfection are always important in any priority dispute, because it is necessary to determine the status of the claimants. UCC § 9-312(1) indicates that sections other than UCC § 9-312 may also be applicable. It specifically mentions "Section 4-208 with respect to the security interests of collecting banks in items being collected; . . . Section 9-103 on security interests related to other jurisdictions; Section 9-114 on consignments." See supra ¶ 7.02.

between secured creditors are resolved by a provision of Section 9-312(5) that incorporates a classic first-in-time priority rule, as follows:

> (5) In all cases not governed by other rules stated in this section (including cases of purchase money security interests which do not qualify for the special priorities set forth in subsections (3) and (4) of this section), priority between conflicting security interests in the same collateral shall be determined according to the following rules:
>
> (a) Conflicting security interests rank according to priority in time of filing or perfection. Priority dates from the time a filing is first made covering the collateral or the time the security interest is first perfected, whichever is earlier, provided that there is no period thereafter when there is neither filing nor perfection.
>
> (b) So long as conflicting security interests are unperfected, the first to attach has priority.

**[i] General Application.** Under the primary rule of Section 9-312(5)(a), as long as both secured creditors are perfected, priority is in the secured creditor who was the first to file *or* the first to perfect. The following examples illustrate this rule:

> **EXAMPLE 1:** Secured creditor *A* files a financing statement covering a debtor's equipment on June 15 and advances money to the debtor. Secured creditor *B* loans money to the debtor and takes an attached non-purchase-money security interest in the debtor's equipment on July 1. On August 1, *A* has the debtor sign a security agreement and thereby obtains an attached non-purchase-money security interest.
>
> *A* has priority even though *B* perfected first.[15] Section 9-312(5)(a) provides that filing *or* perfection controls, whichever is earlier. Here *A* filed before *B* perfected, even though *A* perfected second in time.

> **EXAMPLE 2:** On May 1, secured creditor *A* obtains an attached non-purchase-money security interest in a debtor's collateral. The debtor has possession of the collateral and *A* does not file. On June 1, secured creditor *B* takes an attached non-purchase-money security interest in the same collateral and perfects its interest by taking possession of the collateral.
>
> Here, *B* has priority because it was the first to either perfect or to file.

Official Comment 5 states that the outcome in Example 2 would be the same even if a creditor in the position of *B* had knowledge of *A*'s security interest because Section 9-312(5) is a pure race statute. Most cases agree with that

---

[15] Secured creditor *A* is not perfected until both applicable steps (in this case filing and attachment) come together. UCC § 9-303. Attachment did not occur here until the signing of the security agreement. UCC § 9-203(1)(a).

position.[16] However, some case authority takes the contrary view.[17] If a secured creditor has knowledge of another security interest even though it is not prior in time, the secured creditor is advised to request a subordination by agreement from the other security creditor. Section 9-316 authorizes subordination by agreement by any party entitled to priority.

**EXAMPLE 3:** On April 5, secured creditor *A* loans money to a debtor. *A* properly files a financing statement covering equipment. Secured creditor *B* loans money to the debtor and takes an attached non-purchase-money security interest in the same collateral on July 1. On July 2, *A* has the debtor sign a security agreement, which contains a grant of a security interest in "equipment now owned and hereafter acquired," and thereby obtains an attached non-purchase-money security interest in equipment in which the debtor has property rights. On August 1, the debtor acquires a new bulldozer.

If the bulldozer can be perfected by the filing of a financing statement, *A* has priority. The filing of *A* predates any perfection or filing by *B*. It makes no difference that the collateral is after-acquired; the filing is valid as to the after-acquired collateral as long as such collateral fits within the general description used in the financing statement.

**EXAMPLE 4:** If the bulldozer in Example 3 is a motor vehicle covered by certificate-of-title legislation requiring a notation on the certificate, neither *A* nor *B* is perfected until such notation. The first to obtain the notation has priority. In most states, the filing of a financing statement by *A* is irrelevant because the filing has no effect as to a vehicle covered by a certificate-of-title law.[18] Section 9-312(5)(a), which awards priority to the first to file or perfect, is not meant to award priority to the first to file a financing statement where the filing is not an appropriate manner in which to perfect an interest in the type of collateral at issue.

If neither *A* nor *B* has its interests noted on the certificate of title, neither is perfected and the UCC provides no resolution of a priority dispute between the two. Section 9-312(5)(b) provides that if neither secured creditor is perfected, the first to attach has priority. However, under the facts, both secured creditors' interests would attach at the same time—August 1, when the debtor acquires rights in the bulldozer.[19] The court

---

[16] See, e.g., Todsen v. Runge, 211 Neb. 226, 318 NW2d 88, 33 UCC Rep. Serv. 1541 (1982) and cases cited therein; see also Clark, Law of Secured Transactions ¶ 3.08[1] (Warren, Gorham & Lamont, Inc. 1980); White & Summers, Uniform Commercial Code § 25-4 (West, 2d ed. 1980).

[17] See, e.g., General Ins. Co. of Am. v. Lowry, 412 F. Supp. 12, 23 UCC Rep. Serv. 1058 (SD Ohio 1976), aff'd, 570 F2d 120 (6th Cir. 1978); see also Nickles, "Rethinking Some U.C.C. Article 9 Problems—Subrogation; Equitable Liens; Actual Knowledge; Waiver of Security Interests; Secured Party Liability for Conversion Under Part 5," 34 Ark. L. Rev. 1, 72–103 (1980).

[18] See generally supra ¶ 7.06[6][c].

[19] See UCC § 9-203; supra ¶ 7.04.

should award a pro rata share in such cases. For example, if the debtor owes *A* $40,000 and *B* $60,000, *A* should get 40 percent of the value of the collateral and *B* should get 60 percent.

**[ii] Proceeds.** If a priority dispute under Section 9-312(5) involves proceeds, and the creditor's interest has been continuously perfected in proceeds,[20] the date of filing or perfection as to collateral also is the date of filing or perfection as to proceeds. Thus, in a priority dispute over proceeds between two secured creditors with a perfected security interest in proceeds, priority is won by the secured creditor who is the first to file or to perfect as to the original collateral. This assumes that there is no gap period when the filing or perfection lapses.[21]

**EXAMPLE:** Secured creditor *A* takes an attached non-purchase-money security interest in the inventory of a debtor on April 1 and properly files a financing statement in the Secretary of State's office. On May 1, secured creditor *B* takes an attached security interest in the accounts of the debtor and files a financing statement. On May 5, the debtor sells an item of inventory and receives an account receivable in return.

If perfection of accounts can be obtained by central filing in the Secretary of State's offfice, *A* has priority. The account is proceeds to *A* and is continuously perfected in such a case under Section 9-306(3)(a). Section 9-312(6) provides that the perfection and filing date for the proceeds is the same as the date for *A*'s filing and perfection for the original collateral—April 1. Under Section 9-312(5), *A* has priority because its filing was before *B* either filed or perfected.

**[iii] Future Advances.** Under Section 9-312(7), if future advances are made while a security interest is perfected by filing, or the taking of possession, the security interest has the same priority for the purposes of Section 9-312(5) with respect to the future advances as it does with respect to the first advance.[22]

**EXAMPLE:** Secured creditor *A* loans a debtor $100,000, takes an attached non-purchase-money security interest in the debtor's equipment, and properly files a financing statement on April 1. The security agreement states that the collateral secures any future advances of value as well as the loan of the $100,000. On May 1, secured creditor *B* takes an attached security interest in the same equipment and files a financing statement. On June 1, *A* loans the debtor an additional $50,000 to be secured by the same

---

[20] The meaning of proceeds and perfection in proceeds are discussed at supra ¶ 7.06[7].

[21] UCC § 9-312(6).

[22] The concept of perfection in future advances is discussed at supra ¶¶ 7.04[2][b][vi], 7.06[3][c][x].

equipment pursuant to the original security agreement. In a priority dispute, *B* admits that *A* has priority in the equipment to the extent of any amounts still owing on the original $100,000 advance but denies that *A* has priority to the extent of any amounts still owing on the later advance of $50,000.

Pursuant to Section 9-312(7), *A* has priority to the extent of amounts owing on the first loan *and* later advance—that is, the future advance.[23] The result is the same if the future advance had not been contemplated in the original security agreement and, instead, *A* had the debtor execute a new security agreement upon the date of the later advance indicating that the later advance was to be secured by the equipment.[24]

### [b] Purchase-Money Security Interests in Noninventory Collateral

**[i] General Application.** A creditor who has a purchase-money security interest in collateral other than inventory[25] may be entitled to priority under Section 9-312(4) even if the creditor is not the first to file or to perfect. The purchase-money secured creditor in noninventory collateral must perfect by the time the debtor gets possession or within ten days thereafter.

**EXAMPLE:** Secured creditor *A* obtains an attached non-purchase-money security interest in a debtor's "equipment, now owned and hereafter acquired" and properly files a financing statement on February 15. On March 10, the debtor buys a new machine for his business on credit from secured creditor *B*. *B* takes an attached security interest in the machine and the debtor takes possession of the machine on the same date. On March 15, *B* properly files a financing statement.

*A* is both the first to perfect and to file. The security interest of *A* attaches in the later acquired machine on March 10; the filing suffices to perfect the machine. However, *B* has priority under Section 9-312(4). *B*'s interest is a purchase-money security interest[26] in noninventory collateral and perfection was achieved within ten days after the debtor received possession.

**[ii] Start of the Ten-Day Period.** Under Section 9-312(4), the purchase-money creditor has to perfect within a ten-day period that begins when the "debtor receives possession." If a party is merely negotiating a sale, is that

---

[23] Some jurisdictions recognize a limitation that the second advance must be for the same class of transactions as the first advance. See supra ¶¶ 7.04[2][b][vi], 7.06[3][c][x].

[24] Id.

[25] Purchase-money security interests are defined at UCC § 9-107. See supra ¶ 7.06[5][b].

[26] UCC § 9-107. Purchase-money security interests may also be acquired by a lender who advances value to enable the debtor to acquire goods if the value is in fact so used. See supra ¶ 7.06[5][b].

person a "debtor"? The definition in Section 9-106 of "debtor" indicates that a person negotiating a purchase is not a debtor until the decision to make the purchase is made.

**EXAMPLE:** On March 1, secured creditor *A* obtains an attached non-purchase-money security interest in a debtor's "equipment, now owned and hereafter acquired" and properly files a financing statement. On March 10, the debtor asks to try a machine sold by secured creditor *B*. *B* agrees to allow the debtor to use the machine for up to thirty days on a trial basis. On March 20, the debtor agrees to purchase the machine for his business. *B* takes an attached security interest in the machine and files a financing statement on March 27.

*B* has priority under these facts. Although the debtor received possession of the machine on March 10, she did not become a "debtor" within the meaning of Section 9-105(1)(d) until she became obligated to purchase the machine. This did not occur until March 20 and *B* perfected within ten days of that date.[27]

When an item of equipment or other noninventory goods collateral is to be delivered by individual deliveries of component parts, the date of "possession" is the date when the component parts are delivered.[28] However, if the delivery terms also require assembly of the component parts, the date of possession does not depend upon assembly.[29]

**[iii] Application to Proceeds.** The "super priority" of Section 9-312(4) extends to proceeds arising from the disposition of the collateral in which the secured creditor had a purchase-money security interest.[30]

### [c] Purchase-Money Security Interests in Inventory

**[i] General Application.** A creditor who has a purchase-money security interest in inventory may be entitled to priority under Section 9-312(3) even though he is not the first to file or to perfect. The purchase-money secured creditor must show:

---

[27] See, e.g., Brodie Hotel Supply, Inc. v. U.S., 431 F2d 1316, 8 UCC Rep. Serv. 113 (9th Cir. 1970); see also Commerce Union Bank v. John Deere Indus. Equip. Co., 387 So. 2d 787, 29 UCC Rep. Serv. 1436 (Ala. 1980) (holding that if a true lease is involved and later there is an exercise of option to purchase, the ten-day period does not begin to run until option exercised).

[28] See, e.g., In re Badger Aluminum Extrusion Corp., 7 Bankr. 251, 30 UCC Rep. Serv. 1164 (SDNY 1980).

[29] See, e.g., In re Relpak Corp., 25 Bankr. 148, 35 UCC Rep. Serv. 1022 (EDNY 1982); In re Automated Bookbinding, Inc., 471 F2d 546, 11 UCC Rep. Serv. 897 (4th Cir. 1972).

[30] UCC § 9-312(4).

(1) The purchase-money security interest is perfected at the time the debtor receives possession of the inventory;

(2) The secured party gave written notification to the holder of any conflicting security interest, if the holder had filed a financing statement covering the same types of inventory;

(3) Any required notice was given either:

  (a) Before the date of the filing by the purchase-money secured creditor; or

  (b) Before the beginning of the twenty-one-day period where the purchase-money security interest is temporarily perfected without filing or possession;[31] and

(4) The holder of the conflicting security interest received such notification within five years before the debtor receives possession of the inventory; and[32]

(5) The notification:

  (a) States that the person giving the notice has or expects to acquire a purchase-money security interest in inventory of the debtor; and

  (b) Describes the inventory by item or type.[33]

**EXAMPLE:** On November 1, a debtor borrows money from secured creditor *A* for a business purpose. *A* takes an attached security interest in "all inventory now owned and hereafter acquired."[34] *A* properly files a financing statement on the same date. On December 12, the manufacturer (secured creditor *B*) sells the debtor items that the debtor plans to hold for resale. *B* takes an attached security interest and properly files a financing statement on the same date. Before the debtor gets possession of the inventory, *B* sends a written notification to *A* stating that *B* has acquired a purchase-money security interest in the debtor's inventory. *A* receives the notice ten days after the debtor gets possession of the inventory purchased.

*A* has priority. Each of the previously discussed requirements must be met before *B* gets priority under Section 9-312(3) over another secured creditor who has perfected or filed earlier. All but one of the requirements were met: *A* did not receive the notification before the debtor received possession of the inventory. Therefore, Section 9-312(3) does not operate

---

[31] Such temporary perfection is limited. See supra ¶ 7.06[5][e].

[32] There are two purposes behind this provision: It indicates that (1) the notice must be received before the debtor gets possession, and (2) a notice from the purchase-money secured creditor has a duration of five years. When a debtor gets possession is discussed at supra ¶ 7.06[4][b][ii].

[33] UCC § 9-312(3)(d).

[34] See supra ¶ 7.04[2][b][v] concerning whether the creditor needs to include the after-acquired clause in the security agreement to get attachment with respect to after-acquired inventory. Most courts now hold that the after-acquired clause is not necessary where the collateral is inventory because they feel this is assumed when the collateral is inventory.

to give *B* priority. Instead, Section 9-312(5) applies, because this provision applies when Sections 9-312(3) and 9-312(4) are not operable. Under Section 9-312(5), *A* has priority. The first to file or to perfect has priority.

Recently, a bankruptcy court specifically addressed whether the notice to the holder of the original security interest in inventory must mention that the second secured creditor is taking or expects to take a purchase-money interest in inventory. (The notice at issue in the above example simply indicated that the secured creditor planned to take a security interest in inventory.) After reviewing a number of cases that have required proper form and finding that none of them had specifically answered the question at issue, the court held that a specific reference to a purchase-money interest was not required in the notice.[35]

**[ii] Proceeds.** The "super priority" under Section 9-312(3) for the purchase-money secured creditor with an interest in inventory does not extend to all proceeds arising from the sale of the inventory. Section 9-312(3) provides that the super priority for the purchase-money security interest in inventory extends only to "cash proceeds received on or before the delivery of the inventory to a buyer. . . ."

### [d] Crop Production Loans

Theoretically, a secured creditor who has extended new value to enable crop production may be entitled to priority in the crops under Section 9-312(2) even though the creditor is neither the first to file nor to perfect. However, the provision requires the creditor to meet so many requirements to gain the super priority that, to date, no creditor has successfully received priority status in a reported case. To be entitled to the super priority of Section 9-312(2), a secured creditor must show the following:

(1) The security interest is perfected;
(2) The creditor gave "new value";[36]
(3) The new value was given not more than three months before the crops become growing crops;
(4) The new value was given to enable the debtor to produce crops during the production season; and
(5) Finally, even if the above requirements are met, the priority is valid *only* to the extent that the security interest of the competing secured creditor secures obligations that are more than six months in arrears.[37]

---

[35] In re Daniels, 22 Bankr. 871, 37 UCC Rep. Serv. 967 (WD Okla. 1983).

[36] That means the value cannot be merely the taking as security for, in total or partial satisfaction of, a preexisting claim; the creditor must make a new extension or commitment to extend value not already extended or committed. Value is defined at UCC § 1-102(44).

[37] See U.S. v. Minster Farmers Coop. Exch., Inc., 430 F. Supp. 566 21 UCC Rep. Serv. 1439 (ND Ohio 1977).

## [5] Secured Creditor vs. Buyer of Collateral

### [a] General Rule

The general rule concerning the secured creditor's rights against purchasers of collateral is set out in Section 9-201: The secured creditor has prior rights unless otherwise authorized by Article 9. However, numerous provisions instead give the buyer priority over the secured creditor. There are two important points to remember. First, if the buyer cannot find a section elsewhere in Article 9 that gives the buyer priority, the general rule of Section 9-201 prevails and gives priority to the secured creditor. Second, in Section 9-201 and the other sections of Article 9 that concern the priority of the Article 9 secured creditor, it is presumed that the creditor has an attached security interest in the collateral sold. If that party does not claim attachment of the security interest, the party is not a secured creditor and cannot claim the rights of a secured creditor.[38] Thus, in determining a priority dispute in collateral disposed of by the debtor, it should first be determined whether the party claiming rights under Article 9 as a secured creditor is in fact a secured creditor holding an attached security interest.

Initially, whether the creditor's attached security interest continues in collateral after a sale or other disposition by the debtor depends upon whether the disposition was authorized "in the security agreement or otherwise."[39] If the disposition was so authorized, the security interest does not follow the collateral upon disposition. The issue of authorization may be easy to resolve. Security agreements often clearly state that the parties contemplate sale of the collateral. However, the issue is more difficult when the agreement is silent, the agreement explicitly states that the sale is subject to the security interest, or the agreement places restrictions on disposition by the debtor and the debtor has disposed of the collateral in violation of those restrictions.

When the agreement is silent, the courts will consider whether the trade usage or course of dealing show an authorization—an "or otherwise" authorization. For example, if the security interest is in inventory and its proceeds, and if no restrictions are placed on the sale of the inventory, courts will typically find that sale is authorized and the security interest does not follow the collateral.[40]

If a disposition violates restrictions upon disposition, it typically will not be considered to be authorized, and the security interest will follow the collateral. For example, if the security interest authorizes sales "in the ordinary course of business," the security interest will continue to be attached in the collateral if the sale does not meet that test.[41] Even though a disposition is

---

[38] UCC §§ 9-203, 9-204; see supra ¶ 7.04[1].

[39] UCC § 9-306(2).

[40] See, e.g., Finance Am. Commercial Corp. v. Econo Coach, Inc., 118 Ill. App. 2d 385, 454 NE2d 1127 (1983).

[41] See, e.g., Sterling Nat'l Bank & Trust Co. of New York v. Southwire Co., 713 F2d 684, 36 UCC Rep. Serv. 1383 (11th Cir. 1983) (was not within the ordinary course because it was a transfer in satisfaction of a preexisting debt); Crystal State Bank v. Columbia Heights State Bank, 295 Minn. 181, 203 NW2d 389 (1973) (dictum that bulk

restricted, if the creditor knowingly allows the debtor to make prohibited dispositions, a few courts will find a waiver of the limitation. Such courts find that similar dispositions after the waiver is effective are authorized. Therefore, the security interest does not follow the collateral.[42] Most recent decisions, however, have been very reluctant to find such a waiver.[43]

### [b] Perfected Secured Creditor vs. Buyer

**[i] Buyers in Ordinary Course.** A "buyer in the ordinary course of business," other than a buyer of farm products,[44] has priority over a secured creditor with respect to a security interest if the interest was created by the person who sold to the buyer.[45] This is true even if the buyer in the ordinary course of business has knowledge of the existence of the security interest and even if the security interest is perfected.[46] "Buyer in the ordinary course of business" is defined at Section 1-201(9). To meet the definition, the following requirements must be met:

---

sales, transfers in satisfaction of a preexisting debt, gifts, and the like were examples of sales that would not be authorized when the dispositions were limited to sales "in the ordinary course of business"); North Cent. Kan. Prod. Credit Ass'n v. Washington Sales Co., 223 Kan. 689, 577 P2d 35, 23 UCC Rep. Serv. 1343 (1978) (sale not authorized because of failure to follow condition of sale that payment of sale proceeds be jointly to seller and bank). But see First Nat'l Bank & Trust Co. of Okla. City v. Iowa Beef Processors, Inc., 626 F2d 764, 29 UCC Rep. Serv. 743 (10th Cir. 1980) (security agreement conditioning secured creditor's consent to the sale upon receiving proceeds of resale did not prevent finding of authorization for sale in violation of provision).

[42] See, e.g., Planters Prod. Credit Assn. v. Bowles, 256 Ark. 1063, 511 SW2d 645, 14 UCC Rep. Serv. 1435 (1974).

[43] Security Nat'l Bank v. Belleville Livestock Comm'n Co., 619 F2d 840, 26 UCC Rep. Serv. 528 (10th Cir. 1979); Wabasso State Bank v. Caldwell Packing Co., 308 Minn. 349, 251 NW2d 321, 19 UCC Rep. Serv. 315 (1976). Most of these decisions have concerned whether the continued sale of farm products without the prior permission required in the security agreement constitutes a waiver. Sales of farm products even in the ordinary course do not give the buyer priority under UCC § 9-307(1). Consequently, whether the sale is authorized is critical to the rights of the buyer because the buyer must rely on UCC § 9-306(2) for priority. If the sale is not authorized, and the creditor is perfected, UCC § 9-201 applies to give the creditor priority. See generally Clark, Law of Secured Transactions ¶ 8.04[3] (Warren, Gorham & Lamont, Inc. 1980). But see In re Woods, 25 Bankr. 924, 35 UCC Rep. Serv. 256 (ED Tenn. 1982) (authorization by waiver or estoppel when secured party knew goods were delivered by debtor to a dealer and secured party took no action).

[44] "Farm products" is defined at UCC § 9-109(3); see supra ¶ 7.03[2][b][iii].

[45] UCC § 9-307(1). A buyer does not need to rely on this section if he can show that the sale was authorized "by the security agreement or otherwise." UCC § 9-306(2). See supra ¶ 7.07[5][a]. Neither is UCC § 9-307(1) generally needed by the buyer if the secured creditor is unperfected. UCC §§ 9-301(1)(c), 9-301(1)(d). See infra ¶ 7.07[5][c].

[46] UCC § 9-307(1).

(1) The buyer must be in good faith;[47]

(2) The buyer must not have knowledge that the sale to the buyer is in violation of the security interest;[48]

(3) The purchase must be in the buyer's ordinary course;[49]

(4) The sale must be by a person who is in the business of selling goods of that kind;[50] and

---

[47] Whenever good faith is at issue, the courts may wrestle with whether to apply the subjective test of UCC § 1-201(19)–that is, whether the party was honest in fact–or the objective test of UCC § 2-103(1)(b)–did the party live up to reasonable commercial standards? Most have adopted the subjective standard of UCC § 1-201(19) for the purposes of determining the good faith of the buyer. See, e.g., Martin Marietta Corp. v. New Jersey Nat'l Bank, 612 F2d 745, 27 UCC Rep. Serv. 1153 (3d Cir. 1979); Frank Davis Buick AMC-Jeep, Inc. v. First Ala. Bank of Huntsville, N.A., 423 So. 2d 855, 35 UCC Rep. Serv. 249 (Ala. Civ. App. 1982) (applying subjective standard); Massey-Ferguson, Inc. v. Helland, 105 Ill. App. 3d 648, 434 NE2d 295, 33 UCC Rep. Serv. 1532 (1982) (applying subjective standard); cf. Swift v. J.I. Case Co., 266 So. 2d 379, 11 UCC Rep. Serv. 190 (Fla. Dist. Ct. App. 1972); Hempstead Bank v. Andy's Car Rental Sys., Inc., 35 AD2d 35, 312 NYS2d 317, 7 UCC Rep. Serv. 932 (1970).

[48] Knowledge that there is a security interest is not the same as knowledge that the sale is in violation of the security interest. If the seller is engaged in selling goods of that kind and there is a sale from inventory, the secured creditor with an interest in inventory generally has specifically authorized the sale. See, e.g., In re Woods, 25 Bankr. 924, 35 UCC Rep. Serv. 256 (ED Tenn. 1982). The mere fact that an automobile may be titled and lists the secured creditor does not prevent a buyer from being a "buyer in the ordinary course." Sterling Acceptance Co. v. Grimes, 194 Pa. Super. 503, 168 A2d 600, 1 UCC Rep. Serv. 487 (1961); In re Morristown Lincoln-Mercury, Inc., 25 Bankr. 377, 35 UCC Rep. Serv. 268 (Bankr. ED Tenn. 1982) (although there is dictum in the decision indicating that a different result might be appropriate if the buyer had seen the certificate before purchase).

[49] A few courts have addressed whether a person is a buyer if the sales transaction has not been completed. The majority of courts have not required possession in the buyer. See, e.g., Serra v. Ford Motor Credit Co., 463 A2d 142, 36 UCC Rep. Serv. 1011 (RI 1983); International Harvester Credit Corp. v. Associates Fin. Servs. Co., 133 Ga. App. 488, 211 SE2d 430, 16 UCC Rep. Serv. 396 (1974) (delivery of goods need not be completed). If there is no delivery, a person is a buyer at least by the time of identification of the goods under UCC § 9-501. Serra v. Ford Motor Credit Co., 463 A2d 142, 36 UCC 1011 (RI 1983) (mere retention of title by seller did not prevent person from becoming "buyer"). Some courts have indicated that the person can become a buyer even though specific goods cannot be positively identified by a lack of a serial number or other specific designation. See, e.g., Wilson v. M & W Gear, 110 Ill. App. 3d 538, 442 NE2d 670, 35 UCC Rep. Serv. 685 (1982); Chrysler Credit Corp. v. Sharp, 56 Misc. 2d 261, 288 NYS2d 525, 5 UCC Rep. Serv. 226 (NY Sup. Ct. 1968). Contra Troy Lumber Co. v. Williams, 124 Ga. App. 636, 185 SE2d 580, 9 UCC Rep. Serv. 1144 (1971).

[50] This does not include a pawnbroker. However, all persons who sell minerals or the like (including oil and gas) at the wellhead or minehead are considered to be in the business of selling goods of that kind. UCC § 1-201(9).

Decisions exist in which the seller was found to be in the "business of selling goods of that kind" even though the type of sale at issue was not the primary business of the seller. Tanbro Fabrics Corp. v. Deering Milliken, Inc., 39 NY2d 632, 350 NE2d 590, 385

(5) The "buying"may be for cash or by exchange of other property and includes receiving goods or documents of title under a preexisting contract for sale, but cannot be a transfer in bulk or as security for or in total or partial satisfaction of a money debt.[51]

The limitation of Section 9-307(1)–that the buyer takes free only with respect to a security interest that is "created by his seller"–has tripped up a few buyers.

> **EXAMPLE:** *B*, a buyer in the ordinary course, purchases a used stereo from X's Appliances. X's Appliances had obtained the stereo from *M* who had used the stereo for his personal use. The stereo was subject to a security interest that covered all of *M*'s consumer goods.
>
> Although *B* is a buyer in the ordinary course, *B* does not win under Section 9-307(1). The security interest is not "created by his seller" but by *M*, a third party.[52]

**[ii] Buyers–Priority Rules.** Section 9-307(2) gives the buyer priority over a conflicting secured creditor only if:

(1) The buyer purchases collateral for a personal, family, or household purpose from a seller who was using the goods for a personal, family, or household purpose; and
(2) The secured creditor is not perfected by filing a financing statement.

---

NYS2d 260, 19 UCC Rep. Serv. 385 (1976) (textile "converter" who finished textile into dyed and patterned fabrics was a seller in the ordinary course in selling surplus unfinished fabrics); Finance Am. Commercial Corp. v. Econo Coach, Inc., 118 Ill. App. 2d 385, 454 NE2d 1127 (1983) (seller who was in primary business of leasing recreational vehicles found to meet test with respect to sale of leased vehicles). But see United Carolina Bank v. Capital Automobile Co., 163 Ga. App. 796, 294 SE2d 661, 34 UCC Rep. Serv. 1705 (1982) (sale of leased autos); Hempstead Bank v. Andy's Car Rental Sys., Inc., 35 AD2d 35, 312 NYS2d 317, 7 UCC Rep. Serv. 932 (1970) (sale of leased autos).

[51] See, e.g., Walter E. Heller Western, Inc. v. Bohemia, Inc., 61 Ore. App. 57, 655 P2d 1073, 35 UCC Rep. Serv. 1002 (1982) (transfer of goods by seller to buyer in return for offset of an amount seller owed buyer on another preexisting obligation was not "buying" to the extent of the old value).

[52] See, e.g., Security Pac. Nat'l Bank v. Goodman, 24 Cal. App. 3d 131, 100 Cal. Rptr. 768, 10 UCC Rep. Serv. 529 (1972). Arguably, the buyer has superior rights as against the secured creditor under the entrustment provisions of UCC § 2-403. One case has so held. In re Woods, 25 Bankr. 924, 35 UCC Rep. Serv. 256 (ED Tenn. 1982) (also holding that in facts similar to the example that if the secured creditor knew of its debtor's delivery of goods to the dealer and took no action, then the sale was authorized under UCC § 9-306(2) and the security interest was also lost for that reason). However, another case has held that the entrustment provision of UCC § 2-403 has no applicability to a dispute between the secured creditor and buyer. National Shawmut Bank of Boston v. Jones, 108 NH 386, 236 A2d 484, 4 UCC Rep. Serv. 1021 (1967).

The first limitation means that the sale must be from a consumer to a consumer.[53] The second limitation should encourage secured creditors to file a financing statement to secure an interest in consumer goods of any significant value even if the secured creditor is entitled to automatic perfection under Section 9-302(1)(d).

**[iii] Buyers Not in the Ordinary Course and Future Advances.** If the secured creditor claims a perfected security interest to the extent of future advances of value,[54] the general rule is that a buyer, even though not in the ordinary course, has priority to the extent that the future advances are made: (1) after the secured party acquires knowledge of the purchase, or (2) more than forty-five days after the purchase.[55] If the future advance is made before the knowledge of the purchase or the expiration of the forty-five-day period, the secured creditor has priority.

**[iv] Nonprofessional Buyers of Titled Motor Vehicles.** If a security interest is perfected in a vehicle by a notation on the certificate of title issued by one state (or the interest is perfected in the vehicle in any other manner permitted by the state), and the vehicle is moved to another state, which issues a certificate of title not showing the secured creditor's interest, a buyer of the vehicle in the second state may take free of the security interest. The buyer must not be in the business of selling goods of that kind. Also, the new certificate must not show the secured creditor's interest. If these requirements are met, the nonprofessional buyer takes free of the security interest to the extent the buyer gives value and receives value without knowledge of the security interest.[56]

## [c] Unperfected Secured Creditor vs. Buyers and Transferees

**[i] Buyers and Transferees in Bulk of Goods, Instruments, Documents, and Chattel Paper.** If the collateral is goods, instruments, documents, or chattel paper, certain claimants–buyers, transferees in bulk,[57] and buyers of farm products in the ordinary course of business–have priority over unperfected secured creditors.[58] The buyer or transferee, however, cannot have knowledge

---

[53] See, e.g., New England Merchants Nat'l Bank of Boston v. Auto Owners Fin. Co., 355 Mass. 487, 245 NE2d 437, 6 UCC Rep. Serv. 58 (1969); First Dallas County Bank v. General Motors Acceptance Corp., 33 UCC Rep. Serv. 128 (Ala. Civ. App. 1982).

[54] See supra ¶¶ 7.04[2][vi], 7.06[3][c][x].

[55] See Spector United Employees Credit Union v. Smith, 45 NC App. 432, 263 SE2d 319, 28 UCC Rep. Serv. 310 (1980) (giving priority to creditor because mere refinancing found not to be a future advance).

[56] UCC § 9-103(2)(d); see supra ¶ 7.06[6][c][ii].

[57] See UCC § 6-102.

[58] UCC § 9-301(1)(c). Any party seeking priority under this section cannot also be a party with a security interest in the collateral. Id.

of the security interest.[59] In addition, the priority rights of a transferee in bulk are subject to Section 9-301(2). Under that section, a purchase-money secured creditor who files before or within ten days after the debtor receives possession takes priority over a transferee in bulk whose rights arise between the time of attachment and the filing of the security interest.

**[ii] Transferees of Accounts and General Intangibles.** In the case of accounts and general intangibles, a transferee who is not also a secured party takes priority over an unperfected secured creditor if the transferee gives value without knowledge of the security interest.[60]

### [d] Purchasers of Chattel Paper and Instruments

Purchasers of chattel paper or instruments may gain priority over a secured creditor claiming the same collateral if:

(1) The purchaser gives new value;
(2) The purchaser takes possession of the chattel paper or instrument in the ordinary course of business;
(3) The security interest is either:
   (a) Perfected under Section 9-304 (permissive filing and temporary perfection) or under Section 9-306 (perfection as to proceeds) and the purchaser has no knowledge that the specific paper or instrument is subject to a security interest; or
   (b) Claimed merely as proceeds as inventory without regard to whether the purchaser has knowledge that the specific paper or instrument is subject to a security interest.

**EXAMPLE:** Secured creditor *A* has an attached security interest in all inventory and proceeds of a debtor. The security interest is perfected by the filing of a financing statement. The debtor sells an item of inventory and receives chattel paper in return, which is sold to secured creditor *B*. *B* has knowledge that the chattel paper is subject to a security interest.

In a priority dispute between *A* and *B*, the probable winner will be *B*, the buyer of the chattel paper. However, because *B* has knowledge of the security interest, he will win only if the chattel paper is claimed "merely as proceeds." That seems to be the case here. In inventory financing, the

---

[59] Id.; cf. UCC § 9-307(1), which allows ordinary course buyers, except buyers of farm products, to win unless they have "knowledge that the sale to him is in violation of the . . . security interest." See UCC § 1-201(9) defining "buyer in the ordinary course"; supra ¶ 7.07[5][b][i].

[60] UCC § 9-301(1)(d); cf. UCC § 9-307(1), which allows ordinary course buyers, except buyers of farm products, to win unless they have "knowledge that the sale to him is in violation of the . . . security interest." See UCC § 1-201(9), defining "buyer in the ordinary course"; supra ¶ 7.07[5][b][i].

secured creditor generally looks only to chattel paper and instruments as proceeds generated by sales of inventory.[61]

### [e] Certain Purchasers of Instruments, Negotiable Documents, and Securities

Section 9-309 protects the status of the holder in due course of an instrument,[62] the holder of a negotiable document,[63] and the bona fide purchaser of a document. Although a creditor may perfect a security interest in negotiable documents by filing a financing statement rather than taking possession and may temporarily perfect a security interest in instruments without possession,[64] the potential effect of not having possession is the loss of priority to the intervening holder of the document or holder in due course of the instrument.

## [6] Security Interests in Returned or Repossessed Goods

Section 9-312(5) is concerned with two issues. First, if a secured creditor, *A*, has a security interest in goods that are sold by the debtor and the goods are later returned to the debtor or repossessed by the debtor, is the security interest attached and perfected with respect to such goods? Second, if the sale by the debtor resulted in an account or chattel paper that is transferred to another secured party, *B*, who has priority in the goods returned or repossessed: the secured creditor whose initial security interest was in the goods, *A*, or the second secured creditor, *B*, whose interest initially was in accounts or chattel paper?

With respect to the issue of perfection in returned or repossessed goods, if the goods are still unpaid, *A*, the creditor holding a security interest in the goods before disposition, has an attached security interest in the goods sold that are later returned or repossessed. The interest is perfected if the security interest was perfected when the goods were first sold. If the security interest was originally perfected by a filing that is still effective, nothing further is required. If not, the secured party must take possession of the goods or file.[65]

Priority disputes over the returned or repossessed goods may arise between the secured creditor and a purchaser of accounts or chattel paper (from the debtor) who is claiming the goods as proceeds. The resolution of this priority dispute depends upon whether the debtor transferred accounts or transferred chattel paper. If the debtor disposed of goods covered by *A*'s security interest and the debtor took chattel paper from its buyer and transferred the chattel

---

[61] See, e.g., Bank of Beulah v. Chase, 231 NW2d 738, 17 UCC Rep. Serv. (ND 1975). No appellate case has found that an inventory financier has claimed chattel paper other than as "mere proceeds." But see Official Comment 3 to UCC § 9-308, indicating that a lender may, by separating its transactions, make such a showing.

[62] See UCC § 3-302.

[63] UCC § 7-104.

[64] UCC §§ 9-304(4), 9-304(5); see supra ¶ 7.06[5].

[65] UCC § 9-312(5).

paper to *B*, *B* has a security interest in the repossessed or returned goods. If *B*'s interest in the *chattel paper* is perfected, *B*'s interest in the goods is prior to the interest of *A*.[66] If the debtor disposed of goods covered by *A*'s security interest and the debtor transferred an *account* arising from the sale to *B, B* has a security interest in the repossessed or returned goods. However, *B*'s security interest in the repossessed or returned goods is subordinate to that of *A*.

**EXAMPLE 1:** Secured creditor *A* has a security interest in a debtor's inventory. The interest is perfected by filing. The debtor sells an item of inventory. The buyer gives the debtor a conditional sales contract that contains both an obligation to pay the debtor and a grant of a security interest in the item purchased. The debtor assigns the conditional sales contract to secured creditor *B* who thereby gets a security interest in chattel paper. The debtor repossesses the item sold when the buyer fails to pay for it. Both *A* and *B* have security interest in the repossessed item of inventory. If *B* had perfected its interest in the chattel paper (by either possession or filing a financing statement), *B* would have priority.

**EXAMPLE 2:** If, in Example 1, the debtor had received merely the promise to pay on an open account rather than chattel paper, and had given *B* an interest in the open account, *B* would have an interest in an account. Upon repossession by the debtor of the inventory sold, *A* and *B* would have a security interest in the repossessed goods. Priority in the goods would be in *A* even if *B* had perfected its security interest in the account.

## [7] Secured Creditor vs. Statutory Lienholder

In all states, law outside Article 9 provides for liens for materialmen, warehouse owners, and others who repair, maintain, or store goods. Generally, these liens are provided by statute.[67] When a lienholder and a secured creditor claim priority in the same item of goods, priority is determined by Section 9-310. Priority is given to the lienholder, even if the secured creditor is perfected, to the extent of any claim for services or materials if:[68]

(1) The lienholder has possession of the goods; and

(2) If the lien is statutory, the statute does not expressly provide that the secured creditor has priority.[69]

---

[66] UCC §§ 9-306(5)(b), 9-306(5)(d); see, e.g., Crocker Nat'l Bank v. Clark Equip. Credit Corp., 724 F2d 696, 37 UCC Rep. Serv. 673 (8th Cir. 1984).

[67] See, e.g., Ga. Code Ann. § 44-14-320.

[68] As always the rules set out are those in the official version. There are a number of nonuniform amendments in the various states. See, e.g., Wash. Rev. Code § 62A.9-310, interpreted in In re Tacoma Aviation Center, Inc., 23 Bankr. 326, 35 UCC Rep. Serv. 298 (WD Wash. 1982).

[69] See, e.g., Ga. Code Ann. § 67-2003, discussed in Newton Ford Tractor Co., Inc. v. J.I. Case Credit Corp., 163 Ga. App. 497, 294 SE2d 723, 34 UCC Rep. Serv. 1753 (1982); see also In re Shoup, 34 Bankr. 851, 37 UCC Rep. Serv. 604 (Bankr. WD Pa.

**EXAMPLE:** A debtor takes his auto to *J's Garage*. *J* repairs it, but the debtor refuses to pay for the repairs. *J* retains possession of the auto pursuant to a state statute that gives *J* a lien on the auto for the repairs. The auto is also subject to a perfected security interest held by a secured creditor.

*J* has priority to the extent of the cost of the repairs as long as he retains possession[70] unless the state lien statute under which *J* claims specifically awards priority to a secured creditor.

## [8] Secured Creditor vs. Fixture Claimant

### [a] Definition of Fixture

Fixtures are not specifically defined in the UCC; however, Section 9-313(2) does indicate that goods are not fixtures if they are ordinary building materials incorporated into an improvement on land. Section 9-313 indicates that goods become fixtures when they become "so related to the real estate that an interest in them arises under real estate law." Determination of when this relationship occurs is an issue resolved through the application of law outside Article 9. The major test under such state law typically is whether the intent of the party who attaches the goods to the land is for the goods to become a permanent accession to the land. Intent is determined by a variety of factors, such as the degree of annexation, the adaptation of the goods to the use or purpose of that part of the realty to which it is connected, and the purpose of the party adding the goods.[71] The express intent of the parties in their agreement generally controls even if the other tests, such as the degree of annexation, show a fixture was intended.[72]

### [b] Perfection in Fixtures

Once a secured creditor has an attached security interest in a fixture, perfection may occur by the filing of a financing statement or by a "fixture filing."[73] In addition to other requirements, a fixture filing requires:

---

1983) (state statute provided that priority would be in perfected secured creditor unless the secured creditor had given consent; since there was no consent by holder of security interest, secured creditor had priority).

[70] See U.S. Nat'l Bank v. Atlas Auto Body, 214 Neb. 597, 335 NW2d 288 (1983) (court gave mechanic priority to the extent of money owing for services, but refused to give priority to the extent of money owing for amount of storage charges; three judges dissented).

[71] Bemis v. First Nat'l Bank, 63 Ark. 625, 40 SW 127 (1897).

[72] See, e.g., Bank of Valley v. U.S. Nat'l Bank of Omaha, 215 Neb. 912, 341 NW2d 592, 37 UCC Rep. Serv. 994 (1983); Motorola Communications & Elecs., Inc. v. Dale, 665 F2d 771, 33 UCC Rep. Serv. 761 (5th Cir. 1982). But see Cummings, Inc. v. Beardsley, 271 Ark. 596, 609 SW2d 66, 30 UCC Rep. Serv. 1133 (1980).

[73] The requirements for such a filing are discussed at supra ¶ 7.06[3][c][vii].

(1) A description of real estate;
(2) A direction to the filing officer to file the statement in the real estate records; and
(3) A filing in the office where a mortgage on the real estate would be filed or recorded.[74]

### [c] General Rules Concerning Priority

Disputes between two Article 9 secured creditors claiming priority in fixtures are resolved under Article 9. Priority disputes between two real estate claimants are resolved outside Article 9. If the priority dispute in a fixture is between an Article 9 secured creditor and the owner or an encumbrancer of the real estate, the dispute is resolved under Section 9-313. The general priority rule in such a dispute is that the real estate claimant has priority.[75] There are, however, important exceptions to this general rule, which are discussed below.

### [d] Secured Creditor vs. Prior Real Estate Claimant

Under Section 9-313(4)(a), a secured creditor has priority against a real estate claimant if:

(1) The interest of the real estate claimant arose *before* the goods became fixtures;
(2) The security interest is a purchase-money security interest[76] that is perfected by a "fixture filing"[77] before the goods become fixtures or within ten days thereafter; and
(3) The debtor has an interest of record in the real estate or is in possession of the real estate.

This super priority for the secured creditor who finances the acquisition of fixtures and perfects within a ten-day period is akin to the purchase-money priority rules of Section 9-312(4).

> **EXAMPLE:** Secured creditor *A* obtains an attached purchase-money security interest in an item of equipment purchased by a debtor. *A* files a fixture filing before the item becomes a fixture or within ten days of that date. The debtor is the record owner of the real estate. A real estate encumbrancer claims an interest in the fixture by virtue of a real estate mortgage that includes fixtures as security for the payment of the obligation.
>
> If the real estate claimant's interest predates the date the goods became fixtures, the purchase-money secured creditor wins under these facts.

---

[74] UCC §§ 9-402(5), 9-313(1)(b); see supra ¶ 7.06[3][c][vii].

[75] UCC § 9-313(7).

[76] UCC § 9-107; see supra ¶ 7.06[5][b].

[77] UCC § 9-402(5); see supra ¶ 7.07[8][b].

This super priority of Section 9-313(4)(a) does not exist for the Article 9 secured creditor if: (1) the real estate claimant is the holder of a construction mortgage recorded before the goods become fixtures, and (2) the goods become fixtures before the completion of construction.[78] A mortgage taken to secure the refinancing of a construction loan has the same status as the original construction mortgage.[79]

### [e] Secured Creditor vs. Subsequent Real Estate Claimant

Under Section 9-313(4)(b), the security interest of non-purchase-money secured creditors who have made a "fixture filing" may also be prior if:

(1) The interest of the encumbrancer or owner arises *after* the Article 9 security interest is perfected by the fixture filing;
(2) The Article 9 secured creditor has priority over other conflicting interests of predecessors in title; and[80]
(3) The debtor has an interest of record in the real estate or is in possession of the real estate.

This is simply a version of the basic priority rule that the claimant who is "first in time" wins.[81]

### [f] Security Interests in Certain Readily Removable Fixtures

Under Section 9-313(4)(c), an Article 9 secured creditor who is perfected before the goods become fixtures by any method permitted by Article 9, including fixture filing and standard filing, has priority if the goods are "readily removable." This includes factory or office machines and replacements of domestic appliances that are "consumer goods."

### [g] Secured Creditor vs. Judicial or Equitable Lienholder

Under Section 9-313(4)(d), an Article 9 security interest has priority over liens on the real estate obtained by legal or equitable proceedings if the security interest was perfected before the lien either by a standard filing or a fixture filing. This is similar to the rule at Section 9-301(1)(b), which gives the secured

---

[78] UCC § 9-313(5).

[79] Id.

[80] Official Comment 4(b) to UCC § 9-313 states that this "apparent limitation . . . is not really a limitation, but is an expression of the usual rule that a person must be entitled to transfer what he has." For example, if the fixture security interest is subordinate to the rights of an owner, it is subordinate to the rights of a grantee of the owner and to a subsequent mortgagee of the owner.

[81] See, e.g., Corning Bank v. Bank of Rector, 265 Ark. 68, 576 SW2d 949, 26 UCC Rep. Serv. 1367 (1979).

creditor in nonfixtures priority over lien creditors if the secured creditor is perfected before the lien creditor status arises.

### [h] Subordination Agreements and Effect of Debtor's Right of Removal

Under Section 9-313(6), a security interest in fixtures, whether or not perfected, defeats interests claimed by the real estate claimant if:

(1) The encumbrancer or owner of the real estate has consented in writing to the security interest or has disclaimed an interest in the goods as fixtures; or

(2) The debtor has a right to remove the goods as against the encumbrancer or owner.[82]

### [i] Right to Remove Fixtures

When the secured party has priority over all owners and encumbrancers of the real estate, Section 9-313(8) allows the secured party, upon default of the debtor, to remove the collateral from the real estate. The creditor must follow the provisions of Part 5 of Article 9.[83] The secured creditor must reimburse any encumbrancer or owner of the real estate, who is not the debtor and who has not otherwise agreed, for the cost of repair of any physical damage.[84] However, the real estate claimant is not entitled to reimbursement for any loss in value of the real estate caused merely by the absence of the goods removed or by any necessity of replacing them.[85]

## [9] Secured Creditor vs. Claimant in Accessions

### [a] Definition of Accession

An accession is to personal property what a fixture is to real property. When goods become so attached to personal property that they become accessions is a matter for state law outside Article 9.[86] The general test is whether the person doing the attaching of the goods to personal property intends the

---

[82] UCC § 9-313(5). If the debtor's right terminates, the priority of the security interest continues for a "reasonable time." Id.

[83] These provisions are discussed at supra ¶ 7.05.

[84] A person entitled to reimbursement may refuse permission to remove the accession until the secured party gives adequate security for the performance of this obligation. UCC § 9-313(8).

[85] See, e.g., Motorola Communications & Elecs., Inc. v. Dale, 665 F2d 771, 33 UCC Rep. Serv. 761 (5th Cir. 1982).

[86] UCC § 9-314.

goods to be permanently attached to the personalty.[87] The most common type of accession is accessories added to motor vehicles.[88]

Goods are not accessions if they become so commingled (e.g., as in a manufacturing process) with other goods that their original identity is lost. Priority in commingled goods is covered in Section 9-315.[89]

### [b] Priority Rules

The security interest does *not* take priority over: (1) a subsequent purchaser for value of any interest in the whole;[90] (2) the creditor with a lien on the whole subsequently obtained by judicial proceedings; or (3) a creditor with a prior perfected security interest in the whole to the extent that he makes subsequent advances if these events occur before perfection of the security interest and without knowledge of the security interest.

In other cases, a secured creditor does have priority if:

(1) The security interest attaches before the goods become accessions;[91] or

(2) The security interest attaches after the goods become accessions. (However, this particular priority right is not valid against any person with an interest in the property to which the goods are attached unless such person consents in writing to the security interest or disclaims an interest in the goods as part of the whole.)

### [c] Right of Secured Creditor to Remove Accessions

When the secured party has priority over all other claimants of the personal property to which the accession is attached, Section 9-314(4) allows the secured party, upon default of the debtor, to remove the collateral from the real estate. The creditor must follow the provisions of Part 5 of Article 9.[92] The secured creditor must reimburse any encumbrancer or owner of the whole, who is not the debtor and who has not otherwise agreed, for the cost of repair of any

---

[87] See, e.g., IDS Leasing Corp. v. Leasing Assocs., Inc., 590 SW2d 607, 27 UCC Rep. Serv. 1441 (Tex. Civ. App. 1979).

[88] See, e.g., In re Lyford, 22 Bankr. 222, 34 UCC Rep. Serv. 754 (D. Me. 1982) (accessories added to equip trucks for logging); Johnson v. Conrail-Amtrak Fed. C.U., 37 UCC Rep. Serv. 933 (DC Super. 1983) (engine added to automobile).

[89] See infra ¶ 7.07[10].

[90] This includes a purchaser of the whole at a foreclosure sale other than the holder of a perfected security interest purchasing at his own foreclosure sale. UCC § 9-314(3). The "whole" refers to the item of personalty to which the accession is affixed.

[91] This priority rule is also subject to the commingling and processing rules of UCC § 9-315, discussed at infra ¶ 7.07[10].

[92] These provisions are discussed at supra ¶ 7.05.

physical damage to the whole.[93] However, the real estate claimant is not entitled to reimbursement for any loss in value of the real estate caused merely by the absence of the goods removed or by any necessity of replacing them.

### [10] Secured Creditor vs. Claimant in Commingled Goods and Products

If the goods are commingled or processed, perfection and priority are determined by Section 9-315. Examples of such commingling or processing are the mixture of flour, sugar, and so on, into a cake mix or a cake, or the assembly of components in a machine.[94] Another example would be vegetables that become part of a mass of vegetables in the hands of a debtor-food processor.[95]

If a security interest in goods is perfected and subsequently the goods or a part thereof became part of a product or mass, Section 9-315(1) provides that the security interest continues in the product or mass if:

(1) The goods are so manufactured, processed, assembled, or commingled that their identity is lost in the product or mass; or

(2) A financing statement covering the original goods also covers the product into which the goods have been manufactured, processed, or assembled.[96]

When more than one security interest attaches to the product or mass, the interest rank equally according to the ratio that the cost of the goods to which each interest originally attached bears to the cost of the total product or mass.[97]

### [11] Secured Creditor vs. Article 2 Claimant

A seller of goods who sells on credit generally will take pains to ensure that an Article 9 security interest is created and perfected under the standard rules of Article 9 with respect to the type of collateral. In addition, an Article 9 security interest arises when the seller sells on credit and expressly reserves title

---

[93] A person entitled to reimbursement may refuse permission to remove until the secured party gives adequate security for the performance of this obligation. UCC § 9-314(4).

[94] In the latter case, the secured party has the option to claim under UCC § 9-314 on accessions. See the discussion at supra ¶ 7.07[9][c] and UCC § 9-314(1) discussed below; Official Comment 3 to UCC § 9-315.

[95] See In re San Juan Packers, Inc., 696 F2d 707, 35 UCC Rep. Serv. 661 (9th Cir. 1983). As to whether a security interest in feed would attach to the cow that eats it, see Clark, Law of Secured Transactions ¶ 8.04[6] (Warren, Gorham & Lamont, Inc. 1980).

[96] With respect to the goods under Item 2, the creditor must choose whether to claim under UCC § 9-315 or the accession provision, UCC § 9-314, discussed at supra ¶ 7.07[9][c].

[97] UCC § 9-315(2).

to the goods.[98] In these cases, the seller has a security interest arising under Article 9 and the rights of the seller, including priority rights, are decided by Article 9.

If the seller does not follow the general rules for obtaining a security interest under Article 9, the seller may still obtain a security interest arising solely under Article 2.[99] Under Section 9-113, the holder of such an interest gets these special rights:

(1) No security agreement need be taken;
(2) There is no need to file to perfect;
(3) The priority rules between the seller and other claimants will be determined under the rules of Article 9.[100]

However, these special rules end when the buyer gets possession of the goods. If the buyer gets possession, a seller who wants Article 9 rights must show that he satisfied the standard Article 9 requirements.

Buyers of goods, and other parties, may also be entitled to a security interest arising under Article 2.[101] Such parties are also entitled to the special rights of Section 9-113 but only as long as the "debtor" (the seller, if the buyer has a security interest arising under Article 2) does not get possession of the goods.

### [12] Secured Creditor vs. Trustee in Bankruptcy

A trustee in bankruptcy may have the right to avoid the security interest of the Article 9 secured creditor. Priority disputes between the secured creditor and the trustee are discussed elsewhere in this book.[102]

### [13] Secured Creditor vs. The Internal Revenue Service

The Internal Revenue Service may have the right to take collateral or its value without regard to the secured creditor's interest. Priority disputes between the secured creditor and the holder of a tax lien are discussed elsewhere in this book.[103]

---

[98] UCC § 2-401(1).

[99] See supra ¶ 7.02[2][c].

[100] The rights between the seller and the buyer, however, are determined under Article 2. UCC § 9-113.

[101] See, e.g., UCC §§ 2-707, 2-711; supra ¶ 7.07[2][c].

[102] See ¶¶ 16.02, 16.05.

[103] See ¶ 9.04.

# 8

# Mortgages and Other Secured Transactions in Real Estate

## ¶ 8.01 INTRODUCTION

Consensual real estate security devices are of equal importance to both consensual personal property and fixture security devices.[1] Real estate mortgages and other consensual real estate security devices are considered in this chapter.[2] Because the real estate mortgage is most commonly encountered by the practicing lawyer, principal emphasis is placed on that security device. The mortgage may be defined as "a transfer by a debtor-mortgagor to a creditor-mortgagee of a real estate interest, to be held as security for the performance of an obligation, normally the payment of a debt evidenced by the mortgagor's promissory note."[3]

Unlike Article 9 of the Uniform Commercial Code (UCC), which pertains to secured transactions in personal property and fixtures, there is no uniform law pertaining to consensual security devices in real property. As a result, coverage of real estate security devices on a national scale is somewhat complicated. There are, however, legal principles and issues commonly encountered in every state. This chapter summarizes the law of secured transactions in real estate.

## ¶ 8.02 HISTORICAL DEVELOPMENT OF MORTGAGE LAW

A brief survey of the historical development of real estate mortgage law is helpful in obtaining a proper understanding of modern mortgage law.[1] Early Anglo-Saxon English law and the English common-law mortgage, influenced by the intervention of English Chancery courts, have had the greatest effect upon American mortgage law.

The earliest real property security devices were the Saxon living gage (vivum vadium) and dead gage (mortuum vadium), in which the creditor took possession of the land and profit accruing from it.[2] The gages resembled a pledge of personal property, since the creditor took possession of the property

---

[1] See Chapter 7 for a discussion of UCC Article 9, which covers consensual secured transactions in personal property and fixtures.

[2] See infra ¶ 8.03 for a definition of various types of real estate security devices.

[3] Nelson & Whitman, Real Estate Finance and Development 1 (West 1976).

[1] For an excellent and concise discussion of the historical development of the real estate mortgage, see 7 Debtor-Creditor Law ¶ 31.02[A][2] (Matthew Bender 1982). See also Osborne, Mortgages 2–31 (2d ed. West, 1970); 9 Thompson on Real Property Ch. 58 (Bobbs-Merrill 1958); 3 Powell on Real Property ¶ 438 (Matthew Bender 1981).

[2] See Calamari, Cases and Materials on Real Property Mortgages 1 (C.M. Johnson Co., 2d ed. 1963); 3 Powell on Real Property ¶ 438 (Matthew Bender 1981).

until the debt was satisfied. The English common-law mortgage ultimately evolved in the fourteenth and fifteenth centuries, producing a security device that resembles the modern-day mortgage.[3] The creditor-mortgagee was conveyed legal title in fee simple with the express condition subsequent that the debtor perform the secured obligation at "law day." Law day was simply the due date of the debt; once the debt was paid, the debtor could retake title and re-enter. By the middle of the seventeenth century, the mortgagee gained the right to retain possession upon the slightest default by the mortgagor, causing the creditor's estate in the land to become absolute.

The English Courts of Chancery thereafter began to intervene on behalf of the mortgagor to avoid the harsh effect of the existing mortgage. If the mortgagor had paid the secured debt, Chancery forced the mortgagee to reconvey title to that mortgagor. Additionally, the Chancery Court began to permit late payments if the debtor could establish a proper excuse for the tardiness. This established the roots of the equity of redemption.[4] On the other hand, the mortgagee acquired the right to a decree that specified the time within which the debtor was required to make payment; failure to do so resulted in loss of the right of redemption and the land itself. This procedure established the roots of the strict foreclosure decree, which ultimately led to the development of decrees for foreclosure by sale of the property.[5]

Although most of the basic elements of the modern mortgage had been defined by the mid-eighteenth century, two other matters awaited further development. First, the English mortgage law, which had evolved from the courts of law, began to characterize the mortgage as a transfer of title by the mortgagor to the mortgagee. This title theory of the mortgage relationship found its way to the United States.[6] Most states ultimately adopted a lien theory, which treats the mortgage as a lien instead of an outright transfer of title, a theory that evolved from the English Courts of Chancery.[7]

---

[3] See Osborne, Nelson & Whitman, Real Estate Finance Law § 1.2 (West 1979); 1 Glenn, Mortgages § 2 (Michie Co. 1943); McMichael, How to Finance Real Estate 13 (2d ed. 1953).

[4] See 3 Powell on Real Property ¶ 438 (Matthew Bender 1981); Osborne, Nelson & Whitman, Real Estate Finance Law 7 (West 1979).

[5] See Comment, "Power of Sale Foreclosure after Fuentes." 40 U. Chi. L. Rev. 206 (1972); 3 Powell on Real Property ¶ 438 (Matthew Bender 1981); Dunham, Modern Real Estate Transactions 281–283 (Foundation Press 1958); Kratovil, Modern Mortgage Law and Practice 25 (1972).

[6] See 7 Debtor-Creditor Law ¶ 31.02[A] n.24 (Matthew Bender 1982), which lists the following as "title theory states": Alabama, Arkansas, Connecticut, Maine, Maryland, Massachusetts, New Hampshire, North Carolina, Pennsylvania, Rhode Island, Tennessee, Vermont, Virginia, West Virginia, and, in modified versions, Delaware, Mississippi, and Missouri.

[7] See id. at n.25, which lists the following as "lien theory states": Arizona, California, Colorado, Florida, Georgia, Idaho, Indiana, Iowa, Kansas, Kentucky, Louisiana (civil law), Michigan, Minnesota, Montana, Nebraska, Nevada, New Mexico, New York, North Dakota, Oklahoma, Oregon, South Carolina, South Dakota, Texas, Utah, Washington, Wisconsin, and Wyoming.

Second, the character of the modern mortgage financing relationship underwent significant development in the 1920s and 1930s. Prior to the 1920s, most mortgagees were individuals. Because of the then-developing home mortgage, by the end of World War II mortgages were primarily financed by financial institutions.[8] Until the 1930s, most mortgages were of the "balloon-note" type, involving short-term debts of three to five years; the debtor only made interest payments until the loan came due. During the Depression, many debtors could not make the balloon payments, so lenders, with the encouragement of the Federal Housing Administration (FHA) and federal housing legislation, began to develop the amortized mortgage, by which mortgagors repaid loans over many years in monthly principal and interest payments.[9] These developments have resulted in the modern mortgage, which involves financial institutions and long-term debts.

## ¶ 8.03 TYPES OF REAL ESTATE SECURITY DEVICES

### [1] The Mortgage

The mortgage is the most common real estate security device.[1] As defined previously,[2] a real estate mortgage involves a transfer by a debtor (mortgagor) to a creditor (mortgagee) of an interest in real estate. The interest is held by the mortgagee to secure performance of an obligation to the mortgagor, typically the payment of a debt in the form of a promissory note. The mortgagee's interest is usually described as only a security interest[3] and can exist only if there is an instrument that evidences the debt or obligation[4] and if there is real estate that may serve as the collateral as described in the written mortgage itself.[5]

Considerable terminology describes the particular functions of different types of mortgages. One very important type of mortgage is the purchase-money mortgage, a mortgage in which money is borrowed to buy the land that

---

[8] See Dennis, Fundamentals of Mortgage Lending 11 (Reston 1978); Kratovil, "Mortgage Law Today," 13 J. Mar. L. Rev. 251 (Winter 1980).

[9] See Nelson & Whitman, Real Estate Finance and Development 2 (West 1976).

[1] See 7 Debtor-Creditor Law ¶¶ 81.02[A], 81.02[B] (Matthew Bender 1982), for an excellent basic description of the real estate mortgage and its uses.

[2] See supra ¶ 8.01 and note 3.

[3] See, e.g., Miller v. Federal Land Bank of Spokane, 587 F2d 415, 420 (9th Cir.), cert. denied, 441 US 962 (1978). However, some states still adhere to the title theory of mortgages. See supra ¶ 8.02 note 6.

[4] Of course, without a debt there can be no mortgage. See, e.g., Jaramille v. McLoy, 263 F. Supp. 870 (D. Colo. 1967); Vance v. Fields, 172 So. 2d 613 (Fla. Dist. Ct. App. 1965).

[5] For discussion of how the mortgage is created, see infra ¶ 8.04. See also 59 C.J.S. Mortgages § 71 (1949); cf. Matthews v. Jones Talcott, Inc., 345 F2d 374, 382 (7th Cir.), cert. denied, 382 US 837 (1965).

is used as the mortgage security.[6] The presence of a purchase-money mortgage is particularly important in priority disputes.[7] Mortgages are also described as "senior" or "junior" mortgages, a junior mortgage having a lower priority than a senior mortgage.[8] The terminology used to describe mortgages also serves to depict the nature of the mortgagor-mortgagee financing relationship. Typical of such terminology is the "long-term amortized mortgage," "variable-rate mortgage," "blanket mortgage," "leasehold mortgage," "package mortgage," "participation mortgage," "open-end mortgage," "wraparound mortgage," and "balloon mortgage."[9]

The use of the mortgage to secure numerous obligations provides mortgagees considerable flexibility. For example, some mortgages occasionally include a clause that secures all the mortgagor's instruments of debt that become due to the mortgagee at any time in the future. This type of mortgage is typically referred to as an "open-end mortgage."[10] A similar but broader clause is the "dragnet clause," which covers the extension of credit made at the time the mortgage is executed plus all prior and future indebtedness of the mortgagor. Dragnet clauses have been disfavored by the courts and may have their literal scope limited by case law.[11]

## [2] Mortgage Substitutes

In addition to the mortgage, there are other ways to structure a credit transaction that results in securing an extension of credit with real estate. For

---

[6] See, e.g., Donie State Bank v. Parker, 554 SW2d 858 (Tex. 1977); cf. Loretz v. Cal-Coast Dev. Corp., 249 Cal. App. 2d 176, 57 Cal. Rptr. 188 (1967). See Osborne, Nelson & Whitman, Real Estate Finance Law § 1.1 (West 1979). Obviously, a non-purchase-money mortgage would involve a mortgage on real estate that was *not* purchased with the extension of credit secured by the mortgage.

[7] See infra ¶ 8.09[2][c].

[8] See, e.g., State Mut. Life Assurance Co. of Am. v. Deer Creek Park, 612 F2d 259 (7th Cir. 1979); Omaha Nat'l Bank v. Continental W. Corp., 203 Neb. 264, 278 NW2d 339 (1949).

[9] See 7 Debtor-Creditor Law ¶ 31.02[B][3] (Matthew Bender 1982) for a specific discussion of such terminology.

[10] See Cabot, Cabot & Forbes Land Trust v. First Nat'l Bank of Fort Watton Beach, 369 So. 2d 89 (Fla. Dist. Ct. App. 1979); Georgia R.R. Bank & Trust Co. v. McCullough, 241 Ga. 456, 246 SE2d 313 (1978).

[11] See, e.g., In re Barnard, 1 Bankr. 640 (Bankr. Fla. 1979); Freese Leasing, Inc. v. Union Trust & Sav. Bank, Stanwood, 253 NW2d 921 (Iowa 1977). A matter of collateral importance to the real estate mortgage is that of mortgage guarantees and insurance. In addition to the Federal Housing Administration, the Veterans Administration, and the Farmers Home Administration, private mortgage insurance companies provide mortgage insurance. Basically, the insurance contract provides that if certain events occur, the company will pay the remainder of the mortgaged debt. See 12 USC §§ 1701–1748; 38 USC § 1803; 42 USC § 1487; Rapkin, The Private Insurance of Home Mortgages (1973); Griffith, "Mortgage Guaranty Insurance," 48 Cal. St. B.J. 683 (1973); see also, e.g., Kerrigon v. Unity Sav. Ass'n, 58 Ill. 2d 20, 317 NE2d 39 (1974). See generally 59 C.J.S. Mortgages § 178 (1949).

the most part, a consideration of these "mortgage substitutes" is beyond the scope of this book. Nevertheless, brief note should be made of the variety and nature of these security devices.

One of the most common mortgage substitutes is the deed of trust.[12] Three parties are initially party to the deed of trust. The debtor (grantor), who owns an interest in land, executes and delivers to a third party (trustee) a conveyance stating that the land interest created is to be held as security for payment of a debt by the debtor to the creditor (beneficiary). Although structured differently, the deed of trust is in the nature of a mortgage.[13] In some jurisdictions, however, there are some significant differences between the deed of trust and the mortgage. Enforcement of the real estate mortgage typically involves judicial foreclosure. In contrast, deeds of trust often include power-of-sale clauses; alternatively, the creditor may be provided with that means of enforcement by law. The creditor is thus freed from the requirement of a judicial foreclosure and possibly from the ordinary statutory right of redemption. Further, if a power of sale is exercised, the right to a deficiency judgment may be lost.[14] Throughout discussion of mortgage law in the remainder of this chapter, occasional references are made to deeds of trust, even though discussion usually is limited to real estate mortgages.

A second common mortgage substitute is the land sale contract. The land sale contract is similar in use to a purchase-money mortgage. With purchase-money mortgages, the mortgagor holds title to the real estate and the mortgagee signs a promissory note and the mortgage. In contrast, in the land sale contract the buyer is usually given possession of the property, but the seller retains title to the property. The buyer signs the land sale contract as evidence of the indebtedness for the purchase price of the real property. Consideration of land sale contracts is beyond the scope of this book.[15] Although there are some similarities between the law of mortgages and land sale contracts, enforcement of the latter is "embedded in the doctrines of equity applying to the subject of specific performance of contracts and strongly influenced by ideas of 'freedom of contract' and the inviolability of obligations based upon agreement."[16] Although both modern case law and statutory law may provide otherwise, the traditional chief difference between the land sale contract and the mortgage is that "the vendor in a land contract, on default by the vendee, by summary proceedings . . . may keep the land, all installments paid, and sue

---

[12] For discussion of deeds of trust, see Osborne, Mortgages 26 (West, 2d ed. 1970); Osborne, Nelson & Whitman, Real Estate Finance Law § 1.6 (West 1979); 7 Debtor-Creditor Law ¶ 31.02[A][3] (Matthew Bender 1982).

[13] See, e.g., Yasuna v. Miller, 399 A2d 68 (DC App. 1979).

[14] See infra ¶ 8.08 for an in-depth discussion of enforcement of real estate security interests.

[15] For discussion of law that pertains to land sale contracts, see the following: 3 Powell on Real Property ¶¶ 450–450.1 (Matthew Bender 1981); 8 Thompson on Real Property Ch. 57 (Bobbs-Merrill 1958); "Land Sale Contracts in California: Compared With Mortgages and Trust Deeds," 7 U.C.L.A. L. Rev. 83, 95 (1959).

[16] Osborne, Mortgages 29 (West, 2d ed. 1970); Osborne, Nelson & Whitman, Real Estate Finance Law §§ 3.25–3.32 (West 1979).

for installments due, if the contract so provides, with the vendee having no right of redemption. . . ."[17]

In addition to the trust deed and the land sale contract, other devices are used for real estate security purposes. One of those is the deed absolute, in which the creditor takes a deed from the debtor with the understanding that the realty will be reconveyed upon payment of the debt. If the debtor defaults, the creditor will retain the deed,[18] although some courts treat this arrangement as a mortgage requiring some form of foreclosure and redemption right for the debtor.[19]

Another mortgage substitute is the lease, which becomes a disguised land sale contract when the transaction involves a reservation of rent as installments on a purchase price, with title being retained by the supposed lessor. Title is thus retained for security purposes.[20] This lease arrangement particularly will be found in a sales contract in which the lessee will have the option to purchase the property for a nominal price at the expiration of the lease.

A final mortgage substitute worthy of brief note takes the form of a sale and conveyance with a contract to resell at a higher price. The stated purchase price is in reality a loan and the resale price includes interest charged.[21]

## [3] The Equitable Mortgage

The equitable mortgage is, in a sense, a separate category of real estate security devices.[22] "The term 'equitable mortgage' is used as a catchall term to denote all of the transactions which despite peculiarities of form or the appearance of a nonsecurity deal, are given the effect of a mortgage when examined by a court with equitable powers."[23] The equitable decree recognizing the equitable mortgage defines the true nature and extent of the security interest; thus, previous bona fide interests usually are unaffected by the equitable mortgage.[24]

It is important to understand the circumstances under which an equitable mortgage arises. Generally, a court of equity recognizes an equitable mortgage where it finds that the parties intended to create a mortgage but failed to do so in a commonly recognized form. Examples include outright conveyances by

---

[17] Osborne, Mortgages 29 (West 1970); Osborne, Nelson & Whitman, Real Estate Finance Law §§ 3.25–3.32 (West 1979).

[18] See Osborne, Nelson & Whitman, Real Estate Finance Law § 1.7 (West 1979).

[19] Id. at §§ 3.3–3.15.

[20] See Osborne, Mortgages 31 (West, 2d ed. 1970).

[21] Id.

[22] For discussions of equitable mortgages, see Osborne, Nelson & Whitman, Real Estate Finance Law § 12.6 (West 1979); Osborne, Mortgages Ch. 2 (West, 2d ed. 1970); 3 Powell on Real Property ¶¶ 446–450 (Matthew Bender 1981).

[23] 3 Powell on Real Property 623 (Matthew Bender 1981).

[24] See, e.g., Nissim Hadjes, Inc. v. DiCostanzo, 197 So. 2d 602 (Fla. Dist. Ct. App. 1967); Mooney v. Byrne, 163 NY 86, 57 NE 163 (1900); Segal v. Sounders, 200 SW2d 339 (Tex. Civ. App. 1949); Brinkman v. Jones, 144 Wis. 498 (1878); see also Osborne, Real Estate Finance Law § 12.6, at 755 (West 1979).

deed actually intended to create a security interest;[25] unperformed agreements to give a mortgage on identified land;[26] deposits of title deeds;[27] and contracts for the sale of land with reservation of title in the seller.[28] An equitable mortgage can be categorized as consensual or nonconsensual. One author indicates that

> there are three basic kinds of consensual equitable mortgages: (1) specifically enforceable promises to give a legal mortgage or hold certain property as security; (2) agreements intended to create a security interest but ineffective under conveyancing rules; (3) agreements, in the form of promises or executed transactons, in which the subject matter of the security itself is equitable.[29]

As to nonconsensual equitable mortgage theories, he indicates "[i]t has been asserted that the equitable mortgage . . . rests, not upon principles of specific performance of promises, but upon nonconsensual bases"; however, he notes that "[t]here are strong objections to this view and it is not supported by the authorities."[30]

## ¶ 8.04 CREATION AND FORM OF THE REAL ESTATE MORTGAGE

The creation of the "formal" mortgage, as distinguished from the "equitable" mortgage previously discussed,[1] makes the security interest effective between the mortgagor and the mortgagee. Insofar as most third-party priority disputes are concerned, the mortgage must be both created and recorded to obtain priority.[2] Thus, the creation of the mortgage is analogous to the attachment of the UCC Article 9 security interest,[3] while recordation of the mortgage

---

[25] See, e.g., WL Dev. Corp. v. Trifort Realty, Inc., 44 NY2d 489, 377 NE2d 969, 406 NYS2d 437 (1978); see Bermes v. Sylling, 179 Mont. 448, 587 P2d 377 (1978); 3 Powell on Real Property ¶ 447 (Matthew Bender 1981).

[26] See, e.g., Cauco v. Galante, 8 NJ 233, 84 A2d 712 (1951); 3 Powell on Real Property ¶ 448 (Matthew Bender 1981).

[27] See, e.g., Jennings v. Augir, 215 F. 658 (D. Wash. 1914); Dittman v. Miller, 330 Ill. App. 325, 71 NE2d 186 (1946); 3 Powell on Real Property ¶ 449 (Matthew Bender 1981).

[28] See, e.g., Gamble v. Bryant, 599 SW2d 472 (Ky. Ct. App. 1980); 3 Powell on Real Property ¶ 450 (Matthew Bender 1981).

[29] Osborne, Mortgages 35 (West, 2d ed. 1970).

[30] Id. at 39.

[1] See supra ¶ 8.03[3].

[2] See infra ¶ 8.09[1] for a discussion of recordation of mortgages, and ¶ 8.09[2] for a discussion of priority rules.

[3] See ¶ 7.04 for a discussion of attachment of UCC Article 9 security interests.

is analogous to the perfection of the UCC Article 9 security interest.[4] Once created, the mortgagee's interest may be treated as a lien or title interest, depending upon the position taken on the issue by the applicable jurisdiction.[5]

The creation of the mortgage resembles the creation of an enforceable contract with some additional formalities with which the parties must comply.[6] The law related to creation of the formal mortgage centers on: (1) issues pertaining to the capacity of the mortgagor and mortgagee to hold and to deal with interests in land; (2) the formalities required in executing the instrument; (3) the types of obligations that can be secured by a mortgage; (4) the types of land interests that can be used as security; and (5) the requirement of consideration.[7]

As far as the capacity of the parties to hold and deal with interests in land is concerned, for the most part, nothing unique to mortgages is involved. The same issues related to capacity to hold and transfer interests in land generally are applicable to the mortgage–issues related to aliens, nonresidents, Indians, married persons, infants, mental incompetents, felons, unincorporated groups, private corporations, fiduciaries, and governmental institutions.[8] However, the law will usually allow the mortgagee to enforce his mortgage against minors with interests in mortgaged property.[9]

Because a mortgage is a transfer of a land interest, formalities regarding the execution of real estate instruments generally must be complied with. These formalities vary depending upon the jurisdiction. They relate to signing, sealing, witnessing, and delivery. The mortgage may also encompass chattels located on the real estate, although separate recordings (filings) may be required depending upon the local law.[10] Recall that an error in complying

---

[4] See ¶ 7.06 for a discussion of perfection of UCC Article 9 security interests.

[5] See supra ¶ 8.02 for a discussion of the title and lien theory regarding mortgages, and ¶ 8.02 notes 6 and 7 for a list of the lien and title theory states.

[6] For a discussion of the creation of the real estate mortgage, see 7 Debtor-Creditor Law ¶ 31.02[C] (Matthew Bender 1982); 3 Powell on Real Property ¶¶ 441–445.1 (Matthew Bender 1981).

[7] 3 Powell on Real Property ¶ 441, at 560 (Matthew Bender 1981).

[8] See 1 Powell on Real Property ¶¶ 101–128, 130–168 (Matthew Bender 1981) for a discussion of these capacity issues.

[9] See, e.g., Glenn, Mortgages § 83.1 (Michie Co. 1943); Note, "Foreclosure Suits Against Infants," 28 Va. L. Rev. 1103 (1943); N.Y. Gen. Oblig. Law § 3-101; Kenwood Sav. & Loan Ass'n v. Williams, 220 NE2d 582 (Ohio C.P., Clermont Co. 1966); cf. Sisneros v. Garcia, 94 NM 552, 613 P2d 422 (1980) (minor's "conveyance" of land subject to disaffirmance).

[10] For example, compliance with UCC Article 9 may be necessitated regarding "perfection" of the security interest in the chattels. See ¶ 7.06[3][c][vii]. As to fixtures, consider UCC § 9-402(6), which was included in the 1972 redraft of UCC Article 9:

> "(6) A mortgage is effective as a financing statement filed as a fixture filing from the date of its recording if
>
> "(a) the goods are described in the mortgage by item or type; and

with formalities regarding the execution of the mortgage may not be crucial if the court is willing to find an "equitable mortgage."[11]

The types of obligations that can be secured by a mortgage are basically unlimited, although usually the mortgage is given to secure the mortgagee in his "expectation of being repaid a sum of money which is due to him from the mortgagor."[12] The amount secured may be open-ended; that is, the mortgage may secure future advances to be made by the mortgagee.[13] Indeed, many states have enacted statutes validating the use of the mortgage or trust deed to secure future advances.[14]

Similarly, the type of land interest that can be used as security is basically unlimited. Thus, "[a]ny permissible interest in land, which is transferable, can be used as the subject matter of a mortgage."[15] An interesting issue is whether a mortgage can encompass the mortgagor's after-acquired property interests by using an "after-acquired property clause." At common law, such clauses have been invalid, although between the mortgagor and mortgagee the clause is fully effective as long as the subsequently acquired property has some relation to the property that was originally mortgaged. Between the mortgagee and a creditor of the mortgagor there is a split of authority as to the effectiveness of the clause.[16]

To be enforceable, the mortgage must secure a valid obligation that serves as a consideration for the agreement; because the mortgage is a contract, the concept of contractual consideration is applicable.[17] However, a mortgage is

---

"(b) the goods are or are to become fixtures related to the real estate described in the mortgage; and

"(c) the mortgage complies with the requirements for a financing statement in this section other than a recital that it is to be filed in the real estate records; and

"(d) the mortgage is duly recorded.

"No fee with reference to the financing statement is required other than the regular recording and satisfaction fees with respect to the mortgage."

[11] See, e.g., Beck v. Brooks, 224 Kan. 300, 580 P2d 882 (1978); U.S. v. Canellis, 490 F. Supp. 1125 (D. Ill. 1980); see supra ¶ 8.03[3] for a discussion of equitable mortgages.

[12] 3 Powell on Real Property ¶ 442, at 570 (Matthew Bender 1981).

[13] See, e.g., Central Prod. Credit Ass'n v. Page, 268 SC 1, 231 SE2d 210 (1977); see also Glenn, Mortgages §§ 392–408 (Michie Co. 1943); Osborne, Mortgages 178 et seq. (West, 2d ed. 1970); Osborne, Real Estate Finance Law § 12.8, at 772–776 (West 1979).

[14] See, e.g., Fla. Stat. Ann. § 697.04(1); Ohio Rev. Code Ann. § 5301.232.

[15] 3 Powell on Real Property 577 (Matthew Bender 1981); see also, e.g., Idaho Code § 45-1001; Mont. Code Ann. § 71-1-201; Cal. Civ. Code § 2947.

[16] See 3 Powell on Real Property ¶ 483, at 582–583 (Matthew Bender 1981), and authority cited. As to the mortgagee-mortgagor, see Blair, "Allocation of After Acquired Property," 40 Harv. L. Rev. 222, 228 (1927); Chase Nat'l Bank v. Richmond Cedar Works, 93 F2d 695 (4th Cir. 1938). As to the mortgagee-creditor, see Alaska Rural Rehabilitation Corp. v. Ubert, 10 Alaska 508 (1945). But cf. Bancroft Steel Co. v. Kuniholn Mfg. Co., 301 Mass. 91, 16 NE2d 78 (1938).

[17] See, e.g., In re Ingersoll, 8 Bankr. 912 (Bankr. Wis. 1981); Codo v. Union Nat'l Bank & Trust Co. of Joliet, 54 Ill. App. 810, 370 NE2d 140 (1977); see also Osborne,

valid and enforceable if taken on account of an antecedent debt.[18] The inclusion of the antecedent debt as a validation of a mortgage's creation resembles the concept of "value" required in UCC Article 9 for the creation of an Article 9 security interest.[19] The obligation must be valid and, therefore, a usurious loan may negate the effectiveness of a mortgage in whole or in part.[20] Finally, some jurisdictions do uphold a mortgage given as a gift.[21]

As to the form of the mortgage, the requirements are the subject of statutory regulation and vary materially from state to state. Because consideration of the specific form of each state is beyond the scope of this book, the practitioner should research applicable law carefully.[22] At a minimum the mortgage should "name the parties, manifest the security nature of the instrument, describe with certainty the real property to be subjected to the lien of the mortgage, and set out the obligation to be secured."[23] Other matters that might be included within the mortgage form include: (1) the dates of execution; (2) the effect of the mortgage; (3) the maturity date; (4) clauses that define the termination, extinguishment, release, discharge, or transfer of the parties' interests; (5) the mortgagor's covenants regarding payments, title, and protection of the property; and (6) the mortgagee's right regarding payments, acceleration of the debt, and enforcement of the mortgagee's security interest.[24]

## ¶ 8.05 THE PREFORECLOSURE MORTGAGOR-MORTGAGEE RELATIONSHIP

Before the foreclosure of a mortgage, numerous legal issues may arise that relate to the relationship of the mortgagee and mortgagor,[1] including the following: (1) the parties' rights to possession; (2) matters pertaining to tortious

---

Mortgages §§ 102–108 (West, 2d ed. 1970); Osborne, Nelson & Whitman, Real Estate Finance Law § 2.3, at 21–26 (West 1979).

[18] See, e.g., In re Ingersoll, 8 Bankr. 912, 919 (Bankr. Wis. 1981); O'Neill Prod. Credit Ass'n v. Mitchell, 209 Neb. 206, 307 NW2d 115 (1981).

[19] See UCC §§ 1-204(44), 9-203(1)(b); ¶ 7.04[3].

[20] See, e.g., National Sur. Corp. v. Inland Properties, Inc., 286 F. Supp. 173 (D. Ark. 1968), aff'd, 416 F2d 457 (8th Cir. 1969); Prather, "Mortgage Loans and the Usury Laws," 16 Bus. Law. 181 (1960); Note, "Mortgage Investments and the Usury Problem," 10 Clev.-Mar. L. Rev. 343 (1961).

[21] See 3 Powell on Real Property ¶ 444 n.1 (Matthew Bender 1980). See generally 59 C.J.S. Mortgages § 87 (1949).

[22] See 13 Am. Jur. 2d Legal Forms § 179 (1973) for consideration of the required mortgage and trust deed forms of every state.

[23] Id. at § 179.41.

[24] See id. at § 179.42 for an excellent checklist of matters to be considered when drafting a mortgage. Similarly, as to trust deeds, see id. at § 179.52. The practitioner should develop his own checklist by including matters peculiar to local law.

[1] See Osborne, Mortgages Ch. 6 (West, 2d ed. 1970); Osborne, Nelson & Whitman, Real Estate Finance Law Ch. 4 (West 1979).

injury to the land by the mortgagor or third persons; (3) rights in any "product" of the land; (4) rights to rents from the land; (5) matters pertaining to the mortgagee obtaining possession of the property, including accounting requirements; and (6) acquisition of title upon breach of some duty.

The relationship of the parties before foreclosure can be affected by the status of the relevant jurisdiction as either a title or lien theory state.[2] Recall that some states view the mortgagee as a title holder of the real estate, while other states characterize the mortgagee's interest as a lien.[3] No issue better illustrates the distinction between title and lien theory states than that relating to the right to possess the mortgaged land. In title states the mortgagee technically has the right to possession because the mortgagee is seen as holding title to the land; however, express or implied agreements usually permit the mortgagor to remain in possession. In lien theory states, the mortgagee has only a security interest and the mortgagor holds title with the right to possession, although some states provide the mortgagee the right to possession upon default or broken condition of the mortgage.[4]

Another issue that commonly arises before foreclosure of the mortgage involves injury to the mortgaged land by the mortgagor or some third person. In general, the mortgagor in possession may do with the land that which is reasonable.[5] Damage to the land resulting from improper conduct creates a cause of action in the mortgagee for damages.[6] Recovery is limited to the amount of the mortgaged debt and is applied to it.[7] The same cause of action for damages is available to the mortgagee against a third person who tortiously injures the land.[8] The mortgagor also is given a cause of action to recover for injury tortiously caused by third persons.[9] The mortgagee may also enjoin threatened material waste, and a receiver may even be appointed.[10]

---

[2] See supra ¶ 8.02 for a discussion of the historical development of title and lien theory states.

[3] See supra ¶ 8.02 notes 6 and 7.

[4] See, e.g., Araserv, Inc. v. Bay State Harness Horse Racing & Breeding Ass'n, Inc., 437 F. Supp. 1083 (D. Mass. 1977); cf. Marcon v. First Fed. Sav. & Loan Ass'n, 58 Ill. App. 3d 811, 374 NE2d 1028 (1978). But see Roosevelt Sav. Bank of City of N.Y. v. State Farm Fire & Casualty Co., 27 Ariz. App. 522, 556 P2d 823 (1976); see also Osborne, Mortgages §§ 125–127 (West, 2d ed. 1970); Osborne, Nelson & Whitman, Real Estate Finance Law §§ 4.1–4.3 (West 1979), for a detailed discussion of right to possession in title and lien theory states.

[5] See Florida Bahamas Lines, Ltd. v. Steel Barge Star 800 of Nassau, 433 F2d 1243 (11th Cir. 1970).

[6] See, e.g., Wheeler v. Peterson, 331 SW2d 81 (Tex. Civ. App. 1960).

[7] Kulp v. Trustees of Iowa College, 217 Iowa 310, 251 NW 703 (1933); see Douglas v. Lowery, 130 Ill. App. 2d 910, 266 NE2d 107 (1971).

[8] Cornelison v. Kornbluth, 15 Cal. 3d 590, 124 Cal. Rptr. 557, 542 P2d 981 (1975); Bank of Cal. Nat'l Ass'n v. Twin Harbors Lumber Co., 465 F2d 489 (9th Cir. 1972).

[9] See, e.g., American Sav. & Loan Ass'n v. Leeds, 68 Cal. 2d 611, 440 P2d 933, 68 Cal. Rptr. 453 (1968).

[10] See Osborne, Mortgages 210–222 (West, 2d ed. 1970), particularly note 55 at page 210, which lists the following additional sources for discussion of issues arising in

The mortgaged land may be taken by eminent domain or may be damaged and covered by insurance. Who has the right to the condemnation award or insurance proceeds? Both may be characterized as "product" of the mortgaged land. As to rights in a condemnation award, generally the mortgagee is entitled to the award up to the amount of the debt, with the remainder payable to the mortgagor.[11] As to insurance proceeds, one must first examine whether the typical mortgage clause, which provides that the mortgagor must obtain insurance of both his and the mortgagee's interest, is in effect. If this clause is used and the mortgagor fails to procure such insurance for the mortgagee but does insure his own interest, the mortgagee is given a lien on the amount due the mortgagor under the policy.[12] Assuming the mortgagor has complied with the usual insurance clause of the mortgage, the mortgagee's and the mortgagor's respective interests will be protected pursuant to the single policy's provisions.[13] In the rare event that separate policies are obtained–one for the mortgagee's interest and one for the mortgagor's interest–neither party has an interest in the other's policy.[14] Finally, as to insurance, proceeds reachable by the mortgagee will be applied to the debt; the mortgagee cannot recover on both the debt and the policy.[15] In the United States the typical insurance policy gives the insurer the option of repairing the damaged premises rather than paying the loss in money to the insured.[16]

Rents often will accrue on the mortgaged property, raising the question of whether the mortgagor or mortgagee has the first right to the rents. The rights of the parties may be affected by the status of the jurisdiction as either a lien or

---

connection with tortious injury to the mortgaged land by the mortgagor or third persons: Note, "Mortgagee's Remedy for Damage to or Injury of the Residence," 10 Tex. L. Rev. 475 (1931); Note, "Creditor's Action for Damages to the Security," 17 N.C.L. Rev. 291 (1939); Stocke, "Rights of a Mortgagee and Creditor under Missouri Law When Mortgagor Retains Possession," 11 St. Louis U.L.J. 42 (1925); Denton, "Right of a Mortgagee to Recover Damages From a Third Party for Injury to Mortgaged Property in Ohio," 3 Ohio St. L.J. 161 (1939). See also Osborne, Nelson & Whitman, Real Estate Finance Law § 4.7 (West 1979); Federal Land Bank of New Orleans v. Southmont Mfg. Co., 219 Fla. 447, 122 So. 426 (1929); Fourth Ave. Amusement Co. v. Glenn, 201 F2d 600 (6th Cir. 1953); American Medical Servs., Inc. v. Mutual Fed. Sav. & Loan Ass'n, 52 Wis. 2d 198, 188 NW2d 529 (Wis. 1971); cf. Mutual Benefit Life Ins. Co. v. Frantz Klodt & Son, Inc., 306 Minn. 244, 237 NW2d 350 (1976).

[11] See, e.g., Maxey v. Redevelopment Auth. of Racine, 94 Wis. 2d 575, 288 NW2d 794 (1980); see also Osborne, Mortgages 222–224 (West, 2d ed. 1970); Osborne, Nelson & Whitman, Real Estate Finance Law § 4.12 (West 1979).

[12] See Osborne, Mortgages § 138, at 226 (West, 2d ed. 1970); Osborne, Nelson & Whitman, Real Estate Finance Law 144 (West 1979).

[13] Cf. Farm Bureau Mut. Ins. Co. of Ark. v. Shaw, 269 Ark. 757, 600 SW2d 432 (1980).

[14] See generally 59 C.J.S. Mortgages § 328 (1949).

[15] See, e.g., First Nat'l Bank of Scotia v. Sterling, 71 AD2d 723, 419 NYS2d 220 (1976).

[16] See Osborne, Mortgages 224–231 (West, 2d ed. 1970); Osborne, Nelson & Whitman, Real Estate Finance Law § 4.15 (West 1979).

title theory state. In a lien theory state the mortgagee has no right to rents, although the commencement of foreclosure may result in giving the mortgagee a right to rents.[17] In title theory states, the determination rests largely upon whether the lease precedes or follows the granting of the mortgage. If the lease precedes the mortgage, the mortgagee is said to have the technical right to rents, although this right is rarely exercised before default.[18] If the mortgage precedes the lease, the mortgagee is not in privity with the lessee and may not compel payment of rent to him; instead, the mortgagee must enter into an agreement with the lessee to acquire rights in any rents.[19]

A mortgagee on occasion may obtain possession of the mortgaged property. To obtain possession lawfully, the mortgagee must do so in compliance with the terms of the mortgage and must exercise dominion and control over the property.[20] If he does take possession lawfully, the mortgagee may retain possession until redemption. The mortgagee in possession is, however, liable to third persons if the mortgagee fails to perform any legal duties chargeable to a land owner.[21]

Perhaps the most important issues that arise with regard to a mortgagee in possession pertain to accounting. As a matter of policy, the rules relating to accounting are designed to discourage the mortgagee from taking possession. An "accounting" refers to a "determination on equitable principles of how much of the income received by a mortgagee in possession is to be applied to the debt. It can only be demanded in a foreclosure action or when the mortgagor seeks to pay the debt."[22] The accounting is due the mortgagor, junior mortgagees, and assignees of the redemption interest. The mortgagor's duty to account relates to rents received, with credit for maintenance expenditures (but without credit for some improvements), with credit for expenses related to services he procures that are reasonably necessary for the maintenance of the property (possibly including a commission for himself), and with credit for taxes paid. The excess of rents over the offset of allowable expenses and charges is then applied to the mortgaged debt or interest on the debt with annual "rests"

---

[17] See, e.g., Prudential Ins. Co. of Am. v. Fifty Assocs., 503 F2d 925 (9th Cir. 1974); In re Ventura-Louise Properties, 490 F2d 1141 (9th Cir. 1974).

[18] See In re Perimeter Park Inv. Assoc. Ltd., 1 Bankr. 473 (Bankr. Ga. 1979).

[19] See, e.g., Peoples-Pittsburgh Trust Co. v. Henshaw, 141 Pa. Super. 585, 15 A2d 711 (1940); see also Osborne, Mortgages 231–239 (West, 2d ed. 1970); Osborne, Nelson & Whitman, Real Estate Finance Law §§ 4.23–4.26 (West 1979).

[20] See Aguilar v. Bocci, 35 Cal. App. 3d 475, 114 Cal. Rptr. 91 (1974); Zapata v. Torres, 464 SW2d 926 (Tex. Civ. App. 1971).

[21] See, e.g., Essex Cleaning Contractors, Inc. v. Amato, 127 NJ Super. 364, 317 A2d 411 (1974). But see New York Life Ins. Co. v. Gulf States Utils. Co., 336 So. 2d 320 (La. Ct. App. 1976); see also Osborne, Mortgages 277–285 (West, 2d ed. 1970); Osborne, Nelson & Whitman, Real Estate Finance Law §§ 4.27–4.29 (West 1979).

[22] Osborne, Mortgages 286 (West, 2d ed. 1970); see Nettles v. First Nat'l Bank of Birmingham, 388 So. 2d 916 (Ala. 1980); Landau v. Western Pa. Nat'l Bank, 445 Pa. 217, 282 A2d 335 (1971); see also Osborne, Nelson & Whitman, Real Estate Finance Law § 4.30 (West 1979).

ordered under some circumstances, such as when the net income from the property to the mortgagee exceeds the annual interest.[23]

Two final issues concerning the relationship of the parties to a mortgage pertain to acquisition of title by the mortgagor or mortgagee free of the other's interest. First, a mortgagor or his appointee cannot acquire title free of the mortgagee at either a foreclosure or tax sale occasioned by his breach of duty.[24] Second, a mortgagee cannot cut off the mortgagor's right of redemption by purchase at a tax sale. Similarly, such a purchase would not serve to cut off the interest of prior mortgagees.[25]

## ¶ 8.06 TRANSFER OF THE MORTGAGEE'S OR MORTGAGOR'S INTEREST

The mortgagee or mortgagor may transfer his respective interest. For example, the original mortgagee may wish to discount the mortgaged debt and assign the debt to a third party. Along with the assignment of the debt, the mortgage will also be assigned. On the other hand, the mortgagor may wish to sell any interest the mortgagor has in the mortgaged property to a third-party buyer. Substantial issues often are raised regarding the effect of these transfers on all concerned parties. These issues are examined in the following sections.[1]

### [1] Transfer of the Mortgagee's Interest

The mortgagee may lawfully transfer the mortgagee's interest, although the transfer must satisfy the usual requirements of the applicable jurisdiction

---

[23] See Joliet Fed. Sav. & Loan Ass'n v. Bloomington Loan Co., 131 Ill. App. 2d 619, 265 NE2d 400 (1970); Myers-Macomber Eng'rs v. M.I.W. Constr. Corp., 271 Pa. Super. 484, 414 A2d 357 (1979); see also Osborne, Mortgages 285–304 (West, 2d ed. 1970); Osborne, Nelson & Whitman, Real Estate Finance Law § 4.35 (West 1979).

[24] See generally 59 C.J.S. Mortgages § 577, at 973, n.49, and 1983 Supplement, wherein Home Owners' Loan Corp. v. Guaranty Title Trust Co., 168 Tenn. 118, 76 SW2d 109 (1934) and Dixieland Realty Co. v. Wysor, 272 NC 172, 158 SE2d 7, 10 (1967) are cited.

[25] See Osborne, Mortgages 304–308 (West, 2d ed. 1970); Osborne, Nelson & Whitman, Real Estate Finance Law §§ 4.47–4.49 (West 1979).

[1] Many other sources discuss these issues in some detail. As to transfer of the mortgagee's interest, see, e.g., 3 Powell on Real Property ¶ 455, at 693 (Matthew Bender 1980); Nelson & Whitman, Real Estate Finance and Development 158–189 (West 1976); Osborne, Mortgages Ch. 8, at 440–501 (West, 2d ed. 1970); Osborne, Nelson & Whitman, Real Estate Finance Law §§ 5.27–5.35 (West 1979). As to transfer of the mortgagor's interest, see, e.g., 9 Thompson on Real Property § 477, p. 490 (Bobbs-Merrill 1958); Osborne, Mortgages Ch. 9, at 502–560 (West, 2d ed. 1970); Osborne, Nelson & Whitman, Real Estate Finance Law §§ 5.1–5.26 (West 1979); Cunningham & Tischler, "Transfer of the Real Estate Mortgagor's Interest," 27 Rutgers L. Rev. 24 (1973); Volkmer, "The Application of the Restraints on Alienation Doctrine to Real Property Security Interests," 58 Iowa L. Rev. 747 (1973); Nelson & Whitman, Real Estate Finance and Development 122–158 (West 1976).

regarding conveyances in real property.[2] The mortgagee possesses the right to transfer the complete interest[3] or the partial interest[4] of the mortgagee or may grant a security interest in the mortgagee's interest.[5] If the mortgagee transfers the mortgage without an assignment of the debt, the transaction will be treated as a nullity, as the transferee must receive an interest in the mortgaged debt.[6] In contrast, if the mortgagee transfers only the underlying debt, the mortgage is impliedly assigned, resulting in an effective transfer of the mortgagee's interest.[7]

Even when both the debt and mortgage are transferred, problems can arise. For example,

> When a formal written assignment of a mortgage has been executed and delivered by the mortgagee to his transferee, the transfer may still fail of complete efficacy for any one or more of three reasons; namely, (1) failure to record, (2) failure to notify the mortgagor or his successor in interest of the fact of assignment, or (3) failure of the transferee to take physical possession of the original instrument to secure that which the mortgage was given.[8]

Once an effective transfer of the mortgagee's interest has occurred, the assignee acquires any rights and liabilities that the mortgagee possessed.[9] As a general rule, the assignee remains subject to all defenses of the mortgagor to which the mortgagee was subject.[10] The major exception to this rule arises if the debt is in the form of a negotiable instrument; as a holder in due course, the assignee then would take free of most defenses of the mortgagor.[11] A second

---

[2] See, e.g., Bryan v. Easton Tire Co., 262 Ark. 731, 561 SW2d 79 (1978).

[3] See, e.g., Wipfli v. Bever, 37 Wis. 2d 324, 155 NW2d 71 (1967).

[4] See, e.g., Marine Midland Nat'l Bank v. Roosa Constr. Ass'n, Inc., 28 AD2d 1189, 284 NYS2d 649 (1967); Johnson v. Sowell, 80 NM 677, 459 P2d 839 (1969).

[5] See, e.g., Black v. Sullivan, 48 Cal. App. 3d 557, 122 Cal. Rptr. 119 (1975).

[6] See, e.g., Commercial Prods. Corp. v. Briegel, 101 Ill. App. 2d 156, 242 NE2d 317 (1968); see Osborne, Nelson & Whitman, Real Estate Finance Law § 5.27, at 315 (West 1979).

[7] See, e.g., Barton v. Perryman, 265 Ark. 228, 577 SW2d 596 (1979); Purcel v. Vincent, 211 Ark. 486, 200 SW2d 970 (1947); Miller v. Frederick's Brewing Co., 405 Ill. 591, 92 NE2d 108 (1950); Robertson v. Brown, 75 ND 109, 25 NW2d 781 (1947); see Cal. Civ. Code § 2936: "The assignment of a debt secured by a mortgage carries with it the security."

[8] 3 Powell on Real Property 696.1 (Matthew Bender 1981).

[9] See, e.g., United of Fla., Inc. v. Illini Fed. Sav. & Loan Ass'n, 341 So. 2d 793 (Fla. 1977); Allen v. Wade, 203 Ga. 753, 48 SE2d 538 (1948).

[10] See, e.g., Financial Credit Corp. v. Williams, 246 Md. 575, 229 A2d 712 (1967); FST Corp. v. Onorato, 139 NJ Eq. 195, 50 A2d 467 (1947).

[11] See, e.g., Western Sav. & Loan Ass'n v. Diamond Lazy K Guest Ranch, Inc., 18 Ariz. App. 256, 501 P2d 432 (1972); see also Osborne, Nelson & Whitman, Real Estate Finance Law §§ 5.30, 5.31, 5.32 (West 1979); 3 Powell on Real Property 696.6 (Matthew Bender 1981); UCC § 3-305.

limitation on the general rule is that the assignee may notify the mortgagor of the assignment and thereby prevent subsequent accrual of new defenses.[12] Often as a part of the instrument of assignment, the mortgagee will be required to state the unpaid balance on the mortgaged debt and aver that there are no defenses validly assertable against the mortgagee. In that vein, the mortgagee is often required to provide an estoppel certificate: a statement by the mortgagor of the amount due and the absence of valid defenses.[13] Beyond the assignee's relationship with the mortgagor, the assignment places the assignee in the same position the mortgagee held to third parties with regard to the real property.[14]

Problems develop when a dishonest mortgagee assigns the mortgagee's interest more than once. Which assignee will prevail? As a basic rule, the first assignee prevails, subject to some exceptions. For example, recordation of the first assignment will protect it from subsequent assignees. But failure to record the first assignment may make it subordinate to a subsequent assignee without notice, at least where recordation is mandatory under local law. On the other hand, recordation of a prior assignment has no effect on a subsequent assignee if the latter acquired a negotiable instrument as part of the assignment.[15]

### [2] Transfer of the Mortgagor's Interest

Although at common law the mortgagor had no legal interest to transfer,[16] today the mortgagor has an alienable interest in the mortgaged property.[17] This alienable interest, like any other fee simple interest in real estate, cannot be subjected to direct restraints against alienation. However, two types of restraints have surfaced that have generated much interest. One restraint is the "due-on-sale" clause, which requires satisfaction of the mortgaged debt upon sale of the mortgagor's interest. The second restraint involves the "due-on-encumbrance" clause, which similarly requires full satisfaction of the mortgaged debt if the mortgagor further encumbers the

---

[12] See, e.g., Wood v. Gulf States Capital Corp., 217 So. 2d 257 (Miss. 1968); see Osborne, Nelson & Whitman, Real Estate Finance Law § 5.33 (West 1979).

[13] See, e.g., Harrison v. Gaililee Baptist Church, 427 Pa. 247, 234 A2d 314 (1967). For a discussion of estoppel certificates, see Osborne, Mortgages § 228, at 450 (West, 2d ed. 1970); 3 Powell on Real Property 696.9 (Matthew Bender 1981).

[14] See 3 Powell on Real Property 696.7–696.8 (Matthew Bender 1981). But bona fide purchasers without notice of a third-party right or purchasers of negotiable instruments may take free of latent third-party claims; see, e.g., Perry v. Manal, 110 NJ Eq. 111, 158 A 379 (1932).

[15] For a discussion of successive assignments, see Osborne, Mortgages 483–488 (West, 2d ed. 1970); Osborne, Nelson & Whitman, Real Estate Finance Law § 5.29 (West 1979); cf. Republic Nat'l Life Ins. Co. v. Marquette Bank & Trust Co. of Rochester, 312 Minn. 162, 251 NW2d 120 (Minn. 1977).

[16] See generally 9 Thompson on Real Property § 4777 (Bobbs-Merrill 1958).

[17] See Robar v. Ellingson, 301 NW2d 653 (ND 1981). See generally Osborne, Mortgages § 247 (West, 2d ed. 1970); Osborne, Nelson & Whitman, Real Estate Finance Law § 5.1 (West 1979).

mortgaged property without the consent of the mortgagee. The acceleration of the debt under both clauses is arguably a restraint upon alienation. The enforceability of these clauses under case law has been questionable unless there has been some reasonable basis for exercising the acceleration; in addition, some statutory law has resulted in negating the literal enforcement of these clauses. A recent Supreme Court case and recent federal legislation have had the effect of making due-on-sale clauses, but not due-on-encumbrance clauses, enforceable as a matter of federal law.[18]

The transfer of the mortgagor's interest in the property does not free the mortgagor from performance of the obligation secured by the mortgage.[19] Nor does the transfer terminate the mortgage[20] unless the mortgage is equitable and is cut off by a bona fide purchaser, or unless the mortgage is cut off by an applicable recording statute due to lack of recordation.[21] Thus, the legal relationship of the mortgagee to the mortgagor in regard to the mortgaged property generally remains unaltered by a transfer of the mortgagor's interest without a contrary agreement between the parties.

There are basically three methods by which the mortgagor may sell his interest.[22] First, the purchaser may take the interest in the property subject to the mortgaged debt, but assume no personal obligation to pay it.[23] The mortgagee retains his own interest and still may foreclose on the property, but only has recourse against the mortgagor insofar as personal liability on the debt is concerned. In essence, the mortgagor becomes a surety, necessitating his payment of the obligation to preclude foreclosure on the land. Second, the purchaser may take the mortgagor's interest and assume payment of the obligation. Without a contrary agreement, such assumptions do not

---

[18] See Fidelity Fed. Sav. & Loan Ass'n v. de la Questa, 458 US 141 (1982); Garn-St Germain Depository Institutions Act of 1982, 12 USC § 1701(j-3). For an excellent summary of the law pertaining to due-on-sale and due-on-encumbrance clauses, see also 7 Debtor-Creditor Law ¶ 31.06 (Matthew Bender 1982). See also Volkmer, "The Application of the Restraints on Alienation Doctrine to Real Property Security Interests," 58 Iowa L. Rev. 747 (1973); Tucker v. Lassen Sav. & Loan Ass'n, 12 Cal. 3d 629, 116 Cal. Rptr. 633, 526 P2d 1169 (1974); Cal. Civ. Code § 2949; Comment, "Due on Sale and Due on Encumbrance Clauses in California," 7 Loy. L.A. L. Rev. 306 (1974); Tucker v. Pulaski Fed. Sav. & Loan Ass'n, 252 Ark. 849, 481 SW2d 725 (1972); Connolley v. Harrison, 23 Md. App. 485, 327 A2d 787 (1974); Baker v. Loves Park Sav. & Loan Ass'n, 21 Ill. App. 3d 42, 314 NE2d 306 (1974). See also infra ¶ 8.08[1] for a discussion and cited authority regarding due-on-sale and due-on-encumbrance clauses.

[19] See, e.g., Berg v. Liberty Fed. Sav. & Loan Ass'n, 428 A2d 347 (Del. 1981); see also Osborne, Nelson & Whitman, Real Estate Finance Law § 5.1 (West 1979).

[20] See Osborne, Mortgages § 247 (West, 2d ed. 1970); Malone v. U.S., 326 F. Supp. 106 (D. Miss.), aff'd, 455 F2d 502 (5th Cir. 1971).

[21] See Osborne, Mortgages § 247 (West, 2d ed. 1970); W.W. Planning, Inc. v. Clark, 10 Ariz. App. 86, 456 P2d 406 (1969); Mobley v. Brundidge Banking Co., Inc., 347 So. 2d 1347 (Ala. 1977).

[22] See Osborne, Nelson & Whitman, Real Estate Finance Law § 5.2 at 250 (West 1979).

[23] See, e.g., Fye v. Cox, 263 NW2d 725 (Iowa 1978).

relieve the mortgagor of personal liability to the mortgagee.[24] The mortgagee may either directly or derivatively enforce the assumption promise against the purchaser.[25] If there are successive purchasers of the property, the mortgagee may enforce each purchaser's promise of assumption.[26] Third, the mortgagor may sell the mortgaged property for the property's full value and agree to pay off the mortgage. (Under the first two options, the purchase price would be only equal to the mortgagor's equity in the property.) If this occurs, the mortgagee will lose his own interest in the property once full payment is received. If the mortgagor fails to satisfy the mortgage, the mortgagee retains his own interest and the purchaser has a cause of action against the mortgagor.[27]

## ¶ 8.07 DISCHARGE AND RELEASE OF THE MORTGAGE

Various events may result in discharge or termination of the mortgage thereby freeing the property of the interest of the mortgagee.[1] For example, a merger of the mortgagor's interest with the mortgagee's interest results in termination of the mortgage. The mortgagor may convey his equity of redemption to the mortgagee, resulting in a merger of the two interests in the mortgagee,[2] provided that the entire interest of the mortgagor was conveyed,[3] and that there were no junior interests in the property.[4] Similarly, an assignment by the mortgagee of the mortgagee's interest to the mortgagor effects a merger.[5]

---

[24] See supra ¶ 8.06[2] note 20; Yasuna v. Miller, 399 A2d 68 (DC App. 1979).

[25] See Osborne, Nelson & Whitman, Real Estate Finance Law § 5.9 (West 1979); Ruther v. Thomas, 43 Colo. App. 435, 604 P2d 703 (1979).

[26] See, e.g., Somers v. Avant, 224 Ga. 469, 261 SE2d 334 (1979); Osborne, Nelson & Whitman, Real Estate Finance Law § 5.15 (West 1979).

[27] See Osborne, Nelson & Whitman, Real Estate Finance Law § 5.2 (West 1979); Hernandez v. Leiva, 391 So. 2d 292 (Fla. Dist. Ct. App. 1980).

[1] For discussion of discharge of mortgages, see Osborne, Mortgages Ch. 11, at 598–633 (West, 2d ed. 1970); Osborne, Nelson & Whitman, Real Estate Finance Law Ch. 6 (West 1979); 3 Powell on Real Property ¶¶ 459–461 (Matthew Bender 1981); 9 Thompson on Real Property Ch. 71, at 627–692 (Bobbs-Merrill 1958).

[2] See, e.g., Friedman v. Pohnl, 143 So. 2d 690 (Fla. Dist. Ct. App. 1962); Davis v. Stone, 236 F. Supp. 553 (DDC 1964); Hurlbutt v. Hurlbutt, 6 Conn. Cir. Ct. 314, 272 A2d 146 (1970).

[3] See, e.g., Small v. Cunningham, 120 NW2d 13 (ND 1963); Department of Culture, Recreation & Tourism v. Fort Macons Dev. Corp., 385 So. 2d 1233 (La. Ct. App. 1980).

[4] See, e.g., Barton v. Cannon, 94 Idaho 422, 489 P2d 1021 (1971); Ingraham v. Williams, 173 F. Supp. 1 (ND Cal. 1959).

[5] See, e.g., Hybertsen v. Reimann, 262 Ore. 116, 496 P2d 917 (1972); Harris v. Alaska Title Guar. Co., 510 P2d 501 (Alaska 1973).

The most common occurrence leading to discharge of a mortgage is payment of the entire mortgaged debt.[6] When such a discharge takes place a formal instrument evidencing the discharge will normally be recorded in the real estate records. The instrument may be a deed of release or some form of written acknowledgment of satisfaction of the debt. Equitable relief will be available to the mortgagor to require the mortgagee to provide such an instrument or to simply free the property of the mortgage in an in rem proceeding.[7] Usually the mortgagee's refusal to provide the discharging instrument stems from a controversy concerning whether the mortgaged debt has been paid.[8]

There are other possible means by which a mortgage may be discharged through payment. If the mortgagor tenders payment in full to the mortgagee, it may result in release of the mortgage even though the debt is not actually satisfied.[9] Further, discharge may result by a presumption of payment. In many states it is presumed that the mortgaged debt is paid after twenty years have passed without the mortgagor's recognition of his obligation,[10] although the presumption may be rebuttable.[11] Finally, release of the mortgage or the mortgaged debt by the mortgagee has the same discharging effect as payment.[12]

Statutes of limitation may also result in discharge of the mortgage. These statutes may run on the mortgaged debt itself. Other statutes may run on the enforcement of the mortgage lien. Additionally, as mentioned above, discharge may result from a statute relating to presumption of payment after passage of time without recognition of the mortgaged debt by the mortgagor.[13]

---

[6] See, e.g., 3 Powell on Real Property ¶ 460 (Matthew Bender 1981); Osborne, Mortgages § 293, at 598 (West, 2d ed. 1970); Osborne, Nelson & Whitman, Real Estate Finance Law § 6.4 (West 1979).

[7] See, e.g., MacNeil Bros. Co. v. Cohen, 163 F. Supp. 106 (D. Mass. 1958); Beaton v. Land Court, 267 Mass. 385, 326 NE2d 302 (1975). There may even be statutory penalties assessable against the mortgagee for failure to provide the essential instrument of discharge. See, e.g., Ind. Code Ann. § 32-8-1-2; Mass. Gen. Laws Ann. ch. 183, § 55; Pa. Stat. Ann. tit. 21, § 682; see also Annot., 8 A.L.R.4th 853.

[8] For elaboration of this point, see 3 Powell on Real Property 696.32 (Matthew Bender 1981).

[9] See, e.g., State v. Mobley, 208 Okla. 342, 255 P2d 945 (1949); Mr. U. Inc. v. Mobil Oil Corp., 197 Neb. 612, 249 NW2d 909 (1977).

[10] See, e.g., Northeast Alumni Bldg. & Loan Ass'n v. Schrieber, 398 Pa. 425, 158 A2d 773 (1963); Corn v. Wilson, 365 Pa. 355, 75 A2d 530 (1950); McCrary v. Crumpton, 267 Ala. 484, 103 So. 2d 714 (1958).

[11] See discussion at 3 Powell on Real Property ¶ 460, at 696.36, n.17 (Matthew Bender 1981); Bonner v. Pugh, 376 So. 2d 1354 (Ala. 1979); Kirsner v. Hammond, 256 Md. 570, 261 A2d 159 (1970).

[12] See, e.g., Krukow v. Silvius, 105 Cal. App. 724, 288 P. 684 (1930); Coen v. Gobert, 154 So. 2d 443 (La. Ct. App. 1983); Ott v. Edwards, 161 Colo. 187, 420 P2d 837 (1968).

[13] See 3 Powell on Real Property ¶ 461 (Matthew Bender 1981); see also Osborne, Mortgages §§ 296–299 (West, 2d ed. 1970); Osborne, Nelson & Whitman, Real Estate Finance Law §§ 6.9–6.12 (West 1979).

If the underlying obligation is evidenced by a renewed promissory note, the renewal should not discharge the mortgage.[14] Typically, the mortgagee uses the original note and makes and records it as a renewal, or the mortgagor executes and records a new note, marking the former "paid."[15]

## ¶ 8.08 ENFORCEMENT OF THE MORTGAGE: DEFAULT, RECEIVERSHIP, AND FORECLOSURE

### [1] Default

For the mortgagee to be able to foreclose, the mortgagor must be in default.[1] Additionally, the mortgage must provide for acceleration of the entire debt, enabling the mortgagee to call the entire debt due upon a default. There are many grounds for default. Some of the more common are discussed in this section, with special emphasis placed on the importance of the acceleration clause.

Generally, the mortgagee may foreclose if the mortgagor has failed to comply with the terms of the mortgage. The most common form of default is failure to make payment on the underlying debt or any installment of the debt.[2] However, default can occur by violation of other terms of the mortgage, including the failure to pay taxes and assessments or the failure to maintain insurance protecting the mortgagee's interest.[3]

The acceleration clause contained in most mortgages enables the mortgagee to foreclose upon the mortgagor's default. This clause enables the creditor to foreclose on the mortgage by calling the whole debt due upon a default; acceleration usually is at the mortgagee's option and does not occur automatically.[4] Acceleration may be harsh. There are some limitations, however, upon

---

[14] See Farmers Bank of Clinton, Mo. v. Julian, 383 F2d 314 (8th Cir.), cert. denied, 389 US 1021 (1967); Financial Acceptance Corp. v. Garvey, 6 Mass. App. 610, 380 NE2d 1332 (1978); McGeorge v. Van Meter, 351 SW2d 623 (Tex. Civ. App. 1961), rev'd on other grounds, 358 SW2d 580 (Tex. 1962).

[15] See, e.g., Central Prod. Credit Ass'n v. Page, 268 SC 1, 231 SE2d 210 (1977); McGeorge v. Van Meter, 351 SW2d 623 (Tex. Civ. App. 1961), rev'd on other grounds, 358 SW2d 580 (Tex. 1962); Jackson & Scherer, Inc. v. Washburn, 209 Kan. 321, 496 P2d 1358 (1972).

[1] See 7 Debtor-Creditor Law ¶¶ 31.04–31.06 (Matthew Bender 1982) for discussion of default under a mortgage.

[2] See, e.g., Philmon v. Mid-State Homes, Inc., 245 Ark. 680, 434 SW2d 84 (1968); Kaminski v. London Pub, Inc., 123 NJ Super. 112, 301 A2d 769 (1973).

[3] See, e.g., U.S. Freedom Tower, Inc. v. Citibank, N.A., 372 So. 2d 124 (Fla. Dist. Ct. App. 1979); Bozeman v. Horton, 245 Ga. 188, 263 SE2d 922 (1980).

[4] See, e.g., the following cases that discuss the validity of such acceleration clauses: Occidental Sav. & Loan Ass'n v. Venco Partnership, 206 Neb. 469, 293 NW2d 843 (1980); Ministers & Missionaries Benefit Bd. of Am. Baptist Churches v. Goldsworthy, 253 Pa. Super. 321, 385 A2d 358 (1978).

the ability of the mortgagee to accelerate. For example, acceleration may be waived by a prior pattern of acceptance of late payments.[5] Further, accidental or mistaken default or the doctrine of unconscionability may not enable acceleration.[6] Some state statutory law allows the mortgagor to cure default and thereby avoid acceleration.[7] Finally, the Federal Housing Administration (FHA) and the Veterans Administration (VA) provide guidelines that have the effect of extending the time between default and foreclosure, enabling the mortgagor to cure the default in the interim.[8] However, these guidelines are merely advisory and not binding on the mortgagee.[9]

A matter related to default and acceleration is the due-on-sale or due-on-encumbrance clauses so often found in the modern mortgage form.[10] If sale or encumbrance of the mortgagor's interest occurs without consent of the mortgagee, acceleration of the entire debt may take place pursuant to such clauses.

---

[5] See, e.g., Browne v. Nowlin, 117 Ariz. 73, 570 P2d 1246 (1977). It should be noted that this is not a uniform position taken by the courts; rather, waiver will be judged on a case-by-case basis. See, e.g., First Nat'l Bank of Lincoln v. Brown, 90 Ill. App. 3d 215, 412 NE2d 1078 (1980).

[6] See, e.g., Fed. Home Loan Mtg. Corp. v. Taylor, 318 So. 2d 203 (Fla. Dist. Ct. App. 1975); Delgado v. Strong, 360 So. 2d 73 (Fla. 1978). But see Ciavarelli v. Zimmerman, 122 Ariz. 143, 593 P2d 697 (1979).

[7] See, e.g., Cal. Civ. Code § 2924c; Ill. Ann. Stat. ch. 95, ¶ 57, § 7; Pa. Stat. Ann. tit. 41, § 404.

[8] See, e.g., the following government publications: HUD Handbook FHA G4191.1 (1974); HUD Housing Management Mortgagee Letter 75-10 (Oct. 4, 1975); VA Lenders Handbook ¶ 6011-13.

[9] See, e.g., Roberts v. Cameran-Brown Co., 556 F2d 356 (5th Cir. 1977), citing National Housing Act, § 235, 12 USC § 1715z; Brown v. Lynn, 385 F. Supp. 986 (ND Ill. 1975), later opinion, 392 F. Supp. 559 (ND Ill. 1975), citing 5 USC §§ 553(a)(2), 553(b).

[10] See supra ¶ 8.06[2] and note 18 for a discussion of and authority related to due-on-sale and due-on-encumbrance clauses. See also Ashley, "Use of 'Due-On' Clauses to Gain Collateral Benefits: A Common Sense Defense," 10 Tulsa L.J. 590 (1975); Bonanno, "Due-on-Sale and Prepayment Clauses in Real Estate Financing in California in Times of Fluctuating Interest Rates–Legal Issues and Alternatives," 6 U.S.F.L. Rev. 267 (1976); Hetland, "Real Property and Real Property Security: The Well-Being of the Law," 53 Calif. L. Rev. 151 (1965); Volkmer, "The Application of the Restraints on Alienation Doctrine to Real Property Security Interests," 58 Iowa L. Rev. 747 (1973); Comment, "Mortgages–A Catalogue and Critique on the Role of Equity in the Enforcement of Modern-Day 'Due-on-Sale' Clauses," 26 Ark. L. Rev. 485 (1973); Comment, "Judicial Treatment of the Due-on-Sale Clause: The Case for Adopting Standards of Reasonableness and Unconscionability," 27 Stan. L. Rev. 1109 (1975); Note, "Property–The Device of the Due-on-Sale Clause," 64 Calif. L. Rev. 573 (1976); Note, "Deeds of Trust–Restraints Against Alienation–Due-on-Sale Clause Is an Unreasonable Restraint on Alienation Absent a Showing of Protection of Mortgagee's Legitimate Interests," 47 Miss. L.J. 331 (1976); Note, Mortgages–Use of Due-on-Sale Clause by a Lender Is Not a Restraint on Alienation in North Carolina," 55 N.C.L. Rev. 310 (1977); Note, "Dawn Investment Co., Inc. v. Superior Court of Los Angeles County," 10 Pepperdine L. Rev. 278 (1982).

The enforceability of these clauses is presently in question due to the arguable restraint on alienation that results. The courts have been split on the enforceability of such clauses, often requiring some reasonable basis for having exercised the acceleration right; additionally, there has been statutory regulation of the enforceability of these clauses. A recent U.S. Supreme Court case and recent federal legislation has the effect of making due-on-sale clauses, but not due-on-encumbrance clauses, enforceable as a matter of federal law.[11]

Even if a default has occurred, relief may otherwise be available to the mortgagor.[12] Because foreclosure is an equitable action, the mortgagor will be relieved of a mere technical default if the mortgagee has not been harmed. Additionally, the mortgagor can assert various contractual defenses to foreclosure. These include payment of the debt or even tender of payment under some circumstances.[13] Other defenses include lack of consideration, fraud, and usury. Further, if the FHA or the VA is involved, their guidelines actually encourage forebearance by the mortgagee.[14] Finally, equitable defenses such as laches or unclean hands are available in the foreclosure proceeding, which is equitable in nature.[15]

## [2] Receivership

Although receivership is discussed elsewhere in the book,[16] it has particular importance in the enforcement of mortgages and also must be considered here.[17] Receivership is considered an extraordinary equitable remedy.[18] Nevertheless, in most states it may be used by a mortgagee pending foreclosure. It should be recalled that the mortgagor usually has the right to rents and prof-

---

[11] See Fidelity Fed. Sav. & Loan Ass'n v. de la Questa, 458 US 141 (1982); Garn-St Germain Depository Institutions Act of 1982, 12 USC § 1701(j-3); see also Wellenkamp v. Bank of Am., 21 Cal. 2d 943, 148 Cal. Rptr. 379, 582 P2d 970 (1978), construing Cal. Civ. Code § 771; Miranda v. Macias, 193 Cal. Rptr. 177, 141 Cal. App. 3d 188 (1983); Blongren v. Tinton 763 Corp., 18 AD2d 979, 238 NYS2d 435 (1965).

[12] See, e.g., Nelson v. Orosso, 172 Cal. Rptr. 457 (Cal. App. 1981); see Federal Nat'l Mortgage Ass'n v. Bryant, 62 Ill. App. 25, 378 NE2d 333 (1978); see also 7 Debtor-Creditor Law ¶¶ 31.04[A][2], 31.05 (Matthew Bender 1982) for a discussion of potential relief and defenses to foreclosure.

[13] See supra ¶ 8.07 for a discussion of payment or tender of payment in regard to discharge and release of the mortgage.

[14] See supra ¶ 8.08[1].

[15] See, e.g., Phinney v. Levine, 117 NH 968, 381 A2d 735 (1977).

[16] See ¶ 6.04[4].

[17] For other succinct treatments of the use of receivership in enforcing mortgages, see 7 Debtor-Creditor Law ¶ 81.08[D] (Matthew Bender 1982); 3 Powell on Real Property ¶ 465 (Matthew Bender 1981); Osborne, Mortgages §§ 147–159A, at 239–277 (West, 2d ed. 1970); Osborne, Nelson & Whitman, Real Estate Finance Law §§ 4.36–4.46 (West 1979).

[18] See ¶ 6.04[4][b].

its.[19] The receiver functions after default to preserve these rents and profits and the value of the land and, if possible, to accumulate a fund for application to the claims of the mortgagee and any subordinate interests.[20]

The basis for appointment of a receiver pending foreclosure varies depending upon whether the jurisdiction is a title or lien theory state. In title states the mortgagee must establish that there is a strong danger that the mortgaged real estate will be inadequate without additional rents and profits to cover the underlying debt. Further, consistent with equitable remedial law generally, the mortgagee must establish the inadequacy of his legal remedies.[21] In lien theory states, a receiver usually will be appointed when the security is inadequate in the time between the start of the foreclosure and its completion, although many jurisdictions stress the need to establish either destructive or permissive waste.[22] A few lien theory states view receivership as improper, as it is a means by which the mortgagee circumvents his lack of right of possession.[23] In appointing a receiver there is some authority that it is immaterial whether the owner of the mortgaged land is personally liable for the debt,[24] or whether the plaintiff is merely a junior encumbrancer.[25]

The mortgage form often contains a clause by which the mortgagor authorizes appointment of a receiver without notice and without regard to the value of the land in relation to the amount of the debt. In deciding whether to appoint a receiver, courts do consider such clauses, which can be of particular importance in a lien theory state.[26] However, most courts still require the plaintiff to establish the conditions previously discussed before a receiver will be appointed.[27]

---

[19] See supra ¶ 8.05.

[20] See, e.g., Turner v. Superior Court of Kern County, 72 Cal. App. 3d 804, 140 Cal. Rptr. 475 (1977); Melrose v. Industrial Ass'n, Inc., 136 Conn. 518, 72 A2d 469 (1950).

[21] See, e.g., Mutual Benefit Life Ins. Co. v. Frantz Klodt & Son, Inc., 306 Minn. 244, 237 NW2d 350 (1976); see also Osborne, Mortgages § 148, at 240 (West, 2d ed. 1970).

[22] Osborne, Mortgages § 149 (West, 2d ed. 1970). Examples of cases in which appointment of a receiver is considered include: Hutton v. Rainbow Tower Assocs., 226 Kan. 410, 601 P2d 665 (1979); Manufacturers Small Business Inv. Co. of Conn. v. Empire Auto Body, Inc., 3 Conn. Cir. Ct. 613, 222 A2d 592 (1966). An example regarding the requirement of a showing of waste is Dart v. Western Sav. & Loan Ass'n, 103 Ariz. 170, 438 P2d 407 (1968).

[23] See, e.g., Investors Syndicate v. Smith, 105 F2d 611 (8th Cir. 1939); Wagar v. Stone, 36 Mich. 364 (1867). It should be noted that even in these states a receiver can be appointed if the mortgage itself provides for the appointment. See Michigan Trust Co. v. Lansing Lumber Co., 103 Mich. 392, 61 NW 668 (1894).

[24] See, e.g., Rutherford Realty Co. v. Cook, 198 NY 29, 90 NE 1112 (1910).

[25] See, e.g., Albritton v. Lott-Blachsher Comm'n Co., 167 Ala. 541, 52 So. 653 (1910).

[26] See supra ¶ 8.08[2] note 23.

[27] See, e.g., Davis v. Seay, 247 Ark. 396, 445 SW2d 885 (1969); Riverside Properties v. Teachers Ins. & Annuity Ass'n of Am., 590 SW2d 736 (Tex. Civ. App. 1979).

### [3] Strict Foreclosure

The mortgagee has various methods of foreclosing the mortgage, including: (1) strict foreclosure; (2) judicial foreclosure leading to public sale; (3) nonjudicial foreclosure by a power-of-sale clause in the mortgage; and (4) use of deeds in lieu of foreclosure.

Unlike judicial foreclosure or foreclosure by a power-of-sale clause, in strict foreclosure there is no sale of the property.[28] Rather, "the defaulting mortgagor is given a certain time period by the court in which the debt must be paid; if it is not, title to the mortgaged property vests in the mortgagee without a sale."[29]

Strict foreclosure was the first method of foreclosure that originated in England.[30] It currently is not allowed as the primary mode of foreclosure on the mortgagor's interest in most jurisdictions, particularly in lien theory jurisdictions.[31] At least two title theory states allow for its use as a first resort[32] and Illinois allows strict foreclosure as the principal foreclosure method.[33] A number of states allow for its secondary use under very limited circumstances and for very limited purposes.[34]

Where strict foreclosure is used, it is for the purpose of seeking to perfect the mortgagee's title rather than to apply security to the debt.[35] A prayer for relief in a strict foreclosure does not seek a deficiency judgment. A separate action may be brought after strict foreclosure to obtain a personal deficiency judgment against the mortgagor.[36] The necessity of two actions makes this

---

[28] For discussion of strict foreclosure, see 7 Debtor-Creditor Law ¶ 31.07 (Matthew Bender 1982); Osborne, Mortgages 648–656 (West, 2d ed. 1970); Osborne, Nelson & Whitman, Real Estate Finance Law §§ 7.9, 7.10 (West 1979); 3 Powell on Real Property ¶ 469 (Matthew Bender 1981).

[29] 7 Debtor-Creditor Law 31-98 (Matthew Bender 1982).

[30] See 3 Powell on Real Property ¶ 469 (Matthew Bender 1981).

[31] See Osborne, Nelson & Whitman, Real Estate Finance Law § 7.10, at 443 (West 1979).

[32] Connecticut: see, e.g., Conn. Gen Stat. Ann. ch. 846, § 49-15; Constitution Bank & Trust Co. v. Robinson, 179 Conn. 232, 425 A2d 1268 (1979); Maresca v. Allen, 181 Conn. 521, 436 A2d 14 (198). Vermont: see, e.g., Vt. Stat. Ann. tit. 12, § 4531; see Note, "The Relation of the Equitable Doctrine of Subrogation to Vermont's Strict Foreclosure Law," 7 Vt. L. Rev. 71 (1982).

[33] See, e.g., Great Lakes Mortgage Corp. v. Collymore, 14 Ill. App. 3d 68, 302 NE2d 248 (1973); Prather, "Foreclosure of the Security Interest," 1957 U. Ill. L.F. 420, 446 (1957).

[34] See, e.g., Hermann v. Churchill, 235 Ore. 327, 385 P2d 190 (1963). But see Cooper v. Cooper, 275 Ore. 627, 552 P2d 536 (1976); Iowa Code Ann. §§ 656.1–656.6; Minn. Stat. Ann. § 559.21. See also 3 Powell on Real Property 696.76(32) n.6 (Matthew Bender 1981).

[35] See, e.g., Adair v. Kona Corp., 51 Hawaii 104, 452 P2d 449 (1969); see also 3 Powell on Real Property 696.76(33)–696.76(34) (Matthew Bender 1981).

[36] See, e.g., Pulaski Fed. Sav. & Loan Ass'n v. Woolsey, 242 Ark. 612, 414 SW2d 633 (1967).

method of foreclosure somewhat undesirable, although it retains some usefulness in foreclosing upon subordinate interests in the real estate that might have been overlooked in a prior judicial foreclosure.[37]

### [4] Judicial Foreclosure Leading to Public Sale

One of the most common methods of enforcing a mortgage involves a judicial proceeding whereby the mortgagee seeks to obtain a decree foreclosing the mortgagor's interest and all joined junior interests in the property, along with a judgment against the mortgagor in the amount of the outstanding debt. The decree orders sale of the property subject to the mortgagor's or junior interest's right to redeem the property. The proceeds derived from sale are ultimately applied to the mortgaged debt. The mortgagor remains personally liable, as a general rule, for any deficiency.[38]

A fundamental aspect of judicial foreclosure leading to a public sale involves who may or must be the plaintiff and defendant. As a general rule, the proper plaintiff in foreclosure should be the real and beneficial owner of the debt secured, together with any others who are jointly interested in the security.[39] This includes a mortgagee, assignee,[40] or personal representative.[41] The mortgagee's heirs may not foreclose on the mortgage; the proper party to foreclose is the personal representative of the mortgagee's estate.[42] If there is more than one mortgagee, the mortgagees can bring the foreclosure either jointly or individually. If the latter occurs, it results in a foreclosure of that mortgagee's fractional interest.[43]

The question of who is the necessary and proper defendant is substantially more complicated. As a guideline, the foreclosing mortgagee will want to join as defendants all who have interests in the equity of redemption, all claiming under the owners of the equity of redemption, and all persons who have an interest in the mortgage itself, in order that the property may be sold with a clear title subject only to claims that have higher priority than the mortgagee's interest. Additionally, all who are liable on the mortgaged debt should be

---

[37] See 7 Debtor-Creditor Law ¶ 31.07[B] (Matthew Bender 1982).

[38] Id. at ¶ 31.08.

[39] See 7 Debtor-Creditor Law ¶ 31.08[C], at 31–106, n.15 (Matthew Bender 1982); 59 C.J.S. Mortgages § 625 (1949).

[40] See, e.g., Laing v. Cainey Builders, Inc., 184 So. 2d 897 (Fla. Dist. Ct. App. 1966).

[41] See, e.g., Swinton v. Coffman, 139 Ark. 121, 213 SW 409 (1919). But see Darling v. Darling, 122 Neb. 153, 239 NW 727 (1932), where the court held legatees who received mortgage and note from executor to be proper plaintiffs.

[42] See 3 Powell on Real Property ¶ 452 (Matthew Bender 1981); 7 Debtor-Creditor Law ¶ 31.08[B] (Matthew Bender 1982); 59 C.J.S. Mortgages § 513 (1949); cf. Smith v. Turner, 112 Ga. 533, 37 SE 705 (1900); Mills v. Hamilton, 121 Fla. 435, 163 So. 857, (1935); Houston v. Carlson, 219 Ark. 665, 244 SW2d 151 (1951).

[43] See, e.g., Decker v. Boice, 83 NY 215 (1880); Ex parte Perry, 22 Pa. 43 (1853); see 7 Debtor-Creditor Law ¶ 31.08[B] (Matthew Bender 1982).

joined so that they will have a deficiency judgment entered against them.[44] Necessary defendants are those who have interests in the mortgaged property that must be eliminated to enable passage of the mortgagee's title to the purchaser at sale;[45] those who may be liable on the debt, such as a guarantor, are proper, although not necessary, defendants to clear title as a general rule,[46] but they may be necessary to establish deficiency liability. Those with interests in the property that are superior to the interest of the foreclosing mortgagee cannot be joined in a foreclosure action without their consent.[47] The effect of failing to join a party who possesses an interest in the premises is that the party's interest is not foreclosed; that is, the interest is not terminated by the foreclosure action.[48]

Although the joining of all parties who have subordinate interests in the subject property will clear the title as to interests existing before the commencement of the foreclosure, what of interests that arise after the action is filed—must those later be joined? These interests do not have to be joined, at least if the mortgagee takes advantage of lis pendens statutes that enable the mortgagee to record public notice of the pendency of the foreclosure action. In most states the lis pendens notice is essential to the commencement of the foreclosure action.[49] Any interest that is acquired after the notice is filed is subordinate to and will be terminated by the mortgagee's interest.

Even though judicial foreclosure procedure varies depending upon the jurisdiction in which the action is brought, a few basic comments to describe typical foreclosing pleadings are appropriate. The foreclosure pleading must set forth certain essential elements to state a cause of action. These essential allegations can be summarized as follows:[50]

---

[44] See 7 Debtor-Creditor Law ¶ 31.08[B][2], at 31-109 (Matthew Bender 1982).

[45] See Grady v. Utica Mut. Ins. Co., 69 AD2d 668, 419 NYS2d 565 (1979); see also 7 Debtor-Creditor Law ¶ 31.08[B][2][b] (Matthew Bender 1982); Wiltsie, Mortgage Foreclosures § 329 (Matthew Bender, 5th ed. 1938).

[46] See, e.g., River Edge Sav. & Loan Ass'n v. Clubhouse Assocs., Inc., 178 NJ Super. 177, 428 A2d 544 (1981); see also 7 Debtor-Creditor Law ¶ 31.08[B][2][c] (Matthew Bender 1982).

[47] See 7 Debtor-Creditor Law ¶ 31.08[B][3] (Matthew Bender 1982); see also Osage Oil & Ref. Co. v. Muber Oil Co., 43 F2d 306, 308 (10th Cir. 1930); Doinciana Hotel of Miami Beach, Inc. v. Kasden, 370 So. 2d 399 (Fla. Dist. Ct. App. 1979); Plaza Corp. v. Alban Tractor Co., 219 Md. 570, 151 A2d 170 (1950).

[48] As to owners, see Wayne Sav. & Loan Co. v. Young, 49 Ohio App. 2d 35, 358 NE2d 1380 (1976); compare John Stepp, Inc. v. First Fed. Sav. & Loan Ass'n of Miami, 379 So. 2d 384 (Fla. Dist. Ct. App. 1980). As to junior lienors, see National Acceptance Co. of Am. v. Mardigian, 259 F. Supp. 612 (D. Mich. 1966); Lenexa State Bank & Trust Co. v. Dixon, 221 Kan. 238, 559 P2d 776 (1977).

[49] See, e.g., Wash. Rev. Code § 4.28.320; see 138 A.L.R. 1454 (necessity of filing notice of lis pendens in suit to foreclose mortgage); Reuther, "Lis Pendens—Due Process of Law, United Savings and Loan Ass'n v. Scruggs, 436 A.2d 559," 12 Seton Hall L. Rev. 699–701 (Summer 1982). For further discussion of lis pendens generally, see ¶ 6.05[3][b].

[50] 7 Debtor-Creditor Law ¶ 31.08[D][2] (Matthew Bender 1982).

(1) The operative facts that gave rise to the original obligation and the accompanying mortgage;
(2) An accurate description of the land affected;
(3) Any subsequent changes in ownership of the mortgagor's liability or the mortgagee's claim;
(4) The facts that allegedly constitute a default with or without acceleration of the due date of other amounts;
(5) The fact that no other action has been brought on the mortgage debt;
(6) The reasons for joining various parties as defendants; and
(7) The prayers for relief, including a directed sale, personal judgments for any deficiency, and the demand that the defendants and persons claiming under them be foreclosed of all right, title, claim, lien and equity of redemption in and to the said mortgaged premises.

Of course, the lawyer is well advised to carefully consult applicable local law related to foreclosure procedure. Additionally, in most states excellent mortgage foreclosure pleading forms to be used as guidelines are available to the practitioner from various sources. Other facets of foreclosure procedure include the ability to obtain deficiency judgments, the foreclosure sale that concludes the judicial foreclosure, and the right of redemption.[51]

## [5] Power-of-Sale Foreclosures

A power-of-sale foreclosure is an extrajudicial procedure that is a simplified form of foreclosure. It is a contractural right provided by a clause in the mortgage or implied by statute that grants to the mortgagee the legal ability to sell the mortgaged property upon the mortgagor's default. The sale may be public or private but may not occur until the notice requirements of the applicable jurisdiction have been satisfied.[52] Power-of-sale foreclosures are permitted in about one half of the states.[53]

Although less expensive than a judicial foreclosure leading to sale, foreclosure by power of sale has some drawbacks. The foreclosure does not have the benefit of close judicial scrutiny and, as a result, may lead to errors resulting in

---

[51] See infra ¶¶ 8.08[8] (deficiency judgments), 8.08[9] (redemption), 8.08[10] (foreclosure sales).

[52] See Comment, "Power of Sale Foreclosures After Fuentes," 40 U. Chi. L. Rev. 206 (1972); Osborne, Mortgages § 337 (West, 2d ed. 1970); Osborne, Nelson & Whitman, Real Estate Finance Law §§ 7.19–7.30 (West 1979); 7 Debtor Creditor Law ¶ 31.09 (Matthew Bender 1982); 3 Powell on Real Property ¶ 468 (Matthew Bender 1981).

[53] The following states permit power-of-sale foreclosures: Alabama, Alaska, California, District of Columbia, Georgia, Hawaii, Idaho, Maryland, Massachusetts, Michigan, Minnesota, Mississippi, Missouri, Montana, Nevada, New Hampshire, North Carolina, Oregon, Rhode Island, South Dakota, Tennessee, Texas, Virginia, Washington, West Virginia, and Wyoming.

the transfer of defective title to the purchaser or in the sale being set aside.[54] The ultimate effect of foreclosure by power of sale is the same as a judicial foreclosure leading to sale: The equity of redemption is eliminated and title is granted to the foreclosure sale purchaser, which is equivalent to that title held by the mortgagee. The principal difference in ultimate effect between power-of-sale foreclosures and judicial foreclosures is that the judicial foreclosure results in judgment on the mortgaged debt against the mortgagee and other obligated parties. When a power-of-sale foreclosure occurs, the deficiency judgment must be obtained by separate judicial proceeding.[55]

Procedures related to power-of-sale foreclosures center on notification requirements. The object of these requirements is to notify the mortgagor, all other parties with interests in the mortgaged property, and the public at large that the foreclosure is pending and that a forced sale of the mortgaged property will occur at a specified time and place. The notice requirements vary substantially among the jurisdictions that recognize power-of-sale foreclosures. Usually the public notice must state the amount due, a description of the premises, the time and place of the sale, and other matters provided by either the mortgage or applicable statute.[56] In some states, the statute sets forth the notice form itself.[57] The public notice usually is given by advertisement in newspapers but the mortgagee may also be required to personally serve the mortgagor and other interested parties with the notice.[58]

The notice provides the mortgagor and other affected parties with the opportunity to scrutinize the proceeding. In addition, it creates public interest in purchasing the property. This is important to the integrity of the power-of-sale foreclosure, since the "prospect of an equity proceeding brought by any aggrieved person to set aside the sale and to adjudicate the rights of the party restrains the mortgagee from exercising his powers of sale in an improper manner or without proper cause."[59]

Power-of-sale foreclosures have been attacked on the grounds that they fail to protect the affected party's constitutional guaranty to due process of law. These attacks have found varied success. The potential violation of the due process of law provisions of the Fourteenth Amendment is present because no

---

[54] See, e.g., Ames v. Pardue, 389 So. 2d 927 (Ala. 1980); McHugh v. Church, 583 P2d 210 (Alaska 1978); see also 7 Debtor-Creditor Law ¶ 31.09[D] (Matthew Bender 1982).

[55] See, e.g., Nevada Lands & Mortgage Co. v. Hidden Wells Ranch, Inc., 83 Nev. 501, 435 P2d 198 (1967); Osborne, Nelson & Whitman, Real Estate Finance Law § 8.1 (West 1979).

[56] See 3 Powell on Real Property ¶ 468 (Matthew Bender 1981) and 7 Debtor-Creditor Law ¶ 37.09[B] (Matthew Bender 1982) for a discussion of the typical notice requirements. Specific codes containing such requirements are Cal. Civ. Code § 2924; Mich. Comp. Laws Ann. § 600.3204; Tex. Rev. Civ. Stat. Ann. art. 3810.

[57] See, e.g., Va. Code § 55-62.

[58] See, e.g., N.Y. Real Prop. Acts. Law § 1402; N.D. Cent. Code § 35-22-19(160).

[59] 3 Powell on Real Property 696.76(29) (Matthew Bender 1981).

personal notice or hearing is required before the sale.[60] However, for due process rights to be engendered, there must be some state action. Since the proceeding is extrajudicial, attacks on the constitutional validity on power-of-sale foreclosures have failed with courts that have found no state action.[61] There are, however, plausible arguments supporting the conclusion that state action is indeed present.[62] When state action has been found to be present, at least two federal cases have held that mere public notice is insufficient to satisfy the mortgagor's due process rights.[63] To be safe, personal notice (at least by mail) should be given to all parties whose interest in the property is affected by the foreclosure even though it is not required by statute and even though no state action may be present.[64] The lack of opportunity for a judicial hearing before taking the debtor's property also raises due process issues,[65] even though the affected party could initiate a suit to enjoin the foreclosure.[66] Finally, it has been argued that mortgage clauses that provide for power-of-sale foreclosure constitute valid waivers of the mortgagor's right to prior notice or prior hearings. However, these waiver arguments have met with little success in recent years.[67]

---

[60] For an excellent summary discussion of due process and the power-of-sale foreclosure, see 7 Debtor-Creditor Law ¶ 31.09[C] (Matthew Bender 1982).

[61] See, e.g., Charmicor, Inc. v. Deaner, 572 F2d 694 (9th Cir. 1978); Warren v. Government Nat'l Mortgage Ass'n. 611 F2d 1229 (8th Cir.), cert. denied, 449 US 847 (1980).

[62] These arguments place emphasis on the involvement of any state official, if such is present. See Turner v. Blackburn, 389 F. Supp. 1250 (WDNC 1975). The arguments could also assert that state power of sale statutes encourage objectionable private action and the encouragement is sufficient state action. See Garne v. Tri-State Dev. Co., 382 F. Supp. 377 (ED Mich. 1974); cf. Reitman v. Mulkey, 387 US 369 (1967). Additionally, it could be argued that the mortgagee who forecloses by power of sale is performing a function that is essentially governmental in nature; thus, state action is present in effect. See Marsh v. Alabama, 326 US 501 (1946). Finally, under a pervasive theory it may be argued that state action exists when statutory regulation of the power-of-sale foreclosure governs conduct that otherwise would be private. But see Jackson v. Metropolitan Edison Co., 419 US 345 (1974), which seems to reject this argument.

[63] Ricker v. U.S., 417 F. Supp. 133 (D. Me. 1976); Turner v. Blackburn, 389 F. Supp. 1250 (WDNC 1975).

[64] See, e.g., U.S. v. White, 429 F. Supp. 1245 (ND Miss. 1977); Ricker v. U.S., 417 F. Supp. 133 (D. Me. 1976). But see Wuchter v. Pizzuti, 276 US 13 (1928).

[65] See, e.g., Turner v. Blackburn, 389 F. Supp. 1250 (WDNC 1975).

[66] See, e.g., id.; Northrip v. Federal Mut. Mortgage Ass'n, 372 F. Supp. 594 (ED Mich. 1974). One court, however, saw the right to sue for injunction as saving the procedure in this regard. See Young v. Ridley, 309 F. Supp. 1308 (DDC 1970).

[67] See, e.g., Rau v. Cavenaugh, 500 F. Supp. 204 (DSD 1980); U.S. v. White, 429 F. Supp. 1245 (ND Mass. 1977); Ricker v. U.S., 417 F. Supp. 133 (D. Me. 1976); Turner v. Blackburn, 389 F. Supp. 1250 (WDNC 1975); Garner v. Tri-State Dev. Co., 382 F. Supp. 377 (ED Mich. 1974); Low v. U.S., 366 F. Supp. 1233 (ND Ga. 1973).

### [6] Deeds in Lieu of Foreclosure

A deed in lieu of foreclosure is a means of enforcing the mortgage by simply terminating the mortgagor's right of redemption. In this procedure, the mortgagor reconveys his equity of redemption in the property by deed in consideration for the mortgagee's promise not to sue on the debt or foreclose on the security. There are both advantages and disadvantages from the mortgagor's and mortgagee's point of view regarding the use of such deeds.[68]

The deed serves a number of purposes for the mortgagor: It promptly terminates his obligation to pay taxes and assessments on the property, protects his credit, resolves the matter extrajudicially with minimum adverse publicity, avoids the possibility of having foreclosure costs charged to him, and saves him from incurring personal liability on the note.[69] The deed also can fulfill some of the mortgagee's purposes if he wishes to aid a mortgagor who is faced with financial problems, avoid the delays that accompany foreclosure, eliminate foreclosure costs, or be recognized as the owner of record for tax and assessment purposes.[70]

The use of the deed in lieu of foreclosure also carries with it some distinct disadvantages for the mortgagee. These include the fact that junior lienholders' rights will not be eliminated and the priority of the noteholder's lien may be lost on a resale of the property by the noteholder. In addition, the deed in lieu of foreclosure may be construed as a mortgage rather than a reconveyance, and the benefits of the noteholder's title insurance may not be treated the same way as in foreclosure. The deed in lieu of foreclosure may be set aside on the basis that it constitutes a transfer in fraud of creditors or on the basis of fraud or undue influence. The rights of those who have an interest in the property or who are liable for the debt also may be disposed of by a deed in lieu of foreclosure to which they are not a party or that they have not approved.[71]

In most jurisdictions, use of the deed in lieu of foreclosure is closely scrutinized by the courts. For example, the mortgagee must rebut any presumption of fraud. The deed may even be seen as a mere mortgage that the debtor may redeem.[72] If this is the case, a court may examine the adequacy of consideration, the ongoing relationship of the parties, subsequent possession of the property, improvements by the grantor in possession, and payment of taxes and other acts by the grantor indicative of continued ownership.[73]

---

[68] See 3 Powell on Real Property ¶ 469.1 (Matthew Bender 1981), for an excellent and practical discussion of the advantages and disadvantages of using deeds in lieu of foreclosure and for discussion of the law relating thereto.

[69] Id. at 696.76(35).

[70] Id.

[71] Id. at 696.76(38).

[72] See, e.g., Davis v. Stone, 236 F. Supp. 553 (DDC 1964); Alden Hotel Co. v. Kanin, 88 Misc. 2d 546, 387 NYS2d 948 (NY Sup. Ct. 1976).

[73] See, e.g., Koch v. Wasson, 161 NW2d 173 (Iowa 1968); Davis v. Davis, 256 NC 468, 124 SE2d 130 (1962); Rendleman, "Absolute Conveyance as a Mortgage in Iowa," 18 Drake L. Rev. 197 (1969); Fogelman, "The Deed Absolute as a Mortgage in New York," 32 Fordham L. Rev. 299 (1963); 59 C.J.S. Mortgages §§ 35–47 (1949).

If these problems can be avoided, and if the use of the deed in lieu of foreclosure is desirable, the mortgagee can sell the property as title holder after the mortgagee receives the deed. It is hoped that the proceeds from the sale will satisfy the underlying debt. The primary objective of a foreclosure thus is accomplished by the deed in lieu of foreclosure.

### [7] Election of Remedies

Assuming default by the mortgagor, a mortgagee usually will foreclose on the land first and concurrently attempt to obtain a deficiency judgment for the amount owed after applying the proceeds received from the foreclosure sale to the underlying debt.[74] However, there are other means of satisfying the debt. For example, the mortgagee might pursue the two alternatives separately–one at law in an action on the debt and the other in equity to foreclose the mortgage.[75]

These separate courses can be taken as a general rule.[76] However, the mortgagee should carefully consult local applicable law, which may have a one-action rule under which the mortgagee may not be able to pursue separate actions at the same time, but must first exhaust the option of foreclosure on the land.[77] Additionally, the parties may have agreed that the mortgagee shall look only to the land for payment and that the debtor will not be personally liable. Such agreements will be enforced, in which case the mortgagee may not elect alternate courses of action.[78]

### [8] Deficiency Judgments

If foreclosure has occurred but the proceeds derived from the foreclosure sale do not satisfy the entire underlying debt, the mortgagee will wish to obtain a deficiency judgment and thereafter execute on other assets of the mortgagor.[79] A deficiency judgment is "an imposition of personal liability upon a

---

[74] For other discussions of election of remedies, see 10 Thompson on Real Property §§ 5127-5128 (Bobbs-Merrill 1958); 7 Debtor-Creditor Law ¶¶ 31.03[C], 11.11 (Matthew Bender 1982).

[75] See, e.g., Williams v. Henderson, 580 SW2d 37 (Tex. 1979); Capp v. Sands Point Marina, Inc., 17 NY2d 291, 217 NE2d 654, 270 NYS2d 599 (1966).

[76] See, e.g., Smith v. Certified Realty Corp., 41 Colo. App. 170, 585 P2d 293, aff'd, 198 Colo. 222, 597 P2d 1043 (1978); Grier v. Milt C. Realty Corp., 274 So. 2d 21 (Fla. 1971).

[77] See, e.g., Utah Mortgage & Loan Co. v. Black, 618 P2d 43 (Utah 1980); N.Y. Real Prop. Acts. Law § 1301(3); Cal. Civ. Proc. Code §§ 580a, 726; see also 3 Powell on Real Property ¶ 463 (Matthew Bender 1981); infra ¶ 8.08[8].

[78] See, e.g., Murren v. Southern Coal & Mining Co., 117 Mo. App. 600, 160 SW 835 (1913); cf. Vreeland v. Dawson, 55 NJ Super. 456, 151 A2d 63 (1959).

[79] For other discussions of deficiency judgments, see 7 Debtor-Creditor Law ¶ 31.11[A] (Matthew Bender 1982); 3 Powell on Real Property ¶¶ 467, 473 (Matthew Bender 1981).

mortgagor for an unpaid balance of a secured obligation after foreclosure of the mortgage has failed to yield the full amount of the underlying debt."[80] The principal question for the parties is whether the deficiency judgment will be allowed. If so, it will be enforced as any other judgment on an unsecured debt.[81]

As an initial principle, the mortgagee can obtain a deficiency judgment after a judicial foreclosure, power-of-sale foreclosure, or even after a strict foreclosure,[82] provided the local prerequisites for obtaining a deficiency judgment have been satisfied.[83] However, the mortgagee must be aware of two impediments to obtaining a deficiency judgment: one-action rules and anti-deficiency judgment legislation.

The subject of one-action rules, in large part, is election of remedies.[84] In the event of default by the mortgagor, a one-action rule provides that the mortgagee must pursue foreclosure as his only remedy, asserting any claim for a deficiency judgment as a part of that proceeding.[85] This is the only way the mortgagee may obtain a deficiency judgment. One-action rules thus have the effect of protecting the mortgagor from multiple actions and compelling the mortgagee to exhaust his security before attempting to reach unmortgaged property in satisfaction of his claim.[86]

Anti-deficiency judgment legislation represents a more formidable obstacle for the mortgagee in obtaining a deficiency judgment. Anti-deficiency judgment legislation is "a recognition of the modern shift in mortgage theory from a personal relationship predicated upon acquaintance and the believed solvency of the borrower, to an investment device largely handled by corporations."[87] Anti-deficiency judgment legislation has taken various forms. Some statutes

---

[80] In re Pittsburgh-Duquesne Dev. Co., 482 F2d 243 (3d Cir. 1973); see, e.g., Perpetual Bldg. & Loan Ass'n of Anderson v. Braun, 270 SC 338, 242 SE2d 407 (1978).

[81] See Chapter 6 for a discussion of judicial collection of unsecured debts.

[82] As to judicial foreclosures, see, e.g., In re Langlais, 11 Bankr. 485 (Bankr. Cal. 1981), citing Mich. Comp. Laws Ann. § 600.3150; McKnight v. U.S., 259 F2d 540 (9th Cir. 1958); Fla. Stat. Ann. § 702.06. As to power-of-sale foreclosures, see, e.g., Surety Managers, Inc. v. Stanford, 633 F2d 709 (5th Cir. 1980), cert. denied, 454 US 828. But see U.S. v. Haddon Haciendas Co., 541 F2d 777 (9th Cir. 1976), citing Cal. Civ. Proc. Code § 580d. See also Mich. Comp. Laws Ann. § 600.3280. As to strict foreclosures, see, e.g., Tefft, "The Myth of Strict Foreclosure," 4 U. Chi. L. Rev. 575, 594 (1937).

[83] For example, the deficiency judgment if not taken concurrently with the foreclosure decree, may have to be obtained within certain time limits after the foreclosure sale. See, e.g., International Paper Co. v. Whitson, 595 F2d 559 (10th Cir. 1979), citing Okla. Stat. tit. 12, § 686; N.Y. Real Prop. Acts. Law § 1371; Ohio Rev. Code Ann. § 2329.08.

[84] See supra ¶ 8.08[7].

[85] See, e.g., Cal. Civ. Proc. Code § 726; Idaho Code § 6-101; Nev. Rev. Stat. § 40.430; Utah Code Ann. § 78-37-1.

[86] See, e.g., Keever v. Nicholas Beers Co., 96 Nev. 509, 611 P2d 1079 (1980); see also 7 Debtor-Creditor Law ¶ 31.11[B], at 31-161 (Matthew Bender 1982). Note that the mortgagor cannot waive this rule. See, e.g., Woodruff v. California Republic Bank, 75 Cal. App. 3d 108, 141 Cal. Rptr. 915 (1977).

[87] 3 Powell on Real Property 696.76(67) (Matthew Bender 1981).

simply prohibit a deficiency judgment under particular circumstances; for example, where power of sale has been exercised and where there is no right of redemption.[88] Of these statutes that flatly prohibit deficiency judgments some have a much broader application: Some states prohibit any deficiency judgment in the case of purchase-money mortgages.[89] Other less direct forms of anti-deficiency judgment legislation fall short of absolute prohibition. For example, some statutes require a court to determine the property's fair value, which is then used to compute the deficiency, instead of using the actual sale price of the land.[90] Other states simply combine limits on the amount of a deficiency with restrictions on bringing an action on the debt alone.[91]

### [9] Redemption: Equitable and Statutory

Even though the mortgagor may be in default, a foreclosure may be averted before or after foreclosure sale if the mortgagor successfully exercises an equitable or statutory right to redemption.[92] The equitable right of redemption exists before foreclosure sale while the statutory right to redeem commences upon foreclosure sale.

Regardless of whether or not he is in default, the mortgagor has the right of equitable redemption which allows him to reobtain title to property free of the mortgage upon payment of his debt.[93] The equitable-redemption right originally was a protective creation of the English chancery courts that enabled the mortgagor to regain title that had been lost to the mortgagee on law day.[94] The courts carefully protected the right by prohibiting any efforts to "clog" the equity of redemption; that is, a clause in the mortgage or other documentation could not cut off the right to redeem.[95] Under modern law, the equitable right

---

[88] See, e.g., Cal. Civ. Proc. Code § 580d; see also supra ¶ 8.08[8] note 82.

[89] See, e.g., N.C. Gen. Stat. § 45-21-38; Cal. Civ. Proc. Code § 580(b); Mont. Code Ann. § 93-6008; see also Nev. Rev. Stat. § 40-457; Ore. Rev. Stat. § 88.070; Utah Code Ann. § 57-1-32; N.D. Cent. Code § 32-19-06.

[90] See, e.g., N.Y. Real Prop. Acts. Law § 1371.

[91] See, e.g., N.J. Stat. Ann. § 2A:50-2.

[92] For succinct discussion of the right of redemption, see 7 Debtor-Creditor Law ¶¶ 31.02[D][4], 31.03[E] (Matthew Bender 1982); 3 Powell on Real Property ¶ 470 (Matthew Bender 1981); Osborne, Mortgages §§ 6–8 (West, 2d ed. 1970); Osborne, Nelson & Whitman, Real Estate Finance Law §§ 7.1–7.5 (West 1979); see also ¶ 6.06[4][c].

[93] See, e.g., John Stepp, Inc. v. First Fed. Sav. & Loan Ass'n of Miami, 379 So. 2d 384 (Fla. Dist. Ct. App. 1980); Gay v. Tompkins, 385 So. 2d 973 (Ala. 1978); Chicago Title & Trust Co. v. National Bank of Albany Park in Chicago, 17 Ill. App. 3d 721, 307 NE2d 656 (1974).

[94] See 7 Debtor-Creditor Law ¶ 31.02[D] (Matthew Bender 1982); Osborne, Mortgages § 6 (West, 2d ed. 1970); see also supra ¶ 8.02 for discussion of the historical evolution of the redemption right.

[95] See Williams, "Clogging the Equity of Redemption," 40 W. Va. L.Q. 31 (1933); Wyman, "The Clog on the Equity of Redemption," 21 Harv. L. Rev. 459 (1908); Kane, "The Mortgagee's Option to Purchase Mortgaged Property," Financing Real Estate in

to redeem may be terminated only by foreclosure.[96] To exercise this equitable-redemption right, the mortgagor typically must assert the right in equity.[97] Assuming the redeeming party successfully establishes a right to redeem, the court will issue a decree giving the mortgagor a specified period of time within which to redeem. The redeeming party must pay the mortgagee the entire amount due including the principal debt and any applicable interest, costs, and taxes.[98] The mortgagor is obviously a proper party to redeem,[99] but many other parties also may be eligible to exercise the equitable-redemption right.[100]

The statutory right to redeem property from foreclosure commences upon occurrence of the foreclosure sale and runs thereafter for the statutorily prescribed time period. The time period varies from three months to one year depending upon the jurisdiction.[101] If the mortgagor or other appropriate redeeming party pays the foreclosure sale purchaser the foreclosure sale price and costs within the statutorily prescribed time period, the title to the property is successfully redeemed. The statutory right of redemption is available in approximately one half of the states.[102] The mortgagor and his assignee and successors may redeem, although some states may also allow other parties whose interests in the property were adversely affected by the foreclosure to redeem.[103] Otherwise, the availability of the statutory right to redeem varies significantly from state to state depending on such factors as the amount of the

---

the 80's 123 (A.B.A. 1981); Strum, "Current Trends of Institutional Financing of Real Estate in the United States," Real Property, Probate and Trust Journal 486 (Oct. 1980); Humble Oil & Ref. Co. v. Doer, 123 NJ Super. 530, 303 A2d 898 (1973).

[96] See, e.g., Wayne Sav. & Loan Co. v. Young, 49 Ohio App. 2d 35, 358 NE2d 1380 (1976); Madison Properties, Inc. v. U.S., 375 F2d 740 (9th Cir. 1967); Trauner v. Lowrey, 369 So. 2d 531 (Ala. 1979).

[97] See, e.g., Burroughs v. Garner, 43 Md. App. 302, 405 A2d 301 (1979).

[98] See, e.g., Rowe v. Tucker, 38 Colo. App. 532, 560 P2d 843 (1977); Sun First Nat'l Bank of Orlando v. RGC, 348 So. 2d 620 (Fla. Dist. Ct. App. 1977).

[99] See, e.g., John Stepp, Inc. v. First Fed. Sav. & Loan Ass'n of Miami, 379 So. 2d 384 (Fla. Dist. Ct. App. 1980); Kaplan v. Sleep E Hollow Motel Co., 112 NJ Super. 296, 271 A2d 12 (1970).

[100] All other parties whose interest is terminated by the foreclosure may exercise the equitable right of redemption. This includes junior lienors. Additionally, parties omitted from a judicial foreclosure, purchasers of the equity of redemption, heirs or devisees, tenants for life or certain lessees, holders of easements, and joint tenants may also redeem. See 7 Debtor-Creditor Law ¶ 31.08[E] (Matthew Bender 1982); Trauner v. Lowrey, 369 So. 2d 531 (Ala. 1979).

[101] See, e.g., N.J. Stat. Ann. § 2A:50-4; Mich. Comp. Laws Ann. §§ 600.3240(2), 600.3240(3), 600.3240(4), 600.3240(5); Cal. Civ. Proc. Code § 725a; Wash. Rev. Code § 6.24.140.

[102] These states include, Alabama, Alaska, Arizona, Arkansas, California, Colorado, Florida, Idaho, Illinois, Kansas, Kentucky, Maine, Michigan, Minnesota, Missouri, Montana, New Jersey, New Mexico, North Dakota, Oregon, South Dakota, Tennessee, Utah, Vermont, Washington, and Wyoming. See 7 Debtor-Creditor Law 31-49 n.94 (Matthew Bender 1982).

[103] See, e.g, Cal. Civ. Proc. Code § 725a; Wash. Rev. Code § 6.24.130 (1961).

debt, the type of real estate, and whether a deficiency judgment has been obtained. Additionally, if the federal government has an interest in the mortgage, a federal court may provide other limitations.[104]

### [10] Foreclosure Sales

Legal principles commonly associated with execution and judicial sales were previously discussed in this book.[105] The basic conduct of the mortgage foreclosure sale and particular problems that sometimes arise with regard to the sale and its effect on the interested parties are considered in this section of the book.[106] The attorney is cautioned to carefully consult local applicable law to determine the specific rules related to foreclosure sales in that jurisdiction.

As is the case with execution and judicial sales generally, both legislation and case law require the mortgage foreclosure sale to be a public sale.[107] In contrast to the execution sale, the judicial foreclosure mortgage sale is conducted under the close scrutiny of the court.[108] For example, the sale must be confirmed by the court and the highest bidder has no rights to the property before confirmation.[109] On the other hand, the highest bidder or the mortgagee can demand confirmation in the absence of legal reason for refusing it.[110] A deed, without warranties, ultimately is given to the purchaser. This deed transfers to the purchaser all of the interest of the mortgagee, mortgagor, and others who have had notice of sale or were joined in the foreclosure action.[111] Thereafter, the purchaser may take possession of the property. The statutory right of redemption, however, may still be exercised.[112]

---

[104] See, e.g., U.S. v. Stadium Apartments, Inc., 425 F2d 358 (9th Cir.), cert. denied, 400 US 926 (1970).

[105] See ¶ 6.06.

[106] See also 7 Debtor-Creditor Law ¶ 31.10 (Matthew Bender 1982); 3 Powell on Real Property ¶¶ 466–468 (Matthew Bender 1981).

[107] Numerous examples of such law may be cited. See, e.g., Wash. Rev. Code §§ 6.24.020, 6.24.060; National Reserve Life Ins. Co. v. Kemp, 184 Kan. 648, 339 P2d 368 (1959); Cal. Civ. Proc. Code § 726(e); N.Y. Real Prop. Acts. Law §§ 1351(1), 1351(2), 1351(3).

[108] See, e.g., National Reserve Life Ins. Co. v. Kemp, 184 Kan. 648, 339 P2d 368 (1959); 7 Debtor-Creditor Law ¶ 31.10[A] (Matthew Bender 1982).

[109] See, e.g., Econo-Travel Motor Hotel Corp. v. Foreman's Inc., 44 NC App. 126, 260 SE2d 661 (1980); Southern Realty & Utils. Corp. v. Belmont Mortgage Corp., 186 So. 2d 24 (Fla. 1966); Wash. Rev. Code §§ 6.24.100, 6.24.220.

[110] See, e.g., Cheak v. Savannah Valley Prod. Credit Ass'n, 244 Ga. 768, 262 SE2d 90 (1979); Allen v. Martin, 61 Miss. 78 (1883). As to reasons why confirmation would be denied, a court in its equitable power can refuse to confirm sale, see Arban v. Rogers, 262 Md. 738, 279 A2d 457 (1971); Wash. Rev. Code 6.24.100.

[111] See, e.g., Ryan v. Fitzsimmons, 57 AD2d 922, 395 NYS2d 49 1977); Cooley v. Marx, 11 Mich. App. 470, 169 NW2d 655 (1969); Valley Nat'l Bank of Ariz. v. Arco Dev. Co., 14 Ariz. 56, 480 P2d 671 (1971); Gem Valley Ranchers, Inc. v. Small, 92 Idaho 232, 440 P2d 352 (1968).

[112] See supra ¶ 8.08[9].

The foreclosure sale may bring an inadequate price for the property from the mortgagor's viewpoint. In the absence of a statute, a court will not set aside a sale because of inadequate price,[113] unless the inadequacy is so gross that the court finds it to be unconscionable,[114] or unless there is some other irregularity of a material nature in the sale procedure that was followed by the parties.[115] However, in a judicial foreclosure, some statutory and case law requires or enables a court to establish an "upset price."[116] Typically, sale of the property, whether pursuant to judicial foreclosure or power of sale, must be by parcel as opposed to sale in bulk.[117]

Matters pertaining to the time of sale have caused problems in a power-of-sale foreclosure. The sale sometimes occurs at a time not advertised or at an otherwise unusual hour. If the mortgagor is prejudiced thereby, the sale may be invalidated.[118] Also, in power-of-sale foreclosures the mortgagee and trustee (in deeds of trust) usually may not be purchasers.[119]

If the sale proceeds do not satisfy the debt, a deficiency results and the mortgagee will seek a deficiency judgment.[120] If the price exceeds the debt, a surplus results and must be distributed. All interests junior to the foreclosing

---

[113] See ¶ 6.06[4][a]; United Growth Corp. v. Kelly Mortgage & Inv. Co., 86 Mich. App. 82, 272 NW2d 340 (1978).

[114] See, e.g., Garland v. Hill, 277 Md. 710, 357 A2d 374 (1976); Arban v. Rogers, 262 Md. 738, 279 A2d 457 (1971); First Wis. Nat'l Bank of Oshkosh v. KSW Investments, Inc., 71 Wis. 2d 359, 238 NW2d 123 (Wis. 1976); see 30 Am. Jur. 2d Executions § 733 (1967).

[115] See, e.g., Boyce v. Hughes, 241 Ga. 357, 245 SE2d 308 (1978); Kouros v. Sewell, 225 Ga. 487, 169 SE2d 816 (1969).

[116] See, e.g., Suring State Bank v. Giese, 210 Wis. 489, 246 SW 556 (1933); Michigan Trust Co. v. Kutmers, 265 Mich. 651, 252 SW 478 (1934); Mich Comp. Laws Ann. § 600.3155 (1978); Wash. Rev. Code § 61.12.060. Note that a court will scrutinize more carefully the adequacy of price if it is relevant to computation of a deficiency as opposed to mere confirmation of the sale. See, e.g., Fara Mfg. Co. v. First Fed. Sav. & Loan Ass'n of Miami, 366 So. 2d 164 (Fla. Dist. Ct. App. 1979); Davis v. Sheffield, 123 Ga. App. 228, 180 SE2d 263 (1971).

[117] See, e.g., Metropolitan Life Ins. Co. v. Foote, 95 Mich. App. 399, 290 NW2d 158 (1980), citing Mich. Comp. Laws Ann. § 600.3165; see Wash. Rev. Code 6.24.020; J.H. Morris, Inc. v. Indian Hills, Inc., 282 Ala. 443, 212 So. 2d 831 (1968).

[118] See Bering v. Republic Bank of San Antonio, 581 SW2d 806 (Tex. Civ. App. 1979); see also 7 Debtor-Creditor Law ¶ 31.10[C] (Matthew Bender 1982).

[119] As to mortgagees, since they conduct the sale, their purchase is improper. See, e.g., Dieffenbach v. Buckley, 464 F. Supp. 670 (DNH 1979). There are exceptions such as where the mortgage otherwise provides or state law otherwise provides. See Valley Int'l Properties, Inc. v. Ray, 586 SW2d 898 (Tex. Civ. App. 1979); Southern Trust & Mortgage Co. v. Daniel, 143 Tex. 321, 184 SW2d 465 (1943); Mich. Comp. Laws Ann. § 600.3216. As to trustees, since they are a fiduciary for the debtor and creditor, their purchase also may be improper. See, e.g., Whitlow v. Mountain Trust Bank, 215 Va. 149, 207 SE2d 837 (1974). But see Home Fed. Sav. & Loan Ass'n of Chicago v. Zarkin, 89 Ill. 2d 232, 432 NE2d 841 (1980).

[120] See supra ¶ 8.08[8].

mortgagee's will receive the surplus according to their priority,[121] but interests superior to the foreclosing mortgagee's receive nothing as their interests are unaffected by the foreclosure.[122] Any surplus remaining after distribution is then given to the mortgagor.[123]

## ¶ 8.09 PRIORITY PRINCIPLES

### [1] Recording Statutes

#### [a] Generally

Priority disputes may arise between the mortgagee and a creditor of the mortgagor or other parties who claim an interest through the mortgagor, all of whom may have valid claims to the mortgaged real property. The mortgaged real property may be the only realistic means of satisfying debts due to the creditors of the mortgagor. Thus, the mortgagee must seek to obtain priority over the conflicting claimants to the real estate. To ensure that the mortgage obtains its highest priority, the mortgagee will record the mortgage. The recordation of the mortgage is analagous to the perfection of a UCC Article 9 security interest in personal property.[1] Because mortgages are recorded, as are other transfers of interests in real estate, real property recordation statutes and related law should be reviewed before a consideration of specific mortgage priority rules.[2]

Modern recording statutes have their origin in a colonial Massachusetts ordinance of 1640.[3] Today, all states, except Louisiana,[4] have approximately the same type of recording systems. Recordation is not essential to either passage of title, in the case of a deed, or the creation of a lien, in the case of a mortgage.[5] Rather, the recordation relates to third parties and the priority of

---

[121] See, e.g., Banks-Miller Supply Co. v. Smallridge, 154 W. Va. 360, 175 SE2d 446 (1970); Western Sav. Fund Soc'y of Philadelphia v. Goodman, 103 NJ Super. 307, 247 A2d 151 (1968). Priority rules are discussed at infra ¶ 8.09.

[122] See, e.g., U.S. v. Sage, 566 F2d 1114 (9th Cir. 1977); Armands Eng'g, Inc. v. Town & Country Club, Inc., 113 RI 515, 324 A2d 334 (1974).

[123] See, e.g., Armands Eng'g, Inc. v. Town & Country Club, Inc., 113 RI 515, 324 A2d 334 (1974).

[1] See ¶ 7.06 for discussion of perfection of UCC Article 9 security interests.

[2] For discussion of recording statutes as applied to mortgages, see Osborne, Mortgages 338–380 (West, 2d ed. 1970); Osborne, Nelson & Whitman, Real Estate Finance Law §§ 9.1–9.3 (West 1979).

[3] See Beale, "The Origin of the System of Recording Deeds in America," 19 Green Bag 335 (1907).

[4] For discussion of Louisiana related law, see Redmann, "The Louisiana Law of Recordation: Some Principles and Some Problems," 39 Tul. L. Rev. 491–512 (1965); Dainow, "Mortgages–Public Records Doctrine," 27 La. L. Rev. 492 (1967).

[5] See Osborne, Mortgages § 195 (West, 2d ed. 1970).

their interest vis-à-vis the recorded mortgage in the subject real estate. The recordation gives to the public constructive notice of the claimed interest in the real estate described in the recorded documents. Thus "[p]rompt recording is induced by (1) loss of priority of unrecorded transfers to a later grantee; (2) preservation of priority through recordation which gives public notice."[6]

Recordation basically involves copying the instrument into books kept for that purpose by public recordation offices. Recording usually occurs at the county seat in which the real property is located. The document to be recorded usually must be acknowledged before a public official such as a notary before it is eligible for recordation. Once recorded, public notice is accomplished.

### [b] Chain of Title

Only instruments that are recorded within the chain of title are validly recorded. The instrument is in the chain of title if it can be discovered by a reasonable search.[7] Since most state recordation offices provide only grantor and grantee indexes,[8] the recorded mortgage, to be discoverable by a reasonable search, must be traceable through the system to be regarded as within the chain of title. In short, the mortgage must be traceable back to a common grantor.[9]

### [c] Defective or Erroneous Recordings

Although the mortgage may have been in proper form,[10] the act of recording itself may have been done improperly. Thus, the error may have been committed by the recording officer and not the recording mortgagee. The question then exists of who will bear the loss occasioned by the recording error as between the mortgagee and a subsequent claimant with whom the mortgagee is engaged in a priority dispute in the mortgaged property.[11] Traditionally, most statutes have provided that recordation of a mortgage is complete so as to give notice when it is delivered to the recording officer.[12] However, if there is an

---

[6] Id. at p. 343.

[7] Id. at § 197; see also Philbrick, "Limits of Record Search and Therefore of Notice," 93 U. Pa. L. Rev. 125 (1945).

[8] Most states do not, for example, use plat systems. See, e.g., In re Cushman Bakery, 526 F2d 23 (1st Cir. 1975).

[9] See Osborne, Mortgages § 199 (West, 2d ed. 1970); see, e.g., Truitt v. Grandy, 115 NC 54, 20 SE 293 (1894). The same rule applies as to a recorded purchase-money mortgage given by the vendee under a recorded deed. See, e.g., Dobbins, Inc. v. Economic Gas Co., 183 Cal. 616, 189 P 1073 (1920). For discussion of chain of title problems generally, see Osborne, Mortgages §§ 197–202 (West, 2d ed. 1970).

[10] See supra ¶ 8.04, which considers the form of the mortgage.

[11] As to this issue, see Osborne, Mortgages § 203 (West, 2d ed. 1970).

[12] Id. at p. 352; see, e.g., New Jersey Bank v. Azco Realty Co., Inc., 148 NJ Super. 159, 372 A2d 356 (1977); Pease & Elliman Realty Trust v. Gaines, 160 Ga. 125, 286 SE2d 448 (1981).

error in the actual transcription of the mortgage, some courts hold that the mortgage is not validly recorded so as to give constructive notice and thus the loss between the recording mortgagee and a subsequent party is borne by the mortgagee.[13] On the other hand, today most courts would place the loss on the subsequent party.[14] The party who is to bear the loss probably would have a cause of action against the filing officer.

The mortgagee may be the party who committed the error in recording the mortgage. In general, if the error is material, the recording fails to impart constructive notice. An example of this arises in the case of a mortgage that is unacknowledged. If such a defective recordation takes place, subsequent parties who acquire claims to the subject real estate without actual knowledge of the defectively recorded interest may be unaffected by the mortgage.[15]

### [d] Non-Record Notice

The basic policy underlying recording statutes is for the public to be given notice of the existing claim in the subject real estate and for subsequent mortgagees and other purchasers to be treated just as though they had actual knowledge of the recorded instrument.[16] If an instrument is unrecorded or defectively recorded but, nevertheless, a party knows of the interest in the real estate, is that party subject to the instrument even though there is no valid recordation?[17]

In most states, a subsequent party with non-record notice or knowledge of the existence of the unrecorded interest cannot obtain priority over it.[18] In some states, however, actual knowledge will not have that effect.[19] As to the general rule that actual knowledge is effective to supplant the need for valid

---

[13] See Annot., 70 A.L.R. 595 (1931).

[14] See, e.g., New Jersey Bank v. Azco Realty Co., Inc., 148 NJ Super. 159, 372 A2d 356 (1977); Pease & Elliman Realty Trust v. Gaines, 160 Ga. 125, 286 SE2d 448 (1981); Osborne, Mortgages § 203 (West, 2d ed. 1970).

[15] See, e.g., Northridge Bank v. Lakeshore Commercial Fin. Corp., 48 Ill. App. 3d 82, 365 NE2d 382 (1977); Air Flow Heating & Air Conditioning, Inc. v. Baker, 326 So. 2d 449 (Fla. Dist. Ct. App. 1976). But see Prudential Ins. Co. of Am. v. Holliday, 191 Neb. 144, 214 NW2d 273 (1974) wherein the court found constructive notice existed even though not all mortgagors that were required to acknowledge the mortgage did so. See also Osborne, Mortgages § 205 (West, 2d ed. 1970).

[16] See, e.g., Exchange Place Corp. v. Tarvan Realty Inc., 44 Misc. 2d 980, 255 NYS2d 1002 (NY Sup. Ct. 1964); Gribble v. Mauerhan, 188 Cal. App. 2d 221, 10 Cal. Rptr. 296 (1961); Farm Bureau Fin. Co., Inc. v. Carney, 100 Idaho 745, 605 P2d 509 (1980); see also Osborne, Mortgages 357 (West, 2d ed. 1970).

[17] See, e.g., Farm Bureau Fin. Co., Inc. v. Carney, 100 Idaho 745, 605 P2d 509 (1980).

[18] Osborne, Mortgages §§ 196, 206 (West, 2d ed. 1970).

[19] See Patton on Titles § 8 (West, 2d ed. 1957); cf. Mellon Nat'l Mortgage Co. of Ohio v. Jones, 54 Ohio App. 2d 45, 374 NE2d 666 (1977).

recordation, the policy basis seems to be that actual notice is equivalent to recording in that it effectuates the purpose of recording.[20] The actual knowledge rule is typically applied where property subject to a mortgage is in the possession of someone other than the mortgagor,[21] or where an effective prior instrument was invalidly recorded but actually seen by the mortgagee,[22] or where the mortgage was given by quit claim deed.[23]

The issue of "knowledge" is crucial to the law that declares knowledge to be effective in lieu of valid recordation. The issue concerns whether actual knowledge of the hostile unrecorded conveyance is required (a subjective test), or whether the person as a reasonable person is placed on a duty of inquiry that would reveal the hostile conveyance (an objective test). Authority is split on this issue, with many decisions resting on specific recording statute terminology.[24]

### [e] Burden of Proof

When a prior-in-time interest is not validly recorded, a subsequent mortgagee should take free of the interest as long as he has no knowledge of the interest and has given value. Who has the burden of proof regarding the bona fide nature of the later mortgagee? One position taken by the jurisdictions is that the subsequent mortgagee has the burden of proof.[25] There is, however, contrary authority that places the burden of proof on the prior unrecorded interest.[26] The practitioner therefore is advised to research local law as to this burden of proof issue.[27]

---

[20] See Philbrick, "Limits of Record Search and Therefore of Notice," 93 U. Pa. L. Rev. 259, 270 (1945).

[21] See, e.g., Williams v. Floyd County Wildlife Ass'n, 215 Ga. 789, 113 SE2d 626 (1960); Mellon Nat'l Mortgage Co. of Ohio v. Jones, 54 Ohio App. 2d 45, 374 NE2d 666 (1977); see also Rollison, "Priorities in the Law of Mortgages," 8 Notre Dame Law. 28 (1932).

[22] See, e.g., Meyer, Kasindorf & Mancino, Architects v. Lafayette Bank & Trust Co., 34 Conn. Supp. 84, 377 A2d 861 (1977).

[23] See Osborne, Mortgages 363 (West, 2d ed. 1970); cf. In re American Ventures, Inc., 340 F. Supp. 279, aff'd, 457 F2d 974 (D. Ga. 1971).

[24] See, e.g., Bank of Cave City v. Hill, 266 Ark. 727, 587 SW2d 833 (1979); compare City Bank & Trust Co. v. Caneco Constr., Inc., 341 So. 2d 1331 (La. Ct. App. 1976). See also First Ala. Bank of Huntsville v. Key, 394 So. 2d 67 (Ala. 1981); Myhra v. Rustad, 58 ND 258, 225 SW 796 (1929); compare Brinkman v. Jones, 44 Wis. 498 (1878).

[25] See, e.g., Berge v. Fredericks, 95 Nev. 183, 591 P2d 246 (1979); Corey v. United Sav. Bank Mut., 52 Ore. App. 263, 628 P2d 739 (1981).

[26] See, e.g., Leedy v. First Fed. Sav. & Loan Ass'n of Cocoa, 142 So. 2d 99 (Fla. Dist. Ct. App. 1966); Cessna v. Hulce, 322 Ill. 589, 153 NE 679 (1926).

[27] See also Osborne, Mortgages § 208 (West, 2d ed. 1970).

## [2] Priority Rules

### [a] Subordination Agreements

A potential lender who wishes to rely on the debtor's real estate as security for a loan will be reluctant to extend credit if the real estate is subject to any encumbrances. This reluctance results from the legitimate concern of the potential lender that his later-in-time mortgage may be subordinate to an existing interest.[28] To induce the potential lender to extend credit, a reversal of normally resulting priorities may occur by way of "subordination."[29] Subordination establishes priority between different existing encumbrances on the same realty by means other than the basic rule of first in time[30] or the automatic priority accorded purchase-money mortgages.[31]

There are two intentional methods of accomplishing the subordination. First, the parties can enter into an express subordination agreement. However, courts sometimes are reluctant to enforce written subordination agreements.[32] Therefore, as a second method of subordination, lenders often prefer to record the subordinated lien subsequent to the senior lien.[33] This form of subordination has received favorable treatment by the courts.[34]

Subordination can also occur unintentionally by the use of estoppel. If a prior encumbrancer makes statements of intention relied upon by a subordinate encumbrancer in changing his position, these statements may

---

[28] Discussion of some special priority rules occurs in other portions of the text and will not be repeated here. As to statutory liens, see ¶ 9.02[5]; as to federal tax liens, see ¶ 9.04[6]; as to bankruptcy, see Chapters 14 and 17; as to future advances by the mortgagee, see supra ¶ 8.04; as to after-acquired property, see supra ¶ 8.04; as to judgment liens, see ¶ 6.05[2][f]; as to fixtures, see ¶ 7.07[8].

[29] For succinct discussion of subordination, see 7 Debtor-Creditor Law ¶ 31.03[B][3] (Matthew Bender 1982). For a more detailed discussion of subordination, see Osborne, Mortgages § 212 (West, 2d ed. 1970); Osborne, Nelson & Whitman, Real Estate Finance Law § 12.9 (West 1979).

[30] See infra ¶ 8.09[2][b] for discussion of the basic priority rule.

[31] See infra ¶ 8.09[2][c] for discussion of the purchase-money mortgage priority rule. For the definition of "subordination," see 7 Debtor-Creditor Law 31-43 (Matthew Bender 1982); Middlebrook-Anderson Co. v. Southwest Sav. & Loan Ass'n, 18 Cal. App. 3d 1023, 96 Cal. Rptr. 338, 341 (1971).

[32] This is particularly the case if the subordination agreement is unfair to a seller. See, e.g., Eisenhardt, "Subordination of Purchase-Money Security," 52 Cal. L. Rev. 157 (1964); Gluskin v. Atlantic Sav. & Loan Ass'n, 23 Cal. App. 3d 307, 108 Cal. Rptr. 318 (Cal. App. 1973); Handy v. Gordon, 65 Cal. 2d 578, 422 P2d 329, 55 Cal. Rptr. 726 (1967).

[33] This is known as "automatic subordination."

[34] See, e.g., Middlebrook-Anderson Co. v. Southwest Sav. & Loan Ass'n, 18 Cal. App. 3d 1023, 96 Cal. Rptr. 338 (1971); Kirkeby Corp. v. Cross Bridge Towers, Inc., 91 NJ Super. 126, 219 A2d 343 (1966); In re American Pile Fabric Co., 85 F2d 961 (3d Cir. 1936).

estop the prior encumbrancer from asserting his priority. Thus, a subordination may unintentionally result by this estoppel route.[35]

### [b] Basic Priority Rule—"First in Time, First in Right"

"First in time, first in right" is the basic priority rule regarding interests in real estate, including mortgages. The time at which the encumbrance is recorded typically sets the priority date of that encumbrance with later encumbrances and other interests being subordinate.[36] Thus, the creation of the mortgage usually does not attain a priority for the mortgagee; rather, the mortgage must be recorded, as previously discussed.[37] Priority rules pertaining to mortgages are found in both statutory[38] and case law.[39] It should also be recalled that subordination agreements may alter the effect of such priority rules.[40] In determining priority based upon the first-in-time rule, the courts may even be forced to determine when in a particular day recordings took place, thus making fractions of a day crucial.[41] The first-in-time, first-in-right rule applies to resolving not only priority disputes between mortgages,[42] but also to disputes between a mortgagee and another form of interest or encumbrance.[43]

As to the first-in-time priority rule, one source comments that "[a] problem arises . . . when one mortgage secures many notes which have been sold to numerous persons."[44] The priority of note holders among themselves is dealt with by the various jurisdictions in three different ways. Some courts have held that each holder of a note possesses an independent mortgage with priority

---

[35] See, e.g., Byron J. Myers, Inc. v. Bradbury, 595 SW2d 724 (Mo. 1980); Mutual Life Ins. Co. of N.Y. v. Grissett, 500 F. Supp. 159 (D. Ala. 1980); Liberty Nat'l Bank & Trust Co. of Okla. City v. Kaibab Indus., Inc., 591 P2d 692 (Okla. 1978).

[36] See Debtor-Creditor Law ¶ 31.03[B][1] (Matthew Bender 1982) for discussion of this basic priority rule.

[37] See supra ¶ 8.09[1] for discussion of recordation.

[38] See, e.g., Wash. Rev. Code 65.08.070; Tex. Rev. Civ. Stat. Ann. art. 6627.

[39] See, e.g., Midland-Guardian Co. v. McElroy, 563 SW2d 752 (Ky. Ct. App. 1978); Baron v. Aiello, 319 So. 2d 198 (Fla. Dist. App. 1975); Middlebrook-Anderson Co. v. Southwest Sav. & Loan Ass'n, 18 Cal. App. 3d 1023, 96 Cal. Rptr. 338 (1971).

[40] See supra ¶ 8.09[2][a] for discussion of subordination agreements.

[41] See Kratovil, Modern Mortgage Law and Practice 153 (Prentice-Hall, Inc. 1972). Literal reading of "first in time" statutes support this point. But see Hood v. Landreth, 207 NC 621, 178 SE 222 (1935), wherein mortgages filed on same day were given *equal* priority notwithstanding fact that one was placed on index register first.

[42] See, e.g., Omaha Nat'l Bank v. Continental W. Corp., 203 Neb. 264, 278 NW2d 339 (1979); Savings & Loan Ass'n v. Berberich, 24 AD2d 187, 264 NYS2d 989 (1965).

[43] See, e.g., Giffin Indus. of Jacksonville, Inc. v. Southeastern Assoc., Inc., 357 So. 2d 217 (Fla. 1978); Robert v. First Fed. Sav. & Loan Ass'n of Manatee City, 222 So. 2d 32 (Fla. Dist. Ct. App. 1969).

[44] 7 Debtor-Creditor Law 31-41 (Matthew Bender 1982); see 59 C.J.S. Mortgages § 213 (1949).

determined in order of the maturity of the note.[45] At least one state provides that if the mortgagee sells some and retains others of the mortgaged notes, the selling mortgagee is subordinate to the other purchasers of the notes, particularly if the mortgagee has guaranteed payment.[46] Finally, some states hold that all the notes have equal priority.[47]

### [c] Purchase-Money Mortgages

A notable example of case-made priority rules is the rule according extraordinary priority to a purchase-money mortgage.[48] The purchase-money mortgage arises when a seller conveys title to property to a buyer on credit and

---

[45] Illinois, Florida, and Ohio are examples of such states. See 7 Debtor-Creditor Law 31-41 n.33 (Matthew Bender 1982); Wright v. Merdes, 98 Fla. 859, 124 So. 448 (1929); In re Lalla, 362 Ill. 621, 1 NE2d 50 (1936); Kratovil, Modern Mortgage Law and Practice 154 (Prentice-Hall, Inc. 1972).

[46] Pennsylvania is such a state. See 7 Debtor-Creditor Law 31-41 n.34 (Matthew Bender 1982); In re Phillippi, 329 Pa. 581, 198 A 16 (1938).

[47] North Carolina, Iowa, and South Carolina are such states. See 7 Debtor-Creditor Law 31-41 n.35 (Matthew Bender 1982); Sanders v. Hamilton, 233 NC 175, 63 SE2d 187 (1951); Templeton v. Stephens, 212 Iowa 1064, 233 NW 704 (1931); Hibbitt v. Charleston Heights Co., 163 SC 327, 161 SE 499 (1932).

One other priority issue involves "circuity of liens." It occasionally occurs that the "first claimant has priority over the second, the second over the third, and the third over the first." Osborne, Mortgages 366 (West, 2d ed. 1970). These circuitous lien priority problems usually arise in one of three different settings. First the circuity may result from the fault or neglect of one party to do some act that would have prevented it, normally by charging subsequent lien claimants with notice. Second, the problem of priority may arise by reason of the operation of certain rules of law independent of any element of fault or neglect by one of the parties. Finally, waiver of other agreements or rules of law creating subrogation rights in one of the claimants to another claimant's priority may create the circuitous priority problem: How will the subject property be apportioned to the various claimants, and in which order of priority? Detailed consideration of the solutions devised to resolve the circuitous priority problem is beyond the scope of this text. Many solutions have been devised placing the duty upon counsel to carefully consult applicable law when faced with such a circuity of lien problem. Discussion of various solutions can be found in many sources, including the following: Osborne, Mortgages § 209 (West, 2d ed. 1970), particularly at page 366, note 8, which includes an excellent listing of sources. The sources include Benson, "Circuity of Lien–A Problem in Priorities," 19 Minn. L. Rev. 139 (1935); Campbell, "Protection Against Indirect Attack," Harv. Legal Essays 3, 16, 20 (1934); Note, "Circuity of Liens–A Proposed Solution," 38 Colum. L. Rev. 1267 (1938); Kocourck, "A First Rate Legal Puzzle–A Problem in Priorities," 29 Ill. L. Rev. 952 (1935); White, "A Problem in Priorities," 25 Ohio L. Bull. & Rep. 116 (1926); Tucker, "The Deeds of Trust Puzzle," 1 Va. L. Reg. 4 (1895); Moon, "The Deeds of Trust Puzzle–A Reply," 1 Va. L. Reg. 254 (1895); Kellog, "Priorities Puzzle Under Ship Mortgage Act," 2 Wash. L. Rev. 117 (1927); Note, 8 Va. L. Rev. 550 (1922); Note, 15 Va. L. Rev. 90, 94 (1928); Note, 26 Yale L.J. 129, 134 (1926); Gilmore, Security Interests in Personal Property," § 39.1 (1965).

[48] For discussion of the purchase-money mortgage priority, see Osborne, Mortgages § 213 (West, 2d ed. 1970); Osborne, Nelson & Whitman, Real Estate Finance Law

receives back a promissory note and a mortgage on the sold property.[49] Similarly, if a third-party lender extends credit to enable purchase of real estate and acquires the mortgage in the purchased property, the lender has acquired a purchase-money mortgage.[50] From early on, purchase-money mortgages have been given a special "super-priority" over existing interests and encumbrances.[51] The purchase-money mortgage takes precedence over any prior or subsequent claim or lien attaching to the property through the mortgagor.[52] On the other hand, the purchase-money mortgage must be recorded to receive priority as to subsequent transfers made by the mortgagor.[53]

There are at least two priority problems regarding purchase-money mortgages. First, if a mortgagor holds title to land subject to a purchase-money mortgage and wishes to construct an improvement thereon, the construction lender will wish to have priority over the existing purchase-money mortgage. "In the absence of an explicit reversal of priorities, the law everywhere presumes that the purchase money mortgage is entitled to have priority."[54] Because national banks[55] and federal savings and loan associations[56] have been required by law, or otherwise desire to obtain first liens to secure real estate loans, and because most states apply similar requirements to state-chartered institutions, these construction lenders often will obtain subordination agreements from the prior purchase-money mortgagee.[57]

The second priority problem that may arise with regard to purchase-money mortgages is where more than one purchase-money mortgage is held on the same real estate. For example, a house may be purchased in part with a loan from a commercial lender and in part with an extension of credit from the seller. If both are given mortgages, they both will possess a purchase-money

---

§§ 9.1–9.3 (West 1979); 7 Debtor-Creditor Law ¶ 31.03[B] (Matthew Bender 1982); 59 C.J.S. Mortgages § 231 (1949); 36 Am. Jur. 2d Mortgages § 230 (1971).

[49] See, e.g., Lipps v. Lipps, 87 NE2d 823 (Ohio 1949); see Kratovil, Modern Mortgage Law and Practice 159 (Prentice-Hall, Inc. 1972).

[50] See, e.g., Crystal Ice Co. of Columbia, Inc. v. First Colonial Corp., 273 SC 306, 257 SE2d 496 (1979); County of Pinellas v. Clearwater Fed. Sav. & Loan Ass'n, 214 So. 2d 525 (Fla. Dist. Ct. App. 1968); Lipps v. Lipps, 87 NE2d 823 (Ohio 1949).

[51] See, e.g., Holbrook v. Finney, 4 Mass. 569, 3 Am. Dec. 243 (1808); Star v. Tift, 15 Johns (N.Y.) 458, 8 Am. Dec. 266 (1818); Crystal Ice Co. of Columbia, Inc. v. First Colonial Corp., 273 SC 306, 257 SE2d 496 (1979).

[52] See, e.g., Associates Discount Corp. v. Gomes, 338 So. 2d 552 (Fla. 1979); Note, "Priority of Purchase-Money Mortgages," 29 Va. L. Rev. 491 (1943).

[53] See, e.g., Royal Bank of Can. v. Clarke, 373 F. Supp. 599 (1974); see Osborne, Nelson & Whitman, Real Estate Finance Law 578–582 (West 1979); see also Osborne, Mortgages 392–393 (West, 2d ed. 1970).

[54] Nelson & Whitman, Real Estate Finance and Development 613 (West 1976); see also Osborne, Mortgages § 213 (West, 2d ed. 1970); Osborne, Nelson & Whitman, Real Estate Finance Law § 9.2 (West 1979); Cal. Civ. Code § 2898.

[55] 12 USC § 371(a) as amended October 15, 1982. It no longer requires per se *first* liens. But see 12 CFR §§ 7.2000–7.2700.

[56] 12 USC § 1464(c), as amended March 31, 1980; see 12 CFR §§ 7.2000–7.2700.

[57] See supra ¶ 8.09[2][a] for discussion of subordination agreements.

mortgage. Generally, the vendor's mortgage is given priority absent an agreement among the parties.[58] Subordination agreements would seem to supply the practical answer to this priority problem.[59] or to similar priority problems, particularly where neither of the parties is a vendor of the subject real estate.

---

[58] See Nelson & Whitman, Real Estate Finance and Development 416, at n.2 (West 1976); see also Osborne, Mortgages 393 (West, 2d ed. 1970); Osborne, Nelson & Whitman, Real Estate Finance Law § 9.2 (West 1979); Fecteau v. Fryes, 253 Mich. 51, 234 NW 113 (1931); cf. Hand Trading Co. v. Daniels, 126 Ga. App. 342, 190 SE2d 560 (1972).

[59] See supra ¶ 8.09[2][a] for a discussion of subordination agreements.

# 9

# Common-Law, Statutory, and Equitable Liens

## ¶ 9.01 DEFINITIONS OF COMMON-LAW, STATUTORY, AND EQUITABLE LIENS

### [1] Introduction

As previously discussed, it is important for a creditor to obtain liens in a debtor's assets; the creditor then is able to liquidate assets, to use the proceeds to satisfy the debt, and to obtain priority over other third-party claims to the debtor's assets.[1] Consensual methods and nonconsensual judicial methods of obtaining such liens have been explored elsewhere in the text.[2] There are other nonconsensual methods of obtaining liens that do not require the use of judicial process. These methods result in liens that are typically categorized as "common-law," "statutory," and "equitable" liens,[3] all of which are considered in this chapter. For the most part, these liens are created by state courts and legislatures. Thus, there is a great variety of these liens nationwide. Extensive coverage of the individual types of common-law, statutory, and equitable liens is beyond the scope of this text. Rather, the principles and issues common to the law that pertain to these liens are considered. Special emphasis is placed on the federal tax lien.[4]

### [2] Common-Law and Statutory Liens

The common-law lien, as its name reflects, is a creature of the courts. Originally, it was defined as the right of one person to retain possession of the property of another person until certain demands of the person in possession are satisfied.[5] In the debtor-creditor context, if a creditor has improved the property of the debtor by rendering a service or providing materials and has not been paid by the debtor, the court provides the creditor with the common-law lien as a means of coercing payment of the debt. The lien developed on a case-by-case basis, setting precedent for who could claim the lien, under what

---

[1] See, e.g., ¶¶ 6.03, 6.05.

[2] For discussion of judicial liens, see Chapter 6; for discussion of consensual UCC Article 9 security interests in personal property and fixtures, see Chapter 7; for discussion of real estate mortgages, see Chapter 8.

[3] See also ¶ 8.03[3] for discussion of the equitable mortgage in real estate.

[4] See infra ¶ 9.04.

[5] See, e.g., U.S. v. Hart, 545 F. Supp. 470 (DND 1982), aff'd, 701 F2d 749 (8th Cir. 1983); Shearer v. Bill Garlic Motors, Inc., 59 Ohio App. 2d, 394 NE2d 1014 (1977); Williamson v. Winningham, 199 Okla. 393, 186 P2d 644 (1947).

circumstance, what property can be claimed, and so on. State legislatures ultimately codified some of these common-law liens[6]—sometimes altering the nature of the lien—and went on to create additional liens that did not exist at common law.[7] These "statutory liens" have proliferated over the years in the states. Because of the close relationship between common-law and statutory liens, they are considered together in this chapter.[8]

### [3] Equitable Liens

Equitable liens are difficult to define and categorize. As its name implies, an equitable lien is a creation of the courts of equity. Although equitable liens may arise from agreements between debtors and creditors, they also may be granted by a court of equity to prevent unjust enrichment of the owner of the property in question. In general, the equitable lien is a right to have property subjected to the payment of a claim and is thus in the nature of a lien.[9] Because equitable liens cut across the categories of consensual and nonconsensual liens, they are considered separately in this chapter.[10]

## ¶ 9.02 COMMON-LAW AND STATUTORY LIENS

### [1] Creation of Possessory and Nonpossessory Common-Law and Statutory Liens

#### [a] Creation of Common-Law Liens

The common-law lien is created upon the occurrence of two conditions.[1] First, the lien claimant must be in possession of the property. Second, the lien claimant must have increased the property's value by rendering services or by providing additional materials to the property.

**[i] Possession of the Property.** The lien is created and only can continue to exist if the person claiming the lien has independent and exclusive

---

[6] See, e.g., Auto Owners Fin. Co. v. Evirs, 94 NH 180, 49 A2d 507 (1946); Grusin v. Stutz Motor Car Co. of Am., 206 Ind. 296, 187 NE 382 (1933); Olsen v. Kidman, 120 Utah 443, 235 P2d 510 (1951).

[7] See, e.g., Fox v. Seal, 89 US (22 Wall) 424 (1875).

[8] See infra ¶ 9.02. But, as to federal tax liens, see infra ¶ 9.04.

[9] See, e.g., Robinson v. Robinson, 100 Ill. App. 3d 433, 429 NEd 183 (1981); Monegan v. Pacific Nat'l Bank of Wash., 16 Wash. App. 280, 556 P2d 226 (1976); Farmers & Merchants Bank, Ceresco, Nebraska v. Comm'r, 175 F2d 846 (8th Cir. 1949).

[10] See infra ¶ 9.03.

[1] For specific and concise discussion of creation of common-law liens, see Raushenbush, Brown on Personal Property § 13.2 (Callaghan & Co., 3d ed. 1975).

possession of the property.[2] A particularly descriptive and troublesome circumstance involving the prerequisite of possession arises when an employee furnishes services that improve the property that is on the premises of his employer. If the employee is not paid for the services he renders, the question is raised as to whether he may assert a common-law lien in the subject property. Usually the employee is denied a right to assert a common-law lien because the employer possesses the personal property that is located on its premises.[3]

**[ii] Value of the Property.** The common-law lien is based on "the enhancement of the value of the property by reason of labor performed and materials provided by the lienholder."[4] There are some limitations as to the value-added requirement. For example, there are some common-law liens that are given to a worker who performs a service for the goods in his possession even though the market value of the goods has not increased.[5] On the other hand, if materials are added and the value of the principal good is increased, and if the materials are additions that retain their individual identity, the artisan is not provided a lien in the principal good.[6]

### [b] Creation of Statutory Liens

The creation of statutory liens is, of course, regulated by statute. As previously noted, statutory liens are either codifications of common-law liens[7] or are newly created liens without direct common-law lien origin.[8] If the statutory lien is a codification of a common law lien, the statute will be construed consistently with common-law principles.[9]

Specifically, in reference to the creation of the statutory lien, possessory and nonpossessory liens can be created. If possessory, the creation and continued existence of the lien rests on the possession of the property by the creditor, in addition to the satisfaction of any other prerequisite specified by the individ-

---

[2] See, e.g., Associates Fin. Servs. Co. v. O'Dell, 262 Pa. Super. 584, 396 A2d 1324, aff'd, 491 Pa. 1, 417 A2d 604 (1979); Ahlswede v. Schoneveld, 87 Nev. 449, 488 P2d 908 (Nev. 1981); Central Contractors Serv., Inc. v. Ohio County Stone Co., 255 SW2d 17 (Ky. 1953).

[3] See, e.g., Atlantic Coast Line R.R. v. Baker, 118 Ga. 809, 45 SE 673 (1903); W. Raushenbush, Brown on Personal Property 397 (Callaghan & Co., 3d ed. 1975).

[4] 6 Debtor-Creditor Law 26-13 (Matthew Bender 1982); see, e.g., Apartment Owners & Managers Comm. of State College Area Chamber of Commerce v. Brown, 252 Pa. Super. 539, rev'd, 487 Pa. 548, 410 A2d 747 (1977); Ferrante Equip. Co. v. Foley Mach. Co., 49 NJ 432, 231 A2d 208 (1967).

[5] See, e.g., U.S. v. Toys of the World Club, Inc., 288 F2d 89 (2d Cir. 1961); Philadelphia Nat'l Bank v. K&G Speed Assocs., 43 Pa. D. & C.2d 241, 4 UCC Rep. Serv. 970 (1967).

[6] See, e.g., Griggs v. Stone, 51 NJL 549, 18 A 1094 (1890).

[7] See, e.g., Olsen v. Kidman, 120 Utah 443, 235 P2d 510 (1951).

[8] See, e.g., Fox v. Seal, 89 US (22 Wall) 424 (1875).

[9] See, e.g., Fruehauf Corp. v. Huntington Moving & Storage Co., 217 SE2d 907 (W. Va. 1975); Beck v. Neutrodynamics, Inc., 77 NJ Super. 448, 186 A2d 715 (1962).

ual statute.[10] Most statutes do not require that enhancement of the property's value must have occurred.[11] Thus, for the most part, the creation of the statutory possessory lien parallels the creation of the common-law lien.

In contrast, the creation of nonpossessory statutory liens is quite different. These liens often are based upon the services rendered to a person without regard to specific property of the debtor.[12] The lien by statute may affect property of a particular type[13] or even may be a general lien that is not related to a specific property type.[14] In general, the only major prerequisite to the creation of the nonpossessory statutory lien is that a debt is due to a creditor who falls within a statutorily defined class from a debtor who falls within a statutorily defined class.[15]

## [2] Subject Matter of Common-Law and Statutory Liens

The subject matter of the common-law lien cannot be defined by property type. Rather, if one has extended credit and has possession of property of the debtor that has been enhanced in value because the creditor has rendered a service or has provided additional material, that possessed property is the subject matter of the lien, regardless of its type.[16]

The statutory lien, by contrast, has developed on a piecemeal basis nationwide, resulting in a great variety of liens with respect to their subject matter.[17] The lien generally is referred to in the statute by the name or the title of the class of the lienholder; the specific subject matter of the lien is defined within the statute.[18]

From an economic standpoint, one of the more important types of statutory liens is the mechanic's (construction) lien. Although the mechanic's lien has common-law origins, today the lien is purely statutory.[19] The term "mechanic" refers to laborers or suppliers of material who participate in con-

---

[10] See, e.g., Cal. Civ. Code § 3051.

[11] Id.

[12] See, e.g., Ill. Ann. Stat. ch. 82, §§ 97–101.

[13] See, e.g., Domingue v. Huval, 261 So. 2d 88 (La. Ct. App. 1972); Smith v. Atlantic Boat Builder Co., 356 So. 2d 359 (Fla. Dist. Ct. App. 1978) (construing Fla. Stat. Ann. § 713.60).

[14] See, e.g., Tex. Rev. Civ. Stat. Ann. art. 5506a.

[15] See, e.g., id.; N.J. Stat. Ann. §§ 2A:44-35–2A:44-46.

[16] See supra ¶ 9.02[1] and ¶ 9.02 notes 2–6.

[17] See 6 Debtor-Creditor Law § 26.03 (Matthew Bender 1982) for detailed discussion of the subject matter of specific statutory liens.

[18] Examples include liens given on animals to feed suppliers, stock breeders, and the like; on clients' causes of action given to attorneys; on crops given to crop dusters; on surveys given to engineers; to hospitals and physicians; to bankers, landlords, and the like.

[19] See, e.g., Browning v. Allied Helicopter Serv., Inc., 309 F2d 712 (10th Cir. 1962); Brann & Stuart Co. v. Consolidated Sun Ray, Inc., 433 Pa. 574, 253 A2d 105 (1969).

struction projects. These persons are given liens in the real property on which construction is occurring to secure any extension of credit related to the project made by the laborer or the supplier for which they are not paid.[20] The questions of who is given the lien, against whom the lien is assertible, the amount of the lien, and its relative priority must be resolved by careful review of applicable local law.[21]

### [3] Termination of Common-Law and Statutory Liens Before Enforcement

Common-law and statutory liens may intentionally or inadvertently be terminated before their enforcement.[22] If the creation and continued existence of the lien rests upon the creditor's possession of the property, then loss of possession terminates the lien.[23] This is true whether the property is given to the debtor or to a third party.[24] Once possession is lost, the lien cannot be subsequently restored by retaking possession.[25]

However, there are exceptions to these principles. For example, if the loss of possession was not voluntary, the lien is not terminated, and the lienor may exercise remedies of replevin or conversion against the wrongful taker.[26] Additionally, if the lienor relinquishes possession to the debtor under an agreement that the lien is to continue, the lien is not terminated between the lienor and the debtor.[27] However, if subsequent parties take interests in the property without knowledge of the lien, the lien will be subordinated.[28]

---

[20] See, e.g., Halowich v. Amminiti, 190 Pa. Super. 314, 154 A2d 406 (1959); Efficient Energy Sys., Inc. v. J. Hoyt Kniveton, Inc., 631 SW2d 538 (Tex. Civ. App. 1982); see also Goulden & Dent, "More on Mechanics Liens, Stop Notice and the Like," 54 Cal. L. Rev. 179 (1966).

[21] For a discussion of mechanic's liens, with particular application to the states of California, Florida, Illinois, Michigan, New Jersey, New York, Ohio, Pennsylvania, and Texas, see 6 Debtor-Creditor Law Ch. 25 (Matthew Bender 1982).

[22] For discussion of termination of liens, see Raushenbush, Brown on Personal Property §§ 14.3–14.9 (Callaghan & Co., 3d ed. 1975); 6 Debtor-Creditor Law ¶ 26.02[F] (Matthew Bender 1982).

[23] See, e.g., Murray v. Eisenberg, 29 Wash. App. 42, 627 P2d 146 (1981); Ahlswede v. Schoneveld, 87 Nev. 449, 488 P2d 908 (Nev. 1971); Agnew v. American Ice Co., 2 NJ 291, 66 A2d 330 (1949).

[24] See, e.g., Eastern Airlines Employees Fed. Credit Union v. Lauderdale Yacht Basin, Inc., 334 So. 2d 175 (Fla. Dist. Ct. App. 1976); Auto Owners Fin. Co. v. Evirs, 94 NH 180, 49 A2d 507 (1946).

[25] See, e.g., Martinez v. Therma-King Sales & Serv. Div. of Transport Refrigeration, 346 So. 2d 798 (La. Ct. App.), writ denied, 349 So. 2d 844 (1977); Mahomet v. Hartford Ins. Co., 3 Wash. App. 560, 477 P2d 191 (1970).

[26] See, e.g., McCafferty v. Gilbank, 249 Cal. App. 2d 569, 57 Cal. Rptr. 695 (1967); Beck v. Neutrodynamics, Inc., 77 NJ Super. 448, 186 A2d 715 (1962).

[27] See, e.g., In re Carter, 21 F2d 587 (1927); North End Auto Park v. Petringa Trucking Co., 337 Mass. 618, 150 NE2d 735 (1958).

[28] See, e.g., Lanterman v. Luby, 96 NJL 255, 114 A 325 (1921).

Possessory and nonpossessory common-law and statutory liens also are terminated when the debt is paid.[29] In other less obvious cases where a lienor refuses tender of payment, the lien is terminated.[30] However, tender must be made with "money in hand" to be effective.[31]

A common-law or statutory lien may be terminated by a waiver or estoppel.[32] Usually the waiver or estoppel is limited to loss of lien and does not preclude the creditor from suing on the debt.[33] A waiver includes situations in which the lienor expressly relinquishes a lien or does something that impliedly involves a relinquishment. Estoppel, by contrast, involves conduct by a potential lienor that impliedly precludes him from enforcing his lien.[34] Typically, waiver or estoppel occurs in those circumstances where a creditor makes a claim that is inconsistent with his right of lien[35] or makes a claim in bad faith for an excessive amount.[36] A waiver also may occur when the creditor accepts other security for the debt, although opinion is divided on whether the lien will be extinguished, with the issue often revolving around the intent of the parties.[37] Finally, if the debtor makes a demand for the property, the lien is waived if the lienor fails to assert the lien.[38]

---

[29] See, e.g., Harbour Village at Saga Bay, Inc. v. Dahm, 367 So. 2d 1100 (Fla. Dist. Ct. App. 1979); Jordan v. Manor, 593 P2d 1049 (Mont. 1979); Green v. American Nat'l Ins. Co., 452 SW2d 1 (Tex. Civ. App. 1970).

[30] See, e.g., Segars v. Classen Garage & Serv. Co., 612 P2d 293 (Okla. 1980); Power Transmission Equip. Corp. v. Beloit Corp., 55 Wis. 2d 540, 201 NW2d 13 (1972).

[31] See, e.g., Segars v. Classen Garage & Serv. Co., 612 P2d 293 (Okla. 1980); Sokol v. Harde, 247 AD 193, 286 NYS 656 (1936), aff'd, 273 NY 569, 7 NE2d 696 (1937).

[32] As to possessory liens, loss of possession is actually a form of waiver of a lien. For discussion of the effect of loss of possession, see supra this paragraph.

[33] See, e.g., Vorrath v. Garrelts, 49 Mich. App. 142, 211 NW2d 536 (1973); Sullins v. Sullins, 65 Wash. 2d 283, 396 P2d 886 (1964).

[34] For discussion of waiver and estoppel as terminating common law and statutory liens, see 6 Debtor-Creditor Law ¶¶ 26.02[F][2], 26.02[F][3], 26.02[F][6], 26.02[F][7] (Matthew Bender 1982); Raushenbush, Brown on Personal Property §§ 14.6, 14.8 (Callaghan & Co., 3d ed. 1975). As to waiver, see also Ford Motor Credit Co. v. Parsons, 155 Ga. App. 46, 270 SE2d 230 (1980); Colvis Nat'l Bank v. Thomas, 77 NM 554, 425 P2d 726 (1967). As to estoppel, see Thrifty Supply Co. of Seattle v. Deverian Builders, Inc., 3 Wash. App. 425, 475 P2d 905 (1970).

[35] See, e.g., Engler Bros. Constr. Co. v. L'Allier, 280 Minn. 208, 159 NW2d 183 (1968); Thrifty Supply Co. of Seattle, Inc. v. Deverian Builders, Inc., 3 Wash. App. 425, 475 P2d 905 (1970); Susi v. Belle Acton Stables, Inc., 360 F2d 704 (2d Cir. 1966).

[36] See, e.g., Engler Bros. Constr. Co. v. L'Allier, 280 Minn. 208, 159 NW2d 183 (1968); Power Transmission Equip. Corp. v. Beloit Corp., 55 Wis. 2d 540, 201 NW2d 13 (1972).

[37] See, e.g., Webster Drilling Co. v. Walker, 286 F2d 114 (10th Cir. 1974); Mousel v. Daringer, 190 Neb. 77, 206 NW2d 579 (1973); Blumin v. Ellis, 186 So. 2d 286 (Fla. Dist. Ct. App. 1966).

[38] See, e.g., Power Transmission Equip. Corp. v. Beloit Corp., 55 Wis. 2d 540, 201 NW2d 13 (1972); Enfield v. Huffman Motor Co., 117 Cal. App. 2d 800, 257 P2d 458 (1953).

If the lienor acquires title to the property subject to the lien, the lien merges with the greater title interest and thus is terminated. In other words, one cannot possess a lien against one's own property.[39] However, this "merger" concept may be subject to some exceptions: (1) when the intent of the parties indicates that the lien will not be terminated; (2) when the lienor's interest cannot be protected without the lien; or (3) when there are intervening liens that would subordinate the priority of the lien.[40]

The tort of conversion can overlap with the termination of common-law or statutory liens. In general, a conversion involves the unlawful exercise of dominion and control by one over the property of another.[41] If a person who claims a lien in the property of another otherwise exerts dominion and control over this property contrary to the lawful rights of its owner, the lien may be lost. This may occur where the lienor improperly uses the liened goods for his own purposes or refuses to relinquish possession upon proper demand.[42] The effect of the conversion is to estop that creditor from enforcing the lien.

Three other related situations in which a lien may be terminated should be noted. Obviously, if the property that is subject to the lien is destroyed, the lien terminates.[43] Similarly, if the property that is subject to the lien is sold by a lienor who has no right to sell the property, the lien will be lost not only in the property, but also in the proceeds of the sale.[44] Such a sale is actually a conversion of the property. Finally, liens may be extinguished by lapse of time.[45]

## [4] Enforcement of Common-Law and Statutory Liens

The common-law lien traditionally does not lead to the sale of the asset. The enforcement of the statutory lien does result in the sale of the property, either through an extrajudicial summary process or through a judicial foreclosure.

---

[39] See, e.g., Phoenix Mut. Life Ins. Co. v. Harden, 596 P2d 888 (Okla. 1979); Penn Mut. Life Ins. Co. v. Finkel, 428 Pa. 11, 235 A2d 396 (1967); Kaczenski v. Kaczenski, 118 Ohio App. 225, 193 NE2d 731 (1962).

[40] See, e.g., Gardena Valley Airport, Inc. v. All Am. Sports Enters., Inc., 230 Cal. App. 2d 478, 41 Cal. Rptr. 93 (1964); McGreevy v. Constitutional Life Ins. Co., 238 Cal. App. 2d 364, 47 Cal. Rptr. 711 (1965).

[41] See Prosser, The Law of Torts § 15 (West, 4th ed. 1971).

[42] See, e.g., Wilson Motor Co. v. Dunn, 129 Okla. 211, 264 P 194 (1928); Seaboard Air Line Ry. v. Roberds, 43 Ga. App. 558, 159 SE 742 (1931).

[43] See, e.g., U.S. v. Salerno, 222 F. Supp. 664 (D. Nev. 1963), modified on other grounds sub nom. Mutual Life Ins. Co. of N.Y. v. U.S., 343 F2d 71 (9th Cir. 1965).

[44] See, e.g., Lily Pond Lane Corp. v. Technicolor, Inc., 98 Misc. 2d 853, 414 NYS2d 596 (NY Sup. Ct. 1979); Carnegie Fin. Corp. v. Akron Nat'l Bank & Trust Co., 49 Ohio App. 2d 321, 361 NE2d 504 (1976).

[45] See, e.g., Waterways Marine, Inc. v. Brooks Liquid Transport, Inc., 291 F. Supp. 703 (1968); Mills v. Reneau, 411 P2d 516 (Okla. 1965).

Common-law liens are possessory liens of distraint.[46] The lienor has the right to retain possession of the property in question but has no power of sale.[47] If the right to force a sale is present, it is conferred by statute.[48]

For statutory or common-law liens, where provided by statute, enforcement that leads to a forced sale may be provided for the creditor through a summary extrajudicial procedure or by a judicial foreclosure. The extrajudicial procedure leading to a forced sale traditionally has been conducted in an ex parte fashion. However, a filing of notice of lien might be required, with the actual notice of sale being given to the debtor. Such notices to the debtor are usually sent by certified mail.[49] The notice usually must contain statutorily prescribed information related to the property; claim of lien; date, time, and place of sale; right of redemption; and so on.[50]

Because of the summary nature of the extrajudicial sale, there have been successful challenges to the constitutionality of these procedures. These challenges are based upon the due process clause of the Fourteenth Amendment of the U.S. Constitution, since prior notice and the opportunity for a prior judicial hearing, or both, are not provided to the debtor before a loss of property takes place.[51]

---

[46] See supra ¶¶ 9.01, 9.02[1].

[47] See, e.g. In re Southwest Restaurant Sys's, Inc. v. Stockton & Hing, 607 F2d 1243 (9th Cir. 1979); Lily Pond Lane Corp. v. Technicolor, Inc., 98 Misc. 2d 853, 414 NYS2d 596 (1979); Smyth v. Fidelity & Deposit Co. of Md., 326 Pa. 391, 192 A 640 (1937). However, there is some authority that courts of equity could enforce common-law liens. See, e.g., Perera Co. v. Goldstone, 491 F2d 386 (9th Cir. 1974) (especially by sale where the court acquired jurisdiction for other purposes); Marshall v. Wabash Ry., 201 Mich. 167, 167 NW 19 (1918).

[48] See, e.g., Swiggett v. Watson, 441 F. Supp. 254 (D. Del. 1977).

[49] See, e.g., Cal. Civ. Code § 3072.

[50] See 6 Debtor-Creditor Law ¶ 26.05[A] (Matthew Bender 1982) for specific discussion of statutorily required contents of notices.

[51] See, e.g., Mason v. Garris, 364 F. Supp. 452 (ND Ga. 1973); Parks v. "Mr. Ford," 556 F2d 132 (3d Cir. 1977); Sharrock v. Dell Buick-Cadillac, Inc., 45 NY2d 152, 408 NYS2d 39, 379 NE2d 1169 (1978). Similarly, some challenges of extrajudicial summary enforcement procedure have occurred successfully under Title 42, Section 1983, set forth below:

> "Civil action for deprivation of rights.
>
> "Every person who, under color of any statute, ordinance, regulation, custom, or usage, of any State or Territory, or the District of Columbia, subjects, or causes to be subjected, any citizen of the United States or other person within the jurisdiction thereof to the deprivation of any rights, privileges, or immunities secured by the Constitution and laws, shall be liable to the party injured in an action at law, suit in equity, or other proper proceeding for redress."

The jurisdictional counterpart to Title 42, Section 1983, is Title 28, Section 1343 (1976). It states, in relevant part:

> "Civil rights and elective franchise.
>
> "(a) The district courts shall have original jurisdiction of any civil action authorized by law to be commenced by any person:

Statutory liens and common-law liens, where provided by statute, also are enforced judicially. The action is in the nature of a foreclosure.[52] If a lien statute fails to provide for a method of enforcement, the lienor may foreclose in a court of equity.[53] Jurisdiction depends upon statutes, and, if authorized, a lien may be enforced upon a property in one jurisdiction, even though someone residing in another jurisdiction possesses an interest in it.[54] The lienor brings the action by pleading the existence of the lien and by joining all persons having interests in the property who will be affected by the foreclosure.[55] If the lienor obtains a successful judgment, it forecloses all subordinate interests, orders the property to sale, and, in some jurisdictions, may award a money judgment on the debt.[56] The sale is conducted with the proceeds first distributed to the costs and the lienor's claim, then distributed to junior interests. Any surplus is returned to the owner.[57]

## [5] Priority Rules

Beyond the satisfaction of the debt through a liened asset, the statutory or common-law lien can serve a second function for the lienor. It may be that other creditors and purchasers also are claiming interests in the debtor's property. The acquisition of a common-law or statutory lien may give the lienor priority in the property over claimants. This priority function is particularly crucial if the debtor is insolvent.[58]

When considering general priority principles the traditional treatment of common-law liens, as opposed to that of statutory liens, first must be distinguished. Common-law liens traditionally have been given priority over both

---

"(3) To redress the deprivation, under color of any State law, statute, ordinance, regulation, custom, or usage, of any right, privilege or immunity secured by the Constitution of the United States or by any Act of Congress providing for equal rights of citizens or of all persons within the jurisdiction of the United States."

[52] See, e.g., Cal. Civ. Code § 3068; Ohio Rev. Code Ann. § 1333.41; Ill. Ann. Stat. ch. 82, § 45.

[53] See, e.g., Dewing v. Davis, 117 So. 2d 747 (Fla. Dist. Ct. App. 1960); Moral Ins. Co. v. Cooksey, 285 P2d 223 (Okla. 1955).

[54] See, e.g., Equitable Life Assurance Soc'y of the U.S. v. U.S., 331 F2d 29 (1st Cir. 1964); Shuford v. Anderson, 352 F2d 755 (10th Cir. 1965), cert. denied, 383 US 935 (1966).

[55] These persons would include the debtor, title holders, junior lienors, any persons with an interest subsequent to the lienholder, assignees of the property, and heirs of the owner. See, e.g., Lenexa State Bank & Trust Co. v. Dixon, 221 Kan. 238, 559 P2d 776 (1977); J.R. Dunaway Rig & Lumber Co. v. Blessing, 274 SW2d 90 (Tex. Civ. App. 1954). Prior lienholders need not be joined, since their interest would not be affected. See, e.g., Rogers v. Gonzales, 252 Ala. 313, 40 So. 2d 858 (1949).

[56] See, e.g., Huntley v. Drummond, 226 Miss. 753, 85 So. 2d 188 (1956); Ill. Ann. Stat. ch. 82, § 45; N.Y. Lien Law § 208.

[57] See NY Lien Law § 206; see also ¶ 6.06 regarding judicial sales.

[58] See ¶ 17.06 for discussion of treatment of statutory liens under federal bankruptcy law.

existing and subsequent interests in the property.[59] As a general rule, statutory liens are subject to existing interests in the property, but they have priority over subsequent interests obtained in the property.[60] In other words, state common-law liens often have been given a "super priority," whereas state statutory liens fall within the usual priority rule of "first-in-time, first-in-right." If a federal lien is in conflict with a state lien, the priority is decided according to federal law.[61]

In a sense, setting forth the above rules begs the question. The rule of first-in-time, first-in-right is not useful unless the priority date of the lien can be pinpointed. The priority date of a lien by common law is set as the date of attachment of the lien, which is the time that the lien is created.[62] Recent statutes and case law often have required that the subsequent claimed interest have constructive or actual notice of the earlier lien before that lien will obtain a priority.[63] This notice may be given by registration, filing, or recording of the common law or statutory lien in some public place.[64] If liens are acquired on the same day, fractions of days may be considered.[65] Truly concurrent liens are given equal dignity and rank in the subject asset.[66]

## [6] Exceptions to Priority Rules

These basic priority principles are subject to at least three categories of exceptions. First, the conflicting claimants in the same property might order their priorities by subordination agreements. In essence, these agreements are contracts whereby a junior lienor is given priority over a superior interest in return for a given consideration. These contracts are binding and enforceable.[67]

---

[59] See, e.g., Whitefield Village Fire Dist. v. Bobst, 93 NH 229, 39 A2d 566 (1944); Nichelsen v. Kilbuck, 145 Ore. 203, 26 P2d 828 (1933).

[60] See, e.g., Midland Guardian Co. v. McElroy, 563 SW2d 752 (Ky. Ct. App. 1978); Conklin v. Long, 18 AD2d 246, 239 NYS2d 193 (1963).

[61] See, e.g., Bellegarde Custom Kitchens v. Select-A-Home, Inc., 385 F. Supp. 318 (SD Me. 1974); U.S. v. Bednar Motors, Inc., 219 F. Supp. 34 (DND 1963); U.S. v. Kimbell Foods, Inc., 440 US 715 (1979); U.S. v. Ray Thomas Gravel Co., 380 SW2d 576 (Tex. 1964).

[62] See, e.g., Universal C.I.T. Credit Corp. v. Borough of Paramus, 90 NJ Super. 435, 217 A2d 905 (1966); Southold Sav. Bank v. Finkelstein, 40 Misc. 2d 381, 243 NYS2d 397 (Nassau County Ct. 1963); In re Hiawatha Do It Yourself, Inc., 82 NJ Super. 399, 197 A2d 715 (1964). See supra ¶ 9.02[1] for discussion of creation of common-law and statutory liens.

[63] See, e.g., White Motor Credit Corp. v. Sapp Bros. Truck Plaza, Inc., 197 Neb. 421, 249 NW2d 489 (1977).

[64] See, e.g., Cleveland Trust Co. v. Ousley Sod Co., 351 So. 2d 58 (Fla. Dist. Ct. App. 1977); Continental Radio Co. v. Continental Bank & Trust Co., 369 SW2d 359 (Tex. Civ. App. 1963); N.Y. Lien Law, § 10.

[65] See, e.g., German Sec. Bank v. Campbell, 99 Ala. 249, 12 So. 436 (1893).

[66] See, e.g., Jones v. Howard, 99 Ga. 451, 27 SE 765 (1896).

[67] See, e.g., Vahlsing Christina Corp. v. First Nat'l Bank of Hobbs, 491 SW2d 954 (Tex. Civ. App. 1973); Collins v. Home Sav. & Loan Ass'n, 205 Cal. App. 2d 86, 22 Cal. Rptr. 817 (1962).

A second category of exceptions involves statutory provisions that alter the first-in-time, first-in-right rule of priority. However, in the absence of an applicable priority statute, the first-in-time rule applies.[68] The various state legislatures occasionally conclude that the basic rule—for certain policy reasons—should not apply. Counsel must carefully research local relevant law to determine if such a priority statute is applicable.[69] Mechanic's (construction) lien statutes are particularly likely to have special detailed priority rules that may alter the basic first-in-time, first-in-right principle.[70]

A final category of exceptions to the basic priority principle involves the intervention of equity. Usually the courts will not interfere with the operation of basic common law or statutory priority principles. On the other hand, courts of equity may interfere if they feel it is appropriate, based upon equitable principles.[71]

## ¶ 9.03 EQUITABLE LIENS

Equitable liens owe their existence to the equity courts that originally created them.[1] To a large degree, equitable liens defy definition.[2] Although disfavored in some jurisdictions,[3] they are recognized in many states.[4] The lien may arise from an express agreement, by implication from the conduct of the par-

---

[68] See, e.g., Midland-Guardian Co. v. McElroy, 563 SW2d 752 (Ky. Ct. App. 1978); City & County Sav. Bank v. Oakwood Holding Corp., 88 Misc. 2d 198, 387 NYS2d 512 (NY Sup. Ct. 1976); Smith v. Atlantic Boat Builders Co., 356 So. 2d 359 (Fla. Dist. Ct. App. 1978).

[69] See, e.g., Cal. Civ. Code § 2898; UCC § 9-310, discussed at ¶ 7.07[7].

[70] See 6 Debtor-Creditor Law ¶ 25.17 (Matthew Bender 1982) for discussion of mechanic's lien priority rules.

[71] See, e.g., Del Conte Masonry Co. v. Lewis, 16 Cal. App. 3d 678, 94 Cal. Rptr. 439 (1971); Nicolette v. Lizzoli, 124 Cal. App. 3d 361, 177 Cal. Rptr. 685 (1981); Continental Radio Co. v. Continental Bank & Trust Co., 369 SW2d 359 (Tex. Civ. App. 1963).

[1] For another source dealing with equitable liens, see 4 Pomeroy, Equity Jurisprudence Ch. 7, at 691–786 (Lawyers' Coop. Publishing Co., 5th ed. 1941). For discussion of the equitable mortgage in real estate, see ¶ 8.03[3].

[2] See, e.g., In re Donner's Estate, 364 So. 2d 742 (Fla. Dist. Ct. App. 1978); Warren Tool Co. v. Stephenson, 11 Mich. App. 274, 161 NW2d 133 (1968); Farmers & Merchants Bank v. Comm., 175 F2d 846 (8th Cir. 1949).

[3] See, e.g., Covington County Bank v. R.J. Allen & Assoc., Inc., 462 F. Supp. 413 (ND Ala. 1977); Mansfield Hardwood Lumber Co. v. Johnson, 268 F2d 317 (5th Cir. 1959). Note also that the drafters of UCC Article 9 attempted to do away with equitable liens in personal property as a remedy for creditors who do not obtain a written security agreement. See UCC § 9-203, Official Comment 5. But see In re Czebotar, 5 Bankr. 379 (Bankr. 9th Cir. 1980); Warren Tool Co. v. Stephenson, 11 Mich. App. 274, 161 NW2d 133 (1968).

[4] See, e.g., General Ins. Co. of Am.. v. Lowry, 570 F2d 120 (6th Cir. 1978); Bankers Trust Co. v. Chicago Title & Trust Co., 89 Ill. App. 3d 1014, 412 NE2d 660 (1980);

ties, or by other circumstances. The lien usually is defined as a right not recognized by law to have a fund or specific property, or its proceeds, applied to the payment of a debt or an obligation.[5] In contrast to common-law liens, equitable liens usually are nonpossessory.

In order to be given an equitable lien, a creditor must establish that there is no adequate remedy by law.[6] Once that prerequisite to equitable relief is satisfied, an equitable lien may be recognized by equity, assuming that there is a valid debt or obligation due the creditor[7] and that there is identifiable property against which the debt or obligation may be charged.[8] Finally, the court of equity must find that there is an intent that the property is to serve as security for the payment of the debt or obligation.[9]

This intention may be found in the express agreement of the parties[10] or it may be implied from their conduct and the general surrounding circumstances.[11] It will be implied particularly to avoid unjust enrichment,[12] or in situations in which the "debtor" unlawfully retains property of the "creditor."[13] The intention also may be found from the failure of the parties to properly create a lien (through express agreement) upon the equitable maxim that

---

Fort Lupton State Bank of Murata, 626 P2d 757 (Colo. Ct. App. 1981); Marshall Sav. & Loan Ass'n v. Chicago Nat'l Bank, 56 Ill. App. 2d 372, 206 NE2d 117 (1965).

[5] See, e.g., Sisco v. New Jersey Bank, 151 NJ Super. 363, 376 A2d 1287 (1977); Goldrick v. Goldrick, 99 Misc. 2d 749, 417 NYS2d 410 (1979); Morrison Flying Serv. v. Deming Nat'l Bank, 404 F2d 856 (10th Cir. 1968), cert. denied, 393 US 1020 (1969).

[6] See, e.g., In re Merts Equip. Co., 438 F. Supp. 295 (MD Ga. 1977); Northern Commercial Co. v. E.J. Hermann Co., 22 Wash. App. 963, 593 P2d 1332 (1979); Yedinak v. Yedinak, 283 Mich. 409, 175 NW2d 706 (1970).

[7] See, e.g., Hartog v. Siegler, 615 SW2d 632 (Mo. Ct. App. 1981); R.M. Shoemaker Co. v. Southeastern Pa. Economic Dev. Corp., 275 Pa. Super. 594, 419 A2d 60 (1980); Calacurcio v. Levson, 68 Ill. App. 2d 260, 215 NE2d 839 (1966).

[8] See, e.g., Spring Constr. Co., Inc. v. Harris, 562 F2d 933 (4th Cir. 1977); P.H. Broughton & Sons v. Muller & Allen Realty Co., 40 Ill. App. 3d 776, 353 NE2d 30 (1976); Oregon Mut. Ins. Co. v. Cornelison, 214 Ore. 501, 330 P2d 161 (1958).

[9] See, e.g., U.S. v. Mill Ass'n, Inc., 480 F. Supp. 3 (EDNY 1979); Young v. J.A. Young Mach. & Supply Co., 203 Okla. 595, 224 P2d 971 (1950).

[10] See, e.g., Hueg v. Sunburst Farms (Glendale) Mut. Water & Agricultural Co., 122 Ariz. 284, 594 P2d 538 (1979); Bradley v. Straus-Frank Co., 414 SW2d 504 (Tex. Civ. App. 1967).

[11] See, e.g., Ford v. Guarantee Abstract & Title Co., Inc., 220 Kan. 244, 553 P2d 254 (1976); Equitable Trust Co. v. Imbesi, 412 A2d 96 (Md. Ct. Spec. App. 1980); Frega v. Northern N.J. Mortgage Ass'n, 51 NJ Super. 331, 143 A2d 885 (NJ Super. Ct. App. Div. 1958).

[12] See, e.g., U.S. v. Harris, 480 F. Supp. 3 (EDNY 1978); Parslow v. Parslow, 47 NC App. 84, 266 SE2d 746 (1980); Blumin v. Ellis, 186 So. 2d 286 (Fla. Dist. Ct. App. 1966).

[13] See, e.g., Shipley v. Metropolitan Life Ins. Co., 25 Tenn. App. 452, 158 SW2d 739 (1942).

"equity heeds substance, not form" or upon the maxim that "equity treats as done that which ought to be done."[14]

If equity recognizes an equitable lien, it will treat the lien as an encumbrance on the subject property. In other words, the equitable lienor may seek satisfaction of the debt or obligation through the property in equity. This will occur through an equitable order to sell the property, with proceeds used to satisfy the debt.[15]

The other general function of liens—obtaining priority over third-party claims to the debtor's assets—presents peculiar problems when applied to equitable liens. This is the case because equitable liens most often do not afford third parties with actual or constructive notice. Generally, "reliance creditors," such as bona fide purchasers and consensual lienors, will be accorded priority, over equitable lienors; a "nonreliance creditor," such as a judicial lienor, will be subordinate if the equitable lien arises before its own lien.[16]

## ¶ 9.04 FEDERAL TAX LIENS

### [1] Creation of the Federal Tax Lien

The most important creditor (or, at least, the largest) is the federal government. The federal government may be either an unsecured or a secured creditor. For example, if an agency of the federal government extends credit and obtains a security interest in the personal property of the debtor, it will be treated as a secured creditor. If it fails to obtain a lien in the debtor's assets, it will be treated as an unsecured creditor. The Internal Revenue Service (IRS) is given a particularly important means of obtaining a secured status in a taxpayer's property on behalf of the federal government in order to collect taxes. Like other liens discussed in this chapter, the federal tax lien is statutory.[1]

The federal tax lien is created in the taxpayer's property[2] when "any person liable to pay any tax neglects or refuses to pay the same after demand. . . ."[3] Three conditions must precede the creation of the federal tax lien: assessment, demand, and failure to pay.

---

[14] See, e.g., American Prods. Co. v. Mangless, 287 F. Supp. 744 (ED Okla. 1974); Warren Tool Co. v. Stephenson, 11 Mich. App. 274, 161 NW2d 133 (1968); Oregon Mut. Ins. Co. v. Cornelison, 214 Ore. 501, 330 P2d 161 (1958).

[15] See, e.g., Phelps v. Higgins, 120 So. 2d 633 (Fla. Dist. Ct. App. 1960); Dasher v. Bruno, 5 Ill. App. 2d 500, 126 NE2d 404 (1955).

[16] See, e.g., IFC Collateral Corp. v. Commercial Units, Inc., 51 Wis. 2d 41, 186 NW2d 214 (1971).

[1] The federal tax lien is found principally at 26 USC §§ 6321–6323. For detailed discussion of the federal tax lien see Saltzman, IRS Practice and Procedure Chs. 14–16 and 1983 Supp. (Warren, Gorham & Lamont, Inc. 1981); Plumb, Federal Tax Liens (ALI/ABA, 3d ed. 1972).

[2] See infra ¶ 9.04[3] for discussion of the property subject to the tax lien.

[3] 26 USC § 6321.

### [a] Assessment

Assessment basically occurs by two methods. The first occurs immediately when a taxpayer files a return indicating tax liability.[4] In this case, assessment occurs by the simple notation of the acknowledged tax liability on a list in the office of the District Director of the IRS.[5] The second method of assessment is a more complicated procedure that begins when the taxpayer understates his tax liability on his return. In this case, the return first must be audited and subjected to administrative review. Usually, the assessment occurs after a notice of deficiency is sent to the taxpayer that allows him ninety days to petition for redetermination.[6] The petition is filed with the Tax Court. This action further delays assessment until a tax court judgment against the taxpayer occurs and until all appeals have been waived or otherwise exhausted.[7] Assessment then will occur by notation on a list in the office of the District Director of the IRS.[8]

### [b] Demand

Once assessment takes place, demand must occur as a second prerequisite to creation of the tax lien. Demand must occur as soon as practicable, but, in any event, within sixty days after assessment.[9] The notice given to the taxpayer must state the amount due, must make a demand for that amount, and must be left either at the dwelling or business of the taxpayer or be mailed to the taxpayer's last known address.[10] Although an official form of demand notice is not required,[11] such a form normally is used. If the demand notice is not given to each taxpayer, the tax lien cannot be created.[12]

### [c] Nonpayment

The final prerequisite to creation of the tax lien is nonpayment. If the taxpayer neglects or refuses to make payment upon the expiration of ten days after he receives the demand notice, the tax lien is created in the taxpayer's

---

[4] 26 USC § 6201(a)(1).

[5] 26 USC § 6203.

[6] 26 USC §§ 6212, 6213(a).

[7] There are situations in which assessment will not be delayed by petition with the Tax Court and appeals thereafter. This is the case where collection of the tax would be jeopardized by delay, or where there is a receivership or bankruptcy. See 26 USCA §§ 6213(a), 6851, 6861, 6871.

[8] 26 USC § 6203.

[9] 26 USC § 6303.

[10] Id.

[11] See, e.g., U.S. v. Lorson Elec. Co., 480 F2d 554 (2d Cir. 1973); Laing v. U.S., 364 F. Supp. 469, 472 n.6 (D. Vt. 1973), aff'd on other grounds, 496 F2d 853 (2d Cir. 1974), rev'd on other grounds, 423 US 161 (1976).

[12] See, e.g., Bauer v. Foley, 404 F2d 1215 (2d Cir. 1968), on rehearing, 408 F2d 1331 (2d Cir. 1969).

property *as of the date of assessment.*[13] Even though the tax lien occurs without being publicly recorded it may not be effective against some third parties in a priority dispute.[14]

### [2] Distinguishing the Federal Tax Lien From the Federal Priority Rule (Revised Statute 3466)

The federal priority rule, commonly known as Revised Statute 3466,[15] applies to every kind of debt due to the United States and gives priority to the federal government over competing creditors. It thus overlaps with the tax lien. However, Revised Statute 3466 provides the federal government only with a priority, not a lien. Furthermore, it is a priority that only applies in limited situations. As a result, it is not of great consequence, particularly as applied to tax collections.

For the priority to apply, one of these four situations must occur:

(1) The debtor is insolvent and makes a voluntary assignment of property;

(2) Property of the debtor has been attached;

(3) An act of bankruptcy has been committed;[16] or

(4) The property is the insolvent estate of a deceased or living taxpayer and a representative of the estate has been appointed.

This apparent absolute priority has been limited. For example, case law provides that administrative expenses have a priority over the federal government.[17] Choate liens (liens that are specific as to the identity of the lienor, the amount of the lien, and the property to which it attaches) that are perfected

---

[13] 26 USC § 6322.

[14] See infra ¶ 9.04[6].

[15] Revised statute 3466 is 31 USC § 3713. It is as follows:

"(a)(1) A claim of the United States Government shall be paid first when—

"(A) a person indebted to the Government is insolvent and—

"(i) the debtor without enough property to pay all debts makes a voluntary assignment of property.

"(ii) property of the debtor, if absent, is attached; or

"(iii) an act of bankruptcy is committed; or

"(B) the estate of a deceased debtor, in the custody of the executor or administrator, is not enough to pay all debts of the debtor.

"(2) This subsection does not apply to a case under Title 11.

"(b) A representative of a person or an estate (except a trustee acting under title 11) paying any part of a debt of the person or estate before paying a claim of the Government is liable to the extent of the payment for unpaid claims of the Government."

[16] Section 3 of the Bankruptcy Act of 1898 lists six acts of bankruptcy. The Bankruptcy Reform Act of 1978 does not use the concept of acts of bankruptcy.

[17] See, e.g., Bowes v. U.S., 127 NJ Eq. 132, 11 A2d 720 (1940); Martin v. Dennett, 626 P2d 473 (Utah 1981); U.S. v. Wiesburn, 48 F. Supp. 393 (ED Pa. 1943).

before the government's priority attaches also have priority over the federal governmental priority of Revised Statute 3466.[18] In addition, the priority of Revised Statute 3466, by its very terms, does not apply to a federal bankruptcy that arises under Title 11 of the United States Code.

In sum, as to the collection of taxes in particular, Revised Statute 3466 is of little consequence. This is due to the substantially more effective federal tax lien and the previously mentioned limitations placed on the federal priority.

### [3] Property Subject to the Federal Tax Lien

Assuming assessment, demand, and failure to pay taxes has taken place,[19] the tax lien reaches all property and rights to property, whether real or personal, belonging to the taxpayer.[20] The question of what constitutes the taxpayer's property is resolved by reference to applicable state law.[21] Concurrent ownership of real property provides an excellent example of how state law controls the determination of whether the taxpayer holds an interest in property that is reachable by the tax lien.[22] The same can be said for certain types of personal property that have created difficulties in determining whether they satisfy the requirements of property that can be subjected to the tax lien.[23]

---

[18] See U.S. v. Oswald & Hess Co., 225 F. Supp. 607 (WD Pa. 1964); In re Xelco Corp., 28 Wash. App. 878, 626 P2d 1013 (1981); U.S. v. Gilbert Assocs., Inc., 345 US 361 (1953).

[19] See supra ¶ 9.04[1] for discussion of assessment, demand, and failure to pay as conditions precedent to creation of the tax lien.

[20] 26 USC § 6321.

[21] See, e.g., Shaw v. U.S., 331 F2d 493 (9th Cir. 1964); U.S. v. Taylor, 254 F. Supp. 752 (ND Cal. 1966); Aquilino v. U.S., 363 US 509 (1960).

[22] See Saltzman, IRS Practice and Procedure ¶ 14.08[2][b], at 14-37–14-40 (Warren, Gorham & Lamont, Inc. 1981). Generally, the tax lien will reach the taxpayer's interest in property held as tenants in common. See Rev. Rul. 79-55, 1979-1 CB 400. The same is true as to the taxpayer's interest in a joint tenancy. See, e.g., Edwards v. U.S., 215 F. Supp. 382 (D. Kan. 1963); U.S. v. Kocher, 468 F2d 503 (2d Cir. 1972), cert. denied, 411 US 931 (1973). There is a split of authority as to tenants by the entirety. See, e.g., Cole v. Cardoza, 441 F2d 1337 (6th Cir. 1971); Payne v. U.S., 247 F2d 481, cert. denied, 355 US 923 (1975); U.S. v. Ragsdale, 206 F. Supp. 613 (WD Tenn. 1962). The ability of the tax lien to reach community property varies significantly depending upon the community-property state involved. See Babb v. Schmidt, 496 F2d 957 (9th Cir. 1974); Eaves v. U.S., 433 F2d 1296 (10th Cir. 1970); see also Saltzman, supra, at 14-39. As to partnership property, the taxpayer partner's individual interest in the partnership is subject to the tax lien but not specific partnership property. See Rev. Rul. 73-24, 1973-1 CB 602.

[23] Troublesome types of personal property interests include accounts and executory contracts, alimony, bank accounts, suits against third parties, insurance claims, lienors and franchisers, and trusts. See Saltzman, IRS Practice and Procedure ¶ 14.08[3] (Warren, Gorham & Lamont, Inc. 1981) for specific discussion and citations of primary authority.

The tax lien does not grant the government any greater rights in property than those that the taxpayer possesses.[24] Thus, if a taxpayer holds a life estate in real property, the tax lien will attach only to the life interest of the taxpayer and cannot reach the interest of the remainder if, for example, the taxpayer has died.[25] Similarly, if a taxpayer holds a lease interest in a property, the tax lien attaches only to the leasehold and terminates upon the termination of the lease.[26]

The tax lien only reaches property of the taxpayer as of the assessment date. Transfer of property before the assessment date insulates the property from the tax lien as long as the transfer is not, in effect, a fraudulent conveyance.[27] The tax lien does reach property acquired by the taxpayer after the assessment date.[28]

Almost all property is subject to the tax lien. In this regard, it attaches to literally all property of the taxpayer—state and nontax federal exemptions have no effect.[29] However, some property is exempt from administrative levy.[30] It has been asserted that the tax lien can be foreclosed upon this exempt property, even though the property cannot be subjected to levy.[31]

## [4] Termination of the Federal Tax Lien

A tax lien continues until the liability is satisfied or otherwise released, or until the lien becomes unenforceable by lapse of time.[32] The federal govern-

---

[24] See, e.g., Avco Delta Corp. Can., Ltd. v. U.S., 459 F2d 436 (7th Cir. 1972); State of N.J. v. Moriarity, 268 F. Supp. 546 (DNJ 1967); Carolina Apartment Investors "A" v. U.S., 1977-1 USTC ¶ 9262 (CD Cal. 1977).

[25] See, e.g., U.S. v. United Banks of Denver, 542 F2d 819 (9th Cir. 1976).

[26] See, e.g., Carolina Apartment Investors "A" v. U.S., 1977-1 USTC ¶ 9262 (CD Cal. 1977).

[27] See, e.g., St. Louis Union Trust Co. v. U.S., 617 F2d 1293 (8th Cir. 1980); GM Leasing Corp. v. U.S., 429 US 338 (1977).

[28] See, e.g., Rice Inv. Co. v. U.S., 625 F2d 565 (5th Cir. 1980); Texas Oil & Gas Corp. v. U.S., 466 F2d 1040 (5th Cir. 1972), cert. denied, 410 US 929 (1972). A similar issue involves the taxpayer's existing right to a future interest in real property. The tax lien does attach to the future interest and need not await the acquisition of the interest itself. See, e.g., In re Lackey, 72-2 USTC ¶ 9578 (MDNC 1972). However, if the future interest is contingent upon the occurrence of some condition precedent, the tax lien may not attach. See, e.g., In re Rosenberg's Will, 62 Misc. 2d 12, 308 NYS2d 51 (NY Sur. Ct. 1970); see also Saltzman, IRS Practice and Procedure 14-37 (Warren, Gorham & Lamont, Inc. 1981).

[29] See, e.g., Rostykus v. Rostykus, 385 F. Supp. 470 (D. Okla. 1974); U.S. v. Fidelity & Deposit Co., 214 F2d 565 (5th Cir. 1954). See also ¶ 6.07[1] for discussion of exemption law.

[30] Enforcement (by levy) of the tax lien is considered at infra ¶ 9.04[5]. The assets exempt from levy are found at 26 USC § 6334.

[31] See Saltzman, IRS Practice and Procedure 14-33 (Warren, Gorham & Lamont, Inc. 1981); Plumb, Federal Tax Lien 20–21 (ALI/ABA, 3d ed. 1972).

[32] 26 USC § 6322

ment must resort to collection within six years after the assessment of the tax, or prior to the expiration of any period agreed upon in writing by the government and the taxpayer before the expiration of six years.[33] The lien will not otherwise be vulnerable on an equitable theory of laches.[34] If, within the six-year period, the federal government reduces the tax liability to judgment, the term for collection and the lien apparently is extended indefinitely.[35] Statutes of limitation do not otherwise affect either the tax lien or a judgment obtained by the government.[36] If the government merely levies within a six-year period but fails to fully collect the tax, the issue appears unresolved as to whether the tax lien expires or continues indefinitely.[37]

The duration of the initial six-year period from the assessment date may be suspended under another provision of the Internal Revenue Code. Circumstances that suspend the running of the six-year period include the following:

(1) The property of the taxpayer is in the control of a court;
(2) Soldiers' and sailors' relief is available;
(3) The taxpayer is absent from the country for at least six months; or
(4) The government has mistakenly seized someone else's property to pay the tax.[38]

In addition, the taxpayer may waive the running of the six-year period.[39]

Within the six-year period from the date of assessment, the tax lien may be terminated under some circumstances. First, the government may release the lien. The Internal Revenue Code authorizes a release of lien in these situations: (1) when the tax has been paid; (2) when the tax claim is no longer enforceable; or (3) when a bond is furnished guaranteeing payment of the tax lien.[40] Second, partial discharge of a tax lien can occur, which frees particular items of property from the tax lien, under certain circumstances: (1) when the value of the remaining property is twice the amount of the tax liability; (2) when payment is made in an amount equal to the value of the government's interest in the released property; or (3) when the government's interest in the released

---

[33] 26 USC § 6502(a)

[34] See, e.g., U.S. v. Weintraub, 613 F2d 612 (6th Cir. 1977); U.S. v. Herman, 186 F. Supp. 98 (EDNY 1960).

[35] See, e.g., 26 USC § 6322; U.S. v. Pack, 288 F. Supp. 901 (D. Del. 1968); U.S. v. Overman, 424 F2d 1142 (9th Cir. 1970).

[36] See, e.g., U.S. v. Fidelity Philadelphia Trust Co., 459 F2d 771 (3d Cir. 1972); U.S. v. Overman, 424 F2d 1142 (9th Cir. 1970).

[37] See Saltzman, IRS Practice and Procedure ¶ 14.07 (Warren, Gorham & Lamont, Inc. 1981); see, e.g., U.S. v. Weintraub, 613 F2d 612 (6th Cir. 1979).

[38] 26 USC § 6503.

[39] See, e.g., U.S. v. Moyer, 308 F. Supp. 754 (WD Pa. 1968), aff'd, 420 F2d 375 (3d Cir. 1970), cert. denied, 400 US 819 (1970); U.S. v. Tager, 436 F. Supp. 549 (WD Mo. 1977). See also Plumb, Federal Tax Liens 49 (ALI/ABA, 3d ed. 1972).

[40] 26 USC § 6325(b).

property is valueless.[41] Additionally, the tax lien can be discharged under an agreement enabling sale of the subject property, with the tax lien attaching to the proceeds.[42] A final means of freeing property from the tax lien is by certificate of nonattachment. This may occur when a person other than the taxpayer may be injured by the attachment of the tax lien. The certificate merely clarifies that the tax lien has no effect on the property of a person who is not the delinquent taxpayer, and it usually is used to clarify confusion that arises because of a similarity in names.[43]

### [5] Enforcement of the Federal Tax Lien

There are basically two methods the government may use to enforce the tax lien: collection by administrative levy or collection through judicial proceedings. The administrative levy is the least expensive and least time-consuming method of enforcement from the government's point of view. As is the case with the creation of the tax lien,[44] levy may take place if there has been an assessment of tax due, demand for payment, and neglect or refusal to pay by the taxpayer.[45] Any levy that occurs before the occurrence of these conditions is void.[46]

A levy is simply a form of administrative seizure of the taxpayer's property. Seizure may occur by the physical taking of the property or by notice and padlocking.[47] A levy may reach all property of the taxpayer, but it is subject to some exceptions.[48] Any person in possession of the property must honor the levy or face personal liability and potential penalty.[49]

The object of the levy is to enable the government to sell the property. Generally, the sale must occur quickly and within specified time limits after proper notice has been given.[50] The taxpayer may redeem the property. For real property, redemption may occur before the sale or within 180 days thereafter.[51] For personal property, redemption may take place only before the sale.[52] The redemption price prior to the sale is the amount due plus the costs of the sale; if redemption of real estate occurs after the sale, the redemption

---

[41] Id.

[42] Reg. § 301.6325-1(b)(3).

[43] 26 USC § 6325(e); Reg. § 301.6325-1(e).

[44] See supra ¶ 9.04[1] for discussion of creation of the tax lien.

[45] 26 USC § 6331(a).

[46] See, e.g., Shapiro v. Secretary of State, 499 F2d 527 (DC Cir. 1974), aff'd, Martinez v. U.S., 669 F2d 568 (9th Cir. 1981); L.O.C. Indus., Inc. v. U.S., 423 F. Supp. 265 (MD Tenn. 1976).

[47] See, e.g., GM Leasing Corp. v. U.S., 429 US 338 (1977); Freeman v. Mayer, 253 F2d 295 (3d Cir. 1958).

[48] 26 USC § 6334.

[49] 26 USC § 6332.

[50] 26 USC § 6335. Special rules apply to perishable goods. See 26 USC § 6336.

[51] 26 USC § 6337.

[52] Id.

price is the amount paid by the purchaser plus interest at the rate of 20 percent per year.[53]

There may be circumstances in which the government prefers to pursue judicial remedies. The government may be forced to use judicial procedures if they are instituted by others and if the government believes its involvement is necessary to protect its own interests.[54] Assuming the judicial proceeding is deemed desirable by the government, one of two types of procedures usually is followed. First, the foreclosure of the tax lien may be pursued.[55] In contrast to an administrative levy, the foreclosure does serve the purpose of clarifying priorities before the sale. Alternatively, the government simply may bring an action for a judgment in the amount of the tax claim. This is done only when there is no property or at least no sufficient property on which to levy or foreclose.

## [6] Priorities

### [a] General Priority Principles

The tax lien performs the same general functions for the federal government as do liens for creditors. The tax lien enables the government to efficiently liquidate the taxpayer's property and thereby satisfy the tax claim. However, if the taxpayer is failing to pay his taxes, it is likely that he also is failing to pay other creditors. These creditors may assert interests in the taxpayer's estate. Additionally, the taxpayer may have sold property to a third party. From the government's point of view, the tax lien may serve to provide the government a priority over these third-party claimants.[56]

In general, the tax lien has priority over all third-party claimants, except those creditors who obtain "choate" liens before the federal tax lien arises[57] or those parties who are protected by the Federal Tax Lien Act of 1966.[58] The tax lien may obtain priority in some instances without the need for public filing or recordation. In other instances, filing is essential.

### [b] Filing of the Notice of Tax Lien

It should be recalled that the tax lien is created after assessment, demand, and failure to pay the tax.[59] Thus, the creation of the tax lien does not require a

---

[53] Id.

[54] See Plumb, Federal Tax Liens 250 (ALI/ABA, 3d ed. 1972).

[55] 26 USC § 7403.

[56] For two excellent treatments of tax lien priority, see Plumb, Federal Tax Liens Chs. 2–6 (ALI/ABA, 3d ed. 1972) and Saltzman, IRS Practice and Procedure Ch. 16 (Warren, Gorham & Lamont, Inc. 1981).

[57] See infra ¶ 9.04[6][b] for discussion of this priority principle.

[58] See infra ¶ 9.04[6][c] for discussion of priority principles under the Federal Tax Lien Act of 1966.

[59] See supra ¶ 9.04[1].

filing of public notice. The government will, however, file a notice of the tax lien to assure that the lien attains its maximum priority. In other words, an unfiled tax lien, at the least, is still effective between the government and the taxpayer; the filing only relates to priority.

Filing of the notice of tax lien is expressly provided for in the Internal Revenue Code.[60] For real property, the notice is filed in the office designated by state law.[61] The same is true for personal property.[62] If state law fails to properly designate a place for filing, the government is directed to file notice of the tax lien in the office of the clerk for the federal district court in the district in which the property is located.[63] The location of real property is deemed to be at its physical location.[64] The location of personal property is deemed to be at the residence of the taxpayer at the time the notice of tax lien is filed.[65] The filing is effective for a period of six years and can be extended by a refiling if the refiling is done within the one-year period ending thirty days after the expiration of the six-year period.[66]

### [c] Prior Choate Liens

As a general rule, all interests in the taxpayer's property acquired after the assessment date of the tax will be subordinate to the tax lien. This is true regardless of whether or not a notice of tax lien is filed.[67] The choate lien doctrine provides an exception to that rule, since prior choate liens may attain priority over the tax lien.[68] The choateness doctrine initially arose under Revised Statute 3466.[69] The case law thereunder defined a choate lien as a perfected lien in which the identity of the lienor, the amount of the lien, and the property to which the lien is attached have been established.[70] U.S. Supreme

---

[60] 26 USC § 6323(f).

[61] 26 USC § 6323(f)(1)(A)(i).

[62] 26 USC § 6323(f)(1)(A)(ii).

[63] 26 USC § 6323(f)(1)(B). If the property is in the District of Columbia, filing occurs in the Office of the Recorder of Deeds of the District of Columbia. 26 USC § 6323(f)(1)(C).

[64] 26 USC § 6323(f)(2)A.).

[65] 26 USC § 6323(f)(2)(B). The residence of a corporation or partnership is deemed to be the place of the principal executive office of the business. If a taxpayer has a residence outside the United States, his residence is deemed to be in the District of Columbia.

[66] 26 USC § 6323(g)(3)(A).

[67] See infra ¶ 9.04[6][c], which considers the impact of the Federal Tax Lien Act of 1966 on this general principle.

[68] See, e.g., Iowa Fair Plan v. U.S. Internal Rev. Dep't, 257 NW2d 626 (Iowa 1977); Northwestern Nat'l Ins. Co. v. William G. Wetherall, Inc., 272 Md. 642, 325 A2d 869 (1974); U.S. v. Security Trust & Sav. Bank, 340 US 47 (1950).

[69] See supra ¶ 9.04[2] for discussion of Revised Statute 3466.

[70] See, e.g., U.S. v. Jenison, 484 F. Supp. 747 (DRI 1980); Creditors Exch. Serv., Inc. v. U.S., 277 F. Supp. 885 (SD Tex. 1967); In re Rosenberg's Will, 62 Misc. 2d 12,

Court cases to date have found most liens to be inchoate,[71] although some cases have found the liens to be choate.[72] Again, if a lien is inchoate, even though it is acquired before the assessment date of the tax that ultimately gave rise to the tax lien, the inchoate lien will be subordinate to the tax lien.

### [d] The Federal Tax Lien Act of 1966

The Federal Tax Lien Act of 1966 materially alters the basic priority rules of tax liens.[73] The priority rules place great emphasis upon filing the notice of tax lien.[74] The 1966 Act sets forth basic priority rules based upon the "first-in-time, first-in-right" principle,[75] priority rules that give later-in-time claimants a "super priority,"[76] and special rules that relate to certain creditors with either "after-acquired property" security interests[77] or "future advance" security interests.[78]

**[i] Section 6323(a)—Priority for Prefiling Parties.** Section 6323(a) grants priority to certain parties whose interest is acquired after the tax lien is created but before the notice of tax lien is filed. These prefiling parties who receive priority are purchasers, holders of security, judgment lien creditors, and mechanic's lienors. To fully understand who the protected parties are and how they obtain priority, the definitional section of the 1966 Act must be carefully consulted.[79] The "purchaser" of the taxpayer's property is defined as one who has given adequate and full consideration for the interest obtained, which must be effective under local law against subsequent purchasers without actual notice.[80] The "holder of security" possesses a security interest in the taxpayer's property. This includes any interest that is acquired by contract to secure the payment or the performance of an obligation that is, in effect, perfected under local law.[81] The term "judgment lien creditor" is not defined by the 1966 Act.

---

308 NYS2d 51 (NY Sur. Ct. 1970); In re Xelco Corp., 28 Wash. App. 878, 626 P2d 1013 (1981). Cases also suggest that the creditor must have possession of specific property for the lien to be choate. See U.S. v. Gilbert Assocs., 345 US 361 (1953).

[71] See, e.g., U.S. v. Equitable Life Assurance Soc'y of the U.S., 384 US 323 (1966); U.S. v. Pioneer Ins. Co., 374 US 84 (1962); U.S. v. Scovil, 348 US 218 (1955).

[72] See, e.g., U.S. v. Harris, 249 F. Supp. 221 (WD La. 1966); U.S. v. City of New Britain, 347 US 81 (1954); U.S. v. Vermont, 377 US 351 (1964).

[73] The principal section of the Internal Revenue Code affected by the Federal Tax Lien Act of 1966 is 26 USC § 6323.

[74] 26 USC § 6323(f). Filing of the notice of tax lien was discussed at supra ¶ 9.04[6][a].

[75] 26 USC § 6323(a).

[76] 26 USC § 6323(b).

[77] 26 USC § 6323(c).

[78] 26 USC § 6323(d).

[79] 26 USC § 6323(h).

[80] Note that "purchaser" includes a lessee of property. 26 USC § 6323(h)(6)(A).

[81] 26 USC § 6323(h)(1). For example, see supra ¶ 7.06 for a discussion of perfection of a UCC Article 9 security interest.

However, it appears that a judgment lien creditor includes a person who has obtained a valid judgment in a court of record and of competent jurisdiction for the recovery of specific property or a sum of money and who has obtained some form of judicial lien.[82] Finally, a "mechanic's lienor" is any person who, under local law, has a lien on real property for services, labor, or materials furnished in connection with the construction or improvement of the property.[83] If any of these interests are obtained in the taxpayer's property before the notice of tax lien is filed, the party holding the interest obtains priority over the tax lien.

**[ii] Section 6323(b)—"Super Priority" Rules.** Section 6323(b) sets forth "super priority" rules. These rules grant a priority over the tax lien to a party who attains an interest in the taxpayer's property after notice of the tax lien is filed. There are ten super priority classes. Most of them involve casual, everyday transactions of small amounts in situations in which the conflicting claimant should not be expected to check for filed tax liens. A typical example is the purchaser of tangible personal property at retail. Such purchasers take free of a federal tax lien even though it is filed against the retailer.[84] Most of the super priorities are lost, however, if the conflicting claimant has actual notice or knowledge of the existence of the tax lien.

**[iii] Sections 6323(c), 6323(d)—Security Interests in After-Acquired Property and Future Advances.** Sections 6323(c) and 6323(d) relate primarily to Uniform Commercial Code (UCC) Article 9 security interests in after-acquired property (the floating lien) and future advances. Article 9 security interests are often floating liens,[85] in that security agreements commonly contain after-acquired property clauses providing, for example, that the debt is secured by all of the debtor's inventory, now owned or thereafter acquired. Similarly, future advance clauses are common, providing, for example, that the collateral secures all the debtor's debts to the secured party whenever they are incurred.

Section 6323(c) governs the priority of a secured party for property acquired by the taxpayer after the federal tax lien is filed. Basically, the secured party attains priority if:

(1) It obtained and perfected its security interest before the federal tax lien was filed;
(2) The collateral is commercial financing security (accounts, chattel paper, or inventory, not equipment);[86] and
(3) The property is acquired within forty-five days of the federal tax lien filing.

---

[82] Reg. § 301.6323(h)-1(g).

[83] 26 USC § 6323(h)(2).

[84] 26 USC § 6323(b)(3).

[85] See supra ¶¶ 7.04[b][v], 7.06 [3][c][ix] for discussion of UCC Article 9 floating liens.

[86] See 26 USC § 6323(c)(2). The priority rule can also involve "real property construction or improvement financing" agreements. See 26 USC § 6323(c)(3).

Sections 6323(c) and 6323(d) both apply to future advances made after the notice of the federal tax lien is filed. The future advance will attain priority over the federal tax lien if the secured party has obtained and perfected its security interest before the federal tax lien is filed and if the extension of credit occurred within forty-five days of the federal tax lien filing or before the creditor obtained knowledge of the federal tax lien filing, whichever occurs first. The future advance priority is not limited to "commercial financing security."

One might question whether the choate lien doctrine[87] has any remaining effect, in light of the Federal Tax Lien Act of 1966. The authorities to date disagree about the answer to that question.[88] Arguably, to the extent of Section 6323 does not apply, the choate lien doctrine is still applicable.[89]

### [e] Priority in a Bankruptcy of the Taxpayer

In a bankruptcy case, it is often crucial that a creditor hold a secured claim in the bankrupt's assets. This is the case, since the secured claimant normally will be able to satisfy the claim due the claimant directly from the asset without sharing the asset with other creditors.[90] From the federal government's point of view, the tax lien could be crucial to its success in collecting the tax within the taxpayer's bankruptcy. However, because such tax liens historically have consumed the bankrupt estate through tax lien priority,[91] the Bankruptcy Code subordinates the tax lien to other secured claims and five other classes of unsecured claims.[92] On the other hand, most taxes are not dischargeable in bankruptcy, thus enabling the federal government to seek to collect taxes after the bankruptcy.[93]

---

[87] See supra ¶ 9.04[6][b].

[88] See, e.g., Texas Oil & Gas Corp. v. U.S., 466 F2d 1040 (5th Cir. 1972), cert. denied, 410 US 929 (1973); Donald v. Madison Indus., Inc., 483 F2d 837 (10th Cir. 1973).

[89] See Saltzman, IRS Practice and Procedure 16-8 (Warren, Gorham & Lamont, Inc. 1981). But see Plumb, Federal Tax Liens 100–108 (ALI/ABA, 3d ed. 1971). See also U.S. v. Globe, 113 Ariz. 44, 546 P2d 11 (1976); Note, "The Continuing Use of Choateness in Determining Priority of Tax Liens," 12 Tex. Tech L. Rev. 959 (1981).

[90] See infra ¶¶ 13.05, 15.10, and Chapter 17 for detailed discussion of the treatment of secured claims in bankruptcy.

[91] See Weinstein, The Bankruptcy Law of 1938, 144–145 (1938).

[92] 11 USC § 724(b). The five unsecured claims include administrative expenses; claims that arose in the period between the filing of an involuntary petition in bankruptcy and the granting of an order for relief; wage claimants to a limited amount; unpaid contributions to employee benefit plans to a limited amount; and certain consumer deposits made for the purchase, lease, or rental of property or services, limited in amount. See 11 USC §§ 503, 507, 726. See Chapter 15 for discussion of priorities in distribution in bankruptcy.

[93] 11 USC § 523(a)(1). See ¶ 16.06[2][a] for discussion of discharge of tax claims in bankruptcy.

# IV

# FEDERAL BANKRUPTCY

# 10

# Bankruptcy as a Method of Dealing With Insolvency



## ¶ 10.01 HISTORICAL DEVELOPMENT OF BANKRUPTCY LAW IN THE UNITED STATES

Far from being a recent innovation, bankruptcy as a method for dealing with the problem of insolvent debtors has been known since biblical times as a means for the forgiveness or discharge of debts. In the United States, bankruptcy as a method of dealing with insolvent debtors has been legally recognized since early enactments of some colonial states.

In large part, our system of bankruptcy (and much of our common law) has its roots in the English legal system. When the U.S. Constitution was adopted, bankruptcy was recognized by Article 1, Section 8, Clause 4, which granted to Congress the power "to establish . . . uniform law on the subject of bankruptcies throughout the United States." It was not until 1800, however, that the first Bankruptcy Act was enacted by the Federalists. It was later repealed by the Jeffersonian Republicans in 1803.[1] During most of the existence of the United States, there has been a federal bankruptcy law, although there have been short periods when no federal bankruptcy legislation was in effect. Since 1898, however, there has been continuous federal bankruptcy legislation. From 1898 until 1978, the Bankruptcy Act of 1898 (the 1898 Act)[2] was the basic federal bankruptcy legislation. A major amendment to the 1898 Act was made by the Chandler Act in 1938,[3] and several less extensive amendments were subsequently made to the 1898 Act. In general, however, until 1978, the basic structure of American bankruptcy was established by the 1898 Act. In 1978, the Bankruptcy Reform Act[4] was passed. Although it borrowed heavily from the 1898 Act and the Chandler Act, the Bankruptcy Reform Act made extensive and far-reaching changes in the structure and detail of federal bankruptcy.

This chapter focuses on the development and the general outline of federal bankruptcy as it exists today as a method of dealing with insolvent debtors. As is discussed, insolvency as it has been traditionally defined—either the equity definition of "inability to pay debts as they mature" or the bankruptcy "balance sheet" definition that requires liabilities to be greater than assets—is not necessarily involved or required in every case under the Bankruptcy Reform Act.

## ¶ 10.02 CHARACTERISTICS OF BANKRUPTCY

### [1] Bankruptcy as a Federal System for Dealing With Insolvency

Bankruptcy is a federal system for dealing with problems of insolvency and is regulated by federal statutes. In part, these statutes provide a procedural system or framework for dealing with insolvency. To a large extent, they incorporate substantive rights of creditors and debtors created or existing under state or other nonbankruptcy law. The state-law rights of creditors (for example, the rights of secured creditors) and the rights of debtors are respected to a large extent in federal bankruptcy statutes. In addition, federal bankruptcy law does more than provide a procedural system for dealing with insolvency, it creates many substantive rights not provided for by state law. For example, the trustee in bankruptcy is given very broad avoiding powers to upset certain transfers, fraudulent conveyances, and preferences that occur shortly before bankruptcy. These rights may not be available under nonbankruptcy law. The debtor also is given broad power to discharge debts, claim certain exemptions, avoid certain transactions, and reduce and extend payment of debts. Generally speaking, states are free to regulate and to make provisions with respect to such

---

[1] Hanna & MacLachlan, Cases & Materials on Creditors' Rights and Corporate Reorganization 291 (Foundation Press, 5th ed. 1957).

[2] Act of July 1, 1898, ch. 541, § 40, 30 Stat. 544.

[3] Act of June 22, 1938, ch. 575, 52 Stat. 840.

[4] Pub. L. No. 95-598, 92 Stat. 2549 (1978).

matters as execution, garnishment, attachment, execution and sheriff's sales, liens on personal and real property, receiverships, and assignments for the benefit of creditors. To the extent that state insolvency laws are "bankruptcy laws," however, they are superseded by the supremacy of the federal bankruptcy law. The line between permissible state insolvency laws and nonpermissible bankruptcy laws is hazy nonetheless.[1] Occasionally, questions still arise about whether or not a state enactment is a bankruptcy law.[2]

### [2] "Fresh Start" for the Debtor Through Discharging Debts

Today bankruptcy has several prominent features. The first and most prominent is the idea that bankruptcy is designed to give a debtor a "fresh start." This is accomplished in large part by discharging most, if not all, of the debts and claims against the debtor that exist when the petition in bankruptcy is filed and by permitting the debtor to begin a new life unencumbered by old debts. There are occasions, however, when a debtor will not be granted a discharge because of certain misconduct or wrongdoing, which for assorted reasons of policy has been determined to be conduct that justifies barring a discharge.[3] Even though a discharge may be granted, certain debts or claims against the debtor-bankrupt may not be discharged for policy reasons because of misconduct on the part of the debtor or the nature of the claim.[4] The nature of the discharge may vary, depending upon whether a Chapter 7, 11, or 13 bankruptcy proceeding is used, and whether the debtor is an individual or another entity.[5]

### [3] Equality of Distribution

A second prominent feature of bankruptcy is the concept of "equality of distribution." In general, the assets of the debtor that are available for distribution to creditors are shared or distributed equally or pro rata, at least to the general creditors. This generality that all creditors share equally overstates the reality of bankruptcy, since certain creditors for policy reasons are given priority in payment; in other words, some creditors are more equal than others.[6]

---

[1] See, e.g., Mayer v. Hellman, 91 US 496 (1875); Boese v. King, 108 US 379 (1883); International Shoe Co. v. Pinkus, 278 US 261 (1929); Stellwagen v. Clum, 245 US 605 (1918); Pobreslo v. Joseph M. Boyd Co., 287 US 518 (1933); Johnson v. Star, 287 US 527 (1933); see also MacLachlan, Handbook of the Law of Bankruptcy 22 (West 1956); Comment, "Effect of National Bankruptcy Act on State Insolvency Statutes," 49 Yale L.J. 1090 (1940).

[2] See, e.g., Carlson's For Music, Inc. v. Gould, 176 Colo. 172, 489 P2d 1038 (1971).

[3] For discussion of the grounds for denial of discharge, see ¶ 15.04.

[4] For discussion of nondischargeable debts, see ¶ 15.07.

[5] See generally Chapter 15 and infra ¶ 10.04[3].

[6] Even between general unsecured creditors, there may not be equality or a pro rata distribution because of the priority distribution scheme established by the Bank-

The statement is generally true, however, if limited to general creditors and creditors whose claims fall in the same class with respect to priority of distribution. The general rule also overstates the case if viewed from the perspective of a general unsecured creditor vis-à-vis a creditor whose claim is secured by an interest that will withstand attack by the trustee in bankruptcy; the ultimate amount received by two such creditors (each with the same claim amount) is not on the basis of equality with respect to the amount of their claim. Creditors with valid security for their claims generally receive at least the value of their secured claim (and perhaps a pro rata distributive share on any unsecured portion), while general unsecured creditors frequently receive something less through their pro rata distribution. Furthermore, in Chapter 11 and 13 cases creditors do not necessarily share equally, depending upon the terms of the confirmed plan, although creditors within the same class of claims generally must be treated equally.

## [4] Trustee's Avoiding Power

A third prominent feature of bankruptcy is the avoiding power given to the trustee.[7] Under various sections of the Bankruptcy Code (the Code), the trustee is given the power to set aside or avoid and recover for the debtor's estate certain prepetition payments, transfers, fraudulent conveyances, preferences, certain security interests, and liens.[8] These provisions are designed in part to reclaim for the debtor's estate property that may have been fraudulently conveyed by the debtor and to make this property available to creditors generally. These provisions also are designed to assist in assuring that some property can be made available for general distribution. They permit the recovery for distribution to creditors of last-minute "grabbing" of property by creditors or of preferential transfers made to creditors by the debtor on the eve of or shortly before formal bankruptcy proceedings. Without these avoiding powers, if left undisturbed, the last-minute grabbing of property by creditors or the preferring of creditors might leave little to be distributed to other general creditors, and would enable some creditors to receive more than their fair share.[9]

## [5] The Automatic Stay

A fourth important characteristic of bankruptcy is that generally all of the debtor's property that is owned when the petition in bankruptcy is filed (and in some limited circumstances, property acquired after the petition is filed)

---

ruptcy Code. Some claims have been determined to be deserving of payment in full before other claims receive anything. See ¶ 14.09.

[7] In a Chapter 11 case these avoiding powers may be exercised by the debtor in possession if there is no trustee; in a Chapter 13 proceeding, they may be exercised by the debtor to a limited extent. See ¶¶ 16.01[1], 17.06.

[8] In some limited circumstances transfers made by the debtor after the filing of the petition may also be recovered. See ¶ 16.10.

[9] For discussion of these avoiding powers, see generally Chapter 16.

becomes part of the debtor's estate.[10] With the filing of the petition in bankruptcy, the debtor and the debtor's estate are given the protection of an "automatic stay" against practically all creditor collection activity.[11] For individual debtors, certain property may be claimed as exempt, either under the federal bankruptcy exemptions or under applicable state exemptions, and in effect does not become a part of the debtor's estate.[12]

## ¶ 10.03 THE BANKRUPTCY REFORM ACT OF 1978: THE CURRENT BANKRUPTCY CODE

### [1] Legislative History

The Bankruptcy Reform Act was the result of what has been called a "model legislative process"[1] as well as one "filled with controversy and intrigue,"[2] extending over more than a decade.

Although from time to time since 1898 Congress had revised or amended the 1898 Act, most notably in the Chandler Act of 1938,[3] the prime forces that gave momentum to the reform movement appeared in the 1960s. Professor Frank R. Kennedy identified three significant forces that played a major role in the push for reform in the 1960s.[4] One of these was the National Bankruptcy Conference, which had a long-standing concern for a restructuring of the bankruptcy court system, bankruptcy administration, and other bankruptcy matters. A second group that played a very prominent role consisted of the referees in bankruptcy; later, in the early 1970s they came to be called bankruptcy judges. Along with other matters, the bankruptcy judges were concerned with the problems of discharge, the quality of the fresh start for consumer bankrupts,

---

[10] For discussion of property of the debtor's estate, see Chapter 13.

[11] This automatic stay applies in cases under Chapters 7, 11, and 13. For discussion of the automatic stay, see ¶ 12.05.

[12] For discussion of exemptions, see ¶ 13.07.

[1] Kennedy, "Forward: A Brief History of the Bankruptcy Reform Act," 58 N.C.L. Rev. 667, 669 (1980). However, it is clear that despite the model "process," many persons and groups do not view the resulting Bankruptcy Code as a model bankruptcy bill and this view may be held without denigrating the outstanding work, study, thought, and accomplishment that the Code represents. It seems inevitable that with the many competing viewpoints, the differing values and policies involved, and the necessary compromises, that many would not find it to be the ideal or model bill. Many who have come into contact or been exposed to the Code, although generally satisfied with the result, can perceive its shortcomings and are critical of some of its portions. Perhaps this is indicative of the Code's overall strength and of the fact that no particular viewpoint, value, or approach completely dominated the result.

[2] See Klee, "Legislative History of the New Bankruptcy Law," 2 Appendix, Collier on Bankruptcy vi (Matthew Bender, 15th ed. 1981) (hereafter cited as Klee).

[3] See supra ¶ 10.01 note 3.

[4] Kennedy, "Forward: A Brief History of the Bankruptcy Reform Act," 58 N.C.L. Rev. 667, 669 (1980) (hereafter cited as Kennedy).

and enhancement of the status and quality of the bankruptcy court.[5] A third prominent force was provided by a task force of the Brookings Institution, which focused particularly on the operation and effectiveness of consumer bankruptcy.[6] Many other factors undoubtedly played a role in the push for reform, including changes and developments in commercial legislation such as the Uniform Commercial Code (UCC), the great expansion in consumer use of credit, the administrative problems encountered under the existing 1898 Act, and the increased number of bankruptcies.

In 1968 Congress began hearings to determine whether there was a need for a study of the bankruptcy laws.[7] Two years later it established a Commission on Bankruptcy Laws to "study, analyze, evaluate, and recommend change in the bankruptcy laws in the light of 'technical, financial, and commercial' developments of the last twenty years and more."[8] After extensive study, in July 1973 the Commission issued its report, which included a proposed draft of a new bankruptcy act.[9] The proposed draft contained many changes and proposed, "the creation of a new executive agency, the United States Bankruptcy Administration, to perform most of the nonjudicial functions of the bankruptcy process."[10] This Bankruptcy Commission report is an important part of the formal legislative history of the 1978 Bankruptcy Reform Act.[11]

The Commission's proposed bankruptcy act subsequently was introduced in both houses of Congress.[12] The National Conference of Bankruptcy Judges opposed significant portions of the Commission bill, however. In 1974 the National Conference introduced its own bill in Congress, which came to be known as the "judges' bill." The judges' bill followed the Commission bill in many respects but rejected the proposed creation of a U.S. Bankruptcy Administration and the projected role of the bankruptcy judges, private trustees, private counsel, and the Securities and Exchange Commission (SEC), and proposed a structure much closer to the existing system.[13]

---

[5] Kennedy at 669.

[6] The work of the Brookings Institution resulted in its report published in 1971, Stanley & Girth, "Bankruptcy: Problem, Process, Reform" (Brookings Institution 1971).

[7] Kennedy at 671.

[8] Id.

[9] Communication from the Executive Director, Commission on the Bankruptcy Laws of the United States Transmitting a Report of the Commission on the Bankruptcy Laws of the United States, H.R. Doc. No. 137, Parts I, II, III, 93d Cong., 1st Sess. (July 1973) (hereafter cited as the Commission Report).

[10] Kennedy at 673.

[11] The Commission Report is reprinted in 2 Appendix, Collier on Bankruptcy (Matthew Bender, 15th ed. 1981).

[12] Kennedy at 673. It was introduced in the House by Representatives Edwards and Wiggins in 1973 and in the Senate by Senator Burdick.

[13] See id; see also Lee, "A Critical Comparison of the Commission's Bill and the Judges' Bill for the Amendment of the Bankruptcy Act," 49 Am. Bankr. L.J. 1 (1975).

During the following years, both the Commission bill and the judges' bill were considered by subcommittees of both the House and the Senate, resulting in an extensive record of hearings, witnesses, and statements.[14]

In January, 1977 a new bill was introduced in the House. This House bill (H.R. 6) was the work of the Subcommittee on Civil and Constitutional Rights of the House Judiciary Committee and represented ideas from the Commission bill, the judges' bill, and other hearings and meetings.[15] Although the House bill basically adopted the approach of the Commission,[16] Professor Kennedy has pointed out that it departed from the Commission proposal in two important respects:

> (1) H.R. 6 proposed the denomination of the bankruptcy courts as Article III courts, with judges having tenure during good behavior, and (2) H.R. 6 did not adopt the Commission's recommendation for the establishment of the United States Bankruptcy Administration but did propose the establishment of a new office of the United States trustee in the executive branch to perform certain administrative functions but with a substantially more limited role than the Commission's proposed United States Bankruptcy Administration.[17]

The proposal to create an Article III bankruptcy court encountered strong opposition from the Judicial Conference of the United States and was one of the significant areas in which the House and Senate had great difficulty in reaching an agreement.[18]

A new version of a bankruptcy bill (H.R. 8200) was passed by the House on February 1, 1978.[19] A new version of a Senate bankruptcy bill (S. 2266), introduced by Senator DeConcini on October 31, 1977, was passed by the Sen-

---

[14] Professor Kennedy, Executive Director of the Bankruptcy Commission, stated:

> "The Bankruptcy Judges' bill followed the Commission's bill in most respects but significantly departed from it in rejecting the proposed creation of the United States Bankruptcy Administration and the Commission's projections of the future role of bankruptcy judges, private trustees, private counsel, the Securities and Exchange Commission. The judges' version proposed a structure and allocation of functions much closer to those of the then existing Bankruptcy Act than did the Commission's bill."

Kennedy at 673. However, the constitutionality of both the judges' bill and the Commission's bill was questioned because of their failure to give the judges life tenure. See Klee at ix.

[15] Klee at x.

[16] See Kennedy at 675.

[17] Id.

[18] See Klee at xii. At one point, the Danielson-Railsback Amendment was offered to eliminate the Article III status of bankruptcy judges and to make them adjuncts of the district courts as under the 1898 Act. Klee at xv. The amendment was passed by the House but later deleted. Id. at xvi–xvii.

[19] See Klee at xvii. H.R. 8200 had evolved from H.R. 6. Klee at xi.

ate on September 7, 1978.[20] There were more than 300 differences between these two bills, including such areas as exemptions, reaffirmation of discharged debts, and the treatment of public companies in reorganization cases. The two bills differed on the question of the status of the bankruptcy court. The House bill provided for an independent Article III bankruptcy court in which judges would have tenure during good behavior and administration of cases supervised by U.S. Trustees. The Senate bill provided for a bankruptcy court as an adjunct to the district court in which the bankruptcy judges would be appointed for a term of twelve years and without provisions for U.S. Trustees.[21] During the period between September 7 and October 6, 1978, extensive efforts were made to resolve the differences between the two bills.[22] The final version of this negotiation process passed in both the House and the Senate on October 6, 1978. In the bill that was finally enacted, the Senate's bill "largely prevailed with respect to the structure of the court, but the Senate managers deferred to the House with respect to most other matters."[23] Despite opposition to the bill in its final form by the Chief Justice, the SEC, the consumer credit industry, and other interests,[24] the bill was signed by President Carter on November 6, 1978, the last day on which the bill could be signed into law.[25] The Bankruptcy Reform Act generally became effective on October 1, 1979, with deferral of the effective date of some provisions until April 1, 1984.[26]

---

[20] See Kennedy at 676; Klee at xix.

[21] See Kennedy at 675–676; Klee at xix–xx.

[22] Professor Kennedy points out that the conventional method of resolving differences in bills—a conference committee—was not used. Kennedy at 675–677. Klee states that it was apparent that a conference committee would not be fruitful. Klee at xxi. However, a final version was developed between the House and Senate managers of the two bills, with the staff members of the two subcommittees heavily involved in the process and with various special interest groups playing an active part. See Kennedy at 676–677. Professor Kennedy also points out that certain changes and additions to what became the enacted legislation did not merely represent a reconciliation of diverse views in the two bills but were in effect last-minute additions.

[23] Kennedy at 677; see also Klee at xxiv. Because the House version was more closely followed in the final bill, Professor Kennedy suggests that House Report No. 595, 95th Cong., 1st Sess. (1977), which accompanied H.R. 8200, is more useful than the Senate Report, although both are an important part of the legislative history. Reprints of these two reports are found in 2 Appendix, Collier on Bankruptcy (Matthew Bender, 15th ed. 1981), which also contains the statements of Congressman Edwards and Senator DeConcini explaining the final bill when it was introduced. These statements are particularly important with respect to changes and additions made during the negotiating period.

[24] See Kennedy at 677.

[25] See Klee at xxv. Klee also has important comments on the very complicated legislative history and how it can best be used. See Klee at xxv–xxix.

[26] As discussed in Chapter 11, as a result of the *Marathon* case and the constitutional crisis resulting from it, this transition period, pending resolution of the stalemate resulting from *Marathon*, was extended on several occasions and finally expired on June 27, 1984. As discussed in Chapter 12, as a result of the *Marathon* decision, significant

## [2] Organization

The Bankruptcy Reform Act contains four titles.[27] Title I codified and enacted the "substantive" bankruptcy provisions as Title 11 of the U.S. Code. Section 101 of the Bankruptcy Reform Act, for example, became Section 101 of Title 11 of the U.S. Code. Title 11 of the U.S. Code thus contains the "substantive law" applicable to all bankruptcy cases begun after September 30, 1979.[28] Title II of the Bankruptcy Reform Act contains a series of amendments to Title 28 of the U.S. Code that establishes the bankruptcy courts and grants them jurisdiction, with venue and removal provisions.[29] Title II also has sections that define the appellate route, provide for staff, and describe other integral portions of the bankruptcy system.[30] Title III amends other federal laws to conform to provisions in the Bankruptcy Reform Act. Title IV repeals the Bankruptcy Act of 1898 and contains effective-date provisions.[31]

Title I of the Bankruptcy Code (Title 11 of the U.S. Code) is divided into Chapters 1, 3, 5, 7, 9, 11, 13, and 15. The counterpart of "straight bankruptcy" under the 1898 Bankruptcy Act is now Chapter 7 (liquidation) under the Code. The "chapter proceedings" under the 1898 Act (that is, old Chapters X, XI, and XII) are now consolidated under Chapter 11 (reorganization) of the Code; old Chapter XIII (wage-earner plans) is now Chapter 13 (adjustment of debts of an individual with regular income). Chapter 9 of the Code covers the adjustment of debts of a municipality.

A bankruptcy case is filed under either Chapter 7, 9, 11, or 13, with certain provisions made for conversion of a case from one chapter to another. The provisions of Chapter 1 (general provisions; the "100 series" of sections), Chapter 3 (case administration; the "300 series" of sections), Chapter 5 (creditors, the debtor and the estate; the "500 series" of sections) apply generally to all Chapter 7, 11, and 13 cases.[32] Thus, for "straight" (liquidation) proceedings,

---

amendments to the Bankruptcy Reform Act were made by the Bankruptcy Amendments and Federal Judgeship Act of 1984, Pub. L. No. 98-353.

[27] Pub. L. No. 95-598, 92 Stat. 2549.

[28] The 1898 Act continued to apply to all cases commenced before October 1, 1979.

[29] As discussed in Chapter 11, many of these original provisions were significantly changed by the 1984 Amendments.

[30] The appellate procedure was substantially changed by the 1984 Amendments. See ¶¶ 11.03[3], 11.03[4].

[31] Title IV originally contained provisions and rules for the governance of the bankruptcy system during a period of transition until implementation of the new court system established by the Bankruptcy Reform Act and provisions for a study during the transition to determine the number of bankruptcy judges needed under the new system. As noted above, as a result of the *Marathon* decision this transition period was extended on several occasions and the bankruptcy court system originally envisioned by the Bankruptcy Reform Act never came into existence. In its place the 1984 Bankruptcy Amendments established a significantly different bankruptcy court system. For detailed discussion, see Chapter 11.

[32] See 11 USC § 103(a).

Chapters 1 through 7 are applicable. Chapter 7 provisions (i.e., the "700 series" of sections) apply only in Chapter 7 proceedings, Chapter 13 provisions (the "1300 series" of sections) apply only in Chapter 13 cases, and Chapter 11 provisions generally apply only in Chapter 11 cases (although some provisions of Chapter 11 apply in Chapter 9 cases).[33]

Chapter 3 of the Code deals with the administration of a case. The chapter is subdivided into four subchapters. Subchapter I deals with the commencement of the case; Subchapter II is concerned with the officers, their eligibility, their agents, and compensation; Subchapter III deals with administration; and Subchapter IV deals with various administrative powers. The three subchapters of Chapter 5 are concerned with the creditors and their claims, the debtor's duties and benefits, and the estate, including provisions covering the gathering or marshalling of assets. Chapter 7 deals with the liquidation process, including the general administration by the trustee (the focus of Subchapter I), and collection and distribution of the estate (covered in Subchapter II). Subchapters III and IV of Chapter 7 contain special provisions for stockbrokers and commodity-broker liquidations.

As is the case with many codes and statutory systems, important sections of the Code contain definitions that must be examined carefully. For example, many important terms are defined in Sections 101 and 102. In addition, in some other sections of the Code, certain terms are defined for the limited purposes of a particular section.[34]

## ¶ 10.04 TYPES OF BANKRUPTCY CASES UNDER THE BANKRUPTCY CODE

Although the Code provides for four types of bankruptcy cases, only Chapters 7, 11, and 13 are commonly used.[1]

---

[33] See 11 USC § 103.

[34] See, e.g., 11 USC § 547(a). (Unless otherwise specified in the text, "Section" refers to a section of the Bankruptcy Code.) Another important feature of the Bankruptcy Code is Section 102, which gives several rules of construction to be applied in use of the Code. Of particular note is the rule given in Section 102(1), which in effect defines "after notice and a hearing" as meaning

> "after such notice as is appropriate in the particular circumstances, and such opportunity for a hearing as is appropriate in the particular circumstances; but authorizes an act without an actual hearing if such notice is given properly and if (i) such a hearing is not requested timely by a party in interest; or (ii) there is insufficient time for a hearing to be commenced before such act must be done, and the court authorizes such act."

Thus, "after notice and a hearing" requires a hearing only if a party in interest timely requests a hearing after notice.

[1] Chapter 9, which covers adjustment of debts of a municipality, is rarely used.

### [1] Straight Bankruptcy: Liquidation Under Chapter 7

Chapter 7 cases differ significantly from cases under either Chapter 11 or 13. Chapter 7 contemplates that there will be a liquidation of the debtor's nonexempt property and, after liquidation, a distribution of the assets of estate under the distribution scheme established by the Code.[2] Generally, for a creditor to participate in the distribution of the Chapter 7 estate, proof of claim must be filed in a timely manner.[3] Chapters 11 and 13 do not contemplate liquidation of the debtor's estate; rather, they contemplate that a plan for repayment will be worked out and that the plan will be confirmed by the bankruptcy court.[4] Frequently, such plans provide for payment of only a portion of debts and extend the payment over a period of time, although there is broad flexibility in devising a plan under both Chapters 11 and 13. With some minor exceptions, Chapter 7 generally is available to all debtors–individuals, corporations, partnerships, and other entities. With some exceptions, Chapter 7 may be voluntary (i.e., invoked by the debtor who files a petition) or involuntary (invoked by an appropriate number of creditors that force the debtor into liquidation under Chapter 7).[5] Shortly after the petition is filed, in a involuntary case (or after the order for relief in an involuntary case), a meeting of creditors is required to be held,[6] at which the debtor must appear and submit to examination under oath.[7] A Chapter 7 trustee is appointed or elected to marshall, liquidate, and distribute the estate,[8] and is given broad avoiding powers.[9] With the filing of the petition, all property the debtor owns when the petition is filed (and some property the debtor acquires after the petition is filed) becomes a part of the debtor's estate and must be turned over to the trustee.[10] Individual debtors are entitled to certain property exemptions provided by the federal bankruptcy exemption or applicable state exemptions.[11] In addition, the Chapter 7 trustee may be permitted to assume, assign, or reject certain executory contracts and leases.[12]

In a Chapter 7 case, an individual debtor (but not a corporation or partnership) may obtain a general discharge of prepetition debts (and some very limited postpetition debts).[13] However, a discharge may be denied for certain

---

[2] See generally Chapter 14.

[3] See discussion at ¶¶ 14.03, 14.04.

[4] A Chapter 11 plan may be a plan for liquidation. See infra ¶ 10.04[3].

[5] For a discussion of eligibility and voluntary and involuntary petitions, see ¶ 12.03.

[6] For a discussion of the meeting of creditors, see ¶ 12.06.

[7] 11 USC § 343; see discussion at ¶ 12.06[1].

[8] For a discussion of selection of the trustee, see ¶ 12.06[2].

[9] See generally Chapter 16.

[10] 11 USC § 541. For a discussion of the property of the estate and turnover of property of the estate, see ¶¶ 13.04, 13.05.

[11] 11 USC § 522. For a discussion of exemptions, see ¶ 13.07.

[12] 11 USC § 365; see ¶ 13.09.

[13] For a discussion of discharge, see Chapter 15.

stated grounds,[14] and even though a discharge is granted, certain debts may be nondischargeable; they may be excepted from the effect of the discharge.[15] Certain restrictions and limitations are placed on reaffirmation by the debtor of dischargeable debts.[16]

With the filing of the petition under Chapter 7, the debtor and the debtor's estate are given protection by an automatic stay from practically all creditor collection activity.[17] The Chapter 7 debtor is also protected under Section 366 from termination of services by a utility solely on the basis of the commencement of the bankruptcy case or because a debt owed by the debtor to the utility for service rendered before the order for relief was not paid when due. A utility may refuse service, however, if the debtor does not provide adequate assurance of payment for future services within twenty days after the order for relief.[18] Furthermore, the debtor is protected from governmental discrimination based solely on the fact that the debtor has invoked bankruptcy or has discharged debts in bankruptcy[19] and from similar discrimination by private employers with respect to employment.[20]

The end result of most Chapter 7 cases is a "fresh start" for the debtor. This is particularly true for an individual debtor who obtains a discharge and who has few or no nondischargeable debts. However, an individual debtor generally comes out of a Chapter 7 case with only exempt property and future earning capacity to begin his new life.

### [2] Adjustment of Debts of an Individual With Regular Income Under Chapter 13

Chapter 13 is designed to provide an individual debtor with an alternative to liquidation under Chapter 7. Chapter 13 cases differ significantly from Chapter 7 cases. Chapter 13 is not designed for the liquidation of the debtor's nonexempt property; rather, it envisions that a plan of repayment of creditors will be approved under which creditors will be paid out of the debtor's regular income.[21] In part, the theory behind Chapter 13 is that under such a plan creditors frequently receive more than they would have received in a Chapter 7 liquidation. To encourage the use of Chapter 13, in some circumstances the debtor may obtain a broader discharge in a Chapter 13 proceeding than he would obtain under Chapter 7.[22]

---

[14] See ¶ 15.04.

[15] See ¶ 15.07.

[16] See discussion at ¶ 15.08.

[17] For a discussion of the automatic stay, see ¶ 12.05.

[18] For a discussion of Section 366, see ¶ 15.03.

[19] 11 USC § 525(a); see discussion at ¶ 15.03.

[20] 11 USC § 525(b); see discussion at ¶ 15.03.

[21] Chapter 13 cases are discussed in detail in Chapter 17.

[22] See discussion of the Chapter 13 discharge at ¶¶ 17.01[2], 17.12.

Frequently the plan is a composition plan, which provides for payment of only a certain percentage on the debts, with payments to be made over an extended period, generally not exceeding three years. The plan also may provide for full payment of the creditors' claims over an extended period. Unlike Chapter 7, Chapter 13 may be used only by an individual or an individual and spouse (joint petitions are permitted) and may only be a voluntary proceeding.[23] Corporations and partnerships may not use Chapter 13, although an individual who is in business (but not a partnership) may use it if his debt does not exceed the debt limit for eligibility for Chapter 13.[24] As in a Chapter 7 case, the debtor and the debtor's estate are given the protection of the automatic stay from practically all creditor collection activity as soon as the Chapter 13 petition is filed.[25] In addition, certain codebtors of the Chapter 13 debtor are given limited protection from creditor collection activity.[26] The Chapter 13 debtor is also protected under Section 366 from termination of services by a utility solely on the basis of the commencement of the bankruptcy case or because a debt owed by the debtor to the utility for service rendered before the order for relief was not paid when due. However, a utility may refuse service if the debtor does not provide adequate assurance of payment for future services within twenty days after the order for relief.[27] Furthermore, the debtor is protected from governmental discrimination based solely on the fact that the debtor has invoked bankruptcy or has discharged debts in bankruptcy[28] and from similar discrimination by private employers with respect to employment.[29]

Shortly after the petition is filed, a meeting of creditors is required to be held[30] at which the debtor must appear and submit to examination under oath.[31]

Unlike the Chapter 7 debtor, the Chapter 13 debtor remains in possession of his property, even though it has become a property of the estate.[32] Also, unlike the Chapter 7 estate, the Chapter 13 estate includes the postpetition earnings from services of the debtor during the operation of the plan.[33] These earnings usually are the source of the debtor's payments under the plan. Funding of a Chapter 13 plan is not limited to the debtor's wages or earnings; it also

---

[23] For discussion of commencement of the case, see ¶ 17.03.

[24] To be eligible for Chapter 13, an individual's (or an individual and spouse's) unsecured debt must be less than $100,000 and the secured debts must be less than $350,000. 11 USC § 109(e). For additional discussion, see ¶ 17.02.

[25] 11 USC § 362. For discussion of the automatic stay, see ¶ 12.05.

[26] See ¶ 17.07[1].

[27] For a discussion of Section 366, see ¶ 15.03.

[28] 11 USC § 525(a); see discussion at ¶ 15.03.

[29] 11 USC § 525(b); see discussion at ¶ 15.03.

[30] For a discussion of the meeting of creditors, see ¶ 12.06.

[31] 11 USC § 343; see discussion at ¶ 12.06[1].

[32] 11 USC § 1306(b).

[33] 11 USC § 1306(a); see discussion at ¶ 17.04. By making the postpetition earnings or wages of the debtor property of the estate, these earnings are protected by the automatic stay from creditor collection activity while they are being used to make payments under the plan.

may come from other regular income.[34] A debtor "engaged in business" (as defined in Section 1304(a)) may continue to operate the business unless the court orders otherwise,[35] and under certain circumstances may use, sell, or lease property of the estate.[36]

Unlike a Chapter 7 trustee, the Chapter 13 trustee generally is not concerned with marshalling the assets of the estate and exercising his avoiding powers. Chapter 13 trustees generally function as collecting and disbursing agents, receiving the payments made by the debtor and disbursing the funds under the terms of the confirmed plan.[37]

In a Chapter 13 case only the debtor may propose a plan. Creditor acceptance is not required for confirmation; only the approval and confirmation of the bankruptcy court is required.[38] For a plan to be confirmed, certain statutory requirements must be met, but additional optional provisions may be included in a plan.[39] These requirements and optional provisions afford great flexibility in tailoring the plan to meet the needs of a particular debtor. There are several basic requirements for confirmation:

(1) The debtor must have a regular income to fund the plan;[40]

(2) Under the plan, general unsecured creditors must not receive less than they would receive in a liquidation under Chapter 7;[41]

(3) The plan must be feasible;[42]

(4) The plan must be proposed in good faith;[43]

(5) Payments under the plan cannot exceed three years without court approval and may in no event exceed five years;[44]

(6) Priority claims must be paid in full under the plan, although payment may be made by deferred cash payments;[45] and

(7) Fees and other charges must be paid.[46]

---

[34] See discussion at ¶ 17.02.

[35] 11 USC § 1304(b).

[36] See discussion at ¶ 17.06.

[37] For discussion of the Chapter 13 trustee, see ¶ 17.05. Frequently, there is a "standing" Chapter 13 trustee who serves as trustee for all Chapter 13 cases.

[38] This is in contrast to Chapter 11. Under Chapter 11, after an exclusive period within which only the debtor may propose a plan, any party in interest may file a plan. Generally, in a Chapter 11 case certain creditor approval is required in addition to confirmation by the court. See discussion at infra ¶ 10.04[3].

[39] See discussion at ¶¶ 17.08, 17.09. For example, certain executory contracts and leases may be rejected or assumed in the plan. See ¶ 17.08[2][e].

[40] See discussion at ¶ 17.02.

[41] This is the "best-interests-of-creditors" requirement. See discussion at ¶ 17.09[5].

[42] See discussion at ¶ 17.09[7].

[43] See discussion at ¶ 17.09[4].

[44] See ¶ 17.09[8].

[45] 11 USC § 1322(a)(2); see discussion at ¶ 17.08[1].

[46] See discussion at ¶ 17.09[3].

Confirmation of a plan binds the debtor and each creditor, regardless of whether a claim is provided for by the plan or whether a creditor has objected to, accepted, or rejected the plan.[47] Confirmation vests all property of the estate in the debtor, except as otherwise provided for in the plan or the order confirming the plan.[48]

A plan may be modified at any time after confirmation to change the amount of payments and to extend or reduce the payment period. However, the modified plan must meet the requirements for confirmation; for example, it must meet the "best-interests-of-creditors" test.[49]

Generally, for creditors' claims to be allowed under the plan, proof of claim must be timely filed.[50]

Upon completion of the payments under the confirmed plan, the Chapter 13 debtor is entitled to a discharge.[51] In certain circumstances, even though the debtor does not complete payments under the plan, a more limited "hardship" discharge may be obtained.[52] In some circumstances, a discharge obtained by completing payments under a Chapter 13 plan discharges debts that could not have been discharged in a Chapter 7 case.[53] Certain restrictions and limitations are placed on the debtor's reaffirmation of dischargeable debts.[54]

Because of its flexibility and broader discharge provisions, Chapter 13 is an attractive alternative to Chapter 7 for individuals. Under the terms of the confirmed plan, however, the debtor may have to survive on a restricted budget.

## [3] Reorganization Under Chapter 11

The reorganization provisions of the 1898 Bankruptcy Act were contained in Chapters X, XI, and XII. Each chapter had somewhat different characteristics and was designed for different or specialized types of business reorganization. The Bankruptcy Reform Act of 1978 consolidated all types of reorganization other than Chapter 13 cases for the adjustment of debts of an individual[55] under one type of case under Chapter 11.[56] The reorganization provisions of

---

[47] 11 USC § 1327(a); see discussion at ¶ 17.09[1].

[48] Id.

[49] 11 USC § 1329(c). For discussion of modification of the plan, see ¶ 17.10.

[50] See ¶ 17.04[1].

[51] For detailed discussion of the Chapter 13 discharge, see ¶ 17.12.

[52] See discussion at ¶ 17.12[2].

[53] For discussion of advantages and disadvantages of Chapter 13 vis-à-vis Chapter 7, see ¶ 17.01[2].

[54] See ¶ 15.08.

[55] See supra ¶ 10.04[2].

[56] In addition, the Code contains a Chapter 9 proceeding for adjustment of debts of a municipality. Chapter 11 also contains special provisions in Subchapter IV for railroad reorganization; Chapter 7 contains special provisions in Subchapter III for liquidation of stockbrokers and in Subchapter IV for commodity-broker liquidations.

Chapter 11 are much more complex than those of Chapter 13, and for an individual who is eligible for a Chapter 13 case, Chapter 13 normally is a more attractive option. For an eligible individual, Chapter 13 normally is less expensive and complicated. Frequently, confirmation of the Chapter 13 plan may be obtained more readily and with less expense than in a Chapter 11 case, which generally requires at least some creditor approval in addition to court approval and confirmation. Chapter 13 only requires court approval and confirmation of a repayment plan.[57] Because of the limitations on the amount of debt that can be owed by a debtor using Chapter 13, however, it may not be available for many individuals who are engaged in business.[58]

In describing reorganization under the 1898 Act, the House Report accompanying the bill that eventually became a part of the Bankruptcy Reform Act stated the purpose of business reorganization in these terms:

> The purpose of a business reorganization case, unlike a liquidation case, is to restructure a business's finances so that it may continue to operate, provide its employees with jobs, pay its creditors, and produce a return for its stockholders. The premise of a business reorganization is that assets that are used for production in the industry for which they were designed are more valuable than those same assets sold for scrap. Often, the return on assets that a business can produce is inadequate to compensate those who have invested in the business. Cash flow problems may develop, and require creditors of the business, both trade creditors and long-term lenders, to wait for payment of their claims. If the business can extend or reduce its debts, it often can be returned to a viable state. It is more economically efficient to reorganize than to liquidate, because it preserves jobs and assets.
>
> Most business arrangements, that is, extensions or compositions (reduction) of debts, occur out-of-court. The out-of-court procedure, sometimes known as a common law composition, is quick and inexpensive. However, it requires near universal agreement of the business's creditors, and is limited in the relief it can provide for an over-extended business. When an out-of-court arrangement is inadequate to rehabilitate a business, the bankruptcy laws provide an alternative. An arrangement or reorganization accomplished under the Bankruptcy Act binds nonconsenting creditors, and permits more substantial restructuring of a debtor's finances than does an out-of-court work-out.
>
> The procedure under the Bankruptcy Act is relatively simple in its bare outlines, and the basic principles are the same for all rehabilitation chapters of the Bankruptcy Act. When a petition is filed, all creditor actions against the debtor are stayed. The stay gives the debtor the opportunity to bring all of its creditors together for discussion, explanation of the debtor's financial problems, and negotiation. Creditors are prevented from acting

---

[57] For detailed discussion of Chapter 13 and some of its advantages, see generally Chapter 17.

[58] For discussion of these limitations, see ¶ 17.02.

unilaterally to gain an advantage over other creditors or to pressure the debtor into action.

An initial question in a reorganization case is whether the management of the debtor should be left in possession to operate the business, or whether an independent trustee, representing the creditors' and equity security holders' interests, should be appointed to replace the management. If a trustee is appointed, the management is completely ousted, although occasionally a trustee hires former management to handle day-to-day operations. The trustee is put completely in control of the business. If a trustee is not appointed, then business continues as usual, subject, however, to court supervision over the debtor's actions.

The purpose of the reorganization or arrangement case is to formulate and have confirmed a plan of reorganization or arrangement for the debtor. The plan determines how much creditors will be paid, and in what form (cash, property, or securities, for example); whether the stockholders will continue to retain any interest in the company; and in what form the business will continue (without several unprofitable divisions, for example).

In addition to certain other requirements, the Bankruptcy Act requires that the plan be accepted by a certain percentage of affected creditors and stockholders before it may be confirmed and put into operation. The consent requirement necessitates negotiation among management, creditors and stockholders. Negotiation is usually accomplished through committees. The result of the negotiations, the plan, is sent to all affected creditors and stockholders for consent. If they agree, and if all of the other requirements of the law are met, the court confirms the plan, and the debtor comes out of the case as a reorganized company.

During the progress of the case, the business of the debtor continues to operate. The trustee, or if the debtor remains in possession, the debtor, does what is necessary to reduce the business' losses, by selling unprofitable divisions, by closing certain plants or stores, by reducing the workforces, or by rejecting or renegotiating burdensome contracts. The debtor is relieved during the case from having to pay its prepetition debts. The additional cash flow thus freed is used to meet current operating expenses.[59]

In contrast to Chapter 13, Chapter 11 is primarily designed for more complex business reorganizations but is flexible enough to accommodate both relatively simple and extremely complicated reorganizations. Reorganization under Chapter 11 is not restricted to corporations, partnerships, and businesses, however; it may be used by individuals as well.[60] As is the case with Chapter 7 cases, Chapter 11 cases may be voluntary or involuntary.[61]

---

[59] H.R. Rep. No. 595, 95th Cong., 1st Sess. 220–221 (1977). Reorganization under the new consolidated Chapter 11 generally follows the description given in the report.

[60] For discussion of eligibility under the various chapters, see ¶ 12.03.

[61] 11 USC §§ 109, 301, 303. For discussion of voluntary and involuntary cases, see ¶ 12.03.

Generally, Chapter 11 is designed to permit a debtor to work out a plan for dealing with creditors while being afforded protection from creditor collection activity, lawsuits, and foreclosure on property. It contemplates that the business of the debtor generally will be continued. A Chapter 11 plan, however, may provide for the liquidation of the debtor.[62] One of the assumptions underlying Chapter 11 is that if the debtor is afforded a "breathing spell," with protection from creditors, to negotiate and work out arrangements with creditors and other claimants (perhaps by extending the time of payments on debts, reducing the amount to be paid, or both), then creditors, other claimants, and perhaps the equity security holders of the debtor ultimately may receive more than would be received if the debtor were liquidated in a Chapter 7 proceeding. To afford the debtor an opportunity to work out an arrangement with creditors, the Chapter 11 debtor who files a petition in bankruptcy[63] is given the protection of an automatic stay against practically all creditor collection activity, foreclosure proceedings and lawsuits.[64] Within a relatively short period after the Chapter 11 petition is filed, a meeting of creditors is required to be held[65] at which the debtor must appear and submit to examination under oath.[66]

As soon as possible after the order for relief,[67] the court must appoint a creditors' committee, which ordinarily consists of the seven largest unsecured creditors or unsecured members of a committee organized before the commencement of the case if that committee was fairly chosen and is representative of the different kinds of claims to be represented.[68] Based upon a request of a party in interest, the court may appoint additional committees of creditors or equity security holders if necessary to assure that they are adequately represented.[69] The debtor in possession (or the trustee) and the creditors' committee, with court approval, may employ attorneys, accountants, and other professional persons to assist and to represent them.[70]

In a Chapter 11 case a trustee is not appointed as a matter of course (unlike a Chapter 7 case) and the debtor as "debtor in possession," subject to

---

[62] See generally Anderson & Wright, "Liquidating Plans of Reorganization," 56 Am. Bankr. L.J. 29 (1982).

[63] For discussion of commencement of the case, see generally Chapter 12.

[64] With the filing of the petition under Chapter 11, the debtor is protected from practically all creditor collection activity by the automatic stay of Section 362. For a discussion of the automatic stay, see ¶ 12.05. In some circumstances, creditors may obtain relief from the automatic stay. See ¶ 12.05[4].

[65] For discussion of the meeting of creditors, see ¶ 12.06.

[66] 11 USC § 343; see discussion at ¶ 12.06[1].

[67] For a discussion of the order for relief, see ¶ 12.01[1].

[68] 11 USC §§ 1102(a)(1), 1102(b)(2).

[69] 11 USC § 1102(a)(2). In districts with a U.S. trustee, the trustee appoints the various creditors' committees. 11 USC § 151102.

[70] 11 USC §§ 1107, 327, 1103.

restriction by the court, generally has the rights and powers of a trustee.[71] If a trustee is appointed at any time before the plan is confirmed, the court may terminate the trustee's appointment on the request of a party in interest and restore the debtor in possession to management and operation of the debtor's business.[72] Unless the court orders otherwise, the debtor in possession may operate the debtor's business.[73] In the course of the operation of the business, the debtor in possession (or the trustee, if one is appointed) may use, sell, or lease property of the debtor's estate (including collateral of a secured creditor), subject to the conditions and restrictions stated in Section 363,[74] and may obtain credit under the restrictions stated in Section 364.[75] The debtor in possession or the trustee also is protected under Section 366 from termination of services by a utility solely on the basis of the commencement of the bankruptcy case or because a debt owed by the debtor to the utility for service rendered before the order for relief was not paid when due. A utility may refuse service, however, if the debtor in possession or the trustee does not provide adequate assurance of payment for future services within twenty days after the order of relief.[76] Furthermore, the debtor is protected from governmental discrimination based solely on the fact that the debtor has invoked bankruptcy or has discharged debts in bankruptcy[77] and from similar discrimination by private employers with respect to employment.[78]

Although in some instances a debtor may file a Chapter 11 petition solely to delay and obtain the benefit of the automatic stay, with no intent of filing or proposing a plan or little realistic expectation that a plan can be confirmed, the ultimate goal for the Chapter 11 debtor is to obtain approval and confirmation of a plan for dealing with creditors and other claimants. Initially, during the first 120 days after the order for relief,[79] the debtor is given the exclusive right

---

[71] 11 USC § 1107(a). The debtor in possession does not have the trustee's duties, stated in Sections 1106(a)(2), 1106(a)(3), 1106(a)(4). 11 USC § 1107(a). Under certain conditions, the court may appoint a trustee (11 USC § 1104(a)), and in appropriate circumstances where a trustee has not been appointed, may appoint an examiner to conduct an investigation of the debtor with respect to fraud, dishonesty, incompetence, misconduct, mismanagement, or irregularity in the management of the affairs of the debtor and to investigate the desirability of continuance of the debtor's business. The examiner is required to file a report of the investigation. 11 USC §§ 1104(b), 1106(b). In a district with a U.S. trustee, the U.S. trustee appoints the trustee or examiner, subject to court approval. See 11 USC § 151104. For discussion of the U.S. trustee, see ¶ 13.02[3].

[72] 11 USC § 1105.

[73] 11 USC §§ 1107(a), 1108.

[74] See discussion at ¶ 13.11.

[75] Id.

[76] For a discussion of Section 366, see ¶ 15.03.

[77] 11 USC § 525(a); see discussion at ¶ 15.03.

[78] 11 USC § 525(b); see discussion at ¶ 15.03.

[79] For a discussion of the order for relief, see ¶ 12.01[1].

to file a plan.[80] If a trustee has been appointed, the debtor has not filed a plan within the 120-day period, or the debtor has filed a plan within the 120 days that has not been accepted by each of the impaired classes of claims or interests within 180 days after the order for relief, then any party in interest may file a plan.[81] Thus, after the exclusive period, more than one plan may be filed, although only one plan may be confirmed.[82] On request of a party in interest made within the respective periods, the court for cause may reduce or increase the 120- or 180-day period.[83] On request of a party in interest and after notice and a hearing, the court may dismiss the Chapter 11 case or convert it to a Chapter 7 case for cause, including failure to file or propose a plan in a timely manner or denial of confirmation of all proposed plans.[84]

Section 1123 states detailed mandatory requirements for the contents of a plan as well as optional provisions that a plan may contain. Within these mandatory and optional provisions there is great flexibility in fashioning a plan to meet the circumstances of a particular debtor. Other sections contain details about the acceptance of the plan and the requirements for confirmation of the plan by the court.[85] In general, a plan must designate classes of claims and classes of interests, such as priority claims, secured claims, unsecured claims, and equity interests, and must indicate whether each class of claims or interests is impaired or unimpaired by the plan.[86] In a plan, a particular class may contain only substantially similar claims or interests.[87] For administrative convenience, however, a plan may create a separate class for small unsecured claims.[88] The plan also must "provide the same treatment for each claim or interest of a particular class, unless the holder of a particular claim or interest agrees to a less favorable treatment of such particular claim or interest."[89] A plan may

---

[80] 11 USC § 1121(b).

[81] 11 USC § 1121(c). A "party in interest" includes the debtor, the trustee, a creditors' committee, an equity security holders' committee, a creditor, an equity security holder, and an indenture trustee.

[82] 11 USC § 1129(c).

[83] 11 USC § 1121(d).

[84] 11 USC §§ 1112(b)(2), 1112(b)(4), 1112(b)(5).

[85] See 11 USC §§ 1126 (acceptance of the plan), 1128 (confirmation hearing), and 1129 (confirmation of the plan).

[86] 11 USC §§ 1123(a)(1)–1123(a)(3). The determination of whether a claim or interest is impaired is made under the provisions of Section 1124. In general, under Section 1124(1) a claim or interest is unimpaired if the plan "leaves unaltered the legal, equitable, and contractual rights" of the claim or interest. See also Sections 1124(2) through 1124(3) for additional conditions under which a claim will not be considered impaired.

[87] 11 USC § 1122(a). For example, secured and unsecured claims may not be placed in the same class, nor may interests (e.g., those of stockholders) be placed in a class with creditors.

[88] 11 USC § 1122(b).

[89] 11 USC § 1123(a)(4).

impair or leave unimpaired any class of claims, secured or unsecured, or class of interests.[90]

Generally, in order to be confirmed, the plan must be proposed in good faith;[91] in addition to other requirements,[92] each class of claims or interests must have accepted the plan or be a class that is not impaired by the plan.[93] In some circumstances, under the so-called cram-down provisions of Section 1129(b), a plan may be confirmed without acceptance by each impaired class if the relatively restrictive and detailed conditions of that section are met. Even under the cram-down provisions, however, if a class of claims is impaired under the plan, at least one class of impaired claims must accept the plan.[94] In addition, for confirmation, each holder of a claim or interest who is in an impaired class must either accept the plan or receive or retain under the plan property whose value on the effective date of the plan is not less than the amount the holder would have received in a Chapter 7 liquidation on the effective date of the plan.[95]

---

[90] 11 USC § 1123(b)(1). This means that properly designated classes do not necessarily have to be treated equally, although significant differences in treatment of different classes may affect the ability to obtain the required acceptance of all classes. Subject to the provisions of Section 365, the plan also may provide for the assumption, rejection, or assignment of executory contracts and leases that have not previously been rejected. 11 USC § 1123(b)(2). For a discussion of assumption and rejection of executory contracts and leases, see ¶ 13.09. For rejection of collective bargaining agreements in Chapter 11 cases, see Section 1113 as amended by 1984 Amendments § 541; see also ¶ 13.09[9]. For a discussion of the changes made by the 1984 Amendments for rejection of collective bargaining agreements, see Gibson, "The New Law on Rejection of Collective Bargaining Agreements in Chapter 11: An Analysis of 11 U.S.C. § 1113," 58 Am. Bankr. L.J. 325 (1984).

[91] 11 USC § 1129(a)(3).

[92] See 11 USC § 1129.

[93] 11 USC § 1129(a)(8). Acceptance of a plan by a class of claims generally requires that the holders of at least two thirds in amount and more than one half in number of the allowed claims in the class accept the plan. 11 USC § 1126(c). Acceptance by a class of interests requires acceptance by the holders of at least two thirds in amount of the allowed interests in the class. 11 USC § 1126(d). A class that is unimpaired (and each holder of a claim or interest in that class) is conclusively presumed to have accepted the plan. 11 USC § 1126(f). For details with respect to solicitation and the disclosure statement required for postpetition solicitation of acceptance of the plan, see Section 1125. For details on prepetition solicitation of acceptances, see Section 1126(b).

[94] 11 USC § 1129(a)(10). For discussion of these provisions, see generally Klee, "All You Ever Wanted to Know About Cram Down Under the New Bankruptcy Code," 53 Am. Bankr. L.J. 133 (1979); Pachulski, "The Cram Down and Valuation Under Chapter 11 of the Bankruptcy Code," 58 N.C.L. Rev. 925 (1981); Miller, "Bankruptcy Code Cramdown Under Chapter 11: New Threat to Shareholder Interests," 62 B.U.L. Rev. 1059 (1983); Epling, "Cramdown Under the Bankruptcy Code of 1978: Effect Upon the Soft Collateral Lender," 12 Loy. U. Chi. L.J. 627 (1982); Comment, "From Debtor's Shield to Creditor's Sword: Cram Down Under the Chandler Act and the Bankruptcy Reform Act," 55 Chi.-Kent. L. Rev. 713 (1979).

[95] 11 USC § 1129(a)(7).

For confirmation, the plan must provide that the holders of priority administrative claims under Section 507(a)(1) and certain "involuntary gap" claims specified in Section 507(a)(2) will be paid in cash on the effective date of the plan.[96] Certain other priority claims may receive somewhat different treatment and may in some circumstances be given deferred cash payments whose value on the effective date of the plan is equal to the allowed amount of the claims.[97] To confirm a plan, the court also must determine that the plan is feasible; that is, that "confirmation of the plan is not likely to be followed by the liquidation, or the need for further financial reorganization, of the debtor or any successor to the debtor under the plan, unless such liquidation or reorganization is proposed in the plan."[98]

If a plan is confirmed,

> the provisions of a confirmed plan bind the debtor, any entity issuing securities under the plan, any entity acquiring property under the plan, and any creditor, equity security holder of, or general partner in, the debtor, whether or not the claim or interest of such creditor, equity security holder, or general partner is impaired under the plan and whether or not such creditor, equity security holder, or general partner has accepted the plan.[99]

Unless otherwise provided in the plan or the order confirming the plan,

(1) Confirmation of the plan vests all the property of the estate in the debtor;[100]
(2) After confirmation, all property dealt with by the plan is free and clear of all claims and interests of creditors, equity security holders, and general partners in the debtor;[101]
(3) Confirmation discharges the debtor from
   (a) Any debt that arose before the date of confirmation;
   (b) Debts arising from the rejection of an executory contract or lease;
   (c) Claims arising from the recovery of property; and
   (d) Certain tax claims specified in Section 502(i).[102]

These debts are discharged whether or not proof of claim was filed or deemed filed or the claim was allowed or if the holder of the claim accepted the plan.[103]

---

[96] 11 USC § 1129(a)(9)(A). For discussion of priority claims, see ¶ 14.09.

[97] 11 USC §§ 1129(a)(9)(B), 1129(a)(9)(C).

[98] 11 USC § 1129(a)(11).

[99] 11 USC § 1141(a).

[100] 11 USC § 1141(b).

[101] 11 USC § 1141(c).

[102] 11 USC § 1141(d)(1)(A).

[103] Id. Note that, by confirmation of a plan, Chapter 11 permits discharge of a corporation or a partnership that may not receive a discharge in a Chapter 7 liquidation.

Note, however, that confirmation of an individual debtor's Chapter 11 plan does not discharge any debt excepted from discharge under Section 523.[104] Thus, Chapter 13 may offer the individual debtor a more attractive option if dischargeability of debts is a consideration.[105] Furthermore, if the Chapter 11 plan for an individual or corporation is a plan of liquidation, the debtor does not engage in business after consummation of the plan, and the debtor would be denied a discharge under Section 727(a) in a Chapter 7 proceeding, then confirmation of the plan is not a discharge.[106] This means that a corporation or a partnership under such circumstances is not eligible for a discharge, since only individuals may receive a discharge in Chapter 7.[107]

---

See 11 USC § 727(a)(1) and discussion at ¶ 15.04[1]. Corporations and partnerships also are not eligible for Chapter 13. See 11 USC § 109(e) and discussion at ¶ 12.03.

[104] 11 USC § 1141(d)(2). For discussion of Section 523, see ¶ 15.07. For additional discussion of the Chapter 11 discharge, see ¶ 15.01.

[105] For discussion of the broader discharge available in Chapter 13, see ¶ 17.12.

[106] 11 USC § 1141(d)(3). For additional discussion, see ¶ 15.01.

[107] 11 USC § 727(a)(1).

# 11

# The Bankruptcy Court System

## ¶ 11.01 EVOLUTION OF THE BANKRUPTCY COURT SYSTEM

### [1] Bankruptcy Act of 1898

At the time of the enactment of the Bankruptcy Reform Act of 1978[1] (the current Bankruptcy Code), the court system for handling bankruptcy matters was the product of some eighty years of development under the Bankruptcy Act of 1898 (the 1898 Act).[2] By the early 1970s, when new bankruptcy legislation was being considered, nearly all cases, matters, and proceedings in bankruptcy were handled by bankruptcy judges[3] who were salaried officers of the federal district courts and were appointed by the judges of the district courts for six-year terms.[4] Technically, the federal district courts were the "bankruptcy courts," but all bankruptcy cases were automatically referred to the bankruptcy judges and all proceedings were conducted before the bankruptcy judges. Their orders were final unless reviewed on appeal and reversed by a judge of the district court.[5] In its report on proposed legislation, the House Judiciary Committee in 1977 summarized the status of the bankruptcy courts under the 1898 Act in these terms:

> The result of these developments in the law has been to recognize the bankruptcy judge as a regular judicial official that handles only bankruptcy cases. Thus, bankruptcy judges today comprise a de facto specialized court system within the district courts. District judges become involved very little in the administration of or decisions in bankruptcy cases. Approximately 190 full-time and 30 part-time bankruptcy judges throughout the country handle the approximately 250,000 cases now pending in the courts with little direct supervision from the district judges.
>
> As the system has evolved, district judges have removed themselves further and further from the consideration of bankruptcy matters. The area has become too specialized and requires too much expertise to be able to be handled on an ad hoc basis by a generalist. The district court bench has generally recognized this fact and left bankruptcy matters to the bankruptcy judges. The only control the district judges still retain is in the appointment and removal process, in hearing appeals of bankruptcy

---

[1] Bankruptcy Reform Act of 1978, Pub. L. No. 95-598, 92 Stat. 2549 (hereinafter cited as the Bankruptcy Reform Act).

[2] For a summary of the evolution of the bankruptcy court system as it existed when the Bankruptcy Reform Act was enacted, see H.R. Rep. No. 595, 95th Cong., 1st Sess. 7–11 (1977).

[3] These "bankruptcy judges" formerly were called "referees." However, under the Bankruptcy Rules promulgated by the U.S. Supreme Court in 1973, the referees were given the title of bankruptcy judges, in recognition of the evolution that had taken place in the role, function, and status of the referees. By that time, most of the administrative duties of the referees had been removed. See H.R. Rep. No. 595, 95th Cong., 1st Sess. 7 (1977).

[4] See id.

[5] See id. at 7–8.

judges' decisions, and in the exercise of certain powers reserved to the district court by statute.[6]

Generally, the bankruptcy court had jurisdiction with respect to the following:

(1) Administration of the estate;
(2) Conduct of the creditors' meeting;
(3) Determination of exemptions and claims;
(4) Sale of assets;
(5) Distribution of proceeds of the estate;
(6) Granting or denial of discharge; and
(7) Confirmation of plans.

Also, the bankruptcy court had jurisdiction of disputes affecting property that was in the custody of the court, including property that was in the actual or constructive possession of the bankrupt on the date the petition was filed. In addition, in some circumstances the bankruptcy court might have jurisdiction based on consent or waiver. However, under the Bankruptcy Act of 1898, not all matters relating to the bankruptcy case could be heard by the bankruptcy court in the exercise of its "summary jurisdiction," and some matters relating to the bankruptcy proceeding had to be determined by a nonbankruptcy court, such as a state or federal court, in what were called plenary proceedings. For example, if the trustee was attempting to recover assets for the estate by using Section 60 of the 1898 Act (voidable preference) absent consent, waiver, or possession of the property, the proceeding had to be brought in some nonbankruptcy forum, such as the federal district court or a state court. In addition to the expense and delay frequently encountered in determining whether the bankruptcy court had jurisdiction, delay also was frequently encountered in the nonbankruptcy forum, which in turn delayed administration of the bankruptcy case. Under the 1898 Act, the question of the jurisdiction of the bankruptcy court was one of the most troublesome and complex areas encountered in bankruptcy cases and one of the most litigated issues. A House Report gave this summary of the situation:

> Under the current bankruptcy law, the jurisdiction of the bankruptcy [court] is limited by the concept of possession, either actual or constructive, or consent, either express or implied. An enormous case law has developed around this provision. Volumes have been written on what constitutes adequate possession to give the bankruptcy court jurisdiction, and on what constitutes adequate consent. The Bankruptcy Rules promulgated by the Supreme Court take the position that a failure to object to jurisdiction constitutes consent. One bankruptcy judge has termed this "jurisdiction by ambush." The issue of the jurisdiction of the bankruptcy court has been litigated in every volume of the Federal Reporter. Intervening

[6] Id. at 9.

amendments to the Bankruptcy Act have not significantly affected the volume of this litigation. In an area of law in which time is of the essence, the delay attendant upon litigation over jurisdiction is needless and expensive.[7]

## [2] Bankruptcy Reform Act of 1978

In the early 1970s, the Commission on Bankruptcy Laws of the United States was established to study the bankruptcy system. It described the problems that limited bankruptcy jurisdiction had created:

> The first and most important objection to the present dispensation is the division of labor between the bankruptcy court and other courts. . . .
>
> There are several objectionable results to the division of jurisdiction of the judicial business generated by bankruptcy cases. The first is delay. Not only are the proceedings in non-bankruptcy courts likely to be paced more slowly with longer intervals between successive steps, but the dockets of the nonbankruptcy courts are likely to be more crowded and commencement of the trials more likely to be postponed in such courts than in bankruptcy courts. Delay is critical in cases under the Bankruptcy Act, particularly in the business cases where litigation is most likely to occur. This is true because of the prejudicial effect it might have on prospects for rehabilitating an enterprise in financial distress and the aggravated risk of deterioration of the estate in the course of liquidation.
>
> Another objection to the division of jurisdiction is the extra expense entailed by the estate in litigating outside the bankruptcy court. The expense differential is likely to be most pronounced when it is necessary for the trustee to sue the adversary party in a distant court. . . . Nonetheless, it is common knowledge that trustees have often forgone litigation to recover assets of estates because of the potential expense and other difficulties of litigating in distant courts, having limited resources with which to wage such litigation. What is needed is a system which diminishes the handicaps imposed on litigation by the trustee in the bankruptcy court by the jurisdictional limitations, while providing a mechanism for assuring convenience to all parties to particular litigation and ensuring that the more general public interest in a fair and expeditious disposition of the litigation will be appropriately balanced in the final selection of a forum.
>
> The most serious objection to the division of jurisdiction is the frequent, time-consuming, and expensive litigation of the question whether the bankruptcy court has jurisdiction of a particular proceeding. As Professor MacLachlan has observed, "When a 'summary' proceeding in the bankruptcy court is appropriate and when a plenary suit is required is one of the most involved and controversial questions in the entire field of bank-

---

[7] Id. at 43. For additional discussion, see Report of the Commission on the Bankruptcy Laws of the United States, H.R. Doc. No. 137, Part I, 93d Cong., 1st Sess. 85–106 (1973) (hereinafter cited as the Commission Report).

> ruptcy." Generally, time is on the side of the defendant. If he can subject the plaintiff trustee to the necessity of suing in another court, he can gain the additional time which that necessity imposes on the trustee. Similarly, the extra expense entailed by the estate when the trustee is forced to sue elsewhere gives his adversary a counter for bargaining with him. Even when the trustee is likely to prevail in a contest over whether the bankruptcy court has jurisdiction, the adversary by merely litigating the issue of jurisdiction may gain most of the advantages he would get if he won on the jurisdictional issue, viz., time and bargaining leverage against the trustee. . . .[8]

To remedy this situation, the Bankruptcy Commission proposed a solution in the Commission Report:

> A comprehensive grant of jurisdiction to the bankruptcy courts over all controversies arising out of any bankruptcy or rehabilitation case would greatly diminish the basis for litigation of jurisdictional issues which consume so much time, money, and energy of the bankruptcy system and of those involved in the administration of debtors' affairs. It would foster the development of a more uniform, cohesive body of substantive and procedural law which would be applicable to the administration of estates under the Bankruptcy Act. The withdrawal from state and federal district courts of jurisdiction of the so-called plenary proceedings, when coupled with the establishment of uniform federal standards and rules, as proposed by the Commission for adoption and application in lieu of the diverse state laws governing debtors' and creditors' rights, should eliminate a source of uncertainty and division of authority which has characterized bankruptcy law.[9]

To accomplish these ends and to create a comprehensive unified system in which practically all matters relating to the bankruptcy case could be heard by the bankruptcy court, the Bankruptcy Reform Act dealt with these troublesome problems in a relatively direct manner. It gave the bankruptcy court sweeping and pervasive jurisdiction of practically all bankruptcy matters, eliminating the vexing problems of whether the matter had to be decided under an exercise of "plenary" jurisdiction in some other state court or in the federal district court (sitting as a district court rather than as a bankruptcy court).[10]

### [3] The Bankruptcy Amendments and Federal Judgeship Act of 1984

The resolution of the jurisdiction and court-structure questions of the Bankruptcy Reform Act was not arrived at without strong disagreement in

---

[8] Commission Report at 88–90; see also H.R. Rep. No. 595, 95th Cong., 1st Sess. 43–48 (1977).

[9] Commission Report at 90–91; see also H.R. Rep. No. 595, 95th Cong., 1st Sess. 46 (1977).

[10] See former 28 USC § 1471; see also Kennedy, "The Bankruptcy Court Under the New Bankruptcy Law: Its Structure and Jurisdiction," 55 Am. Bankr. L.J. 63 (1981).

Congress. The final compromise solution of the Bankruptcy Reform Act later produced a constitutional crisis and a period of extreme uncertainty in bankruptcy administration in the United States when this broad delegation of judicial power to bankruptcy judges was held to be unconstitutional in *Northern Pipeline Co. v. Marathon Pipe Line Co.*[11] The subsequent but long-delayed congressional attempt to resolve this constitutional crisis and to establish a constitutional bankruptcy court system was the Bankruptcy Amendments and Federal Judgeship Act of 1984 (the 1984 Amendments).[12] In the view of many, however, the system for bankruptcy administration and the court structure created by the 1984 Amendments does not improve the situation that existed under the 1898 Act. Rather, it reintroduces all the problems of delay and expense due to litigation over jurisdiction and similar matters. Indeed, in the view of some observers, the system created by the 1984 Amendments is far worse than what existed under the 1898 Act; in addition to reintroducing some of the old problems that existed under the 1898 Act, it has introduced other areas sure to be litigated with additional expense and delay. According to one early commentary:

> Constitutional issues aside, it cannot be reasonably disputed that the new bankruptcy court system multiplies the delay and expense of bankruptcy litigation and may jeopardize the rehabilitation of financially troubled companies that need expeditious resolutions of issues or lack funds for extensive litigation. In place of the summary-plenary litigation that interested parties of all persuasions wanted to do away with, Congress has now substituted:
>
> litigation as to the constitutionality of the new court system
>
> litigation as to what is a core proceeding and what is a noncore proceeding
>
> litigation in respect of permissive abstention
>
> litigation in respect of mandatory abstention
>
> duplicative litigation in noncore proceedings whereby all facts found by the bankruptcy court may be retried by the district court upon timely motion
>
> litigation over revoking the reference on mandatory and discretionary bases
>
> uncoordinated litigation in bankruptcy courts, district courts, and state courts.
>
> If there is one area that mandates a minimization of the proliferation of litigation and attendant expenditure of time and money that is drowning our judicial system, it is certainly the administration of bankruptcy law and the protection of debtors, creditors, and shareholders who have

---

[11] 458 US 50 (1982). The *Marathon* decision is discussed below.

[12] Bankruptcy Amendments and Federal Judgeship Act of 1984, Pub. L. No. 98-353, 98 Stat. 333 (hereinafter cited as the 1984 Amendments).

> already suffered losses. They should not be saddled with a court system that by any account maximizes litigation time and expense.[13]

However, the problems created by the 1984 Amendments unfortunately are not limited to those of court structure and jurisdiction.[14] Professor Lawrence King, a prominent bankruptcy scholar, has reportedly stated that the 1984 Amendments constitute "one of the sloppiest jobs Congress has ever done enacting a law. It is rife with errors, incomplete sentences, and nonconforming and inconsistent numbers."[15]

### [4] Legislative Reactions to Structure and Nature of Bankruptcy Court

To appreciate the 1984 Amendments, it is helpful to understand what led up to this legislation as well as to the 1978 Bankruptcy Code. Throughout the 1970s, when Congress was considering bankruptcy legislation, one of the focal points of disagreement was the structure and nature of the bankruptcy court. During this extended period when various proposals were being considered, the Senate, supported by the Judicial Conference and others, generally opposed the establishment of Article III bankruptcy courts with bankruptcy judges having life tenure. The House of Representatives, on the other hand, generally favored Article III bankruptcy courts with life tenure for bankruptcy judges. However, in the final reconciliation of differences between the House and Senate versions of bankruptcy legislation in 1978, the managers for the House bill, apparently fearing all would be lost at least for that session of Congress, agreed to the Senate view of how the bankruptcy court should be structured. This system was approved by the House in the final bill.[16] In the final version of the bill, the

---

[13] Miller & Bienenstock, "Analysis and Perspective–Bankruptcy," 7 Legal Times 39 (July 30, 1984).

[14] For additional critical views on the 1984 Amendments, see "Lawscope–Bad Law? Brickbats for Bankruptcy Code," 70 A.B.A. J. 28 (Dec. 1984).

[15] Id. The American Bar Association Journal further stated:

> "When Congress was working on the changes, it was pressured by many different lobbying groups. 'The consumer credit industry, shopping center owners, farmers, fishermen, unions, the securities industry, and trial lawyers all put in their two cents,' said King. 'They all affected the way the code came out,' said King, adding: 'It was not a matter of public policy but of who had the loudest voice and the greatest pull.' "

Id. For additional background and information with respect to the lobbying and the frenzied approach taken in passage of the 1984 Amendments, see also Easton, "For Three Months, Bankrupt Beggars Can Be Choosers," 7 Legal Times 1 (July 16, 1984); Arthurs, "Technical Provision Sets Off Bankruptcy Bar Lobbying War," 7 Legal Times 1 (July 30, 1984).

[16] Klee, "Legislative History of the New Bankruptcy Law," 28 De Paul L. Rev. 941, 955 (1979). An earlier version of this article is found in Collier on Bankruptcy v–xxix Appendix Vol. 1 (Matthew Bender, 15th ed. 1981). The article contains extremely helpful information with respect to the legislative history of the Bankruptcy Reform Act and how this legislative history should be used.

Bankruptcy Reform Act of 1978, a new Chapter 6 was added to Title 28 of the U.S. Code. These new provisions of Title 28 provided for the creation of bankruptcy courts as "adjuncts" of the district courts[17] with bankruptcy judges to be appointed for fourteen-year terms by the President of the United States by and with the advice and consent of the Senate.[18] However, these new bankruptcy courts were not to come into existence until April 1, 1984.[19] Under the Bankruptcy Reform Act, the federal district courts were given original and exclusive jurisdiction of "all cases under title 11" (i.e., Title 11 of the U.S. Code, bankruptcy cases) and original but not exclusive jurisdiction of "civil proceedings arising under title 11 or arising in or related to cases under title 11."[20] However, the pervasive jurisdiction granted to the district courts under Title 28, Sections 1471(a) and 1471(b), was to be exercised by the bankruptcy court for the district in which a case under Title 11 was commenced.[21] Thus, under the Bankruptcy Reform Act, new federal bankruptcy courts, with judges appointed by the President, were to come into existence on April 1, 1984. As "adjuncts" of the federal district courts, they would exercise the pervasive jurisdiction granted to the district courts under Sections 1471(a) and 1471(b).[22] In addition, the broad and pervasive jurisdiction granted by Section 1471 was to be exercised not only by the restructured federal bankruptcy courts beginning on April 1, 1984, but was to be exercised beginning on October 1, 1979 (the effective date of the 1978 Bankruptcy Reform Act) and during the interim "transition period" by the bankruptcy courts that were in existence on the effective date of the 1978 Act.[23] As a result of *Marathon*, this transition period

---

[17] 28 USC § 151.

[18] 28 USC §§ 153(a), 152. The President was admonished to give "due consideration to the recommended nominee of the Judicial Council of the Circuit within which an appointment is to be made."

[19] See Bankruptcy Reform Act § 402(b). Pending congressional resolution of the *Marathon* crisis, this transition period was subsequently extended on several occasions and finally expired on June 27, 1984. See infra ¶ 11.01[4] n.34.

[20] See former (1978 Bankruptcy Code) 28 USC §§ 1471(a), 1471(b). Generally, under the Bankruptcy Act of 1898, the bankruptcy court had "summary jurisdiction" over matters internal to the bankruptcy system, such as the bankrupt's status and administrative matters involved in collecting, liquidating, and distributing assets. However, summary jurisdiction over disputes between the estate (trustee) and adverse claimants generally depended on "possession" of the property by the trustee or the estate or consent to jurisdiction by the adverse claimant. However, under the Bankruptcy Reform Act, the bankruptcy court was given jurisdiction of all these matters under its pervasive grant of jurisdiction of the whole bankruptcy case and of "all civil proceedings arising under title 11 or arising in or related to" a bankruptcy case.

[21] 28 USC 1471(c) provided: "The bankruptcy court for the district in which a case under title 11 is commenced shall exercise all of the jurisdiction conferred by this section on the district courts."

[22] 28 USC § 151.

[23] Under the 1978 Act, there was a "transition period" from October 1, 1979 (the effective date for most of the Code) to March 31, 1984, during which certain transitional provisions applied. Although the Bankruptcy Reform Act repealed the 1898 Act, the

was extended on several occasions pending resolution of the constitutional crisis but finally expired on June 27, 1984. However, as a result of the 1984 Amendments and the long-delayed congressional resolution of the *Marathon* crisis, the bankruptcy courts as originally contemplated by the Bankruptcy Reform Act did not come into existence at the end of the transition period. A substantially different bankruptcy court system and jurisdictional structure was substituted in its place.

Under Section 1471(e) of the 1978 Act, the bankruptcy court in which a case was commenced also was given exclusive jurisdiction of all the property of the debtor, wherever located, as of the commencement of the case. Former Title 28, Section 1481, also provided that "[a] bankruptcy court shall have the powers of a court of equity, law, and admiralty, but may not enjoin another court or punish a criminal contempt not committed in the presence of the judge of the court or warranting a punishment of imprisonment." In addition, the bankruptcy court was given the power to "issue any order, process, or judgment that is necessary or appropriate to carry out the provisions of this title."[24] However, the bankruptcy court could not appoint a receiver in a case under the new 1978 Bankruptcy Code (the Code).[25]

For a period of time after the Bankruptcy Reform Act became effective, the Code operated as intended, with the existing bankruptcy courts exercising the broad pervasive jurisdiction given by Section 1471. Not long after the effective date of the new Code, however, challenges were made to the constitutionality of the conferral of jurisdiction on the bankruptcy courts.[26] Briefly, the grant of jurisdiction to the bankruptcy courts was challenged as an unconstitutional delegation of Article III judicial power to a non-Article III judge.

Such a challenge was not wholly unexpected. During the legislative process there had been debate about the constitutionality of conferring this power on non-Article III judges who did not have life tenure and whose salary was subject to being diminished. In *Northern Pipeline Co. v. Marathon Pipe Line Co.*,[27] the U.S. Supreme Court, in a plurality decision with two concurring opinions, decided the question and struck down this broad grant of jurisdiction as an unconstitutional delegation to non-Article III judges. Partly because of the

---

restructuring of the bankruptcy courts was not to take effect until April 1, 1984. During the transition period, the existing bankruptcy courts were continued and were given the same jurisdiction and power that the bankruptcy courts were to have at the end of the transition period. Bankruptcy Reform Act §§ 405(a), 405(b). During this transition period, the Director of the Administrative Office of the U.S. Courts was directed to make a study to determine the number of bankruptcy judges that would be needed for the new bankruptcy court at the end of the transition period. Bankruptcy Reform Act § 406.

[24] 11 USC § 105.

[25] 11 USC § 105(b).

[26] See, e.g., Northern Pipe Line Constr. Co. v. Marathon Pipeline Co., 12 Bankr. 946 (D. Minn. 1981); In re Segarra, 14 Bankr. 870 (Bankr. DPR 1981); In re Marin Oil Co., Inc., 16 Bankr. 822 (Bankr. DNJ 1982); In re Seatrain Lines, Inc., 16 Bankr. 540 (Bankr. DNJ 1981).

[27] 458 US 50 (1982).

numerous opinions in the case and uncertainty about its scope and meaning, the decision in *Marathon* produced a constitutional bankruptcy crisis and a period of confusion, uncertainty, stopgap measures, and legislative stalemate with respect to the status of the bankruptcy courts and resolution of the crisis. However, two years after the *Marathon* decision, after numerous compromises, Congress responded to the crisis by passing the Bankruptcy Amendments and Federal Judgeship Act of 1984 on June 29, 1984, which was signed by President Reagan on July 10, 1984.

In its decision in *Marathon* on June 28, 1982, the U.S. Supreme Court in an unusual (but understandable) procedure stayed the judgment in the case until October 4, 1982 to "afford Congress an opportunity to reconstitute the bankruptcy courts or to adopt other valid means of adjudication, without impairing the interim administration of the bankruptcy laws."[28] Congress failed to act; however, the U.S. Solicitor General asked for an extension of the stay, and an extension to December 24, 1982 was granted by the U.S. Supreme Court on October 4, 1982. Throughout this period, numerous challenges and questions were raised concerning the meaning, scope, and effect of *Marathon*, with the lower courts expressing various views and holdings. In December 1982, when it became clear that Congress would not act before expiration of the second stay, the U.S. Solicitor General again requested an extension of the stay. However, the U.S. Supreme Court refused to extend the stay. Faced with what appeared to be an imminent collapse of the whole bankruptcy system, the Judicial Conference of the United States earlier had requested the Director of the Administrative Office of the United States Courts to provide each circuit with a proposed rule "which [would] permit the bankruptcy system to continue without disruption in reliance upon jurisdictional grants remaining in the law as limited by" *Marathon*. On September 27, 1982, the Director of the Administrative Office of the United States Courts provided such an "emergency rule." When the second stay expired in December 1982, this emergency rule was adopted by each of the district courts as a stopgap measure.

The emergency rule essentially provided for a referral by the district court to the bankruptcy court of "all cases under Title 11 and all civil proceedings arising in or related to cases under Title 11." Under the rule, reference to a bankruptcy court could be withdrawn by the district court on its own motion or on timely motion by a party, and certain matters were subject to review by the district court. However, this emergency rule did not end the confusion but only added fuel to the controversy emanating from *Marathon*. Almost immediately after its adoption, the emergency rule was challenged on several grounds. One substantial challenge was made to the power of the district court to promulgate the emergency rule. Somewhat simplified, one argument was that after the *Marathon* decision, the district court had no basis for bankruptcy jurisdiction, and since it could not delegate what it did not have, the emergency rule under *Marathon* was an unconstitutional delegation to a non-Article III

---

[28] Id. at 88.

court.[29] However, the federal courts of appeals consistently upheld the emergency rule,[30] and on several occasions the U.S. Supreme Court declined to hear challenges to the rule.[31] In addition, as a part of the fallout of the *Marathon* case, the validity of other provisions of the Code, including the constitutionality of the three-judge Bankruptcy Appellate Panels, was brought into question.[32]

Congressional resolution of the jurisdictional crisis was in part stymied by the recurring strong differences over whether bankruptcy judges should be Article III judges with life tenure or something less. Powerful political forces were aligned on both sides of the issue. Other factors also played a major role in delaying resolution of the court-jurisdiction issue. There was significant opinion in Congress that in some respects the new Code was too liberal in favor of debtors and that it had produced abuses and practices that should be remedied, particularly in the area of consumer credit and consumer bankruptcy. Other interests, representing business, credit, and lending interests, and consumer and other special interests, proposed their own changes or amendments or sought to prevent any further changes. To a large extent, the resolution of the court-jurisdiction question was held hostage to the resolution of these other issues.

In February 1984, the situation was further complicated when the U.S. Supreme Court decided *NLRB v. Bildisco & Bildisco,*[33] in which the Court held that a debtor in possession in a Chapter 11 case could unilaterally modify a collective bargaining agreement without court approval and that the test to be

---

[29] See, e.g., In re Color Craft Press, Ltd., 27 Bankr. 392 (Bankr. D. Utah 1983), and In re Richardson, 27 Bankr. 407 (Bankr. D. Utah 1983), both rev'd in In re Color Craft Press, Ltd., 27 Bankr. 962 (D. Utah 1983); In re Seven Springs Apartments, Phase II, 33 Bankr. 458 (Bankr. ND Ga. 1983); In re South Portland Shipyard, 31 Bankr. 770 (Bankr. D. Me. 1983); In re Johnson County Gas Co., 30 Bankr. 690 (Bankr. ED Ky. 1983); In re Wildman, 30 Bankr. 133 (Bankr. ND Ill. 1983); In re United Grocers Corp., 29 Bankr. 309 (Bankr. DNJ 1983); In re Williamson, 28 Bankr. 276 (Bankr. MD Ga. 1983); In re Jorges Carpet Mill, Inc., 27 Bankr. 333 (Bankr. ED Tenn. 1983); In re Conley, 26 Bankr. 885 (Bankr. MD Tenn. 1983); Winters Nat'l Bank & Trust Co. v. Schear Group, 25 Bankr. 463 (Bankr. SD Ohio 1982); In re Motion to Dismiss: Constitutionality of Jurisdiction of the Bankruptcy Courts, 23 Bankr. 334 (Bankr. ND Ga. 1982).

[30] See In re Kaiser, 722 F2d 1574 (2d Cir. 1983); Coastal Steel Corp. v. Tilghman Wheelabrator-Frye, Inc., 709 F2d 190 (3d Cir. 1983); Gold v. Johns-Manville Sales Corp., 723 F2d 1068 (3d Cir. 1983); In re Braniff Airways, Inc., 700 F2d 214 (5th Cir. 1983); White Motor Corp. v. Citibank, N.A., 704 F2d 254 (6th Cir. 1983); In re UNR Indus., Inc., 725 F2d 1111 (7th Cir. 1984); In re Hansen, 702 F2d 728 (8th Cir. 1983); Oklahoma Health Servs. Fed. Credit Union v. Webb, 726 F2d 624 (10th Cir. 1984).

[31] See, e.g., In re Braniff Airways, Inc., 700 F2d 214 (5th Cir. 1983), cert. denied, 103 S. Ct. 2122 (1983); In re Hansen, 702 F2d 728 (8th Cir.), cert. denied, 103 S. Ct. 3539 (1983).

[32] See, e.g., In re Dartmouth House Nursing Home, Inc., 30 Bankr. 56 (Bankr. App. Pan. 1st Cir. 1983), aff'd, 726 F2d 26 (1st Cir. 1984); In re Burley, 738 F2d 981 (9th Cir. 1984); In re Wallen, 34 Bankr. 785 (Bankr. App. Pan. 9th Cir. 1983).

[33] 104 S. Ct. 1188 (1984). For additional discussion see ¶ 13.09[9].

applied in determining whether a Chapter 11 debtor should be permitted to reject a collective bargaining agreement should be a "balancing of the equities" test. This decision produced an immediate response from organized labor, and an attempt to overturn the decision by legislation was introduced in Congress. Of course, there were other interests that supported the *Bildisco* decision and opposed the efforts to overrule *Bildisco*. The resolution of these competing views was tied to resolution of the court and jurisdictional questions. By late March, 1984, however, the congressional stalemate on the *Marathon* crisis had not been resolved. The "transition period" was due to expire on April 1, 1984, when the new bankruptcy court system was to be implemented, although this system largely had been invalidated by *Marathon*. At this juncture, the bankruptcy courts were faced with what appeared to be an imminent collapse of the system. In a last-minute measure, Congress authorized a stopgap continuation of the existing bankruptcy courts for thirty days. With congressional resolution of the crisis still impossible, Congress again on several occasions extended the transition period, with the final extension due to expire on June 27, 1984.[34]

During this period, significantly different bankruptcy bills were working their ways through the House and the Senate, and a conference committee had been appointed. However, the conference committee was not able to report a compromise bill to both houses until after the expiration of the June 27, 1984 transition period extension. Finally, without an additional extension of the transition period and after a conference committee was able to reconcile differences between the Senate and the House versions of the bill, Congress passed the Bankruptcy Amendments and Federal Judgeship Act of 1984[35] on June 29, 1984, which was signed by President Reagan on July 10, 1984. However, the transition period had expired on June 27, 1984, and during the interim before the Act was signed there was great uncertainty and confusion about the status of the bankruptcy courts, whether they even existed, and whether bankruptcy judges had any authority to act. At least one bankruptcy court reportedly was closed for a period of time and other bankruptcy judges took a vacation or "went fishing." Under an emergency authorization from the Judicial Conference, some former bankruptcy judges served as magistrates handling bankruptcy matters.

Due to the expiration of the transition period on June 27, 1984 and arguably with it the expiration of the appointments of the sitting bankruptcy judges on that date, Congress attempted to deal with the problem in the 1984 Amendments by retroactively appointing the bankruptcy judges who were sitting on June 27, 1984 (the expiration date of the transition period) to serve during the period between the expiration date and the date of the Act's enactment. Then, upon enactment of the bill, those judges who were serving on the date of the enactment would be appointed (or "folded in") to serve a term as bankruptcy

---

[34] On March 31, 1984, Public Law 98-249, § 1(a), substituted "May 1, 1984" for "April 1, 1984"; on April 30, 1984, Public Law 98-271, § 1(a), substituted "May 26, 1984" for "May 1, 1984"; on May 25, 1984, Public Law 98-299, § 1(a), substituted "June 21, 1984" for "May 26, 1984"; on June 20, 1984, Public Law 98-325, § 1(a), substituted "June 28, 1984" for "June 21, 1984."

[35] Pub. L. No. 98-353, 98 Stat. 333.

judges under the new 1984 Amendments. The mechanics were as follows: Section 121(e) of the 1984 Amendments provided that the term of office of the bankruptcy judges sitting on June 27, 1984 (the expiration date of the transition period) would be "extended to and [would] expire at the end of the day of the enactment of this Act [July 10, 1984]."[36] Section 106 of the 1984 Amendments then extended the term of office of each bankruptcy judge serving on the date of the enactment of the 1984 Amendments to the later of October 1, 1986, or four years after the date of his last appointment. The constitutionality of these provisions has been questioned in several cases; both the Justice Department and the Administrative Office of the United States Courts have questioned the legality of these retrospective provisions. One early decision upheld the constitutionality of the appointment of the bankruptcy judges.[37]

However, the 1984 Amendments did significantly more than deal with bankruptcy jurisdiction and the structure of the bankruptcy courts. They made important substantive changes in many areas, along with a great number of technical amendments.[38]

## ¶ 11.02 STRUCTURE OF THE BANKRUPTCY COURT UNDER THE BANKRUPTCY REFORM ACT AND THE 1984 AMENDMENTS

The 1978 Bankruptcy Reform Act blended many interests and represented compromises on many questions. One of the more significant compromises concerned the status of the bankruptcy courts and the bankruptcy judges. In considering bankruptcy reform in the 1970s, the House and the Senate differed significantly in their approach to a solution, although the two bodies recognized the need for functional independence of the bankruptcy court. The House generally favored an independent bankruptcy court with life-tenured Article III bankruptcy judges, while the Senate generally opposed Article III status for the bankruptcy judges and supported establishment of a bankruptcy court as an adjunct to the district court.

As originally enacted, Title II of the 1978 Bankruptcy Reform Act amended portions of Title 28 of the U.S. Code and added a new Chapter 6 to Title 28. Under these provisions, on April 1, 1984 a new federal bankruptcy

---

[36] Section 122(c) of the 1984 Amendments stated that Section 121(e) "shall take effect on June 27, 1984."

[37] In re Benny, 12 BCD 495 (ND Cal. 1984); see also In re Tom Carter Enters., 12 BCD 536 (CD Cal. 1985); In re Baldwin-United Corp., 12 BCD 913 (Bankr. SD Ohio 1985), in which the appointment of both the bankruptcy judges and their jurisdiction has been challenged. Developments in this area must be watched.

[38] The formal legislative history for the 1984 Amendments is not extensive, nor is it particularly helpful. The Conference Committee report on the final bill is in H.R. Rep. 882, 98th Cong., 2d Sess. (1984). Statements made by various members of Congress when the conference report was submitted in some instances add some enlightenment as to what was intended. These statements are found in the Cong. Rec. S8887–8900 (daily ed. June 29, 1984).

court was to come into existence as an adjunct to each federal district court. These bankruptcy courts were to be courts of record and, although adjuncts to the district courts, were to be functionally independent. The bankruptcy judges were to be appointed by the President, with the advice and consent of the Senate, for terms of fourteen years. The federal district courts were given original and exclusive jurisdiction of "all cases under title 11"[1] and "original but not exclusive jurisdiction of all civil proceedings arising under title 11 or arising in or related to cases under title 11."[2] However, the bankruptcy court for the district in which a case was commenced was to exercise all of the jurisdiction given to the district courts under Title 28, Sections 1471(a) and 1471(b).[3] In other words, the pervasive jurisdiction granted to the district courts was to be exercised by the bankruptcy courts. During the transition period until the new bankruptcy courts were to come into existence on April 1, 1984, the existing bankruptcy courts were authorized to exercise this broad jurisdiction. However, as noted earlier, this provision was held to be an unconstitutional delegation of Article III judicial power to a non-Article III judge in *Northern Pipeline Co. v. Marathon Pipe Line Co.*,[4] and ultimately resulted in the 1984 Amendments and in a restructuring of the bankruptcy system very different from that originally contemplated by the Bankruptcy Reform Act.[5]

---

[1] 28 USC § 1471(a).

[2] 28 USC § 1471(b).

[3] 28 USC § 1471(c). In effect, this meant that in bankruptcy matters the district court served only in an appellate capacity.

[4] 458 US 50 (1982).

[5] Apparently as a mistake, there is a conflict between two of the provisions in the 1984 Amendments. Section 402(b) of the 1978 Act provided that, with certain exceptions, Title II of the Bankruptcy Reform Act (including 28 USC §§ 1471–1482 and the new bankruptcy court provisions) would take effect at the end of the transition period. Section 113 of the 1984 Amendments amended Section 402(b) of the Bankruptcy Reform Act to provide that these provisions "shall not become effective." The apparent intent was to repeal the provisions of the 1978 Act that provided for the establishment of the new bankruptcy court at the end of the transition period. However, in what appears to be an oversight, Section 121(a) of the 1984 Amendments also amends Section 402(b) of the Bankruptcy Reform Act to state that the section becomes effective on the date of the enactment of the 1984 Amendments. Standing alone, Section 121(a) of the 1984 Amendments states that the sections of Title II of the 1978 Act to be made effective under Section 402(b) are still effective. However, this clearly seems inconsistent with the apparent attempt of Congress to remedy the problems of *Marathon*. For detailed discussion of these conflicting provisions, see In re Long, 43 Bankr. 692 (Bankr. ND Ohio 1984). The court in *Long* held that Section 121(a) of the 1984 Amendments, enacting Section 402, should not be given effect (at least with respect to the 1978 removal provision, 28 USC § 1478) because it enacted provisions that were declared unconstitutional in *Marathon*. For more detailed discussion of this question and *In re Long*, see infra ¶ 11.03[5]. Hereafter, Sections 1471 through 1482 contained in the Bankruptcy Reform Act are referred to as "former" sections, although under Section 121(a) of the 1984 Amendments they arguably are still effective. Presumably, at some point a technical amendments bill to the 1984 Amendments will be passed to take care of this and other technical oversights.

Under new Title 28, Section 151,[6] the bankruptcy judges in each judicial district will constitute a unit of the district court to be known as the bankruptcy court for that district. The bankruptcy judges are to be appointed by the federal court of appeals, after considering the recommendations of the Judicial Conference, for a term of fourteen years and serve as judicial officers of the district court.[7] Bankruptcy judges may be removed from office only by the vote of the majority of the judicial council of the circuit for incompetence, misconduct, neglect of duty, or physical or mental disability.[8]

On April 1, 1984, the new bankruptcy court system originally provided for by the Bankruptcy Reform Act was to have come into existence and the terms of the sitting judges were to have expired on that date.[9] However, because the stalemate resulting from the *Marathon* decision that had invalidated that system, pending resolution of the crisis, Congress on several occasions temporarily extended the terms of the sitting bankruptcy judges by extending the transition period. The final extension of the transition period and the term of the bankruptcy judges expired on June 27, 1984 before Congress passed the 1984 Amendments on June 29, 1984, and before it was signed by the President on July 10, 1984. Thus, it appeared that the terms of the sitting bankruptcy judges had expired before the bill was passed and signed into law by President Reagan. In an attempt to deal with this situation, Congress provided that the term of any bankruptcy judge serving on June 27, 1984 was extended to and expired at the end of the day of the enactment of the 1984 Amendments.[10] By Section 106(a) of the 1984 Amendments, Congress provided that the term of office of bankruptcy judges who were serving on the date of the enactment of the Act (July 10, 1984, the date the interim "retroactive" term under Section 121(e) would expire) was extended and expires on the later of four years after the date the judge was last appointed to office, or on October 1, 1986. However, a seri-

[6] 1984 Amendments § 104. The section provides:

> "In each judicial district, the bankruptcy judges in regular active service shall constitute a unit of the district court to be known as the bankruptcy court for that district. Each bankruptcy judge, as a judicial officer of the district court, may exercise the authority conferred under this chapter with respect to any action, suit or proceeding and may preside alone and hold a regular or special session of the court, except as otherwise provided by law or by rule or order of the district court."

[7] 28 USC § 152(a), added by 1984 Amendments § 104. If a majority of the judges of any court of appeals cannot agree upon the appointment of a bankruptcy judge, the chief judge of the circuit shall make the appointment. 28 USC § 152(a)(3). New 28 USC § 152(a)(2) specifies the number of bankruptcy judges for the various districts. In making the appointments, Congress in Section 120(a)(2) of the 1984 Amendments stated:

> "It is the sense of the Congress that the courts of appeals should consider for appointment . . . to the first vacancy which arises after the date of the enactment of this Act . . . the bankruptcy judge who holds such office immediately before such vacancy arises, if such bankruptcy judge requests to be considered for such appointment."

[8] 28 USC § 152(e), added by 1984 Amendments § 104.

[9] See supra ¶ 11.01[4].

[10] 1984 Amendments § 121(e).

ous question has been raised as to whether Congress, under the appointments clause of the U.S. Constitution,[11] had the power to make the appointments for the interim period by "folding in" the existing bankruptcy judges.[12]

## ¶ 11.03 JURISDICTION

As previously noted, the Bankruptcy Reform Act had originally given the federal bankruptcy courts, which were to become effective on April 1, 1984, very broad, pervasive jurisdiction, with exclusive jurisdiction over bankruptcy cases under Title 11 of the Code. It also gave original but not exclusive jurisdiction over all civil proceedings arising in or related to bankruptcy cases.[1] The existing bankruptcy courts that were continued in the transition period were also given this jurisdiction. However, as the result of the *Marathon* decision that invalidated this broad grant of judicial power to non-Article III judges, the 1984 Amendments made significant changes in bankruptcy jurisdiction and the administration of bankruptcy proceedings. Unfortunately, it appears that the 1984 Amendments, because of many compromises, provisions for special interests, and other changes, may have created a system that not only reintroduces some old problems but that also introduces a number of additional questions and issues.[2] Many of these issues and questions appear certain to be litigated. They have the potential for harmful delay and for expensive and time-consuming litigation of questions of jurisdiction and bankruptcy administration that the Bankruptcy Reform Act had sought to eliminate.

In bankruptcy matters, questions of jurisdiction generally arise within two areas. First, they arise with respect to the court in which the bankruptcy petition may be filed; that is, which court has subject matter jurisdiction over bankruptcy cases.[3] Questions of jurisdiction of this type generally present few problems, although venue may present slightly more questions. Second, questions of jurisdiction arise with respect to where suits or proceedings within or related to the bankruptcy case may be brought. These include objections to discharge, a request for determination of dischargeability, and requests for relief from the stay and such matters as civil proceedings or lawsuits by the estate (the trustee or the debtor in possession in a Chapter 11 case) based on claims against third parties, claims of third parties against the debtor (e.g., for personal injury), or actions by the trustee (or debtor in possession) to set aside fraudulent conveyances or to recover preferences. Questions arise as to whether

---

[11] Article II, clause 2.

[12] See supra ¶ 11.01[3].

[1] Former 28 USC § 1471(b).

[2] For a listing of some of these new problem areas, see supra ¶ 11.01.

[3] Of course, this is different from the question of venue or which court with subject matter jurisdiction is the appropriate court in which to exercise this jurisdiction. Venue is discussed at infra ¶ 11.04. Eligibility for a particular type of bankruptcy (e.g., Chapter 7, 11, or 13) in a sense may also be viewed as a question of subject matter jurisdiction. Eligibility is discussed at ¶ 12.03.

such proceedings or actions may or must be heard and determined by the bankruptcy judge, by the federal district judge, or in an appropriate nonbankruptcy forum such as a state court or federal district court. Jurisdiction questions of this second type present difficult questions under the exceedingly complex system created by the 1984 Amendments. There are many areas where the answers are unclear and offer great potential for litigation on questions of consequent delay, expense, and noncentralized administration of the whole bankruptcy case and related proceedings, which the Bankruptcy Reform Act had sought to eliminate by concentrating all proceedings in the bankruptcy court.

The 1984 Amendments added new Title 28, Section 1334.[4] Section 1334(a) grants the federal district courts exclusive and original jurisdiction of all bankruptcy cases under Title 11. This essentially represents no change from the Bankruptcy Reform Act, and thus all bankruptcy petitions still must be filed in a federal district court.[5] In addition, under Section 1334(b) the district courts are also given "original but not exclusive jurisdiction of all civil proceedings arising under title 11, or arising in or related to cases under title 11."[6] The district court in which a bankruptcy case is commenced or is pending is also given jurisdiction over all property, wherever located, of the debtor as of the commencement of the case, and of property of the estate.[7] Thus, the district court potentially has subject matter jurisdiction of not only the "case," but also of all "civil proceedings arising under title 11 or arising in or related to" a bankruptcy case. However, as will be discussed later, there are substantial restrictions or conditions placed on the exercise of this jurisdiction and on when this power may be exercised by a bankruptcy judge rather than the district judge. The 1984 Amendments clearly contemplate that most matters within this broad bankruptcy jurisdiction will not be handled by the district court but will routinely be referred by the district court judges to the judges of the bankruptcy unit of the district court.[8] However, the 1984 Amendments do much more than provide a restatement of the broad pervasive jurisdiction formerly contained in Title 28, Section 1471, with elimination of the direct statutory delegation of the exercise of this jurisdiction to the bankruptcy court formerly contained in Section 1471(c), the section declared unconstitutional in *Marathon*. Substantial restrictions are placed on the exercise of this jurisdiction

---

[4] 1984 Amendments § 101. Section 1334 is practically identical to former 28 USC § 1471 except that Section 1471(c), which authorized the bankruptcy court to exercise the bankruptcy jurisdiction, is omitted from Section 1334.

[5] This represents a slight change in the sense that the bankruptcy court is no longer a separate "adjunct" of the district. It instead is now a "unit" of the district court, and the petition is filed with the district court rather than the "bankruptcy court," since the bankruptcy court "unit" is no longer a separate court of record.

[6] Sections 1334(a) and 1334(b) are identical to former Sections 1471(a) and 1471(b) of the Bankruptcy Reform Act.

[7] Section 1334(d) is identical in most respects to former Section 1471(e) except that the jurisdiction over such property is given to the "district court" rather than the "bankruptcy court" in keeping with the changes made in the court structure.

[8] See 28 USC § 157(a).

not only by the bankruptcy court but also by the district court. One area of significant change is with respect to abstention.

## [1] Abstention

Under Section 1334(c),[9] the district court is permitted discretion ("permissive abstention"), and in certain circumstances is required ("mandatory abstention") to abstain from exercising the broad jurisdiction given by Sections 1334(a) and 1334(b).[10] Although Section 1334(c) does not specify what abstention means in this context, it appears to mean that the district court may either dismiss or remand the matter to an appropriate state court or administrative agency, or perhaps in appropriate circumstances, to stay proceedings in the district (bankruptcy) court.[11] In contrast to mandatory abstention, for the court to exercise its permissive abstention power, a case or proceeding does not have to be commenced or pending in another court. In circumstances where abstention is mandatory, because of the requirement that a case or proceeding be commenced or pending, it appears to be appropriate for the district court to remand the proceeding,[12] since the question of abstention likely would arise after the proceeding had been removed to the district court from the state court pursuant to Title 28, Section 1452(a).[13]

---

[9] 28 USC § 1334(c); 1984 Amendments § 101.

[10] The mandatory-abstention provisions are not applicable to cases pending on the date of enactment of the 1984 Amendments (July 10, 1984), or to proceedings arising in or related to such cases. 1984 Amendments § 122(b). However, the permissive-abstention provisions of Section 1334(c)(1) do apply to cases pending on the date of the enactment (July 10, 1984) of the 1984 Amendments. See 1984 Amendments § 122(a); In re Dakota Grain Sys., Inc., 41 Bankr. 749 (Bankr. DND 1984). Section 1334(c)(1) parallels the abstention provisions of former Section 1471(d).

[11] For example, assume that the trustee or debtor in possession has begun an adversary proceeding by filing a complaint in the district court, and the proceeding has been automatically referred to the bankruptcy "unit" or judge. The defendant/third party by appropriate timely motion requests withdrawal of the reference and asks the district court to exercise its permissive-abstention power. If there is no state proceeding pending, as a result of the decision to abstain, must the district court dismiss the proceeding or merely stay the district court (bankruptcy) proceeding pending timely resolution of the proceeding in an appropriate state forum? It appears that "staying" the bankruptcy proceeding should be appropriate. (If there is a state proceeding pending, mandatory abstention might be required.) Or assume, for example, that the debtor has an action pending in state court against a third party at the time the petition in bankruptcy is filed. After the petition is filed, the debtor (or trustee) removes the action to the district court. (See 28 USC § 1452.) The third party then timely moves for mandatory abstention. If the district court determines that abstention is required under Section 1334(c)(2), it appears that the appropriate action for the district court is to remand the proceeding to the appropriate state court pursuant to Section 1452(b).

[12] See 28 USC § 1452(b) and discussion at infra ¶ 11.03[5].

[13] For discussion of removal, see infra ¶ 11.03[5]. If the matter has been removed to the district court and then referred to the bankruptcy court, a motion to abstain because the claim is based on state law may have to be combined with a motion for

### [a] Permissive Abstention

Under Section 1334(c)(1) the district court may abstain from hearing a "particular proceeding arising under title 11 or arising in or related to a case under title 11" in "the interest of justice, or in the interest of comity with state courts or respect for state law."[14] The scope of the "permissive abstention" is quite broad. By use of the language "proceeding arising under title 11 or arising in [a bankruptcy case]" it seems clear that "core proceedings"[15] as well as proceedings "related to a case" fall within the permissive-abstention provision.[16] In contrast to "mandatory abstention,"[17] there is no requirement that a proceeding be pending in a state court or other forum to which the district court must, in effect, defer. Thus, in the case of permissive abstention where no state action is pending, it appears appropriate for the district court to merely stay proceedings in the district court pending timely resolution of the matter in an appropriate state forum.

The determination to abstain is to be made by the district court, not the bankruptcy judge.[18] However, the district court should not abstain if there is no other appropriate forum to hear the matter.[19] Traditional abstention doctrine indicates that abstention is appropriate when the matter under consideration brings into question the construction or validity of a state statute that has not been construed by the state court. However, it seems clear from the terms "in the interest of justice," or in the "interest of comity with state courts or respect for state law" that Section 1334(c)(1) does not limit permissive abstention to such circumstances.

Note also that permissive abstention (as well as "mandatory abstention") goes beyond a mere concern that related proceedings involving state law not be determined by a nontenured bankruptcy judge—one of the concerns expressed

---

withdrawal of reference. See 28 USC § 157(d). For discussion of withdrawal of reference, see discussion at infra ¶ 11.03[2][c].

[14] Section 1334(c)(1) provides: "Nothing in this section prevents a district court in the interest of justice, or in the interest of comity with State courts or respect for State law, from abstaining from hearing a particular proceeding arising under title 11 or arising in or related to a case under title 11."

[15] For discussion of core proceedings, see infra ¶ 11.03[2][a].

[16] This is in contrast to the language in the mandatory-abstention section (28 USC § 1334(c)(2)), which requires abstention only on a state cause of action "related to a case under title 11 but not arising under title 11 or arising in a case under title 11" (i.e., only on "related proceedings"). See discussion at infra ¶ 11.03[1][b].

[17] See discussion at infra ¶ 11.03[1][b].

[18] 28 USC § 1334(c)(1).

[19] The legislative history to former Section 1471(d) of the Bankruptcy Reform Act, which was similar to new Section 1334(c)(1), indicates that this power to abstain should not be exercised where no other federal, state, or local court would have jurisdiction over the proceeding in question. H.R. Rep. No. 595, 95th Cong., 1st Sess. 446 (1977); cf. Thompson v. Magnolia Petroleum Co., 309 US 478 (1940).

in *Marathon*—and expresses a "state's rights" view that such claims should not even be determined by a life-tenured, Article III district court judge.[20]

However, Section 1334(c)(1) does not authorize abstention from the bankruptcy case as contrasted to a "proceeding arising under title 11 or arising in or related to a case under title 11." Abstention by the court with respect to a particular "case" is covered by Title 11, Section 305. Under the circumstances specified in Section 305, the court, after notice and a hearing, may dismiss a bankruptcy case or suspend all proceedings if the "interests of creditors and the debtor would be better served by such dismissal or suspension."[21] Dismissal or refraining from exercise of jurisdiction with respect to a bankruptcy case might occur, for example, if an out-of-court workout were feasible, adequate, and less expensive[22] or if an insolvency or liquidation proceeding were pending in a foreign country.[23] To illustrate the scope of Sections 305 and 1334(c)(1), abstention on a petition for bankruptcy under, for example, Chapter 7 of Title 11 (a "straight" liquidation case) would have to be justified under Section 305, not under Title 28, Section 1334(c)(1). In contrast, abstention on an adversary claim by the trustee asserting a preference claim under Section 547, or abstention on a cause of action asserted by the trustee (or a debtor in possession) as a claim of the debtor that passed to the estate, would have to be justified under Title 28, Section 1334(c), or perhaps under Section 305.

---

[20] For some, however, this provision did not go far enough. Senator Hatch, a member of the conference committee on the 1984 Amendments, stated:

> "I have only one regret as I reflect upon this conference product. It involves the deletion of the Senate passed mandatory abstention provision. With its deletion, purely State law claims which do not arise under the Bankruptcy Code are allowed to be tried in State [sic] courts. This presents an important constitutional concern. State tort or contract cases in which one party happens to be bankrupt are still State law claims. They are not Federal questions. Thus, there is no Federal jurisdiction for these claims. The Constitution only grants Federal jurisdiction to cases 'arising under' Federal law and diversity cases. This is neither."

130 Cong. Rec. S8891 (daily ed. June 29, 1984). Senator Hatch further expressed the view that substantial constitutional issues are raised:

> "Although the conference remedied the flaws discerned by the Supreme Court in the Marathon case, its failure to adhere to the Senate-passed bill may create constitutional problems of the same magnitude as those resolved by the bill. These problems arise because the conference bill retains the broad jurisdictional language allowing a bankruptcy court to adjudicate any case 'related to' a bankruptcy claim. This means that a purely State law case could be litigated in a Federal Court without the Federal question jurisdiction necessary under the constitution for Federal court adjudication.... Thus, the provision allowing any case 'related to' bankruptcy to be adjudicated in Federal court violates article III. Purely State law claims cannot be adjudicated in a Federal court."

Id. at 8893.

[21] 11 USC § 305(a)(1). Such a dismissal or suspension, or a decision not to do so, is "not reviewable by appeal or otherwise." 11 USC § 305(c).

[22] See, e.g., In re Colonial Ford, Inc., 24 Bankr. 1014 (Bankr. D. Utah 1982).

[23] See 11 USC § 305(a)(2).

It appears that the district court's discretionary decision to abstain is not reviewable by appeal or otherwise. The language dealing with no appeal of the decision to abstain is contained in Section 1334(c)(2) (the mandatory-abstention provision) but states that "any decision to abstain made under this *subsection* is not reviewable by appeal or otherwise." (Emphasis added.) However, there is some ambiguity as to whether the language "this subsection" refers only to Section 1334(c)(2) by its placement within (c)(2), or whether it refers to Section 1334(c) as a whole, including (c)(1). It also should be observed that the language of the section denies the right of appeal only of a *decision to abstain;* the language does not preclude appeal of a decision not to abstain.[24]

### [b] Mandatory Abstention

Under some circumstances the district court must abstain from hearing certain proceedings.[25] Section 1334(c)(2) provides:

> Upon timely motion of a party in a proceeding based upon a state law claim or state law cause of action, related to a case under title 11 but not arising under title 11 or arising in a case under title 11, with respect to which an action could not have been commenced in a court of the United States absent jurisdiction under this section, the district court shall abstain from hearing such proceeding if an action is commenced, and can be timely adjudicated, in a state forum of appropriate jurisdiction. Any decision to abstain made under this subsection is not reviewable by appeal or otherwise. This subsection shall not be construed to limit the applicability of the stay provided for by section 362 of title 11, United States Code, as such section applies to an action affecting the property of the estate in bankruptcy.

It should be observed that this mandatory abstention is based upon timely motion of a party to the proceeding[26] and that Section 1334(c)(2) does not authorize the district court to abstain on its own motion. In addition to a timely motion, five other requirements must be met. The first requirement is that the proceeding be based upon a state-law claim or a state-law cause of action. Second, this claim or cause of action must be "related to" a bankruptcy case, but not be a proceeding "arising under title 11 or arising in a case under

---

[24] This is in contrast to former 28 USC § 1471(d), which stated that "such abstention, or a decision not to abstain, is not reviewable by appeal or otherwise." Compare also 11 USC § 305(c). From this it appears that the omission of the language "or decision not to abstain" was deliberate, and the inference may be drawn that decisions not to abstain (permissive and mandatory) were intended to be appealable. However, this question will have to be resolved by the courts.

[25] 28 USC § 1334(c)(2). The mandatory-abstention provisions are not applicable to cases pending on the date of enactment of the 1984 Amendments (July 10, 1984) or to proceedings arising in or related to such cases. 1984 Amendments § 122(b).

[26] The statute and the Bankruptcy Rules do not specify when a motion for abstention must be made.

title 11." Although in many instances it may be clear whether a particular proceeding is one "arising under title 11 or arising in a case," there undoubtedly will be circumstances where it will be difficult to determine whether a proceeding falls in that category or is a "related proceeding." These terms are not self-defining and therefore offer the potential for litigation, with consequent delay and expense. A third requirement is that the proceeding could not otherwise have been commenced in a federal court apart from Section 1334 (i.e., if there had been no bankruptcy case).[27] For example, if, absent bankruptcy, the proceeding could have been brought in a federal district court based on diversity or some other basis for federal jurisdiction, the district court is not required to abstain. Fourth, an action must have been commenced in a state court and, fifth, the state proceeding must be one that can be timely adjudicated in the state forum of appropriate jurisdiction.

In determining the scope of the mandatory-abstention provision, the question arises as to what types of state-law claims satisfy the first requirement. Note that Section 1334(c)(2), at least by its language, is not limited to state-law claims of the debtor against third parties but appears to include prepetition state-law claims[28] (and, arguably, counterclaims) by a creditor against the debtor.[29] It is clear that the 1984 Amendments were designed in part to deal with problems related to *Marathon* and the Supreme Court's concern that state-law claims asserted by the debtor against third parties not be determined by non-Article III (non-life-tenured) judges. The mandatory-abstention provision seems to respond at least in part to that concern. [30] If the intent of the section were to deal only with the *Marathon*-type problem (i.e., a state-law claim asserted by the debtor against a third party), then this would indicate that mandatory abstention should be limited to claims of the estate or debtor against third parties. However, the section itself indicates that the concern was broader than just a concern that such claims should be heard by a life-tenured judge to meet the constitutional infirmity recognized in *Marathon*. If this were the only concern, then it could have been met by the mandatory-abstention provision simply requiring that *Marathon*-type state-law claims be heard by an Article III district judge. If the concern were to have such state-law claims heard by life-tenured judges, then the irony is that the mandatory-abstention provision requires such claims to be handled by a state court judge who rarely, if ever, is appointed for life. It seems clear that Section 1334(c)(2) represents

[27] 28 USC § 1334(c)(2).

[28] Note that postpetition claims are not covered, since they appear to arise "under title 11" or "in a case under title 11."

[29] In most instances it seems likely that if the trustee (or debtor in possession) sues on a claim against a third party after the petition is filed and wants a federal forum, the suit will be filed in the district court under Section 1334(b) as a "related proceeding" and the mandatory-abstention provision will not apply if there is no state proceeding that has been "commenced." On the other hand, if the debtor or trustee files in a state court, of course, the question of abstention under Section 1334(c)(2) will not arise unless for some reason the case is removed to the district court pursuant to 28 USC § 1452.

[30] However, as previously noted, it does not meet the constitutional concern raised by Senator Hatch. See supra ¶ 11.03[1][a].

not merely a constitutional concern for insuring that *Marathon*-type state claims are heard by life-tenured judges but represents a broader "state's rights" concern for deference to and respect for state courts (as well as opposition to "encroaching federalism") to the extent that such deference can be made consistent with orderly and timely bankruptcy administration.[31] If this is the basic policy of the section, then the mandatory-abstention provision should apply not only to the debtor's state-law claims against third parties, but to state-law claims against the debtor.[32] However, if one follows this rationale, one is then confronted by the fact that most creditor claims (and counterclaims) against a debtor are based purely on state law and in many of these there will be no independent basis, apart from bankruptcy, for federal jurisdiction.[33] If such claims can be "timely adjudicated," as frequently may be the situation, then the district court may be required to abstain if the other requirements for mandatory abstention are present. However, at this point the question must also confront the second requirement: whether the determination of the third party's state-law claim[34] against the debtor is, for abstention purposes, a "related claim" (and thus subject to mandatory abstention), or whether it is a "proceeding arising under title 11 or arising in a case under title 11" (and thus not subject to mandatory abstention). Clearly the allowance or disallowance of claims against the estate are "core proceedings" that can be determined by the bankruptcy judge and are not required to be heard by the district court.[35] Are core proceedings then never "related proceedings" and thus not subject to mandatory abstention, or may some core proceedings also be related proceedings and thus subject to mandatory abstention?[36]

---

[31] However, the mandatory-abstention provision is in a sense a very limited deference to state courts and state jurisdiction. It does not require abstention if there is no proceeding "commenced" in the state court. Arguably, if full deference was given to state jurisdiction, this limitation should not be imposed as long as the matter could be timely adjudicated in a state forum and not unduly delay bankruptcy administration; the "timely adjudicated" restriction alone should be sufficient.

[32] Apart from this indication from the policy of the section, there are indications in Section 1334(c)(2) itself that claims against the estate were intended to be within mandatory abstention. See discussion in the following paragraphs.

[33] See the views of Senator Hatch given at supra ¶ 11.03[1][a] note 20, which suggest constitutional problems are also raised by this approach.

[34] In this context, the type of claim that would raise this question is either one by the third party that was filed before the petition in bankruptcy was filed or one filed by the claimant after the petition and relief from the stay are obtained.

[35] 28 USC § 157(b)(2)(B). See discussion of core proceeding at infra ¶ 11.03[2][a].

[36] Section 157(b)(2)(B) expressly excludes from core proceedings the "liquidation or estimation of contingent or unliquidated personal injury tort or wrongful death claims against the estate for purposes of distribution." However, such noncore proceedings are not subject to the mandatory-abstention provisions. Section 157(b)(5), by expressly excluding such claims from mandatory abstention, certainly suggests that otherwise such claims would be subject to those provisions and, in turn, supports the view that third-party claims against the debtor are subject to mandatory abstention under Section 1334(c)(2).

The question of whether a core proceeding can also be a related proceeding and therefore subject to mandatory abstention can be answered in the negative if Title 28, Section 157(b)(2), which lists core proceedings, is read as implying that core proceedings are not "related proceedings" but are proceedings that arise "in" or "under" Title 11. Section 157(b)(1) states in part: "Bankruptcy judges may hear and determine . . . all core proceedings arising under title 11, or arising in a case under title 11. . . ." Section 157(b)(3) also tends to support the view that core proceedings are not related proceedings by requiring the bankruptcy judge to determine whether a "proceeding is a core proceeding . . . or is a proceeding that is otherwise related to a case under title 11." Countering the implications of Sections 157(b)(1) and 157(b)(3) and tending to suggest that third-party claims against the estate may be both core proceedings and related proceedings and therefore subject to mandatory abstention, is Section 1334(c)(2), which concludes by stating: "This subsection shall not be construed to limit the applicability of the stay provided for by Section 362 of title 11, United States Code, as such section applies to an action affecting the property of the estate in bankruptcy." This sentence seems to clearly indicate that mandatory abstention does apply to claims against the debtor. Otherwise, if Section 1334(c)(2) dealt only with claims by the debtor against third parties, there would be no need to deal with the effect of abstention on the Section 362 stay, which restrains creditor action against the debtor, the estate, or property of the debtor but not actions by the debtor (trustee).

However, perhaps this detailed analysis is unnecessary if what Congress intended was a very straightforward interpretation of the section: that abstention (out of deference to a state court, federalism, comity, or whatever one chooses to label it) is required if:

(1) A suit is pending in a state court by or against the debtor that is based on a state-law claim;

(2) Apart from bankruptcy there would have been no independent basis for federal court jurisdiction; and

(3) The claim can be timely adjudicated.

If, however, a claim (other than the personal injury tort or wrongful death claim) against the debtor is, for purposes of allowance, a core proceeding and in some circumstances also a related proceeding (subject to mandatory abstention), then generally it can be assumed the matter will have been referred to the bankruptcy judge. However, the determination of abstention must be made by the district court. Thus, it would seem that the motion to abstain must be made to the district court, perhaps coupled with a motion for withdrawal of the reference. If the district court determines that it must abstain with respect to a claim against the debtor because the conditions have been met, the question then arises as to whether a decision to abstain is tantamount to relief from the stay of Section 362 or whether the creditor in addition must justify relief from the stay under Section 362[37] to proceed with the case or to proceed against prop-

---

[37] See 11 USC §§ 362(d), 363(f).

erty of the debtor or the estate. [38] An unlikely conclusion is that the statute requires the district court to abstain (the core proceeding presumably having been withdrawn from the bankruptcy judge) from determining the allowability of the third party's claim but leaves the claimant in the possible position of being unable to justify relief from the stay to pursue the claim unless the determination to abstain is tantamount to relief from the stay or "cause" for lifting the stay under Section 362. It seems more likely that the courts will deal with the problem by lifting the stay to permit the claimant to proceed with the case when the decision of both permissive and mandatory abstention is made. However, Section 1334(c)(2) concludes by stating: "This subsection shall not be construed to limit the applicability of the stay provided for by section 362 of title 11, United States Code, as such section applies to an action affecting the property of the estate in bankruptcy."[39] The meaning of this sentence is not clear. What is an action "affecting the property of the estate"? Any action to determine the validity or amount of a claim against the debtor ultimately seems to affect at least the distribution of the property of the estate. Does the sentence mean that even though the circumstances for mandatory abstention exist, the claimant must independently justify relief from the stay under Section 362? Or is the implication that if it is not an action directly affecting property of the estate (such as an action to reclaim or foreclose on collateral or to acquire a lien), relief from the stay is unnecessary? The implication may be that if the court determines it must or may abstain the third party is free from the automatic stay at least to proceed against the debtor, for example, to determine liability. However, the section appears to say that the determination to abstain does not in and of itself remove the automatic stay with respect to the claimant proceeding against the property of estate (e.g., a proceeding to foreclose a security interest or enforce the claim against property of the estate). One can speculate that this indeed is the intention: to permit the claimant to liquidate or establish the claim while requiring any action to satisfy the claim from property of the estate to be in the bankruptcy proceeding, absent relief from the stay to proceed against property of the estate. [40] This appears to be a sensible reading

---

[38] The court could determine to exercise its permissive-abstention power, which is limited neither to circumstances where a state court action is pending nor to related proceedings, but which includes proceedings "arising under or arising in or related to a case under title 11." In cases of permissive abstention, the same questions will arise with respect to whether abstention is tantamount to relief from the stay and to what extent it is a relief from the stay.

[39] Again, the problem arises as to whether the language "this subsection" (being placed in Section 1334(c)(2)) applies only to mandatory abstention under Section 1334(c)(2) or also to permissive abstention under Section 1334(c)(1). In passing, it should be observed that this phrase seems to indicate clearly that mandatory abstention does apply to claims against the debtor; otherwise, if Section 1334(c)(2) dealt only with claims by the debtor against third parties, there would be no need to deal with the effect of abstention on the stay of Section 362, since it does not restrain the debtor (trustee), but applies to creditor action against the debtor, the estate, or property of the debtor.

[40] Under this view, it is somewhat curious that the language is limited to "an action affecting the property of the *estate*," and does not include property of the debtor.

of the section and consistent with the idea of permitting the state court to determine state claims if it can be timely done.

The fourth and fifth requirements for mandatory abstention are that "an action is commenced, and can be timely adjudicated, in a state forum of appropriate jurisdiction."[41] This apparently requires that, at the time the district court makes the determination that abstention is required,[42] a proceeding must have been commenced in a state court (or other state forum).[43] For example, assume that at the time the petition in bankruptcy was filed the debtor had a contract claim pending against a third party in a state court and the third party has asserted various counterclaims. Following the filing of the bankruptcy petition, the trustee (or debtor in possession) then moves pursuant to new Title 28, Section 1452,[44] to remove the state proceeding to the federal district court for the district where the civil action is pending. The mandatory-abstention provisions of Section 1334(c)(2) appear to apply here and the district must abstain if the claim or cause of action can be "timely adjudicated" in the state forum. In another example, assume that prior to the filing of the bankruptcy petition a third party had a contract claim against the debtor pending in a state court.

---

Does this mean that the creditor, if the court determines to abstain, may proceed against property of the debtor, or must relief from the stay also be obtained to proceed against such property?

[41] Does abstention mean that the bankruptcy court cannot proceed to estimate the third-party claim (e.g., for administrative purposes such as voting for a trustee in Chapter 7 or confirmation of a plan in Chapter 11)? Or does it mean that the district court or bankruptcy court cannot finally liquidate or determine liability or the extent of liability? It seems that mandatory abstention should not preclude the bankruptcy court from estimating a claim for purely administrative purposes, other than allowance of the claim, but is this problem resolved in making the determination of whether the state court action can be timely adjudicated? Does "timely adjudicated" mean for bankruptcy administrative purposes or for final allowance purposes? If mandatory abstention is for purposes of final allowance of the claim, it appears to apply even if determination of the claims may be more expensive in a state court and depends, in part, on the fortuitous circumstance of whether the state case is "commenced" in a state court.

[42] As previously noted, permissive abstention under Section 1334(c)(1) does not require a state court proceeding to be commenced or pending.

[43] If the third party's action is commenced in the state court before the filing of the petition, the automatic stay of Section 362 would prevent the third-party claimant from pursuing the claim unless relief from the stay was obtained. For discussion of the automatic stay, see ¶ 12.05.

However, a question may be raised as to whether the mandatory-abstention provision is limited to those related proceedings that have been commenced in a state forum at the time the petition is filed or at the time the district court is requested to abstain. Can the words "is commenced" be read to mean "can be commenced" so that abstention is required (assuming the other elements are present) if the claim can be "timely adjudicated" even though not then pending in a state court? The language of Section 1334(c)(2), however, does not require that reading.

[44] 1984 Amendments § 103. When the action is removed to the district court under Section 1452, the court may remand the case "on any equitable ground." 28 USC § 1452(b). For discussion of removal, see infra ¶ 11.03[5].

With the filing of the bankruptcy petition, the automatic stay[45] would prevent prosecution of the case in the state court. However, if the third party obtained relief from the stay to prosecute the action in the state court and the trustee (or debtor in possession) sought to remove the case to the appropriate district court, again it would appear, on timely motion, that this proceeding would be subject to the mandatory abstention if the action could be timely adjudicated in the state court.[46] Another situation where the section may apply would be where, after the bankruptcy petition is filed, the third party obtains relief from the stay to file suit on a prepetition claim against the debtor and then files the suit in a state court.[47] The trustee or debtor in possession then attempts to remove the case to the district court, and the third party timely requests the district court to abstain. Again it appears that this proceeding would be subject to the mandatory provisions of Section 1334(c)(2). However, as suggested earlier, it may be argued that allowance and disallowance of claims is not a related proceeding but a core proceeding under Title 28, Section 157(b)(2)(B) (except for personal injury tort or wrongful death claims against the estate).

The fifth mandatory-abstention requirement that the state-law claim can be "timely adjudicated" in the state forum in which the action has been commenced will require amplification by the courts; if the claim cannot be timely adjudicated in the state forum, the district court is not required to abstain. The courts must determine the meaning of "timely adjudicated": With respect to what must the state action be able to be timely adjudicated? Assuming a court can determine with any reasonable certainty how long a proceeding will take in a state court, what is the basis for determining "timeliness"? Does it mean "timely" so as not to unduly interfere with the administration of the case? With respect to which aspects of administration of the case must the claim be timely adjudicated? Allowance of the claim (if claims against the estate are included within the mandatory-abstention provision)? For distribution of the estate? For determination of the feasibility or confirmation of a plan? Timely so as not to interfere with the effective reorganization of the debtor in a Chapter 11 case? The aspect against which "timeliness" is to be measured is not clear and appears to require a case-by-case determination in light of the type and nature of the proceeding for which abstention is sought.

The decision of the district court to abstain under Section 1334(c)(2) is not reviewable by appeal or otherwise.[48] Observe that the language of the section

---

[45] 11 USC § 362.

[46] This assumes that third-party claims against the estate are subject to mandatory abstention, and that such an action is a related proceeding that is subject to the mandatory-abstention provisions rather than a core proceeding arising "in" or "under" Title 11 (i.e., the allowance of a claim under Section 157(b)(2)(B) is a core proceeding), which arguably is not a "related proceeding." See previous discussion.

[47] A postpetition claim against the debtor (or trustee) appears to be excluded from the mandatory-abstention provisions under the excluding language "but not arising under title 11 or arising in a case under title 11" of Section 1334(c)(2).

[48] 28 USC § 1334(c)(2).

denies the right of appeal only of a decision to abstain; the language does not preclude appeal of a decision not to abstain.[49]

It should be noted that the liquidation or estimation of contingent or unliquidated personal injury tort or wrongful death claims against the estate for purposes of distribution are "noncore proceedings"; that is, they cannot be determined finally by the bankruptcy judge,[50] and are not subject to the mandatory-abstention provisions of Section 1334(c)(2).[51] Section 157(b)(5) also provides:

> The district court shall order that personal injury tort and wrongful death claims shall be *tried* in the district court in which the bankruptcy case is pending, or in the district court in which the claim arose, as determined by the district court in which the bankruptcy case is pending [emphasis added]."

Furthermore, Title 28, Section 1412(a), states: "Except as provided in subsection (b) of this section, this chapter and title 11 do not affect any right to trial by jury that an individual has under applicable nonbankruptcy law with regard to a personal injury or wrongful death tort claim." Read together, what do these sections mean? Do they mean that liquidation or estimation of such claims must be made by the district court unless the district court, exercising its permissive abstention power and granting relief from the stay, permits the claimant to proceed in state court? This appears to be the thrust of these sections, which for such claims in effect override Section 502(c) (which permits, for purpose of allowance, estimation of contingent or unliquidated claims if fixing or liquidation would unduly delay administration of the case). A related question also arises as to whether the district court may refer such personal injury tort or wrongful death claims to the bankruptcy court under Section 157(c)(1) for proposed findings of facts or conclusion of law, with the district court making the final determination, subject to de novo review on matters to which any party has timely and specifically objected.

## [2] Procedure for Exercise of Bankruptcy Jurisdiction: 28 USC § 157

Although the bankruptcy jurisdiction provided for in Section 1334 is granted to the district court, the 1984 Amendments contemplate that most, if not all, bankruptcy matters will be handled by the judges in the "bankruptcy

---

[49] This is in contrast to former 28 USC § 1471(d), which stated that "such abstention, or a decision not to abstain, is not reviewable by appeal or otherwise." See also 11 USC § 305(c). From this it appears that the omission of the language "or decision not to abstain" was deliberate and the inference may be drawn that decisions not to abstain were intended to be subject to review by appeal. However, case law will be required to determine the issue.

[50] 28 USC § 157(b)(2)(B). However, the section does permit the bankruptcy court to estimate such claims for purposes of confirming a plan under Chapter 11 or 13. For discussion of core proceedings, see infra ¶ 11.03[2][a].

[51] 28 USC § 157(b)(4).

unit" of the district court. To accomplish this in the restructuring of the court system in the wake of *Marathon*, the 1984 Amendments added a new Section 157 to Title 28 of the U.S. Code,[52] which set forth the procedure for exercise of the bankruptcy jurisdiction given to the district courts under Title 28, Sections 1334(a) through 1334(b). Although Section 157 itself does not grant jurisdiction to either the bankruptcy judges or to the district court, it is an integral part of the new system of bankruptcy administration and contains provisions or procedures, with certain limitations, for the exercise of this bankruptcy jurisdiction. Section 1334 must be read together with Section 157 to appreciate the new bankruptcy system. Section 157 authorizes the district court to refer bankruptcy matters to bankruptcy judges (the bankruptcy unit of the district court) and, at least in some areas, spells out the capacity in which bankruptcy judges may act and establishes limits on their authority with respect to some referred matters. Section 157(a) authorizes each district court to refer to the bankruptcy judges for the district "any or all *cases* under title 11 and any and all proceedings arising under title 11 or arising in or related to a case under title 11." However, even though all cases and proceedings can (and probably automatically will) be referred to the bankruptcy judges,[53] this does not mean that the bankruptcy judge may in all proceedings fully determine all matters or fully exercise all of the jurisdictional power granted by Section 1334; in some circumstances the bankruptcy judge may be restricted to acting in a limited capacity. Under Section 157 some matters may not be finally determined by the bankruptcy judge and in some areas it is unclear what the bankruptcy judges may do and the extent to which they, as officers of the district court, can exercise the jurisdiction granted to the district court under Section 1334.[54]

With respect to matters that are referred to bankruptcy judges, it is important to distinguish between core proceedings and noncore proceedings. Under Section 157(b)(1), bankruptcy judges may hear and determine "all cases under title 11 and all core proceedings arising under title 11, or arising in a case under title 11" that have been referred to them and may enter appropriate orders and judgments, subject to review under Section 158.[55] Thus, for "cases" and "core proceedings" the bankruptcy judge will make the final determination and orders subject to review ("appeal") under Section 158. The power of the bankruptcy judge to make such determinations with respect to the case presumably includes such matters as the determination of the eligibility of a debtor for the particular type of bankruptcy case;[56] determinations with respect to involuntary petitions under Section 303, including questions as to the appropriate

---

[52] 1984 Amendments § 104.

[53] It is assumed that all district courts will adopt a general or a standing order automatically referring some or all bankruptcy matters to the bankruptcy judges. These local orders or rules should, of course, be consulted.

[54] Section 157(b)(1) does not say anything with respect to what a bankruptcy judge may or may not do in noncore proceedings, which under Section 157(a) may be referred to the bankruptcy judge.

[55] For discussion of appeals under Section 158, see infra ¶¶ 11.03[3], 11.03[4].

[56] See 11 USC § 109. For discussion of eligibility, see ¶ 12.03.

number of petitioning creditors;[57] if an involuntary petition is contested, determination of whether the debtor is not generally paying his debts;[58] questions with respect to payment of filing fees, and other matters relating to the petition.[59]

For noncore proceedings "otherwise related to a case under title 11" that are referred to the bankruptcy judge, the bankruptcy judge acts in a much more limited capacity than in core proceedings and, with some exceptions noted below, in most instances does not make the final determination.[60]

### [a] Core Proceedings

As previously noted, the bankruptcy judge may make final determinations and may enter appropriate orders and judgments with respect to core proceedings. Although Section 157 does not define core proceedings, it does state that core proceedings include, but are not limited to, the following:[61]

"(A) *Matters concerning the administration of the estate.*"[62]

Among other things, this appears to include matters relating to the hiring of professionals, payment of attorney fees and other professionals' fees, relief from the stay, and confirmation of a plan in Chapter 11 or 13. How broadly or restrictively the clause "matters concerning the administration of the estate" will be read by the courts remains to be seen, but it may have an important effect on the work of the bankruptcy court.

"(B) *Allowance or disallowance of claims against the estate or exemptions from property of the estate, and estimation of claims or interest for the purposes of confirming a plan under chapter 11 or 13 of title 11 but not the liquidation or estimation of contingent or unliquidated personal injury tort or wrongful death claims against the estate for purposes of distribution in a case under title 11.*"[63]

This passage seems to state clearly that allowance and disallowance of claims is within the bankruptcy court "core jurisdiction."[64] Note that liquidation or estimation of "personal injury tort or wrongful death claims" for pur-

---

[57] See ¶ 12.03[1][b].

[58] See 11 USC § 303.

[59] Some of these arguably may also be core proceedings.

[60] 28 USC § 157(c).

[61] 28 USC §§ 157(b)(2)(A)–157(b)(2)(O). Some "proceedings" may well fall under one or more of the categories in this list.

[62] 28 USC § 157(b)(2)(A).

[63] 28 USC § 157(b)(2)(B).

[64] See also 11 USC § 502(c), which permits, for purposes of allowance, estimation of contingent or unliquidated claims if fixing or liquidation would unduly delay administration of the case. This estimation, with the exception for personal injury tort and wrongful death claims, appears to be within the core jurisdiction of the bankruptcy judge.

poses of distribution cannot be made by the bankruptcy court as a core proceeding.[65] The apparent intent (probably representing the lobbying efforts of personal injury lawyers) is to require that liquidation or estimation of such claims for purposes of distribution, at least as a final determination, be made by the district court.[66] Although Section 157(b)(2)(B) precludes estimation by

---

[65] This exclusion from core proceedings does not exclude tort claims for property damage.

[66] It is not clear whether the district court can refer, for purposes of distribution, such claims to the bankruptcy court for proposed findings of fact and conclusions of law under Section 157(c)(1). Are such claims ones that are "otherwise related" to a case and that can be referred to the bankruptcy court for proposed findings of fact and conclusions of law under Section 157(c)(1)? Also, as previously mentioned, Sections 157(b)(2)(B), 157(b)(5), and 1411(a) (preserving the right of jury trial for personal injury tort and wrongful death claims) arguably were intended to preclude an estimation of such claims under Section 502(c). The ostensible purpose of these sections also was to preclude the district court from referring such claims to the bankruptcy court for proposed findings of fact and conclusions of law under Section 157(c)(1). Note that Section 157(b)(5) (which requires the district court to order that personal injury tort and wrongful death claims "shall be tried" in the district court in which the bankruptcy case is pending or in the district where the claim arose) suggests that such claims must be tried by the district court and may not be referred to the bankruptcy court. One district court has held that Section 157(b)(5) clearly requires that personal injury (asbestos) claims must be tried in the district court rather than the bankruptcy court. In re UNR Indus., Inc., 53 USLW 2258 (ND Ill. 1984). The court also concluded that with respect to the asbestos claims, Section 157(b)(5), which directs that such personal injury tort and wrongful death claims must be tried in the district court, implicitly means that such claims are relieved from the effect of the Section 362 automatic stay or that the district court has the duty to lift the stay. The court stated: "If Congress enacts a statute which, though not referring to the automatic stay section, can only be carried out by lifting that stay, then this court's duty would be to lift the stay and give effect to the statute." Id. The court also pointed out that the express terms of Section 157(b)(2)(B) do not exclude from the definition of core proceedings the estimation of personal injury tort and wrongful death claims for all purposes, but only for "purposes of distribution" and that estimation of such claims for other purposes, such as confirming a plan, apparently remains a core proceeding for the bankruptcy judges. Id.

In addition, note that Section 157(b)(5) by its language is not limited to claims against the estate (as is the case in Section 157(b)(2)(B) ) but seems to include claims by the debtor against third parties. It also suggests that such claims by the estate must be tried by the district court and not referred to the bankruptcy court for proposed findings of fact and conclusions of law. This interpretation that Section 157(b)(5) also covers personal injury tort and wrongful death claims by the debtor does not conflict with Section 502(c), which deals only with estimation of claims against the estate.

If Section 157(b)(5) is construed to require such claims by the debtor against third parties to be heard in the district court, these claims appear to be subject to the mandatory-abstention provisions of Section 1334(c)(2) (if the case has been commenced). On the other hand, such personal injury tort and wrongful death claims against the debtor are not subject to mandatory abstention by the express terms of Section 157(b)(4), which specifically exempts only claims under Section 157(b)(2)(B) (claims against the estate) from the mandatory-abstention provisions of Section 1334(c)(2).

the bankruptcy court of such claims against the estate for purposes of distribution, it does permit the bankruptcy court to estimate such claims for the purposes of confirming a plan.

"(C) *Counterclaims by the estate against persons filing claims against the estate.*"[67]

Read literally, Section 157(b)(2)(C) seems to say that if a creditor has filed proof of claim, as will be required in a Chapter 7 or 13 case for the claim to be allowed,[68] the creditor has in effect submitted to the "core jurisdiction" of the bankruptcy judge with respect to counterclaims. The section appears to be based on *Katchen v. Landy*,[69] which has generally been read broadly to stand for the proposition that a creditor, by filing proof of claim, has consented to the jurisdiction of the bankruptcy court to grant an affirmative judgment against the claimant. As under *Katchen v. Landy*, a question that seems likely to arise with respect to Section 157(b)(2)(C) is whether the creditor by filing proof of claim has submitted to the core jurisdiction with respect to both mandatory and permissive counterclaims.[70] Questions with respect to the scope of this forced waiver and the meaning of *Katchen v. Landy* are likely to reappear.[71]

"(D) *Orders in respect to obtaining credit.*"[72]

Section 157(b)(2)(D) appears to say that proceedings by the debtor to obtain credit under Section 364 that require court authorization (or at least "after notice and hearing") before incurring or obtaining credit are core proceedings and may be authorized by the bankruptcy judge.[73] By implication it appears to mean that all court proceedings that are necessary under Section 364 for obtaining credit are core proceedings. Where the debtor in a Chapter 13 case, the debtor in possession in a Chapter 11 case, or the trustee in a Chapter 7 case is authorized to operate the business,[74] the debtor or trustee is authorized to obtain credit in the ordinary course of business unless the court orders otherwise; an order restricting the obtaining of such credit could be issued by the

---

Note that under Section 157(b)(5) personal injury tort claims and wrongful death actions will not necessarily be tried in the "home court," but may be tried in the district court for the district where the claim arose.

[67] 28 USC § 157(b)(2)(C).

[68] See ¶ 14.03. In a Chapter 11 case, a creditor is not required to file proof of claim unless the claim is listed as disputed, contingent, or unliquidated. See 11 USC § 1111(a).

[69] 382 US 323 (1966).

[70] See, e.g., In re Behring & Behring, 445 F2d 1096 (5th Cir. 1971); In re Carnell Constr. Corp., 424 F2d 296 (3d Cir. 1979); In re Los Angeles Trust Deed & Mortgage Exch., 464 F2d 1136 (9th Cir. 1972). For discussion of *Katchen v. Landy* and the question of consent to counterclaims, see Rochelle & King, "Summary Jurisdiction in Bankruptcy: *Katchen v. Landy* and Questions Left Unanswered," 1966 Duke L.J. 669.

[71] See, e.g., Miller & Bienenstock, "Analysis and Perspective–Bankruptcy," 7 Legal Times 39 (July 30, 1984).

[72] 28 USC § 157(b)(2)(D).

[73] For discussion of Section 364, see ¶ 13.11.

[74] For discussion of this in a Chapter 13 case, see ¶ 17.06.

bankruptcy judge in the exercise of its core jurisdiction. Obtaining credit other than in the ordinary course of business may be authorized by the court under Section 364(b)(c)(d), after notice and hearing, and is within the core-proceeding jurisdiction of the bankruptcy judge.

"(E) *Orders to turn over property of the estate.*"[75]

A question that may be raised with respect to Section 157(b)(2)(E) is whether the court will distinguish between a turnover of tangible and intangible property (such as accounts receivables). Under the 1898 Bankruptcy Act a distinction was sometimes drawn between tangibles and intangibles with respect to the summary jurisdiction of the bankruptcy court. However, under Title 28, Section 1334(d), the district court in which the case is commenced or is pending is given exclusive jurisdiction of all the property of the debtor and of the estate, wherever located.

"(F) *Proceedings to determine, avoid, or recover preferences.*"[76]

This includes actions brought by the trustee or the debtor in possession to recover preferences under Section 547.[77]

"(G) *Motions to terminate, annul, or modify the automatic stay.*"[78]

This appears to include all proceedings with respect to the automatic stay within the core-proceeding jurisdiction.[79]

"(H) *Proceedings to determine, avoid, or recover fraudulent conveyances.*"[80]

This appears to include actions by the trustee or debtor in possession to set aside fraudulent conveyances under Sections 548[81] and 544.[82] Where the trustee or debtor in possession proceeds under Section 544(b) by asserting the right of an actual creditor to set aside a fraudulent conveyance under state law, a question may be raised as to whether this is a "related proceeding" and the type of state-law claim that under *Marathon* could not be heard by a non-Article III bankruptcy judge. However, in response it may be argued that an action by the trustee under Section 544(b) is not based solely on state law. The trustee under that section may assert *Moore v. Bay* (federal bankruptcy case law) and is not limited to avoiding the fraudulent transfer to the extent of the actual creditor's claim but may avoid the entire transaction.[83] In contrast to the summary jurisdiction of the bankruptcy court under the 1898 Bankruptcy Act, for core jurisdiction under Section 157(b)(2), possession of the property by the debtor or the estate is not required.

---

[75] 28 USC § 157(b)(2)(E).

[76] 28 USC § 157(b)(2)(F).

[77] For discussion of Section 547, see ¶ 16.04.

[78] 28 USC § 157(b)(2)(G).

[79] For discussion of the automatic stay, see ¶ 12.05.

[80] 28 USC § 157(b)(2)(H).

[81] See discussion at ¶ 16.05.

[82] See discussion at ¶¶ 16.02, 16.03.

[83] For discussion of Moore v. Bay, 284 US 4 (1931), see ¶ 16.02[1].

"(I) *Determinations as to the dischargeability of particular debts.*"[84]

Under Section 157(b)(2)(I), proceedings to determine the nondischargeability of debts under Section 523 are core proceedings, and the determination can be made by the bankruptcy judge. This includes the determination with respect to those types of nondischargeable claims that require, in order for the debt not to be discharged, a request for determination of dischargeability to be made in the bankruptcy court within specific time limits under Section 523(c).[85]

"(J) *Objections to discharges.*"[86]

Under this section objections to a general discharge under Section 727 are core proceedings and may be determined by the bankruptcy judge.[87]

"(K) *Determinations of the validity, extent, or priority of liens.*"[88]

Note that in contrast to the summary jurisdiction of the bankruptcy court under the 1898 Act, Section 157(b)(2)(K) (stating that the determination of the validity, extent, and priority of liens is a core proceeding) is not limited to circumstances where the debtor or the estate has possession of the property or the creditor has consented by filing proof of claim. A question may be raised as to whether possession of the property is necessary under this section to constitute a "core proceeding." If the proceeding for determination of the validity of a lien (e.g., as a fraudulent conveyance) is determined to be a related proceeding, then the proceeding is subject to the mandatory-abstention provisions of Section 1334(c)(2).

"(L) *Confirmations of plan.*"[89]

Confirmation of a plan in a Chapter 11 or 13 case under Section 1129 or 1325 is a core proceeding and the determinations on confirmation may be made by a bankruptcy judge.[90]

---

[84] 28 USC § 157(b)(2)(I).

[85] For discussion of dischargeability, see ¶ 15.07. One court has held that under the 1984 Amendments to Section 1334, the district court and the bankruptcy court have concurrent jurisdiction to determine dischargeability. "It is the opinion of this court that jurisdiction to determine the dischargeability of particular debts lies concurrently with bankruptcy judges and the district court." In re Lagrotteria, 12 BCD 467 (Bankr. ND Ill. 1984). In *Lagrotteria*, the bankruptcy court modified the stay to permit an action pending against the debtor in the district court to proceed; the court took the view that this would permit the district court (with concurrent jurisdiction with respect to dischargeability) to determine both liability and dischargeability, resulting in a conservation of judicial resources.

[86] 28 USC § 157(b)(2)(J).

[87] For discussion of objections to discharge, see ¶ 15.04.

[88] 28 USC § 157(b)(2)(K).

[89] 28 USC § 157(b)(2)(L).

[90] For discussion of confirmation in a Chapter 13 case, see ¶ 17.09.

"(M) *Orders approving the use or lease of property, including the use of cash collateral."*[91]

If the business of the debtor is authorized to be operated,[92] the trustee (or debtor or debtor in possession) may sell, lease, or use property of the estate in the ordinary course of business without notice or hearing.[93] However, absent consent by the secured party, cash collateral may not be sold, used, or leased unless the court, after notice and a hearing, authorizes such use.[94] Under Sections 157(b)(2)(M) and 157(b)(2)(N),[95] authorization of such use is a core proceeding and may be approved by the bankruptcy judge. In addition, the trustee or debtor in possession may use, sell, or lease property of the estate other than in the ordinary course of business after notice and a hearing. If, after notice, there is an objection to such use, it appears that the hearing to determine whether such use should be authorized would be a core proceeding and the bankruptcy judge would be authorized to enter an order authorizing or denying such use. If, after notice, no objection is made by an interested party, authorization of the court is not required.[96] By implication, Sections 157(b)(2)(M) and 157(b)(2)(N) appear to mean that all court proceedings that are necessary under Section 363 for the use, sale, or lease of property or cash collateral are core proceedings.

"(N) *Orders approving the sale of property other than property resulting from claims brought by the estate against persons who have not filed claims against the estate."*[97]

As previously noted, by implication Sections 157(b)(2)(M) and 157(b)(2)(N) appear to mean that all court proceeding that are necessary under Section 363 are core proceedings, and where court authorization is required the bankruptcy judge may authorize or deny such use, lease, or sale. The meaning of the qualification "other than property resulting from claims brought by the estate against persons who have not filed claims against the estate" is not clear.

"(O) *Other proceedings affecting the liquidation of the assets of the estate or the adjustment of the debtor-creditor or the equity security holder relationship, except personal injury tort or wrongful death claims."*[98]

An application by a creditor for equitable subordination of a creditor's claim under Section 510 has been held to be a core proceeding:

---

[91] 28 USC § 157(b)(2)(M).

[92] See 11 USC §§ 721, 1108, 1304.

[93] 11 USC § 363(c)(1).

[94] 11 USC § 363(c)(2).

[95] Section 157(b)(2)(M) speaks only in terms of "use or lease" of property, while Section 157(b)(2)(N) speaks in terms of orders approving the "sale" of property with a qualification.

[96] See ¶ 13.11; see also 11 USC § 102(1).

[97] 28 USC § 157(b)(2)(N).

[98] 28 USC § 157(b)(2)(O).

> The instant equitable subordination action is clearly a 'core' proceeding as defined in the act. In it, the general creditors seek the court-ordered subordination of the claim of a secured creditor. It thus falls within 28 U.S.C. § 157(b)(2)(o), which includes among core proceedings other proceedings affecting the liquidation of the assets of the estate or the adjustment of the debtor-creditor or the equity security holder relationship, except personal injury tort or wrongful death claims.[99]

The bankruptcy judge, on his own motion or on timely motion of a party, makes the determination of whether a particular proceeding is a core proceeding or is a "proceeding that is otherwise related to a case."[100] However, the determination that a proceeding is not a core proceeding is not to be made solely of the basis that its resolution may be affected by state law.[101] The statute does not state when such a determination must be made. In many cases it may be clear that the proceeding is a core proceeding. In cases where there is a question or it is unclear whether the proceeding is a core proceeding, it seems that the bankruptcy judge is likely to make the determination early in the proceeding, since the determination will affect the capacity in which the bankruptcy judge acts. If the proceeding is a noncore proceeding but "otherwise related to a case," the bankruptcy judge is limited to submitting proposed findings of fact and conclusions of law to the district court.[102] Also, the responsibilities of counsel for the parties may be different depending upon whether the proceeding is a core proceeding or a noncore proceeding. For example, if it is a noncore proceeding, counsel may be responsible for preparing proposed findings of fact and conclusions of law for consideration by the bankruptcy judge.

### [b] Noncore Proceedings

Bankruptcy judges are also authorized to hear and to act in a limited capacity with respect to noncore proceedings that are "otherwise related" to a case under Title 11 and are referred by the district court to the bankruptcy judge.[103] The bankruptcy judge may hear such proceedings, but must submit proposed findings of fact and conclusions of law to the district court. Any final order or judgment must be entered by the district judge after considering the proposed findings and conclusions and after a de novo review of "those matters to which any party has timely and specifically objected."[104] However, if all

---

[99] In re Osborne, 42 Bankr. 988, 993 (WD Wis. 1984).

[100] 28 USC § 157(b)(3).

[101] Id.

[102] 28 USC § 157(c)(1); see discussion at infra ¶ 11.03[3][b]. As subsequently discussed, the district court, with consent of all parties, may refer a noncore related proceeding to a bankruptcy judge to hear and determine and to enter an appropriate judgment or order. 28 USC § 157(c)(2).

[103] 28 USC § 157(c)(1).

[104] 28 USC § 157(c)(1). Any applicable local rules should be consulted with respect to objections, proposed findings of fact, and the like.

parties to the proceeding consent, the district court may refer noncore related proceedings to a bankruptcy judge to hear and determine and to enter appropriate orders and judgments, subject to review under Section 158.[105]

As previously discussed, it is unclear whether a district court, absent consent of all the parties, may under Section 157(c)(1) refer to the bankruptcy judge the claim of a third party against the debtor for personal injury tort or wrongful death.[106]

### [c] Withdrawal of Reference

As previously noted, presumably all district courts will make, as they are authorized to do, provision for automatic reference of all bankruptcy cases and proceedings to the bankruptcy judges for the particular district. The district court, on its own motion or on timely motion of any party, for cause shown, may withdraw in whole or in part "any *case* or *proceeding*" that has been referred to the bankruptcy judge.[107] In some circumstances withdrawal of reference is mandatory. On timely motion of a party, the district court must withdraw the referral "if the court determines that resolution of the proceeding requires consideration of both title 11 and other laws of the United States regulating organizations or activities affecting interstate commerce."[108] For example, assume that a creditor files proof of claim on a loan made to the debtor and the debtor asserts as a counterclaim or defense that in connection with the loan there was a truth-in-lending violation or perhaps an antitrust violation. Is the proceeding, upon timely motion, subject to mandatory withdrawal?[109] Arguably, it would seem so, since resolution of the proceeding appears to require consideration of not only Title 11 but of other federal laws regulating organizations or activities that affect interstate commerce. In what appears to be the first decision construing this section, *In re White Motor Corp.*,[110] the court, in addressing the issues raised with respect to withdrawal of reference under Section 157(d), held that the section applies to core proceedings as well as noncore related proceedings.[111] Further, the court held that the controversy in that case (between a trustee acting under a confirmed plan in a Chapter 11 case and the Pension Benefit Guaranty Corporation regarding the debtor's pension-plan liability under the Employee Retirement Income Security Act of 1974 (ERISA) ) was not subject to the mandatory withdrawal of reference provisions of Section 157(b)(2)(B). The court stated:

---

[105] 28 USC § 157(c)(2).

[106] See discussion at supra ¶ 11.03[2][a].

[107] 28 USC § 157(d).

[108] Id.

[109] In In re White Motor Corp., 42 Bankr. 693, 701 (ND Ohio 1984), the parties agreed that the Internal Revenue Code and ERISA were "laws of the United States regulating organizations or activities affecting interstate commerce" within the meaning of Section 157(c).

[110] 42 Bankr. 693 (ND Ohio 1984).

[111] Id. at 701.

> Section 157(d) must therefore be read to require withdrawal not simply whenever non-Code federal statutes will be considered but rather only when such consideration is necessary for the resolution of a case or proceeding. The preceding analysis of legislative history and the Code's structure demonstrates the importance of the observations during the House debate that § 157(d) was not intended to become "an escape hatch through which most bankruptcy matters will be removed to the district court" . . . and in the Senate debate that district courts "should not allow a party to use this provision to require withdrawal where such laws are not material to the resolution of the proceeding. . . ." Consequently, in light of the congressional goal of having expert bankruptcy judges determine complex Code matters to the greatest extent possible, PBGC's motion to withdraw reference should be granted only if the current proceedings before the bankruptcy court cannot be resolved without substantial and material consideration of ERISA and IRC provisions.[112]
>
> . . . .
>
> But the amendments as a whole and § 157(d) in particular must be read to require withdrawal of the proceedings from the Bankruptcy Court only if this Court [district court] can make an affirmative determination that resolution of the claims will require substantial and material consideration of those non-Code statutes. On the present record, no such determination is possible.[113]

### [3] Appeals and Judicial Review Under the 1978 Bankruptcy Reform Act Prior to the 1984 Amendments

The Bankruptcy Reform Act made significant changes in the manner in which appeals from a decision of the bankruptcy court were handled. Generally, under the 1898 Act, appeals from a bankruptcy judge's decision and order were to the federal district court and from there to the federal court of appeals.[114] Although previously the procedure was somewhat different, with the adoption of the Bankruptcy Rules in 1973, the bankruptcy judge in effect became a trial judge, and the district court became an appellate tribunal whose function was to affirm, modify, or reverse a bankruptcy judge's judgment or order, or to remand with instructions for further proceedings.[115] The findings of fact by the bankruptcy judge were accepted unless clearly erroneous.[116] The district judge was not free to review orders sua sponte and, like most appellate

---

[112] Id. at 703–704.

[113] Id. at 705.

[114] See 1898 Act §§ 39(c), 24(a)(9); Former B. Rules 801–814 (1973).

[115] See Former B. Rule 810 (1973).

[116] See id.

courts, did not take new evidence on appeal.[117] If a bankruptcy judge's decision was not timely appealed, it became final.[118] In the movement for bankruptcy reform, there was widespread dissatisfaction with the existing appellate procedure, particularly with the idea of one trial judge (the district judge) reviewing the decisions of another trial judge (the bankruptcy judge), especially where the reviewing judge was responsible for appointing the person whose decisions were being reviewed. However, the House and Senate in earlier bills had taken different approaches to dealing with questions of appeals; the appellate procedure that was adopted by the Bankruptcy Reform Act represented a compromise.

Under the Bankruptcy Reform Act as originally enacted, during the "transition period" from October 1, 1979 until the new bankruptcy courts were to be established beginning on April 1, 1984,[119] the same appellate procedures were used as those that were to have been utilized after the new bankruptcy courts were to have been established on April 1, 1984.[120] Under the original Bankruptcy Reform Act, an appeal from the bankruptcy court could take one of three routes: (1) to the federal district court; (2) to a three-judge appellate panel appointed by the senior judge for the circuit court of appeals for that district; or (3) directly to the circuit court of appeals.[121]

### [a] Appellate Panels

Under former Title 28, Section 160, if the "circuit council"[122] of a circuit elected to establish an appellate panel for a particular district within the circuit and so ordered, the chief judge of the circuit was authorized to designate panels of three bankruptcy judges to hear appeals from judgments, orders, and decrees of the bankruptcy court for the district concerned.[123] These panels were composed of bankruptcy judges from within the circuit in which the appeal arose. However, the bankruptcy judge from whom the appeal was taken could not be

---

[117] See Former B. Rules 83, 810 (1973).

[118] See 1898 Act § 83(c); Former B. Rule 803 (1973). For additional detail with respect to the appeals process under the 1898 Act, see H.R. Rep. No. 595, 95th Cong., 1st Sess. 39–40 (1977).

[119] As previously noted, this transition period was extended on several occasions pending resolution of the *Marathon* impasse and the transition period expired on June 27, 1984. See discussion at supra ¶ 11.01.

[120] See Bankruptcy Reform Act § 405.

[121] For discussion of the appeals process under the 1978 Act, see generally Levin, "Bankruptcy Appeals," 58 N.C.L. Rev. 967 (1981).

[122] Apparently, this referred to the "Judicial Council" of the circuit. See 28 USC § 332.

[123] The Courts of Appeals for the First and Ninth Circuits had established such appellate panels. For discussion of these appellate panels, see George, "The Bankruptcy Appellate Panels: An Unfinished Experiment," 1982 B.Y.U. L. Rev. 20 (1982).

a member of the reviewing panel.[124] If an appellate panel was established for a particular district, the panel had jurisdiction of appeals from "all final judgments, orders and decrees of bankruptcy courts" and, by leave of such panel, "jurisdiction of appeals from interlocutory judgments, orders and decrees."[125] Further appeal from a decision of an appellate panel was to the court of appeals.[126] Even if a panel was established for a particular district, the parties, by agreement, could bypass the appellate panel and take an appeal of a final judgment, order, or decree directly to the circuit court of appeals.[127]

After the decision in *Northern Pipeline Co. v. Marathon Pipe Line Co.,*[128] the validity and constitutionality of the three-judge bankruptcy appellate panels was questioned.[129]

As noted in the following sections, judicial review and appellate procedure is significantly changed under the 1984 Amendments.

### [b] Appeal to the United States District Court

Under the Bankruptcy Reform Act prior to the 1984 Amendments, in districts in which no appellate panel had been established pursuant to Section 160, the federal district courts had jurisdiction to hear appeals from all final judgments, orders, and decrees of bankruptcy courts and, by leave of the district court, of appeals from interlocutory orders and decrees.[130] Further appeal from the final decision of the district court was to the circuit court of appeals.[131]

### [c] Appeal to the Circuit Court of Appeals

Before the 1984 Amendments, former Title 28, Section 1293, granted the circuit court of appeals jurisdiction to hear appeals from final decisions of appellate panels established under Section 160 or of district courts, and from final judgments, orders, or decrees of the bankruptcy courts if the parties agreed to a direct ("bypass") appeal to the circuit court of appeals.

---

[124] See former 28 USC § 160(b).

[125] Former 28 USC § 1482.

[126] See former 28 USC § 1293. Such subsequent appeals were governed by the Federal Rules of Appellate Procedure.

[127] See former 28 USC § 1293(b). These direct appeals were governed by the Federal Rules of Appellate Procedure.

[128] 458 US 50 (1982).

[129] See, e.g., In re Dartmouth House Nursing Home, Inc., 30 Bankr. 56 (Bankr. App. Pan. 1st Cir. 1983), aff'd on other grounds, 726 F2d 26 (1st Cir. 1984); In re Burley, 738 F2d 981 (9th Cir. 1984); In re Wallen, 34 Bankr. 785 (Bankr. App. Pan. 9th Cir. 1983).

[130] 28 USC § 1334(a)–1334(b).

[131] 28 USC § 1293(b). Such appeals were governed by the Federal Rules of Appellate Procedure.

## [4] Appeals Under the 1978 Bankruptcy Reform Act After the 1984 Amendments

In resolving the crisis resulting from the *Marathon* decision and in restructuring the bankruptcy court system, the 1984 Amendments made significant changes in the appeals process and jurisdiction for appeals.

As previously discussed,[132] the bankruptcy court may hear and determine all referred cases and all core matters and may enter appropriate orders and judgments subject to review under Title 28, Section 158.[133] In general, final judgments or orders of the bankruptcy judge are appealed to the district court. The district court, by Section 158, is given jurisdiction to hear appeals from final judgments, orders, decrees, and, with leave of the court, from interlocutory orders of bankruptcy judges entered in cases and proceedings referred to the bankruptcy judge. Thus, for final judgments or orders of the bankruptcy judge in core proceedings, and in noncore related proceedings where the parties have consented to the bankruptcy court determining the matter,[134] the district court is an appellate court.[135] The district court also has jurisdiction to hear appeals from interlocutory orders and decrees of bankruptcy judges.[136] Appeals from a final decision of the bankruptcy judge are taken to the federal district court for the district in which the bankruptcy judge is serving.[137] Appeals to the district court and to appellate panels are taken in the same manner as appeals in civil proceedings generally are taken: to the circuit court of appeals from the district court.[138]

With consent of all the parties, appeals from the bankruptcy judge may be taken to an appellate panel if one has been established for that district.[139] Section 158(b) authorizes, but does not require, the judicial council of a circuit to establish a bankruptcy appellate panel to hear, upon consent of all the parties, an appeal.[140] The appellate panel is to be made up of three bankruptcy judges from within the circuit establishing such panels.[141] However, appeals may not

---

[132] See discussion at supra ¶ 11.03[2].

[133] 28 USC § 157(b)(1).

[134] Under Section 157(c)(2), with consent of all the parties to a proceeding, the district court may refer a noncore related proceeding to the bankruptcy judge to hear and determine and to enter appropriate orders. These presumably include final orders and judgments, subject to review under Section 158. However, where the parties consent to such a determination by the bankruptcy court for noncore related proceedings, there is no right of de novo review by the district court, which otherwise would be available under Section 157(c)(1) for such noncore related proceedings.

[135] 28 USC § 158.

[136] Id.

[137] 28 USC § 158(a).

[138] 28 USC § 158(c). For discussion of the time within which an appeal must be taken, see infra ¶ 11.03[4][a].

[139] 28 USC § 158(b)(1).

[140] Id.

[141] Id.; 28 USC § 158(b)(3).

be referred to an appellate panel unless the district judges for the district, by majority vote, authorize the referral of such appeals originating within the district.[142] Note that the appellate panel hears, by consent, only appeals from the bankruptcy court and not from orders or judgments of the district court. In a district for which an appellate panel has been established, by consent the parties may elect to have the first level of appeal heard by a bankruptcy appellate panel rather than a district judge. The requirement that the parties consent to the appeal to the appellate panel is an apparent attempt to avoid the types of constitutional questions raised after *Marathon* with respect to the appellate panels as originally established under the Bankruptcy Reform Act.[143]

A bankruptcy judge serving on an appellate panel may not hear an appeal originating in the district for which he is appointed or designated; that is, a panel must be made up of bankruptcy judges from districts other than the district from which an appeal is taken.[144] Further appeals from the district court or from an appellate panel are then to the court of appeals.[145]

For noncore related proceedings that are referred to a bankruptcy judge, the bankruptcy judge is authorized only to submit proposed findings of fact

---

[142] 28 USC § 158(b)(2). This provision permits the district judges within a given district to elect not to permit appeals from their district to be heard by an appellate panel. It remains to be seen whether the district judges will "opt out" and elect to assume the appeals caseload for bankruptcy judges' decisions that otherwise might be handled by the appellate panel if one were established.

[143] Under the original Bankruptcy Reform Act, the appellate panels were composed of non-Article III bankruptcy judges; the exercise of the appellate power by such judges under *Marathon* was arguably an unconstitutional exercise of Article III judicial power. See In re Dartmouth House Nursing Home, Inc., 30 Bankr. 56 (Bankr. App. Pan. 1st Cir. 1983), aff'd, 726 F2d 26 (1st Cir. 1984); In re Burley, 738 F2d 981 (9th Cir. 1984); In re Wallen, 34 Bankr. 785 (Bankr. App. Pan. 9th Cir. 1983).

[144] 28 USC § 158(b)(3).

[145] 28 USC § 158(d). This section only grants the court of appeals "jurisdiction of appeals from all final decisions, judgment, orders and decrees entered under subsections (a) and (b)" of Section 158. Thus, it covers only bankruptcy judges' decisions that are appealed to the district judge or to an appellate panel whose decision in turn is appealed. However, Section 158 is silent with respect to appeals of orders and judgments originally entered by the district court in related proceedings and in core proceedings that have been withdrawn from the bankruptcy court. It appears that appeals from such orders, judgments and decrees are (like other nonbankruptcy judgments and orders) to the court of appeals under 28 USC §§ 1291 and 1292 (interlocutory orders), and will be governed by the Federal Rules of Appellate Procedure. See, e.g., Fed. R. App. P. 3–6. Generally, notice of the appeal must be filed within thirty days after the date of entry of the judgment or order appealed from. See Fed. R. App. P. 4(a); see also 28 USC § 2107.

Section 158(c) does not cover appeals from such original orders or judgments of the district court, since it refers to appeals under Sections 158(a)–158(b) that are appeals from the bankruptcy judge, not from the district court.

Observe also that the provision of former Section 1293(b) that permitted the parties, by consent, to bypass the district court and to take an appeal directly to the court of appeals was not carried forward into new Section 158.

and conclusions of law, and the district court enters any final order or judgment after considering the bankruptcy judge's proposed findings of fact and conclusions of law.[146] In such proceedings, to obtain de novo review by the district judge on any matter, a party must timely and specifically object.[147] Final orders or judgments of the district court with respect to such noncore related proceeding may be appealed to the circuit court.[148] If noncore related proceedings are referred to a bankruptcy judge with the consent of all parties, the bankruptcy judge may enter appropriate final orders and judgments. Such final orders or judgments (and interlocutory orders with leave of the district court) may then be appealed to the district court under Section 158.[149]

Note that a district court decision to abstain from hearing a proceeding based on a state-law claim or cause of action under Title 28, Section 1334(c)(2), is not reviewable by appeal or otherwise.[150]

Sections 157 and 158 of Title 28 do not expressly establish the standard of review that is to be applied by either the district court (or an appellate panel) in reviewing bankruptcy court judgments and orders or by the circuit court in reviewing the final decisions and judgments of the district court.[151] To the extent that Bankruptcy Rule 8013 is controlling on appeals from the bankruptcy judge to the district court or to an appellate panel, the standard appears to remain a "clearly erroneous" standard with respect to findings of fact. In *In re Osborne*,[152] the defendant/secured creditor challenged the application of the clearly erroneous standard of review of Bankruptcy Rule 8013 in light of *Marathon*. In holding that the standard did apply to review of core proceedings after the 1984 Amendments, the district court stated:

> After these arguments were made, Congress enacted the Bankruptcy Amendments and Federal Judgeship Act of 1984, P.L. No. 98-353. Section 104(a) of the Act amends Title 28 of the United States Code by adding a

---

[146] 28 USC § 157(c)(1).

[147] Id.

[148] As previously noted, Section 158 is silent with respect to such appeals. However, it appears that such appeals will be covered under Sections 1291 and 1292, and will be governed by the Federal Rules of Appellate Procedure.

[149] 28 USC § 158(c)(2).

[150] 28 USC § 1334(c)(2). Observe that the language of the section denies the right of appeal only of a decision to abstain; it does not preclude appeal of a decision not to abstain. This is in contrast to former 28 USC § 1471(d), which stated that "such abstention, or a decision not to abstain, is not reviewable by appeal or otherwise." See also 11 USC § 305(c). From this it appears that the omission of the language "or decision not to abstain" was deliberate, and the inference may be drawn that decisions not to abstain were intended to be subject to review by appeal. However, case law will be required to determine the issue.

[151] For noncore related proceedings that are referred to a bankruptcy judge for proposed findings of fact and conclusions of law under Section 157(c)(1), there is a right of de novo review only on matters to which any party has timely and specifically objected. See In re Osborne, 42 Bankr. 988 (WD Wis. 1984).

[152] 42 Bankr. 988 (WD Wis. 1984).

new chapter 6, including provisions dealing with bankruptcy procedures and appeals. 28 U.S.C. § 157 now enumerates a number of "core proceedings" and provides for *de novo* review only for proceedings which are not "core proceedings." 28 U.S.C. § 157(c)(1). 28 U.S.C. § 158 also provides that appeals from decisions of bankruptcy judges "shall be taken in the same manner as appeals in civil proceedings generally are taken to the courts of appeals from the district courts. . . ." 28 U.S.C. § 158(c). Since Rule 52(a), Federal Rules of Civil Procedure applies the clearly erroneous standard to appeals taken from district courts to courts of appeals, the clear implication of both § 158(c) and the special *de novo* review procedure of § 157(c)(1) is that Congress intended that the clearly erroneous standard apply in appeals from decisions of bankruptcy judges in "core" proceedings.[153]

With respect to the standard of review to be applied by a circuit court to judgments and orders of the district court in noncore proceedings, Rule 52(a) of the Federal Rules of Civil Procedure applies and the "clearly erroneous" standard applies to finding of fact by the district court.

### [a] Time for Taking an Appeal

Appeals to the district court (or to an appellate panel if one has been established pursuant to Section 158(b)) from judgments, orders, and decrees of bankruptcy judges in cases and proceedings referred to bankruptcy judges under Section 157 are taken in the same manner as appeals in civil proceedings. These appeals generally are taken to the courts of appeals from the district court and must be made within the time provided for by Bankruptcy Rule 8002,[154] which provides that notice of an appeal must be filed with the clerk of the bankruptcy court[155] within ten days of the date of entry of the judgment, order, or decree appealed from. The rule also permits the bankruptcy judge to extend the time for filing the notice of appeal for a period not exceeding twenty days if a request to extend the time is made before the expiration of the original

---

[153] In re Osborne, 42 Bankr. 992–993 (WD Wis. 1984). The court held further that use of the clearly erroneous standard under the 1984 Amendments for core proceedings was constitutionally permissible under Northern Pipeline Constr. Co. v. Marathon Pipe Line Co., 458 US 50 (1982). "The limited application of the clearly erroneous standard to 'core' proceedings does not violate either the holding or the rationale of *Northern Pipeline*. The amendments reserve to the district court 'most, if not all, of the essential attributes of the judicial power,' [citations omitted] and limit application of the clearly erroneous standard to proceedings within the core of the federal bankruptcy power. Accordingly, I conclude that the proper standard of review is the clearly erroneous standard adopted in Bankruptcy Rule 8013 and approve implicitly in the Bankruptcy Amendments of 1984." Id. at 994.

[154] 28 USC § 158(c).

[155] This presumably is now the clerk of the district court, since technically there is no longer a bankruptcy court as a separate court of record, but only a "unit" of the district court composed of the bankruptcy judges who "shall constitute a unit of the district court to be known as the bankruptcy court." See 28 USC § 151.

period. Note, however, that an appeal from a judgment, order, or decree of the district court is governed by the Federal Rules of Appellate Procedure. This includes appeals from an original judgment of the district court (e.g., in a noncore proceeding) or a judgment or order of the district court in the second instance that is, in effect, an appellate court judgment. Under Rule 4(a) of the Federal Rules of Appellate Procedure, notice of appeal generally must be filed with the district court clerk within thirty days after the date of entry of the order or judgment appealed from.[156]

## [5] Removal to District Court

Any claim or cause of action in a civil action may be removed to the district court for the district where the action is pending if the district court has jurisdiction of the claim or cause of action under Title 28, Section 1334.[157] This means that civil proceedings arising under Title 11, or arising in or related to a case under Title 11, may be removed to the district court.[158] It should be observed that the removal under new Title 28, Section 1452, is to the district court, not to the bankruptcy court as was the case under the predecessor to Section 1452, former Title 28, Section 1478. In *In re Long*,[159] the court held that the 1984 Amendments applied to an application (made on July 12, 1984, after the 1984 Amendments were enacted) to remove a civil action pending in a district court (having previously been removed from a state court) at the time of the enactment of the 1984 Amendments (July 10, 1984). The court further held that after enactment of the 1984 Amendments there is no authorization for removal to a *bankruptcy* court, since new Section 1452 authorizes removal only to the *district* court. The argument was made that Title 28, Section 1478, enacted by Section 241 of the 1978 Act, which authorized removal of a case to the *bankruptcy* court and arguably was not invalidated by *Marathon*, was still effective after the 1984 Amendments. The argument was based on an apparent mistake and contradiction in the 1984 Amendments and a very involved interplay of various sections of the Bankruptcy Reform Act and the 1984 Amendments. Section 113 of the 1984 Amendments amended Section 402(b) of the Bankruptcy Reform Act to provide that, with certain exceptions, the Amendments made by Title 2 of the Bankruptcy Reform Act (containing among other provisions, the jurisdictional provisions in Title 28, Sections 1471 through 1481) "shall not be effective." The practical effect of this was to repeal Sections 201 and 241 of the Bankruptcy Reform Act; pursuant to original Section 402(b), Sections 201 (establishing the new bankruptcy court) and 241 (contain-

---

[156] For appeals of interlocutory orders of the district court, Rule 5(a) of the Federal Rules of Appellate Procedure requires that the petition for permission to appeal be filed with the clerk of the court of appeals within ten days after entry of the order.

[157] 28 USC § 1452(a). However, a proceeding before the U.S. Tax Court or a civil action by a governmental unit to enforce its police or regulatory power is not removable. Id.

[158] For discussion of jurisdiction under Section 1334, see ¶ 11.03.

[159] 43 Bankr. 692 (Bankr. ND Ohio 1984).

ing the jurisdictional provisions of Sections 1471 through 1481) were to take effect at the expiration of the transition period. However, Section 121(a) of the 1984 Amendments also amended Section 402(a) of the Bankruptcy Reform Act to provide that, with stated exceptions, the amendments made by Title 2 of the Bankruptcy Reform Act "shall take effect on the date of the enactment" of the 1984 Amendments. Standing alone, the effect of Section 121 of the 1984 Amendments was to enact the jurisdictional provisions of Sections 1471 through 1481 of the Bankruptcy Reform Act as of the date of the enactment of the 1984 Amendments. The party seeking to remove in the *Long* case thereby argued that Section 1478 permitting removal to the bankruptcy court was still effective. In confronting this argument and concluding that Section 1478 should not be viewed as effective after the 1984 Amendments despite Section 121 of the 1984 Amendments, the court stated:

> Obviously, only one of these contradictory provisions can be given effect. Upon considering the 1984 Act as a whole, this court concludes that the purported amendment of section 402(b) of the 1978 Act by section 121(a) of the 1984 Act cannot be given effect.
>
> Section 121(a) of the 1984 Act would make effective sections 201 and 241 of the 1978 Act. Section 241, in turn enacts the jurisdictional provision, 28 U.S.C. section 1471(c), the exercise of which the Supreme Court found unconstitutional in *Northern Pipeline*. Certainly Congress would not want to enact legislation which has already been declared unconstitutional.
>
> Furthermore, the 1984 Act creates a new bankruptcy court system which was obviously meant to supersede the bankruptcy courts created by section 201 of the 1978 Act. Section 104 of the 1984 Act enacts Chapter 6 of Title 28 of the United States Code, 28 U.S.C. Sections 151-158. Unlike the stillborn court of section 201, this new bankruptcy court is not an independent and separate court; it is instead a "unit" of the district court. Obviously, Congress could not have intended to create two distinct bankruptcy court systems, each with different powers. It is just as obvious that the 28 U.S.C. section 151 et. seq. enacted by section 201 of the 1978 Act cannot coexist with 28 U.S.C. section 151 et. seq. enacted by section 104 of the 1984 Act. To hold otherwise would result in chaos.
>
> The bankruptcy courts created by the new 28 U.S.C. section 151 as enacted by section 104 of the 1984 Act do not have an independent grant of jurisdiction. Instead these courts may exercise jurisdiction over only those cases which are referred to them by the district court. 28 U.S.C. section 157(a) and (d). The authority for these bankruptcy courts is much more limited than that contemplated by the 1978 Act. See 28 U.S.C. section 157(b) as enacted by section 104 of the 1984 Act. Obviously, the circumscribed jurisdiction of the new Act cannot coexist with the broad grant of jurisdiction found in section 241 of the 1978 Act.
>
> Upon considering the 1984 Act as a whole, it is clear that Congress intended that sections 201 and 241 of the 1978 Act should be repealed. This court, therefore, will not give effect to section 121(a) of the 1984 Act to the extent that said section is in conflict with both section 113 of the

> 1984 Act and the manifest intent of Congress. The court hopes that Congress will enact legislation which will correct this apparent contradiction.
>
> It follows that this court cannot have jurisdiction over an action purportedly removed to it under the no longer effective 28 U.S.C. section 1478. Furthermore, the court finds that there is no other statute which would confer jurisdiction upon this court by removal.[160]

The district court to which such a civil action is removed may remand based on any equitable ground, and any decision to remand or not to remand is not reviewable by appeal or otherwise.[161]

Upon removal of a case to the district court, the other procedural provisions of Title 28, Section 157 (regarding mandatory abstention, withdrawal of reference, limitations on the role of the bankruptcy judge in referred noncore "otherwise related" proceedings, parties consenting to noncore related proceedings being determined by the bankruptcy judge, and the like) apply, as well as Section 158 with respect to appeals and judicial review.

## ¶ 11.04 VENUE

As a preliminary matter, it should be observed that under the Bankruptcy Code, venue questions (i.e., determining the appropriate court to exercise the subject matter jurisdiction granted by Title 28, Section 1334) arise in two ways.[1] First, venue questions arise in determining in which district court a case may be commenced (i.e., in which court a petition in bankruptcy, under Chap-

---

[160] In re Long, 43 Bankr. 445 (Bankr. ND Ohio 1984).

[161] 28 USC § 1452(b). One bankruptcy court has ruled, where a removed case had been referred to the bankruptcy judge, that it is not appropriate for the bankruptcy judge, as a non-Article III judge, to make the decision to remand or not to remand in light of the fact that such a decision is not subject to review. However, the bankruptcy judge made a report to the district court recommending remand. In re Nilsson, 42 Bankr. 587 (Bankr. CD Cal. 1984). Compare In re Long, 43 Bankr. 692 (Bankr. ND Ohio 1984), which held that removal jurisdiction by the express language of Section 1452(a) is limited to the district court. However, does this necessarily mean that once the case has been removed to the district court it cannot be referred to the bankruptcy judge under Section 157(a)? It seems to not necessarily follow since all of the bankruptcy jurisdiction is in the district court under new Section 1334, and it is only consistent to have the removal jurisdiction to the only court with bankruptcy jurisdiction. However, Section 157 does permit bankruptcy cases and "proceedings arising under title 11 or arising in or related to a case under title 11" to be referred to the bankruptcy judge, subject to the other procedural limitations imposed by Section 157 on the exercise of this jurisdiction by the bankruptcy judge.

[1] The venue provisions of the 1984 Amendments are similar in most respects to those contained in the original 1978 Act in former 28 USC §§ 1472 and 1473. The changes are largely ones of renumbering, with the new venue provisions now referring to the "district court" rather than to the "bankruptcy court," reflecting the 1984 changes that placed bankruptcy jurisdiction in the district courts under Section 1334 resulting from the changes required by *Marathon*. See discussion at supra ¶¶ 11.01, 11.02.

ter 7, 11, or 13, may be filed by or against a person or entity). The venue provisions with respect to filing the petition are in Title 28, Section 1408.[2] Second, venue questions arise when determining in which district court lawsuits or proceedings arising in or related to the bankruptcy case may be brought. Frequently, these lawsuits are adversary proceedings "arising in or related to a case under title 11,"[3] such as suits by or against the debtor's estate. For example, this type of venue question arises where the trustee is pursuing a claim or cause of action owned by the debtor-bankrupt that has passed to or became a part of the estate under Section 541. A venue question of this type may also arise when the trustee is suing to recover a fraudulent conveyance under Section 544 or 548, or to set aside and recover a preference under Section 547. It also arises where a claim is brought against the debtor's estate. Venue questions of this type "arising under or related" to a bankruptcy case are covered by Title 28, Section 1409.[4]

### [1] Venue for Bankruptcy Cases: Where to File a Petition

In general, proper venue for filing a petition is the district court for the district where the debtor has either a domicile, residence, principal place of business, or his principal assets for the 180 days or the greater portion thereof immediately preceding the petition.[5] The district court may transfer a case or proceeding under Title 11 to a district court for another district "in the interest of justice or for the convenience of the parties."[6] However, under former Title 28, Section 1477[7] (apparently deleted from and with no counterpart in the 1984 Amendments), the court in which the petition was filed was given power "in the

---

[2] Added by 1984 Amendments § 102. Section 1408 supersedes Section 1472 and is identical to Section 1472 except that "district court" is substituted for "bankruptcy court."

[3] Under the Bankruptcy Reform Act as originally enacted, the bankruptcy courts were given jurisdiction to hear such matters by Section 1471(c). This section was at the heart of the *Marathon* dispute and, as previously discussed, was invalidated in that case. Section 1334 now grants the district court original and exclusive jurisdiction of all cases, and original but not exclusive jurisdiction of all civil proceedings arising under Title 11, or arising in or related to cases under Title 11.

[4] Added by 1984 Amendments § 102. Section 1409 supersedes Section 1473.

[5] See 28 USC § 1408, which should be consulted for additional detail. See ¶ 12.02 for additional discussion of venue for commencement of the case. 28 USC § 1410, added by 1984 Amendments § 102, contains the venue provisions for cases ancillary to foreign proceedings.

[6] 28 USC § 1412, added by 1984 Amendments § 102. 28 USC § 1412 supersedes 28 USC § 1475.

[7] Former 28 USC § 1477 (cure or waiver of defects) provided:

> "(a) the bankruptcy court of a district in which is filed a case or proceeding laying venue in the wrong division or district may, in the interest of justice and for the convenience of the parties, retain such case or proceeding, or may transfer, under section 1475 of this title, such case or proceeding to any other district or division.

interest of justice and for the convenience of the parties" to either *retain* or transfer the case, even though the petition may have been filed in a bankruptcy court that was not proper venue under former Title 28, Section 1472.[8] A section that may apply, although it is not clear that it does, is Title 28, Section 1406.[9]

As can be seen, Section 1406 is similar to Section 1477, except that Section 1406 permits the district court to dismiss or transfer, but not retain, the case as did former Section 1477.[10] The omission of a counterpart to Section 1477 in the 1984 Amendments may have been based on the assumption that Section 1406 would apply in bankruptcy cases and was adequate to deal with bankruptcy petitions filed in the wrong venue. However, there is no indication from the legislative history that this is what was intended. In addition, if Section 1406 is applicable, it may be questionable whether the word "case" as used in Section 1406(a) includes civil proceedings arising in or related to a bankruptcy case.

Title 28, Section 1412, added by the 1984 Amendments, does authorize the district court to transfer (but not retain) a case or proceeding to another district in the interest of justice or for the convenience of the parties. However, the section does not address cases or proceedings filed in the wrong venue as did Title 28, Section 1477, of the original Bankruptcy Reform Act.

## [2] Venue for Proceedings Arising Under Title 11 or Arising in, or Related to, Cases Under Title 11

Title 28, Section 1409, contains the venue provisions for civil suits and proceedings arising under Title 11 or arising in or related to a case under Title 11. In general, such proceedings may be commenced in the district court in

---

"(b) nothing in this chapter shall impair the jurisdiction of a bankruptcy court of any matter involving a party who does not interpose timely and sufficient objection to the venue."

[8] 28 USC § 1477(a); see also B. Rule 1014(a)(2). Objection to improper venue or a motion for change of venue, of course, had to be timely made by a party in interest. See 28 USC § 1477(b); B. Rule 1014(a)(2). The case could be transferred only after "hearing on notice to the petitioners and to other persons as directed by the court." B. Rule 1014(a)(2).

[9] 28 USC § 1406 provides in part:

"(a) The district court of a district in which is filed a case laying venue in the wrong division or district shall dismiss, or if it be in the interest of justice, transfer such case to any district or division in which it could have been brought.

"(b) nothing in this chapter shall impair the jurisdiction of a district court of any matter involving a party who does not interpose timely and sufficient objection to the venue."

[10] Bankruptcy Rule 1014(a)(2) appears to be no longer effective, since it is based on Section 1477(a).

which the bankruptcy *case* is pending (i.e., the "home court").[11] However, there are exceptions to this general rule. A trustee seeking to recover a judgment for certain small debts and for consumer debts may have to proceed in a federal district court for the district in which the defendant resides. A trustee may commence a proceeding "arising in or related to [a bankruptcy] case" to recover a money judgment of or property worth less than $1,000 or a consumer debt[12] of less than $5,000 *only* in the district court for the district in which the defendant resides.[13] This provision is designed to prevent the defendant owing a small claim or consumer debt from being compelled to defend the action in some remote district where the creditor-debtor's bankruptcy case is pending. Compelling the defendant to appear in a remote forum might entail an undue hardship and default where otherwise valid defenses might be available. Also, for claims arising *after* the commencement of the case from the operation of the debtor's business, the trustee may proceed only in the district court for the district where a state or federal court action on such claim, under applicable nonbankruptcy venue provisions, could be brought.[14] Where the trustee is acting or proceeding as the statutory successor to the debtor under Section 541 (property of the estate) or the successor to rights of creditors under Section 544(b) (the trustee as representative of actual creditors), the proceeding may be commenced in the federal district court for the district where the state or federal court sits in which, under applicable nonbankruptcy venue provisions, the debtor or creditors, as the case may be, could bring the action had the bankruptcy case not been commenced.[15]

A proceeding based on a claim *against* the estate arising *after* the commencement of the bankruptcy case from the operation of the business of the debtor may be commenced either in the district court where the bankruptcy case is pending or in the district court for the district where the state or federal court sits in which the party commencing such action, under applicable nonbankruptcy venue provisions, could have brought an action on such claim.[16]

As previously noted, Title 28, Section 1477, of the 1978 Act, which authorized the bankruptcy court "in the interest of justice and for the convenience of the parties" to retain or transfer "a case or *proceeding*" filed in the wrong venue, has no counterpart in the 1984 Amendments. Presumably Section 1477 was not carried forward into the 1984 Amendments because of Section 1406, which is similar to Section 1477 in most respects. However, Section 1406 only authorizes the district court to dismiss or transfer the case and does not authorize retaining the case filed in the wrong district. Further, Section 1406(a) speaks

---

[11] 28 USC § 1409. This section is identical to former Section 1473 with the substitution of "district court" for "bankruptcy court."

[12] "Consumer debt" is defined in Section 101(7).

[13] 28 USC § 1409(b).

[14] 28 USC § 1409(d).

[15] 28 USC § 1409(c). However, claims of this type for less than $1,000 or consumer debts of less than $5,000 are subject to the provisions of Section 1409(b) and must be brought in the district court where the defendant resides.

[16] 28 USC § 1409(e).

in terms of "a case," and there may be some question whether this will include "proceedings arising in or related to" bankruptcy cases.

As discussed below, Title 28, Section 1412, added by the 1984 Amendments, does authorize the district court to transfer (but not retain) a proceeding to another district in the interest of justice or for the convenience of the parties. However, the section does not address cases or proceedings filed in the wrong venue, as did Title 28, Section 1477, of the original Bankruptcy Reform Act.

### [3] Change of Venue

In the interest of justice or for the convenience of the parties, the district court may transfer a case or proceeding under Title 11 to a district court for another district.[17] Note, however, that Section 1412 does not address cases or proceedings filed in the wrong venue, as did former Title 28, Section 1477, of the original 1978 Bankruptcy Reform Act.

## ¶ 11.05 JURY TRIALS

Title 28, Section 1411,[1] provides:

> (a) Except as provided in subsection (b) of this section, this chapter and title 11 do not affect any right to trial by jury that an individual has under applicable nonbankruptcy law with regard to a personal injury tort or wrongful death claim.
>
> (b) The district court may order the issues arising under section 303 of title 11 to be tried without a jury.

The apparent intent of subsection (a) of Section 1411 is to preserve for personal injury tort or wrongful death claims any right of trial by jury that might exist under nonbankruptcy law. As previously noted, such claims were expressly excepted from the core jurisdiction of the bankruptcy judge,[2] and under Title 28, Section 157(b)(5), arguably such claims must be determined by

---

[17] 28 USC § 1412, added by 1984 Amendments § 102. This section is almost identical to former Section 1475 except that "bankruptcy court" is changed to "district court." There is a difference also in that former Section 1475 stated that the bankruptcy court in the interest of justice and for the convenience of the parties could "transfer a case under title 11 or a proceeding arising under or *related* to such a case," whereas the new Section 1412 states that the district court "may transfer a case or proceeding under title 11" but does not refer to a *related* proceeding. Whether or not this difference is significant is not clear.

[1] As added by 1984 Amendments § 102.

[2] See 28 USC § 157(b)(2)(B) and discussion at supra ¶ 11.03[2][a].

the district court[3] and are not subject to the mandatory-abstention provisions.[4] It is not clear that the bankruptcy judge may conduct jury trials.[5]

Section 1411(b) permits, but does not require, the district court to order that issues arising with respect to an involuntary petition under Section 303 be determined without a jury. This includes, if the involuntary petition is timely controverted, the determination of such issues as whether the debtor is generally not paying his debts as they become due and whether a custodian has been appointed within 120 days of the filing of the petition.[6]

## ¶ 11.06 BANKRUPTCY RULES

Under the 1898 Act, the U.S. Supreme Court had the power to promulgate bankruptcy rules that, to the extent they did not abridge or modify substantive rights, superseded other laws that were in conflict therewith.[1] In 1973, Bankruptcy Rules were adopted for "straight" Chapter VII liquidation bankruptcy and subsequently rules were adopted for other "chapter" proceedings. In many areas these rules superseded provisions of the 1898 Act. To a large extent these Bankruptcy Rules, with adaptation to fit the bankruptcy situation, were patterned after, and in some instances incorporated by reference, the Federal Rules of Civil Procedure. This was particularly true for the 700 series of Bankruptcy Rules governing "adversary proceedings."

Section 247 of the Bankruptcy Reform Act[2] amended Title 28, Section 2075; as a result, the Bankruptcy Rules that were in effect on September 30, 1979 (i.e., the existing rules promulgated in 1973) continued to apply to cases

---

[3] See discussion at supra ¶ 11.03[2][a].

[4] 28 USC § 157(b)(4); see discussion at supra ¶ 11.03[1][b].

[5] In In re UNR Indus., Inc., 52 USLW 2258 (ND Ill. 1984), the court held that Section 157(b)(5) clearly requires that personal injury (asbestos) claims be tried in the district court rather than the bankruptcy court. Id. The court also concluded that with respect to the asbestos claims, Section 157(b)(5), mandating that such personal injury tort and wrongful death claims be tried in the district court, implicitly means that such claims are relieved from the effect of the Section 362 automatic stay or that the district court has the duty to lift the stay. The court stated: "If Congress enacts a statute which, though not referring to the automatic stay section, can only be carried out by lifting that stay, then this court's duty would be to lift the stay and give effect to the statute." Id. But see In re Gibbons Constr., Inc., 12 BCD 463 (ED Ky. 1984). In *Gibbons* the court considered a motion for withdrawal of reference on the ground that the bankruptcy court (judge) could not conduct a jury trial. The court overruled the motion in a very cryptic opinion, without specifying the basis other than Section 157, holding that the bankruptcy court may hold a jury trial. The court apparently felt that Section 157, which authorizes the district court to refer all cases arising under or arising in or related to a case under Title 11 (except for personal injury tort or wrongful death claims) to the bankruptcy judge, also authorizes the bankruptcy judge to conduct jury trials.

[6] For discussion of Section 303 and the involuntary petition, see ¶ 12.03[2].

[1] Former 28 USC § 2075.

[2] Pub. L. No. 95-598, 92 Stat. 2549 (1978).

under the new Code "to the extent not inconsistent" with the new Code until the "former rules" were repealed or superseded by new rules promulgated pursuant to Section 2075 as amended by the Bankruptcy Reform Act.[3] However, under amended Section 2075, new rules to be adopted for use under the Code may no longer supersede other conflicting laws.[4] In March 1979, Chief Justice Burger appointed an Advisory Committee on Bankruptcy Rules to draft new rules for use under the new Code. In August 1979, this committee published Suggested Interim Rules to serve as guidelines, until final new rules were adopted, in applying the former rules under the new Code and in filling gaps in the former rules created by the new legislation. In effect, these Interim Rules were supplemental rules, but were not binding until adopted as local rules by a particular bankruptcy court. Generally, the bankruptcy courts adopted these Interim Rules, sometimes with local modifications and additional local rules. Subsequently, in early 1982, the Advisory Committee submitted Proposed Bankruptcy Rules to cover all proceedings under the various bankruptcy chapters. On April 25, 1983 pursuant to Section 2075, these proposed rules were adopted by the U.S. Supreme Court and became effective on August 1, 1983.[5] The Advisory Committee's notes to the Proposed Rules are extremely helpful.[6] Presumably, the 1983 Bankruptcy Rules continue to apply after the 1984 Amendments to the extent that they are not inconsistent with any of the provisions of the 1984 Amendments. It seems clear that in the long run the Bankruptcy Rules will have to be revised to reflect the substantial changes made in jurisdiction and the bankruptcy court structure;[7] therefore, care must be exercised in using the Bankruptcy Rules. In addition, local rules and standing or general orders of the district courts must be consulted as undoubtedly there will be some that are relevant to the 1984 changes.

In addition to the Bankruptcy Rules, a number of bankruptcy courts have adopted additional local bankruptcy rules. These, of course, must be consulted and generally should be available from the local bankruptcy court or district clerk.[8]

### [1] Official Forms

Pursuant to Bankruptcy Rule 9009 adopted by the U.S. Supreme Court in 1983, the Judicial Conference of the United States has prescribed Official Forms to be observed and used with appropriate alterations. The Advisory

---

[3] See Bankruptcy Reform Act § 405(d).

[4] See Bankruptcy Reform Act § 247(2).

[5] These bankruptcy rules may be found in standard works such as Collier on Bankruptcy, Collier Bankruptcy Practice Guide, and Lawyer's Edition Bankruptcy Service, and are published in pamphlet form by various law publishers.

[6] The Advisory Committee continues work; in August 1984 it submitted a Preliminary Draft of Proposed Amendments to Bankruptcy Rules 5002 and 5004.

[7] In the 1984 Amendments Congress made changes in Bankruptcy Rules 2002 and 3001. 1984 Amendments §§ 321, 354.

[8] Some of these local rules are available in Collier Bankruptcy Practice Guide.

Committee on Bankruptcy Rules had recommended that the Official Forms be promulgated by the Judicial Conference rather than by the U.S. Supreme Court. There are Official Forms for petitions, to which petitions should substantially conform.[9] Printed Official Forms are generally available through suppliers of legal forms.[10]

---

[9] See B. Rules 1002, 1003, Official Forms 1 and 11. In the 1984 Amendments, Congress prescribed a change in Official Form 1 to reflect changes made by the 1984 Amendments. See 1984 Amendments § 322.

[10] In addition, the forms are reprinted in such works as Collier on Bankruptcy (15th ed.); Collier Bankruptcy Practice Guide; Lawyer's Edition Bankruptcy Service; Collier, Pamphlet Edition, Bankruptcy Rules, and other bankruptcy works.

# 12

# Bankruptcy: Commencement of Proceedings

## ¶ 12.01 INTRODUCTION

A bankruptcy case is begun by filing a petition with the bankruptcy court under the appropriate bankruptcy chapter—Chapter 7, 9, 11, or 13. Several sections of the Bankruptcy Code (the Code) are important with respect to the commencement of a case.[1] Section 109[2] specifies who is eligible for bankruptcy and which chapter the case may be filed under. Section 301[3] deals with the filing of a voluntary petition while Section 303[4] covers involuntary petitions. Section 302[5] covers joint petitions by spouses. There are Official Forms for petitions; the petitions should substantially conform to the Official Forms.[6] The federal Bankruptcy Rules, as well as any local bankruptcy rules, must be consulted on such details as filing the petition, caption of the petition, number of copies of the petition, signing, verification, filing fees.[7] The petition must be accompanied by the filing fee.[8]

Bankruptcy cases may be either voluntary (i.e., initiated by the debtor filing a petition) or involuntary (i.e., initiated by an appropriate number of creditors filing a petition against a debtor).[9] Note, however, that although there may be involuntary Chapter 7 or 11 cases there cannot be involuntary Chapter 13 cases.[10]

In both voluntary and involuntary cases, the filing of the petition is the "commencement of the case"[11] and is a significant term or point in time used in many sections of the Code.[12] Generally speaking, the dividing line between

---

[1] "Bankruptcy Code" refers to the Bankruptcy Reform Act of 1984, Pub. L. No. 95-598, as amended by the Bankruptcy Amendments and Federal Judgeship Act of 1984, Pub. L. No. 98-353. In general, the provisions of these two acts are codified in Titles 11 and 28 of the U.S. Code.

[2] 11 USC § 109. Unless otherwise specified in the text, "Section" refers to a section of the Bankruptcy Code (Title 11 of the U.S. Code).

[3] 11 USC § 301.

[4] 11 USC § 303.

[5] 11 USC § 302.

[6] Bankruptcy Rules (B. Rules) 1002, 1003; see Official Forms 1 and 11. Printed official forms are generally available through suppliers of legal forms. In addition, the forms are reprinted in such works as Collier on Bankruptcy (Matthew Bender, 15th ed. 1981); Collier Bankruptcy Practice Guide (Matthew Bender 1984); Bankruptcy Service, Lawyers Edition (Lawyers' Coop. Publishing Co. 1979); and Collier Bankruptcy Rules (Matthew Bender, pamphlet ed. 1985). The 1984 Amendments to the Bankruptcy Code required some changes in some forms (e.g., Official Form 1); the forms used should reflect these changes.

[7] Generally, Part 1 of the Bankruptcy Rules are of concern in filing the petition and commencement of the case. For discussion of the Bankruptcy Rules, see ¶ 11.06.

[8] B. Rule 1006. See discussion of filing fees at infra ¶ 12.04[3].

[9] There are Official Forms for both types of petitions. See Official Forms 1 (as amended in 1984) and 11.

[10] 11 USC § 303; see discussion at infra ¶ 12.03[2].

[11] See 11 USC §§ 301, 303(b).

[12] See, e.g., 11 USC §§ 362, 541(a), 544, 547.

the debtor's old life and his "fresh start" begins with the filing of the petition and commencement of the case. With some exceptions, property acquired after the petition is filed does not become property of the bankruptcy estate.[13] Debts incurred before the petition are discharged, but those incurred by the debtor after the petition, with some exceptions, are not discharged.[14] With some exceptions, only claims against the debtor that exist at the time the petition is filed will share in distribution of the estate.[15]

## [1] The Order for Relief

In a voluntary case, the filing of the petition—"commencement of the case"—constitutes an "order for relief."[16] This is the equivalent of an "adjudication" of bankruptcy under the 1898 Bankruptcy Act (the 1898 Act), although the Code does not use either the term "adjudication" or "bankrupt," substituting for those terms "order for relief" and "debtor" respectively.

In contrast, in an involuntary case, the filing of the petition does not automatically result in an "order for relief." In the case of an involuntary petition, entry of an "order for relief" necessarily occurs some time after the petition is filed.[17] This interim period between the filing of the involuntary petition and the order for relief commonly is referred to as the "involuntary gap." The term "order for relief" is used throughout the Code.[18]

Before the commencement of a case by an individual whose obligations are primarily consumer debts, the clerk must give written notice to the individual that informs the debtor of each chapter (e.g., Chapter 7, 11, or 13) under which he may proceed.[19]

Section 342(a) directs that "there shall be given such notice as is appropriate, including notice to any holder of a community claim, of an order for relief in a case under this title."[20] Bankruptcy Rule 2002(f) requires the clerk of the bankruptcy court to give notice by mail of the order for relief to the debtor, all creditors, and indenture trustees. Common practice is to send out notice of the order for relief with notice given under Section 342 of the meeting of creditors held pursuant to Section 341. Included with this notice is notice of the time for filing objections to discharge and for filing complaints to determine dis-

---

[13] See discussion at ¶ 13.04. For discussion of the Chapter 13 estate, which includes postpetition earnings of the Chapter 13 debtor, see ¶ 17.04.

[14] See discussion at ¶ 15.07.

[15] See ¶ 14.02.

[16] 11 USC § 301. Under Section 102(6), "order for relief" means entry of an order for relief.

[17] See 11 USC § 303(h); see also Official Form 14.

[18] See, e.g., 11 USC §§ 101(9), 348, 365(d), 366, 502(f).

[19] 11 USC § 342(b), as amended by Bankruptcy Amendments and Federal Judgeship Act of 1984, Pub. L. No. 98-353, § 302 (hereafter referred to as "the 1984 Amendments"). "Consumer debt" is defined in Section 101(7).

[20] 11 USC § 342(a), as amended by 1984 Amendments § 435. "Community claim" is defined in Section 101(6).

chargeability of certain debts, notice of the automatic stay, and time for filing proof of claim.[21] Bankruptcy Rule 2002(n), added by the 1984 Amendments, in a voluntary case commenced by an individual whose debts are primarily consumer debts, requires that notice by mail of the order for relief must be given not more than twenty days after the entry of the order.[22]

## ¶ 12.02 VENUE AND COMMENCEMENT OF THE CASE

As previously discussed,[1] the Code gives broad pervasive jurisdiction to the district courts (and the bankruptcy judges as the "bankruptcy unit" of the district court) to deal with most matters relating to bankruptcy: claims by and against the debtor's estate, distribution of assets, actions by the trustee to recover property for the estate or to recover fraudulent conveyances, preferences, and other proceedings arising in or related to bankruptcy cases.[2] The question of venue is important in determining which district court (or by referral, which bankruptcy unit) is the appropriate forum to exercise this broad pervasive jurisdiction in with respect to any given matter or issue.[3] Under the Code, venue questions can arise in two ways.[4] First, venue questions arise in

---

[21] See Official Form 16. Note, however, that the rule does not specify the time within which the notice must be given. Congress, in August 1983, in Pub. L. No. 98-91 amended Bankruptcy Rule 2002(f) by inserting after the word "clerk" the additional language "or some other person as the Court may direct." The purpose of this change was to authorize the bankruptcy clerk to contract with mailing agencies to provide mailing service for giving notices and to permit the cost of such services to be treated as an administrative cost to be borne by the estate.

[22] 1984 Amendments § 321. In a Chapter 7 case, the court is directed to promptly appoint an interim trustee after the order for relief. See 11 USC § 701(a); see also discussion at ¶ 13.02.

[1] See ¶ 11.03.

[2] For a discussion of the broad, pervasive jurisdiction originally granted under the Bankruptcy Reform Act of 1978 and the significant complicating changes made by the 1984 Amendments as a result of the *Marathon* decision, see generally ¶¶ 11.02, 11.03. Under the 1984 Amendments, all of the bankruptcy jurisdiction is granted to the federal district courts. See 28 USC § 1334. However, bankruptcy matters generally are referred to bankruptcy judges as the bankruptcy "unit" of the district court "known as the bankruptcy court." See 28 USC §§ 151, 1334. Certain core proceedings may be heard and determined by bankruptcy judges, while other bankruptcy matters or proceedings related to the bankruptcy case must be heard or finally determined by the district court. In some instances, however, the district court may be required to abstain and defer to a state court.

[3] For additional discussion of venue, see ¶ 11.04.

[4] The venue provisions of the 1984 Amendments are similar in most respects to those contained in the original 1978 Bankruptcy Reform Act in Title 28, Sections 1472, 1473. The changes are largely ones of renumbering, with the new venue provisions now referring to the "district court." This reflects the 1984 changes, which placed bankruptcy jurisdiction in the district courts under Title 28, Section 1334, resulting from changes

determining the district court in which a case may be commenced (i.e., where may a petition in bankruptcy, under either Chapter 7, 11 or 13, be filed by or against a person or entity). Section 1408 of Title 28 of the U.S. Code contains the venue provisions with respect to filing the petition.[5] Second, venue questions arise when determining the court in which lawsuits within the bankruptcy case or proceedings related to the bankruptcy case may be brought. Frequently these lawsuits will be proceedings "arising in or related to a case under Title 11,"[6] such as suits by or against the debtor's estate. For example, this second type of venue question arises when the trustee is pursuing a claim or cause of action owned by the debtor-bankrupt that has passed to or become a part of the estate under Section 541. Venue questions of this type also can arise when the trustee is suing to recover a fraudulent conveyance under Section 544 or 548 or to set aside and recover a preference under Section 547. Such questions also arise in situations in which a claim is brought against the debtor's estate. Venue questions of this type "arising under or related to" a bankruptcy case are covered by Section 1409 of Title 28 of the U.S. Code.[7]

In general, proper venue for filing a petition is the district court for the district where the debtor has his domicile, residence, principal place of business, or principal assets for the 180 days or the greater portion thereof immediately preceding the petition.[8] The district court may transfer a case or proceeding under Title 11 to a district court for another district "in the interest of justice or for the convenience of the parties."[9] Thus, if a petition is filed in a court that is not proper venue under Section 1408 of Title 28 of the U.S. Code, the court in which the petition was filed has the power to transfer the case "in the interest of justice and for the convenience of the parties."[10] A

---

required by the *Marathon* decision invalidating the broad grant of judicial power to non-Article III judges under the original grant of bankruptcy jurisdiction in former Title 28, Section 1471.

[5] Title 28, Section 1408, was added by 1984 Amendments § 102; it supersedes and is identical to former Title 28, Section 1472, except that "district court" is substituted for "bankruptcy court."

[6] The district courts are given jurisdiction to hear such matters by Title 28, Section 1334, added by the 1984 Amendments. For more detailed discussion, see ¶ 11.03. Under the 1978 Bankruptcy Reform Act as originally enacted, the bankruptcy courts were given jurisdiction to hear such matters by Title 28, Section 1471(c). This section was at the heart of the *Marathon* dispute and, as previously discussed, was invalidated in that case. Title 28, Section 1334, now grants the district courts original and exclusive jurisdiction of all cases and original but not exclusive jurisdiction of all civil proceedings arising under Title 11, or arising in or related to cases under Title 11.

[7] Title 28, Section 1409, was added by 1984 Amendments § 102; it supersedes former Title 28, Section 1473.

[8] See 28 USC § 1408, which should be consulted for additional detail. For additional discussion of venue for bankruptcy cases, see ¶ 11.04[1].

[9] 28 USC § 1412, added by 1984 Amendments § 102. Title 28, Section 1424, supersedes former Title 28, Section 1475.

[10] 28 USC § 1412(a); B. Rule 1014(a)(2). For additional discussion of petitions filed in a court that is not proper venue, see infra ¶ 12.02[1].

motion for change of venue must be made in a timely manner by a party in interest.[11]

## [1] Transfer and Consolidation

Even if a petition is filed in a district court that is proper venue under Section 1408 of Title 28 of the U.S. Code, the court may, upon timely motion of a party in interest and after a hearing with notice to the petitioner(s) and other parties, transfer the case to another district court "in the interest of justice and for the convenience of the parties."[12]

If a petition is filed by or against a debtor in more than one bankruptcy district, the court in which the first petition is filed may, upon a filed motion, determine "for the convenience of the parties and witnesses in the interest of justice the court or courts in which the case or cases should proceed."[13] The determination of where the case(s) is to proceed is to be made after a hearing on notice to the petitioner(s) and other persons as directed by the court. Unless otherwise ordered by the court in which the first petition is filed, proceedings on the other petitions are stayed until the determination is made by the court in which the first petition is filed.[14]

If two or more petitions are pending in the same court by or against the same debtor, Bankruptcy Rule 1015(a) permits consolidation of the cases. This will include the situation where more than one petition is pending in the same court due to a transfer from another court.

An individual and spouse may commence a case under an appropriate chapter[15] by a single petition.[16] After commencement of the case, the court determines whether, and to what extent, the debtors' estates will be consolidated.[17] As in other voluntary cases, the filing of a joint petition constitutes an

[11] See B. Rule 1014(a)(1).

[12] 28 USC § 1412; B. Rule 1014(a)(1).

[13] B. Rule 1014(b). The Rule also covers a situation where petitions are filed in more than one bankruptcy district against (1) a partnership and one or more of its general partners, (2) two or more general partners, or (3) a debtor and an affiliate. "Affiliate" is broadly defined in Section 101(2).

[14] B. Rule 1014(b).

[15] A joint voluntary petition may be filed under either Chapter 7, 11, or 13 by an individual and spouse who are otherwise eligible under the particular chapter. 11 USC § 302(a). However, there may not be a joint involuntary petition. See King v. Fidelity Nat'l Bank of Baton Rouge, 712 F2d 188 (5th Cir. 1983); Collier on Bankruptcy ¶ 303.07[a] (Matthew Bender, 15th ed. 1981).

[16] 11 USC § 302(a). There is one filing fee, which may be paid in installments. See 28 USC § 1980. For discussion of filing fees, see infra ¶ 12.04[2]. The spouses need not be insolvent in either the "equity" sense (failure to pay debts as they mature) or "bankruptcy" sense (assets less than liabilities).

[17] 11 USC § 302(b). One court held that an unmarried couple who had lived together for a period of three years, had incurred joint debts, and had joint assets (although precluded from filing a joint petition under Section 302 because they were not spouses), and who had filed separate Chapter 13 petitions, was entitled to joint adminis-

order for relief under the chapter under which the petition is filed.[18] If consolidated, the husband's and wife's assets and liabilities will be combined into a single pool to pay creditors.[19]

Joint administration and consolidation should be distinguished. In joint administration, the assets and debts of the debtors are not pooled; the two cases are merely handled together for administrative purposes. For example, there may be one trustee, a keeping of one docket, joint notices, and combined meetings of creditors. Consolidation, on the other hand, treats the consolidated estates as one and may affect the substantive rights of creditors.[20] Generally, certain conditions must be established to justify substantive consolidation:

> The power to consolidate should be used sparingly because of the possibility of unfair treatment of creditors of a corporate debtor who have dealt solely with that debtor without knowledge of its interrelationship with others. Yet in the rare case such as this, where the interrelationships of the group are hopelessly obscured and the time and expense necessary even to attempt to unscramble them so substantial as to threaten the realization of any net assets for all the creditors, equity is not helpless to reach a rough approximation of justice to some rather than deny any to all.[21]

Bankruptcy Rule 1015(b) also authorizes the court to order joint administration where two or more petitions are pending in the same court by or against any of the following parties:

(1) A husband and wife

(2) A partnership and one or more of its general partners

---

tration, but the court denied a request for consolidation. In re Coles, 14 Bankr. 5 (Bankr. ED Pa. 1981).

[18] 11 USC § 302(a); see also B. Rule 1015(b).

[19] H.R. Rep. No. 595, 95th Cong., 1st Sess. 321 (1977); S. Rep. No. 989, 95th Cong., 2d Sess. 32 (1978); Kennedy, "The Commencement of a Case Under the New Bankruptcy Code," 36 Wash. & Lee L. Rev. 977, 996 (1979). The House and Senate reports indicate that among the factors to be considered in consolidation are the extent of jointly held property and the amount of joint debts. Section 302 is designed mainly for ease of administration and, as the legislative reports indicate, is not to be taken as a license to consolidate in order to avoid other provisions of the Code to the detriment of either the creditors or debtors.

[20] See Collier on Bankruptcy ¶ 302.05, at 302–308 (Matthew Bender, 15th ed. 1981); see also B. Rules 1015 and 2009, which deal with procedural consolidation (i.e., joint administration) and not with substantive consolidation. Collier on Bankruptcy ¶ 302.05, at 302–309 (Matthew Bender, 15th ed. 1981).

[21] In re Coles, 14 Bankr. 5, 6 (Bankr. ED Pa. 1981), quoting from Chemical Bank N.Y. Trust Co. v. Kheel, 369 F2d 845, 847 (2d Cir. 1966); see also Sampsell v. Imperial Paper & Color Corp., 313 US 215 (1941); In re Flora Mir Candy Corp., 432 F2d 1060 (2d Cir. 1970).

(3) Two or more general partners
(4) A debtor and an affiliate.[22]

If joint administration is ordered by the court pursuant to Bankruptcy Rule 1015(b), the creditors may elect a single or separate trustees for the estates being jointly administered.[23] This applies only in Chapter 7 cases, since trustees are not elected under the other chapters.[24]

## ¶ 12.03 ELIGIBILITY TO BECOME A DEBTOR

Section 109 specifies who may be a debtor under each chapter of the Bankruptcy Code. Generally, only a "person" who resides or has a domicile, place of business, or property in the United States[1] may be a debtor under Chapter 7, 11, or 13.[2] As defined in Section 101(33), "person" includes an individual, a partnership, and a corporation but not a "governmental unit."[3]

The broad definition in Section 101(8) of a "corporation" (which is included in the definition of a "person") should be noted because it includes many forms of business organization not formally organized as corporations:[4]

(1) Associations having the power or privilege possessed by private corporations, but not by individuals or partnerships;

---

[22] In such circumstances, whether consolidation of the various cases involving two or more separate debtors is appropriate depends on other substantive considerations. See Levy, "Joint Administration and Consolidation," 85 Com. L.J. 538 (1980).

[23] B. Rules 2009(a), 2009(b).

[24] See discussion at ¶ 13.02. The rule also makes provision for separate trustees in jointly administered estates under other chapters. See B. Rule 2009(c).

[1] A foreign company with deposits in a United States bank is eligible to be a debtor as a person with property in the United States even though for some tax purposes the situs of personal property may be the owner's domicile. Bank of Am. N.T. & S.A. v. World of English, 23 Bankr. 1015 (ND Ga. 1982).

[2] 11 USC § 109(a).

[3] A "municipality," defined in Section 101(32) as a "political subdivision or public agency or instrumentality of a State," is included in the definition of "governmental unit" in Section 101(24) and thus is not a "person" under Section 109(a) and may not be a debtor under Chapter 7, 11, or 13. A municipality may file only under Chapter 9. See 11 USC §§ 109(a), 109(c).

[4] A dissolved corporation that, under state law, continues in existence for a period of three years for the purpose of winding up its financial affairs is eligible for an involuntary case under Chapter 7. See In re Liberal Mack Sales, Inc., 24 Bankr. 707 (Bankr. D. Kan. 1982); see also Chicago Title & Trust Co. v. Forty-One Thirty-Six Wilcox Bldg. Corp., 302 US 120 (1937), holding that whether a dissolved corporation can avail itself of bankruptcy laws depends on whether, under the law of the state of incorporation, the corporation continues in existence after dissolution. But see In re S & T Terry Contractors, Inc., 6 Bankr. 84 (Bankr. ND Ill. 1980), holding that a dissolved Illinois corporation was not eligible for a Chapter 11 case.

(2) Partnership associations organized under a law that makes only the capital subscribed responsible for the debts of the association;

(3) Joint-stock companies;

(4) Unincorporated companies or associations and business trusts.[5]

The term "corporation," however, does not include a limited partnership.[6]

A "person" generally is eligible for a Chapter 7, 11, or 13 case without any requirement that a specific amount or number of debts be owed. The "person" need not be insolvent, either in the "bankruptcy" or "equity" sense.[7] In contrast to an involuntary case under the 1898 Act, an "act" of bankruptcy is not required for an involuntary case under the Code.[8] Not every "person" is eligible for each type of bankruptcy, however.[9] For example, railroads,[10] domestic insur-

---

[5] "Business trust" is not defined in the Code. In In re Tru Block Concrete Prods., Inc., 27 Bankr. 486 (Bankr. SD Cal. 1983), a trust that was formed solely to liquidate a corporation and that was controlled to a substantial degree by the beneficiaries, and that was considered to be engaged in business under California tax law, was held to be a "business trust" and thus was eligible as a "corporation" for purposes of Chapter 11. However, the court acknowledged that under the U.S. Internal Revenue Code the trust would be considered a "simple" nonbusiness trust. An Illinois land trust has been held not to be a "business trust" and thus not eligible for a Chapter 11 case. In re North Shore Nat'l Bank of Chicago, 17 Bankr. 867 (Bankr. ND Ill. 1982); see also In re Old Second Nat'l Bank of Aurora, 7 Bankr. 37 (Bankr. ND Ill. 1980); In re Treasure Island Land Trust, 2 Bankr. 332 (Bankr. MD Fla. 1980); In re Citizens Bank & Trust Co. of Park Ridge, 8 Bankr. 812 (Bankr. ND Ill. 1981); In re Cohen, 4 Bankr. 201 (Bankr. SD Fla. 1980). In In re Dreske Greenway Trust, 14 Bankr. 618 (Bankr. ED Wis. 1981), the court held that a trust created for the specific purpose of engaging in business and used for such purposes was a "business trust."

[6] 11 USC § 101(8)(B).

[7] For a Chapter 13 case, Section 109(e) may be read to require that a debtor owe both secured and unsecured debts. See Kennedy, "The Commencement of a Case Under the New Bankrupcy Code," 36 Wash. & Lee L. Rev. 977, 983 (1979).

[8] As pointed out at infra ¶ 12.03[2][d], if an involuntary petition is contested by the debtor, one of two conditions must be established for the petition to be successful: (1) the debtor is generally not paying his debts as they become due, or (2) a custodian was appointed within 120 days of the filing of the petition. In this sense, an "act" of bankruptcy may be required for a petition in an involuntary case to succeed under the Code. In part, the requirement of an "act" of bankruptcy was abolished to eliminate the heavy burden of proof in establishing such acts (many acts required proof of insolvency) and to permit earlier filing of a petition to prevent deterioration of the debtor's estate and perhaps to permit an attempt at rehabilitation before the debtor's condition reaches the point where there is little realistic chance for rehabilitation. See Kennedy, "The Commencement of a Case Under the New Bankruptcy Code," 36 Wash. & Lee L. Rev. 977, 1013 (1979).

[9] Chapter 9 is reserved for a municipality. See 11 USC §§ 109(a), 109(c).

[10] "Railroad" is defined in Section 101(36). A railroad may be a debtor under Chapter 11, with the Subchapter IV provisions applying to railroad reorganizations. 11 USC § 109(d).

ance companies,[11] banks, savings banks, cooperative banks, savings and loan associations, building and loan associations, homestead associations, and credit unions are not eligible for Chapter 7.[12] Also excluded from Chapter 7 eligibility are foreign insurance companies, banks, savings banks, cooperative banks, savings and loan associations, building and loan associations, homestead associations and credit unions that are engaged in such business in the United States. If such a financial institution is not doing such a business in the United States but does own property here, then it may be eligible for Chapter 7 or 11.[13] The Code does not define such terms as "bank," "insurance company," and "savings bank," used in Sections 109(b)(2) and 109(b)(3), and "neither the Code nor the legislative history undertakes to resolve the question whether the terms should be given a uniform meaning or whether they should depend on the state or other non-bankruptcy law."[14] Any "person" who is eligible for Chapter 7, except a stockbroker or a commodity broker,[15] is eligible for Chapter 11.[16]

Only individuals with a "regular source of income" may use Chapter 13. There are also limitations on the amount of debt, secured and unsecured, that a

---

[11] A health maintenance organization (HMO) has been held to be an "insurance company" within the meaning of Section 109(b)(2) and thus not eligible for Chapter 7 or Chapter 11. See In re Portland Metro Health, Inc., 15 Bankr. 102 (Bankr. D. Ore. 1981). In determining whether the exclusions of Section 109(b) applied, the court in *Portland Metro Health* indicated that the debtor's status under a "state classification test" was an important, but not the sole, test. In concluding that the HMO was an insurance company, the court considered such factors as (1) the extent of regulation of the debtor, (2) whether there were express statutory procedures for nonbankruptcy liquidation of the debtor, (3) whether the nature of the debtor's business was public or quasi-public and involved interests other than those of creditors, and (4) whether there was an underwriting of and spreading of risk.

[12] 11 USC § 109(b)(2).

[13] 11 USC § 109(b)(3). However, note that there are provisions in Section 303(k) permitting involuntary petitions against a foreign bank not engaged in such business in the United States only under Chapter 7. Compare Israel-British Bank (London) Ltd. v. FDIC, 536 F2d 509 (2d Cir. 1976). A foreign banking or insurance company that is not doing business in the United States is permitted to become a debtor because there otherwise would be no nonbankruptcy law governing liquidation or rehabilitation of such businesses. Kennedy, "The Commencement of a Case Under the New Bankruptcy Code," 36 Wash. & Lee L. Rev. 977, 990 (1979).

[14] See id. at 977, 989 for discussion of the varying approaches taken by the courts under the 1898 Act.

[15] These terms are defined in Sections 101(46) and 101(5). Special subsections of Chapter 7 apply to stockbrokers and commodity brokers. An individual employed by a stock brokerage firm as an account executive at a fixed salary was held not to be a "stockbroker" as defined in former Section 101(40) (now Section 101(46)) and therefore was eligible for Chapter 13. See In re Berry, 22 Bankr. 950 (Bankr. ND Ohio 1982). In In re Co Petro Marketing Group, Inc., 680 F2d 566 (9th Cir. 1982), the court held that a debtor who sold contracts for future delivery of petroleum and undertook to resell the contracts for the purchasers where no officially designated or regulated market existed was not a "commodity broker."

[16] 11 USC § 109(d). In addition, a railroad is eligible for Chapter 11. Id.

debtor may have under Chapter 13.[17] Only an individual, or an individual and spouse, owing less than $100,000 of unsecured debt and less than $350,000 of secured debt is eligible for Chapter 13.[18] In addition, a stockbroker or commodity broker may not use Chapter 13.[19]

New Section 109(f)[20] of the 1984 Amendments added a new condition of eligibility or disqualifying factor for individuals under any of the chapters of bankruptcy. Under Section 109(f), an individual is not eligible to be a debtor under Title 11 (Chapter 7, 11, or 13) if the individual has been a debtor in a case under Title 11 within the preceding 180 days and (1) the case was dismissed for willful failure of the debtor to abide by orders of the court or to appear before the court in proper prosecution of the case; or (2) the debtor requested and obtained a voluntary dismissal of the case following the filing of a request for relief from the automatic stay provided by Section 362. If the debtor has been a debtor in such a bankruptcy case, this may mean that the filing of a new petition will have to be delayed until the expiration of the 180-day period.

Finally, it should be noted that eligibility for relief under the Code is a question of subject matter jurisdiction and may be raised at any time.[21]

## [1] Voluntary Bankruptcy

A voluntary petition may be filed by an eligible "person" under bankruptcy Chapter 7, 11, or 13. The filing constitutes an order for relief.[22] For a

---

[17] 11 USC § 109(e). For additional discussion of eligibility for Chapter 13, see ¶ 17.02. There may not be an involuntary Chapter 13 case, and a Chapter 7 case can be converted to Chapter 13 only if the debtor requests a conversion. 11 USC § 706(c).

[18] 11 USC § 109(e). Note that when calculating these debt limits, contingent and unliquidated debts are not considered. One court has held that the obligation of the debtor as an accommodation comaker of a note was not a contingent debt and must be counted in determining debt eligibility under Section 109(e). Under state law, the debtor as maker of the note was bound without prior recourse to the principal. In re Marchetto, 24 Bankr. 967 (Bankr. App. Pan. 1st Cir. 1982).

An unsecured claim based on contract, although disputed, is not excluded in determining whether the $100,000 unsecured debt limitation is exceeded, because only contingent or unliquidated debt is excluded in the view of a Bankruptcy Appellate Panel for the Ninth Circuit. The fact that a claim is subject to defenses or counterclaims in excess of the creditors' claims does not prevent it from being liquidated. However, the court must determine the liquidated amount of any disputed claim prior to making the determination required by Section 109(e). In re Sylvester, 19 Bankr. 671 (Bankr. App. Pan. 9th Cir. 1982). Contra In re King, 9 Bankr. 376 (Bankr. D. Ore. 1981).

[19] 11 USC § 109(e).

[20] 11 USC § 109(f), as added by 1984 Amendments § 301. Section 109(f) was designed to limit the ability of an individual to file successive petitions (i.e., "back-to-back" bankruptcies) in a relatively short period.

[21] In re Citizen Bank & Trust Co. of Park Ridge, 8 Bankr. 812 (Bankr. ND Ill. 1981); In re Dreske Greenway Trust, 14 Bankr. 618 (Bankr. ED Wis. 1981); In re Associated Developers Trust, 10 BCD 406 (Bankr. D. Mass. 1976).

[22] 11 USC § 301.

voluntary petition, the debtor is not required to be insolvent in either the bankruptcy or equity sense.[23] A voluntary petition cannot be contested.[24]

### [2] Involuntary Bankruptcy

An involuntary petition may be filed only under Chapters 7 and 11 and may not be filed under Chapter 9 or 13.[25] Only persons eligible for voluntary bankruptcy under the particular chapter involved are eligible for involuntary bankruptcy.[26] Thus, a railroad may be forced into a Chapter 11 case but may not be forced into a Chapter 7 case.[27] Insurance companies, banks, and other financial institutions mentioned in Section 109(b) may not be forced into a Chapter 7 or 11 case.[28] However, some persons who are eligible to file a voluntary petition may not be forced into bankruptcy by an involuntary petition. A

---

[23] Under Chapter 9, a municipality must show insolvency or inability to pay its debts. See 11 USC §§ 109(c)(1), 109(c)(3); see also Kennedy, "The Commencement of a Case Under the New Bankruptcy Code," 36 Wash. & Lee L. Rev. 977, 983 (1979), suggesting that Section 109(e) may be read as requiring for purposes of Chapter 13 that the debtor must owe both secured and unsecured debts, although there is no minimum amount that must be owed. As previously noted, there are limits on the amount of secured and unsecured debt that can be owed in order to remain eligible for Chapter 13 relief.

[24] Kennedy, "The Commencement of a Case Under the New Bankruptcy Code," 36 Wash. & Lee L. Rev. 977, 982 (1979); Collier on Bankruptcy ¶ 301.19[4] (Matthew Bender, 15th ed. 1981). Collier suggests there may be some exceptions. Note, however, that "eligibility" for a particular chapter (i.e., subject matter) can be raised. See, e.g., In re Citizens Bank & Trust Co. of Park Ridge, 8 Bankr. 812 (Bankr. ND Ill. 1981); In re Dreske Greenway Trust, 14 Bankr. 618 (Bankr. ED Wis. 1981); In re Liberal Mack Sales, Inc., 24 Bankr. 707 (Bankr. D. Kan. 1982); In re Co Petro Mktg. Group, 680 F2d 566 (9th Cir. 1982); In re Old Second Nat'l Bank of Aurora, 7 Bankr. 37 (Bankr. ND Ill. 1980); In re Cohen, 4 Bankr. 201 (Bankr. SD Fla. 1980); In re Treasure Island Land Trust, 2 Bankr. 332 (Bankr. MD Fla. 1980); Bank of Am. N.T. & S.A. v. World of English, 23 Bankr. 1015 (ND Ga.1982).

Questions concerning the authority of the party acting on behalf of a corporate debtor, such as the authority of corporate officer to file the petition, may also be raised. See In re Penny Saver, Inc., 15 Bankr. 252 (Bankr. ED Pa. 1981) and cases cited therein; In re Al-Wyn Food Distribs., Inc., 8 Bankr. 42 (Bankr. MD Fla. 1980); In re American Int'l Indus., Inc., 10 Bankr. 695 (Bankr. SD Fla. 1981). In *Penny Saver*, the court said the burden of proof is on the objecting party and held that the objector had failed to show that the party filing on behalf of the corporation did not act with proper authority.

[25] 11 USC § 303(a). Official Form 11 or a petition substantially conforming to Form 11 should be used. See B. Rule 1003(a). Service of the petition and summons is made pursuant to B. Rule 1010.

[26] 11 USC § 303(a).

[27] 11 USC §§ 109(d), 303(a).

[28] 11 USC §§ 109(b), 109(d), 303(a).

farmer[29] and a "corporation" that is not a "moneyed, business or commercial corporation" may not be involuntarily thrown into a Chapter 7 or 11 case.[30]

There are no provisions for a joint involuntary petition; thus, a joint involuntary petition may not be filed against spouses.[31] An involuntary petition may be filed against a foreign bank not engaged in banking business in the United States only under Chapter 7 and only if a foreign proceeding concerning that bank is pending.[32]

### [a] Effect of an Involuntary Petition

An "involuntary gap" exists between the filing of an involuntary petition and the entry of the order for relief. The filing of the petition, however, does not end all activities of the debtor during this involuntary gap. Unless the court orders otherwise, the debtor may continue to operate any business during this gap and may continue to use, acquire, or dispose of property as if the case had

---

[29] "Farmer" is defined in Section 101(17) as a person who has received more than 80 percent of his gross income for the taxable year immediately preceding the taxable year in which the case is commenced from a farming operation owned or operated by such person. "Farming operation" is defined in Section 101(18). "Person" includes a partnership or corporation (see 11 USC § 101(33)); thus, an agribusiness falls within this definition. This represents an expansion of protection for "farmers" from that given under the 1898 Act. Farmers are protected from involuntary bankruptcy because of the cyclical nature of their business; one bad year due to low prices or weather should not subject a debtor to involuntary bankruptcy. See H.R. Rep. No. 595, 95th Cong., 1st Sess. 322 (1977); S. Rep. No. 989, 95th Cong., 2d Sess. 32 (1978).

[30] 11 USC § 303(a). This includes "eleemosynary" institutions such as churches, schools, and charitable organizations. H.R. Rep. No. 595, 95th Cong., 1st Sess. 322 (1977); S. Rep. No. 989, 95th Cong., 2d Sess. 32 (1978). Such organizations, although protected from involuntary bankruptcy, may voluntarily invoke either Chapter 7 or 11. One author suggests that in determining what is included within the phrase "moneyed, business or commercial corporation," there is no reason to consult state law but that the phrase probably does not include all "nonprofit organizations." Kennedy, "The Commencement of a Case Under the New Bankruptcy Code," 36 Wash. & Lee L. Rev. 977, 1001 (1979). Professor Kennedy states that similar language under the 1898 Act did not insulate produce marketing cooperatives, and that it is not clear that Congress intended to include within the term all fraternal and social organizations.

In In re Mandalay Shores Coop. Hous. Ass'n, 22 Bankr. 202 (Bankr. MD Fla. 1982), a nonprofit corporation, formed by tenants to acquire an apartment complex to prevent sale of the complex, which likely would have resulted in conversion of the apartment to a condominium, was held to be a "non-moneyed, non-business, non-commercial" corporation and thus not subject to involuntary conversion from Chapter 11 to 7. The court noted that in making such a determination, other courts have looked to the provisions of state law, the articles of incorporation, and the actual character and activities of the corporation. Id. at 206.

[31] See King v. Fidelity Nat'l Bank of Baton Rouge, 712 F2d 188 (5th Cir. 1983); Collier on Bankruptcy ¶ 303.07[a] (Matthew Bender, 15th ed. 1981).

[32] 11 USC § 303(k).

not been commenced.[33] To enable the debtor to operate during this uncertain period, claims of creditors that arise in the ordinary course of business and that are incurred during the involuntary gap (or before the appointment of a trustee if earlier than the order for relief) are treated as if they arose before the petition was filed and are given second priority claim status.[34] Also, transfers of property by the debtor during the involuntary gap and before the order for relief are valid and may not be set aside by the trustee to the extent that the transfer is made for value given after the commencement of the case.[35] These transfers are valid notwithstanding the fact that the transferee had notice or knowledge of the commencement of the case.[36]

During the involuntary gap and before entry of the order for relief, the court may appoint an interim trustee, if necessary, to preserve the property of the estate or to prevent loss to the estate. This appointment occurs only upon request by a party in interest.[37]

### [b] Petitioning Creditors

An involuntary petition filed under either Chapter 7 or 11 requires at least one petitioning creditor. In most cases, three or more petitioning creditors are required. If the debtor has twelve or more creditors, at least three petitioning creditors are required; if there are fewer than twelve creditors, one petitioning creditor may be sufficient.[38] In either case, the claims of the petitioning creditor(s), which may not be either contingent as to liability[39] or be the subject of a

---

[33] 11 USC § 303(f).

[34] See 11 USC §§ 507(a)(2), 502(f), and discussion at ¶¶ 14.06[1], 14.09[2].

[35] 11 USC §§ 549(a), 549(b). For additional discussion, see ¶ 16.10. Section 549(b) specifically provides that satisfaction of or securing of a debt that arose before the commencement of the case is not "value" within the meaning of this section.

[36] 11 USC § 549(b).

[37] 11 USC § 303(g). In "pilot districts" the U.S. Trustee will make the appointment. See 11 USC § 15303. For discussion of the U.S. Trustee in "pilot districts," see ¶ 13.02[3].

[38] 11 USC § 303(b). See generally Taube, "Involuntary Bankruptcy: Who May Be a Petitioning Creditor?" 21 Hous. L. Rev. 339 (1984).

[39] A contingent claim is

> "one which the debtor will be called upon to pay only upon the occurrence or happening of an extrinsic event which will trigger the liability of the debtor to the alleged creditor and if such triggering event or occurrence was one reasonably contemplated by the debtor and creditor at the time the event giving rise to the claim occurred."

In re B.D. Int'l Discount Corp., 701 F2d 1071, 1073 n.2 (2d Cir. 1983), cert. denied, 104 S. Ct. 108 (1983), quoting In re All Media Properties Inc., 5 Bankr. 126, 133 (Bankr. SD Tex. 1980); see also In re North County Chrysler Plymouth, Inc., 13 Bankr. 393 (Bankr. WD Mo. 1981); In re Longhorn 1979-II Drilling Program, 32 Bankr. 923 (Bankr. WD Okla. 1983) (claims of petitioners who had purchased partnership interests in the debtor and had sued for rescission and damages were not contingent); In re Dill, 30 Bankr. 546, 550 (Bankr. App. Pan. 9th Cir. 1983) ("[C]reditor holding an unadjudicated and dis-

bona fide dispute,[40] must aggregate at least $5,000 in excess of any lien securing the claim(s).[41]

Some case law under the 1898 Act had held that a secured creditor could not act as a petitioning creditor unless the security was waived. A petitioning creditor with security must be aware of the hazard of a "waiver" of security by acting as a petitioning creditor and should take steps to negate any suggestion of waiver in filing the petition.[42] Some authority suggests that a fully secured creditor may act as one of the petitioning creditors for purposes of obtaining the required number of petitioning creditors if the other petitioning creditors' unsecured claims aggregate $5,000.[43]

In determining whether a debtor has fewer than twelve creditors, creditors who are employees or "insiders" of the debtor, as well as persons who have received certain voidable transfers, are excluded from the count.[44] A creditor

---

puted tort claim is not barred as a petitioner by 11 U.S.C. § 303(b)(1). The only limiting factor under that section is contingency, and a tort claim is not contingent."). An unmatured obligation is not contingent as to liability. See In re All Media Properties, Inc., 5 Bankr. 126, 133 (Bankr. SD Tex. 1980).

[40] The 1984 Amendments added the requirement that the petitioning creditor(s) claim may not also be the subject of a bona fide dispute. 1984 Amendments § 426.

[41] 11 USC § 303(b). Note that although a fully secured creditor's claim does not qualify for meeting the $5,000 aggregate claim requirement, the claim of a partially secured creditor, who under Section 506 has both a secured claim and an unsecured claim, will be counted to the extent of the deficiency of the collateral. See 11 USC § 506.

[42] Cf. In re American Gypsum Co., 31 Bankr. 187 (Bankr. DNM 1983).

[43] In re Crabtree, 32 Bankr. 837 (Bankr. ED Tenn. 1983), quoting Collier on Bankruptcy: "Secured creditors may act as petitioning creditors if they intentionally waive their security . . . or if the other petitioning creditors' claims aggregate at least $5,000.00 over the value of any lien as provided for in § 303(b)(1)." Id. at 839.

[44] 11 USC § 303(b)(2). "Insider" is defined in Section 101(28) quite broadly; for individual debtors the term includes, among others, certain "relatives" (defined in Section 101(37)), partners, and a corporation of which the debtor is a director or officer or a person in control. Where the debtor is a corporation, an "insider" includes a director or officer of the corporation and a person in control of the debtor. The rationale for the exclusion of employees and insiders from the creditor count is that they might be sympathetic to the debtor and, by refusing to join in the petition, might frustrate other creditors in obtaining a sufficient number of petitioning creditors. The rationale for exclusion of persons who have received voidable transfers is similar; these persons are likely to be unwilling to act as petitioning creditors for a case that may have the result of upsetting a preference or other voidable transfer they have received. Their refusal to join as a petitioning creditor might frustrate the legitimate interests of other creditors. See In re Rassi, 701 F2d 627 (7th Cir. 1983).

There is an ambiguity in Section 303(b)(2) as to whether secured creditors and contingent claims are to be excluded in determining whether there are twelve or fewer creditors. The ambiguity is caused by the word "such" in the first clause of Section 303(b)(2), which reads "if there are fewer than 12 *such* holders"; this causes uncertainty as to whether "such" should be read to include all or only part of the preceding subsection 303(b)(1). The court in In re Skye Mktg. Corp., 11 Bankr. 891, 898–899 (Bankr. EDNY 1981) appeared to assume that creditors with contingent claims would not be counted. See also In re Hoover, 32 Bankr. 842, 851 (Bankr. WD Okla. 1983).

may be entitled to discovery to determine whether the list of creditors filed by the debtor is accurate as to the number of creditors and to determine whether any creditors should be excluded from the count.[45]

Under the 1898 Act, authority was divided on the question of whether small de minimis claims, such as recurrent utility bills, should be counted for purposes of determining whether a debtor had twelve or fewer creditors.[46] Neither the Code nor the legislative history makes clear whether small claims are to be excluded in counting the number of creditors.[47] One case under the Code has held that small de minimis claims should not be counted,[48] while other courts, including the Court of Appeals for the Seventh Circuit, have held that bona fide small recurring claims must be included in the count.[49]

At any time before dismissal of the case or entry of an order for relief, a creditor who qualifies as a petitioning creditor may join in the petition with the same effect as if the creditor had been an original petitioning creditor.[50] Thus, if there is an insufficient number of original petitioning creditors or if some creditors are disqualified, others may join in the petition to ensure that there are sufficient petitioning creditors in number and amount.

Under Bankruptcy Rule 1003(c), a person who has either transferred or acquired a claim for the purpose of commencing a Chapter 7 or 11 case is not qualified to act as a petitioning creditor.[51] An indenture trustee who represents holders of unsecured, noncontingent claims is expressly authorized to act as a petitioning creditor.[52] Under Section 303(b), as originally enacted in 1978, a number of cases held that a creditor was not disqualified from acting as a petitioning creditor because the claim was disputed.[53] However, a 1984 amendment to Section 303(b) requires that the petitioning creditor's claim be one that

---

[45] In re Rassi, 701 F2d 627 (7th Cir. 1983).

[46] The split of authority developed even though there was no express statutory authority for disregarding small claims. See, e.g., Grigsby-Grunow Co. v. Hieb Radio Supply Co., 71 F2d 113 (8th Cir. 1934) (small claims included); In re Okamoto, 491 F2d 496 (9th Cir. 1974) (small claims included); Denham v. Shellman Grain Elevator, Inc., 444 F2d 1376 (5th Cir. 1971) (small claims excluded).

[47] See H.R. Rep. No. 595, 95th Cong., 1st Sess. 322 (1977); S. Rep. No. 989, 95th Cong., 2d Sess. 33 (1978); In re Blaine Richards & Co., 10 Bankr. 424, 430–431 (Bankr. EDNY 1981).

[48] See In re Blaine Richards & Co., Inc., 10 Bankr. 424 (Bankr. EDNY 1981).

[49] In re Rassi, 701 F2d 627 (7th Cir. 1983); In re Hoover, 32 Bankr. 842 (Bankr. WD Okla. 1983); In re Skye Mktg. Corp., 11 Bankr. 891, 899 n.5 (Bankr. EDNY 1981) (dictum).

[50] 11 USC § 303(c).

[51] Kennedy, "The Commencement of a Case Under the New Bankruptcy Code," 36 Wash. & Lee L. Rev. 977, 1005 n.150 (1979), raises the question of whether such a rule is inconsistent with the Code, which itself does not contain such a procedural limitation.

[52] 11 USC § 303(b)(1).

[53] In re Covey, 650 F2d 877 (7th Cir. 1981); In re B.D. Int'l Discount Corp., 13 Bankr. 635 (Bankr. SDNY 1981); In re All Media Properties, Inc., 5 Bankr. 126 (Bankr. SD Tex. 1980); In re Kreidler Import Corp., 4 Bankr. 256 (Bankr. D. Md. 1980); see

is not the subject of a bona fide dispute, and thus overrules these cases.[54] It is not clear that the Code requires a petitioning creditor to be free of the "taint" of a preferential transfer or other voidable transfer.[55] The case law under the 1898 Act, which generally required an "act" of bankruptcy for a successful involuntary petition, held that a creditor who had received a voidable preference could qualify as a petitioning creditor only if the voidable transfer was surrendered.[56] One bankruptcy court has found nothing in the Code or legislative history requiring a departure from this case law. The court held that a creditor who had received a postpetition voidable preference, but had not surrendered the preference, could not join as a petitioning creditor.[57] The same court also held that a bona fide counterclaim that exceeds the amount of a claim extinguishes the claim for the purpose of filing a petition.[58]

Although employees and "insiders" are expressly excluded from the count in determining the number of creditors, these parties are not expressly disqualified from acting as petitioning creditors.[59]

If the petition is dismissed on grounds other than consent of all the petitioners and the debtor, the court may grant judgment against the petitioners and in favor of the debtor for costs and attorney fees. In cases where a trustee has been appointed, damages caused by the trustee taking possession of the debtor's property may be awarded.[60] If the petition was filed in bad faith, an award against the petitioners may be made for damages caused by the filing, and in appropriate cases, punitive damages may be awarded.[61] Petitioning creditors may be required to gave a bond to indemnify the debtor against costs and damages.[62] If the petitioners are successful in their petition, however, their

---

also Taube, "Involuntary Bankruptcy: Who May Be a Petitioning Creditor?" 21 Hous. L. Rev. 339, 345–358 (1984).

[54] 1984 Amendments § 426.

[55] Transferees of certain voidable transfers are not to be included in determining whether a debtor has twelve creditors.

[56] In re Kreidler Import Corp., 4 Bankr. 256 (Bankr. D. Md. 1980); Collier on Bankruptcy ¶ 59.06[1.2], at 573 (Matthew Bender, 14th ed. 1977).

[57] In re Kreidler Import Corp., 4 Bankr. 256 (Bankr. D. Md. 1980).

[58] Id. at 259.

[59] 11 USC § 303(b)(2).

[60] 11 USC § 303(i)(1).

[61] 11 USC § 303(i)(2); see In re Ramsden, 17 Bankr. 59 (Bankr. ND Ga. 1981). The House and Senate reports stated:

> "These damages may include such items as loss of business during and after the pendency of the case, and so on. 'Or' is not exclusive in this paragraph. The court may grant any or all of the damages provided for under the provision. Dismissal in the best interests of creditors under section 305(a)(1) would not give rise to a damages claim."

H.R. Rep. No. 595, 95th Cong., 1st Sess. 424 (1977); S. Rep. No. 989, 95th Cong., 2d Sess. 34 (1978).

[62] 11 USC § 303(e).

actual and necessary expenses and attorney fees have priority as administrative expenses.[63]

### [c] Involuntary Partnership Cases

An involuntary petition may be filed against a partnership by the appropriate number of creditors under either Section 303(b)(1) or 303(b) (2).[64] In addition, under Section 303(b)(3), an involuntary petition may be filed against a partnership by one or more but fewer than all of the general partners. In either situation, if the petition is timely contested, the appropriate basis for entry of an order for relief must be established: Either the debtor must have been generally not paying debts as they became due or there must have been an appointment of a custodian.[65] Also, if an order for relief has been entered against all of the general partners, then a general partner, the trustee of a general partner, or a holder of a claim against the partnership may file an involuntary petition against the partnership.[66]

### [d] Opposing the Petition

Section 303(d) expressly provides that the debtor may file an answer to the petition. In the case of a petition against a partnership, a general partner who has not acted as a petitioning creditor may file an answer.[67] There is no express authorization for other parties answering the involuntary petition, but the general view, with possible exceptions, is that other parties may not oppose the petition.[68]

In opposing or making an answer to the petition, the applicable rules must be consulted.[69] Defenses and objections to the petition must be filed and served within twenty days after service of summons.[70] If no pleading or other

---

[63] 11 USC §§ 503(b)(3)(A), 503(b)(4), 507.

[64] See generally Hanley, "Partnership Bankruptcy Under the New Act," 31 Hastings L.J. 149 (1979).

[65] 11 USC § 303(h) and discussion at infra ¶ 12.03[2][d].

[66] 11 USC § 303(b)(3).

[67] The effect of this partnership provision is that a petition by less than all of the general partners is treated as an involuntary petition that may be answered by a nonpetitioning general partner. See H.R. Rep. No. 595, 95th Cong., 1st Sess. 322–23 (1977); S. Rep. No. 989, 95th Cong., 2d Sess. 33 (1978); see also B. Rule 1011.

[68] See Collier on Bankruptcy ¶ 303.20 (Matthew Bender, 15th ed. 1981); see also Kennedy, "The Commencement of a Case Under the New Bankruptcy Code," 36 Wash. & Lee L. Rev. 977 (1979). It seems clear, however, that other parties in interest may raise the question of whether the debtor is eligible for the particular chapter under which the case is filed. See supra ¶ 12.03[1]; see also Collier on Bankruptcy ¶ 301.20[1] (Matthew Bender, 15th ed. 1981).

[69] See also B. Rule 1011.

[70] Id. If service is made by publication on a debtor or partner not residing within the state in which the bankruptcy court sits, the court must fix a time for filing and serving the response.

defense to a petition is filed within the time provided for in Bankruptcy Rule 1011, the court is directed to enter an order for relief on the next day or as soon thereafter as practicable.[71] If the petition is timely controverted, the court, after trial, may enter an order for relief only if one of two conditions is established: (1) the debtor is generally not paying debts as they become due unless such debts are the subject of a bona fide dispute,[72] or (2) a custodian or receiver has been appointed within 120 days before the filing of the petition.[73]

If the involuntary petition alleges that the debtor is generally not paying his debts as they become due[74] and the debtor denies the allegation, discovery is available pursuant to Bankruptcy Rule 1012 and Federal Rules of Civil Procedure 26 through 37. Examination of the debtor and other parties may be ordered pursuant to Bankruptcy Rule 2004.[75] Also, a creditor may be entitled to discovery to determine whether the list of creditors filed by the debtor is accurate as to the number of creditors and to determine whether any creditors should be excluded from the count.[76]

### [e] Jury Trial

In contrast to the 1898 Act,[77] the Code eliminates the right to a jury trial with respect to a contested involuntary petition. Even if a jury trial is properly requested, the district court has the discretion, sua sponte or on motion, to dispense with a jury on issues arising under Section 303.[78] This elimination of the right to a jury trial on issues arising out of the involuntary petition does not

---

Service of a motion under Federal Rule of Civil Procedure 12(b) extends the time for filing and serving a responsive pleading. B. Rule 1011(c). Also, no pleadings other than an answer or such motion are permitted unless the court orders a reply to the answer. B. Rule 1011(e).

[71] B. Rule 1013(b).

[72] 11 USC § 303(h)(1), as amended by 1984 Amendments § 426.

[73] See 11 USC § 303(h)(1) and discussion at infra ¶ 12.03[2][f]. This does not include a receiver who is appointed or authorized to take charge of less than substantially all of the debtor's property for the purpose of enforcing a lien against such property. 11 USC § 303(h)(2).

[74] See discussion at infra ¶ 12.03[2][f].

[75] B. Rule 1012; see generally Viar, "Discovery in Bankruptcy Cases," 17 U.C.C.L.J. 22 (1984).

[76] In re Rassi, 701 F2d 627 (7th Cir. 1983).

[77] Under Section 19 of the 1898 Act (former Title 11, Section 42), a person against whom an involuntary petition was filed was entitled upon timely request to a jury trial with respect to the question of insolvency and "acts" of bankruptcy. An "act" of bankruptcy as a requirement for an involuntary petition has been eliminated under the Code.

[78] 28 USC § 1411(b), added by 1984 Amendments § 101; see also B. Rule 9015(b)(3). Title 28, Section 1411, replaces former Title 28, Section 1480. Title 28, Section 1411(b), is identical to former Title 28, Section 1480(b).

appear to involve a constitutional issue, since there was no right to a jury trial in bankruptcy case under the English common law in 1789.[79]

### [f] Grounds for Relief

The Code eliminates the 1898 Act requirement that there be an "act" of bankruptcy for a successful involuntary petition. In one sense, however, the Code may be viewed as retaining the requirement of an "act" of bankruptcy if the involuntary petition is "timely controverted."[80] If the petition is controverted, the court, after trial, may enter an order for relief only if one of two grounds is shown to exist.[81] First, the court may enter an order for relief if "the debtor is generally not paying such debtor's debts as they become due unless such debts that [sic] are the subject of a bona fide dispute."[82] The statute does not set forth guidelines, tests, or the factors to be considered in determining when a debtor is "generally not paying his debts."[83] For example, how widespread must the failure to pay debts be? Is failure to pay a small number or even one large debt owed to a creditor sufficient to meet the test even if payment is being made to a majority of the creditors?[84] Should the determination be based upon a percentage test? If so, should the percentage be applied to the

---

[79] Kennedy, "The Commencement of a Case Under the New Bankruptcy Code," 36 Wash. & Lee L. Rev. 977, 1015 (1979). See generally Levy, "Trial by Jury Under the Bankruptcy Reform Act of 1978," 12 Conn. L. Rev. 1 (1979).

[80] See discussion at supra ¶ 12.03[2][d] on when the petition must be contested.

[81] 11 USC § 303(h).

[82] 11 USC § 303(h)(1), as amended by 1984 Amendments § 426. The amendment added the language "unless such that [sic] are the subject of a bona fide dispute."

As noted previously, if the petition alleges this ground and it is denied by the debtor, discovery is available pursuant to Bankruptcy Rule 1012 and Federal Rules of Civil Procedure 26 through 37. Examination of the debtor and other parties may also be ordered pursuant to Bankruptcy Rule 2004.

[83] One court has stated that the language is "woefully lacking in clarity" and that "[t]he legislative history sheds a limited amount of light." See In re B.D. Int'l Discount Corp., 701 F2d 1071, 1075 (2d Cir. 1983), cert. denied, 104 S. Ct. 108 (1983). Congress appears to have thought this "equity insolvency test" would be one that "the bankruptcy courts should have no difficulty in applying. . . ." See H.R. Rep. No. 595, 95th Cong., 1st Sess. 323 (1977). The view also was expressed that this "generally not paying his debts" test was more workable and could "more easily be determined than acts of bankruptcy." See Report of the Commission on the Bankruptcy Laws of the United States, H.R. Doc. No. 137, 93d Cong., 1st Sess. 75 (1973).

[84] See, e.g., In re Hill, 8 Bankr. 779 (D. Minn. 1981) (failure to pay three large debts constituted failure to pay debts "generally"); In re Kreidler Import Corp., 4 Bankr. 256 (Bankr. D. Md. 1980) (failure to pay a claim constituting over 97 percent of debtor's total obligation was "generally not paying debts as they became due"); In re International Teldata Corp., 12 Bankr. 879 (Bankr. D. Nev. 1981) (nonpayment of a small number of relatively large longterm obligations was "generally not paying debts as such become due," even though all other small, periodic debts were being paid). For discussion of the test, see generally Comment, "Involuntary Bankruptcy: The Generally Not Paying Standard," 33 Mercer L. Rev. 903 (1982).

number of creditors whose debt is not paid, or should it be applied to the amount of debt not paid, or both?[85] Before the 1984 Amendments to Section 303(h)(l), a question was raised as to whether the fact that a claim was not being paid because it was disputed should be considered in making the determination of whether the debtor was generally paying his debts as they became due. In the leading case on whether disputed claims should be examined to determine whether the debtor was generally paying his debts as they became due, the Court of Appeals for the Seventh Circuit refused to adopt a per se rule and adopted the following test:

> Thus, disputed debts should be excluded from the "generally paying debts" determination only under the following circumstances: 1) the dispute is whether any claims exist, not merely regarding the amount of a claim; 2) the dispute can be examined without substantial litigation of legal and factual questions; and 3) the interests of the debtor in defeating an order of involuntary bankruptcy outweigh creditors' interests in achieving a somewhat more rapid determination of the involuntary bankruptcy question.[86]

The Court of Appeals for the Seventh Circuit further indicated that if the debtor prevailed under the above test, then the bankruptcy court should examine the merits of the claim and if "the debtor does establish that the entire debt is barred or otherwise invalid," then the disputed debt should be excluded from the "generally paying debts" calculation.[87] As previously mentioned, however, the 1984 amendment to Section 303(h)(1) now provides that debts that are the "subject of a bona fide dispute" are not to be considered in making the "generally paying debts" determination.

It is probably safe to predict that no clear-cut test for "generally paying debts" will be generally accepted and that determinations will be on a factual,

---

[85] At one point in the legislative process, Senate bill S.2266 contained the following language: "[I]f the debtor is generally unable to pay or has failed to pay a major portion of his debts as such debts become due"; however, this language apparently was eliminated in the legislative compromise. See Kennedy, "The Commencement of a Case Under the New Bankruptcy Code," 36 Wash. & Lee L. Rev. 977, 1009 (1979), for helpful discussion on this point. See also In re B.D. Int'l Discount Corp., 701 F2d 1071 (2d Cir. 1983). In In re All Media Properties, Inc., 5 Bankr. 126 (Bankr. SD Tex. 1980), a 51 percent or "majority of debts" test was rejected. In In re Reed, 11 Bankr. 755 (Bankr. SD W. Va. 1981), the court said that a purely mechanical test is not to be used, that the amount of indebtedness is not the only factor, and that "the factors of number, amount and materiality of non-payment must be viewed in the context of the debtor's overall handling of his financial affairs." Id. at 760.

[86] In re Covey, 650 F2d 877, 883–884 (7th Cir. 1981); see also In re B.D. Int'l Discount Corp., 15 Bankr. 755 (Bankr. SDNY 1981), aff'd, 701 F2d 1071 (2d Cir. 1983), cert. denied, 104 S. Ct. 108 (1983). However, the Court of Appeals for the Second Circuit declined to adopt, at that early stage, the "elaborate gloss" of the guidelines set forth in the *Covey* case.

[87] In re Covey, 650 F2d 883 (7th Cir. 1981).

case-by-case basis.[88] There is substantial authority that an order for relief may be granted on an involuntary petition even if there is only one creditor. With only a single debt, however, it can be argued that no case exists of the debtor "generally not paying debts" as mandated in Section 303(h))(1).[89] In single-creditor cases, the courts have generally granted an order for relief under "special circumstances": (1) if the sole creditor would be without an adequate remedy in nonbankruptcy law, or (2) if there is a showing of special circumstances amounting to fraud, trick, artifice, or scam on the part of the debtor.[90]

The second ground for relief is if a "custodian" was appointed or took possession of the debtor's property within 120 days before the filing of the involuntary petition.[91] Adequate grounds exist for entry of an order for relief if certain conditions exist within 120 days before the filing of the petition:

(1) A receiver or trustee of *any* property of the debtor is appointed in a nonbankruptcy proceeding; or
(2) There is a general assignment for the benefit of creditors; or
(3) A trustee or receiver is appointed or authorized to take possession of substantially all of the debtor's property for the purpose of enforcing a lien against the property (a receiver or trustee appointed or authorized to foreclose on less than substantially all of the debtor's property does not qualify).[92]

---

[88] See In re B.D. Int'l Discount Corp., 15 Bankr. 755 (Bankr. SDNY 1981), aff'd, 701 F2d 1071, 1076–1077, (2d Cir. 1983), cert. denied, 104 S. Ct. 108 (1983). In this case, where a creditor had a claim for $7.2 million, about 98 percent of the total debt, the bankruptcy court stated that "the 'generally not paying test' is satisfied where there is nonpayment of any single claim which represents an 'overwhelming portion' of the total debt, even if the claim is disputed." 15 Bankr. at 762. See also In re Blaine Richards & Co., 16 Bankr. 362 (Bankr. EDNY 1982); In re Hill, 5 Bankr. 79 (Bankr. D. Minn. 1980).

[89] See, e.g., In re LeSher Int'l, Ltd., 32 Bankr. 1 (Bankr. SDNY 1982), and cases cited therein holding that failure to pay a single creditor does not indicate that the debtor is "generally not paying debts as they become due." See also Collier on Bankruptcy ¶ 303.12[4] (Matthew Bender, 15th ed. 1981).

[90] See In re B.D. Int'l Discount Corp., 13 Bankr. 635 (Bankr. SDNY 1981); In re 7H Land & Cattle Co., 6 Bankr. 29 (Bankr. D. Nev. 1980); In re Arker, 6 Bankr. 632 (Bankr. EDNY 1980); In re B.D. Int'l Discount Corp., 15 Bankr. 755 (Bankr. SDNY 1981). Cf. In re LeSher Int'l, Ltd., 32 Bankr. 1 (Bankr. SDNY 1982).

[91] 11 USC § 303(h)(2). "Custodian" is defined in Section 101(10) to include (1) a receiver or trustee, appointed in a nonbankruptcy proceeding, of any property of the debtor; (2) an assignee under a general assignment for the benefit of creditors; and (3) a trustee, receiver, or agent appointed or authorized to take charge of property for purposes of enforcing a lien against the property or for the purpose of general administration of such property for the benefit of creditors.

[92] 11 USC § 303(h)(2). For discussion of this "custodian" test, see Kennedy, "The Commencement of a Case Under the New Bankruptcy Code," 36 Wash. & Lee L. Rev. 977, 1011 (1979). See also In re B.D. Int'l Discount Corp., 15 Bankr. 755 (Bankr. SDNY 1981) (establishment of custodial escrow account with attorney in which all cash assets were placed was not shown to be type of "custodian" contemplated by statute, as it was

If bankruptcy ensues following appointment of a custodian, the custodian has a duty to turn over to the trustee the debtor's property and account for that property.[93]

## ¶ 12.04 FILING THE PETITION

A case under any of the chapters of the Code is begun by filing a petition under the appropriate chapter with the district court. Official Forms for the petition or a petition that conforms substantially to the Official Form should be used.[1]

### [1] Schedules of Assets and Liabilities, Current Income and Expenditures, and List of Creditors

Section 521(1) requires the debtor to file a list of creditors and, unless the court orders otherwise, a schedule of assets and liabilities, a schedule of current income and current expenditures, and a statement of the debtor's financial affairs.[2] This section is applicable in all types of cases.[3] The Bankruptcy Rules must be consulted for important details with respect to filing the list of creditors and schedules of assets and liabilities.[4]

In a voluntary case, the debtor generally is required to file with the petition a list of the names and addresses of all the creditors unless the petition is accompanied by a schedule of liabilities or a Chapter 13 Statement.[5] In an involuntary case, the debtor is required to file a list of creditors within fifteen days after entry of the order for relief unless a schedule of liabilities has been filed.[6]

Extensions of time for filing such lists may be granted only on motion, for cause shown, and with notice to any trustee and other parties, as directed by the court.[7]

---

not shown that attorney had responsibility for liquidating property); In re North County Chrysler Plymouth, Inc., 13 Bankr. 393 (Bankr. WD Mo. 1981) (auctioneer was not a "custodian" because he had no responsibility for paying debtor's debts).

[93] 11 USC § 543(b); see discussion at ¶ 13.05[3].

[1] See B. Rules 1002, 1003 and Official Forms 1, 11. In the 1984 Amendments, Congress prescribed a change in Official Form 1 to reflect changes made by the 1984 Amendments. See 1984 Amendments § 322.

[2] 11 USC § 521(1), as amended by 1984 Amendments § 305. See also 11 USC § 343 and B. Rule 4002 for other duties of the debtor.

[3] 11 USC § 103(a).

[4] In addition to B. Rule 1007, see, e.g., B. Rules 1008 (Verification) and 1009 (Amendments of Voluntary Petitions, Lists, Schedules, and Statements of Financial Affairs).

[5] B. Rule 1007(a)(1).

[6] B. Rule 1007(a)(2).

[7] B. Rule 1007(a)(4).

In addition to the items already discussed, debtors in a Chapter 7 or 11 case must file with the court schedules of assets and liabilities, a statement of financial affairs, and a statement of executory contracts prepared as prescribed by Official Form 6 and either Official Form 7 or 8. In a Chapter 13 case, the debtor must file a Chapter 13 Statement (Official Form 10) and, if engaged in business, a Statement of Financial Affairs (Official Form 8).[8] In a voluntary case, schedules must be filed with the petition, unless the petition is accompanied by the list of creditors, in which case the schedules must be filed within fifteen days. In an involuntary case, the schedules must be filed within fifteen days after the entry of the order for relief.[9] In addition, in a Chapter 11 case, the debtor must file a list of the name and address of the twenty largest unsecured creditors, excluding "insiders."[10]

Under Section 521(2)(A), added by the 1984 Amendments,[11] if an individual debtor's schedule of assets and liabilities includes consumer debts that are secured by property of the estate, within thirty days after the filing of a petition under Chapter 7 (or before the date of the meeting of creditors, if earlier), the debtor must file with the clerk a statement of his intention with respect to retention or surrender of the property. The debtor must also specify whether the property is claimed as exempt, whether he intends to redeem the property, or whether he intends to reaffirm the debt secured by the property.[12] Furthermore, within forty-five days after filing this notice of intent (or within such additional time as the court, for cause, fixes), the debtor must "perform his intention with respect to such property."[13]

## [2] Filing Fees and Attorney Fees

Upon application, individuals filing a voluntary petition may be permitted to pay the filing fee in installments.[14] The Bankruptcy Commission had recommended an in forma pauperis proceeding that is permitted in other federal courts under Title 28, Section 1915. As finally enacted, however, Title 28, Section 1930(a), specifically excludes the bankruptcy filing fees from the application of the in forma pauperis provisions of Section 1915 of Title 28 of the U.S.

---

[8] B. Rule 1007(b).

[9] B. Rule 1007(c).

[10] B. Rule 1007(d).

[11] 1984 Amendments § 305.

[12] The court may within this period, for cause, extend the time for filing the statement. Id.

[13] 11 USC § 521(2)(B).

[14] 28 USC § 1930(a); B. Rule 1006(b). The filing fees are set forth in Title 28, Section 1930: $60 for Chapter 7 or Chapter 13, $200 for nonrailroad filings under Chapter 11, and $500 for Chapter 11 filings concerning a railroad. If paid in installments, the filing fee must be paid in not more than four installments and the fee must be paid in full not later than 120 days after filing of the petition unless the court extends the time to not more than 180 days. B. Rule 1006(b)(2); see also Official Form 2, "Application to Pay Filing Fee in Installments."

Code.[15] The filing fee may not be paid in installments if attorney fees in connection with the case have been paid in advance.[16] If the filing fee is not paid, the petition may be dismissed.[17]

Any attorney representing a debtor in a bankruptcy case must file with the bankruptcy court a statement of the compensation paid or agreed to be paid for services rendered or to be rendered in connecton with the case.[18] This statement must be filed with the bankruptcy court on or before the first date set for the meeting of creditors unless another time is fixed by the court.[19] To the extent such compensation exceeds the reasonable value of the services, the court may cancel the agreement or order return of any excess payment.[20] The bankruptcy court on its own initiative or on motion by a proper party, after notice and a hearing, may determine if attorney fees paid by the debtor before or after the commencement of the case are excessive.[21]

### [3] Service of the Petition and Process

The details with respect to service of the involuntary petition and summons are covered by Bankruptcy Rule 1010.

## ¶ 12.05 AUTOMATIC STAY

The filing of a petition under any of the chapters of the Code operates as a very broad automatic stay against practically any creditor collection action against the debtor or property of the estate.[1] The stay applies to both secured and unsecured creditors[2] and covers the following:

(1) Commencement or continuation of judicial or administrative proceedings against the debtor;

---

[15] See Kennedy, "The Commencement of a Case Under the New Bankruptcy Code," 36 Wash. & Lee L. Rev. 977, 993–994 (1979), for discussion of the irony of requiring filing fees in bankruptcy cases but permitting in forma pauperis in other civil proceedings. See also Report of the Commission on the Bankruptcy Laws of the United States, H.R. Doc. No. 137, 93d Cong., 1st Sess. 9 (1973). The constitutionality of requiring a filing fee was upheld under the 1898 Act in U.S. v. Kras, 409 US 434 (1973). Cf. Boddie v. Connecticut, 401 US 371 (1971).

[16] B. Rule 1006(b).

[17] 11 USC § 707(a); B. Rule 1017(b).

[18] 11 USC § 329(a); B. Rule 2016(b).

[19] B. Rule 2016(b).

[20] 11 USC § 329(b); B. Rule 2017(a).

[21] B. Rule 2017.

[1] 11 USC § 362.

[2] In re Holtkamp, 669 F2d 505 (7th Cir. 1982).

(2) Employment of process to recover on a prepetition claim or to enforce a judgment obtained before the commencement of the case;

(3) Any act to obtain possession of property of the estate or to create, perfect, or enforce any lien against property of the estate;[3]

(4) Any act to collect, assess, or recover a claim that arose before the commencement of the case or to set off against a prepetition debt.[4]

Examples of conduct that constitutes a violation of the stay include the following:

(1) Unauthorized postpetition eviction of the debtor;[5]

(2) Failure by a credit union to stop payroll deductions for loan repayment after the filing of the petition;[6]

(3) Recording of a mortgage shortly after the filing of the petition;[7]

(4) Suing for reclamation of collateral before relief from stay has been granted;[8] and

(5) Attempted cancellation after the filing of the petition of a bond issued to a corporation-debtor.[9]

Specifically included within the scope of the stay is the commencement or continuation of a case before the U.S. Tax Court concerning the debtor.[10]

---

[3] With the filing of the petition, all of the debtor's nonexempt property becomes property of the estate. See 11 USC § 541 and discussion at ¶ 13.04.

[4] In addition to the automatic stay, the court has injunctive power under Section 105, as amended by 1984 Amendments § 118. As amended, Section 105(a) states: "The court may issue any order, process, or judgment that is necessary or appropriate to carry out the provisions of this title." The 1984 Amendments deleted the word "bankruptcy" before "court," reflecting the 1984 changes made in the grant of bankruptcy jurisdiction to the district court resulting from the *Marathon* decision. See discussion at ¶¶ 11.02, 11.03. On the question of the extent to which the bankruptcy judges may exercise the power given by Section 105(a), Section 105(c) (added by the 1984 Amendments) states:

> "The ability of any district judge or other officer or employee of a district court to exercise any of the authority or responsibilities conferred upon the court under this title shall be determined by reference to the provisions relating to such judge, officer, or employee set forth in title 28. This subsection shall not be interpreted to exclude bankruptcy judges and other officers or employees appointed pursuant to Chapter 6 of title 28 from its operation."

[5] In re Lowry, 25 Bankr. 52 (Bankr. ED Mo. 1982).

[6] In re Holland, 21 Bankr. 681 (Bankr. ND Ind. 1982).

[7] In re Funket, 27 Bankr. 640 (Bankr. MD Pa. 1982).

[8] In re Codesco, Inc., 24 Bankr. 746 (Bankr. SDNY 1982).

[9] In re Advent Corp., 24 Bankr. 612 (Bankr. App. Pan. 1st Cir. 1982).

[10] 11 USC § 362(a)(8). For more extensive treatment of the automatic stay, see Kennedy, "The Automatic Stay in Bankruptcy," 11 U. Mich. J.L. Rev. 175 (1978); Martin, "Creditor Alternatives to Obtain Relief From Automatic Stays in Bankruptcy," 98 Banking L.J. 525 (1981); Aaron, "Bankruptcy Stays of Environmental Regulation: Harvest of Commercial Timber as an Introduction to a Clash of Policies," 12 Envtl. L. Rev.

Violation of the stay may lead to a finding of contempt not only for the creditor but also for the creditor's attorney,[11] and it also may expose the creditor to potential liability for damages.[12] Section 362(h), added by the 1984 Amendments,[13] permits an individual who is injured by a willful violation of a stay to recover actual damages, including costs and attorney fees, and in appropriate circumstances, punitive damages.

There is some difference in the case law as to whether a party may be held in contempt for violation of the automatic stay without a showing of a willful and knowing violation or at least a knowing violation.[14] Action taken in violation of the stay generally is held to be void.[15]

## [1] Exceptions to the Automatic Stay

The automatic stay that arises upon the filing of the petition does not operate as a stay of eleven types of action specified in Section 362(b).[16] One

---

1 (1981); Groschadl, "Freezing the Debtor's Bank Account: A Violation of the Automatic Stay?" 57 Am. Bankr. L.J. 75 (1983); Comment, "Automatic Stay Under the 1978 Bankruptcy Code: An Equitable Roadblock to Secured Creditor Relief," 17 San Diego L. Rev. 113 (1981); Comment, "The Automatic Stay in Bankruptcy: An Analysis of the Braniff Chapter 11 Proceeding," 14 Tex. Tech L. Rev. 433 (1983); Note, "When is a Governmental Unit's Action to Enforce Its Police or Regulatory Power Exempt From the Automatic Stay?" 9 Fla. St. U.L. Rev. 369 (1981); Annot., 53 A.L.R. Fed. 622 (1981).

[11] See, e.g., In re Bazan, 6 Bankr. 937 (Bankr. ND Ill. 1980); In re Carter, 691 F2d 390 (8th Cir. 1982); cf. In re Dennis, 17 Bankr. 558 (Bankr. MD Ga. 1982). In *Dennis*, although refusing to hold the creditor's attorney in contempt, the court held that the creditor's attorney had an affirmative duty to dismiss a garnishment proceeding against the debtor upon notification of the filing of the bankruptcy petition. For extensive discussion of the contempt power, see In re Reed, 11 Bankr. 258 (Bankr. D. Utah 1981).

[12] In re Lowry, 25 Bankr. 52 (Bankr. ED Mo. 1982). But see In re Jones, 27 Bankr. 374 (Bankr. SD Ohio 1983). See generally Comment, "Monetary Awards to the Debtor for Violations of the Automatic Stay," 11 Fla. St. U.L. Rev. 423 (1983).

[13] 1984 Amendments § 304.

[14] For cases holding that there must be a willful and knowing violation, see, e.g., In re Tom Powell & Son, Inc., 22 Bankr. 657 (Bankr. WD Mo. 1982); In re Holland, 21 Bankr. 681 (Bankr. ND Ind. 1982); In re Berger, 16 Bankr. 236 (Bankr. SD Fla. 1981); cf. In re Carter, 691 F2d 390 (8th Cir. 1982); In re Sandmar Corp., 12 Bankr. 910 (Bankr. DNM 1981). For extensive discussion and survey of the cases, see In re Reed, 11 Bankr. 258 (Bankr. D. Utah 1981). Contra In re Lohnes, 26 Bankr. 593 (Bankr. D. Conn. 1983).

[15] See, e.g., In re Young, 14 Bankr. 809 (Bankr. ND Ill. 1981); In re Johnson, 18 Bankr. 755 (Bankr. SD Ohio 1982); In re Holland, 21 Bankr. 681 (Bankr. ND Ind. 1982); In re Funket, 27 Bankr. 640 (Bankr. MD Pa. 1982); In re Advent Corp., 24 Bankr. 612 (Bankr. App. Pan. 1st Cir. 1982).

[16] 11 USC § 362(b), as amended by 1984 Amendments §§ 363, 392, 441. In an apparent mistake in renumbering, there are now two Sections numbered 362(b)(9), and new Section 362(b)(10) apparently should be Section 362(b)(11).

exception provides that the stay does not affect "the commencement or continuation of a criminal action or proceeding" against the debtor.[17] A significant number of cases have dealt with this exception. Some of the cases have held that the automatic stay does apply to a criminal prosecution in which the criminal action is merely being used to collect a debt, while other courts have enjoined these proceedings by use of the injunctive power of Section 105.[18]

Another important exception to the stay is "collection of alimony, maintenance, or support from property that is not property of the estate."[19] Thus, a nondischargeable claim for alimony and support that exists when the petition is filed can be asserted against property of the debtor that does not become a part of the estate property. This includes property acquired by the debtor after the petition is filed, or exempt property if subject to the claim.

In very limited circumstances, Section 362(b)(3)[20] permits perfection of a security interest after the petition is filed. If postpetition perfection is permitted against the trustee under Sections 546(b) or 547(e)(2)(a), such perfection is not subject to the automatic stay.[21]

The stay also does not cover the commencement or continuation of an action or proceeding by a "governmental unit" to enforce its police or regulatory power or to enforce a nonmoney judgment obtained to enforce police or regulatory power.[22] Another exception to the stay is made for certain foreclosures of mortgages or deeds of trust by the Secretary of Housing and Urban

---

[17] 11 USC § 362(b)(1).

[18] For cases where action was stayed or enjoined, see In re Alan I.W. Frank Corp., 19 Bankr. 41 (Bankr. ED Pa. 1982); In re Caldwell, 5 Bankr. 740 (Bankr. WD Va. 1980); In re Herman Hassinger, Inc., 20 Bankr. 517 (Bankr. ED Pa. 1982); In re Whitaker, 16 Bankr. 917 (Bankr. MD Tenn. 1982); In re Taylor, 16 Bankr. 323 (Bankr. D. Md. 1981); In re Ohio Waste Servs., Inc., 23 Bankr. 59 (Bankr. SD Ohio 1982); In re Ryan, 15 Bankr. 514 (Bankr. D. Md. 1981); In re Kaping, 13 Bankr. 621 (Bankr. D. Ore. 1981). For cases where action was not enjoined or stayed, see In re Wagner, 18 Bankr. 339 (Bankr. WD Mo. 1982); Barnette v. Evans, 673 F2d 1250 (11th Cir. 1982); Johnson v. Lindsey, 16 Bankr. 211 (Bankr. MD Fla. 1981); In re C.H. Stuart, Inc., 12 Bankr. 85 (Bankr. WDNY 1981); In re Magnifico, 21 Bankr. 800 (Bankr. D. Ariz. 1982); In re H. Cohen Caterers, Inc., 26 Bankr. 1 (Bankr. WD Ky. 1981); In re Richardello, 28 Bankr. 344 (Bankr. D. Mass. 1983); In re Wilson, 30 Bankr. 91 (Bankr. ED Tenn. 1983); In re Tenpins Bowling, Ltd., 32 Bankr. 474 (Bankr. MD Ga. 1983).

[19] 11 USC § 362(b)(2).

[20] 11 USC § 362(b)(3), as amended by 1984 Amendments § 441.

[21] Section 546(b) limits the avoiding power of the trustee under several sections, including Sections 544 (the "strong arm" clause), 547 (preferences), and 548 (fraudulent conveyances). It also permits postpetition perfection of a security interest as against the challenge of the trustee under those sections if nonbankruptcy law permits perfection of the security interest after a lien creditor's interest has arisen. This essentially contemplates a "grace period" statute that permits, within a certain period, the security interest to be perfected and to relate back and be good against an intervening lien creditor. An example of this is the ten-day grace period given for perfection of purchase-money security interests under UCC Section 9-301(2).

[22] 11 USC §§ 362(b)(4), 362(b)(5). See 11 USC § 101(24) for a definition of "governmental unit."

Development on certain multi-family living units.[23] Nor does the automatic stay apply to the issuance of a notice of tax deficiency by a governmental agency.[24] The 1984 Amendments added three new exceptions for conduct that is not within the automatic stay:

(1) Certain setoffs by a "repo participant" under certain repurchase agreements;[25]

(2) The presentation, giving of notice of dishonor, and protest of a negotiable instrument;[26] and

(3) An act by a lessor of the debtor to obtain possession of property under a lease of nonresidential real property that has terminated by the expiration of the stated term of the lease before the commencement of or during a case under Title 11.[27]

## [2] Stay of Proceedings Against Codebtors

In a Chapter 7 or 11 case, the automatic stay does not operate as a stay of proceedings against nonfiling codebtors or other parties who may be liable with the debtor on the particular claim, such as a guarantor or surety.[28] In appropriate circumstances, however, proceedings against a codebtor may be enjoined or the scope of the stay extended under Section 105.[29]

Section 362 also applies in Chapter 13 cases;[30] in addition, Section 1301 has provisions that deal with the stay of proceedings or collection actions

---

[23] 11 USC § 362(b)(8), as renumbered by the 1984 Amendments.

[24] 11 USC § 362(b)(9), as renumbered by the 1984 Amendments.

[25] 11 USC § 362(b)(7), added by 1984 Amendments § 392. "Repo participant" is defined in Section 101 (38); "repurchase agreement" is defined in Section 101(39).

[26] 11 USC § 362(b)(10), added by 1984 Amendments § 441.

[27] 11 USC § 362(b)(9), added by 1984 Amendments § 363.

[28] See, e.g., Wedgeworth v. Fibreboard Corp., 706 F2d 541 (5th Cir. 1983); In re Johns-Manville Corp., 26 Bankr. 405 (Bankr. SDNY 1983); In re Related Asbestos Cases, 23 Bankr. 523 (ND Cal. 1982); In re UNR Indus., Inc., 23 Bankr. 144 (Bankr. ND Ill. 1982); see also H.R. Rep. No. 595, 95th Cong., 1st Sess. 340 (1977); S. Rep. No. 989, 95th Cong., 2d Sess. 54–55 (1978). There is some authority that the stay does not include the debtor's liability carrier. See Wedgeworth v. Fibreboard Corp., 706 F2d 541 (5th Cir. 1983). But see In re Johns-Manville Corp., 26 Bankr. 405 (Bankr. SDNY 1983); Williford v. Armstrong World Indus., Inc., 715 F2d 124 (4th Cir. 1983) (joint tortfeasors in an asbestos liability suit could not avail themselves of the automatic stay provisions applicable to defendants who had filed for reorganization).

[29] See, e.g., Wedgeworth v. Fibreboard Corp., 706 F2d 541 (5th Cir. 1983); In re Johns-Manville Corp., 26 Bankr. 405 (Bankr. SDNY 1983); Royal Truck & Trailer v. Armadora, Etc., 10 Bankr. 488 (ND Ill. 1981). However, when the injunctive power given by Section 105 is invoked, other requirements come into play. See Fed. R. Civ. P. 65; B. Rule 7065; see also Spagnol Enters., Inc. v. Atlantic Fin. Fed. Sav. Ass'n, 33 Bankr. 129 (WD Pa. 1983).

[30] 11 USC § 103(a).

against certain individual codebtors of a Chapter 13 debtor.[31] Under Section 1301, after the order for relief, collection proceedings against individual codebtors are stayed if the debt is a consumer debt,[32] and if the individual codebtor did not become liable or secure the debt in the ordinary course of business.[33] The stay against individual codebtors does not prevent a creditor from presenting or giving notice of dishonor on a negotiable instrument.[34] Furthermore, the Chapter 13 claimant may obtain relief from the stay to proceed against the codebtor (1) if the codebtor received the consideration for the claim held by the creditor, or (2) to the extent the Chapter 13 plan does not propose payment of the claim, or (3) to the extent the creditor's interest would be irreparably harmed by the stay.[35]

### [3] Termination of the Stay

In determining when the Section 362 stay terminates, a distinction must be drawn between when the stay terminates with respect to property of the estate and when it terminates with respect to any other action, including action against the debtor or against property of the debtor. Unless relief from the stay is obtained earlier, the automatic stay, with respect to collection action against property of the estate, terminates when the property is no longer property of the estate.[36] With respect to any other action based on a prepetition debt or claim, such as commencing an action or attempting to enforce a judgment against the debtor, telephoning, and dunning, all of which are covered by the stay, or attempting to enforce a lien or security interest in property of the debtor, the stay does not terminate until the time the case is closed or dismissed

---

[31] For additional discussion of the codebtor stay of Section 1301, see discussion at ¶ 17.07.

[32] "Consumer debt" is defined in Section 101(7) as a debt incurred by an individual primarily for a personal, family, or household purpose.

[33] 11 USC § 1301(a). The effect of these sections is to require the creditor to share with other creditors to the extent provided for in the plan; his rights against the codebtor are not impaired but may be delayed.

[34] 11 USC § 1301(b).

[35] 11 USC § 1301(c).

[36] 11 USC § 362(c)(1). For example, the stay will terminate when the property is sold by the estate; if it is sold subject to a security interest, then after the sale the secured creditor is free to proceed against the property even though the debt might be dischargeable. Note, however, that abandonment of property by the trustee does not necessarily mean that the automatic stay has terminated and that a creditor who has a valid security interest in the abandoned property can then, without obtaining relief from the stay, proceed to realize on the abandoned collateral. Although upon abandonment the property is no longer property of the estate, the abandoned property generally revests in the debtor and the stay of proceedings against property of the debtor continues under Section 362(c)(2) until the earlier of the time the case is closed or dismissed or, in the case of an individual, the time a discharge is granted or denied. Before this time, relief from the stay must be obtained by a secured creditor before proceeding to repossess or realize on a valid security interest in the abandoned property. For more detailed discussion and authority, see ¶ 13.06[1].

or a discharge is granted or denied, whichever occurs earlier.[37] At the time the discharge is granted, however, there is a permanent injunction with respect to any collection efforts for discharged debts. For debts that are discharged, which generally includes most of the prepetition claims against the debtor, a discharge voids any judgment obtained on a discharged debt and operates as an injunction against any action to collect such debt as a personal liability of the debtor, whether or not discharge of such debt is waived.[38] However, a security interest or a lien (the in rem rights) that has not been avoided by the trustee will survive even though the debt is discharged and Section 524(a) does not prevent enforcement of such in rem rights.[39]

### [4] Relief From the Stay

Section 362(d) provides that on request of a party in interest and after "notice and hearing"[40] the court may grant relief from the stay under certain specified conditions. A request for relief from the stay may be made by motion pursuant to Bankruptcy Rules 4001 and 9014.[41] Relief from the stay may be granted by either terminating, annulling, modifying, or conditioning the stay.[42] Relief may be granted "for cause, including the lack of adequate protection of an interest in property" or "if the debtor does not have an equity in such property" and "such property is not necessary to an effective reorganization."[43] The phrase "including the lack of adequate protection" indicates that relief from

---

[37] 11 USC § 362(c)(2).

[38] 11 USC §§ 524(a), 524(b), as amended by 1984 Amendments §§ 308, 455.

[39] See In re Fitzgerald, 20 Bankr. 27 (Bankr. NDNY 1982); Long v. Bullard, 117 US 617 (1886). "The rule of Long v. Bullard is accepted with respect to the enforcement of valid liens on nonexempt property as well as on exempt property." H.R. Rep. No. 595, 95th Cong., 1st Sess. 361 (1977); S. Rep. No. 989, 95th Cong., 2d Sess. 76 (1978); see also In re Weathers, 15 Bankr. 945 (Bankr. D. Kan. 1981) and cases cited therein.

[40] "Notice and hearing" is a defined term and does not necessarily require a hearing; if proper notice is given, and no interested party requests a hearing, then no hearing is required. See 11 USC § 102(1).

[41] Under the "new" bankruptcy rules a request for relief from the stay is a "contested matter" rather than an "adversary proceeding." Before the new bankruptcy rules were adopted on August 1, 1983, there was authority that relief from the stay had to be obtained, not by motion, but by a complaint filed as an adversary proceeding that entailed a $60 filing fee. See, e.g., In re Northwest Recreational Activities, 8 Bankr. 5 (Bankr. ND Ga. 1980); In re UNR Indus., Inc., 23 Bankr. 144 (Bankr. ND Ill. 1982). The constitutionality of the filing fee for such an adversary complaint was unsuccessfully challenged on due process and equal protection grounds. See In re South, 689 F2d 162 (10th Cir. 1982); In re Bradford, 14 Bankr. 722 (Bankr. ND Ill. 1981); see also In re Mullins, 10 Bankr. 346 (Bankr. App. Pan. 9th Cir. 1980) (entry of order approving stipulation by parties relieving creditor from automatic stay without filing an adversary proceeding could be made by paying $3 for filing stipulation). Under the prior rules, one court held that the trustee was a necessary party to a complaint seeking relief from the stay. In re Dibona, 7 Bankr. 798 (Bankr. ED Pa. 1980).

[42] 11 USC § 362(d).

[43] 11 USC §§ 362(d)(1), 362(d)(2).

the stay for cause is not limited to lack of adequate protection.[44] The parameters of "for cause" are still being determined, however. Section 362(f) and the implementing provisions of Bankruptcy Rule 4001(c) that cover "ex parte relief from the stay" clearly recognize that "immediate and irreparable injury, loss, or damage" may be cause for relief.[45] Under Bankruptcy Rule 4001(c), in appropriate circumstances and on a proper showing, relief may be granted without prior notice to adverse parties, subject to the right of the adverse party to move for reinstatement of the stay.[46] Since the decision on whether to lift the stay is in the discretion of the bankruptcy judge, the decision may be overturned only upon a showing of abuse of discretion.[47] Parties who are interested in obtaining relief from the stay often are holders of secured claims who are prevented by the stay from realizing on their collateral.

Granting relief from the stay is a final order that can be appealed[48] under Section 158(a) of Title 28 of the U.S. Code.[49] If relief from the stay is requested, the request must be disposed of with relative dispatch; otherwise, the stay will be terminated. Thirty days after the request for relief, the stay will be terminated as to the requesting party unless the court, after "notice and a hearing," orders the stay continued pending conclusion of a final hearing, or unless the court orders the stay continued as a result of a final hearing and determination.[50] It appears that at least a preliminary hearing must be held within the thirty days after the request for relief is made, and that a final hearing must be commenced within thirty days of the preliminary hearing.[51] The court is directed to continue the stay pending conclusion of the final hearing if there is reasonable likelihood that the party opposing relief will prevail at the final hearing.[52]

---

[44] See rules of construction, 11 USC § 102(3).

[45] 11 USC § 362(f), as amended by 1984 Amendments § 441, permits the court, upon request of a party in interest, with or without a hearing, to grant such relief from the stay as is necessary to prevent irreparable damage to the interest of an entity in property, if irreparable harm will occur before there is an opportunity for notice and a hearing.

[46] B. Rule 4004(c); see also 11 USC § 102(1).

[47] In re Holtkamp, 669 F2d 505 (7th Cir. 1982); In re Frigitemp Corp., 8 Bankr. 284 (SDNY 1981). Under Title 28, Section 157(b)(2)(G), motions to terminate, annul, or modify the automatic stay are core proceedings and may, upon referral, be determined by the bankruptcy judge. For discussion of core proceedings, see ¶ 11.03[2].

[48] In re Comer, 716 F2d 168 (3d Cir. 1983).

[49] Title 28, Section 158(a), was added by 1984 Amendments § 104.

[50] 11 USC § 362(e), as amended by 1984 Amendments § 441.

[51] Id. Note that the statute requires only commencement, and not completion, of the final hearing within the thirty days after the preliminary hearing. However, B. Rule 4001(b) provides that the stay will terminate within thirty days after the final hearing is commenced unless the court has previously denied the motion for relief. The effect of the Rule is to require the court to complete the final hearing within thirty days after the preliminary hearing; otherwise, the stay is terminated.

[52] Id. Where the stay is inadvertently terminated under Section 362(e) because of the lapse of the thirty-day period, the court may use its injunctive power to enjoin action against property of the debtor. However, under Section 105 different requirements come

There is some authority that a bankruptcy court other than the one in which the petition is filed (the "home court") may grant relief from the stay.[53]

In a hearing on a request for relief from the stay, the party requesting relief has the burden of proof on the issue of the debtor's equity in the property. The party opposing relief has the burden of proof on all other issues, such as whether the property is necessary for an effective reorganization.[54]

## ¶ 12.06 MEETING OF CREDITORS

Section 341 requires that "within a reasonable time after the order for relief" a meeting of creditors must be held.[1] Bankruptcy Rule 2003(a) implements this section by providing that the meeting shall be held not less than twenty and not more than forty days after the order for relief. Bankruptcy Rule

---

into play. See Spagnol Enters., Inc. v. Atlantic Fin. Fed. Sav., 33 Bankr. 129 (WD Pa. 1983) and cases cited therein; see also Fed. R. Civ. P. 65; B. Rule 7065.

[53] See In re Rapco Foam, Inc., 16 Bankr. 765 (Bankr. WD Mo. 1982) (Missouri bankruptcy court had jurisdiction to grant relief from stay as to personal injury claim that had been removed from Missouri state court to Missouri bankruptcy court and bankruptcy petition had been filed in South Carolina); In re Rapco Foam, Inc., 23 Bankr. 692 (Bankr. WD Wis. 1982) (Wisconsin bankruptcy court had jurisdiction to grant relief from stay imposed by Chapter 11 petition filed in South Carolina to permit adversary proceeding based on negligence and strict liability); In re Coleman Am. Cos., 6 Bankr. 251 (Bankr. D. Colo. 1980) (Colorado bankruptcy court granted relief from stay as to property located in Colorado, even though petition was previously filed in Kansas bankruptcy court). But see In re Coleman Am. Cos., 8 Bankr. 384 (Bankr. D. Kan. 1981), holding that the creditor who sought relief from stay in the non- "home court" in Colorado was in violation of the automatic stay and subject to contempt. The Kansas "home court" took the view that it had exclusive jurisdiction of all of the debtor's property wherever located, pursuant to Title 28, Section 1471(e) (now Title 28, Section 1334(d)). See also In re Ashley, 18 Bankr. 216 (Bankr. D. Del. 1982) (based on venue provisions, party seeking relief from stay must file action in bankruptcy court where case is commenced). But see In re Dew Mortgage Co., 10 Bankr. 242 (Bankr. MD Fla. 1981) (proper venue for relief from stay is in nonfiling court where property is located). One court has held that where the complaint seeking relief from the stay is filed in a court other than the "home court," the complaint should be transferred to the "home court" as the appropriate venue. In re Zaleta, 13 Bankr. 144 (Bankr. SD Fla. 1981). See also In re Whitehorn, 9 Bankr. 404 (Bankr. ND Ga. 1981). B. Rule 4001, which now provides that relief from the stay is sought by motion, not by an adversary proceeding, may suggest that the request by motion should be made where the case is pending.

[54] 11 USC § 362(g); see, e.g., In re East Redley Corp., 4 Bankr. 288 (Bankr. ED Pa. 1980) (where debtor offered no testimony that would support a finding that property was necessary for an effective reorganization, debtor had failed to carry burden of proof, and creditor seeking relief was entitled to relief from stay after carrying its burden of showing no equity).

[1] Notice of the date set for this meeting of creditors generally will be included with the initial notice sent to creditors giving notice of the order for relief, notice of the time for filing objections to discharge, notice of time for filing proof of claim, and other appropriate notices.

2002(a)(1) requires that notice of the meeting of creditors must be given by mail to the debtor, the trustee, all creditors, and indenture trustees not less than twenty days prior to the meeting.

In a significant change from the practice under the 1898 Act,[2] the bankruptcy judge is prohibited from presiding at or attending a meeting of creditors.[3] There are two main purposes for excluding the bankruptcy judge from creditor meetings. First, this provision insulates the judge from testimony or other information that might be inadmissible in subsequent hearings before the judge. Second, it relieves the judge from this administrative responsibility. Generally, the meeting will be presided over by the clerk of the bankruptcy court unless the court designates another person, such as the interim trustee,[4] or unless the creditors entitled to vote designate a presiding officer.[5] The debtor is required to appear at the meeting of creditors, and to submit to examination under oath;[6] failure to appear imposes the risk that the case may be dismissed.[7]

### [1] Examination of the Debtor

At the meeting of creditors, the debtor may be examined under oath;[8] any examination under oath is to be recorded electronically,[9] and may be conducted by creditors, any indenture trustee, or any examiner or trustee in the case.[10] The scope of the examination of the debtor may relate only to "the acts, conduct, or property or to the liabilities and financial condition of the debtor, or to any matter which may affect the administration of the debtor's estate, or to the debtor's right to a discharge."[11]

---

[2] See, e.g., Former B. Rules 204, 205.

[3] 11 USC § 341(c).

[4] 11 USC § 701.

[5] See B. Rule 2003(b)(1). In a Chapter 11 case, if a chairman has been selected by a creditors' committee, the chairman or his designee may preside. Id. In a Chapter 11 case, a creditors' committee is appointed pursuant to Section 1102. In a U.S. trustee "pilot" district, the U.S. trustee or his designee presides at the meeting of creditors. B. Rule X-1006(b)(1).

[6] 11 USC § 343. This section applies in Chapter 7, 11, and 13 cases. See 11 USC § 103(a).

[7] See, e.g., In re Rust, 1 Bankr. 656 (Bankr. MD Tenn. 1979).

[8] 11 USC § 343. The presiding officer is authorized to administer oaths. See B. Rule 2003(b)(1).

[9] B. Rules 2003(b)(1), 2003(c).

[10] 11 USC § 343.

[11] B. Rule 2004(b). In addition to examination at the meeting of creditors, the court, for cause shown, may order the debtor to appear to be examined at any time or place designated. See B. Rule 2004(d). In specified circumstances, B. Rule 2005 authorizes the bankruptcy court to issue an order for the apprehension of a debtor to compel his attendance for examination. The bankruptcy court is authorized to issue a writ of habeas corpus to bring a person before the court for examination under Title 28, Section 2256.

In a Chapter 11 or 13 case, the scope of the examination may relate to the operation of any business, the desirability of its continuance, the source of funds or property for fulfilling the plan, and any other matter relevant to formulation of the plan.[12]

If the debtor is required to submit to examination, immunity may be granted from self-incrimination in appropriate circumstances.[13]

### [2] Selection of a Trustee

At the meeting of creditors in a Chapter 7 case, the creditors entitled to vote[14] may elect a trustee if a request for an election of a trustee is made by the appropriate number of creditors.[15]

There are no provisions for the election of a trustee under either Chapter 11 or 13.[16] In Chapter 11 cases, at any time before the confirmation of a plan, upon application of a party in interest, the court for "cause" or in the "interest of creditors" may appoint a trustee.[17] Appointment of a trustee is not automatic in Chapter 11, however, and in many cases there is no trustee.[18] In Chapter 13 cases, pursuant to Section 1302(a), if there is no standing Chapter 13 trustee, the court appoints the trustee.

---

[12] See B. Rule 2004(b). B. Rule 2004 is not limited to examination of debtors and covers examination of "any person" and provides for compelling attendance and production of documentary evidence.

[13] See 11 USC § 344. See generally Kurland, "A Debtor's Prism: Immunity for Bankrupts Under the Bankruptcy Reform Act of 1978 (Pt. 1)," 55 Am. Bankr. L.J. 177 (1981); Note, "Self-Incrimination Under the New Bankruptcy Code: An Analysis of § 344," Ann. Survey of Bankr. L. 211 (1980).

[14] Only a creditor with an allowable, undisputed, fixed, liquidated, unsecured, nonpriority claim who does not have an interest materially adverse (other than an equity interest) to the interests of the general unsecured creditors, and who is not an "insider," is entitled to vote in an election of a trustee. See 11 USC § 702(a), as amended by 1984 Amendments § 472. In addition, B. Rule 2003(b)(3) requires that a creditor must, at or before the meeting, file a proof of claim or a writing setting forth facts evidencing a right to vote pursuant to Section 702(a). If objection is made to the amount or allowability of a claim for voting, the court, after notice and hearing, may temporarily allow, "in an amount that seems proper," the claim for voting purposes. Disqualifying "insiders" eliminates relatives, persons in control of the debtor, and others closely related to the debtor from voting. "Insider" is defined in Section 101(28).

[15] 11 USC § 702(b); B. Rule 2003(b)(1). For election of a trustee, creditors holding at least 20 percent in amount of all of the claims entitled to vote, must vote, and a candidate must receive a majority in amount of the claims voted to be elected. B. Rule 2006 covers the solicitation and voting of proxies in Chapter 7 cases.

[16] Section 702 is applicable only in Chapter 7. See 11 USC § 103(a).

[17] 11 USC §§ 1104(a)(1), 1104(a)(2). See 11 USC § 1163 for appointment of a trustee in a railroad reorganization case.

[18] If no trustee is appointed in a Chapter 11 case, the "debtor in possession" has all of the rights, powers, functions, and duties of the trustee. See 11 USC § 1107(a).

In a Chapter 7 case, after the order for relief the court is required to appoint an interim trustee from the panel of private trustees established under Title 28, Section 604(f). The service of the interim trustee terminates when a trustee is elected or otherwise designated under Section 702.[19] In an involuntary Chapter 7 case, in the "involuntary gap" after the commencement of the case but before the order for relief, the court, on request of a party in interest and after notice to the debtor and a hearing, may appoint an interim trustee if necessary to protect the property of the estate or to prevent loss.[20] If a trustee is not elected, then the interim trustee serves as trustee in the case.[21]

## ¶ 12.07 CONVERSION OF A CASE AND ITS EFFECTS

The Code contains specific provisions for conversion of a case filed or proceeding under one chapter to a case under another chapter.[1] Several generalizations may be made about these sections.[2] First, these sections permit the debtor one absolute right to convert to another chapter. Second, a case may be converted only to a chapter for which the debtor is eligible. Third, upon the request of a party in interest, the court in its discretion, for cause and after notice and a hearing, may convert the case to another chapter. Fourth, an individual who is in a Chapter 7 or 11 case may be converted to Chapter 13 only upon the request of the debtor; there is no involuntary conversion to Chapter 13. This is consistent with the idea that only voluntary Chapter 13 cases are permitted.

Under the Bankruptcy Rules, proceedings to convert a case to another chapter are treated as "contested matters" governed by Bankruptcy Rule 9014 and the moving party proceeds by a motion pursuant to Bankruptcy Rule 9014.[3]

Sections 706(a) and 706(d) authorize a debtor to convert a Chapter 7 case at any time to either a Chapter 11 or 13 case if the debtor is eligible for the chapter to which the conversion is to be made, and provided that the case has not previously been converted from either Chapter 11 or 13.[4] This means, for example, that a debtor who is a corporation could not convert to Chapter 13

---

[19] 11 USC § 701. In the case of a conversion from a reorganization case to Chapter 7, a trustee already serving in the case may be appointed interim trustee. See 11 USC § 701(a). In a "pilot district" with a U.S. trustee, under Section 15701 the U.S. trustee appoints the interim trustee.

[20] 11 USC § 303(g); B. Rule 2001(a).

[21] 11 USC § 702(d).

[1] See 11 USC §§ 706, 1112, 1307.

[2] Of course, one must be alert to the details of these sections.

[3] See B. Rule 1017(d). When a case is converted from Chapter 11 or 13 to Chapter 7, B. Rule 1019 supplies important details with respect to filing lists, inventories, schedules, filing of claims, etc. See also 11 USC § 348 and discussion at infra ¶ 12.04[1].

[4] 11 USC §§ 706(a), 706(d). The legislative history indicates this is an absolute right. See H.R. Rep. No. 595, 95th Cong., 1st Sess. 380 (1977); S. Rep. No. 989, 95th

because only "individuals" are eligible for that chapter. At the request of a party in interest, after "notice and a hearing," the court may convert a Chapter 7 case to Chapter 11.[5]

A Chapter 11 debtor may convert to Chapter 7 if he is a debtor in possession, unless the Chapter 11 case originally was begun as an involuntary case or the case has been converted to Chapter 11 at the request of someone other than the debtor.[6] To convert to Chapter 7, however, the debtor must be eligible for Chapter 7.[7] On request of a party in interest and after notice and a hearing, a Chapter 11 or 13 case may be converted to Chapter 7 if it is in the best interest of the creditors and for cause, provided the debtor could be forced into an involuntary Chapter 7 case under Section 303. Thus, a "farmer" or a "corporation" that is not a "moneyed, business or commercial corporation" cannot be converted to Chapter 7 unless the debtor requests the conversion.[8] A case can be converted from Chapter 11 to 13 only if the debtor is eligible for Chapter 13 and only if the debtor requests the conversion and has not been discharged under Section 1141(d).[9]

A debtor may convert a Chapter 13 case to a Chapter 7 case at any time; a waiver of this right is unenforceable.[10] At any time before a Chapter 13 plan is confirmed, upon request of a party in interest and after notice and a hearing, the court may convert a Chapter 13 case to Chapter 11 if the debtor is eligible

---

Cong., 2d Sess. 94 (1978). A waiver of this right by the debtor is unenforceable. See 11 USC § 706(a).

[5] The legislative history indicates this is within the sound discretion of the court. See H.R. Rep. No. 595, 95th Cong., 1st Sess. 380 (1977); S. Rep. No. 989, 95th Cong., 2d Sess. 94 (1978). However, a case may be converted to a Chapter 13 case only on the request of the debtor. See 11 USC § 706(c). Only individuals are eligible for Chapter 13. See 11 USC § 109(e). Under Section 706(c) there can be no involuntary Chapter 13 by conversion. This is consistent with Section 303(a), which does not permit an involuntary Chapter 13 case.

[6] 11 USC § 1112(a). The legislative history indicates this is an absolute right of the debtor. See H.R. Rep. No. 595, 95th Cong., 1st Sess. 405 (1977); S. Rep. No. 989, 95th Cong., 2d Sess. 117 (1978).

[7] 11 USC § 1112(e); see also 11 USC § 109(b).

[8] 11 USC §§ 1112(b), 1112(c), 1307(c), 1307(e). Section 1112(b) sets forth nine factors that may, among other reasons, constitute "cause"; Section 1307(c), as amended by 1984 Amendments §§ 315, 527, sets forth eight factors. In In re Mandalay Shores Coop. Hous. Ass'n, 22 Bankr. 202 (Bankr. MD Fla. 1982), a nonprofit corporation was formed by tenants to acquire an apartment complex to prevent sale of the complex, which probably would have resulted in conversion of the apartment to a condominium. The corporation was held to be a "non-moneyed, non-business, non-commercial" corporation and thus not subject to involuntary conversion from Chapter 11 to 7. The court noted that in making such a determination other courts have looked to the provisions of state law, the articles of incorporation, and the actual character and activities of the corporation. Id. at 206.

[9] 11 USC §§ 1112(d), 1112(e). This is consistent with the idea that there may not be an involuntary Chapter 13 case.

[10] 11 USC § 1307(a).

for Chapter 11. In the case of a farmer, the case may be converted only if the farmer requests the conversion.[11]

Conversion may be made irrespective of whether the original petition was voluntary or involuntary, and the statutes do not require that a party in interest who seeks conversion must qualify as a petitioning creditor.[12]

Important details with respect to the effect of converting a case from one chapter to another are covered in Section 348 and Bankruptcy Rule 1019. Where there is a conversion from either Chapter 11 or 13 to Chapter 7, Bankruptcy Rule 1019 should be consulted for details with respect to filing schedules, inventories, notice of the order for conversion, claims filed in the superseded case, and so forth.

Within twenty days after entry of an order converting a case from Chapter 11 or 13 to Chapter 7, notice of the order must be given to all creditors.[13] Conversion constitutes an order for relief under the chapter to which the case is converted but, with some important exceptions spelled out in the statute, does not change the date of the filing of the petition, the commencement of the case, or the order for relief. The date for these events in the converted case remains the date of the event under the original case except for the listed exceptions.[14]

Claims against the estate or the debtor that arise after the original order for relief but before the conversion are treated as if they had arisen immediately before the filing of the petition.[15]

Conversion of a case terminates the services of any trustee or examiner who was serving in the case before the conversion.[16]

## ¶ 12.08 ABSTENTION

Under circumstances specified in Section 305, a bankruptcy court, after notice and a hearing, may dismiss a bankruptcy case or suspend all proceedings in a case if, for example, "the interests of creditors and the debtor would be better served by such dismissal or suspension." This dismissal or suspension, or decision not to dismiss or suspend, is "not reviewable by appeal or otherwise."[1] Dismissal or abstention under this section is a dismissal or suspension of the

---

[11] 11 USC §§ 1307(d), 1307(e), 1307(f).

[12] Kennedy, "The Commencement of a Case Under the New Bankruptcy Code," 36 Wash. & Lee L. Rev. 977, 1019 (1979).

[13] B. Rule 1019(2).

[14] 11 USC § 348(a). The exceptions generally apply to the date of the order for relief.

[15] 11 USC § 348(d). There is an important exception to this for certain administrative claims specified in Section 503(b). Upon conversion to a Chapter 7 case, administrative claims of Chapter 7 have priority over the administrative claims of Chapter 11. See 11 USC § 726(b) and discussion at ¶ 14.09[1].

[16] 11 USC § 348(e).

[1] 11 USC § 305(c).

entire case.[2] In contrast, under Title 28, Section 1334(c),[3] the district court may abstain ("permissive abstention") with respect to a particular proceeding arising under Title 11, or arising in or related to a case under Title 11.[4] In some circumstances where a proceeding related to a bankruptcy case is based on a state-law claim or cause of action, the district court may be required to abstain ("mandatory abstention").[5] It should be observed, however, that Title 28, Section 1334(c), deals with abstention with respect to proceedings and not with respect to the bankruptcy case. For example, abstention on a petition for bankruptcy filed under Chapter 7 is controlled by Title 11, Section 305, not Title 28, Section 1334(c). It is appropriate for the court to abstain under Section 305 in a case where the creditors have negotiated an arrangement outside of bankruptcy that better serves the interests of those involved in the case and that is less expensive than bankruptcy administration.[6] On the other hand, abstention on a proceeding (e.g., a claim by the trustee in bankruptcy to set aside a preference under Section 547) must be justified under Title 28, Section 1334.

Section 305 provides that a second ground for abstention is if a foreign proceeding is pending, and if the factors specified in Section 304(c) justify dismissal or suspension.[7]

Although Section 305 speaks only in terms of dismissal or suspension of a case, the statutory language should not preclude a court from conditioning a dismissal or suspension.[8]

Finally, Bankruptcy Rule 1017(c) provides that a petition should not be dismissed or suspended under Section 305 before a hearing on notice as provided in Bankruptcy Rule 2002(a), which requires not less than twenty days' notice by mail.

## ¶ 12.09 DISMISSAL OF THE CASE

Several sections in the Code deal with dismissal of a case. In a Chapter 7 case, Section 707 authorizes the court to dismiss a case only after notice and a hearing and only for cause, including, but not limited to, unreasonable delay by the debtor that is prejudicial to creditors, and for nonpayment of filing fees and

---

[2] H.R. Rep. No. 595, 95th Cong., 1st Sess. 325 (1977); S. Rep. No. 989, 95th Cong., 2d Sess. 35 (1978).

[3] Title 28, Section 1334(c), was added by 1984 Amendments § 101.

[4] 28 USC § 1334(c)(1). For detailed discussion of "permissive abstention," see ¶ 11.03[1][a].

[5] 28 USC § 1334(c)(2). For detailed discussion of "mandatory abstention," see ¶ 11.03[1][b].

[6] H.R. Rep. No. 595 Cong., 1st Sess. 325 (1977); S. Rep. No. 595, 95th Cong., 2d Sess. 34–36 (1978); see also In re Colonial Ford, Inc., 24 Bankr. 1014 (Bankr. D. Utah 1982), which contains an extensive discussion of Section 305.

[7] 11 USC § 305(a)(2).

[8] Kennedy, "The Commencement of a Case Under the New Bankruptcy Code," 36 Wash. & Lee L. Rev. 977, 1023–1024 (1979).

charges required under Title 28, Section 123.[1] The section does not contemplate, however, that the ability of the debtor to repay his debt in whole or in part constitutes adequate cause for dismissal.[2] However, the 1984 Amendments added a new Section 707(b),[3] which authorizes the court on its own motion to dismiss a case filed under Chapter 7 by an individual debtor whose debts are primarily consumer debts if the court finds that granting of relief would be a substantial abuse of Chapter 7. There is a statutory presumption in favor of granting the relief requested by the debtor. New Section 707(b) does not indicate what factors are to be considered in making the determination of substantial abuse.

Bankruptcy Rule 1017(a) implements Section 707 by providing that a petition, except for a dismissal by the petitioner in a Chapter 13 case, may not be dismissed on motion of the petitioner or for want of prosecution or other cause or by consent of the parties prior to a hearing on notice to all creditors, as provided for in Bankruptcy Rule 2002(a).[4] Not less than twenty days' notice by mail is required. For failure to pay the filing fee, the court may dismiss the petition after hearing on notice to the debtor and the trustee.[5]

The debtor in a Chapter 13 case may dismiss the case at any time before conversion of the case to a Chapter 11 or 7 case.[6]

A Chapter 11 case may be dismissed pursuant to Section 1112(b), after notice and a hearing, for cause, including but not limited to nine grounds for cause listed in the section. Under Bankruptcy Rule 1017(a), the case may not be dismissed before a hearing on notice to all creditors as provided for in Bankruptcy Rule 2002(a), which requires not less than twenty days' notice by mail.

---

[1] For discussion of filing fees, see supra ¶ 12.04[2].

[2] H.R. Rep. No. 595, 95th Cong., 1st Sess. 380 (1977); S. Rep. No. 989, 95th Cong., 2d Sess. 94 (1978).

[3] 11 USC § 707(b), as added by 1984 Amendments § 312, which provides:

> "After notice and a hearing, the court, on its own motion and not at the request or suggestion of any party in interest, may dismiss a case filed by an individual debtor under this chapter whose debts are primarily consumer debts if it finds that the granting of relief would be a substantial abuse of the provisions of this chapter. There shall be a presumption in favor of granting the relief requested by the debtor."

[4] See also B. Rule 1017(c).

[5] B. Rule 1017(b)(1).

[6] 11 USC § 1307(b). Note that such a dismissal is excepted from the hearing on notice requirement of B. Rule 1017(a). For additional discussion of dismissal in Chapter 13 cases, see ¶ 17.11[2].

# 13

# The Bankruptcy Estate

## ¶ 13.01 INTRODUCTION

This chapter deals primarily with the property of the estate as it relates to Chapter 7 liquidation proceedings, although portions of the material covered are applicable in other chapters as well.

In general, all of the property that the debtor owns when the petition is filed becomes a part of the debtor's estate. The estate also includes property that is brought back into the estate by the exercise of the avoiding powers of the trustee.[1] With some exceptions covered later in this chapter, property acquired by the debtor after the petition is filed does not become property of the estate.[2] With the filing of the petition, the automatic stay of Section 362, with some very limited exceptions, prevents creditors from attempting to reach property of the estate or from enforcing judgments against, realizing on, or creating or perfecting security interests in property of the debtor or of the estate. Practically all collection efforts by creditors are covered by the automatic stay.[3] In addition, the district court in which the petition is filed is given exclusive jurisdiction over all of the property of the debtor wherever located as of the "commencement of the case."[4] Generally, in a Chapter 7 case the trustee will assemble and liquidate the property of the estate and then make distribution of the estate to creditors according to the distribution scheme set forth in the Bankruptcy Code (the Code).[5] Although initially a part of the debtor's

---

[1] See discussion of the trustee's avoiding powers in Chapter 16.

[2] See infra ¶ 13.04[3].

[3] For discussion of the automatic stay, see ¶ 12.05, infra ¶ 13.03.

[4] See 28 USC § 1334(d), added by the Bankruptcy Amendments and Federal Judgeship Act of 1984, Pub. L. No. 353, 98 Stat. 333, § 101 (hereafter cited as the 1984 Amendments).

[5] See Chapter 14. Unless otherwise indicated, "Code" as used in this chapter refers to the Bankruptcy Reform Act of 1978, as amended.

estate, property that is effectively claimed as exempt by the debtor will not be liquidated or otherwise be subject to the claims of creditors in the bankruptcy proceeding.[6]

It should be noted that property of the debtor that is encumbered by a valid lien or security interest does become a part of the "debtor's estate," and the secured creditor is subject to the automatic stay even though the lienor or secured party has possession of the property. If a security interest or other lien can be avoided by the trustee,[7] then generally the effect of this avoidance will be to place the collateral in the debtor's estate unencumbered by the security interest or lien. If the security interest is not avoided by the trustee, the property remains in the debtor's estate subject to the valid security interest or other lien. In addition, unless sold by the trustee free and clear of the security interest in the liquidating process, the valid security interest or lien will remain on the property and pass through the bankruptcy proceeding with the security interest intact. This is so, even though the personal liability of the debtor is discharged for the debt or claim represented by the security interest or lien.

Property of the estate may be abandoned by the trustee where there is no value or benefit to be realized from the property by the estate. Abandonment is quite common where, for example, the debt secured by the property exceeds the value of the property and there is no value or equity to be realized for the estate.

## ¶ 13.02 SELECTION OF THE TRUSTEE

Under the Bankruptcy Act of 1898 (the 1898 Act), the bankruptcy judge frequently selected the trustee, who later would appear before the same judge in formal as well as informal proceedings relating to the administration of the estate. In an effort to relieve the bankruptcy judge from administrative duties and to eliminate the situation that existed under the 1898 Act, the process of selecting a trustee was significantly changed under the Code. Under the Code, in "nonpilot" bankruptcy districts[1] the Director of the Administrative Office of the U.S. Courts establishes, maintains, and supervises a list of qualified per-

---

[6] Exempt property may, however, be subject to the claims of some creditors who exist at the time the petition is filed. For example, a claim for support, maintenance, and alimony is nondischargeable, is not subject to the automatic stay, and may be enforced against property that has been claimed as exempt in bankruptcy. See infra ¶ 13.07[3]. Very commonly under state law, exemptions may not be asserted against claims for support, maintenance, and alimony.

[7] See Chapter 16 for a discussion of the trustee's avoiding powers.

[1] "Non-pilot districts" refers to bankruptcy districts that do not have the pilot U.S. trustee discussed at infra ¶ 13.02[3]. Pilot districts are districts that do have a U.S. trustee, at least until September 30, 1986 when the pilot system is due to expire unless the pilot program is extended by Congress. Originally the pilot program was to expire on April 1, 1984 (Pub. L. No. 95–598, § 408(c)), but was extended to September 30, 1986 by 1984 Amendments § 323.

sons to serve as private trustees.[2] In pilot districts, the U.S. trustee has the responsibility for establishing, maintaining, and supervising the panel of private trustees.[3]

As noted previously, a trustee may be elected only in a Chapter 7 case, and it is quite common in Chapter 7 cases for the creditors not to elect a trustee. In effect, by default, the interim trustee, who in most cases will have been selected from the panel of private trustees, will typically serve as trustee in the case.[4] In a Chapter 13 case, if there is a standing Chapter 13 trustee, then that person serves as the trustee; if there is no standing Chapter 13 trustee, then a trustee is appointed.[5] In Chapter 11, there is no automatic appointment of a trustee and commonly there will be no appointment of a trustee. In such a case, the "debtor in possession" will be responsible for the estate and, unless the court orders otherwise, the "debtor in possession" will have all of the duties and powers given to the trustee, with some limited exceptions.[6] However, at any time after the commencement of the case but before the confirmation of a plan, upon request of a party in interest and after notice and a hearing, the court may appoint a trustee in a Chapter 11 case, for cause or if it is in the best interests of the creditors, of any equity security holders, and of other interests of the estate.[7]

## [1] Duty, Powers, and Compensation

In a Chapter 7 case, the trustee is the representative of the estate and has the capacity to sue and be sued.[8] The essential duties of the trustee in a liquidation case are listed in Section 704.[9] The principal duties are to collect

---

[2] See 28 USC § 604(f). The number and qualifications of such persons are determined by rules and regulations adopted by the Director. Individuals named to this panel of private trustees must reside or have an office in the state served by the bankruptcy court or in an adjacent state; for a corporation to serve on the panel it must have an office in the state served by the bankruptcy court. Note that there is a discrepancy between Title 28, Section 604(f), and the residency requirements of Section 321(a) for qualification of a trustee in a particular case. See infra ¶ 13.02[2]. The Director may for cause remove a person from this panel.

[3] 28 USC § 586(a)(1). In pilot districts the U.S. Attorney General appoints the U.S. trustee (28 USC § 581(a)) and prescribes the qualifications of persons to serve on the panel of private trustees. 28 USC § 586(d).

[4] For additional detail and discussion of the selection of the trustees and qualifications, see ¶ 12.02[2].

[5] 11 USC § 1302(a). For a discussion of the Chapter 13 trustee, see ¶ 17.05.

[6] 11 USC § 1107(a).

[7] See 11 USC § 1104(a). In a pilot district if the court determines that a trustee should be appointed, then the U.S. trustee makes the appointment after consultation with parties in interest and subject to court approval. See 11 USC § 151104(c).

[8] 11 USC § 323.

[9] A very helpful work for trustees and debtors in possession is Sulmeyer, Lynn & Rochelle, Collier Handbook for Trustees and Debtors in Possession (Matthew Bender 1982).

the property of the estate and to reduce it to money, so as to be able to close the estate as expeditiously as possible. The trustee is authorized to deposit or invest money of the estate to "yield the maximum reasonable net return on such money, taking into account the safety of such deposit or investment."[10] The entity with which funds are deposited or invested may be required to give a performance bond with a surety.[11] The trustee is accountable for all property received, is directed to investigate the financial affairs of the debtor, and, when a purpose would be served, to examine proofs of claim and to object to the allowance of any claim that is improper.[12] The trustee also has the duty, if advisable, to oppose the discharge of the debtor.[13] The 1984 Amendments imposed an additional duty on the trustee to "ensure that the debtor shall perform his intention as specified in section 521(2)(B)."[14] Under Section 521(2)(A),[15] if an individual debtor's schedule of assets and liabilities includes consumer debts that are secured by property of the estate, within thirty days after the filing of a petition under Chapter 7 (or before the date of the meeting of creditors, if earlier) the debtor must file with the clerk a statement of his intention with respect to retention or surrender of such property and specify whether (1) the property is claimed as exempt, (2) the debtor intends to redeem the property, or (3) the debtor intends to reaffirm the debt that the property secures. Under Section 521(2)(B), within forty-five days after filing of this notice of intent (or within whatever additional time the court, for cause, fixes), the debtor must "perform his intention with respect to such property."[16]

Although generally in a Chapter 7 liquidation case the duty of the trustee is to liquidate the estate as soon as possible, on occasion the trustee may need to continue the business of the debtor, at least for a relatively short period, to facilitate the liquidation of the estate and to best realize on the assets. For example, it may be in the best interest of the estate to finish manufacturing raw materials or to complete partially finished goods. In such situations, the court may authorize the trustee to operate the business for a limited period of time if it is in the "best interest of the estate and consistent with the orderly liquidation of the estate."[17] If authorized to continue the business, the trustee must file (1) periodic reports of the operation of the business, including a statement of receipts and disbursements with the court and (2) appropriate reports with governmental tax agencies.[18] Bankruptcy Rule 2015 contains additional

---

[10] 11 USC § 345(a).

[11] 11 USC § 345(b).

[12] 11 USC § 704.

[13] 11 USC § 704(5).

[14] 11 USC § 704(3), added by 1984 Amendments § 311.

[15] Added by 1984 Amendments § 305.

[16] 11 USC § 521(2)(B), added by 1984 Amendments § 305.

[17] 11 USC § 721.

[18] 11 USC § 704(8), as renumbered by 1984 Amendments § 311.

important details with respect to the duties of the trustee, including record keeping, filing reports, giving notice of the case, and other duties. This rule should be examined carefully.[19]

In the course of performing the principal duties, the trustee may (1) examine the debtor to determine whether assets have been improperly disposed of or concealed;[20] (2) assume or reject executory contracts or unexpired leases;[21] (3) expand the estate by recovering certain voidable prepetition or postpetition transactions and transfers of the debtor and by avoiding certain statutory liens;[22] and (4) abandon property that is burdensome or of inconsequential value.[23]

In performing these duties, the trustee is authorized, subject to court approval, to employ one or more attorneys, accountants, appraisers, auctioneers, or other professional persons who do not hold or represent an interest adverse to the estate and who are "disinterested persons."[24] Under some exceptional circumstances, this "disinterested person" restriction is not applicable. For example, where the trustee is authorized to operate the business of the debtor under Chapter 7, the trustee may, if necessary for operation of the business, retain professional persons previously employed by the debtor.[25] Limitations on compensation of professional persons employed by the trustee are set forth in Section 328.[26] The court may authorize the trustee to act as attorney or accountant for the estate if such authorization is in the "best interest" of the estate.[27] Limits on the compensation of the trustee are set forth in Section 326,[28] which contains a maximum fee schedule based on decreasing percentages of increasing amounts of money distributed by the trustee. Where the trustee also serves as attorney or accountant, the limit on compensation for such services is controlled by Section 328.[29]

---

[19] With regard to the bond of the trustee, see 11 USC § 322, B. Rule 2010, and Official Forms 23, 24, 25; see also B. Rule 9025. Other Code provisions relevant to the trustee should be consulted.

[20] 11 USC § 343; see discussion at ¶ 12.06[1].

[21] 11 USC § 365(a); see discussion at infra ¶ 13.09.

[22] 11 USC §§ 544, 545, 547–549. For a discussion of these avoiding powers, see Chapter 16.

[23] 11 USC § 554; see infra ¶ 13.06.

[24] 11 USC § 327(a). "Disinterested person" is defined in Section 101(13). See also Bankruptcy Rule 2014 for important details with respect to employment of professionals. See generally Annot., 66 A.L.R. Fed. 259 (1984).

[25] For the details of these exceptions, see 11 USC § 327, as amended by 1984 Amendments § 430.

[26] See also Annot., 69 A.L.R. Fed. 644 (1984).

[27] 11 USC § 327(d).

[28] 11 USC § 326, as amended by 1984 Amendments § 430.

[29] 11 USC § 328, as amended by 1984 Amendments § 431. See also Annot., 69 A.L.R. Fed. 644 (1984).

## [2] Eligibility of Trustee

Any individual person may serve as a trustee in a case under Title 11 if that individual is competent to perform the duties of a trustee and provided that, in a Chapter 7 or 13 case, the individual resides or has an office in the judicial district where the case is pending or in an adjacent judicial district.[30] A corporation may serve as trustee if the corporation is authorized by its charter or bylaws to act as trustee and, in a Chapter 7 or 13 case, has an office in the judicial district in which the case is pending or in an adjacent judicial district.[31]

However, a person who has served as an examiner in the case may not serve as a trustee in the same case.[32]

After selection,[33] to qualify as trustee the person selected must, within five days after selection, and before beginning official duties, give a bond in favor of the United States, conditioned on the faithful performance of official duties.[34] The court determines the amount of the bond and the sufficiency of the surety on the bond.[35]

A suit or proceeding on the trustee's bond must be brought within two years after the trustee's discharge.[36]

## [3] The U.S. Trustee

The Bankruptcy Commission, in one of its innovative but controversial suggestions, had proposed that a new U.S. Bankruptcy Administration be established in the executive branch of the government to handle the adminis-

---

[30] 11 USC § 321(a)(1). Section 321 is applicable in Chapters 7, 11, and 13. See 11 USC § 103(a). Note that there is an inconsistency between Section 321(a), which requires the individual to reside in or have an office in the judicial *district* in which the case is pending or in an adjacent district, and Title 28, Section 604(f), which deals with the establishment of the private panel of trustees by the Director of the Administrative Office of the U.S. Courts and permits an individual trustee to reside or have an office in the state served by the bankruptcy court in which the case is pending or in an adjacent state.

[31] 11 USC § 321(a)(2). Again, there is an inconsistency between Section 321(a)(2) and Title 28, Section 604(f), which permits a corporation to serve as trustee if it has an office in the state served by the bankruptcy court.

[32] 11 USC § 321(b), as amended by 1984 Amendments § 428.

[33] The clerk of the bankruptcy court is directed to immediately notify the trustee of his selection. Within five days after receipt of this notice, the person selected must notify the court in writing of the acceptance or rejection of the office. B. Rule 2008.

[34] 11 USC § 322(a), as amended by the 1984 Amendments § 429; see also B. Rule 2010 and Official Form 25 for important details. Under Bankruptcy Rule 2010, the court may authorize a blanket bond to cover a person who qualifies as trustee in a number of cases or a number of trustees each of whom qualifies in a different case.

[35] In pilot districts, the U.S. trustee determines the amount and sufficiency of the bond. See 11 USC § 15322. If the U.S. trustee is serving as trustee in the case, no bond is required. See 11 USC § 15322(a).

[36] 11 USC § 322(d); see also B. Rule 2010(d).

tration of bankruptcy cases.[37] One of the perceived problems with bankruptcy practice under the 1898 Act was that, in many cases, the trustee was appointed by the judge before whom the trustee might later have to appear with respect to administration of the estate or in litigation affecting the bankruptcy case. This created at least an appearance that the judge might not be impartial and some appearance of potential lack of independence on the part of the trustee. In addition, bankruptcy judges under the 1898 Act had significant administrative and supervisory responsibilities along with their judicial roles. For example, the judge conducted the first meeting of the creditors and the examination of the debtor that took place during that meeting. Frequently, the judge had significant contact with the trustee in the course of the administration of the estate and sometimes in the conduct of the business of the debtor, particularly in business reorganization cases. These factors, along with others, had resulted in a practice that was viewed as requiring correction. One commentator states:

> It was not uncommon for a bankruptcy judge to be unable to recall, when called upon to resolve a dispute or find facts after a trial, whether the information on which he was basing a decision was heard at the first meeting of creditors, during the judge's extensive ex parte contacts with the trustee and with counsel during the administration of the case, or during the actual trial on an issue presented for decision.[38]

Furthermore, from the contact with the debtor in the first meeting of creditors, the judge may have gained impressions that might have in some way affected him. In the view of the Bankruptcy Commission, one of the purposes of the proposed bankruptcy administration was to assume responsibility for the administrative detail then handled by the bankruptcy judges (formerly referees) and to insulate the judges from dealing in an administrative capacity with matters that the judge might later have to determine in a judicial capacity. Also, the proposed bankruptcy administration was to function somewhat as a social service agency for debtors, particularly consumer debtors. This Commission proposal, however, encountered strong opposition from various quarters, and it was not adopted in the Bankruptcy Reform Act. However, as a legislative compromise and as a step in the direction of removing the bankruptcy judges from the administrative responsibilities and insulating them from the influences resulting from an active role in the administration and supervision of cases, the Code established in eighteen judicial districts a U.S. trustee pilot program. In explaining the purpose of this pilot program, Senator DeConcini stated:

> Under present law bankruptcy judges are required to both resolve disputes and supervise the administration of bankruptcy cases. The main purpose of the U.S. trustee is to remove administrative duties from the bankruptcy judge leaving the bankruptcy judge free to resolve disputes untainted by

---

[37] Report of the Commission on the Bankruptcy Laws of the United States, H.R. Doc. No. 137, Part I, 93d Cong., 1st Sess. 117 (1973).

[38] Collier on Bankruptcy ¶ 6.01[3], at 6-20 (Matthew Bender, 15th ed. 1981).

knowledge of matters necessary to a judicial determination. The U.S. trustee is responsible for supervising panels of private trustees in the district or districts covered by the pilot program. The U.S. trustee, rather than the court, in a pilot district will appoint trustees, supervise administration of bankruptcy cases, and exercise any other function prescribed by the Attorney General, such as presiding at first meetings of creditors, related to bankruptcy administration. In addition, in no-asset cases where private trustees may be unwilling to serve or in chapter 13 cases under title 11 where no standing trustee may be willing to serve the U.S. trustee is required to serve as trustee or standing trustee in the case.[39]

The pilot program was established by the Bankruptcy Reform Act. It amended Title 28 of the U.S. Code by adding a new "Chapter 39–United States Trustees," which included nine new sections, 581 through 589. The pilot program created for the eighteen judicial districts[40] was created under "sunset legislation." The provisions of Chapter 15 of Title 11 (which contains the provisions relating to the U.S. trustee that were originally in the bill when the U.S. trustee was proposed for all districts but as enacted apply only in the pilot districts) and Chapter 39 of Title 28 were to be repealed, and all references to "U.S. trustee" in Title 28 deleted on March 31, 1984 unless renewed by Congress prior to that date.[41] However, in the 1984 Amendments Congress extended the pilot program to September 30, 1986.[42]

During this experimental period the U.S. Attorney General was directed to study and evaluate the U.S. trustee system. Not later than January 3, 1984, the Attorney General was to submit a report and recommendations to Congress, the President, and the Judicial Conference of the United States as to the desirability and method of proceeding with implementation of the U.S. trustee system in all judicial districts.[43] At the time of this writing, there is no clear indication of how Congress will respond and whether the pilot U.S. trustee program will be abolished, or permanently established and perhaps expanded.

Under the pilot program, the U.S. trustees for the eighteen judicial districts are appointed by, and are under the general supervision of, the U.S. Attorney General.[44] They are a part of the executive branch. No qualifications

---

[39] Statement of Senator DeConcini to Senate on October 6, 1978. 124 Cong. Rec. S17,424 (daily ed. Oct. 6, 1978).

[40] The eighteen judicial districts are: Northern District of Alabama, Central District of California, District of Colorado, District of Delaware, District of District of Columbia, Northern District of Illinois, District of Kansas, District of Maine, District of Massachusetts, District of Minnesota, District of New Hampshire, District of New Jersey, Southern District of New York, District of North Dakota, District of Rhode Island, District of South Dakota, Northern District of Texas, and Eastern District of Virginia. See 28 USC § 581.

[41] Bankruptcy Reform Act of 1978, Pub. L. No. 95-598, § 408(c), 92 Stat. 2549.

[42] 1984 Amendments § 323.

[43] Bankruptcy Reform Act § 408(c).

[44] 28 USC §§ 586, 584.

for U.S. trustees are set forth in the Chapter 39 of Title 28, and the qualifications to serve as a U.S. trustee are in the sole discretion of the Attorney General.[45] The U.S. trustee is, however, always eligible to serve as trustee in a particular case.[46] The term of office of the U.S. trustee is for seven years, and upon expiration of the term, the trustee continues to serve until a successor is appointed and qualifies.[47] However, as previously noted, under the "sunset legislation," unless extended by Congress, the office of all U.S. trustees will terminate on September 30, 1986.[48]

The duties and powers of the U.S. trustee are set forth in Title 28, Section 586. Generally, the U.S. trustee is concerned only with the administrative aspects of a case and not with the judicial aspects. Also, he is not involved in the administration of the bankruptcy courts.[49] One of the principal duties of the U.S. trustee is to establish, maintain, and supervise a panel of private trustees to serve in Chapter 7 liquidation cases.[50] In addition, he is responsible for supervising the administration of cases under Chapter 7, 11, or 13.[51] Where the Chapter 13 caseload in a particular judicial district warrants, the U.S. trustee may, subject to the approval of the Attorney General, appoint a standing trustee for Chapter 13.[52] Also, in the pilot districts, it is the duty of the U.S. trustee to preside at the meeting of creditors held pursuant to Section 341.[53]

---

[45] 28 USC § 581; see also Collier on Bankruptcy ¶ 6.03[3], at 6-33 (Matthew Bender, 15th ed. 1981).

[46] See 11 USC § 15321; Collier on Bankruptcy ¶ 6.03[3], at 6-33 (Matthew Bender, 15th ed. 1981). The U.S. trustee may be removed from office for "cause" by the U.S. Attorney General. 28 USC § 581(c). See discussion in Collier on Bankruptcy ¶ 6.03[6], at 6-35 (Matthew Bender, 15th ed. 1981). However, it appears that the bankruptcy court has the power to disqualify the U.S. trustee from acting in a particular case, as distinguished from removing a U.S. trustee from office. See Collier on Bankruptcy ¶ 6.04[1][e], at 6-40 (Matthew Bender, 15th ed. 1981).

[47] 28 USC § 581(b).

[48] Bankruptcy Reform Act § 408(c), as amended by 1984 Amendments § 323. Thus, unless Congress extends the pilot program in the pilot districts, there will be a vacancy in the office of trustee in every Chapter 7 case where the U.S. trustee is serving as trustee in the case. See Collier on Bankruptcy ¶ 6.03[5], at 6-34. (Matthew Bender, 15th ed. 1981).

[49] Collier on Bankruptcy ¶ 6.08[1], at 6-44, 6-45, 6-46 (Matthew Bender, 15th ed. 1981).

[50] 28 USC § 586(a)(1). The qualifications of persons for this panel of trustees are established by the U.S. Attorney General. 28 USC § 586(d). The U.S. Attorney General has adopted interim rules in this regard. Collier on Bankruptcy ¶ 6.08[2][b], at 6-48 (Matthew Bender, 15th ed. 1981).

[51] 28 USC § 586(a)(3).

[52] 28 USC § 586(b).

[53] See B. Rule X-1006(b). The U.S. trustee may designate another party to preside at this meeting. (Bankruptcy Rules with the prefix "X" are for use only in the pilot districts with a U.S. trustee.) See B. Rule X-1001(b) and corresponding Advisory Committee Note.

Another duty of the U.S. trustee is to serve as and perform the duties of a trustee in a case under Title 11 when required to serve as trustee.[54] Essentially, this means that in a Chapter 7 case if no person from the panel of private trustees is willing to serve as interim trustee, then the U.S. trustee must serve.[55] Thus, if the creditors fail to elect a trustee in the case under Section 702, then the interim (U.S.) trustee continues as trustee in the case if no member of the private panel is willing to serve.[56]

As noted previously, in an involuntary Chapter 7 case, at any time before the order for relief the court may appoint an interim trustee to take possession of property of the estate and to operate any business of the debtor, if necessary, in order to preserve the property of the estate or to prevent loss to the estate. The court may act only on the request of any party in interest and only after notice to the debtor and a hearing.[57] In a pilot district, the U.S. trustee will make this appointment from the panel of private trustees, although he does not make the determination whether a trustee should be appointed.[58] The U.S. trustee may also object in a Chapter 7 proceeding to discharge of the debtor under Section 727(a),[59] and on request of a party in interest, the court may order the U.S. trustee to examine the acts and conduct of the debtor to determine whether grounds exist for denial of discharge.[60] In addition, the U.S. trustee may examine the debtor at the meeting of creditors held pursuant to Section 341(a).[61]

## ¶ 13.03 THE AUTOMATIC STAY

As noted previously, the filing of a petition, under any of the chapters, operates as a very broad "automatic stay" against practically any creditor collection action against the debtor or property of the estate.[1] The stay applies to both secured and unsecured creditors. The stay covers (1) the commencement or continuation of judicial or administrative proceedings against the debtor; (2) employment of process to recover on a prepetition claim or to enforce a judgment obtained before the commencement of the case; (3) any act to obtain

---

[54] 28 USC § 586(a)(2).

[55] In pilot districts, in a Chapter 7 case upon entry of an order for relief the U.S. trustee is directed to appoint an interim trustee from the panel of private trustees. See 11 USC §§ 701(a), 15701(a). In non-pilot districts the bankruptcy court makes the appointment.

[56] 11 USC § 702(d), as amended by 1984 Amendments § 472.

[57] 11 USC § 303(g).

[58] 11 USC §§ 15303, 303(g).

[59] 11 USC § 15727(a)(1).

[60] 11 USC § 15727(a)(2).

[61] 11 USC § 15343.

[1] 11 USC § 362, as amended by 1984 Amendments §§ 304, 363, 392, 441.

possession of property of the estate or to create, perfect, or enforce any lien against property of the estate; and (4) any act to collect, assess, or recover a claim that arose before the commencement of the case or to set off against a prepetition debt. There are exceptions to the automatic stay, and in certain circumstances a creditor may obtain relief from the stay.[2]

## ¶ 13.04 PROPERTY OF THE ESTATE

With the filing of either a voluntary or involuntary petition under Chapter 7, 11, or 13, the "debtor's estate" is created. Section 541 of the Code treats as property of the estate "all legal or equitable interests of the debtor in property as of the commencement of the case," wherever the property may be located.[1] There are minor exceptions specified in Sections 541(b), 541(c)(2), and 541(d). The 1984 Amendments added new Section 541(b)(2), which provides that property of the estate does not include

> any interest of the debtor as a lessee under a lease of nonresidential real property that has terminated at the expiration of the stated term of such lease before the commencement of the case under this title, and ceases to include any interest of the debtor as a lessee under a lease of nonresidential real property that has terminated at the expiration of the stated term of such lease during the case.

Property of the estate includes tangible and intangible property as well as causes of action. Also, in a change from the 1898 Act, exempt property becomes a part of the estate until properly claimed as exempt.[2] Such property becomes a part of the estate, subject to valid encumbrances that cannot be upset under the avoiding powers of the trustee, although in some cases certain liens and security interests may be avoided by the debtor.[3] The district court in which the petition is filed is given exclusive jurisdiction of the property of the debtor and of the estate, wherever it is located.[4]

---

[2] For detailed discussion of the automatic stay, see ¶ 12.05. The effect of abandonment of property on the automatic stay is discussed at infra ¶ 13.06.

[1] 11 USC § 541, as amended by 1984 Amendments §§ 363, 456.

[2] The House and Senate reports stated:

> "Paragraph (1) has the effect of overruling *Lockwood v. Exchange Bank*, 190 U.S. 294 (1903), because it includes as property of the estate all property of the debtor, even that needed for a fresh start. After the property comes into the estate, then the debtor is permitted to exempt under proposed 11 U.S.C. § 522, and the court will have jurisdiction to determine what property may be exempted and what remains as property of the estate."

H.R. Rep. No. 595, 95th Cong., 1st Sess. 368 (1977); S. Rep. No. 989, 95th Cong., 2d Sess. 82–83 (1978).

[3] See infra ¶ 13.07[3].

[4] 28 USC § 1334(d), added by 1984 Amendments § 101.

Under the avoiding powers of the trustee, the estate may be enhanced by recovering fraudulent conveyances, preferential transfers made by the debtor, and other voidable transfers or setoff. Section 541(a)(3) provides that interests recovered by the trustee under Section 550 become property of the estate. Recovery under Section 550 includes:

(1) Transfers voidable under Section 544 (the "strong arm" clause and the rights of actual creditors);[5]
(2) Voidable statutory liens under Section 545;[6]
(3) Voidable preferences under Section 547;[7]
(4) Fraudulent conveyances under Section 548;[8] and
(5) Certain postpetition transactions voidable under Section 549.[9]

In addition, Section 541(a)(3) brings into the estate:

(1) Property recovered by turnover from a custodian;[10]
(2) Certain prepetition setoffs recovered under Section 553;[11] and
(3) In the case where the debtor is a partnership, property recovered from the general partners under Section 723.

The estate also includes certain interests in property that are preserved for the benefit of, or are ordered transferred to, the estate.[12]

Although generally only property owned by the debtor at the time the petition is filed will become property of the estate in a Chapter 7 case,[13] certain interests in property acquired by the debtor after the commencement of the case also become property of the estate. Property acquired by the debtor within 180 days after the filing of the petition by bequest, devise, or inheritance, or as beneficiary of a life insurance policy or a death benefit plan or under a property settlement, becomes a part of the debtor's estate.[14]

---

[5] See discussion at ¶ 16.02.

[6] See discussion at ¶ 16.06.

[7] See discussion at ¶ 16.04.

[8] See discussion at ¶ 16.05.

[9] See discussion at ¶ 16.10.

[10] 11 USC § 543; see discussion at infra ¶ 13.05[3].

[11] See discussion at ¶ 16.08.

[12] 11 USC §§ 541(a)(4), 510(c), 551.

[13] In a Chapter 13 case, in addition to the property of the kind specified in Section 541, all property that would be included in the estate under Section 541 (including earnings from services performed by the debtor) that the Chapter 13 debtor acquires after commencement of the case but before conversion, dismissal, or closing of the case is also property of the estate. See 11 USC § 1306; H.R. Rep. No. 595, 95th Cong., 1st Sess. 428 (1977). For a discussion of the Chapter 13 estate, see ¶ 17.04.

[14] 11 USC § 541(a)(5); see discussion at infra ¶ 13.04[3].

### [1] Property of the Estate

The statute, as written, is without qualification: "[T]he estate is comprised of all the following *property*, wherever located and by whomever held: . . . all legal or equitable interests in property. . . ."[15] However, some attention must be paid to the use of the word "property," since the term *may* carry with it some judicial gloss that had been placed on the term as it was used in the 1898 Act. In a series of cases under the 1898 Act, the U.S. Supreme Court made clear that what was property for purposes of the 1898 Act was not to be determined by state property law but was a question of federal bankruptcy law. It stated further that the determination was to be made in light of the purposes of bankruptcy, including a fresh start for the debtor-bankrupt.[16] In *Segal v. Rochelle*, resolving a split of authority in the circuits, the U.S. Supreme Court held that a claim for tax refunds, due to loss-carrybacks to prior years of losses incurred in the tax year in which the bankruptcy petition was filed, was property of the bankrupt estate. In *Segal*, the Court said:

> To this end the term "property" has been construed most generously and an interest is not outside its reach because it is novel or contingent or because enjoyment must be postponed. . . . However, limitations on the term do grow out of other purposes of the Act; one purpose which is highly prominent and is relevant in this case is to leave the bankrupt free after the date of his petition to accumulate new wealth in the future. Accordingly, future wages of the bankrupt do not constitute "property" at the time of bankruptcy nor, analogously, does an intended bequest to him or a promised gift—even though state law might permit all of these to be alienated in advance.[17]

Subsequently, in *Lines v. Frederick*, in determining that a wage earner's vacation pay, accrued but unpaid at the time of the filing of the petition, was not property that passed to the bankruptcy estate, the Court said: "The most important consideration limiting the breadth of the definition of 'property' lies in the basic purpose of the Bankruptcy Act to give the debtor a 'new opportunity in life and a clear field for future effort, unhampered by the pressure and discouragement of pre-existing debt.' "[18] In the third case, *Kokoszka v. Belford*, in holding that an income tax refund was "property" of the estate, the Court noted that the term "property" had never been given a precise or universal definition and said that the income tax refund did not "relate conceptually to future wages and it is not the equivalent of future wages for the purpose of giving the bankrupt a 'fresh start,' " and was "sufficiently rooted in the pre-bankruptcy past" to be property.[19] It is not clear

---

[15] 11 USC § 541(a), as amended by 1984 Amendments § 456.

[16] These cases were Segal v. Rochelle, 382 US 375 (1966); Lines v. Frederick, 400 US 18 (1970); Kokoszka v. Belford, 417 US 642 (1974).

[17] 382 US at 379–380 (1966).

[18] 400 US 19 (1970).

[19] 417 US 647 (1974).

the extent to which the approach of these cases in defining what is "property" will be carried over into the Code.[20] The legislative history does indicate, although property is not defined in the Code, that *Lines v. Frederick* is overruled but that *Segal v. Rochelle* is followed.[21] There is some indication that courts are still looking at whether an interest is transferable or reachable by creditors.

One area where it is clear that the Code has made a change is with respect to certain causes of action. Under the 1898 Act, causes of action passed to the estate if, prior to the petition, they could be transferred "by any means" or could "have been levied upon and sold under judicial process." However, rights of action ex delicto for libel, slander, or injuries to the person of the debtor or a relative passed to the estate only if they could be reached by legal process, such as attachment, execution, or garnishment.[22] The Code does not contain such qualifications for determining whether causes of action pass to the debtor's estate. Thus, under the Code, causes of action that are "property" should pass to the debtor's estate without reference to whether such claims under state law are assignable, transferable, or can be reached by creditors.[23]

> Though this paragraph [§ 541(a)] will include choses in action and claims by the debtor against others, it is not intended to expand the debtor's rights against others more than they exist at the commencement of the case. For example, if the debtor has a claim that is barred at the time of the commencement of the case by the statute of limitations, then the trustee would not be able to pursue that claim because he too would be barred.[24]

---

[20] Collier on Bankruptcy ¶ 541.02, at 541-10 (Matthew Bender, 15th ed. 1981). Under the 1898 Act, in addition to being considered to be "property" under the Act, for "property" to become a part of the bankruptcy estate, generally the property had to be an interest "transferable by any means" by the debtor *or* an interest that could have been reached by a creditor by judicial process. See 1898 Act § 70(a); 11 USC § 110. These requirements were important issues in determining whether property passed to the estate under the 1898 Act. See, e.g., Segal v. Rochelle, 382 US 375 (1966). Note that the Code eliminated these "transferable" and "reachable" requirements for determining whether property becomes a part of the debtor's estate.

[21] H.R. Rep. No. 595, 95th Cong., 1st Sess. 367–368 (1977); S. Rep. No. 989, 95th Cong., 2d Sess. 82–83 (1978).

[22] See 1898 Act § 70(a)(5); 11 USC § 110(a)(5).

[23] Cases such as Carmona v. Robinson, 336 F2d 518 (9th Cir. 1964) and Saper v. Delgado, 146 F2d 714 (2d Cir. 1945) no longer apply to the extent that they turned on the question of whether a claim for personal injury was subject to the claims of creditors under state law. In addition, the debtor may be able to claim as exempt some causes of action that otherwise would become part of the estate. See, e.g., 11 USC §§ 522(d)(11)(B), 522(d)(11)(D), 522(d)(11)(E), and discussion of exemptions at infra ¶ 13.07.

[24] H.R. Rep. No. 595, 95th Cong., 1st Sess. 367–368 (1977); S. Rep. No. 989, 95th Cong., 2d Sess. 82 (1978).

If, however, the statute of limitations has not run on the claim at the time of the filing of the petition, Section 108[25] provides for a tolling of the statute of limitations and gives the trustee a period of time to determine whether the claim should be pursued or perhaps abandoned. If at the time the petition in bankruptcy is filed the statute of limitations has not run on a claim or cause of action of the debtor that becomes a part of the estate, then the trustee may commence an action on the claim before the time period for bringing such action or within two years after the order for relief, whichever is later.[26] For other types of actions not covered by Section 108(a), such as filing a pleading, demand, notice, proof of claim or loss (such as an insurance claim), action to cure a default or perform any other similar act, the trustee has sixty days from the order for relief or the end of such period, whichever is later.[27]

In a number of cases where the debtor had a right to redeem property[28] (e.g., from a mortgage foreclosure sale), and the time period for redemption had not run at the time the petition was filed, the issue has been raised about whether the running of the redemption period is controlled by the tolling period of Section 108, or whether the automatic stay of Section 362, during the period it is in effect, tolls the running of the redemption period. On this question the courts are divided.[29]

With respect to claims or causes of action that become a part of the estate, the claim in the hands of the estate has no greater rights than the debtor had at the time of the commencement of the case. Also, where the debtor has only

---

[25] 11 USC § 108, as amended by 1984 Amendments § 424.

[26] 11 USC § 108 (a); H.R. Rep. No. 595, 95th Cong., 1st Sess. 318 (1977); S. Rep. No. 989, 95th Cong., 2d Sess. 30 (1978); see, e.g., In re T.C.I. Ltd., 21 Bankr. 876 (Bankr. ND Ill. 1982) (Section 108(a) tolled the state statute of limitations on a mechanic's lien that had not run at the time the petition was filed). Accord, see In re Reliable Drywall, Inc., 20 Bankr. 386 (Bankr. D. Ariz. 1982).

[27] 11 USC § 108(b); H.R. Rep. No. 595, 95th Cong., 1st Sess. 318 (1977); S. Rep. No. 989, 95th Cong., 2d Sess. 30 (1978).

[28] The right to redeem is property of the estate under Section 541. In re Sapphire Invs., 19 Bankr. 492 (Bankr. D. Ariz. 1982); In re Martinson, 26 Bankr. 648 (DND 1983).

[29] For cases holding that the automatic stay does not toll the statutory period for redemption, see In re Murphy, 22 Bankr. 663 (Bankr. D. Colo. 1982); In re Bank of Commonwealth, 13 Bankr. 989 (ED Mich. 1981); In re Martinson, 26 Bankr. 648 (DND 1983). For cases holding that the automatic stay of Section 363 does toll the statutory period for redemption, see In re Johnson, 8 Bankr. 371 (Bankr. D. Minn. 1981); In re Jenkins, 19 Bankr. 105 (D. Colo. 1982); In re Sapphire Invs., 19 Bankr. 492 (Bankr. D. Ariz. 1982); see also In re Hellenschmidt, 5 Bankr. 758 (Bankr. D. Colo. 1980) (automatic stay does not affect notice requirements for redemption; lienor who had wished to redeem was required to give notice within the statutory period even if petition for bankruptcy had been filed or the creditor had agreed to lengthen the debtor's time to redeem); In re Bank of Commonwealth, 13 Bankr. 989 (ED Mich. 1981) (court may use discretionary power under Section 105 to lengthen the redemption period following foreclosure on debtor's property).

bare legal title but no beneficial interest, only the bare legal title goes to the estate.[30]

Any power that the debtor can only exercise solely for the benefit of an entity other than the debtor does not become property of the estate.[31] Thus, a power of appointment created by a will or trust and held by the debtor would not be a part of the estate if the debtor may exercise the power only for the benefit of others. However, if, for example, it is a general power of appointment and could be exercised for the benefit of the holder-debtor, the power would be property of the estate. The rationale is that if the power can be exercised for the debtor's benefit, it should also be available to creditors. In one case, a debtor's right to revoke a trust, under which the debtor held legal title to the real property with the beneficial interest in her son, was held to be property of the estate because the power was exercisable not "solely for the benefit of an entity other than the debtor."[32]

Under the 1898 Act, a life insurance policy under which the debtor-insured had the right to change the beneficiary and to surrender the policy and receive the cash surrender value was held to pass to the trustee as part of the estate, if not otherwise exempt under state law, even though the power was deemed to be personal to the insured. Collier suggests the same result should prevail under Section 541(b), since such a power would not be within the exception of "solely for the benefit of an entity other than the debtor."[33] Exempt property becomes a part of the estate property until it is properly claimed and set apart as exempt.[34]

Generally, property in which the debtor has an interest and that otherwise would become property of the estate will become property of the estate, despite restrictions or conditions on the transfer of the property by the debtor, since such provisions are rendered ineffective by the Code.[35] Furthermore, the interest of the debtor in property will become property of the estate, even though the interest of the debtor may be terminated, forfeited, or modified upon certain conditions, such as the financial status or insolvency of the debtor, the commencement of bankruptcy proceedings, or the appointment of a trustee or

---

[30] 11 USC § 541(d). In explaining this provision, Senator DeConcini stated: "To the extent such an interest is limited in the hand of the debtor, it is equally limited in the hands of the estate, except to the extent that defenses which are personal against the debtor are not effective against the estate." 124 Cong. Rec. S17,413 (daily ed. Oct. 6, 1978). However, this statement is qualified by the provisions of Section 541(c), which invalidate certain conditions and restrictions on property when it becomes property of the estate.

[31] 11 USC § 541(b), as amended by 1984 Amendments § 363. "Entity" is defined in Section 101(14). For a summary of the types of powers that had been held to be within a similar provision of the 1898 Act, see Collier on Bankruptcy ¶ 541.21, at 541-96 (Matthew Bender, 15th ed. 1981).

[32] In re O'Connor, 32 Bankr. 626 (Bankr. ED Pa. 1983).

[33] Collier on Bankruptcy ¶ 541.21, at 541-98 (Matthew Bender, 15th ed. 1981).

[34] H.R. Rep. No. 595, 95th Cong., 1st Sess. 360 (1977); S. Rep. No. 989, 95th Cong., 2d Sess. 75–76 (1978).

[35] 11 USC § 541(c)(1)(A), as amended by 1984 Amendments § 456.

custodian.[36] However, spendthrift trust provisions are enforceable to the extent they are enforceable under the applicable nonbankruptcy law.[37]

A significant provision is Section 558,[38] which gives the estate the benefit of any defense available to the debtor against other parties, including statutes of limitations and statutes of frauds, usury, and other personal defenses and makes it clear that the trustee as representative of the estate[39] may use such defenses.[40] A waiver of such defenses by the debtor after the commencement of the case is ineffective against the estate.[41]

Note should be taken of the provisions of Section 541(d), which were drafted to assist in the functioning of the secondary mortgage market. For example, an originator of a loan secured by a mortgage or deed of trust may sell the note and mortgage on the secondary market. However, for purposes of servicing or supervising the mortgage, the originator of the loan may retain legal title to the note and mortgage. Under Section 541(a)(1), the legal title of the originator-debtor becomes a part of the debtor's estate. However, Section 541(d) provides that in a situation where the debtor holds only legal title but no beneficial interest, it becomes property of the estate only to the extent of the legal title but not to the extent of any equitable interest that the debtor does not own. The purpose of this provision was to make "certain that the secondary mortgage market sales as they are currently structured are not subject to challenge by bankruptcy trustees and that purchasers of mortgages will be able to obtain the mortgages or interests in mortgages which they have purchased from

---

[36] 11 USC § 541(c)(1)(B), as amended by 1984 Amendments § 456. The House and Senate Reports stated: "The provisions invalidated are those that . . . are conditioned on the insolvency or financial condition of the debtor, on the commencement of a bankruptcy case, or on the appointment of a custodian of the debtor's property." H.R. Rep. No. 595, 95th Cong., 1st Sess. 369 (1977); S. Rep. No. 989, 95th Cong., 2d Sess. 83 (1978); see, e.g., In re Bell, 8 Bankr. 549 (Bankr. ED Mich. 1981). Note also that such provisions will not prevent sale of such property by the estate. See 11 USC § 363(1), as amended by 1984 Amendments § 442. If the property is abandoned by the trustee, however, there is authority that Section 541(c)(1) is no longer operable and a clause in a security agreement making bankruptcy a condition of default is then enforceable even if the debtor had not defaulted in any payments under the security agreement. In re Bell, 700 F2d 1053 (6th Cir. 1983); see also In re Schweitzer, 19 Bankr. 860 (Bankr. EDNY 1982). In *Bell*, the Court of Appeals for the Sixth Circuit indicated that to retain the property the debtor must elect either redemption or reaffirmation, taking the view that these are the exclusive rights given under the Code. However, there is significant authority to the contrary. See In re Ballance, 33 Bankr. 89 (Bankr. ED Va. 1983) and cases cited therein.

[37] 11 USC § 541(c)(2); see In re Goff, 706 F2d 574 (5th Cir. 1983).

[38] 11 USC § 558, added by 1984 Amendments § 470. The provisions of Section 558 were formerly in Section 541(e), but were moved to new Section 558 without change by the 1984 Amendments.

[39] See 11 USC § 323(a).

[40] H.R. Rep. No. 595, 95th Cong., 1st Sess. 367–368 (1977); S. Rep. No. 989, 95th Cong., 2d Sess. 82–83 (1978).

[41] 11 USC § 558.

trustees without the trustees asserting that a sale of mortgages is a loan from the purchaser to the seller."[42]

## [2] Community Property

The Code has specific provisions that deal with community property. With the commencement of the case, all interests of the debtor and the debtor's spouse in community property that is under the sole, equal, or joint management of the debtor, or is liable for an allowable claim against the debtor, or for allowable claims against both the debtor and the debtor's spouse, to the extent that such interest is so liable, becomes property of the estate.[43] The effect of this is that generally the community property interests of both spouses will become a part of the property of the estate even though only one of the spouses is in bankruptcy.[44] However, community creditors of both spouses may share in the community property of the estate under Section 726(c),[45] which requires segregation of the community and noncommunity property. The community property, or the proceeds of such property after liquidation, is then distributed under a "marshalling" distribution scheme specified in Section 726(c). The distribution is made first to such administrative expenses as the interest of justice requires; second, to the community claims (other than allowed administrative expenses) of the debtor or debtor's spouse, observing the priority rules of Section 507 between such community creditors, except to the extent that such property is liable solely for the debts of the debtor; third, to the extent that community debts are not paid, the community claims are paid from community property that is solely liable for debts of the debtor. If any community claims against the debtor or the debtor's spouse are unpaid under the preceding provisions, they are paid from all remaining property of the estate. After the discharge of the debtor, community creditors of the nonbankrupt spouse are barred from moving against community property acquired after bankruptcy.[46]

## [3] Property Acquired After the Filing of the Petition

Although generally the debtor's estate only includes property owned by the debtor at the time of commencement of the case, there are some important

---

[42] See 124 Cong. Rec. S17,413 (daily ed. Oct. 6, 1978). However, Section 541(d) did not solve all of the problems that the secondary mortgage market encounters in bankruptcy. See Krasnowiecki, Miller & Ziff, "The Kennedy Mortgage Co. Bankruptcy Case: New Light Shed on the Position of Mortgage Warehousing Banks," 56 Am. Bankr. L.J. 325 (1982).

[43] 11 USC § 541(a)(2). The separate property of the nondebtor spouse does not become part of the estate of the debtor-spouse. See generally Pedlar, "Community Property and the Bankruptcy Reform Act of 1978," 11 St. Mary's L.J. 349.

[44] Collier on Bankruptcy ¶ 541.15, at 541-76 (Matthew Bender, 15th ed. 1981).

[45] 11 USC § 726(c), as amended by 1984 Amendments § 479.

[46] See Weintraub & Resnick, Bankruptcy Law Manual ¶ 4.03[3] (Warren, Gorham & Lamont, Inc. 1980).

exceptions, and some property acquired by the debtor after the petition is filed will become property of the estate. Included in the estate will be any interest in property that would have been a part of the estate had the debtor owned it on the date of the filing of the petition and that the debtor acquires or becomes entitled to within 180 days after the filing of the petition by bequest, devise, or inheritance or as a result of a property settlement with a spouse, or as a beneficiary of a life insurance policy or a death benefit plan.[47] For example, if within 180 days after the filing of the petition, the debtor's rich uncle dies leaving a bequest to the debtor, the bequest becomes a part of the estate; or if the uncle dies within the time period and the debtor is the beneficiary under a life insurance policy insuring the uncle, the proceeds of the policy become property of the estate.[48] Under Bankruptcy Rule 1007(h), the debtor is required within ten days after knowledge of such property, or such additional time as the court may allow, to file a supplemental schedule with respect to such property. If the debtor wants to claim any of this property as exempt, it must be claimed on the supplemental schedule. The duty to file such a supplemental schedule continues, notwithstanding the closing of the case.[49]

In addition, all proceeds, product, offspring, and rents and profits of property of the estate that accrue after the filing of the petition are part of the estate.[50] However, this does not include earnings from services performed by the individual debtor after the commencement of the case. Such earnings are the property of the debtor.[51] Note that the term "proceeds" as used in this section is not to be read in the confining sense as defined in the UCC, but is intended to be a broad term to encompass all proceeds of property of the estate.[52] A qualification on this imposed by Section 552 should be mentioned. Under Section 552(a), property acquired by the estate or the debtor after the petition is filed is not subject to any lien resulting from any security agreement, including one with after-acquired property coverage, entered into by the debtor before the commencement of the case.[53] In effect,

---

[47] 11 USC § 541(a)(5).

[48] The debtor may be able to claim the proceeds as exempt. For a discussion of exemptions, see infra ¶ 13.07.

[49] Note also that the debtor has a duty to surrender such property of the estate to the trustee. 11 USC § 521(4), as amended by 1984 Amendments §§ 303, 452. Concealing or transferring such property may be grounds for blocking the discharge. See 11 USC § 727(a)(2).

[50] 11 USC § 541(a)(6), as amended by 1984 Amendments § 456.

[51] Id. In contrast, in a Chapter 13 proceeding, earnings for services performed, along with property acquired after the filing of the petition but before the case is closed, dismissed, or converted, do become a part of the estate under Section 1306(a)(2). In a Chapter 13 case these earnings generally are the property that will be used to make payments under the plan. Note also that, unless otherwise provided for in a confirmed plan or order confirming the plan, the Chapter 13 debtor remains in possession of all property of the estate. 11 USC § 1306(b).

[52] H.R. Rep. No. 595, 95th Cong., 1st Sess. 368 (1977); S. Rep. No. 989, 95th Cong., 2d Sess. 83 (1978).

[53] 11 USC § 552(a).

with the filing of the petition, the UCC Article 9 "floating lien" stops floating and does not pick up property acquired thereafter by the debtor or the debtor's estate. However, if the property acquired after the petition consists of proceeds, product, offspring, or rent or profits of collateral acquired before the petition is filed, the security interest does extend to such after-acquired property to the extent provided for by the security agreement, except to the extent that the court, after notice and a hearing, based on the equities, orders otherwise.[54] Thus, in such circumstances the after-acquired property of the estate would be subject to the security interest in these "proceeds." Of course, if the security interest in the collateral acquired before the petition were voidable under one of the trustee's avoiding powers, the security interest in the "proceeds" also would be voidable.

## ¶ 13.05 TURNOVER OF PROPERTY TO ESTATE

To assist the trustee in his duties of assembling and liquidating the property of the estate, Section 542 requires any entity, other than a custodian,[1] in possession, custody, or control of property of the estate during the case, to deliver the property or its value to the trustee if the trustee may use, sell, or lease the property, or if the debtor may exempt the property under Section 522,[2] unless the property is of inconsequential value or benefit to the estate.[3] In addition, Section 542(a) requires these parties to give an accounting for any property of the debtor that has been under their custody, possession, or control.

If the entity in possession of the property has an interest in the property, there is some question as to whether that entity must turn over the property immediately or whether the party has the right to demand "adequate protection" for the interest as a condition of turnover. Collier suggests that the better view is that turnover must be tendered immediately after commencement of the case. If demanded by the creditor, however, adequate protection is a condition precedent to turnover.[4]

The U.S. Supreme Court has held that property of the debtor seized prior to the commencement of a Chapter 11 case by the Internal Revenue Service

[54] 11 USC § 552(b), as amended by 1984 Amendments § 466.

[1] "Custodian" is defined in Section 101(10); the responsibility of a custodian to turn over property is covered in Section 543. See discussion at infra ¶ 13.05[3].

[2] In a Chapter 11 case in which there is no trustee, the property must be delivered to the debtor in possession.

[3] The use of the term "benefit" is intended to convey the idea that even though the property may have inconsequential monetary value, it may still have significant use value for the estate and should be turned over to the estate. H.R. Rep. No. 595, 95th Cong., 1st Sess. 369 (1977); S. Rep. No. 989, 95th Cong., 2d Sess. 84 (1978). See In re Belize Airways Ltd., 6 Bankr. 157 (Bankr. SD Fla. 1980), where a creditor was required to turn over a computer printout containing business information of the debtor.

[4] Collier on Bankruptcy ¶ 542.02, 542-6 (Matthew Bender, 15th ed. 1981).

(IRS), pursuant to a levy based on a federal tax lien claim, is property of the estate, and that the IRS is subject to a turnover order pursuant to Section 542. The Court did acknowledge the right of the IRS to adequate protection of its interest under Section 363(e).[5] The Court in dictum also stated that a secured party that had repossessed prior to bankruptcy but that had not fully foreclosed on the property would still be subject to turnover under Section 542 since the debtor's title and interest had not been fully extinguished.[6] The scope of the interest the debtor or the debtor's estate must have to be entitled to turnover is not limited to possessory interests.[7]

Furthermore, an entity that owes a debt that is property of the estate must pay such debt to the trustee if the debt is matured, payable on demand or payable on order except to the extent that the debt may be offset under Section 553.[8]

Finally, the provisions of Section 542(e) should be noted. The section states: "Subject to any applicable privilege, after notice and hearing, the court may order an attorney, accountant, or other person that holds recorded information, including books, documents, records, and papers, relating to the debtor's property or financial affairs, to turn over or disclose such recorded information to the trustee."[9] Such material, if property of the debtor, is required to be turned over to the trustee under Section 542(a). This section appears to provide a means of obtaining information from the mentioned sources even though these sources are not property of the estate, subject, of course, to any applicable privilege.[10]

In addition to the exception for property of inconsequential value or use, there are two other important exceptions where parties holding property of the estate may not be required to turn over the property to the trustee.

---

[5] U.S. v. Whiting Pools, Inc., 103 S. Ct. 2309 (1983). The Court in *Whiting* very carefully pointed out that although the turnover provisions of Section 542(a) are applicable in Chapters 7 and 13, "our analysis in this case depends in part on the reorganization context in which the turnover order is sought. We express no view on the issue whether § 542(a) has the same broad effect in liquidation or adjustment of debt proceedings." 103 S. Ct. at 2315 n.17. See generally Nowak, "Turnover Following Prepetition Levy of Distraint Under Bankruptcy Code § 542," 55 Am. Bankr. L.J. 313 (1981).

[6] 103 S. Ct. at 2314.

[7] Id.

[8] 11 USC § 542(b). For discussion of setoff, see infra ¶ 16.08.

[9] 11 USC § 542(e), as amended by 1984 Amendments § 457.

[10] The House and Senate Reports have this to say about the section: "It is a new provision that deprives accountants and attorneys of the leverage that they have today, under State law lien provisions, to receive payment in full ahead of other creditors when the information they hold is necessary to the administration of the estate." H.R. Rep. No. 595, 95th Cong., 1st Sess. 369–370 (1977); S. Rep. No. 989, 95th Cong., 2d Sess. 84 (1978).

A portion of the legislative history also stated: "The extent to which the attorney client privilege is valid against the trustee is unclear under current law and is left to be determined by the courts on a case by case basis." 124 Cong. Rec. H11,097 (daily ed. Sept. 28, 1978); S17,413 (daily ed. Oct. 6, 1978).

### [1] Good Faith Transfers Made Without Knowledge of the Bankruptcy Proceeding

A party that has neither actual notice nor actual knowledge of the commencement of the case may transfer property of the estate or pay a debt owing to the debtor to an entity other than the trustee with the same effect as if the case had not been commenced.[11] Section 542(c) codifies the holding in *Bank of Marin v. England*,[12] which held that a bank was not liable for payment made after the filing of the petition on checks drawn by the bankrupt before the filing, where the bank had no knowledge or notice of the bankruptcy proceeding.[13] It should be observed, however, that Section 542(c) only protects the good faith transferor and does not protect the transferee.[14] The transferee in such cases is covered under Sections 549 and 550. Under Section 549, in some cases the property or its value may be recovered from the transferee as a postpetition preference.[15] It should be noted that in this postpetition period, setoff is not permitted, even though, for example, the bank offsetting against the debtor's balance has no knowledge of the commencement of the case.[16] It should also be noted that the protection given by Section 542(c) to good faith payment or transfers is not limited to banks.

### [2] Automatic Deduction of Life Insurance Premiums

A life insurance company may, after the petition is filed, transfer to itself property of the estate or property of the debtor, if the transfer is made in good faith to pay a premium or is made to carry out a nonforfeiture insurance option and if such transfer or payment is required to be made automatically.[17] The purpose of this section is to provide protection to life insurance companies that are required by contract to make automatic premium loans from property that might otherwise be property of the estate, such as the loan or cash surrender value of the policy.[18] This exception to the turnover requirement applies only to life insurance policies entered into before the commencement of the case.

---

[11] 11 USC § 542(c).

[12] 385 US 99 (1966).

[13] See H.R. Rep. No. 595, 95th Cong., 1st Sess. 369 (1977); S. Rep. No. 989, 95th Cong., 2d Sess. 84 (1978).

[14] 124 Cong. Rec. S17,413 (daily ed. Oct. 6, 1978); 124 Cong. Rec. H11,097 (daily ed. Sept. 28, 1978).

[15] See discussion at ¶ 16.10.

[16] Section 542(c) is expressly subject to the automatic stay of Section 362(a)(7) against postpetition setoff.

[17] 11 USC § 542(d).

[18] H.R. Rep. No. 595, 95th Cong., 1st Sess. 369 (1977); S. Rep. No. 989, 95th Cong., 2d Sess. 84 (1978).

### [3] Turnover of Property by a Custodian

A "custodian"[19] having or acquiring property of the estate is expressly excluded from the turnover provisions of Section 542(a). However, he is covered by the provisions of Section 543,[20] which require the custodian to turn over to the trustee (or debtor in possession) any property of the debtor that is in the custodian's possession, custody, or control on the date the custodian acquires knowledge of the commencement of the case.[21] Upon acquiring this knowledge, the custodian may not make any disbursement from, or take any action with respect to, the debtor's property that is in the custodian's possession or control, except any action that is necessary to preserve the property.[22] In addition to turning over the property, the custodian must promptly file an accounting of any property of the debtor (or proceeds, product, offspring, rents, or profits thereof) that at any time came into his possession, custody, or control.[23] Section 543(c) also requires the bankruptcy court to protect any obligations incurred by the custodian with respect to property of the debtor and to surcharge the custodian for any improper or excessive disbursement unless it has been approved by a court of competent jurisdiction.[24] After notice and a hearing, the bankruptcy court may, in the interest of creditors, and if the debtor is not insolvent, of equity security holders, permit the custodianship to continue and excuse compliance with the turnover, accounting, and other provisions of Sections 543(a), 543(b), and 543(c).[25] Also, after notice and a hearing, the bankruptcy court must excuse an assignee for the benefit of the debtor's creditors who were appointed or took possession more than 120 days before the filing of the petition in compliance with Sections 543(a) (prohibiting disbursement after knowledge of the commencement of the bankruptcy case) and 543(b) (requiring turnover of property transferred to the debtor), unless compliance with these sections is necessary to prevent fraud or injustice.[26]

---

[19] "Custodian" is defined in Section 101(10).

[20] 11 USC § 543, as amended by 1984 Amendments § 458.

[21] "Property of the debtor" includes property that was property of the debtor at the time the custodian took the property, but whose title passed to the custodian, or proceeds of such property that were in the custodian's possession, custody, or control on the date the custodian acquired knowledge of the commencement of the case. 11 USC § 543(b); H.R. Rep. No. 595, 95th Cong., 1st Sess. 370 (1977); S. Rep. No. 989, 95th Cong., 2d Sess. 84 (1978).

[22] 11 USC § 543(a), as amended by 1984 Amendments § 458.

[23] 11 USC § 543(b)(2), as amended by 1984 Amendments § 458; B. Rule 6002.

[24] H.R. Rep. No. 595, 95th Cong., 1st Sess. 370 (1977); S. Rep. No. 989, 95th Cong., 2d Sess. 84 (1978); see also B. Rule 6002(b). The surcharge provisions do not apply to an assignee for the benefit of creditors who was appointed or took possession more than 120 days before the date of filing of the petition.

[25] 11 USC § 543(d), as amended by 1984 Amendments § 458.

[26] 11 USC § 543(d)(2), added by 1984 Amendments § 458.

## ¶ 13.06 ABANDONMENT OF PROPERTY

Under the 1898 Act, there were no express provisions dealing with the power of the trustee to abandon property of the estate that, for example, was burdensome or of no value to the estate or that might be encumbered by a valid security interest for a debt in excess of the value of the collateral. However, the right to abandon property was generally recognized under the 1898 Act. The Code expressly authorizes abandonment in Section 554, which, to a large extent, codifies the case law and practice under the 1898 Act.[1] The trustee, or the debtor in possession in a Chapter 11 case, after notice and a hearing, may abandon any property of the estate that is burdensome to the estate or is of inconsequential value and benefit to the estate.[2] Unless otherwise directed by the court, the trustee or debtor in possession must give notice of a proposed abandonment to all creditors, indenture trustees, and appointed or elected committees.[3] Objection to such abandonment may be filed by a party in interest within fifteen days of the mailing of such notice, or within the time fixed by the court.[4] If an objection to abandonment is timely filed, the court must set a hearing on the objection, with notice given to such persons as the court may direct; the objection is the equivalent of a request for a hearing.[5] If no objection to abandonment is filed, there does not have to be a hearing on abandonment.[6] However, although there is some difference of opinion on whether a formal order of abandonment is necessary where the trustee proposes abandonment, for purposes of title insurance in some cases it may be necessary to obtain a formal order.[7]

By motion, a party in interest may request that property be abandoned and the court, after notice and a hearing, may order the trustee to abandon property of the estate that is burdensome or of inconsequential value and benefit to the estate.[8] Property that is abandoned by the trustee or upon request of a

---

[1] Collier on Bankruptcy ¶ 554.01, at 554-6 (Matthew Bender, 15th ed. 1981). Section 554 is applicable in Chapters 7, 11, and 13.

[2] 11 USC § 554(a), as amended by 1984 Amendments § 468.

[3] B. Rule 6007(a).

[4] Id.

[5] See Bankruptcy Rule 6007(c) and the Advisory Committee Note thereto.

[6] "Notice and hearing" does not require a hearing unless there is a request or objection. See 11 USC § 102(1); In re Peninsula Roofing & Sheet Metal, Inc., 9 Bankr. 257 (Bankr. WD Mich. 1981); see also In re Motley, 10 Bankr. 141 (Bankr. MD Ga. 1981), which indicates that if there is no objection to abandonment the trustee may abandon property without court approval or an order of abandonment although the holding in *Motley* may turn on a local bankruptcy rule regarding abandonment.

[7] Sulmeyer, Lynn & Rochelle, Collier Handbook for Trustees and Debtors in Possession ¶ 11.01[4], at 11-5 (Matthew Bender 1983).

[8] 11 USC § 554(b); B. Rules 6007(b), 6007(c). Where the request for abandonment is made by a party other than the trustee under Section 554(b) (e.g., such as a secured creditor), the statute clearly contemplates that a formal order will be entered by the court directing abandonment by the trustee. A motion requesting abandonment under Section 554(b) is not an adversary proceeding. See B. Rule 7001(1).

party in interest may apparently be abandoned to any party with a possessory interest in it.[9] For example, if a secured creditor requests abandonment based on the fact that there is no equity in the property, it could be abandoned to the secured creditor if the creditor has a possessory interest. To whom the property is abandoned may be significant with respect to whether the automatic stay is still applicable.[10] Under case law, if the order of abandonment does not state to whom the property is abandoned, it appears that property will be deemed to be abandoned to the debtor.[11]

In addition to the "formal" abandonment discussed above, unless the court orders otherwise, any property that is listed on the schedule of assets required to be filed by the debtor,[12] but that is not administered before the case is closed, is deemed to be abandoned to the debtor and deemed to be administered for purposes of Section 350.[13] However, if property is not scheduled or administered and has not been otherwise formally abandoned either by the trustee or upon request of a party in interest, then it is not deemed to be abandoned and remains property of the estate unless the court orders otherwise.[14] This includes, for example, property of the debtor that is undiscovered during administration and before the close of the case. When discovered, if the property is of inconsequential value, the court could then order abandonment without the necessity of reopening the case; if of value, it would remain property of the estate. If property is discovered after the case is closed and it has not been abandoned, the trustee may reopen the case and administer the property as part of the estate.[15] Generally, abandonment is not to be lightly inferred, and the burden of showing abandonment rests on the party relying on it.[16]

---

[9] H.R. Rep. No. 595, 95th Cong., 1st Sess. 377 (1977); S. Rep. No. 989, 95th Cong., 2d Sess. 92 (1978); see also In re Cruseturner, 8 Bankr. 581 (Bankr. D. Utah 1981).

[10] See discussion at infra ¶ 13.06.

[11] See In re Gassaway, 28 Bankr. 842 (Bankr. ND Miss. 1983). In many of the cases dealing with abandonment by the trustee, it has not been clear from the facts given whether there was a formal order of abandonment, and in practically all cases the court has treated the property, at least for purposes of termination of the stay, as if it had been abandoned to the debtor.

[12] See 11 USC § 521(1).

[13] 11 USC § 554(c), as amended by 1984 Amendments § 468. See H.R. Rep. No. 595, 95th Cong., 1st Sess. 377 (1977); S. Rep. No. 989, 95th Cong., 2d Sess. 92 (1978).

[14] See 11 USC § 554(d), as amended by 1984 Amendments § 468.

[15] In re Medley, 29 Bankr. 84 (Bankr. MD Tenn. 1983).

[16] See In re Peninsula Roofing & Sheet Metal, Inc., 9 Bankr. 257 (Bankr. WD Mich. 1981) and cases cited therein. In *Peninsula Roofing* the court held that although the trustee had abandoned "all accounts receivable," this did not include an amount of $3,250 that had not been listed on the schedules as an account receivable. An abandonment, the court stated, does not revest title in a debtor "as to unscheduled assets of which the trustee was ignorant and had an opportunity to make an election." Id. at 260.

As a general rule, abandonment once made is irrevocable, even though subsequently it may turn out that the property has significant value.[17] The bankruptcy court, however, retains jurisdiction over all abandoned property.[18]

There has been and continues to be confusion with respect to the effect that abandonment of property has on the automatic stay.[19] For example, if the trustee abandons property, is the secured creditor or lienholder then free to repossess or otherwise realize on its security interest without obtaining relief from the automatic stay? Close attention must be paid to Section 362(c)(1), which states that the stay against "property of the estate" continues until the property is no longer property of the estate. From this, it may too readily be thought that, upon abandonment of property, which may occur relatively early in the bankruptcy case, the stay is terminated, at least with respect to the property involved.[20] However, the automatic stay does not terminate with respect to any creditor action against "property of the debtor" until one of the events specified in Section 362(c)(2) occurs: the time the case is closed or dismissed, whichever is earlier, or, in the case of an individual, when a discharge is granted or denied. Thus, if property is abandoned to the debtor, the stay does not terminate with respect to acts to create, perfect, or enforce liens against such property until the case is closed or dismissed, whichever is earlier, or, in the case of an individual, a discharge is granted or denied.[21] Before this time, if the property is abandoned to the debtor, the secured creditor must obtain relief from the stay to realize on the collateral.[22] Continuation of the stay for such aban-

---

[17] In re Enriquez, 22 Bankr. 934 (Bankr. D. Neb. 1982); In re (NMI) Sutton, 10 Bankr. 737 (Bankr. ED Va. 1981) (abandonment of a residence thought to have no equity was irrevocable even though subsequent foreclosure sale realized substantial equity where value was not concealed and property was scheduled); Collier on Bankruptcy ¶ 554.02[2], at 554-8 (Matthew Bender, 15th ed. 1981).

[18] In re Fitzgerald, 29 Bankr. 41 (Bankr. ED Va. 1983); In re Bennett, 13 Bankr. 643 (Bankr. WD Mich. 1981).

[19] For discussion of the automatic stay, see ¶ 12.04.

[20] Indeed, the Administrative Office of the U.S. Courts apparently took this view at one time: "In fact, if the property in question is exempt or abandoned, it is no longer property of the estate and therefore not subject to the provisions of Section 362." Information and Management Bulletin, Vol. 29 (July 1980) of the Administrative Office of the U.S. Courts, as quoted in In re Cruseturner, 8 Bankr. 581, 589 (Bankr. D. Utah 1981).

[21] See 11 USC §§ 362(c)(2), 362(a)(5).

[22] See In re Cruseturner, 8 Bankr. 581 (Bankr. D. Utah 1981); see also In re Bell, 700 F2d 1053 (6th Cir. 1983) (citing Cruseturner); In re Motley, 10 Bankr. 141 (Bankr. MD Ga. 1981); In re Doyle, 11 Bankr. 110, 111 n.4 (Bankr. ED Pa. 1981); In re Gassaway, 28 Bankr. 842 (Bankr. ND Miss. 1983); In re Fitzgerald, 29 Bankr. 41 (Bankr. ED Va. 1983); In re Tummillo, 14 Bankr. 736 (Bankr. EDNY 1981); In re Bennett, 13 Bankr. 643 (Bankr. ED Mich. 1981) In re Berry, 11 Bankr. 886 (Bankr. WD Pa. 1981); In re Quinlan, 12 Bankr. 516 (Bankr. WD Wis. 1981).

Similarly, where property is claimed as exempt by the debtor, the property revests in the debtor and the automatic stay with respect to such exempt property does not terminate under Section 362(c)(2) until the earlier of the time the case is closed or dismissed or a discharge is granted or denied. See In re Berry, 11 Bankr. 891 (Bankr. WD

doned property enables the debtor to exercise the right to redeem by acquiring financing, by otherwise gathering the necessary funds, or by negotiating a reaffirmation.[23] It also protects other rights of the debtor, such as the right to a discharge, to exemptions, and to lien avoidance under Section 522.[24] However, there is authority that holds that if the debtor is a corporation, the automatic stay does not continue after the voluntary abandonment by the trustee of property to the secured creditor. This is so because the reasons for the continuation of the stay do not exist; only an individual debtor may be discharged in Chapter 7 and only an individual debtor is entitled to exemptions or the avoidance of liens under Section 522. In addition, only an individual debtor is entitled to redeem abandoned consumer goods under Section 722.[25]

On the other hand, if property is abandoned to the secured party or lienholder,[26] as, for example, when the order of abandonment indicates that the property is abandoned to the secured party,[27] it is not clear that the stay is terminated with respect to that secured party. It may be argued that the property is no longer property of the estate; thus, the stay terminates with respect to property of the estate under Section 362(c)(1). Furthermore, if the property is no longer considered to be property of the debtor, Section 362(a)(5) does not apply.[28] However, unless all of the debtor's interest has been foreclosed, the debtor *may* retain a property interest sufficient to retain the protection of Section 362(a)(5) even though the property is abandoned to the secured creditor. Abandonment of property to the secured creditor thus may not necessarily mean that the debtor no longer has a property interest protected by the stay. In addition, at least in the case of an individual debtor, all of the reasons for continuation of the stay would exist (i.e., to give the debtor an opportunity to redeem or to negotiate a reaffirmation, etc.). Until the case law clearly resolves the question of whether the stay is terminated with abandonment of property

---

Pa. 1981); In re Williams, 9 Bankr. 228 (Bankr. D. Kan. 1981); see also In re Cruseturner, 8 Bankr. 581 (Bankr. D. Utah 1981).

[23] See id. at 592. If additional time is needed by the debtor, continuation of the stay may be requested for cause under Section 362(d)(1) or an injunction against creditor action may be requested under Section 105(a). Id. at 592. However, the creditor may move for relief from the stay.

[24] See In re D'Annies Restaurant, Inc., 15 Bankr. 828 (Bankr. D. Minn. 1981).

[25] Id. The court indicated that the stay would not survive abandonment if the debtor also were a partnership. Id. at 831.

[26] The legislative history indicates that property may be abandoned to any party with a possessory interest. H.R. Rep. No. 595, 95th Cong., 1st Sess. 377 (1977); S. Rep. No. 989, 95th Cong., 2d Sess. 92 (1978).

[27] If the order of abandonment does not state to whom the property is abandoned, it will be considered to be abandoned to the debtor and still subject to the stay. See In re Gassaway, 28 Bankr. 842 (Bankr. ND Miss. 1983); In re D'Annies Restaurant, Inc., 15 Bankr. 828 (Bankr. D. Minn. 1981). If the property is not formally abandoned by an order, but is scheduled and not administered, then it is deemed abandoned to the debtor and the stay will not be terminated. H.R. Rep. No. 595, 95th Cong., 1st Sess. 377 (1977); S. Rep. No. 989, 95th Cong., 2d Sess. 92 (1978).

[28] Cf. In re D'Annies Restaurant, Inc., 15 Bankr. 828 (Bankr. D. Minn. 1981).

to the secured party, a secured creditor seeking abandonment should, in addition, seek relief from the stay before attempting to realize on the collateral. Otherwise, repossession, realization, or sale of the collateral may be in violation of the stay and the sale is void.[29] Moreover, creditors must be aware that relief from the stay by one creditor is not relief from the stay for other creditors.[30]

## ¶ 13.07 EXEMPTIONS

The Code made significant changes with respect to exemptions in bankruptcy. Under the 1898 Act, an individual debtor was essentially entitled to the exemptions given by the state law, but there were no provisions in the 1898 Act itself that created exemptions.[1] The result of this approach, caused by the wide discrepancies among the states, was that the exemptions available to bankrupts varied widely depending on the state, with very liberal exemptions available in some states but only very limited exemptions available in others. This disparity of result, caused by state exemptions that were commonly archaic and had not been changed or modernized for many years, had been of great concern and had received a great amount of critical comment before the adoption of the Code in 1978.[2] In order to deal with these problems and to provide uniformity, the Bankruptcy Commission recommended establishing a federal bankruptcy exemption. It stated that "the reference to nonbankruptcy law to determine the exemptions is abandoned to

---

[29] See In re Motley, 10 Bankr. 141 (Bankr. MD Ga. 1981), where the trustee abandoned real property that was subject to a first and second mortgage. After abandonment the holder of the second mortgage obtained relief from the stay and foreclosed on its second mortgage. Subsequently, without obtaining relief from the stay, the holder of the first mortgage foreclosed; however, the bankruptcy court set aside the sale as void because it was in violation of the automatic stay. See also In re Gassaway, 28 Bankr. 842 (Bankr. ND Miss. 1983); cf. In re Tummillo, 14 Bankr. 736 (Bankr. EDNY 1981). Also, proceeding against abandoned property without obtaining relief from the stay may mean that the creditor (and perhaps even the debtor's attorney) will be held in contempt. See In re Coronado, 11 Bankr. 8 (Bankr. D. Ariz. 1981); Cf. In re Estes, 15 Bankr. 25 (Bankr. SD Ohio 1981).

[30] See In re Motley, 10 Bankr. 141 (Bankr. MD Ga. 1981).

[1] See 1898 Act § 6; 11 USC § 24. Of course, in some cases a bankrupt might be able to claim exemptions created or given under nonbankruptcy federal law exempting certain federal benefits or property; however, under the 1898 Act, generally only state exemptions were available.

[2] See Countryman, "For a New Exemption Policy in Bankruptcy," 14 Rutgers L. Rev. 678 (1960); Countryman, "Consumer Bankruptcy–Some Recent Changes and Some Proposals," 19 U. Kan. L. Rev. 165 (1971); Resnick, "Prudent Planning or Fraudulent Transfer? The Use of Nonexempt Assets to Purchase or Improve Exempt Property on the Eve of Bankruptcy," 31 Rutgers L. Rev. 615 (1978); Marier, "Bankruptcy Exemptions: A Full Circle Back to the Act of 1800?" 53 Cornell L. Rev. 663 (1968); Kennedy, "Limitation of Exemptions in Bankruptcy," 45 Iowa L. Rev. 445 (1960); Joslin, "Debtor's Exemption Laws: Time for Modernization," 34 Ind. L.J. 355 (1959).

eliminate diversity, reduce the amount of litigation having no direct relationship to the policy underlying exemptions, and because state exemption laws seem generally archaic and unduly generous in some states and exceedingly niggardly, particularly as to urban residents, in others."[3]

## [1] State "Opt-Out" Power

Because of opposition to establishing a uniform federal bankruptcy exemption, the result in the Code was a legislative compromise. Under Section 522,[4] a specific "federal bankruptcy exemption" was created, but a state is permitted by specific legislation adopted after the Code to "opt out" or to override the federal bankruptcy exemption and to permit a debtor to take only the exemptions given under the state exemption law. At present, there is a clear indication that this legislative compromise will ultimately, if it has not already done so, revert to the condition that the Bankruptcy Commission sought to avoid: lack of uniformity of exemptions in the federal bankruptcy system, with archaic and very limited exemptions available to some debtors and overly generous exemptions available to others. This has occurred because at present more than half of the states have opted out of the federal bankruptcy exemptions.[5]

The basic approach of the legislative compromise on exemptions embodied in Section 522 is that, under Section 522(b), an *individual* debtor may exempt from property of the estate either the "federal bankruptcy" exemptions specified in Section 522(d) or, alternatively, property that is exempt under the state law of the debtor's domicile and in addition, any property that is exempt under non-bankruptcy federal law.[6] However, Section 522(b)(1) permits a state to "opt out" of the federal bankruptcy exemption given by Section 522(d) by specific legislation enacted after the Code was adopted. As noted previously, more than thirty states have opted out. The specific "opt-out" language of Section 522(b)(1) is

---

[3] Report of the Commission on the Bankruptcy Laws of the United States, H.R. Doc. No. 137, 93d Cong., 1st Sess. 127 (1973).

[4] 11 USC § 522, as amended by 1984 Amendments §§ 306, 453.

[5] See Bankruptcy Service, Lawyers Edition § 22.120-172 (Lawyers Coop. Publishing Co. 1979); Koffler, "The Bankruptcy Clause and Exemption Laws: A Reexamination of the Doctrine of Geographic Uniformity," 58 N.Y.U. L. Rev. 22 (1983); see also Rhodes v. Stewart, 705 F2d 159, 162 n.2 (6th Cir. 1983); In re Brooks, 31 Bankr. 302, 303 (Bankr. SDNY 1983).

[6] Some of the items that may be exempted under federal laws other than Title 11 include: (1) Social Security payments (42 USC § 407); (2) Foreign Service Retirement and Disability payments (22 USC § 1104); (3) injury or death compensation payments from war risk hazards (42 USC § 1717); (4) wages of fishermen, seamen, and apprentices (46 USC § 601); (5) Civil Service retirement benefits (5 USC §§ 729, 2265); (6) Longshoremen's and Harbor Workers' Compensation Act death and disability benefits (33 USC § 916); (7) Railroad Retirement Act annuities and pensions (45 USC § 228(L)); (8) veterans' benefits (38 USC § 352 (E)); (9) special pensions paid to winners of the Congressional Medal of Honor (38 USC § 3101); (10) federal homestead lands on debts contracted before issuance of the patent (43 USC § 175).

that the debtor may choose the "federal bankruptcy exemption" of Section 522(d) "unless the State law that is applicable to the debtor under paragraph (2)(A) of this subsection specifically does not so authorize." The state opt-out power is thus limited to denying the debtor the right to choose the federal bankruptcy exemptions under Section 522(d) and arguably does not give the state the power to override other provisions of Section 522, such as Section 522(f) or 522(m).[7] Thus, if a state has not opted out of the federal bankruptcy exemptions of Section 522(d), the debtor may choose either the federal bankruptcy exemptions or the exemptions given by the state law that are applicable on the date of the filing of the petition at the place where the debtor's domicile was located for the 180 days, or the greater portion thereof, immediately preceding the date of filing the petition.[8] In a non-"opt-out" state, the debtor has the choice of choosing the exemption that will protect the greatest amount of property. In a state that has validly opted out of the federal bankruptcy exemption, however, the debtor may exempt only the property that may be exempt under the applicable state law. This result is, with some exceptions, a reversion to the exemption situation as it existed under the 1898 Act.

It should be pointed out that exemptions, whether state or federal bankruptcy exemptions, are claimed in the value of the property over and above any valid liens or security interests. "Property may be exempted even if it is subject to a lien, but only the unencumbered portion of the property is to be counted in computing the 'value' of the property for the purposes of exemption. Thus, for example, a residence worth $30,000 with a mortgage of $25,000 will be exemptable to the extent of $5,000."[9] If there is value in the property claimed as exempt that is in excess of the valid liens and the claimed exemption, and if the debtor does not redeem the property under Section 722,[10] then the trustee can sell the property and the debtor will receive the value of the exemption from the proceeds of sale.

As a result of legislative compromise, Section 522(b) provides:

> Notwithstanding section 541 of this title, an individual debtor may exempt from property of the estate the property listed in either paragraph (1) or, in the alternative, paragraph (2) of this subsection. . . . (1) property that is specified under subsection (d) of this section, unless the State law that is applicable to the debtor under paragraph (2)(A) of this subsection specifically does not so authorize. . . .[11]

On its face, the statute seems to empower a state only to "opt out" of the federal bankruptcy exemptions of Section 522(b) (i.e., the federal bankruptcy

---

[7] See discussion at infra ¶ 13.07[1].

[8] If the state exemptions are chosen, the debtor also may claim any exemptions under federal laws other than Title 11. 11 USC § 522(b)(2).

[9] See H.R. Rep. No. 595, 95th Cong., 1st Sess. 360–361 (1977); S. Rep. No. 989, 95th Cong., 2d Sess. 75–76 (1978).

[10] See infra ¶ 13.08.

[11] 11 USC § 522(b), as amended by 1984 Amendments § 306.

exemptions specified in Section 522(d)) and to substitute state exemptions for the federal bankruptcy exemptions.[12] However, it is unclear how much beyond this a state may go to negate the other provisions of Section 522 and to limit the exemptions available to a debtor in bankruptcy. May, for example, a state negate Section 522(m), which, in a joint case, gives both spouses the benefit of Section 522 and permits both to claim exemptions?[13] May a state undermine the "spirit" of Section 522? Or may a state negate the effect of Section 522(f), permitting a debtor to avoid nonpossessory, nonpurchase-money security interests in property that he could otherwise claim as exempt? A number of cases have dealt with the extent to which a state may opt out and, not surprisingly, have arrived at different results. It is unclear from the cases how far the opt-out power of the state extends.

One argument that has been used to attack the constitutionality of Section 522(b) is that, by allowing the states to limit their citizens to exemptions that differ from state to state, Congress has failed to establish uniform bankruptcy laws.[14] The U.S. Supreme Court, in a decision under the 1898 Act, had held, in *Hanover National Bank v. Moyses*,[15] that the uniformity provision of the bankruptcy clause required only "geographical uniformity" rather than "true uniformity"; that is, true uniformity that does not allow any state-by-state variations in bankruptcy law is not required. Instead, only geographic uniformity is necessary, which allows state-by-state variations in exemptions. The "opt-out" provision of Section 522(b) of the Code has been unsuccessfully challenged as unconstitutional on the basis of the "uniformity requirement."[16] Although the

---

[12] Although Section 522(b) was amended by the 1984 Amendments, the opt-out power given to a state under Section 522(b)(1) remained unchanged. The cases discussed in the following paragraphs with respect to the power of the state to opt out do not appear to be affected by the 1984 changes.

[13] 11 USC § 522(m), as amended by 1984 Amendments § 306. It should be noted that the 1984 amendment to Section 522(b) to an extent limits the right of a husband and wife in a joint case (whose estates are administered jointly) to both claim exemptions under Section 522(m). In a husband-and-wife joint case, under amended Section 522(b), both debtors must claim the same exemption; one debtor may not claim the federal bankruptcy exemption and the other debtor the state exemption. If the state has not opted out of the federal bankruptcy exemptions, both must take either the state or federal exemption; if the state has validly opted out, it appears that both debtors must elect the state exemption. In addition, amended Section 522(b) provides that if the husband and wife in a joint case cannot agree on the alternative to be selected, they are deemed to have elected the federal bankruptcy exemptions where the state has not opted out of the federal bankruptcy exemptions.

[14] The argument is based on the "bankruptcy clause" of the U.S. Constitution, article 1, section 8, clause 4, which provides that Congress is "[t]o establish . . . uniform Laws on the subject of bankruptcies throughout the United States." For discussion of this and other arguments, see Comment, "Bankruptcy Exemptions: Whether Illinois's Use of the Federal 'Opt Out' Provision Is Constitutional," 1981 S. Ill. U.L.J. 65; Koffler, "The Bankruptcy Clause and Exemption Laws: A Reexamination of the Doctrine of Geographic Uniformity," 58 N.Y.U. L. Rev. 22 (1983).

[15] 186 US 181 (1902).

[16] In re Sullivan, 680 F2d 1131, 1138 (7th Cir. 1982); In re Lausch, 16 Bankr. 162 (MD Fla. 1981); Rhodes v. Stewart, 705 F2d 159 (6th Cir. 1983); see also Comment,

Court of Appeals for the Seventh Circuit in *In re Sullivan* indicated that the argument against the constitutionality based on the uniformity requirement was forceful, it felt bound by the holding in *Moyses* that only geographic uniformity, not personal uniformity, was required.[17] In addition, an argument that Section 522(b) is an unconstitutional delegation of congressional power to the states has been rejected.[18] Another argument that has been used to attack the opt-out provisions is that of preemption. It has been argued that because the Code provided a "highly detailed scheme of bankruptcy exemptions ... Congress clearly has preempted state law with regard to the exemption of property interests in bankruptcy cases."[19] The countering argument is that "Congress clearly did not intend to preempt the area of bankruptcy exemptions ... since it left the ultimate determination of available bankruptcy exemptions to the states."[20]

Some courts have held that the states have an unlimited right to provide whatever exemptions the state desires to provide, whether or not the state scheme of exemptions varies drastically from the federal exemptions provided for in Section 522(d).[21] Other courts have held that, when a state opts out of the federal exemptions, the state exemptions provided must not be inconsistent with the federal exemptions and must be adequate to provide debtors with a "fresh start."[22] Under this approach, the courts have tended to compare the state exemptions concerned with the federal exemptions in order to determine whether the state exemptions involved are adequate to give the debtor a "fresh start." For example, the Colorado exemption scheme was upheld, even though

---

"Bankruptcy Exemptions: Whether Illinois's Use of the Federal 'Opt Out' Provision is Constitutional," 1981 S. Ill. U.L.J. 65; In re Goering, 23 Bankr. 1010 (Bankr. ND Ill. 1982). In *Goering* the court rejected arguments based on the "supremacy clause" and on equal protection.

[17] In re Sullivan, 680 F2d 1134 (7th Cir. 1982).

[18] Id. at 1131, 1138; In re Lausch, 16 Bankr. 162, 165 (MD Fla. 1981). For development of this argument, see Comment, "Bankruptcy Exemptions: Whether Illinois's Use of the Federal 'Opt Out' Provision Is Constitutional, 1981 S. Ill. U.L.J. 65, 88.

[19] In re Rhodes, 14 Bankr. 629, 631 (Bankr. MD Tenn. 1981). However, the bankruptcy court was reversed in Rhodes v. Stewart, 705 F2d 159 (6th Cir. 1983).

[20] In re Lausch, 16 Bankr. 162, 165 (MD Fla. 1981); In re Sullivan, 680 F2d 1131, 1136 (7th Cir. 1982); Rhodes v. Stewart, 705 F2d 159 (6th Cir. 1983); In re McManus, 681 F2d 353 (5th Cir. 1982).

[21] In re Sullivan, 680 F2d 1131, 1138 (7th Cir. 1982) (upholding an Illinois exemption even though it provided an unmarried debtor without dependents a $300 allowance for a homestead and certain "wild card" exemptions, while the federal exemption under Section 522(d)(1) provided for a $7,500 exemption); In re Goering, 23 Bankr. 1010 (Bankr. ND Ill. 1982); In re Wilson, 22 Bankr. 146 (Bankr. D. Ore. 1982); In re Lausch, 16 Bankr. 162, 165 (MD Fla. 1981); Foster v. City Loan & Sav. Co., 16 Bankr. 467, 469 (ND Ohio 1981). The court in *Foster* also indicated that a state could provide no exemption if it so chose. Id. at 469.

[22] Cheeseman v. Nachman, 656 F2d 60, 64 (4th Cir. 1981); In re Parrish, 19 Bankr. 331, 334–335 (Bankr. D. Colo. 1982); In re Balgemann, 16 Bankr. 780, 782 (Bankr. ND Ill. 1982); In re Rhodes, 14 Bankr. 629, 634 (Bankr. MD Tenn. 1981).

it provided exemptions in lower dollar amounts in some areas than did the federal exemption scheme. This was permissible because the Colorado scheme also provided higher dollar amounts in some areas than did the federal exemption scheme. These allowances were found to balance each other and to enable the debtor to be left with some assets in order to make a fresh start.[23] On the other hand, a Maryland scheme of exemptions was struck down because it failed to provide exemptions for nonhomeowners that were available to homeowners. The court found this inconsistent with the federal scheme of exemptions that provides a similar exemption to both homeowners and nonhomeowners and thus found the Maryland provisions did not provide an adequate fresh start for its citizens.[24]

Concerning the question of whether states may include provisions in their exemption schemes that prevent debtors from taking advantage of the lien avoidance provisions of Section 522(f), once state exemptions are selected, a majority of the courts have held that state statutes may not prevent debtors from taking advantage of Section 522(f).[25] Other courts have held that states do have the power to preclude use of the lien avoidance provisions of Section 522(f).[26] One court has found that where the state has not opted out, the state exemption scheme may preclude debtors from using the Section 522(f) lien avoidance provisions.[27]

Another question with respect to state power is whether a state may require a debtor to comply with state procedures in order to claim exemptions. Some courts have held that imposing preconditions, such as proof of a debtor's good faith attempt to pay creditors, is impermissible.[28] Other courts have held that states may impose preconditions on the debtor, such as residency or filing requirements.[29]

An additional area of controversy is whether states may preclude debtors in a joint bankruptcy case from independently selecting state or federal exemptions as provided for in Section 522(m).[30] Several courts have found it uncon-

---

[23] In re Parrish, 19 Bankr. 331 (Bankr. D. Colo. 1982).

[24] In re Locarno, 23 Bankr. 622 (Bankr. D. Md. 1982).

[25] In re Dahdah, 20 Bankr. 665 (Bankr. App. Pan. 9th Cir. 1982); In re McKelvey, 20 Bankr. 405 (Bankr. D. Ariz. 1982); In re Latulippe, 13 Bankr. 528 (Bankr. D. Vt. 1981); In re Fredrickson, 12 Bankr. 506 (Bankr. DSD 1981); In re Meadows, 9 Bankr. 882 (Bankr. ND Ga. 1981); In re Fisher, 6 Bankr. 206 (Bankr. ND Ohio 1980); In re Storer, 13 Bankr. 1 (Bankr. SD Ohio 1980); In re Dubrock, 5 Bankr. 353 (Bankr. WD Ky. 1980); cf. In re Thacker, 5 Bankr. 592 (Bankr. WD Va. 1980).

[26] In re McManus, 681 F2d 353 (5th Cir. 1982); Foster v. City Loan & Sav. Co., 16 Bankr. 467 (ND Ohio 1981).

[27] In re Falck, 12 Bankr. 835 (Bankr. CD Cal. 1981).

[28] In re Davis, 16 Bankr. 62 (Bankr. D. Md. 1981).

[29] Zimmerman v. Morgan, 689 F2d 471 (4th Cir. 1982); In re Collins, 24 Bankr. 485 (Bankr. ED Va. 1982); In re Lowe, 7 Bankr. 248 (Bankr. ED Wash. 1980); see also White v. Stump, 266 US 310 (1924).

[30] 11 USC § 522(m), as amended by 1984 Amendments § 306. Section 522(m) permits a husband and wife in a joint case to separately claim exemptions under Section 522; that is, both may claim exemptions. However, the amendments to Sections 522(m)

stitutional where states have required joint debtors to join together in selecting state exemptions if either debtor desires to select the state exemption scheme.[31] Other courts have arrived at an opposite result.[32]

## [2] Federal Bankruptcy Exemptions: Section 522(d)

The exemptions given by this section may be summarized as follows:[33]

*Homestead.* An exemption may be claimed in property not to exceed $7,500 in real or personal property that the debtor or a dependent uses as a residence or as a burial plot. This type of "homestead" may include an interest in a cooperative and may include a homestead in personal property, such as a mobile home.

*Motor vehicle.* The exemption may not exceed $1,200 in value in one motor vehicle.

*Household furnishings, appliances, wearing apparel, and other items.* The debtor may claim an exemption not to exceed $200 in value in *any* particular item or $4,000 in aggregate value of household furnishings, household goods, wearing apparel, appliances, books, animals, crops, or musical instruments that are held primarily for personal, family, or household use of the debtor or a dependent of the debtor. This means that any of the specified items may be exempt up to the value of $200. If an item exceeds that value, the debtor would appear to still have the right to claim an exemption in the item and have the right to redeem the property under Section 722.[34]

*Jewelry.* Jewelry used for personal, family, or household use of the debtor or a dependent may be exempt to an aggregate value not exceeding $500.

---

and 522(b) (as amended by 1984 Amendments § 306) to an extent limit the right of a husband and wife in a joint case (whose estates are administered jointly) to both claim exemptions under Section 522(m). In a husband-and-wife joint case, under amended Section 522(b), both debtors must claim the same exemption; one debtor may not claim the federal bankruptcy exemption and the other debtor the state exemption. If the state has not opted out of the federal bankruptcy exemptions, both must take either the state or federal exemption; if the state has validly opted out, it appears that both debtors must elect the state exemption. In addition, amended Section 522(b) provides that if the husband and wife in a joint case cannot agree on the alternative to be elected, they are deemed to have elected the federal bankruptcy exemptions where the state has not opted out of the federal bankruptcy exemptions.

[31] In re Stacy, 24 Bankr. 97 (Bankr. SD Cal. 1982); In re Lee, 22 Bankr. 977 (Bankr. CD Cal. 1982); In re Gustinis, 16 Bankr. 108 (Bankr. ED Va. 1981); In re Ageton, 14 Bankr. 833 (Bankr. App. Pan. 9th Cir. 1981); cf. In re Jones, 31 Bankr. 20 (Bankr. WD Wash. 1983); In re Brooks, 31 Bankr. 302 (Bankr. SDNY 1983).

[32] In re Brooks, 31 Bankr. 302 (Bankr. SDNY 1983); In re Skipwith, 9 Bankr. 730 (Bankr. SD Cal. 1981).

[33] 11 USC § 522(d), as amended by 1984 Amendments § 306. This summary of necessity lacks precision; the statute must be consulted for specifics.

[34] See discussion of redemption at infra ¶ 13.08.

*"Wild-card" exemption.*[35] The debtor may claim an aggregate exemption in *any* property not to exceed $400 *plus* up to $3,750 of any of the unused portion of the $7,500 homestead exemption. Under the 1984 Amendments, the maximum "wild-card" exemption is thus $4,150. For example, if the debtor only has $2,500 of equity in a homestead that was claimed as exempt, then $3,750 of the unused portion of $5,000 plus the $400 could be claimed in any property of the debtor not claimed under any of the other exemptions. In another example, if the debtor had $5,000 of unused homestead exemption and owned a car valued at $3,000 in excess of any lien, then a $1,200 exemption could be claimed under the motor vehicle exemption and $1,800 of the wild-card exemption could be claimed in the car. This would leave a $2,350 wild-card exemption to be claimed in other property not otherwise exempt under Section 522(d).

*Tools of the trade.* The debtor may claim an aggregate exemption not to exceed $750 in any implements, professional books, or tools of the trade of the debtor or of a dependent of the debtor. If the debtor has tools of the trade in excess of this value, the wild-card exemption might be used.

*Life insurance policies.* All unmatured life insurance policies owned by the debtor, other than credit life insurance contracts, may be exempted. Note that this refers to the life insurance contract itself and does not encompass any other rights under the contract, such as the right to borrow on the loan value that otherwise becomes property of the estate. However, Subsection 522(d)(8) permits the debtor to exempt up to $4,000 of loan value, accrued dividend, or interest under a life insurance policy owned by the debtor, provided that the insured is the debtor or an individual of whom the debtor is a dependent. If the loan value exceeds this $4,000 exemption, the wild-card exemption might be used or the debtor might redeem the cash surrender value under Section 722.[36]

*Health aids.* All professionally prescribed health aids for the debtor or a dependent of the debtor are exempt.

*Certain benefits and wage substitutes.* The debtor may claim as exempt the right to receive (1) Social Security benefits; (2) unemployment compensation; (3) local public assistance benefits; (4) veterans' benefits; (5) disability, illness, or unemployment benefits; (6) alimony, support, or maintenance to the extent reasonable necessary for support of the debtor or of any dependent of the debtor; and (7) certain payments under pension or profit-sharing plans payable for illness, disability, death, age, or length of service to the extent reasonably necessary for the support of the debtor.

*Miscellaneous "compensation" types of payments.* The debtor may claim as exempt either the right to receive property or property that is *traceable* to (1) certain payments under crime victim's reparation laws; (2) payments on account of wrongful death of an individual or under a life insurance policy of

---

[35] 11 USC § 522(d)(5), as amended by 1984 Amendments § 306.

[36] See discussion at infra ¶ 13.08.

an insured of whom the debtor was a dependent; or (3) payments for personal injury or other compensation for loss of future earnings.

If the state in which the debtor has been domiciled for the greater portion of the 180 days immediately preceding the filing of the petition has opted out of the federal bankruptcy exemptions, then the debtor is limited to the state exemptions. However, there are additional provisions in Section 522 that are important to the debtor with respect to exemptions and that are applicable in states that have or have not opted out.[37]

In a joint case involving spouses, Section 522(m) provides: "Subject to the limitation in subsection (b), this section shall apply separately with respect to each debtor in a joint case."[38] Section 522(m) has been construed to mean that, in a joint case, both husband and wife may claim exemptions. Thus, in effect, there may be double exemptions. Before the 1984 Amendments, cases had held that, in states where the federal exemptions are available, one spouse may claim the federal bankruptcy exemptions under Section 552(d) and the other spouse may claim the state exemption under Section 522(b)(2), or that both could claim either the state or the federal bankruptcy exemptions.[39] However, the 1984 Amendments to Sections 522(b) and 522(m) limit the right of a husband and wife in a joint case (whose estates are administered jointly) to both claim exemptions under Section 522(m). In a husband-and-wife joint case under amended Section 522(b), both debtors must claim the same exemption; one debtor may not claim the federal bankruptcy exemption and the other debtor the state exemption. If the state has not opted out of the federal bankruptcy exemptions, both must take either the state or federal exemption; if the state has validly opted out, it appears that both debtors must elect the state exemption. In addition, amended Section 522(b) provides that if the husband and wife in a joint case cannot agree on the alternative to be elected, they are deemed to have elected the federal bankruptcy exemptions where the state has not opted out of the federal bankruptcy exemptions. This means that in a non-"opt-out" state, there may be a double homestead exemption in a joint case, and if, for example, both spouses choose the federal exemption, $15,000 of homestead property could be exempt under Section 522(d)(1) by use of Section 522(m).

It is unclear the extent to which a state under the opt-out power may negate the double exemption provisions of Section 522(m). It seems clear

---

[37] Some states that have opted out have attempted to negate some of the additional provisions of Section 522. The extent to which a state has the power to negate these provisions is unclear under the decided cases. See discussion at supra ¶ 13.07[1].

[38] 11 USC § 522(m), as amended by 1984 Amendments § 306. (The 1984 Amendments added to the section "Subject to the limitation in subsection (b).")

[39] See, e.g., In re Cannady, 653 F2d 210 (5th Cir. 1981); In re Barnes, 14 Bankr. 788 (Bankr. ND Tex. 1981); In re Lee, 22 Bankr. 977 (Bankr. CD Cal. 1982); In re Pearl, 28 Bankr. 492 (Bankr. EDNY 1983); In re Alvarez, 14 Bankr. 940 (Bankr. D. Colo. 1981); In re Collins, 5 Bankr. 675 (Bankr. ND Cal. 1980). But see First Nat'l Bank of Mobile v. Norris, 701 F2d 902 (11th Cir. 1983). Cf. In re Jones, 31 Bankr. 20 (Bankr. WD Wash. 1983); In re Brooks, 31 Bankr. 302 (Bankr. SDNY 1983).

enough that in Section 522(b)(1) the states were given power to specifically provide that a debtor may not elect the "federal bankruptcy exemptions." On its face, the language of Section 522(b)(1) seems to confer only the power to forbid use of the Section 522(d) federal bankruptcy exemptions. As noted previously, however, the extent to which a state may opt out or negate the other subsections of Section 522 is unclear from the decided cases.[40]

Note that if the debtor elects the state exemption, any interest that the debtor has in property held as a tenant by the entirety or joint tenant, to the extent such interest is exempt from process under applicable nonbankruptcy law, may be claimed as exempt.[41]

### [3] Protection of the Debtor's Exemptions

The Code has several provisions that are designed to ensure that the debtor receives the benefit of any exemptions and that the exempt property will be available to assist the debtor in a fresh start.

Generally, Section 522(c)[42] provides that exempt property will not be liable, during or after the case, for any debt that arose or is deemed to have arisen before the commencement of the case.[43] This means that nondischargeable debts generally cannot be satisfied with exempt property. However, there are two exceptions.[44] First, exempt property is subject to claims for nondischargeable taxes and for nondischargeable claims for alimony, maintenance, or support.[45] Second, liens on exempt property that are not avoided, as well as certain tax liens, may be enforced against exempt property.[46] Such claimants must be concerned with when they are free to proceed against such property.[47] If the property is claimed as exempt, this revests the property in the debtor; the automatic stay is still effective and is not terminated under Section 362(c)(2) until the case is closed or dismissed, or, in the case of an individual, a discharge is

---

[40] See discussion at supra ¶ 13.07[1]. Cf. In re Jones, 31 Bankr. 20 (Bankr. WD Wash. 1983); In re Brooks, 31 Bankr. 302 (Bankr. SDNY 1983). For discussion, see Comment, "Bankruptcy Exemptions: Whether Illinois's Use of the Federal 'Opt Out' Provision Is Constitutional," 1981 S. Ill U.L.J. 65; Comment, "Controversy Surrounding Exemption Uniformity: The Opt Out Provision of Section 522 of the New Bankruptcy Code," 13 U. Tol. L. Rev. 1111 (1982).

[41] See 11 USC § 522(b)(2)(B); cf. Chippenham Hosp. Inc. v. Bondurant, 716 F2d 1057 (4th Cir. 1983).

[42] 11 USC § 522(c), as amended by 1984 Amendments § 453.

[43] Certain claims, although arising after the petition, are treated as if they arose before the petition. See ¶ 14.06.

[44] Most debts will be discharged an unenforceable after bankruptcy. See Chapter 15.

[45] 11 USC §§ 522(c)(1), 523(a)(1), 523(a)(5).

[46] 11 USC § 522(c)(2).

[47] See 11 USC §§ 362 and 524 and discussion of the automatic stay at ¶ 12.05.

granted or denied.[48] Thus, the creditor must generally obtain relief from the stay.

Significant protection to ensure that exemptions are available to the debtor is given by Section 522(e), which makes unenforceable any waiver of exemption in favor of an unsecured creditor,[49] and renders unenforceable any waiver of the debtor's avoiding powers given by Sections 522(f) and 522(h) and certain other powers.[50]

One of the most significant protections given for exemptions is a new section[51] of the Code giving the debtor the power to avoid judicial liens and certain security interests in property that may be claimed as exempt.[52] As noted previously, exemptions are claimed in the value of the property in excess of any valid liens. If most of the debtor's property is fully encumbered, however, realistically there are no exemptions. In an attempt to permit exemptions in such cases, in limited circumstances, the Code gives the debtor the power to avoid certain liens on property of the debtor that might otherwise be claimed as exempt under either the federal bankruptcy or the state exemptions, as the case may be.[53] If this avoiding power is successfully invoked, the effect of this provision is to reduce the lienholder to an unsecured status to the extent necessary for the debtor to claim the exemption; an otherwise valid lien is "confiscated" to the extent the property may be claimed as exempt. Only certain liens may be avoided under this section. First, judicial liens[54] on any property that the debtor might claim as exempt may be avoided to the extent the property may be claimed as exempt.[55] A lien obtained by a confession of judgment note has been held to be a judicial lien within the meaning of this section.[56] If there is value in the property in excess of the claimed exemption, the lien will still be valid to that extent and the debtor may then be able to redeem the property from the lienholder for the value of the lien on the property above the exemption.[57] There is no time limit within which the judicial lien must have arisen, that is, the judicial lien can arise at any time before the petition is filed.

---

[48] See In re Cruseturner, 8 Bankr. 581 (Bankr. D. Utah 1981).

[49] 11 USC § 522(e), as amended by 1984 Amendments § 453. This section applies to both federal and state exemptions. H.R. Rep. No. 595, 95th Cong., 1st Sess. 362 (1977); S. Rep. No. 989, 95th Cong., 2d Sess. 76 (1978).

[50] 11 USC § 522(e). For a discussion of the debtor's avoiding powers, see ¶ 16.09.

[51] One court has suggested that Section 522(f) is not entirely new, but had a counterpart, at least with respect to avoiding judicial liens, in Section 67(a) of the 1898 Act. In re Ashe, 669 F2d 105 (3d Cir. 1982).

[52] 11 USC § 522(f). To avoid such interests under Section 522(f) the debtor may proceed by a motion under Bankruptcy Rule 9014. See B. Rule 4003(d).

[53] 11 USC § 522(f). This provision is available only to individual debtors.

[54] "Judicial lien" is defined in Section 101(30).

[55] 11 USC § 522(f)(1). See generally Annot., 47 A.L.R. Fed. 937 (1980).

[56] In re Ashe, 669 F2d 105 (3d Cir. 1982); Gardner v. Commonwealth of Pa. Dep't of Pub. Welfare, 685 F2d 106 (3d Cir. 1982) (lien avoidance provision of Section 522(f) applies against governmental agency).

[57] See discussion of redemption at infra ¶ 13.08.

Second, nonpossessory, non-purchase-money security interests may be avoided in household furnishings and goods, wearing apparel, appliances, crops, and other specified items held primarily for personal family or household use. Nonpossessory, non-purchase-money security interests in implements, professional books, and tools of the trade of the debtor or a dependent, or in professionally prescribed health aids, may also be avoided under this section.[58]

If the debtor avoids such judicial liens or nonpossessory, non-purchase-money security interests, the debtor may then claim an exemption in the property.[59]

There is a significant body of case law that has developed with respect to what is a purchase-money security interest within the meaning of this section. In a number of cases, the trend has been to take a restrictive view. If the secured party has added in debt other than that which represents the purchase price or loan, then the interest may be held not to be a purchase-money security interest. In addition, some cases have held that, if property other than that acquired with the purchase-money loan or extension of credit is included in the security agreement, the interest does not qualify as a purchase-money security interest and may be avoided by the debtor.[60] However, there is authority to the contrary.[61]

Exemptions also may be claimed in property that is recovered for the estate by the trustee under the avoiding powers[62] if the voidable transfer was not a voluntary transfer of the property by the debtor and the debtor did not conceal the property.[63] If there is a transfer that could be avoided by the trustee, but the trustee does not attempt to avoid it, the debtor may avoid the transfer to the extent he could have exempted the property, recover the property for the estate, and then claim an exemption in the property if the debtor did not voluntarily transfer the property and conceal it.[64] The debtor may use

---

[58] 11 USC § 522(f)(2). See generally Annot., 55 A.L.R. Fed. 353 (1981).

[59] 11 USC § 522(i).

[60] In re Kelley, 17 Bankr. 770 (Bankr. ED Tenn. 1982); In re Calloway, 17 Bankr. 212 (Bankr. WD Ky. 1982); In re Rosen, 18 Bankr. 723 (Bankr. DSC 1981); In re Ashworth, 16 Bankr. 645 (Bankr. CD Cal. 1981); In re Slater, 19 Bankr. 954 (Bankr. D. Md. 1982); In re Jones, 5 Bankr. 655 (Bankr. MDNC 1980).

[61] In re Russell, 29 Bankr. 270 (Bankr. WD Okla. 1983); Stevens v. Associates Fin. Servs., 24 Bankr. 536 (Bankr. D. Colo. 1982); In re Conn, 16 Bankr. 454 (Bankr. WD Ky. 1982); In re Gibson, 16 Bankr. 257 (Bankr. D. Kan. 1981); In re Holland, 16 Bankr. 83 (Bankr. ND Ohio 1981); In re Matthews, 20 Bankr. 654 (Bankr. App. Pan. 9th Cir. 1982); In re Moore 33 Bankr. 72 (Bankr. D. Ore. 1983); In re Hunter, 32 Bankr. 437 (Bankr. WD Pa. 1983).

[62] As discussed in Chapter 16, the trustee may avoid and recover for the estate transfers voidable under Sections 544 (the "strong arm" clause), 545 (certain statutory liens), 547 (preferences), 548 (fraudulent conveyances), and 549 (certain postpetition transfers).

[63] 11 USC § 522(g).

[64] 11 USC §§ 522(h), 522(i).

these sections only to the extent he has not otherwise exempted his full federal or state exemption of this type of property under Section 522(b).[65]

The rights of the debtor under these subsections are cumulative, and the debtor is not required to choose which subsections he may use to gain an exemption. Instead, the debtor may use more than one subsection in any particular instance, just as the trustee's avoiding powers are cumulative.[66]

Exempt property in not liable for payment of any administrative expenses of the estate, except for the aliquot share of the costs and expenses of the trustee in avoiding a transfer of property that the debtor later claims as exempt under Section 522(g). Another exception includes any costs and expenses of avoiding a transfer by the debtor that he has not already paid.[67]

### [4] Claiming the Exemption

In order to claim property as exempt, the debtor must file a list of all property claimed as exempt. Unless a party in interest objects, the property claimed as exempt is deemed exempt.[68] The Code does not specify when the exemption must be claimed. However, Bankruptcy Rule 4003 requires the debtor to list the property claimed as exempt on the schedule of assets that are required to be filed by Bankruptcy Rule 1007.[69] If the debtor fails to claim the exemption or to file the schedules within the time prescribed by Bankruptcy Rule 1007,[70] a dependent of the debtor may claim the exemptions within thirty days thereafter.[71]

---

[65] See 11 USC § 522(j). Note also the debtor may avoid such transfers only to the extent the trustee could avoid them under the sections specified. H.R. Rep. No. 595, 95th Cong., 1st Sess. 360, 363 (1977); S. Rep. No. 989, 95th Cong., 2d Sess. 75, 77 (1978). Bankruptcy Rule 4003(d) provides that an action by the debtor to avoid a lien or transfer under Section 522(f) may be by motion pursuant to Bankruptcy Rule 9014 as a contested matter. However, Bankruptcy Rule 4003(d) does not state that the debtor action under Sections 522(h) and 522(i) may be by motion rather than by an adversary proceeding.

[66] H.R. Rep. No. 595, 95th Cong., 1st Sess. 363 (1977); S. Rep. No. 989, 95th Cong., 2d Sess. 77 (1978).

[67] 11 USC § 522(k); see also H.R. Rep. No. 595, 95th Cong., 1st Sess. 363 (1977); S. Rep. No. 989, 95th Cong., 2d Sess. 77 (1978).

[68] 11 USC § 522(1).

[69] See ¶ 12.04[1]; see also Official Bankruptcy Form 6.

[70] Unless the court extends the time for cause, in a voluntary case the schedules must be filed with the petition or within fifteen days thereafter, and in an involuntary case, within fifteen days of entry of the order for relief. See discussion at ¶ 12.04[1] and B. Rule 1007 for more detail.

[71] 11 USC § 522(1); B. Rule 4003(a). "Dependent" includes a spouse whether or not actually dependent; it is not, however, limited to a spouse. See 11 USC § 102(3).

### [a] Amendment of the List of Exemptions

Bankruptcy Rule 1009 permits a debtor, at any time before the case is closed, to amend the list and schedule of property and exemptions.[72] In order to amend the schedules of exemptions, Bankruptcy Rule 1009 requires that the debtor give notice to the trustee and any entity affected thereby. However, a significant number of cases have refused to permit amendment of exemptions.[73]

### [b] Objections to Claim of Exemptions

The trustee or any creditor may file objections to the list of property claimed as exempt within thirty days after the meeting of creditors.[74] Within this thirty-day period, the court may extend the time for filing objections.[75] Copies of the objections to the exemptions must be mailed or delivered to the trustee and to the debtor or dependent who filed the list of exemptions and his attorney.[76] If an objection to an exemption is filed, the court, after hearing on notice, must determine if the exemption is to be allowed. However, the objecting party has the burden of proving that the exemption is not properly claimed.[77]

## [5] Converting Nonexempt Property Into Exempt Property Prior to Bankruptcy

In some circles, it is considered sound "bankruptcy planning" to advise an individual contemplating the filing of a petition in bankruptcy to convert nonexempt assets into exempt assets before filing the petition. Although converting nonexempt assets into exempt assets is generally not considered to be a fraudulent conveyance[78] (and indeed, Congress clearly acknowledged this[79]), a

---

[72] See In re Doan, 672 F2d 831 (11th Cir. 1982), holding that absent bad faith of the debtor or prejudice to creditors, former Bankruptcy Rule 110 permitted the debtor as a matter of course to amend the schedule of exemptions at any time before the close of the case. See also Redmond v. Tuttle, 698 F2d 414 (10th Cir. 1983).

[73] See, e.g., In re Eldridge, 15 Bankr. 594 (Bankr. SDNY 1981); In re Korff, 14 Bankr. 189 (Bankr. DRI 1981); In re Selman, 7 Bankr. 889 (Bankr. DNM 1980); cf. B. Rule 4003.

[74] See discussion at ¶ 12.06.

[75] B. Rule 4003(b).

[76] Id.

[77] B. Rule 4003(c).

[78] See Weintraub & Resnick, Bankruptcy Law Manual ¶ 4.09, at 4-33 (Warren, Gorham & Lamont, Inc. 1980).

[79] The House and Senate Reports stated: "As under current law, the debtor will be permitted to convert non-exempt property into exempt property before filing a bankruptcy petition. The practice is not fraudulent as to creditors, and permits the debtor to make full use of the exemptions to which he is entitled under the law." H.R. Rep. No. 595, 95th Cong., 1st Sess. 361 (1977); S. Rep. No. 989, 95th Cong., 2d Sess. 76 (1978).

caveat must be raised. There is significant case law to indicate that, in advising a client in this regard, an attorney must be somewhat cautious and not take this general rule too literally.[80] If actual fraud is found in converting nonexempt property into exempt property shortly before bankruptcy, a discharge may be denied or the exemption may be denied.[81]

## ¶ 13.08 REDEMPTION

In a Chapter 7 liquidation case, the property of the debtor is generally liquidated by sale of the property. However, in some instances, property may be partially exempt and perhaps subject to a valid security interest. Except for those circumstances discussed previously where the nonpossessory, non-purchase-money security interest or judicial lien may be avoided under Section 522(f), any exemption must be claimed over and above any valid security interest or lien. If the property has value in excess of such liens and any exemption that might be claimed in the property, this represents property value that the trustee normally will want to realize for the estate. Thus, the property normally will not be abandoned unless it is of inconsequential value. However, because of the forced sale nature of the liquidation, frequently the true value of the property may not be realized for the estate. Moreover, the value realized by the estate may not correspond to the replacement value of the property to the debtor. Section 722 therefore permits an individual debtor to redeem property in certain circumstances.[1] This section is applicable only to individual debtors in Chapter 7 cases,[2] and only tangible personal property intended primarily for personal, family, or household use may be redeemed. Furthermore, only property that is claimed as exempt under Section 522 or that has been abandoned

---

[80] For discussion of this problem, see Resnick, "Prudent Planning or Fraudulent Transfer? The Use of Nonexempt Assets to Purchase or Improve Exempt Property on the Eve of Bankruptcy," 31 Rutgers L. Rev. 615 (1978); Weintraub & Resnick, Bankruptcy Law Manual ¶ 4.09 (Warren, Gorham & Lamont, Inc. 1980).

[81] In re Reed, 700 F2d 986 (5th Cir. 1983), noted in 14 Tex. Tech L. Rev. 648 (1983); 24 S. Tex. L.J. 909 (1983); see also In re Wallace, 30 Bankr. 5 (Bankr. CD Ill. 1983) (debtor was denied an exemption in cash surrender value of life insurance policies, where shortly before bankruptcy the debtor had repaid loans on the policies with nonexempt proceeds from a certificate of deposit, with actual intent to defraud creditors; the court was influenced by a state statute that created a presumption that the cash surrender value was acquired in contemplation of bankruptcy when acquired within six months of filing the petition in bankruptcy).

[1] See generally Butler, "Section 722: A Redeeming Aspect of the Bankruptcy Code," 88 Com. L.J. 462 (1983). For a good discussion of the development of Section 722 and its relationship to the "reaffirmation" provisions of Section 524(c), see In re Cruseturner, 8 Bankr. 581 (Bankr. D. Utah 1981).

[2] 11 USC §§ 722, 103(b). In Chapter 13, under Section 1325(a)(5) a debtor may in effect force redemption upon a secured creditor and may do so by installment payments, which may be spread out over not more than three years or, with court approval, not more than five years.

under Section 554 may be redeemed, and the redemption may only be from a lien that is securing a dischargeable consumer debt.[3] The right to redeem given by Section 722 in effect gives the debtor the "right of first refusal" on the property that otherwise might be repossessed or sold;[4] the right to redeem extends to the whole of the property, not just to the debtor's exempt interest in it.[5]

Redemption is made by paying to the holder of the lien the amount of the allowed *secured* claim of such holder.[6] This means that the debtor may redeem by paying only the secured portion of the creditor's claim, not the entire claim, in the event the debt exceeds the value of the collateral. For example, assume that the dischargeable consumer debt owed to a finance company is $3,000 and that the value of the car securing the claim is only $2,000. Under Section 506, the finance company would have an allowable secured claim for $2,000 and an unsecured claim for $1,000; the debtor would be able to redeem by paying the finance company $2,000, not $3,000, if the property were abandoned by the trustee.[7] The $1,000 deficiency would be allowable as an unsecured general claim. In another example, suppose that the car is valued at $3,000 and the lien of the finance company secured a debt of only $2,000. The debtor then could redeem the car by paying the finance company $2,000 if the remaining equity or interest of the debtor in the car of $1,000 was claimed as exempt under Section 522 using either the federal bankruptcy exemption or the state exemption. Assume further that the value of the car is $5,000, the secured claim of the finance company is $2,000, and the individual debtor claims an exemption of $1,200, leaving the estate with a property value of $1,800. In these circumstances, the trustee should not abandon the property because of the substantial value to the estate. What may the debtor do? Under these circumstances, the debtor should be able to obtain abandonment of the property by paying the trustee the value of the estate's interest ($1,800) and then redeeming the property from the lienholder finance company.

There is authority holding that the valuation of the collateral, for purposes of determining the amount of the secured claim and hence the redemption

[3] "Consumer debt" is defined as a "debt incurred by an individual primarily for a personal, family, or household purpose." 11 USC § 101(7).

[4] In re Hobdy, 18 Bankr. 70 (Bankr. WD Ky. 1982); In re Zimmerman, 4 Bankr. 739 (Bankr. SD Cal. 1980); H.R. Rep. No. 595, 95th Cong., 1st Sess. 380–381 (1977); S. Rep. No. 989, 95th Cong., 2d Sess. 95 (1978). Section 722 is based on the redemption rights given to a debtor under UCC Section 9-506 but is intended to be broader than that section. Id.

[5] H.R. Rep. No. 595, 95th Cong., 1st Sess. 381 (1977). The right to redeem is personal to the debtor and not assignable. S. Rep. No. 989, 95th Cong., 2d Sess. 95 (1978).

[6] Where the value of the collateral, a motor vehicle, was less than the amount of the first lien, the debtor was permitted to redeem from a second lien, which the court viewed as having no value, by paying only the cost of filing with the appropriate agency notice that the lien had been discharged. In re Altenburg, 6 BCD 331 (Bankr. SD Fla. 1980).

[7] In re Williams, 9 Bankr. 83 (Bankr. MD Tenn. 1981) (debtor was permitted to redeem even though there was no equity in which exemption could be claimed and even though trustee had not formally abandoned the property).

amount, is to be made as of the date of the redemption hearing.[8] However, there is also authority holding that the valuation for redemption is to be made as of the time of the filing of the petition.[9]

An important question of practical importance to the debtor is the question of whether redemption under Section 722 may be made in installment payments or whether it must be made by a lump-sum payment. Although there is a split of authority, the greater number of cases hold that redemption may not be made by installments but must be made by a lump-sum payment.[10] However, there appears to be nothing to prevent a secured party from agreeing to a redemption in installments, although such an agreement is subject to the provi-

---

[8] In re Van Holt, 28 Bankr. 577 (Bankr. WD Mo. 1983) (valuation computed as if the creditor disposed of the collateral, a car, in a normal commercial fashion at wholesale); In re Pierce, 5 Bankr. 346 (Bankr. D. Neb. 1980) (normally the time of valuation is the date of the redemption proceeding unless secured creditor can show undue delay, gross negligence, or other acts of the debtor that unreasonably diminish value of collateral); compare In re Klein, 10 Bankr. 657 (Bankr. EDNY 1981); In re Klein, 20 Bankr. 493 (Bankr. ND Ill. 1982) (where a Chapter 13 case had been converted to Chapter 7, a car purchased during the Chapter 13 proceeding could be redeemed at value established by the NADA used-car valuation publication on the date that the claim was filed and deemed allowed; the court refused to use the repurchase value established in the repurchase agreement).

[9] See In re Kinser, 17 Bankr. 468 (Bankr. ND Ga. 1981). For additional cases on the time and method of valuation, see Butler, "Section 722: A Redeeming Aspect of the Bankruptcy Code," 88 Com. L.J. 462 (1983).

[10] For cases holding that redemption may not be by installments, see In re Bell, 700 F2d 1053 (6th Cir. 1983); In re Cruseturner, 8 Bankr. 581 (Bankr. D. Utah 1981) (the court gave the debtor thirty days to make the lump-sum redemption; the case contains an outstanding discussion of the legislative development of "redemption" and its relationship to the reaffirmation provisions of Section 524(c)); In re Schweitzer, 19 Bankr. 860 (Bankr. EDNY 1982); In re Carroll, 11 Bankr. 725 (Bankr. App. Pan. 9th Cir. 1981) (reversing a bankruptcy court holding that redemption could be by installments); In re Hart, 8 Bankr. 1020 (NDNY 1981); In re Kinser, 17 Bankr. 468 (Bankr. ND Ga. 1981); In re Whatley, 16 Bankr. 394 (Bankr. ND Ohio 1982); In re Zimmerman, 4 Bankr. 739 (Bankr. SD Cal. 1980); In re Miller, 4 Bankr. 305 (Bankr. ED Mich. 1980); In re Stewart, 3 Bankr. 24 (Bankr. ND Ohio 1980); cf. In re Rose, 21 Bankr. 272, 278 (Bankr. DNJ 1982) (dicta). But see In re Davis, 15 Bankr. 118 (Bankr. CD Ill. 1981); In re Hall, 11 Bankr. 3 (Bankr. WD Mo. 1980); In re Clark, 10 Bankr. 605 (Bankr. CD Ill. 1981). See also Butler, "Section 722: A Redeeming Aspect of the Bankruptcy Code," 88 Com. L.J. 462 (1983); Dye, "An Overview of Chapter 13–Its Uses and Abuses," 43 Mont. L. Rev. 35, 50 n.134 (1982). In a Chapter 13 case the debtor under the "cram-down" provisions may, in effect, force a secured creditor to take a forced redemption under Section 1325(a)(5) and the payments may be made in installments over not more than three years or, with court approval, not more than five years. Similarly, in a Chapter 11 case under Section 1129(b)(2)(A) a secured creditor may be compelled to take what in effect may be a redemption by installments. See, e.g., In re Bell, 700 F2d 1053 (6th Cir. 1983); In re Cruseturner, 8 Bankr. 581 (Bankr. D. Utah 1981); In re Thompson, 17 Bankr. 748 (Bankr. WD Mich. 1982). For an individual debtor unable to make a lump-sum redemption or to arrive at an installment reaffirmation with the secured creditor, Chapter 11 or 13 may offer an alternative to accomplish an "installment redemption."

sions of Section 524(c) and the provisions of that section must be complied with.[11] In contrast to reaffirmation, redemption may be made without the consent of, and over the objection of, the lienholder. Any waiver by the debtor of the right to redeem given by Section 722 is unenforceable.[12]

If the debtor is not in default in making the payments due or is not otherwise in default under the security agreement, other than under an ipso facto bankruptcy clause, there is disagreement in the cases as to whether the debtor must either redeem or reaffirm in order to retain possession of the property, or whether the debtor may retain possession by making payments and performing all other obligations required under the security agreement, such as maintaining insurance. The Court of Appeals for the Sixth Circuit has held that even though the debtor may not be in default in making payments or in meeting other conditions of the security agreement, upon abandonment of the property, an ipso facto clause is operable and the exclusive options available to the debtor under the Code to retain possession are either redemption or reaffirmation. In the view of the Sixth Circuit, the debtor is not entitled to retain possession merely by making installment payments as they become due, which, in effect, would be redemption by installment.[13] However, there is significant authority to the contrary.[14]

In order to obtain authorization from the court to redeem, the debtor may proceed by motion pursuant to Bankruptcy Rules 6008 and 9014. Reasonable notice and opportunity for a hearing must be afforded the secured party or other lienholder from whom redemption is sought. Service of the motion must be made pursuant to Bankruptcy Rule 7004. In addition, local bankruptcy rules also should be consulted. The Code does not specify when redemption must be made and when applicable local rules must be consulted.[15]

## ¶ 13.09 ASSUMPTION, ASSIGNMENT, AND REJECTION OF UNEXPIRED LEASES AND EXECUTORY CONTRACTS

The 1898 Bankruptcy Act contained brief specific provisions dealing with the assumption and rejection of leases and executory contracts to which the

---

[11] See In re Cruseturner, 8 Bankr. 581 (Bankr. D. Utah 1981); see also In re Kinser, 17 Bankr. 468 (Bankr. ND Ga. 1981); In re Bell, 8 Bankr. 549 (Bankr. ED Mich. 1981). If the creditor agrees to permit "redemption" by installment payment, this is generally labeled a "reaffirmation" and is subject to the provisions of Section 524(c), as amended by the 1984 Amendments. For a discussion of reaffirmation, see ¶ 15.08. However, reaffirmation may not be forced upon the creditor. See In re Cruseturner, 8 Bankr. 581, 587 (Bankr. D. Utah 1981).

[12] 11 USC § 722.

[13] In re Bell, 700 F2d 1053 (6th Cir. 1983).

[14] See In re Perry, 729 F2d 982 (4th Cir. 1983); In re Ballance, 33 Bankr. 89 (Bankr. ED Va. 1983), and cases cited therein.

[15] Some bankruptcy courts, by local rule, apparently require a certificate of service of the motion and that the motion for redemption be filed with the court at least three working days before the debtor's scheduled discharge hearing. See Butler, "Section 722: A Redeeming Aspect of the Bankruptcy Code," 88 Com. L.J. 462, 464 (1983).

debtor-bankrupt was a party.[1] In general, under the 1898 Act these contracts and leases became property of the estate and could be rejected by the trustee; in some cases, they could be assumed and assigned by the trustee. The Code continues this general pattern, and Section 365 specifically, and in much greater detail, deals with the assumption, assignment, and rejection of executory contracts and unexpired leases.[2] However, there are significant changes in the treatment of executory contracts and unexpired leases under the Code.[3]

With some minor exceptions,[4] Section 365(a) permits the trustee, subject to court approval, to assume or reject any executory contract or unexpired lease of the debtor.[5]

The 1984 Amendments added significant qualifications with respect to nonresidential (commercial) leases of real property. Under Section 365(c)(3),[6] the trustee (or debtor in possession) cannot assume or assign a lease on nonresidential real property that has been terminated under applicable nonbankruptcy law prior to the order for relief.[7] In addition, the 1984 Amendments made

---

[1] See 1898 Act § 70(b). The classic work on this section is Countryman, "Executory Contracts in Bankruptcy: Part I," 57 Minn. L. Rev. 439 (1973) and "Part II," 58 Minn. L. Rev. 479 (1974).

[2] 11 USC § 365, as amended by 1984 Amendments § 362,402–404. Bankruptcy Rule 1007(b) requires that the debtor in a Chapter 7 or 11 case file a statement of executory contracts unless the court orders otherwise.

[3] Helpful articles include Shanker, "The Effect of the Bankruptcy Code Amendments on Contracts," 31 Prac. Law. 13 (1985); Fogel, "Executory Contracts and Unexpired Leases in the Bankruptcy Code," 64 Minn. L. Rev. 341 (1980); Shanker, "The Treatment of Executory Contracts and Leases in the 1978 Bankruptcy Code," 25 Prac. Law. 11 (1979); Levy, "Impact of the New Bankruptcy Code on Article 2 Sales," 14 U.C.C. L.J. 307 (1982); Ehrlich, "The Assumption and Rejection of Unexpired Real Property Leases Under the Bankruptcy Code—A New Look," 32 Buffalo L. Rev. 1 (1983); Epling, "Treatment of Land Sales Contracts Under the New Bankruptcy Code," 1981 Ariz. St. L.J. 852; Nimmer, "Executory Contracts in Bankruptcy: Protecting the Fundamental Terms of the Bargain," 54 U. Colo. L. Rev. 507 (1983); Simpson, "Leases and the Bankruptcy Code: The Protean Concept of Adequate Assurance of Future Performance," 56 Am. Bankr. L.J. 233 (1982); Simpson, "Leases and the Bankruptcy Code: Tempering the Rigors of Strict Performance," 38 Bus. Law. 61 (1983); Note, "Rejection of Unexpired Oil and Gas Leases in Bankruptcy Proceedings (In re J.H. Land & Cattle Co.)," 19 Tulsa L.J. 68 (1983).

[4] 11 USC § 365(a). The exceptions relate to commodity broker liquidations. See 11 USC §§ 765, 766.

[5] In a Chapter 11 case, the debtor in possession has the powers of the trustee and may exercise the powers given under Section 365. See 11 USC §§ 1107(a), 103. Different time periods for assumption or rejection apply in Chapters 11 and 13 than in Chapter 7. See infra ¶ 13.09[2].

[6] 11 USC § 365(c)(3), added by 1984 Amendments § 362. Note that for purposes of Section 365, leases of real property include "any rental agreement to use real property." 11 USC § 365(m), added by 1984 Amendments § 362.

[7] Section 541(b)(2), added by 1984 Amendments § 363, also provides that the debtor's estate does not include any interest of the debtor as lessee under a lease of nonresidential real property that has terminated before the commencement of the case and the debtor's estate ceases to include "any interest of the debtor as a lessee under a

significant changes with respect to assumption by the trustee (or the debtor in possession) of real estate leases in shopping centers.[8]

## [1] The Executory Contract

A threshold question in the application of Section 365 is: What is an executory contract? Although at one point in the development of the Code an attempt was made to define an executory contract, when the Code was adopted the term was intentionally left undefined.[9] The House and Senate reports stated:

> Though there is no precise definition of what contracts are executory, it generally includes contracts on which performance remains due to some extent on both sides. A note is not usually an executory contract if the only performance that remains is repayment. Performance on one side of the contract would have been completed and the contract is no longer executory.[10]

In *NLRB v. Bildisco & Bildisco*, in discussing what is an executory contract the U.S. Supreme Court stated:

> The Bankruptcy Code furnishes no express definition of an executory contract, see 11 U.S.C § 365, but the legislative history to § 365 indicates that Congress intended the term to mean a contract "on which performance is due to some extent on both sides." H.R. Rep. No. 95-595, p. 347 (1977), see S. Rep. No. 95-989, p. 58 (1977). We reject the argument of amicus United Mine Workers of America that a collective-bargaining agreement is not an executory contract within the meaning of § 365. Under their labor contract both Bildisco and the Union had reciprocal obligations, and at any point during the life of the contract, performance was due by both parties.[11]

Professor Morris Shanker has raised the question of whether the Supreme Court in *Bildisco*, by stressing "reciprocal obligations," may have shifted the focus in determining what is an executory contract. Professor Shanker stated:

> This definition seems contrary to the historical definition of an executory contract, which focused on whether future duties, other than the payment of money, were to be performed on the part of the bankrupt. If these

---

lease of nonresidential real property that has terminated at the expiration of the stated term of such lease during the case."

[8] See discussion at infra ¶ 13.09[4].

[9] See Report of the Commission on the Bankruptcy Laws of the United States, H.R. Doc. No. 137, 93d Cong., 1st Sess. 199 (1973); In re Booth, 19 Bankr. 53, 55 (Bankr. D. Utah 1982).

[10] H.R. Rep. No. 595, 95th Cong., 1st Sess. 347 (1977); S. Rep. No. 989, 95th Cong., 2d Sess. 58 (1978).

[11] 104 S. Ct. 1188, 1194 n.6 (1984). For additional discussion of *Bildisco*, see infra ¶ 13.09[9].

future duties were required only on the part of the nonbankrupt, then the contract was not executory for bankruptcy purposes. Rather, future performances due from the nonbankrupt were simply assets of the estate. To repeat, the primary focus was on whether there were future duties to be performed by the bankrupt, not whether there were any reciprocal duties to be performed by the nonbankrupt. *Bildisco*, however, speaks of reciprocal obligations in an executory contract. Is the Court suggesting that this is the only time that an executory contract that is governed by section 365 exists?[12]

Although the cases under the 1898 Act left a great deal of ambiguity as to what would be considered an executory contract, the following definition by Professor Countryman was followed in a number of cases. He stated that "A contract under which the obligation of both the bankrupt and the other party to the contract are so far unperformed that the failure of either to complete performance would constitute a material breach excusing performance of the other."[13] In general, this definition of an executory contract has been followed under the Code.[14] However, one bankruptcy court in a Chapter 11 proceeding held that the "Countryman test" is not always the appropriate test for determining what is an executory contract. It also held that the debtor's interest as the vendee under an installment sales contract for the purchase of real estate (a contract for deed) is not an interest in an executory contract.[15] The court acknowledged, as it had previously held,[16] that the debtor-vendor's interest under a real estate installment sales contract is treated as an executory contract by the Code.[17] Thus, for an installment sales contract of real property, whether the contract is "executory" may depend upon whether the debtor is the vendor or the vendee.[18]

---

[12] Shanker, "The Effect of the 1984 Bankruptcy Code Amendments on Contracts," 31 Prac. Law. 5, 23–24 (1985).

[13] Countryman, "Executory Contracts in Bankruptcy, Part I," 57 Minn. L. Rev. 439, 460 (1973).

[14] See, e.g., In re Alexander, 670 F2d 885 (9th Cir. 1982). In *Alexander*, a Chapter 13 proceeding, the debtor-vendor under a "deposit receipt sales contract" of real property was permitted to reject. The contract remained executory even though the purchaser had tendered full performance on the closing date but still had to pay the remainder of the purchase price and the vendor-debtor had refused to give up possession and convey title. In the view of the court, the contract remained executory: "The contract did not cease to be executory when there was a tender of performance. Performance or the rendering of performance, not just tender of performance, is required." Id. at 887.

[15] In re Booth, 19 Bankr. 53 (Bankr. D. Utah 1982); accord In re Cox, 28 Bankr. 588 (Bankr. D. Idaho 1983).

[16] See In re Summit Land Co., 13 Bankr. 310 (Bankr. D. Utah 1981).

[17] See In re Booth, 19 Bankr. 53, 61 (Bankr. D. Utah 1982).

[18] In addition to *Booth*, *Summit Land*, and *Cox*, see In re Chi-Feng Huang, 23 Bankr. 798 (Bankr. App. Pan. 9th Cir. 1982).

## [2] Timetable for Rejection or Assumption of an Executory Contract or Unexpired Lease

In a Chapter 7 case, if the trustee does not assume or reject an executory contract or unexpired lease of the debtor within sixty days after the order for relief, the lease or contract is deemed rejected.[19] For cause, within the sixty-day period, the court may extend the period for rejection or assumption.

In a Chapter 11 or 13 case, the trustee or debtor in possession may assume or reject an executory contract or unexpired lease of the debtor at any time before the confirmation of the plan. However, on request of any party to the contract or lease, the court may order the trustee within a specified period of time to reject or assume the contract or lease.[20] However, the 1984 Amendments added new provisions for nonresidential (commercial) leases of real property.[21] In a case under either Chapter 7, 11, or 13, if the trustee (or debtor in possession) does not assume or reject an unexpired lease of nonresidential real property under which the debtor is the lessee within sixty days after the order for relief (or within such additional time as the court may allow for cause), then the lease is deemed rejected. If the lease is rejected under such circumstances, the trustee must immediately surrender the property.[22] The purpose of the 1984 Amendments with respect to nonresidential leases of real property was to reduce for the nondebtor lessor (particularly in a Chapter 11 case) the period of uncertainty as to whether the commercial lease will be assumed or rejected.[23] Furthermore, with respect to these unexpired leases of nonresidential real property, the trustee (or debtor in possession) must timely perform the obligations of the debtor arising from and after the order for relief until the lease is assumed or rejected.[24]

In addition, in Chapter 11 and 13 cases, executory contracts or unexpired leases not previously rejected may be rejected by the plan of reor-

---

[19] 11 USC § 365(d)(1), as amended by 1984 Amendments § 362. Bankruptcy Rule 6006(a) provides that proceedings to assume, reject, or assign an executory contract or unexpired lease shall be made by motion (a "contested matter") under Bankruptcy Rule 9014.

[20] 11 USC § 365(d)(2). Bankruptcy Rule 6006(b) provides that a party to the executory contract or unexpired lease may proceed by motion under Bankruptcy Rule 9014 to require the trustee to determine whether to assume or reject a contract or lease.

[21] 11 USC § 365(d)(4), as added by 1984 Amendments § 362.

[22] 11 USC § 365(d)(4).

[23] For discussion, see Shanker, "The Effect of the 1984 Bankruptcy Code Amendments on Contracts," 31 Prac. Law. 5, 25–27 (1985).

[24] 11 USC § 365(d)(3), added by 1984 Amendments § 362. The apparent impact of this provision is to keep the nonresidential lease in effect until the lease is assumed or rejected and the trustee (or debtor in possession) must perform the obligations under the lease until he assumes or rejects the lease. See Shanker, "The Effect of the 1984 Bankruptcy Code Amendments on Contracts," 31 Prac. Law. 5, 26–27 (1985). Section 365(d)(3) by its terms is not restricted to a debtor-lessee and may apply to a debtor who is the lessor. This is in contrast to Section 365(d)(4), which by its terms is limited to a debtor-lessee under a commercial lease.

ganization or by the Chapter 13 plan.[25] However, in the case of nonresidential leases of real property where the debtor is the lessee, Section 365(d)(4) practically means that the lease, except in the rare case, will be rejected or assumed prior to confirmation of the Chapter 11 or 13 plan. Note that for purposes of Section 365, leases of real property include "any rental agreement to use real property."[26]

### [3] The Test for Rejecting Executory Contracts or Unexpired Leases

Although there is some disagreement over the proper test to be applied by the court in approving a request by the trustee or the debtor in possession to reject an executory contract or unexpired lease, the test generally applied is the "business judgment test."[27] However, some other cases have applied a "burdensome" test, that is, rejection should be permitted only if the contract or lease is burdensome or onerous to the estate.[28]

In cases dealing with the rejection of a collective bargaining agreement, there had been a strong debate on the standard to be applied. In February 1984, the U.S. Supreme Court decided the question in *NLRB v. Bildisco & Bildisco* and determined that a "balancing of the equities" test should be

---

[25] 11 USC §§ 1123(b)(2), 1322(b)(7). Rejection by a Chapter 13 plan does not require approval of the rejection by the court. In re Alexander, 670 F2d 885, 888–889 (9th Cir. 1982). Note, however, that Section 1322(b)(7) was amended by the 1984 Amendments to state that the rejection, assumption, or assignment of an executory contract or lease by a Chapter 13 plan is "subject to Section 365."

[26] 11 USC § 365(m), added by 1984 Amendments § 362.

[27] See NLRB v. Bildisco & Bildisco, 104 S. Ct. 1188 (1984); In re Alexander, 670 F2d 885 (9th Cir. 1982); In re Chi-Feng Huang, 23 Bankr. 798 (Bankr. App. Pan. 9th Cir. 1982). In *Huang*, the court said:

> "What are the standards that are to guide the court and trustee in exercising their 'business judgment?' Stated differently: 'What are the criteria which the court and trustee should legitimately consider in exercising their 'business judgment?' The primary issue is whether rejection would benefit the general unsecured creditors. This may involve a balancing of interests."

Id. at 801. The court also stated that

> "[t]he fact that the expectations of a vendee are disappointed is not sufficient grounds standing alone to deny the trustee permission to reject. Any rejection will inevitably entail the disappointment of legitimate expectations. A basic policy of the Bankruptcy laws is to spread the burdens evenly among both those who may have loaned the debtor money and those who might have obtained a profit from dealing with him."

Id.

[28] See discussion in In re Summit Land Co., 13 Bankr. 310 (Bankr. D. Utah 1981); Collier on Bankruptcy ¶ 365.03, at 365-14 (Matthew Bender, 15th ed. 1981); Krasnowiecki, "The Impact of the New Bankruptcy Reform Act on Real Estate Development and Financing," 53 Am. Bankr. L.J. 363, 382 (1979).

applied in a Chapter 11 case.[29] The 1984 Amendments, however, added new Section 1113, which specifically deals with the rejection of collective bargaining agreements in Chapter 11 cases.[30]

### [4] Assumption of Executory Contracts or Unexpired Leases

In some circumstances, it may be in the best interests of the debtor's estate for the trustee in a Chapter 7 case, or the debtor in possession in a Chapter 11 case, to assume an executory contract or unexpired lease. For example, in a Chapter 7 case, if the trustee has obtained permission from the bankruptcy court to continue the business for a limited period of time in order to liquidate the business, it may be beneficial for the estate to have the trustee assume a contract of the debtor for the sale of goods in order to realize the contract price of the goods. This may be a better alternative than selling the goods at a bankruptcy sale.[31] Also, it may be in the best interest of the debtor's estate to assume an unexpired lease if, for example, the lease can be sold and assigned to a third party or if the leased property can be beneficially used by the debtor in possession. Section 365 permits, subject to court approval, assumption of executory contracts or unexpired leases. If the contract is assumed by the trustee or the debtor, it must be assumed cum onere (i.e., with the benefits and burdens of the contract or unexpired lease); the trustee cannot assume only the benefits and reject the burdens.[32] If the contract or lease is assumed by the trustee, a claim arising against him for failure to perform under the assumed contract will be an administrative expense priority claim.[33] However, if there has been a default in an executory contract or unexpired lease, the trustee may not assume the executory contract or unexpired lease unless, at the time of the assumption, he cures or provides adequate assurance that he will promptly cure the

---

[29] 104 S. Ct. 1188 (1984). The Court left open the question of whether the same standard should be applied in a Chapter 7 case. See discussion at infra ¶ 13.09[9].

[30] 11 USC § 1113, added by 1984 Amendments § 541. See discussion at infra ¶ 13.09[9].

[31] See Levy, "Impact of the New Bankruptcy Code on Article 2 Sales," 14 U.C.C. L.J. 307, 319–320 (1982).

[32] See NLRB v. Bildisco & Bildisco, 104 S. Ct. 1188 (1984); In re Johns, 5 BCD 1074 (Bankr. D. Nev. 1979); In re Pin Oaks Apartments, 7 Bankr. 364 (Bankr. SD Tex. 1980). Sections 365(e)(1) and 365(f) give the trustee the power in assuming or assigning a lease or contract to ignore anti-assignment clauses and "ipso facto" bankruptcy clauses. The House and Senate reports state:

> "The unenforceability of ipso facto or bankruptcy clauses proposed under this section will require the courts to be sensitive to the rights of the nondebtor party to executory contracts and unexpired leases. If the trustee is to assume a contract or lease, the courts will have to insure that the trustee's performance under the contract or lease gives the other contracting party the full benefit of his bargain."

H.R. Rep. No. 595, 95th Cong., 1st Sess. 348 (1977); S. Rep. No. 989, 95th Cong., 2d Sess. 59 (1978).

[33] See 11 USC §§ 507(a)(1), 726(a)(1).

default.[34] Furthermore, in order to assume, the trustee must compensate or provide adequate assurance that he will promptly compensate for any actual pecuniary loss resulting from the default.[35] In addition, he must provide adequate assurance of future performance under the contract or lease.[36] The so-called ipso facto or bankruptcy clauses that, for example, automatically terminate or give the nonbankrupt party the right to terminate or modify the contract or lease in the event of bankruptcy of the other party are not enforceable in bankruptcy[37] and do not prevent assumption of the lease or executory contract.[38] However, the trustee may not assume or assign an executory contract or unexpired lease if applicable nonbankruptcy law excuses the other party from performance to someone other than the debtor, unless the other party consents.[39] This includes personal service contracts. Contracts to make a loan or to extend debt financing or to issue securities of the debtor may not be assumed or assigned.[40]

---

[34] 11 USC § 365(b)(1)(A). Defaults relating to insolvency of the debtor, commencement of a bankruptcy proceeding, or the appointment of a custodian or of a trustee in bankruptcy do not have to be cured. See 11 USC § 365(b)(2).

[35] 11 USC § 365(b)(1)(B).

[36] 11 USC §§ 365(b)(1)(B)–365(b)(1)(C). These requirements of "cure" and adequate assurance apply only if there is a default under the lease or contract. In the case of leases of real property in shopping centers, Section 365(b)(3) contains specific provisions as to factors that are included in the requirement for adequate assurance for future performance. Substantial additions to these requirements were made by the 1984 Amendments. See 11 USC § 365(b)(3), as amended by 1984 Amendments § 362. For a discussion of these changes, see Shanker, "The Effect of the 1984 Bankruptcy Code Amendments on Contracts," 31 Prac. Law. 5, 28 (1985). For a discussion of adequate assurance, see Simpson, "Leases and the Bankruptcy Code: The Protean Concept of Adequate Assurance of Future Performance," 56 Am. Bankr. L.J. 233 (1982); Simpson, "Leases and the Bankruptcy Code: Tempering the Rigors of Strict Performance," 38 Bus. Law. 61, 72 (1982).

[37] This represents a change from the 1898 Act, which generally gave effect to such clauses. H.R. Rep. No. 595, 95th Cong., 1st Sess. 348 (1977); S. Rep. No. 989, 95th Cong., 2d Sess. 59 (1978); see also 1898 Act § 70(b).

[38] 11 USC § 365(e)(1). The House and Senate Reports stated:

> "This subsection does not limit the application of an ipso factor or bankruptcy clause to a new insolvency or receivership after the bankruptcy case is closed. That is, the clause is not invalidated in toto, but merely made inapplicable during the case for the purposes of disporition [sic] of the executory contract or unexpired lease."

H.R. Rep. No. 595, 95th Cong., 1st Sess. 349 (1977); S. Rep. No. 989, 95th Cong., 2d Sess. 59 (1978).

[39] 11 USC §§ 365(c)(1)(A), 365(c)(1)(B).

[40] 11 USC § 365(c)(2). The House and Senate Reports stated:

> "This prohibition applies only in the situation in which applicable law excuses the other party from performance independent of any restrictive language in the contract or lease itself. The purpose of this subsection, at least in part, is to prevent the trustee from requiring new advances of money or other property. The section per-

### [5] Assignment of Executory Contracts or Unexpired Leases

Notwithstanding a provision in the executory contract or unexpired lease that prohibits, restricts, or conditions assignment, the trustee may assign a lease or contract if certain conditions are met.[41] The trustee may assign the lease or contract only if he (or debtor in possession) assumes the lease or contract[42] and provides adequate assurance of future performance by the assignee.[43]

If the trustee assigns a contract or unexpired lease that has been assumed, the trustee and the estate are relieved from any breach of the contract or lease that occurs after the assignment.[44] However, if an unexpired lease is assigned under which the debtor was the lessee, the lessor may require a deposit, or other security for the performance of the debtor's obligations under the lease, that is substantially the same as would have been required by the landlord upon the initial leasing to a similar tenant.[45]

### [6] Rejection of Executory Contracts or Unexpired Leases

The trustee, subject to court approval, may reject any executory contract or unexpired lease of the debtor.[46] However, rejection by the trustee of such a

---

mits the trustee to continue to use and pay for property already advanced, but is not designed to permit the trustee to demand new loans or additional transfers of property under lease commitments. Thus under this provision, contracts such as loan commitments and letters of credit are nonassignable, and may not be assumed by the trustee."

H.R. Rep. No. 595, 95th Cong., 1st Sess. 348 (1977); S. Rep. No. 989, 95th Cong., 2d Sess. 59 (1978).

[41] 11 USC § 365(f). The House and Senate Reports stated:

"Subsection (f) partially invalidates restrictions on assignment of contracts or leases by the trustee to a third party. . . . Paragraph (3) of the subsection invalidates contractual provisions that permit termination or modification in the event of an assignment, as contrary to the policy of this subsection."

H.R. Rep. No. 595, 95th Cong., 1st Sess. 349 (1977); S. Rep. No. 989, 95th Cong., 2d Sess. 59 (1978).

[42] See supra ¶ 13.09[4] for the requirements for assumption.

[43] 11 USC § 365(f)(2). Collier suggests that in most cases for adequate assurance of future performance by the assignee "there must be both an assumption of the contract or lease by the assignee and some demonstration of ability to perform." Collier on Bankruptcy ¶ 365.07, at 365-40 (Matthew Bender, 15th ed. 1981).

[44] 11 USC § 365(k).

[45] 11 USC 365(l), added by 1984 Amendments § 362.

[46] 11 USC § 365(a). As noted at supra ¶ 13.09[2], in a Chapter 7 case, if the trustee does not timely reject or assume an executory contract or lease, then such contract is deemed rejected. See 11 USC § 365(d)(1). Similarly, in any case under Chapters 7, 11, or 13, if the trustee does not assume or reject an unexpired lease of nonresidential real property under which the debtor is the lessee within sixty days after the order for relief, then the lease is deemed rejected. See 11 USC § 365(d)(4), added by 1984 Amendments § 362. See also discussion at supra ¶ 13.09[2].

contract or lease constitutes a breach of the contract or lease, and the breach relates back to immediately before the filing of the petition.[47] Any claim for damages arising from the rejection, rather than being an administrative claim, is allowable under Section 502(g) as if the claim had arisen before the filing of the petition. In the case of a claim for damages arising from the rejection of a contract for employment or from the rejection of a lease of real property, there are specific limitations on the damages that may be allowable.[48]

In the unusual circumstance where the trustee rejects an executory contract or lease that had previously been assumed in a bankruptcy proceeding, special rules apply to the time that the breach is deemed to have occurred. These special rules are contained in Section 365(g)(2), which appears to sanction the rejection of contracts previously assumed.[49]

### [7] Rejection of the Debtor's Executory Contracts for the Sale of Real Property

Not infrequently, a debtor is the vendor of real property under a real estate installment sales contract. Less frequently, the debtor may be the vendor for the sale of a timeshare interest under a timeshare plan.[50] If such contracts are executory,[51] the trustee of the debtor-vendor, subject to court approval, may reject the contract.[52] If the contract for the sale of real property or the timeshare is rejected by the trustee of the debtor-vendor, a purchaser who is in possession may either treat the contract as terminated or, alternatively, may remain in possession of the real property or timeshare interest.[53] If the purchaser elects to remain in possession, he must continue to make the payments due under the contract. However, he may offset against these payments any damages that occur after rejection of the contract caused by the nonperformance of the debtor-vendor. In addition, the purchaser may not assert against the estate a claim, other than by offset, for any postrejection default by the

---

[47] 11 USC § 365(g)(1).

[48] See 11 USC §§ 502(b)(6)–502(b)(7). For discussion of these limitations see ¶¶ 14.05[6], 14.05[7].

[49] Collier states: "While a contrary view based on necessity to the rehabilitative effort could also be made, it now seems clear from the wording of Section 365(g)(2)(A) that a contract or lease may be assumed in, for example, a chapter 11 case and later rejected in the same chapter." Collier on Bankruptcy ¶ 365.08, at 365-42 (Matthew Bender, 15th ed. 1981).

[50] "Timeshare plan" is defined in Section 101(47).

[51] Under the test that is generally applied for determining whether a contract is executory, this means that performance is still due on both sides. See discussion at supra ¶ 13.09[1].

[52] 11 USC §§ 365(a), 365(i), as amended by 1984 Amendments §§ 402, 403. The provisions concerning timeshares were added by the 1984 Amendments.

[53] 11 USC § 365(i)(1), as amended by 1984 Amendments § 404.

debtor-vendor.[54] In effect, by electing to remain in possession, the vendee has elected to forgo any affirmative claim for damages against the estate for post-rejection nonperformance by the debtor of the contractual undertakings.[55] When the purchaser complies with the terms of the contract, he is entitled to a conveyance of title by the trustee.[56] On the other hand, a purchaser in possession who elects to treat the contract as terminated by the rejection, or a party who is *not* in possession and whose executory contract is rejected, will not, of course, be entitled to a conveyance of title. However, such a purchaser will have a lien on the debtor's interest in the property to the extent of the purchase price that has been paid.[57]

A purchaser under an executory contract for the sale of real property who is "not in possession" does not have the option to remain in possession and, upon compliance with the contract, to receive title to the real estate. He only has a right to a lien on the debtor's interest in the property to the extent of the purchase price paid.[58] Thus, a purchaser's rights, upon rejection of the contract for sale by the debtor-vendor's trustee, will differ significantly, depending on whether the purchaser is in possession.[59] This phrase is not defined in the Code and will undoubtedly be a source of litigation.[60] However, where the debtor is the seller of a timeshare interest and the contract is rejected, the purchaser of the timeshare may (1) treat the timeshare plan as terminated by the rejection, where the disaffirmance by the trustee amounts to a breach that would entitle the timeshare purchaser to treat the plan as terminated by its own terms or under applicable nonbankruptcy law, or (2) remain in possession of the timeshare interest.[61] If the timeshare purchaser remains in possession, he may offset against any payment due under the plan any damages occurring after the date of rejection caused by the nonperformance of any obligation of the debtor under the timeshare plan. However, the timeshare purchaser may not assert against the estate a claim, other than by setoff, for any postrejection default by the debtor-vendor.[62]

In contrast to the situation where the debtor is the vendor, if the debtor-bankrupt is the vendee under a contract for the purchase of real estate, there is

---

[54] 11 USC §§ 365(i)(1)–365(i)(2), as amended by 1984 Amendments § 404. However, for any prerejection nonperformance by the debtor the purchaser will have a claim for any damages against the estate.

[55] 11 USC § 365(i)(2)(A).

[56] 11 USC § 365(i)(2)(B).

[57] 11 USC § 365(j).

[58] Id.

[59] See, e.g., In re Summit Land Co., 13 Bankr. 310 (Bankr. D. Utah 1981).

[60] In In re Summit Land Co., 13 Bankr. 310 (Bankr. D. Utah 1981), the court held that the purchaser under a "real estate contract" of an "interest" in a shared-use recreational park was not "in possession" and therefore not entitled to the protection of Section 365(i). The court viewed the purchaser's interest as essentially a recreational-use permit.

[61] 11 USC § 365(h)(1), as amended by 1984 Amendments § 402.

[62] 11 USC § 365(h)(2), as amended by 1984 Amendments § 403.

a substantial question whether the debtor-vendee's interest will be considered an "executory contract."[63]

### [8] Rejection of the Debtor-Lessor's Unexpired Leases of Real Property

Where the debtor is the lessor under an unexpired lease of real property,[64] the trustee may, with court approval, reject the lease. The effect of such a rejection is covered by Section 365(h).[65] Somewhat simplified, for bankruptcy purposes a lease of real property is viewed in two aspects. First, a lease of real property is a conveyance or creation of an estate in the property in the lessee; second, the lease is viewed in its contractual undertakings or covenants. If the trustee of the debtor-lessor (or the debtor in possession in a rehabilitation proceeding) rejects the unexpired lease, the lessee has two options. Rejection of the lease by the trustee does not deprive the lessee of the estate in the property, and the lessee may elect to remain in possession for the balance of the term and any enforceable renewal or extension thereof.[66] However, by rejecting the lease, the trustee, in effect, states that the contractual undertakings or covenants of the lessor will not be performed and will be breached, even though the lessee may retain the estate created by the lease. Alternatively, upon rejection, the lessee may treat the lease as terminated by the rejection where the disaffirmance by the trustee amounts to a breach that would entitle the lessee to treat the lease as terminated by the terms of the lease or under applicable nonbankruptcy law[67] and will have a claim under Section 502 for any damages arising from the rejection. The rejection is deemed to have occurred just before the filing of the petition and is thus an allowable claim against the estate under Section 502(g).[68] If the lessee elects to remain in possession, retaining its estate, he may offset against the rent due under the lease any damages that occur *after* the rejection

---

[63] See In re Booth, 19 Bankr. 53 (Bankr. D. Utah 1982), holding that the debtor-vendee's interest under a contract for deed (real estate installment sale contract) was not an "executory contract" and could not be rejected. The court rejected the Countryman definition of an "executory contract" as being the appropriate test to be applied in all cases, and viewed the vendor's interest as essentially the interest of a mortgagee or the holder of a lien. Accord In re Cox, 28 Bankr. 588 (Bankr. D. Idaho 1983).

[64] Note that for purposes of Section 365, leases of real property include "any rental agreement to use real property." 11 USC § 365(m), added by 1984 Amendments § 362.

[65] 11 USC § 365(h), as amended by 1984 Amendments §§ 402, 403. As amended, Section 365(h) also covers the effect of rejection of a timeshare interest under a timeshare plan where the debtor is the timeshare interest seller. Where the trustee of the debtor-seller of the timeshare interest rejects the interest, the holder of the timeshare interest has the same rights that a lessee of real property has upon rejection by the trustee of the debtor-lessor. For additional discussion of rejection of such timeshare interests, see supra ¶ 13.09[7].

[66] 11 USC § 365(h).

[67] Id.

[68] 11 USC § 365(g).

caused by the nonperformance of any obligation of the debtor-lessor, such as a rejected covenant or a contractual undertaking to supply utilities. However, the lessee does not have any affirmative claim against the estate for any postrejection nonperformance of the contractual undertakings of the lessor under the lease, being limited to offset against the rent. To illustrate this, assume that under the lease the lessor-debtor is obligated by contract or covenant to provide utilities valued at $1,000 per month and that the trustee rejects the contract. However, the lessee elects to remain in possession of the premises. The lessee could offset the damages ($1,000 per month) for failure of the lessor to provide utilities after the rejection against the rent due. However, damages for failure to provide the utilities before the rejection could be asserted against the estate.

### [9] Rejection of Collective Bargaining Agreements

In a number of cases under the 1898 Act, the question had been raised as to whether a collective bargaining agreement could be rejected by a debtor-employer as an executory contract and if so, what standard or test was to be used by the court in approving rejection. This question has also been raised with increasing frequency under the Code, generally in Chapter 11 rehabilitation cases. There was great debate on the standard that the court should apply in approving rejection of such contracts.[69] In *NLRB v. Bildisco & Bildisco*,[70] a Chapter 11 case, the U.S. Supreme Court held that a debtor-employer's collective bargaining agreement with a union was an executory contract that could be rejected under Section 365 by the debtor in possession. The Court held that rejection should be permitted by the bankruptcy court, not under the "business judgement" test generally applied for other executory contracts, but under a stricter standard. The Court stated: "[T]he Bankruptcy Court should permit rejection of a collective-bargaining agreement under § 365(a) of the Bankruptcy Code if the debtor can show that the collective-bargaining agreement burdens the estate, and that after careful scrutiny, the equities balance in favor of

---

[69] See, e.g., Bordewieck & Countryman, "The Rejection of Collective Bargaining Agreements by Chapter 11 Debtors," 57 Am. Bankr. L.J. 293 (1983); Cherry, "The Collective Bargaining Agreement in Bankruptcy: Rejection and Its Consequences," 36 Ark. L. Rev. 469 (1983); Pulliam, "The Rejection of Collective Bargaining Agreements Under Section 365 of the Bankruptcy Code," 58 Am. Bankr. L.J. 1 (1984); Comment, "The Labor-Bankruptcy Conflict: Rejection of a Debtor's Collective Bargaining Agreement," 80 Mich. L. Rev. 134 (1981); Comment, "The Accommodation of the Bankruptcy and Labor Acts in Chapter 11 Reorganizations," 16 Creighton L. Rev. 859 (1983); Note, "The Bankruptcy Law's Effect on Collective Bargaining Agreements," 81 Colum. L. Rev. 391 (1981); Comment, "Collective Bargaining Agreements and the Bankruptcy Reform Act: What Test Should the Bankruptcy Court Use in Deciding Whether to Allow a Debtor to Reject a Collective Bargaining Agreement?" 51 U. Cin. L. Rev. 862 (1982); Note, "Rejection of Collective Bargaining Agreements as Executory Contracts in Bankruptcy-Receiver's Authority to Unilaterally Assume or Adopt Collective Bargaining Agreements," 27 Wayne L. Rev. 1601 (1981); Note, "Rejection, Assumption, and Modification of Collective Bargaining Agreements, 1981 Ariz. St. L.J. 311.

[70] 104 S. Ct. 1188 (1984).

rejecting the labor contract."[71] The Court indicated several factors that should be considered in balancing the equities, and also held that the debtor did not commit an unfair labor practice by unilaterally modifying the contract before court approval of the rejection. However, on this point the Court was divided in a five-to-four split. Immediately after the decision in *Bildisco*, legislation was introduced in Congress to overturn the decision. As a result of the *Bildisco* decision, Congress in the 1984 Amendments enacted a new Section 1113,[72] regulating the rejection of collective bargaining agreements in Chapter 11 cases. To a large extent, Section 1113 adopts the test for rejection that the U.S. Supreme Court adopted in *Bildisco*. However, Section 1113 contains other important details with respect to rejection of collective bargaining agreements and should be carefully examined.[73]

## ¶ 13.10 RECLAMATION BY SELLERS

The position of an unpaid seller of goods with respect to goods delivered to a buyer has always been somewhat precarious with regard to lien creditors, the trustee in bankruptcy of the buyer, purchasers of the goods from the buyer, and other third parties claiming some interest in the goods. It is not uncommon for an unpaid seller to deliver goods to a buyer only to discover shortly thereafter that the debtor is insolvent or is in bankruptcy. Also, the seller might discover that a judgment creditor of the buyer has levied on the goods, that the goods have been sold to a third party, or that a third party claims a security interest in the goods. Indeed, the seller may have delivered the goods to the buyer based on false and material representations by the buyer as to the buyer's financial condition or as a result of some other type of fraud. In such circumstances, determining the relative rights of the seller in the goods sold vis-à-vis the competing claims of levying creditors, the trustee in bankruptcy, and perhaps other parties, such as purchasers, has presented difficult questions. These circumstances have produced a number of cases, with varying approaches and results,[1] and have produced perhaps even a greater body of comment and discussion of the problems.[2]

---

[71] 104 S. Ct. at 1188, 1196 (1984).

[72] 11 USC § 1113, added by 1984 Amendments §§ 541, 553. Section 1113 is applicable only in Chapter 11 cases. See 11 USC § 103(f).

[73] For discussion of new Section 1113, see Shanker, "The Effect of the 1984 Bankruptcy Code Amendments on Contracts," 31 Prac. Law. 13 (1985); Gibson, "The New Law on Rejection of Collective Bargaining Agreements in Chapter 11: An Analysis of 11 U.S.C. § 1113," 58 Am. Bankr. L.J. 325 (1984).

[1] See, e.g., In re Kravitz, 278 F2d 820 (3d Cir. 1960); In re Mel Golde Shoes, Inc., 403 F2d 658 (6th Cir. 1968); In re Federal's, Inc., 553 F2d 509 (6th Cir. 1977); In re Samuels & Co., 526 F2d 1238 (5th Cir. 1976), cert. denied, Stowers v. Mahon, 429 US 834 (1976); Los Angeles Paper Bag Co. v. James Talcott, Inc., 604 F2d 38 (9th Cir. 1979). For additional cases, see the references given in the following note.

[2] For an excellent detailed treatment of this whole area, including exhaustive references to the great body of commentary, see Mann & Phillips, "The Reclaiming Seller

## [1] Seller's Right to Reclaim Goods From Debtor's Bankruptcy Estate

In a bankruptcy context, an important question for the unpaid seller is whether he may reclaim the goods from the debtor's bankruptcy estate or whether he will be relegated merely to pursuing his unsecured claim in the bankruptcy proceeding. If the unpaid seller is so fortunate as to have retained a valid, perfected security interest in the goods delivered, and this security interest is not subject to successful challenge under the trustee's avoiding powers, then the unpaid seller will be a secured creditor, at least to the extent of the value of the goods covered by the security interest.[3] However, if the unpaid seller has not retained a valid security interest in the goods sold or otherwise secured the unpaid purchase price, the position of the unpaid seller in bankruptcy is far from clear. If the unpaid seller sold the goods on credit, or if it was a "cash sale" and for some reason the seller was not paid (e.g., a check given in payment was dishonored), may the unpaid seller reclaim the goods from the debtor's bankruptcy estate? Or suppose the unpaid seller had sold the goods based on some false representations, perhaps in a written financial statement, as to the buyer's solvency or creditworthiness; may the seller reclaim the goods from the bankruptcy estate? Under the 1898 Act, the answers to these questions were not clear and consistent. The Code, in Section 546(c), in a limited but important area, attempts to provide some answers with respect to the reclamation rights of an unpaid seller; however, many other questions with respect to the rights of the unpaid seller in bankruptcy are not expressly addressed in the Code.[4]

---

Under the Bankruptcy Reform Act: Resolution or Renewal of an Old Conflict?" 33 Vand. L. Rev. 1 (1980). For a shorter version of this, see Mann & Phillips, "Section 546(c) of the Bankruptcy Reform Act: An Imperfect Resolution of the Conflict Between the Reclaiming Seller and the Bankruptcy Trustee," 54 Am. Bankr. L.J. 239 (1980); see also Weintraub & Resnick, "From the Bankruptcy Courts: A Seller's Right to Reclaim Goods Under the Bankruptcy Code–A Look at Current Cases," 14 U.C.C. L.J. 376 (1982); Romans, "Seller's Right of Reclamation Under the Bankruptcy Code," 41 La. L. Rev. 1159 (1981); Wallach, "The Unpaid Seller's Right to Reclaim Goods: The Impact of the Uniform Commercial Code and the Bankruptcy Acts of 1898 and 1978," 34 Ark. L. Rev. 252 (1980); Levy, "Impact of the New Bankruptcy Code on Article 2 Sales," 14 U.C.C. L.J. 307 (1982); Marshak, "The Return of the Reclaiming Seller: New Decisions Under the Bankruptcy Code and the Uniform Commercial Code," 16 U.C.C. L.J. 187 (1984).

[3] This does not mean, however, that the unpaid seller-secured party will be able to reclaim the goods without obtaining relief from the stay.

[4] For good discussion of this area, see Mann & Phillips, "The Reclaiming Seller Under the Bankruptcy Reform Act: Resolution or Renewal of an Old Conflict?" 33 Vand. L. Rev. 1 (1980); Wallach, "The Unpaid Seller's Right to Reclaim Goods: The Impact of the Uniform Commercial Code and the Bankruptcy Acts of 1898 and 1978," 34 Ark. L. Rev. 252 (1980); Romans, "Seller's Right of Reclamation Under the Bankruptcy Code," 41 La. L. Rev. 1159 (1981); Levy, "Impact of the New Bankruptcy Code on Article 2 Sales," 14 U.C.C. L.J. 307 (1982). Counsel for an unpaid seller will find these articles extremely helpful.

Before turning to Section 546(c) of the Code, it is helpful to examine briefly Section 2-702 of the UCC, since these two sections are related.[5] Section 2-702 of the UCC provides that if, in a credit sale, the seller discovers that the buyer has received goods while insolvent,[6] the goods may be reclaimed if a demand[7] is made within ten days after receipt of the goods.[8] However, the right to reclaim is subject to the rights of a buyer in ordinary course or of other good faith purchasers under UCC Section 2-403, and, in those states that have not adopted the 1966 amendments to UCC Section 2-702(3), it is subject to rights of lien creditors.[9] It should be observed that, under UCC Section 2-702(2), if a misrepresentation has been made in writing to the particular seller within three months before delivery, the demand for reclamation does not have to be made within ten days of receipt of the goods.[10] In addition, the last sen-

---

[5] The House and Senate Reports stated: "The purpose of the provision [§ 546(c)] is to recognize, in part, the validity of section 2-702 of the Uniform Commercial Code, which has generated much litigation, confusion, and divergent decisions in different circuits." H.R. Rep. No. 595, 95th Cong., 1st Sess. 372 (1977); S. Rep. No. 989, 95th Cong., 2d Sess. 86–87 (1978).

[6] Note that UCC Section 1-201(23) defines "insolvency" in a slightly different way than does Section 101(29) of the Bankruptcy Code.

[7] What is sufficient as a demand is not entirely clear. See Mann & Phillips, "The Reclaiming Seller Under the Bankruptcy Reform Act: Resolution or Renewal of an Old Conflict?" 33 Vand. L. Rev. 1, 9–10 (1980).

[8] UCC Sections 2-702(2) and 2-702(3) provide:

> "(2) Where the seller discovers that the buyer has received goods on credit while insolvent he may reclaim the goods upon demand made within ten days after the receipt, but if misrepresentation of solvency has been made to the particular seller in writing within three months before delivery the ten-day limitation does not apply. Except as provided in this subsection the seller may not base a right to reclaim goods on the buyer's fraudulent or innocent misrepresentation of solvency or of intent to pay.
>
> "(3) The seller's right to reclaim under subsection (2) is subject to the rights of a buyer in ordinary course or other good faith purchaser [or lien creditor] under this Article (Section 2-403). Successful reclamation of goods excludes all other remedies with respect to them."

Note that as originally proposed by the drafters of the UCC and as generally adopted by the states, UCC Section 2-702(3) contained the words "or lien creditor" as indicated by the brackets above. As a result of the *Kravitz* case, the official version of UCC Section 2-702(3) was amended by the drafters in 1966 and the words "or lien creditor" were deleted. Subsequently a number of states adopted this amendment although a substantial number of states have not amended the section to delete "or lien creditors."

[9] Note that UCC Section 2-702(3) does not state what the rights of a lien creditor are. This question is at the heart of the *Kravitz* controversy: What are the rights of a lien creditor of the buyer in such circumstances, and should non-UCC law be referred to for those rights? See Braucher, "Reclamation of Goods from A Fraudulent Buyer," 65 Mich. L. Rev. 1281 (1967).

[10] Although the statute speaks in terms of a written representation "made" within three months, Comment 2 to UCC Section 2-702 speaks in terms of one "dated" within three months of the delivery.

tence of UCC Section 2-702(2) states that the rights given by the subsection are the exclusive reclamation right of the seller based on the buyer's fraudulent or innocent misrepresentation of solvency or of intent to pay.[11] Further, UCC Section 2-702(3) provides that successful reclamation of the goods excludes all other remedies with respect to them. This means that if the seller is successful in reclaiming the goods from the debtor's estate under Section 546(c), by use of UCC Section 2-702(2) the reclaiming seller will not have a claim in bankruptcy based upon the fraudulent representation as to solvency.

In an attempt to deal with the reclamation rights of an unpaid seller, at least in a limited fashion, the Code in Section 546(c) provides:[12]

> [T]he rights and powers of a trustee under sections 544(a), 545, 547, and 549 of this title are subject to any statutory or common-law right of a seller of goods that has sold goods to the debtor, in the ordinary course of such seller's business, to reclaim such goods if the debtor has received such goods while insolvent, but–
>
> (1) such a seller may not reclaim any such goods unless such seller demands in writing reclamation of such goods before ten days after receipt of such goods by the debtor; and

---

[11] Thus, if the unpaid credit seller bases a claim for reclamation on a fraudulent misrepresentation of solvency or intent to pay that does not fall within UCC Section 2-702(2) (e.g., the written representation is made more than three months before delivery), under the UCC there is no right to reclaim and the "exclusive remedy" language of UCC Section 2-702(2) excludes any common-law right to rescind the contract and reclaim the goods. This may be important for Section 546(c), which speaks in terms of "any statutory or common-law" right of a seller to reclaim. However, Mann & Phillips suggest that the "or common-law right" provision of Section 546(c) may be read to give, under the supremacy clause, the unpaid seller a common-law right to reclaim if the "received while insolvent" test of Section 546(c) can be met. See Mann & Phillips, "The Reclaiming Seller Under the Bankruptcy Reform Act: Resolution or Renewal of an Old Conflict?" 33 Vand. L. Rev. 1, 49 (1980), where the authors state: "Section 546(c) also allows the reclaiming seller a common-law right of recovery in bankruptcy despite the exclusivity of U.C.C. section 2-702(2). The legislative history of this section tends to suggest that recovery based on pre-Code fraud rules was intended." Mann & Phillips also point out that the language of Section 546(c), "if the debtor has received such goods while insolvent," may be read in two ways. The language may be read to

> "incorporate statutory or common-law rights which are themselves contingent on the receipt of goods while insolvent. The section could, however, be read as including any statutory right or common-law right of a seller, in the ordinary course of such seller's business, of goods to the debtor to reclaim such goods, such right being effective against the trustee only if the debtor has received such goods while insolvent. In the first case, insolvency assists in defining the right incorporated; in the second, it acts as a bankruptcy-specific limitation on the reach of rights more generally defined."

Id. at 48 n.283. This construction problem may be important with respect to rights of a *cash* seller. Id.

[12] 11 USC § 546(c), as amended by 1984 Amendments §§ 351, 461.

(2) the court may deny reclamation to a seller with such a right of reclamation that has made such a demand only if the court—

(A) grants the claim of such a seller priority as [an administrative expense]; or

(B) secures such claim by a lien.

Several observations should be made regarding this section, since it is not identical to UCC Section 2-702. First, it should be noted that it is a limitation on certain avoiding powers of the trustee.[13] The section is designed to protect any statutory or common-law right of reclamation of a seller against the avoiding power of the trustee under Sections 544(a) ("the ideal lien creditor"),[14] 545 (avoiding statutory liens),[15] 547 (preferences), and 549 (postpetition transfers).[16] Second, the section applies if the debtor received the goods while insolvent. In this regard, Section 546(c) parallels UCC Section 2-702, although, as noted earlier, the two acts define insolvency in different terms; in some rare cases, this may be significant.[17] Third, the statutory or common-law rights to reclaim recognized by the section must arise from a sale in the ordinary course of the seller's business.[18] Fourth, the seller must make a written demand for

---

[13] Several courts, however, have read the section as not merely being a limitation on the rights of the trustee but as stating the exclusive reclamation rights of a seller under the Bankruptcy Code.

[14] Note that the protection of Section 546(c) is not given against the avoiding power under Section 544(b), which permits the trustee to assert the rights of an actual creditor with an allowable, unsecured claim. Section 544(b) is the counterpart of Section 70(e) of the 1898 Act.

[15] Under the 1898 Act, trustees had argued that UCC Section 2-702 was an invalid statutory lien. See Weintraub & Resnick, Bankruptcy Law Manual ¶ 5.13, at 5-44 (Warren, Gorham & Lamont, Inc. 1980).

[16] For discussion of these sections, see Chapter 16. The 1898 Act counterparts to these sections had been the most troublesome for reclaiming sellers. See Wallach, "The Unpaid Seller's Right to Reclaim Goods: The Impact of the Uniform Commercial Code and the Bankruptcy Acts of 1898 and 1978," 34 Ark. L. Rev. 252, 271 (1980). Wallach suggests that there are at least three other avoiding powers—subordination (11 USC § 510(c)), fraudulent conveyances (11 USC § 548), and preservation of avoided transfer (11 USC § 550)—against which Section 546(c) does not protect, but that these avoiding powers do not seem to be a significant risk to the reclaiming seller. Id. at 272. Collier on Bankruptcy ¶ 546.04, at 546-12 (Matthew Bender, 15th ed. 1981) also states that Section 546(c) does not protect against the avoiding power under Sections 544(b) (trustee as representative of actual creditors), 548 (fraudulent conveyances), 550 (preservation of avoided transfer), and 553 (setoff).

[17] Mann & Phillips have raised the question of whether the "common-law rights to reclaim" that are preserved or given by the section must themselves be based on receipt of the goods while insolvent, or whether common-law rights to reclaim (e.g., on the grounds of fraud that is not based on insolvency of the debtor) may be afforded the protection of Section 546(c) if the debtor receives the goods while insolvent.

[18] Bulk sales, sales by a non-merchant, and sales by a merchant unrelated to the seller's ordinary business appear not to be within the protection of Section 546(c). See

reclamation within ten days after receipt of the goods.[19] The proper method for computing the ten-day time period is not specified by the statute, although there is authority that Federal Rule of Civil Procedure 6(a) (or Bankruptcy Rule 9006(a) based on that rule) should apply by analogy.[20] There is authority that the automatic stay of Section 362 does not prevent the seller from making the ten-day written demand required by Section 546(c) after the petition is filed.[21]

In addition, Section 546(c) does not expressly recognize the unpaid seller's right to reclaim given by UCC Section 2-702(2), even though no demand is made within ten days of receipt of the goods, when the representation had been made in writing within the three-month period before delivery. In such circumstances it is arguable that the unpaid seller would have the right to reclaim under Section 546(c) as a "statutory right," if the goods were received while insolvent.[22] However, this depends upon the "exclusivity issue"; that is, may a seller reclaim only if the requirements of Section 546(c) are met?[23] What will be a sufficient "demand in writing" is not clear and will have to determined by case law. If the writing is sent before the end of the ten-day period but is

---

Mann & Phillips, "The Reclaiming Seller Under the Bankruptcy Reform Act: Resolution or Renewal of an Old Conflict?" 33 Vand. L. Rev. 1, 48 (1980). In contrast, UCC Section 2-702(2) covers a "seller" and is not limited to a seller in the ordinary course of business.

[19] In contrast, under UCC Section 2-702 the demand, although required to be made within ten days of receipt, is not required to be in writing. However, under UCC Section 2-702(2) the ten-day demand is not applicable where a written misrepresentation has been made within three months before delivery.

[20] See Action Indus., Inc., v. Dixie Enters., Inc., 22 Bankr. 855 (Bankr. SD Ohio 1982). In *Action Industries* the goods had been delivered on Thursday, September 24, 1981; on Monday, October 5, 1981 by mailgram the seller demanded return of the goods. Counting from September 25, since the tenth day fell on Sunday, October 4, the court held that the demand made on the following Monday was timely, relying on Federal Rule of Civil Procedure 6(a) and a similar state statute that stated that if the last day of a time period fell on Sunday, the period ran until the end of the next day.

[21] See In re Production Steel, Inc., 21 Bankr. 951, 953–954 (Bankr. MD Tenn. 1982), in which the court stated:

> "Section 362(a)(3) stays 'any act to obtain possession of property of the estate or property from the estate.' It is the opinion of this court that the giving of a notice of a seller's intention to seek reclamation of goods is not itself an 'act to obtain possession of property' subject to the stay of § 362(a)(3). Such a demand does not affect the debtor's right to possession of the property. . . . A seller making timely demand for reclamation would, of course, still have to seek relief from the stay to take postpetition possession of the goods. The making of demand for reclamation merely puts the debtor on notice of the seller's intent to seek reclamation."

Compare In re Hellenschmidt, 5 Bankr. 758 (Bankr. D. Colo. 1980) (junior lienor was not barred by automatic stay from filing notice of intent to claim statutory right to redeem property of debtor that had been sold under deed of trust).

[22] See Mann & Phillips, "The Reclaiming Seller Under the Bankruptcy Reform Act: Resolution or Renewal of an Old Conflict?" 33 Vand. L. Rev. 1, 51–53 (1980).

[23] See discussion at infra ¶ 13.10[1] note 30.

received after, the court will have to determine whether the writing is effective on dispatch or when received.[24] Fifth, even though a proper written demand is made within the ten-day period, the right to reclaim the goods is not absolute; the bankruptcy court has the power to deny reclamation and, in lieu of reclamation, grant the unpaid seller a priority claim as an administrative expense or to otherwise secure the claim of the unpaid seller.[25] Sixth, unlike UCC Section 2-702, Section 546(c) is not limited to a credit seller.[26]

With this brief look at both the Code and the UCC, what is the position of the unpaid seller under the new Code? Where the unpaid seller can meet both the requirements of UCC Section 2-702(2) and Section 546(c) of the Code, it seems sufficiently clear that the unpaid credit seller is entitled to reclamation. Alternatively, he may be entitled to a priority administrative claim or to security for the claim, unless the unpaid seller's right of reclamation can be avoided under a section of the Code from which section 546(c) gives no protection.

A seller attempting to assert the right to reclaim in bankruptcy, even though a timely ten-day demand is made, must act promptly to reclaim the goods and cannot wait until the goods are commingled and sold by the debtor in the ordinary course of business and then claim an administrative priority.[27] In order to successfully reclaim, the goods must be identifiable and in possession of the debtor on the day of demand.[28] The right to reclaim is of the goods and not of the proceeds from the goods.[29]

However, assume that the unpaid credit seller meets the requirements of UCC Section 2-702(2) for reclamation but does not meet all of the requirements of Section 546(c). For example, assume that the seller made an appropriate demand within the ten-day period, but that the demand was not in writing as required by Section 546(c),[30] or that the sale was not made in the ordinary course of the seller's business but under circumstances that permit reclamation under UCC Section 2-702(2). Suppose that the seller delivered goods to a buyer based on a false written financial statement given within three months of delivery, and under UCC Section 2-702(2) the ten-day demand rule is not applicable. Further assume that the seller does not make a written demand within ten days of delivery but does so twenty days later. In such circumstances, may the

---

[24] See Mann & Phillips, "The Reclaiming Seller Under the Bankruptcy Reform Act: Resolution or Renewal of an Old Conflict?" 33 Vand. L. Rev. 1, 47 n.279 (1980).

[25] 11 USC § 546(c)(2).

[26] See discussion at infra ¶ 13.10[1] note 34.

[27] See Action Indus., Inc., v. Dixie Enters., 22 Bankr. 855 (Bankr. SD Ohio 1982); see also In re Landy Beef Co., 30 Bankr. 19 (Bankr. D. Mass. 1983). But see In re Davidson Lumber Co., 22 Bankr. 775 (Bankr. SD Fla. 1982) (seller was granted an administrative claim where the debtor had sold goods after demand made but before petition in bankruptcy was filed).

[28] In re Flagstaff Foodservice Corp., 14 Bankr. 462 (Bankr. SDNY 1981); In re Landy Beef Co., 30 Bankr. 19 (Bankr. D. Mass. 1983).

[29] See id. and cases cited therein.

[30] See, e.g., In re A.G.S. Foods Sys., Inc., 14 Bankr. 27 (Bankr. DSC 1980) (a prepetition oral demand made within ten days of delivery was sufficient).

unpaid seller still reclaim the goods from the buyer who is in bankruptcy? Section 546(c) does not expressly address such circumstances, and there is considerable difference of opinion as to whether Section 546(c) sets forth the "exclusive" circumstances under which a seller may reclaim (i.e., unless there is compliance with Section 546(c) there is no right to reclaim). In addition, may a seller, having either a statutory or common right to reclaim, reclaim without meeting the requirements of Section 546(c), unless the trustee can avoid such rights under one of the avoiding powers? Professor Wallach has suggested that where UCC Section 2-702(2) has been complied with, but Section 546(c) has not, the seller does not automatically lose its reclamation rights. Although not expressly acknowledged by Section 546(c), it is possible that the seller will be able to reclaim if the right survives challenge under the trustee's avoiding power. In other words, Section 546(c) should not be read as stating that the unpaid seller can reclaim only if the seller meets the requirements of Section 546(c). It should be viewed as protecting reclamation rights falling within its conditions against challenge by the trustee under the specified sections and such that other common-law or statutory reclamation rights are still available if not avoidable by the trustee.[31] Professors Mann and Phillips take a similar view and suggest that, although Section 546(c) may be read as stating the only conditions under which the reclaiming seller may prevail against the trustee under the mentioned sections, "underlying this view of Section 546(c) is the idea that it is intended to resolve the dispute between the Code seller and the trustee in bankruptcy by explicitly stating the conditions under which such a seller can defeat the trustee, and by implicitly providing that only under those conditions can the seller prevail."[32] However, Mann and Phillips, like Professor Wallach, reject the view that Section 546(c) should be read to give only a reclaiming seller who complies with its requirements the power to defeat the trustee. Supporting authority for this nonexclusive view of Wallach and Mann and Phillips may be found in *In re A.G.S. Foods Systems, Inc.*[33] However, this does not appear to be the view of the section that most courts are taking:

> Any common law or statutory right to reclaim goods sold in the ordinary course of business is contingent upon the (seller) making a written demand within ten days of the debtor's receipt of the goods. . . . [citations omitted]

---

[31] The most significant challenge from the trustee is likely to come under Section 544(a) (the "strong arm" clause), 545 (statutory lien), or 547 (preferences), or be based on the argument that UCC Section 2-702(2) is an attempt to create an invalid priority. For discussion, see Wallach, "The Unpaid Seller's Right to Reclaim Goods: The Impact of the Uniform Commercial Code and the Bankruptcy Acts of 1898 and 1978," 34 Ark. L. Rev. 252, 272 (1980); Wallach, The Law of Sales Under the Uniform Commercial Code ¶ 7.04[4] (Warren, Gorham & Lamont, Inc. 1981); Mann & Phillips, "The Reclaiming Seller Under the Bankruptcy Reform Act: Resolution or Renewal of an Old Conflict?" 33 Vand. L. Rev. 1, 51–65 (1980).

[32] Id. at 52.

[33] 14 Bankr. 27 (Bankr. DSC 1980); see also Collier on Bankruptcy ¶ 546.04[2], at 546-11 (Matthew Bender, 15th ed. 1981).

This section provides the exclusive remedy for a creditor attempting to reclaim such goods.[34]

Another important question that is not clear from the language of Section 546(c) is whether any statutory or common-law reclamation right of an unpaid *cash* seller is preserved. Unlike UCC Section 2-702(2), Section 546(c) speaks in terms of "any statutory or common law right of a seller" and is not limited to a credit seller. This suggests that the language was intended to include a cash seller.[35] One Bankruptcy Appellate Panel has also taken this view: "We also conclude that Section 546(c) was intended to include cash transactions. Nowhere, either expressly or by implication do we see any intent to limit its applicability to credit sales. The legislative history supports this view."[36] However, in many cash sales where the seller is unpaid because a "bad" check is not paid, the seller is very likely to be unable to comply with the ten-day written demand of Section 546(c) if that is required under the "exclusivity" view of Section 546(c).

---

[34] In re Koro Corp., 20 Bankr. 241, 243 (Bankr. App. Pan. 1st Cir. 1982). The *Koro* court appeared to hold that a seller who does not comply with the ten-day written demand requirement of Section 546(c) automatically loses reclamation rights apart from any showing that the reclamation right was avoidable by the trustee or debtor in possession in a Chapter 11 proceeding. One court has explicitly rejected the Mann & Phillips view that Section 546(c) is not the exclusive right of the unpaid seller and rejected the view that the section provides a "non-exclusive safe harbor." See In re Contract Interiors, Inc., 14 Bankr. 670 (Bankr. ED Mich. 1981); see also In re Original Auto Parts Distribs., 9 Bankr. 469 (Bankr. SD NY 1981); In re L.T.S., Inc., 32 Bankr. 907 (Bankr. D. Idaho 1983); In re Kentucky Flush Door Corp., 28 Bankr. 808 (Bankr. WD Ky. 1983); In re Deephouse Equip. Co., 22 Bankr. 255 (Bankr. D. Conn. 1982) (failure to make written demand for reclamation within ten days bars relief); In re Alla-Ohio Valley Coals, Inc., 22 Bankr. 336 (Bankr. DC 1982); In re Ateco Equip., Inc., 18 Bankr. 917 (Bankr. WD Pa. 1982); In re Production Steel, Inc., 21 Bankr. 951 (Bankr. MD Tenn. 1982); Marshack, "The Return of the Reclaiming Seller: New Decisions Under the Bankruptcy Code and the Uniform Commercial Code," 16 U.C.C. L.J. 187, 199 (1984); White & Summers, Uniform Commercial Code § 24-9 (West, 2d ed. 1980). White and Summers, acknowledging the "nonexclusivity" argument of Section 546(c), state: "Thus we would read a negative implication into section 546(c), namely that a 2-702(2) reclaiming seller who does not fit section 546(c) is intended by Congress to be subordinate to the trustee's claims under section 544 et seq." Id. at 1027.

[35] For extensive discussion of this, see Mann & Phillips, "The Reclaiming Seller Under the Bankruptcy Reform Act: Resolution or Renewal of an Old Conflict?" 33 Vand. L. Rev. 1, 48 n.283 (1980). Under the UCC the cash seller's right to reclaim in the case of a bounced check is generally based on UCC Sections 2-507(2) and 2-511(3). Mann & Phillips suggest that the legislative history indicates that a cash seller was intended to be included and, although acknowledging that there is some doubt on the question, conclude: "Despite this uncertainty, the better view is to read § 546(c) as including both the Code [see UCC §§ 2-507(2) and 2-511(3)] and the common-law cash sale reclamation rights." Id. at 50.

[36] In re Koro Corp., 20 Bankr. 241, 243 (Bankr. App. Pan. 1st Cir. 1982); see also Levy, "Impact of the New Bankruptcy Code on Article 2 Sales," 14 U.C.C. L.J. 307, 335–336 (1982).

Mann and Phillips also suggest that Section 546(c) may give an unpaid seller a common-law right of recovery (e.g., based on fraudulent misrepresentation of solvency not falling within UCC Section 2-702(2)), despite the exclusivity language of UCC Section 2-702(2).[37] Mann and Phillips maintain that the legislative history of Section 456(c) suggests that recovery based on pre-UCC fraud rules was intended, although common-law reclamation rights are limited by the Section 546(c) requirement of insolvency.[38] Some support for this view of Section 546(c) as "revitalization" of state common law (seemingly abolished by UCC Section 2-702(2)) may be found in *In re Auto Original Parts Distributors, Inc.*[39] In commenting on this view, Levy has asserted:

> This court [in *Original Parts*] believes that Section 546(c) would give a seller who complied with its notice requirement a common-law right of reclamation which existed under applicable state law prior to its adoption of the U.C.C. by the state but which was abolished by the 'exclusivity' provision of Section 2-702(2)! It makes no sense whatsoever for the seller to have greater reclamation rights against the buyer's trustee than were available against the buyer immediately prior to bankruptcy.[40]

Even though an unpaid seller may qualify under both UCC Section 2-702(2) and Code Section 346(c), the seller may be unable to reclaim from a secured party, claiming an interest in the goods under the floating lien of an after-acquired property clause and claiming priority over the seller under UCC Section 2-702(3), as a good faith purchaser or buyer in ordinary course.[41]

The 1984 Amendments in new Section 546(d)[42] provided additional protection to some grain producers and fishermen who have sold grain or fish to a debtor-bankrupt. Briefly, if a producer of grain has sold, in his ordinary course of business, grain to a grain storage facility owned or operated by the debtor, or a U.S fisherman in the ordinary course of his business has sold fish to a fish-processing facility owned or operated by the debtor, the rights and powers of

---

[37] The last sentence of UCC Section 2-702(2) states: "Except as provided in this subsection the seller may not base a right to reclaim goods on the buyer's fraudulent or innocent misrepresentation of solvency or of intent to pay."

[38] Mann & Phillips, "The Reclaiming Seller Under the Bankruptcy Reform Act: Resolution or Renewal of an Old Conflict?" 33 Vand. L. Rev. 1, 49 (1980).

[39] 9 Bankr. 469, 471 (Bankr. SDNY 1981). Compare In re National Sugar Ref. Co., 27 Bankr. 565 (SDNY 1983) with In re Fabric Buys, 34 Bankr. 471 (Bankr. SDNY 1983).

[40] Levy, "Impact of the New Bankruptcy Code on Article 2 Sales," 14 U.C.C. L.J. 307, 332 (1982).

[41] See Action Indus. Inc., v. Dixie Enters. Inc., 22 Bankr. 855 (Bankr. SD Ohio 1982); In re Davidson Lumber Co., 22 Bankr. 775 (Bankr. SD Fla. 1982). UCC Section 2-702(3) states in part: "The seller's right to reclaim under subsection (2) is subject to the rights of a buyer in ordinary course or other good faith purchaser under this Article (Section 2-403)."

[42] 11 USC § 546(d), added by 1984 Amendments § 351.

the trustee under Sections 544(a), 545, 547, and 549 are subject to any statutory or common-law right of the grain producer or fisherman to reclaim the grain or fish if the debtor received the goods while insolvent. To reclaim, however, the grain producer or fisherman must make a written demand within ten days of receipt of the fish or grain by the debtor. Reclamation may be denied by the court if the seller's claim is secured.[43]

## [2] Seller's Right to Stop Goods in Transit or to Withhold Delivery

The UCC recognizes in certain circumstances the right of the seller to withhold delivery or to stop delivery of goods that are in transit and that have not yet been delivered, actually or constructively (such as by attornment by the carrier or warehouseman), to the buyer.[44] The Code poses several questions with respect to the buyer's assertion of these rights to withhold delivery or to stop goods in transit.[45] Two cases have held that the right to stoppage in transit under UCC Sections 2-702(1) and 2-705, although not expressly recognized in Section 546(c), is available to a seller under the Code.[46] An important issue is whether assertion of these rights, for example, to stop goods in transit under UCC Section 2-705 upon discovery that the buyer is insolvent and in bankruptcy, is subject to the automatic stay of Section 362. Professor Levy suggests that in such circumstances if the courts view the goods as still being in the possession of the seller, absent attornment of the carrier or warehouseman, the use of a stop order should not be within the automatic stay, since the seller already in possession is not attempting to gain possession.[47] One court has held that exercise of the right to stoppage in transit, pursuant to UCC Sections 2-702(1) and 2-705, is not a violation of the automatic stay.[48] Another court rejected the view that stoppage in transit is a "transfer" that might, in appropriate circumstances, be a voidable preference under Section 547.[49]

---

[43] Id.

[44] See UCC §§ 2-702, 2-703, 2-705. For general discussion of these sections see Wallach, The Law of Sales Under the Uniform Commercial Code §§ 7.01, 7.02 (Warren, Gorham & Lamont, Inc. 1981); Nordstrom, Law of Sales, § 164 (West 1970); Dusenberg & King, Sales & Bulk Sales Transfers Under the Uniform Commercial Code § 13.03 (Matthew Bender 1983).

[45] For discussion of these issues, see Levy, "Impact of the New Bankruptcy Code on Article 2 Sales," 14 U.C.C. L.J. 307, 340–343 (1982).

[46] In re National Sugar Ref. Co., 27 Bankr. 565 (SDNY 1983); In re Fabric Buys, 34 Bankr. 471 (Bankr. SDNY 1983).

[47] Levy, "Impact of the New Bankruptcy Code on Article 2 Sales," 14 U.C.C. L.J. 340 (1982).

[48] In re National Sugar Ref. Co., 27 Bankr. 565 (SDNY 1983).

[49] The court in In re Fabric Buys, 34 Bankr. 471 (Bankr. SDNY 1983), held that a seller who stopped goods being shipped to a debtor within the ninety-day preference period preceding bankruptcy had not received a voidable preference because there had been no "transfer" of property. See also Levy, "Impact of the New Bankruptcy Code on

Another potential attack on such rights is that they may be challenged as an invalid statutory lien under Section 545.[50]

## ¶ 13.11 LIQUIDATION OF THE ESTATE: SALE, USE OF PROPERTY, AND OBTAINING CREDIT

Detailed treatment of the procedures and methods of liquidating the estate in a Chapter 7 case is beyond the scope of this book.[1] However, the basic procedure and statutory structure will be outlined.

The trustee, in a Chapter 7 liquidation proceeding, is directed to collect and reduce to money the property of the estate as expeditiously as is compatible with the best interest of the parties in interest.[2] In the ordinary case, where the Chapter 7 trustee is not authorized to conduct the business of the debtor, the trustee may sell property of the estate "after notice and a hearing."[3] If there is an objection to the proposed sale by a party in interest, ordinarily there must be a hearing.[4] If there is no objection to the proposed sale, the trustee may sell the property; the Code does not require an order from the court approving the sale.[5] However, in the case of real property, for title insurance purposes, apparently it is the practice of some title insurance companies to require, before issuance of a title policy, a court order authorizing the sale.[6] The sale by the trustee may be by a private sale or by a public auction sale. The sale by the trustee may be free and clear of any interest in the property (e.g., a valid security interest in the property) if the holder of such interest consents or if the applicable non-bankruptcy law permits sale of the property free and clear of the interest. It

---

Article 2 Sales," 14 U.C.C. L.J. 307, 340–343 (1982); In re Ault, 6 Bankr. 58 (Bankr. ED Tenn. 1980). For discussion of preferences, see ¶ 16.04.

[50] The court in In re National Sugar Ref. Co., 27 Bankr. 564 (SDNY 1983) held that the right to stoppage of goods in transit under UCC Sections 2-702(1) and 2-705 was not a statutory lien available under Section 545, and was not avoidable under Section 544(a) (the "strong arm" clause).

[1] For a very useful detailed guide for trustees in performing their duties in liquidation and administration of estates, see Sulmeyer, Lynn & Rochelle, Collier Handbook for Trustees and Debtors in Possession (Matthew Bender 1982), which contains many helpful practice aids and forms. See also Collier, Bankruptcy Practice Guide (Matthew Bender 1984).

[2] 11 USC § 704(1).

[3] 11 USC § 363(b). "After notice and a hearing" does not require a hearing if no request for a hearing is made by a party in interest. See rule of construction in Section 102(1); Novellino, "After Notice and a Hearing," 55 Am. Bankr. L.J. 293 (1981).

[4] Under extraordinary circumstances, such as a "wasting" or perishable asset, Section 102(1)(B) permits dispensing with the hearing if there is insufficient time for a hearing.

[5] 11 USC § 363(b).

[6] See Sulmeyer, Lynn & Rochelle, Collier Handbook for Trustees and Debtors in Possession ¶ 11.02[4] (Matthew Bender 1982).

may also be sold free and clear of the interest if a lien and the price at which the property is to be sold is greater than the aggregate value of all liens on the property.[7] If the secured creditor purchases the collateral at a sale that is free and clear of its interest, it may offset the amount of its allowed claim against the purchase price.[8] However, "cash collateral"[9] may not be used or sold unless the party having an interest in the cash collateral consents or the court after notice and a hearing authorizes the use or sale.[10]

In Chapter 11 cases, where generally the business will be continued, ordinarily the debtor in possession will want to sell, use, lease, or otherwise dispose of property of the estate and, in some cases, collateral of a secured party, in the ordinary course of the business and not in the ordinary course. Such use, or sale, is subject to the restrictions set forth in Section 363, and obtaining credit is regulated by Section 364. Generally, unless the court orders otherwise, the debtor in possession may obtain unsecured credit in the ordinary course of business without notice and a hearing or court approval.[11] However, to obtain credit, other than in the ordinary course of business, such credit must be authorized by the court after notice and a hearing.[12] If the debtor in possession is unable to obtain unsecured credit, the court may, after notice and a hearing, authorize the obtaining of secured credit under Section 364(c) as a "super priority" administrative expense that may be secured by unencumbered property

---

[7] 11 USC § 363(f), as amended by 1984 Amendments § 442.

[8] 11 USC § 363(k), as amended by 1984 Amendments § 442. The secured creditor is permitted to bid at the sale unless the court orders otherwise. Id.

A part of the legislative history of Section 363(k) stated:

> "The provision indicates that a secured creditor may bid in the full amount of the creditor's allowed claim, including the secured portion and any unsecured portion thereof in the event the creditor is undersecured, with respect to property that is subject to a lien that secures the allowed claim of the sale of the property."

124 Cong. Rec. H11,093 (daily ed. Sept. 28, 1978); 124 Cong. Rec. S17,409 (daily ed. Oct. 6, 1978).

In some cases, the trustee in Chapter 7 may be authorized to continue the business for purposes of most efficiently liquidating the estate, although this is the exception rather than the general rule. In such cases, unless the court orders otherwise, the trustee may sell, lease, or use property of the estate in the ordinary course of business without notice or hearing or court approval. 11 USC § 363(c)(1).

[9] "Cash collateral" is defined in Section 363(a) as "cash, negotiable instruments, documents of title, securities, deposit accounts, or other cash equivalents whenever acquired in which the estate and an entity other than the estate have an interest and includes the proceeds, products, offspring, rents, or profits of property subject to a security interest as provided in Section 552(b) of this title, whether existing before or after a commencement of a case under this title." 11 USC § 363(a), as amended by 1984 Amendments § 442.

[10] 11 USC § 363(c)(2). "After notice and a hearing" does not require a hearing if no request for a hearing is made by a party in interest. See rule of construction in Section 102(1); Novellino, "After Notice and a Hearing," 55 Am. Bankr. L.J. 293 (1981).

[11] 11 USC § 364(a). This debt will be an administrative expense of the estate.

[12] 11 USC § 364(b).

of the estate or by a junior lien on property of the estate that is subject to a lien.[13] If credit is not otherwise available under the previously mentioned conditions, after notice and a hearing, the court may authorize the obtaining of credit with a "super priority" over existing secured creditors; that is, the new credit may be given priority over, or "prime," an existing secured party if the terms of Section 365(d) are complied with and if the existing secured party who is primed by the "super priority" is given "adequate protection" for its security interest.[14] Note that a party in interest, objecting and desiring to appeal a decision of the bankruptcy court authorizing the obtaining of credit or debt (e.g., with a "super priority administrative claim" or a "super priority secured claim") must stay such authorization and the incurring of debt pending appeal. Otherwise, reversal or modification on appeal of the authorization to obtain credit or incur debt or a grant of priority does not affect the validity of any debt so incurred.[15] In a Chapter 7 case, where the trustee is authorized to conduct the business, obtaining credit, although probably not common, is controlled by these same provisions of Section 364.[16]

## ¶ 13.12 REOPENING CLOSED ESTATES

After a case is closed, it may be reopened in the court in which it was closed in order to administer assets, to accord relief to the debtor, or to adjudicate for other cause.[1] Although the court may permit reopening of a case so that the trustee may exercise an avoiding power, laches may constitute a bar to an action that has been delayed too long.[2] Under Bankruptcy Rule 5010, a case may be reopened on motion of the debtor or other party in interest. Bankruptcy Rule 9024, which incorporates Federal Rule of Civil Procedure 60, exempts motions to reopen cases from the one-year limitation of Rule 60(b).

The decision to reopen is in the sound discretion of the court.[3] In a no-asset case, where notice had been given pursuant to former Bankruptcy Rule

[13] 11 USC § 364(c).

[14] 11 USC § 364(d). For a good discussion of these provisions, see "Structuring and Documenting Business Financing Transactions Under the Federal Bankruptcy Code of 1978," 35 Bus. Law. 1645 (1980).

[15] 11 USC § 364(e).

[16] For a discussion of the debtor's right in a Chapter 13 case to use or sell property of the estate or to obtain credit, see ¶ 17.06.

[1] 11 USC § 350(b).

[2] H.R. Rep. No. 595, 95th Cong., 1st Sess. 338 (1977); S. Rep. No. 989, 95th Cong., 2d Sess. 49 (1978); see in In re Sarafini, 30 Bankr. 606 (Bankr. WD Pa. 1983). In *Sarafini*, the court denied the debtor's petition to reopen the case a second time to file a petition to avoid a lien of a charging order against the debtor's partnership interest filed fourteen months before the bankruptcy petition. The case previously had been reopened to add additional creditors to the schedules.

[3] See In re Sarafini, 30 Bankr. 606 (Bankr. WD Pa. 1983) and cases cited therein.

202(b) that no filing of claims was necessary, the Court of Appeals for the Seventh Circuit held that a debtor should be permitted to reopen the case to add an omitted creditor where there was no evidence of fraud or intentional design.[4]

---

[4] In re Stark, 717 F2d 322 (7th Cir. 1983) The court pointed out that if assets were available later, the added creditor could then timely file proof of claim. See B. Rule 2002(e).

# 14

# Distribution of the Estate

## ¶ 14.01 INTRODUCTION

This chapter deals primarily with distribution of the estate in a Chapter 7 liquidation case, although some attention is given to claims of creditors and others in Chapters 11 and 13. In Chapter 11 and 13 cases, distribution to creditors essentially follows the terms of the confirmed plan. In contrast, as previously discussed,[1] the trustee in a Chapter 7 liquidation case has the duty to collect the assets of the estate, to liquidate the property by reducing it to money,[2] and to distribute the proceeds to creditors under the distribution scheme established by the Bankruptcy Code.[3] In Chapter 7 cases, unsecured creditors generally must look to the distribution or "dividend" they receive in the liquidation as the sole source of satisfying their claims, since in most instances creditors' claims against individual debtors will be discharged.[4] In the case of a corporate debtor, the corporation practically will cease to exist or

[1] See Chapter 13.

[2] 11 USC § 704(1); see also 11 USC § 363.

[3] 11 USC § 726. See generally infra ¶¶ 14.04–14.09. The effect of a discharge is that the creditor's claim will not be enforceable after bankruptcy, and assets of the debtor acquired after the filing of the petition in bankruptcy will not be subject to claims of creditors whose claims are discharged.

[4] If reaffirmation of a debt is obtained, the creditor may be able to enforce the claim against property acquired by the debtor after the petition was filed. However, there are certain restrictions on reaffirmation. See ¶ 15.08.

will be merely a shell with no assets. In contrast, in a Chapter 11 or Chapter 13 case, the assets of the debtor generally are not liquidated[5] and creditors, claimants, and shareholders in most instances receive in satisfaction of their claims only what is provided for in the confirmed plan.

Only creditors with claims existing at the time the petition was filed are entitled to share in distribution of the estate.[6] In a Chapter 7 case, to share in distribution of the liquidated estate, a creditor must file a proof of claim; in addition, the claim must be "allowed" as a claim entitled to share in the distribution.[7] All allowed claims are not of equal rank, however, since the Bankruptcy Code (the Code) establishes a priority for payment of claims. Certain priority claims must be paid, and paid in full, before other junior claims receive a distribution.[8] Within a given priority class, creditors share equally or pro rata in the event there are insufficient assets to satisfy in full all claims within the same class.[9]

## ¶ 14.02 CREDITORS WHO MAY SHARE IN DISTRIBUTION OF THE ESTATE

For purposes of distribution of the estate, two defined terms are important. "Creditor" is broadly defined as an "entity that has a *claim* that arose at the time of or before the order for relief."[1] Note that "claim" is defined

---

[5] Note, however, that there may be a plan for liquidation in Chapter 11. See Anderson & Wright, "Liquidating Plans of Reorganization," 56 Am. Bankr. L.J. 29 (1982). A Chapter 13 plan may also be funded in part from liquidation of property. See ¶ 17.02.

[6] This is due to the definition of "creditor" in Section 101(9), which is restricted to an "entity" with a claim "that arose at the time of or before the order for relief." Note also that "community claims" (defined in Section 101(6) ) must arise before the "commencement of the case." There are some important exceptions for allowance of certain postpetition claims, such as for administrative expenses, "involuntary gap" creditors, claimants of rejected executory contracts and leases, and claims based on property recovered under the trustee's avoiding powers. See 11 USC §§ 101(9)(B), 502(g), 502(h), 502(i); infra ¶ 14.06.

[7] Note that the Bankruptcy Code has eliminated the concept of "provability" that existed under the 1898 Bankruptcy Act. Under the 1898 Act, to receive a dividend a claim had to be "allowed" and only "provable" claims were "allowable." See 1898 Act §§ 63, 65(a), 57(d). In addition, claims that were not "provable" were not discharged, since only "provable" claims were discharged. See 1898 Act § 17. "Provability" under the 1898 Act depended upon whether the claim fit within the specific categories of "provable" claims of the statute. See 1898 Act § 63(a).

[8] 11 USC § 726(a); see discussion at infra ¶ 14.09.

[9] 11 USC § 726(b).

[1] 11 USC § 101(9). An "entity" includes a person, estate, trust, and governmental unit. 11 USC § 101(4). "Creditor" also includes an entity with a "community claim." 11 USC §§ 101(9)(C), 101(6). Note that "creditor" is defined in terms of when the order for relief is entered and distribution is made to allowable claims as of the date of the filing

broadly to include not only a "right to payment, whether or not such right is reduced to judgment, liquidated, unliquidated, fixed, contingent, matured, unmatured, disputed, undisputed, legal, equitable, secured or unsecured," but also includes a "right to an equitable remedy for breach of performance if such breach gives rise to a right to payment."[2] Also, certain claims that arise after the commencement of the case are treated as if they arose before the filing of the petition; holders of these claims may share in the distribution of the estate.[3]

In the case of an involuntary petition, there is a period of time between the filing of the petition and the order for relief.[4] Certain creditors who extend credit to the debtor between the filing of the petition and the earlier of the appointment of a trustee or the order for relief (the "involuntary gap") will be treated for allowance of their claim as if their claim arose before the filing of the petition.[5] The claims of obligees under executory contracts and leases that are rejected by the trustee pursuant to Section 365 are treated as if they arose before the petition is filed for purpose of allowance, although the rejection occurs after the petition is filed.[6] Claims arising after the petition from recovery of property by the trustee under the avoiding powers are determined and allowed as if they had arisen before the filing of the petition.[7]

Administrative expenses arising after the petition also are allowable priority claims.[8]

## ¶ 14.03 PROOF OF CLAIM

In Chapter 7 and 13 cases, a proof of claim must be filed for a claim to be allowed.[1] In a Chapter 11 case, proof of claim is deemed "filed" if the claim appears on the schedules. If, however, the claim is scheduled as disputed, con-

---

of the petition. 11 USC § 502(b). In a voluntary petition case, the "filing" and "order for relief" occur at the same time. 11 USC § 301. In an involuntary case, there is a gap between the filing and order for relief. See discussion at ¶ 12.01[1]. However, certain involuntary gap claims are allowable. See infra ¶ 14.06[1]. See also generally Weintraub & Resnick, "Allowance of Claims and Priorities Under the New Bankruptcy Code," 12 U.C.C. L.J. 291 (1980).

[2] 11 USC §§ 101(4)(A)–101(4)(B).

[3] 11 USC §§ 101(9)(B), 501(d).

[4] See discussion at ¶ 12.01[1].

[5] 11 USC §§ 101(9), 502(f). See infra ¶ 14.06[1]. Some involuntary gap claims may be discharged under Section 727(b) as debts that arose before the order for relief, but are not allowable under Section 502(f) because they did not occur in the ordinary course of business.

[6] See infra ¶ 14.06[2]. A claim arising from rejection of an executory contract or lease must be filed within the time set by the court. B. Rule 3002(c)(4).

[7] 11 USC §§ 101(9)(B), 502(h); see infra ¶ 14.06[3].

[8] 11 USC §§ 727(a)(1), 507(a)(1); see infra ¶ 14.09[1].

[1] 11 USC §§ 726, 501(a), 502(a); B. Rule 3002.

tingent, or unliquidated, proof must be filed.[2] Without checking the schedules, however, a creditor will not know if the claim is scheduled or is listed as disputed, contingent, or unliquidated. Thus, from the creditor's viewpoint, it is prudent to file a proof of claim unless the schedules are checked.[3] After conversion of a case from Chapter 11 to Chapter 7, proof of claim must be filed on a claim that was not listed as disputed, contingent, or unliquidated and would have been deemed filed in the Chapter 11 case; upon conversion, the claim is not deemed to be filed.[4]

Applicable rules should be consulted for important details with respect to proof of claim.[5] For example, the statutes do not set the time for filing proof of claim. Under the present Bankruptcy Rules, the proof of claim must be in writing and be executed by the creditor or an authorized agent unless the proof of claim is filed by the trustee, the debtor, or a codebtor.[6] In addition, the proof must set forth facts showing the claim is free from any charge forbidden by applicable law.[7] If the claim is founded on a writing, the original or a duplicate must be filed with the proof of claim unless the writing has been lost or destroyed. A statement of the circumstances of the loss or destruction must be filed with the claim.[8] If a claim is filed as a secured claim, documentary evidence of the perfection of the security interest must be submitted with the proof of claim.[9] If proof of claim is filed without evidence of perfection of the

[2] 11 USC § 1111(a); B. Rules 3001(a), 3003(b), 3003(c); see also H.R. Rep. No. 595, 95th Cong., 1st Sess. 405 (1977); S. Rep. No. 989, 95th Cong., 2d Sess. 117 (1978).

[3] See, e.g., In re Fabric Buys, 28 Bankr. 513 (Bankr. SDNY 1983). An unsigned statement of an account balance with no declaration of authorization was insufficient as a proof of claim under Interim Rule 3001(b)(5). In addition, even though the debt may not be scheduled as disputed, contingent, or unliquidated, "an attorney-in-fact may want to file a proof of claim so that notices and dividends will be sent directly to the attorney-in-fact." Weintraub & Resnick, "Allowance of Claims and Priorities Under the New Bankruptcy Code," 12 U.C.C. L.J. 291, 295 (1980). See Official Bankruptcy Forms 17, 18.

[4] In re Humblewit Farms, Inc., 23 Bankr. 703 (Bankr. SD Ill. 1982). Under such circumstances the court permitted a late filing. But see B. Rule 1019(4) (dealing with conversion of a Chapter 11 or 13 case to a Chapter 7 case), which states: "All claims filed in the superseded case shall be deemed filed in the chapter 7 case." The Advisory Committee Note to the Rule states: "Paragraph (4) renders it unnecessary to file anew claims that had been filed in the chapter 11 or 13 case before conversion to chapter 7." Does Bankruptcy Rule 1019(4) change *Humblewit*? Is a claim deemed filed in the Chapter 11 case one that was "filed" in the superseded case, and therefore one that does not have to be filed in the Chapter 7 case?

[5] See discussion at ¶ 11.06 regarding Bankruptcy Rules.

[6] B. Rule 3001. A creditor may appoint an attorney-in-fact by filing a general or special power of attorney (see Official Bankruptcy Forms 17, 18), which may be filed with the proof of claim.

[7] B. Rule 3001(a).

[8] B. Rule 3001(c).

[9] B. Rule 3001(d); see In re Salsbury, 23 Bankr. 615 (Bankr. ED Mich. 1982) (proof of claim with attached copy of security agreement and stamped application for

security interest, there is the risk that the claim may be treated as unsecured.[10] Proof of claim generally will be made using one of the Official Bankruptcy Forms,[11] although something less may be sufficient.[12] Amendment of proof of claim may be permitted.[13] Filing proof of claim by a governmental unit waives sovereign immunity.[14]

## [1] When Proof of Claim Must Be Filed

The Code does not specify a time for filing proof of claim; thus the applicable bankruptcy rules control the time for filing proof of claim.[15] In general, in a Chapter 7 or 13 case, proof of claim must be filed within ninety days after the first date set for the meeting of creditors.[16] Upon motion made before the expiration of the ninety days, for cause shown, the court may grant a reasonable extension to a federal or state agency.[17] In some exceptional circumstances,

---

issuance of certificate of title, which had been returned by secretary of state, was sufficient evidence of perfection in a Chapter 13 case).

[10] In re Leon W. Louie, 10 Bankr. 928, (Bankr. ED Mich. 1981). Failure to timely file the claim as a secured claim may also forfeit its secured status. See In re Adams, 17 Bankr. 742, 744 n.5 (Bankr. ED Pa. 1982); In re Rebuelta, 27 Bankr. 137 (Bankr. ND Ga. 1983) (failure to timely file proof of claim forfeits secured status for purposes of distribution under Chapter 13 plan and for purposes of the automatic stay and adequate protection, but does not avoid lien); In re Hines, 20 Bankr. 44 (Bankr. SD Ohio 1982) (failure to timely file proof in Chapter 13 forfeits secured status for purposes of distribution but does not avoid lien or right to seek adequate protection).

[11] See Official Bankruptcy Forms 19, 20, 21. If a formal "official" proof of claim is not used, what will pass as or constitute a proof of claim is not clear from the cases to date. The question has been considered generally in the context of amendment of an "informal" proof of claim. See discussion of amendment of proof of claim at infra ¶ 14.03[1].

[12] A letter sent by the creditor's attorney to the trustee setting forth the existence, nature, and amount of the debt was held to be a sufficient proof of claim in In re Evanston Motor Co., 20 Bankr. 550 (Bankr. ND Ill. 1982). See also In re Davis, 20 Bankr. 519 (Bankr. MD Ga. 1982).

[13] See In re Evanston Motor Co., 20 Bankr. 550 (Bankr. ND Ill. 1982); In re Hart Ski Mfg. Co., 5 Bankr. 326 (Bankr. D. Minn. 1980); In re Myers, 24 Bankr. 37 (Bankr. SD Ill. 1982); In re Sapienza, 27 Bankr. 526 (Bankr. WDNY 1983) (IRS is not permitted to amend tax claim in Chapter 13 more than seven months after confirmation of plan); In re Lanman, 24 Bankr. 741 (Bankr. ND Ill. 1982) (based on equitable factor of prejudice to other creditors, claimant not permitted to amend timely filed unsecured claim to a priority administrative claim); cf. In re Rite Autotronics Corp., 27 Bankr. 599 (Bankr. App. Pan. 9th Cir. 1982); In re Davis, 20 Bankr. 519 (Bankr. MD Ga. 1982).

[14] Id. at 519, 522 (filing of a proof of claim is not required for waiver of sovereign immunity under Section 106).

[15] H.R. Rep. No. 595, 95th Cong., 1st Sess. 351 (1977); see B. Rules 3001, 3002.

[16] B. Rule 3002(c).

[17] B. Rule 3002(c)(1).

other time limits may control.[18] Bankruptcy Rules 9006(b)(1) through 9006(b)(3) authorize bankruptcy courts to enlarge the time periods for filing proof of claim "only to the extent and under the conditions stated" in Bankruptcy Rule 3000(c). It is unclear whether the bankruptcy court has equitable power or discretion beyond these rules to permit untimely filing. The Advisory Committee Note to Bankruptcy Rule 9006(b) indicates, "If a rule is included in paragraph (3), an extension may not be granted under paragraph (1)." In a Chapter 7 case, notice of the time for filing proofs of claims normally will be included with the first notice sent to creditors, which informs them of the filing of the petition and of the date set for the meeting of creditors. This notice also sets the date by which objections to the discharge must be filed and the deadline for the filing of complaints to determine the dischargeability of specific debts.[19]

Under Bankruptcy Rules 2002(e) through 2002(f), a different procedure may be followed in "no asset" cases, if it appears from the schedules of assets filed by the debtor that there will be no distribution. To obviate the filing of proofs of claim that serve no purpose, creditors may be notified that it is unnecessary to file proof. However, if there subsequently are sufficient assets for a distribution, notice will be given of that fact, and proof of claim must be filed within ninety days after the mailing of the notice.[20]

It is not clear that bankruptcy courts have the equitable power or discretion to extend the time period and permit an untimely filing of proof of claim. Even if such power exists, there is uncertainty regarding the circumstances under which it should be exercised.[21] However, substantial authority indicates that the bankruptcy court has some discretion to permit late filing, particularly

---

[18] See B. Rule 3002(c). For calculation of time periods, see B. Rule 9006.

[19] See Chapter 15.

[20] B. Rule 3002(c)(5).

[21] See, e.g., In re Pigott, 684 F2d 239 (3d Cir. 1982), a decision under the 1898 Act holding that the bankruptcy court has no equitable power to extend the deadlines for filing proof of claim established by Section 57(n) of the 1898 Act and old Bankruptcy Rule 302. See also In re Mellen Mfg. Co., 287 F2d 37 (3d Cir. 1961); In re Breezewood Acres, Inc., 28 Bankr. 36 (Bankr. MD Pa. 1982) (a decision under the Bankruptcy Act); In re Popular Fruit & Produce, Inc., 21 Bankr. 185 (Bankr. SDNY 1982) (creditor's lack of knowledge of bankruptcy not sufficient to permit late filing); In re Bortzel, 18 Bankr. 523 (Bankr. ED Pa. 1982) (where creditor had no notice of the filing date and acted promptly to file upon receiving actual notice; late filing was permitted); In re Sems Music Co., 24 Bankr. 376 (Bankr. MD Tenn. 1982); In re Brown, 27 Bankr. 771 (Bankr. ND Ill. 1983) (a Chapter 13 case); In re Foster, 11 Bankr. 476 (Bankr. SD Cal. 1981) (late filing not allowed in Chapter 13 case even though creditor did not receive notice of bankruptcy within the time for filing proof of claim); In re Francis, 15 Bankr. 998 (Bankr. EDNY 1981) (claim disallowed for failure to timely file proof of claim although debtor's Chapter 13 plan proposed paying the claim); In re Rebuelta, 27 Bankr. 137 (Bankr. ND Ga. 1983); In re Hines, 20 Bankr. 44 (Bankr. SD Ohio 1982); In re Phillips, 27 Bankr. 95 (Bankr. D. Va. 1983); In re Williams, 8 Bankr. 802 (Bankr. SD Fla. 1981) (proof of claim, which was filed late due to creditor's reliance on erroneous instructions given by the bankruptcy court clerk as to the deadline, was deemed timely filed due to the reliance on the erroneous instructions).

where the filing may be viewed as an "amendment."[22] To permit amendment of "informal proof" after the time for filing proof of claim, some authority suggests that the purported informal proof must state an explicit demand, evidencing an intention to hold the estate liable.[23] In general, where no formal proof of claim has been timely filed, courts appear to have permitted an untimely amendment only when something in the record constitutes an amendable claim that must have been filed within the requisite time and evidences some positive conduct by the creditor. The informal proof of claim must state an explicit demand against the estate evidencing an intent to hold the estate liable.[24] Equitable factors also will be considered by the court.[25]

---

[22] See In re Corbett, 27 Bankr. 442 (Bankr. WD Mo. 1983) (unsecured claim not timely filed in Chapter 13 but filed before case is closed may be allowed, absent a showing of prejudice on part of debtor; the court concluded that mandatory language of the then Bankruptcy Rule 13-302(e)(2) was not consistent with the Code); In re Rite Autotronics Corp., 27 Bankr. 599 (Bankr. App. Pan. 9th Cir. 1982). In permitting a late filing in a Chapter 11 case, the court in In re Hart Ski Mfg. Co., 5 Bankr. 326, 328 (Bankr. D. Minn. 1980), stated:

> "Collier on Bankruptcy (14th Ed.) ¶ 57.11(3) states: 'It is well settled that if there is upon the record in the bankruptcy proceedings, within the six months prescribed by § 57n, anything sufficient to show the existence, nature and amount of a claim, it may be amended even after the expiration of the period.' This court believes that in the interest of equity this rule should continue under the new Code."

See also In re Alsted Automotive Warehouse, Inc., 16 Bankr. 924 (Bankr. EDNY 1982); cf. In re Evanston Motor Co., 20 Bankr. 550 (Bankr. ND Ill. 1982) (letter sent to trustee by creditor's attorney was sufficient proof of claim to permit "amendment" after time for filing proof of claim); In re Dialysis Serv. Co., 19 Bankr. 940 (Bankr. D. Colo. 1982) (letter sent within filing period from creditor's general counsel to trustee's attorney referring to creditor as "a major creditor of the bankruptcy" sufficient to permit amendment by formal proof of claim outside the time for filing proof of claim as amendment did not alter status of original claim). See also In re Myers, 24 Bankr. 37 (Bankr. D. Vt. 1982) (a Chapter 13 case). In In re Humblewit Farms, Inc., 23 Bankr. 703 (Bankr. SD Ill. 1982), the court held that upon conversion from a Chapter 11 to a Chapter 7 case, proof of claim had to be filed even though the claim had been scheduled in the Chapter 11 case as undisputed (and hence proof of claim had not been required). In this situation the court permitted a late filing of proof of claim.

[23] See In re Alsted Automotive Warehouse, Inc., 16 Bankr. 924 (Bankr. EDNY 1982) (nunc pro tunc filing of proof of claim by secured creditor not permitted because of equitable considerations); In re Dialysis Serv. Co., 19 Bankr. 940 (Bankr. D. Colo. 1982); In re Sems Music Co., 24 Bankr. 376 (Bankr. MD Tenn. 1982); In re Lanman, 24 Bankr. 741 (Bankr. ND Ill. 1982).

[24] In re Sems Music Co., 24 Bankr. 376 (Bankr. MD Tenn. 1982) (no amendment permitted since there was no document to be found that could be amended, and the trustee's knowledge of the claim was not sufficient). Standing alone, neither the trustee's knowledge of the claim nor the scheduling of the debt by the trustee nor the mere pendency of litigation is sufficient to permit amendment or late filing of claim. See cases cited at id.

[25] See In re Alsted Automotive Warehouse Inc., 16 Bankr. 924 (Bankr. EDNY 1982) (amendment not permitted where this would prejudice parties who had compromised and settled with the trustee based on projected distribution that did not include

Code Sections 501(b) and 501(c) provide that if a creditor does not "timely" file proof of claim, then debtors, trustees, codebtors, sureties, and guarantors that are liable to the creditor, or persons who have secured the creditor (a "real surety") may file proof on the claim.[26] However, in one case a bankruptcy court held that where the Internal Revenue Service (IRS) had failed to "timely file" a proof of claim, the debtor could not file the claim under Section 501(c). In the view of the court, the claim was not allowable since Section 726 does not provide for payment of tardily filed claims under Section 501(c).[27] Thus, to be safe, it appears that proof of claim should be filed by the codebtor before expiration of the time for filing to avoid possible barring of the claim.[28] A proof of claim subsequently timely filed by the creditor will then supersede the proof of the codebtor. The debtor is advised to follow the same approach, particularly where the claim upon which no proof of claim is filed is nondischargeable; to the extent a dividend is paid on the nondischargeable claim, the surviving claim will be reduced by that amount. Otherwise, the debtor's assets will be distributed without reducing that claim.[29]

In a Chapter 7 case, where the debtor is solvent or the estate has substantial assets, it is advisable for a limited partner of the debtor or a shareholder (as an "equity security holder") of the debtor to file proof of his interest in the event that a distribution is made to such interests after all allowed claims are paid in full.[30]

## [2] Place of Filing

Bankruptcy Rule 3002(b) provides that proof of claim shall be filed in the place prescribed by Bankruptcy Rule 5005, which directs that proofs of claims are to be filed with the clerk of the court in which the case is pending. The bankruptcy judge may permit papers to be filed with him.[31]

---

the claim of the creditor seeking to amend); In re Belize Airways Ltd., 20 Bankr. 817 (Bankr. SD Fla. 1982) (where creditor delivered a proper proof of claim to employee of debtor as trustee's agent, a late proof of claim that was identical was considered timely filed).

[26] See discussion at infra ¶ 14.07. If the third party (e.g., the codebtor) files a proof of claim and subsequently the creditor also files a proof of claim, the creditor's proof of claim supersedes the proof of the codebtor or other third party.

[27] In re Harold F. Thompson, 12 Bankr. 122 (Bankr. D. Nev. 1981).

[28] Note that the new Bankruptcy Rules make no provision for such filing *before* the ninety days. The rule does permit the codebtor to file proof of claim within thirty days after the expiration of the ninety days. See B. Rule 3005. However, under the *Thompson* analysis there is no provision for distribution under Section 726 for tardily filed claims filed by codebtors under Section 501(b).

[29] Bankruptcy Rule 3004 permits the debtor to file proof if the creditor fails to file proof of claim on or before the first day set for the meeting of creditors.

[30] See Weintraub & Resnick, "Allowance of Claims and Priorities Under the New Bankruptcy Code," 12 U.C.C. L.J. 291, 297 (1980).

[31] B. Rule 5005(a).

## [3] Errors in Filing

Situations may arise in which a proof of claim is intended to be filed but is erroneously delivered to the trustee, the attorney for the trustee, a bankruptcy judge, a district judge, or the clerk of the district court. In such circumstances, Bankruptcy Rule 5005(b) directs that the proof, after the date of its receipt has been noted thereon, should be transmitted to the clerk of the bankruptcy court. In the interest of justice, the court may order the proof of claim to be filed as of the original delivery date.[32]

In one case where an error was made in recording the amount of a proof of claim on the bankruptcy clerk's claims docket, the proof of claim was held to be controlling.[33]

## [4] Withdrawal of Proof of Claim

Before certain events occur, a creditor may as of right withdraw a proof of claim by filing a notice of withdrawal. After an objection is filed to the proof of claim, or a complaint against the creditor is filed in an adversary proceeding, or after the creditor participates significantly in the case, the creditor may withdraw only upon application or motion with notice to the trustee and on order of the court on such terms and conditions as the court deems proper.[34]

# ¶ 14.04 ALLOWANCE OF CLAIMS

To receive a distribution or dividend, a claim must be allowed.[1] A claim on which a proof of claim has been filed is deemed allowed unless an objection is made by a "party in interest."[2] A properly filed proof of claim constitutes prima facie evidence of the validity and amount of the claim.[3]

---

[32] The term "erroneously delivered" includes not only misdelivery to a wrong party or misdelivery due to mechanical error, but also a letter intentionally mailed in good faith to a wrong party, such as the trustee. The purpose of the rule is "to allow creditors unskilled in bankruptcy procedure, who have submitted a claim to an officer of the court, to rely on those good faith efforts." In re Evanston Motor Co., 20 Bankr. 550, 553 (Bankr. ND Ill. 1982); see also In re Dialysis Serv. Co., 19 Bankr. 940 (Bankr. D. Colo. 1982) (delivery to trustee's attorney was sufficient "filing"). Where the creditor delivers a proper proof of claim to an employee of the debtor as trustee's agent, a late proof of claim that is identical will be considered timely. In re Belize Airways Ltd., 20 Bankr. 817 (Bankr. SD Fla. 1982).

[33] In re Stuart, C.H., Inc., 28 Bankr. 360 (Bankr. WDNY 1983).

[34] B. Rule 3006; see also Advisory Committee Note thereto.

[1] 11 USC §§ 726(a)(2)–726(a)(4), 507(a)(1)–507(a)(7), as amended by the Bankruptcy Amendments and Federal Judgeship Act of 1984, Pub. L. No. 98-353, §§ 350, 449, 98 Stat. 333 (hereafter cited as the 1984 Amendments).

[2] 11 USC § 502(a), as amended by 1984 Amendments § 445.

[3] B. Rule 3001(f). The court in In re Coleman Am. Cos., 26 Bankr. 825, 830 (Bankr. D. Kan. 1983) stated:

## [1] "Parties in Interest"

For purposes of determining who may object to a claim, other than indicating that a "creditor of a general partner in a partnership that is a debtor in a case under Chapter 7" is a party in interest,[4] the Code does not specify who is a "party in interest." It seems clear that the trustee is a party in interest since the trustee is specifically given the duty to object to claims.[5] It is uncertain whether a creditor is a "party in interest" who may object to allowance of claims. It appears that a creditor has an obvious interest in having another claim disallowed; disallowance of one claim may mean a larger distribution for the allowed claims. However, objections to claims may be used for purposes of delay and also may be abused. For this reason, the prevailing view under the 1898 Bankruptcy Act may have been that a creditor could not object.[6] Some commentators have suggested this is the position of creditors under the Code.[7] If a creditor may not formally object to allowance of a claim, then the recourse of a creditor is to bring the basis for the objection to the attention of the trustee and urge that the trustee object to allowance of the claim.[8] Should the trustee refuse to perform his duty to object to claims, this might be the basis for an action to compel the trustee to fulfill his duty.[9]

Also, it is not clear that the debtor is a "party in interest" who may object to allowance of claims.[10] In any event, should the debtor have a basis for disallowance of a claim, such as a defense to the claim, it should be brought to the attention of the trustee who then has the duty of objecting to allowance on that basis.

---

> "In bankruptcy proceedings, the burden is on the objecting party to go forward with the evidence establishing the basis of the objections. The court then determines whether the proof has overcome the prima facie case. If the objecting party succeeds, the claimant has the burden of persuasion to prove the validity of the claim by the preponderance of the evidence."

1 Norton, Bankruptcy Law and Practice § 28.06 (Callaghan 1981). See also In re Breezewood Acres, Inc., 28 Bankr. 32, 34 (Bankr. MD Pa. 1982) (a decision under the 1898 Act); In re Mobile Steel Co., 563 F2d 692 (5th Cir. 1977); In re Good Hope Indus., Inc., 16 Bankr. 719 (Bankr. D. Mass. 1982) (a decision under the 1898 Act).

[4] 11 USC § 502(a), as amended by 1984 Amendments § 445.

[5] 11 USC §§ 704(5), 1106(a)(1) (as amended by 1984 Amendments § 311), 1302(b)(1) (as amended by 1984 Amendments § 314). The debtor has a duty to cooperate with the trustee with respect to objections and allowance of claims. See 11 USC § 521(3), as amended by 1984 Amendments § 305.

[6] See Collier on Bankruptcy ¶ 57.17[2] (Matthew Bender, 14th ed. 1977); see also Collier on Bankruptcy ¶ 502.01[2] (Matthew Bender, 15th ed. 1981).

[7] See id.; Norton, Bankruptcy Law and Practice § 28.07 (Callaghan 1981); Cohen, Bankruptcy, Secured Transactions and Other Debtor-Creditor Matters 147 (Michie–Bobbs-Merrill 1981). The Advisory Committee Note to Bankruptcy Rule 3007 seems to acknowledge that creditors may make objections to allowance of claims.

[8] See Collier on Bankruptcy ¶ 502.01[2] (Matthew Bender, 15th ed. 1981).

[9] Id.

[10] Id.

### [2] Objections to Allowance of Claims

Objections to allowance of claims must be in writing and filed with the court. A copy of the objection, with notice of the hearing thereon, must be mailed or delivered to the claimant, the debtor, and the trustee at least thirty days before the hearing.[11] However, note that the statute and rules do not specify a time period within which objections to claims must be made, and there is authority under the Bankruptcy Reform Act that objection may be made any time before allowance of the claim.[12] The doctrine of laches may preclude a belated objection to a proof of claim, although mere lapse of time usually is not sufficient to bar the claim. Laches generally is invoked only when there is prejudice to a party's position,[13] and Bankruptcy Rule 3008 permits a party in interest to move for reconsideration of an order allowing or disallowing a claim.

The filing of an objection generally results in a "contested matter" governed by Bankruptcy Rule 9014. However, if the objection is joined with a claim covered by Bankruptcy Rule 7001, such as a counterclaim by the trustee, then the filing commences an "adversary proceeding," which is then subject to Part VII of the Bankruptcy Rules.[14]

### [3] Reconsideration of Claims

Under Section 502(j),[15] a claim that has been allowed or disallowed may be reconsidered for cause, and, upon reconsideration, allowed or disallowed according to the equities of the case. Reconsideration of a claim does not affect the validity of any payment or transfer made to a holder of an allowed claim that is not reconsidered. However, if a reconsidered claim is allowed and is of the same class as claims not reconsidered and that have received payment, the claims in the same class that are not reconsidered are not entitled to receive any additional payment or transfer from the estate until the holder of the reconsidered-allowed claim receives payment on his claim proportionate in value to that already received by the holders of the allowed claims not reconsidered. In other words, other allowed claims in the same class are not entitled to additional distributions until the reconsidered-allowed claim receives a proportionate distribution.[16]

---

[11] B. Rule 3007.

[12] In re Good Hope Indus., Inc., 16 Bankr. 719 (Bankr. D. Mass. 1982).

[13] See In re Mikart, Inc., 9 Bankr. 144 (Bankr. ND Ga. 1981) (a decision under the 1898 Act).

[14] See B. Rule 3007 and the Advisory Committee Notes thereto.

[15] 11 USC § 502(j), as amended by 1984 Amendments § 445. Prior to the 1984 Amendments, Section 502(j) provided: "Before a case is closed, a claim that has been allowed may be reconsidered for cause, and reallowed or disallowed according to the equities of the case."

[16] 11 USC § 502(j), as amended by 1984 Amendments § 445. One court has indicated that reconsideration is appropriate where a contingent claim that has been esti-

## ¶ 14.05 DISALLOWANCE OF CLAIMS

If proper objection to allowance of a claim is made, the claim will not be allowed to the extent the claim falls within nine specific statutory grounds for disallowance.[1]

### [1] Claims Unenforceable Under Nonbankruptcy Law

A claim will not be allowed to the extent that, at the time the petition is filed, it is "unenforceable against the debtor, and unenforceable against property of the debtor, under any agreement or applicable law for a reason other than because such claim is contingent or unmatured."[2] For example, a valid defense that the debt had been paid, a defense of usury, or a statute of limitations may be asserted to disallow a claim.[3]

There are two major exceptions to this general rule that claims unenforceable at the time the petition is filed are not allowable. First, unmatured claims, although not due when the petition is filed, are allowable. The commencement of the case operates as an acceleration of the principal amount, even though the amount is due in the future. However, there is no acceleration of unmatured interest.[4] Second, contingent claims are allowable. If fixing the amount of any contingent or unliquidated claim will unduly delay closing of the estate, the court must estimate the amount of the claim. The Bankruptcy Amendments and Federal Judgeship Act of 1984 (the 1984 Amendments) substituted "unduly delay administration of the case" for "unduly delay closing of the case."[5]

---

mated is subsequently liquidated before the close of the case. See In re Nova Real Estate Inv. Trust, 23 Bankr. 62 (Bankr. ED Va. 1982); cf. In re Langlais, 11 Bankr. 485 (Bankr. SD Cal. 1981).

[1] 11 USC § 502(b), as amended by 1984 Amendments § 445.

[2] 11 USC § 502(b)(1), as amended by 1984 Amendments § 445. Despite this provision, the court in In re Spanish Trails Lanes, Inc., 16 Bankr. 304 (Bankr. D. Ariz. 1981) allowed the claim of an unlicensed contractor, although the claim was unenforceable under Arizona state law in Arizona courts. The court took the view that the Arizona statutes did not make the claim void ab initio, and in exercise of its equitable powers allowed the claim, noting that the debtor had been enriched by the work and had acquiesced in the continued performance of the contractor after being put on notice that he was unlicensed.

[3] 11 USC § 558, added by 1984 Amendments § 470. Under Section 558, such defenses pass to the trustee in bankruptcy, and after the petition has been filed the debtor may not waive such defenses. The provisions of new Section 558 formerly were contained in Section 541(e).

[4] 11 USC § 502(b)(2). Whether interest is matured or unmatured on the date of bankruptcy is to be determined without reference to any ipso facto or bankruptcy clause in the agreement creating the claim. H.R. Rep. No. 595, 95th Cong., 1st Sess. 352–354 (1977); S. Rep. No. 989, 95th Cong., 2d Sess. 62–65(1978).

[5] 11 USC § 502(c), as amended by 1984 Amendments § 445; see also H.R. Rep. No. 595, 95th Cong., 1st Sess. 354 (1977); S. Rep. No. 989, 95th Cong., 2d Sess. 65 (1978). In a Chapter 13 case, In re Langlais, 11 Bankr. 485 (Bankr. SD Cal. 1981), the

## [2] Unmatured Interest

As a general rule, although the commencement of a case accelerates the principal amount of all claims,[6] it does not accelerate unmatured interest and postpetition interest is not allowed.[7]

There are two important exceptions to this general rule. First, under Section 506(b), a creditor with an allowed secured claim who is oversecured may recover postpetition interest to the extent the value of the collateral exceeds the value of the claim. He may do this provided interest is covered by the security agreement. To the extent the collateral is sufficient to cover both principal and interest, postpetition interest is recoverable, as are reasonable fees, costs, and charges provided for in the security agreement.[8]

The second exception is the rare event in which there are sufficient funds after all claims have been paid. In this case, interest will then be paid on all claims.[9]

## [3] Property Tax Claims

Property tax claims assessed against property of the estate are disallowed to the extent the tax exceeds the value of the interest of the estate in the property.[10] For example, if the accrued property tax against certain property is

---

debtor-mortgagor apparently had sold the mortgaged property and under the applicable state law would only be liable for a deficiency upon default on the mortgage note if the foreclosure sale did not realize enough to satisfy the loan. The court disallowed the claim, determining that the value of the property was in excess of the unpaid amount of the note and therefore the contingent claim of the noteholder against the debtor was valueless. The court's classification of the claim as contingent may be questioned; however, important facts are not brought out in the opinion.

In another Chapter 11 case, although the creditor had obtained relief from the automatic stay, the court estimated the claim of a developer-creditor, since to wait for the outcome of the litigation in a state court would unduly delay the case and jeopardize the debtor's plan of reorganization. The court indicated, however, that upon liquidation of the claim the creditor, under Section 502(j), could ask for reconsideration of the claim "for cause" as long as the case had not been closed. In re Nova Real Estate Inv. Trust, 23 Bankr. 62, 66 (Bankr. ED Va. 1982). Note that Section 502(j), as amended by 1984 Amendments § 445, no longer speaks in terms of reconsideration of claims "before a case is closed."

[6] Collier on Bankruptcy ¶ 502.02[2], at 502-35 (Matthew Bender, 15th ed. 1981); H.R. Rep. No. 595, 95th Cong., 1st Sess. 352–353 (1977); S. Rep. No. 989, 95th Cong., 2d Sess. 62–63 (1978); see also in re Schweitzer, 19 Bankr. 860, 868 (Bankr. EDNY 1982).

[7] 11 USC § 502(b)(2).

[8] 11 USC § 506(b), as amended by 1984 Amendments § 448. There is a substantial question whether interest is payable at the contract rate or some other rate. See infra ¶ 14.10.

[9] 11 USC § 726(a)(5). Under this section, interest is payable at the legal rate.

[10] 11 USC § 502(b)(3), as renumbered by 1984 Amendments § 445. Prior to the 1984 Amendments, Section 502(b)(3) provided that a creditor's claim was not allowable to the extent that the debtor had a claim or mutual debt against the claimant that could

$12,000, but the interest of the debtor's estate in the property is valued at only $10,000, then the tax claim is allowed only to the extent of $10,000.

### [4] Services of an Insider or Attorney of the Debtor

Claims of an insider[11] or of an attorney of the debtor for personal service are not allowed to the extent the claims exceed the reasonable value of the services, as determined by the court.[12] This limitation appears to be a safeguard against persons who may be in a position of influence or leverage over the debtor, or who through collusive conduct may assist in diverting assets to a person who is close to the debtor.[13]

### [5] Unmatured Claims for Postpetition Alimony, Maintenance, and Support

The commencement of the case does not accelerate claims for alimony, maintenance, and support. These unmatured claims, which are also excepted from discharge under Section 523(a)(5), are not allowable.[14] To the extent these postpetition claims are nondischargeable, the spouse or former spouse may be able to go against exempt property or pursue property acquired by the debtor after the filing of the petition.[15]

### [6] Claims of Lessors of Real Property

Section 502(b)(7) sets ceilings or limitations on the amount that may be allowed on landlord's claims for damages resulting from termination of a lease of real property.[16] Allowable claims of a landlord for damages may not

---

be set off under Section 553. Former Section 502(b)(3) was probably redundant, because under Section 506(a) a claim is treated as a secured claim to the extent that the creditor has a right of setoff. See Collier on Bankruptcy ¶ 502.02, at 502-37 (Matthew Bender, 15th ed. 1981).

[11] "Insider" is a defined term. See 11 USC § 101(28).

[12] 11 USC § 502(b)(4), as renumbered by 1984 Amendments § 445; see 11 USC § 329(b); In re Smith, 5 Bankr. 92 (Bankr. DDC 1980), rev'd in part, In re Devers, 507 F. Supp. 468 (DDC 1981) (ethical conduct of attorney can be taken into account in determining fee).

[13] See Weintraub & Resnick, "Allowance of Claims and Priorities Under the New Bankruptcy Code," 12 U.C.C. L.J. 291, 301 (1980).

[14] 11 USC § 502(b)(5), as renumbered by 1984 Amendments § 445.

[15] Note that claims for such future support and alimony are not subject to the "automatic stay" of Section 362 with respect to property that is not a part of the debtor's estate. For example, some property that is exempt in the bankruptcy proceeding may still be subject to claims for alimony or support. 11 USC § 362(b)(2); see also ¶ 12.05[1].

[16] 11 USC § 502(b)(6), as renumbered by 1984 Amendments § 445. Under the 1898 Act, there were differences in the ceilings on such damages recoverable by land-

exceed: (1) the total unpaid rent to the earlier of the date the petition was filed or the date the lessor repossessed or the lessee surrendered the property, *and* (2) future rent that is the greater of one year's rent reserved by the lease or 15 percent of the rent due under the remaining terms of the lease not to exceed three years following the earlier of the filing the petition, or the date the lessor repossessed or the lessee surrendered the property.[17] In other words, the maximum in damages that a landlord may recover is the accrued unpaid rent, without acceleration, at the earlier of the filing of the petition or repossession or surrender plus the greater of one year's rent or 15 percent of the rent reserved for the balance of the term. The 15 percent, however, may not exceed the three-year limit.[18] It should be pointed out that recovery of the above amounts is not automatic. By use of the term "damages," it seems that the principle of mitigation of damages, to the extent applicable, must be taken into account; consequently, the above ceilings apply after any mitigation of damages is considered.[19] For example, if the lessor is able to re-lease the premises within six months after the petition is filed, on terms at least as favorable as the debtor's, the lessor should not be able to recover, as future rent damages, an amount greater than the rent reserved for the six-month period. Alternatively, if the lessor is unable to rent the premises until fifteen months after the petition was filed, the landlord is not entitled to damages for future rent in an amount exceeding the rent for the fifteen months.

Note that if the lessor's claim for rent is secured by a state statutory lien, this lien may be avoided by the trustee under Sections 545(3) and 545(4).

The legislative history indicates that the limitations of Section 502(b)(6)[20] were not intended to apply to "financing leases," which in reality are security devices rather than leases.[21] For example, this might be the case where the

---

lords between Chapter VII and Chapter XI proceedings. The limitations of Section 502(b)(7) of the current Bankruptcy Code, however, apply in Chapter 7, 11, and 13 cases. Note also that acceleration clauses triggered by bankruptcy, so-called ipso facto clauses, are no longer enforceable in bankruptcy under Section 502(b)(7)(A). See also 11 USC §§ 363(c)(1), 365(b)(2), 365(e), 365(f)(3), 541(c)(1); In re Schweitzer, 19 Bankr. 860 (Bankr. EDNY 1982).

[17] 11 USC § 502(6).

[18] The 15 percent limit applies where the unexpired term exceeds 6⅔ years, and the three-year cap on the 15 percent is operative when the unexpired term exceeds twenty years. See Cohen, Bankruptcy, Secured Transactions and Other Debtor-Creditor Matters ¶ 13–310.22[7.1] (Michie–Bobbs-Merrill 1981).

[19] See generally 3 Thompson on Real Property § 1064 (Bobbs-Merrill, replacement vol. 1981); Restatement (Second) of Property § 21.1 (1977); 5 Corbin on Contracts § 1053, at 314 (West 1963). In In re Weeks, 28 Bankr. 958 (Bankr. WD Okla. 1983), where the debtor had surrendered the leasehold before the expiration of the lease, and the lessor had obtained a default judgment in the state court some months prior to the debtor filing a Chapter 11 case, the claim of the lessor under the judgment was held to be subject to the limitations of Section 502(b)(7) (now Section 502(b)(6)).

[20] Formerly 11 USC § 502(b)(7).

[21] S. Rep. No. 989, 95th Cong., 2d Sess. 64 (1978).

lease contains an option that may be exercised for nominal or no additional consideration, and the economic substance of the lease is really a purchase-security device.[22] The legislative history also indicates that a security deposit given to the lessor is to be applied to the allowed claim. To the extent the deposit exceeds the allowed claim, the excess must be turned over to the trustee as part of the estate.[23] Note that any claim that the lessor has against the estate for postpetition rent as an administrative claim due to occupancy of the leased premises by the trustee or the debtor in possession is not subject to the limitations of Section 502(b)(6).

### [7] Claims of Employees Under Employment Contracts

The allowance of a claim of an employee for damages resulting from termination of an employment contract is limited to (1) unpaid compensation to the earlier of the filing of the petition, or the date the employer directed the employee to terminate or the employee terminated, plus (2) compensation due under the contract for one year following the earlier of the filing of the petition or termination by the employer or the employee.[24] Thus, for termination of an employment contract, an employee's allowable claim for loss after the date of bankruptcy or termination of employment may not exceed compensation for more than one year at the contract rate. Again, the general contract principle of mitigation of damages should be applicable. Some, if not all, of the employee's claim may be a priority claim under Section 507(a)(3).[25]

### [8] Limitations on the Allowability of Certain Tax Claims

Tax claims for employment taxes on wages, salaries, or commissions resulting from a reduction in tax credits due to late payment are not allowable.[26] For example, certain federal tax credits are given for state employment taxes; if, however, the state tax is paid late, the federal tax credit is disallowed, which may result in an increased federal tax claim. Such claims are not allowed under Section 502(b)(8).[27]

---

[22] Id.

[23] H.R. Rep. No. 595, 95th Cong., 1st Sess. 353–354 (1977); S. Rep. No. 989, 95th Cong., 2d Sess. 63–64 (1978); cf. In re Standard Furniture Co., 3 Bankr. 527 (Bankr. SD Cal. 1980) (trustee can set off the security deposit against the claim of the lessor for rent due as an administrative expense).

[24] 11 USC § 502(b)(7), as amended and renumbered by 1984 Amendments § 445.

[25] See infra ¶ 14.09[3].

[26] 11 USC § 502(b)(8), as renumbered by 1984 Amendments § 445.

[27] See Cowans, Bankruptcy Law and Practice 313 (West, interim ed. 1983); Weintraub & Resnick, "Allowance of Claims and Priorities Under the New Bankruptcy Code," 12 U.C.C. L.J. 291, 302 (1980).

### [9] Claims of Transferees of Voidable Transfers

Any claim of a creditor who has received a transfer voidable or recoverable under Sections 542, 543, 550, 553, 522(f), 522(h), 544, 545, 547, 548, 549, and 721(a)[28] will not be allowed unless the transferee has paid the amount or turned over to the estate the property for which the claimant is liable.[29] The claim is disallowed only until the order is complied with.[30]

This section applies to the *claimant*, not to the claim. For example, assume that the creditor has two claims against the debtor. On the first claim, the creditor receives a preference voidable under Section 547; on the second claim, the creditor does not receive a transfer voidable or recoverable under any of the specified sections. The creditor's proof of claim on the second claim, as well as on the first claim, will not be allowed until creditor relinquishes the preference received on the first claim. In some cases, this presents a helpful tool to the trustee in recovering such voidable transfers.

If the trustee, along with an objection to the claim on the basis of the claimant receiving an avoidable transfer, makes a demand against the claimant based on the claimant's liability to the estate, the matter will be an adversary proceeding.[31]

## ¶ 14.06 ALLOWANCE OF POSTPETITION CLAIMS

As a general rule, only claims that exist when the petition is filed are allowable. There are several important exceptions to this rule and certain claims that arise after the filing of the petition may be allowable.

### [1] "Involuntary Gap" Claims

In the gap between the filing of an involuntary petition and the entry of an order for relief, the debtor is permitted to continue business, unless the court orders otherwise.[1] Claims that arise in the ordinary course of the debtor's business after the filing of an involuntary petition, but before the earlier of the appointment of a trustee or the entry of an order for relief, are treated as if they had arisen before the filing of the petition and are allowed.[2] These claims also are second-priority claims under Section 507(a)(2), ranking behind only administrative expenses.[3]

---

[28] For discussion of these avoiding powers, see Chapter 17.

[29] 11 USC § 502(d).

[30] See Cowans, Bankruptcy Law & Practice 315 (West, interim ed. 1983).

[31] See Weintraub & Resnick, "Allowance of Claims and Priorities Under the New Bankruptcy Code," 12 U.C.C. L.J. 291, 309 (1980); B. Rule 3007.

[1] 11 USC § 303(f).

[2] 11 USC § 502(f).

[3] See infra ¶¶ 14.09[1]–14.09[2].

### [2] Claims Arising From Rejection of Executory Contracts or Leases

As discussed elsewhere,[4] executory contracts or leases of the debtor may be rejected by the trustee under Section 365 or by a Chapter 11[5] or 13 plan.[6] If this power is exercised, which of necessity occurs after the filing of the petition, the claim arising from such rejection is treated as if it arose before the filing of the petition. These claims are subject to the limitations on allowability contained in Sections 502(b)(6) and 502(b)(7).

### [3] Claims Arising From the Trustee's Recovery of Property

If the trustee in a Chapter 7 or 11 case or the debtor in possession in a Chapter 11 case recovers property from a creditor[7] under Section 522,[8] 550,[9] or 553,[10] then the creditor's claim resulting from the recovery, although arising after the petition, is determined and allowed as if it had arisen before the filing of the petition. For example, if the trustee recovers a voidable preference from the creditor, the creditor's claim to the extent of the recovery is allowable under this section. As previously noted, the creditor, having received a voidable preference, must surrender the preference to have any claim allowed.[11]

### [4] Certain Tax Claims Arising After the Commencement of the Case

Certain tax claims arising after the commencement of the case are treated as if they arose before the filing of the petition for purposes of allowance. The details are covered in Section 502(i).

### [5] Certain Expenses Incurred by the Trustee

Expenses incurred by the trustee or the debtor in possession after the petition is filed that qualify as administrative expenses are allowed as priority claims.[12]

---

[4] See ¶ 13.09.

[5] 11 USC § 1123(b)(2), as amended by 1984 Amendments § 507.

[6] 11 USC § 1322(b)(7), as amended by 1984 Amendments § 528.

[7] 11 USC § 502(h), as amended by 1984 Amendments § 445.

[8] Sections 522(h)–522(i) permit the debtor to exercise the avoiding powers of the trustee and to recover property to the extent that the debtor can claim an exemption in the property if the trustee does not attempt to exercise the avoiding power. See discussion at ¶ 13.07[3].

[9] Section 550 includes the avoiding power given to the trustee under the following sections: 544 (the "strong arm" clause and the avoiding powers of actual creditors); 547 (preferences); 545 (statutory liens); 548 (fraudulent conveyances); 549 (certain postpetition transfers); and 724(a).

[10] Section 553 permits the trustee to recover certain prepetition setoffs. See discussion at ¶ 16.08.

[11] See supra ¶ 14.05[9].

[12] See discussion at infra ¶ 14.09[1].

### [6] Certain Expenses Incurred by Creditors After the Petition Is Filed

Certain expenses incurred by creditors after the petition is filed may also be allowed as administrative expenses. For example, the expenses of a creditor who files an involuntary petition against the debtor may be entitled to administrative expense priority. Expenses of creditors who with court approval recover property for the estate are also entitled to administrative expense priority.[13]

## ¶ 14.07 CLAIMS OF CODEBTORS, SURETIES, AND GUARANTORS

As used in this section, the term "codebtors" includes comakers of notes or other obligations, guarantors, sureties, and other persons who have secured the debtor's obligations–so-called real sureties. The basic concept here is that such a codebtor, or the property in the case of a real surety, is liable for the obligation for which he is a codebtor, even though the debtor may receive a discharge of that obligation.[1] Further, except in some circumstances in a Chapter 13 case,[2] the codebtor is not protected by the automatic stay of Section 362.[3] The codebtor, remaining liable for the obligation, thus has a great interest in seeing that a proof of claim is properly filed on the obligation because the ultimate liability or exposure of the codebtor to that creditor will be reduced to the extent that a payment or dividend is received by the creditor from the estate.[4] However, a creditor may be inclined not to properly and timely file proof of claim on the obligation, relying on the ultimate responsibility of the codebtor or the property of the real surety. If this occurs, no dividend will be received to reduce the liability of the codebtor. Further, any contingent right by way of reimbursement, subrogation, or contribution the codebtor might have

---

[13] 11 USC §§ 503(b)(3)(A), 503(b)(3)(B).

[1] See 11 USC § 524(e) and discussion at Chapter 15.

[2] In a Chapter 13 case, the stay does extend to certain individual codebtors for consumer debts, at least to the extent the claim is to be paid under the plan. See 11 USC § 1301 and discussion at ¶ 17.07[1].

[3] See, e.g., In re Smith, 14 Bankr. 956 (Bankr. D. Conn. 1981); In re Aboussie Bros. Constr. Co., 8 Bankr. 302 (Bankr. ED Mo. 1981); In re Lamar Estates, Inc., 5 Bankr. 328 (Bankr. EDNY 1980); In re Kash & Karry Wholesale, Inc., 28 Bankr. 66 (Bankr. DSC 1982). Although the automatic stay is not applicable against guarantors, in appropriate circumstances proceedings against guarantors may be enjoined under Section 105. See, e.g., In re Brentano's, 27 Bankr. 90 (Bankr. SDNY 1983); In re Kash & Karry Wholesale, Inc., 28 Bankr. 66, 72 (Bankr. DSC 1982); Pitts v. Unarco Indus., Inc., 698 F2d 313 (7th Cir. 1983) (automatic stay does not apply to nonbankrupt codefendant in asbestos-related litigation); see also discussion of the "automatic stay" at ¶ 12.05.

[4] This will be true where the codebtor (e.g., a guarantor) is liable for the entire debt. Where the codebtor is liable for only a part of the debt (e.g., the debt is $50,000 and the codebtor is liable for only $20,000 of the debt), or in the case of the "real surety" where the value of the security is $20,000, the dividend received by the creditor reduces the liability of the codebtor only when it exceeds $30,000.

against the debtor, as a contingent claim, will be discharged if the debtor receives a discharge. Thus, to protect the codebtor, the Code permits the codebtor to file proof of claim if the creditor does not timely file proof of claim.[5] In a Chapter 7 or 13 case, under Bankruptcy Rule 3002(c), the creditor must file proof of claim within ninety days after the first date set for the meeting of creditors. Bankruptcy Rule 3005(a), implementing Section 501(b), provides that within thirty days after the expiration of the ninety days the codebtor may file a proof of claim in the name of the debtor, if known; if unknown, the codebtor may file in his own name. The creditor may thereafter file proof of claim, which will supersede the proof of claim of the codebtor.[6]

### [1] Claims for Reimbursement and Contribution and the Right of Subrogation

If the codebtor has paid the claim of the creditor before the petition is filed, to the extent of any rights against the debtor for reimbursement, contribution, or subrogation, the codebtor will have a claim against the debtor's estate.[7] If the claim has been paid in full, then the creditor is satisfied and has no claim against the debtor's estate.

If, after the petition is filed, the codebtor pays the creditor's claim,[8] he also has important rights covered under Sections 502(e) and 509, in addition to his right to file the creditor's claim previously discussed. The legislative history indicates that these two sections, which must be read together, offer codebtors a choice of action.[9] Section 502(e) deals with the claim of a codebtor for reimbursement or contribution, while Section 509 covers the codebtor's right of subrogation.

First, it should be noted that the codebtor's right to reimbursement or contribution, which becomes fixed after the commencement of the case, is treated as if it became fixed before the filing of the petition.[10] Second, with respect to the codebtor's right to reimbursement or contribution, the codebtor's

---

[5] 11 USC § 501(b); B. Rule 3005.

[6] B. Rule 3005(a).

[7] Claims for reimbursement and contribution are covered in Section 502(e), as amended by 1984 Amentment § 445. Subrogation is covered in Section 509. For discussion of the legislative history of this section, see Collier on Bankruptcy ¶ 509.01 (Matthew Bender, 15th ed. 1981).

[8] It appears that this also is the case where the codebtor has paid some but not all of the creditor's claim before the petition. There generally must be some payment by the codebtor for any of these rights of reimbursement, contribution, or subrogation to arise. See generally Restatement of Security §§ 104–106, at 275–281 (1941); Simpson, Handbook on the Law of Suretyship § 48, at 224–237 (West 1950).

[9] See Collier on Bankruptcy ¶ 502.05, at 502-79, 502-80 (Matthew Bender, 15th ed. 1981); 124 Cong. Rec. S17,413 (daily ed. Oct. 6, 1978); 124 Cong. Rec. H11,097 (daily ed. Sept. 28, 1978).

[10] See 11 USC § 502(e)(2). Section 502(e)(1)(B) must be read together with Section 502(e)(1). It appears that under Section 502(e)(1)(B), a codebtor's claim that has not

claim is not allowed to the extent that the creditor's claim is not allowed, if disallowed for a reason other than payment; the codebtor or surety's claim is entitled to no better stature than the creditor's.[11] Third, the codebtor's claim for reimbursement is allowed only to the extent he has paid the creditor's claim at the time of allowance.[12] Fourth, if the codebtor also requests subrogation under Section 509, his claim for reimbursement or contribution is not allowed.[13] Fifth, an important limitation imposed by Section 509[14] is that the codebtor's claim is subordinated to the creditor's claim until the creditor's claim has been paid in full.[15]

The other option available to the codebtor who makes payment to the creditor, irrespective of whether the payment is before or after the petition,[16] is the right of subrogation under Section 509. To the extent that the codebtor makes payment to the creditor, the codebtor is subrogated to the rights of the creditor.[17] There are important limitations on this right, however. First, although subrogated to the creditor's claim to the extent of the payment by the codebtor, the codebtor's claim by way of subrogation is subordinated to the claim of the creditor until the creditor's claim is paid in full either by the bankruptcy proceeding or by other means, such as by the codebtor. As previously noted, this subordination is for the "benefit" of the creditor; the codebtor

---

become fixed by payment at the time of the determination of the allowance of the claim will not be allowed.

[11] 11 USC § 502(e)(1)(A). For example, if the creditor had received a voidable preference or a fraudulent transfer and his claim would not be allowed under Section 502(d) until the transfer was surrendered, then the codebtor's claim for reimbursement or contribution would not be allowed. Collier on Bankruptcy ¶ 502.05, at 502-82 et seq. (Matthew Bender, 15th ed. 1981).

[12] See Weintraub & Resnick, Bankruptcy Law Manual ¶ 5.06 n.102. (Warren, Gorham & Lamont, Inc. 1980). This limitation appears to arise from the principle that the right to reimbursement or contribution arises only to the extent that the "surety" has paid the creditor's claim.

[13] 11 USC § 502(e)(1)(C), as amended by 1984 Amendments § 445.

[14] 11 USC § 509, as amended by 1984 Amendments § 450.

[15] See 11 USC § 509(c). This is consistent with the general principle of suretyship that the surety cannot compete with the creditor for whom he is a surety until the creditor is paid in full. This subordination is for the "benefit" of the creditor, which means that the codebtor has no right to share in the distribution of the estate and his distributive share will be paid to the creditor until the creditor is paid in full. See Collier on Bankruptcy ¶ 502.05, at 505-79 (Matthew Bender, 15th ed. 1981).

[16] The language of Section 509 does not speak in terms of whether payment is made before or after the petition. See also Collier on Bankruptcy ¶ 509.02, at 509-10 (Matthew Bender, 15th ed. 1981). If the claim is paid in full before the petition, the codebtor generally "owns" the claim either by subrogation or by an assignment and files proof of claim in his own right. Cf. UCC § 3–415(5).

[17] 11 USC § 509(a). Implicit in the scheme of subrogation provided by the Code is that if the creditor's claim is not allowable, then the codebtor's claim by way of subrogation also is not allowable. See Collier on Bankruptcy ¶ 509.02, at 509-11 (Matthew Bender, 15th ed. 1981).

receives no distribution from the estate until the creditor has has been paid in full.[18] Furthermore, the codebtor is not subrogated to the rights of the creditor to the extent that (1) the codebtor's claim for reimbursement or contribution on such claim is allowed under Section 502,[19] (2) the codebtor's claim is disallowed, other than under Section 502,[20] or (3) the codebtor's claim is subordinated under Section 510.[21] Additionally, the codebtor will not be subrogated if he received the consideration for the claim of the creditor.[22] This includes the situation in which the codebtor actually is the principal or obtained the benefit of the debt incurred by the debtor and himself. For example, this is the case where the maker of a note is an accommodation maker for the guarantor or endorser who actually receives the benefit of the proceeds of the loan for which the note is given.

Whether the codebtor should choose to pursue the claim for reimbursement or contribution or to pursue the right of subrogation depends upon the circumstances. Frequently the choice turns on whether either of the claims is secured.[23] The details of filing claim by the codebtor are covered by Section 501(b) and the related Bankruptcy Rules.[24]

---

[18] The codebtor's share is paid to the creditor until the creditor has been paid in full by the bankruptcy or otherwise. See Collier on Bankruptcy ¶ 509.04, at 509-17, 509-18 (Matthew Bender, 15th ed. 1981). Note that Section 509(c) does not disallow the codebtor's claim or deny subrogation but merely postpones the codebtor's right to receive his share, appropriating it for the creditor until he is paid; the codebtor's claim is not subordinated vis-à-vis other creditors. See Weintraub & Resnick, Bankruptcy Law Manual ¶ 5.07, at 5-22 (Warren, Gorham & Lamont, Inc. 1980).

[19] 11 USC § 509(b)(1)(A). In a sense, this prevents double recovery; the choice for the codebtor enters here. Where the codebtor has elected to file a claim for reimbursement, and it is allowed under Section 502(e), he thereby elects to forgo subrogation.

[20] 11 USC § 509(b)(1)(B). For example, if the codebtor's claim were unenforceable under state law and therefore not allowable under Section 502(b)(1).

[21] 11 USC § 509(b)(1)(C). Note that subordination under Sections 509(c) and 509(b)(1)(C) is not the same. See Collier on Bankruptcy ¶ 509.03, at 509-15 (Matthew Bender, 15th ed. 1981).

[22] 11 USC § 509(b)(2).

[23] Weintraub and Resnick state:

> "The answer to this question may depend on whether there is collateral securing the claim. If the creditor's claim is secured by the debtor's assets, the co-debtor will be put in a more favorable position by asserting subrogation rights. Since the creditor's claim is secured, the codebtor may obtain through subrogation a secured claim against the estate. Assume, however, that the creditor's claim is unsecured, but that the surety's rights against the debtor are secured; that is, the debtor and the surety have agreed that the debtor's assets will secure the surety's right to reimbursement. In this situation, the surety should file a proof of claim seeking allowance of a secured claim for reimbursement. If the surety relied on the right of subrogation alone, the surety would have only the unsecured claim of the creditor."

Weintraub & Resnick, Bankruptcy Law Manual ¶ 5.07, at 5-22 (Warren, Gorham & Lamont, Inc. 1980).

[24] See supra ¶ 14.03.

The subrogation rights of the codebtor under Section 509 are also subject to the restrictions of Section 507(d), which in most cases denies subrogation to any priority claim status of the creditor.[25] In other words, a codebtor's claim by subrogation generally is not given the priority status of the creditor's claim to which the codebtor is subrogated.

## ¶ 14.08 CONTINGENT AND UNLIQUIDATED CLAIMS

The Bankruptcy Code made a significant change in the treatment of unliquidated and contingent claims. Under the old Act, unliquidated and contingent claims were not allowed unless they could be liquidated or reasonably estimated without unreasonable delay of the administration of the case.[1] Under Section 502(c) of the Code,[2] if fixing or liquidating of unliquidated or contingent claims will unduly delay the administration of the case,[3] then the value of the claims must be estimated.[4] Equitable claims for breach of performance that give rise to a right to payment are treated in the same manner.[5]

The 1984 Amendments appear to have imposed a limitation on this power to estimate unliquidated claims with respect to unliquidated personal injury tort or wrongful death claims. Under new Section 157 of Title 28, the liquidation or estimation of such claims for purposes of distribution is expressly excluded from the "core proceeding" jurisdiction of the bankruptcy judge. Section 157(b)(5) of Title 28 further provides that the "district court shall order that personal injury tort and wrongful death claims shall be tried in the district court in which the bankruptcy case is pending, or in the district court in which the claim arose." Furthermore, Section 1411 of Title 28 provides that "except as provided in subsection (b) of this section, this chapter and title 11 do not affect any right to trial by jury that an individual

---

[25] See discussion at infra ¶ 14.09[8].

[1] See 1898 Act §§ 57(d), 63(d). If such claims were disallowed because they could not be estimated or liquidated without unreasonable delay, they were deemed to be "nonprovable" and hence nondischargeable because only "provable" debts were dischargeable under old Section 17. The new Bankruptcy Code eliminates the concept of "provable" claims.

[2] 11 USC § 502(c), as amended by 1984 Amendments § 445.

[3] The 1984 Amendments changed the test from one of "unduly delaying closing of the case" to one of "unduly delaying the administration of a case." Whether this change will produce differences in results remains to be seen.

[4] See, e.g., In re Langlais, 11 Bankr. 485 (Bankr. SD Cal. 1981); In re Nova Real Estate Inv. Trust, 23 Bankr. 62 (Bankr. ED Va. 1982). In *Nova*, the court indicated that where the claim is estimated but subsequently liquidated, the creditor can request reconsideration of the claim for cause under Section 502(j). See also Weintraub & Resnick, "Treatment of Contingent and Unliquidated Claims Under the Bankruptcy Code," 15 U.C.C. L.J. 373 (1983); Comment, "Procedures for Estimating Contingent or Unliquidated Claims in Bankruptcy," 35 Stan. L. Rev. 153 (1983).

[5] 11 USC § 502(c)(2).

has under applicable nonbankruptcy law with regard to a personal injury or wrongful death claim." The clear implication of these sections is that, at least for purposes of distribution (although perhaps not for other administrative purposes), unliquidated personal injury tort or wrongful death claims may not be estimated.[6]

## ¶ 14.09 PRIORITY CLAIMS

As previously mentioned, after liquidation of the estate, distribution is made only to allowed claims, and although the general principle in bankruptcy is that creditors share equally, some creditors take priority over others. Some creditors, in effect, are more equal than others. Two key sections deal with the order of distribution in a Chapter 7 case: Sections 726[1] and 507. Section 726(a)(1) directs that distribution is to be made in the following order:

(1) Allowed unsecured "priority" claims, in the order set forth in Section 507;[2]

(2) Allowed unsecured claims with some qualifications.[3] This includes most general unsecured creditors;

(3) Certain allowed but tardily filed unsecured claims;[4]

(4) Certain allowed claims for fines and penalties that are not compensation for pecuniary loss;[5]

(5) Interest at the legal rate on claims paid in the prior four classes. This will be postpetition interest on the claims;[6]

(6) The debtor.[7] This, of course, is a rare occurrence.

All creditors within a priority class must be paid in full before any distribution is made to creditors in a lower class. If all creditors within a particular class cannot be paid in full, then payments are made pro rata among claims within a particular class.[8] The order for payment of "priority claims" is specifically set forth in Section 507.

---

[6] For additional discussion, see ¶ 11.03[2][a].

[1] Note that Section 726 does not apply in a Chapter 11 or 13 case. See 11 USC § 103(b).

[2] 11 USC § 726(a)(1).

[3] 11 USC § 726(a)(2).

[4] 11 USC § 726(a)(3).

[5] 11 USC § 726(a)(4).

[6] 11 USC § 726(a)(5).

[7] 11 USC § 726(a)(6).

[8] 11 USC § 726(b), as amended by 1984 Amendmenents § 479.

## [1] First Priority: Administrative Expenses

Certain claims that are allowed administrative expenses under Section 503 are given first priority in distribution.[9] Determination of when administrative expenses are to be paid is within the discretion of the bankruptcy court.[10] Administrative expenses include the actual, necessary costs and expenses of preserving the estate, including wages, salaries, or commissions for services rendered after the commencement of the case.[11] These administrative expenses include compensation for the trustee, attorneys, accountants, appraisers, and other professionals appointed with approval of the court.[12] In addition, certain taxes incurred by the estate such as taxes on, measured by, or withheld from administrative priority wage, salary, or commission claims, share in this priority.[13] If the trustee is authorized by the court to operate the business in order to

---

[9] The debtor's "withdrawal liability" to certain pension plans under the Multi-Employer Pension Plan Amendments Act of 1980 has been held not to be entitled to administrative expense priority since there was no benefit to the estate and the liability was based on prepetition services. In re Kessler, 23 Bankr. 722, 724 (Bankr. SDNY 1982). The court indicated, however, that severance pay for employees would be treated as an administrative expense. Id. at 726.

[10] In re Verco Indus., 20 Bankr. 665 (Bankr. App. Pan. 9th Cir. 1982); In re Standard Furniture Co., 3 Bankr. 527 (Bankr. SD Cal. 1980).

[11] 11 USC § 503(b)(1)(A).

[12] Payments to paraprofessionals employed by the trustee or the debtor's attorney are administrative expenses since they are expressly included under Section 330(a)(1) (as amended by 1984 Amendments §§ 433, 434) as compensation of the trustee or the attorney of the debtor.

[13] 11 USC § 503(b)(1)(B). See H.R. Rep. No. 595, 95th Cong., 1st Sess. 355 (1977); S. Rep. No. 989, 95th Cong., 2d Sess. 99 (1978). Otte v. U.S., 419 US 43 (1974) is codified in part by this section.

Personal property taxes arising after the petition is filed are entitled to priority. In re South Shore Vending, Inc., 25 Bankr. 111, 114 (Bankr. D. Mass. 1982). State cigarette taxes paid after the order for relief by the debtor's guarantor were held not to be entitled to administrative priority as expenses "incurred during the administration of the estate" because the tax liability was incurred before the petition was filed; additionally, the tax was excluded as an administrative expense under Sections 503(b)(1)(B) and 507(a)(6)(E)(ii) (now Section 507(a)(7)(E)(ii)). In re Melino Cigar & Candy Co., 22 Bankr. 703 (Bankr. DRI 1982).

One court has held that the liability for unpaid unemployment taxes incurred by a debtor after a Chapter 11 petition had been filed and after confirmation of a Chapter 11 plan, but before the conversion of the case to Chapter 7, were not taxes "incurred by the estate." Therefore, the taxes were not entitled to priority in the Chapter 7 case as administrative expenses under Section 503(b)(1)(B)(i), but instead were prepetition taxes entitled to lower priority under Section 507(a)(6) (now Section 507(a)(7)). In re Westholt Mfg., Inc., 20 Bankr. 368 (Bankr. D. Kan. 1982). But see In re EMC Indus., Inc., 27 Bankr. 696 (Bankr. DSC 1983), which may be contra in holding that the liability for withholding, sales, and use taxes incurred by the Chapter 11 debtor in possession after commencement of the case was entitled to administrative expense priority upon conversion to Chapter 7. However, it is not clear from the opinion that a Chapter 11 plan had been confirmed, which appeared to be a significant factor to the court in *Westholt*.

complete work in process, then the wages, salaries, and other expenses incurred in the business may be allowed as administrative expenses.[14]

It is not uncommon for the trustee in a Chapter 7 case or the debtor in possession in a Chapter 11 proceeding to continue to occupy or use property that had been leased by the debtor. The liability for rent incurred by the trustee or the debtor in possession during their occupancy of leased premises is allowable as an administrative expense.[15]

Actual and necessary expenses incurred by creditors who file a petition in an involuntary case have priority as an administrative expense,[16] as well as expenses of creditors who, after court approval, recover for the benefit of the estate property transferred or concealed by the debtor.[17] After notice and a hearing, reasonable compensation for services rendered and costs and expenses incurred by a "custodian" may be allowed as administrative expenses.[18]

---

[14] 11 USC § 503(b)(1)(A).

[15] See, e.g., In re Lanman, 24 Bankr. 741 (Bankr. ND Ill. 1982); In re Standard Furniture, 3 Bankr. 527, 530 (Bankr. SD Cal. 1980). Where a lease of the debtor is eventually assumed by the trustee (or the debtor in possession), the estate becomes liable for the rent reserved under the lease. However, where the lease is ultimately rejected the amount of rent allowable as an administrative expense is measured by the period of actual occupation and use by the trustee of the premises and the amount is for the reasonable value, which is ordinarily, but not necessarily, determined by the rent reserved in the lease. See also Collier on Bankruptcy ¶ 503.04[1][a], at 505-15 (Matthew Bender, 15th ed. 1981); In re Arzola, 11 Bankr. 762, 765 (Bankr. DPR 1981) (the liability of the trustee for rent as an administrative claim begins with "adjudication" (order for relief) and continues until the premises are returned to the landlord and does not extend to the time for rejection or assumption of the lease); In re Standard Furniture, 3 Bankr. 527, 530 (Bankr. SD Cal. 1980). In *Arzola*, the landlord was also allowed an administrative claim for damage to the leased premises occurring during the custody and control of the trustee. Expenses of cleaning the premises may also be allowed as an administrative claim. See In re Standard Furniture, 3 Bankr. 532 (Bankr. SD Cal. 1980).

However, new Section 365(d)(3) of the 1984 Amendments (for nonresidential leases of real property) appears to modify the rule mentioned above that the trustee (or debtor in possession) is liable for the reasonable value prior to assumption or rejection of the lease. Section 365(d)(3) provides that "the trustee shall timely perform all of the obligations of the debtor, except those specified in section 365(b)(2), arising from and after the order for relief under any unexpired lease of nonresidential real property, until such lease is assumed or rejected, notwithstanding section 503(b)(1) of this title." The effect of this appears to be that the estate is liable as a priority administrative expense for the rent reserved under such a lease for the period before assumption or rejection of the unexpired lease on nonresidential real estate. The reasonable-value rule appears to continue to apply for nonresidential leases of realty and personal property.

[16] 11 USC §§ 507(a)(1), 503(b)(3)(A).

[17] 11 USC § 503(b)(3)(B).

[18] See 11 USC §§ 503(b)(3)(E), 543(c)(2). Generally, the custodian will be required to turn over the property to the trustee or debtor in possession. See discussion at ¶ 13.05[3]. "Custodian" is defined in Section 101(10) to include a receiver, trustee, assignee under a general assignment for the benefit of creditors or trustee or a receiver appointed or authorized to enforce a lien against property. A state court wage earner receiver has been held to be a "custodian"; however, the state court award of compensa-

Where a case is converted from either Chapter 11 or 13 to a Chapter 7 case, the administrative expenses of the Chapter 7 case have priority over the carryover administrative expenses of the Chapter 11 or 13 case.[19] For parties in Chapter 11 or 13 cases who may be relying on their administrative expense priority in that proceeding, Section 726 subordinates those expenses to the new administrative expenses. This subordination, particularly in a Chapter 11 case, poses a hazard. For example, a secured party who is lending to the Chapter 11 debtor may, in part, be relying on an administrative priority as part of the security.[20] However, if the Chapter 11 case is converted to a Chapter 7 case, the administrative priority given to the secured lender will be subordinated to the Chapter 7 administrative expenses.

Also allowable as an administrative expense is the claim of a secured party who has been given "adequate protection" under either Section 362, 363, or 364 to secure or protect the value of the secured party's collateral. If the "adequate protection" turns out to be inadequate to protect that value, this inadequacy results in an administrative claim that has priority over all other administrative expenses.[21] For example, this could occur when the secured party has sought relief from the stay, the value of his secured claim has been determined, and the secured party has been given adequate protection in the form of substitute security. The substitute security turns out, however, to be insufficient to protect the value of the secured claim. An administrative expense priority could also occur when the secured party's collateral is to be used or sold by the trustee or the debtor in possession in a Chapter 11 case pursuant to Section 363 or 364. The secured party is given "substitute collateral" as part of the adequate protection, but this substitute security turns out to be inadequate to protect the value of the secured claim. In such cases, the secured party would then have a "super priority" administrative claim under Section 507(b).

## [2] Second Priority: "Involuntary Gap" Claims

As previously mentioned, in the case of an involuntary petition there is a period of time between the filing of the petition and entry of the "order for relief".[22] Claims arising in the ordinary course of the debtor's business or financial affairs during this "involuntary gap" (i.e., after the commencement of

---

tion to such a receiver was not res judicata with respect to the bankruptcy court's determination of the reasonable compensation allowable to the receiver-custodian as an administrative expense. In re Gomes, 19 Bankr. 9 (Bankr. DRI 1982).

[19] 11 USC § 726(b), as amended by 1984 Amendments § 479.

[20] See 11 USC §§ 364(b), 364(c). See generally "Structuring and Documenting Business Financing Transactions Under the Federal Bankruptcy Code of 1978," 35 Bus. Law. 1645 (1980).

[21] 11 USC § 507(b). This is commonly referred to as a "super priority" administrative claim.

[22] See ¶ 12.01[1].

the proceeding but before either the appointment of a trustee or the order for relief) are allowable as second-priority claims.[23]

### [3] Third Priority: Wage, Salary, and Related Claims

The "wage claim" priority in the Code is significantly broader than the comparable section under the old Bankruptcy Act.[24] In addition to covering unsecured "wages" and "commissions," Section 507(a)(3) expressly covers "salaries," thus including some claims that arguably would not have been covered under the Act. In addition, wage- or employment-related claims for vacation, severance, and sick leave, which today are so common and constitute a vital part of many workers' wages, are expressly included in this priority class.

However, this priority claim for wages, vacation, and sick pay is limited to the amount earned by an *individual* within the ninety days before the filing of the petition or the date of cessation of the debtor's business, whichever occurs first, with a ceiling on these priority claims of $2,000 per individual.[25] Claims for wages earned before the ninety-day period or in excess of the $2,000, although not entitled to priority, will be allowable as general claims. One court has held that a creditor who cashed the worthless payroll check of an employee of the debtor was entitled, as assignee, to the employee's wage priority position.[26]

### [4] Fourth Priority: Claims of Employee Benefit Plans

This priority had no counterpart under the 1898 Bankruptcy Act; the new Code recognizes that employment compensation now frequently includes not only direct wages but other significant "fringe benefits."[27] Unsecured claims for contributions to employee benefit plans are given fourth priority to the extent that they arise for services rendered by covered employees within 180 days of the earlier of the filing of the petition or the date of cessation of the debtor's business. These claims are closely related to and share, in part, the third priority for wages. In most instances, this priority for employee benefit plans is asserted by the administrator of the benefit plan, if one exists, and not by the individual employee.

---

[23] 11 USC § 507(a)(2).

[24] See 1898 Act § 64(a)(2).

[25] 11 USC § 507(a)(3); see In re Stunzi U.S.A., Inc., 7 Bankr. 401 (Bankr. WD Va. 1980) (claims of employees for money wages, for authorized deductions for bonds not purchased and delivered, and for severance pay were entitled to priority as were claims for vacation pay; this was so even though the employees had been terminated on April 4th when debtor closed the business, and the collective bargaining agreement provided that employees discharged prior to June 1st would not be entitled to vacation pay).

[26] In re Missionary Baptist Found. of Am., Inc., 12 Bankr. 570 (Bankr. ND Tex. 1981), aff'd, 667 F2d 1244 (5th Cir. 1982).

[27] See H.R. Rep. No. 595, 95th Cong., 1st Sess. 357 (1977); S. Rep. No. 989, 95th Cong., 2d Sess. 69 (1978).

The priority is limited to an amount equal to the number of employees covered by the plan multiplied by $2,000, less the aggregate amount paid to the employees under the wage (third) priority (i.e., the unused portion of the wage priority), less the aggregate amount paid by the estate on behalf of the employees to any other employee benefit plan.

The term "employee benefit plan," while not defined in the Code, has been construed as not being limited to fringe benefits that are the result of a collective bargaining agreement. A plan can include an informal health, life, and disability insurance plan maintained by an employer as a benefit for employees. Earned but unpaid premiums owed to the insurer under such a plan at the time of the petition are held to be "contributions" entitled to priority under Section 507(a)(4).[28]

In *In re Shearon*,[29] the court held that the claim of a union for employer contributions to vacation and holiday trusts was subject to the ninety-day limitation of the wage (third) priority even though the contributions were payable to a trustee rather than directly to the employees. The court also held that the union's claim for union dues and contributions to pension and education trusts was entitled to fourth priority.

### [5] Fifth Priority: Claims of Grain Producers and Fishermen

The 1984 Amendments created a new fifth priority for certain unsecured claims of grain producers and fishermen.[30] Allowed unsecured claims of an individual grain producer[31] against a debtor who owns or operates a grain storage for grain or the proceeds of grain are entitled to fifth priority in distribution to the extent of $2,000.[32] Likewise, allowed unsecured claims of individual U.S. fishermen against a debtor engaged in operating a fish producing or processing facility are entitled to fifth priority to the extent of $2,000.[33]

### [6] Sixth Priority: Consumer Deposits

A limited priority has been created to protect individuals who before commencement of the case have made deposits or down payments for the purchase of property or services. For each individual, allowed unsecured claims for deposits made before the commencement of the case in connection with the purchase, lease, or rental of property, or the purchase of services for personal,

---

[28] In re Saco Local Dev. Corp., 23 Bankr. 644, 646 (Bankr. D. Me. 1982). In construing the Bankruptcy Code, the court looked to the use of the term "employee benefit plan" as used in the Employee Retirement Income Security Act of 1979 (ERISA), 29 USC §§ 1001 et seq.

[29] 10 Bankr. 626 (Bankr. D. Neb. 1981).

[30] 11 USC § 507(a)(5), as added by 1984 Amendments § 350.

[31] "Grain producer" is defined in Section 557(b).

[32] 11 USC § 507(a)(5)(A).

[33] 11 USC § 507(a)(5)(B).

family, or household use are given priority to the extent of $900. The priority applies only for deposits made for property or services that were not delivered or provided and does not include deposits that are made for commercial purposes.[34]

Note that purchase price payments made under executory real estate contracts are protected by being given lien status under Section 365(j) to the extent of the debtor's interest in the property. To the extent there is a lien on the debtor's property for such payments, the claim is secured and thus does not share in this fifth priority.[35] However, to the extent these payments exceed the value of the debtor's interest in the property, they will be unsecured and the portion that is not secured would appear to qualify for the priority.

### [7] Seventh Priority: Certain Governmental Tax Claims

There are no dollar limitations on the priority for governmental tax claims although there are certain time-period limitations.[36] The priority is limited to unsecured claims, and to the extent that a governmental claim, although otherwise qualifying for the priority, is secured (e.g., by a tax lien on the debtor's property), it does not qualify for the priority.[37]

Bankruptcy courts may determine the amount or legality of any tax unless the amount or legality "was contested before and adjudicated by a judicial or administrative tribunal of competent jurisdiction before the commencement of the case."[38] A default judgment entered by a state court on a tax claim has been held not to be "contested and adjudicated" within the meaning of this section, and the amount and validity of the tax could be determined by the bankruptcy court.[39]

Determination of whether fees, levies, and the like are taxes is a federal question to be determined by the bankruptcy court.[40] Note that not all governmental charges and fees are "taxes."[41]

---

[34] 11 USC § 507(a)(6), as renumbered by 1984 Amendments § 350.

[35] 11 USC §§ 507(a)(6), 506.

[36] 11 USC § 507(a)(7), as renumbered by 1984 Amendments § 350.

[37] Note, however, that under Section 724(b) the tax lien may be subordinated to certain priority claims.

[38] 11 USC § 505(a).

[39] In re Tapp, 16 Bankr. 315 (Bankr. D. Alaska 1981). Cases pending before the Tax Court are subject to the automatic stay of Section 362 until the stay is removed. See 11 USC § 362(a)(8). Action to assess or collect taxes is also stayed. 11 USC § 362(a)(6). For a summary of the Code provisions dealing with the determination of tax liabilities, see Weintraub & Resnick, "Allowance of Claims and Priorities Under the New Bankruptcy Code," 12 U.C.C. L.J. 291, 319 (1980).

[40] In re Beaman, 9 Bankr. 539, 540-541 (Bankr. D. Ore. 1980); In re King, 19 Bankr. 936 (Bankr. ED Tenn. 1982).

[41] For a discussion of what characterizes a "tax," see In re Lorber Indus. of Cal. Inc., 675 F2d 1062 (9th Cir. 1982); In re South Atl. Packers Ass'n, Inc., 28 Bankr. 80 (Bankr. DSC 1983); In re Payne, 27 Bankr. 809 (Bankr. D. Kan. 1983).

Characterization of a particular tax is important, not only for purposes of distribution priority because of the different priority limits for the various classifications of taxes, but also for purposes of discharge. For example, certain tax claims are nondischargeable to the extent they are unpaid in the bankruptcy proceeding. Thus, from the debtor's viewpoint it is in his best interest to have the tax claims paid to the fullest extent possible in the bankruptcy proceeding.[42] Characterization of tax claims is also important in Chapter 11, because to be confirmed the plan must provide for cash payment of all Section 507(a)(6) priority tax claims.[43] Again, the amount of the tax priority may depend upon the characterization of the tax because of the different priority limits.

The seventh priority includes the following taxes in the order given.

### [a] Income and Gross Receipt Taxes

Income and gross receipt taxes are included in this priority for taxable years that ended on or before the filing of the petition and for which any required return was last due, including any extensions, after three years before the filing of the petition.[44]

---

[42] See, e.g., In re Tapp, 16 Bankr. 315 (Bankr. D. Alaska 1981), where characterization of the tax involved was critical for discharge purposes because of the differences in the limits on the priority for the various taxes.

Unsecured taxes or customs duties arising during the "involuntary gap" and having priority under Section 507(a)(2) are nondischargeable under Section 523(a)(1). Tax claims that have priority under Section 507(a)(6) also are nondischargeable under Section 523(a)(1). These exceptions to the effect of the discharge apply in Chapter 7, 11, or 13 proceedings. For discussion of nondischargeable claims, see Chapter 15. Note that the 1984 Amendments added new Section 507(a)(5), which gives fifth-priority status to certain claims of grain producers and fishermen, and redesignated former Section 507(a)(6) (dealing with priority tax claims) as Section 507(a)(7). Former Section 507(a)(5) (dealing with consumer deposits) was redesignated as Section 507(a)(6). In an apparent oversight, however, Section 523(a)(1)(A) was not amended to conform to this change; that is, the reference to "section 506(a)(6)" was not changed to read "section 507(a)(7)." Thus, as the statute presently reads, priority tax claims under new Section 507(a)(7) are not excepted from the effect and would appear to be dischargeable. Presumably, this oversight will be taken care of by a technical amendment and in the interim the courts may have to deal with the oversight and perhaps find some way of circumventing it.

[43] See 11 USC § 1129(a)(9)(C). Such cash payments may, however, be paid over a period not exceeding six years. Where cash payment is deferred, the deferred payments must be of a value, as of the effective date of the plan, equal to the allowed amount of the claim. In other words, because the payments are deferred, a "discount" may have to be added so that the total of the future payments is greater than the amount of the allowed claim. Deferred payments in an amount equal to the allowed claim would not give the claimant the present value of its claim, since a future payment is worth less than a present one.

Note that Section 1129(a)(9)(C) refers to Section 507(a)(6) (now the consumer deposit priority) and apparently should have been changed to Section 507(a)(7) (priority tax claims) to reflect renumbering by the 1984 Amendments.

[44] 11 USC § 507(a)(7)(A), as renumbered by 1984 Amendments § 350.

### [b] Property Taxes

Property taxes, if unsecured, have priority if they meet two requirements. First, they must be assessed before the petition; second, the last day on which payment could be made without penalty must be later than one year before the date the petition in bankruptcy was filed.[45] In many cases, real property taxes are secured by liens on the property of the debtor and thus are not covered by this priority.[46] Water and sewer taxes, which under state law were in the nature of property taxes, have been held to be entitled to this priority.[47]

### [c] Taxes Required to Be Collected or Withheld

Priority is given without limit to unsecured "taxes required to be collected or withheld and for which the debtor is liable in whatever capacity."[48] This category includes Social Security taxes, federal withholding taxes, and perhaps some state sales taxes.

One bankruptcy court has held that the liability for state sales taxes, which the debtor had assumed in a property settlement with her former husband, was not for taxes falling within the priority of Section 507(a)(6)(C) (now Section 507(a)(7)(C)), which has no limitation. Instead, it was a liability for an "excise" tax within Section 507(a)(6)(E) (now Section 507(a)(7)(E)), which has a time limitation on the priority.[49]

### [d] Certain Employment Taxes on Wages, Salary, or Commissions

Certain employment taxes on wages, salary, or commissions earned before the date of filing the petition are given priority, without limitation, under Section 507(a)(7)(D).[50]

---

[45] 11 USC § 507(a)(7)(B), as renumbered by 1984 Amendments § 350.

[46] If the tax lien can be avoided by the trustee under one of his avoiding powers (e.g., 11 USC § 545–statutory lien), then the tax agency should be entitled to priority. Cf. In re Garden Inn Steak House, Inc., 22 Bankr. 830 (Bankr. ND Ohio 1982).

[47] See In re Adams, 17 Bankr. 742 (Bankr. ED Pa. 1982), where failure to timely file proof of claim as a secured claim precluded consideration of the claim as a secured claim. Id. at 744 n.5.

[48] 11 USC § 507(a)(7)(C), as renumbered by 1984 Amendments § 350.

[49] In re Tapp, 16 Bankr. 315 (Bankr. D. Alaska 1981). The taxes in question, falling outside the three-year limit of Section 507(a)(6)(E), were thus not priority claims and not excepted from the effect of the discharge under Section 523(a)(1).

[50] In a Chapter 11 case, the claim of the state for unemployment taxes, which were secured by a lien that was avoided by the debtor in possession, was held to be a priority claim under this section. As a priority tax claim under Section 507(a)(6), the claim had to be paid in full under the plan for the plan to be confirmed under Section 1129(a)(9). In re Garden Inn Steak House, Inc., 22 Bankr. 830 (Bankr. ND Ohio 1982).

### [e] Excise Taxes

If a tax return is required, the priority for excise taxes[51] is limited to the tax on transactions for which a return was required to be filed within the three years before filing of the petition. If no tax return is required, the priority is limited to the tax on transactions within the three years before filing of the petition.

A state sales tax has been held to be an "excise tax" within Section 507(a)(7)(E),[52] as have mine reclamation fees under the Surface Mining Control and Reclamation Act of 1977.[53] The claim of a state for reimbursement from an employer for payments made under the State Industrial Accident Fund to injured employees has also been held to be an excise tax.[54] However, fees charged by the South Carolina Department of Agriculture for grading poultry to be shipped in interstate commerce were held not to be "excise taxes" and thus were not entitled to priority.[55]

### [f] Custom Duties

Certain custom duties with limits are given priority under Section 507(a)(7)(F). For example, custom duties arising out of the importation of merchandise entered for consumption within one year before the filing of the petition are priority claims under Section 507(a)(7)(F). This section should be consulted for details on other custom duties that fall within this priority.

### [g] Penalties That Are Compensation for Actual Loss

Certain penalties that are compensation for actual pecuniary loss are given priority under Section 507(a)(7)(G).[56]

A penalty assessed against a debtor for failure to file a report with respect to unpaid contributions to a state unemployment fund has been held to be a "forfeiture" and not a penalty to compensate for pecuniary loss within the Sec-

---

[51] 11 USC § 507(a)(6)(E), as renumbered by 1984 Amendments § 350.

[52] In re Tapp, 16 Bankr. 315 (Bankr. D. Alaska 1981).

[53] 30 USC §§ 1201 et seq.; see In re King, 19 Bankr. 936 (Bankr. ED Tenn. 1982). Such "fees," although not denominated by the Reclamation Act as a "tax," were held to be nondischargeable under Section 523(a)(1) as a priority "excise" tax.

[54] In re Beaman, 9 Bankr. 539 (Bankr. D. Ore. 1980). But see In re Payne, 27 Bankr. 809 (Bankr. D. Kan. 1983) (employer's obligation to Insurance Commission under Kansas Worker's Compensation Act not a priority tax under Section 507(a)(6) (now Section 507(a)(7)).

[55] In re South Atl. Packers Ass'n, Inc., 28 Bankr. 80 (Bankr. DSC 1983). The court held that the fees were not "taxes" because of their voluntary character: "[I]nvoluntariness is a fundamental characteristic of taxes." Id. at 82. See also In re Lorber Indus. of Cal., Inc., 675 F2d 1062 (9th Cir. 1982).

[56] 11 USC § 507(a)(7)(G), as renumbered by 1984 Amendments § 350.

tion 507(a)(6)(G) (now Section 507(a)(7)(G)) priority.[57] IRS tax penalties that do not represent actual pecuniary loss also do not qualify for this priority.[58]

### [8] Subrogation to Priority Status

In general, because of a specific provision in the Bankruptcy Code, the priority status of a creditor's claim does not pass to a subrogee of that claim. If a creditor has a third, fourth, fifth, or sixth priority claim, a party who is subrogated to the rights of that creditor, such as a codebtor or guarantor who pays the claim, does not receive the priority status of the creditor.[59] For example, in one case a debtor's former business partner paid partnership taxes for which the debtor had assumed liability. The former partner's subrogation claim under Section 509 was not entitled to the priority status of the IRS under Section 507(a)(6) (now Section 507(a)(7)) because of the express restriction of Section 507(d).[60] Similarly, an insurance company that, as surety for the debtor, had paid the debtor's state tax liability was denied Section 507(a)(6) (now Section 507(a)(7)) priority although the company had received an assignment from the state of its claim.[61] It is not clear whether a party that takes an assignment of a priority claim stands in the priority position of the assigning creditor or is to be treated as one "subrogated" within the meaning of Section 507(d) and thus barred from priority status by that section.[62] In *Woerner*, the court indicated that where the right to subrogation exists, an assignment adds nothing. The court further stated however, that "[i]t may be true that if an entity is truly an assignee § 507(d) would not bar assignment of the priority claim,"[63] citing *In re Missionary Baptist Foundation of America, Inc.*[64] In *Missionary Baptist*, a bankruptcy court held that a supermarket that had cashed payroll checks for employees of the debtor that subsequently were dishonored was entitled to assert as assignee, and not as subrogee, the employees' wage priority. This decision was affirmed on appeal.[65]

---

[57] In re Federal Insulation Dev. Corp., 14 Bankr. 362 (Bankr. SD Ohio 1981). As a "forfeiture" the claim would be entitled to distribution in the order prescribed by Section 726(a)(4), ranking below all claims except those for interest accruing during the case (i.e., postpetition interest).

[58] In re Coleman Am. Cos., 26 Bankr. 825 (Bankr. D. Kan. 1983).

[59] 11 USC § 507(d). This represents a change, at least for subrogees, from the prior law under the 1898 Act. See In re Missionary Baptist Found. of Am., 667 F2d 1244 (5th Cir. 1982). Note, however, that Section 507(d) does not bar subrogation with respect to administrative claims and "involuntary gap claims." See remarks of Senator DeConcini, 124 Cong. Rec. S17,411 (daily ed. Oct. 6, 1978); remarks of Representative Edwards, 124 Cong. Rec. H11,095 (daily ed. Sept. 28, 1978).

[60] In re DuBose, 22 Bankr. 780 (Bankr. ND Ohio 1982).

[61] In re Woerner, 19 Bankr. 708 (Bankr. D. Kan. 1982).

[62] See Collier on Bankruptcy § 507.07, at 507-49 (Matthew Bender, 15th ed. 1981).

[63] 19 Bankr. 712 (Bankr. D. Kan. 1982).

[64] 12 Bankr. 570 (Bankr. ND Tex. 1981).

[65] 667 F2d 1244 (5th Cir. 1982).

Although the subrogee may be barred from subrogation to the priority status of the creditor, *Woerner* held that the subrogee does succeed to the non-dischargeable quality of the creditor's claim.[66]

## ¶ 14.10 SECURED CLAIMS

Under the Code, it is more accurate to speak in terms of secured and unsecured claims rather than in terms of secured and unsecured *creditors*, since a given claim may be both secured and unsecured. Under Section 506, an allowed claim is a secured claim to the extent that it is secured by a valid lien on property of the estate and is an unsecured claim to the extent the amount of the claim exceeds the value of the collateral.[1] Note that an allowed claim is also secured to the extent that the creditor under Section 553 may set off a mutual debt owed by the creditor to the debtor's estate against the claim the creditor has against the estate.[2]

To be allowed as a secured claim, proof of claim must be properly and timely filed[3] and must include the written documents or duplicates thereof and proof of the perfection of the security interest. Failure to properly file proof of claim as a secured claim very likely means that the claim will be treated as an unsecured claim.[4] If the security interest is avoided by the trustee or the debtor in possession under one of the avoiding powers, the claim will be treated as an unsecured claim.[5]

Valuation of the security is to be "determined in light of the purpose of the valuation and the proposed disposition or use of such property and in conjunction with any hearing on such disposition or use or on a plan affecting such creditor's interest."[6]

---

[66] 19 Bankr. 712 (Bankr. D. Kan. 1982). The court acknowledged there was a split of authority under the 1898 Act.

[1] "Lien" is defined under Section 101(31) to include consensual security interests defined in Section 101(43) such as a real estate mortgage or a security interest in personal property. "Lien" also includes Section 101(30) nonconsensual judicial liens, such as judgment liens or liens created by execution, and Section 101(45) statutory liens, such as mechanic's or materialmen's liens.

[2] See discussion of setoff at ¶ 16.08.

[3] See supra ¶ 14.03[1]. In a Chapter 11 case the secured creditor will not be permitted to vote on a plan of reorganization unless the claim is allowed under Section 1126(a), although the claim is deemed allowed unless scheduled as disputed, contingent, or unliquidated.

[4] See, e.g., In re Adams, 17 Bankr. 742, 744 n.5 (Bankr. ED Pa. 1982).

[5] See Chapter 16.

[6] 11 USC § 506(a). Valuation of collateral for one purpose should not, at least theoretically, be binding for other purposes. See Weintraub & Resnick, "Allowance of Claims and Priorities Under the New Bankruptcy Code," 12 U.C.C. L.J. 291, 329 (1980); H.R. Rep. No. 595, 95th Cong., 1st Sess. 326 (1977).

The holder of a secured claim should recognize that after the filing of the petition in bankruptcy the creditor is subject to the "automatic stay" of Section 362, which is applicable in Chapter 7, 11, and 13 cases.[7] Any attempt to repossess or realize on the collateral, even though the secured claim may be in default, and even though the secured claimant may be in possession of the collateral,[8] is in violation of the stay and the creditor and perhaps even the counsel for the creditor may be held in contempt of court. Under the old Bankruptcy Act, in most cases if the secured party had acquired possession of the collateral before filing of the petition, then the bankruptcy court did not have summary jurisdiction over the property, and generally the secured creditor could proceed to realize on the collateral. However, under the Bankruptcy Code, after the filing of the petition, the district court has exclusive jurisdiction over the property of the debtor wherever the property is located.[9] Generally, after the petition is filed, any action by a secured claimant to collect, enforce, foreclose, perfect, or otherwise realize on its security will be subject to the stay regardless of who has possession of the collateral. In some cases an important exception in Section 362(b)(3)[10] permits perfection of a security interest after the petition is filed. If state law permits perfection of a security interest to relate back against parties that acquired an interest in the collateral before its perfection (a "grace period"), then the creditor may perfect its security interest after the petition is filed.[11] For example, for purchase-money security interests under the Uniform Commercial Code (UCC), Section 9-301(2) permits a ten-day grace period for perfection by filing. If the security interest is perfected by filing within that period, it is good against the rights of a lien creditor that arise between the time the security interest attaches and the time of filing of the financing statement.[12] This purchase-money security interest appears to be the type that could be perfected after the petition in bankruptcy is filed. The 1984 Amendments added an additional exception to the stay for the perfection of an interest "to the extent that such act is accomplished within the period provided under section 547(e)(2)(A)."[13] Section 547(e)(2)(A) speaks in terms of perfection of a transfer within ten days after the time the transfer takes effect between the transferor and the transferee. Thus, the 1984 addition to Section 362(b)(3) seems to except from the effect of the stay the perfection of a security interest if

---

[7] For a discussion of the automatic stay, see ¶ 12.05. The automatic stay does not apply to a codebtor, guarantor, or a surety, except in Chapter 13 for some consumer debts and where the codebtor or guarantor is an individual. See ¶¶ 12.05[2], 17.07[1]. Thus, where a creditor has "security" in the form of a nonbankrupt surety or guarantor, the creditor may enforce the claim against that party, including "affiliates" and subsidiaries. See Collier on Bankruptcy ¶ 362.04[1] (Matthew Bender, 15th ed. 1981).

[8] In re Murray, 5 Bankr. 732 (Bankr. D. Md. 1980).

[9] 28 USC § 1334(d), as added by 1984 Amendments § 101.

[10] 11 USC § 362(b)(3), as amended by 1984 Amendments § 441.

[11] See also 11 USC § 546(b).

[12] The ten-day grace period is from the time the debtor receives possession of the collateral.

[13] 11 USC § 362(b)(3), as amended by 1984 Amendments § 441.

it is made within ten days after the transfer takes effect between the parties. Note that under Section 547(e)(3), a transfer does not take effect until the debtor has acquired rights in the property transferred.

A secured party may seek relief from the stay under the provisions of Section 362(d). The stay terminates with respect to action against the property when the property is no longer property of the estate, for example, when the property has been abandoned or sold subject to the security interest or lien.[14]

If the security interest of the secured claimant is avoided by the trustee under one of the avoiding powers,[15] the claim is then treated as an unsecured claim[16] even though the claim arises after the petition is filed. If the lien is not avoided, the security interest or lien continues unless the secured claim is disallowed.[17] After termination of the stay, the security interest may be enforced, and relief from the stay does not have to be obtained.[18]

In some circumstances, particularly in a Chapter 11 case but also perhaps in a Chapter 7 case in which the trustee is permitted to continue the business for a limited purpose, the trustee may be permitted to use, sell, or lease collateral of the secured party.[19] To do so, however, the debtor in possession or the trustee may have to provide the secured party with "adequate protection" to protect the "value" of the secured claim. In effect, the secured creditor is given substitute collateral (i.e., "adequate protection") for the collateral used or sold. In the event the "adequate protection" (substitute collateral) turns out to be inadequate to protect the value of the secured party's collateral, the Code provides that the secured claimant is given an "administrative claim" for this inad-

---

[14] 11 USC § 362(c)(1). The stay terminates with respect to all other acts upon the earlier of the dismissal of the case or the time the discharge is granted or denied or the closing of the case. 11 USC § 363(c)(2). The secured creditor who is subject to the stay, however, may request and is entitled to "adequate protection" for the value of its collateral during the stay. See 11 USC § 362(a)(4). The trustee or the debtor in possession may be permitted to use, lease, or sell the collateral in the ordinary course of business or, with permission of the court and subject to certain restrictions, may sell, use, or lease property other than in the ordinary course of business. See 11 USC §§ 363, 364, and discussion at ¶ 13.11. For a discussion of the "automatic stay," see ¶ 12.05; for a discussion of the effect of "abandonment" on the stay, see ¶ 13.06.

[15] See generally Chapter 16.

[16] See 11 USC § 502(h) and discussion at supra ¶ 14.06[3].

[17] 11 USC § 506(d)(1); Weintraub & Resnick, "Allowance of Claims and Priorities Under the New Bankruptcy Code," 12 U.C.C. L.J. 328 (1980). In some rare circumstances, the lien may survive even though the secured claim is disallowed. See 11 USC §§ 506(d)(1), 506(d)(2), as amended by 1984 Amendments § 448.

[18] See In re Andrews, 22 Bankr. 623 (Bankr. D. Del. 1982); In re Nason, 22 Bankr. 690 (Bankr. D. Me. 1982); In re Grimes, 7 BCD 576 (Bankr. D. Kan. 1980.) Note that in Chapter 11, although confirmation of the plan discharges the debtor, subject to some exceptions (see Section 541(d)), after confirmation of the plan, the property dealt with by the plan is free and clear of all claims and interests of creditors except as provided for in the plan. In other words, after confirmation of the plan, secured creditors have no interest in the property except that given by the plan. See 11 USC § 1141(c), as amended by 1984 Amendments § 513.

[19] See 11 USC §§ 363, 364; see also discussion at ¶ 13.11.

equacy that has priority over all other administrative claims. In effect, the inadequately protected secured party is given a "super priority" administrative claim.[20]

An oversecured creditor (i.e., one whose collateral value exceeds the debt) is entitled to interest on the claim for the period that the claim is unpaid.[21] There is dispute, however, whether such interest is to be paid at the contract rate or some other rate such as the legal rate. Section 506(b) provides:

> To the extent that an allowed secured claim is secured by property the value of which, after any recovery under (c) of this section, is greater than the amount of such claim, there shall be allowed to the holder of such claim, interest on such claim, and any reasonable fees, costs, or charges provided [for] under the agreement under which such claim arose.[22]

The dispute is produced by the language and punctuation of Section 506(b). Does the clause "provided [for] under the agreement under which such claim arose" modify "interest on such claim" or only "reasonable fees, costs or charges"? At least two courts have held that the section does not require payment of interest at the contract rate.[23]

---

[20] 11 USC § 507(b); see Collier on Bankruptcy ¶ 507.05 (Matthew Bender, 15th ed. 1981). Collier suggests that where the case has been converted from a Chapter 11 or 13 case to Chapter 7 case, these carryover "inadequacy administrative claims" from the Chapter 11 or 13 case have priority over the Chapter 7 administrative claims.

[21] 11 USC § 506(b). This section has been held to be applicable in Chapter 13. See In re Brooks, 24 Bankr. 447 (Bankr. D. Kan. 1982) and cases cited therein; In re Caudle, 13 Bankr. 29 (Bankr. WD Tenn. 1981).

[22] 11 USC § 505(b), as amended by 1984 Amendments § 448. The bracketed word "for" indicates the addition made by the 1984 Amendments. The 1984 change does not appear to clear up the dispute over whether interest is to be paid at the contract rate or at some other rate.

[23] In In re Marx, 11 Bankr. 819, 820 (Bankr. SD Ohio 1981) the court said:

> "This statutory language is curiously and significantly, it seems, punctuated. The phrase 'interest on such claim' is set off by commas, and grammatically such separation leads to the conclusion that the following phrase–'reasonable fees, costs, or charges provided under the agreement under which such claim arose'–is meant to be separately considered. Thus, while 'interest' on such 'claim' is to be allowed in the situation where the property securing the claim is of greater value than the amount of the claim, it does not follow that such interest is to be that provided under the agreement. In other words, the modifier 'provided under the agreement' refers only to fees, costs, or charges, and not to interest."

The court in *Marx* held that the secured creditor was entitled to receive interest at the legal rate. See also In re Minguey, 10 Bankr. 806 (Bankr. WD Wis. 1981). In *Minguey* the court posed the construction problem in these terms: "Does the clause 'provided under the agreement under which such claim arose' identify the interest on such claim or only the "reasonable fees, costs or charges?" Id. at 808. In concluding that equitable principles should apply in determining the amount of interest the court stated:

> "Upon the conviction that by its enactment, § 506(b) was intended to be a codification and not a modification of the existing law, I am compelled to conclude that

In determining the appropriate interest rate, the courts have taken a variety of approaches and found various rates to be appropriate: the contract rate; the market rate the secured creditor would have been able to obtain on a similar transaction; the legal rate of interest; the appropriate rate in light of equitable considerations; or an average of some of these preceding rates.[24]

An oversecured creditor is also entitled to reasonable fees, costs, or charges provided for in the security agreement.[25] A prior secured party is entitled to interest even though this decreases the amount of security or proceeds available to a subordinate secured creditor and thereby increases the deficiency of the junior creditor.[26] Postpetition interest is payable to the senior oversecured creditor before prepetition interest is payable to a junior secured creditor.[27]

The trustee may recover from property that secures an allowed secured claim the reasonable and necessary costs and expenses of preserving or disposing of the property. These costs are recoverable to the extent of any benefit to the holder of the security interest.[28]

---

> the clause 'provided under the agreement under which such claim arose' does not modify the word interest and applies only to 'reasonable fees, costs, or charges.' "

Id. at 809. But see In re Elmwood Farm, Inc., 19 Bankr. 338 (Bankr. SDNY 1982) (interest payable according to rate provided for in the mortgage note); In re Brooks, 24 Bankr. 447 (Bankr. D. Kan. 1982) ("§ 506(b) only requires that the oversecured creditor receive some rate of interest. It doesn't require the contract rate of interest. . . ."). Cf. In re Evans, 20 Bankr. 175, 176–177 (Bankr. ED Pa. 1982) and cases cited therein dealing with the question of what interest rate or discount must be paid on deferred payments under Section 1325(a)(5) to secured claims under Chapter 13 plans to ensure that the secured creditor receives the "value" of his secured claim as of the effective date of the plan.

[24] See cases cited in In re Evans, 20 Bankr. 175, 176–177 (Bankr. ED Pa. 1982); Memphis Bank & Trust Co. v. Whitman, 692 F2d 427 (6th Cir. 1982). Similar questions have been raised in Chapter 11 decisions as to the appropriate "discount" to be given on certain claims to insure that the deferred payment gives the present economic "value" of the claim on the effective date of the plan as required under Section 1129. See, e.g., In re Nite Lite Inns, 17 Bankr. 367 (Bankr. SD Cal. 1982), and cases cited therein; In re Moore, 25 Bankr. 131 (Bankr. ND Tex. 1982); In re Bay Area Serv., 26 Bankr. 811 (Bankr. MD Fla. 1982); In re Barrington Oaks Gen. Partnership, 15 Bankr. 952, 964 (Bankr. D. Utah 1981).

[25] 11 USC § 506(b); see, e.g., In re Brooks, 24 Bankr. 447 (Bankr. D. Kan. 1982); cf. In re Roberts, 20 Bankr. 914 (Bankr. EDNY 1982) (under a strict construction of the term "agreement," attorney fees for pursuing a claim in bankruptcy were held not to be covered by the agreement).

[26] In re Anderson, 28 Bankr. 231 (Bankr. ND Ga. 1983).

[27] Wolohan Lumber Co. v. Robbins, 21 Bankr. 747 (Bankr. SD Ohio 1982).

[28] 11 USC § 506(c); see, e.g., In re Elmwood Farm, Inc., 19 Bankr. 338 (Bankr. SDNY 1982) (secured creditor's claim constituted 66 percent of the total allowed secured claims; therefore, the secured creditor should bear 66 percent of the total expense of preserving and liquidating the secured collateral).

## ¶ 14.11 SUBORDINATION OF CLAIMS

Although the old Bankruptcy Act did not have an an express statutory provision on subordination, the principle of equitable subordination was well recognized in case law.[1] Legislative history indicates that Section 510(c) was intended to codify this case law and that the bankruptcy court remains a court of equity.[2] The courts have frequently stated that the following conditions are necessary for equitable subordination:

(1) The claimant must have engaged in some type of inequitable conduct;
(2) The misconduct must have resulted in injury to the creditors of the bankrupt or conferred an unfair advantage on the claimant; and
(3) Equitable subordination of the claim must not be inconsistent with the provisions of the old Bankruptcy Act.[3]

A claim, however, should be subordinated only to the extent necessary to offset the unfair advantage or the harm suffered by the creditor on account of the inequitable conduct.[4] Actual fraud need not be established.[5] Dominant actual control by a creditor pursuant to a security agreement may be sufficiently inequitable conduct to justify subordination if it results in unfair advantage or harm to other creditors.[6] In one case, a creditor had paid twice for goods purchased from the debtor due to duplicate invoices and sought priority over other creditors based on the mistake in overpayment. Under the circumstances, however, the court held that subordination of other creditors was not justified.[7]

---

[1] See, e.g., Pepper v. Litton, 308 US 295 (1939); Taylor v. Standard Gas & Elec. Co., 306 US 307 (1939); In re Mobile Steel Co., 563 F2d 692 (5th Cir. 1977).

[2] See Collier on Bankruptcy ¶ 510.4 (Matthew Bender, 15th ed. 1981).

[3] See, e.g., In re Goodman Indus., Inc., 21 Bankr. 512, 523 (Bankr. D. Mass. 1982); In re Formaggio Mfg., Inc., 23 Bankr. 688, 692 (Bankr. DRI 1982); In re Bellucci, 24 Bankr. 493 (Bankr. D. Mass. 1982), aff'd, 29 Bankr. 814 (Bankr. App. Pan. 1st Cir. 1983) (application for equitable subordination of tax claim to claims of clients of attorney-debtor was denied); In re Lockwood, 14 Bankr. 374 (Bankr. EDNY 1981); In re Weeks, 28 Bankr. 958 (Bankr. WD Okla. 1983). For a discussion of equitable subordination, see generally Note, "Equitable Subordination of Shareholder Debt to Trade Creditors: A Reexamination," 61 B.U.L. Rev. 433 (1981); Note, "Deep Rock in the Deep South—Equitable Subordination of Claims in Fifth Circuit Bankruptcy Proceedings," 11 Cum. L. Rev. 619 (1980); Herzog & Zweibel, "The Equitable Subordination of Claims in Bankruptcy," 15 Vand. L. Rev. 83 (1961).

[4] In re T.E. Mercer Trucking Co., 16 Bankr. 176, 189 (Bankr. ND Tex. 1981).

[5] Id. at 189. The conduct of a telephone company in disconnecting the telephone service of a debtor in "violation of the language and spirit" of the automatic stay provisions of Sections 362 and 366 has been held to be sufficient to subordinate the claim of the company under Section 510(c)(1). In re Sayman's Inc., 15 Bankr. 229 (Bankr. ND Ga. 1981).

[6] In re T.E. Mercer Trucking Co., 16 Bankr. 176 (Bankr. ND Tex. 1981).

[7] In re David A. Rosow, Inc., 13 Bankr. 203 (Bankr. D. Conn. 1981).

Since equity will not enforce a penalty, subordination should not be granted where doing so operates only to penalize the claimant.[8]

Insiders such as corporate officers, directors, shareholders, or relatives who use their position to gain unfair advantage over other creditors may be subjected to equitable subordination.[9] Loans of "insiders" to the debtor (e.g., a loan by the sole stockholder to the corporation) are often examined carefully to determine if the "loan" in fact is a capital contribution that justifies subordination of the insider claim to the claims of other creditors.[10] In insider loan cases, the burden of proof for equitable subordination apparently requires that the challenge be more than a formal objection and that it be based on some "substantial factual basis." The insider is required to justify the loan only after such a showing has been made.[11]

The Code expressly sanctions the enforcement of subordination agreements.[12] It also broadly authorizes courts "after notice and a hearing,"[13] under

---

[8] In re Lockwood, 14 Bankr. 374, 381 (Bankr. EDNY 1981); In re Westgate-Cal. Corp., 642 F2d 1174 (9th Cir. 1981).

[9] See, e.g., In re Formaggio Mfg., Inc., 23 Bankr. 688 (Bankr. DRI 1982) (claim of officer and sole stockholder of debtor who siphoned off corporate money for bogus "salary" and "rent" that were not owed was subordinated under Section 510(c)).

[10] See, e.g., In re Rego Crescent Corp., 23 Bankr. 958, 963 (Bankr. EDNY 1982), where the court, quoting from *Pepper v. Litton*, said:

> "So called loans or advances by the dominant or controlling stockholder will be subordinated to claims of other creditors and thus treated in effect as capital contributions by the stockholder . . . where the paid in capital is purely nominal, the capital necessary for the scope and operations of the company being furnished by the stockholder as a loan."

Id. at 963. In addition, the court pointed out that "ordinarily the mere fact that a loan is from an insider will not justify subordination of the debt arising from that loan" and that additional equitable factors must exist. Id. at 964.

[11] See In re Rego Crescent Corp., 23 Bankr. 958, 967 (Bankr. EDNY 1982).

[12] 11 USC § 510(a); see also In re Cormarc, Inc., 29 Bankr. 569 (Bankr. SD Fla. 1983); Citibank, N.A. v. Smith Jones, Inc., 17 Bankr. 128 (Bankr. D. Minn. 1982) (intercreditor subordination agreement applied to and remained valid with respect to postpetition as well as prepetition debt). See generally Lopes, "Contractual Subordination and Bankruptcy," 97 Banking L.J. 204 (1980).

The House and Senate Reports stated:

> "A subordination agreement will not be enforced, however, in a reorganization case in which the class that is the beneficiary of the agreement has accepted, as specified in proposed 11 U.S.C. § 1126, a plan that waives their right under the agreement. Otherwise, the agreement would prevent just what chapter 11 contemplates; that seniors may give up rights to juniors in the interest of confirmation of a plan and rehabilitation of the debtor."

H.R. Rep. No. 595, 95th Cong., 1st Sess. 359 (1977); S. Rep. No. 989, 95th Cong., 2d Sess. 74 (1978).

[13] See 11 USC § 102(1), "Rules of Construction," which in effect defines the phrase. Note that the "after notice and a hearing" does not in all circumstances require a hearing. See, e.g., In re Hanline, 8 Bankr. 449 (Bankr. ND Ohio 1981). If no objection is made, no hearing is required.

principles of equitable subordination, and for purposes of distribution to subordinate allowed claims in whole or in part to other allowed claims.[14] One court has held that the debtor does not have standing to request equitable subordination, only a creditor or the trustee.[15]

For purposes of distribution, a claim for damages or for rescission arising from the purchase or sale of a security[16] of the debtor or an affiliate of the debtor[17] is subordinated to all other claims that are senior or equal to the security from which the claim for rescission or damages arises.[18] For example, if the claim for rescission or damages relates to a subordinated debenture, the claim is subordinated to other debt claims that are senior or equal to the debenture. In a claim for damages based on the purchase of an equity security (stock), the claim is subordinate to the claims of all creditors, and would be treated as the claim of an equity security holder. In effect, the claim for damages or rescission with respect to a security is derivative of the security to which it relates.[19]

---

The House and Senate reports stated:

> "Thus, hearing will not be necessary in every instance. If there is no objection to the proposed action, the action may go ahead without court action. This is a significant change from present law, which requires affirmative approval of the bankruptcy judge for almost every action. The change will permit the bankruptcy judge to stay removed from the administration of the bankruptcy or reorganization case, and to become involved only when there is a dispute about a proposed action, that is, only when there is an objection."

H.R. Rep. No. 595, 95th Cong., 1st Sess. 315 (1977); S. Rep. No. 989, 95th Cong., 2d Sess. 27 (1978).

[14] 11 USC § 510(c), which permits subordination of "claims" to "claims," and 'interests" to "interests," but does not authorize subordination of "claims" to "interests." See Collier on Bankruptcy ¶ 510.14 (Matthew Bender, 15th ed. 1981).

[15] In re Weeks, 28 Bankr. 958 (Bankr. WD Okla. 1983); cf. In re Lockwood, 14 Bankr. 374, 381 (Bankr. EDNY 1981).

[16] "Security" is defined in Section 101(41).

[17] "Affiliate" is defined in Section 101(2).

[18] 11 USC § 510(b) as amended by 1984 Amendments § 451.

[19] H.R. Rep. No. 595, 95th Cong., 1st Sess. 359 (1977); S. Rep. No 989, 95th Cong., 2d Sess. 74 (1978). For a thorough discussion, see also H.R. Rep. No. 595, 95th Cong., 1st Sess. 194–196 (1977).

# 15

# Bankruptcy: Discharge

## ¶ 15.01 INTRODUCTION

For individuals and for some corporations and other debtors in Chapter 11 rehabilitation proceedings, the ultimate benefit of bankruptcy proceedings frequently is a discharge of debts, which permits the debtor a "fresh start" unencumbered by most prebankruptcy obligations.[1] For individuals, discharge may be accomplished either through a "straight" Chapter 7 liquidation proceeding or through a Chapter 13 proceeding.[2] Discharge may even be accomplished through a Chapter 11 proceeding if that appears to be more appropriate for an individual than Chapter 13.[3] For a corporation, Chapter 11 presents the only opportunity for obtaining a discharge; only individuals may obtain a discharge in Chapter 7, and a corporation is not eligible for Chapter 13.[4]

The nature of how a discharge is obtained for an individual in a Chapter 13 proceeding differs significantly from discharge in a Chapter 7 proceeding. In a Chapter 7 case, the debtor's nonexempt assets are liquidated and distributed to the creditors. In the normal course of this proceeding, the debtor obtains a general discharge of most debts owed at the time the petition was filed. In many Chapter 7 cases, the discharge is granted as a matter of course if no objection is properly made to the discharge. If there is no objection to discharge, the discharge is generally granted in a relatively short period of time. Even though a general discharge is granted, however, certain debts may be excepted from the effect of the discharge or are nondischargeable. In contrast, in a Chapter 13 case, the discharge does not result as a matter of course following the filing of the petition. In a Chapter 13 case, the debtor must obtain approval of a plan, which might propose, for example, to pay 50 percent on all debts over the life of the

---

[1] See 11 USC § 727(b).

[2] See discussion of Chapter 13 proceedings at Chapter 17.

[3] As previously noted in ¶ 12.03, there are limits on the amount of secured and unsecured debt that an individual or an individual and spouse may owe and still be eligible for Chapter 13.

[4] See discussion at ¶ 12.03.

plan with the payments to be made out of the future earnings or other regular income of the debtor. Upon completion (not merely confirmation) of the Chapter 13 plan, the debtor is then discharged from the debts covered by the plan. In some circumstances even though the Chapter 13 debtor does not complete payment under the plan, he may obtain a "hardship" discharge.[5] In either case, however, discharge for an individual in Chapter 13 is based on payment of some portion of the discharged debts through the future earnings or other regular source of income of the debtor. In contrast, the Chapter 7 discharge is, in effect, the result of liquidation and payment of creditors through the nonexempt assets of the debtor existing at the time the petition is filed.

Discharge for individuals, corporations, and other debtors in Chapter 11 differs from discharge under both Chapters 7 and 13. A Chapter 11 proceeding normally does not involve a liquidation proceeding but rather a reorganization of the debtor's affairs, with the intention of rehabilitating the debtor through restructuring of the debt and other claims against the debtor. Frequently, this is accomplished by stretching out debt payments and paying less than the full amount of the general claims; payment may be made in various ways and over extended periods of time. In a Chapter 11 proceeding, a plan of reorganization is proposed that sets forth how the creditors will be dealt with and what they will receive. Unless the plan or the order confirming the plan provides otherwise, confirmation of a Chapter 11 plan discharges prepetition debts and certain debts that arose after the petition was filed but that are treated as if they arose before the petition.[6] Confirmation of a plan discharges debts regardless of whether proof of claim is filed or whether the claim is allowed.[7] Note, however, that confirmation of the plan is not a discharge if the Chapter 11 plan for an individual, corporation, or a partnership is a plan of liquidation and the debtor does not engage in business after consummation of the plan and if the debtor would be denied a discharge under Section 727(a) in a Chapter 7 proceeding.[8] Under these circumstances, a corporation or a partnership is not eligible for a discharge since only individuals are permitted to receive a discharge

---

[5] See Chapter 17 for more detailed discussion. The Chapter 13 discharge based on full performance discharges all debts except debts nondischargeable under Section 523(a)(5) (support, maintenance, and alimony) and certain long-term obligations. 11 USC § 1328(a). A "hardship" discharge is a more limited discharge and does not discharge secured claims or any debts that are nondischargeable under Section 523(a). 11 USC § 1328(c).

[6] 11 USC § 1141(d)(1). For an individual debtor, note that confirmation of the Chapter 11 plan does not discharge any debt that is excepted from discharge under Section 523 ("nondischargeable debts"). 11 USC § 1141(d)(2). For corporations, partnerships, and other nonindividual debtors, however, the dischargeability or nondischargeability of debts under Section 523 is of no importance. Debts are discharged by confirmation of the plan even if they are the type of debt that would be nondischargeable for an individual under Section 523. Nondischargeable debts are discussed at infra ¶ 15.07.

[7] 11 USC § 1141(d)(1)(A).

[8] 11 USC § 1141(d)(3). Note that, unless otherwise specified, "Section" refers to a section of the Bankruptcy Code (Title 11 of the U.S. Code).

in Chapter 7.[9] This provision is intended to prevent a debtor who otherwise would be unable to obtain a discharge in a Chapter 7 liquidation from obtaining a discharge by a Chapter 11 plan of liquidation by not engaging in business after consummation of the plan. If the individual debtor does engage in business after consummation of the plan, a discharge may be obtained after a Chapter 11 liquidation if the individual is otherwise eligible for a discharge under Section 727(a).[10] However, as previously noted, the individual debtor would not be discharged of nondischargeable debts. In a Chapter 11 case, discharge is based on confirmation of the plan and not on performance of the plan (or the excuse of performance due to "hardship"), as is the case in Chapter 13 proceedings.

In addition to the sections already mentioned, Sections 727 and 523 of the Bankruptcy Code (the Code) deal with discharge and are of primary importance to the debtor. Section 727 sets forth the grounds for denial of a general discharge; Section 523 sets forth the types of debts that are nondischargeable—that is, debts that are excepted from the effect of the discharge.[11] If one of the grounds given in Section 727 for denial of discharge is successfully asserted, no debts are discharged and a determination of the nondischargeability of debts under Section 523 does not have to be made. In these circumstances, all that has been accomplished for the debtor is a liquidation of his nonexempt property and a satisfaction of creditors to the extent that they have received a distribution from the estate. However, even though a general discharge is granted, this does not mean that all debts will be discharged since some debts may be nondischargeable. If properly and successfully invoked, Section 523 means only that the specific debt determined to be nondischargeable is enforceable after the discharge. In exceptional cases where the creditor has grounds for both objecting to a discharge under Section 727 and for having a claim determined to be nondischargeable under Section 523, it generally is to his advantage to assert Section 523 rather than Section 727. If the discharge is denied, the creditor then may have to compete with all of the other creditors for postbankruptcy assets. On the other hand, if a discharge is granted and the creditor's claim is nondischargeable, there may be less competition from other creditors for these assets. Note, however, that the trustee or another creditor may be able to assert the Section 727 grounds and block a general discharge.

---

[9] 11 USC § 727(a)(1).

[10] 11 USC § 1141(d)(3).

[11] In many respects these two sections are quite similar to their counterparts under the 1898 Bankruptcy Act, Sections 14 and 17. Thus some case law under the 1898 Act is relevant under the Code, particularly with respect to specific debts that are excepted from the effect of the discharge under Section 523. There is a rapidly developing body of case law under the new sections, however. Additional materials that deal with discharge include Rendleman, "The Bankruptcy Discharge: Toward A Fresher Start," 58 N.C.L. Rev. 723 (1980); Ayers, "Reforming the Reform Act: Should the Bankruptcy Reform Act of 1978 Be Amended to Limit the Availability of Discharge to Consumers?" 17 New Eng. L. Rev. 719 (1982); Lander, "An Analysis and Comparison of the Nondischargeability Provisions of Chapter 11 and Chapter 13 of the Bankruptcy Code," 27 St. Louis U.L.J. 639 (1983); Sullivan, Warren, & Westbrook, "Limiting Access to Bankruptcy Discharge: An Analysis of the Creditors' Data," 1983 Wis. L. Rev. 1091.

In counseling the client on the advisability of a Chapter 7 "straight" liquidation case, counsel must be aware of when a discharge may not be obtained, or if it is obtained, which debts may be excepted from the effect of the discharge. From the viewpoint of a debtor-client, little more than liquidation of the debtor's nonexempt property may occur if a discharge is not obtained or if the most pressing debts (such as alimony, child support, tax claims, or perhaps willful and malicious tort claims) are not affected by a discharge. On the other hand, from the viewpoint of a creditor-client, it is equally important to know when and how a discharge may be blocked and what claims may be excepted from the effect of the discharge. Counsel for creditors also must be aware of the procedures for properly and timely obtaining a determination of the dischargeability of a debt. Knowledge of the discharge aspects of bankruptcy may be extremely important for both debtors and creditors in prebankruptcy negotiation and bargaining.

In some circumstances, a discharge of some but not all of the debtor's obligations may make it easier for the debtor to deal with the nondischargeable debts after bankruptcy. In other circumstances, where discharge of pressing debts is unlikely either because a discharge may not be granted or important debts will be excepted from the discharge, an option other than Chapter 7 may be a more appropriate alternative. As previously noted, some individuals may be able to use either Chapter 11 or 13. Chapter 13 generally is a more attractive alternative because of its relative simplicity, greater flexibility, and easier method of obtaining confirmation of a payment plan without creditor approval.[12] In considering the possibility of bankruptcy, counsel is advised to carefully review with the client both Sections 727 and 523 before arriving at a decision on which alternative is more appropriate. In the past, debtors have filed "straight" bankruptcy petitions but failed to obtain a discharge or to discharge a primary obligation as a result of the attorney's failure to carefully consider the dischargeability questions at the counseling and decision-making stage. This chapter deals primarily with Sections 727 and 523 as they relate to Chapter 7 proceedings. Certain material, however, is also relevant to discharge in Chapter 11 and Chapter 13 cases.

## ¶ 15.02 NATURE AND EFFECT OF DISCHARGE

A discharge under Chapter 7 relieves the debtor of liability for all scheduled and dischargeable debts that arose before the date of the order for relief.[1] In addition, debtors will be relieved of some debts that are incurred after the

---

[12] See discussion in Chapter 17. See generally Moller, "It Isn't Only For Wage Earners Anymore: The Individual in Business and Chapter 13 of the Bankruptcy Code," 17 Hous. L. Rev. 331 (1980); Lander, "An Analysis and Comparison of the Nondischargeability Provisions of Chapter 11 and Chapter 13 of the Bankruptcy Code," 27 St. Louis U.L.J. 639 (1983); Van Baalen, "Bankruptcy Code Chapter 13—What Price the 'Better Discharge'?" 35 Okla. L. Rev. 455 (1982).

[1] 11 USC § 727(b).

filing of the petition but that are treated as if they arose before the filing under Section 502(f).[2] The discharge voids any judgment obtained at any time on any debt that is discharged, whether or not discharge of the debt is waived.[3] In addition, the discharge operates as an injunction against commencement or continuation of an action to collect, recover, or offset any discharged debt as a personal liability of the debtor.[4] Under Section 523, however, some debts are expressly made nondischargeable.[5] Unless excepted from the discharge, debts are discharged even if no proof of claim is filed under Section 501 and whether or not the debt is allowed under Section 502.[6] In the case of a secured claim, unless the security interest is avoided under one of the avoiding powers of the trustee or of the debtor, the lien or security interest continues even though the debt is discharged.[7]

For an individual debtor, if no objection to discharge is timely filed, the discharge is granted as a matter of course without the necessity of an application for discharge. If a timely objection to discharge is made, the bankruptcy

---

[2] 11 USC § 727(b). As reported in the *Congressional Record*: "The provision makes clear that the debtor is discharged from all debts that arose before the date of the order for relief under Chapter 7 in addition to any debt which is determined under section 502 as if it were a prepetition claim. Thus, if a case is converted from Chapter 11 or Chapter 13 to a case under Chapter 7, all debts prior to the time of conversion are discharged, in addition to debts determined after the date of conversion of a kind specified in section 502 that are to be determined as prepetition claims." 124 Cong. Rec. H11,098 (daily ed. Sept. 28, 1978); 124 Cong. Rec. S17,415 (daily ed. Oct. 6, 1978).

[3] 11 USC § 524(a)(1).

[4] 11 USC § 524(a)(2). The Bankruptcy Amendments and Federal Judgeship Act of 1984, Pub. L. No. 98-353, §§ 308, 455, 98 Stat. 333 (hereafter referred to as the 1984 Amendments), made the following changes in Section 524(a)(2). Bracketed material indicates deletion by the 1984 Amendments; italicized material indicates added material.

> "(a) A discharge in a case under this title–
>
> (2) operates as an injunction against the commencement or continuation of an action, the employment of process, or [any act] *an act*, to collect, recover or offset any such debt as a personal liability of the debtor, [or from property of the debtor,] whether or not discharge of such debt is waived;"

Deletion of the words "or from property of the debtor" appears to be designed to state, in effect, that the permanent injunction of Section 524 does not apply to enforcement against property of the debtor, after discharge, of a lien or security interest that has survived bankruptcy even though the debt is discharged.

[5] See discussion at infra ¶ 15.07[3].

[6] 11 USC §§ 727(b), 524(a)(2). Proof and allowance of claims are covered in Chapter 14.

[7] Cowans, Bankruptcy Law & Practice § 5.3, at 257 (West, interim ed. 1983). As noted at supra ¶ 15.02 note 4, deletion of "property of the debtor" from coverage of the permanent injunction of Section 524 appears to be designed to permit a secured party to realize on the security interest without the necessity, after discharge, of obtaining relief from the permanent injunction, at least with respect to property that the debtor has claimed as exempt or that has been abandoned.

court must then determine whether a discharge will be granted. In either situation, after the court has determined whether or not to grant a discharge, the court, pursuant to Section 524(d), must hold what is often referred to as the "discharge hearing." At the discharge hearing, the court must inform the debtor either that a discharge has been granted or the reason why it has not been granted. If the debtor wishes to reaffirm a debt that is discharged, then the court must inform the debtor at the discharge hearing that reaffirmation is not required. It also must explain the legal effect and consequences of the reaffirmation agreement.[8] The debtor is required to attend this discharge hearing,[9] should be advised of his duty to attend, and should be warned that failure to attend may result in dismissal of the case or refusal to grant a discharge.[10]

However, the requirement presents real practical problems if the debtor has moved or if his attendance at the hearing means the loss of work. The debtor may be unable to attend for other substantial reasons. In exceptional circumstances, some courts have waived the requirement that the debtor attend the discharge hearing or have adopted other practical adjustments, such as permitting the debtor to transfer the discharge hearing to another bankruptcy court in the debtor's new location.[11]

---

[8] 11 USC § 524(d). For more detailed discussion of reaffirmation, see infra ¶ 15.08.

[9] 11 USC § 524(d). The statute speaks in terms of "a hearing at which the debtor shall appear in person."

[10] See, e.g., In re Martin, 12 Bankr. 319 (Bankr. SD Ala. 1981). In *Martin*, the court dismissed the bankruptcy petition of a man permanently confined to a nursing home as a result of a crippling stroke because of failure to attend the discharge hearing. Another court commented on *Martin*:

> "The court in *In re Martin* was unable to find in the statute 'any room for the application of equity,' and held that to grant an excuse in the absence of statutory latitude would be 'nothing more or less than judicial legislation.' The case stands for the proposition, we may presume, that a poor man should avoid having a stroke in the Southern District of Alabama."

In re Rennels, 37 Bankr. 81, 84 (Bankr. WD Ky. 1984).

[11] See In re Killett, 2 Bankr. 273 (Bankr. ED Va. 1980) (serviceman who had been transferred to England was excused from required attendance at the reaffirmation-discharge hearing); In re Edwards, 2 Bankr. 103 (Bankr. SD Fla. 1979). In *Edwards*, the wife had also filed a petition and her case had been consolidated with her husband's case. The court held that the wife's appearance was sufficient attendance for the husband, who was unable to attend because of military service. See also In re Garber, 4 Bankr. 684 (Bankr. CD Cal. 1980); In re Keefe, 7 Bankr. 270 (Bankr. ED Va. 1980); In re Mensch, 7 Bankr. 804 (Bankr. SDNY 1980) (excusing a disabled stroke victim from attending the discharge hearing). In In re Rennels, 37 Bankr. 81 (Bankr. WD Ky. 1984), the court found much more latitude in the statute and held that where motions to be excused from the discharge hearing were uncontested and there were no substantive issues to be determined at the hearing, the debtor's attendance was permissive and not mandatory. In these circumstances, the court said debtors will be excused from the discharge hearing upon a showing that:

(1) They have no motions of a substantive nature to bring before the court;

## ¶ 15.03 ENSURING THE "FRESH START": PROTECTING THE DEBTOR FROM DISCRIMINATORY TREATMENT

Even though a debtor receives a discharge in bankruptcy, consequences may be attached to the discharge that inhibit the debtor in making a "fresh start" and that may to some extent frustrate the effect of the discharge. Of course, the adverse consequences of bankruptcy are not limited to situations in which the debtor obtains a discharge and may be visited on the debtor-bankrupt even though no discharge is granted. Section 525 gives some limited protection to debtors against some consequences or action that might be imposed or inflicted upon the debtor because bankruptcy has been invoked.[1] Section 525 provides that "a governmental unit[2] may not deny, revoke, suspend, or refuse to renew a license, permit, charter, franchise, or other similar grant to, condition such a grant to, discriminate with respect to such a grant against, deny employment to, terminate the employment of, or discriminate with respect to employment against" a person solely because the person is or has been a debtor under the Code (or the 1898 Bankruptcy Act).[3] In addition, governmental discrimination is prohibited if it is made solely on the basis of insolvency before or during the case but before discharge is granted or denied, or on the basis that the debtor has not paid a debt discharged in bankruptcy. This provides very broad protection from discriminatory treatment by governmental agencies.[4]

---

(2) They have been fully and completely advised by their counsel of their rights and duties outlined in Section 524(d) and have received an emphatic warning of the postbankruptcy consequences of any reaffirmation agreement;
(3) Their counsel has advised them with reference to their individual case in the absence of any creditors;
(4) They fully and completely understand the advice given and still do not wish for any reason to attend; and
(5) Their counsel will officially report to the court that he has given the required advice and will stand accountable to the court for his failure to do so.

[1] See generally Comment, "Protection of a Debtor's 'Fresh Start' Under the New Bankruptcy Code," 29 Cath. U.L. Rev. 843 (1980).

[2] "Governmental unit" is defined in Section 101(24) to include federal, state, and municipal agencies. The Bankruptcy Commission had proposed including discrimination by private parties as well. See H.R. Rep. No. 595, 95th Cong., 1st Sess. 367 (1977); S. Rep. No. 989, 95th Cong., 2d Sess. 81 (1978).

[3] Section 525(a) contains an exception for action taken pursuant to the Perishable Agricultural Commodities Act of 1930, 7 USC §§ 499(a)–499(s); the Packers and Stockyards Act of 1921, 7 USC §§ 181–229; and Section 1 of a 1944 appropriations act for the Department of Agriculture, 7 USC § 204.

[4] The legislative history to Section 525 stated: "It [Section 525] does not prohibit consideration of other factors, such as future financial responsibility or ability, and does not prohibit imposition or requirements such as net capital rules, if applied non-discriminatorily." H.R. Rep. No. 595, 95th Cong., 1st Sess. 366–367 (1977); S. Rep. No. 989, 95th Cong., 2d Sess. 81 (1978). See generally Annot., 68 A.L.R. Fed. 137.

The 1984 Amendments to the Code added new Section 525(b), which provides additional protection to debtors. Under this Section,[5] a private employer is prohibited from terminating the employment of or discriminating with respect to employment against an individual who has been a debtor under either the Code or the 1898 Bankruptcy Act (or has been associated with such a debtor or bankrupt) solely on the basis that the person has been a debtor-bankrupt or has been insolvent before or during the bankruptcy case or has not paid a debt discharged in bankruptcy.

Section 525(a) codifies the result of *Perez v. Campbell*,[6] which held that a state would frustrate the congressional policy of a fresh start for a debtor if it were permitted to refuse to renew a driver's license as a result of a tort judgment from an automobile accident being unpaid due to a discharge in bankruptcy.[7] The legislative history indicates that Section 525 was not intended to be exhaustive, to permit other forms of discrimination, nor to prevent further case development.[8]

Several cases have dealt with the implications of *Perez* and the extent to which a discharge in bankruptcy can be considered in determining whether a debtor is entitled to practice law, particularly as it relates to "moral character." In *Florida Board of Bar Examiners Re Groot*,[9] the court held that an applicant for admission to the bar who had discharged student loans in bankruptcy could be admitted because default was justified by the surrounding circumstances. However, the court did not squarely address the constitutional issue of denying employment licenses on the basis of bankruptcy.[10] In the recent similar case of *Ex parte Gahan*,[11] the Supreme Court of Minnesota was confronted with an

---

[5] 1984 Amendments § 309.

[6] 402 US 637 (1971).

[7] H.R. Rep. No. 595, 95th Cong., 1st Sess. 366–367 (1977); S. Rep. No. 989, 95th Cong., 2d Sess. 81 (1978).

[8] The legislative history to Section 525 states:

> "The courts have been developing the *Perez* rule. This section permits further development to prohibit actions by governmental or quasi-governmental organizations that perform licensing functions, such as a State bar association or a medical society, or by other organizations that can seriously affect the debtor's livelihood or fresh start, such as exclusion from a union on the basis of a discharge of a debt to the union's credit union."

H.R. Rep. No. 595, 95th Cong., 1st Sess. 367 (1977); S. Report No. 989, 95th Cong., 2d Sess. 81 (1978).

[9] 365 So. 2d 164 (Fla. 1978).

[10] This case and an earlier Florida case, Florida Bd. of Bar Examiners Re G.W.L., 364 So. 2d 454 (Fla. 1978), in which a student who had discharged student loans was denied admission to the bar, are discussed in Note, "Constitutional Law–Florida Bar Admission Rule Requiring Good Moral Character Does Not Defeat the Purpose of the Federal Bankruptcy Act in Violation of the Supremacy Clause of the United States Constitution," 7 Fla. St. U.L. Rev. 587 (1979). See also Comment, "Evaluation of A Bar Applicant's Moral Character: May a State Consider the Circumstances Surrounding a Discharge in Bankruptcy?" 56 Ind. L.J. 703 (1981).

[11] 279 NW2d 826 (Minn. 1979); see also Annot., 4 A.L.R.4th 436 (1981).

applicant for admission to the bar who had discharged student loans in bankruptcy. Although the court expressed reservations as to whether it was constitutionally permissible to "consider the morality of any motivations for filing bankruptcy," it had no difficulty in concluding that federal law did not preclude it from evaluating the financial responsibility of an applicant and from considering the circumstances of the default. The court said:

> We hold that applicants who flagrantly disregard the rights of others and default on serious financial obligations, such as student loans, are lacking in good moral character if the default is neglectful, irresponsible, and cannot be excused by a compelling hardship that is reasonably beyond the control of the applicant.[12]

In denying admission of the applicant, the court further stated:

> Consistent with Gahan's Federal bankruptcy rights, we expressly state that our decision is in no way influenced by any assessment of Gahan's motivation in seeking bankruptcy. Nor are we interested in whether Gahan has any present willingness or ability to reaffirm the debts. We have based our decision solely on the circumstances surrounding Gahan's default on the student loan and the resulting failure to satisfy this important obligation. Gahan's subsequent conduct of obtaining discharge in bankruptcy and release from the default is of no concern to us.[13]

In a more recent case, the Supreme Court of Washington considered an application for reinstatement of an attorney who had been disbarred for misappropriation of client trust funds and criminal charges resulting therefrom.[14] Following disbarment, in a bankruptcy proceeding under the Code, the attorney had discharged the claims arising from the misappropriation of funds as well as certain income tax liabilities. The attorney had reaffirmed the obligations representing the misappropriated funds but had not reaffirmed the discharged tax liabilities. In permitting reinstatement of the attorney, the court held that reinstatement could not be conditioned on the attorney's repaying the discharged taxes. The court stated:

> The present case seems to be controlled by *Perez*, since any requirement that Mr. Batali repay debts discharged in bankruptcy would similarly contravene the federal policy of giving discharged debtors a fresh start. Further, Mr. Batali's case is distinguishable from *Gahan* in that Mr. Batali was forced to seek bankruptcy because of insufficient funds to immediately satisfy the full income tax obligation and because Mr. Batali has now voluntarily reaffirmed the other debts arising from his misconduct.[15]

---

[12] Ex parte Gahan, 279 NW2d 831 (Minn. 1979).

[13] Id. at 832.

[14] In re Batali, 98 Wash. 2d 610, 657 P2d 775 (1983).

[15] 98 Wash. 2d 618, 657 P2d 780 (1983).

Problems similar to those raised in *Perez* also have arisen in cases where educational institutions withheld college transcripts from students who discharged student loans.[16]

Section 366 provides additional protection to a debtor who invokes bankruptcy. Under this section, a utility may not alter, refuse, or discontinue service to a debtor, and it may not discriminate against a debtor (or the trustee) solely because a bankruptcy case has been commenced or a debt owed by the debtor to the utility for service rendered before the order for relief was not paid when due.[17] A utility may, however, refuse or discontinue service if the debtor does not within twenty days after the order for relief furnish adequate assurance or security for service after the date of the order for relief.[18] The effect of this provision is that for the first twenty days after the order for relief, the utility may not unilaterally alter, refuse, or discontinue service to the debtor. However, once the twenty-day period has expired, the utility may alter or refuse service unless the debtor has furnished adequate assurance of payment demanded by the utility. If the debtor is not satisfied with the "adequate assurance" demanded by the utility, he may apply to the bankruptcy court, and the court, after notice and a hearing, may order a reasonable modification of the amount of the deposit or other security for payment.[19]

## ¶ 15.04 GROUNDS FOR DENIAL OF DISCHARGE

Unless an objection to discharge is timely filed, an individual debtor in a Chapter 7 case will receive a discharge in the normal course of events; an individual does not need to request a discharge. Section 727 of the Code[1] sets forth ten grounds for denying discharge of a debtor in a Chapter 7 liquidation proceeding. As enacted, the Code makes several significant changes in the 1898

---

[16] See Comment, "Student Loans and the Withholding of Transcripts Under the Bankruptcy Reform Act of 1978," 30 U. Kan. L. Rev. 265 (1982); Note, "Bankruptcy–Private College May Withhold Transcripts From Students Whose Educational Loan Debts Were Discharged," 22 How. L.J. 155 (1979).

[17] 11 USC § 366(a), as amended by 1984 Amendments § 443.

[18] 11 USC § 366(b).

[19] Id. For an application of this section, see In re Stagecoach Enters., Inc., 1 Bankr. 732 (Bankr. MD Fla. 1979). The House Report on this section states:

> "This subsection will prevent a utility from terminating service until there is a court hearing, if there is a dispute over what is adequate assurance. The court is required, however, to hold the hearing as soon as practicable, but in any event within 30 days after the commencement of the case. If an estate is sufficiently liquid, the guarantee of an administrative expense priority may constitute adequate assurance of payment for future services. It will not be necessary to have a deposit in every case."

H.R. Rep. No. 595, 95th Cong., 1st Sess. 350 (1977).

[1] Title 11, Section 727, is the counterpart to Section 14 of the 1898 Act.

Bankruptcy Act (the 1898 Act). First, failure to pay filing fees is no longer a ground for barring a discharge; however, failure to pay filing fees may be a ground for dismissal of the case.[2] Second, under Section 14(c)(3) of the 1898 Act, obtaining money or property for a business on credit (or an extension or renewal of credit) by means of a false statement in writing, was grounds for barring a discharge. Under the Code, this has been eliminated as a ground for denying discharge. However, as discussed below, this conduct may be the basis for having a debt excepted from the effect of the discharge under Section 523(a)(2). Third, as noted below, a corporation or partnership cannot obtain a discharge in a Chapter 7 proceeding under the Code; only an individual may do so. Section 727(a) directs that the court shall grant a discharge unless one of the following ten grounds for denial of a discharge exists.

### [1] The Debtor Is Not an Individual: Section 727(a)(1)

Only an individual may receive a discharge in a Chapter 7 case. Other debtors, including corporations, associations, and partnerships, are not permitted to receive a discharge under Chapter 7. This restriction was designed to prevent trafficking in corporate shells and bankrupt partnerships.[3] As previously noted, however, these entities may obtain a discharge in a Chapter 11 proceeding if a plan is confirmed.[4]

### [2] Fraudulent Conveyance: Section 727(a)(2)

A discharge may be denied if the debtor within one year before the filing of the petition in bankruptcy has transferred, removed, destroyed, mutilated, or concealed his property with intent to hinder, delay, or defraud a creditor, or has permitted such action to take place. After the petition is filed, if the debtor transfers, conceals, destroys, or removes property of the estate with the intent to hinder, delay, or defraud a creditor or an officer of the estate (such as the trustee), this also constitutes grounds for denial of the discharge.

### [3] Unjustified Failure to Keep or Preserve Business or Financial Books, Documents, and Records of the Debtor: Section 727(a)(3)

A discharge may be denied if the debtor has "concealed, destroyed, mutilated, falsified, or failed to keep or preserve any recorded information, including books, documents, records, and papers from which the debtor's financial condition or business transactions might be ascertained, unless such act or fail-

---

[2] 11 USC § 707. See discussion of filing fees at ¶ 12.04[2].

[3] H.R. Rep. No. 595, 95th Cong., 1st Sess. 384 (1977); S. Rep. No. 989, 95th Cong., 2d Sess. 98 (1978). This change has little practical significance, since most of these entities cease to exist after bankruptcy.

[4] See 11 USC § 1141(d).

ure to act was justified under all of the circumstances."[5] Note, however, that this section does not require that every debtor must keep books, particularly if the debtor is a consumer or a nonbusiness debtor.[6] Generally, the courts have applied a test of reasonableness in light of the type and complexity of the business and the standards of the debtor's business community.[7] This section also denies discharge for falsification, destruction, or concealment of financial and business records, and requires the debtor to be responsible for maintaining records.

### [4] Knowingly and Fraudulently Making a False Oath or Presenting a False Claim: Section 727(a)(4)

If the debtor knowingly and fraudulently makes a false oath or account or presents or uses a false claim in connection with the bankruptcy case, this may be the basis for denial of a discharge. This includes a knowing and fraudulent statement in connection with the filing of the petition, and the schedules and statement of affairs that the debtor must file under oath. This also includes the examination of the debtor under oath at the meeting of creditors held pursuant to Section 341 as well as any other examination of the debtor.

In addition, if the debtor in connection with the case knowingly and fraudulently gives, offers, receives, or attempts to obtain money, property, or advantage or a promise of such, for acting or forbearing to act, this may be the basis for denial of discharge.[8] Similarly, knowingly and fraudulently withholding from an officer of the estate any recorded information, such as financial and business records, to which the officer is entitled to possession is grounds for denial of discharge.[9]

### [5] Failure to Satisfactorily Explain Any Loss of Assets or Deficiency of Assets to Meet the Debtor's Liabilities: Section 727(a)(5)

A discharge may be denied if the debtor had substantial assets before bankruptcy but no longer has such assets at the time of bankruptcy and can offer no reasonably satisfactory explanation of what was done with the assets. Cowans has suggested that "satisfactory explanation" is an objective rather than subjective test in the sense that the court must be convinced of the truth of the debtor's explanation and not of the wisdom of his expenditures or dispositions. The court cannot sit in moral judgment of the debtor.[10]

---

[5] 11 USC § 727(a)(3).

[6] Cowans, Bankruptcy Law & Practice §§ 5.28, 5.29, at 296–297 (West, interim ed. 1983).

[7] Id. at § 5.29, 297–298.

[8] 11 USC § 727(a)(4)(C).

[9] 11 USC § 727(a)(4)(D).

[10] Cowans, Bankruptcy Law & Practice § 5.43, at 315 (West, interim ed. 1983).

### [6] Refusal to Obey a Lawful Court Order or to Testify: Section 727(a)(6)

A discharge also may be denied if the debtor in the bankruptcy case has refused to obey any lawful order of the court other than an order to respond to a material question or to testify.[11] Thus, counsel for a debtor must stress to the debtor the importance of obeying the orders of the court, such as an order to turn over property, to appear for examination, or to appear at a hearing on an objection of discharge.[12] Failure to comply with the statutory duties imposed on the debtor by Section 521[13] does not appear to constitute "failure to obey a court order" unless there has been a court order directing the debtor to perform the statutory duty.[14]

In addition, discharge may be denied if the debtor has refused, on the grounds of the privilege against self-incrimination, to respond to a material question approved by the court or refuses to testify after immunity has been granted with respect to the matter on which the privilege was invoked. This means that a debtor cannot be denied a discharge for properly invoking the right against self-incrimination unless the debtor "has been granted immunity with respect to the matter concerning which such privilege was invoked."[15]

The House and Senate Reports summarized the changes made by Section 727(a)(6) in these terms:

> Part V is a significant departure from current law. Under section 7a(10) of the Bankruptcy Act, a debtor is required to testify in all circumstances, but any testimony he gives may not be used against him in any criminal proceedings, except testimony given in any hearing on objections to discharge. With that exception, section 7a(10) amounts to a blanket grant of use immunity to all debtors. Immunity for other witnesses in bankruptcy courts today is governed by part V of title 18.
>
> The consequences of a claim of privilege by a debtor under proposed law and current law differ as well. Under section 14(c)(6) of current law,

---

[11] 11 USC § 727(a)(6)(A).

[12] For extensive discussion, see Cowans, Bankruptcy Law & Practice §§ 5.49–5.54 (West, interim ed. 1983).

[13] Section 521 requires the debtor to file a list of creditors, schedules of assets and liabilities, a schedule of current income and expenditures, and a statement of financial affairs; to cooperate with the trustee, surrender property and records; and to appear at the discharge hearing required under Section 524(d) where the debtor is informed that the discharge has been granted and a "Miranda" warning given with respect to reaffirmation.

[14] Cowans, Bankruptcy Law & Practice § 5.52, at 325 (West, interim ed. 1983).

[15] 11 USC § 727(a)(6)(B). Under Section 344, immunity for the debtor or other persons required to submit to examination or to testify or to provide information in a bankruptcy case is to be granted under Part V of Title 18 of the U.S. Code. Under Title 18, for immunity (use immunity, not transactional immunity) to be granted by the federal district court, a request for immunity must be made by the U.S. attorney for the district (with the U.S. Attorney General's approval). See 18 USC § 6003.

any refusal to answer a material question approved by the court will result in the denial of a discharge, even if the refusal is based on the privilege against self-incrimination. Thus the debtor is confronted with the choice between losing his discharge and opening himself up to possible criminal prosecution.

Under section 727(a)(6) of the proposed title 11, a debtor is only denied a discharge if he refuses to testify after having been granted immunity. If the debtor claims the privilege and the United States attorney does not request immunity from the district courts, then the debtor may refuse to testify and still retain his right to a discharge. It removes the Scylla and Charibdis choice for debtors that exists under the Bankruptcy Act.[16]

### [7] Commission of Acts Mentioned in Sections 727(a)(2)–727(a)(6): Section 727(a)(7)

A discharge may be denied if the debtor committed, within one year before the filing of the petition, any of the following acts in connection with another bankruptcy case concerning an insider:[17]

(1) Made a fraudulent conveyance or fraudulently concealed property of the estate;
(2) Failed to keep or destroyed business or financial records;
(3) Committed a bankruptcy crime such as making a false oath or statement;
(4) Failed to satisfactorily explain the loss of assets;
(5) Refused to obey a lawful court order; or
(6) Refused to testify after having been given immunity.

Discharge also may be denied the debtor if he at any time during his own case has committed any other act covered by Sections 727(a)(2) through 727(a)(6).

### [8] Prior Discharge in a Case Commenced Within Six Years of Filing the Petition: Sections 727(a)(8)–727(a)(9)

If the debtor has received a discharge in a prior Chapter 7 or 11 case that was commenced within six years of filing the petition, a discharge will be denied.[18] If the debtor has received a discharge in a prior Chapter 13 case commenced within six years of filing the petition, a discharge may not be granted unless payments under the prior Chapter 13 plan totaled at least 100

---

[16] H.R. Rep. No. 595, 95th Cong., 1st Sess. 332–333 (1977); S. Rep. No. 989, 95th Cong., 2d Sess. 43–44 (1978).

[17] "Insider" is defined in Section 101(28).

[18] Similar limitations apply if the prior bankruptcy and discharge was under the 1898 Act. See 11 USC §§ 727(a)(8)–727(a)(9). See generally Comment, "Toward a Reform of the Six-Year Bar to Discharge in Bankruptcy," 97 Harv. L. Rev. (1984).

percent of the allowed unsecured claims in the case, or 70 percent of such claims, and the plan was proposed in good faith and represented the debtor's best effort.[19] For example, if the prior Chapter 13 case was commenced three years earlier and the debtor received a discharge through completion of a full payment plan or received a "hardship" discharge after paying 70 percent of the allowed unsecured claims, a discharge could be obtained. Note that the six-year time period runs from the commencement of the prior case in which the discharge was granted, and not from the time the discharge was granted. In other words, the six-year period runs from filing to filing.[20]

### [9] Waiver of Discharge: Section 727(a)(10)

The debtor may be denied a discharge if the court approves a written waiver of discharge that is executed by the debtor after the order for relief.[21]

## ¶ 15.05 OBJECTIONS TO DISCHARGE

An objection to discharge is made by a complaint and is an adversary proceeding covered by Part VII of the Bankruptcy Rules.[1] The complaint should be filed in the court in which the case is pending.[2] Under Bankruptcy Rule 4005, the plaintiff has the burden of proof at a trial on a complaint objecting to a discharge. If called as a witness, the debtor is required to attend the hearing on a complaint objecting to discharge.[3]

### [1] Who May Object to Discharge

Either the trustee (the U.S. trustee in districts with a "pilot program")[4] or a creditor may object to granting of a discharge on one or more of the stated grounds.[5] Under Section 704(6), the trustee has the duty to "if advisable, oppose the discharge of the debtor."[6] On request of a party in interest, the court may order the trustee to examine the debtor's acts and conduct to determine whether a ground exists for denial of discharge.[7]

---

[19] This six-year bar resulting from a prior discharge does not apply in Chapter 13 proceedings since Section 727(a) applies only to Chapter 7 proceedings.

[20] 11 USC §§ 727(a)(8)–727(a)(9).

[21] 11 USC § 727(a)(10).

[1] See B. Rules 4004(c)–4004(d), 7003.

[2] B. Rule 5005(a).

[3] B. Rule 4002; see also 11 USC § 521. As previously mentioned, denial of discharge may result if the debtor refuses to submit to appropriate examination.

[4] 11 USC § 15727.

[5] 11 USC § 727(c)(1).

[6] Use of the term "if advisable" seems to suggest that some discretion is given to the trustee as to whether to object to discharge.

[7] 11 USC § 727(c)(2).

### [2] When an Objection Must Be Made

The Code does not specify when objections to discharge must be filed. However, Bankruptcy Rule 4004 provides that in a Chapter 7 case, objections to discharge must be filed no later than sixty days after the first date set for the meeting of creditors held pursuant to Section 341. The bankruptcy court must give not less than twenty-five days' notice of the time fixed for filing of complaints objecting to the discharge.[8] In a Chapter 11 case, complaints objecting to the discharge must be filed no later than the first date set for the hearing on confirmation.[9] Generally, notice of the time for filing objections to the discharge is given with the notice of the order for relief and notice of the date set for the meeting of creditors.[10] On motion of a party in interest filed before the original period expires, the court, after hearing on notice, may for cause extend the time for filing a complaint objecting to discharge.[11] If no complaint objecting to discharge is timely filed, on expiration of the time for filing objections, the court is directed to grant the discharge unless the debtor is not an individual or the debtor has filed a waiver of discharge.[12] After the final order of discharge, notice of the discharge must be promptly sent to all creditors and to the trustee and his attorney.[13] A certified copy of the order of discharge may be registered in any other district by filing with the clerk of the bankruptcy court for the district. When the copy is registered, it has the same effect as the order of the court where registered.[14]

## ¶ 15.06 REVOCATION OF DISCHARGE

On request of the trustee (the U.S. trustee in a pilot district) or of a creditor, and after notice to the debtor and an opportunity for a hearing, the court may revoke a discharge if it was obtained through the debtor's fraud and the requesting party did not know of the fraud until after the discharge was

---

[8] B. Rule 4004(a); see also B. Rule 2002(f).

[9] B. Rule 4004(a).

[10] See Official Form 16; B. Rule 2002.

[11] B. Rule 4004(b).

[12] B. Rule 4004(c); Official Form 27. Upon motion of the debtor, however, the court may defer entry of an order granting discharge for thirty days. B. Rule 4004(c). This provision apparently is intended to permit the debtor time to perhaps settle, by reaffirmation, a nondischargeability complaint filed on a specific debt. For discussion of reaffirmation, see infra ¶ 15.08. To be enforceable, however, a reaffirmation agreement must be entered into before the discharge is granted. By deferring the discharge, the debtor may obtain time needed to negotiate settlement and reaffirmation. See Weintraub & Resnick, Bankruptcy Law Manual ¶ 3.04[5], at 3-19 (Warren, Gorham & Lamont, Inc. 1980).

[13] B. Rule 4004(g).

[14] B. Rule 4004(f).

granted.[1] The discharge also may be revoked if the debtor knowingly and fraudulently failed to report acquisition of or entitlement to property that should have been included in the estate or failed to deliver or surrender this property to the trustee.[2] Furthermore, the discharge may be revoked if the debtor committed one of the other acts specified in Section 727(a)(6), such as refusing to obey a lawful court order or to answer questions after having been granted immunity. A request for revocation of discharge based on fraud must be made within one year of the granting of the discharge. If a request is based on other grounds, it must be made within one year of the granting of discharge or the date of the closing of the case, whichever is later.[3]

The request for revocation of discharge is made by a complaint in an adversary proceeding under Bankruptcy Rule 7001 and is governed by Part VII of the Bankruptcy Rules.

## ¶ 15.07 EXCEPTIONS TO THE EFFECT OF DISCHARGE: NONDISCHARGEABLE DEBTS

Even though a debtor obtains a general discharge, some debts or claims against him may be nondischargeable if they fall within certain exceptions listed in Section 523. As discussed in the following paragraphs, in some cases the creditor must act in a timely manner to have the determination of nondischargeability made in the bankruptcy court; otherwise, the debt will be discharged. For other debts, the determination of discharge may be made at any time and the determination may be made by the bankruptcy court or any other appropriate nonbankruptcy court. The question of the nondischargeability of debts, however, arises only if the debtor obtains a discharge; if a discharge is not granted, it is unnecessary to determine whether any debts are excepted from the effect of the discharge.

As previously mentioned, in some circumstances a creditor may have a basis for objecting either to the general discharge or for having a specific claim excepted from the effect of the discharge. In these cases, it may be to the creditor's advantage not to object to the discharge but to have the debt determined

---

[1] 11 USC §§ 727(d)(1), 15727(b).

[2] 11 USC § 727(d)(2).

[3] 11 USC § 727(e). Bankruptcy Rule 9024 also makes it clear that a complaint to revoke a discharge in a Chapter 7 proceeding may be filed only within the time allowed by Section 727(e). The rule provides that a complaint to revoke an order confirming a Chapter 11 or 13 plan may be filed only within the time allowed by Section 1144 or 1330. The Advisory Committee Notes to the rule indicate that the purpose of the rule was to make it clear that the time periods of Sections 727(e), 1144, and 1330 could not be circumvented by the invocation of Federal Rule of Civil Procedure 60(b). Confirmation of the plan in Chapter 11 operates as a discharge, and under both Sections 1144 and 1330 the request for revocation must be made within 180 days of entry of the order of confirmation. In a Chapter 13 case, the request for revocation, based on a discharge obtained by the debtor through fraud, must be made within a year after the discharge is granted. 11 USC § 1328(e).

to be nondischargeable. This permits the creditor to enforce the nondischargeable claim against the debtor's postpetition assets without having to compete with other creditors whose claims have been discharged. Of course, it must be recognized that the trustee or other creditors still may block the general discharge. From a counseling viewpoint, an attorney who is exploring with a client the feasibility of filing a Chapter 7 petition or perhaps a petition under Chapter 11 or 13 must be concerned not only with the question of whether the debtor will receive a discharge but also must be concerned with the question of which debts are nondischargeable. From the perspective of the debtor, if the debtor's principal debts are nondischargeable in a Chapter 7 proceeding, Chapter 7 may prove to be little more than a liquidation proceeding without providing the debtor relief from the most pressing debts. Thus, in considering the feasibility of bankruptcy for a client, an attorney should take care to determine, to the extent possible, not only whether a discharge will be granted, but also which debts are important for a discharge, whether or not these debts are nondischargeable, and the likelihood of a creditor successfully invoking the nondischargeability provisions. Counsel should impress upon the debtor the importance of these considerations and the necessity for frank and full disclosure with respect to factors that are important in arriving at informed judgments on these questions. In some circumstances, because of the dischargeability questions, a Chapter 13 proceeding or perhaps even Chapter 11 may be a more attractive alternative for an individual than Chapter 7. In some instances, debts that are nondischargeable in a Chapter 7 proceeding may be discharged in a Chapter 13 case. The Chapter 13 discharge is discussed in greater detail in Chapter 17 of this book.

The exceptions to discharge or nondischargeable debts listed in Section 523 represent policy judgments that certain debts (such as support, alimony, and tax claims) should not be discharged because of the nature of the debts, despite the basic bankruptcy policy of providing the debtor with a "fresh start." To a large extent, the basic policy reflected by the exceptions is that discharge should be for the "poor but honest debtor."

## [1] Determining Dischargeability: Procedural Aspects

As in the case of objections to the general discharge under Section 727, creditors must be concerned with the procedural aspects of how, when, and in which court they must proceed to have a specific debt determined to be nondischargeable or excepted from the effect of the discharge under Section 523. These procedural details are critically important to creditors; in some cases, if the creditor does not act in a timely manner, nondischargeable debts will be discharged. For certain nondischargeable debts, the determination must be made in the bankruptcy court that has exclusive jurisdiction to determine nondischargeability of the claims and a complaint for determination of dischargeability must be filed within a specified time limit. For debts that are nondischargeable under Section 523(a)(2) (debts obtained by fraud or a false statement in writing), Section 523(a)(4) (embezzlement, larceny, fraud, or defalcation in a fiduciary capacity), or Section 523(a)(6) (willful and malicious injury), the determination of dischargeability must be made in the bankruptcy court (after notice and a hearing). If a complaint for determination of dischargeability is not timely filed, these debts will be discharged.[1]

If a creditor files a request for determination of dischargeability of a consumer debt under Section 523(a)(2) and the creditor is unsuccessful (i.e., the debt is held to be dischargeable), the court must award the debtor costs and reasonable attorney fees if the court finds that the position of the creditor was not substantially justified. An award may not be made if special circumstances make the award unjust as provided by Section 307(a)(3)

Generally, the first notice sent to creditors notifying them of the order for relief and setting the date for the first meeting of creditors also will fix deadlines for filing objections to discharge under Section 727 and for filing complaints for determination of dischargeability under Section 523(c).[2] In a Chapter 7 or 11 case, Bankruptcy Rule 4007(c) provides that a complaint to determine the dischargeability of any debt pursuant to Section 523(c) must be filed not later than sixty days after the first date set for a meeting of creditors and that the court must give not less than thirty days' notice of this deadline.[3] On motion made before the expiration of this period, after hearing on notice, the court for cause may extend the time for filing complaints.[4]

For other nondischargeable debts,[5] the determination of nondischargeability may be made either by the bankruptcy court or in another appropriate nonbankruptcy forum. The determination may be made at any time and need not be asserted within any time limit.[6] Bankruptcy Rule 4007(b) provides

---

[1] 11 USC § 523(c). If these debts are not scheduled in time to permit a timely filing of a request for a determination of dischargeability, the debt will not be discharged unless the creditor had notice or actual knowledge of the case in time for filing the request. 11 USC § 523(a)(3)(B).

[2] See B. Rule 2002(f).

[3] In a Chapter 13 case, on motion by a debtor for a discharge under Section 1328(b), the court must fix a time for filing of complaints to determine dischargeability under Section 523(c) and give not less than thirty days' notice of the deadline.

[4] B. Rule 4007(c).

[5] "Other nondischargeable debts" refers to debts specified in Sections 523(a)(1), 523(a)(3), 523(a)(5), and 523(a)(7)–523(a)(9). Note that due to a mistake in numbering in the 1984 Amendments, there are two Sections numbered 523(a)(9).

[6] If a complaint for such a determination were filed in a state court, it appears that the action could be removed to the federal district court under new Title 28, Section 1452(a) (added by 1984 Amendments § 101); the district court could then refer the matter to the bankruptcy court under Title 28, Section 157(a). However, the district court also could remand under Title 28, Section 1452(b) and the decision to remand or not to remand is not reviewable by appeal or otherwise. Upon removal and referral of the proceeding to the bankruptcy court, under Title 28, Section 157(b)(2)(I), the determination of dischargeability appears to be a "core proceeding." For discussion of removal in these circumstances under former Title 28, Section 1478 (identical in most respects to new Title 28, Section 1452), see Collier on Bankruptcy ¶¶ 523.06[13], 523.14[2], 523.15[6] (Matthew Bender, 15th ed. 1981).

that a complaint for determination of dischargeability that is not made under Section 523(c) (those nondischargeable claims that do not fall within the exceptions of Sections 523(a)(2), 523(a)(4), and 523(a)(6)) may be filed with the bankruptcy court at any time and the case may be reopened for the purpose of filing a complaint.[7]

The debtor or any creditor may file a complaint with the bankruptcy court. Filing the complaint commences an adversary proceeding under Bankruptcy Rule 7001 and is governed by Part VII of the Bankruptcy Rules.[8]

## [2] Questions of Res Judicata and Collateral Estoppel

With some frequency, the claim or debt for which a determination of dischargeability is sought will be represented by a judgment that has been obtained before bankruptcy in a nonbankruptcy court. In these cases, questions of res judicata and collateral estoppel are raised. For example, assume that the creditor had obtained a judgment against the debtor before bankruptcy and that the creditor asserts that the claim is nondischargeable under the "willful and malicious injury" exception.[9] In making the dischargeability determination, may the bankruptcy court look behind the judgment, the pleadings, findings of fact, and so on to determine the dischargeability issue? If the issue of whether an injury was "willful and malicious" was determined (or could have been determined) in the prior case, is the bankruptcy court bound by principles of collateral estoppel? These were issues of concern under the 1898 Act, which also have been raised in a number of cases under the Code.[10]

In *Brown v. Felsen*,[11] the U.S. Supreme Court considered the question of "whether a bankruptcy court may consider evidence extrinsic to the judgment and record of a prior state suit when determining whether a debt previously reduced to judgment is dischargeable under Section 17 of the Bankruptcy Act."[12] In

---

[7] See also 11 USC § 350(b).

[8] B. Rule 4007(e). Although the rule speaks in terms of "any creditor" filing a complaint for determination of dischargeability, Section 523(c) speaks in terms of the determination of dischargeability under that section being "on request of the creditor to whom such debt is owed." It is doubtful whether the rule is intended to confer "standing" on one creditor to obtain a determination of dischargeability of another creditor's claim. It would seem that the rule should be read to mean that any creditor may file a complaint for a determination of the debtor's own, not another's, obligation.

[9] 11 USC § 523(a)(6).

[10] See generally Comment, "Res Judicata and Collateral Estoppel in Bankruptcy Discharge Proceedings," 37 Wash. & Lee L. Rev. 281 (1980); Ferriell, "The Preclusive Effect of State Court Decisions in Bankruptcy," 58 Am. Bankr. L.J. 349 (1984).

[11] 442 US 127 (1979).

[12] Id. at 127–128.

*Brown v. Felsen*, a guarantor of a loan had been sued in a state court, along with the principal debtor. The guarantor had cross-complained against the principal debtor and alleged that the guaranty had been obtained "by misrepresentation and nondisclosures of material facts" by the principal debtor. However, the suit was settled by stipulations, which provided that the guarantor should have judgment against the principal debtor. Neither the stipulations nor the resulting judgment indicated the cause on which the principal debtor's liability was based. Subsequently, the principal debtor filed a petition in bankruptcy and the guarantor sought in the bankruptcy court to have his claim determined to be nondischargeable as a claim obtained by fraud, deceit, and malicious conversion.[13] The principal debtor-bankrupt contended that res judicata barred relitigation of the bankrupt's debt even though the application of Section 17 of the 1898 Act had not been in issue in the state proceeding. The bankruptcy court had confined its consideration to the judgment, pleadings, and exhibits that were in the state court record and declined to hear other evidence. The bankruptcy court had concluded that neither the judgment nor the record showed that misrepresentation was the basis for the judgment. The claim, therefore, was dischargeable. The case was affirmed on appeal by the Court of Appeals for the Tenth Circuit. However, the U.S. Supreme Court held that res judicata did not apply and that "the bankruptcy court is not confined to a review of the judgment and record in the prior state-court proceedings when considering the dischargeability of the respondent's debt." The Court reasoned in part that certain dischargeability questions, including those raised in this case,[14] were in the exclusive jurisdiction of the bankruptcy court. To apply res judicata would be inconsistent with the policy of this exclusive jurisdiction and adoption of a policy of res judicata would in effect force these questions back into the state courts.

However, with respect to the question of collateral estoppel the Court in *Brown v. Felsen* stated:

---

[13] 1898 Act §§ 17(a)(2), 17(a)(4). The case arose under the 1898 Act.

[14] Prior to 1970, the determination of the dischargeability of debts (i.e., whether a debt was excepted from the effect of the discharge) could be made in a state court. These determinations generally were made by a state court when the creditor, after bankruptcy, pursued a claim. The debtor asserted as an affirmative defense the discharge in bankruptcy and the creditor then relied on the nondischargeability of the specific claim. However, particular problems and alleged abuse by creditors arose with respect to the dischargeability of three types of claims: (1) claims based on obtaining money or property by false representations or by a false statement in writing, (2) claims based on fraud or defalcation in a fiduciary capacity, and (3) claims for willful and malicious injury. In 1970, the 1898 Act was amended to place the determination of the dischargeability of these three types of claims within the exclusive jurisdiction of the bankruptcy court. See 1898 Act § 17(c)(2). With some refinement, these are essentially the three types of nondischargeable claims that are placed within the exclusive jurisdiction of the bankruptcy court under Section 523(c) of the Code.

This case concerns res judicata only, and not the narrower principle of collateral estoppel. Whereas res judicata forecloses all that which might have been litigated previously, collateral estoppel treats as final only those questions actually and necessarily decided in a prior suit. [Citations omitted.] If, in the course of adjudicating a state-law question, a state court should determine factual issues using standards identical to those of § 17, then collateral estoppel, in the absence of countervailing statutory policy would bar relitigation of those issues in the bankruptcy court.

Because respondent does not contend that the state litigation actually and necessarily decided either fraud or any other question against petitioner, we need not and therefore do not decide whether a bankruptcy court adjudicating § 17 question should give collateral estoppel effect to a prior state judgment. In another context the Court has held that a bankruptcy court should give collateral estoppel effect to a prior decision. [Citation omitted.] The 1970 amendments to the Bankruptcy Act, however, has [sic] been interpreted by some commentators to permit a contrary result. [Citations omitted.][15]

## [3] Nondischargeable Debts

Section 523(a) sets forth ten classes or types of debts that are nondischargeable.[16] As just discussed, for debts of the type specified in Sections 523(a)(2), 523(a)(4), and 523(a)(6), the determination of dischargeability must be made by the bankruptcy court. A complaint requesting the determination must be filed within the time limits set by Bankruptcy Rule 4007.[17] The ten classes of nondischargeable debts are considered below.

### [a] Taxes and Custom Duties: Section 523(a)(1)

A debtor generally may not discharge the liability for most taxes because of the exception provided in Section 523(a)(1). A debtor may not discharge

---

[15] 442 US 139 n.10 (1979). For a case applying res judicata where the trial court had made specific findings of fact, see In re Manitta, 1 Bankr. 393 (Bankr. CD Cal. 1979).

[16] As originally enacted, the 1978 Bankruptcy Reform Act contained nine types of nondischargeable debts. However, the 1984 Amendments added an additional type of nondischargeable debt: judgments or consent decrees for a liability incurred as a result of the debtor's operation of a motor vehicle while legally intoxicated. See new 11 USC § 523(a)(9); 1984 Amendments § 371. In an apparent oversight, the new Section 523(a)(9) was added by the 1984 Amendments and the existing Section 523(a)(9) was not renumbered. For a discussion of the existing Section 523(a)(9), which deals with claims not discharged in a prior bankruptcy proceeding, see infra ¶ 15.07[3][i]. Thus, at present, there are two Sections numbered 523(a)(9).

[17] For discussion of acquiescence as a defense, see Comment, "Creditor Acquiescence as a Defense to an Exception to Discharge in Bankruptcy," 58 Ind. L.J. 319 (1982).

income and gross receipt taxes that are unsecured[18] and are priority claims under either Section 507(a)(2) (second priority) or Section 507(a)(6) (sixth priority).[19] These claims are nondischargeable even if no proof of claim is filed, regardless of whether or not the claim is allowed.[20] However, it normally is to the debtor's advantage to file proof of claim for the nondischargeable taxes if the taxing agency does not. To the extent that the nondischargeable taxes are paid by distribution from the estate, the nondischargeable postbankruptcy liability will be reduced. If the taxing agency does not file proof of claim, either the debtor or the trustee may do so.[21] Under Section 507(a)(2), claims for income and gross receipt taxes that arise in the ordinary course of the debtor's business during the "involuntary gap" (i.e., before the order for relief or the appointment of a trustee, whichever is earlier) are priority claims and thus are not dischargeable. Under Section 507(a)(6),[22] unsecured claims of governmental units[23] for income or gross receipt taxes for which a return was due in the three years before the filing of the petition are given priority and thus are also nondischargeable.[24] In addition, income or gross receipt taxes assessed within 240 days of filing the petition are nondischargeable.[25] Included in this priority class are property tax claims (to the extent they are unsecured)[26] that are

---

[18] If the taxes are secured, for example, by a valid tax lien, they are not priority tax claims and will not be covered by this exception but will be satisfied from the lien.

[19] Section 523(a)(1)(A) states that debts for a tax or custom duty of the kind specified in Section 507(a)(2) or 507(a)(6) are nondischargeable. The 1984 Amendments added new Section 507(a)(6), giving fifth-priority status to certain claims of grain producers and fishermen, and redesignated former Section 507(a)(6) (dealing with priority tax claims) as Section 507(a)(7) and former Section 507(a)(5) (dealing with consumer deposits) as Section 507(a)(6). However, in an apparent oversight, Section 523(a)(1)(A) was not amended to conform to this change; that is, the reference to "Section 507(a)(6)" was not changed to read "Section 507(a)(7)." Thus, as the statute presently reads, priority tax claims under new Section 507(a)(7) are not excepted from the effect and would appear to be dischargeable. Presumably, this oversight will be taken care of by a technical amendment. In the interim, the courts may have to deal with the oversight and find some way of circumventing it. The discussion in this section assumes that this oversight will be corrected and that priority tax claims under new Section 507(a)(7) are intended to be nondischargeable, as was the case before the 1984 Amendments.

[20] 11 USC § 523(a)(1)(A).

[21] 11 USC § 501(c); see discussion at ¶ 14.03.

[22] As previously noted, this should read "Section 507(a)(7)"; see supra ¶ 15.07[3][a] note 19.

[23] "Governmental unit" is defined in Section 101(24) to include federal, state, and municipal governments and other agencies of these governments.

[24] 11 USC § 507(a)(7)(A)(i) (formerly 11 USC § 507(a)(6)(A)(i)). Of course, to the extent that these taxes are paid through distribution of the estate, they will be discharged.

[25] 11 USC § 507(a)(7)(A)(ii) (formerly 11 USC § 507(a)(6)(A)(ii)).

[26] Real property tax claims frequently are secured by a valid lien on property of the estate. To that extent, they are not priority claims but are satisfied by the lien.

assessed before filing the petition. If these claims were last payable without penalty within the year before filing the petition, they are considered to be nondischargeable.[27] In addition, the debtor may not discharge as a priority tax claim his liability for taxes that were required to be collected or withheld and for which he is liable in any capacity.[28] For example, this includes claims against a debtor who is a responsible officer of a corporation and is liable for income withholding taxes and FICA taxes that are required to be withheld and properly remitted; if this is not done, certain officers may be personally liable for the taxes.[29] In addition, certain employment and excise taxes and custom duties are nondischargeable.[30] Tax penalties relating to any of the nondischargeable tax claims of Section 507(a)(7) (formerly Section 507(a)(6)) that are compensation for actual pecuniary laws are also nondischargeable.[31]

In addition to the above nondischargeable priority taxes, taxes are nondischargeable for which a return was required to be filed, if the return was not filed or if it was filed after the date the return was due and within two years of filing the petition.[32] If the debtor made a fraudulent return with respect to a tax or willfully attempted to evade or defeat a tax, these taxes are nondischargeable.[33]

### [b] Claims for Money, Property, or Services, or an Extension or Renewal of Credit Obtained by Fraud or False Pretenses: Section 523(a)(2)

Claims against the debtor for money, property, services, or an extension or renewal or refinancing of credit are nondischargeable to the extent they are obtained by false pretenses, false representation, or actual fraud.[34] If the property, money, services, or the extension or renewal of credit was obtained by a statement in writing, the claim arising therefrom is nondischargeable if the creditor can establish certain elements. It must be shown that the written state-

---

[27] 11 USC § 507(a)(7)(B) (formerly 11 USC § 507(a)(6)(B)).

[28] 11 USC § 507(a)(7)(D) (formerly 11 USC § 507(a)(6)(D)).

[29] See 26 USC § 6672; Cowans, Bankruptcy Law & Practice § 6.15, at 385 (West, interim ed. 1983); see also Note, "Dischargeability of Corporate Withholding Taxes in the Personal Bankruptcy Suit of a Responsible Officer," 16 Wake Forest L. Rev. 103 (1980).

[30] See 11 USC §§ 507(a)(7)(D)–507(a)(7)(F) (formerly 11 USC §§ 507(a)(6)(D)–507(a)(6)(F)).

[31] 11 USC § 507(a)(7)(G) (formerly 11 USC § 507(a)(6)(G)).

[32] 11 USC § 523(a)(1)(B).

[33] 11 USC § 523(a)(1)(C).

[34] 11 USC § 523(a)(2)(A). It is important to observe that nondischargeability of claims under this section must be asserted in the bankruptcy court and within the time limits set by Bankruptcy Rule 4007. If a complaint for determination of dischargeability is not timely filed, these claims are discharged. See Section 523(c) and discussion at supra ¶ 15.07[1].

ment was materially false respecting the debtor's (or an insider's) financial condition, that the creditor reasonably relied on the false statement, and that the debtor caused the written statement to be made or published with intent to deceive.[35]

The 1984 Amendments added new Section 523(a)(2)(C),[36] under which a consumer debt[37] that is incurred on or within forty days before the order for relief is presumed to be nondischargeable if it is owed to a single creditor and totals more than $500 for "luxury goods or services." Cash advances totaling more than $1,000 that are extensions of consumer credit under an open-end credit plan[38] and obtained by an individual on or within twenty days before the order for relief are presumed to be nondischargeable under Section 523(a)(2)(A). This provision creates the presumption that these debts were obtained by false pretenses, a false representation, or actual fraud. Under Federal Rule of Evidence 301, which applies in bankruptcy proceedings, this presumption is rebuttable and does not shift the burden of proof from the creditor but puts the burden on the debtor of going forward with the evidence to rebut the presumption. In order for this presumption to apply under the new section, note that the claim arising under an open-end credit plan must be for cash advances that are extensions of consumer credit under the plan. The use of the term "cash advances [that are] extensions of consumer credit" clearly seems to indicate that mere extensions of credit by a credit purchase under an open-end credit plan that do not constitute "cash advances" do not have the benefit of the presumption. From a policy viewpoint, it is difficult to see why cash advances should be given the benefit of the presumption while extensions of credit are not; however, the section appears to have this effect.[39] Although "luxury goods or services" are not otherwise defined, the statute does state that they do not "include goods or services reasonably acquired for the support or maintenance of the debtor or a dependent of the debtor."[40]

If a creditor files a request for determination of dischargeability of a consumer debt under Section 523(a)(2) and the creditor is unsuccessful (i.e., the

---

[35] 11 USC §§ 523(a)(2)(B)(i)–523(a)(2)(B)(iv). See generally Zaretsky, "The Fraud Exception to Discharge Under the New Bankruptcy Code," 53 Am. Bankr. L.J. 253 (1979).

[36] 1984 Amendments § 307(a)(3).

[37] "Consumer debt" is defined in Section 101(7) as "debt incurred by an individual primarily for a personal, family or household purpose."

[38] Section 523(a)(2)(C) provides: "An extension of consumer credit under an open end credit plan is to be defined for purposes of this subparagraph as it is defined in the Consumer Credit Protection Act (15 USC 1601 et seq.)."

[39] Some claims for credit purchases may have the benefit of the presumption, if they fall within the "luxury goods or services" provision, which has the lower dollar threshold and longer period preceding the bankruptcy (order for relief). The twenty- and forty-day periods offer potential for "bankruptcy planning" for the debtor by delaying the filing of the voluntary petition to avoid the presumption.

[40] 11 USC § 523(a)(2)(C).

debt is held to be dischargeable), the court must award the debtor costs and reasonable attorney fees if the court finds that the position of the creditor was not substantially justified. An award may not be made, however, if special circumstances make the award unjust.[41]

### [c] Unscheduled Claims: Section 523(a)(3)

Claims that have not been listed or scheduled on the schedules that the debtor is required to file[42] are not discharged under certain conditions. This exception, of course, makes it quite important for the debtor and his attorney to ensure that all claims and creditors are listed on the schedules so that unscheduled claims are not excepted from the discharge. One purpose of listing the creditors is to provide the creditors with notice of the bankruptcy proceeding, notice of the time for filing proof of claim, and notice of the deadline for filing complaints objecting to discharge under Section 727 or for determination of dischargeability of claims under Section 523(c). If creditors are not aware of or fail to receive notice of the bankruptcy cases, they could be prejudiced if rights were foreclosed (e.g., by failure to timely file proof of claim or to timely file a complaint to determine dischargeability of a particular debt). To prevent this injury, if the creditor is prejudiced by lack of notice of the case with respect to filing proof of claim or a request for determination of dischargeability, the claim generally will not be discharged. Specifically, if a claim is neither scheduled nor listed and is not a nondischargeable claim under Section 523(a)(2) (obtaining money or property by fraud or a false statement in writing), Section 523(a)(4) (claims arising from larceny, embezzlement, defalcation in a fiduciary capacity), or Section 523(a)(6) (willful and malicious injury), the claim will not be discharged unless it was scheduled or listed in time to permit the creditor to timely file proof of claim. However, if the creditor had sufficient notice or actual knowledge of the bankruptcy case to timely file proof of claim, the debt will be discharged.[43] If a claim is nondischargeable under Section 523(a)(2), 523(a)(4), or 523(a)(6) and is not scheduled in time for the creditor to timely file proof of claim and a timely request for a determination of the dischargeability,[44] the claim will not be discharged unless the creditor had sufficient notice or actual knowledge of the case for timely filing proof of claim and a timely request for determination of dischargeability.[45] The mere fact that the creditor is not formally scheduled and notified does not mean that the debt will be nondischargeable if the creditor knew or had notice of the case in time to

---

[41] 11 USC § 523(d), as amended by 1984 Amendments § 307(a)(3).

[42] 11 USC § 521(1).

[43] 11 USC § 523(a)(3)(A).

[44] As previously discussed, for claims excepted from discharge under Sections 523(a)(2), 523(a)(4), and 523(a)(6), the determination of the dischargeability must be made in the bankruptcy court based on a timely filed complaint.

[45] 11 USC § 523(a)(3)(B).

take timely action with respect to filing proof of claim or a request for determination of dischargeability.

### [d] Claims Arising From Defalcation in a Fiduciary Capacity or From Embezzlement or Larceny: Section 523(a)(4)

Claims arising from larceny or embezzlement are nondischargeable, as are claims arising from fraud or defalcation that occurs while the debtor acts in a fiduciary capacity.[46] A number of cases have dealt with the question of the meaning of "acting in a fiduciary capacity." Generally, the cases have held that the debtor must have been acting in a technical trust capacity.[47] In a recent decision under the 1898 Act, the Court of Appeals for the Fifth Circuit stated:

> The Court made clear that the technical trust required by *Chapman* must exist prior to the act creating the debt and without reference to that act. See *Upshur v. Briscoe*, 138 U.S. 365, 378 . . . As the Court stated in *Davis v. Aetna Acceptance Co.,* 293 U.S. 328, 333 . . . "It is not enough that by the very act of wrongdoing out of which the contested debt arose, that the bankrupt has become chargeable as a trustee *ex maleficio*. He must have been a trustee before the wrong and without reference thereto."[48]

A number of cases have dealt with the question of whether certain statutory provisions that impose obligations on parties (such as a statute requiring a contractor to use funds only for the construction for which it is advanced) also create a "fiduciary" relationship within the meaning of that term for dischargeability purposes. Although the cases are not consistent, a number have held that these provisions do create a "fiduciary" capacity.[49]

---

[46] It is important to observe that nondischargeability of claims under this section must be asserted in the bankruptcy court and within the time limits set by Bankruptcy Rule 4007. If a complaint for determination of dischargeability is not timely filed, these claims are discharged. See 11 USC § 523(c) and discussion at supra ¶ 15.07[1].

[47] See, e.g., Chapman v. Forsyth, 2 US 202 (1844) and cases discussed in In re Angelle, 610 F2d 1335, 1338–1341 (5th Cir. 1980).

[48] Id. at 1338.

[49] See In re Romero, 535 F2d 618 (10th Cir. 1976). In *Romero*, funds advanced to a contractor were not used for construction for which the advance was made. The court held that the contractor was acting in a fiduciary capacity based on a state statute that provided for revocation of the contractor's license if funds were not properly applied. The court took the view that the statute imposed a fiduciary duty. For a similar holding, see also In re Kawczynski, 442 F. Supp. 41 (WDNY 1977). For a case holding that there was no "fiduciary capacity" under a specific statute, see In re Thornton, 544 F2d 1005 (9th Cir. 1976). In *Thornton*, an employer violated a written agreement and failed to remit funds deducted from employees' wages to a vacation-savings fund. The employer was held not to be a "fiduciary" even though a state statute made such conduct unlawful. See also In re Dloogoff, 600 F2d 166 (8th Cir. 1979); In re Angelle, 610 F2d 1335, 1338 (5th Cir. 1980).

### [e] Claims for Alimony, Maintenance, or Support: Section 523(a)(5)

Claims of a spouse, former spouse, or child of the debtor for alimony, maintenance, or support are nondischargeable.[50] However, to the extent that the claim for alimony, maintenance, and support has been assigned to a third party (voluntarily or by operation of law or otherwise), the claim is dischargeable unless the assignment was made pursuant to Section 402(a)(2b) of the Social Security Act or the claim was assigned to the federal government, a state, or any political subdivision of a state.[51]

Characterization or determination of what constitutes "alimony, maintenance, or support," in contrast to what is a "property settlement," is a federal bankruptcy question, although the bankruptcy court will look to state law to determine the rights of the parties.[52]

---

[50] 11 USC § 523(a)(5). See generally Annot., 69 A.L.R. Fed. 403 (1984); Schiffer, "The New Bankruptcy Reform Act: Its Implications for Family Law Practitioners," 19 J. Fam. L. 1 (1980); Comment, "Congressional Intent in Excepting Alimony, Maintenance, and Support From Discharge in Bankruptcy," 21 J. Fam. L. 525 (1983); Comment, "The Bankruptcy Reform Act of 1978: Dischargeability of Obligations Incurred Under Property Settlements, Separation Agreements, and Divorce Decrees," 12 U. Balt. L. Rev. 520 (1982); Comment, "Discharge of Post-Marital Support Obligations Under the New Bankruptcy Code," 4 Harv. Women's L.J. 177 (1981); Note, "Dischargeability of Divorce Related Expenses Under 11 U.S.C. § 523(a)(5)," 35 Okla. L. Rev. 799 (1982).

[51] As a condition of receiving certain Social Security benefits, such as benefits received under the Aid for Dependent Children program, a person may be required to assign support and alimony to the agency proving the assistance. If the assignment is made pursuant to Section 402(A)(2b) of the Social Security Act, it would not render the assigned claim of the agency dischargeable. As originally adopted, Section 523(a)(5) did not contain this provision relating to assignment under the Social Security Act but was amended in 1981 to prevent discharge of such assignments. Omnibus Budget Reconciliation Act of 1981, Pub. L. No. 97-35, 95 Stat. 863, 11 USC § 523(a)(5). See Williams v. Department of Social & Health Servs., 529 F2d 1264 (9th Cir. 1976). In In re Glidden, 653 F2d 85 (2d Cir. 1981), the court upheld the constitutionality of discharging under Section 523(a)(5)(A) claims assigned to the state as a condition of eligibility for public assistance. The 1981 amendment now makes such claims nondischargeable and, in effect, overrules *Glidden*. The 1984 Amendments to Section 523(a)(5)(A) further broadened the exception from discharge to include any claim for alimony, maintenance, or support that "has been assigned to the Federal Government or to a State or any political subdivision of such state." 1984 Amendments § 454(b)(2).

[52] The legislative history to Section 523(a)(5) stated:

> "What constitutes alimony, maintenance, or support will be determined under the bankruptcy laws, not State law. Thus, cases such as *In re Waller*, 494 F2d 447 (6th Cir. 1974); Hearings, pt. 3, at 1308-10 are overruled, and the result in cases such as *Fife v. Fife*, 1 Utah 2d 281, 265 P.2d 642 (1952) is followed."

H.R. Rep. No. 595, 95th Cong., 1st Sess. 364 (1977); S. Rep. No. 989, 95th Cong., 2d Sess. 79 (1978); see also In re Calhoun, 715 F2d 1103 (6th Cir. 1983); In re Warner, 5 Bankr. 434 (Bankr. D. Utah 1980); In re Pelikant, 5 Bankr. 404 (Bankr. ND Ill. 1980); In re Allen, 4 Bankr. 617 (Bankr. ED Tenn. 1980); Stamper v. Stamper, 17 Bankr. 216 (Bankr. SD Ohio 1982); In re Romeo, 16 Bankr. 531 (Bankr. DNJ 1981).

A claim labeled as "support, maintenance and alimony" is dischargeable to the extent that it is determined to be a "property settlement." It is clear from the decided cases that the mere label is not determinative.[53] One question that has arisen frequently is whether attorney fees that are to be paid pursuant to a divorce, property settlement, or custody arrangement are nondischargeable as "support, maintenance and alimony." The cases on this point are divided, although the great majority of the cases have held that these claims are nondischargeable since they are in the nature of support, maintenance, or alimony.[54]

Mortgage and loan payments that are required to be made under a property settlement have been found in some cases to be in the nature of support or alimony and therefore nondischargeable.[55]

### [f] Claims for Willful or Malicious Injury: Section 523(a)(6)

Claims for willful and malicious injury by the debtor to an entity or property of another entity are nondischargeable.[56] The 1898 Act made a similar

---

[53] See, e.g., In re Warner, 5 Bankr. 434 (Bankr. D. Utah 1980); In re Newman, 15 Bankr. 67 (Bankr. MD Fla. 1981); In re King, 15 Bankr. 127 (Bankr. D. Kan. 1981); In re Carrigg, 14 Bankr. 658 (Bankr. DSC 1981); In re Calhoun, 715 F2d 1103 (6th Cir. 1983); cf. In re Coil, 680 F2d 1170 (7th Cir. 1982) (husband's agreement to hold former wife harmless for debts incurred during marriage held nondischargeable as in the nature of alimony, maintenance, or support).

[54] For cases holding that these fees are dischargeable, see, e.g., In re Crawford, 8 Bankr. 552 (Bankr. D. Kan. 1981) (dischargeable even though debtor's former spouse had paid fees and then sought reimbursement based on the divorce decree that obligated debtor to pay attorney fees); In re Allen, 4 Bankr. 617 (Bankr. ED Tenn. 1980); In re King, 15 Bankr. 127 (Bankr. D. Kan. 1981). For cases holding these fees to be nondischargeable, see, e.g., In re Catlow, 663 F2d 960 (9th Cir. 1981) (attorney fees awarded to debtor's former spouse in a postdivorce child custody proceeding were nondischargeable under Section 17 of the Bankruptcy Act); In re Spong, 661 F2d 6 (2d Cir. 1981) (attorney fees were nondischargeable as in the nature of alimony even though they were payable directly to the former spouse's attorney); In re Wells, 8 Bankr. 189 (Bankr. ND Ill. 1981) (attorney fees are nondischargeable even if payable to attorney as long as fees are in the nature of support or maintenance); In re Bell, 5 Bankr. 653 (Bankr. WD Okla. 1980); In re Lekvold, 18 Bankr. 663 (Bankr. DNM 1982); In re Gwinn, 20 Bankr. 233 (Bankr. App. Pan. 9th Cir. 1982) (attorney fees awarded in postdivorce litigation over child support were nondischargeable even though payable directly to the attorney; the attorney had standing to raise the nondischargeability issue); In re Glover, 16 Bankr. 213 (Bankr. MD Fla. 1981).

[55] In re Maitlen, 658 F2d 466 (7th Cir. 1981); In re Calhoun, 715 F2d 1103 (6th Cir. 1983); Stamper v. Stamper, 17 Bankr. 216 (Bankr. SD Ohio 1982); In re Newman, 15 Bankr. 67 (Bankr. MD Fla. 1981). But see In re Hobbs, 30 Bankr. 586 (Bankr. D. Nev. 1983).

[56] Observe that nondischargeability of claims under this section must be asserted in the bankruptcy court and within the time limits set by Bankruptcy Rule 4007. If a complaint for determination of dischargeability is not filed in a timely manner, these claims are discharged. See 11 USC § 523(c) and discussion at supra ¶ 15.07[1].

exception to discharge for willful and malicious injuries.[57] However, the House and Senate Reports indicate that some change from the application of the term under the 1898 Act was intended: "Under this paragraph 'willful' means deliberate or intentional. To the extent that *Tinker v. Colwell,* 139 U.S. 473 (1902), held that a looser standard is intended, and to the extent that other cases relied on *Tinker* to apply a 'reckless disregard' standard, they are overruled."[58] Several cases have dealt with the question of the dischargeability of claims against a debtor arising from driving while intoxicated.[59]

### [g] Claims for Fines, Penalties, or Forfeitures: Section 523(a)(7)

The debtor may not discharge claims of a governmental unit for a fine, penalty, or forfeiture that is not compensation for actual pecuniary loss. Tax penalties are also nondischargeable if the underlying tax for which the penalty was imposed is also nondischargeable.[60]

### [h] Claims for Educational Loans: Section 523(a)(8)

A debtor may not discharge educational loans that are made, insured, or guaranteed by a governmental unit or made under a program funded by a governmental unit or nonprofit institution,[61] unless the loan first became due more than five years before filing of the bankruptcy petition (exclusive of any applicable suspension of the repayment). However, provision has been made for an "undue hardship" discharge if the debtor can establish that denying the discharge of the student loan would impose an undue hardship on the debtor and his dependents. A number of cases have dealt with this hardship discharge.[62]

---

[57] See 1898 Act § 17(a)(8).

[58] H.R. Rep. No. 595, 95th Cong., 1st Sess. 365 (1977); S. Rep. No. 989, 95th Cong., 2nd Sess. 79 (1978).

[59] For cases holding that such claims are not dischargeable, see, e.g., In re Wooten, 30 Bankr. 357 (Bankr. ND Ala. 1983); In re Cloutier, 33 Bankr. 18 (Bankr. D. Me. 1983). For cases holding such claims are dischargeable, see, e.g., In re Oakes, 24 Bankr. 766 (Bankr. ND Ohio 1982); In re Naser, 7 Bankr. 116 (Bankr. ND Wis. 1980).

[60] 11 USC § 523(a)(7); see S. Rep. No. 989, 95th Cong., 2d Sess. 79 (1978).

[61] Before the 1984 Amendments, Section 523(a)(8) excepted from discharge "an educational loan, made, insured, or guaranteed by a governmental unit, or made under any program funded in whole or in part by a governmental unit or a non-profit institution *of higher education* . . ." (emphasis added). However, the 1984 Amendments deleted the language "of higher education" and the nonprofit institution is no longer required to be an institution of higher education. See 1984 Amendments § 454(a)(2).

[62] See Annot., 63 A.L.R. Fed. 570 (1983); see also Kosel, "Running the Gauntlet of 'Undue Hardship'–The Discharge of Student Loans in Bankruptcy," 11 Golden Gate U.L. Rev. 457 (1981); Comment, "A Fresh Start Through Bankruptcy: Fact or Frustration for the Student Loan Debtor?" 2 U. Puget Sound L. Rev. 365 (1979); Comment, "Student Loan Bankruptcy: Establishing 'Undue Hardship' in South Dakota," 27 S.D.L. Rev. 282 (1982); Note, "Discharging Student Loans in

### [i] Claims That Were Not Discharged in a Prior Bankruptcy Case: Section 523(a)(9)

Generally, if the debtor in a prior bankruptcy case has either waived discharge or been denied a discharge under Sections 727(a)(2) through 727(a)(7), debts that were or could have been listed or scheduled in the previous case will not be discharged in a later case. However, if the earlier general discharge was denied because of the six-year bar to discharge (i.e., the debtor in a still earlier case had obtained a discharge in a case commenced within six years),[63] the exception does not apply and debts that were not discharged in the previous proceeding will not be excepted from discharge under Section 523(a)(9) in a later case.

Where there has been a prior bankruptcy proceeding and some debts were excepted from discharge, certain previously nondischargeable debts may be discharged in a later case.[64] Debts that were excepted from discharge in the previous case under Section 523(a)(1) (tax claims), 523(a)(3) (unscheduled debts), or 523(a)(8) (educational loans) may be discharged in a later case if they otherwise would be dischargeable in the later case under Section 523(a)(9).[65] For example, a student loan may have been nondischargeable in the previous case because it was not first due more than five years before the petition was filed in that case or because the debtor could not establish "undue hardship." However, the loan would be dischargeable in a still later case begun more than five years after the loan first became due or if the debtor could establish "undue hardship" in a later case. Similarly, tax claims may have been nondischargeable in a previous case because the claims accrued within three years of the filing of the petition but could be discharged in a later case filed more than three years after the tax claims accrued.[66] However, for these claims to be discharged in the later case, note that the debtor must be able to obtain a general discharge in the later case and that six years must have elapsed between the commencement of the previous case in which a discharge was obtained and the filing of the petition in the later case.[67]

---

Bankruptcy: The Bankruptcy Court Test of 'Undue Hardship'," 26 Ariz. L. Rev. 445 (1984).

A related question is whether transcripts may be withheld of students who have discharged student loans. See generally Comment, "Student Loans and the Withholding of Transcripts Under the Bankruptcy Reform Act of 1978," 30 U. Kan. L. Rev. 265 (1982); Note, "Bankruptcy—Private College May Withhold Transcripts From Students Whose Educational Loan Debts Were Discharged," 22 How. L.J. 155 (1979). See also discussion at supra ¶ 15.03.

[63] See discussion at supra ¶ 15.04[8].

[64] 11 USC § 523(b).

[65] Id.

[66] With respect to the dischargeability of taxes under Section 523(a)(1), see caveat in discussion at supra ¶ 15.07[3][a] with respect to the oversight and failure to redesignate the reference in Section 523(a)(1) from "§ 507(a)(6)" to "§ 507(a)(7)."

[67] See 11 USC §§ 727(a)(8)–727(a)(9) and discussion at supra ¶ 15.04[8].

### [j] Judgment or Consent Decree Representing Liability for Operation of a Motor Vehicle While Legally Intoxicated: Section 523(a)(9)

The 1984 Amendments to the Code added an additional type of nondischargeable debt in new Section 523(a)(9).[68] The debtor may not discharge claims against a debtor that are represented by a judgment or a consent decree based on liability for the debtor's operation of a motor vehicle while legally intoxicated. Note that the statute speaks in terms of a judgment or consent decree; therefore, it seems clear that a judgment entered before filing the petition that represents liability for drunken driving would be nondischargeable. However, it appears that the questions of res judicata and collateral estoppel previously discussed are likely to be encountered here as well.[69] Assume that a creditor has a claim or cause of action against the debtor for personal injury or property damage caused by the debtor's operation of a motor vehicle while legally intoxicated but the cause of action has not been reduced to a judgment at the time the petition is filed. Based on the language of new Section 523(a)(9), the cause of action would not be excepted from discharge under that section since it is not represented by a judgment or consent decree, as is required by the statute. However, if relief from the automatic stay can be obtained, may the creditor proceed to obtain a judgment and render the claim nondischargeable? The answer to this and other questions will have to await case law development. Even if the claim or cause of action has not been reduced to judgment, arguably it may be nondischargeable under the "willful and malicious injury" exception of Section 523(a)(6).[70]

---

[68] As originally enacted, the 1978 Bankruptcy Reform Act contained nine types of nondischargeable debts. However, the 1984 Amendments added an additional type of nondischargeable debt: judgments or consent decrees representing a liability incurred as a result of the debtor's operation of a motor vehicle while legally intoxicated. See new 11 USC § 523(a)(9). In an apparent oversight, the new Section 523(a)(9) was added by the 1984 Amendments and the existing Section 523(a)(9) was not renumbered. For a discussion of former Section 523(a)(9), which deals with claims not discharged in a prior bankruptcy case, see discussion at supra ¶ 15.07[3][i]. Thus, at present, there are two sections numbered 523(a)(9). The new Section 523(a)(9) states that a discharge does not discharge an individual debtor from any debt

> "to any entity, to the extent that such debt arises from a judgment or consent decree entered in a court of record against the debtor wherein liability was incurred by such debtor as a result of the debtor's operation of a motor vehicle while legally intoxicated under the laws or regulations of any jurisdiction within the United States or its territories wherein such motor vehicle was operated and within which such liability was incurred."

1984 Amendments § 371.

[69] See Brown v. Felsen, 442 US 127 (1979), and discussion at supra ¶ 15.07[2].

[70] A determination of nondischargeability under Section 523(a)(6) is, however, within the exclusive jurisdiction of the bankruptcy court. See 11 USC § 523(c). The legislative history to new Section 523(a)(9) indicates: "Subtitle D [Section 371 of the 1984 Act, new Section 523(a)(9)] clarifies present law relating to the nondischargeability of debts incurred by drunk drivers. Debts incurred by persons driving while intoxicated are

## ¶ 15.08 REAFFIRMATION

Under the 1898 Act, the reaffirmation of debts was a recurring problem that generated much comment.[1] Frequently, creditors were able to frustrate the debtor's discharge by obtaining reaffirmation of discharged debts; that is, the debtor agreed to pay or be bound on the discharged debt or obligation. Even though a debtor may have obtained a general discharge, the benefit of the discharge and the opportunity for a "fresh start" was negated to the extent that the debtor reaffirmed a part of his debts. These reaffirmations occurred with some frequency and generally were enforceable. It was suggested that reaffirmation frequently was not necessarily in the best interests of the debtor but occurred as a result of pressure, subtle or otherwise, that was placed on the debtor. The reaffirmation may have been the result of duress, unequal bargaining power, or lack of knowledge on the part of the debtor. In its report, the Bankruptcy Commission stated:

> Substantial evidence of the use of reaffirmations to nullify discharges has come to the Commission's attention. To the extent reaffirmations are enforceable, the 'fresh start' goal of the discharge provisions is frustrated. Reaffirmations are often obtained by improper methods or result from the desire of the discharged debtor to obtain additional credit or continue to own property securing a discharged debt.[2]

During the legislative development of the Code, proposals were made to bar reaffirmation or renewal of discharged debts.[3] However, in recognizing that there may be appropriate uses of reaffirmation, Congress took a compromise approach in the Code in Sections 524(c) through 524(d). These sections do not impose a "blanket" bar to reaffirmations but instead place important restrictions on their use and provide substantial protections to the debtor in an

---

presumed to be willfully and maliciously incurred under this provision." 130 Cong. Rec. H7,489 (daily ed. June 29, 1984). The question may be raised whether this can be taken as an expression of congressional intent that claims based on liability for drunken driving, although not reduced to judgment, are presumed to be or should be considered to be willful and malicious and, in effect, an expression of disapproval of those cases holding to the contrary. A number of cases have dealt with the question of the dischargeability of claims against a debtor arising from driving while intoxicated. For cases holding that such claims are not dischargeable, see, e.g., In re Wooten, 30 Bankr. 357 (Bankr. ND Ala. 1983); In re Cloutier, 33 Bankr. 18 (Bankr. D Me. 1983). For cases holding such claims are dischargeable, see, e.g., In re Oakes, 24 Bankr. 766 (Bankr. ND Ohio 1982) ; In re Naser, 7 Bankr. 116 (Bankr. ND Wis. 1980).

[1] See, e.g., Boshkoff, "The Bankrupt's Moral Obligation to Pay His Discharged Debts: A Conflict Between Contract Theory and Bankruptcy Policy," 47 Ind. L.J. 36 (1971).

[2] Report of the Commission on the Bankruptcy Laws of the United States, H.R. Doc. No. 137, 93d Cong., 1st Sess. 177 (1973).

[3] See 124 Cong. Rec. H11,096 (daily ed. Sept. 28, 1978); 124 Cong. Rec. S17,413 (daily ed. Oct. 6, 1978). For an extended discussion of the legislative development of the reaffirmation provisions, see In re Blount, 4 Bankr. 92 (Bankr. MD Tenn. 1980).

attempt to prevent some perceived abuses of reaffirmation.[4] In addition, the 1984 Amendments made significant changes with respect to reaffirmation.

First, an agreement for which the consideration, in whole or in part, is based on a debt that is dischargeable in bankruptcy is enforceable only to the extent that it is enforceable under applicable nonbankruptcy law.[5] Nonbankruptcy law generally does permit enforcement of these reaffirmations.[6] Second, the reaffirmation agreement must be made before the granting of the discharge under Section 727, 1141, or 1328.[7] Third, the reaffirmation agreement must contain a clear and conspicuous statement advising the debtor of the right to rescind at any time before discharge or within sixty days after the agreement is filed with the court, whichever is later, by giving notice of rescission to the holder of the claim.[8] This means that within this "cooling off" period (i.e., before discharge or sixty days after the agreement is filed with the court, whichever is later), the debtor by notice to the holder of the claim may rescind the reaffirmation agreement.[9] Fourth, the agreement must be filed with the court and, if the debtor was represented by an attorney during the course of negotiating the reaffirmation agreement, the agreement must be accompanied by the attorney's affidavit stating that the agreement represents a fully informed and voluntary agreement by the debtor and does not impose an undue hardship on the debtor or a dependent of the debtor.[10] If the debtor was not represented by an attorney during the negotiation of the reaffirmation agreement, the court must approve the agreement and determine that it does not impose an undue hardship on the debtor or a dependent of the debtor and is in the best interest of the debtor.[11] However, court approval is not required if the reaffirmed debt

---

[4] For additional treatment of reaffirmation, see Ahart, "Obtaining Reaffirmation of Individual Debts Under the New Bankruptcy Code," 97 Banking L.J. 153 (1980); DeWoskin, "A Warning to Attorneys: Reaffirmation Under the New Bankruptcy Code," 85 Com. L.J. 296 (1980); Comment, "Reaffirmation Agreements: A Fight for Enforceability Under the New Bankruptcy Code," 12 Cum.-Sam. L. Rev. 431 (1982).

[5] 11 USC § 524(c).

[6] The Restatement (Second) of Contracts § 83 (1979) states the general rule: "An express promise to pay all or part of an indebtedness of the promisor, discharged or dischargeable in bankruptcy proceedings begun before the promise is made, is binding." Some states may impose formal requirements such as requiring that the reaffirmation agreement be in writing. As a practical matter, before the 1984 changes this was probably required for approval by the bankruptcy court. See, e.g., In re Vinson, 5 Bankr. 32 (Bankr. ND Ga. 1980). The 1984 Amendments clearly contemplate that there will be a written reaffirmation agreement that is filed with the court and that such agreement must contain a statement advising the debtor of his right to rescind. See 11 USC §§ 524(c)(2)–524(c)(3), as added by 1984 Amendments § 308(b).

[7] 11 USC § 524(c)(1).

[8] 11 USC § 524(c)(2), as added by 1984 Amendments § 308(b).

[9] 11 USC § 524(c)(4), as added by 1984 Amendments § 308(b).

[10] 11 USC § 524(c)(3), as amended by 1984 Amendments § 308(b).

[11] 11 USC § 524(c)(6)(A), as amended by 1984 Amendments § 308(b).

is a consumer debt secured by real property.[12] For example, court approval is not required for reaffirmation of a mortgage debt on the debtor's home. Fifth, for a reaffirmation agreement to be enforceable, a discharge and reaffirmation hearing must be held pursuant to Section 524(d).[13] After the determination to grant a discharge has been made, Section 524(d) requires that the court must hold a hearing at which the debtor must appear in person.[14] At this hearing, the court must explain that a discharge has been granted (or explain the reason why a discharge has not been granted) and give the debtor a debtor's "Miranda" warning. If the debtor wishes to make a reaffirmation agreement, the court must inform the debtor that such an agreement is not required[15] and explain the legal effect and consequences, including default, of the agreement.[16] At this hearing, the court must also determine that the reaffirmation agreement does not impose an undue hardship and is in the debtor's best interests if it was made by an individual who was not represented by an attorney during the negotiation of the reaffirmation agreement and if it is reaffirmation of a consumer debt not secured by real property.[17]

---

[12] 11 USC § 524(c)(6)(B), as amended by 1984 Amendments § 308(b). "Consumer debt" is defined in Section 101(7) as a "debt incurred by an individual primarily for personal, family, or household purpose." Before the 1984 Amendments, under repealed Section 524(c)(4), in the case of an individual, if the reaffirmation was of a "consumer debt" that was not secured by real property of the debtor, for the reaffirmation to be enforceable the court had to approve the agreement as (1) not imposing an undue hardship on the debtor (or the debtor's dependents) and as being in the debtor's best interest, or (2) being an agreement entered into in good faith and in settlement of litigation regarding the nondischargeability of a debt under Section 523 or an agreement providing for redemption of property under Section 722. For discussion of redemption, see ¶ 13.08.

[13] 11 USC § 524(c)(5), as renumbered by 1984 Amendments § 308(b).

[14] B. Rule 4008 requires that this Section 524(d) meeting must be held not more than thirty days after the entry of an order granting or denying a discharge or confirming a plan in a Chapter 11 case. No less than ten days notice of this meeting must be given to the debtor and the trustee. The rule also requires that a motion by the debtor for approval of a reaffirmation agreement must be filed before or at the hearing.

[15] 11 USC § 524(d)(1)(A).

[16] 11 USC § 524(d)(1)(B). In commenting on this section, one court stated:

> "It is apparent that Congress desired that debtors understand their listed debts were discharged, unless excepted by a previously filed action; that debtors know creditors can not seek to collect those debts; that debtors be aware there is no obligation to renew any debt; and that if the debtors voluntarily renew the obligation, the consequences of such renewal. The debtors must understand renewal would negate the benefits of discharge and would subject them to the usual collection procedures."

In re Blount, 4 Bankr. 92, 93 (Bankr. MD Tenn. 1980).

[17] 11 USC § 524(d)(2). There appears to be a slight inconsistency in amended Section 524(c)(6), which appears to require court approval of all reaffirmation agreements (except consumer debts secured by real property) where the debtor was not represented by counsel during the negotiation. That is, Section 524(c)(6) is not restricted to consumer debts, whereas Section 524(d)(2) seems to require at the "discharge hearing" that

A number of cases have dealt with the issue of what is "in the debtor's best interest." In general, many bankruptcy courts appear to have taken a protective attitude with respect to what represents the debtor's "best interests" and frequently have refused to approve reaffirmation agreements.[18] For example, in *In re Avis*,[19] the court refused to approve reaffirmation where the sole purpose was to protect codebtors on the obligation for which reaffirmation was sought. The court stated:

> In this case, the debtors have stated that their sole reason for agreeing to the reaffirmation was the existence of co-debtors. The amount of the proposed reaffirmation is more than one third of the total listed unsecured claims against them. Another claim with co-debtors obligated ($5,000.00), is not proposed for reaffirmation. Approval of the submitted reaffirmation would violate the basic principles guiding bankruptcy relief, the effectiveness of discharge would be weakened; and all creditors would not be treated substantially alike. No sufficient reasons have been presented to justify approval or to override the debtors' financial consideration.[20]

In a similar case, another court refused to approve reaffirmation of a debt secured by property owned by the mother of the debtor. The debtor, by reaffirmation, sought to avoid collection of the discharged debt from the mother, who acted as a guarantor of the debt.[21]

---

the court determine only that *consumer debts* under Section 524(c)(6) do not impose an undue hardship and are in the debtor's best interest. Before the 1984 Amendments, for reaffirmation of consumer debts the court was required to determine that reaffirmation of the consumer debt (not secured by real estate) did not impose an undue hardship and was in the debtor's best interest or that the agreement was entered into in good faith and in settlement of dischargeability litigation under Section 523. To make the two sections compatible, it appears that the word "consumer" should have been deleted from Section 523(d)(2).

[18] Note that these cases arose before the 1984 Amendments. Under the 1984 Amendments, it is likely that the courts will be required to make these determinations with less frequency. As previously noted, under the 1984 Amendments court approval is not required in those cases in which the debtor is represented by an attorney during the negotiation of the reaffirmation agreement. Although the attorney must file an affidavit with the agreement that it does not impose an undue hardship, the determination of what is in the debtor's best interest in such cases in effect is left to the debtor, presumably with advice of counsel ("a fully informed and voluntary agreement"), rather than to the court. Under the 1984 Amendments, however, where the debtor is not represented by an attorney during the negotiation of the agreement, the court still must make a determination of whether the agreement is in the debtor's best interest in the case of reaffirmation of debts (other than those secured by real property). 11 USC §§ 524(c)(6), 524(d)(2).

[19] 3 Bankr. 205 (Bankr. SD Ohio 1980).

[20] Id. at 207.

[21] In re Berkich, 7 Bankr. 483 (Bankr. ED Pa. 1980). Discharge of the debtor does not affect the liability of any other party on, or the property of any other party for, such discharged debt. 11 USC § 524(e).

Prior to the 1984 Amendments, under Section 524(c)(4)(B) (now repealed) the court was required in some circumstances to determine if the reaffirmation agreement was entered into in good faith and in settlement of dischargeability litigation under Section 523 or as a provision for redemption under Section 722. In the case of *In re Blount*,[22] the court refused to approve an agreement under which the debtor proposed payments on a debt of $1,820.25, secured by collateral valued at $600, where the monthly payments and terms of the reaffirmation agreement were the same as those of the original agreement. In another case, the court refused to approve under Section 524(c)(4)(B) a reaffirmation agreement that resulted from the creditor's unfounded objection to dischargeability of the debt. The court found that settlement of the dischargeability complaint was not in good faith, as required by the statute.[23] The court stated:

> A creditor's motivation in initiating a § 523 proceeding could be an honest belief that on the facts and the law, the debt may be nondischargeable. On the other hand, a creditor's action could be initiated without any merit as a mere subterfuge for the purpose of using the § 523 proceedings as a hammer or leverage in obtaining reaffirmation of an otherwise dischargeable debt. A § 523 complaint which on its face has little or no chance of success can have no purpose but that of a bargaining tool. The Court believes that commencement of a § 523 action solely for bargaining purposes does not constitute good faith, but rather shows an intent to gain an improper advantage and any reaffirmation exacted in settlement of such litigation could not have been entered into in good faith.[24]

One bankruptcy court held that no reaffirmation could be entered into "in settlement of litigation under section 523" (nondischargeable claims) where the creditor had not filed a complaint to determine dischargeability and where the time for filing a complaint by the creditor under Section 523(c) had expired. The court stated:

> When no complaint has been filed, the Court cannot approve a reaffirmation agreement under § 524(c)(4)(B), because that subsection mandates that a lawsuit actually be pending between the parties concerning the dischargeability of a debt at the time the Debtor reaffirms that debt. It follows *a fortiori* that a reaffirmation agreement is not to be approved by a bankruptcy court when the dischargeability action required by § 524(c)(4)(B)(ii) is barred by an order under Bankruptcy Rule 409(a)(2) and Local Bankruptcy Rule 4003. Furthermore, because no complaint was filed the Court does not have a sufficient means of determining whether the reaffirmation agreement was entered into in good faith within the meaning of § 524(c)(4)(B)(i).[25]

---

[22] 4 Bankr. 92 (Bankr. MD Tenn. 1980).

[23] In re Hinkle, 9 Bankr. 283 (Bankr. D. Md. 1981).

[24] Id. at 285.

[25] In re Leonard, 12 Bankr. 91, 93 (Bankr. D. Md. 1981).

However, since the 1984 Amendments have eliminated the provisions of Section 524(c)(4), which required a finding of good faith, it remains to be seen whether courts, where court approval is required, will read an element of "good faith" into the determination of what is in the debtor's "best interest."

After discharge a debtor may be permitted to modify a reaffirmation agreement before the expiration of the "cooling off" period or rescission period of Section 524(c)(4)[26] where the modification terms are more favorable to the debtor than those of the original agreement.[27] In *In re Sholos,*[28] the court held that reaffirmation of a secured debt, where the collateral exceeded the debt, could include reasonable attorney fees provided for in the secured note. However, the court indicated that if the collateral was worth less than the debt and the attorney fees, it would be difficult to find that the reaffirmation was in the "best interest" of the debtor. In one case, the debtor was disabled, unemployed, and her entire monthly income consisted of a $300 Social Security payment. No public transportation was available to the debtor to reach food, medical care, and other necessary services.[29] To retain a car valued at $2,400 as transportation, the debtor sought approval of reaffirmation of a $4,119.91 debt, with monthly payments of $171.43, which represented more than half of the debtor's monthly gross income of $300. The court recognized the dilemma faced by the debtor:

> In these circumstances, virtually the only basis for determining that reaffirmation would not impose an *undue* hardship on the debtor, within the meaning of section 524(c)(4)(A)(i), is that a disabled person deprived of her only means of transportation may experience even greater hardship than reaffirmation represents. For a disabled chapter 7 debtor with $300 monthly gross income, it is almost inescapable that basic self-support will represent a real hardship. What is an 'undue hardship' for such a debtor?[30]

Although declining to approve or disapprove reaffirmation, the court suggested that an attempt should be made to redeem the property under Section 722 by paying the amount of the allowed secured claim. The court stated:

> Absent a showing that redemption is either unavailable or inappropriate in the circumstances, the court will not approve a reaffirmation agreement as being in the best interest of the debtor under Bankruptcy Code § 524(c)(4)(A)(ii).
>
> Accordingly, counsel for the debtor is directed, within twenty days, either to initiate redemption proceedings under Bankruptcy Code § 722, or

---

[26] As amended by 1984 Amendments § 308(b).

[27] In re Sacks, 8 Bankr. 249 (Bankr. D. Md. 1981). The case arose under the thirty-day rescission period of Section 524(c)(2) prior to the 1984 Amendments.

[28] 11 Bankr. 782 (Bankr. WD Pa. 1981).

[29] In re Delano, 7 Bankr. 72 (Bankr. D. Me. 1980).

[30] Id. at 72–73.

to make a sufficient written showing that redemption is unavailable or inappropriate in the circumstances.[31]

Bankruptcy Rule 4008 contemplates that the request for approval of the reaffirmation will be made by the debtor and not by the creditor.[32] However, in *In re Vinson*,[33] the court held that a debtor in an adversary proceeding could not unilaterally require a creditor to agree to a proposed reaffirmation agreement. The court stated that Section 524(c) "clearly anticipates an executed, '*voluntary agreement*' between the debtor and creditor prior to the application for approval by the Bankruptcy Court. . . ."[34] As previously noted, under the 1984 Amendments to Section 524(c), court approval is not required if the debtor is represented by an attorney during the course of negotiating the reaffirmation agreement and the agreement is filed with the court with the appropriate attorney's affidavit. Hence, the number of reaffirmation agreements requiring court approval may be substantially reduced.

An additional clarification made by the 1984 Amendments is that even though a debt is discharged (and apart from any valid reaffirmation), the discharge does not prevent a debtor from voluntarily repaying any debt.[35]

---

[31] Id. at 73.

[32] Cf. In re Newsome, 3 Bankr. 626 (Bankr. WD Va. 1980).

[33] 5 Bankr. 32 (Bankr. ND Ga. 1980).

[34] In re Vinson, 5 Bankr. 33 (Bankr. ND Ga. 1980).

[35] 11 USC § 524(f), added by 1984 Amendments § 308(d).

# 16

# The Trustee's Avoiding Powers and Recovery of Assets for the Estate

## ¶ 16.01 INTRODUCTION

In representing the creditors of the debtor's estate and in collecting the assets of the estate, the trustee is given very substantial rights to assert. The avoiding powers are designed in part to upset and prevent the last-minute use of "grab law," preferences, and collusive or fraudulent transfers, and are designed to promote one of the central concepts of bankruptcy–equality of distribution. In many instances, the avoiding powers given to the trustee permit assets to be brought back into the estate, increasing the distribution to the creditors. For example, the trustee may avoid and recover for the estate certain fraudulent transfers made by the debtor prior to bankruptcy, certain "preferential" transfers, and certain liens and security interests. In effect, the trustee may reduce the lienholder or secured party to an unsecured status.

One of the most powerful avoiding powers given to the trustee is the so-called "strong arm clause" of Section 544 (a) of the Bankruptcy Code (the Code).[1] Under the strong arm clause, as of the commencement of the case, the trustee is given the status of a hypothetical lien creditor. In effect, the trustee is treated as if he extended credit at the time the petition was filed, obtained a judgment at that time, and by execution levied on all of the debtor's property, that could be reached by such an execution creditor under applicable nonbankruptcy law. In other words, all property of the debtor and all transfers and encumbrances (including creation of security interests) that, as of the commencement of the case, could have been reached or avoided by a judicial lien creditor may be avoided by the trustee and recovered for the estate. Under Section 544(a)(3), the trustee also is given the rights of a bona fide purchaser of real property from the debtor. In addition, Section 544(b)[2] gives the trustee the rights of actual creditors who have allowable unsecured claims; under this power, the trustee may avoid transfers of the debtor that would be avoidable by these creditors. Section 547 gives the trustee an extremely important power to

---

[1] 11 USC § 544(a), as amended by the Bankruptcy Amendments and Federal Judgeship Act of 1984, Pub. L. No. 98-353, § 459 (hereafter cited as the 1984 Amendments). Section 544(a) is the counterpart of Section 70(c) of the 1898 Bankruptcy Act (the 1898 Act). Unless otherwise specified, "Sections" refer to Sections of the Bankruptcy Code (Title 11 of the U.S. Code).

[2] Section 544(b) is the counterpart of Section 70(e) of the 1898 Act.

avoid and recover certain preferences[3] made to creditors within ninety days before the filing of the petition. In the case of "insiders"[4] the trustee may avoid certain preferences made within one year before the filing of the petition. In addition, certain prepetition setoffs that have a preferential effect may be avoided under Section 553.[5] Section 548 gives the trustee the power to avoid fraudulent conveyances made within one year of the filing of the bankruptcy petition.[6] Certain statutory liens[7] may be avoided by the trustee under Section 545 and certain unauthorized postpetition transfers of property may be recovered under Section 549.[8] In some cases, liens securing claims for penalties, fines, and forfeitures may be avoided under Section 724.[9] If any of these avoiding powers are successfully invoked by the trustee, the assets that are available for distribution to creditors will be increased.[10]

To the extent that a transfer is avoidable under Section 544, 545, 547, 548, 549, or 724(a), the trustee may recover the transferred property, or if the court so orders, the value of the property from the initial transferee or a subsequent transferee.[11] However, the trustee may not recover from a subsequent transferee who takes for value (including securing or satisfaction of a present or antecedent debt), in good faith, and without knowledge of the voidability of the transfer,[12] or from a good faith transferee of such a person who in effect takes by shelter.[13] In some cases, this means that the trustee may recover the value of the voidable transfer only from the initial transferee.[14] However, in those cases where the trustee may recover from both the initial transferee and a subsequent transferee, the trustee is entitled to only a single satisfaction.[15] A good faith transferee from whom the trustee may recover, including the initial transferee and a subsequent transferee, has a lien on the property to the extent of (1) the cost of any improvement made in the property, or (2) the increase in the value of the property as a result of the improvement, whichever is less.[16] If an avoid-

---

[3] 11 USC § 547, as amended by 1984 Amendments §§ 301, 462. Section 547 is the counterpart of Section 60 of the 1898 Act, but has significant changes.

[4] "Insider" is defined in Section 101(28). See discussion at infra ¶ 16.04[10].

[5] See 11 USC § 553, as amended by 1984 Amendments §§ 395, 467.

[6] 11 USC § 548, as amended by 1948 Amendments §§ 394, 463.

[7] "Statutory lien" is defined in Section 101(45).

[8] 11 USC § 549, as amended by 1984 Amendments § 464.

[9] 11 USC § 724, as amended by 1984 Amendments § 477.

[10] See 11 USC § 551.

[11] Note that in some cases (e.g., under 11 USC § 549 or 548) the trustee may be able to avoid a transfer only in part.

[12] 11 USC § 550(b)(1).

[13] 11 USC § 550(b)(2). Such a third-level good faith transferee, apparently without having to give value, takes in effect by shelter from the prior subsequent good faith transferee for value, and thus is protected from recovery by the trustee.

[14] Cf. In re Belize Airways, Ltd., 7 Bankr. 601 (Bankr. SD Fla. 1980).

[15] 11 USC § 550(c).

[16] 11 USC § 550(d), as amended by 1984 Amendments § 465; see also H.R. Rep. No. 595, 95th Cong., 1st Sess. 376 (1977); S. Rep. No. 989, 95th Cong., 2d Sess. 90 (1978).

ing power under Section 544, 545, 547, 548, 549, 553, or 724(a) is successfully invoked by the trustee, the claim of the creditor arising from the avoidance and recovery is treated as if it were a prepetition claim for the purpose of allowance of the claim, even though the claim arises after the petition is filed.[17]

If a creditor has received a transfer voidable under one of the specified sections, the voidable transfer must be surrendered before *any* claim of the creditor will be allowed.[18] In some instances this provision means that the trustee will be able to recover a voidable transfer without bringing an adversary proceeding to recover the voidable transfer; if the voidable transfer is not surrendered by the creditor, no claim of the creditor will be allowed. In most cases, however, to exercise the avoiding power and recover the transfer, the trustee must initiate, by a complaint, an adversary proceeding under Part VII of the Bankruptcy Rules.[19] Venue for these actions currently is covered by Title 28, Section 1409.[20]

The avoiding powers of Sections 544 (strong arm clause and rights of actual creditors), 545 (statutory liens), 547 (preferences), 548 (fraudulent conveyances), and 553 (setoff) are subject to the limitations of Section 546.[21]

## [1] Who May Exercise the Avoiding Powers

In a Chapter 7 case, the avoiding powers are normally exercised by the trustee. However, in very limited circumstances, the debtor may exercise the avoiding powers if the trustee does not exercise them. Under the circumstances set forth in Section 522(h), the debtor may use the avoiding powers given to the trustee under Section 544, 545, 547, 548, 549, or 724(a) to avoid a transfer of property that the debtor may claim as exempt if (1) the property was not voluntarily transferred by the debtor, (2) the debtor did not conceal the property, and (3) the trustee does not attempt to avoid the transfer. The concept of Section 522(h) is that if the property has been involuntarily transferred under circumstances that would make it voidable by the trustee under one of the named sections but the trustee does not exercise the power to recover the voidable transfer, the debtor may exercise the power and exempt the property.[22] This section is designed primarily to give the debtor the rights the trustee could, but did not, pursue. This right given to the debtor may be exercised in Chapter 7, 11, and 13 cases.[23]

---

[17] 11 USC § 502(h); see discussion at ¶ 14.06[3].

[18] 11 USC § 502(d); see discussion at ¶ 14.05[9].

[19] See B. Rule 7001.

[20] Added by 1984 Amendments § 102.

[21] The limitations placed on the trustee's avoiding powers by Section 546(c) are discussed at ¶ 13.10.

[22] See also 11 USC § 522(i).

[23] 11 USC § 103(a). Only an individual debtor may claim exemptions under Section 522 in Chapter 7, 11, or 13; therefore, use of Section 522(h) is limited to individuals. For additional discussion, see infra ¶ 16.09.

In a Chapter 11 case, the debtor in possession has the powers of the trustee and may exercise the avoiding powers given to the trustee.[24] Where the term "trustee" is used in the Bankruptcy Code sections dealing with the avoiding powers, "trustee" generally can be read to include the "debtor in possession" in a Chapter 11 case. The same meaning can be inferred in the following discussion. It has been pointed out, however, that there is some uncertainty as to whether a trustee appointed in a Chapter 11 proceeding may exercise the avoiding powers.[25]

### [2] When the Avoiding Powers Must Be Invoked

Actions by the trustee or the debtor in possession to avoid transfers under Section 544, 545, 547, 548, or 553 must be commenced within two years after the appointment of a trustee, or before the case is closed or dismissed, whichever is earlier.[26] One bankruptcy court in a Chapter 7 case has held this to mean that action must be brought within two years after appointment of the permanent trustee, not of the interim trustee.[27] The court noted that the interim trustee serves by virtue of Section 701, and the permanent trustee is appointed under Section 702. The court held that the specific reference in Section 546(a)(1) that actions must be brought within two years "after the appointment of a trustee under section 702" indicated that the date of the appointment of the permanent trustee was the appropriate date for measuring the time period. Additionally, the court noted that the interim trustee is primarily responsible for preserving property of the estate and generally takes little affirmative action until after the election or designation of the permanent trustee, except for those situations where perishable property needs to be sold or action must be taken to preserve assets of the estate.

## ¶ 16.02 THE "STRONG ARM" CLAUSE: THE TRUSTEE AS A HYPOTHETICAL LIEN CREDITOR OR BONA FIDE PURCHASER

Section 544(a)[1] of the Code is the counterpart to Section 70(c) of the 1898 Bankruptcy Act (the 1898 Act) and generally follows the pattern of that section with some important clarification and additions. Under Section 544(a), the trustee as of the "commencement of the case"[2] is given three distinct status

---

[24] 11 USC §§ 1107(a) (as amended by 1984 Amendments § 503), 103(a); see, e.g., In re Naudain, Inc., 32 Bankr. 871 (Bankr. ED Pa. 1983).

[25] Cowans, Bankruptcy Law and Practice § 10.1, at 503–504 (West 1983).

[26] 11 USC § 546(a), as amended by 1984 Amendments § 461. Section 546(a)(1) states that an action may not be commenced after the earlier of "two years after the appointment of a trustee under section 702, 1104, 1163, or 1302 of this title."

[27] In re Killian Constr. Co., 24 Bankr. 848 (Bankr. D. Idaho 1982).

[1] 11 USC § 544(a), as amended by 1984 Amendments § 459.

[2] "Commencement of the case" means the filing of the petition in bankruptcy. See 11 USC §§ 301, 303.

positions. Under each of these positions, the trustee is given the status without regard to any knowledge of the trustee or of any creditor; that is, any knowledge of the trustee or of any creditor is not imputed to the trustee in the exercise of these powers. Under Section 544(a)(1), the trustee is given the status of a hypothetical lien creditor, under Section 544(a)(2) he is given the status of a judgment lien creditor with an unsatisfied execution, and under Section 544(a)(3) he is given the position of a bona fide purchaser of real property (other than fixtures) from the debtor.

### [1] The Trustee as a Hypothetical Lien Creditor: Section 544(a)(1)

Under Section 544(a)(1), as of the commencement of the case the trustee is given the status of a hypothetical lien creditor. In effect, the trustee is treated as if he extended credit at the time the petition was filed, obtained judgment at that time, and levied on all of the property of the debtor that could be reached by an execution creditor under applicable nonbankruptcy law. In other words, the trustee may avoid and recover for the estate all property of the debtor and all transfers and encumbrances, including creation of security interests, that as of the commencement of the case could have been reached or avoided by a judicial lien creditor. The basic concept is that property that could have been reached by and that was available to lien creditors at the time the petition was filed should be available to the debtor's estate for distribution to the creditors. Note that the rights and attributes of the trustee are created as of the commencement of the case; that is, the trustee cannot be given rights or attributes before the filing of the petition. This limitation is a codification of *Lewis v. Manufacturers National Bank*,[3] in which the Court held that the trustee could not, as a hypothetical lien creditor under the strong arm clause, be given an attribute such as extending credit before the filing of the petition. Under Section 544(a), all the attributes of the trustee as a hypothetical lien creditor, such as extending credit, obtaining judgment, and levying execution, must be hypothesized as having occurred at the time of filing of the petition and cannot be hypothesized as having occurred before that time. Section 544(a) also makes it clear that the trustee's status as a hypothetical lien creditor exists whether or not such a creditor exists. This language overrules the decision of the Court of Appeals for the Ninth Circuit in *Pacific Finance Corp. v. Edwards*.[4] Despite

---

[3] 364 US 603 (1961). In *Lewis*, a chattel mortgage had been given but had not been recorded until four days later. Under applicable Michigan law, such a chattel mortgage was void as against creditors unless filed. Five months later, the borrower filed a voluntary petition in bankruptcy. Although there was no showing that any creditor had extended credit to the borrower during the period that the chattel mortgage was unrecorded, the trustee argued that under state law a creditor who had extended credit during the interim when the chattel mortgage was unrecorded would have priority. It was argued that the trustee as a hypothetical lien creditor could be given the attribute of a creditor who had extended credit during the gap, and who could on the date the petition was filed, levy on and prevail over the unrecorded interest and therefore could avoid the chattel mortgage under Section 70(c) of the 1898 Act.

[4] 304 F2d 224 (9th Cir. 1962). A part of the legislative history to Section 544(a) stated: "In particular, section 544(a)(1) overrules *Pacific Finance Corp. v. Edwards* . . .

language in Section 70(c) of the 1898 Act that seemed to indicate a contrary conclusion,[5] the court held that the hypothetical lien creditor status of the trustee under Section 70(e) could be invoked only if at the time of bankruptcy a creditor existed who could, but did not, avoid the transaction.

In hypothesizing the trustee's status as a lien creditor at the time of filing the petition, the trustee is created "without regard to any knowledge of the trustee or of any creditor."[6] This language is apparently intended to have the effect of not imputing to the trustee in his official capacity any knowledge of any creditor or any knowledge that the trustee may personally have. For example, if a particular transaction could only be avoided by a "judgment lien creditor without knowledge" of a particular fact, and if one of the creditors or the trustee personally had such knowledge, this knowledge would not be imputed to the trustee in his official capacity to preclude avoiding the transaction. However, despite this language, there is some question as to whether "constructive notice" will be imputed to the trustee.[7]

Security interests covered by Article 9 of the Uniform Commercial Code (UCC) that are unperfected upon the commencement of the case are voidable by the trustee under Section 544(a)(1) by use of UCC Section 9-301(1)(b). This is true both in those states that have adopted the 1972 Amendments to Article

---

and *In re Federals, Inc.,* 553 F2d 509 (6th Cir. 1977), insofar as those cases held that the trustee did not have the status of a creditor who extended credit immediately prior to the commencement of the case." 124 Cong. Rec. H11,097 (Sept. 28, 1978); S17,413 (Oct. 6, 1978).

[5] In *Pacific Finance*, under the applicable Washington state statute, a conditional sales contract had to be recorded within ten days after execution. If not recorded within the ten-day period, the contract could not be perfected by a late filing and was void, even if later filed, as to subsequent creditors whether or not they extended credit before or after the contract was filed. The trustee sought to avoid the chattel mortgage in his status as a hypothetical lien creditor under Section 70(c) of the 1898 Act. Although the court conceded that the conditional sales contract was subject to attack by a creditor up to the date of bankruptcy, the court held that

> "[u]nder our construction of § 70, sub. c the Trustee is empowered to exercise the powers given him even if no actual creditor has obtained a lien, but he cannot do so if no actual creditor could have obtained a lien. In the instant case, as presented to us, there was in existence at the date of bankruptcy no actual subsequent creditor of the bankrupt who could have obtained a lien on the Cadillac automobile at the date of bankruptcy. For such reason, the Trustee could not acquire the hypothetical status of a creditor holding a lien because the existence of an actual creditor who could have obtained a lien is a condition to the acquisition by the Trustee of the status of a creditor holding a lien."

304 F2d 224, 228. The court further stated: "In our view, § 70, sub. c grants to the Trustee the status of a lien creditor whenever an actual creditor exists who could have become a lien creditor but did not do so." Id. at 230. *Pacific Finance* had been criticized as being incorrectly decided under the 1898 Act. See King, "Pacific Finance Corp. v. Edwards: Another Misreading of Section 70(c) of the Bankruptcy Act," 63 Colum. L. Rev. 232 (1963). *Pacific Finance* had implicitly been overruled by the U.S. Supreme Court in U.S. v. Speers, 382 US 266 (1965).

[6] See 11 USC § 544(a).

[7] See infra ¶ 16.02[3].

9 as well as in those few states that have not yet adopted the 1972 Amendments.[8]

However, there is an important, but very limited, exception to the rule that a security interest that is unperfected at the time of the filing of the petition is voidable by the trustee under Section 544(a)(1). If the security interest unperfected on the date that the petition is filed is a purchase-money security interest, perfection after the petition is filed may be effective if made within ten days after the debtor receives possession and if perfection is made pursuant to the ten-day grace period of UCC Section 9-301(2). For purchase-money security interests, UCC Section 9-301(2) gives a ten-day grace period, running from the time the debtor receives possession of the collateral. If the purchase-money security interest is perfected within that period, the perfection relates back as against an interim lien creditor. This provision is recognized in the Code.[9] Furthermore, perfection of such a purchase-money security interest within the ten-day grace period (e.g., by filing a financing statement) is excepted from the automatic stay provisions of Section 362.[10]

Under Section 544(a)(1), the trustee may take advantage of an Article 9 secured lender's mistakes, including failure to perfect by filing a financing statement in the proper place, a lapse in perfection by expiration of a financing statement, inadequate description or lack of a debtor's signature or address in

---

[8] The 1962 version of UCC § 9-301(1)(b), as originally adopted by most states, provided that an unperfected security interest was subordinate to the rights of "a person who becomes a lien creditor without knowledge of the security interest and before it is perfected." Under the 1972 Amendments to UCC § 9-301(1)(b), now adopted by a majority of the states, the requirement that the lien creditor be "without knowledge" was deleted. Under either version, the trustee as a hypothetical lien creditor without knowledge should prevail over an unperfected security interest and may prevail over an unperfected Article 9 security interest without regard to whether there is "knowledge." Section 544(a) makes it clear that the trustee does not have knowledge "without regard to any knowledge of the trustee or of any creditor."

[9] 11 USC § 546(b), as amended by 1984 Amendments § 461. Section 546(b) provides that the trustee's avoiding powers under Sections 544, 545, and 549 are subject to "any generally applicable law that permits perfection of an interest in property to be effective against an entity that acquires rights in such property before the date of such perfection." The legislative history states:

> "For example, many State laws, under the Uniform Commercial Code, permit perfection of a purchase-money security interest to relate back to defeat an earlier perfected non-purchase money security interest if the former was perfected within ten days. U.C.C. § 9-301(2). Such perfection would then be able to defeat a hypothetical judicial lien creditor on the date of the filing of the petition."

H.R. Rep. No. 595, 95th Cong., 1st Sess. 371 (1977); S. Rep. No. 989, 95th Cong., 2d Sess. 86 (1978).

[10] See 11 USC § 362(b)(3), as amended by 1984 Amendments § 441; see also additional discussion at ¶ 12.05[1]. One bankruptcy court has held that Sections 546(b) and 363(b)(3) permitted a creditor to file a materialman's lien after the petition was filed where the state law permitted the materialman's lien to relate back to the time the creditor first began work or supplied materials. In re Design Builders, Inc., 18 Bankr. 392 (Bankr. D. Idaho 1981). Accord In re Yobe Elec., Inc., 728 F2d 207 (3d Cir. 1984).

the financing statement,[11] and inadequate or lack of possession of collateral where possession is relied on as the method of perfecting the security interest.[12] Security interests that are unenforceable because the Article 9 statute of frauds has not been complied with[13] may be avoided by the trustee under Section 544(a)(1) since the security interest would be unenforceable against a lien creditor under UCC Section 9-203.[14]

Leases and consignments of personal property that are not "true leases" or "consignments" under Article 9 of the UCC, but are "intended as security"[15] may be successfully challenged by the trustee in his status as a lien creditor under Section 544(a) and UCC Section 9-301(1)(b) if there has been no proper perfection by filing a financing statement.[16] Additionally, if the lease or consignment is intended as security and the lessor or consignor (secured party) does not have a writing or writings statement that will pass as a written security

---

[11] See UCC § 9-401 for requirements of a financing statement. Under the UCC, in many cases a financing statement must be filed in the proper filing office to perfect a security interest.

[12] A Washington case of significant note is Freeborn v. Seattle Trust, 94 Wash. 2d 336, 617 P2d 424 (1980), involving two bankruptcy cases certified from the federal district court. The Washington Supreme Court held that the vendor's right to receive payments under an executory real estate contract is personal property, and that when such an interest is assigned to secure a loan, the transaction is covered by Article 9 of the UCC and must be perfected by an Article 9 filing to be valid against the trustee in bankruptcy and that recording a "deed and seller's assignment of real estate contract" was not sufficient. The court pointed out:

> "We further hold that where the vendor in a real estate contract executes a 'Deed and Seller's Assignment of Real Estate Contract' by which he or she (a) assigns the contract and (b) conveys the real estate (legal title) . . . the assignee-grantee must both file pursuant to U.C.C. Article 9 . . . and record pursuant to RCW 65.08.070 in order to have priority over subsequent lien creditors, purchasers and encumbrancers."

94 Wash. 2d 344, 617 P2d 429.

[13] See UCC Section 9-203, which requires either a signed security agreement or possession of the collateral by the secured party pursuant to agreement for a security interest to be enforceable, both between the parties and against third parties. If the secured party does not have possession of the collateral, in the absence of a formal signed security agreement, what will be sufficient as a "signed security agreement" may be a critical issue between the secured party and a trustee in bankruptcy who challenges the security interest as unenforceable and therefore voidable under Section 544(a)(1) by the use of UCC Section 9-203.

[14] In addition, the defense of the debtor that the security interest is unenforceable is a defense available to the trustee in bankruptcy under Section 558 (added by 1984 Amendments § 470). Under Section 558, the trustee may also assert other defenses and claims of the debtor, such as rescission based on fraud, mutual mistake, and undue influence.

[15] See UCC § 1-201(37).

[16] See UCC §§ 1-201(37), 9-302, 9-301(1)(b), 2-326.

agreement, the trustee may be able to successfully challenge the lease or consignment security interest on that basis.[17]

Under Section 544(a)(1), the trustee may assert such claims as whether a specific debt is covered by a security agreement. For example, the trustee may question whether a future advance was "intended" to be covered by a broad "future advance clause."[18] Where a security interest is avoided under Section 544(a) or 544(b), payments made to a secured party within the preference period may be recoverable as a voidable preference under Section 547.[19]

Mortgages, deeds of trust, and real estate installment sales contracts that the debtor has granted, but that are unrecorded at the time the petition in bankruptcy is filed may be avoidable under Section 544(a), depending upon the applicable real estate recording act and whether a lien creditor may prevail and have priority over such unrecorded interests. If under the applicable recording act a lien creditor has priority over the unrecorded interest, then the trustee can avoid such interest. If under the applicable recording act and state law only a bona fide purchaser can prevail or have priority over such unrecorded interests, then the trustee's challenge is not under Section 544(a)(1) but in the trustee's status as a bona fide purchaser of real property under Section 544(a)(3). Under Section 544(a)(3), however, a relevant issue may be whether the trustee is to be charged with constructive notice, for example, of the rights of a party in possession.[20]

In some cases, the trustee may also be able to avoid under Section 544(a)[21] transfers that are voidable under, for example, a state Uniform Fraudulent Conveyance Act (UFCA) or a similar fraudulent conveyance law based on the Statute of Elizabeth, if these transfers are voidable as to subsequent creditors of the fraudulent grantor-debtor. For example, under Section 7 of UFCA, a transfer that is made with actual intent to hinder, delay, or defraud creditors is fraudulent as to both present and future creditors. Thus, the trustee as a future creditor (but not having the attribute of having extended credit or of becoming a creditor before the petition) could avoid the fraudulent conveyance by use of the state law if the state statute of limitation on the fraudulent conveyance had not expired. In many cases, the trustee could use Section 548,[22] which essen-

---

[17] See UCC § 9-203; cf. In re Walter W. Willis, Inc., 313 F. Supp. 1274 (ND Ohio 1970).

[18] See, e.g., In re Antuna, 4 Bankr. 25 (Bankr. WD Mo. 1980), where an original security agreement covered "all accounts" as collateral, with a broad future advance clause covering "all debts." Later, a second security agreement covering only specified accounts was executed when there was no outstanding debt. The court held that advances under the second security agreement were "not intended" to be covered by the first security agreement and that the specific accounts covered by the second security agreement had been collected by the debtor.

[19] Cf. In re Kelley, 3 Bankr. 651 (Bankr. ED Tenn. 1980). See discussion of preferences at infra ¶ 16.04.

[20] See discussion of this issue under Section 544(a)(3) at infra ¶ 16.02[3].

[21] Under Section 544(b), the trustee could also assert the right of actual creditors to set aside transfers that are fraudulent under state law.

[22] See discussion at infra ¶ 16.05.

tially restates UFCA with minor changes. However, Section 548 has a one-year statute of limitation. If this year period expires and the applicable state fraudulent conveyance law has a longer statute of limitation, the trustee might have to proceed under Section 544(a) using the state fraudulent conveyance law and statute of limitation. If under the applicable state law a particular fraudulent conveyance is voidable only as to creditors existing at the time of the fraudulent conveyance, the trustee cannot use Section 544(a)(1) but must proceed under Section 544(b) if an actual creditor who existed at the time of the transfer has a provable claim in the bankruptcy proceeding.

### [2] The Trustee as a Judgment Creditor With an Execution Returned Unsatisfied

In addition to the "ideal lien creditor" status given by Section 544(a)(1), the trustee is given the rights of a creditor who extends credit to the debtor at the time of the commencement of the case and obtains an execution against the debtor that is returned unsatisfied at such time, whether or not such a creditor exists.[23] This section is designed to give the trustee the rights under state law that unsatisfied execution creditors have under state law. For example, in some states it may be necessary to obtain a return of a writ of execution nulla bona to proceed against real property or to file a "creditor's bill" to set aside a fraudulent conveyance. The trustee is given this status under Section 544(a)(2).

### [3] The Trustee as a Bona Fide Purchaser of Real Property

In Section 544(a)(3), the trustee also is given the status of a bona fide purchaser of real property (other than fixtures) from the debtor at the time of the commencement of the case, whether or not such a purchaser exists.[24] It seems relatively well-established by case law that although the trustee's status under this section is conferred by federal bankruptcy law, his rights regarding other parties are to be determined by reference to state law.[25] For example, the trustee may avoid unrecorded conveyances, mortgages, deeds of trusts, real estate installment sales contracts, and leases that would not be valid under the applicable state recording act against a bona fide purchaser from the debtor.[26] Although Section 544(a) speaks in terms of a "bona fide purchaser" of real

[23] 11 USC § 544(a)(2).

[24] 11 USC § 544(a)(3), as amended by 1984 Amendments § 459; see also H.R. Rep. No. 595, 95th Cong., 1st Sess. 370 (1977); S. Rep. No. 989, 95th Cong., 2d Sess. 85 (1978).

[25] See, e.g., In re Morse, 30 Bankr. 52 (Bankr. App. Pan. 1st Cir. 1983) and cases cited therein.

[26] See, e.g., In re Kelly, 29 Bankr. 708 (Bankr. D. Me. 1983); In re Harter, Inc., 31 Bankr. 1015 (D. Kan. 1983) (trustee was permitted to use Section 544(a)(3) to avoid debtor's unrecorded reconveyance of real property back to grantor even though the grantor was in open and obvious possession of the property). In both *Kelly* and *Harter*, under local law constructive notice did not defeat the rights of a bona fide purchaser.

property (other than fixtures) "without regard to any knowledge," a serious question has been raised as to whether this also means that the trustee is to be regarded as being without "constructive knowledge" or inquiry notice that would preclude the existence of a bona fide purchaser with superior rights under applicable state law. For example, assume that a purchaser from the debtor under an unrecorded real estate installment sales contract is in possession of the property and that under the applicable state recording act a bona fide purchaser for value has priority over the unrecorded real estate contract. Under that particular state law, however, possession of the property by the purchaser serves as constructive notice to any purchaser from the debtor-vendor. May the trustee of the vendor, as a bona fide purchaser without knowledge, avoid the contract purchaser's interest under Section 544(a)(3), or will constructive notice defeat the trustee?[27] At present, the great weight of case law has held that constructive notice that will defeat a bona fide purchaser under applicable state law will be imputed to the trustee. In *McCannon v. Marston*,[28] perhaps the leading case on this subject, the Court of Appeals for the Third Circuit held that "constructive notice" given by possession of the real estate by the contract purchaser, which would defeat a bona fide purchaser under applicable state law,[29] would prevent the trustee from avoiding under Section 544(a)(3) the interest of a purchaser under an unrecorded contract for the sale of real property. A Ninth Circuit Bankruptcy Appellate Panel also held that the trustee under Section 544(a)(3) may be charged with constructive notice given by a lis pendens that gave constructive notice to all subsequent purchasers under applicable California law.[30] The court stated:

> The provision of Bankruptcy Code § 544(a)(3) that the trustee takes the powers of a bona fide purchaser of real property, "without regard to any knowledge of the trustee or any creditor," does not override provisions of state law which impute notice of claims to real estate, such as lis pendens, to all the world.[31]

---

[27] Note that if under local recording acts or state law possession or other constructive notice does not prevent a bona fide purchaser from attaining priority, then the trustee should be able to avoid the unrecorded interest. See In re Kelly, 29 Bankr. 708 (Bankr. D. Me. 1983); In re Harter, Inc., 31 Bankr. 1015 (D. Kan. 1983).

[28] 679 F2d 13 (3d Cir. 1982).

[29] The court made a determination as to the applicable state law:

> "We believe that were the Pennsylvania Supreme Court asked to consider whether a subsequent purchaser of a condominium building had a duty to make inquiry as to the rights of persons in possession of apartments in that building, it would hold that such possession provides constructive notice, as matter of law, no different than in the case of possession of a single family home."

Id. at 17. The Pennsylvania recording act specifically required that the bona fide purchaser be without "actual or constructive notice." See id. at 15 n.1.

[30] In re Gurs, 27 Bankr. 163 (Bankr. App. Pan. 9th Cir. 1983).

[31] Id. at 164. For additional cases supporting the view that constructive notice may be imputed to the trustee, see In re Richardson, 23 Bankr. 434 (Bankr. D. Utah 1982); In re Fitzpatrick, 29 Bankr. 701 (Bankr. WD Wis. 1983); In re Elin, 20 Bankr. 1012

Unless the mortgagee is in possession, constructive notice is much less likely to be an issue in the case of an unrecorded mortgage or deed of trust than it would be in an unrecorded real estate contract or lease situation where the purchaser or lessee is in possession, which may constitute constructive notice.

## ¶ 16.03 THE TRUSTEE AS REPRESENTATIVE OF ACTUAL CREDITORS

Under Section 544(b) (the counterpart to Section 70(e) of the 1898 Act), the trustee is authorized to avoid any transfer of an interest of the debtor in property or any obligation incurred by the debtor that is avoidable by an actual creditor who has an allowable unsecured claim in the bankruptcy proceeding. This section clarifies a point on which there had been some dispute under the 1898 Act and makes it clear that the trustee may assert only the rights of unsecured creditors. The legislative history also indicates that the doctrine of *Moore v. Bay*[1] is to be followed.[2] In *Moore v. Bay*, one of the more famous bankruptcy cases, the Court held that in asserting the right of an actual creditor to avoid a transaction, the trustee is not limited to the amount of the claim of the actual creditor's right that the trustee is asserting, but may avoid the entire transaction. Further, the recovery is for the benefit of all the creditors and not merely for the benefit of the creditor whose right is asserted.[3] For example, assume that a debtor had made a fraudulent conveyance of property valued at $100,000 or had given a security interest in real property worth $100,000 and that the conveyance or security interest was voidable as to creditor *A*, whose claim was for $10,000.[4] In asserting the right of creditor *A* to avoid the fraudulent transfer or security interest, the trustee would not be limited under Section 544(b) to setting aside the fraudulent transfer or voidable security interest to

---

(DNJ 1982); In re Jones, 20 Bankr. 988 (Bankr. ED Pa. 1982); In re Lewis, 19 Bankr. 548 (Bankr. D. Idaho 1982); In re Hardway Restaurant Inc., 31 Bankr. 322 (Bankr. SDNY 1983).

[1] 284 US 4 (1931).

[2] H.R. Rep. No. 595, 95th Cong., 1st Sess. 370 (1977); S. Rep. No. 989, 95th Cong., 2d Sess. 85 (1978).

[3] For extensive discussion of *Moore v. Bay*, see Collier on Bankruptcy ¶ 70.95 (Matthew Bender, 14th ed. 1978). "Since the decision in the *Bay* case, no dissenting voice has been raised by the courts. The accepted rule is that in a suit under § 70(e) if the transfer or obligation is voidable at all, it is voidable in toto." Id. at ¶ 70.95, p. 1111.

[4] In the case of the transfer of the security interest in real property, assume, for example, that the transfer was subject to a recording act, perhaps not common, that permitted a general creditor who extended credit while a mortgage was unrecorded to set aside or have priority over the unrecorded mortgage. However, if the recording act required a creditor to become a lien creditor before the mortgage was recorded, and a creditor did become a lien creditor before the mortgage was recorded, the trustee could not use the rights of the lien creditor under Section 544(b) because the lien creditor would be a secured creditor and under Section 544(b) the trustee is limited to asserting the rights of unsecured creditors.

the extent of $10,000, but could avoid the entire fraudulent transfer or security interest and recover it for the estate. However, in cases of security interests in personal property covered by UCC Article 9, the doctrine of *Moore v. Bay* is no longer of any practical consequence. Under UCC Section 9-301(1)(b), a lien creditor is the only type of creditor who may have priority over an unperfected security interest. A lien creditor under the Code is a secured creditor; under Section 544(b) the trustee may not assert the rights of a secured creditor. Thus, if the security interest is perfected before bankruptcy, the trustee cannot assert under Section 544(b) the priority rights of a lien creditor who became a lien creditor before perfection of the security interest. If the Article 9 security interest is unperfected at the time of the filing of the petition, then the trustee may avoid the security interest in his status as a lien creditor under Section 544(a). However, there are two areas where the doctrine of *Moore v. Bay* is still potentially applicable. The first is with respect to a bulk transfer that is covered by Article 6 of the UCC.[5] If there is a covered bulk transfer and the requirements of Article 6 are not met,[6] the transfer, for a limited period of six months, is "ineffective"[7] as to "creditors" (not limited to lien creditors, as is the case with secured transactions under UCC Section 9-301). Thus, if the trustee asserted under Section 544(b) the right of a creditor who had a claim for $1,000 to set aside a bulk transfer of $100,000 of inventory, the trustee could assert the creditor's right if the creditor were not secured, the trustee could use *Moore v. Bay* to avoid the transfer to the full extent of $100,000. The other area in which *Moore v. Bay* is still potentially applicable is with respect to unrecorded transfers of real property under some recording acts. If, as in the example given above, a subsequent general creditor could set aside or avoid a transfer of realty, regardless of whether the transfer was recorded, the trustee under Section 544(b) could avoid the transfer in its entirety using *Moore v. Bay* if such an actual creditor existed with an allowable unsecured claim in bankruptcy.[8]

---

[5] See In re Verco Indus., 10 Bankr. 347 (Bankr. App. Pan. 9th Cir. 1981).

[6] Generally, this requires compiling a schedule of the property being transferred, compiling a list of creditors of the transferor, and giving notice to the creditors prior to the transfer. If notice is not properly given, the bulk transfer is void as to creditors of the transferor even if later, after the transfer is made, notice is given to creditors and the Act is otherwise complied with. See UCC §§ 6-101–6-111.

[7] This probably equates to "voidable" for bankruptcy purposes. Cf. In re Verco Indus., 10 Bankr. 347 (Bankr. App. Pan. 9th Cir. 1981).

[8] This could occur under a type of recording act that, for example, makes an unrecorded mortgage voidable as to a creditor who extends credit while the mortgage is "off record" even though the mortgage is subsequently recorded. If the applicable realty recording act makes the transfer voidable as to subsequent creditors for example, because the mortgage is not promptly recorded (i.e., late recording does not protect even as to subsequent general creditors if the mortgage is not promptly recorded), then the trustee can avoid it under Section 544(a)(1) as a subsequent lien creditor and need not invoke *Moore v. Bay*. However, it is questionable whether such recording acts exist. Generally if "creditors" are protected by recording acts (creditors are generally not considered "purchasers" under such acts), it appears they generally must be "lien creditors" to prevail over the unrecorded interests. See 4 American Law of Property § 17.29, at

As previously noted, where the one-year statute of limitation on avoiding fraudulent conveyances under Section 548 has expired, the trustee may, by using the right of an existing unsecured creditor, be able to take advantage of a longer state statute of limitation to set aside a fraudulent conveyance.[9]

## ¶ 16.04 PREFERENCES UNDER SECTION 547

Along with the "strong arm" clause, one of the most important avoiding powers given to the trustee is the power to avoid certain preferences under Section 547.[1] Generally, outside of bankruptcy, a preference (i.e., giving or paying one creditor more on his claim than other creditors) is not considered a fraudulent conveyance and in the absence of a specific statute, it is not voidable by other creditors even though the favored creditor may be preferred with all of the debtor's assets. However, in a bankruptcy context, certain preferences are avoidable in keeping with the general bankruptcy policy of equality of distribution. If a debtor were permitted to prefer certain creditors, perhaps even with all of the debtor's assets, and then shortly thereafter resorted to bankruptcy, equality of distribution would have little meaning if there were no assets to be distributed. Similarly, if certain creditors by use of "grab law" were permitted to appropriate most, if not all, of the debtor's assets and bankruptcy then ensued, equality of distribution would again be meaningless. To promote the concept of equality of distribution, to prevent seizing of the debtor's assets by creditors, and to prevent the debtor from favoring some creditors to the exclusion of others, in bankruptcy certain preferential transfers made within the ninety-day period before the filing of the bankruptcy petition may be avoided and recovered for the estate. In the case of "insider" preferences, transfers made within a year of filing may also be avoided and recovered for the estate.[2]

---

610; § 71.32 (Little, Brown 1952). The trustee under Section 544(b) may not assert the rights of a lien (secured) creditor.

[9] See discussion at supra ¶ 16.02[1].

[1] For helpful discussion of preferences, see Kaye, "Preferences Under the New Bankruptcy Code," 54 Am. Bankr. L.J. 197 (1980); Young, "Preferences Under the Bankruptcy Reform Act of 1978," 54 Am. Bankr. L.J. 221 (1980); Ellis, "Preferential Payments by Check: At What Point Is Payment Made?" 16 U.C.C. L.J. 46 (1983); Pitts, "Insider Guaranties and the Law of Preferences," 55 Am. Bankr. L.J. 343 (1981); Phillips, "Insider Provisions of the New Bankruptcy Code," 55 Am. Bankr. L.J. 363 (1981); Tait & Williams, "Bankruptcy Preference Laws: The Scope of Section 547(c)(2)," 99 Banking L.J. 55 (1982); Clark, "Preferences Under the Old and New Bankruptcy Acts," 12 U.C.C. L.J. 154 (1979); Nimmer, "Security Interests in Bankruptcy: An Overview of Section 547 of the Code," 17 Hous. L. Rev. 289 (1981).

[2] 11 USC §§ 547 (as amended by 1984 Amendments §§ 310, 462), 550 (as amended by 1984 Amendments §§ 465, 551).

To a large extent, the basic concept of voidable preferences under Section 547 of the Code remains the same as it was under Section 60 of the 1898 Act. However, the following significant changes have been made:[3]

(1) The concept of "insider" preferences is new;
(2) Not all preferential transfers made within the preference period are voidable; that is, there are express exceptions to the avoiding powers;
(3) There is a presumption of insolvency during the ninety days immediately preceding the filing of the petition;
(4) The elimination of the requirement that the creditor who receives the preferential transfer have "reasonable cause to believe the debtor is insolvent at the time of the transfer";
(5) Some important case law under Section 60 of the 1898 Act is overruled by Section 547.

A preliminary look at the organization of Section 547 is helpful. First, Section 547(a) contains important definitions of terms used in section 547.[4] These definitions should be carefully examined.[5] Section 547(b)[6] contains the basic definition or elements of a preference. Section 547(c)[7] contains exceptions to the rule that all preferences are voidable by the trustee; certain specified transfers that meet the elements of a preference set out in Section 547(b) are not voidable by the trustee. Section 547(e)[8] contains important and complex details as to when, for purposes of Section 547, a "transfer" will be deemed to have been made or will be recognized. These rules as to when a transfer is deemed to have occurred are critical to the operation of Section 547.

The basic definition of a preference is given in Section 547(b): any transfer of an interest of the debtor in property to or for the benefit of a creditor, for or on account of an antecedent debt made while the debtor was insolvent, made

---

[3] Some of these changes were made by the 1984 Amendments to Section 547.

[4] 11 USC § 547(a), as amended by 1984 Amendments § 462.

[5] "Inventory" is defined as "personal property leased or furnished, held for sale or lease, or to be furnished under a contract for service, raw materials, work in process, or materials used or consumed in a business, including farm products such as crops or livestock, held for sale or lease." 11 USC § 547(a)(1). This definition is broader than the UCC definition of inventory (see UCC § 9-109(4)) and may include property that would be classified under UCC § 9-109(3) as "farm products."

"Receivable" is defined as the "right to payment, whether or not such right has been earned by performance." This definition is probably broader than "accounts receivable" as customarily used and is broader than "accounts" as defined in UCC Section 9-106 (both in the 1962 and 1972 versions of the UCC). In addition to "accounts" the definition may include "instruments," "chattel paper," and "general intangibles," as defined in the UCC. See UCC §§ 9-105, 9-106. Also, "receivables" as used in the Code is not limited to payments for goods sold or leased or for services rendered (as is an "account" under the UCC), and could include rent for use of realty.

[6] 11 USC § 547(b), as amended by 1984 Amendments § 462.

[7] 11 USC § 547(c), as amended by 1984 Amendments §§ 310, 462.

[8] 11 USC § 547(e), as amended by 1984 Amendments § 462.

on or within ninety days before the date of filing the petition, and that enables the creditor to receive more than he would have received if the transfer had not been made and the case were a liquidation case under Chapter 7. The elements of this definition will be considered individually. However, there are significant changes from Section 60 of the 1898 Act that are worth noting before turning to a more detailed treatment of the elements under Section 547.

First, the basic preference period is reduced from four months to ninety days before filing of the petition; for transfers to "insiders,"[9] the preference period is one year before filing the petition. For transfers within the ninety-day period, the requirement of showing that the creditor had "reasonable cause to believe the debtor was insolvent at the time of the transfer" was eliminated under the Code.[10] However, under the 1978 Bankruptcy Reform Act as originally enacted, the requirement was retained for transfers to insiders in the period between ninety days and one year before filing the petition. The 1984 Amendments to Section 547 eliminated this "reasonable cause to believe the debtor was insolvent" requirement entirely and it is no longer an element for any type of preference.[11] Determination of when the transfer is deemed to have been made under Section 547(e) is, of course, important. The application of the transfer rules of Section 547(e) in some cases pushes the date of "transfer" closer to the date of bankruptcy and perhaps makes it easier to establish the insolvency requirement. In some cases, it may place the "transfer" date within one of the preference periods.[12]

There is a statutory presumption of insolvency during the ninety days before filing the petition, which is designed to simplify the trustee's burden of proof.[13]

## [1] Transfer of Property of the Debtor

"Transfer" is defined very broadly in Section 101(48) to include "every mode, direct or indirect, absolute or conditional, voluntary or involuntary, of disposing of or parting with property or with an interest in property, including retention of title as a security interest and foreclosure of the debtor's equity of redemption."[14] As can be seen, practically any means of transferring or dispos-

---

[9] This is a new concept under Section 547. "Insider" is defined in Section 101(28).

[10] This element was required for all voidable preferences under Section 60(b) of the 1898 Act.

[11] Under the Code, prior to the 1984 Amendments, for an "insider preference" this element had to have been shown to have existed at the time the transfer was made.

[12] For example, the transfer may "in fact" or "actually" be made outside of the applicable preference period but because of the operation of the "transfer rules" be deemed to be made within the preference period. See discussion at infra ¶ 16.04[1].

[13] See discussion at infra ¶ 16.04[4].

[14] 11 USC § 101(48), as amended by 1984 Amendments § 421(i). The 1984 Amendments added the final phrase "and foreclosure of the debtor's equity of redemption." This 1984 addition is significant for Durrett v. Washington Nat'l Ins. Co., 621 F2d 201 (5th Cir. 1980), and other cases following it that held that for purposes of

ing of an interest in property will be a "transfer" whether made voluntarily by the debtor or involuntarily, such as by the creation of a lien by a levy of execution.[15] The most common preferences occur, of course, where there is a transfer by payment of an antecedent debt or where a previously unsecured debt is secured within the preference period.

A number of cases have involved the question of when a transfer occurs when a check is involved.[16] Checks commonly are considered the equivalent of cash; however, in theory under the UCC, an ordinary check is treated as a conditional payment.[17] Arguably no transfer of funds is made until the check is honored by the drawee bank, or perhaps is certified or accepted. However, for bankruptcy purposes, the courts have different views as to when the transfer

---

Section 548 a foreclosure may in some circumstances be a fraudulent conveyance and avoidable by the trustee. The *Durrett* case and the significance of the change is discussed at infra ¶ 16.05. The express inclusion of "foreclosure of the debtor's equity of redemption" as a transfer may be significant for Section 547 preferences as well. Assume, for example, the *Durrett* type of case. Within the preference period, the secured creditor, with a secured debt of $115,000 that is in default, forecloses on a mortgage or deed of trust on property valued at $200,000 and the creditor purchases the property for $115,000 at the foreclosure sale. Under *Durrett* and other cases, this may be a voidable fraudulent conveyance under Section 548. See discussion at infra ¶ 16.05. Is it also a voidable preference under Section 547? Under the 1984 addition to the definition of transfer, clearly the foreclosure is a transfer. If the transfer is within the preference period and the debtor is insolvent at that time, arguably there is a preference if the transfer enables the creditor to receive more than he would receive in a Chapter 7 liquidation. In the example given, arguably the foreclosing creditor has received more than he would have received in a Chapter 7 liquidation. In a Chapter 7 liquidation the creditor would be entitled to receive the amount of his secured claim, $115,000. Yet by the foreclosure the creditor received property valued at $200,000 and arguably received more than he would have received in a Chapter 7 case. Furthermore, the "equity" or excess value (i.e., the difference between the debt and the value of the property) is transferred to the creditor to the detriment of other unsecured creditors. It remains to be seen whether the courts will accept this argument. In jurisdictions that follow the *Durrett* case, it may not be necessary to make this preference argument if the *Durrett* requirements can be satisfied. That is, the margin between the debt and the value of the foreclosed property is sufficient; if not, then the preference argument may be an additional way in which such foreclosure may be challenged.

[15] For example, an assignment of an interest in a lawsuit is a transfer. In re Sun Railing, Inc., 5 Bankr. 538 (Bankr. SD Fla. 1980).

[16] This is important not only as to whether the transfer occurs within the ninety-day period but also with respect to the "substantially contemporaneous" exception of Section 547(c)(1) and the "payment in the ordinary course of business" exception of Section 547(c)(2). However, the 1984 Amendments to the "payment in the ordinary course of business" exception eliminated the requirement that to qualify for the exception the payment had to be made within forty-five days of the time the debt was incurred. With the elimination of this forty-five-day restriction, the time at which payment by a check occurs will be less important for the exception. See discussion at infra ¶¶ 16.04[7][a], 16.04[7][b]. For a helpful survey of the cases, see Ellis, "Preferential Payments by Check: At What Point Is Payment Made?" 16 U.C.C. L.J. 46 (1983).

[17] See UCC § 3-802 and Official Comment 3.

or payment occurs when a check is used. Some courts have taken the view that payment is deemed to occur when the check is delivered.[18] Other courts have taken the view that payment is deemed to occur when the drawee bank honors the check, not when the creditor receives it.[19] In *In re Duffy*,[20] a postdated check was delivered to a creditor outside the ninety-day period but was honored and paid by the drawee within the ninety-day period. The court held that this was a "transfer when paid." Since the transfer was not within the "contemporaneous exchange" exception of Section 547(c)(1), it was a voidable preference.

The rules set out in Section 547(e)[21] for determining when a transfer will be deemed to have occurred or will be recognized for purposes of Section 547 are extremely important and make significant changes in the preference law that generally prevailed under the 1898 Act.[22]

---

[18] In re Hoover, 32 Bankr. 842, 849 (Bankr. WD Okla. 1983). In *Hoover*, the court took the view that payment of a debt by means of a check is the equivalent of a cash payment unless the check is dishonored, and that for purposes of Sections 547(c)(1) and 547(c)(2) payment is considered to be made when the check is delivered. The court relied in part on the legislative history. See 124 Cong. Rec. H11,097 (Sept. 28, 1978); S17,414 (Oct. 6, 1978).

[19] See In re Naudain, Inc., 32 Bankr. 871 (Bankr. ED Pa. 1983) and cases cited therein; In re Mailbag Int'l, Inc., 28 Bankr. 905 (Bankr. D. Conn. 1983) and cases cited therein. In *Mailbag*, the court held that the "transfer" occurred for a certified check when the check was delivered, and not on the date of certification.

[20] 3 Bankr. 263 (Bankr. SDNY 1980).

[21] 11 USC § 547(e), as amended by 1984 Amendments § 462.

[22] Section 547(e) provides:

"(1) For purposes of this section–

(A) a transfer of real property other than fixtures, but including the interest of a seller or purchaser under a contract for the sale of real property, is perfected when a bona fide purchaser of such property from the debtor against whom applicable law permits such transfer to be perfected cannot acquire an interest that is superior to the interest of the transferee; and

(B) a transfer of a fixture or property other than real property is perfected when a creditor on a simple contract cannot acquire a judicial lien that is superior to the interest of the transferee.

(2) For the purposes of this section, except as provided in paragraph (3) of this subsection, a transfer is made–

(A) at the time such transfer takes effect between the transferor and the transferee, if such transfer is perfected at, or within 10 days after, such time;

(B) at the time such transfer is perfected, if such transfer is perfected after such 10 days; or

(C) immediately before the date of the filing of the petition, if such transfer is not perfected at the later of–

(i) the commencement of the case; or

(ii) 10 days after such transfer takes effect between the transferor and the transferee.

The transfer rules of Section 547(e) are somewhat artificial and in some cases the "transfer" for preference purposes is deemed to have occurred at a time other than when the transfer actually occurred. However, there is reason underlying these artificial rules. Initially, it may be helpful to examine the structure of the subsection itself. Note first that Section 547(e) sets forth rules applicable only for Section 547; it does not apply to other sections of the Code. Section 547(e)(1) gives "perfection rules" as to when a transfer of property is "perfected" for Section 547 purposes. Section 547(e)(2), using "perfection" as defined in Section 547(e)(1), then sets forth detailed "transfer rules" as to when a transfer is deemed to have been made or is recognized for purposes of Section 547. Finally, Section 547(e)(3) states that a transfer "is not made until the debtor has acquired rights in the property transferred."[23] Determining when a "transfer" occurs under Section 547(e)(2) requires a three-step analysis:

(1) When was the transfer perfected under the "perfection rules" of Section 547(e)(1)–the "perfection date or time"?

(2) When was the transfer "effective" between the parties, i.e., effective between the debtor-transferor and the transferee–the "effective date or time"?

(3) When did the debtor-transferor acquire "rights" in the property transferred?

Under Section 547(e)(3), the transfer can occur no earlier than the time the transfer is effective between the parties and the transferor-debtor has acquired rights in the property transferred. If at the time the transfer is "effective" between the parties, the transfer is "perfected" as defined in Section 547(e)(1) or if "perfected" within ten days of the "effective date" (by relation back), the transfer is deemed to have occurred on the "effective date."[24] If not perfected within ten days of the "effective" date, there is no relation back and the transfer will be deemed to be made when the transfer is perfected beyond the ten-day grace period.[25]

Turning to the "perfection rules" for real property (not including fixtures), transfers are "perfected" at the time when a bona fide purchaser of such property from the transferor cannot acquire priority over the transferee.[26] Under

---

(3) For the purpose of this section, a transfer is not made until the debtor has acquired rights in the property transferred."

[23] Section 547(e)(3) overrules the theory of the *Dubay* case or what Professor Countryman calls the "abracadabra" or "the-transfer-occurred-before-it-occurred" theory. See discussion at infra ¶ 16.04[9].

[24] 11 USC § 547(e)(2)(A). Perfection within the ten-day period permitted by Section 547(e)(2)(A) is not subject to the automatic stay of Section 362. See 11 USC § 362(b)(3), as amended by 1984 Amendments § 441.

[25] 11 USC § 547(e)(2)(B).

[26] 11 USC § 547(e)(1)(A). This test is consistent with the "bona fide purchaser" test for real property in Section 544(a)(3). The Code clears up a point of uncertainty under Section 60 of the 1898 Act as to whether, for purposes of when the "transfer" would be recognized, "fixtures" would fall under the "bona fide purchaser" test for

many recording acts, this generally occurs when the transfer (e.g., the deed, mortgage, deed of trust, or real estate contract) is recorded; a bona fide purchaser generally has priority over prior unrecorded conveyances. Under Section 547(e)(2), the transfer then is deemed to have been made at the time the real property transfer was "perfected" (recorded), if the debtor-transferor had "rights" in the property at that time and the transfer was effective between the transferor and the transferee. To illustrate, assume that on May 1, the debtor gives the creditor a mortgage on real estate then owned by the debtor to secure a loan made to the debtor on that date, but the mortgage is not recorded until August 10. The debtor then files a petition in bankruptcy on September 20. Assume also that the applicable real property recording act requires that mortgages be recorded, and if not recorded, a bona fide purchaser from the debtor-grantor will have priority. Assume further that there is no basis for any "constructive" notice to defeat a bona fide purchaser.[27] Although the transfer in fact occurred on May 1,[28] and thus was not for an antecedent debt and also was not made within the ninety-day preference period, the transfer by operation of Sections 547(e)(1)(A) and 547(e)(2) will be deemed to have occurred when the mortgage was recorded on August 10. The transfer will then be within the preference period and also be a transfer for an antecedent debt, the debt having been incurred on May 1.[29] In such circumstances, the effect of the operation of Sections 547(e)(1)(A) and 547(e)(2) on the delayed recording is to "split" the debt from the security transfer and to translate what in fact was a transfer for a present consideration into a transfer for an antecedent debt. Note also that even if the real property conveyance is promptly recorded but covers after-acquired property of the debtor-grantor, the transfer cannot occur before the debtor-grantor acquires rights in such property.[30]

---

realty or whether they would fall under the "lien creditor" test for personal property. Section 547(e)(1)(A) makes it clear that the "lien creditor" test applies for fixtures. The section also makes it clear that the interest of a purchaser under a contract for the sale of real property is treated as "real property."

[27] See discussion at supra ¶ 16.02[3] dealing with constructive notice of the trustee in his status as a bona fide purchaser under Section 544(a). As noted at supra ¶ 16.02[3], a number of cases have held that despite the "bona fide purchaser without knowledge" status of the trustee under Section 544(a)(3) with respect to real property, constructive notice may nevertheless defeat the trustee under that section. It would seem that under appropriate circumstances "constructive notice" may well be argued to apply under Section 547(e).

[28] Assume that under local law the mortgage was good between the parties without recording.

[29] The creditor might still argue that the mortgage falls within the "substantially contemporaneous" exception of Section 547(c)(1), although with such a long delay in recording it seems unlikely that this argument would prevail. For discussion of the substantially contemporaneous exception, see infra ¶ 16.04[7][a].

[30] In appropriate circumstances, one of the exceptions of Section 547(c) may be applicable, such as the "enabling loan" or "purchase money" exception of Section 547(c)(3). See discussion at infra ¶ 16.04[7][c].

For personal property and fixtures,[31] Section 547(e)(1)(B) states that transfers are "perfected" for Section 547 purposes "when a creditor on a simple contract cannot acquire a judicial lien that is superior to the interest of the transferee" (i.e., when the transfer is protected from a lien creditor).[32] For personal property security interests covered by UCC Article 9, this means "perfection" in an Article 9 sense by one of the appropriate methods of perfection.[33]

Therefore, until the property is put beyond the reach of lien creditors, the transfer is not recognized as "perfected" for preference purposes.[34] Under Section 547(e)(3), a "transfer is not made until the debtor has acquired rights" in the property transferred. For security interests, this means that the transfer for Section 547 purposes can occur no earlier than when the debtor acquires "rights" in the collateral. This is particularly significant with respect to after-acquired collateral and the Article 9 floating lien.[35] If at the time the transfer is effective between the parties, the transfer is perfected as defined in Section 547(e)(1) or if perfected within ten days of the "effective date," then the transfer, by relation back, is deemed to have occurred on the effective date. If not perfected within ten days of the effective date, there is no relation back but the transfer will be deemed to be made when the transfer is perfected beyond the ten-day grace period.

Under Section 547(e)(2), a transfer cannot take place earlier than the time such "transfer takes effect between the transferor and the transferee"; that is, before the security interest is "enforceable" and "attaches" as defined in Article 9.[36]

---

[31] As previously noted, the Code clears up a point of uncertainty under Section 60 of the 1898 Act and makes it clear that fixtures are subject to the transfer rules applicable to personal property, not the "bona fide purchaser" test for real property.

[32] A "Judicial lien" means "lien obtained by judgment, levy, sequestration, or other legal or equitable process or proceeding." 11 USC § 101(30).

[33] Technically this is somewhat inaccurate and perhaps should be equated to having taken the "steps" necessary to perfect, such as filing or possession. Perfection under the UCC means taking the necessary steps, such as filing, possession, or automatic perfection, *plus* attachment, which means that there is an enforceable security agreement, value has been given, and the debtor has acquired rights in the collateral. See UCC §§ 9-303, 9-203(2). Under the UCC, the steps for perfection, such as filing, might have been taken, but the security interest might not be perfected as the debtor had not yet acquired rights in the collateral.

[34] The transfer rules of Section 547(e)(2) discussed above also apply to transfers of personal property and fixtures and interrelate with the perfection rules of Section 547(e)(1)(B). Under Section 547(e)(2), the transfer can occur no earlier than the time the transfer is effective between the parties and the transferor-debtor has acquired rights in the property transferred.

[35] See discussion at infra ¶ 16.04[9].

[36] Under UCC Section 9-203(1), a security interest is not enforceable between the parties or against third parties until the secured party either has possession of the collateral pursuant to agreement or has a signed written security agreement. A security interest cannot attach until a security agreement is enforceable and the debtor has acquired rights in the collateral. UCC § 9-203(2).

If a transfer is not perfected at the time the petition in bankruptcy is filed, the transfer is deemed to be made just before the petition is filed,[37] and if the other elements are present, there will be a voidable preference. However, in most cases where the security interest or transfer is unperfected on the date the petition is filed, the trustee will also be able to avoid the security interest under Section 544(a)(1). Note also that Section 547(e)(2)(C), which deems the security interest to be perfected just before the petition is filed, is only for purposes of Section 547 and does not mean the security interest will be perfected just before the petition for purposes of Section 544(a).

Some specific examples help to illustrate the operation of Section 547(e). First, assume that on May 1, the debtor borrowed $50,000 from the creditor, and to secure the loan, properly executed a security agreement covering all of "debtor's inventory and equipment, now owned and hereafter acquired." The creditor properly filed on the same date a financing statement covering the collateral. Assume also that on August 10, the debtor repaid $10,000 of the loan; on September 20, the debtor filed a voluntary petition in bankruptcy. As discussed below, if the creditor were fully secured, the August 10 payment would not be a preference, since it does not permit the creditor to receive more than would have been received in liquidation.[38] If the creditor were not secured or only partially secured, the August 10 payment would be a transfer for an antecedent debt and a preference (to the extent of the unsecured debt) if the other elements were present. Assume, however, that the creditor failed to file the financing statement covering the collateral until August 10. Under Section 547(e), the transfer would be deemed to have been made on August 10 when the enforceable security interest was perfected and thus protected against a lien creditor. Although in fact the transfer occurred when the loan was made, since the security interest was enforceable and was not for an antecedent debt, the transfer would be deemed to be made on August 10 within ninety days of the petition and for an antecedent debt. The delayed perfection has the same effect as the payment in the unsecured situation.

Changing the facts slightly, assume that the financing statement was filed on the date of the loan, May 1, but that the creditor neglected to obtain a written security agreement until August 20 and did not have possession of the collateral. Even though there initially was a filing, the security interest would not be enforceable ("effective" between the parties) until August 20 and would not be good against a lien creditor under UCC Section 9-203 until that time. Thus, under Section 547(e)(2), the transfer would be deemed to have been made on August 10 and would be a transfer within the ninety-day preference period and would be for an antecedent debt.[39]

To illustrate another aspect of Section 547(e), assume that the creditor made the loan on May 1 and took a properly executed security agreement on

---

[37] 11 USC § 547(e)(2)(C).

[38] See discussion at infra ¶ 16.04[6].

[39] Again, the creditor might argue that the transaction falls within one of the exceptions, such as a "substantially contemporaneous exchange." Under such circumstances, would it be held to be "in fact substantially contemporaneous"?

the same date but did not file the financing statement until May 8. Under Section 547(e)(2)(A), since the security interest was "effective between the parties" when the security agreement and loan were made, and was perfected within ten days of that time, the "transfer" date would relate back to May 1 and the transfer would not be for an antecedent debt. However, if the filing were not made until May 13, which would be outside the ten-day grace period, the "transfer" for Section 547 purposes would be deemed to be made on May 13, for an antecedent debt. If bankruptcy ensues within ninety days and the other elements are present, this transfer could be a voidable preference if it does not fall within any of the exceptions of Section 547(c).

For a transfer to be a preference, it must be a transfer of an interest of the debtor in property.[40] For example, a relative paying or securing a debt of the debtor would not be a preference. In a sense, the favored creditor has not been preferred at the expense of the debtor's other creditor by use of the debtor's property.

One bankruptcy court has held that wages that had been paid into a municipal court's statutory trusteeship before the ninety-day preference period but disbursed to a creditor within the ninety-day period were not property of the debtor and thus not a voidable preference.[41]

## [2] Transfer to or for the Benefit of a Creditor

For a transfer to be a preference, it must be made to or for the benefit of a creditor. A "creditor" is an entity with a claim against the debtor that arose before filing the petition.[42] "Claim" is very broadly defined to include a "right to payment, whether or not such right is reduced to judgment, liquidated, unliquidated, fixed, contingent, matured, unmatured, disputed, undisputed, legal, equitable, secured, or unsecured," and includes a right to an equitable remedy, if the breach gives rise to a right to payment.[43] As the language "to or for the benefit of a creditor" suggests, the transfer does not have to be made directly to the creditor. Thus a guarantor, surety, or an indorser of an obligation of the debtor (e.g., of a note made by the debtor) may be a "creditor." A transfer (such as by paying or securing of a previously unsecured debt) to the creditor within the preference period may be a preference not only to the creditor but also to the surety, guarantor, or indorser of the obligation. By paying the debt (or securing the previously unsecured debt), the debtor decreases the potential liability of the indorser (the surety or guarantor) to the creditor; to that extent, the indorser's contingent claim against the debtor is decreased. Thus, the indorser benefits from the payment or securing of the debt.[44]

[40] 11 USC § 547(b).

[41] In re Hayes, 5 Bankr. 676 (Bankr. SD Ohio 1980).

[42] 11 USC § 101(9).

[43] 11 USC § 101(4).

[44] Collier on Bankruptcy ¶ 547.18 (Matthew Bender, 15th ed. 1981); see also Pitts, "Insider Guaranties and the Law of Preferences," 55 Am. Bankr. L.J. 343 (1981).

### [3] Transfer for or on Account of an Antecedent Debt

The Code does not define an antecedent debt other than to say that the transfer must be for or on account of an antecedent debt[45] owed by the debtor before the transfer was made. In some cases a debt may be incurred at one time and the transfer of property may occur after that time (e.g., by creating or giving a security interest). The transfer, however, is not a voidable preference if the transaction meets the requirement of the "contemporaneous exchange" or one of the other exceptions of Section 547(c)(1).

Of course, it is important to determine when a debt is incurred. Case law dealing with the issue generally has been concerned with when the debt was incurred for purposes of determining whether payment was made within the exception of Section 547(c)(2).[46] One court observed:

> The determination of when a debt is actually "incurred" is critical. One view is that the debt is not incurred until an invoice is sent or demand for payment is made. The probably better view is that the debt is incurred whenever the debtor obtains a property interest in the consideration exchanged giving rise to the debt. Thus if goods are identified for shipment, unless the special agreement otherwise provides, the debtor has a special property interest and the debt is "incurred." Certainly when a debtor uses a utility the debt is incurred at the time the resource is consumed rather than when the invoice is sent.[47]

The court in *Naudain* held that a debt was incurred each time electricity was consumed, and cited with approval a statement from *In re Valley Mechanical Industries, Inc.*[48] that "incurred" does not necessarily imply "due."[49]

---

[45] "Debt" is defined in Section 101(11) as liability on a "claim," which is broadly defined in Section 101(4).

[46] Prior to the 1984 Amendments, the "payment in the ordinary course" exception of Section 547(c)(2) required that the payment be made within forty-five days of the time that the debt was incurred. However, the 1984 Amendments to Section 547(c)(2) eliminated this requirement for the "payment in ordinary course of business" exception. See 1984 Amendments § 462. With elimination of the "payment within forty-five days" requirement, in determining whether the exception applies, the focus now is less likely to be on when the debt was incurred or payment made and more on whether the payment was made in the ordinary course of both the creditor and debtor's business and according to ordinary business terms. See discussion at infra ¶ 16.04[7][b].

[47] In re Naudain, Inc., 32 Bankr. 871, 873 (Bankr. ED Pa. 1983) (quoting from Collier on Bankruptcy ¶ 547.39, at 547-121 (Matthew Bender, 15th ed. 1981)).

[48] 20 Bankr. 350 (Bankr. ND Ga. 1982).

[49] 32 Bankr. 873 (Bankr. ED Pa. 1983); cf. In re Emerald Oil Co., 695 F2d 833 (5th Cir. 1983), holding that a debt is incurred for the purposes of the Section 547(c)(2) exception

> "when the debtor becomes obligated to pay it, not when the creditor chooses to invoice the debtor for his work or goods. This view is in accord with the most logical meaning of the statutory language in the light of statutory definitions in the

## [4] Transfer Made While the Debtor Was Insolvent

To be a voidable preference, the transfer must be made when the debtor is insolvent.[50] In determining when insolvency must be established (i.e., the date of the transfer), the transfer rules of Section 547(e) are important. Insolvency must be established on the date the transfer is deemed to be made, and not on the "actual" date of the transfer. For example, assume that a creditor makes a loan to a debtor on March 1 and at the same time takes an enforceable security interest in the debtor's accounts. However, the creditor delays filing a financing statement to perfect the security interest until April 10. Under the transfer rules of Section 547(e)(2), the transfer would be deemed to be made on April 10, with the effect that not only is the transfer for an antecedent debt (the loan made on March 1), but the date for establishing insolvency would be April 10.

For purposes of avoiding a preferential transfer, the "debtor is presumed to have been insolvent on and during the 90 days immediately preceding the date of the filing of the petition" in bankruptcy.[51] However, the presumption is a rebuttable one and the burden of proof (risk of nonpersuasion) on the issue of insolvency remains on the trustee.[52] The presumption, representing a change from the 1898 Act, was created "to simplify the trustee's former burden of reconstructing the debtor's books and records, even though it was unusual that a debtor was not insolvent for the 90 days before the bankruptcy petition was filed."[53] The presumption of insolvency does not apply in the period between

---

> Code as a whole, as well as with the apparent general Congressional intent in creating the exception."

Id. at 837.

[50] "Insolvent" is defined for an individual, a corporation, or an entity other than a partnership as the "financial condition such that the sum of such entity's debts is greater than all of such entity's property, at a fair valuation" exclusive of property fraudulently conveyed or concealed and exempt property. 11 USC § 101(29)(A). A somewhat different definition is used for partnerships. See 11 USC § 101(29)(B), as amended by 1984 Amendments § 421.

[51] 11 USC § 547(f).

[52] The Court of Appeals for the Fifth Circuit stated:

> "[A]s expressly indicated in the legislative reports and in legislative amendments clarifying the application of the Federal Rules of Evidence to bankruptcy proceedings, the intent of the presumption was to be governed by Fed. R. Evid. 301; thus, to require the party against whom directed (here, the creditor Wilson) to come 'forward with evidence to rebut or meet the presumption,' but not to shift the burden of proof or nonpersuasion to him, which burden remains against the party (here, the trustee) who had the original burden to prove insolvency in order to avoid a transfer as preferential."

In re Emerald Oil Co., 695 F2d 833, 837–838 (5th Cir. 1983); see also In re Zuni, 6 Bankr. 449 (Bankr. DNM 1980).

[53] 695 F2d 838 n.5 (5th Cir. 1983), citing Collier on Bankruptcy ¶ 547.03[5], at 547-24 (Matthew Bender, 15th ed. 1981).

ninety days and one year before the petition is filed. In "insider" preferences, the trustee must carry the burden of proof on insolvency unaided by the presumption.[54]

### [5] Transfer Made on or Within Ninety Days Before Filing of the Petition

Except in the case of insiders, the transfer must occur on or within ninety days before the petition in bankruptcy is filed. Note that the transfer of the interest in property is the event that must occur within the preference period of ninety days. In the case of an insider, the transfer must occur within a year before filing the petition. As long as the debt is antecedent to the transfer, it does not matter whether the debt is incurred within the preference period; only the "transfer" must occur within that period.

There is some difference of opinion as to how the ninety-day preference period should be computed. The Code does not specify in Section 547 how time periods are to be calculated.[55] In *In re Grimaldi*, a lien had been acquired by attachment on August 7 and the petition in bankruptcy was filed on November 5. The creditor contended that both November 5 and August 7 should be counted, which would make August 7 the ninety-first day. The trustee argued that only November 5 should be excluded, thus placing August 7 within the ninety-day period. The court noted that Section 31 of the 1898 Act provided that "days shall be computed by excluding the first and including the last," but that the Code does not contain a section comparable to Section 31. The court held that Bankruptcy Rule 906(a)[56] was still applicable and provided for application of Federal Rule of Civil Procedure 6(a), which states "in computing any period of time prescribed . . . by any applicable statute, the day of the act, event, or default from which the designated period of time begins to run shall not be included." Therefore, the court concluded that the transfer was made within the ninety-day period and that Section 547 requires that the transfer must occur "on or within 90 days before the date of the filing of the petition."

---

[54] The 1984 Amendments to Section 547(b) eliminated the requirement that the insider have reasonable cause to believe that the debtor was insolvent for transfers made between ninety days and one year before the petition is filed. See 11 USC § 547(b), as amended by 1984 Amendments § 462. For discussion of insider preferences, see infra ¶ 16.04[10].

The 1984 Amendments added a new Section 547(g), which provides:

> "For the purposes of this section, the trustee has the burden of proving the avoidability of a transfer under subsection (b) of this section, and the creditor or party in interest against whom recovery or avoidance is sought has the burden of proving the nonavoidability of a transfer under subsection (c) of this section."

11 USC § 547(g), added by 1984 Amendments § 462.

[55] In re Grimaldi, 3 Bankr. 533 (Bankr. D. Conn. 1980).

[56] This is now Bankruptcy Rule 9006.

Although there seems to be agreement in case law that Federal Rule of Civil Procedure 6(a) should be followed,[57] and although Bankruptcy Rule 9006(a) now expressly states the same rule, this has not resolved all the problems encountered in unusual cases. Opinion is divided on whether the starting point for counting should be the date of the "transfer" and counted forward or whether the starting point should be the date of filing the petition and counted back. The issue has been described in these terms:

> As noted by the Court in *Sid Kumins, Inc., v. Wolf* (*In re Wolf*), 13 B.R. 167, 169, ... "there exists some disagreement among the authorities whether it is the date the petition is filed or the date of the attachment [or, in this case, the garnishment] which is to be considered the 'event' and thereby excluded from the calculation." Collier takes the position that "the day the alleged transfer is effected will not be counted," citing *Bell v. West*, 44 F.2d 161 (4th Cir. 1930) and *Whitley Grocery Co. v. Roach*, 115 Ga. 918, 42 S.E. 282 (1902). 4 Collier on Bankruptcy ¶ 547.28 at 547-109 (15th ed. 1981). This view is not persuasive because of the language of Section 547(b)(4)(A), which indicates that the event from which the 90 day period begins to run is the date of the filing of the petition. Under Rule 6(a), the date of the filing of the petition should be excluded and the 90 day period calculated by beginning with the day before the filing of the petition as the first day and counting back until the 90th day. [Citations omitted]. Whether the petition date or the transfer date is excluded makes a difference in some cases. In this case if the petition date is excluded, transfers on October 15 [1980] would fall within the 90 day preference period. If a transfer occurred on October 15 and that date is excluded, the transfer would fall outside the preference period.[58]

---

[57] See, e.g., Harbor Nat'l Bank of Boston v. Sid Kumins, Inc., 696 F2d 9 (1st Cir. 1982); In re Grimaldi, 3 Bankr. 533 (Bankr. D. Conn. 1980); In re Wolf, 13 Bankr. 167 (Bankr. D. Mass. 1981); In re B & M Contractors, Inc., 2 Bankr. 110 (Bankr. ND Alaska 1979); In re Mailbag Int'l, Inc., 28 Bankr. 905 (Bankr. D. Conn. 1983); In re Larson, 21 Bankr. 264 (Bankr. D. Utah 1982); In re Utility Stationery Stores, Inc., 12 Bankr. 170 (Bankr. ND Ill. 1981); see also Collier on Bankruptcy ¶ 547.28, at 547-109 (Matthew Bender, 15th ed. 1981). Federal Rule of Civil Procedure 6(a) provides in part:

> "In computing any period of time prescribed ... by any applicable statute, the day of the act, event, or default from which the designated period of time begins to run shall not be included. The last day of the period so computed shall be included, unless it is a Saturday, a Sunday, or a legal holiday, in which event the period runs until the end of the next day which is not a Saturday, Sunday, or a legal holiday."

[58] In re Larson, 21 Bankr. 264, 267 n.2 (Bankr. D. Utah 1982). In *Larson* the petition had been filed on January 13, 1980. For contrary authority holding that the computation should start with the transfer and go forward, see In re Mailbag Int'l, Inc., 28 Bankr. 905 (Bankr. D. Conn. 1983). In Harbor Nat'l Bank of Boston v. Sid Kumins, Inc., 696 F2d 9 (1st Cir. 1982), the court found it unnecessary to decide the issue.

### [6] Transfer That Enables Creditor to Receive More Than Would Be Received in a Chapter 7 Liquidation

Section 547(b)(5) codifies *Palmer Clay Products Co. v. Brown*,[59] which held that the preferential effect of the transfer depends not upon what would have been its effect on creditors if the debtor's assets had been liquidated and distributed at the time of the transfer, but upon the actual effect on creditors during the ensuing bankruptcy. In other words, the time to determine the preferential effect is at the time of bankruptcy, and not at the time of the transfer.[60]

For a fully secured creditor who receives payment on the loan within the preference period there is no preference.[61] Such payments do not permit the fully secured creditor to receive more than he would have received without the payment; being fully secured, the creditor will receive full payment in a liquidation proceeding. Moreover, it may be viewed as "buying back" security; that is, to the extent the debt is paid, collateral is released and there is a present exchange for value. However, payments to a partially secured creditor within the preference period may be a preference at least to the extent of the unsecured debt. In the absence of agreement otherwise, payments on a partially secured debt generally will be taken as applied to the unsecured portion.[62]

### [7] Exceptions to the Avoiding Power

Although a transfer may meet all of the requirements of Section 547(b), it may not be avoidable by the trustee if it falls within one of the seven exceptions given in Section 547(c).[63] The legislative history indicates that these exceptions are cumulative: "If a creditor can qualify under any one of the exceptions, then he is protected to that extent. If he can qualify under several, he is protected by each to the extent he can qualify under each."[64]

The 1984 Amendments added a new Section 547(g)[65] which provides:

---

[59] 297 US 227 (1936). See Kaye, "Preferences Under the New Bankruptcy Code," 54 Am. Bankr. L.J. 197, 199 n.3 (1980).

[60] But see White & Summers, Uniform Commercial Code § 24-4, at 1004–1005 (West, 2d ed. 1980), who seem to suggest in an example a contrary view that the preferential effect is determined at the time of the transfer.

[61] See, e.g., Barash v. Public Fin. Corp., 658 F2d 504 (7th Cir. 1981); In re Rogers Refrigeration, 33 Bankr. 58, 60 (Bankr. D. Ore. 1983); In re Debmar Corp., 21 Bankr. 858, 862 (Bankr. SD Fla. 1982); Collier on Bankruptcy ¶ 547.21 (Matthew Bender, 15th ed. 1981).

[62] Barash v. Public Fin. Corp., 658 F2d 504 (7th Cir. 1981); see In re McCormick, 5 Bankr. 726 (Bankr. ND Ohio 1980), where in absence of proof to the contrary, the court assumed that the payments were credited to the unsecured portion.

[63] 1984 Amendments § 310 added the seventh exception in Section 547(c)(7) for certain small preferences in individual consumer cases (discussed at infra ¶ 16.04[7][f]).

[64] H.R. Rep. No. 595, 95th Cong., 1st Sess. 373–374 (1977); S. Rep. No. 989, 95th Cong., 2d Sess. 88 (1978).

[65] 11 USC § 547(g), added by 1984 Amendments § 462.

> For the purposes of this section, the trustee has the burden of proving the avoidability of a transfer under subsection (b) of this section, and the creditor or party in interest against whom recovery or avoidance is sought has the burden of proving the nonavoidability of a transfer under subsection (c) of this section.

### [a] Substantially Contemporaneous Exchanges

If the preferential transfer was intended by the debtor and the creditor to be a contemporaneous exchange for "new value" given to the debtor and was in fact a substantially contemporaneous exchange, the transfer is not avoidable by the trustee.[66] This exception is the codification of case law that had developed under the 1898 Act.[67] From a planning perspective, reliance on this exception by a secured party is unwise and invites litigation by the trustee in the event of bankruptcy. A secured party is advised to avoid any "gap periods" of unperfection or periods when the security interest is unenforceable, in which the "transfer" rules might operate as illustrated in the previously given examples and turn what in fact was not a transfer for an antecedent debt into such a transfer by the date the transfer is deemed to be made. However, in some instances where delayed perfection or delayed enforceability has occurred, the substantially contemporaneous exception may be the only method of salvaging the transfer.[68]

The scope of the "substantially contemporaneous" exception is far from clear and leaves several areas open for dispute. For example, what is the meaning of "substantially contemporaneous" or "intended to be"? If a loan initially is "intended to be" a secured loan, how long may the delay be between the giving of the new value and the execution or perfection of the security interest and still qualify as "substantially contemporaneous"? If the security agreement is executed at the time the new value is given and perfection occurs within the ten-day grace period of Section 547(e)(2), the transfer will relate back and there will be no preference since there is no antecedent debt. But how long after the new value is given may a secured party delay in obtaining a written security agreement and still qualify for the exception?[69] May a secured party who takes a written security agreement and gives new value at the same time delay filing (and hence perfection) beyond the ten-day grace period of Section 547(e)(2) and still qualify for the exception? Note that the ten-day grace period of Sec-

---

[66] "New value" is defined in Section 547(a)(2).

[67] See, e.g., Dean v. Davis, 242 US 438 (1917); National City Bank of N.Y. v. Hotchkiss, 231 US 50 (1913); Kaye, "Preferences Under the New Bankruptcy Code," 54 Am. Bankr. L.J. 197, 198 (1980).

[68] See generally Duncan, "Delayed Perfection of Security Interests in Personal Property and the Substantially Contemporaneous Exchange Exception to Preference Attack," 62 Neb. L. Rev. 201 (1983).

[69] As discussed earlier, under the transfer rules of Section 547(e)(2) the transfer cannot occur earlier than the time the security interest is effective between the parties (i.e., until there is a written security agreement if the secured party does not have possession of the collateral).

tion 547(e)(2) suggests that a delay beyond the ten-day period in obtaining either a written security agreement to make the interest enforceable or in filing to perfect is certainly questionable, although Section 547(e)(2) does not expressly state that the ten-day grace period is the outer limit for the substantially contemporaneous exception. In one case, the loan was made and the security agreement was taken on June 12, but not perfected until around the first of August. The transfer therefore was not deemed to have been made until then and the court held that the transfer was not "substantially contemporaneous" in fact.[70]

The legislative history of Section 547(c)(1) indicates that the exception was intended to cover an important area where property is sold and paid for by check. Although checks commonly are thought to be the same as cash, under the theory of the UCC, a check is conditional payment and, in theory at least, no funds are transferred until the check is honored. Thus, where a check is given in payment for goods purchased and the check is paid later, arguably it could be said to be a transfer for an antecedent debt. However, the legislative history indicates that if a check is given for new value and is paid or honored later, it is considered to be a substantially contemporaneous exchange as long as the check is honored within thirty days.[71]

Another issue that has been raised by one commentator is whether the exception includes a "substantially contemporaneous substitution" of collateral.[72]

### [b] "Payment in the Ordinary Course" Rule

This exception is designed to cover the routine payment of monthly bills such as rent, utility, and other ordinary trade credit that is kept current[73] and

---

[70] In re Kelley, 3 Bankr. 651 (Bankr. ED Tenn. 1980).

[71] The House and Senate reports stated:

> "Normally, a check is a credit transaction. However, for the purposes of this paragraph, a transfer involving a check is considered to be 'intended to be contemporaneous,' and if the check is presented for payment in the normal course of affairs, which the Uniform Commercial Code specifies as 30 days, U.C.C. § 3-503(2)(a), that will amount to a transfer that is 'in fact substantially' contemporaneous."

H.R. Rep. No. 595, 95th Cong., 1st Sess. 373 (1977); S. Rep. No. 989, 95th Cong., 2d Sess. 88 (1978).

[72] See Kaye, "Preferences Under the New Bankruptcy Code," 54 Am. Bankr. L.J. 197, 199–201 (1980). Even if a substantially contemporaneous substitution of collateral is permissible, an argument can be made that substitution of an appreciating asset for a depreciating asset, even if they are of equal value at the time of the substitution, may be preferential if the substituted asset permits the debtor to receive more at the time of liquidation than would have been received at that time from the released depreciating asset. Id. To the extent that the substituted collateral permits the creditor to receive more at the time of liquidation, arguably there is a preference.

[73] Levin, "An Introduction to the Trustee's Avoiding Powers," 53 Am. Bankr. L.J. 173, 186 (1979). For helpful discussion, see Tait & Williams, "Bankruptcy Preference Laws: The Scope of Section 547(c)(2)," 99 Banking L.J. 55 (1982).

"to leave undisturbed normal financial relations."[74] Under this exception, payment of a debt is not a voidable preference if the payment meets the following criteria:

(1) It is of a debt incurred in the "ordinary course" of the "business or financial affairs" of both the debtor and the transferee;[75]
(2) It is made in the ordinary course of business or financial affairs of both the debtor and the transferee; and
(3) It is made according to ordinary business terms.

The use of the term "or financial affairs" was intended to include a consumer and payment of such monthly bills as utility bills.[76]

As noted previously, for application of Section 547(c)(2) it is critical in some instances to determine when the debt is incurred.[77] Is it incurred when the debt first becomes legally owing or on the billing or invoice date? When is the obligation for rent "incurred"? One court has held that on an installment note payable monthly, the debt was incurred when the note was executed and not when the monthly payments became due.[78] Revolving charge accounts present additional problems with respect to the application of payments—to which purchase should a payment be applied?[79] For example, assume that item *A* is purchased on January 1 for $100 and item *B* is purchased on February 2 for

---

[74] H.R. Rep. No. 595, 95th Cong., 1st Sess. 373 (1977); S. Rep. No. 989, 95th Cong., 2d Sess. 88 (1978).

[75] Prior to the 1984 Amendments, the "payment in the ordinary course" exception of Section 547(c)(2) required that the payment be made within forty-five days of the time that the debt was incurred. However, the 1984 Amendments to Section 547(c)(2) eliminated this requirement. See 1984 Amendments § 462. With elimination of the "payment within forty-five days" requirement, in determining whether the exception applies, the focus now is less likely to be on when the debt was incurred or payment made and more on whether the payment was made in the ordinary course of both the creditor and debtor's business and according to ordinary business terms.

[76] H.R. Rep. No. 595, 95th Cong., 1st Sess. 373 (1977); S. Rep. No. 989, 95th Cong., 2d Sess. 88 (1978).

[77] This determination may be less critical after the 1984 amendment that deleted the requirement that the payment be made within forty-five days of the time the debt was incurred. However, determination of the time the debt is incurred may still be relevant in determining whether payment is made in the ordinary course and according to ordinary business terms.

[78] In re Bowen, 3 Bankr. 617 (Bankr. ED Tenn. 1980); see also In re McCormick, 5 Bankr. 726 (Bankr. ND Ohio 1980) (holding that an installment debt that was payable monthly was not "incurred" as the monthly payments became due but when the debtor originally assumed the obligation to pay); Barash v. Public Fin. Corp., 658 F2d 504 (7th Cir. 1981). But see Henson, "The Uniform Commercial Code and the New Bankruptcy Act: Some Problem Areas," 35 Bus. Law. 83, 96 (1979).

[79] The addition by the 1984 Amendments of new Section 547(c)(7), containing an exception to voidability for certain small preferences in cases of individual consumer debtors, makes this question less likely to arise. For discussion of this new exception, see infra ¶ 16.04[7][g].

$100. Billing is sent out on the fifteenth of each month. A payment of $50 is made on March 10 and the petition in bankruptcy is filed on April 1 by the purchaser-debtor. Does the $50 apply to item *A* or item *B*? Prior to the elimination of the "payment within forty-five days" requirement, if applied to item *A* payment would not have been made within the forty-five-day period of the ordinary-course rule of Section 547(c)(2).[80] After the elimination of the forty-five-day rule, the issue is now whether the payment is made in the ordinary course of business of the debtor and creditor, and made according to ordinary business terms.

Prior to the 1984 Amendments deleting the "payment within forty-five days" requirement, a number of cases had arisen under this exception where checks were given and the issue was raised as to when payment had been made for purposes of the forty-five-day period. Is payment made when the check is delivered or when the check is honored and paid? With some exceptions, in the case of an ordinary check, the courts have held that payment is made when the check is paid, and not on delivery.[81]

To come within the "payment in ordinary course" rule, a payment must meet the requirements of all subsections of Section 547(c)(2).[82]

### [c] Enabling Loans

The exception contained in Section 547(c)(3)[83] is designed to give protection to purchase-money loans. For example, assume that a loan or advance is made to enable the debtor to purchase the collateral, a security agreement is given covering the collateral, and a financing statement is filed promptly. Sometime later, after the loan is made, the collateral is acquired. Under Section 547(e)(3), because the transfer cannot occur before the debtor acquires rights in

---

[80] See In re Williams, 5 Bankr. 706 (Bankr. SD Ohio 1980), where charges had been made under a Sears charge account; the court held that a state statute directed that payment should be applied to the first charges. Absent a controlling statute, if there is an express agreement as to the application of payments, the agreement should control. If there is no express agreement and the debtor does not direct how the payments are to be applied, the bankruptcy court will have to make the determination as to how the payment is to be applied.

[81] See discussion at supra ¶ 16.04[1].

[82] In re Naudain, Inc., 32 Bankr. 871 (Bankr. ED Pa. 1983). In rejecting an argument that to come within the exception of Section 547(c)(2) it was not necessary to comply with all four subsections (after the 1984 Amendments there are only three subsections), the court stated:

> "Met-Ed states that it is 'aware of no authority' which stands for the proposition that the four elements of section 547(c)(2) must be read in the conjunctive. Simply put, the relevant case law does not support that interpretation. In *Matter of Donny*, 11 B.R. 451 (Bkrtcy. W.D. Wis. 1981), the court held that 'the exception found in § 547(c)(2) requires all four elements, (A) through (D), to be satisfied in order to prevent avoidance of a preferential transfer of § 547(b).' " [Citations omitted.]

Id. at 874.

[83] 11 USC § 547(c)(3), as amended by 1984 Amendments § 462.

the collateral, the transfer (via the attaching of the security interest) will be for an antecedent debt. If the other requirements of Section 547(b) are met, the transfer will be a voidable preference unless it falls within one of the exceptions of Section 547(c). However, not all purchase-money security interests will meet the requirements of Section 547(c)(3). To come within the "enabling loan" exception, a security interest must be taken for value given to enable the debtor to acquire, and in fact be used to acquire, the collateral. The new value also must be given at or subsequent to the signing of a security agreement describing the collateral and the security agreement must be perfected within ten days after the debtor receives possession of the collateral.[84] Note that this exception requires the secured party to show that in fact the new value was used to acquire the collateral. Establishing that a loan in fact enabled the debtor to acquire the collateral may be a factual showing that will be difficult to establish in some instances. For example, if the new value funds were given directly to the debtor and are not traceable to the collateral, there may be difficulty in meeting the requirement. On the other hand, if the disbursement is made by check directly to the seller of the collateral or by a check made payable jointly to the debtor and the seller, this should be sufficient to establish that the funds in fact were used to acquire the collateral. If the seller is the secured party financing the acquisition of the collateral by extending credit (e.g., under a conditional sales contract), this also should satisfy the requirement. Note that the ten-day grace period runs from the time the debtor receives possession of the collateral.[85] If the purchase-money security interest is not perfected within this ten-day period, the security interest will not be within the "enabling loan" exception and will be a transfer for an antecedent debt and voidable unless it falls within one of the other exceptions.[86]

### [d] Setoff

Section 547(c)(4) is the counterpart of Section 60(c) of the 1898 Act and codifies the "net result rule."[87] Section 547(c)(4) provides that any preferential payment or transfer received by a creditor is to be set off against any subse-

---

[84] "New value" is defined in Section 547(a)(2).

[85] Prior to the 1984 amendment to Section 547(c)(3), the ten-day grace period ran from the time the security interest attached, not from the date the debtor received possession of the collateral. The 1984 amendment apparently was made to conform to the ten-day grace period for perfecting purchase-money security interests under UCC Section 9-301(2) that runs from the date that the debtor receives possession. Prior to the 1984 changes to Section 547(c)(3), in some cases, depending on when the debtor acquired rights in the collateral, the security interest may have attached before the debtor received possession of the collateral and the ten-day grace period may have expired before the debtor received possession.

[86] See, e.g., In re Kelley, 3 Bankr. 651 (Bankr. ED Tenn. 1980).

[87] H.R. Rep. No. 595, 95th Cong., 1st Sess. 374 (1977); S. Rep. No. 989, 95th Cong., 2d Sess. 88 (1978).

quent unsecured transfer the creditor makes to the debtor.[88] In other words, a creditor who receives a preference, but who subsequently gives new value to the debtor that is unsecured, has a nonavoidable preference to the extent the debtor's estate, temporarily depleted by the transfer to the creditor, is subsequently replenished by unsecured new value.[89]

### [e] "Improvement of Position" Test

The exception given by Section 547(c)(5)[90] is extremely important with respect to the UCC Article 9 floating lien. For property that is acquired by the debtor within the preference period and is picked up by the floating lien of an after-acquired property clause in a valid perfected security agreement, the transfer is deemed under Section 547(e)(3) to have been made when the debtor acquires rights in the collateral. If the elements of Section 547(b) are met, the transfer is a voidable preference unless it falls within one of the exceptions. The main exception designed to give limited protection to after-acquired property covered by a UCC Article 9 floating lien is the "improvement in position" exception of Section 547(c)(5). The exception is limited, however, to inventory and receivables and the proceeds of either. These terms are defined in Section 547(a) and are somewhat broader in scope than comparable terms under the UCC.[91] The exception does not cover other collateral not falling within the bankruptcy definition of "inventory" and "receivables," such as "equipment" as defined by UCC Article 9. For such collateral, acquired within the preference period and covered by the floating lien of a perfected security agreement, the transfer is deemed to occur when the security interest attaches upon acquisition of rights by the debtor and is not protected under the "improvement in position" exception unless the equipment is shown to be "proceeds" of "inventory" or "receivables."[92] In some instances, the transfer may fall within another exception such as the "enabling loan" or "substantially contemporaneous" exception.

### [f] Nonavoidable Statutory Liens

Transfers brought about by the fixing of a statutory lien within the preference period are not avoidable under Section 547 if the statutory lien is not

---

[88] For helpful discussion, see Comment, "The Running-Account Creditor and Section 547(c)(4) of the New Bankruptcy Code," 16 Wake Forest L. Rev. 959 (1981).

[89] See In re Hygrade Envelope Corp., 393 F2d 60 (2d Cir. 1968).

[90] 11 USC § 547(c)(5), as amended by 1984 Amendments § 462.

[91] See discussion at supra ¶ 16.04.

[92] "Proceeds" is not defined in the Code but presumably will include at least "identifiable proceeds" as defined in UCC Sections 9-306(1) through 9-306(2). To what extent tracing theories will be applied is not apparent from the statute and will have to be developed in case law. See, e.g., Kaye, "Preferences Under the New Bankruptcy Code," 54 Am. Bankr. L.J. 198, 211 (1980).

avoidable under Section 545.[93] However, not all statutory liens are valid under Section 545.[94]

### [g] Small Preferences in Consumer Debtor Cases

The 1984 Amendments added a new Section 547(c)(7),[95] which created an additional exception to voidability of certain transfers that might otherwise be voidable under Section 547(b). In a case filed by an individual debtor whose debts are primarily consumer debts,[96] if the aggregate value of the preferential transfer is less than $600, the preference may not be avoided. Thus, small payments or preferences by a consumer debtor may not be avoided. Note that the small preferences falling within the exception do not have to be consumer debts if the individual's obligations are primarily consumer debts. If the individual debtor's obligations are not primarily consumer debts (e.g., are business debts), the small preference exception does not apply but some other exception (e.g., the "payment in ordinary course" exception) may apply.

## [8] Judicial Liens as Preferences

The creation of a lien by judicial proceedings, such as by garnishment, attachment, execution, or a judgment lien against real property (created by obtaining a judgment or docketing of a judgment where required), is a "transfer."[97] If acquired within the preference period by a previously unsecured creditor, the lien may be a preference.[98] However, if the lien or transfer is obtained outside the preference period, it is not a preference.[99] State law generally deter-

---

[93] 11 USC § 546(c)(6). "Statutory lien" is defined as a

> "lien arising solely by force of a statute on specified circumstances or conditions, or lien of distress for rent, whether or not statutory, but does not include security interest or judicial lien, whether or not such interest or lien is provided by or is dependent on a statute and whether or not such interest or lien is made fully effective by statute."

11 USC § 101(45).

[94] For discussion of the avoiding power under Section 545, see infra ¶ 16.06. For additional discussion of avoiding federal tax liens as preferences under Section 547, see infra ¶ 16.11.

[95] Added by 1984 Amendments § 310.

[96] "Consumer debt" is defined as "debt incurred by an individual primarily for a personal, family, or household purpose." 11 USC § 101(7).

[97] See 11 USC § 101(48).

[98] See, e.g., In re Levine, 6 Bankr. 54 (Bankr. SD Fla. 1980); In re Larson, 21 Bankr. 264 (Bankr. D. Utah 1982); In re Riverfront Food & Beverage Corp., 29 Bankr. 846, 851 (Bankr. ED Mo. 1983).

[99] See, e.g., Harbor Nat'l Bank of Boston v. Sid Kumins, Inc., 696 F2d 9 (1st Cir. 1982); In re Jordan, 5 Bankr. 59 (Bankr. DNJ 1980) (judgment lien on realty); In re Bradford, 5 Bankr. 18 (Bankr. D. Nev. 1980).

mines when the lien is acquired.[100] In the case of a writ of garnishment served outside the preference period but covering wages earned within the preference period, case law is divided as to whether this constitutes a voidable preference. The better view is that for wages earned within the preference period, the transfer occurs when the debtor acquires rights in the wages by earning them and thus may be a voidable preference if the other elements are present.[101] Other courts have taken the view that after service of the writ of garnishment outside the preference period, the debtor no longer has rights in the wages earned thereafter and therefore no transfer occurs within the preference period. These cases appear to turn largely upon the local garnishment law.[102]

## [9] The Uniform Commercial Code Article 9 "Floating Lien"

With certain exceptions not applicable to "inventory" and "receivables" as defined in the Bankruptcy Code, UCC Section 9-204 sanctions the use in security agreements of after-acquired property clauses. Generally, these clauses are given effect by nonbankruptcy courts. If a security agreement is properly worded (e.g., "all inventory and accounts, now owned and hereafter acquired"), then as new collateral falling within the collateral description is acquired, it automatically becomes security for the obligations covered by the security agreement and is covered by the so-called floating lien. In effect, the security interest attaches to the after-acquired property. Note that UCC Section 9-204(3) also permits "future advance coverage." To the extent that property is acquired within the preference period—ninety days or one year for insiders—and to which the Article 9 floating lien attaches and secures an antecedent debt, there is potentially a voidable preference. A transfer occurs by means of the floating lien that attaches when the property is acquired to secure an antecedent debt. In effect, it is analogous to the situation where security is given within the preference period for a previously unsecured or partially secured debt.[103]

The floating lien was generally upheld against attack under Section 60 of the 1898 Act,[104] and four theories were advanced to sustain the floating lien

---

[100] See, e.g., In re Larson, 21 Bankr. 264 (Bankr. D. Utah 1982) and cases discussed therein.

[101] In re Larson, 21 Bankr. 264 (Bankr. D. Utah 1982).

[102] For discussion of the numerous cases in this area, see id.

[103] For helpful discussion, see Harrington, "Insecurity for Secured Creditors: The Floating Lien and Section 547 of the Bankruptcy Act," 63 Marq. L. Rev. 447 (1980); Cohen, "Value Judgments: Accounts Receivable Financing and Voidable Preferences Under the New Bankruptcy Code," 66 Minn. L. Rev. 639 (1982); Duncan, "Preferential Transfers, The Floating Lien, and Section 547(c)(5) of the Bankruptcy Reform Act of 1978," 36 Ark. L. Rev. 1 (1983); Breitowitz, "Article 9 Security Interests as Voidable Preferences: Part II—the Floating Lien," 4 Cardozo L. Rev. 1 (1983).

[104] See DuBay v. Williams, 417 F2d 1277 (9th Cir. 1969); In re King-Porter Co., 446 F2d 722 (5th Cir. 1971); Grain Merchants of Ind., Inc., v. Union Bank & Sav. Co., 408 F2d 209 (7th Cir. 1969); Rosenberg v. Rudnick, 262 F. Supp. 635 (D. Mass. 1967); In re Nunnemaker Transp., 456 F2d 28 (9th Cir. 1972); Owen v. McKesson & Robbins Drug Co., 349 F. Supp. 1327 (ND Fla. 1972).

against attack by the trustee as a preference.[105] One theory was the "res" theory, otherwise known as the "Mississippi River" theory or "unitary" theory.[106] Under this theory, inventory and receivables were viewed as unitary, not changing; the increase or decrease or change in the collateral within the preference period was ignored. This clearly was a fiction used to avoid the reality that new inventory or receivables might be acquired within the preference period and that the secured position might change.

The dominant theory perhaps was the "transfer occurred at perfection (filing) theory," or what Professor Countryman labeled the "abracadabra" or "the-transfer-occurred-before-it-occurred" theory.[107] For bankruptcy purposes, it was theorized that the "transfer" occurred upon filing of the security interest because at that time the security interest was protected against subsequent lien creditors, and not when the property was acquired within the preference period and the security interest attached. Thus, if perfection (filing) occurred outside the preference period or at the time value was given, there was no preference.

The floating lien might also have been upheld against preference attack under a "substitution theory." Under this view, to the extent that acquisition of new collateral within the preference period could be matched with or considered to be a substitute for the release of old collateral, the acquisition or transfer of the new collateral would not be for an antecedent debt. Instead, the acquisition would be for "new value"; (i.e., the release of the old collateral, at least to the extent there was no enhancement of the secured position by the substitution).[108] In part, the theory was that, due to the substitution, there was no depletion of the debtor's estate. Successful use of this theory by a secured party to sustain the floating lien might require a certain amount of policing to establish the substantially contemporaneous nature of the release and substitution.

The UCC itself provided a theory under which the floating lien might have been upheld. This theory might be labeled the "UCC Section 9-108 theory" or "outdeeming-the-Bankruptcy-Act theory." UCC Section 9-108 provides that if a secured party gives new value (e.g., by way of an advance, incurring an obligation, or releasing of a perfected security interest) that is to be secured by a security interest in after-acquired property, the security interest in the after-acquired property is deemed to be "for new value and not as security for an antecedent debt" if the collateral is acquired in the ordinary course of the debtor's business or under a contract of purchase made pursuant to the security

---

[105] These theories are discussed in detail in Countryman, "Code Security Interests in Bankruptcy," 4 U.C.C. L.J. 35 (1971); the following material in this text is borrowed from that source. See also Kaye, "Preferences Under the New Bankruptcy Code," 54 Am. Bankr. L.J. 197 (1980). The apt and descriptive labels used for these theories below are those of Professor Countryman.

[106] See, e.g., Rosenberg v. Rudnick, 262 F. Supp. 635 (D. Mass. 1967).

[107] See DuBay v. Williams, 417 F2d 1277 (9th Cir. 1969); In re King-Porter Co., 446 F2d 722 (5th Cir. 1971); Grain Merchants of Ind., Inc., v. Union Bank & Sav. Co., 408 F2d 209 (7th Cir. 1969).

[108] Compare the Code definition of "new value" in Section 547(a)(1).

agreement. In effect, UCC Section 9-108 attempts to relate the value forward to the time of acquisition of the collateral; when the transfer occurs on attachment of the security interest, the transfer is not for an antecedent debt and hence is not a preference.[109] The chief point of contention with respect to this theory is whether the UCC can make such an end run around the federal bankruptcy law.[110] Most courts faced with the floating lien preference issue under the 1898 Act avoided the supremacy issue posed by UCC Section 9-108 and did not rely on the section.[111]

How viable is the Article 9 floating lien under the Bankruptcy Code? If under the provisions of Section 547(e) the transfer is deemed to occur within the preference period and the transfer is for an antecedent debt, then potentially there is a preference problem. As discussed previously, if there is delayed perfection or delayed enforceability that does not coincide with the giving of value or the extension of credit, the transfer may be for an antecedent debt and a preference. In the case of a floating lien, where the loan is made, an enforceable security agreement is obtained, and a filing is made at the same time, but part or all of the collateral is acquired within the preference period, under Section 547(e)(3) the transfer is deemed to occur when the debtor acquires rights in the collateral. As in the case of delayed perfection or delayed enforceability, the transfer cannot take place earlier than when the debtor acquires rights in the collateral and the security interest is perfected and enforceable. The reasoning underlying the *DuBay v. Williams* and *Grain Merchants* cases, and the "transfer-occurred-before-it-occurred" theory is effectively overruled by Section 547(e)(3).[112] It also appears that the "res," "unitary," or "Mississippi River" theory is overruled since Section 547 seems to demand a determination of when rights in separate items of collateral, including inventory and receivables, are acquired.

The substitution theory is not expressly overruled and appears to be a viable basis for upholding a floating lien, if the appropriate factual basis is established. "New value" as defined in Section 547(a)(2) appears to include release of collateral. Arguably, as old collateral is released and new value is given, if this new value can be matched up with the acquisition of new collateral acquired under the floating lien, it may not be a transfer for antecedent debt. If the transfer is considered to be for an antecedent debt, it may be protected under the substantially contemporaneous exception.[113] However, whether this theory will be applied, and to what extent it will be applied under the Code, is not clear at present.

---

[109] UCC § 9-108 is similar in some respects to the "enabling" exception of Section 547(c)(3) but is without some of its restrictions.

[110] See Countryman, "Code Security Interests in Bankruptcy," 4 U.C.C. L.J. 35, 52 (1971).

[111] But see In re King-Porter Co., 446 F2d 722 (5th Cir. 1971), which relied in part on this theory. See also In re White, 283 F. Supp. 208 (SD Ohio 1967).

[112] H.R. Rep. No. 595, 95th Cong., 1st Sess. 374 (1977); S. Rep. No. 989, 95th Cong., 2d Sess. 89 (1978).

[113] See discussion at supra ¶ 16.04[7][a].

The "UCC Section 9-108 theory" is not expressly overruled by Section 547(e)(3) but serious doubts remain as to its validity under the supremacy clause. As to validity of the Article 9 floating lien with respect to property acquired within the preference period, it tentatively may be concluded that it is subject to a preference attack unless preserved under one of the six exceptions of Section 547(c). The floating lien may perhaps be preserved under the "substitution theory," which may be preserved under Section 547(c)(1), or under UCC Section 9-108, if that section is viable under the Bankruptcy Code. However, the main hope for sustaining the floating lien against a preference attack is found in Section 547(c)(5), the "improvement of position" exception. As noted previously, this exception is limited to "inventory" and "receivables," as defined in Section 547(a). Section 547(a)(5) will not protect collateral, such as "equipment," as defined by the UCC,[114] that might, in an appropriate case, fall under one of the other exceptions.

However, the "improvement of position" exception of Section 547(c)(5) is limited and does not give blanket protection to the floating lien on all collateral or even on all receivables and inventory acquired within the preference period. To be protected under Section 547, the floating lien on receivables and inventory and their proceeds must be perfected. If perfected, under Section 547(c)(5), even if the after-acquired security interest in the receivables and inventory is a transfer when the debtor acquires rights in them,[115] and even if the property is acquired within the preference period, there is a voidable preference only to the extent that, measured from a date ninety days before the petition is filed (or in the case of an insider, one year before the petition) to the date the petition is filed, these transfers (judged only from these two points) have resulted in a reduction of the unsecured debt. In other words, there is a voidable preference only to the extent that from the ninetieth day to the date of bankruptcy, without looking at the intervening periods, there has been a reduction in the unsecured debt by the change in the inventory and receivables and the proceeds thereof or by reduction in the debt.

The following examples illustrate the scope of Section 547(c)(5).

**EXAMPLE 1:** On January 2, a secured party, *S* makes a loan to a debtor, *D* secured by "equipment now owned and hereafter acquired" and properly files a financing statement on the same date. On that date, *D* owns only Item 1 of equipment. On April 1, *D* acquires Item 2 of equipment. For purposes of Section 547, the transfer of Item 2 is deemed to have occurred on April 1 and is for an antecedent debt. If bankruptcy occurs within ninety days (or within one year, if *S* is an insider), the transfer will be subject to challenge as a preference if the debt is not fully secured by Item 1 and if the transfer does not fall within one of the exceptions of Section 547(c); such a transfer is not within the Section 547(c)(5) exception.

Two additional examples illustrate the operation of Section 547(c)(5) with respect to receivables and inventory.

---

[114] See UCC § 9-109(2).

[115] See 11 USC § 547(e)(3).

**EXAMPLE 2:**

| | *Ninety days before bankruptcy* | *At date of bankruptcy petition* |
|---|---|---|
| Outstanding debt | $20,000 | $30,000 |
| Collateral (receivables and inventory) | 17,000 | 29,000 |
| Unsecured debt | −3,000 | −1,000 |

Preference = $2,000 (unsecured debt reduced by $2,000)

**EXAMPLE 3:**

| | *Ninety days before bankruptcy* | *At date of bankruptcy petition* |
|---|---|---|
| Outstanding debt | $ 5,000 | $10,000 |
| Collateral (receivables and inventory) | 3,000 | 8,000 |
| Unsecured debt | −2,000 | −2,000 |

No preference—no reduction of unsecured debt although there has been an increase in the collateral by the floating lien.

For an insider, the critical beginning date is one year before the date the petition is filed. Alternatively, if the secured party has not given value on the ninetieth day before the petition is filed (or for an insider, one year before filing), then the beginning date for determining whether there is a reduction in the unsecured debt is the date on which new value (the loan, for example) is first given.[116] If the debtor first borrows from the secured party on the seventy-fifth day before bankruptcy, with the secured party taking a security interest in the debtor's receivables and inventory, then the seventy-fifth day is the beginning date from which the determination is made as to whether there had been a decrease in the unsecured position on the date the petition in bankruptcy was filed. Note that if the secured party is fully secured "by the value of all security interest for such debt" on the beginning date of the preference period (or the alternative date when new value is first given), there will be no preferential buildup due to an increase in receivables and inventory. In other words, if on the beginning date there is no unsecured debt, there can be no reduction of the unsecured debt at the date of bankruptcy, and the intervening secured positions (e.g., of being only partially secured on the fiftieth day) are ignored.

Another important limitation is placed on the floating lien by Section 552, which deals with property acquired after the petition is filed.[117] Under Section 552(a), the floating lien of a security agreement entered into before bankruptcy stops floating with respect to property acquired by the debtor or the estate after the filing of the petition in bankruptcy. However, there is an exception. To the extent that "proceeds, product, offspring, rents or profits" are derived from a nonavoidable security interest in property acquired before the commencement

[116] See 11 USC § 547(c)(5)(B).

[117] 11 USC § 552, as amended by 1984 Amendments § 466.

of the case, the secured party is entitled to such proceeds arising after bankruptcy "except to the extent that the court, after notice and a hearing and based on the equities of the case, orders otherwise."[118]

## [10] Insider Preferences

The Code added the concept of insider preferences, which did not exist under the 1898 Act.[119] Under the insider preference provisions, the trustee may avoid a transfer made in the period between ninety days and one year before the filing of the petition by establishing, in addition to the six elements given above, an additional element: that the transfer was to an insider.[120] The transfer and perfection rules of Section 547(e) previously discussed also apply with respect to insider preferences. However, in the period from more than ninety days but less than one year before filing the petition, the presumption of insolvency created by Section 547(f) is not applicable and the trustee has the burden of establishing insolvency at the time of the transfer without benefit of the presumption.

"Insider" is defined in Section 101(28) but leaves areas of uncertainty that will have to be filled in by case law.[121] This is particularly true for the criteria for determining who is a "person in control"; these criteria are not set forth in the statute and are likely to involve factual determinations. For example, when will restrictions in loan and security agreements, such as management retention, stock control, policing of the debtor's expenditures, and incurring of debt, constitute being in control and make one an insider?

---

[118] 11 USC § 552(b).

[119] For helpful discussion, see Phillips, "Insider Provisions of the New Bankruptcy Code," 55 Am. Bankr. L.J. 363 (1981); Pitts, "Insider Guaranties and the Law of Preferences," 55 Am. Bankr. L.J. 343 (1981); Comment, "The Term 'Insider' Within Section 547(b)(ii)(B) of the Bankruptcy Code," 57 Notre Dame Law. 726 (1982); Winship, "Banks as Insiders Within the New Bankruptcy Code," 9 J. Contemp. L. 244 (1983).

[120] Prior to the 1984 Amendments to Section 547(b), an additional element was required to avoid an insider preference; the trustee had to establish that the insider-creditor had reasonable cause to believe the debtor was insolvent at the time of the transfer. See former 11 USC § 547(b)(4)(B). However, the requirement was eliminated by 1984 Amendments § 462.

[121] 11 USC § 101(28), as renumbered by 1984 Amendments § 421. For an individual debtor, an "insider" includes a "relative" (defined in Section 101(37)); a partnership in which the debtor is a general partner; a general partner of the debtor; or a corporation of which the debtor is a director, officer, or "person in control." For a corporation debtor, an "insider" includes a director or officer of the debtor; a person in control of the debtor; a general partner; a partnership in which the debtor is a general partner; and a relative of a general partner, director, officer, or person in control of the debtor. If the debtor is a partnership, an "insider" includes a general partner of the debtor; a general partner in the debtor; a person in control of the debtor; and a partnership in which the debtor is a relative of a general partner in, general partner of, or person in control of the debtor. See also Annot., 71 A.L.R. Fed. 197 (1984).

Affiliates of the debtor and managing agents are considered to be insiders.[122] Section 101(2) defines an "affiliate" as any entity that directly or indirectly owns, controls, or holds the power to vote 20 percent or more of the voting securities of the debtor. This does not include, however, a fiduciary that does not have the sole discretionary power to vote such securities, and it does not include a pledgee of stock to secure a debt if the pledgee has not in fact exercised the power to vote.[123] Likewise, the term "affiliate" includes a corporation in which the debtor owns, controls, or holds the power to vote 20 percent or more of the voting securities of the corporation, with the same exceptions for fiduciaries and pledgees who have not exercised the power to vote.[124]

## ¶ 16.05 AVOIDING FRAUDULENT CONVEYANCES

The Code, in Section 548, enacted with minor changes the Uniform Fraudulent Conveyance Act (UFCA).[1] Section 548 permits the trustee to avoid fraudulent conveyances or obligations that were made or incurred on or within one year before the date of filing the petition. Under Section 548(a)(1), the trustee may avoid transfers or obligations that were made with "actual intent to hinder, delay, or defraud" existing or future creditors of the debtor. Like UFCA, certain transfers that are "constructively" fraudulent may also be avoided by the trustee without a showing of actual intent to hinder, delay, or defraud creditors. Under the constructive-fraud provisions, the trustee may avoid a transfer that is made for less than a "reasonably equivalent value"[2] if the debtor was insolvent on the date of the transfer or became insolvent as a result of the transfer. Furthermore, a transfer for less than reasonably equivalent value may be avoided if the debtor was engaged in business or was about to engage in business for which any property remaining with the debtor was unreasonably small capital, or if the debtor intended to incur debts that were beyond his ability to pay.[3] If the debtor is a partnership, the trustee may avoid any transfer of property of the debtor, made within one year before filing the petition, to a general partner in the debtor, if the debtor was insolvent at the time of the transfer or was rendered insolvent as a result of the transfer.[4]

A significant development with respect to fraudulent conveyances and the "reasonably equivalent value" requirement is a line of bankruptcy cases that have resulted from a case in the Court of Appeals for the Fifth Circuit, *Durrett*

---

[122] H.R. Rep. No. 595, 95th Cong., 1st Sess. 311 (1977); S. Rep. No. 989, 95th Cong., 2d Sess. 25 (1978).

[123] See 11 USC § 101(2)(A).

[124] See 11 USC § 101(2)(B).

[1] 11 USC § 548, as amended by 1984 Amendments §§ 394, 463.

[2] "Value" for purposes of Section 548 is defined in Section 548(d)(2) to include paying or securing an antecedent debt but does not include an unperformed promise to furnish support to the debtor or a relative of the debtor.

[3] 11 USC § 548(a)(2)(B).

[4] 11 USC § 548(b).

*v. Washington National Insurance Co.*[5] Under a somewhat simplified interpretation, *Durrett* has been said to stand for the proposition that a mortgage foreclosure at which the purchaser does not pay "reasonably equivalent value" for the property purchased at the foreclosure sale may be a voidable fraudulent conveyance under Section 548(a)(2).[6] For example, assume that the mortgage debt is $115,400, the property foreclosed is valued at $200,000, and the holder of the mortgage note purchases at the foreclosure sale for the amount of the mortgage debt.[7] The argument based on *Durrett* is that there has been a fraudulent transfer for less than "reasonably equivalent value," and if the transfer or foreclosure is within the one-year period of Section 548, it may be avoided by the trustee in bankruptcy.[8] Other bankruptcy cases have followed the *Durrett* approach and some have even suggested, based on language in *Durrett*, that a foreclosure sale that does not realize 70 percent of the value of the property is fraudulent.[9] However, two cases have rejected or avoided application of the

---

[5] 621 F2d 201 (5th Cir. 1980). *Durrett* was decided under the 1898 Act and the action to set aside the foreclosure sale as a fraudulent conveyance was brought by the Chapter 11 debtor in possession. For discussion of the *Durrett* problem, see Henning, "An Analysis of Durrett and Its Impact on Real and Personal Property Foreclosures: Some Proposed Modifications," 63 N.C.L. Rev. 257 (1984); Alden, Gross & Borowitz, "Real Property Foreclosure As a Fraudulent Conveyance: Proposals on Solving the Durrett Problem," 38 Bus. Law. 1605 (1983); Zinman, Houle & Weiss, "Fraudulent Transfers According to Alden, Gross and Borowitz: A Tale of Two Circuits," 39 Bus. Law. 977 (1984); Coppel & Kann, "Defanging Durrett: The Established Law of Transfer," 100 Banking L.J. 676 (1983); Comment, "Regularly Conducted Non-Collusive Mortgage Foreclosure Sales: Inapplicability of Section 548 (a)(2) of the Bankruptcy Code," 52 Fordham L. Rev. 261 (1983); Comment, "Mortgage Foreclosure as Fraudulent Conveyance: Is Judicial Foreclosure an Answer to the Durrett Problem?" 1984 Wis. L. Rev. 195; Note, "Nonjudicial Foreclosure Under Deed of Trust May Be a Fraudulent Transfer of Bankrupt's Property," 47 Mo. L. Rev. 345 (1982).

[6] It seems clear that the theory of *Durrett* is applicable not only to mortgage foreclosures but also to deed of trust foreclosures, foreclosures of security interests in personal property, forfeiture of real estate contracts, and execution sales. For discussion of the cases applying *Durrett* to such actions, see Henning, "An Analysis of Durrett and Its Impact on Real and Personal Property Foreclosures: Some Proposed Modifications," 63 N.C.L. Rev. 257 (1984). *Durrett* has been applied in Chapter 7, 11, and 13 cases. Id.

[7] These were the amounts involved in the *Durrett* case. The court noted that the purchase price was only 57.7 percent of the fair market value of the property.

[8] A debtor in possession in a Chapter 11 case, having the powers of the trustee, might also be able to invoke the theory as well as a Chapter 13 debtor. See In re Smith, 24 Bankr. 19 (Bankr. WDNC 1982); In re Alsop, 22 Bankr. 1017 (D. Alaska 1982); In re Peridido Bay Country Club Estates, Inc., 23 Bankr. 36 (Bankr. SD Fla. 1982); In re Berge, 33 Bankr. 642 (Bankr. WD Wis. 1983); In re Coleman, 21 Bankr. 832 (Bankr. SD Tex. 1982); In re Marshall, 15 Bankr. 738 (Bankr. WDNC 1981); In re Wheeler, 34 Bankr. 818 (Bankr. ND Ala. 1983).

[9] See, e.g., In re Coleman, 21 Bankr. 832 (Bankr. SD Tex. 1982); In re Thompson, 18 Bankr. 67 (Bankr. ED Tenn. 1982); In re Wheeler, 34 Bankr. 818 (Bankr. ND Ala. 1983). See also cases cited at supra ¶ 16.05 note 8; Henning, "An Analysis of Durrett and Its Impact on Real and Personal Property Foreclosures: Some Proposed Modifications," 63 N.C.L. Rev. 257 (1984).

*Durrett* theory, at least in part, taking the view that for bankruptcy purposes the transfer takes place upon execution and perfection of the security instrument.[10] In *In re Madrid*, at a foreclosure of a second deed of trust, the property had been purchased for 67 percent of the value of the property. The bankruptcy court had set aside the sale as a fraudulent conveyance. However, the Bankruptcy Appellate Panel for the Ninth Circuit had reversed,[11] stating:

> The law of foreclosure should be harmonized with the law of fraudulent conveyances. Compatible results can be obtained by construing the reasonably equivalent value requirement of Code § 548(a)(2) to mean the same as the consideration received at a non-collusive and regularly conducted foreclosure sale. Thus, in the absence of defects, such foreclosure withstands avoidance as a fraudulent conveyance.[12]

However, the Court of Appeals for the Ninth Circuit took a different approach and held that the only relevant transfer occurred at the time the deed of trust was perfected under state law, not upon foreclosure, and therefore the transfer was outside the one-year period and not voidable as a fraudulent conveyance. The Ninth Circuit, after examining the legislative history of Section 548 and its predecessors, concluded that Section 548 was not intended to affect the enforcement of a valid lien. On the other hand, the Court of Appeals for the Eighth Circuit in *In re Hulm*[13] rejected the approach of the Ninth Circuit and held that foreclosure did effect a transfer of the debtor's interest at the time of the foreclosure.[14] The 1984 Amendments made two significant changes that appear to affect the *Durrett* question. First, the definition of "transfer" in Section 101(48) was amended to specifically include "foreclosure of the debtor's equity of redemption."[15] On its face, this appears to overrule the reasoning of the Ninth Circuit in *Madrid*. Second, Section 548(a) was amended to expressly state that voluntary and involuntary transfers made by the debtor within one year of the petition may be avoided by the trustee.[16] This change on its face clearly rejects the suggestion that had been made that Section 548 was not intended to cover involuntary transfers (at least noncollusive ones).[17] The 1984 Amendments do not deal with the approach used by the Appellate Panel in

---

[10] See In re Madrid, 725 F2d 1197 (9th Cir. 1984); In re Alsop, 14 Bankr. 982 (Bankr. D. Alaska 1981), aff'd, 22 Bankr. 1017 (D. Alaska 1982).

[11] 21 Bankr. 424 (Bankr. App. Pan. 9th Cir. 1982).

[12] 21 Bankr. 424, 427 (Bankr. App. Pan. 9th Cir. 1982).

[13] 738 F2d 323 (8th Cir. 1984).

[14] See also In re Richardson, 23 Bankr. 434 (Bankr. D. Utah 1982).

[15] See 1984 Amendments § 421(i).

[16] Section 548(a), as amended by 1984 Amendments § 463, states in part: "The trustee may avoid any transfer of an interest of the debtor in property . . . that was made or incurred on or within one year before the date of the filing of the petition, [if the debtor voluntarily or involuntarily] . . ." The bracketed material indicates the addition made by the 1984 Amendments.

[17] See, e.g., the concurring opinion of Judge Farris in In re Madrid, 725 F2d 1197 (9th Cir. 1984).

*Madrid*,[18] which, although apparently accepting the view that a transfer took place upon foreclosure, took the view that the price paid at a regularly conducted noncollusive foreclosure sale was conclusively presumed to be for "reasonably equivalent" value for purposes of Section 548. However, as pointed out by Judge Volinn, dissenting in *Madrid*,[19] this approach functionally would preclude consideration of the question of the adequacy of the consideration.

If a conveyance or transfer is avoided by the trustee under Section 548, a transferee who takes for value and in good faith has a lien on the property transferred (or may retain any interest transferred) to the extent that he gave value to the debtor in exchange for the transfer.[20] This includes the situation where the good faith transferee gives some value but less than reasonably equivalent value.

For purposes of the one-year limitation on the avoiding power of the trustee under Section 548 that runs from the time the transfer was made, transfers are deemed to have been made when the transfer becomes so far perfected that a bona fide purchaser from the debtor cannot acquire priority over the interest of the fraudulent transferee. If the transfer is not perfected before filing of the petition, the transfer is deemed to have been made immediately before the filing.[21] If the one-year limitation of Section 548 has passed, the trustee by use of Section 544 may, in some circumstances, be able to avoid a fraudulent conveyance by using the state Uniform Fraudulent Conveyance Act or other fraudulent conveyance law if the state statute of limitation on the fraudulent conveyance has not expired at the time the petition is filed.[22]

## ¶ 16.06 AVOIDING STATUTORY LIENS

The trustee may avoid certain statutory liens that have been "fixed" against property of the debtor before filing of the petition.[1] A statutory lien is

---

[18] 21 Bankr. 424 (Bankr. App. Pan. 9th Cir. 1982).

[19] 21 Bankr. 424, 428 (Bankr. App. Pan. 9th Cir. 1982).

[20] 11 USC § 548(c), as amended by 1984 Amendments § 463.

[21] 11 USC § 547(d)(1), as amended by 1984 Amendments § 463.

[22] In re Bethune, 18 Bankr. 418 (Bankr. ND Ala. 1982); In re Copter, Inc., 19 Bankr. 588 (Bankr. ED Pa. 1982); In re Famous State Fair Meat Prods., Inc., 19 Bankr. 48 (Bankr. ED Pa. 1982); In re Flanzbaum, 10 Bankr. 420 (Bankr. SD Fla. 1981). But see Ackerman v. Gladwin Leasing, Inc., 725 F2d 37 (3d Cir. 1984), holding that a trustee could not invoke, as "applicable law" under Section 544(b), a Pennsylvania statute providing for the recovery of preferential transfers within four months of "proceedings in insolvency." The court pointed out that the state statute was intended for state insolvency proceedings and that there was no indication that the Pennsylvania legislature intended the statute to apply in bankruptcy.

[1] 11 USC § 545, as amended by 1984 Amendments § 460. "Statutory lien" is defined in Section 101(45); it includes a lien of distress for rent whether or not the lien is statutory.

avoidable if the lien first becomes effective on the occurrence of certain specified events:

(1) The filing of a petition under the Code;
(2) The commencement of a nonbankruptcy insolvency proceeding;
(3) When a custodian is appointed or authorized to take or takes possession;[2] or
(4) When the debtor becomes insolvent, or the debtor's financial condition fails to meet a specified standard, or first becomes effective upon execution against property of the debtor.[3]

Statutory liens for rent or liens of distress for rent also are avoidable,[4] as are statutory liens that are not perfected or enforceable against a bona fide purchaser at the time of the commencement of the case.[5] Legislative history also indicates that "the trustee may avoid a transfer of a lien under this section even if the lien has been enforced by sale before the commencement of the case."[6]

## ¶ 16.07 PRESERVING AVOIDABLE LIENS AND TRANSFERS

If a transfer is avoided under Section 522 (avoiding liens on exempt property), 544 ("strong arm" clause), 545 (statutory liens), 547 (preferences), 548 (fraudulent conveyances), 549 (postpetition transfers), 724(a) (lien securing fines and penalties), and 506(d) (avoiding security interest securing disallowed claims), the lien is automatically preserved for the benefit of the estate.[1] The operation of Section 551 is automatic although a preserved lien may be abandoned by the trustee under Section 554 if the preservation does not benefit the estate.[2] Preservation of the avoided lien for the benefit of the estate prevents

---

[2] "Custodian" is defined in Section 101(10) and includes the appointment of a receiver or an assignee under a general assignment for the benefit of creditors.

[3] 11 USC § 545(1). For helpful discussion, see Schneyer, "Statutory Liens Under the New Bankruptcy Code–Some Problems Remain," 55 Am. Bankr. L.J. 1 (1981).

[4] 11 USC §§ 545(3), 545(4).

[5] 11 USC § 545(2), as amended by 1984 Amendments § 460. If the lienholder is able to perfect under Section 546(b), which in some limited situations permits perfection of interests after the petition is filed, and that perfection relates back to an earlier date, then despite the filing of the bankruptcy petition, the trustee will not be able to defeat the lien because the lien will be perfected and enforceable against a bona fide purchaser of the property on the date of the filing of the petition. H.R. Rep. No. 595, 95th Cong., 1st Sess. 371 (1977); S. Rep. No. 989, 95th Cong., 2d Sess. 85–86 (1978).

[6] H.R. Rep. No. 595, 95th Cong., 1st Sess. 371 (1977); S. Rep. No. 989, 95th Cong., 2d Sess. 85 (1978).

[1] 11 USC § 551.

[2] H.R. Rep. No. 595, 95th Cong., 1st Sess. 376 (1977); S. Rep. No. 989, 95th Cong., 2d Sess. 91 (1978).

junior lienors from improving their position at the expense of the estate when a senior lien is avoided.[3]

## ¶ 16.08 TRUSTEE'S POWER TO RECOVER PREPETITION SETOFF

Although is does not create such rights, Section 553(a) expressly recognizes the right of a creditor to offset a mutual prepetition debt owed by the creditor to the debtor against a prepetition claim that the creditor has against the debtor.[1] Questions of setoff commonly arise in connection with a debtor who owes money to a bank but who is also a creditor of the bank based on deposits of the debtor with the bank. Questions of setoff are not limited, however, to such circumstances and may arise where there are mutual debts between a debtor and a nonbank creditor.[2] Debts are generally considered to be mutual when they are due between the same parties acting in the same capacity.[3] Both mutual debts generally must be mature and liquidated.[4] However, even if debts are mutual, Section 553 places limitations on the kinds of claims against the debtor that the creditor may offset. In part, these limitations prevent parties who owe debts to the debtor from acquiring claims against the debtor for the purpose of setting off and reducing the amount owed to the debtor. Section 553 does not permit a creditor to offset a claim against the

---

[3] H.R. Rep. No. 595, 95th Cong., 1st Sess. 376 (1977); S. Rep. No. 989, 95th Cong., 2d Sess. 91 (1978).

[1] One writer has observed:

> "Unlike Section 68 of the Act, Section 553 of the Code is not an independent source of law authorizing setoff. The right under the Code will have to be established by reference to statutory provisions of the individual states and precedents in decision law. Thus, there is a potential for varying results in various jurisdictions."

Freeman, "Setoff Under the New Bankruptcy Code: The Effect on Bankers," 97 Banking L.J. 484, 488 (1980).

[2] Helpful articles dealing with setoff include Ahart, "Bank Setoff Under the Bankruptcy Reform Act of 1978," 53 Am. Bankr. L.J. 205 (1979); Freeman, "Setoff Under the New Bankruptcy Code: The Effect on Bankers," 97 Banking L.J. 484 (1980) (containing a good discussion of setoff in general as well as a comparison of Section 68 of the 1898 Act and Section 553); Lopes, "The Improvement Offset Under the New Bankruptcy Act," 96 Banking L.J. 868 (1979); Hammon, "Setoff in Bankruptcy: Is the Creditor Preferred or Secured?" 50 U. Colo. L. Rev. 511 (1979).

[3] See Ahart, "Bank Setoff Under the Bankruptcy Reform Act of 1978," 53 Am. Bankr. L.J. 205, 215 (1979); Freeman, "Setoff Under the New Bankruptcy Code: The Effect on Bankers," 97 Banking L.J. 484, 492 (1980).

[4] See id. at 492–493, which suggests, however, that an argument can be made that the maturity and liquidated requirement is not a part of the Code. The author nevertheless concludes that this was not the legislative intention.

debtor if the creditor's claim is disallowed,[5] or if the claim was transferred by a third party to the creditor after the filing of the petition,[6] or transferred by a third party to the creditor within the ninety days before filing the petition while the debtor was insolvent.[7] These sections are designed "to discourage trafficking in claims of insolvents for the purpose of using those claims to set off debts owed by the insolvent."[8] In addition, if the debt owed by the creditor to the debtor was incurred within ninety days before filing the petition, while the debtor was insolvent and for the purpose of obtaining a right of setoff, it may not be set off by the creditor.[9] For purposes of Section 553, the debtor is presumed to be insolvent on and during the ninety days before the petition is filed.[10]

If a setoff by the creditor has occurred within ninety days before filing the petition, the trustee may be able to recover from the creditor a part of the setoff under Section 553(b).[11] This section is new, applies only to prepetition setoffs, and did not have a counterpart in Section 68 of the 1898 Act. To recover under this section, the trustee does not have to show insolvency of the debtor during the ninety-day period. The amount that may be recovered by the trustee depends upon a determination of the "insufficiency" at two points in time. "Insufficiency" is defined as the "amount, if any, by which a claim against the debtor exceeds a mutual debt owing to the debtor."[12] For example, if the debtor owes the creditor $10,000 and the creditor owes the debtor $5,000, there is an insufficiency of $5,000. To determine the amount that can be recovered by the trustee, the insufficiency must be determined at two points: the date of the prepetition offset, and the ninetieth day before filing the petition. If there was no insufficiency on the ninetieth day, the insufficiency must be determined on the first day thereafter on which there was an insufficiency. If the insufficiency on the date of the setoff is less than the insufficiency on the ninetieth day (or the next day thereafter on which there was an insufficiency), the trustee may

---

[5] 11 USC § 553(a)(1). Section 502(b) specifies which claims will not be allowed. For discussion of nonallowable claims, see ¶ 14.05.

[6] 11 USC § 553(a)(2)(A).

[7] 11 USC § 553(a)(2)(B).

[8] Freeman, "Setoff Under the New Bankruptcy Code: The Effect on Bankers," 97 Banking L.J. 484, 496 (1980).

[9] 11 USC § 553(a)(3). The statute is not clear as to whether it is the creditor or debtor who must intend to incur the debt for the "purpose" of obtaining a setoff. Freeman suggests that there must be a showing that the creditor so intended. Freeman, "Setoff Under the New Bankruptcy Code: The Effect on Bankers," 97 Banking L.J. 484, 497–498 (1980).

[10] 11 USC § 553(c).

[11] This section does not apply to certain setoffs by a commodity broker, forward contract merchant, stockbroker, or securities clearing agency; neither does it apply to setoffs by a lessee where the trustee of the debtor-lessor has rejected the lease but the lessee remains in possession. See 11 USC § 365(h). For discussion of the possibilities of the meaning of "recover," see Freeman, "Setoff Under the New Bankruptcy Code: The Effect on Bankers," 97 Banking L.J. 484, 499–500 (1980).

[12] 11 USC § 553(b)(2).

recover to the extent that the insufficiency was less on the date of the setoff. To illustrate, assume the following:

> **EXAMPLE:** A year before the petition in bankruptcy is filed, the debtor borrows $100,000 from the bank in which the debtor also maintains a demand or checking account. On the ninetieth day before the petition is filed, the debtor still owes the bank $100,000 and has $50,000 on deposit with the bank. At that point, there is a $50,000 insufficiency. On the fiftieth day before the bankruptcy petition is filed, when the debtor has $60,000 in his deposit account with the bank, the bank sets off against the $100,000 debt owed by the debtor the $60,000 owed to the debtor (the $60,000 balance in the debtor's account with the bank). At the time of setoff, the insufficiency of the bank was $40,000. Due to the increase in the debtor's account from $50,000 to $60,000, there is a $10,000 decrease in the insufficiency and that amount could be recovered by the trustee.

Assume alternatively that the deposit account on the date of setoff remains at $50,000 but the debt owing to the bank at the time of the setoff was only $80,000 (reduced from $100,000 on the ninetieth day with an insufficiency at that time of $50,000). In this case the insufficiency at the time of setoff would be $30,000 ($80,000 less $50,000) and the decrease in insufficiency from the ninetieth day of $20,000 ($50,000 less $30,000) would be recoverable by the trustee. If there is an increase in the insufficiency from the ninetieth day (or the next day thereafter on which there is an insufficiency) to the date the setoff is exercised, there is no enhancement of the creditor's setoff position and no recovery by the trustee.[13] If the trustee does recover the amount of the decrease in insufficiency from the creditor under Section 553(b), the creditor's allowable claim is then increased by the amount of the recovery.[14]

Setoff by a creditor after filing of the petition is stayed by the automatic stay of Section 362.[15] Some exceptions permit postpetition setoff by a commodity broker, forward contract merchant, stockbroker, or a securities clearing

---

[13] Additional helpful examples and discussion of questions raised by Section 553 are found in Ahart, "Bank Setoff Under the Bankruptcy Reform Act of 1978," 53 Am. Bankr. L.J. 205, 215 (1979); Freeman, "Setoff Under the New Bankruptcy Code: The Effect on Bankers," 97 Banking L.J. 484, 492 (1980). As pointed out by Freeman and others, where a prepetition setoff has occurred, the time of the filing of the petition can be critical in determining the ninety-day benchmark. Freeman states:

> "The provision sets the stage for a very interesting match between (1) the debtor who will arrange to file his petition after the creditor bank has set off on that day following setoff which will result in the greatest recovery for the DIP and the estate and (2) the creditor bank which will attempt to ascertain when a filing is going to be made and will attempt to set off in such a manner as to reduce the recovery by the estate."

Id. at 503.

[14] Under Section 502(h), the claim for recovery is treated as if it arose before the petition is filed. See discussion at ¶ 14.06[3].

[15] 11 USC § 362(a)(7).

agency.[16] To exercise the right of setoff after the petition is filed, the creditor must request and obtain relief from the stay under Section 362(d).[17] Even though a creditor or bank may not exercise a right of setoff after the petition is filed, the creditor's claim is treated as a secured claim under Section 506(a) to the extent of the right of setoff. However, a debtor in possession or the trustee who is authorized to continue the business in a Chapter 7 case may not use such funds (e.g., a bank account) unless the creditor consents or the court, after notice and a hearing, authorizes use of the funds under Section 363. In this event, the creditor, upon request, is entitled to "adequate protection."[18]

## ¶ 16.09 AVOIDING POWERS AFFECTING EXEMPT PROPERTY

In very limited circumstances, the debtor may exercise the avoiding powers if the trustee does not exercise them. Under the circumstances set forth in Section 522(h), the debtor may use the avoiding powers given to the trustee under Section 544, 545, 547, 548, 549, or 724(a) to avoid a transfer of property, which the debtor may claim as exempt if (1) the property was not voluntarily transferred by the debtor; (2) the debtor did not conceal the property, and (3) the trustee does not attempt to avoid this transfer. The concept of Section 522(h) is that if the property (which might be claimed as exempt) has been involuntarily transferred under circumstances that would make it voidable by the trustee under one of the named sections but the trustee does not exercise the power to recover the voidable transfer, the debtor may exercise the power and exempt the property.[1] This section is designed primarily to give the debtor the rights the trustee could, but did not, pursue. This right given to the debtor may be exercised in Chapter 7, 11, and 13 cases.[2]

---

[16] 11 USC § 362(b)(6).

[17] For discussion of obtaining relief from the stay in such circumstances, see Ahart, "Bank Setoff Under the Bankruptcy Reform Act of 1978," 53 Am. Bankr. L.J. 205, 207–208 (1979). Ahart points out that the rationale for the stay of postpetition setoff by a bank is "to prevent the frustration of an attempted reorganization, such as would occur if a bank seized the cash in the debtor's deposit accounts needed to implement the reorganization plan." Id. at 212. However, the automatic stay applies in both liquidation and reorganization cases even though the "frustration" rationale does not apply in a liquidation case. Id.

There is a substantial question whether a bank may put an "administrative hold" on or "freeze" the debtor's bank account without violating the automatic stay. See Groschadl, " 'Freezing' the Debtor's Bank Account: A Violation of the Automatic Stay?" 57 Am. Bankr. L.J. 75 (1983).

[18] 11 USC §§ 363(c)(2), 363(e).

[1] See also 11 USC § 522(i).

[2] See 11 USC § 103(a). Only an individual debtor may claim exemptions under Section 522 in Chapter 7, 11, or 13 cases; therefore, use of Section 522(h) is limited to individuals. For discussion of cases dealing with whether the debtor in a Chapter 13 case may invoke Section 522(f) to avoid nonpossessory, non-purchase-money security inter-

## ¶ 16.10 AVOIDING POSTPETITION TRANSFERS OF PROPERTY OF THE ESTATE

Section 549 deals with the problems of postpetition transfers of both personal and real property, the effect of notice, knowledge, and good faith purchasers.[1] Section 549, although not easily appreciated on first reading, is an improvement over Sections 70(d) and 21(g) of the 1898 Act, which covered some of the same areas. Section 549 complements the fraudulent conveyance provisions of Section 548 and the preference provisions of Section 547.

In general, under Section 549 the trustee may avoid all postpetition transfers of personal or real property of the estate unless the trustee or debtor in possession is authorized to make the transfer by a provision of the Code[2] or the transfer has been authorized by the court. However, there are two major exceptions to this general rule. First, in an involuntary case, a transfer of real or personal property made in the involuntary gap between the filing of the petition and the order for relief is not avoidable, notwithstanding any notice or knowledge of the bankruptcy case on the part of the transferee, to the extent that it is made for postpetition value.[3] Even though transfers during the involuntary gap in some cases may be authorized under Section 303(f), these authorized transfers may be avoided by the trustee under Section 549(a)(2) although the purchaser may be protected to the extent of postpetition value.[4] If the transfer is for less than fair postpetition value, it is avoidable under Section 549 as a fraudulent conveyance.[5] If the postpetition transfer is made for prepetition value, then it is avoidable under Section 549 as, in effect, a postpetition preference for an antecedent debt. In this sense, Section 549 complements Section 547.

Second, a transfer of real property to a good faith purchaser without knowledge of the commencement of the case, for present fair equivalent value, cannot be avoided if the transfer is perfected against a bona fide purchaser[6] before a copy or notice of the bankruptcy petition is filed in the real estate

---

ests in property that may be claimed as exempt, see ¶ 17.06. Generally, the Chapter 13 debtor has been permitted to assert the avoiding power under Section 522(f).

[1] 11 USC § 549, as amended by 1984 Amendments § 464.

[2] See, e.g., 11 USC §§ 363, 364. See discussion at ¶ 13.11.

[3] 11 USC § 549(b). "Value" includes services but does not include "satisfaction or securing of a debt that arose before the commencement of the case."

[4] 11 USC § 549(b). During the involuntary gap, unless the court orders otherwise, the debtor is authorized to continue business and dispose of property during the "gap" as if the case had not been commenced. See 11 USC § 303(f). Section 303(f) is intended to protect the transferor and not the transferee. 124 Cong. Rec. S17,413 (daily ed. Oct. 6, 1978); 124 Cong. Rec. H11,097 (daily ed. Sept. 28, 1978); Collier on Bankruptcy ¶ 549.02, at 549-6 (Matthew Bender, 15th ed. 1981).

[5] This results from the language of Section 549(b), which states that an involuntary-gap transfer is valid against the trustee "to the extent any value" is given after the commencement of the case.

[6] Under most recording acts this probably means recording the conveyance.

recording office.[7] If a copy or notice of the bankruptcy petition is filed in the real estate recording office before the transfer is perfected (e.g., by recording) against a bona fide purchaser, then the transfer may be avoided, since the purchaser takes with constructive notice of the bankruptcy case. If a good faith purchaser without knowledge of the commencement of the case gives less than present fair equivalent value, he has a lien on the property to the extent of the present value given unless a copy of the notice of the petition was filed before the transfer was perfected.[8]

Actions to set aside transfers that are voidable under Section 549 must be brought within two years after the date of the transfer that is sought to be avoided, or before the case is closed or dismissed, whichever is earlier.[9] In addition to recovering the types of authorized and unauthorized transfers mentioned above, one additional type of postpetition transfer that is authorized to be made by the transferor may also be recovered from the transferee by the trustee under Section 549(a). This is the result of the interaction of Sections 549(a)(2) and 542(c). Section 549(a)(2) states that the trustee may avoid a postpetition transfer of property that is authorized only under Section 542(c). In turn, Section 542(c) provides that an entity that has neither actual notice nor actual knowledge of the commencement of a case may in good faith transfer property of the estate or pay a debt owed to the debtor to someone other than the trustee, with the same effect as if the bankruptcy case had not been commenced.[10] This permits, for example, a bank to honor a check or draft of the debtor and make payment after the commencement of the case if the bank does so in good faith and without actual notice or knowledge of the filing of the petition.[11] However, the trustee may recover the transfer from the transferee under Section 549(a), unless one of the exceptions is available to the transferee.[12] For example if after filing the petition a bank honors and pays a check of the debtor given in payment of an obligation incurred by the debtor before filing of the petition, this, in effect, is a postpetition preference and is recoverable from the creditor-transferee under Section 549.

---

[7] 11 USC § 549(c). This section does not protect purchasers of personal property. Purchasers of personal property are protected only under Section 549(b).

[8] 11 USC § 549(c).

[9] 11 USC § 549(d).

[10] Section 542(c) is designed to afford protection to the transferor but not the transferee. Collier on Bankruptcy ¶ 549.02, at 549-6; ¶ 549.03, at 549-8 (Matthew Bender, 15th ed. 1981). For additional discussion, see ¶ 13.05[1].

[11] Section 542 is a codification in part of Bank of Marin v. England, 385 US 99 (1966). Section 542, however, does not authorize setoff in violation of the automatic stay, even if the bank offsetting the debtor's balance has no knowledge of the case. H.R. Rep. No. 595, 95th Cong., 1st Sess. 369 (1977); S. Rep. No. 989, 95th Cong., 2d Sess. 84 (1978).

[12] For example, if the transfer is made during the involuntary gap, the Section 549(b) exception may apply. Otherwise, the only exception will be for a purchaser of real property falling within Section 549(c). There is no exception for a postpetition transfer of personal property that is not made within the involuntary gap.

## ¶ 16.11 AVOIDING FEDERAL TAX CLAIMS AND LIENS AND OTHER MISCELLANEOUS LIENS

Section 724(a) gives the trustee the power to avoid liens that secure claims for any fine, penalty, or forfeiture, or for multiple, exemplary, or punitive damages to the extent that such fine, penalty, forfeiture, or damages are not compensation for pecuniary loss suffered by the holder of the lien. For a lien to be avoided under this section, the claim secured by the lien must arise before the order for relief or the appointment of a trustee, whichever is earlier.[1] This provision is substantially broader than former Section 57(j) of the 1898 Act.[2] The legislative history states:

> The subsection follows the policy found in section 57j of the Bankruptcy Act of protecting unsecured creditors from the debtor's wrongdoing, but expands the protection afforded. The lien is made voidable rather than void in chapter 7, in order to permit the lien to be revived if the case is converted to chapter 11, under which penalty liens are not voidable. To make the lien void would be to permit the filing of a chapter 7, the voiding of the lien, and the conversion to a chapter 11, simply to avoid a penalty lien, which should be valid in a reorganization case.[3]

To the extent that tax liens are for penalties, they may be avoided under this section. However, the section is not limited to liens of governmental agencies. If liens representing fines and penalties are avoided under this section, they are automatically preserved for the benefit of the estate under Section 551. Avoided liens are preserved to preclude subordinate lienors from improving their position at the expense of the estate when the prior lien is avoided.[4]

If a Chapter 7 case is dismissed, any lien avoided under Section 724(a) is reinstated.[5]

A federal tax lien that has not been filed at the time of filing of the petition in bankruptcy[6] may be avoided by the trustee in his lien creditor status under Section 544(a).[7] With respect to an unfiled federal tax lien on real property, it appears that the trustee can also avoid the tax lien in his status of a bona fide

---

[1] 11 USC §§ 724(a), 726(a)(4).

[2] For comparison of Sections 724(a) and 57(j), see Collier on Bankruptcy ¶ 724.02 (Matthew Bender, 15th ed. 1981).

[3] H.R. Rep. No. 595, 95th Cong., 1st Sess. 382 (1977); S. Rep. No. 989, 95th Cong., 2d Sess. 96 (1978).

[4] See Collier on Bankruptcy ¶ 551.01, at 551-2 (Matthew Bender, 15th ed. 1981).

[5] 11 USC § 349(b)(1)(B).

[6] Under 26 USC §§ 6321, 6322, if a taxpayer fails to pay any federal tax after demand, a "secret lien" arises at the time of the assessment. This secret lien is a lien on all property and rights to property, whether real or personal, belonging to the taxpayer. However, this secret lien is not good against certain parties, including a "purchaser" (defined in 28 USC § 6323(h)(6)) and a judgment lien creditor, until an appropriate tax lien notice is filed. See 26 USC §§ 6323(a), 6323(f).

[7] U.S. v. Speers, 382 US 266 (1965).

purchaser of real property under Section 544(a)(3) and as an avoidable statutory lien under Section 545.[8]

A question that has been raised in several cases is whether the filing of a federal tax lien within the preference period constitutes a voidable preference under Section 547. Courts generally have held that the mere filing of the federal tax lien within the preference period is not a voidable preference but is a statutory lien protected by the exception of Section 547(c)(6).[9] However, where realization on the lien occurs within the preference period, such as by sale of the property subject to the lien, there is a substantial question as to whether this constitutes an avoidable preference[10] and also whether the federal tax lien claim, although protected by the exception of Section 547(c)(6), is still subject to subordination under Section 724(b).[11] One argument that satisfying the valid tax may be a preference states:

> However the argument is made that the satisfaction of a federal tax lien can have a preferential effect. The theory is that if there were a liquidation under Chapter 7 of the Bankruptcy Code, the property would be distributed first to claimants accorded priority by § 507(a)(1)-(5) and only then to the payment of the federal tax lien; in other words, the tax lien would be subordinated to those priority claims. . . . Thus, the IRS conceivably could get more of its claim paid by keeping the pre-petition payment than if it surrendered the payment and was paid in accordance with § 724(b).[12]

---

[8] See Collier on Bankruptcy ¶ 545.04, at 545-21 (Matthew Bender, 15th ed. 1981).

[9] See In re Rogers Refrigeration, Inc., 33 Bankr. 59 (Bankr. D. Ore. 1983); In re Riverfront Food & Beverage Corp., 29 Bankr. 846 (Bankr. ED Mo. 1983); In re Debmar Corp., 21 Bankr. 858 (Bankr. SD Fla. 1982); In re Community Hosp. of Rockland County, 15 Bankr. 785 (Bankr. SDNY 1981).

[10] Nowak has stated:

> "The mere fixing of a tax lien by notice and filing is not a preference. Such statutory liens are excepted from the preference provisions by section 547(c)(6). It is important to note, however, that this exception extends only to the 'fixing' of a lien and not to its satisfaction by levy."

Nowak concludes that the legislative history of Section 546 indicates that the satisfaction of the lien was intended to be brought within Section 547. See Nowak, "Turnover Following Prepetition Levy of Distraint Under Bankruptcy Code § 542," 55 Am. Bankr. L.J. 318 (1981).

[11] As mentioned previously, Section 724(b) subordinates the tax lien to the expenses of administration and to claims given priority in Sections 507(a)(1) through 507(a)(5).

[12] In re Debmar Corp., 21 Bankr. 858 (Bankr. SD Fla. 1982). Although expressing doubt as to this argument and as to whether "Congress intended to require the IRS to disgorge payments received within the preference period," the court did not find it necessary to determine the issue. Id. at 862. See also Collier on Bankruptcy ¶ 547.42, at 547-131 (Matthew Bender, 15th ed. 1981); Norton, Bankruptcy Law and Practice § 32.26 (Callaghan 1981); In re Community Hosp. of Rockland County, 15 Bankr. 785, 788–789 (Bankr. SDNY 1981); In re R & T Roofing Structures, 42 Bankr. 980 (Bankr. D. Nev. 1984).

One bankruptcy court has held that, where sale of the property pursuant to the federal tax lien occurred before bankruptcy, there was no preference and the trustee could not recover any of the proceeds from the IRS to distribute to higher classes of priority creditors.[13] In another bankruptcy court decision where goods were sold at an auction sale and the IRS obtained and filed a tax lien on the proceeds of the sale prior to bankruptcy, the court upheld the tax lien as within the statutory lien exception of Section 547(c)(6). However, the court held that the IRS' claim to such funds was subject to the subordination provisions of Section 724(b) and to the specified priority claims; therefore, the trustee was entitled to the funds from the sale.[14]

One bankruptcy court has held that a seizure of property by the IRS within the preference period pursuant to a valid tax lien is a voidable preference under Section 547.[15]

---

[13] In re Rogers Refrigeration, Inc., 33 Bankr. 59 (Bankr. D. Ore. 1983). The court distinguished the case from the situation in U.S. v. Whiting Pool, Inc., 103 S. Ct. 2309 (1983), where the IRS was required to turn over to the estate property seized, but not sold, pursuant to a tax levy made prior to bankruptcy. In *Rogers* the court stated:

> "The general rule is that turning over before bankruptcy to a secured creditor collateral securing such loan is not a preferential transfer. IRS was such a secured creditor. Nor can the proceeds be recovered by the trustee to distribute to higher classes of priority creditors since such classes are preferred over IRS only where the tax lien on those assets still existed at the time of bankruptcy."

In re Rogers Refrigeration, Inc., 33 Bankr. 59, 60–61 (Bankr. D. Ore. 1983).

[14] In re Riverfront Food & Beverage Corp., 29 Bankr. 846 (Bankr. ED Mo. 1983).

[15] In re R & T Roofing Structures, 42 Bankr. 980 (Bankr. D. Nev. 1984). In *Roofing Structures*, the tax lien notice had been filed outside the ninety-day preference period by the IRS. Within the ninety-day period, the IRS had realized on the tax lien by levying and seizing property (cash) of the debtor-taxpayer. Although the court acknowledged that the creation or fixing of the lien was protected from attack as a preference by the express exception in Section 547(c)(6), it held that the levy and seizure was a transfer of the debtor's property to a creditor on account of an antecedent debt, made within ninety days of the filing of the petition and while the debtor was insolvent. Furthermore, the court found that the seizure permitted the IRS to obtain more than it would have received in liquidation because of the operation of Section 724(b). Under Section 724(b) the secured tax claim of the IRS was subordinated to certain priority claims. In the view of the court, because of this subordination the IRS would receive less in a Chapter 7 liquidation than it did through its prepetition levy. Therefore the court concluded that the levy and seizure was a voidable preference under Section 547.

# 17

# Chapter 13 Plans: Debt Adjustment for Individuals

## ¶ 17.01 INTRODUCTION

Chapter XIII of the Bankruptcy Act of 1898 provided for "wage earner" plans, under which a debtor who qualified as a "wage earner" could pay off his debts out of future earnings if the plan was approved by the appropriate number of creditors and if it received court approval. The "wage earner" plan could be an "extension" plan, under which the debtor paid in full the debts covered by the plan over a limited period of time. Alternatively, the plan could be a composition plan, which paid only a certain percentage on the claims covered by the plan. Use of Chapter XIII "wage earner" plans varied widely, with significant use in some areas of the country. In areas where the plans received relatively little use, most debtors used "straight" or liquidation proceedings under Chapter VII. Under the Bankruptcy Reform Act of 1978, the new Chapter 13 proceeding for "individuals with a regular source of income" differs significantly from the 1898 Bankruptcy Act and is widely used throughout the country because of its expanded scope and flexibility. The new Chapter 13 debt adjustment for individuals is no longer limited to individuals who are "wage earners" and now applies as well to self-employed individuals and those with regular income from other sources, such as investments, pensions, public assistance, social security, and trust income. Because of its more liberal discharge provisions, Chapter 13, in some instances, may offer a more attractive alternative for individuals than Chapter 7. However, Chapter 13 may only be invoked by individuals, and there are limits on the amount of secured and unsecured debt that an individual may owe and still be eligible for Chapter 13. Chapter 13 proceedings may only be voluntary, and a case may be converted from Chapter 7 or Chapter 11 to Chapter 13 only on request of the debtor.[1]

---

[1] See ¶ 12.07.

Under Chapter 13, plans may take the form of either "extension" or "composition." Unlike the 1898 Bankruptcy Act, creditor approval is not required for confirmation of the plan. For a plan to be confirmed, the debtor must have a "regular income"[2] from which payments or distribution under the plan will be made. The plan must also meet other statutory requirements for confirmation.

This chapter deals with the details of Chapter 13 plans for individuals with a regular source of income. For qualified individuals, Chapter 13 provides several advantages and affords flexibility in devising a plan to meet individual circumstances.

## [1] Overview and Purpose of Chapter 13

For individual debtors with a regular source of income, Chapter 13 provides an alternative to liquidation under Chapter 7. In part, the new version of Chapter 13 is designed to encourage debtors to pay creditors out of future income, if this is reasonably feasible, rather than resorting to a liquidation proceeding, in the belief that creditors will frequently receive more than they would in a liquidation proceeding. Chapter 13 also is intended to assist debtors who believe they should attempt to pay their creditors to the extent reasonably possible, but who need protection from creditor collection action while doing so. Chapter 13 is designed to provide a formal procedure to meet these aims. Note, however, that there may only be voluntary Chapter 13 cases. Chapter 13 offers advantages over a liquidation proceeding under Chapter 7 in some circumstances. In an apparent attempt to encourage further use of Chapter 13, the 1984 Amendments to the Bankruptcy Code added a new Section 707(b), which authorizes the court, after notice and a hearing, on its own motion to dismiss a Chapter 7 case filed by an individual whose debts are primarily consumer debts, if the court finds that granting of relief would be a substantial abuse of Chapter 7.[3] However, there is a presumption in favor of granting Chapter 7 relief.[4]

Under Chapter 13, a debtor is given protection from his creditors while operating and paying creditors under a plan that has been confirmed by the bankruptcy court. In addition, some codebtors who are obligated with the

---

[2] See generally Annot., 57 A.L.R. Fed. 339 (1982).

[3] Bankruptcy Amendments and Federal Judgeship Act of 1984, Pub. L. No. 98-353, § 312 (hereafter referred to as "the 1984 Amendments"). The factors to be considered in determining whether granting relief would be a "substantial abuse" are not specified in the statute. However, in a 1984 addition to Section 521(1), the debtor is now required to file a schedule of current income and current expenditures. Should this information be considered by the court in determining whether there is "substantial abuse"? If the debtor's schedule of income and expenditures indicates that a substantial portion of the debts could be paid off under a Chapter 13 proceeding, does this indicate a substantial abuse to invoke Chapter 7? Section 320 of the 1984 Amendments authorizes the U.S. Supreme Court to prescribe rules for the practice and procedure to be followed under new Section 707(b).

[4] 11 USC § 707(b).

debtor on consumer debts are given protection from creditor collection action. Unlike "wage earner" plans under the Bankruptcy Act, confirmation of a Chapter 13 debt adjustment plan under the Bankruptcy Code (the Code) does not require creditor approval. However, certain statutory requirements must be met for a plan to be confirmed by the court. A plan may only be proposed by the debtor. If a plan is confirmed, payments generally are made to the Chapter 13 trustee, who then disburses the payments to the creditors according to the terms of the plan. Generally, the plan will be funded out of the wages or earnings of the debtor, but the required "regular source of income" is not limited to wages or salary and may come from other sources. If a debtor does not have a "regular source" of income, this eliminates Chapter 13 as an option.[5] Payment of claims in full generally is not required, and secured creditors may be covered by the plan. However, priority claims must be paid in full under the plan. Generally, the plan cannot extend over a period of more than thirty-six months, except with court approval, and in no event may a plan last more than five years. The debtor generally retains all of his property while operating under the Chapter 13 plan. Under a Chapter 13 plan, a debtor may also reject executory contracts and unexpired leases. If the debtor fully performs on the plan, he will receive a discharge. In certain cases where the debtor is unable to complete the plan, the debtor may receive a "hardship discharge." However, the hardship discharge is a more limited discharge. The debtor may dismiss the Chapter 13 case or convert the case to a Chapter 7 case at any time.

Chapter 13 encourages debtors whose income exceeds the level necessary for living purposes to attempt to pay out of future income at least a part of the debt owed to creditors. It is hoped that creditors will receive more than they otherwise would have received if the debtor's property were liquidated. However, Chapter 13 may not be attractive or well-suited for a debtor with little regular income or whose income barely exceeds the level needed for support and essential obligations and if the debtor is unconcerned about nondischargeable debts. In situations in which the debtor has few assets but large liabilities, Chapter 13 may not be an attractive option. In some circumstances, such as where the debtor has substantial tax liabilities and is having difficulty in working out a satisfactory payment plan with the taxing authorities, Chapter 13 may provide an option for paying taxes under a confirmed plan and may offer a more satisfactory solution for the debtor.

## [2] Comparison and Contrast With Chapter 7 Liquidation: Advantages and Disadvantages

To encourage its use, several features of Chapter 13 make it more attractive to a debtor than Chapter 7, under certain circumstances. First, in contrast to Chapter 7, the debtor does not have to give up all of his nonexempt property.[6] Second, some debts that are nondischargeable under Chapter 7 may be

[5] See generally Annot., 57 A.L.R. Fed. 339 (1982).

[6] Section 1306(b) provides that "except as provided in a confirmed plan or order confirming a plan, the debtor shall remain in possession of all property of the estate." In

discharged under Chapter 13.[7] Additionally, in a Chapter 7 case, discharge may be denied for any one of ten grounds set forth in Section 727.[8] However, Section 727 does not apply in Chapter 13 cases.[9] For example, if a debtor has received a discharge in a proceeding commenced within the past six years, a discharge may not be obtained in a Chapter 7 case, although this would not bar obtaining a discharge under Chapter 13.[10] A discharge in a prior Chapter 7 or Chapter 13 case does not bar a later Chapter 13 proceeding or bar obtaining a discharge under Chapter 13.[11] Further, if a discharge is obtained in a Chapter 13 case through a full payment plan (i.e., 100 percent of the allowed unsecured claims were paid), or if a "hardship" discharge is obtained[12] and the debtor paid at least 70 percent of the allowed unsecured claims, and this represented his best efforts, then the six-year bar to discharge in a later Chapter 7 proceeding is not applicable.[13]

The scope of protection afforded by the stay against creditor collection activity also is broader in a Chapter 13 proceeding than it is under Chapter 7. With the filing of the petition for relief under Chapter 13, the debtor is given the protection of the "automatic stay" of Section 362.[14] In addition, certain codebtors (such as comakers, endorsers, or guarantors) of the debtor's consumer debts are protected from collection efforts by the stay of Section 1301.[15] A Chapter 7 proceeding does not afford this protection to codebtors. In many cases, the filing of a petition under Chapter 7 is likely to compel the creditor to pursue collection efforts against the codebtor. Thus, a debtor concerned about codebtor responsibility may find Chapter 13 attractive because of the Section 1301 stay.

Chapter 13 may be attractive for a debtor with a regular source of income who is in default, for example, on his home mortgage and is being threatened

---

addition, except as otherwise provided in the plan or in the order confirming the plan, confirmation of the plan vests all property of the estate in the debtor, and the property is free and clear of any claim or interest of creditors. 11 USC §§ 1327(b), 1327(c); H.R. Rep. No. 595, 95th Cong., 1st Sess. 430 (1977); S. Rep. No. 989, 95th Cong., 2d Sess. 142 (1978).

[7] See discussion at infra ¶ 17.12.

[8] See discussion at ¶ 15.04.

[9] 11 USC § 103(b).

[10] For discussion of the six-year bar, see ¶ 15.04[8].

[11] However, Section 109(f), added by 1984 Amendments § 301, does preclude an individual from becoming a debtor under any of the chapters (of Title 11) if the individual has been a debtor in a case under Title 11 within the preceding 180 days, if the case was dismissed for willful failure of the debtor to abide by orders of the court or to appear before the court in proper prosecution of the case, or if the debtor requested and obtained a voluntary dismissal of the case following the filing of a request for relief from the automatic stay provided by Section 362.

[12] See discussion at infra ¶ 17.12[2].

[13] See 11 USC § 727(a)(9) and discussion at ¶ 15.04[8].

[14] See discussion of automatic stay at ¶ 12.05.

[15] For discussion of this stay for codebtors, see infra ¶ 17.07.

with or is at the point of foreclosure. Chapter 13 may stay the foreclosure and also provide a means of curing the default. In circumstances where the debtor has substantial nonexempt property, Chapter 13 also provides an opportunity for the debtor to retain the property and to avoid liquidation, which would be necessary if Chapter 7 were invoked. Additionally, if the creditor's claim exceeds the value of the collateral securing the debt, Chapter 13 may offer a means of redeeming the collateral by paying the value of the collateral over the duration of the plan.[16] Although property that is exempt or abandoned may be redeemed in a Chapter 7 proceeding, under case law the property generally must be redeemed by a lump-sum payment.[17] In Chapter 13, in some cases, collateral may in effect be redeemed by paying the present value of the collateral over the life of the plan.[18]

As discussed previously,[19] most taxes generally are nondischargeable in a Chapter 7 liquidation and, depending upon the type of discharge obtained in Chapter 13, tax claims may not be discharged in a Chapter 13 case.[20] Chapter 13 does provide a procedure for paying off these tax obligations and other claims over a period of time while providing court protection from creditor collection efforts.

In some instances, a debtor may be eligible for both Chapter 13 and Chapter 11 proceedings. Ordinarily, if a debtor is eligible for both, Chapter 13 will be preferable because it is less complex and more flexible. In comparison to Chapter 11, which has much more elaborate procedures and requirements, Chapter 13 is relatively uncomplicated. For this reason, Chapter 13 proceedings generally will be less expensive and time-consuming; in many cases, it will be easier to formulate a payment plan that can be confirmed and that may be less expensive to implement. Chapter 13 requires only court approval and confirmation, in contrast to Chapter 11 where certain creditor approval is required for confirmation of the plan. Creditor approval is difficult to obtain at best and frequently is a time-consuming process. In addition, there is no creditors' committee in Chapter 13 as there is in Chapter 11. This eliminates additional complications and expenses. Furthermore, in contrast to Chapter 11, a disclosure statement is not required in Chapter 13. Under a Chapter 13 plan, secured creditors may be satisfied by a transfer of the collateral to the secured creditor, by deferred cash payments, or by a combination of these two methods. Also, by successfully completing payment on a plan, an individual debtor may discharge

---

[16] See discussion at infra ¶ 17.09[6].

[17] See discussion at ¶ 13.08.

[18] See discussion at infra ¶ 17.09[6].

[19] See ¶ 15.07[2][a].

[20] See infra ¶ 17.12. If a "completion" discharge is obtained in Chapter 13, tax claims will be discharged, since only claims nondischargeable under Section 523(a)(5) are excepted from the "completion discharge." See 11 USC § 1328(a). To the extent that the tax claims were priority claims, they will have been paid in full by completion of the plan, since priority claims must be paid in full for a plan to be confirmed. 11 USC § 1322(a)(2). See discussion at infra ¶ 17.08[1]. A Chapter 13 "hardship discharge" will not discharge priority tax claims, however, since a hardship discharge does not discharge any of the claims nondischargeable under Section 523(a). See 11 USC § 1328(c).

most debts, except debts for alimony, maintenance, or support that would not be dischargeable in a Chapter 11 case.[21]

As mentioned previously, an additional advantage of a Chapter 13 proceeding is that certain codebtors of the Chapter 13 debtor are given protection by the stay of Section 1301; codebtors in Chapter 11 are not provided with similar protection. There is an additional factor that may be important but somewhat hard to predict. For an individual debtor who wants to continue business after filing a petition in bankruptcy, there is some risk in Chapter 11 that the "debtor in possession" may be displaced by a trustee.[22] In a Chapter 13 proceeding, only the debtor may file a plan; however, in Chapter 11, after the expiration of the exclusive period within which only the debtor may file a plan (and any extension of that period), creditors may propose plans for confirmation.[23] Creditor approval of a plan is not required for confirmation in Chapter 13, while, generally, certain creditor approval is required in Chapter 11.[24]

## ¶ 17.02 ELIGIBILITY: WHO MAY FILE UNDER CHAPTER 13

Only an individual or an individual and spouse may use Chapter 13, although an individual who is in business and otherwise qualifies may use Chapter 13.[1] The Bankruptcy Code does not define who is an "individual"; however, under Section 101(33), the definition of "person" includes an "individual, partnership, and corporation, but does not include governmental unit." By negative implication, this suggests that a corporation or a partnership is not included, and the accepted view is that partnerships or corporations may not use Chapter 13. A husband and wife who conduct a business as a partnership have been held to be ineligible for Chapter 13.[2] A number of cases have held

[21] Confirmation of a Chapter 11 plan for an individual does not discharge a debtor of any claim nondischargeable under Section 523. 11 USC § 1141(d)(2). For general discussion of discharge, see Chapter 15 and for discussion of Chapter 13 discharge, see infra ¶ 17.12. See generally Lander, "An Analysis and Comparison of the Non-Dischargeability Provisions of Chapter 11 and Chapter 13 of the Bankruptcy Code," 27 St. Louis U.L.J. 639 (1983).

[22] See 11 USC § 1104.

[23] See 11 USC § 1121.

[24] See 11 USC § 1129.

[1] 11 USC § 109(e).

[2] See In re Krokos, 12 Bankr. 520 (Bankr. SDNY 1981); cf. In re Ward, 6 Bankr. 93 (Bankr. MD Fla. 1980). The House Report stated:

> "Whether a small business operated by a husband and wife, the so-called 'mom and pop grocery store,' will be a partnership and thus excluded from Chapter 13, or a business owned by an individual, will have to be determined on the facts of each case. Even if partnership papers have not been filed, for example, the issue will be whether the assets of the grocery store are for the benefit of all creditors of the debtor or only for business creditors, and whether such assets may be the sub-

that an estate may not use Chapter 13.[3] In addition, a "stockbroker" or "commodity broker" is not eligible for Chapter 13.[4]

To be eligible for Chapter 13, the individual (or individual and spouse) must be "an individual with regular income."[5] Of course, this requirement is intended to ensure that there is a source from which payments under the plan can be made. However, a "regular source of income" is not limited to wages and may come from other sources, including a trust or pension,[6] disability payments,[7] welfare payments,[8] child support payments,[9] social security,[10] unem-

---

ject of a Chapter 13 proceeding. The intent of the section is to follow current law, that a partnership by estoppel may be adjudicated in bankruptcy and therefore would not prevent a Chapter 13 debtor from subjecting assets in such a partnership to the reach of all creditors in a Chapter 13 case. However, if the partnership is found to be a partnership by agreement, even informal agreement, then a separate entity exists and the assets of that entity would be exempt from a case under Chapter 13."

H.R. Rep. No. 595, 95th Cong., 1st Sess. 320 (1977).

[3] In re Jarrett, 19 Bankr. 413 (Bankr. MDNC 1982); In re Brown, 16 Bankr. 128 (Bankr. DDC 1981).

[4] 11 USC § 109(e). An individual employed by a stock brokerage firm as an account executive at a fixed salary has been held not to be a "stockbroker," as defined in Section 101(40) (after the 1984 Amendments, now Section 101(46)), and therefore was eligible for Chapter 13. In re Berry, 22 Bankr. 950 (Bankr. ND Ohio 1982). See also In re Co Petro Mktg. Group, Inc., 680 F2d 566 (9th Cir. 1982), where the court held that a debtor who sold contracts for future delivery of petroleum and undertook to resell the contracts for the purchasers where no officially designated or regulated market existed, was not a "commodity broker" as defined in Section 101(5).

[5] 11 USC § 109(e). "Individual with regular income" is defined in Section 101(27) (as renumbered by the 1984 Amendments) to mean an "individual whose income is sufficiently stable and regular to enable such individual to make payments under a plan under chapter 13 of this title. . . ." See generally Annot., 57 A.L.R. Fed. 339 (1982).

[6] Regan v. Ross, 691 F2d 81 (2d Cir. 1982) (monthly state retirement pension benefits could be used to fund plan despite state law prohibiting assignment of such benefits); In re Wood, 23 Bankr. 552 (Bankr. ED Tenn. 1982) (monthly benefits from a qualified ERISA pension plan could be used to fund plan despite antiassignment provisions of ERISA; pursuant to Section 1325(b), the court may order the retirement plan to pay the debtor's benefits directly to the trustee since the Code implicitly amends ERISA to except such an order from the trust's antiassignment provisions).

[7] In re Howell, 4 Bankr. 102 (Bankr. MD Tenn. 1980); In re Dawson, 13 Bankr. 107 (Bankr. MD Ala. 1981).

[8] In re Iacovoni, 2 Bankr. 256 (Bankr. D. Utah 1980); In re Hammonds, 23 Bankr. 674 (Bankr. MD Ga. 1982) (Aid For Dependent Children payments).

[9] In re Taylor, 15 Bankr. 596 (Bankr. D. Ariz. 1981).

[10] In re Buren, 4 Bankr. 109 aff'd, 6 Bankr. 744 (MD Tenn. 1980); In re Penland, 11 Bankr. 522 (Bankr. ND Ga. 1981); In re Hughes, 7 Bankr. 791 (Bankr. ED Tenn. 1980); U.S. v. Devall, 704 F2d 1513 (11th Cir. 1983). In these Social Security cases, the courts held that the provisions of Section 207 of the Social Security Act (42 USC § 407) making such benefits nonassignable, nontransferable, and not subject to bankruptcy law, were implicitly repealed by the Code and that Social Security payments could be

ployment benefits,[11] and the like.[12] Section 1322(b)(8) permits the debtor to repay creditors with property of the estate. However, in one case, a debtor was unable to make monthly payments out of wages and proposed a plan under which single payments would be made to creditors from liquidation of the debtor's property. The court held that this plan would render meaningless Section 109(e), which requires a regular source of income. The plan would also eliminate the distinction between a Chapter 13 case and a Chapter 7 liquidation.[13] In the view of the court, Section 1322(b) permits proceeds from the sale of property to supplement, but not to replace, payments from future income. In another case where the plan was to be funded in part by a loan, the plan was rejected.[14]

There are limits on the amount of secured and unsecured debt that can be owed by an individual using Chapter 13. To be eligible, on the date of filing the petition the individual (or individual and spouse) must have "noncontingent, liquidated, unsecured debts of less than $100,000 and noncontingent, liquidated, secured debts of less than $350,000."[15] The debt limits are the same if there is a joint petition by spouses.[16] However, if the spouses individually are within the debt limits, they may be able to file separately and then move to consolidate the cases. However, if most of the debt is the joint liability of the spouses, they may individually still exceed the debt limits and be ineligible.

---

voluntarily assigned pursuant to a Chapter 13 plan. The cases further held that the Social Security Administration could be ordered to make such payments to the Chapter 13 trustee under Section 1325(b). However, subsequent to these decisions, Congress amended Section 207 of the Social Security Act (42 USC § 407) to provide that "No other provision of law, enacted before, on, or after the date of the enactment of this section, may be construed to limit, supersede, or otherwise modify the provisions of this section except to the extent that it does so by express reference to this section." Social Security Reform Act, Pub. L. No. 98-21, 97 Stat. 65, 130 (Apr. 20, 1983). The legislative history, referring to the cases ordering the Social Security Administration to pay such benefits to the Chapter 13 trustee, indicated that under the amendment "[Social Security] benefits may not be assigned notwithstanding any other provisions of law, including P.L. 95-598, the 'Bankruptcy Reform Act of 1978.' " 129 Cong. Rec. H1765-1766 (daily ed. Mar. 24, 1983). The amendment to the Social Security Act applies with respect to benefits payable or rights existing under the Social Security Act on or after April 20, 1983.

[11] In re Overstreet, 23 Bankr. 712 (Bankr. WD La. 1982); In re McMonagle, 30 Bankr. 899 (Bankr. DSD 1983).

[12] In re Williams, 20 Bankr. 154 (Bankr. ED Ark. 1982) (seaman's wages may be used to fund plan despite the provisions of 46 USC § 601, which preclude attachment of such wages).

[13] In re Gavia, 24 Bankr. 573 (Bankr. App. Pan. 9th Cir. 1982).

[14] See In re Safka, 18 Bankr. 196 (Bankr. D. Vt. 1982); In re McGowan, 24 Bankr. 73 (Bankr. ND Ohio 1982).

[15] 11 USC § 109(e).

[16] Joint petitions may be filed under Section 302.

The 1984 Amendments in new Section 109(f)[17] added an additional disqualifying factor. An individual is not eligible for Chapter 13 if he has been a debtor in a case under Title 11 within the preceding 180 days and (1) the case was dismissed for the debtor's willful failure to abide by orders of the court or to appear before the court in proper prosecution of the case, or (2) the debtor requested and obtained a voluntary dismissal of the case following the filing of a request for relief from the automatic stay provided by Section 362. If the debtor has been a debtor in such a bankruptcy proceeding, this may mean that the filing of a new petition will have to be delayed until the expiration of the 180-day period.

## ¶ 17.03 COMMENCEMENT OF THE CASE

The federal district courts are given jurisdiction for cases under Chapter 13 by Title 28, Section 1334(a), as added by the 1984 Amendments.[1] The venue provisions are contained in new Title 28, Section 1408,[2] which provides that a case may be commenced in the district court for the district in which the domicile, residence, principal place of business, or principal assets have been located for the 180 days immediately preceding the filing or for the greater portion of the 180-day period.[3] The debtor commences a Chapter 13 case[4] by filing a petition using Official Form 1 or a form that substantially conforms to the official form.[5] The Bankruptcy Rules and any local rules must be consulted for details concerning the filing of the petition and commencement of the case.[6] There may be a joint petition by the debtor and the debtor's spouse under Section 302. In appropriate circumstances, the court may decide to consolidate the cases by combining the two estates into a single pool, rather than merely

---

[17] 11 USC § 109(f), added by 1984 Amendments § 301.

[1] 1984 Amendments § 101. Prior to the amendment, the jurisdictional statute was Title 28, Section 1471, which granted jurisdiction to the district courts but provided that the jurisdiction was to be exercised by the bankruptcy court. The new Section 1334(a) is the result of the constitutional problems raised by the decision in Northern Pipeline Co. v. Marathon Pipe Line Co., 458 US 50 (1982). For a discussion of this decision see ¶ 11.02.

[2] As added by 1984 Amendments § 102. The new Title 28, Section 1408, is identical to the prior venue section, Title 28, Section 1472.

[3] For discussion of venue for commencing a case, see ¶ 12.02.

[4] As noted previously, there may only be a voluntary Chapter 13 case. Section 303 provides for the filing of an involuntary petition but does not authorize filing of an involuntary petition under Chapter 13. Also, a case may be converted from Chapter 7 or 11 only on request of the debtor. See infra ¶ 17.11.

[5] See B. Rule 1002(a).

[6] The commencement of the case is discussed in Chapter 12. See ¶ 12.04[2] for details concerning the filing fee.

administering the estates jointly. However, due consideration must be given to the effect of consolidation on the rights of creditors.[7]

Along with the petition, the debtor must file a list with the name and address of each creditor unless the petition is accompanied by a schedule of liabilities or a Chapter 13 statement.[8] The debtor also must file with the bankruptcy court a Chapter 13 Statement conforming to Official Form 10. If the debtor is "engaged in business,"[9] he must file a statement of financial affairs prepared as prescribed by Official Form 8.[10] If the schedules and statements are not filed with the petition, they must be filed within fifteen days of the filing of the petition if the petition is accompanied by a list of the debtor's creditors and their addresses.[11] The 1984 Amendments to Section 521(a) also require an individual debtor to file a schedule of current income and current expenditures.[12] The debtor is required to file a plan for payment of creditors[13] with the petition or within fifteen days of filing the petition.[14] The time may be extended only for cause shown and on notice as the court directs.[15]

The filing of the petition constitutes an order for relief[16] and vests the district court with exclusive jurisdiction over all of the debtor's property, wherever located, as of the commencement of the case.[17] With the filing of the petition, the automatic stay of Section 362 begins, staying practically all creditor collection activity against the debtor, the debtor's property, or property of the estate.[18] In addition, after the order for relief, the stay protecting codebtors from collection activity is operative.[19] With the filing of the petition, Section 366 gives the debtor protection against termination of services by a public utility.[20] Section 362(a)(7) prevents a utility from setting off a security deposit

---

[7] H.R. Rep. No. 595, 95th Cong., 1st Sess. 321 (1977); S .Rep. No. 989, 95th Cong., 2d Sess. 32 (1978). For discussion of consolidation, see ¶ 12.02[1].

[8] B. Rule 1007(a); see Official Forms 6–8, 10.

[9] Section 1304(a) states that "a debtor that is self-employed and incurs trade credit in the production of income from such employment is engaged in business."

[10] B. Rule 1007(b).

[11] B. Rule 1007(c).

[12] 1984 Amendments § 305. The statute does not state when this schedule must be filed, but it would appear that the time limits set by Bankruptcy Rule 1007(c) should be observed.

[13] 11 USC § 1321.

[14] B. Rule 3015.

[15] Id.

[16] 11 USC § 301.

[17] 28 USC § 1334(d), as added by 1984 Amendments § 101(a).

[18] For discussion of the automatic stay, see ¶ 12.05.

[19] See discussion at infra ¶ 17.07.

[20] For discussion of the details of Section 366, see ¶ 15.03. As noted there, a utility may terminate services if the debtor does not furnish adequate assurance of payment for postpetition services within twenty days after the order for relief.

against a prepetition debt for services to the debtor unless relief from the stay is obtained. In addition, the debtor is given certain protection from discriminatory treatment by a governmental agency solely on the basis that the debtor has been a debtor under the Code or has not paid a discharged debt.[21] Section 525(b), added by the 1984 Amendments,[22] also protects a debtor from discrimination by a private employer with respect to employment solely because the debtor has been a debtor under the Bankruptcy Code or has not paid a discharged debt.[23]

Section 341 of the Code requires a meeting of creditors to be held "within a reasonable time after the order for relief." Generally, notice of the date set for this meeting of creditors will be included with the initial notice sent to creditors giving notice of the order for relief and notice of the time for filing proof of claims. The debtor is required to appear at the meeting of creditors and to submit to examination under oath;[24] failure to appear imposes the risk that the case may be dismissed.[25]

## ¶ 17.04 THE CHAPTER 13 ESTATE

The "commencement of the case" by the filing of the petition creates the Chapter 13 estate.[1] In addition to the property specified in Section 541,[2] the Chapter 13 estate includes all property of the kind specified in Section 541 that the debtor acquires *after* the commencement of the case but before the case is closed, dismissed, or converted to a case under Chapter 7 or 11, whichever occurs first.[3] The property that is included in the estate under Section 541 is important in determining whether a plan meets the "best interest of creditors test." For confirmation of a plan, this requires that

---

[21] 11 USC § 525(a). See discussion at ¶ 15.03.

[22] 1984 Amendments § 309.

[23] See discussion at ¶ 15.03.

[24] 11 USC § 343.

[25] See In re Rust, 1 Bankr. 656 (Bankr. MD Tenn. 1979). For additional discussion of the meeting of creditors, examination of the debtor, and the like, see ¶ 12.06.

[1] 11 USC § 541.

[2] Generally, Section 541 (with the exceptions contained in Sections 541(b) and 541(c)(2)) includes (1) all "legal or equitable interests of the debtor in property as of the commencement of the case" (and this may include certain community property); (2) property acquired by the estate after the commencement of the case, and property that is a proceed, product, offspring, rent, or profit from property of the estate (except earnings for services performed by the individual debtor after the commencement of the case); (3) postpetition property acquired within 180 days after the filing of the petition by bequest, devise, or inheritance, or by a property settlement or divorce decree, or as beneficiary of a life insurance policy or a death benefit plan; and (4) property recovered through the trustee's avoiding powers. For discussion of Section 541 and property of the estate, see ¶ 13.04.

[3] 11 USC § 1306(a)(1).

unsecured creditors receive at least the present value of what they would have received if there had been a hypothetical liquidation under Chapter 7.[4] Also included in the Chapter 13 estate are all earnings from services performed by the debtor after the commencement of the case but before the case is closed, dismissed, or converted, whichever occurs first.[5] Thus, the Chapter 13 estate will include practically all of the property acquired by the debtor after the filing of the petition but before dismissal, closing, or conversion of the case.[6] In contrast, the Chapter 7 estate, with some limited exceptions, does not include property acquired by the debtor after the filing of the petition. Because the Chapter 13 estate includes property acquired by the estate and the debtor (including the earnings of the debtor) after the filing of the petition, this property is protected by the automatic stay of Section 362 from collection efforts of creditors until the case is closed, the case is dismissed, a discharge is granted or denied, or the stay is otherwise terminated.[7] Section 542(a), which requires turnover by parties holding property of the estate, is also applicable in Chapter 13[8] as well as Section 542(c), which provides protection to a party who, in good faith without actual notice or actual knowledge of the commencement of the case, transfers property of the estate or pays a debt owing to the debtor to an entity other than the trustee.[9] However, it should be observed that unless the court orders otherwise, the debtor remains in possession of all property of the estate.[10] Upon confirmation of the plan, unless otherwise provided for in the plan or in the order confirming the plan, all property of the estate vests in the debtor[11] and vests free and clear of any claim or interest of any creditor provided for by the plan, unless otherwise provided in the plan or the order confirming the plan.[12]

## [1] Filing and Allowance of Claims

Sections 501 (filing proof of claim), 502 (allowance of claims), 503 (allowance of administrative expenses), 506 (determination of secured status), 507 (priority claims), 509 (claims of codebtors), and 510 (subordination of claims)

---

[4] For discussion of the "best interest of creditors test," see infra ¶ 17.09[5].

[5] 11 USC § 1306(a)(2).

[6] Two notable exceptions of property that will not become a part of the estate are contained in Sections 541(b) and 541(c)(2).

[7] 11 USC § 362(c). For additional discussion of the scope and termination of the stay, see ¶ 12.05.

[8] For discussion of Section 542, see ¶ 13.05.

[9] For discussion of Section 542(c), see ¶ 16.10.

[10] 11 USC § 1306(b). The plan may provide for distribution of the property as a method of payment under the plan. See infra ¶ 17.08[2][i].

[11] 11 USC § 1327(b).

[12] 11 USC § 1327(c).

are all applicable in Chapter 13 proceedings.[13] It should be emphasized, however, that for a claim to be allowed and to share in the distribution under the Chapter 13 plan, proof of claim must be timely filed.[14] Bankruptcy Rule 3002(c) requires that proof of claim in a Chapter 13 case must be filed within ninety days after the first date set for the meeting of creditors called pursuant to Section 341(a).[15] As discussed previously, if proof of claim is timely filed and no objection to the claim is timely made, then the claim is deemed to be allowed.[16] In addition to claims against the debtor that exist at the time the petition is filed, proof of claim may be filed on certain postpetition claims for taxes and "consumer debts."[17] These claims are allowed or disallowed under Section 502[18] as if they arose before the filing of the petition. However, they are determined as of the date the claim arises.[19] First, proof of claim may be filed for taxes that become payable to a governmental agency while the case is pending.[20] Second, Section 1305(a)(2) permits proof of claim and allowance of a postpetition "consumer debt"[21] that is for property or services necessary for the debtor's performance under the plan. However, these consumer debts are not allowable if the holder of the claim knew or should have known that prior approval by the trustee of the debtor's incurring the obligation was practicable and was not obtained.[22] These provisions disallowing consumer debts if the creditor knew or should have known trustee approval was practicable and was not obtained, and nondischargeability, if obtaining approval was practicable but not obtained, are designed to encourage both the creditor and the debtor to obtain prior approval of the trustee if practicable.[23] Priority claims must be paid in full under the plan for the plan to be confirmed.[24]

---

[13] See 11 § USC 103(a). Details with respect to filing proof of claim, allowance and disallowance of claims, priority claims, secured claims, and subordination are considered in detail in Chapter 14.

[14] 11 USC § 502(a); B. Rule 3002(a).

[15] For additional details, see ¶ 14.03[1].

[16] 11 USC § 502(a). For discussion of objections to proof of claim, see ¶ 14.04[2].

[17] 11 USC § 1305(a).

[18] See discussion at ¶¶ 14.04, 14.05, 14.06.

[19] 11 USC § 1305(b).

[20] 11 USC § 1305(a)(1).

[21] "Consumer debt" is defined in Section 101(7) as a "debt incurred by an individual primarily for a personal, family, or household purpose."

[22] 11 USC § 1305(c). For discussion of dischargeability of consumer debts, see infra ¶ 17.12. If claims are disallowed, generally they are discharged by a Chapter 13 discharge. See 11 USC §§ 1328(a), 1328(c), and discussion at infra ¶ 17.12. However, if a consumer debt is not allowed, the creditor may still be able to collect the claim from the debtor if the claim is not discharged by the Chapter 13 discharge. Such consumer debts will not be discharged by either a "completion of payment" discharge or a "hardship discharge" if prior approval by the trustee of the debtor's incurring such debt was practicable and was not obtained. 11 USC § 1328(d). See discussion at infra ¶ 17.12.

[23] See Drake & Morris, Chapter 13 Practice and Procedure § 8.18, at 8-22, 8-23 (Shepard's/McGraw-Hill 1983).

[24] 11 USC § 1322(a)(2); see infra ¶ 17.08[1].

## ¶ 17.05 THE CHAPTER 13 TRUSTEE

Unlike Chapter 7, the trustee in Chapter 13 may not be elected by creditors.[1] If the number of cases in a particular judicial district so warrants, the court may appoint one or more individuals to serve as standing trustees for Chapter 13 cases.[2] If there is a standing trustee, the standing trustee will serve as trustee in the case.[3] If there is no standing trustee, the court appoints a trustee for the case.[4] The eligibility and bonding requirements for qualifying to serve as a trustee were discussed previously in this book.[5] Limits on the annual compensation of a standing trustee are established by Section 1302(e).[6]

The Chapter 13 trustee serves as disbursing agent by collecting the income paid to the trustee under the plan and by making the payments to creditors as provided for in the plan.[7] In addition, he has the responsibility to advise the debtor, on matters other than legal matters, and to assist the debtor in performance under the plan.[8] This affords the debtor the benefit of the counsel and experience of the trustee, which may be valuable in the case of a standing trustee.

The trustee is accountable for all property received[9] and has the following duties:

(1) To investigate the financial affairs of the debtor;[10]
(2) If any purpose would be served, to examine proofs of claims and object to the allowance of any improper claim;[11]
(3) If advisable, to oppose the discharge of the debtor;[12]

---

1 Section 702, providing for the election of a trustee, is not applicable in Chapter 13. See 11 USC § 103(b).

2 11 USC § 1302(d). In a "pilot district" with a U.S. trustee (see discussion at ¶ 13.02[3]), the U.S. trustee, subject to the approval of the U.S. Attorney General, may appoint an individual as standing trustee for Chapter 13 if the caseload so warrants. 28 USC § 586(b). If there is a standing trustee who has qualified, then the standing trustee serves in the case. 11 USC § 151302(a). In such districts, the U.S. trustee has the responsibility of supervising the standing trustee in the performance of his duties. If there is no standing Chapter 13 trustee in a "pilot district," the U.S. trustee must serve as the Chapter 13 trustee or appoint a disinterested person to serve. 11 USC § 151302(a), as amended by 1984 Amendments § 534.

3 11 USC § 1302(a).

4 Id.

5 See ¶ 13.02[2].

6 See Title 28, Section 586(e), for limits on annual compensation of a standing trustee in a "pilot district."

7 11 USC §§ 1322(a)(1), 1326.

8 11 USC § 1302(b)(4), as amended by 1984 Amendments § 525.

9 11 USC §§ 1302(b), 704(2).

10 11 USC §§ 1302(b), 704(4), as amended by 1984 Amendments § 311.

11 11 USC §§ 1302(b), 704(5), as amended by 1984 Amendments § 311.

12 11 USC §§ 1302(b), 704(6), as amended by 1984 Amendments § 311.

(4) To furnish information concerning the estate and the estate's administration as requested by a party in interest;[13] and

(5) Make a final report and accounting on the estate.[14]

If the debtor is "engaged in business," unless the court orders otherwise, the trustee has the additional duties stated in Sections 1106(a)(3)–1106(a)(4) to investigate the debtor's acts, conduct, assets, liabilities and financial condition, the operation of the debtor's business, and the desirability of continuing the business. He must also file a statement concerning this investigation.[15] The trustee is charged with the duty of ensuring that the debtor begins making timely payments as required under Section 1326.[16] Failure of the debtor to make these payments may be the basis for dismissing the case.[17]

The trustee is required to attend and to be heard at any hearing concerning the value of property that is subject to a lien. He is also required to attend any confirmation hearing or any hearing on modification of a confirmed plan.[18]

Under Section 327, the court may authorize the trustee to employ professionals such as attorneys, appraisers, and accountants, and, in some cases, the trustee may be authorized to act as attorney or accountant for the estate.[19] At any time before confirmation of the plan, the Chapter 13 trustee may assume or reject an executory contract or unexpired lease of residential real property or of personal property of the debtor.[20] Upon request by a party in interest, the court may order the trustee to assume or reject such leases or executory contracts before a specified time.[21]

The trustee as representative of the estate may "sue and be sued."[22] In addition, the Chapter 13 trustee has the avoiding powers given by Sections 547

---

[13] 11 USC §§ 1302(b), 704(7), as amended by 1984 Amendments § 311.

[14] 11 USC §§ 1302(b), 704(9), as amended by 1984 Amendments § 311.

[15] 11 USC § 1302(c).

[16] 11 USC § 1302(5), as added by 1984 Amendments § 314. Under new Section 1326(a), unless the court orders otherwise, the debtor must begin making the payments proposed by the plan within thirty days after the plan is filed. Such payments are to be retained by the trustee until confirmation or denial of confirmation. If the plan is confirmed, the trustee must distribute such payments according to the plan; if the plan is not confirmed, the payments are to be returned to the debtor. 11 USC § 1326(a), as added by 1984 Amendments § 318.

[17] 11 USC § 1307(c)(4), as amended by 1984 Amendments § 315.

[18] 11 USC § 1302(b)(2).

[19] For discussion of the employment of professionals by the trustee under Section 327, see ¶ 13.02[1]. See also Annot., 69 A.L.R. Fed. 644 (1984).

[20] 11 USC § 365(d)(2), as amended by 1984 Amendments § 361.

[21] Id.

[22] 11 USC § 323; H.R. Rep. No. 595, 95th Cong., 1st Sess. 326 (1977); S. Rep. No. 989, 95th Cong., 2d Sess. 37 (1978).

(preferences), 548 (fraudulent conveyances), 544 (strong arm clause and rights of actual creditors), 545 (statutory liens), and 549 (postpetition transfers).[23]

## ¶ 17.06 RIGHTS AND POWERS OF THE DEBTOR

The Chapter 13 debtor must perform the following duties imposed by Section 521[1]:

(1) File a list of creditors, and unless the court orders otherwise, a schedule of assets and liabilities, a schedule of current income and current expenditures, and a statement of the debtor's financial affairs;

(2) Cooperate with the trustee as necessary to enable the trustee to perform his duties;

(3) Appear at the discharge hearing required by Section 524(d); and

(4) Surrender to the trustee all property of the estate and any recorded information, including books, documents, and records, relating to the property of the estate whether or not immunity has been granted under Section 344.

In the case of the Chapter 13 debtor, the duty to turn over property to the trustee is qualified by Section 1306(b), which states that "except as provided in a confirmed plan or order confirming a plan, the debtor shall remain in possession of all property of the estate." Thus, unless the confirmed plan or the order of confirmation directs otherwise, the Chapter 13 debtor retains possession rather than turning over the property to the trustee as in a Chapter 7 case. Unless the court orders otherwise, the debtor must begin making the payments proposed by the plan within thirty days after the plan is filed.[2]

Section 1303 provides: "Subject to any limitations on a trustee under this chapter, the debtor shall have, exclusive of the trustee, the rights and powers of a trustee under sections 363(b), 363(d), 363(e), 363(f), and 363(l), of this title."

---

[23] See 11 USC § 103(a); In re Johnson, 26 Bankr. 381 (Bankr. D. Colo. 1982); In re Colandrea, 17 Bankr. 568 (Bankr. D. Md. 1982); In re Walls, 17 Bankr. 701 (Bankr. SD W. Va. 1982); In re Reeves, 17 Bankr. 383 (Bankr. WD La. 1982). See also In re Carter, 2 Bankr. 321 (Bankr. D. Colo. 1980). For discussion of these avoiding powers, see Chapter 16. These avoiding powers are subject to the provisions of Section 546, which in some cases limit the avoiding powers. See discussion in Chapter 16. See also Drake & Morris, Chapter 13 Practice and Procedure § 6.01, at 6-3, 6-4 (Shepard's/McGraw-Hill 1983). However, there is a question of whether, and to what extent, the debtor may exercise the avoiding powers. See discussion at infra ¶ 17.06.

[1] As amended by 1984 Amendments §§ 305, 452.

[2] 11 USC § 1326(a)(1), as added by 1984 Amendments § 318. Such payments are to be retained by the trustee until the plan is confirmed or denied. If the plan is confirmed the trustee is to distribute the payments pursuant to the plan; if the plan is not confirmed, the payments are to be returned to the debtor. 11 USC §§ 1326(a)(2), 1326(c). Failure to make such payments may be the basis for dismissing the case. See 11 USC § 1307(c)(4), as amended by 1984 Amendments § 315.

These rights and powers are given exclusively to the debtor and may not be exercised by the trustee.[3] The listed powers deal primarily with the power of the debtor to use, sell, or lease property other than in the ordinary course of the debtor's business.[4] However, the sections specified in Section 1303 do not authorize the sale, use, or lease of property of the estate in the ordinary course of business.[5] Section 363(b) permits the Chapter 13 debtor, after notice and a hearing,[6] to use, sell, or lease property of the estate other than in the ordinary course of business. Generally, if a Chapter 13 debtor who is not engaged in business wants to sell property of the estate, for example, a car or home, it may be sold only after notice and a hearing.[7] However, this use or sale of property may not be inconsistent with any relief from the stay obtained by a creditor under Section 362(c), 362(d), 362(e), or 362(f).[8] On request of a party with an interest in the property (such as the holder of a security interest) that is to be sold, used, or leased, the court, with or without a hearing, must prohibit or condition such use or sale on the provision of adequate protection for the interest.[9] With some restrictions, Section 363(l) gives the debtor the power to sell, use, or lease property of the estate, notwithstanding any provision in a contract, a lease, or applicable law that effects, or gives an option to effect, a forfeiture, modification, or termination of the debtor's interest on the basis of the insolvency or financial condition of the debtor, the commencement of a bankruptcy proceeding, or the appointment of a receiver.[10] Thus, property of the estate may be sold despite bankruptcy or ipso facto clauses that otherwise might ter-

---

[3] H.R. Rep. No. 595, 95th Cong., 1st Sess. 427 (1977).

[4] For additional discussion of these sections, see ¶ 13.11.

[5] However, if the debtor is "engaged in business" (as defined in 11 USC § 1304(a)), and is authorized to continue business, then the debtor may sell, use, or lease property in the ordinary course of business subject to the restrictions of Section 363(c).

[6] "After notice and a hearing" does not require a hearing if no request for a hearing is made by a party in interest. See rule of construction in Section 102(1). See generally Novellino, "After Notice and a Hearing," 55 Am. Bankr. L.J. 293 (1981).

[7] For the procedural details of notice, time for objecting, and the like, with respect to use, sale, or lease of property, see Bankruptcy Rule 6004.

[8] 11 USC § 363(d).

[9] 11 USC § 363(e), as amended by 1984 Amendments § 442(c). The 1984 Amendments deleted from Section 363(e) the following language: "In any hearing under this section, the trustee [debtor] has the burden of proof on the issue of adequate protection." The intended effect of this deletion is not clear; is the burden now on the creditor to establish that there is not "adequate protection"?

[10] 11 USC § 363(1), as amended by 1984 Amendments § 442(h). Section 363(1) provides:

> "Subject to the provisions of section 365, the trustee may use, sell, or lease property under subsection (b) or (c) of this section, or a plan under Chapter 11 or 13 of this title may provide for the use, sale, or lease of property, notwithstanding any provision in a contract, a lease, or applicable law that is conditioned on the insolvency or financial condition of the debtor, on the commencement of a case under this title concerning the debtor, or on the appointment or the taking of possession by a trustee in a case under this title or a custodian, and that effects, or gives an

minate the debtor's interest or that might work a forfeiture or modification of that interest.[11]

In addition to the right to sell or use property other than in the ordinary course pursuant to Section 1303, a Chapter 13 debtor who is "engaged in business" is given additional powers.[12] Unless the court orders otherwise, a debtor who is "engaged in business" may continue to operate the business after filing the petition.[13] Subject to any restrictions that may be imposed by the bankruptcy court, debtors engaged in business have, exclusive of the trustee, the rights and powers given to the trustee under Sections 363(c) and 364.[14] Thus, a Chapter 13 debtor who is authorized to do business, unless the court orders otherwise, may sell, use, or lease property of the estate in the ordinary course of business without notice or hearing or court approval.[15] Use or sale of property, however, may not be inconsistent with any relief from the stay obtained by a creditor under Section 362(c), 362(d), 362(e) or 362(f).[16] "Cash collateral"[17] may not be sold or used unless the party having an interest in the "cash collateral" consents or unless the court "after notice and a hearing" authorizes the use or sale.[18] This right to sell or use property of the estate in the ordinary course of business or to sell or use "cash collateral" is subject to the right of a party with an interest in the property, such as a holder of a security

---

option to effect, a forfeiture, modification, or termination of the debtor's interest in such property."

[11] H.R. Rep. No. 595, 95th Cong., 1st Sess. 346 (1977); S. Rep. No. 989, 95th Cong., 2d Sess. 57 (1978).

[12] "A debtor that is self-employed and incurs trade credit in the production of income from such employment in engaged in business." 11 USC § 1304(a). A creditor who is engaged in business but operates solely on a cash basis and does not incur "trade credit" would not be "engaged in business" and thus would not have the powers given by Section 1304. The term "trade credit" is not defined.

[13] 11 USC § 1304(b).

[14] Id.

[15] 11 USC § 363(c)(1).

[16] 11 USC § 363(d).

[17] "Cash collateral" is defined in Section 363(a) as

"cash, negotiable instruments, documents of title, securities, deposit accounts, or other cash equivalents whenever acquired in which the estate and an entity other than the estate have an interest and includes the proceeds, products, offspring, rents, or profits subject to a security interest as provided in section 552(b) of this title whether existing before or after the commencement of a case under this title."

11 USC § 363(a), as amended by 1984 Amendments § 442. It should be observed that if a secured party has a security interest, for example, in the debtor's inventory or accounts, then proceeds from collateral, such as cash, checks, and instruments, would be "cash collateral" and thus subject to the restrictions on the use of "cash collateral." In addition, the debtor is required to segregate and account for any cash collateral that comes into the debtor's possession, custody, or control. 11 USC § 363(c)(4).

[18] 11 USC § 363(c)(2). A request for use of cash collateral may be made by a motion as a contested matter pursuant to Bankruptcy Rule 9014. See B. Rule 4001(a).

interest, to require, by request at any time, adequate protection for its interest in the property or collateral.[19]

Section 364 gives the Chapter 13 debtor who is engaged in business the ability to obtain credit after the petition is filed under the conditions and restrictions stated in that section. Generally, unless the court orders otherwise, the debtor may obtain unsecured credit in the ordinary course of business without notice and hearing or court approval.[20] This permits the debtor to obtain trade credit for utilities, materials, and supplies for the business and to purchase goods for resale. However, to obtain credit other than in the ordinary course of business, the credit must be authorized by the court after notice and a hearing.[21] If the debtor is unable to obtain unsecured credit, the court may, after notice and a hearing, authorize the obtaining of secured credit under Section 364(c) as a "super priority" administrative expense that may be secured by unencumbered property of the estate or by a junior lien on property of the estate that is subject to a lien.[22] If credit is not otherwise available under the previously mentioned conditions, after notice and a hearing, the court may authorize the obtaining of credit with a "super priority" over existing secured creditors. The new credit may be given priority over or "prime" an existing secured party if the terms of Section 364(d) are complied with and if the existing secured party who is primed by the "super priority" is given "adequate protection" for its security interest.[23] The debtor has the burden of proof on the issue of "adequate protection."[24] Note that a party in interest objecting to and desiring to appeal a decision of the bankruptcy court authorizing the obtaining of credit or incurring debt (including, e.g., obtaining credit with a "super priority administrative claim" or a "super priority secured claim") must stay the authorization and the incurring of debt pending appeal. Otherwise, reversal or modification on appeal of the authorization to obtain credit or to incur debt or a grant of priority does not affect the validity of any debt so incurred.[25]

A Chapter 13 debtor who is engaged in business and who is authorized to continue business also has the duty to file periodic reports and summaries of the operation of the business, including a statement of receipts and disbursements, and other information that the court requires. He must file these reports

---

[19] 11 USC § 363(e). The court "with or without a hearing, shall prohibit or condition such use, sale, or lease as is necessary to provide adequate protection of such interest." Id., as amended by 1984 Amendments § 442(c).

[20] 11 USC § 364(a).

[21] 11 USC § 364(b). This debt will be an administrative expense of the estate under Section 503(b)(1).

[22] 11 USC § 364(c).

[23] 11 USC § 364(d). For helpful discussion of these provisions, see "Structuring and Documenting Business Financing Transactions Under the Federal Bankruptcy Code of 1978," 35 Bus. Law. 1645 (1980).

[24] 11 USC § 364(d)(2).

[25] 11 USC § 364(e).

with the court and with any governmental agency charged with the responsibility for collecting or determining any tax arising out of the business operation.[26] Filing of these reports does not relieve the debtor from filing other types of reports, such as tax returns, that may be required by applicable nonbankruptcy law for a debtor engaged in business.

Bankruptcy Rule 2015(b) should be consulted for details on the duty of the Chapter 13 debtor (business and nonbusiness debtor) and the trustee to file an inventory of property of the debtor; to keep records of receipts and disbursements; to file reports; and to give notice of the case to banks, savings and loan associations, utilities, landlords (security deposits), to all other persons holding money or property of the debtor, and to any insurance company that has issued a policy having a cash surrender value payable to the debtor. Bankruptcy Rule 2015(b) and the Code do not specify when the reports must be filed with the court, but the court may fix the time by local rule or order.[27] Thus, any applicable local bankruptcy rules should be consulted.

As previously noted, Section 1322(b)(7) authorizes the debtor to assume or reject (by the Chapter 13 plan) executory contracts or unexpired leases that have not previously been rejected under Section 365.

With respect to Section 1303, it has been questioned whether the specific listed powers given to the debtor under Section 1303 (e.g., to sell or use property under Section 363(b)) are the exclusive powers given to the debtor, as might be suggested by the failure to specifically mention other powers.[28] May the Chapter 13 debtor exercise other avoiding powers of the trustee, such as the avoiding powers given under Sections 542–553? One court has concluded that a Chapter 13 debtor may not use these avoiding powers.[29] However, the avoiding power under Section 522(f) is available to the Chapter 13 debtor.[30] In the case of *In re Saberman*,[31] the court held that, to the extent a mechanic's lien impaired the Chapter 13 debtor's exemption, the debtor under Sections 522(g) and 522(h) could assert the trustee's avoiding power.

---

[26] 11 USC § 1304(c); 11 USC § 704(8), as amended by 1984 Amendments § 311; see also B. Rule 2015(b).

[27] See Advisory Committee report to Bankruptcy Rule 2015.

[28] 11 USC § 1303 states: "Subject to any limitations on a trustee under this chapter, the debtor shall have, exclusive of the trustee, the rights and powers of a trustee under sections 363(b), 363(d), 363(e), 363(f), and 363(l) of this title."

[29] In re Carter, 2 Bankr. 321 (Bankr. D. Colo. 1980); see also In re Walls, 17 Bankr. 701 (Bankr. SD W. Va. 1982). But cf. In re Reeves, 17 Bankr. 383 (Bankr. WD La. 1982).

[30] In re Jordan, 5 Bankr. 59 (Bankr. DNJ 1980); In re Snow, 8 Bankr. 113 (Bankr. SD Ohio 1980); In re Drummond, 17 Bankr. 494 (Bankr. ED Ark. 1981); In re Hagerman, 9 Bankr. 412 (Bankr. WD Mo. 1981); In re Lantz, 7 Bankr. 77 (Bankr. SD Ohio 1980); In re Brahm, 7 Bankr. 253 (Bankr. SD Ohio 1980); In re Cowart, 43 Bankr. 110 (Bankr. MD Fla. 1984). For discussion of Section 522(f), see ¶ 16.09.

[31] 3 Bankr. 316 (Bankr. ND Ill. 1980).

## ¶ 17.07 AUTOMATIC STAY AND PROTECTION FOR CODEBTORS

From the filing of the petition, the automatic stay of Section 362 stays practically all creditor collection activity against the Chapter 13 debtor or against property of the estate.[1] Protection to some codebtors is provided by Section 1301.

### [1] Protections for Codebtors

Under Section 1301, after the order for relief, a creditor may not commence or continue any civil action or act to collect all or any part of a consumer debt[2] of the debtor from any individual that is liable on the debt with the debtor (such as an endorser, comaker, guarantor, or surety) or that secured the debt, unless the codebtor became liable or secured the debt in the ordinary course of the individual codebtor's business.[3] The stay terminates when the case is either closed, dismissed, or converted to a case under Chapter 7 or 11.[4] The Section 1301 stay does not cover business debts or debts where the codebtor is not an individual or where the codebtor becomes liable on the debt or secures the debt in the ordinary course of business. The stay basically is designed to protect friends and relatives of the debtor who otherwise might be called on to make good on the debt or from whom collection might be sought. It insulates the debtor from indirect pressure applied by his creditors, which may be exerted through friends or relatives who may have cosigned an obligation of the debtor.[5]

The stay does not prevent a creditor from presenting a negotiable instrument or from giving notice of dishonor on a negotiable instrument.[6] This permits the creditor to preserve his substantive rights against the codebtor as

---

[1] See discussion at ¶ 12.05.

[2] "Consumer debt" is defined in Section 101(7) as a "debt incurred by an individual primarily for a personal, family, or household purpose."

[3] 11 USC § 1301(a)(1).

[4] 11 USC § 1301(a)(2).

[5] The House Report states:

> "It [Section 1301] is designed to protect a debtor operating under a Chapter 13 individual repayment plan case by insulating him from indirect pressure from his creditors exerted through friends or relatives that may have cosigned an obligation of the debtor. The protection is limited, however, to ensure that the creditor involved does not lose the benefit of the bargain he made for a cosigner. He is entitled to full compensation, including any interest, fees, and costs provided for by the agreement under which the debtor obtained his loan. The creditor is simply required to share with other creditors to the extent that the debtor will repay him under the chapter 13 plan. The creditor is delayed, but his substantive rights are not affected."

H.R. Rep. No. 595, 95th Cong., 1st Sess. 426 (1977).

[6] 11 USC § 1301(b).

required by applicable nonbankruptcy law.[7] Even though a creditor is stayed from collection action against a codebtor, in specified circumstances the creditor may obtain relief from the stay.

### [2] Relief From the Stay

On request of a party in interest and after notice and a hearing, the bankruptcy court may grant relief from the stay imposed by Section 1301(a). Although Bankruptcy Rule 4001 does not specifically state that it covers action under Section 1301 to obtain relief from the codebtor stay, it appears that this rule does apply. Under the rule, the creditor may proceed to seek relief by a motion as a contested matter under Bankruptcy Rule 9014.[8] If a creditor files a request for relief from the stay, twenty days after the request is filed the stay will be terminated with respect to the requesting party unless the debtor or codebtor files and serves a written objection to the request for relief.[9]

There are three grounds for obtaining relief. First, relief from the stay may be obtained to the extent that the codebtor received the consideration for the claim held by the creditor.[10] For example, the Chapter 13 debtor may have been the maker of a note (representing a loan for consumer purposes) and the nonbankrupt codebtor was a comaker or endorser of the note. However, the codebtor actually received a part of, or all of, the proceeds of the loan. This would be the case, for example, where the Chapter 13 debtor was merely an accommodation party. Under these circumstances, the creditor may get relief from the stay to proceed against the codebtor to the extent necessary to protect the creditor's interest. Second, if the plan filed by the debtor does not propose to pay the claim for which there is a codebtor, then the creditor by request may obtain relief from the stay to the extent necessary.[11] For example, the debtor may propose to pay under the plan only a certain percentage of the claim for which there is a codebtor; to the extent that the claim will not be paid, the creditor is entitled to relief from the stay.[12] Even if the plan proposes to pay 100 percent of the amount of the allowed claim, this may not constitute full payment of the claim. For example, to the extent that postpetition interest is not paid, the creditor under the plan may be receiving less than the creditor would be entitled to under applicable nonbankruptcy law. To the extent of this

---

[7] H.R. Rep. No. 595, 95th Cong., 1st Sess. 426 (1977).

[8] See B. Rule 4001(a).

[9] 11 USC § 1301(d), as added by 1984 Amendments § 313.

[10] 11 USC § 1301(c)(1).

[11] 11 USC § 1301(c)(2).

[12] H.R. Rep. No. 595, 95th Cong., 1st Sess. 426 (1977). However, in some circumstances it may be difficult to determine how much is to be paid under the plan for purposes of determining whether the creditor is entitled to relief from the stay. See Drake & Morris, Chapter 13 Practice and Procedure § 501, at 5-37 (Shepard's/McGraw-Hill 1983).

additional amount, the creditor may be entitled to relief from the stay.[13] Finally, the creditor may obtain relief from the stay if the creditor's interests will be irreparably harmed by continuation of the stay.[14]

## ¶ 17.08 FORMULATION OF THE PLAN

As mentioned previously, the debtor must file a plan that proposes how creditors will be paid out of "regular income." The plan, if not filed with the petition, must be filed within fifteen days after the filing of the petition unless an extension is granted for cause.[1] In a Chapter 13 case, the debtor has the exclusive right to file a plan.[2]

### [1] Requirements

To be confirmed by the bankruptcy court, a Chapter 13 plan must meet certain statutory requirements set forth in Section 1322(a). In addition, Section 1322(b) lists a number of other optional provisions that may be included in a plan. However, the plan does not have to be approved by creditors. This represents a change from Chapter XIII of the 1898 Bankruptcy Act.

Section 1322(a) lists three provisions that each plan must contain. First, the debtor must propose a plan that provides for submission of a sufficient portion of future earnings or other future income of the debtor to the supervision and control of the trustee as is necessary for the execution of the plan.[3]

---

[13] See In re Bradley, 705 F2d 1409, 1412 (5th Cir. 1983); In re Johnson, 12 Bankr. 894 (Bankr. D. Me. 1981).

[14] 11 USC § 1301(c)(3), as amended by 1984 Amendments § 524. The House Report stated:

> "Finally, the court must grant relief to the extent that the creditor's interest would be irreparably harmed by the stay, for example, where the co-debtor filed bankruptcy himself, or threatened to leave the locale, or lost his job."

H.R. Rep. No. 595, 95th Cong., 1st Sess. 426 (1977). The Senate Report stated:

> "Under subsection (c), if the codebtor has property out of which the creditor's claim can be satisfied, the court can grant relief from the stay absent the transfer of a security interest in that property by the codebtor to the creditor. Correspondingly, if there is reasonable cause to believe that property is about to be disposed of by the codebtor which could be used to satisfy his obligation to the creditor, the court should lift the stay to allow the creditor to perfect his rights against such property. Likewise, if property is subject to rapid depreciation or decrease in value the stay should be lifted to allow the creditor to protect his rights to reach such property. Otherwise, the creditor's interest would be irreparably harmed by such stay."

S. Rep. No. 989, 95th Cong., 2d Sess. 139 (1978).

[1] B. Rule 3015.

[2] 11 USC § 1321.

[3] 11 USC § 1322(a)(1).

Unless the court orders otherwise, the debtor must begin making the payments proposed by the plan within thirty days after the plan is filed.[4] Second, the plan must provide for full payment, in deferred cash payment, of all claims that have priority under Section 507 (such as taxes and wage claims) unless the holder of the claim agrees to different treatment.[5] However, the plan may propose less than full payment of other unsecured creditors subject to the "good faith" and "best interest of creditors" tests discussed below. Third, if the plan classifies claims, it must provide the same treatment for each claim within a particular class.[6] The plan may not provide for payments over a period of more than three years unless the court, for cause, approves a longer period not to exceed five years.[7]

## [2] Optional Provisions

In addition to the required provisions, a plan may have a number of optional provisions subject to the provisions of Section 1322(b). These optional provisions provide great flexibility in formulating a plan to meet the individual requirements of a debtor.

### [a] Classes of Creditors

A plan may, but is not required to, designate or create a class or classes of unsecured claims; however, it may not discriminate unfairly against any class so designated.[8] If the plan creates classes of creditors, each claim within a particular class must be given the same treatment.[9] The Bankruptcy Code does not specify how claims may be classified for Chapter 13 purposes beyond stating in Section 1322(b)(1) that "the plan may (1) designate a class or classes of unsecured claims, as provided in section 1122 of this title. . . ." At present there is disagreement as to how claims may be classified for Chapter 13 purposes, and the courts differ significantly on this question. Frequently, debtors have attempted to create classes of creditors so that unsecured creditors in one class

---

[4] 11 USC § 1326(a)(1), as added by 1984 Amendments § 318. Such payments are to be retained by the trustee until the plan is confirmed or denied. If the plan is confirmed, the trustee is to distribute the payments pursuant to the plan; if the plan is not confirmed, the payments are to be returned to the debtor. 11 USC §§ 1326(a)(2), 1326(c). Failure to make such payments may be the basis for dismissing the case. See 1307(c)(4), as amended by 1984 Amendments § 315.

[5] 11 USC § 1322(a)(2). For discussion of priority claims, see ¶ 14.09.

[6] 11 USC § 1322(a)(3).

[7] 11 USC § 1322(c).

[8] 11 USC § 1322(b)(1). See generally Annot., 50 A.L.R. Fed. 694 (1980). Bankruptcy Rule 3013 provides: "For the purposes of the plan and its acceptance, the court may, on motion after hearing on notice as the court may direct, determine classes of creditors and equity security holders pursuant to sections 1122 and 1322(b)(1) of the Code."

[9] 11 USC § 1322(a)(3).

may be treated more favorably than creditors in another class. One court has suggested that, in effect, the debtor is unrestricted in creating classes of unsecured creditors, as long as all creditors, including those treated the least favorably, receive what they would receive in a Chapter 7 liquidation.[10] In contrast, another court took a more restrictive view, in rejecting a plan that proposed that debts for which there were codebtors should be placed in a separate class that would receive more favorable treatment than other unsecured claims. It held that the only exception permitted to the uniform classification of unsecured creditors is set forth in Section 1122(b), which permits the classification of small claims for the purpose of "administrative convenience."[11] In part, the court, in *Iacovoni*, based its holding on the reasoning that claims with the same legal rights must receive the same treatment. In the court's view, with respect to claims against the debtor's assets, claims secured by codebtors were the same as those of other unsecured creditors. Therefore, the proposed classification was arbitrary and inconsistent with Section 1322(b)(1), which requires equal treatment of claims within the same class. In part, *Iacovoni* is overruled by a new provision in Section 1322(b)(1), added by the 1984 Amendments, which permits claims for a consumer debt for which there is an individual codebtor to be treated differently from other unsecured claims.[12] With this exception, *Iacovoni* arguably is still correct in its view that claims with the same legal rights must receive the same treatment.[13] Other courts have also held

---

[10] In re Sutherland, 3 Bankr. 420 (Bankr. WD Ark. 1980).

[11] In re Iacovoni, 2 Bankr. 256 (Bankr. D. Utah 1980); see also In re Crago, 4 Bankr. 483 (Bankr. SD Ohio 1980); In re Cooper, 3 Bankr. 246 (Bankr. SD Cal. 1980); In re Wade, 4 Bankr. 483 (Bankr. MD Tenn. 1980); In re McKenzie, 4 Bankr. 88 (Bankr. WDNY 1980); cf. Cowans, Bankruptcy Law and Practice § 19.22, at 921 (West, interim ed. 1983). For extensive discussion of *Iacovoni, Sutherland*, and other cases dealing with classification of claims, see Drake & Morris, Chapter 13 Practice and Procedure §§ 9.05(b)–9.05(e) (Shepard's/McGraw-Hill 1983). For additional discussion of Chapter 13 classification cases, see Blair, "Classification of Unsecured Claims in Chapter 11 Reorganization," 58 Am. Bankr. L.J. 197 (1984); Vihon, "Classification of Unsecured Claims: Squaring a Circle?" 55 Am. Bankr. L.J. 143 (1981).

[12] 1984 Amendments § 313. In relevant part, the new section provides: "[h]owever, such plans may treat claims for a consumer debt of the debtor if an individual is liable on such consumer debt with the debtor differently than other unsecured claims."

[13] But see In re Wolff, 22 Bankr. 510 (Bankr. App. Pan. 9th Cir 1982), which held that *Iacovoni* is too narrow and followed the test adopted in In re Dziedzic, 9 Bankr. 424 (Bankr. SD Tex. 1981):

> "The test is (1) whether the discrimination has a reasonable basis; (2) whether the debtor can carry out a plan with discrimination; (3) whether the discrimination is proposed in good faith; and (4) whether the degree of discrimination is directly related to the basis or rationale for the discrimination. Restating the last element, does the basis for the discrimination demand that the degree of differential treatment be imposed?"

Id. at 512.

that claims may be classified only on the basis of the legal right of the claims,[14] while other courts have permitted claims to be classified on the basis of being secured by a codebtor.[15] Courts also have permitted certain creditors to be placed in a favored class, such as creditors with whom the debtor may wish to do business after the filing of the Chapter 13 petition or to whom the debtor must look for medical services. In addition, the courts have permitted debtors to create separate classes for holders of nondischargeable debts.[16]

An additional issue that has been raised is whether creditors may be paid "outside the plan."[17] Providing for payments to be made "outside the plan" appears in some cases to be in part an attempt to avoid the trustee's fee (Section 1302(e)) on such payments.[18] The term "payment outside the plan" is ambiguous and has produced some confusion.[19] In the decided cases, it has not always been clear in what sense the term was used.[20] In some cases, it appears that payment "outside the plan" was used to refer to situations where claims were covered by the Chapter 13 plan, but the disbursements were to be made by the debtor directly to the creditor rather than through the Chapter 13 trustee (i.e., the debtor was to be the disbursing agent).[21] Payment "outside the plan" apparently has also been used to mean that a claim is not covered or to be paid under the plan (and not merely that the debtor is the disbursing agent).[22] Generally, the courts have held that Chapter 13 does permit direct disbursements

---

[14] See, e.g., In re Montano, 4 Bankr. 535, 537 (Bankr. DDC 1980) (claims may be classified only on the basis of the legal rights of the claims, except for small claims that may be treated separately for administrative convenience); In re McKenzie, 4 Bankr. 88 (Bankr. WDNY 1980); In re Cook, 21 Bankr. 650 (Bankr. DNM 1982).

[15] See, e.g., In re Hill, 4 Bankr. 694 (Bankr. D. Kan. 1980); In re Garcia, 6 Bankr. 35 (Bankr. D. Kan. 1980); cf. In re Wolff, 22 Bankr. 510 (Bankr. App. Pan. 9th Cir. 1982); In re Hosler, 12 Bankr. 395 (Bankr. SD Ohio 1981). As noted above, amended Section 1322(b)(1) does permit different treatment for consumer debts for which there is an individual codebtor.

[16] See, e.g., In re Wolff, 22 Bankr. 510 (Bankr. App. Pan. 9th Cir. 1982), and In re Hosler, 12 Bankr. 395 (Bankr. SD Ohio 1981), which suggest that such classification will be permitted if the debtor meets the burden of proof for classification under the test set forth in In re Dziedzic, 9 Bankr. 424 (Bankr. SD Tex. 1981). For discussion of these and other cases, see Drake & Morris, Chapter 13 Practice and Procedure §§ 9.05(b)–9.05(e) (Shepard's/McGraw-Hill 1983).

[17] See Drake & Morris, Chapter 13 Practice and Procedure § 9.05(a) (Shepard's/McGraw-Hill 1983). See generally Annot., 50 A.L.R. Fed. 694 (1980).

[18] See, e.g., In re Foster, 670 F2d 478 (5th Cir. 1982); In re Case, 11 Bankr. 843 (Bankr. D. Utah 1981); In re Hines, 7 Bankr. 415 (Bankr. DSD 1980).

[19] See In re Foster, 670 F2d 478 (5th Cir. 1982).

[20] "Payment outside" the plan is not used or defined in the Code and is a carry-over from a practice that had developed under Chapter XIII of the 1898 Bankruptcy Act to deal with secured claims. See In re Blevins, 1 Bankr. 442, 443 (Bankr. SD Ohio 1979); In re Foster, 670 F2d 478, 485 (5th Cir. 1982).

[21] See, e.g., In re Hines, 7 Bankr. 415 (Bankr. DSD 1980); cf. In re Foster, 670 F2d 478 (5th Cir. 1982).

[22] See, e.g., In re Glasper, 28 Bankr. 9 (Bankr. App. Pan. 9th Cir. 1983).

by the debtor to creditors covered by the plan, although reasonable justification for such disbursement may be required[23] and permitting such direct payments is in the discretion of the court.[24] If the debtor is permitted to be the disbursing agent for claims covered by the plan, the courts generally have held that the trustee's fees must be paid on such payments, although the fee may be reduced in appropriate circumstances.[25]

Although in many cases it is difficult to discern what is meant by "payment outside the plan," the other sense in which the term appears to have been used covers the situation where the disbursements will be made directly by the debtor and the claim is not treated or covered by the terms of the plan or is not to be paid under the plan.[26]

Without clearly indicating in many cases what was meant by payment "outside the plan," a number of courts have refused to permit payments "outside the plan," while a greater number of courts have approved such payments. Generally, the courts that have refused to approve payments outside the plan have done so on the theory that these payments to unsecured creditors constituted an improper classification under Section 1322(a)(3), which requires equal treatment of each claim within a particular class. Furthermore, they constituted unfair discriminatory treatment under Section 1322(b)(1).[27] Generally, it is to the debtor's advantage to pay all allowed claims "under the plan." Oth-

---

[23] See, e.g., In re Case, 11 Bankr. 843 (Bankr. D. Utah 1981); In re Foster, 670 F2d 478, 486 (5th Cir. 1982); In re Hines, 7 Bankr. 415 (Bankr. DSD 1980); In re Centineo, 4 Bankr. 654 (Bankr. D. Neb. 1980); In re Wittenmeier, 4 Bankr. 86 (Bankr. MD Tenn. 1980); In re Glasper, 28 Bankr. 6 (Bankr. App. Pan. 9th Cir. 1983) (concurring opinion of Judge Hughes).

[24] In re Case, 11 Bankr. 843 (Bankr. D. Utah 1981); In re Foster, 670 F2d 478, 486 (5th Cir. 1982).

[25] In re Foster, 670 F2d 478, 492 (5th Cir. 1982); In re Case, 11 Bankr. 843 (Bankr. D. Utah 1981); In re Hines, 7 Bankr. 415 (Bankr. DSD 1980). *Hines* also suggested the debtor may negotiate with the trustee the amount of the fee on such direct payments.

[26] See, e.g., In re Glasper, 28 Bankr. 6 (Bankr. App. Pan. 9th Cir. 1983) (plan did not specify what was to be paid to creditor); In re Foster, 670 F2d 478, 492 (5th Cir. 1982); In re Case, 11 Bankr. 843 (Bankr. D. Utah 1981).

[27] In re Weeden, 7 Bankr. 106 (Bankr. DRI 1980); In re Blevins, 1 Bankr. 442 (Bankr. SD Ohio 1979); In re Tatum, 1 Bankr. 445 (Bankr. SD Ohio 1979); In re Fizer, 1 Bankr. 400 (Bankr. SD Ohio 1979). See also In re Dziedzic, 9 Bankr. 423 (SD Tex. 1981). But see In re Bradley, 705 F2d 1409 (5th Cir. 1983) (fully secured claim may be paid outside the plan); In re Foster, 670 F2d 478 (5th Cir. 1982) (although fully secured claims may, in some instances, be dealt with outside a Chapter 13 plan, a plan may not provide for the making of the current payments on a mortgage claim outside the plan while "curing" the arrearage on that claim under the plan pursuant to Section 1325(b)(5)); accord, In re Glasper, 28 Bankr. 6 (Bankr. App. Pan. 9th Cir. 1983). See also In re Wittenmeier, 4 Bankr. 86 (Bankr. MD Tenn. 1980) (claim secured by home mortgage could be paid outside the plan, although it appears to be a holding that disbursements could be made by debtor); cf. In re Centineo, 4 Bankr. 654 (Bankr. D. Neb. 1980) (disbursement may be made by debtor directly to secured party but trustee is entitled to fee); In re Berry, 5 Bankr. 515 (Bankr. SD Ohio 1980); In re Case, 11 Bankr. 843 (Bankr. D. Utah 1981); In re Blevins, 1 Bankr. 442 (Bankr. SD Ohio 1979); In re

erwise, claims paid outside the plan may be considered as not "provided for" under the plan and thus are not discharged under either a completion of payment discharge (Section 1328(a)) or a "hardship discharge" (Section 1328(b)). However, there is authority to the effect that payments "outside of the plan," in the sense that the disbursement is made directly by the debtor to the creditor (rather than through the trustee) do not make the claim one that is not "provided for by the plan." If, however, the claim is to be paid "fully outside the plan," it will not be dischargeable.[28] For purposes of determining the "feasibility" of a plan,[29] the court may require disclosure of payments that are to be made "outside the plan."[30]

### (b) Modifying the Rights of Unsecured Creditors

The plan may modify the rights of holders of unsecured creditors,[31] for example, by paying the unsecured creditors a certain percentage of their claim and stretching out the payments over the term of the plan. However, to be confirmed, at a minimum the plan must pay unsecured creditors the value of what they would have received in a Chapter 7 liquidation.[32] However, the rights of creditors do not have to be modified, and the plan may leave unaffected the rights of holders of any class of claims.[33]

### [c] Treatment of Secured Claims

The plan may modify the rights of holders of secured claims, other than a claim secured "only by a security interest in real property that is the debtor's principal residence."[34] The modification of secured claims is subject to the requirements of Section 1325(a)(5) on confirmation. In general, Section 1325(a)(5) requires that the secured creditor retain its lien and receive, through payments under the plan, the *present value* of its allowed secured claim unless the secured creditor accepts some other treatment under the plan or the debtor

---

Hines, 7 Bankr. 415 (Bankr. DSD 1980). See also Drake & Morris, Chapter 13 Practice and Procedure § 9.06, at 9-29 (Shepard's/McGraw-Hill 1983).

[28] See In re Case, 11 Bankr. 843 (Bankr. D. Utah 1981).

[29] See discussion at infra ¶ 17.09[7].

[30] See In re Case, 11 Bankr. 843 (Bankr. D. Utah 1981); In re Foster, 670 F2d 478 (5th Cir. 1982).

[31] 11 USC § 1322(b)(2).

[32] See Section 1325(a)(4) and discussion of the "best interest of creditors" requirement at infra ¶ 17.09[5].

[33] 11 USC § 1322(b)(2), as amended by 1984 Amendments § 528(b). As previously noted, priority claims must be paid in full.

[34] 11 USC § 1322(b)(2). If the holder of a secured claim is secured only by a security interest in real property that is the principal residence of the debtor, then the claim may not be affected other than as provided for by 1322(b)(5). Section 1322(b)(5) permits curing of a default within a reasonable time while payments are maintained if the last payment on the secured claim is due after the final payment under the plan.

surrenders the collateral to the creditor.[35] Thus, a secured claim (other than one secured only by real property that is the principal residence of the debtor), could be "stretched out" over the life of the plan by modifying the original payment schedule, as long as the creditor receives in payments the present value of the allowed secured claim.[36] This ability to modify the rights of secured and unsecured claims provides the debtor with flexibility in reducing payments and in extending the time of payments and is one of the attractive features of Chapter 13.

### [d] Curing of Default

The plan may also provide for curing or waiving of any default.[37] Generally, this concerns the curing of default on a claim secured by property of the debtor or property of the estate that is personal or real property, excluding the debtor's principal residence. For example, if, at the time the petition is filed, the debtor is in default on an installment loan secured by a car and the lender has invoked an acceleration clause declaring the total amount due, the default could be cured by making payments on the amount in default over a reasonable period of time, thereby preventing acceleration of the debt.[38] In addition, subject to the confirmation requirements of Section 1325(a)(5), the plan could also modify rights of the secured creditor under Section 1322(b)(2).[39] For example, the payments could be stretched out over a period of time, as long as the secured creditor receives the present value of the allowed secured claim and the secured creditor retains its lien.[40]

---

[35] See discussion at infra ¶ 17.09[6]. Note that if a secured creditor does not timely file proof of claim as a secured creditor, it may be treated as an unsecured claim. See Cowans, Bankruptcy Law and Practice § 19.22, at 922–923 (West, interim ed. 1983). However, a 1984 amendment to Section 506 provides that failure to file proof of claim is not a basis for avoiding the lien under Section 506(d). See Section 506(d)(2), as amended by 1984 Amendments § 448.

[36] Unsecured claims may be stretched out as well, although there is no requirement that unsecured creditors must receive any specific amount under the plan as long as they receive at least the amount they would have received in a Chapter 7 liquidation and the plan meets the "good faith" requirement. See discussion at infra ¶¶ 17.09[4], 17.09[5].

[37] 11 USC § 1322(b)(3).

[38] The Code does not specify a time within which defaults must be cured. It appears that courts apply a test of what is reasonable and fair under the circumstances. See Cowans, Bankruptcy Law and Practice, § 19.22, at 923 (West, interim ed. 1983); Drake & Morris, Chapter 13 Practice and Procedure § 9.09, at 9-38 (Shepard's/McGraw-Hill 1983).

[39] See discussion at infra ¶ 17.09[6].

[40] Note that Section 1322(b)(2) does not authorize the modification of the rights of a holder of a secured claim that is secured only by a security interest in the debtor's principal residence. However, for such a security interest, if it is a "long-term debt" (i.e., the last payment is due after the date on which the final payment under the plan is due),

### [e] Rejection or Assumption of Executory Contracts or Unexpired Leases

Subject to Section 365, the plan may provide for the assumption, rejection, or assignment of any executory contract or unexpired lease of the debtor not previously rejected under section 365.[41] The Chapter 13 trustee has the authority to assume or reject an executory contract or unexpired lease of the debtor at any time before the confirmation of the plan.[42] Upon request of a party in interest, the court may order the trustee to assume or reject an executory contract or unexpired lease within a specified period of time.[43] Where the debtor assumes or rejects the contract or unexpired lease as permitted by Section 1322(b)(7), the question has been raised whether the restrictions and conditions that are imposed by Section 365 are applicable.[44] In the case of *In re Alexander*, the Ninth Circuit held that when the debtor assumes or rejects in a Chapter 13 plan, Section 365 is not applicable and court approval is not required.[45] However, the 1984 Amendments to Section 1322(b)(7) appear to overrule *Alexander* by expressly providing that rejection or assumption by a plan is "subject to section 365."[46]

### [f] Provisions for Payment

The plan may provide for payments on any unsecured claim to be made concurrently with payments on any secured or unsecured claim.[47]

### [g] Treatment of Long-Term Debt

Section 1322(b)(5) states that a plan may "notwithstanding paragraph (2) of this subsection, provide for the curing of any default within a reasonable time and maintenance of payments while the case is pending on any unsecured claim or secured claim on which the last payment is due after the date on which

---

a default may be cured under Section 1322(b)(5) with maintenance of payments while the case is pending. See discussion at infra ¶ 17.08[2][g].

[41] 11 USC § 1322(b)(7), as amended by 1984 Amendments § 528. For discussion of what is an "executory contract" and the right to assume or reject under Section 365, see ¶ 13.09.

[42] 11 USC § 365(d)(1).

[43] 11 USC § 365(d)(2).

[44] For discussion of Section 365, see ¶ 13.09.

[45] In re Alexander, 670 F2d 885 (9th Cir. 1982). For discussion and criticism of this case, see Drake & Morris, Chapter 13 Practice and Procedure § 9.10, at 9-42 et seq. (Shepard's/McGraw-Hill 1983).

[46] 11 USC § 1322(b)(7), as amended by 1984 Amendments § 528, in relevant part provides that the plan may, "*subject to section 365 of this title*, provide for the assumption, rejection, or assignment of any executory contract or unexpired lease of the debtor not previously rejected under such section." (Italicized words added by the amendment.)

[47] 11 USC § 1322(b)(4).

the final payment under the plan is due."[48] As mentioned previously, Section 1322(b)(2) does not authorize the modification of the rights of a holder of a secured claim that is secured only by a security interest in the debtor's principal residence. However, if this security interest is a "long-term debt,"[49] Section 1322(b)(5) permits the curing of any default within a reasonable time and maintenance of payments while the case is pending.[50] For example, default may be cured on a long-term mortgage debt on the debtor's principal residence, for which the last payment is due five years after completion of payments under the plan. Acceleration may be prevented by paying the amount of the default or arrearage within a reasonable time period under the plan while maintaining the original payments. There is case authority that holds that the maintenance of the current payments must be made under the plan and cannot be made by payments "outside the plan."[51] After completion of the plan, the remaining payments extending beyond the plan are not discharged and will still be due under the terms of the original debt after completion of the plan.[52] Note, however, that the cure of default and maintenance of payments on long-term debt under Section 1322(b)(5) is not limited to long-term debt secured by the debtor's principal residence but includes other secured and unsecured long-term debt.

### [h] Provision for Postpetition Claims

Provision may be made in the plan for the payment of certain postpetition claims that are allowable under Section 1305.[53] Section 1305(a) permits the filing of proof of claim on two kinds of postpetition claims against the debtor: (1) claims against the debtor for taxes that become payable to a governmental unit while the case is pending[54] and (2) consumer debt claims that arise after the date of filing the petition for property or services that are necessary for the

---

[48] See generally Annot., 63 A.L.R. Fed. 309 (1983).

[49] "Long-term debt," as used here and elsewhere, means a debt on which the last payment is due after the date on which the final payment under the plan is due.

[50] If the final payment on the debt is due before the final payment under the plan, such debt appears not to be covered by Section 1322(b)(5). For helpful discussion of the treatment of "long-term debt," see Drake & Morris, Chapter 13 Practice and Procedure § 9.08 (Shepard's/McGraw-Hill 1983).

[51] In re Case, 11 Bankr. 843 (Bankr. D. Utah 1981); In re Foster, 670 F2d 478 (5th Cir. 1982); In re Glasper, 28 Bankr. 6 (Bankr. App. Par. 9th Cir. 1983). In *Glasper*, quoting from *Foster*, the court said: "Although Chapter 13 may allow some fully secured claims to be treated outside of a plan, a plan may not provide for the making of the current payment on a mortgage claim outside the plan while curing the arrearage on that claim under the plan pursuant to § 1322(b)(5). . . . So, too for the arrearage on a mortgage claim to be cured under § 1322(b)(5), the current mortgage payments while the case is pending must be provided for in the plan.." 28 Bankr. at 7.

[52] 11 USC §§ 1328(a)(1), 1328(c)(1). For discussion of Chapter 13 discharge, see infra ¶ 17.12.

[53] 11 USC § 1322(b)(6).

[54] 11 USC § 1305(a)(1).

debtor's performance under the plan.[55] For example, the second type of claim includes medical bills or car repairs that are necessary to enable the debtor to get to work.[56] Both types of claims are allowable under Section 1305(b) as if they had arisen before filing the petition. However, they are determined as of the time the claims arise. Claims for property or service necessary for the debtor's performance under the plan are not allowable if the holder of the claim knew or should have known that prior approval of the debtor's incurring of the obligation was practicable and was not obtained.[57]

### [i] Other Optional Provisions

The plan may provide for payments of claims to be made from property of the estate or property of the debtor.[58] For example, a creditor's claim could be paid in full or in part by a transfer to the creditor of property of the estate or of the debtor's exempt property. Alternatively, a secured creditor's claim could be paid by surrendering the collateral to the creditor.[59] The plan also may provide for the vesting of the property of the estate, on confirmation of the plan or at a later time, in the debtor or in any other entity.[60] Finally, the plan may include any other appropriate provision not inconsistent with the provisions of the Code.[61]

## ¶ 17.09 CONFIRMATION OF THE PLAN

After notice has been given to creditors, the bankruptcy court must hold a hearing on confirmation of the plan.[1] Under Bankruptcy Rule 2002(b), not less than twenty-five days' notice of the hearing must be given to the debtor, the trustee, and all creditors of the time for filing objections to the plan and of the hearing to consider confirmation of the plan.[2] The trustee is required to attend and to be heard at the confirmation hearing.[3] Any party in interest may object to confirmation of the plan based on the failure of the plan (or on the procedures employed before confirmation) to conform to the requirements of Chap-

[55] 11 USC § 1305(a)(2).

[56] H.R. Rep. No. 595, 95th Cong., 1st Sess. 427-428 (1977).

[57] 11 USC § 1305(c); see also H.R. Rep. No. 595, 95th Cong., 1st Sess. 428 (1977); S. Rep. No. 989, 95th Cong., 2d Sess. 140 (1978).

[58] 11 USC § 1322(b)(8).

[59] See 11 USC § 1325(a)(5)(C).

[60] 11 USC § 1322(b)(9).

[61] 11 USC § 1322(b)(10).

[1] 11 USC § 1324.

[2] The House Report states that Section 1324 requires a hearing on confirmation "after notice to all parties in interest." H.R. Rep. No. 595, 95th Cong., 1st Sess. 429 (1977).

[3] 11 USC § 1302(b)(2).

ter 13.[4] Objections to confirmation of the plan must be filed with the bankruptcy court within the time fixed for filing objections and must be served on the debtor, the trustee, any committee appointed under the Code, and on any other entity designated by the court.[5] An objection to confirmation is a contested matter and is governed by Bankruptcy Rule 9014.[6] If no objection is timely filed, the bankruptcy court may find, without receiving evidence, that the plan has been proposed in good faith and not by any means forbidden by law.[7] However, this does not mean that the court must confirm the plan without determining that the requirements for confirmation have been complied with.[8] Under new Section 1325(b) added by the 1984 Amendments,[9] if the trustee or the holder of an unsecured claim objects to confirmation, the court may not approve the plan unless (1) the value of the property to be distributed under the plan on account of the claim is not less than the amount of the claim or (2) the plan provides that all of the debtor's projected "disposable income"[10] to be received in the three-year period beginning on the date that the first payment is due under the plan will be applied to make payments under the plan. This means that if an unsecured creditor objects to confirmation and the creditor's claim is not to be paid in full under the plan, the plan may not be confirmed unless the debtor's projected "disposable income" for the next three years is devoted to payments under the plan.[11] If the trustee may object generally to confirmation on behalf of all unsecured creditors who will not receive full payment (which seems to be contemplated by the section), then the practical effect of this provision is to require the debtor to commit three years of "disposable income" to the plan. Otherwise, if there is objection by the trustee (or an unsecured creditor who is not paid in full), the plan cannot be confirmed without full payment of all claims. It should be observed that if all of the "dis-

---

[4] S. Rep. No. 989, 95th Cong., 2d Sess. 142 (1978). This objection to the confirmation is distinguished from merely rejecting the plan. Id.

[5] B. Rule 3020(b)(1).

[6] Id.

[7] B. Rule 3020(b)(2).

[8] Id. The order of confirmation must conform to Official Form 31, and notice of entry of the order must be sent promptly to the debtor, creditors, and other parties in interest. B. Rule 3020(c).

[9] 1984 Amendments § 317.

[10] "Disposable income" is defined as "income which is received by the debtor and which is not reasonably necessary to be expended (A) for the maintenance or support of the debtor or a dependent of the debtor; or (B) if the debtor is engaged in business, for the payment of expenditures necessary for the continuation, preservation, and operation of such business." 11 USC § 1325(b)(2), as added by 1984 Amendments § 317.

[11] It appears that if only one creditor whose claim is not to be paid in full objects, then, unless the plan can be modified to pay this claim in full, the debtor will have to modify the plan to meet the three-year disposable income test. Whether the plan can be modified to pay the one objecting unsecured creditor in full may be questionable in many cases because of the limitations on creation of class and unfair discrimination between classes and the requirement that claims within a class must receive equal treatment.

posable income" for three years is committed to the plan, this new section does not mean that unsecured claims must be paid in full for confirmation. The section is designed to compel debtors who have "disposable income" to use the income to fund the plan if claims are not to be paid in full. In part, Section 1325(b) is a response to the consumer credit industry, which claimed that consumer credit frequently is extended on the basis of the debtor's anticipated future earnings and that these earnings should, within reason, be available in bankruptcy to pay creditors.

## [1] The Effect of Confirmation

A confirmed plan binds the debtor and each creditor, regardless of whether the creditor's claim is provided for by the plan, or whether the creditor has objected to, accepted, or rejected the plan.[12] Confirmation also vests all property of the estate in the debtor, unless otherwise provided for in the plan or in the order of confirmation.[13] In the absence of other provisions, in the plan or confirming order, the property vests in the debtor free and clear of any claim or interest of any creditor provided for by the plan.[14] After confirmation, the court may order any entity from whom the debtor receives income to pay all or part of the income to the trustee.[15] Except as provided in Section 1325(b), Section 1325(a) states that the court *shall* confirm a plan if it meets the six criteria listed in Section 1325(a); if one of these requirements is not satisfied, the plan cannot be confirmed.[16] If the requirements are met, the court must confirm the plan and does not have the discretion to reject the plan.[17] The six requirements for confirmation are considered in the following discussion.

## [2] Compliance With Chapter 13 and the Bankruptcy Code

To be confirmed, the plan must comply with the provisions of Chapter 13 and with other applicable provisions of the Bankruptcy Code.[18] For example, the plan cannot be confirmed if it does not meet the requirement of Section

---

[12] 11 USC § 1327(a).

[13] 11 USC § 1327(b).

[14] 11 USC § 1327(c).

[15] 11 USC § 1325(c), as amended by 1984 Amendments § 317. "Entity" includes governmental agencies. 11 USC § 101(14); see, e.g., Regan v. Ross, 691 F2d 81 (2d Cir. 1982); U.S. v. Devall, 704 F2d 1513 (11th Cir. 1983).

[16] Section 1325(b) is the three-year "disposable income" rule. In addition to the six requirements of Section 1325(a), the requirements of Section 1325(b) must be met for confirmation if that section is applicable due to objection to confirmation by an unsecured creditor or by the trustee.

[17] In re Estus, 695 F2d 311 (8th Cir. 1982); Barnes v. Whelan, 689 F2d 193 (DC Cir. 1982); In re Markman, 5 Bankr. 196 (Bankr. EDNY 1980).

[18] 11 USC § 1325(a)(1).

1322(a)(2) that all priority claims must be paid in full,[19] or if it does not provide for equal treatment for each claim within a particular class. In addition, if the debtor is not eligible for Chapter 13, the plan should not be confirmed.[20]

### [3] Payment of Filing Fees and Other Charges

A plan cannot be confirmed if any fee or charge that is required to be paid under Chapter 123 of Title 28 of the U.S. Code or that is required by the plan has not been paid.[21] This includes the filing fee of $60. As noted elsewhere, the debtor may be permitted to pay the filing fees in not more than four installments, and the last installment must be paid within 120 days of filing the Chapter 13 petition.[22] Thus, since the statute permits payment in installments, where the debtor has obtained approval to pay the filing fee in installments, the filing fee does not have to have been paid in full for confirmation. However, if a debtor is in default on an installment payment, this may be sufficient to deny confirmation.[23]

### [4] Proposed in "Good Faith"

Section 1325(a)(3) requires that the plan must be proposed in "good faith" and not by any means forbidden by law. Good faith is not defined in the Code, and the legislative history does not shed any light on the intended meaning in this context. The good faith requirement has given the bankruptcy courts difficulty in application and, as might be expected, there are differences in approach as to what constitutes good faith. Indeed, the requirement has produced a fair amount of comment.[24] Much of the dispute over the good faith requirement centers on the question of what percentage, or how much, the

---

[19] See, e.g., In re Davis, 25 Bankr. 177 (Bankr. ND Ga. 1982).

[20] See 11 USC § 109. For discussion of eligibility requirements, see supra ¶ 17.02.

[21] 11 USC § 1325(a)(2).

[22] For discussion of filing fees, see ¶ 12.04[2].

[23] See Weintraub & Resnick, Bankruptcy Law Manual ¶ 9.14[2] (Warren, Gorham & Lamont, Inc. 1980); see also Drake & Morris, Chapter 13 Practice and Procedure § 11.03 (Shepard's/McGraw-Hill 1983).

[24] See generally Cyr, "The Chapter 13 'Good Faith' Tempest: An Analysis And Proposal for Change," 55 Am. Bankr. L.J. 271 (1981); Note, " 'Good Faith' and Confirmation of Chapter 13 Composition Plans: Analysis and a Proposal," 65 Minn. L. Rev. 659 (1981); Kelley, "Good Faith and Chapter 13," 36 Q. Rep. 8 (1982); Note, "Chapter 13 de Minimis Plans: Toward a Consensus on 'Good Faith,' " 9 Hofstra L. Rev. 593 (1981); Comment, "Good Faith in Chapter 13: A New Wild Card for Bankruptcy," 8 Ohio N.U.L. Rev. 102 (1981); Note, "Good Faith, Zero Plans, and the Purposes of Bankruptcy Code Chapter 13: A Legislative Solution to the Controversy," 61 B.U.L. Rev. 773 (1981); Case Note, "Chapter 13–Good Faith Requirement Does Not Require Substantial Repayment of Unsecured Creditors." (Goeb v. Heid [In re Goeb])," 52 Miss. L.J. 957 (1982). For discussion of some of the cases, see Cowans, Bankruptcy Law and Practice § 19.23, at 927–932 (West, interim ed. 1983).

debtor must propose paying on unsecured claims. As mentioned in the following discussion, for confirmation a plan must meet the "best interest of creditors" test and pay, over the term of the plan, at least the value of what unsecured creditors would receive in a Chapter 7 liquidation.[25] However, in many liquidation proceedings, there is no distribution to general unsecured creditors because there are no assets for distribution. Once this minimal requirement is met, how much more, if anything, must the debtor propose to pay to be acting in good faith? May a debtor propose a zero payment plan and still be acting in good faith? Or does good faith require at least some minimum payment? For example, may a plan that proposes to pay only 10 percent on unsecured claims (or perhaps a one percent or a zero payment plan) be confirmed as proposed in good faith? Or must a greater percentage be paid to evidence good faith? Is it sufficient to propose paying only what unsecured creditors would receive under the "best interests" test, even though in many cases this may be a zero payment?[26] In addition, does good faith require a "meaningful attempt"? Or a significant payment? Or represent the debtor's best efforts, as some courts have suggested?[27] Generally, the circuit courts that have dealt with the good faith issue have held that it does not require a substantial payment and that determination of good faith should be made on a case-by-case approach considering all of the circumstances. The courts have pointed out that meeting the "best interests of creditors" test does not automatically indicate that the plan is proposed in good faith.[28] Representative of this general approach is that of the Court of Appeals for the Eighth Circuit in *In re Estus.*[29]

> We agree with the above-discussed circuit court opinions that subsection (a)(3) good faith does not impose a rigid and unyielding requirement of substantial payment to unsecured creditors. A per se minimum payment requirement to unsecured creditors as an element of good faith would infringe on the desired flexibility of Chapter 13 and is unwarranted. Nor should the courts perfunctorily conclude that good faith is achieved whenever the minimum requirements of subsection (a)(4) have been met. The good faith requirement demands a separate, independent determination. As indicated, in determining whether a debtor's plan meets the section 1325(a)(3) confirmation require-

---

[25] See infra ¶ 17.09[5].

[26] See, e.g., In re Sadler, 3 Bankr. 536 (Bankr. ED Ark. 1980) (approving a zero payment plan); In re Harland, 3 Bankr. 597 (Bankr. D. Neb. 1980). But see In re Iacovoni, 2 Bankr. 256 (Bankr. D. Utah 1980).

[27] See, e.g., In re Heard, 6 Bankr. 876 (Bankr. WD Ky. 1980); In re Long, 10 Bankr. 880 (DSD 1981); In re Fredrickson, 5 Bankr. 199 (Bankr. MD Fla. 1980); In re Thorson, 6 Bankr. 678 (Bankr. DSD 1980); In re Burrell, 6 Bankr. 360 (Bankr. ND Cal. 1980); In re Iacovoni, 2 Bankr. 256 (Bankr. D. Utah 1980).

[28] In re Kitchens, 702 F2d 885 (11th Cir. 1983); In re Estus, 695 F2d 311 (8th Cir. 1982); Deans v. O'Donnell, 692 F2d 968 (4th Cir. 1982); Barnes v. Whelan, 689 F2d 193 (DC Cir. 1982); In re Goeb, 675 F2d 1386 (9th Cir. 1982); In re Rimgale, 669 F2d 426 (7th Cir. 1982).

[29] 695 F2d 311, 316–317 (8th Cir. 1982).

ment of good faith, we believe the proper inquiry should follow the analysis adopted by the Fourth Circuit: whether the plan constitutes an abuse of the provisions, purpose or spirit of Chapter 13. The bankruptcy court must utilize its fact-finding expertise and judge each case on its own facts after considering all the circumstances of the case. . . .

Certainly an important factor the courts must weigh in their analysis is the percentage of payment to unsecured creditors which the plan proposes. . . . However, the amount of the proposed repayment to unsecured creditors is only one of the many factors which the courts must consider in determining whether the plan meets the statutory good faith requirement. . . .

We make no attempt to enumerate all relevant considerations since the factors and the weight they are to be given will vary with the facts and circumstances of the case. However, in addition to the percentage of repayment to unsecured creditors, some of the factors that a court may find meaningful in making its determination of good faith are: (1) the amount of the proposed payments and the amount of the debtor's surplus; (2) debtor's employment history, ability to earn and likelihood of future increases in income; (3) the probable or expected duration of the plan; (4) the accuracy of the plan's statements of the debts, expenses and percentage of repayment of unsecured debt and whether any inaccuracies are an attempt to mislead the court; (5) the extent of preferential treatment between classes of creditors; (6) the extent to which secured claims are modified; (7) the type of debt sought to be discharged and whether any such debt is nondischargeable in Chapter 7; (8) the existence of special circumstance such as inordinate medical expenses; (9) the frequency with which the debtor has sought relief under the Bankruptcy Reform Act; (10) the motivation and sincerity of the debtor in seeking Chapter 13 relief; and (11) the burden which the plan's administration would place upon the trustee.

## [5] Best Interest of Creditors Test

For confirmation, Section 1325(a)(4) requires that the value, as of the effective date of the plan, of property to be distributed under the plan on account of each allowed unsecured claim, must be no less than the amount that would be paid on the claim if the estate of the debtor were liquidated under Chapter 7 on that date. This requirement is commonly referred to as the "best interest of creditors test" and, in effect, requires that unsecured creditors receive not less than they would receive in a liquidation case. The bankruptcy court must make a hypothetical determination of what unsecured creditors would receive in a liquidation of the nonexempt assets of the debtor and then determine whether the value of the payments under the plan, as of the effective date of the plan, at least equals that amount.[30] Generally, since payments will be made over a period of time, the unsecured creditors are entitled to receive

---

[30] The effective date of the plan generally is the date of confirmation, although the plan may provide that the plan will be effective at a later time.

not merely payments totaling the amount they would have received in a liquidation, but also an appropriate interest or "discount" factor that must be added to the liquidation amount to give the creditor the present value by future payments. In other words, the future payments must be discounted in order to determine the present value of the future payments as of the effective date of the plan.[31] As might be expected, courts have not been consistent in determining the appropriate interest rate to be used in discounting future installment payments to arrive at their present value.[32] Determination of the amount that unsecured creditors would receive in a Chapter 7 liquidation may require the court to determine not only the value of the property of the estate and of exemptions but also to make other determinations as well.[33] In some instances, to determine how much will be distributed to unsecured creditors, the court may have to determine the value of property that might be recovered for the estate under the avoiding powers or from a cause of action that belongs to the estate. A determination of the priority claims and administrative expenses also may have to be made.[34]

A related issue is whether the Chapter 13 plan must provide for full payment of claims that would be nondischargeable in a Chapter 7 case. Creditors have argued that they would receive their distributive share in the liquidation and that they also would have an enforceable right against the debtor for the unpaid balance. Generally, the courts have rejected this argument and held that these creditors are not entitled to full payment, reasoning that Section 1325(a)(4) requires that the creditor receive the *value* of what would be distributed in Chapter 7 and not what might be recovered from the debtor apart from the liquidation.[35]

---

[31] For example, assume that the amount the unsecured creditor would receive in a liquidation case is $1,000. A plan proposing to make monthly payments of $50 for twenty months would not afford the creditor a present value of $1,000 because the future payments would have to be discounted by some appropriate discount factor. To give the present value, an appropriate "interest" factor would have to be added to the twenty monthly payments to give a present value of $1,000.

[32] Weintraub & Resnick, Bankruptcy Law Manual ¶ 9.14[5], at S9-17 (Warren, Gorham & Lamont, Inc. 1983). The paragraph reference cited contains a helpful discussion of the approaches and the cases. See also Drake & Morris, Chapter 13 Practice and Procedure § 11.07, at 11-22–11-25 (Shepard's/McGraw-Hill 1983).

[33] In Chapter 7, the net proceeds from liquidation of property of the estate (excluding exempt property) generally will go to the unsecured creditors, and some, if not all, of the net proceeds must be used to pay priority claims. Some of the estate property may also be subject to valid security interests or liens as well; thus, it may not be available for distribution to unsecured creditors. In some cases, determinations with respect to such factors may have to be made by the court to arrive at a liquidation amount for unsecured creditors. Of course, in a great many cases, it will be clear that there is nothing that would be distributed to creditors because there are no nonexempt assets.

[34] See generally Drake & Morris, Chapter 13 Practice and Procedure § 11.05 (Shepard's/McGraw-Hill 1983).

[35] Drake & Morris, Chapter 13 Practice and Procedure § 11.05, at 11-18 (Shepard's/McGraw-Hill 1983).

## [6] Treatment of Secured Claims

A Chapter 13 plan may be confirmed only if each of the allowed secured claims provided for by the plan is dealt with in one of the three methods specified in Section 1325(a)(5).[36] First, the holder of an allowed secured claim may accept the plan.[37] Second, the collateral may be surrendered to the holder of the secured claim.[38] By surrender of the collateral, the secured claimant receives the value of the secured claim. The third method for treatment of a secured claim under a plan is governed by the "cram-down" provisions of Chapter 13.[39] Under the "cram-down" provisions, the rights of the holder of the secured claim may be modified, with the secured creditor forced to take stretched-out payments equal to the present value of the secured claim.[40] Specifically, if the plan provides for retention of the lien by the holder of the secured claim, the secured creditor may be forced to accept payments or property whose value, as of the effective date of the plan, at least equals the amount of the allowed secured claim.[41] In effect, by the use of Section 1325(a)(5)(B), an installment redemption of the property may be "crammed down" or forced upon the secured creditor despite objection to, or rejection of, the plan by the creditor.

Note that Section 1325(a)(5) deals only with allowed secured claims that are dealt with or provided for by the plan. If a claim is not an allowed secured claim or is not dealt with by the plan, the provisions of Section 1325(a)(5) are not applicable.

---

[36] If a proper proof of claim is not timely filed on the claim as a secured claim, the claim will not be an allowed secured claim and thus will not be entitled to the protection given by Section 1325(a)(5) to "allowed secured claims." If proof of claim is properly filed on a secured claim, a creditor who holds a claim that is undersecured will have both a secured claim to the extent of the value of the collateral and an unsecured claim to the extent of the deficiency. See Section 506 and discussion at ¶ 14.10. On the unsecured portion the creditor is entitled to receive at least the present value of the liquidation distribution, and in such circumstances only the allowed secured claim is entitled to the treatment provided for by Section 1325(a)(5). If the amount of the debt is less than the value of the collateral, the claim is a secured claim only to the extent of the debt. See 11 USC § 506(a). The valuation and method of evaluation will, of course, be important in determining the amount of the allowed secured claim. See ¶ 14.10. See also Drake & Morris, Chapter 13 Practice and Procedure § 11.07, at 11-22 (Shepard's/McGraw-Hill 1983) for discussion of valuation for Section 1325(a)(5) purposes.

[37] 11 USC § 1325(a)(5)(A). Acceptance of the plan by a secured creditor must be made within the time set by the court and must be in writing, must identify the plan accepted, must be signed by the creditor or his authorized agent, and must conform to Official Form 30. B. Rules 3018(a), 3018(c).

[38] 11 USC § 1325(a)(5)(C).

[39] 11 USC § 1325(a)(5)(B).

[40] Id.

[41] In determining the present value of the future payments, the "stretched out" payments must be discounted by an appropriate discount factor to arrive at their present value. See discussion at supra ¶ 17.09[5].

### [7] Feasibility

One of the more important requirements for confirmation is that the court must find that the plan is feasible; that is, it must find that "the debtor will be able to make all payments under the plan and to comply with the plan."[42] The determination of feasibility of the plan is in the discretion of the court.[43] In determining feasibility, courts have looked at the cushion in the plan or the margin between the debtor's expenses and income;[44] the failure to take into account inflation;[45] or the failure to provide adequately for medical expenses,[46] family living expenses,[47] and unforeseen expenses.[48] For purposes of determining the feasibility of a plan, the court may require disclosure of payments that are to be made "outside the plan."[49]

### [8] Duration of the Plan

The plan may not provide for payments over a period that is longer than three years, unless the court for cause approves a longer period that is not to exceed five years.[50]

### [9] Ordering Third Parties to Make Payments to the Trustee

After confirmation of the plan, the court may order any entity from whom the debtor receives income to pay all or a part of the income to the trustee who will serve as the disbursing agent under Section 1326.[51] An entity who disre-

---

[42] 11 USC § 1325(a)(6).

[43] In re Anderson, 18 Bankr. 763 (Bankr. SD Ohio 1982); In re Hockaday, 3 Bankr. 254 (Bankr. SD Cal. 1980).

[44] In re Howard, 3 Bankr. 75 (Bankr. SD Cal. 1980); In re Hockaday, 3 Bankr. 254 (Bankr. SD Cal. 1980); In re Perskin, 9 Bankr. 626 (Bankr. ND Tex. 1981); In re Barnes, 5 Bankr. 376 (Bankr. DDC 1980), aff'd, 689 F2d 193 (DC Cir. 1980).

[45] In re Barnes, 5 Bankr. 376 (Bankr. DDC 1980), aff'd, 689 F2d 193 (DC Cir. 1982); In re Lucas, 3 Bankr. 252 (Bankr. SD Cal. 1980); In re Washington, 6 Bankr. 226 (Bankr. ED Va. 1980).

[46] In re Hockaday, 3 Bankr. 254 (Bankr. SD Cal. 1980); In re Lucas, 3 Bankr. 252 (Bankr. SD Cal. 1980); In re Washington, 6 Bankr. 226 (Bankr. ED Va. 1980).

[47] In re Washington, 6 Bankr. 226 (Bankr. ED Va. 1980); In re Hockaday, 3 Bankr. 254 (Bankr. SD Cal. 1980); In re Barnes, 5 Bankr. 376 (Bankr. DDC 1980), aff'd, 689 F2d 193 (DC Cir. 1982).

[48] In re Street, 17 Bankr. 787 (Bankr. ND Ill. 1982); In re Perskin, 9 Bankr. 626 (Bankr. ND Tex. 1981).

[49] In re Case, 11 Bankr. 843 (Bankr. D. Utah 1981); In re Foster, 670 F2d 478 (5th Cir. 1982).

[50] 11 USC § 1322(c).

[51] 11 USC § 1325(c), as amended by 1984 Amendments § 317. "Entity," as defined in Section 101(14), includes governmental agencies, and such agencies are subject to such an order. See, e.g., Regan v. Ross, 691 F2d 81 (2d Cir. 1982); U.S. v. Devall, 704

gards this order may be held in contempt or be subject to other enforcement action by the bankruptcy court, such as an order to pay the amount that should have been remitted to the trustee.[52]

Unless the court orders otherwise, the debtor must begin making the payments proposed by the plan within thirty days after the plan is filed.[53] Failure to make payments may be the basis for dismissing the case.[54]

## ¶ 17.10 MODIFICATION OF THE PLAN

### [1] Modification of the Plan Before Confirmation

The debtor may modify the plan at any time before confirmation. However, the plan as modified must meet the mandatory and permissive requirements of Section 1322 discussed previously,[1] as well as meet the requirements for confirmation set forth in Section 1325. Bankruptcy Rule 3015 requires that the modification (as well as the original) must be dated. After the filing of the modification, the plan as modified becomes the plan.[2] Any holder of a secured claim who has accepted or rejected the plan is deemed to have accepted or rejected the modified plan unless the modification changes the rights of the holder. If the rights of an accepting or rejecting holder of a secured claim are changed by the modification, then the holder may change its previous rejection or acceptance.[3]

---

F2d 1513 (11th Cir. 1983); In re Latchaw, 24 Bankr. 457 (Bankr. ND Ohio 1982); S. Rep. No. 989, 95th Cong., 2d Sess. 142 (1978).

[52] In re Bradley, 7 BCD 99 (Bankr. ND Ala. 1980). In *Bradley*, the employer had paid the wages directly to the employee despite an order of the bankruptcy court to remit a part of the debtor's wages to the trustee. The court ordered the employer to pay to the trustee the wages that should have been remitted and, in addition, ordered the employer to pay the fees and costs of the trustee's attorney, which were incurred in filing the action to recover the unpaid wages.

[53] 11 USC § 1326(a)(1), as added by 1984 Amendments § 318. Such payments are to be retained by the trustee until the plan is confirmed or denied. If the plan is confirmed, the trustee is to distribute the payments pursuant to the plan; if the plan is not confirmed, the payments are to be returned to the debtor. 11 USC §§ 1326(a)(2), 1326(c).

[54] 11 USC § 1307(c)(4), as added by 1984 Amendments § 315.

[1] 11 USC § 1323(a). This means that the plan as modified must have the three mandatory requirements of Section 1322(a): (1) submission of sufficient income to the control and supervision of the trustee; (2) provision for full payment in cash for all priority claims; and (3) if classes of creditors are created, provision for equal treatment for all claims within the class. The provisions of Section 1322(b) that are applicable to optional provisions apply to modifications as well.

[2] 11 USC § 1323(b).

[3] 11 USC § 1323(c). H.R. Rep. No. 595, 95th Cong., 1st Sess. 429 (1977); S. Rep. No. 989, 95th Cong., 2d Sess. 142 (1978); see also B. Rule 3019.

### [2] Modification of the Plan After Confirmation

A creditor operating under a Chapter 13 plan may find that modification is necessary after confirmation of the plan for a number of reasons, including loss of a job, reduced income, medical needs, unexpected expenses, or perhaps merely unrealistic expectations with respect to income or expenses.[4] On request of the debtor, the trustee, or the holder of an allowed unsecured claim, at any time after confirmation of the plan but before the completion of payments, a Chapter 13 plan may be modified to:

(1) Increase or reduce the amount of payments on claims of a particular class provided for by the plan;

(2) Extend or reduce the time for payments; or

(3) Alter the amount of the distribution to a creditor whose claim is provided for by the plan, to the extent necessary to take account of any payment of the claim other than under the plan.[5]

However, the plan as modified may not contain any provision that could not be included in an original plan as prescribed by Section 1322(a) or 1322(b).[6] In addition, the plan must meet the requirements for confirmation set out in Section 1325(a).[7] For example, if the modification proposes to reduce payments or to reduce the payments to the amount already paid to creditors under the plan, it can not be approved if the payments to unsecured creditors do not meet the "best interest of creditors" test; that is, unsecured creditors must receive at least the present value of what they would have received in a Chapter 7 liquidation. Holders of secured claims who have previously rejected or accepted a plan have the right given under Section 1323(c) to change a prior rejection or acceptance if the modification changes the rights of the creditor. If the modification does not affect the rights of a creditor who has previously rejected or accepted the plan, the creditor will be deemed to have rejected or accepted, as the case may be.[8]

---

[4] One of the requirements for obtaining a "hardship discharge" under Section 1328(b) is that modification is not practicable.

[5] 11 USC §§ 1329(a)(1)–1329(a)(3), as amended by 1984 Amendments § 319. The amendment added the language in Section 1329(a) stating that modification can be "upon request of the debtor, the trustee or the holder of an allowed unsecured claim." It is not clear whether this change was intended to permit a creditor to compel a modification of the plan to increase the debtor's payments where, for example, the debtor's income has increased and there is additional "disposable income."

[6] See discussion at supra ¶¶ 17.08[1], 17.08[2]. This means that the plan as modified must meet the three mandatory requirements of Section 1322(a): (1) submission of sufficient income to the control and supervision of the trustee; (2) provision for full payments in cash for all priority claims; and (3) if classes of creditors are created, provision for equal treatment for all claims within the class. The provisions of Section 1322(b) that are applicable to optional provisions, apply to modifications as well.

[7] 11 USC § 1329(b)(1).

[8] 11 USC §§ 1323(c), 1329(b)(1).

The plan as modified becomes the plan, unless the court, after notice and a hearing, disapproves the modification.[9] The modified plan may not provide for payments beyond three years from the time the first payment was due under the original confirmed plan, unless the court, for cause, approves a longer period not exceeding five years from the time the first payment was due under the original plan.[10]

If additional postpetition claims arise that are allowable under Section 1305,[11] modification of the plan may be required to include these claims under the plan, and in certain circumstances may require a reduction of payments to other creditors or an increase in the amount paid to the trustee under the plan. Otherwise, without additional income devoted to the plan, the modified plan might not comply with Section 1322(a)(1), which requires that sufficient funds must be provided for execution of the plan.[12]

The trustee is required to appear and to be heard at the modification hearing.[13]

## ¶ 17.11 CONVERSION OR DISMISSAL

A debtor who has initially filed a petition under Chapter 13 may wish to dismiss the case or convert it to either Chapter 7 or 11. Creditors also may seek (e.g., where the debtor has not proposed a plan or proposed a plan that cannot be confirmed) to dismiss the case or to convert it to Chapter 7 or 11. Conversion of a pending Chapter 7 or 11 proceeding to a Chapter 13 proceeding has been discussed earlier in this text.[1] As noted previously, an individual's case may be converted from a Chapter 7 or 11 proceeding to Chapter 13 only upon request of the debtor and only if the debtor is eligible for Chapter 13.[2]

### [1] Conversion of a Chapter 13 Case to Chapter 7 or Chapter 11

A debtor may convert a Chapter 13 case to a Chapter 7 case at any time; a waiver of this right is unenforceable.[3] This gives the debtor the absolute right

---

[9] 11 USC § 1329(b)(2).

[10] 11 USC § 1329(c).

[11] See discussion at supra ¶ 17.04[1].

[12] See In re Nelson, 27 Bankr. 341 (Bankr. MD Ga. 1983). For additional discussion, see Drake & Morris, Chapter 13 Practice and Procedure § 10.02, at 10-5–10-7 (Shepard's/McGraw-Hill 1983).

[13] 11 USC § 1302(b)(2)(C).

[1] See ¶ 12.07.

[2] See 11 USC §§ 706(d), 1112(e).

[3] 11 USC § 1307(a).

to convert to a liquidation case at any time.[4] On request of a party in interest and after notice and a hearing, the court may convert a Chapter 13 case to a case under Chapter 7, or it may dismiss the case, whichever is in the best interests of creditors and the estate, for cause, including, but not limited to,[5] eight specified grounds.[6] The grounds have been specified as follows:

(1) Unreasonable delay by the debtor that is prejudicial to creditors;
(2) Failure to pay filing fees and other charges required under Chapter 123 of Title 28 of the Code;
(3) Failure to timely file a plan;
(4) Failure of the debtor to make timely payments under the plan as required by Section 1326;[7]
(5) Denial of confirmation of a plan and denial of a request for additional time for filing another plan or a modification;
(6) Material default by the debtor under the plan;
(7) Revocation of the order of confirmation and denial of confirmation of a modified plan; and
(8) Termination of a confirmed plan by reason of the occurrence of a condition specified in the plan other than completion of payments under the plan.

At any time before confirmation of the Chapter 13 plan, on request of a party in interest and after notice and a hearing, the court may convert the case to a case under Chapter 11.[8] For example, an individual businessman whose case would more appropriately be handled under Chapter 11 may be converted to that chapter on request of a party in interest. However, a farmer may be converted to Chapter 11 only on request of the debtor.[9]

Finally, no Chapter 13 debtor may be converted to a case under another chapter unless the debtor is eligible to be a debtor under that chapter.[10]

Upon entry of an order for conversion, the clerk must give notice to the debtor and all creditors pursuant to Bankruptcy Rule 2002(f)(4). Bankruptcy

---

[4] H.R. Rep. No. 595, 95th Cong., 1st Sess. 428 (1977); In re Collins, 19 Bankr. 209 (Bankr. SD Fla. 1982); In re Doyle, 11 Bankr. 110 (Bankr. ED Pa. 1981). The debtor also may dismiss the Chapter 13 proceeding at any time with one exception.

[5] "Including," as used in the Code, is not limiting. 11 USC § 102(3).

[6] 11 USC § 1307(c), as amended by 1984 Amendments §§ 315, 527. However, a farmer who is not eligible for an involuntary Chapter 7 proceeding (see 11 USC § 303(a) ), may be converted from a Chapter 13 case to Chapter 7 only upon request of the debtor. 11 USC §§ 1307(c), 1307(e). "Farmer" is defined in Section 101(17).

[7] Unless the court orders otherwise, the debtor must begin making the payments proposed by the plan within thirty days after the plan is filed. 11 USC 1326(a)(1), as added by 1984 Amendments § 315.

[8] 11 USC § 1307(d). This section does not state that the conversion to Chapter 11 must be for cause, nor does it specify grounds for such conversion.

[9] 11 USC §§ 1307(d), 1307(e).

[10] 11 USC § 1307(f); see also 11 USC § 109.

Rule 1019 covers important details with respect to conversion of a Chapter 13 case to Chapter 7 and should be consulted.[11] For example, inventories, schedules, statements of financial affairs, and executory contracts that were previously filed will be deemed filed in the Chapter 7 case unless the court orders otherwise.[12] Notice of the conversion also must be given to all creditors within twenty days after entry of the order of conversion pursuant to Bankruptcy Rule 2002 and must be included in the notice of the meeting of creditors.[13] Claims that were filed in the superseded case will be deemed filed in the Chapter 7 case.[14] If the case was converted from Chapter 7 to Chapter 13 and then reconverted to Chapter 7, and if the time for filing claims or for filing complaints objecting to discharge or to dischargeability of a debt has expired in the original Chapter 7 case before its conversion to Chapter 13, the reconversion to Chapter 7 does not revive or extend the time for filing these claims or complaints.[15] After qualification of the Chapter 7 trustee, the debtor and the Chapter 13 trustee must turn over to the Chapter 7 trustee all records and property of the estate.[16] Each debtor or trustee in the superseded case should file a final report and account with the court within thirty days after entry of the order of conversion, unless the court directs otherwise.[17] In addition, the rule covers details with respect to filing postpetition claims.[18]

Under the Bankruptcy Rules, proceedings to convert a case to another chapter are treated as "contested matters" governed by Bankruptcy Rule 9014, and the moving party proceeds by motion pursuant to Bankruptcy Rule 9014.[19] The effect of conversion is governed by Section 348.[20]

## [2] Dismissal of a Chapter 13 Case

On request of the debtor at any time, if the case has not previously been converted from a Chapter 7 or 11 proceeding, the court must dismiss the Chapter 13 case.[21] A waiver of this right is unenforceable.[22] This gives the Chapter 13 debtor the absolute right to dismiss the case if the case has not previously been converted from a Chapter 7 or 11 case.

---

[11] See also discussion at ¶ 13.07[1].

[12] B. Rule 1019(1).

[13] B. Rule 1019(2).

[14] B. Rule 1019(4).

[15] B. Rule 1019(3).

[16] B. Rule 1019(5).

[17] B. Rule 1019(6).

[18] B. Rule 1019(7).

[19] See B. Rule 1017(d).

[20] See discussion at ¶ 12.07[1].

[21] 11 USC § 1307(b). As noted in ¶ 12.07, a case may be converted from Chapter 7 or 11 to Chapter 13 only upon request of the debtor. This is in keeping with the voluntary nature of Chapter 13 cases.

[22] 11 USC § 1307(b).

In addition, as indicated previously, upon request of a party in interest, after notice and a hearing, the court may dismiss or convert a case to Chapter 7, whichever is in the best interest of creditors and the estate, for cause, including the eight grounds specified in Section 1307(c).[23]

Proceedings to dismiss a case or to convert a case to another chapter are "contested matters" governed by Bankruptcy Rule 9014, and the moving party proceeds by motion pursuant to Bankruptcy Rule 9014.[24] The effect of the dismissal is governed by Section 349. Generally, unless the court for cause orders otherwise, dismissal of the case is without prejudice and does not bar discharge in a later case of debts that were dischargeable in the case dismissed and does not prejudice the debtor with regard to filing a subsequent petition.[25]

Also, unless the court for cause orders otherwise, dismissal reinstates any proceeding or custodianship that was superseded by the case, reinstates any transfer that was avoided under the avoiding powers or any voided lien, and revests the property of the estate in the entity in which the property was vested immediately before the commencement of the case.[26] Generally, this means that the parties will be placed in the position they were in before commencement of the case.

## ¶ 17.12 DISCHARGE

For the debtor, obtaining a discharge generally will be of prime importance. As mentioned previously, one advantage of a Chapter 13 case for a debtor is that, in some instances, debts that are nondischargeable in a Chapter 7 case may be discharged in a Chapter 13 case. The scope of the discharge in Chapter 13, however, depends upon the type of discharge obtained and whether a discharge is obtained under Section 1328(a) by completing all payments under the plan or whether the debtor obtains what is generally referred to as a "hardship discharge" under Section 1328(b).[1] Generally, a discharge obtained under Section 1328(a), by completing all payments under the plan, will discharge the debtor of all debts covered by the plan except those nondischargeable under Sections 523(a)(5) (claims for alimony, maintenance, or sup-

---

[23] See B. Rule 1017.

[24] See B. Rule 1017(d).

[25] 11 USC § 349(a), as amended by 1984 Amendments § 303. However, if the dismissal is due to the willful failure of the debtor to abide by orders of the court, or to appear before the court in proper prosecution of the case, or the case was voluntarily dismissed by the debtor following the filing of a request for relief from the stay of Section 362, the debtor is not eligible to be a debtor under the Code for 180 days after dismissal of the case. See 11 USC § 109(f), as added by 1984 Amendments § 301.

[26] 11 USC § 349(b).

[1] See generally Van Baalen, "Bankruptcy Code Chapter 13—What Price the Better Discharge?" 35 Okla. L. Rev. 455 (1982); Lander, "An Analysis and Comparison of the Nondischargeability Provisions of Chapter 11 and Chapter 13 of the Bankruptcy Code," 27 St. Louis U.L.J. 639 (1983).

port) and 1322(b)(5) ("long-term debt"). However, a "hardship discharge" obtained under Section 1328(b) is more limited and discharges all unsecured debts covered by the plan except those nondischargeable under Sections 523(a) and 1322(b)(5).[2]

Section 727, which gives ten grounds for objecting to a discharge in a Chapter 7 case,[3] does not apply in Chapter 13.[4] For example, an individual debtor who had received a discharge in a Chapter 7 case commenced within six years of the commencement of the Chapter 13 case may obtain a Chapter 13 discharge, although a discharge would not be available in Chapter 7 because of the six-year bar. Thus, a debtor who is concerned with the ability to obtain a discharge in Chapter 7, because one or more of the grounds for blocking a discharge exists, may find that Chapter 13 offers an attractive option. Furthermore, as noted previously,[5] if a discharge is obtained in a Chapter 13 case in which the payments totaled 100 percent of the allowed unsecured claims (i.e., an extension plan) or 70 percent of the allowed unsecured claims, and the plan was proposed in good faith and represented the debtor's best effort, the six-year bar is not applicable. Thus, a discharge may be obtained in a subsequent Chapter 7 case even though it is commenced within six years of the commencement of the previous Chapter 13 case. If a debtor is concerned with preserving as a future option the ability to obtain a Chapter 7 discharge within six years after filing the Chapter 13 case, the debtor should be concerned with obtaining a Chapter 13 discharge that will preserve this option. Consequently, consideration should be given to proposing a plan that pays at least 70 percent of the allowed unsecured claims. The plan should be proposed in good faith and represent the debtor's best efforts. If possible, such a determination should be obtained from the bankruptcy court at the time of the confirmation of the plan that provides for at least 70 percent payment. The order of confirmation should include a recital that states that the plan represents the debtor's best efforts. Also, if a hardship discharge is obtained, a similar determination and recital should be placed in the order of discharge, if possible.[6] Finally, neither a Chapter 13 discharge (i.e., a completion discharge or a "hardship discharge") nor a Chapter 7 discharge bars a subsequent Chapter 13 discharge, since Section 727 is not applicable in Chapter 13 cases.[7]

After the determination has been made by the court to grant or deny a discharge, the court must hold the discharge hearing required by Section 524(d), at which time the debtor must appear in person.[8] At this discharge

---

[2] For discussion of nondischargeable debts, see ¶ 15.06.

[3] See discussion at ¶ 15.04.

[4] 11 USC § 103(b).

[5] See ¶ 15.04[8].

[6] Weintraub & Resnick, Bankruptcy Law Manual ¶ 9.17, at 9-36 (Warren, Gorham & Lamont, Inc. 1983); Drake & Morris, Chapter 13 Practice and Procedure ¶ 12.07, at 12-19 (Shepard's/McGraw-Hill 1983).

[7] See, e.g., In re Ciotta, 4 Bankr. 253 (Bankr. EDNY 1980).

[8] 11 USC § 524(d). For discussion of the discharge hearing and cases dealing with waiver of the requirement that the debtor attend, see ¶ 15.02.

hearing, the debtor must also be given the "Miranda" warning with respect to reaffirmation of discharge debts.[9]

In contrast to Chapter 11,[10] the Chapter 13 discharge does not occur with the confirmation of the plan. It occurs at the time of completion of payments under the plan or at the time the hardship discharge is obtained.[11]

### [1] Discharge Where Payments Under the Plan Are Completed: Section 1328(a)

Upon completion of all payments under the confirmed plan, the court must grant the debtor a discharge, unless the court approves a written waiver of discharge by the debtor.[12] The discharge obtained under Section 1328(a) discharges the debtor of all secured and unsecured debts provided for by the plan and all claims disallowed under Section 502.[13] This also means that unsecured or secured claims not provided for by the plan are not discharged. The Code does not define what "provided for by the plan" means, and it has been questioned whether a zero payment plan or one that states that no payment will be made to a particular debt "provides for such debts" within the meaning of the section, hence making the debts nondischargeable. A Bankruptcy Appellate Panel of the Court of Appeals for the Ninth Circuit has held that an unsecured creditor is "provided for by the plan" as long as the creditor is listed on the plan as an unsecured creditor and as long as the plan states that the creditor is to receive nothing under the plan. Thus, the court rejected the view that creditors are provided for only when they receive a benefit under the plan.[14] The Appellate Panel suggested that there is a distinction between claims not listed by the debtor and those that are listed under a plan that states that they will receive no payment.[15] In addition, "long-term debt" that is provided for by the plan[16] and debts for alimony, support, or maintenance that are nondischargeable under Section 523(a)(5)[17] are not discharged by a Chapter 13 completion

[9] For discussion of reaffirmation of debts that have been discharged, see ¶ 15.08. For discussion of the effect of the discharge and the provisions that protect the discharge, see ¶ 15.03.

[10] In Chapter 11, confirmation of the plan operates as a discharge. See 11 USC § 1141(d).

[11] 11 USC §§ 1328(a), 1328(b).

[12] 11 USC § 1328(a). Bankruptcy Rule 4004(g) directs the bankruptcy court clerk to promptly mail a copy of the discharge to all creditors and the trustee and his attorney. Any waiver of discharge must be executed after the order for relief. Id.

[13] See ¶ 14.05 for discussion of disallowance of claims.

[14] In re Gregory, 19 Bankr. 668 (Bankr. App. Pan. 9th Cir. 1982).

[15] Id. at 670.

[16] See supra ¶ 17.08[2][g]. Long-term debt, such as a mortgage debt, may be dealt with by the plan. The plan may provide for curing of default within a reasonable time, with payments being made on the long-term debt while the Chapter 13 plan is pending.

[17] For discussion of this exception and the meaning of "alimony, maintenance or support," see ¶ 15.07[3][e]. Note, however, that if such claims are dischargeable under

discharge obtained under Section 1328(a). Priority claims will have been paid in full as required by Section 1322(a)(2). However, other types of debts that are nondischargeable under Section 523(a) in a Chapter 7 case are discharged by the Chapter 13 payment completion discharge. For example, claims for a student loan, willful or malicious injury, money or property obtained by fraud, and claims arising from defalcation in a fiduciary capacity can be discharged when payments under the Chapter 13 plan are completed, although the plan may not have provided for full payment of these claims. Thus, for an individual concerned with nondischargeable debts, Chapter 13 may be an attractive alternative, and the debtor, of course, will be interested in proposing a plan under which payments can be completed to obtain the broader discharge available under Section 1328(a).

Additionally, any postpetition claim allowed under Section 1305(a)(2)[18] is not discharged if prior approval by the trustee of the debtor's incurring the debt was practicable and was not obtained.[19]

There are no provisions for objecting to a full payment or "completion" discharge.

## [2] Where Payments Under the Plan Are Not Completed: The "Hardship Discharge" Under Section 1328(b)

At any time after the confirmation of the plan and after notice and a hearing, the court may grant a debtor a "hardship discharge," even though payments under the plan have not been completed. However, certain conditions must be met.[20] First, the debtor's failure to complete payment must be due to circumstances for which the debtor should not justly be held accountable.[21] Second, the value, as of the effective date of the plan, of the payments or property distributed under the plan on account of each unsecured claim must not be less than the amount that would have been paid had there been a liquidation under Chapter 7.[22] If any unsecured creditor has not received at least the value of what he would have received in liquidation, then a hardship discharge may not be granted because the "best interest of creditors" requirement has not been met. Third, modification of the plan must be impracticable.[23] In some

---

Section 523(a)(5) because they have been assigned to a third party (other than pursuant to the Social Security Act or to the federal government or a state or state agency), they will be included in the Chapter 13 discharge under Section 1328(a).

[18] Section 1305(a)(2) permits allowance of a postpetition "consumer debt" that is for property or services necessary for the debtor's performance under the plan. However, these claims are not allowable if the holder of the claim knew or should have known that prior approval of the debtor's incurring the obligation was practicable and was not obtained. 11 USC § 1305(c).

[19] 11 USC § 1328(d).

[20] 11 USC § 1328(b).

[21] 11 USC § 1328(b)(1).

[22] 11 USC § 1328(b)(2).

[23] 11 USC § 1328(b)(3). See supra ¶ 17.10 for discussion of modification.

circumstances, although the debtor may meet the first two requirements for a hardship discharge, if the debtor is concerned with discharging debts not dischargeable by the hardship discharge, it may be to the debtor's advantage to modify the plan, if this can be done, to enable the debtor to obtain a full payment (completion) discharge with its broader discharge. This might be accomplished by modifying the plan under Section 1329 to limit payments to those already made under the plan. If the "best interests of creditors" test can be met, the debtor might be able to obtain a full payment or completion discharge.[24] This "hardship discharge" discharges unsecured debts provided for by the plan[25] and all disallowed claims. However, it does not discharge "long-term" debts covered by the plan and any debt that is not dischargeable under Section 523(a).[26] Essentially this means that the hardship discharge does not discharge most taxes[27] and debts obtained by fraud, willful and malicious injury, student loans, and other claims listed in Section 523(a). Of course, nondischargeable claims will be satisfied to the extent of any payments made under the plan. Additionally, any postpetition claim allowed under Section 1305(a)(2), which represents a "consumer debt" necessary for the debtor's performance under the plan, is not discharged if prior approval by the trustee of the debtor's incurring the debt was practicable and was not obtained.[28]

Upon motion by a debtor for a hardship discharge under Section 1328(b), the court, by order, must set a deadline for the filing of a complaint to determine the dischargeability of claims under Section 523(c).[29] All creditors must be given not less than thirty days' notice of the deadline for filing such complaints for determination of dischargeability. On motion of a party in interest made before the time expires, the court, after notice and a hearing, may, for cause, extend the time for filing complaints.[30]

---

[24] For additional discussion, see Drake & Morris, Chapter 13 Practice and Procedure § 10.02, at 10-5–10-7 (Shepard's/McGraw-Hill 1983).

[25] Secured debts are thus excepted from the hardship discharge whether or not they are included in the plan.

[26] 11 USC § 1328(c). See ¶ 15.07 for discussion of nondischargeable debts.

[27] For discussion of the discharge of taxes and the apparent oversight in the 1984 Amendments, which at present appear to make tax claims dischargeable, see ¶ 15.07[3][a].

[28] 11 USC § 1328(d).

[29] B. Rule 4007(d). Section 523(c) gives the bankruptcy court exclusive jurisdiction to determine dischargeability of claims under Section 523(a)(2) (debts obtained by fraud or a false statement in writing), 523(a)(4) (fraud or defalcation in a fiduciary capacity), or 523(a)(6) (willful and malicious injury). If a complaint for determination of dischargeability of such claims is not timely filed in the bankruptcy court, then such debts are discharged. See discussion at ¶ 15.07[1]. The complaint for determination of dischargeability should be filed with the court where the case is pending pursuant to Bankruptcy Rule 5005. Determination of dischargeability of particular debts may be heard and determined by the bankruptcy judge as a "core proceeding." 28 USC § 157(b)(2)(I). For discussion of core proceedings, see ¶ 12.02[2][a].

[30] B. Rule 4007(d).

### [3] Revocation of Discharge

On request of a party in interest, made within a year after the discharge is granted, the court, after notice and a hearing, may revoke the discharge. However, the court may revoke the discharge only on the ground that it was obtained by the debtor through fraud and that the requesting party did not know of the fraud until the discharge was granted.[31] A party in interest seeking to revoke a discharge must proceed by an adversary proceeding under Bankruptcy Rule 7001.

---

[31] 11 USC § 1328(e), as amended by 1984 Amendments § 532.

# TABLES AND INDEX

# Table of USC Sections

[*References are to paragraphs (¶) and notes (n.).*]

[*References are to paragraphs (¶) and notes (n.).*]

[*References are to paragraphs (¶) and notes (n.).*]

[*References are to paragraphs (¶) and notes (n.).*]

[*References are to paragraphs (¶) and notes (n.).*]

[*References are to paragraphs (¶) and notes (n.).*]

[*References are to paragraphs (¶) and notes (n.).*]

[*References are to paragraphs (¶) and notes (n.).*]

[*References are to paragraphs (¶) and notes (n.).*]

[*References are to paragraphs (¶) and notes (n.).*]

[*References are to paragraphs (¶) and notes (n.).*]

[*References are to paragraphs (¶) and notes (n.).*]

[*References are to paragraphs (¶) and notes (n.).*]

[*References are to paragraphs (¶) and notes (n.).*]

## TRUTH-IN-LENDING ACT

15 USC § (TILA)



## FAIR CREDIT BILLING ACT

15 USC § (FCBA)



## CONSUMER LEASING ACT

15 USC §



## FAIR CREDIT REPORTING ACT

15 USC § (FCRA)



## EQUAL CREDIT OPPORTUNITY ACT

15 USC § (ECOA)

[*References are to paragraphs (¶) and notes (n.).*]

[*References are to paragraphs (¶) and notes (n.).*]

[*References are to paragraphs (¶) and notes (n.).*]

*[References are to paragraphs (¶) and notes (n.).]*

# Table of CFR Sections

*[References are to paragraphs (¶) and notes (n.).]*

[*References are to paragraphs (¶) and notes (n.).*]

[*References are to paragraphs (¶) and notes (n.).*]

# Table of 1898 Bankruptcy Act Sections

[*References are to paragraphs (¶) and notes (n.).*]

# Table of 1984 Bankruptcy Amendments and Federal Judgeship Act Sections

[*References are to paragraphs (¶) and notes (n.).*]

[*References are to paragraphs (¶) and notes (n.).*]

# Table of Bankruptcy Rules

*[References are to paragraphs (¶) and notes (n.).]*

[*References are to paragraphs (¶) and notes (n.).*]

[*References are to paragraphs (¶) and notes (n.).*]



## FORMER BANKRUPTCY RULES

# Table of Official Bankruptcy Forms

*[References are to paragraphs (¶) and notes (n.).]*

# Table of Uniform Act Sections

*[References are to paragraphs (¶) and notes (n.).]*

UNIFORM COMMERCIAL CODE

UCC §

1-102(44) .......... 7.07[4][d] n.36
1-103 ............. 7.01[4][a] n.15; 7.05[4][b][ii]; 7.06[6][d][ii]
1-105 .......... 7.06[6][a] & n.133
1-106 ............ 7.05[9][b] n.152
1-108 ................ 7.05[4][b][i]
1-201 .............. 7.01[4][a] n.13
1-201(19) ............ 7.05[4][b][i]; 7.07[5][b][i] n.47
1-201(22) ......... 7.06[7][c] n.184
1-201(23) ..... 6.07[2][c]; 13.10 n.6
1-201(28) ........ 7.06[3][c][ii] n.18
1-201(30) ........ 7.06[3][c][ii] n.18
1-201(32) .......... 7.06[3][j] n.86
1-201(37) ...... 2.04[2][b][iv] n.38; 7.02[2][a][iv] n.16; 7.02[2][b] n.35; 16.02[1] ns. 15, 16
1-201(39) ........... 7.04[2][a][ii]
1-201(44)(a) ......... 7.04[3] n.31
1-201(44)(b) ......... 7.04[3] n.32
1-201(44)(d) ......... 7.04[3] n.30
1-203 ..... 2.01[1][b] n.40; 7.01[4][a] n.16; 7.05[4][b][i]
1-204(44) .............. 8.04 n.19
1-205 .............. 7.01[4][a] n.14
1-208 ...... 4.02[1] n.5; 7.05[4][b][i] ns. 12, 13, 16
1-209(9) ...... 7.07[5][b][i] & n.50; 7.07[5][c][i] n.59; 7.07[5][c][ii] n.60
1-228 .................. 5.05[2][d]
2-103(1)(b) ...... 7.07[5][b][i] n.47
2-103(1)(b) ........ 2.01[1][b] n.40
2-208 ............ 7.05[4][b][ii] n.20
2-209 ............ 7.05[4][b][ii] n.20
2-302 ............. 2.01[1][b] n.40; 3.02[3][a][ii] n.18; 6.02[5][d] n.126
2-313 .............. 2.01[1][b] n.28
2-326 ....... 7.02[2][b] ns. 30, 31; 16.03[1] n.16

UCC §

2-326(3) ........... 7.02[2][b] n.34
2-401 ...... 7.02[2][c] n.42; 7.04[4]
2-401(1) ............ 7.07[11] n.98
2-403 .... 7.07[5][b][i] n.52; 13.10[1] & ns. 8, 41
2-501 .................... 7.04[4]
2-505(1)(a) ........ 7.02[2][c] n.43
2-505(1)(b) ........ 7.02[2][c] n.44
2-506 .............. 7.02[2][c] n.47
2-507(2) ............ 13.10[1] n.35
2-511(3) ............ 13.10[1] n.35
2-701(1) ............ 13.10[2] n.49
2-702 .......... 7.04[4]; 13.10 n.5; 13.10[1] & ns. 13, 15, 19; 13.10[2] n.43
Comment 2 ........ 13.10[1] n.10
2-702(1) ................ 13.10[2]
2-702(2) .... 13.10 ns. 8, 9; 13.10[1] & ns. 11, 18, 19, 31, 34, 37
2-702(3) ...... 13.10[1] & ns. 8, 41
2-703 ...... 7.02[2][c] n.45; 13.10[2] n.43
2-705 .... 7.02[2][c] n.45; 13.10[2] & ns. 43, 49
2-706 .............. 7.02[2][c] n.45
2-707 ...... 7.02[2][c] n.48; 7.07[11] n.101
2-711 .... 3.03[1] n.1; 7.02[2][c] n.46; 7.07[11] n.101
2-714(2) ........... 2.01[1][b] n.28
2-717 ................. 3.03[1] n.1
2-721 .................. 2.01[1][b]
3-104 .... 3.03[1] ns. 3, 7; 3.03[3][a] n.20; 3.03[4] n.54; 7.03[2][c][iii]
3-112(1)(d) ....... 6.02[5][a] n.105
3-202 ............. 3.03[1] ns. 4, 7
3-302 .... 3.03[1] n.5; 3.03[3][a] n.21; 3.03[4][b] ns. 54, 57; 7.07[5][e] n.62
3-305 .... 3.03[1] n.6; 5.05[2][t] n.75; 5.05[2][u] n.76; 8.06[1] n.11

[*References are to paragraphs (¶) and notes (n.).*]

[*References are to paragraphs (¶) and notes (n.).*]

UCC §

9-106 . . . . . . . . . . . 7.02[3] ns. 52, 56; 7.03[2][a] & n.5; 7.03[2][c][iii] n.33; 7.07[4][b][ii]; 16.04 n.5
 Comment . . . . . . 7.03[2][c][iii] n.34
9-107 . . . . 3.02[3][b] n.24; 7.06[5][b]; 7.07[4][b][i] n.26; 7.07[8][d] n.76
9-108 . . . . . . . . . . . 16.04[9] & n.109
9-109 . . . . . 1.02 n.1; 7.03[2][a] & n.3
 Comment 3 . . . . . . . . 7.03[2][b][ii] ns. 19–21
 Comment 5 . . . . 7.03[2][b][iv] n.21
9-109(1) . . . . . . . . . . 3.02[2] ns. 5, 8; 7.03[2][b][i]; 7.06[5][b] n.111
9-109(2) . . . . . . . . 7.03[2][b][iv] n.21; 16.04[9] & n.114
9-109(3) . . . . . . . . 7.07[5][b][i] n.44; 16.04 n.5
9-109(4) . . . . 7.03[2][b][ii] ns. 19, 20; 16.04 n.5
9-110 . . . . 7.04[2][a][iv]; 7.06[3][c][v]
9-113 . . . . 7.02[2][c]; 7.03[2][a] n.11; 7.07[1] & n.100
 Comment 1 . . . . . . . 7.02[2][c] n.45
9-113(b) . . . . . . . . . . 7.06[5][e] n.126
9-114 . . . . 7.02[2][b] & ns. 30, 31, 40; 7.07[4][a] n.14
9-201 . . . . 5.05[2][n]; 7.02[2][b] n.33; 7.07[2] & n.6; 7.07[5][a] & n.43
9-203 . . . . 7.04[1] & n.2; 7.04[2][a][i]; 7.07[2] n.5; 7.07[4][a][i] n.17; 7.07[5][a] n.38; 16.02[1] & ns. 13, 17; 16.04[1]
 Comment 3 . . . . . . 7.04[2][b][i] n.6
 Comment 5 . . . . . . 7.04[2][b][i] n.6; 9.03 n.3
 Note . . . . . . . . . . 7.01[4][b][ii] n.19
9-203(1) . . . . 3.02[2] ns. 4, 6; 7.04[1]; 7.04[2][a][i]; 16.04[1] n.36
9-203(1)(a) . . . . . . . 7.03[2][a] n.17; 7.04[2][a] n.4; 7.06[3][c][v] n.34; 7.06[3][c][vi] n.45; 7.06[4][a] n.96; 7.07[4][a][i] n.15
9-203(1)(b) . . . . . . . . . 7.04[3] n.29; 8.04 n.19
9-203(1)(c) . . . . . . . . . . 7.04[3] n.33
9-203(2) . . . . 3.02[2] n.6; 7.04[1] n.3; 16.04[1] ns. 33, 36
9-204 . . . . . . 3.02[2] n.4; 7.07[2] n.5; 7.07[5][a] n.38; 16.04[9]

UCC §

9-204(1) . . . . . . . . . . . . . . 3.02[2] n.7
9-204(2) . . . . . . . . . . . . . . 3.02[2] n.9; 7.04[2][b][v] n.22
9-204(3) . . . . . . . . . . . . . . . 16.04[9]
9-206 . . . . . . . . . . . . . . . . . 3.03[1] n.8
9-207 . . . . . . 7.05[6][d]; 7.06[4][c] & n.108
9-207(1) . . . . . 7.05[6][d] ns. 61, 62; 7.06[4][c] ns. 105, 106
9-207(2)(a) . . . . . . . 7.05[6][d] n.63; 7.06[4][c] n.107
9-207(2)(b) . . . . . . . 7.05[6][d] n.65; 7.06[4][c] n.109
9-207(2)(d) . . . . . . . 7.05[6][d] n.63; 7.06[4][c] n.107
9-207(3) . . . . . . . . . . 7.05[6][d] n.64
9-207(4) . . . . . . . . . . 7.05[6][d] n.63; 7.06[4][c] n.107
9-301 . . . . . . . . 6.04[1][e] n.88; 16.03
9-301(1) . . . . . . . . . . . . . . 7.06[1] n.1
9-301(1)(b) . . . . . . . . . . . 7.07[3][b]; 7.07[8][g]; 16.02[1] & ns. 7, 8; 16.03[1] n.16
9-301(1)(c) . . . . . . 7.01[4][b][i] n.18; 7.07[5][b][i] n.45; 7.07[5][c][i] ns. 58, 59
9-301(1)(d) . . . . . 7.07[5][b][i] n.45; 7.07[5][c][ii] n.60
9-301(2) . . . . . . . . . . 7.07[3][b] n.11; 7.07[5][c][i]; 12.05[1] n.21; 14.10; 16.02[1] & n.8; 16.04[7][c] n.85
9-301(3) . . . . . 7.06[1] n.1; 7.07[3][a]
9-301(4) . . . . . . . . . . 7.07[3][c] n.13
9-302 . . . . . . . . . . . . . . 16.03[1] n.16
 Comment 5 . . . . . . . . . . . 7.06[5][c]; 7.07[4][b][i]
9-302(1) . . . . . . . . . . 7.04[2][b][i] n.7; 7.06[3][a] n.4
9-302(1)(b) . . . . . . 7.06[5][d] n.122
9-302(1)(c) . . . . . . . 7.06[5][f] n.128
9-302(1)(d) . . . . . . 7.06[5][b] n.110; 7.07[5][b][ii]
9-302(1)(e) . . . . . . 6.04[2][e] n.197; 7.06[3][a] n.5; 7.06[5][c] n.116
9-302(1)(f) . . . . . . . 7.06[5][e] n.126; 7.06[5][f] n.130
9-302(1)(g) . . . . . . . 7.06[5][f] n.129
9-302(2) . . . . . . . . . . 7.06[5][f] n.127
9-302(3)(a) . . . . . . . . 7.02[4][a] n.58

[*References are to paragraphs (¶) and notes (n.).*]

[*References are to paragraphs (¶) and notes (n.).*]

[*References are to paragraphs (¶) and notes (n.).*]

## UNIFORM CONSUMER CREDIT CODE



## UNIFORM FRAUDULENT CONVEYANCE ACT



## NATIONAL CONSUMER ACT

# Table of Cited Books and Articles

[*References are to paragraphs (¶) and notes (n.).*]

## Chapter 1: INTRODUCTION TO CONSUMER LAW

### Books

Curran, Trends in Consumer Credit Legislation (U.S. Government Printing Office 1965) . . . . . . 1.03[3][a][i] ns. 87–89, 91, 96

National Commission on Consumer Finance, Consumer Credit in the United States (U.S. Government Printing Office 1972) . . . . . . . . . . 1.03[3][a][i] n.86

National Consumer Finance Association Facts Year Book (American Bar Foundation 1981) . . 1.03[5][a] n.84

Rohner, The Law of Truth in Lending (Warren, Gorham & Lamont, Inc. 1984) . . . . . . . . . . . 1.03[2][a] n.23

Rothschild & Carroll, Consumer Protection: Text and Materials (Anderson Publishing Co., 2d ed. 1977) . . . . . . . . . . . . 1.03[2][c][i] n.33; 1.03[3][a][i] n.97

Sheldon & Zweibel, Survey of Consumer Fraud Law (National Institute of Law Enforcement and Criminal Justice 1978) . . . . . . . . . . 1.03[3][b] n.113

### Notes and Comments

Note, "Regulation of Advertising," 56 Colum. L. Rev. 1018 (1958) . . . . 1.03[3][b] n.112

## Chapter 2: PROBLEMS ARISING BEFORE OR AT THE FORMATION OF THE DEBT

### Articles

Baer, "The Equal Credit Opportunity Act and the 'Effects Test,'" 95 Banking L.J. 241 (1978) . . . . . . . . 2.03[2][e] n.77

Braucher, "Freedom of Contract and the Second Restatement," 78 Yale L.J. 598 (1969) . . . . . . . . . . . . . . . . 2.01[1][b] ns. 38, 49

Craswell, "The Identification of Unfair Acts and Practices by the FTC," 1981 Wis. L. Rev. 107 (1981) . . . . 2.01[2][b][i] ns. 57, 59, 61

Hsia, "Credit Scoring and the Equal Credit Opportunity Act," 30 Hastings L.J. 371 (1978) . . . . . . . . . . . . 2.03[2][e] n.69

Miller, "The Problem of Preemption in Consumer Credit Regulation," 3 Okla. City U.L. Rev. 529 (1979) . . . . . . . . . . . . . 2.03[1][h] n.45

Scalia, "Back to Basics: Making Law Without Making Rules," 1981 Regulation 25 (July-Aug.) . . . . . . . . . . . . 2.01[2][a] n.45

### Books

Clark, The Law of Product Warranties (Warren, Gorham & Lamont, Inc. 1984) . . . . . . . . . . . 2.01[1][b] n.28

Clontz, Equal Credit Opportunity Act (Warren, Gorham & Lamont, Inc. 1984) . . . . . . . . . . . 2.03[2][a] n.50

[*References are to paragraphs (¶) and notes (n.).*]

Clontz, Truth-in-Lending Manual (Warren, Gorham & Lamont, Inc., 5th ed. 1982) ...... 2.04[1] n.13

Farnsworth, Contracts (Little, Brown 1982) .......... 2.01[1][a] n.12; 2.01[1][b] n.39

Posner, Regulation of Advertising by the FTC (American Enterprise Institute 1973) ........ 2.01[2][a] n.52

Rosden, The Law of Advertising (Mathew Bender 1979) .............. 2.01[2][a] n.53

## Chapter 3: REGULATION OF THE SUBSTANTIVE TERMS OF CONSUMER CREDIT TRANSACTIONS

### Articles

Arnold & Rohner, "The 'Most Favored Lender' Doctrine for Federally Insured Financial Institutions—What Are Its Boundaries?" 31 Cath. U.L. Rev. 1 (1981) .... 3.01[3][b] n.19

Burke, "Federal Preemption of Usury Laws," 37 Bus. Law. 747 (1982) ............ 3.01[3][b][i] n.25

Burke & Kaplinsky, "Unraveling the New Federal Usury Law," 37 Bus. Law. 1079 (1982) ............. 3.01[3][b][iv] n.32

Crandall, "The Wisconsin Consumer Act: Wisconsin Consumer Credit Laws Before and After," 1973 Wis. L. Rev. 334 ...... 3.03[3][a] n.13

Littlefield, "Good Faith Purchase of Commercial Paper," 39 S. Cal. L. Rev. 48 (1966) ...... 3.03[2] n.9

Prebble, "Choice of Law to Determine the Validity and Effect of Contracts," 58 Cornell L. Rev. 635 (1973) ... 3.01[3][c][i] n.40

Reese, "Choice of Law: Rules or Approach," 57 Cornell L. Rev. 315 (1971) ........ 3.01[3][c][i] n.40

### Books

Leymaster, Consumer Usury and Credit Overcharges (National Consumer Law Center 1982) ........ 3.01[2] n.9; 3.01[2][b][iv] n.32

### Notes and Comments

Note, "Direct Loan Financing of Consumer Purchases," 85 Harv. L. Rev. 1409 (1972) ........ 3.03[2] n.12

## Chapter 5: EXTRAJUDICIAL DEBT COLLECTION

### Articles

Barron, "An Introduction to the Fair Debt Collection Practices Act," 95 Banking L.J. 500 (1978) ........ 5.09[1] n.1

Berger, "The Bill Collector and the Law — A Special Tort, at Least for a While," 17 DePaul L. Rev. 327 (1968) ........... 5.08[2][a] n.9

Carpenter, "Interference With Contract Relations," 41 Harv. L. Rev. 728 (1928) .......... 5.08[2][d] n.28

Douglas-Hamilton, "Creditor Liabilities Resulting From Improper Interference With the Management of a Financially Troubled Debtor," 31 Bus. Law. 343 (1975) .......... 5.08[2][d] n.32

Evans, "Legal Immunity for Defamation," 24 Minn. L. Rev. 607 (1940) .............. 5.08[2][a] n.15

Fox, "New Hope for the Harassed Consumers: The Federal Fair Debt Collection Practices Act of 1977," 18 Am. Bus. L.J. 19 (1980) ...... 5.09[1] n.1

Fritz, "Actions for Harassment of Debtors," 16 Am. Jur. Trials 619–779 .......... 5.08[2][a] n.9

[*References are to paragraphs (¶) and notes (n.).*]

Gloster, "Abuse of Process and Attachment: Toward a Balance of Power," 30 U.C.L.A. L. Rev. 1218 (1983) .............. 5.08[2][a] n.9

Greenfield, "Alternatives to Bankruptcy for the Business Debtor," 51 Los Angeles B.J. 135 ............ 5.05[2][j] n.45

Greenfield, "Coercive Collection Tactics — An Analysis of the Interests and the Remedies," 1972 Wash. U.L.Q. 1 ........ 5.08[1] ns. 1–8; 5.08[2][c] n.22; 5.08[2][d] n.31; 5.08[2][f] n.42; 5.09[4]

Hagedorn, "Bank Setoff in Washington — Is It a Right Without Restriction?" 15 Gonzaga L. Rev. 989 (1980) ...... 5.05 ns. 1, 6; 5.05[2][n] n.57; 5.05[2][s] n.74

Hamilton, "Getting Out From Under, or Assisting the Consumer-Debtor in Default," 52 Conn. Bar. J. 83, 84 (1978) ............ 5.07 ns. 3, 9

Harris, "Improper Methods of Collecting Debts," 58 Com. L.J. 5 (1953) .............. 5.08[2][a] n.9

Heiser, "Wisconsin Consumer Act — A Critical Analysis," 57 Marq. L. Rev. 389 (1974) .. 5.09[4][b] n.40

Holman, "Contacting Debtor's Employer Regarding a Delinquent Account," 19 Pers. Fin. Q. Rep. 70 (1964) ............ 5.08[2][a] n.9

Hurt, "Debt Collection Torts," 67 W. Va. L. Rev. 201 (1965) ...... 5.08[2][a] n.9

Leff, "Injury, Ignorance and Spite — The Dynamics of Coercive Collection," 80 Yale L.J. 1 (1970) ...... 5.08[2][a] n.9

Murray, "Banks v. Creditors of Their Customers: Setoffs Against Customers' Accounts," 82 Com. L.J. 449 (1977) ............ 5.05[1] n.2; 5.05[2][i] n.36; 5.05[2][n] n.57

National Commission on Consumer Finance, "Summary of Hearings on Debt Collection Practices," 88 Banking L.J. 291 (1971) .... 5.01 n.5; 5.07 n.8

Scott & Strickland, "Abusive Debt Collection — A Model Statute for Virginia," 15 Wm. & Mary L. Rev. 566 (1974) ................ 5.09[4]

Sherwin, "Locating the Missing Judgment Debtor," 21 Prac. Law., No. 3, 13 (1975) .......... 5.02[1] n.1

Sheinfield, "Current Trends in the Restriction of Creditors' Collection Activities," 9 Hous. L. Rev. 615 (1972) ........... 5.08[2][a] n.9

Shimm, "The Impact of State Law of Bankruptcy," 1971 Duke L.J. 879 ....... 5.04[2] n.3; 5.05[2][j] n.45; 5.07 n.2

Skilton, "The Secured Party's Rights in a Debtor's Bank Account Under Article 9 of the Uniform Commercial Code," 120 S. Ill. U.L.J. 197 (1978) ... 5.05[1] n.5; 5.05[2][n] n.57

Smith & Straske, "Collection Procedures and Right of Privacy," 36 Fla. B.J. 1085 (1962) ... 5.08[2][a] n.9

Books

Bailey, Brady on Bank Checks (Warren, Gorham & Lamont, Inc., 5th ed. 1979) .. 5.05[2][g] n.27; 5.06[1] n.3

Cohen, Bankruptcy, Secured Transactions and Other Debtor-Creditor Matters (Bobbs-Merrill 1981) .... 5.08[2][a] n.9; 5.08[2][b] n.20; 5.09[1] n.1

Debtor-Creditor Law (Matthew Bender 1982) ...... 5.06 n.2; 5.06[1] n.6; 5.06[2] ns. 8, 17, 19; 5.06[4] n.28; 5.06[5] n.33; 5.09[1] n.1

Fonseca & Teachout, Handling Consumer Credit Cases (Lawyers' Coop. Publishing Co., 2d ed. 1980) ...... 5.05[2][u] n.79; 5.09[2] n.27; 5.09[4][b] ns. 34, 40, 42

Hawkland, Commercial Paper and Bank Deposits and Collections (Foundation Press 1967) ........ 5.06 n.2

Hawkland & Loiseaux, Debtor-Creditor Relations (Bobbs-Merrill 1979) .... 5.04[2] n.3; 5.07 n.2

[*References are to paragraphs (¶) and notes (n.).*]



Committee and Staff Reports



Notes and Comments

[*References are to paragraphs (¶) and notes (n.).*]

## Chapter 6: JUDICIAL COLLECTION

### Articles

Alexander, "Wrongful Attachment Damages Must Be Fixed in the Original Suit," 5 U.S.F.L. Rev. 38 (1969) .......... 6.04[1][b] n.29

Austin & Nelson, "Attaching and Levying on Corporate Shares," 16 Bus. Law. 336 (1961) .. 6.04[1][e] n.81

Bresnan & Cornelis, "Project, Relief From Default Judgments Under Rule 60(b) — A Study of Federal Case Law," 49 Fordham L. Rev. 956 (1981) .......... 6.02[4][c] n.98

Brown, "Some Incidents of Execution on Florida Judgments," 12 Fla. L.J. 364 (1938) ...... 6.05[3][e] n.235

Bunge & Bunge, "Proceedings in Aid of Execution," 16 Ohio St. L.J. 17 (1955) ......... 6.05[5][c] n.335

Clermont, "Restating Territorial Jurisdiction and Venue for State and Federal Courts," 66 Cornell L. Rev. 411 (1981) .......... 6.02[2][b] ns. 40, 58, 59

Crapo, "Equal Management of Community Property: Creditor's Rights," 13 Idaho L. Rev. 177 (1976) ..... 6.07[5][d] n.255

Felix, "The Effect of the National Bankruptcy Code Upon the Uniform Business Corporation Act," 23 Wash. L. Rev. 60 (1948) ..... 6.04[4][c] n.268

Graubert, "Should Lis Pendens Prevent the Performance of an Executory Contract?" 44 Dick. L. Rev. 59 (1940) .......... 6.05[2][b] n.36

Hagedorn, "Prejudgment Attachment in Washington — A Need for Legislative Action," 16 Gonz. L. Rev. ............ 6.04[1][b] n.12; 6.04[5][a][i] n.272; 6.04[5][a][ii] n.286

Halbach, "Creditor's Rights in Future Interests," 43 Minn. L. Rev. 217 (1958) .......... 6.05[2][d] n.98

Haskins, "Homestead Exemption Laws," 63 Haw. L. Rev. 1289 (1950) .......... 6.07[1][d] n.43

Healey, "The Judgment Creditor Encounters Homestead Problems," 27 L.A.B. Bul. 361 (1952) ......... 6.07[1][d] n.43

Hines, "Personal Property Joint Tenancies: More Law, Fact, and Fancy," 54 Minn. L. Rev. 509 (1970) ..... 6.07[5][b] n.222

Horwitz, "Confession of Judgment Clauses as Violating Federal Truth-In-Lending Where Creditors Have Waived Their Right to Have Liens Placed on Obligator's Residence," 66 Ill. B.J. 688 (1978) ............ 6.02[5][d] n.136

Huber, "Creditor's Rights in Tenancies by the Entireties," 1 B.C. Ind. & Com. L. Rev. 197 (1961) ........ 6.07[5][c] n.225

Hudspeth, "Judgment Liens and Abstracts of Judgments in Texas," 32 Tex. B.J. 520 (1969) ........... 6.07[3] n.191

Joslin, "Debtors' Exemption Laws: Time for Modernization," 34 Ind. L.J. 355 (1959) ...... 6.07[1] n.5

Karlen, "Exemptions from Execution," 22 Bus. Law. 1167 (1967) ....... 6.07[1] ns. 8, 14

Kennedy, "The Rights of Levying Creditors Against Negotiable Property Under the Uniform Commercial Code," 31 Bus. Law. 1517 (1976) ...... 6.04[1][e] ns. 81, 83, 86; 6.05[3][d] n.217

McLesky & McLesky, "Dormancy and Revival of Ohio Judgments," 16 Ohio St. L.J. 81 (1955) ......... 6.07[3] n.190

Mitchell, "Perpetuating the Force of Judgments and Judgment Liens in Texas," 29 Tex. L. Rev. 530 (1951) .............. 6.07[3] n.191

Rich, "Enforcing Money Judgments in Tennessee," 4 Mem. St. U.L. Rev. 65 (1973) ......... 6.05[3][e] n.275

[*References are to paragraphs (¶) and notes (n.).*]



Books

[*References are to paragraphs (¶) and notes (n.).*]



## Committee and Staff Reports

[*References are to paragraphs (¶) and notes (n.).*]

NOTES AND COMMENTS



## CHAPTER 7: SECURED TRANSACTIONS UNDER ARTICLE 9 OF THE UNIFORM COMMERCIAL CODE

ARTICLES

[*References are to paragraphs (¶) and notes (n.).*]

ticle 8 of the Uniform Commercial Code," 92 Harv. L. Rev. 1013 (1979) ......... 7.06[6][b] n.135

DeKoven, "Secured Transactions," 37 Bus. Law. 1033 (1982) .......... 7.06[3][c][ii] n.24

Dolan, "The UCC's Consignment Rule Needs an Exception for Consumer," 44 Ohio St. L.J. 21 (1983) ...... 7.02[2][b] n.34

Kripke, "The 'Last Event' Test for Perfection of Security Interests Under Article 9 of the Uniform Commercial Code," 50 N.Y.U. L. Rev. 47 (1975) ........ 7.06[3][c] n.73; 7.06[6][c][i] n.148

Meyer, "Crops As Collateral Under Article 9," 15 U.C.C. L.J. 3 (1982) ............. 7.02[4][j] n.96

Mooney, "Personal Property Leasing: A Challenge," 36 Bus. Law. 1605 ........ 7.02[2][a][ii] ns. 5, 8

Nickles, "Rethinking Some U.C.C. Article 9 Problems — Subrogation; Equitable Liens; Actual Knowledge; Waiver of Security Interests; Secured Party Liability for Conversion Under Part 5," 34 Ark. L. Rev. 1 (1980) ........ 7.07[4][a][i] n.17

Sanford, "Debtor's Rights in Collateral as a Requirement for Attachment of a Security Interest Under the UCC," 26 S.D.L. Rev. 163 ........ 7.04[4] n.35

Skilton, "Field Warehousing as a Financing Device," 1961 Wis. L. Rev. 221 ............... 7.01[3][a] n.7

BOOKS

Clark, Law of Secured Transactions Under the Uniform Commercial Code (Warren, Gorham & Lamont, Inc. 1980) ............. 7.01[2]; 7.02[4][a][ii] n.63; 7.02[4][g] n.89; 7.02[4][i] n.92; 7.05[3] n.7; 7.05[4][a] n.9; 7.05[4][b][i] n.10; 7.05[6][d] n.65; 7.05[7][a][iii] n.73; 7.05[7][c][iv] n.89; 7.05[7][c][v] n.95; 7.05[9][c] n.156; 7.06[3][b][i] ns. 7, 11; 7.06[4][a] n.98; 7.06[4][c] n.108; 7.07[2] n.6; 7.07[4][a][i] n.16; 7.07[5][a] n.43; 7.07[10] n.95

Gilmore, Security Interests in Personal Property (Little, Brown 1965) .... 7.01[3] n.5; 7.01[3][c] n.9; 7.01[3][d] ns. 10, 11; 7.01[3][f] n.12; 7.02[2][b] n.36; 7.06[7][c] n.192

Henson, Secured Transactions (West, 2d ed. 1979) ...... 7.03[2][a] n.9

White & Summers, Uniform Commercial Code (West, 2d ed. 1980) ............ 7.02[2][b] n.38; 7.03[2][b][v] n.30; 7.02[2][b][i] n.9; 7.05[5][a] n.23; 7.05[7][d][ii] n.104; 7.06[3][c][iii] n.30; 7.06[3][d][i] n.68; 7.06[6][b] n.139; 7.06[6][c][iii] n.152; 7.06[6][d][i] n.157; 7.06[7][c] n.193; 7.07[4][a][i] n.16

## CHAPTER 8: MORTGAGES AND OTHER SECURED TRANSACTIONS IN REAL ESTATE

ARTICLES

Ashley, "Use of 'Due-On' Clauses to Gain Collateral Benefits: A Common Sense Defense," 10 Tulsa L.J. 590 (1975) ............ 8.08[1] n.10

Beale, "The Origin of the System of Recording Deeds in America," 19 Green Bag 335 (1907) .......... 8.09[1][a] n.3

Benson, "Circuity of Lien—A Problem in Priorities," 19 Minn. L. Rev. 139 (1935) ....... 8.09[2][b] n.47

Blair, "Allocation of After Acquired Property," 40 Harv. L. Rev. 222 (1927) ............... 8.04 n.16

[*References are to paragraphs (¶) and notes (n.).*]

[*References are to paragraphs (¶) and notes (n.).*]

## Books



## Notes and Comments

[*References are to paragraphs (¶) and notes (n.).*]



## Chapter 9: COMMON-LAW, STATUTORY, AND EQUITABLE LIENS

### Articles



### Books

[*References are to paragraphs (¶) and notes (n.).*]

NOTES AND COMMENTS

Note, "The Continuing Use of Choateness in Determining Priority of Tax Liens," 12 Tex. Tech L. Rev. 959 (1981) ........ 9.04[6][d][iii] n.89

## CHAPTER 10: BANKRUPTCY AS A METHOD OF DEALING WITH INSOLVENCY

ARTICLES

Anderson & Wright, "Liquidating Plans of Reorganization," 56 Am. Bankr. L.J. 29 (1982) .......... 10.04[3] n.62

Epling, "Cramdown Under the Bankruptcy Code of 1978: Effect Upon the Soft Collateral Lender," 12 Loy. U. Chi. L.J. 713 (1982) ........ 10.04[3] n.94

Gibson, "The New Law on Rejection of Collective Bargaining Agreements in Chapter 11: An Analysis of 11 U.S.C. § 1113," 58 Am. Bankr. L.J. 325 (1984) ........ 10.04[3] n.90

Kennedy, "Forward: A Brief History of the Bankruptcy Reform Act," 58 N.C.L. Rev. 667 (1980) ........ 10.03[1] ns. 1, 4, 5, 7, 8, 10, 12–14, 18, 20–24

Klee, "All You Ever Wanted to Know About Cram Down Under the New Bankruptcy Code," 53 Am. Bankr. L.J. 133 (1979) .... 10.04[3] n.94

Klee, "Legislative History of the New Bankruptcy Law," 2 Appendix, Collier on Bankruptcy (Matthew Bender, 15th ed. 1981) ......... 10.03[1] ns. 2, 14, 15, 18–22, 25

Lee, "A Critical Comparison of the Commission's Bill and the Judges' Bill for the Amendment of the Bankruptcy Act," 49 Am. Bankr. L.J. 1 (1975) ...... 10.03[1] n.13

Miller, "Bankruptcy Code Cramdown Under Chapter 11: New Threat to Shareholder Interests," 62 B.U.L. Rev. 1059 (1983) ... 10.04[3] n.94

Pachulski, "The Cram Down and Valuation Under Chapter of the Bankruptcy Code," 58 N.C.L. Rev. 925 (1981) ............ 10.04[3] n.94

BOOKS

Collier on Bankruptcy (Matthew Bender, 15th ed. 1981) ... 10.03[1] ns. 2, 9, 11, 14, 15 18–23, 25

Hann & MacLachlan, Cases & Materials of Creditors' Rights and Corporate Reorganization (Foundation Press, 5th ed. 1957) ..... 10.01 n.1

MacLachlan, Handbook of the Law of Bankruptcy (West 1956) ........ 10.02[1] n.1

Stanley & Girth, Bankruptcy: Problem, Process, Reform (Brookings Institution 1971) .......... 10.03[1] n.6

COMMITTEE AND STAFF REPORTS

Communication from the Executive Director, Commission on the Bankruptcy Laws of the United States Transmitting a Report of the Commission on the Bankruptcy Laws of the United States, H.R. Doc. No. 137, Parts I, II, III, 93d Congress, 1st Sess. (July 1973) ........... 10.03[1] ns. 9, 11

NOTES AND COMMENTS

Comment, "Effect of National Bankruptcy Act on State Insolvency Statutes," 49 Yale L.J. 1090 (1940) ................ 10.02[1] n.1

Comment, "From Debtor's Shield to Creditor's Sword: Cram Down Under the Chandler Act and the Bankruptcy Reform Act," 55 Chi.-Kent. L. Rev. 713 (1979) ........... 10.04[3] n.94

[*References are to paragraphs (¶) and notes (n.).*]

## CHAPTER 11: THE BANKRUPTCY COURT SYSTEM

### ARTICLES

Arthurs, "Technical Provision Sets Off Bankruptcy Bar Lobbying War," 7 Legal Times 1 (July 30, 1984) .... 11.01[3] n.15

Easton, "For Three Months, Bankrupt Beggars Can Be Choosers," Legal Times 1 (July 16, 1984) ......... 11.01[3] n.15

George, "The Bankruptcy Appellate Panels: An Unfinished Experiment," 1982 B.Y.U. L. Rev. 20 (1982) ........... 11.03[3][a] n.123

Kennedy, "The Bankruptcy Court Under the New Bankruptcy Law: Its Structure and Jurisdiction," 55 Am. Bankr. L.J. 63 (1981) ........... 11.01[2] n.10

Klee, "Legislative History of the New Bankruptcy Law," 28 De Paul L. Rev. 941 (1979) .... 11.01[4] n.16

"Lawscope-Bad Law? Brickbats for Bankruptcy Code," 70 A.B.A. J. 28 (Dec. 1984) ... 11.01[3] ns. 14, 15

Levin, "Bankruptcy Appeals," 58 N.C.L. Rev. 967 (1981) ........ 11.03[3] n.121

Miller & Bienenstock, "Analysis and Perspective Bankruptcy," 7 Legal Times 39 (July 30, 1984) ...... 11.01[3] n.13; 11.03[2][a] n.71

Rochelle & King, "Summary Jurisdiction in Bankruptcy: *Katchen v. Landy* and Questions Left Unanswered," 1966 Duke L.J. 669 ..... 11.03[2][a] n.70

### BOOKS

Collier, Bankruptcy Practice Guide (Matthew Bender 1984) ........ 11.06 ns. 5, 8; 11.06[1] n.10

Collier on Bankruptcy (Matthew Bender, 15th ed. 1981) .......... 11.01[4] n.16; 11.06 n.5; 11.06[1] n.10

### COMMITTEE AND STAFF REPORTS

Report of the Commission on the Bankruptcy Laws of the United States, H.R. Doc. No. 137, Part I, 93d Cong., 1st Sess. 85–106 (1973) ........ 11.01[1] n.7; 11.01[2] ns. 8, 9

## CHAPTER 12: BANKRUPTCY: COMMENCEMENT OF PROCEEDINGS

### ARTICLES

Aaron, "Bankruptcy Stays of Environmental Regulation: Harvest of Commercial Timber as an Introduction to a Clash of Policies," 12 Envtl. L. Rev. 1 (1981) ........ 12.05 n.10

Groschadl, "Freezing the Debtor's Bank Account: A Violation of the Automatic Stay?" 57 Am. Bankr. L.J. 75 (1983) ....... 12.05 n.10

Hanley, "Partnership Bankruptcy Under the New Act," 31 Hastings L.J. 149 (1979) ... 12.03[2][c] n.64

Kennedy, "The Automatic Stay in Bankruptcy," 11 U. Mich. L. Rev. 175 (1978) .......... 12.05 n.10

Kennedy, "The Commencement of a Case Under the New Bankruptcy Code," 36 Wash. & Lee L. Rev. 977, 996 (1979) ........ 12.02[1] n.19; 12.03 ns. 7, 8, 13; 12.03[1] ns. 23, 24; 12.03[2] n.30; 12.03[2][b] n.51; 12.03[2][d] n.68; 12.03[2][e] n.79; 12.03[2][f] ns. 85, 92; 12.04[2] n.15; 12.07 n.12; 12.08 n.8

Kurland, "A Debtor's Prism: Immunity for Bankrupts Under the Bankruptcy Reform Act of 1978 (Pt. 1)," 55 Am. Bankr. L.J. 177 (1981) ...... 12.06[1] n.13

[*References are to paragraphs (¶) and notes (n.).*]

Levy, "Joint Administration and Consolidation," 85 Com. L.J. 538 (1980) ............ 12.02[1] n.22

Levy, "Trial by Jury Under the Bankruptcy Reform Act of 1978," 12 Conn. L. Rev. 1 (1979) ......... 12.03[2][e] n.79

Martin, "Creditor Alternatives to Obtain Relief From Automatic Stays in Bankruptcy," 98 Banking L.J. 525 (1981) .............. 12.05 n.10

Taube, "Involuntary Bankruptcy: Who May Be a Petitioning Creditor?" 21 Hous. L. Rev. 339 (1984) ...... 12.03[2][b] ns. 38, 53

Viar, "Discovery in Bankruptcy Cases," 17 U.C.C. L.J. 22 (1984) ........ 12.03[2][d] n.75

BOOKS

Collier, Bankruptcy Practice Guide (Matthew Bender 1984) ......... 12.01 n.6

Collier on Bankruptcy (Matthew Bender, 15th ed. 1981) ..... 12.01 n.6; 12.02[1] ns. 15, 20; 12.03[1] n.24; 12.03[2] n.31; 12.03[2][b] ns. 43, 56; 12.03[2][d] n.68; 12.03[2][f] n.89

COMMITTEE AND STAFF REPORTS

Report of the Commission on the Bankruptcy Laws of the United States, H.R. Doc. No. 137, 93d Cong., 1st Sess. 9, 75 (1973) .... 12.03[2][f] n.83; 12.04[2] n.15

NOTES AND COMMENTS

Comment, "The Automatic Stay in Bankruptcy: An Analysis of the Braniff Chapter 11 Proceeding," 14 Tex. Tech L. Rev. 433 (1983) ................ 12.05 n.10

Comment, "Automatic Stay Under the 1978 Bankruptcy Code: An Equitable Roadblock to Secured Creditor Relief," 17 San Diego L. Rev. 113 (1981) .............. 12.05 n.10

Comment, "Involuntary Bankruptcy: The Generally Not Paying Standard," 33 Mercer L. Rev. 903 (1982) .......... 12.03[2][f] n.84

Comment, "Monetary Awards to the Debtor for Violations of the Automatic Stay," 11 Fla. St. U.L. Rev. 423 (1983) .......... 12.05 n.12

Note, "Self-Incrimination Under the New Bankruptcy Code: An Analysis of § 344," Ann. Survey of Bankr. L. 211 (1980) ....... 12.06[1] n.13

Note, "When Is a Governmental Unit's Action to Enforce Its Police or Regulatory Power Exempt From the Automatic Stay?" 9 Fla. St. U.L. Rev. 369 (1981) ...... 12.05 n.10

## CHAPTER 13: THE BANKRUPTCY ESTATE

ARTICLES

Bordewieck & Countryman, "The Rejection of Collective Bargaining Agreements by Chapter 11 Debtors," 57 Am. Bankr. L.J. 293 (1983) .............. 13.09[9] n.69

Braucher, "Reclamation of Goods From A Fraudulent Buyer," 65 Mich. L. Rev. 1281 (1967) ...... 13.10[1] n.9

Butler, "Section 722: A Redeeming Aspect of the Bankruptcy Code," 88 Com. L.J. 462 (1983) .......... 13.08 ns. 1, 9, 10, 15

Cherry, "The Collective Bargaining Agreement in Bankruptcy: Rejection and Its Consequences," 36 Ark. L. Rev. 469 (1983) .... 13.09[9] n.69

Countryman, "Consumer Bankruptcy — Some Recent Changes and Some Proposals," 19 U. Kan. L. Rev. 165 (1971) .............. 13.06 n.2

[*References are to paragraphs (¶) and notes (n.).*]

[*References are to paragraphs (¶) and notes (n.).*]



### Books



### Committee and Staff Reports



### Notes and Comments

[*References are to paragraphs (¶) and notes (n.).*]



## CHAPTER 14: DISTRIBUTION OF THE ESTATE

### ARTICLES



### BOOKS

[*References are to paragraphs (¶) and notes (n.).*]

Norton, Bankruptcy Law and Practice (Callaghan 1981) ...... 14.04 n.3; 14.04[1] n.7

Simpson, Handbook on the Law of Suretyship (West 1950) ......... 14.07[1] n.8

Thompson on Real Property (Bobbs-Merrill, replacement vol. 1981) .... 14.05[6] n.19

Weintraub & Resnick, Bankruptcy Law Manual (Warren, Gorham & Lamont, Inc. 1980) ........ 14.07[1] ns. 12, 18, 23

Notes and Comments

Note, "Deep Rock in the Deep South—Equitable Subordination of Claims in Fifth Circuit Bankruptcy Proceedings," 11 Cum. L. Rev. 619 (1980) .................. 14.11 n.3

Note, "Equitable Subordination of Shareholder Debt to Trade Creditors: A Reexamination," 61 B.U.L. Rev. 433 (1981) ........... 14.11 n.3

Comment, "Procedures for Estimating Contingent or Unliquidated Claims in Bankruptcy," 35 Stan. L. Rev. 153 (1983) ............... 14.08 n.4

## Chapter 15: BANKRUPTCY: DISCHARGE

Articles

Ahart, "Obtaining Reaffirmation of Individual Debts Under the New Bankruptcy Code," 97 Banking L.J. 153 (1980) ............... 15.08 n.4

Ayers, "Reforming the Reform Act: Should the Bankruptcy Reform Act of 1978 Be Amended to Limit the Availability of Discharge to Consumers?" 17 New Eng. L. Rev. 719 (1982) .............. 15.01 n.11

Boshkoff, "The Bankrupt's Moral Obligation to Pay His Discharged Debts: A Conflict Between Contract Theory and Bankruptcy Policy," 47 Ind. L.J. 36 (1971) .... 15.08 n.1

DeWoskin, "A Warning to Attorneys: Reaffirmation Under the New Bankruptcy Code," 85 Com. L.J. 296 (1980) ............... 15.08 n.4

Ferriell, "The Preclusive Effect of State Court Decisions in Bankruptcy," 58 Am. Bankr. L.J. 349 (1984) ...... 15.07[2] n.10

Kosel, "Running the Gauntlet of 'Undue Hardship' — The Discharge of Student Loans in Bankruptcy," 11 Golden Gate U.L. Rev. 457 (1981) ............ 15.07[3][h] n.62

Lander, "An Analysis and Comparison of the Nondischargeability Provision of Chapter 11 and Chapter 13 of the Bankruptcy Code," 27 St. Louis U.L.J. 639 (1983) ........ 15.01 ns. 11, 12

Moller, "It Isn't Only for Wage Earners Anymore: The Individual in Business and Chapter 13 of the Bankruptcy Code," 17 Hous. L. Rev. 331 (1980) .......... 15.01 n.12

Rendleman, "The Bankruptcy Discharge: Toward A Fresher Start," 58 N.C.L. Rev. 723 (1980) ........ 15.01 n.11

Schiffer, "The New Bankruptcy Reform Act: Its Implications for Family Law Practitioners," 19 J. Fam. L. 1 (1980) .......... 15.07[3][e] n.50

Sullivan, Warren & Westbrook, "Limiting Access to Bankruptcy Discharge: An Analysis of the Creditors' Data," 1983 Wis. L. Rev. 1091 ......... 15.01 n.11

Van Baalen, "Bankruptcy Code Chapter 13 — What Price the 'Better Discharge'?" 35 Okla. L. Rev. 455 (1982) .............. 15.01 n.12

Zaretsky, "The Fraud Exception to Discharge Under the New Bankruptcy Code," 53 Am. Bankr. L.J. 253 (1979) ........ 15.07[3][b] n.35

[*References are to paragraphs (¶) and notes (n.).*]

BOOKS

Collier on Bankruptcy (Matthew Bender, 15th ed. 1981) . . . 15.07[1] n.6

Cowans, Bankruptcy Law & Practice (West, interim ed. 1983) . . . . . . . . 15.02 n.7; 15.04[3] ns. 6, 7; 15.04[5] n.10; 15.04[6] ns. 12, 13; 15.07[3][a] n.29

Weintraub & Resnick, Bankruptcy Law Manual (Warren, Gorham & Lamont, Inc. 1980) . . . . 15.05[2] n.12

COMMITTEE AND STAFF REPORTS

Report of the Commission on the Bankruptcy Laws of the United States, H.R. Doc. No. 137, Part I, 93d Cong., 1st Sess. (1973) . . 15.08 n.2

NOTES AND COMMENTS

Note, "Bankruptcy — Private College May Withhold Transcripts From Students Whose Educational Loan Debts Were Discharged," 22 How. L.J. 155 (1979) . . . . . 15.03 n.16; 15.07[3][h] n.62

Comment, "The Bankruptcy Reform Act of 1978: Dischargeability of Obligations Incurred Under Property Settlements, Separation Agreements, and Divorce Decrees," 12 U. Balt. L. Rev. 520 (1982) . . 15.07[3][e] n.50

Comment, "Congressional Intent in Excepting Alimony, Maintenance and Support From Discharge in Bankruptcy," 21 J. Fam. L. 525 (1983) . . . . . . . . . 15.07[3][e] n.50

Note, "Constitutional — Florida Bar Admission Rule Requiring Good Moral Character Does Not Defeat the Purpose of the Federal Bankruptcy Act in Violation of the Supremacy Clause of the United States Constitution," 7 Fla. St. U.L. Rev. 587 (1979) . . . . . . . . . 15.03 n.10

Comment, "Creditor Acquiescence as a Defense to an Exception to Discharge in Bankruptcy," 58 Ind. L.J. 319 (1982) . . . . . . . . 15.07[3] n.17

Note, "Dischargeability of Corporate Withholding Taxes in the Personal Bankruptcy Suit of a Responsible Officer," 16 Wake Forest L. Rev. 103 (1980) . . . . . . . . . 15.07[3][a] n.29

Note, "Dischargeability of Divorce Related Expenses Under 11 U.S.C. § 523(a)(5)," 35 Okla. L. Rev. 799 (1982) . . . . . . . . 15.07[3][e] n.50

Comment, "Discharge of Post-Marital Support Obligations Under the New Bankruptcy Code," 4 Harv. Women's L.J. 177 (1981) . . 15.07[3][e] n.50

Note, "Discharging Student Loans in Bankruptcy: The Bankruptcy Court Test of 'Undue Hardship'," 26 Ariz. L. Rev. 445 (1984) . . . . . . . . . . . 15.07[3][h] n.62

Comment, "Evaluation of A Bar Applicant's Moral Character: May a State Consider the Circumstances Surrounding a Discharge in Bankruptcy?" 56 Ind. L.J. 703 (1981) . . . . . . . . . . . . . . . 15.03 n.10

Comment, "A Fresh Start Through Bankruptcy: Fact or Frustration for the Student Loan Debtor?" 2 U. Puget Sound L. Rev. 365 (1979) . . . . . . . . . . . 15.07[3][h] n.62

Comment, "Protection of a Debtor's 'Fresh Start' Under the New Bankruptcy Code," 29 Cath. U.L. Rev. 843 (1980) . . . . . . . . . . . 15.03 n.1

Comment, "Reaffirmation Agreements: A Fight for Enforceability Under the New Bankruptcy Code," 12 Cum.-Sam. L. Rev. 431 (1982) . . . . . . . . 15.08 n.4

Comment, "Res Judicata and Collateral Estoppel in Bankruptcy Discharge Proceedings," 37 Wash. & Lee L. Rev. 281 (1980) . . . . 15.07[2] n.10

Comment, "Student Loan Bankruptcy: Establishing 'Undue Hardship' in

[*References are to paragraphs (¶) and notes (n.).*]

South Dakota," 27 S.D.L. Rev. 282 (1982) .......... 15.07[3][h] n.62

Comment, "Student Loans and the Withholding of Transcripts Under the Bankruptcy Reform Act of 1978," 30 U. Kan. L. Rev. 265 (1982) ............ 15.03 n.16; 15.07[3][h] n.62

Comment, "Toward a Reform of the Six-Year Bar to Discharge in Bankruptcy," 97 Harv. L. Rev. (1984) ............. 15.04[8] n.18

## Chapter 16: THE TRUSTEE'S AVOIDING POWERS AND RECOVERY OF ASSETS FOR THE ESTATE

### Articles

Ahart, "Bank Setoff Under the Bankruptcy Reform Act of 1978," 53 Am. Bankr. L.J. 205 (1979) ......... 16.08 ns. 2, 3, 13, 17

Alden, Gross & Borowitz, "Real Property Foreclosure as a Fraudulent Conveyance: Proposals on Solving the Durrett Problem," 38 Bus. Law. 1605 (1983) .......... 16.05 n.5

Breitowitz, "Article 9 Security Interests as Voidable Preferences: Part II — The Floating Lien," 4 Cardozo L. Rev. I (1983) .... 16.04[9] n.103

Clark, "Preferences Under the Old and New Bankruptcy Acts," 12 U.C.C. L.J. 154 (1979) ....... 16.04 n.1

Cohen, "Value Judgments: Accounts Receivable Financing and Voidable Preferences Under the New Bankruptcy Code," 66 Minn. L. Rev. 639 (1982) ......... 16.04[9] n.103

Coppel & Kann, "Defanging Durrett: The Established Law of Transfer," 100 Banking L.J. 676 (1983) ..... 16.05 n.5

Countryman, "Code Security Interests in Bankruptcy," 4 U.C.C. L.J. 35 (1971) ...... 16.04[9] ns. 105, 110

Duncan, "Delayed Perfection of Security Interests in Personal Property and the Substantially Contemporaneous Exchange Exception to Preference Attack," 62 Neb. L. Rev. 201 (1983) ......... 16.04[7][a] n.68

Duncan, "Preferential Transfers, The Floating Lien, and Section 547(c)(5) of the Bankruptcy Reform Act of 1978," 36 Ark. L. Rev. 1 (1983) ............ 16.04[9] n.103

Ellis, "Preferential Payments by Check: At What Point Is Payment Made?" 16 U.C.C. L.J. 46 (1983) ........ 16.04 n.1; 16.04[1] n.16

Freeman, "Setoff Under the New Bankruptcy Code: The Effect on Bankers," 97 Banking L.J. 484 (1980) ..... 16.08 ns. 1–4, 8, 9, 11, 13

Groschadl, "'Freezing' the Debtor's Bank Account: A Violation of the Automatic Stay?" 57 Am. Bankr. L.J. 75 (1983) .......... 16.08 n.17

Hammon, "Setoff in Bankruptcy: Is the Creditor Preferred or Secured?" 50 U. Colo. L. Rev. 511 (1979) ............... 16.08 n.2

Harrington, "Insecurity for Secured Creditors: The Floating Lien and Section 547 of the Bankruptcy Act," 63 Marq. L. Rev. 447 (1980) ..... 16.04[9] n.103

Henning, "An Analysis of Durrett and Its Impact on Real and Personal Property Foreclosures: Some Proposed Modifications," 63 N.C.L. Rev. 257 (1984) .. 16.05 ns. 5, 6, 9

Henson, "The Uniform Commercial Code and the New Bankruptcy Act: Some Problem Areas," 35 Bus. Law. 83 (1979) ..... 16.04[7][b] n.78

Kaye, "Preferences Under the New Bankruptcy Code," 54 Am. Bankr.

[*References are to paragraphs (¶) and notes (n.).*]



BOOKS



NOTES AND COMMENTS

[*References are to paragraphs (¶) and notes (n.).*]

## Chapter 17: CHAPTER 13 PLANS: DEBT ADJUSTMENT FOR INDIVIDUALS

### Articles

Blair, "Classification of Unsecured Claims in Chapter 11 Reorganization," 58 Am. Bankr. L.J. 197 (1984) .......... 17.08[2][a] n.11

Cyr, "The Chapter 13 'Good Faith' Tempest: An Analysis And Proposal for Change," 55 Am. Bankr. L.J. 271 (1981) ........... 17.09[4] n.24

Kelley, "Good Faith and Chapter 13," 36 Q. Rep. 8 (1982) .. 17.09[4] n.24

Lander, "An Analysis and Comparison of the Non-Dischargeability Provisions of Chapter 11 and Chapter 13 of the Bankruptcy Code," 27 St. Louis U.L.J. 639 (1983) ........ 17.01[2] n.21; 17.12 n.1

Novellino, "After Notice and Hearing," 55 Am. Bankr. L.J. 293 (1981) ................. 17.06 n.6

"Structuring and Documenting Business Financing Transactions Under the Federal Bankruptcy Code of 1978," 35 Bus. Law. 1645 (1980) ................ 17.06 n.23

Van Baalen, "Bankruptcy Code Chapter 13—What Price the Better Discharge?" 35 Okla. L. Rev. 455 (1982) ............... 17.12 n.1

Vihon, "Classification of Unsecured Claims: Squaring a Circle?" 55 Am. Bankr. L.J. 143 (1981) ......... 17.08[2][a] n.11

### Books

Cowans, Bankruptcy Law and Practice (West, interim ed. 1983) ........ 17.08[2][a] n.11; 17.08[2][c] n.35; 17.08[2][d] n.38; 17.09[4] n.24

Drake & Morris, Chapter 13 Practice and Procedure (Shepard's/McGraw-Hill 1983) ........ 17.04[1] n.23; 17.05 n.23; 17.07[2] n.12; 17.08[2][a] ns. 11, 16, 17, 27; 17.08[2][d] n.38; 17.08[2][e] n.45; 17.08[2][g] n.50; 17.09[3] n.23; 17.09[5] ns. 32, 34, 35; 17.09[6] n.36; 17.10[2] n.12; 17.12 n.6; 17.12[2] n.24

Weintraub & Resnick, Bankruptcy Law Manual (Warren, Gorham & Lamont, Inc. 1983 Supp.) .. 17.09[5] n.32; 17.12 n.6

Weintraub & Resnick, Bankruptcy Law Manual (Warren, Gorham & Lamont, Inc. 1980) .... 17.09[3] n.23

### Notes and Comments

Note, "Chapter 13 de Minimis Plans: Toward a Consensus on 'Good Faith,'" 9 Hofstra L. Rev. 593 (1981) ........... 17.09[4] n.24

Note, "Chapter 13 — Good Faith Requirement Does Not Require Substantial Repayment of Unsecured Creditors. (Goeb v. Heid [In re Goeb])," 52 Miss. L.J. 947 (1982) .............. 17.09[4] n.24

Note, "'Good Faith' and Confirmation of Chapter 13 Composition Plans: Analysis and a Proposal," 65 Minn. L. Rev. 659 (1981) .. 17.09[4] n.24

Comment, "Good Faith in Chapter 13: A New Wild Card for Bankruptcy," 8 Ohio N.U.L. Rev. 102 (1981) .............. 17.09[4] n.24

Note, "Good Faith, Zero Plans, and the Purposes of Bankruptcy Code Chapter 13: A Legislative Solution to the Controversy," 6 B.U.L. Rev. 773 (1981) ....... 17.09[4] n.24

# Table of Cases

[*References are to paragraphs (¶) and notes (n.).*]

[*References are to paragraphs (¶) and notes (n.).*]

[*References are to paragraphs (¶) and notes (n.).*]

[*References are to paragraphs (¶) and notes (n.).*]

[*References are to paragraphs (¶) and notes (n.).*]



**B**

[*References are to paragraphs (¶) and notes (n.).*]

[*References are to paragraphs (¶) and notes (n.).*]

[*References are to paragraphs (¶) and notes (n.).*]

[*References are to paragraphs (¶) and notes (n.).*]

[*References are to paragraphs (¶) and notes (n.).*]

*[References are to paragraphs (¶) and notes (n.).]*

*[References are to paragraphs (¶) and notes (n.).]*

[*References are to paragraphs (¶) and notes (n.).*]

[*References are to paragraphs (¶) and notes (n.).*]

## C

[*References are to paragraphs (¶) and notes (n.).*]

[*References are to paragraphs (¶) and notes (n.).*]

[*References are to paragraphs (¶) and notes (n.).*]

[*References are to paragraphs (¶) and notes (n.).*]

[*References are to paragraphs (¶) and notes (n.).*]

[*References are to paragraphs (¶) and notes (n.).*]

[*References are to paragraphs (¶) and notes (n.).*]

[*References are to paragraphs (¶) and notes (n.).*]

[*References are to paragraphs (¶) and notes (n.).*]

[*References are to paragraphs (¶) and notes (n.).*]

[*References are to paragraphs (¶) and notes (n.).*]

*[References are to paragraphs (¶) and notes (n.).]*

*[References are to paragraphs (¶) and notes (n.).]*

[*References are to paragraphs (¶) and notes (n.).*]

[*References are to paragraphs (¶) and notes (n.).*]



## F

[*References are to paragraphs (¶) and notes (n.).*]

[*References are to paragraphs (¶) and notes (n.).*]

[*References are to paragraphs (¶) and notes (n.).*]

[*References are to paragraphs (¶) and notes (n.).*]

[*References are to paragraphs (¶) and notes (n.).*]

[*References are to paragraphs* (¶) *and notes* (*n.*).]



## G

[*References are to paragraphs (¶) and notes (n.).*]

[*References are to paragraphs (¶) and notes (n.).*]

[*References are to paragraphs (¶) and notes (n.).*]

[*References are to paragraphs (¶) and notes (n.).*]

[*References are to paragraphs (¶) and notes (n.).*]

[*References are to paragraphs (¶) and notes (n.).*]

[*References are to paragraphs (¶) and notes (n.).*]

[*References are to paragraphs (¶) and notes (n.).*]

[*References are to paragraphs (¶) and notes (n.).*]

[*References are to paragraphs (¶) and notes (n.).*]



## I

[*References are to paragraphs (¶) and notes (n.).*]



## J

[*References are to paragraphs (¶) and notes (n.).*]

[*References are to paragraphs (¶) and notes (n.).*]

[*References are to paragraphs (¶) and notes (n.).*]



## K

[*References are to paragraphs (¶) and notes (n.).*]

[*References are to paragraphs (¶) and notes (n.).*]

[*References are to paragraphs (¶) and notes (n.).*]

*[References are to paragraphs (¶) and notes (n.).]*

[*References are to paragraphs (¶) and notes (n.).*]

[*References are to paragraphs (¶) and notes (n.).*]



## M

[*References are to paragraphs (¶) and notes (n.).*]

[*References are to paragraphs (¶) and notes (n.).*]

[*References are to paragraphs (¶) and notes (n.).*]

[*References are to paragraphs (¶) and notes (n.).*]

[*References are to paragraphs (¶) and notes (n.).*]

[*References are to paragraphs (¶) and notes (n.).*]

[*References are to paragraphs (¶) and notes (n.).*]

[*References are to paragraphs (¶) and notes (n.).*]



## N

[*References are to paragraphs (¶) and notes (n.).*]

[*References are to paragraphs (¶) and notes (n.).*]

[*References are to paragraphs (¶) and notes (n.).*]



## O

[*References are to paragraphs (¶) and notes (n.).*]



## P

[*References are to paragraphs (¶) and notes (n.).*]

[*References are to paragraphs (¶) and notes (n.).*]

[*References are to paragraphs (¶) and notes (n.).*]

[*References are to paragraphs (¶) and notes (n.).*]

[*References are to paragraphs (¶) and notes (n.).*]

[*References are to paragraphs (¶) and notes (n.).*]

[*References are to paragraphs (¶) and notes (n.).*]

[*References are to paragraphs (¶) and notes (n.).*]

[*References are to paragraphs (¶) and notes (n.).*]



## S

[*References are to paragraphs (¶) and notes (n.).*]

[*References are to paragraphs (¶) and notes (n.).*]

*[References are to paragraphs (¶) and notes (n.).]*

[*References are to paragraphs (¶) and notes (n.).*]

[*References are to paragraphs (¶) and notes (n.).*]

[*References are to paragraphs (¶) and notes (n.).*]

[*References are to paragraphs (¶) and notes (n.).*]

[*References are to paragraphs (¶) and notes (n.).*]

[*References are to paragraphs (¶) and notes (n.).*]



## T

[*References are to paragraphs (¶) and notes (n.).*]

[*References are to paragraphs (¶) and notes (n.).*]

[*References are to paragraphs (¶) and notes (n.).*]



## U

*[References are to paragraphs (¶) and notes (n.).]*



## V

[*References are to paragraphs (¶) and notes (n.).*]

[*References are to paragraphs (¶) and notes (n.).*]

[*References are to paragraphs (¶) and notes (n.).*]

[*References are to paragraphs (¶) and notes (n.).*]

[*References are to paragraphs (¶) and notes (n.).*]

[*References are to paragraphs (¶) and notes (n.).*]

[*References are to paragraphs (¶) and notes (n.).*]



## X



## Y



## Z

[*References are to paragraphs (¶) and notes (n.).*]

# Index

*[References are to paragraphs (¶).]*

[*References are to paragraphs (¶).*]

[*References are to paragraphs (¶).*]

[*References are to paragraphs (¶).*]



## C

[*References are to paragraphs (¶).*]

[*References are to paragraphs (¶).*]



## H



## I

[*References are to paragraphs (¶).*]

[*References are to paragraphs (¶).*]

[*References are to paragraphs (¶).*]

[*References are to paragraphs (¶).*]